SOCIOLOGY

This book is offered to teachers of sociology in the hope that it will help our students understand their place in today's society and, more broadly, in tomorrow's world.

John J. Macionis

what we call "civilization" is relatively recent, indeed, with the first permanent settlements occurring in the Middle East a scant 12,000 years ago. But the written record of our species' existence extends back only half this long, to the time humans invented writing and first farmed with animal-driven plows some 5,000 years B.P.

Sociology came into being in the wake of the many changes to society wrought by the Industrial Revolution over the last few centuries—just the blink of an eye in evolutionary perspective. The lower time line provides a close-up look at the events and trends that have defined **The Modern Era**, most of which are discussed in this text. Innovations in technology are charted in the green panel below the line and provide a useful backdrop for viewing the milestones of social progress highlighted in the blue panel above the line. Major contributions to the development of sociological thought are traced along the very bottom of this time line.

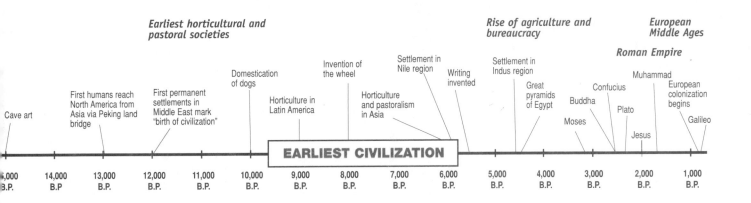

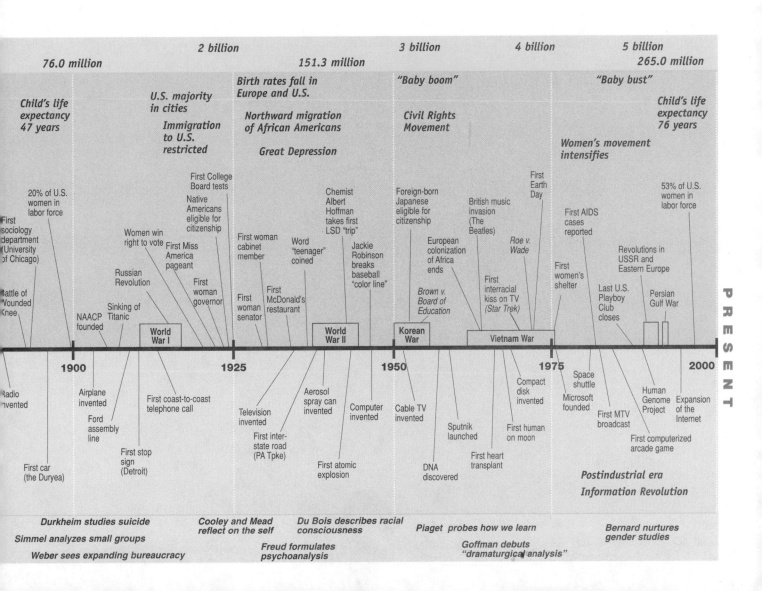

SOCIOLOGY

ANNOTATED INSTRUCTOR'S EDITION

SEVENTH EDITION

John J. Macionis

Kenyon College

Prentice Hall, Upper Saddle River, New Jersey 07458

Senior Acquisitions Editor: John Chillingworth
Editor in Chief: Nancy Roberts
Editorial Director: Charlyce Jones Owen
Editor in Chief of Development: Susanna Lesan
Development Editor: Harriet Prentiss
AVP, Director of Production and Manufacturing: Barbara
    Kittle
Production Editor: Barbara Reilly
Copyeditors: Amy Macionis, Rebecca Donlan
Proofreader: Marianne Peters Riordan
Production Assistants: Kathleen Sleys, Claire Rottino,
    Nicole Tellem
Editorial Assistants: Pat Naturale, Allison Westlake
Manufacturing Manager: Nick Sklitsis
Prepress and Manufacturing Buyer: Mary Ann Gloriande
Director of Marketing: Gina Sluss
Marketing Manager: Christopher De John
Creative Design Director: Leslie Osher

Art Director: Carole Anson
Interior and Cover Designer: Anne DeMarinis
Line Art Coordinator: Guy Ruggiero
Line Art Illustrations: Lithokraft II
Maps: Carto-Graphics
Director, Image Resource Center: Lori Morris-Nantz
Photo Research Supervisor: Melinda Lee Reo
Image Permissions Supervisor: Kay Dellosa
Permissions Coordinator: Debra Hewitson
Photo Researcher: Barbara Salz
Fine Art Researcher: Francelle Carapetyan
Cover Coordinator: Karen Sanatar
Cover Art: Joan Truckenbrod, *Incubation Buffer,* 1995.
    Limited Edition IRIS Print. 32" H × 36" W. Represented
    by The Williams Gallery of Fine Art, Princeton, N.J.
Executive Manager, New Media: Alison M. Pendergast
Senior Project Manager, New Media: John Archer
New Media Assistant: Maurice Murdock

This book was set in 10/11 Janson by Lithokraft II, and was
printed and bound by RR Donnelley & Sons Company. The
cover and endpapers were printed by The Lehigh Press, Inc.

For permission to use copyrighted material, grateful
acknowledgment is made to the copyright holders listed
on pages 684–85, which is considered an extension of this
copyright page.

Printed in the United States of America

10 9 8 7 6 5 4 3 2 1

STUDENT ISBN 0-13-095391-1
AIE ISBN 0-13-095772-0

Prentice-Hall International (UK) Limited, *London*
Prentice-Hall of Australia Pty. Limited, *Sydney*
Prentice-Hall Canada Inc., *Toronto*
Prentice-Hall Hispanoamericana, S.A., *Mexico*
Prentice-Hall of India Private Limited, *New Delhi*
Prentice-Hall of Japan, Inc., *Tokyo*
Simon & Schuster Asia Pte. Ltd., *Singapore*
Editora Prentice-Hall do Brasil, Ltda., *Rio de Janeiro*

Printed on Recycled Paper

BRIEF CONTENTS

CONTENTS

cyber.scope PART II: HOW NEW
TECHNOLOGY IS CHANGING OUR WAY
OF LIFE 232

 SOCIAL
INEQUALITY

PART III

**SOCIAL
CHANGE**

PART V

MAPS

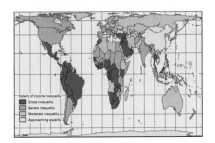

BOXES

EXPLORING CYBER-SOCIETY

SOCIAL DIVERSITY

SOCIOLOGY OF EVERYDAY LIFE

GLOBAL SOCIOLOGY

CRITICAL THINKING

CONTROVERSY & DEBATE

FEATURE ESSAYS

NEW INFORMATION TECHNOLOGY AND SOCIETY

cyber.scope

WE ARE PROUD TO BRING YOU THE

Seventh Edition of
John J. Macionis's *Sociology*

Dear Student,

Get ready! You are about to go on a fascinating trip to study the most amazing creatures on the face of the earth—human beings. People come in all shapes, sizes, colors, and creeds, and have created thousands of different ways of life all over the planet. Understanding our human world is the focus of sociology, which makes this one of the most important courses you can take in college.

As you begin this course, I would like to offer my own greeting. Just as important, let me offer a few suggestions about how you can get the most out of this text. There are three major themes to our story; keeping them in mind will help you organize all your reading assignments. The first theme is this: <u>We must learn about others to understand ourselves</u>. Sections of every chapter deal with societies around the world. As you read about another society, pay attention to not only how other people live, but think about how we live as well. The second theme is: <u>We may be one nation, but we are many, diverse peoples</u>. Pay attention to how social patterns differ for women and men, African Americans and white people, the young and the old, and people of high and low class standing. The third theme of the text is: <u>Good learning means being an active, critical reader. Don't be passive, accepting everything you read as true</u>.

This text is part of an interactive learning package that will involve you in two kinds of new information technology. Inside the back cover of the Student Media Version is a CD-ROM that features author video clips, practice tests, interactive maps, and learning exercises keyed to every chapter. In addition, you are invited to visit our Web sites. One site, www.macionis.com, reviews all the features of this text, gives several recent examples of sociology in the news, and provides links to the sites of dozens of organizations that have provided statistics and other material for this book. The other site, www.prenhall.com/macionis, offers for each text chapter self-grading tests, suggested paper topics, still more interesting Web links, and a chat room. It's all there to help you, and it's all absolutely free. Finally, I would like to hear from you. I teach in the sociology department at Kenyon College in Gambier, Ohio, 43022. But, in this new world of high technology, I am as near as your keyboard. Feel free to drop me a note to let me know what you think of our book, the CD-ROM, or the Web sites. My e-mail address is macionis@kenyon.edu And, if you wish, pass along suggestions for making them better. I <u>will</u> write back! Good luck, and welcome to a new way of looking at the world!

Sincerely,

John J. Macionis

About the Author

John J. Macionis (pronounced ma-SHOW-nis) grew up in Philadelphia, Pennsylvania. He received his bachelor's degree from Cornell University and his doctorate in sociology from the University of Pennsylvania. His publications are wide-ranging, focusing on community life in the United States, interpersonal intimacy in families, effective teaching, humor, and the importance of global education. He and Nijole V. Benokraitis have edited the companion volume to this text, the fourth edition of *Seeing Ourselves: Classic, Contemporary, and Cross-Cultural Readings in Sociology*. John also has written a brief version of this book, *Society: The Basics*, now in its fourth edition, and collaborates on international editions of this text. In addition, he is co-author of a new urban studies text, *Cities and Urban Life*, with Vincent Parillo.

John Macionis is professor of sociology at Kenyon College. During his twenty-year career at Kenyon, he has served as chair of the Anthropology-Sociology Department, director of the college's multidisciplinary program in humane studies, and presided over the college's faculty. He has also been active in academic programs in other countries, having traveled to some fifty nations. In the fall of 1994, he directed the global education course for the University of Pittsburgh's Semester at Sea program, teaching 400 students on a floating campus that visited twelve countries as it circled the globe.

John writes, "I am an ambitious traveler, eager to learn—and, through the texts, I try to share much of what I discover with students, many of whom know so little about the rest of the world. For me, traveling and writing are all dimensions of teaching. First and foremost, I am a teacher—a passion for teaching animates everything I do." Recently, he was named the recipient of the North Central Sociological Association's 1998 Award for Distinguished Contribution to Teaching for his work with textbooks and for pioneering the use of new technology in sociology.

At Kenyon, Macionis teaches a wide range of upper-level courses, but his favorite course is Introduction to Sociology, which he schedules every semester. He  enjoys extensive contact with students, making an occasional appearance on campus with his guitar and each term inviting his students to enjoy a home-cooked meal. The Macionis family—John, Amy, and children McLean and Whitney—live on a farm in rural Ohio. Their home serves as a popular bed and breakfast, where they enjoy visiting with old friends and making new ones. In his free time, John enjoys bicycling through the Ohio countryside, or a warm afternoon might find him sharing an adventure with his two children.

CHAPTER 6

SOCIAL INTERACTION IN EVERYDAY LIFE

Harold and Sybil are on their way to another couple's home in an unfamiliar section of Rochester, New York. They are late because, for the last twenty minutes, they have been driving in circles looking for Creek View Drive. Harold, gripping the wheel ever more tightly, is doing a slow burn. Sybil, sitting next to him, looks straight ahead, afraid to utter a word. Both realize the evening is off to a bad start (Tannen, 1990:62).

Here we have what appears to be a simple case of two people unable to find their friends' home. But Harold and Sybil are also lost in another way: They fail to grasp why they are growing more and more upset with their situation and with each other.

Consider the predicament from Harold's point of view. Like most men, Harold cannot tolerate getting lost, so the longer he drives around, the more incompetent he feels. Sybil, on the other hand, cannot understand why Harold does not pull over and ask someone where Creek View Drive is. If she were driving, she fumes to herself, they already would have arrived and would now be comfortably settled with drink in hand.

Why don't men ask for directions? Because men value their independence, they are uncomfortable asking for help (and also reluctant to accept it). To men, asking for assistance is an admission of inadequacy, a sure sign that others know something they don't. If it takes Harold a few more minutes to find Creek View Drive on his own—and to keep his self-respect in the process—he thinks it's a good bargain.

If men pursue self-sufficiency and are sensitive to hierarchy, women are more attuned to others and strive for connectedness. From Sybil's point of view, sharing information reinforces social bonds. Asking for directions seems as natural to her as searching on his own is to Harold. Obviously, getting lost is sure to generate conflict as long as neither one understands the other's point of view.

Such examples of everyday life are the focus of this chapter. We begin by presenting the building blocks of common experience and then explore the almost magical way in which face-to-face interaction generates reality. The central concept is **social interaction**, *the process by which people act and react in relation to others*. Through social interaction, we create the reality we perceive. And we interact according to particular social guidelines.

SOCIAL STRUCTURE: A GUIDE TO EVERYDAY LIVING

October 21, 1994, Ho Chi Minh City, Vietnam. This morning we leave the ship and make our way along the docks toward the center of Ho Chi Minh City—known to an earlier generation as Saigon. The government security

How do the world's people differ? **Global Sociology** boxes provide a look at an unfamiliar culture and, in the process, help sharpen your understanding of our own way of life.

GLOBAL SOCIOLOGY

Confronting the Yąnomamö: The Experience of Culture Shock

A small aluminum motorboat chugged steadily along the muddy Orinoco River, deep within South America's vast tropical he scarcely noticed the discomfort, so preoccupied was he with the prospect of meeting people unlike any he had ever known.

even more hideous, and strands of dark green slime dripped or hung from their nostrils—strands so long that they clung to their [chests] or

CRITICAL THINKING

The Importance of Gender in Research

Carol Gilligan, an educational psychologist at Harvard University, has demonstrated the importance of gender in our ideas about social behavior. Her early work confident, but their self-esteem slips away as they pass through adolescence.

Why? Gilligan claims that the answer lies in the way our culture defines females. In our society, the ideal woman is calm, controlled, and eager to please. Then, too, as girls move from the elementary grades to secondary school, they encounter fewer women teachers and find that most authority figures are

Do you believe everything you read? **Critical Thinking** boxes help you sharpen your reasoning skills as you learn to ask sociological questions, identify appropriate evidence, and reach logical conclusions.

Do we duck the tough questions? No way! **Controversy & Debate** boxes present several points of view on many of today's most controversial issues. Use the "Continue the debate" questions at the end of each box to assess your own views.

CONTROVERSY & DEBATE

The Bell Curve Debate: Are Rich People Really Smarter?

It is rare when the publication of a new book in the social sciences captures the attention of the public at large. But *The Bell Curve: Intelligence* and 70 percent) is transmitted genetically from one generation to another; the remaining variability is due to environmental factors.

dominated by a "cognitive elite," who are, on average, not only better trained than most people but actually more intelligent.

SOCIOLOGY OF EVERYDAY LIFE

Double Take: Real Headlines That Make People Laugh

Humor is generated by mixing two distinct and opposing realities. Here are several actual headlines from recent newspaper stories. Read each one and identify the

"Squad Helps Dog Bite Victim"

"War Dims Hope for Peace"

"Drunk Gets Nine Months in Violin Case"

"Survivor of Siamese Twins Joins Parents"

"Prostitutes Appeal to Pope"

"Teacher Strikes Idle Kids"

Can you put sociology to work in your own life? **Sociology of Everyday Life** boxes show how to apply the discipline to familiar, everyday experiences.

How is computer technology changing our way of life? A new series of **Exploring Cyber-Society** boxes gives some answers.

EXPLORING CYBER-SOCIETY

Pornography: As Close as Your Computer

The days when customers passed quickly through the door of the adult bookstore—a windowless building near the airport or along the payment before they provide full access. Moreover, software programs (such as Surf Watch and Net Nanny) can be installed to block access to certain sites.

many parents can do to keep their children from finding sexually explicit material on the Web. Especially disturbing to critics is that the most objectionable

SOCIAL DIVERSITY

The Color of Money: Being Rich in Black and White

African American families earn 59 cents for every dollar a white family earns, a fact that $75,000 a year, compared to only 38 percent of affluent African American families (9 percent of all black families).

Families typically contain two employed spouses, perhaps with working children.

Third, affluent African Americans

Do you realize how much people differ right here "at home"? **Social Diversity Boxes** focus on multicultural issues and amplify the voices of people of color and women.

DIVERSITY SNAPSHOT

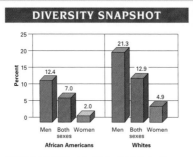

FIGURE 1–2 Rate of Death by Suicide, by Race and Sex, for the United States

Rates indicate the number of deaths by suicide for every 100,000 people in each category for 1994.

Source: U.S. National Center for Health Statistics (1996).

How do people within the United States differ from one another? **Diversity Snapshots** are colorful graphs that point out dimensions of difference within our society.

GLOBAL SNAPSHOT

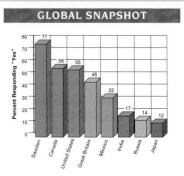

FIGURE 6–2 Happiness: A Global Survey

Survey Question: "We are interested in the way people are feeling these days. During the past few weeks, did you ever 'feel on top of the world,' feeling that life is wonderful?"

Source: *World Values Survey* (1994). Reprinted with permission of the Institute for Social Research Center for Political Studies, The University of Michigan.

WINDOW ON THE WORLD

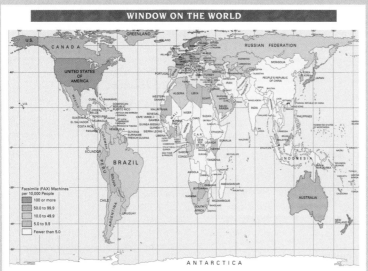

GLOBAL MAP 4–1 High Technology in Global Perspective

Countries with traditional cultures ignore or even resist technological innovation; nations with highly rationalized ways of life eagerly embrace such changes. Facsimile (fax) machines, one common form of high technology, are numerous in high-income countries such as the United States, where 5 million faxes fly along the "information superhighway" every hour. In low-income nations, by contrast, fax machines are unknown to most people. Notice that, in Asia, fax machines are widely available only in Japan, South Korea, Taiwan, and the business centers of Hong Kong and Singapore.

Source: *Peters Atlas of the World* (1990).

How do people in this country differ from people in other countries? **Global Snapshots** offer a quick and insightful comparison between the United States and other nations of the world.

Would you like to learn more about the world? **Window on the World** global maps (twenty-nine in all) highlight contrasts between rich and poor countries on issues such as income disparity, the lives of women, and HIV infection. All the maps use a non-Eurocentric projection by cartographer Arno Peters that accurately shows the relative size of the continents.

SEEING OURSELVES

NATIONAL MAP 6–1
Baseball Fans
Across the United States

One in three U.S. adults claims to follow baseball. The map shows that fans are concentrated in the northern states from New England to the Pacific Northwest. Why? What categories of people have a world view that celebrates this kind of activity? (Hint: Baseball is more likely to appeal to white males over forty years of age who were born in the United States.)

Source: From Michael J. Weiss, *Latitudes & Attitudes: An Atlas of American Tastes, Trends, Politics, and Passions.* Copyright © 1994 by Michael J. Weiss. Reprinted by permission of the author.

Do people on the Plains really differ from those on the West coast? Find out by looking at the **Seeing Ourselves** national maps (a total of twenty-nine) that offer a close-up look at life in the roughly 3,000 U.S. counties, highlighting suicide rates, household income, college attendance, chance of divorce, and more.

PART II
HOW NEW TECHNOLOGY IS CHANGING OUR WAY OF LIFE

Marshall McLuhan (1969) summed up his pioneering research in the study of communications this way: "Any new technology tends to create a new human environment." In other words, technology affects not just how we work, but it shapes and colors our entire way of life. In this second Cyber.Scope, we pause to reflect on some of the ways the Information Revolution is changing our culture and society.

The Information Revolution and Cultural Values

Chapter 3 ("Culture") noted that members of our society attach great importance to material comfort. In fact, throughout our history, many people have defined "success" to mean earning a good income and enjoying the things money will buy, including a home, car, and fashionable clothing.

But some analysts wonder if, as we enter the next century, our values may shift from a single-minded focus on the accumulation of things (the products of industrial technology) to an appreciation of ideas (the products of information technology). "New age" ideas range from experiences (including both travel and virtual reality[1]) to well-being (including the self-actualization that has become popular in recent decades) (Newman, 1991).

[1] For example, "travel" to an Adirondack mountaintop and enjoy the view (http://www.adirondack.net/adnet/bluemt/bluemt4.html) or wander through a Shaker settlement in Massachusetts (http://www.hancockshaker village.org).

Socialization in the Computer Age

Half a century ago, television rewrote the rules for socialization in the United States and, as Chapter 5 ("Socialization") explained, young people now spend more time watching TV than talking to their parents. Today, in the emerging Information Society, screens are not just for television; they are our windows into a cyber-world where computers link, entertain, and educate us. But this trend toward "cyber-socialization" raises several important questions.

First, will the spread of computer-based information erode the regional diversity that distinguishes this country? Will New England no longer be set off from the Deep South, and the Midwest from the West Coast? We know that new information technology is linking our nation with the world, so we might well expect to see a more national culture emerge and, with time, a more global culture as well.

Second, how will this "cyber-culture" affect our children? Will having computers at the center of their lives be good for them? For many children, computer-based images and information already play a significant role in the socialization process. Will this trend lessen the importance of parents in children's lives, as television did? Cyber-socialization can certainly entertain and instruct, but can it meet the emotional needs of children? Will it contribute to their moral development?

Almost unlimited access to information can be a mixed blessing, as parents can well understand. How can we prevent children from gaining access to pornography or other objectionable material on the Internet? Or, should we?

Have you noticed how rapidly the world is changing? **Cyber. Scopes** are a new series of five essays spread throughout the book (one follows each of the text's five parts) that explains new information technology and points out many of the ways the Information Revolution is involved in the issues raised in the chapters you have just finished reading. The Cyber. Scope essays highlight trends both in the United States and throughout the world.

their lives be good for them? For many children, computer-based images and information already play a significant role in the socialization process. Will this trend lessen the importance of parents in children's lives, as television did? Cyber-socialization can certainly entertain and instruct, but can it meet the emotional needs of children? Will it contribute to their moral development?

Third, who will control cyber-socialization? Just as parents have long expressed concern about what their children watch on television, they now worry about what kids encounter as they "surf the 'Net." To date, the federal courts have taken the position that the Internet should operate with minimal governmental interference. Do we—as citizens and as parents—have expectations for the content of "virtual culture"? Should the information industry operate for profit? With standards to ensure some measure of educational content? Who should decide?

The Cyber-Self

A person using the name "VegDiet" enters one of thousands of "chat rooms" found on the Internet, the vast global network described in Chapter 7 ("Groups and Organizations"). Within a few seconds, "Veg-Diet" is actively debating the state of the world with three other people: "MrMaine," "Ferret," and "RedWine."

Computer-chat, which is growing increasingly popular, highlights how online interaction differs from conventional modes

---

next century, our values may shift from a single-minded focus on the accumulation of things (the products of industrial technology) to an appreciation of ideas (the products of information technology). "New age" ideas range from experiences (including both travel and virtual reality[1]) to well-being (including the self-actualization that has become popular in recent decades) (Newman, 1991).

Socialization in the Computer Age

Half a century ago, television rewrote the rules for socialization in the United States and, as Chapter 5 ("Socialization") explained, young

"On the Internet, nobody knows you're a dog."

Peter Steiner ©1993 from *The New Yorker* Collection. All rights reserved.

Use the numbered
Summary to help
review the material you
read in each chapter.

SUMMARY

Gerhard and Jean Lenski

1. Sociocultural evolution explores the societal consequences of technological advance.

2. The earliest hunting and gathering societies were composed of a small number of family-centered nomads. Such societies have all but vanished from today's world.

3. Horticulture began some 10,000 years ago as people devised hand tools for cultivation. Pastoral societies domesticate animals and engage in extensive trade.

4. Agriculture, about 5,000 years old, is large-scale cultivation using animal-drawn plows. This technology allows societies to expand into vast empires, with greater productivity, greater specialization, and increasing inequality.

5. Industrialization began 250 years ago in Europe, as people harnessed advanced energy sources to power sophisticated machinery.

6. In postindustrial societies, production shifts from material things to information, with computers and other information technology replacing the heavy machinery of the industrial era.

Karl Marx

7. Marx's materialist analysis points up conflict between social classes.

8. Conflict in "ancient" societies involved masters and slaves; in agrarian societies, it places nobles and serfs in opposition; in industrial-capitalist societies, capitalists confront the proletariat.

Here's the listing of all
the **Key Concepts**
found at the end of
each chapter.

KEY CONCEPTS

society people who interact in a defined territory and share culture

sociocultural evolution the Lenskis' term for the changes that occur as a society gains new technology

hunting and gathering simple technology for hunting animals and gathering vegetation

horticulture technology based on using hand tools to cultivate plants

pastoralism technology that supports the domestication of animals

agriculture the technology of large-scale farming using plows harnessed to animals or more powerful sources of energy

ndustrialism technology that powers sophisticated machinery with advanced sources of energy

postindustrialism technology that supports an information-based economy

social conflict struggle between segments of society over valued resources

capitalists people who own factories and other productive enterprises

proletariat people who provide the labor necessary to operate factories and other productive enterprises

social institution a major sphere of social life, or societal subsystem, organized to meet a basic human need

false consciousness Marx's term for explanations of social problems in terms of the shortcomings of individuals rather than the flaws of society

class conflict antagonism between entire classes over the distribution of wealth and power in society

**Critical Thinking
Questions** help you
review each chapter's
material and suggest
topics for discussion,
papers, and essay
examinations.

CRITICAL-THINKING QUESTIONS

1. Present evidence that supports and contradicts the assertion that technological advance amounts to "progress."

2. Explain how Marx, as a materialist, took a different view of society than Weber, an idealist.

3. Both Marx and Weber were concerned with modern society's ability to alienate people. How are

their approaches different? How do their notions of alienation compare with Durkheim's concept of anomie?

4. What might each theorist discussed in this chapter say about the changing social standing of women? What issues might a feminist critique of these theories raise?

Learning Exercises,
new to this edition, give
suggestions for doing
"hands on" sociology
on campus, in the local
community, and by
exploring Web sites
throughout the world.

LEARNING EXERCISES

1. Hunting and gathering people mused over stars, and we still know the constellations in terms that were relevant to them—mostly animals and hunters. As a way of revealing what's important to *our* way of life, write a short paper imagining what meaning we would impose on the stars if we were beginning from scratch.

2. Spend an hour going around your home, trying to identify every device that has a computer chip in it. How many did you find? Were you surprised by the number?

3. Rent or watch the television schedule for an old "Tarzan" movie or another film that portrays technologically simpler people. How are they portrayed in the film?

4. Over the next few days, ask a dozen people over the age of twenty-five whether they think our society is getting better or worse, and why they hold their opinion. See how much agreement you find.

SOCIOLOGY, Seventh Edition, Mutimedia Version is offered FREE with the text. Prentice Hall, in association with Modern Age Books, has produced a CD-ROM that brings alive the traditional textbook with a long list of exciting interactive features. Pages spring to life with audio, video, multimedia animations, photos, and graphs, plus a companion Web site for online activities, You can highlight and place your own notes in the CD's electronic text. Reflection questions allow you to monitor your understanding of key concepts online.

Macionis World Wide Web **Companion Web Site,** http://www.prenhall.com/macionis, is menu-driven and easy to use, providing assessment tools for each chapter of the text while giving you a direct gateway to resources on the World Wide Web. Among the features available for every chapter are a chapter overview and learning objectives, suggested paper topics, essay questions, multiple-choice and true-false questions that the server will immediately grade, chapter-relevant Web destinations with learning questions, and much more!

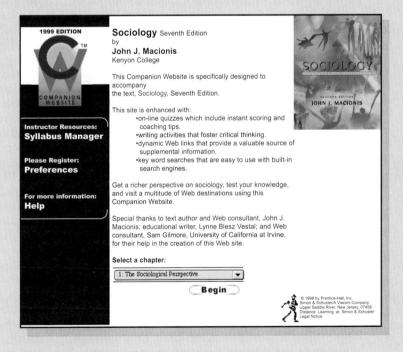

PREFACE

How much the world has changed in just the last few years! And nowhere is the change greater than with regard to new information technology. Back in 1995, when we were preparing the last edition of *Sociology*, this nation was just discovering the Internet. Now, as we stand at the brink of a new century, about half of U.S. adults—and a majority of men and women enrolled in college—have made computers a part of their everyday lives.

To mark the beginning of the new century—and to acknowledge the arrival of the Information Age—we are both proud and excited to present a new, groundbreaking edition of *Sociology*. As you surely have noticed, the seventh edition has a very different look. This new appearance symbolizes the fact that *Sociology* will never stand still or be revised with only superficial changes. On the contrary, *Sociology* enters the new century as the first complete multimedia learning package in sociology.

The heart of this package is, of course, the text. As in the past, this seventh edition of *Sociology* is authoritative, comprehensive, stimulating, and—as daily e-mail messages from students across the country and around the world testify—plain fun to read. This thoroughly updated edition elevates sociology's most popular text to a still higher standard of excellence, and offers an unparalleled resource to today's students as they learn about both our diverse society and the changing world.

But the book is just part of the learning package. Found in the back cover of every copy of *Sociology, Seventh Edition,* Student Media Version, is a CD-ROM, included *at no additional cost to the student*. This CD-ROM offers video author tips to introduce each chapter, practice tests that help students identify sections of chapters where they need additional study, a search engine, profiles of key sociologists, interactive maps, direct Internet access to Web sites, and short video clips that bring to life the key themes of each chapter of the text. In all, the CD-ROM stimulates students' interest as it helps them learn.

In addition, all students using *Sociology, Seventh Edition,* can benefit from the full-featured Web site http://www.prenhall.com/macionis also at no cost to them. For each chapter of the text, this site provides a chapter overview and learning objectives, suggested research paper topics, essay questions as well as multiple-choice and true-false questions that the server will immediately grade, chapter-relevant Web destinations with learning questions, and a chat room where students can discuss sociological issues with others taking the same course.

Textbook, CD-ROM, and Web site: A three-part foundation for sound learning. We invite you to examine all three!

ORGANIZATION OF THIS TEXT

Part I of the textbook introduces the foundations of sociology. Underlying the discipline is the *sociological perspective*—the focus of Chapter 1, which explains how this invigorating point of view brings the world to life in a new and instructive way. Chapter 2 spotlights *sociological investigation*, or the "doing of sociology," and explains how to use the logic of science to study human society. We demonstrate major research strategies in action through well-known examples of sociological work. Learning how sociologists see the world and carry out research, passive readers become active, critical participants in the issues, debates, and controversies that frame our discipline.

Part II surveys the foundations of social life. Chapter 3 focuses on the central concept of *culture*, emphasizing the cultural diversity that makes up our society and our world. Chapter 4 links culture to the concept of *society*, presenting four time-honored models for understanding the structure and dynamics of social organization. This unique chapter provides students with the background to comprehend more deeply the ideas of important thinkers—including Emile Durkheim, Karl Marx, Max Weber, as well as Gerhard and Jean Lenski—that appear in subsequent chapters. The topic of Chapter 5 is *socialization*, an exploration of how we gain our humanity as we learn to participate in society. Chapter 6 provides a micro-level look at the patterns of *social interaction* that make up our everyday lives. Chapter 7 offers full-chapter coverage of *groups and organizations*, two additional and vital elements of social structure. Chapter 8 completes the unit by investigating how the operation of society generates both *deviance and conformity*.

Part III offers unparalleled discussion of social inequality, beginning with three chapters devoted to social stratification. Chapter 9, *social stratification*, introduces major concepts and presents theoretical explanations of social inequality. This chapter richly illustrates the historical changes in stratification and how patterns of inequality vary around the world today. Chapter 10 surveys *social inequality in the United States*, exploring common perceptions of inequality and assessing how well they square with research findings. Chapter 11 extends the analysis with a look at *global stratification*, revealing the gaps in wealth and power that separate rich and poor nations. Both Chapters 10 and 11 pay special attention to how global developments affect stratification in the United States, just as they explore our society's role in global inequality. Chapter 12, *sex and gender*, begins with the biological foundation of sex and sexuality, and goes on to explain how societies transform the distinction of sex into systems of gender stratification. *Race and ethnicity*, additional important dimensions of social inequality both in North America and the rest of the world, are detailed in Chapter 13. *Aging and the elderly*, a topic of increasing concern to "graying" societies such as our own, is addressed in Chapter 14.

Part IV includes a full chapter on each social institution. Chapter 15 leads off investigating *the economy and work*, because most sociologists recognize the economy as having the greatest impact on all other institutions. This chapter highlights the processes of industrialization and postindustrialization, explains the emergence of a global economy, and suggests what such transformations mean for the U.S. labor force. Chapter 16, *politics and government*, analyzes the distribution of power in U.S. society and surveys political systems around the world. It includes discussion of the U.S. military, the threat of war, and the search for peace. Chapter 17, *family*, explains the central importance of families to social organization, and underscores the diversity of family life both here and in other societies. Chapter 18, *religion*, addresses the timeless human search for ultimate purpose and meaning, introduces major world religions, and explains how religious beliefs are linked to other dimensions of social life. Chapter 19, *education*, traces the expansion of schooling in industrial societies. Here again, schooling in the United States comes to life through contrasts with educational patterns in many other countries. Chapter 20, *health and medicine*, shows how health is a social issue just as much as it is a matter of biological processes. This chapter traces the historical emergence of medicine, analyzes current medical issues, and compares U.S. patterns to those found in other countries.

Part V examines important dimensions of global social change. Chapter 21 focuses on the powerful impact of *population growth and urbanization* in the United States and throughout the world. Chapter 22 presents issues of contemporary concern by highlighting the interplay of society and *the natural environment*. Chapter 23 explores forms of *collective behavior* and explains how people seek or resist social change by joining *social movements*. Chapter 24 concludes the text with an overview of *social change* that contrasts *traditional, modern, and postmodern societies*. This chapter rounds out the text by explaining how and why world societies change and by critically analyzing the benefits and liabilities of traditional, modern, and postmodern ways of life.

CONTINUITY: ESTABLISHED FEATURES OF *SOCIOLOGY*

Everyone knows that introductory sociology texts have much in common; but they are not the same. The extraordinary success of *Sociology*—far and away the most widely adopted text of its kind—results from a combination of the following distinctive features:

Unsurpassed writing style. Most important, this text offers a writing style widely praised by students and faculty alike as elegant and inviting. *Sociology* is an enjoyable text that encourages students to read—even beyond their assignments.

Comprehensive coverage that lets instructors choose. No other text matches *Sociology's* twenty-four-chapter coverage of the field. We offer such breadth—at no greater cost—not with the expectation that instructors will assign every chapter, but so that instructors can choose exactly what they wish to teach.

Engaging and instructive chapter openings. One of the most popular features of earlier editions of *Sociology* has been the engaging vignettes that begin each chapter. These openings—for instance, using the tragic sinking of the *Titanic* to illustrate the life-and-death consequences of social inequality, citing the Million Man March to highlight our ability to bring about intentional change, and visiting a vast city dump in the Philippines to bring home the desperate plight of many of the world's poor—spark the interest of readers as they introduce important themes. This revision retains the best chapter-opening vignettes from earlier editions and offers ten new ones as well.

Instructive and varied examples. On virtually every page of *Sociology*, rich, illuminating examples bring concepts and theories to life, demonstrating to students the value of applying sociology to our everyday world.

A celebration of social diversity. *Sociology* invites students from all social backgrounds to discover a fresh and exciting way to see the world and understand themselves. Readers will discover in this text the diversity of U.S. society—people of African, Asian, European, and Latino ancestry, as well as women and men of various class positions, in all parts of the country, and at all points in the life course. Just as important, without flinching from the problems that marginalized people confront, this text does not treat minorities as social problems but notes their achievements.

Inclusive focus on women and men. Beyond devoting a full chapter to the important concepts of sex and gender, *Sociology* mainstreams gender into *every* chapter, showing how the topic at hand affects women and men differently, and explaining how gender operates as a basic dimension of social organization.

A global perspective. *Sociology* has taken a leading role in expanding the horizons of our discipline beyond the United States. Each chapter of this text contains comparative material that explores the social diversity of the entire world. Moreover, this text explains that social trends in the United States—from musical tastes, to the price of wheat, to the growing disparity of income—are influenced by what happens elsewhere. Conversely, students will recognize ways in which social patterns and policies that characterize the United States and other rich countries affect poor nations around the world.

Theoretically clear and balanced. *Sociology* makes theory easy. Chapter 1 introduces the discipline's major theoretical approaches, which systematically reappear in the chapters that follow. The text highlights not only the social-conflict, structural-functional, and symbolic-interaction paradigms, but incorporates feminist theory, social-exchange analysis, ethnomethodology, cultural ecology, and sociobiology.

Chapter 4—unique to this text—provides students with an easy-to-understand introduction to important social theorists *before* they encounter their work in later chapters. The ideas of Max Weber, Karl Marx, Emile Durkheim, as well as Gerhard Lenski's historical overview of human societies, appear in distinct sections that instructors may assign together or refer to separately at different points in the course.

Emphasis on critical thinking. Critical thinking skills include the ability to challenge common assumptions by formulating questions, identifying and weighing appropriate evidence, and reaching reasoned conclusions. This text not only teaches but encourages students to discover on their own.

Recent sociological research. *Sociology* blends classical sociological statements with the latest research as reported in the leading publications in the field. Some 250 new studies inform this revision, and half of 1,500 research citations used throughout the book were published since 1990. From chapter to chapter, the text's statistical data are the most recent available.

Learning aids. This text has many features to help students learn. In each chapter, **Key Concepts** are identified by boldfaced type and following each appears *a precise, italicized definition*. A listing of key concepts with their definitions appears at the end of each chapter, and a complete **Glossary** is found at the end of the book. Each chapter also contains a numbered **Summary** and four **Critical-Thinking Questions** that help students to review material and assess their understanding. In this revision, each chapter ends with a list of **Learning Exercises**, which provides students with activities to do on or near the campus and identifies interesting Web sites on the topic at hand.

Outstanding images: photography and fine art. This book offers the finest and most extensive program of photography and artwork available in any sociology textbook. The seventh edition of *Sociology* displays more than one hundred examples of fine art as well as hundreds of color photographs—more than ever before. Each of these images is carefully selected by the author and appears with an insightful caption. Moreover, both photographs and artwork present people of various social backgrounds and historical periods. For example, alongside art by well-known Europeans such as Vincent Van Gogh and U.S. artists including George Tooker, this edition has paintings by celebrated African American artists Jacob Lawrence and Henry Ossawa Tanner, outstanding Latino artists Frank Romero and Diego Rivera, and the engaging Australian painter and feminist Sally Swain.

Thought-provoking theme boxes. Although boxed material is common to introductory texts, *Sociology, Seventh Edition*, provides a wealth of uncommonly good boxes. Each chapter typically contains four boxes, which fall into six types that amplify central themes of the text. **Global Sociology** boxes provoke readers to think about their own way of life by examining the fascinating social diversity that characterizes our world. **Social Diversity** boxes focus on multicultural issues and amplify the voices of women and people of color. **Critical Thinking** boxes teach students to ask sociological questions about their surroundings and help them to evaluate important, controversial issues. **Exploring Cyber-Society** boxes, new to this edition, explore how computers and other new information technology are changing our lives. **Sociology of Everyday Life** boxes show how to apply sociological insights to familiar, everyday experiences. **Controversy & Debate** boxes conclude each chapter by presenting several points of view on an issue of contemporary importance; "Continue the debate" questions, which end each of these boxes, are sure to stimulate spirited class discussion.

Sociology, Seventh Edition, contains ninety-one boxes in all (on average, about four per chapter), revised and updated as necessary with seventeen boxes new to this revision. A complete listing of this text's boxes appears after the table of contents.

An unparalleled program of fifty-eight global and national maps. Another popular feature of *Sociology* is its program of global and national maps. **"Windows on the World"** global maps—twenty-nine in all and many updated for this edition—are truly sociological maps offering a comparative look at income disparity, favored languages and religions, the extent of prostitution, permitted marriage forms, the degree of political freedom, the incidence of HIV infection, the extent of the world's rain forests, and a host of other issues. **Windows on the World** use a new, non-Eurocentric projection, devised by cartographer Arno Peters, that accurately portrays the relative size of all the continents. A complete listing of the **Windows on the World** global maps follows the table of contents.

"Seeing Ourselves" national maps—twenty-nine in all with seven new to this edition—help to illuminate the social diversity of the United States. Most of these maps offer a close-up look at all of the roughly 3,000 U.S. counties, highlighting suicide rates, median household income, labor force participation, college attendance, divorce rates, most widespread religious affiliation, air quality, and, as measures of popular culture, where baseball fans live or where households consume white bread or croissants. Each national map includes an explanatory caption that poses several questions to stimulate students' thinking about social forces. A complete listing of the **Seeing Ourselves** national maps follows the table of contents.

INNOVATION: CHANGES IN THE SEVENTH EDITION

Each new edition of *Sociology* has broken new ground, one reason that more than 2 million students have learned from this sociological best-seller. A revision raises high expectations, but, after several years of planning and work, we are excited to offer the most dramatically new and improved revision ever. Here is a brief overview of the innovations that define *Sociology, Seventh Edition*:

Sociology, Seventh Edition, offers the first multimedia, interactive learning resource in sociology! Computers and other new information technology are changing the way we learn, and *Sociology, Seventh Edition*, is now a

twenty-first century textbook. The heart of the learning package—the book itself—comes with many new features, which are outlined below. In addition, the text is supported by two new, high technology resources: the CD-ROM and the Web site.

The CD-ROM. A CD-ROM, included inside the back cover of the Student Media Version of the text, provides video-based author tips and learning exercises for every chapter. These videos enhance key themes of the text: social diversity, global comparisons, critical thinking, and applying sociology to our everyday lives. Just as important, students receive the CD-ROM packaged with the text *at no increase in price!*

The Web site. Students using *Sociology* have free access to a freshly revised and full-featured Web site: http://www.prenhall.com/macionis Menu-driven and easy to use, this site follows the chapter flow of the text, providing learning objectives, essay questions and suggested paper topics, multiple-choice and true/false tests, additional Web destinations, and a chat room.

Together with the text, the CD-ROM and the Web site offer more information *and more ways to learn* than ever before. For the latest information on this and all our textbooks, visit our other Web site, http://www.macionis.com

Cyber.Scopes. One of the innovations found within the text itself is the new series of Cyber.Scope essays spread throughout the text with one appearing after each of the book's five parts. Cyber.Scope essays explain what the Information Revolution is all about and show how computers and new information technology are altering the shape of people's lives here and around the world. The five Cyber.Scope essays are titled:

- Part I: Welcome to the Information Revolution!
- Part II: How New Technology Is Changing Our Way of Life
- Part III: New Information Technology and Social Stratification
- Part IV: New Information Technology and Social Institutions
- Part V: New Information Technology and Social Change

These essays, which contain photos, figures, and maps, provide an opportunity for instructors to pause at several points during the course to focus on new information technology or, alternatively, they can be read together as a "chapter" on new technology and society.

Exploring Cyber-Society boxes. The Cyber.Scopes are not the only place to find discussion of new information technology. A new series of Exploring

Cyber-Society boxes highlights ways in which computer technology is linked to specific sociological topics. These new boxes—eight in all—explore the spread of virtual culture (Chapter 3); imagine what Marx, Weber, and Durkheim might have to say about computer technology (Chapter 4); introduce the Internet as the world's largest network (Chapter 7); assess the problem of online pornography (Chapter 12); explore job patterns in the cyber-age (Chapter 15); examine the prospects for computer warfare (Chapter 16); look at how religious organizations are utilizing the Internet (Chapter 18); and evaluate the prospects for online colleges with no campuses at all (Chapter 19). A complete listing of these and all seventh edition boxes appears after the Table of Contents.

Diversity Snapshots. In the last edition, we introduced Global Snapshots—colorful figures that compare social patterns in the United States with those in other nations. In this edition, we have added Diversity Snapshots, figures that highlight the social diversity of our own society by presenting social patterns linked to race, ethnicity, class, gender, and age.

Learning Exercises. *Sociology* is a text that helps transform students into active learners. This edition retains the Critical-Thinking Questions at the end of each chapter and the "Continue the debate" questions that conclude the Controversy & Debate boxes. Also, many of the captions for maps, photographs, and fine art are written as questions that provoke critical thinking.

And, in this seventh edition, *Sociology* includes a new feature: Learning Exercises at the end of each chapter. Some direct students to explore engaging Web sites found around the world. But opportunities to use the sociological perspective are always close at hand (and, of course, many students do not have Internet access). Thus, most of the Learning Exercises involve familiar settings on and around the campus.

A small change in chapter ordering. In this revision, Chapters 12 and 13 have switched places. This change—prompted by suggestions from colleagues as well as my own classroom experiences—places the chapter on race and ethnicity *after* other stratification chapters, including sex and gender. Doing so gives students more experience discussing social inequality before they focus on race, a topic they sometimes find difficult to discuss in class.

A revised time line. Have you ever wished there was a way to locate at a glance important historical periods and key events? The last edition of *Sociology* introduced a time line found inside the front cover. This

edition presents a more complete and improved time line that makes historical patterns even more clear to readers.

A thorough rewriting of the text. For every revision of this text, I have gone through the chapters page by page, line by line, updating and making the discussion as clear and engaging as possible. This time around, I performed this ritual twice, with the goal of identifying and replacing any language that presented unnecessary difficulties to students. The result is, by far, the most accessible and best-reading version of the text ever.

New topics. The seventh edition of *Sociology* is completely updated with new and expanded discussions in every chapter. Here is a partial listing, by chapter:

• **Chapter 1 The Sociological Perspective**: A new section entitled "Marginal Voices" highlights women's contribution to the development of sociology; see the updated discussion on the sociology of W. E. B. Du Bois and C. Wright Mills and the expanded section on applied sociology.

• **Chapter 2 Sociological Investigation**: We've looked at the debate over how the Census Bureau should classify biracial people and expanded the discussion of research ethics.

• **Chapter 3 Culture**: A new chapter opening visits Connecticut's Mohegan Indians; we've added material on U.S. cultural diversity; a new section links culture to information technology; a new Cyber-Society box tracks the rise of virtual culture; and a new journal entry highlights child labor in Morocco.

• **Chapter 4 Society**: A new chapter opening describes the Tuareg nomads of the Sahara; a new Cyber-Society box imagines the classic theorists' view of the Information Revolution.

• **Chapter 5 Socialization**: There is a new discussion of Erik H. Erikson's theory of life course socialization and a new presentation of sexuality and violence in the mass media.

• **Chapter 6 Social Interaction in Everyday Life**: Beyond extensive rewriting, this chapter includes a new Critical Thinking box on the military's use of jargon and a Sociology of Everyday Life box on humorous newspaper headlines.

• **Chapter 7 Groups and Organizations**: New research links organizational behavior to size; notice a considerable increase in discussion of new information technology throughout the chapter as well as a new Cyber-Society box on the Internet; see the updated discussion of organizations, technology, and personal privacy.

• **Chapter 8 Deviance**: A new opening vignette discusses the trend in violent crime in New York City; there are two new National Maps: one shows the distribution of psychiatrists across the United States and the other provides a state-by-state review of death penalty legislation and death row populations; we have added a discussion of projective labeling, made statistical updates on crime and victimization, and added a discussion of community policing.

- **Chapter 9 Social Stratification**: This chapter features an expanded discussion of the Kuznets curve; updates on inequality in South Africa and economic struggle in the former Soviet Union; there is a new Critical Thinking box on social Darwinism that assesses the view of social stratification as "the survival of the fittest."

- **Chapter 10 Social Class in the United States**: A new opening looks at the effect of welfare reform; there are new data on U.S. income distribution; a new Critical Thinking box highlights William Julius Wilson's analysis of inner-city joblessness; the chapter brings students up to date on the new Temporary Assistance to Needy Families (TANF) program and other aspects of the 1996 welfare reforms.

- **Chapter 11 Global Stratification**: A new chapter-opening vignette as well as a new section highlight the reality of global slavery; statistical updates document the extent of inequality among the world's people today; new United Nations data support discussion of world economic development; and a new Global Map shows which nations are making economic progress and which are not.

- **Chapter 12 Sex and Gender**: Note the new chapter ordering, switching gender and race; a new chapter-opening vignette deals with female circumcision; note the reorganized and expanded discussion of human sexuality; a new figure compares women's and men's athletic performance over time; a new Global Map explores women's political clout; there is a new Critical Thinking box on the beauty myth, a new section on women in the military, an update on women's political firsts, and a new Cyber-Society box on cyber-porn.

- **Chapter 13 Race and Ethnicity**: Three updated National Maps in this chapter show the national distribution of this country's African American, Asian American, and Hispanic populations; a new National Map indicates where white Anglo-Saxon Protestants (WASPs) live; the chapter concludes with an update on the affirmative action debate.

- **Chapter 14 Aging and the Elderly**: See the new discussion contrasting the "young old" and the "old old" and the discussion of the ethical issues surrounding death; a new section explores the challenge of finding meaning in old age; a new Global Sociology box looks at euthanasia in the Netherlands; a new Global Map surveys the elderly population in global perspective.

- **Chapter 15 The Economy and Work**: A new chapter-opening vignette looks at corporate downsizing; a new Cyber-Society box describes temporary jobs on the rise in the Information Age; a new section analyzes the personal freedoms provided by different economic models; and, overall, the chapter now has a more critical tone.

- **Chapter 16 Politics and Government**: A new opening looks at U.S. voter apathy; a Marxist model has been added to the discussion of the U.S. political system, and more social-conflict content is found throughout the chapter; a new Social Diversity snapshot looks at voter apathy by income level; the chapter recognizes nongovernmental organizations (NGOs) as important actors on the global political stage; and a new Cyber-Society box assesses the promise and dangers of information warfare.

- **Chapter 17 Family**: Note how the new chapter-opening vignette leads into an updated and expanded discussion of the gay marriage debate; there are new data on the extent of cohabitation; a new Global Sociology box describes arranged marriages in India.

- **Chapter 18 Religion**: Another new chapter-opening vignette examines religious tensions on campus; there is an updated discussion of cults in the United States, an expanded discussion of decline in Jewish culture in North America, and a new Cyber-Society box on religious organizations spreading their messages on the Internet.

- **Chapter 19 Education**: A new Cyber-Society box looks ahead to computer-based learning in the coming century; a new Global Snapshot focuses on functional illiteracy; there is a new discussion of charter schools, as well as an update on the academic performance of U.S. students; one of the chapter's new Learning Exercises takes students to a Web site created by students in a sociology course.

- **Chapter 20 Health and Medicine**: A new Sociology of Everyday Life box characterizes masculinity as a leading cause of death; two new National Maps highlight longevity for U.S. women and men; the chapter provides updates on the leading causes of death in the United States as well as the "right-to-die" debate; and a new Global Snapshot compares cigarette smoking in selected countries.

- **Chapter 21 Population and Urbanization**: A new chapter-opening vignette considers Japan's falling birth rate; discussion focuses on both underpopulation and overpopulation; new data and projections inform the section on global population; note the new section on "edge cities" as well as a new discussion of urban political economy.

- **Chapter 22 Environment and Society**: A new Critical Thinking box describes the birth of trash; see the update on global warming; and one of the new Learning Exercises includes a visit to the Web sites for the Sierra Club and Greenpeace.

- **Chapter 23 Collective Behavior and Social Movements**: Discusses the mutiny on the slave ship *Amistad* as a case of mob behavior or rebellion; investigates new information technology as a medium for rumor; updates data on political involvement of college students; and a Learning Exercise takes students to the NORML home page.

- **Chapter 24 Social Change: Traditional, Modern, and Postmodern Societies**: The discussion of modernity and postmodernity are heavily rewritten to make theory clearer to students; photography and fine art are updated throughout; and there is coverage of the communitarian movement that now includes a Learning Exercise that invites students to explore that organization's Web site.

The latest statistical data. *Sociology* has a reputation for including the very latest available statistical data. The seventh edition continues this tradition, making use of data from the Internet as well as conventional bound publications of various agencies and organizations. The author and Carol A. Singer, a professional government documents librarian at the Department of Justice Law Library, have incorporated new statistics—many 1996, and even 1997 and 1998—throughout. Finally, this revision is informed by some 250 new research findings and uses current events to illustrate discussions, elevating the interest of readers.

A WORD ABOUT LANGUAGE

This text's commitment to representing the social diversity of the United States and the world carries with it the responsibility to use language thoughtfully. In most cases, we prefer the terms *African American* and *person of color* to the word *black*. We use the terms *Hispanic* and *Latino* to refer to people of Spanish descent. Most tables and figures refer to "Hispanics" because the U.S. Bureau of the Census employs this term in collecting statistical data about our population.

Students should realize, however, that many individuals do not describe themselves using these terms. Although the term "Hispanic" is commonly used in the eastern part of the United States, and "Latino" and the feminine form "Latina" are widely heard in the West, across the United States people of Spanish descent identify with a particular ancestral nation, whether it be Argentina, Mexico, some other Latin American country, or Spain or Portugal in Europe.

The same holds for Asian Americans. Although this term is a useful shorthand in sociological analysis, most people of Asian descent think of themselves in terms of a specific country of origin (say, Japan, the Philippines, Taiwan, or Vietnam).

In this text, the term "Native American" refers to all the inhabitants of the Americas prior to contact with Europeans. Here again, however, most people in this broad category identify with their historical society (for example, Cherokee, Hopi, or Zuni). The term "American Indian" designates only those Native Americans who live in the continental United States, not including Native peoples living in Alaska or Hawaii.

Learning to think globally also leads us to use other terminology more carefully. This text avoids the word "American"—which literally designates two continents—to refer to just the United States. Thus, for example, if we are referring to this country, the term "U.S. economy" is more correct than the "American economy." This convention may seem a small point, but it implies the significant recognition that we in this country represent only one society (albeit a very important one) in the Americas.

SUPPLEMENTS

Sociology, Seventh Edition, is the heart of an unparalleled learning package that includes a wide range of proven instructional aids as well as several new ones. As the author of the text, I maintain a keen interest in all of the supplements to ensure their quality and integration with the text. The supplements for this revision have been thoroughly updated, improved, and expanded.

FOR THE INSTRUCTOR

• **The Annotated Instructor's Edition**. The AIE is a complete student text annotated by the author on every page. Annotations—which have been thoroughly revised for this revision—have won praise from instructors for enriching class presentations. Margin notes include summaries of research findings, statistics from the United States or other nations, insightful quotations, information highlighting patterns of social diversity in the United States, and high-quality survey data from the National Opinion Research Center's (NORC) *General Social Survey* and *World Values Survey* data from the Inter-university Consortium for Political and Social Research (ICPSR).

• **Data File**. This is the "instructor's manual" that is of interest even to those who have never used one before. The *Data File* provides far more than detailed chapter outlines and discussion questions; it contains statistical profiles of the United States and other nations, summaries of important developments and significant research, and supplemental lecture material for every chapter of the text. The *Data File* is available in Windows format.

• **Social Survey Software**, **Third Edition**. This is the supplement that is changing the way instructors teach and students learn. *Student CHIP Social Survey Software* is an easy yet powerful program that allows users to investigate U.S. society and other nations of the world by calling on the best source of survey data available, the *General Social Survey*. Two hundred sixty *GSS* items have been transformed into CHIP data sets and linked to the chapters of *Sociology, Seventh Edition*. There is an *Instructor's Manual* that leads students through multivariate analysis of attitudes and reported behavior by sex, race, occupation, level of income and education, and a host of other variables. *Social Survey Software,* which investigators can now manipulate either by keyboard or mouse, also has a new graphing feature. The *Student CHIP* microcomputer program was developed by James A. Davis (Harvard University) and is available in both IBM and Macintosh formats.

• **Test Item File**. A revised test item file is available in both printed and computerized forms. The file contains 2400 items—100 per chapter—in multiple-choice, true-false, and essay formats. Questions are identified as simple "recall" items or more complex "inferential" issues; the answers to all questions are page-referenced to the text. Prentice Hall

Custom Test is a test generator designed to allow the creation of personalized exams. It is available in DOS, Windows, and Macintosh formats. Prentice Hall also provides a test preparation service to users of this text that is as easy as one call to our toll-free 800 number.

• **Core Test Item File, Second Edition.** This general test item file consists of over 350 additional test questions appropriate for introductory sociology courses. All of the questions have been class tested, and an item analysis is available for every question.

• **Film/Video Guide: Prentice Hall Introductory Sociology, Sixth Edition.** This helpful guide describes well over 300 films and videos appropriate for classroom viewing for each of the text's chapters. It also provides summaries, discussion questions, and rental sources for each film and video.

ABCNEWS ABC News/Prentice Hall Video Library for Sociology. Few will dispute that video is the most dynamic supplement you can use to enhance a class. However, the quality of the video material and how well it relates to your course still make all the difference. Prentice Hall and ABC News are now working together to bring you the best and most comprehensive video ancillaries available in the college market

Through its wide variety of award-winning programs—*Nightline, Business World, On Business, This Week, World News Tonight,* and *The Health Show*—ABC offers a resource for feature and documentary-style videos related to the chapters in *Sociology, Seventh Edition.* The programs have high production quality, present substantial content, and are hosted by well-versed, well-known anchors

The authors and editors of Prentice Hall have carefully selected videos on topics that complement *Sociology, Seventh Edition,* and included notes on how to use them in the classroom. An excellent video guide in the *Data File* carefully and completely integrates the videos into your lecture. The guide has a synopsis of each video showing its relation to the chapter and discussion questions to help students focus on how concepts and theories apply to real-life situations.

ABC News/Prentice Hall Video Library, Sociology:
Volume I—Social Stratification
Volume II—Marriages and Families
Volume III—Race and Ethnic Relations
Volume IV—Criminology
Volume V—Social Problems
Volume VI—Introductory Sociology I
Volume VII—Introductory Sociology II
Volume VIII—Introductory Sociology III
Volume IX—Social Problems II
Volume X—Marriages and Families II

• **Prentice Hall Introductory Sociology PowerPoint Transparencies, Version I.** Created by Roger J. Eich of Hawkeye Community College, this PowerPoint slide set combines graphics and text in a colorful format to help you convey sociological principles in a new and exciting way. Created in PowerPoint, an easy-to-use widely available software program,

this set contains over 300 content slides keyed to each chapter in the text.

• **Prentice Hall Color Transparencies: Sociology Series V.** Full-color illustrations, charts, and other visual materials from the text as well as outside sources have been selected to make up this useful in-class tool.

• **Instructor's Guide to Prentice Hall Color Transparencies, Sociology Series V.** This guide offers suggestions for effectively using each transparency in the classroom.

MEDIA SUPPLEMENTS

• **Companion Web site.** In tandem with the text, students and professors can now take full advantage of the World Wide Web to enrich their study of sociology. The Macionis Web site correlates the text with related material available on the Internet. Features of the Web site include chapter objectives and study questions, as well as links to interesting material and information from other sites on the Web that can reinforce and enhance the content of each chapter. **Address:** http://www. prenhall.com/macionis

• **Distance Learning Solutions.** To meet the growing needs of distance learning courses, Prentice Hall is committed to being the leader in using innovative methods to deliver our content to students. For further details, please contact your Prentice Hall representative.

• **Sociology on the Internet.** This brief guide introduces students to the Internet and provides clear strategies for navigating the Internet and the World Wide Web. Exercises within and at the end of chapters allow students to practice searching for the myriad resources available to the student of sociology. This supplementary book is free to students when shrink-wrapped to *Sociology, Seventh Edition.*

• **Sociology: Interactive Edition.** This exciting new electronic version of the text on CD-ROM features point-and-click multimedia presentations, photographs, interactive maps from the text, study questions that strengthen the student's understanding of sociology, interactive essay review questions, and the complete text of *Sociology, Seventh Edition.*

• **Simon & Schuster's NewsLink.** This unique news service brings the leading newspapers of the world to the college campus. For the first time ever, news stories, organized daily by academic subject, are made available to you via the World Wide Web or e-mail. Most articles are hot linked to educational resources on the Web, which puts the day's events in an educational context. Please visit http://www.ssnewslink.com for more information.

FOR THE STUDENT

• **Study Guide.** This complete guide helps students review and reflect on the material presented in Macionis's text. Each of the twenty-four chapters in the Study Guide provides an overview of the corresponding chapter in the student text, summarizes its major topics and concepts, offers applied exercises, and features end-of-chapter tests with solutions.

 The New York Times Supplement, Themes of the Times, for Introductory Sociology. *The New York Times* and Prentice Hall are sponsoring *Themes of the Times*, a program designed to enhance student access to current information relevant to the classroom. Through this program, the core subject matter provided in this text is supplemented by a collection of timely articles from one of the world's most distinguished newspapers, *The New York Times*. These articles demonstrate the vital, ongoing connection between what is learned in the classroom and what is happening in the world around us.

To enjoy the wealth of information of *The New York Times* daily, a reduced subscription rate is available. For information, call toll-free: 1-800-631-1222.

Prentice Hall and *The New York Times* are proud to co-sponsor *Themes of the Times*. We hope it will make the reading of both textbooks and newspapers a more dynamic, involving process.

• **Seeing Ourselves: Classic, Contemporary, and Cross-Cultural Readings in Sociology, Fourth Edition.** Create a powerful teaching package by combining this text with the fourth edition of the best-selling anthology, *Seeing Ourselves*, edited by John J. Macionis and Nijole V. Benokraitis (University of Baltimore). Instructors relish this reader's unique format: Clusters of readings—from classic works to well-rounded looks at contemporary issues and cross-cultural comparisons—correspond to each chapter in *Sociology, Seventh Edition*.

• **Critical Thinking Audiocassette Tape.** In keeping with the text's critical thinking approach, a sixty-minute audio tape is available to help students think and read critically.

IN APPRECIATION

The conventional practice of designating a single author obscures the efforts of dozens of women and men that have resulted in *Sociology, Seventh Edition*. I would like to express my thanks to the Prentice Hall editorial team, including Phil Miller, division president, Charlyce Jones Owen, editorial director, Nancy Roberts, editor-in-chief, and John Chillingworth, senior editor in sociology, for their continual enthusiasm, and for supporting our pursuit of innovation and excellence. Day-to-day work on the book is shared by the author and the production team. Susanna Lesan, developmental editor-in-chief at Prentice Hall, has played a vital role in the development of all my texts for almost fifteen years, coordinating and supervising the editorial process. Barbara Reilly, production editor at Prentice Hall, is another key member of the team. Barbara deserves much of the credit for the attractive page layout of the book; indeed, if anyone "sweats the details" more than the author, it is Barbara! Amy Marsh Macionis, freelance "in house" editor, checks virtually everything, untangling awkward phrases, eliminating errors and inconsistencies in all the statistical data, and generally "getting it right."

I also have a large debt to the members of the Prentice Hall sales staff, the men and women who have given this text such remarkable support over the years. Thanks, especially, to Gina Sluss and Chris DeJohn, who have directed our marketing campaign.

Thanks, too, to Anne DeMarinis for providing the book's interior design, which was coordinated in-house by Art Director Carole Anson. Developmental and copy editing of the manuscript was provided by Harriet Prentiss and Amy Marsh Macionis. Barbara Salz did a wonderful job of researching photographs, and Francelle Carapetyan provided much of the fine art, both under the supervision of Melinda Lee Reo.

It goes without saying that every colleague knows more about some topics covered in this book than the author does. For that reason, I am grateful to the hundreds of faculty and students who have written to me to offer comments and suggestions. More formally, I am grateful to the following people who have reviewed some or all of this manuscript:

Peter Adler, University of Denver
Brent Bruton, Iowa State University
Stanley Capela, St. Francis College
William T. Chute, University of Nebraska at Omaha
Karen Conner, Drake University
Jackie Eller and Tina Deshofels
Ivan T. Evans, University of California at San Diego
Dona Fletcher, Sinclair Community College
Julie Ford, Long Island University
Robin Franck, Southwestern College
Melissa Hardy, Florida State University
Darnell Hawkins, University of Illinois
Phyllis Hay, Alvernia College
Michael Kleiman, University of South Florida
Bonnie Korn Ach, Chapman University
Dale A. Lund, University of Utah
Richard J. Lundman, Ohio State University
Garth Massey, University of Wyoming
Neville M. Morgan, Kentucky State University
C. Leon Pitt, Community College of Beaver County
Scott B. Potter, Marion Technical College
Robert A. Rothman, University of Delaware
John Skvoretz, University of South Carolina
Edward J. Steffes, Salisbury State University
George F. Stine, Millersville University
William Tolone, Illinois State University
Amy Wharton, Washington State University
John Wilson, Duke University

I also wish to thank the following colleagues for sharing their wisdom in ways that have improved this book:

Doug Adams (The Ohio State University), Peter K. Angstadt (Wesley College), Kip Armstrong (Bloomsburg University), Rose Arnault (Fort Hays State University), Grace Auyang (University of Cincinnati, RWC), Paula Barfield (Southwest Texas State University), Scott Beck (Eastern Tennessee State University), Lois Benjamin (Hampton University), Philip Berg (University of Wisconsin, La Crosse), Charlotte Brauchle (Southwest Texas Junior College), Bill Brindle (Monroe Community College), John R. Brouillette (Colorado State University), Valerie Brown (Cuyahoga Community College), Cathryn Brubaker (DeKalb College), Brent Bruton (Iowa State University), Richard Bucher (Baltimore City Community College), Karen Campbell (Vanderbilt University), Joseph Carroll (Colby-Sawyer College), Lynn Chamberlain (Scott Community College), Robert E. Clark (Midwestern State University), Harold Conway (Blinn College), Gerry Cox (Fort Hays State University), Lovberta Cross (Shelby State Community College), Robert Daniels (Mount Vernon Nazarene College), James A. Davis (Harvard University), Nanette J. Davis (Chapman University), Sumati Devadutt (Monroe Community College), Michael Donnelly (University of New Hampshire), Keith Doubt (Northeast Missouri State University), Denny Dubbs (Harrisburg Area Community College), Travis Eaton (Northeast Louisiana State University), Helen Rose Fuchs Ebaugh (University of Houston), John Ehle (Northern Virginia Community College), Roger Eich (Hawkeye Community College), Heather Fitz Gibbon (The College of Wooster), Kevin Fitzpatrick (University of Alabama-Birmingham), Dona C. Fletcher (Sinclair Community College), Charles Frazier (University of Florida), Karen Lynch Frederick (St. Anselm College), Patricia Gagné (University of Kentucky, Louisville), Pam Gaiter (Collin County Community College), Jarvis Gamble (Owen's Technical College), Steven Goldberg (City College, City University of New York), Michael Goslin (Tallahassee Community College), Charlotte Gotwald (York College of Pennsylvania), Norma B. Gray (Bishop State Community College), Rhoda Greenstone (DeVry Institute), Jeffrey Hahn (Mount Union College), Harry Hale (Northeast Louisiana State University), Dean Haledjian (Northern Virginia Community College), Dick Haltin (Jefferson Community College), Marvin Hannah (Milwaukee Area Technical College), Charles Harper (Creighton University), Gary Hodge (Collin County Community College), Elizabeth A. Hoisington (Heartland Community College), Sara Horsfall (Stephen F. Austin State University), Peter Hruschka (Ohio Northern University), Alicia Hughes-Jones (Tabor College), Glenna Huls (Camden County College), Jeanne Humble (Lexington Community College), Harry Humphries (Pittsburg State University), Cynthia Imanaka (Seattle Central Community College), Patricia Johnson (Houston Community College), Ed Kain (Southwestern University), Paul Kamolnick (Eastern Tennessee State University), Irwin Kantor (Middlesex County College), Thomas Korllos (Kent State University), Bonnie Korn Ach (Chapman University), Rita Krasnow (Virginia Western Community College), Donald Kraybill (Elizabethtown College), Michael Lacy (Colorado State University), Michael Levine (Kenyon College), George Lowe (Texas Tech University), Don Luidens (Hope College), Larry Lyon (Baylor University), Li-Chen Ma (Lamar University), Setma Maddox (Texas Wesleyan University), Errol Magidson (Richard J. Daley College), Mary Ann Maguire (Tulane University), Allan Mazur (Syracuse University), Karen E. B. McCue (University of New Mexico, Albuquerque), Meredith McGuire (Trinity College), Patrick McGuire (University of Toledo), Jack Melhorn (Emporia State University), Antonio V. Menéndez-Alarcón (Butler University), George Miller (University of Utah), Ken Miller (Drake University), Michael V. Miller (University of Texas at San Antonio), Richard Miller (Navarro College), Joe Morolla (Virginia Commonwealth University), Craig Nauman (Madison Area Technical College), Toby Parcel (The Ohio State University), Anne Peterson (Columbus State Community College), Marvin Pippert (Roanoke College), Lauren Pivnik (Monroe Community College), Daniel Quinn (Adrian College), Nevel Razak (Fort Hays State College), Jim Rebstock (Broward Community College), George Reim (Cheltenham High School), Virginia Reynolds (Indiana University of Pennsylvania), Laurel Richardson (The Ohio State University), Keith Roberts (Hanover College), Ellen Rosengarten (Sinclair Community College), Howard Schneiderman (Lafayette College), Anne Schulte (Des Moines Area Community College), Ray Scupin (Linderwood College), Steve Severin (Kellogg Community College), Harry Sherer (Irvine Valley College), Walt Shirley (Sinclair Community College), Ree Simpkins (Missouri Southern State University), Anson Shupe (Indiana University-Purdue University at Fort Wayne), Glen Sims (Glendale Community College), Nancy Sonleitner (University of Oklahoma), Larry Stern (Collin County Community College), Randy Ston (Oakland Community College), Verta Taylor (The Ohio State University), Vickie H. Taylor (Danville Community College), Mark J. Thomas (Madison Area Technical College), Len Tompos (Lorain County Community College), Wen-hui Tsai (Indiana University-Purdue University at Fort Wayne), Ronnie E. Turner (Colorado State University), Christopher Vanderpool (Michigan State University), Glenna Van Metre (Wichita State University), Phyllis Watts (Tiffin University), Murray Webster (University of North Carolina, Charlotte), Debbie White (Collin County Community College), Faith Willis (Brunswick College), Marilyn Wilmeth (Iowa University), Stuart Wright (Lamar University), William Yoels (University of Alabama, Birmingham), Dan Yutze (Taylor University), Wayne Zapatek (Tarrant County Community College), and Frank Zulke (Harold Washington College).

Finally, I would like to dedicate this book to my own Information Age children, McLean Johnston Macionis and Whitney Linnea Macionis. Children, of course, are small people who do everything in their power to keep books from being written. But nothing in the world is more precious to me than they!

Albina Kosiec Felski, *The Circus,* 1971

Oil on canvas, 48 × 48 in. (121.19 × 121.9 cm). National Museum of American Art, Smithsonian Institution, Washington, DC/Art Resource, NY.

CHAPTER 1

THE SOCIOLOGICAL PERSPECTIVE

Imagine that someone you have never seen before walks into your classroom and begins telling you and your classmates all about yourselves—how much money your parents make, how much *you* will earn during your lifetime, whether you will marry or not, how long you will live, and even what will cause your death. Who is this? A psychic looking into a crystal ball? No, it's a sociologist. With their knowledge of social patterns and trends, sociologists describe the lives—and even the future—of complete strangers.

First, the simple fact that you are sitting in a college classroom is a clue to your social standing. And *where* you are going to school offers even more information. People who attend private, liberal arts colleges, on average, come from well-to-do families with about twice the national level of income. At a state university? Your classmates are not quite as privileged, although their families' earnings are still above average. At a community college? Most of the students around you are from households of

more modest means, and many are the first in their families to attend college.

Second, regardless of what college or university you attend, more than nine out of ten members of your class will marry at some time in their lives, and about half will divorce at least once. On average, the divorces will occur after seven years of marriage. Most members of your class will have one or two children, and then most (or their partners) will choose to be surgically sterilized.

Third, if you complete a two-year associate's degree, you will earn about $1.5 million (in today's dollars) during your lifetime. Completing a bachelor's degree raises the figure to $2.0 million, and a Ph.D., to about $2.8 million. With a professional degree (in, say, law or medicine), you can expect lifetime earnings to top $3.5 million. But gender also comes into play: Women will trail men in lifetime earnings by about 25 percent.

Fourth, on average, your classmates will live to their mid-seventies. But here the women have an edge: They will outlive the men by six years. And, the odds are that your life will end in a hospital as a result of heart disease, cancer, or stroke.

These are the facts, but we are still left with the question of why—why do human lives seem to follow certain predictable patterns? The truth is that our lives do not unfold according to sheer chance, but neither do we decide for ourselves how to live, acting on what philosophers call "free will." We make many important decisions every day, of course, but always within a larger arena called "society"—a family, a campus, a nation, an entire world. The essential wisdom of sociology is that our social world guides our actions and

Every page of the Annotated Instructor's Edition of *Sociology* contains information and data—substantially revised for this edition—that will enhance the usefulness of the text. The annotations, as well as the separately bound *Data File*, provide supplementary teaching material directly related to the topic at hand. Annotations are of twelve types:

(1) **SUPPLEMENTS:** *Cross-references to material in the* Data File, *video library, or other supplementary material.*

(2) **CYBER:** *Material concerning the social implications of new information technology.*

(3) **THEN AND NOW:** *Data on the extent of change during recent decades.*

(4) **DIVERSITY:** *Comparative data or analysis of the issue in terms of race, ethnicity, age, gender, or class.*

We can easily grasp the power of society over the individual by imagining how different our world would be had we been born in place of any of these children from, respectively, Bolivia, Sri Lanka, South Africa, Botswana, the People's Republic of China, and El Salvador.

life choices just as the seasons influence our activities and clothing. And, because sociologists know a great deal about how society works, they can analyze and predict our behavior with surprising accuracy.

THE SOCIOLOGICAL PERSPECTIVE

The discipline of **sociology** is *the systematic study of human society*. At the heart of sociology is a distinctive point of view called "the sociological perspective."

SEEING THE GENERAL IN THE PARTICULAR

Peter Berger (1963) characterized the sociological perspective as *seeing the general in the particular*. That is, it is possible to identify general patterns in the behavior of particular people. Although every individual is unique, society acts differently on various *categories* of people (children compared to adults, for example, or women compared to men). Therefore, to think sociologically is to realize that the general categories to which we belong shape our particular life experiences.

In this text we look at the power of society to affect our actions, thoughts, and feelings. For instance, children are different from adults in more than just biological maturity. Society attaches meaning to age, so that we experience distinct stages in our lives. As children we are dependent, but as adults we are expected to behave responsibly. Further along the life course, our society defines old age as a time when people lose their social standing and often withdraw from earlier routines. How do we know that society—

and not simply biology—is at work here? We know because we can look back in time or around the world today and see that societies define the stages of life differently. The Native American Hopi, for example, give children surprising independence while, in Abkhasia (part of the Russian Federation), elderly people are powerful and held in high esteem.

A sociological look around us reveals the power of class position as well. Chapter 9 ("Social Stratification") and Chapter 10 ("Social Class in the United States") explain that how we live—and, sometimes, whether we live at all—follow from our position in our society's class hierarchy.

Finally, seeing the world sociologically makes us aware of the importance of gender. As Chapter 12 ("Sex and Gender") discusses, every society attaches meaning to being female or male, by giving women and men different work and family responsibilities. Thus the advantages and opportunities available to us can depend upon whether we are born one sex or the other.

SEEING THE STRANGE IN THE FAMILIAR

At first, using the sociological perspective is a bit like *seeing the strange in the familiar*. This does not mean that sociologists focus on the bizarre elements of society. Rather, looking at life sociologically requires giving up the familiar idea that human behavior is simply a matter of what people *decide* to do in favor of the initially strange notion that society shapes our thoughts and deeds.

For individualistic North Americans, learning to "see" how society affects us may take a bit of practice. For example, asked why you "chose" to enroll at your particular college, you might give one of these reasons:

"I wanted to stay close to home."

"I got a basketball scholarship."

"With a journalism degree from this university I can get a good job anywhere."

"My girlfriend goes to school here."

"I wasn't accepted by the school I *really* wanted to attend."

Such responses certainly seem true to the people expressing them. But do they tell the whole story?

Thinking sociologically about college attendance, we might realize that, in most of the world, college is

Whenever we come upon people whose habits differ from our own, we become more aware of social patterns. This is why travel is an excellent way to stimulate the sociological perspective. But even within the United States there is striking cultural diversity, which prompts us to become conscious of our social surroundings.

all but unavailable. Moreover, had we lived a century or two ago, going to college probably never would have been an option. But even here and now, a look around the classroom shows that social forces still have a great deal to do with college attendance. Typically, college students are relatively young—generally between eighteen and twenty-four. Why? Because in our society attending college is associated with this period of life. But more than age is involved, since less than half of all college-age men and women actually end up on campus.

Another factor is cost. Because higher education is so expensive, college students tend to come from families with above-average incomes. As Chapter 19 ("Education") explains, if you are lucky enough to belong to a family earning more than $75,000, you are three times as likely to go to college than if your family's annual earnings are below $20,000. And, as Figure 1–1 on page 5 shows, because both race and ethnicity are also linked to income, a greater share of white people (63 percent) "choose" to go to college than African

NOTE: Many comedians dropped Jewish-sounding names in favor of more WASPy names; a notable exception is Caryn Johnson who became Whoopi Goldberg.

Q: "For the most part we do not first see then define; we define and then see." U.S. social critic Walter Lippman

Q: C. Wright Mills said that using the sociological perspective is like "waking up in a stranger's house."

THEN AND NOW: The share of U.S. four-year college graduates among adults aged 25 and older, *1960:* 7.7%; *1996:* 23.6%.

DIVERSITY: Regarding Fig. 1–1, the higher a family's income, the more likely a daughter or son is to attend a private rather than a state college or university. Average tuition, room, and board at private schools topped $16,000 in 1997 versus about $4,000 for public institutions.

 ## SOCIAL DIVERSITY

What's in a Name?
How Social Forces Affect Personal Choices

On July 4th, 1918, twins were born to Abe and Becky Friedman in Sioux City, Iowa. They called the first to arrive Esther Pauline Friedman, and her sister, Pauline Esther Friedman. Today, the twins are known to almost everyone in the United States, but as Ann Landers and Abigail ("Dear Abby") Van Buren.

Like thousands of people in our society, Ann Landers and "Dear Abby" changed their names to advance their careers. But isn't choosing a new name simply a matter of personal preference? Consider the following list. All of these people changed their names to advance their careers in the entertainment field.

1. Thomas Mapother
2. Cherilyn Sarkisian
3. Cheryl Stoppelmoor
4. Robert Allen Zimmerman

5. Larry Zeigler
6. Nathan Birnbaum
7. Paul Rubenfeld
8. George Kyriakou Panayiotou
9. Annie Mae Bullock
10. Joan Molinsky
11. Malden Sekulovich
12. Jerome Silberman
13. Milton Supman
14. Karen Ziegler
15. Ramon Estevez
16. Henry John Deutschendorf, Jr.
17. Allen Stewart Konigsberg
18. Patsy McClenny
19. Jacob Cohen
20. William Claude Dukenfield
21. Lee Yuen Kam

22. Raquel Tejada
23. Frederick Austerlitz
24. Sophia Scicoloni

From a sociological point of view, what pattern do you see? Historically, people of various national backgrounds have adopted *English-sounding* names. Why? Because our society attaches high social prestige to an Anglo-Saxon background. Once again, we see personal choice guided by social forces.

1. Tom Cruise, 2. Cher, 3. Cheryl Ladd, 4. Bob Dylan, 5. Larry King, 6. George Burns, 7. Pee Wee Herman, 8. George Michael, 9. Tina Turner, 10. Joan Rivers, 11. Karl Malden, 12. Gene Wilder, 13. Soupy Sales, 14. Karen Black, 15. Martin Sheen, 16. John Denver, 17. Woody Allen, 18. Morgan Fairchild, 19. Rodney Dangerfield, 20. W. C. Fields, 21. Bruce Lee, 22. Raquel Welch, 23. Fred Astaire, 24. Sophia Loren

Americans (51 percent) or Hispanics[1] (54 percent) (U.S. National Center for Education Statistics, 1996).

So society affects what we do. It can even affect who we are, as the examples of name-changing in the box reveal.

INDIVIDUALITY IN SOCIAL CONTEXT

Perhaps the most compelling demonstration of how social forces affect human behavior comes from the study of suicide. What could be a more personal "choice" than deciding to take one's own life? But

Emile Durkheim (1858–1917), a pioneer of sociology writing a century ago, showed that social forces are at work even in an isolated act of self-destruction.

Durkheim began his research by examining suicide records in his native France. The statistics clearly showed that some categories of people were more likely than others to take their own lives. Specifically, Durkheim found that men, Protestants, wealthy people, and the unmarried had significantly higher suicide rates than women, Catholics and Jews, the poor, and married people. Durkheim reasoned that the differences had to do with *social integration*. That is, people with strong social ties had low suicide rates, and more individualistic people had high suicide rates.

In the male-dominated societies that Durkheim studied, men certainly had more freedom than women. But whatever the advantages of autonomy, it

---

[1]Hispanics or Latinos may be of any race; about 85 percent state their race as white. (See "A Word About Language" in the Preface.)

SOCIAL SURVEY: "Does everybody have the opportunity to obtain an education corresponding to their abilities and talents?" (GSS 1983–87, N=1,473; *Codebook*, 1996:99)
"Yes" 69.8%   "No" 27.9%   DK/NR 2.3%
THEN AND NOW: U.S. suicide rate, *1950*: 11.4 per 100,000 people; *1960*: 10.6; *1970*: 11.6; *1980*: 11.9; *1996: 11.6.*

DIVERSITY: Suicide rates rise with advancing age: 15–24-year-olds, 10.9 (1993); 65 and older, 22.8 (U.S. Bureau of the Census, 1997).
GLOBAL: Support for Durkheim's thesis comes from rising suicide rates (especially among the young) in Hong Kong, Singapore, and other Asian countries experiencing rising affluence.
Q: "The farther one travels, the less one knows." George Harrison

contributed to social isolation and a higher suicide rate. Likewise, individualistic Protestants were more prone to suicide than Catholics and Jews, whose rituals foster stronger social ties. The wealthy have much more freedom of action than the poor but, once again, at the cost of a higher suicide rate. Finally, Durkheim found that single people, with weaker social ties than married people, were also at greater risk of suicide.

A century later, statistical evidence still supports Durkheim's analysis. Figure 1–2 shows suicide rates for four categories of the U.S. population. In 1994, there were 12.9 recorded suicides for every 100,000 white people, almost twice the rate for African Americans (7.0). For both races, suicide is more common among men than among women. White men (21.3) are four times more likely than white women (4.9) to take their own lives. Among African Americans, the rate for men (12.4) is six times higher than for women (2.0). Following Durkheim's logic, the higher suicide rate among white people and men reflects their greater wealth and autonomy. Conversely, the lower rate among women and people of color follows from

DIVERSITY SNAPSHOT

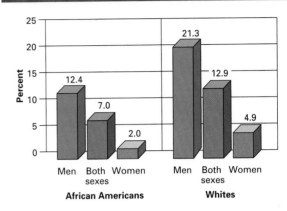

FIGURE 1–2 Rate of Death by Suicide, by Race and Sex, for the United States

Rates indicate the number of deaths by suicide for every 100,000 people in each category for 1994.

Source: U.S. National Center for Health Statistics (1996).

DIVERSITY SNAPSHOT

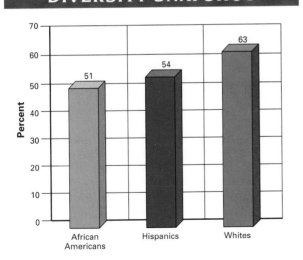

FIGURE 1–1 Share of 1995 High School Graduates Entering College the Following Fall

Source: U.S. National Center for Education Statistics (1996).

their tighter social ties and limited social choices. Just as in Durkheim's day, we can see social patterns in suicide—the most personal of actions.

THE IMPORTANCE OF GLOBAL PERSPECTIVE

December 10, 1994, Fez, Morocco. This medieval city—a web of narrow streets and alleyways, alive with the sounds of children at play, the silence of veiled women, and the steady gaze of men leading donkeys laden with goods—has changed little over the centuries. We stand in northwest Africa, only a few hundred miles from the more familiar rhythms of Europe; yet this place seems a thousand years away. Never have we had such an adventure! Never have we thought so much about home!

As new information technology draws even the farthest reaches of the earth closer to each other, many academic disciplines take a **global perspective,** *the*

Q: "To blandly subsume, say, Ethiopia, India, and Brazil under the one banner of Third Worldhood is as absurd and denigrating as the old assertion that all Chinese look alike." Trinidad-born novelist Shiva Naipaul

DISCUSS: Confronting the strange gives us a new sense of the familiar. Anthropologist Clifford Geertz once commented that nothing made him aware of home as much as being in the world's

most remote places. Have students had similar experiences?
NOTE: Good travel is hard work—note the common root of "travel" and "travail"; "tour," by contrast, refers to simply "going in a circle." For cross-cultural experiences to involve learning rather than simply fun, we need to work at it!
Q: "The world is a book and those who study just their own society read only a single page." Old saying

GLOBAL SOCIOLOGY

The Global Village:
A Social Snapshot of Our World

The earth is home to some 5.9 billion people who live in 191 nations. Imagine for a moment, though, that our planet's population is reduced to a single settlement of 1,000 people. A visit to this "global village" would reveal that more than half (575) the inhabitants are Asians, including 200 citizens of the People's Republic of China. Next, in terms of numbers, we would find 130 Africans, 125 Europeans, and about 100 Latin Americans. North Americans—including people from the United States, Canada, and Mexico—would account for just 65 villagers.

The village is a rich place, with a seemingly endless array of goods and

services for sale. Yet most of the inhabitants can do no more than dream about such treasures, since half of the village's total income is earned by just 150 individuals. In fact, most people do not get enough food. Every year, village workers produce more than enough to feed everyone, yet half the villagers—including most of the children—are poorly nourished, and many go to sleep hungry. The 200 worst-off residents don't even have safe drinking water or secure shelter. They are often unable to work, and many fall victim to life-threatening diseases.

Villagers boast of their community's many schools, including colleges and universities. About 75 inhabitants have

completed a college degree and a few even have doctorates, but half the people cannot read or write.

We in the United States stand among the most prosperous people of the "global village." But before we leap to take credit for our achievements, we should apply the sociological perspective. How much of what we attribute to our personal abilities is the product of our privileged position in the worldwide social system?

Source: United Nations data and calculations by the author.

study of the larger world and our society's place in it. What is the importance of a global perspective for sociology?

First, global awareness is a logical extension of the sociological perspective. Sociology's basic premise is that our place in a society profoundly affects our life experiences. It stands to reason, then, that the position of our society in the larger world system affects everyone in the United States. The box describes a "global village," to show the "social shape" of the world and the place of the United States in it.

Global Map 1–1 shows the relative economic development of the world's countries. The **high-income countries** are *industrialized nations in which most people enjoy material abundance*[2]. High-income countries include the United States and Canada, most

of Western Europe, Israel, Japan, and Australia. Taken together, these forty nations generate most of the world's goods and services and control most of the planet's wealth. On average, individuals in these countries live well, not because they are particularly bright or exceptionally hardworking, but because they had the good fortune to be born in an affluent part of the world.

The world's **middle-income countries** are *nations with limited industrialization and moderate personal income.* Individuals living in any of the roughly ninety nations at this level of economic development—which include the countries of the Middle East, Eastern Europe, and most of Latin America—are more likely to live in rural areas than cities, to walk or ride bicycles, scooters, or animals rather than drive cars, and to receive only a few years of schooling. Most middle-income countries also have marked social inequality so that while some people are extremely rich (the sheiks of oil-producing nations in the Middle East, for example), many more lack safe housing and adequate nutrition.

[2] This text uses this terminology rather than the traditional, but outdated, terms "First World," "Second World," and "Third World." Chapter 11 ("Global Stratification") provides a complete discussion of the issue.

THE MAP: About 15% of the world's people live in high-income countries, one-third live in middle-income nations, and just over half live in low-income countries. Per capita GNP for the world as a whole stands at roughly $4,500.

Q: "One can be an excellent physicist without ever stepping outside of one's society; I know this is not so for a sociologist." Peter Berger (1992)

NOTE: Some students may not know that the world is divided into twenty-four time zones. While the U.S. has four, the highly centralized People's Republic of China, although just as "wide," holds to one (everyone uses Beijing time).

THEN AND NOW: Percent of Japanese households with cars—*1961*, 2.8%; *1994*, 79.7% (Japanese Economic Planning Agency).

WINDOW ON THE WORLD

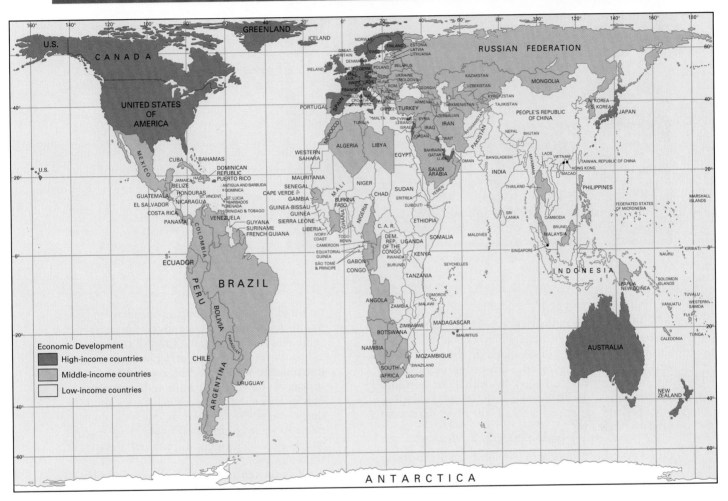

GLOBAL MAP 1–1 Economic Development in Global Perspective*

In high-income countries—the United States, Canada, most of the nations of Western Europe, Israel, Australia, and Japan—industrial technology provides people, on average, with material plenty. Middle-income countries—found throughout Latin America and including the nations of Eastern Europe—have limited industrial capacity. Their people have a standard of living about average for the world as a whole but far below that of most people in the United States. These nations also have a significant share of poor people who barely scrape by with meager housing and diet. In the low-income countries of the world, poverty is severe and extensive. Although small numbers of elites live very well in the poorest nations, most people struggle to survive on a small fraction of the income common in the United States.

*Note: Data for this map are provided by the World Bank and the United Nations. High-income countries have a per capita gross domestic product (GDP) of at least $10,000. Many are far richer than this, however; the figure for the United States exceeds $25,000. Middle-income countries have a per capita GDP ranging from $2,500 to $10,000. Low-income countries have a per capita GDP below $2,500. Figures used here reflect the new United Nations "purchasing power parities" system. Rather than directly converting income figures into U.S. dollars, this calculation estimates the local purchasing power of each domestic currency.

Sources: Prepared by the author using data from United Nations Development Programme (1995) and The World Bank (1995). Map projection from *Peters Atlas of the World* (1990).

GLOBAL: Evidence of ties linking the United States and the rest of the world: Many rock stars sell more records abroad than in the United States; conversely, salsa has replaced ketchup as this nation's favorite condiment.

THEN AND NOW: The number of telephone calls made from the United States to some other country: *1985,* 411 million; *1995,* 2.8 billion (almost a sevenfold increase; FCC data).

Q: "The world belongs to me because I understand it." French writer Honoré de Balzac

Q: "O wad some Power the giftie gie us; To see oursels as ithers see us! It wad frae monie a blunder free us; An' foolish notion." Scottish poet Robert Burns

One important reason to gain a global understanding is that, living in a high-income society, we scarcely can appreciate the suffering that goes on in much of the world. The life of this Rwandan boy has been shredded by civil war. But even in more peaceful nations of Africa, children have less than a fifty-fifty chance to grow to adulthood.

Finally, about half of the world's people live in the sixty **low-income countries**, *nations with little industrialization and severe poverty.* As Global Map 1–1 shows, most of the poorest societies in the world are in Africa and Asia. Here, again, a few people are rich; but the majority struggle to get by with poor housing, unsafe water, too little food, little or no sanitation, and, perhaps most seriously of all, little chance to improve their lives.

Chapter 11 ("Global Stratification") discusses the causes and consequences of global wealth and poverty in detail. But every chapter highlights life beyond our own borders for three important reasons:

1. **Societies the world over are increasingly interconnected.** Separated from Europe and Asia by vast oceans, we in the United States have historically done little more than take passing note of our neighbors to the north (Canada) and south (Mexico and other Latin American nations). Recently, however, the United States and the rest of the world have become linked as never before. Electronic technology now transmits pictures, sounds, and written documents around the globe in seconds.

   One consequence of this new technology, as later chapters explain, is that people all over the world now share many tastes in music, clothing, and food. On the one hand, the United States, with its economic clout, casts a global shadow on other societies whose people eagerly gobble up our hamburgers, dance to our music, and, more and more, speak the English language.

   But even as we project our way of life onto much of the world, the larger world has an impact on us. Almost 1 million documented immigrants entered the United States annually during the 1990s, and we are quick to adopt many of their fashions and foods as our own, which greatly enhances the cultural diversity of this country.

   Commerce across national boundaries has also created a global economy. Corporations manufacture and market goods worldwide, just as global financial markets linked by satellite communication operate around the clock. Stock traders in New York follow the financial markets in Tokyo and Hong Kong, even as wheat farmers in Kansas watch the price of grain in the former Soviet republic of Georgia. With eight out of ten new U.S. jobs involving international trade, global understanding has never been more important.

2. **Many human problems that we face in the United States are far more serious elsewhere.** Poverty is a serious problem in the United States, but, as Chapter 11 ("Global Stratification") explains, poverty is both more widespread and more severe in Latin America, Africa, and Asia. Similarly, women have a lower

social standing than men in the United States, but inequality is much greater in poor countries of the world.

Then, too, some of our toughest problems are global in scope. As we discuss in Chapter 22 ("Environment and Society"), the world is a single ecosystem in which the action (or inaction) of one nation has implications for all others.

3. **Thinking globally is a good way to learn more about ourselves.** We cannot walk the streets of a distant city without becoming keenly aware of what it means to live in the United States. Making global comparisons also leads to unexpected lessons. For instance, in Chapter 11 ("Global Stratification") we visit a squatter settlement in Madras, India. There, despite a desperate lack of basic material comforts, people thrive in the love and support of family members. Why, then, does poverty in the United States produce isolation and anger? Are material goods—so crucial to our definition of a "rich" life—the best way to gauge human well-being?

In sum, in an increasingly interconnected world, we can understand ourselves only to the extent that we comprehend others (Macionis, 1993).

THE SOCIOLOGICAL PERSPECTIVE IN EVERYDAY LIFE

People who are different from us—whether we encounter them in an art museum in Rome, a little village in the Andes, or at a community meeting in our own hometown—remind us of the power of social forces to shape our lives. Two other kinds of everyday situations also prompt us to see our surroundings sociologically, even before we take a first course in sociology.

SOCIOLOGY AND SOCIAL MARGINALITY

From time to time, we are all social "outsiders." For some categories of people, however, being an outsider—not part of the dominant group—is part of daily living. The more acute people's social marginality, the more aware they are of their surroundings and the better able they are to understand the sociological perspective.

No African American, for example, lives for long in the United States without learning how much race affects personal experience. But white people, as the dominant majority, think about race only occasionally and think it affects only people of color, not themselves. The same is true of women, gay people, people with disabilities, and the very old: People relegated to the outskirts of social life typically become aware of social patterns others take for granted. Therefore, to develop a sociological perspective we must step back from our familiar routines and look upon our lives with a new awareness and curiosity.

SOCIOLOGY AND SOCIAL CRISIS

Because social awareness stems from marginality, periods of change or social crisis—when everyone feels a little off balance—allow us to look beyond our personal problems and see the bigger sociological picture. U.S. sociologist C. Wright Mills (1959) illustrated this concept with the Great Depression of the 1930s. As the unemployment rate soared to 25 percent, people out of work could not help but see general social forces at work in their particular lives. Instead of saying, "Something is wrong with me; I can't find a job," they could take a more sociological approach and realize, "The economy has collapsed; there are no jobs to be found!"

Not only can social change foster sociological thinking, but the opposite is true: Sociological thinking often fosters social change. The more we learn about how "the system" operates, the more we may wish to change it in some way. Becoming aware of the power of gender, for example, many women and men have actively tried to reduce the traditional differences that divide men and women.

In short, an introduction to sociology is an invitation to learn a new way of looking at familiar patterns of social life. At this point, we might well consider whether this invitation is worth accepting. In other words, what are the benefits of learning to use the sociological perspective?

BENEFITS OF THE SOCIOLOGICAL PERSPECTIVE

Applying the sociological perspective to our daily lives benefits us in four ways:

1. **The sociological perspective helps us assess the truth of commonly held assumptions.** Thinking sociologically, we may realize that some ideas we take for granted are not true. One good example, noted earlier, is the notion that

Q: Recognizing the power of society to confer or withhold great-ness, Theodore Roosevelt commented, "A man has to take advan-tage of his opportunities, but the opportunities have to come. If there is not the war, you don't get the great general. If there is not the great occasion, you do not get the great statesman. If Lincoln had lived in times of peace, no one would know his name now."

Q: "Knowledge is the antidote of fear." Ralph Waldo Emerson
NOTE: The number of bachelor's degrees in sociology peaked at 35,996 in 1973; it dropped to 14,939 in 1989 and reached 22,368 in 1994.
NOTE: Lewis Coser (1977) notes that Comte first called his new discipline "social physics." Thinking the term stolen by Adolphe Quetelet, Comte renamed the fledgling field "sociology."

we are autonomous individuals who are person-ally responsible for our lives. If we believe the world is filled with people who decide their own fate, we may be quick to praise successful people as superior and consider others with more mod-est achievements personally deficient. A socio-logical approach, by contrast, encourages us to ask whether such beliefs are true, and, to the extent that they are not, why they are so widely held.

2. **The sociological perspective prompts us to assess both the opportunities and the con-straints that characterize our lives.** Sociologi-cal thinking leads us to see that, for better or worse, our society operates in a particular way. Moreover, in the game of life, we may decide how to play our cards, but it is society that deals us the hand. The more we understand the game, then, the better players we will be. Sociology helps us understand what we are likely and unlikely to accomplish for ourselves and how we can pursue our goals more effectively.

3. **The sociological perspective empowers us to participate actively in our society.** If we do not understand how society operates, we are likely to accept the status quo. But the greater our understanding, the more we can take an active hand in shaping social life. The discipline of sociology does not advocate any particular political orientation, and sociologists themselves weigh in at many points across the political spectrum. But evaluating any aspect of social life—whatever your eventual goal—means iden-tifying the social forces at work and assessing their consequences.

   Some thirty years ago, C. Wright Mills claimed that sociology helps people to see their everyday lives in terms of social forces. As the box explains, this "sociological imagination" can empower us to become more active citizens.

4. **The sociological perspective helps us recog-nize human variety and confront the chal-lenges of living in a diverse world.** North Americans represent a scant 5 percent of the world's population, and, as the remaining chap-ters of this book explain, much of the other 95 percent live lives that differ dramatically from ours. Still, like people everywhere, we tend to consider our way of life as "right" and "natural," dismissing other lifestyles. But the sociological perspective encourages us to think critically

about the relative strengths and weaknesses of all ways of life—including our own.

APPLIED SOCIOLOGY

The benefits of sociology go well beyond intellectual growth. Sociologists have played important roles in shaping public policy and law in a host of areas, including school desegregation and busing, pornogra-phy laws, and social welfare programs. The work that family researcher Lenore Weitzman alone (1985) did on the financial hardships facing women after divorce "had a real impact on public policy and resulted in the passage of fourteen new laws in California" (1996:538).

Sociology is also an important source of jobs. According to the American Sociological Association, sociology is sound training for literally hundreds of jobs in various fields, including advertising, banking, criminal justice, education, government, health care, public relations, and research (Billson & Huber, 1993).

Most men and women who continue beyond the bachelor's level to earn advanced degrees in sociology go on to careers in teaching and research. But an increasing number of professional sociologists work in all sorts of applied fields. Clinical sociologists, for example, work with troubled clients much as clinical psychologists do. A basic difference, however, is that, while psychologists focus on the individual, sociolo-gists look at the person's web of social relationships. Another type of applied sociology is evaluation research. In today's cost-conscious climate, govern-ment and corporate administrators must evaluate the effectiveness of virtually every kind of program and policy. Sociologists—especially those with advanced research skills—are in high demand for this kind of work.

THE ORIGINS OF SOCIOLOGY

Like the "choices" made by individuals, major histor-ical events rarely "just happen." They are the products of powerful and complex social forces and are only somewhat predictable. So it was with the emergence of sociology itself. Having described the discipline's distinctive perspective and surveyed some of its bene-fits, we now ask how and why sociology emerged in the first place.

Although we humans have mused about society since the beginning of our history, sociology is of

SOCIOLOGY OF EVERYDAY LIFE

The Sociological Imagination:
Turning Personal Problems Into Public Issues

The power of sociology can be summed up in one sentence: A sociological imagination can transform individual lives as it changes society. As C. Wright Mills saw it, sociology is not some dry academic discipline detached from life. Rather, sociology shows us how to escape from the "traps" of our lives such as poverty and powerlessness. By thinking sociologically, Mills explained, we see that society—not simply people's personal failings—is responsible for many of our problems. And seeing others grapple with the same problems that we do enables us to join together and turn personal *problems* into public *issues*.

Here is a brief excerpt* from Mills's work, *The Sociological Imagination*, in which he explains the need for people to develop the ability to understand their own lives in terms of larger social forces:

When a society becomes industrialized, a peasant becomes a worker; a feudal lord is liquidated or becomes a businessman. When classes rise or fall, a man is employed or unemployed; when the rate of investment goes up or down, a man takes new heart or goes broke. When wars happen, an insurance salesman becomes a rocket launcher; a store clerk, a radar man; a wife lives alone; a child grows up without a father. Neither the life of an individual nor the history of a society can be understood without understanding both.

Yet men do not usually define the troubles they endure in terms of historical change. . . . The well-being they enjoy, they do not usually impute to the big ups and downs of the society in which they live. Seldom aware of the intricate connection between the patterns of their own lives and the course of world history, ordinary men do not usually know what this connection means for the kind of men they are becoming and for the kinds of history-making in which they might take part. They do not possess the quality of mind essential to grasp the interplay of men and society, of biography and history, of self and world. . . .

What they need . . . is a quality of mind that will help them to [see] . . . what is going on in the world and . . . what may be happening within themselves. It is this quality . . . that . . . may be called the sociological imagination.

*In this excerpt, C. Wright Mills uses male pronouns to apply to all people. It is interesting—even ironic—that an outspoken critic of society such as Mills reflected the conventional writing practices of his time as far as gender was concerned.

Source: Mills (1959):3–5.

relatively recent origin. It is among the youngest academic disciplines—far newer than history, physics, or economics, for example. Only in 1838 did the French social thinker Auguste Comte (1798–1857) coin the term *sociology* to describe a new way of looking at the world.

SCIENCE AND SOCIOLOGY

Virtually all the brilliant thinkers of the ancient world pondered the nature of society, including the Chinese philosopher K'ung Fu-tzu or Confucius (551–479 B.C.E.) and the Greek philosophers Plato (c. 427–347 B.C.E.) and Aristotle (384–322 B.C.E.).[3] Later, the Roman emperor Marcus Aurelius (121–180), the medieval thinkers St. Thomas Aquinas (c. 1225–1274) and Christine de Pizan (c. 1363–1431), and the great English playwright William Shakespeare (1564–1616) took up the question. Yet, as Emile Durkheim pointed

[3]Throughout this text, the abbreviation B.C.E. designates "before the common era." We use this terminology in place of the traditional B.C. ("before Christ") in recognition of the religious plurality of our society. Similarly, in place of the traditional A.D. (*anno Domini*, or "in the year of our Lord"), we employ the abbreviation C.E. ("common era").

Q: "Savoir pour prévoir et prévoir pour pouvoir." Auguste Comte (Literally, "Know to foresee and foresee to be able to," or translated more freely, "By knowing the laws of phenomena we can make predictions about them, and change the world to our advantage.")
NOTE: Comte considered sociology the "Queen of the Sciences," which inspired some of his followers to acts of arrogance. A century ago, for example, sociologists at Brown University suggested that their entire university be reorganized under the sociology department.
GLOBAL: Brazil, a country that has long embraced ambitious social planning (consider the building of the new capital, Brasilia, deep in the interior), was guided by Comte's ideas. In fact, the Brazilians adopted for their national flag Comte's slogan, "Order and Progress."

This medieval drawing conveys the mix of apprehension and excitement with which early scientists began to question traditional understandings of the universe. Pioneering sociologists, too, challenged many ideas that people had long taken for granted, explaining that society is neither fixed by God's will nor by human nature. On the contrary, Comte and other sociological pioneers claimed, society is a system that we can study scientifically and, based on what we learn, act deliberately to improve.

out almost a century ago, none of these social thinkers approached society with a sociological point of view.

> Looking back in history . . . we find that no philosophers ever viewed matters [with a sociological perspective] until quite recently. . . . It seemed to them sufficient to ascertain what the human will should strive for and what it should avoid in established societies. . . . Their aim was not to offer us as valid a description of nature as possible, but to present us with the idea of a perfect society, a model to be imitated. (1972:57; orig. 1918)

What, then, sets sociology apart from earlier social thought? Early philosophers and theologians imagined the ideal society. None tried to analyze society as it really was. Sociology was born when pioneers such as Auguste Comte and Emile Durkheim reversed these priorities. Although they were certainly concerned with improving human society, their primary goal was to understand how society actually operates.

The key to understanding society, according to Comte, was to look at it scientifically. This may seem obvious to us, but earlier eras had different frameworks for understanding the world (Comte, 1975; orig. 1851–54). From the beginning of human history through Europe's medieval period (until roughly 1350 C.E.), which Comte termed the *theological stage*, thinking was guided by religion. People saw society as an expression of God's will—at least insofar as humans were capable of fulfilling a divine plan.

With the Renaissance, the theological approach to society gradually gave way to what Comte called the *metaphysical stage*. People came to understand society as a natural, rather than supernatural, phenomenon. The English philosopher Thomas Hobbes (1588–1679), for example, suggested that society reflected not the perfection of God as much as the failings of selfish human nature.

What Comte called the *scientific stage* began with the work of early scientists such as the Polish astronomer Copernicus (1473–1543), the Italian astronomer and physicist Galileo[4] (1564–1642), and the English physicist and mathematician Isaac Newton (1642–1727). Comte's contribution came in applying the scientific approach—first used to study the physical world—to the study of society.

Comte thus favored **positivism,** *an approach to understanding the world based on science.* As a positivist,

---

[4]Comte's three stages are illustrated by the way people through history viewed the planets. To the ancient Greeks and Romans, the planets were gods. Renaissance thinkers believed they were astral influences (giving rise to astrology). But by Galileo's time, people understood the planets as natural objects behaving in orderly ways.

Q: "O, when degree is shak'd,
   Which is the ladder of all high designs,
   The enterprise is sick! . . .
   Take but degree away, untune that string,
   And hark what discord follows!"
Shakespeare (*Troilus and Cressida*) reflecting on the erosion of the

Comte believed that society operates according to certain laws, just as the physical world operates according to gravity and other laws of nature.

Sociology emerged as an academic discipline in the United States at the beginning of the twentieth century when early U.S. sociologists such as Lester Ward (1841–1913) advanced Comte's vision of a scientific sociology. Even today, most sociologists agree that science is a crucial part of sociology. But, as Chapter 2 ("Sociological Investigation") explains, we now realize that human behavior is more complex than the movement of planets or even the actions of other living things. Humans are creatures of imagination and spontaneity, so our behavior can never be fully explained by any rigid "laws of society."

SOCIAL CHANGE AND SOCIOLOGY

Striking transformations in eighteenth- and nineteenth-century Europe led to the rapid development of the new science of sociology. As the social ground trembled under their feet, people understandably focused their attention on society.

First came scientific discoveries that produced a factory-based industrial economy. Second, factories drew millions of people from the countryside, causing an explosive growth of cities. Third, people in these burgeoning industrial cities developed new ideas about democracy and political rights. We will briefly describe each of these three changes.

A New Industrial Economy

During the European Middle Ages (about 600 to 1350 C.E.), people tilled fields near their homes or engaged in small-scale *manufacturing* (a word derived from Latin words meaning "to make by hand"). But by the end of the eighteenth century, inventors applied new sources of energy—first water power and then steam power—to the operation of large machines, which gave birth to factories. Now, instead of laboring at home, workers became part of a large and anonymous industrial work force, toiling for strangers who owned the factories. This change in the system of production separated families and weakened traditions that had guided members of small communities for centuries.

The Growth of Cities

Across Europe, factories became magnets attracting people in need of work. Along with this "pull" came the "push" of the "enclosure movement." Landowners fenced off more and more land, turning farms into grazing pasture for sheep—the source of wool for textile mills. Deprived of their land, countless tenant farmers left the countryside in search of work in the new factories.

Sometimes whole villages were abandoned, while nearby factory towns swelled into big cities. Such urban growth dramatically changed people's lives. Cities churned with strangers, in numbers that overwhelmed available housing. Poverty, disease, pollution, crime, and homelessness were the order of the day. Such widespread social problems further stimulated development of the sociological perspective.

Political Change

During the Middle Ages, when people viewed society as an expression of God's will, royalty claimed to rule by "divine right," and each person up and down the social hierarchy played a part in the holy plan. This theological view of society is captured in lines from the old Anglican hymn "All Things Bright and Beautiful":

> The rich man in his castle,
> The poor man at his gate,
> God made them high and lowly
> And ordered their estate.

But economic development and the rapid growth of cities brought new political ideas. By about 1600, every kind of tradition came under attack. In the writings of Thomas Hobbes, John Locke (1632–1704), and Adam Smith (1723–1790), we see a major shift in focus. People are no longer morally obligated to remain loyal to their rulers. Rather, they are free to pursue individual self-interest. The key phrases in the new political climate were *individual liberty* and *individual rights*. Echoing the thoughts of Locke, our own Declaration of Independence asserts that every individual has "certain unalienable rights," including "life, liberty, and the pursuit of happiness."

The political revolution in France that began in 1789 symbolized the Western world's break with political and social traditions. As the French social analyst Alexis de Tocqueville (1805–1859) declared after the French Revolution, the change in society amounted to "nothing short of the regeneration of the whole human race" (1955:13; orig. 1856). And, on this wave of change, Auguste Comte and other pioneers developed the new discipline of sociology. Sociology flowered in precisely those societies—France, Germany, and England—where change was greatest.

NOTE: The early Industrial Revolution saw the first U.S. courses in sociology. Williams College offered a course in social ethics in 1865; Johns Hopkins taught social science in its opening year, 1876, and that same year William Graham Sumner taught his first sociology course at Yale; Cornell introduced a social science course in 1884; the University of Chicago founded the first formal sociology department in 1892.

NOTE: Harriet Martineau's lifelong activism was guided by a Comtean view of the world as comprehensible and changeable. Her achievements are all the more impressive in light of her almost total deafness from the age of about twelve.

The birth of sociology was prompted by rapid social change. The discipline developed in those regions of Europe where the Industrial Revolution most disrupted traditional ways of life, drawing people from isolated villages to rapidly growing industrial cities.

Sociologists reacted differently to the new social order then, just as they respond differently to changes in society today. Some, including Auguste Comte, feared that people would feel uprooted and overwhelmed by change. Comte took a conservative turn, seeking to shore up the family and traditional morality.

But the German social critic Karl Marx (1818–1883), whose ideas are presented in Chapter 4 ("Society"), took a different view. Marx worried little about the loss of tradition, which he detested. What struck him was the way industrial technology concentrated wealth in the hands of a few, while the masses of people remained hungry and miserable.

Comte and Marx saw the modern world in radically different ways, yet they both believed that society rests on more than individual choice. The sociological perspective animates the work of each, revealing that people's individual lives reflect the broader society in which they live. This lesson, of course, remains as true today as a century ago.

MARGINAL VOICES

Auguste Comte and Karl Marx stand among the giants of sociology. But, especially in recent years, sociologists have come to recognize the important contribution that others—pushed to the margins because they were women living in a male-dominated society—have made to the discipline.

Harriet Martineau (1802–1876), born to a wealthy English family, first made her mark in 1853 by translating the writings of Auguste Comte from French into English. She later became a scholar in her own right, revealing the evils of slavery and arguing for laws to protect factory workers and to advance the standing of women.

In the United States, Jane Addams (1860–1935) was an early sociological pioneer. Trained as a social worker, Addams spoke out on behalf of a million immigrants who were entering this nation each year. In 1889, she founded Hull House, a settlement house in Chicago that provided assistance to immigrant families. She also gathered sociologists and politicians to discuss the urban social problems of the day. For her work on behalf of immigrants, Addams received the Nobel Peace Prize shortly before her death in 1931.

Widespread belief in the social inferiority of women kept Martineau and Addams at the margins of sociology. Many "established" sociologists simply ignored their writings. Looking back with a sociological eye, we can see how the forces of society were at work shaping even the history of sociology itself.

NOTE: The word "theory" is derived from the Greek *theoria*, meaning "a viewing." The Latin root of the word "structure" (*struct*) means "a piling up of."
Q: "Theories should be as simple as possible, but not more so." Albert Einstein
NOTE: Kingsley Davis (1959) pointed out that, since any theoretical approach involves assessing part-whole relationships, every sociologist is a functionalist to some degree.
Q: "[Functional] theory aims at the explanation of anthropological facts at all levels of development by their function, by the part which they play within the integral system of culture, by the manner in which they are related to each other within the system . . ." Anthropologist Bronislaw Malinowski

We can use the sociological perspective to look at sociology itself. All of the most widely recognized pioneers of the discipline were men. This is because, in the nineteenth century, it was all but unheard of for women to be college professors, and few women took a central role in public life. But women, such as Harriet Martineau in England and Jane Addams in the United States, made contributions to sociology that we now recognize as important and lasting.

SOCIOLOGICAL THEORY

Weaving observations into understanding brings us to another dimension of sociology: theory. A **theory** is *a statement of how and why specific facts are related.* Recall that Emile Durkheim observed that some categories of people (men, Protestants, the wealthy, and the unmarried) have higher suicide rates than others (women, Catholics and Jews, the poor, and the married). He explained these observations by developing a theory: A high risk of suicide results from a low level of social integration.

Of course, as Durkheim pondered his observations on suicide, he considered any number of possible theories. But merely linking facts together into a theory does not guarantee that the theory is correct. To evaluate a theory, as the next chapter explains, sociologists use various methods of scientific research to gather evidence. Hard data—facts—allow sociologists to confirm some theories while rejecting or modifying others. As a scientist, Durkheim was not content merely to identify a plausible cause of suicide; he meticulously collected data to determine precisely which categories of people committed suicide with the highest frequency. Then, poring over his data, Durkheim settled on a theory that best squared with all the available evidence. National Map 1–1, on page 16, which displays the recent suicide rate for each of the fifty states, gives you a chance to do some scientific theorizing of your own.

In investigating human society, sociologists face two basic questions: What issues should we study? How should we connect the facts to form theories about society? In answering these questions, sociologists are guided by one or more theoretical "roadmaps" or paradigms (Kuhn, 1970). A **theoretical paradigm** provides *a basic image of society that guides thinking and research.*

We suggested earlier that two of sociology's founders—Auguste Comte and Karl Marx—made sense of the emerging modern society in different ways. Such differences persist today as some sociologists focus on how societies stay the same, while others focus on patterns of change. Similarly, some look to what joins people together, while others investigate how society divides people according to gender, race, ethnicity, or social class. Some sociologists seek to understand the operation of society as it is, while others work towards what they consider desirable social change.

In short, sociologists often disagree about what the most interesting questions are, and even when they agree on the questions, they may disagree in their answers. Nonetheless, sociology is far from chaotic because three major theoretical paradigms guide sociologists' work.

THE STRUCTURAL-FUNCTIONAL PARADIGM

The **structural-functional paradigm** is *a framework for building theory that sees society as a complex system whose parts work together to promote solidarity and stability.* As its name suggests, this paradigm is based, first, on the

Q: ". . . [I]t has historically been the case with white people, in their regard for black people, that even though we might be *with* them, we weren't considered *of* them." Malcolm X

Q: "My life had its significance and its only deep significance because it was part of a problem; but the problem was, I continue to think, the central problem of the greatest of the world's democracies and so the problem of the future world." W. E. B. Du Bois

Q: "The Negro is a sort of seventh son . . . gifted with second sight . . . the sense of always looking at oneself through the eyes of others . . ." W. E. B. Du Bois

NOTE: Theoretical paradigms sometimes overlap. See, for example, Lewis Coser's (1956) analysis of the functions of social conflict.

CRITICAL THINKING

Understanding the Issue of Race

A key contribution to understanding race in the United States was made by one of sociology's pioneers, William Edward Burghardt Du Bois (1868–1963). Born to a poor Massachusetts family, Du Bois showed extraordinary aptitude as a student. After graduating from high school, he went to college, one of only a handful of the young people of his small town (and the only person of African descent) to do so. After graduating from Fisk University in Nashville, Tennessee, Du Bois realized a childhood ambition and enrolled at Harvard, where he ended up earning the first doctorate awarded by Harvard to a person of color.

Like Karl Marx and Jane Addams before him, Du Bois argued that sociologists should work to solve contemporary problems. He therefore spoke out against racial separation and served as a founding member of the National Association for the Advancement of Colored People (NAACP). In addition, he helped his colleagues (and people everywhere) see the deep and bitter racial divisions in the United States. Unlike white people, who can simply be "Americans," Du Bois pointed out, African Americans have a "double consciousness," reflecting their status as Americans who are never able to escape identification based on color.

In his sociological classic, *The Philadelphia Negro: A Social Study* (1899),

Du Bois explored Philadelphia's African American community, highlighting both the strengths and weaknesses of people wrestling with overwhelming social problems. He challenged the widespread belief in black inferiority, attributing the problems of African Americans to white prejudice. But his criticism extended also to successful people of color, whom he scolded for being so eager to win white acceptance that they abandoned all ties with the black community, which needed their help.

Early in his career, Du Bois was optimistic about overcoming racial divisions. By the end of his life, however, he had grown bitter, believing that little had changed. At the age of ninety-three, Du Bois left the United States for Ghana, where he died two years later. The problems of race, of course, remain with us to this day.

Sources: Based, in part, on Baltzell (1967) and Du Bois (1967; orig. 1899).

strive to protect their privileges, while the disadvantaged try to gain more resources for themselves.

A conflict analysis of our educational system might highlight how schooling perpetuates inequality by reproducing the class structure in every new generation. For instance, secondary schools routinely channel incoming students into either college-preparatory or vocational-training programs. From a structural-functional point of view, such "tracking" benefits all of society because students receive training that is appropriate to their academic abilities. But a conflict analysis counters that "tracking" often has less to do with talent than with a student's social background, so that well-to-do children are placed in higher tracks and poor children end up in the lower tracks.

In this way, young people from privileged families gain the best schooling, and, when they leave college, they pursue prestigious, high-income careers. The children of poor families, on the other hand, are not prepared for college, so, like their parents before them, they typically enter low-paying jobs. In both cases, the social standing of one generation is passed on to another, with schools justifying the practice in terms of individual merit (Bowles & Gintis, 1976; Oakes, 1982, 1985).

Social conflict in the United States extends well beyond schools. Later chapters of this book explain, in fact, how inequality based on class, gender, and race is rooted in the organization of society itself.

Many sociologists who use the social-conflict paradigm attempt not just to understand society but to reduce social inequality. This was the goal of W. E. B. Du Bois and also Karl Marx, who has had a singularly important influence on the development of

Q: "Serious differences among social scientists occur not between those who would observe without thinking and those who would think without observing; the differences have rather to do with what kinds of thinking, what kinds of observing, and what kinds of links, if any, there are between the two." C. Wright Mills

NOTE: Herbert Blumer first used the term "symbolic interactionism" in 1937.

NOTE: An interesting illustration of "the human process of attaching meaning to our surroundings": The first act of Adam and Eve in Genesis is to name the elements around them.

Q: "Situations that are defined as real are real in their consequences." W. I. Thomas

the social-conflict paradigm. Marx had little patience with people who tried merely to understand how society works. In a well-known declaration, inscribed on his monument in London's Highgate Cemetery, Marx asserted: "The philosophers have only interpreted the world, in various ways; the point, however, is to change it."

Critical evaluation. The social-conflict paradigm has developed a large following in recent decades but, like other approaches, has come in for its share of criticism. Because this paradigm highlights inequality and division, it largely ignores how shared values and interdependence can generate unity among members of a society. In addition, say critics, to the extent that the social-conflict approach pursues political goals, it cannot claim scientific objectivity. But as Chapter 2 ("Sociological Investigation") explains in detail, conflict theorists do not think science can ever be "objective." They contend that the social-conflict paradigm—and *all* theoretical approaches—have political consequences, albeit different ones.

One final criticism that applies equally to both the structural-functional and social-conflict paradigms is that they envision society in very broad terms, describing our lives in terms of "family," "social class," "race," and so on. A third theoretical paradigm presents society less in terms of abstract generalizations and more as everyday experiences.

THE SYMBOLIC-INTERACTION PARADIGM

Both the structural-functional and social-conflict paradigms share a **macro-level orientation,** meaning *a focus on broad social structures that shape society as a whole.* Macro-level sociology takes in the big picture, rather like observing a city from high above in a helicopter, seeing how highways carry traffic from place to place and noting the striking contrasts between rich and poor neighborhoods. The symbolic-interaction paradigm provides a **micro-level orientation,** meaning *a focus on social interaction in specific situations.* Exploring urban life this way takes place at street level, perhaps observing how boys and girls interact on a school playground or how pedestrians respond to homeless people. The **symbolic-interaction paradigm,** then, is *a framework for building theory that sees society as the product of the everyday interactions of individuals.*

But how does "society" result from the everyday experiences of tens of millions of people? One answer, explained in Chapter 6 ("Social Interaction in Everyday Life"), is that "society" amounts to the shared

The painting Dinner is Served *(1995), by Paul Marcus, presents the essential wisdom of social-conflict theory: Society operates in a way that conveys wealth, power, and privileges to some at the expense of others. Looking closely at the painting, what categories of people does the artist suggest are disadvantaged?*

reality that people construct as they interact with one another. That is, human beings are creatures who live in a world of symbols, attaching *meaning* to virtually everything. "Reality," therefore, is simply what results as we define our surroundings, our own identities, and our obligations toward others.

Of course, any process of definition is subjective and may vary from person to person. For example, one person may define a homeless man as "just a bum looking for a handout" and ignore him, but another might define him as "a fellow human being in need" and offer help. In the same way, one individual may feel a sense of security passing by a police officer walking the beat, while another is seized by nervous anxiety. Sociologists who take a symbolic-interaction approach, therefore, view society as a complex, ever-changing mosaic of subjective meanings.

NOTE: Key thinkers in each paradigm: *functional*, Comte, Durkheim, and Spencer; *conflict*, Marx and Weber; *interactional*, Weber, G. H. Mead, Blumer, Garfinkel. Note that all sociological approaches challenge the utilitarian approach evident in the 18th-century thought of Thomas Hobbes and others (and which is now staging something of a comeback in the form of "rational-choice theory").

NOTE: The idea that sports "build character" was widely expressed at the founding of the Young Men's Christian Association (YMCA) in 1844.
DIVERSITY: The National Collegiate Athletic Association (NCAA) reports that African Americans—5% of all college students—comprise 64% of collegiate basketball players and 46% of collegiate football players.

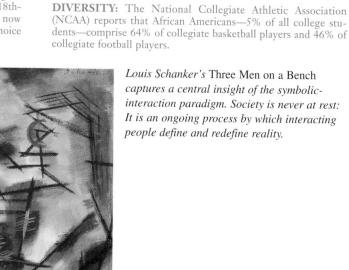

Louis Schanker's Three Men on a Bench *captures a central insight of the symbolic-interaction paradigm. Society is never at rest: It is an ongoing process by which interacting people define and redefine reality.*

The symbolic-interaction paradigm rests, in part, on the thinking of Max Weber (1864–1920), a German sociologist who emphasized the need to understand any social setting from the point of view of the people in it. Chapter 4 ("Society") discusses Weber's ideas in detail.

Since Weber's time, sociologists have developed the basic symbolic-interaction paradigm in a number of ways. Chapter 5 ("Socialization") examines the ideas of U.S. sociologist George Herbert Mead (1863–1931). Mead explored how we build our personalities over time from social experience. Chapter 6 ("Social Interaction in Everyday Life") presents the work of Erving Goffman (1922–1982), whose *dramaturgical analysis* explains how we resemble actors on a stage as we play out our various roles before others. Other contemporary sociologists, including George Homans and Peter Blau, have developed *social-exchange analysis*. In their view, social interaction is a negotiation guided by what individuals stand to gain and lose from others (cf. Molm, 1997). In the ritual of courtship, for example, people typically seek mates who offer at least as much—in terms of physical attractiveness, intelligence, and social background—as they provide in return.

Critical evaluation. The social-interaction paradigm helps correct a bias inherent in all macro-level approaches to understanding society. Without denying the usefulness of abstract social structures such as "the family" and "social class," this approach reminds us that society basically amounts to *people interacting*. Put another way, this micro-approach helps convey how individuals actually experience society.

However, by focusing on day-to-day interactions, the symbolic-interaction paradigm tends to ignore larger social structures. Similarly, by emphasizing what is unique in each social scene, this approach risks overlooking the widespread effects of culture, as well as factors such as class, gender, and race.

Table 1–1 summarizes the important characteristics of the structural-functional paradigm, the social-conflict paradigm, and the symbolic-interaction paradigm. As you read the chapters in this book, keep in mind that each paradigm is helpful in answering particular kinds of questions. By and large, however, the fullest understanding of society comes from linking the sociological perspective to all three, as in the following analysis of sports in the United States.

SPORTS: THREE THEORETICAL PARADIGMS IN ACTION

People in the United States love sports. Soccer moms drive their eight-year-olds to practice, and teens play

DIVERSITY: The summer Olympics features sports (track and field) that are accessible to people of all social backgrounds. The winter Olympics focus on expensive sports (skiing, skating, luge) that are socially exclusive. This fact explains the greater share of white and well-to-do athletes in the winter games.
THEN AND NOW: African Americans in the NBA: *1954*, 5%; *1997*, 79%; Major League Baseball: *1954*, 7%; *1997*, 17%; NFL:

1954, 12%; *1997*, 66%.
DIVERSITY: In 1997, all owners of NBA and NFL teams were white people: 98% men, 2% women. In Major League Baseball, one owner was a Japanese citizen; all others were white; 3% of owners were women.
DIVERSITY: Latinos in Major League Baseball: *1990*, 13%; *1997*, 24%. Latinos are less than 1% of all NBA and NFL players.

TABLE 1–1 The Three Major Theoretical Paradigms: A Summary

Theoretical Paradigm	Orientation	Image of Society	Core Questions
Structural-functional	Macro-level	A system of interrelated parts that is relatively stable because of widespread agreement on what is morally desirable; each part has a particular function in society as a whole.	How is society integrated? What are the major parts of society? How are these parts interrelated? What are the consequences of each part for the overall operation of society?
Social-conflict	Macro-level	A system based on social inequality; each part of society benefits some categories of people more than others; social inequality leads to conflict which, in turn, leads to social change.	How is society divided? What are the major patterns of social inequality? How do some categories of people try to protect their privileges? How do other categories of people challenge the status quo?
Symbolic-interaction	Micro-level	An ongoing process of social interaction in specific settings based on symbolic communications; individual perceptions of reality are variable and changing.	How is society experienced? How do human beings interact to create, maintain, and change social patterns? How do individuals try to shape the reality that others perceive? How does individual behavior change from one situation to another?

pick-up basketball after school. Weekend television is filled with sporting events of all kinds, and a large share of the daily news covers the scores of recent games. In short, sports in the United States is a multibillion-dollar industry. What sociological insights can the three theoretical paradigms reveal about this familiar part of everyday life?

The Functions of Sports

A structural-functional approach directs attention to the ways sports help society operate. The manifest functions include recreation, physical conditioning, and a relatively harmless way to "let off steam." Sports have important latent functions as well, from fostering social relationships to generating countless jobs. Perhaps most important, though, sports encourage competition and the pursuit of success, both of which are central to our way of life.

Sports also have dysfunctional consequences, of course. For example, universities intent on fielding winning teams sometimes recruit students for their athletic ability rather than their academic aptitude. Not only does this practice pull down the academic standards of a school, it shortchanges athletes who devote little time to their academic work.

Sports and Conflict

A social-conflict analysis of sports might begin by pointing out that sports reflect social inequality. Some sports—including tennis, swimming, golf, and skiing—are expensive, so participation is largely limited to the well-to-do. Football, baseball, and basketball, however, are accessible to people of all income levels. In short, the games people play are not simply a matter of choice; they also reflect social standing.

Throughout history, sports have been oriented primarily toward males. The first modern Olympic Games held in 1896, for example, excluded women from competition; in the United States, until recently, even Little League teams in most parts of the country barred girls from the playing field. Such exclusion has been defended by unfounded notions that girls and women lack the strength or the stamina to play sports or that women risk losing their femininity if they do. Thus our society encourages men to be athletes while expecting women to be attentive observers and cheerleaders. More women now play professional sports than ever before, yet they continue to take a back seat to men, particularly in sports that offer the most earnings and social prestige.

Although our society long excluded people of color from big league sports, the opportunity to earn high

African-American artist Jacob Lawrence recognized that sports are more than mere diversion and entertainment. On the contrary, through sports we acknowledge the importance of individualism and competition to our way of life.

Lawrence, Jacob. American, b. 1917. *Munich Olympic Games*, Poster, 1972. Courtesy of the artist and Francine Seders Gallery, Seattle. Photo: Spike Mafford.

incomes in professional sports has expanded in recent decades. Major League Baseball first admitted African American players when Jackie Robinson broke the "color line" in 1947. By 1997, African Americans (12 percent of the U.S. population) accounted for 17 percent of Major League Baseball players, 66 percent of National Football League (NFL) players, and 79 percent of National Basketball Association (NBA) players (Center for the Study of Sport in Society, 1998).

One reason for the increasing proportion of people of African descent in professional sports is the fact

that athletic performance—in terms of a batting average or number of points scored per game—can be precisely measured, and is thus not diminished by white prejudice. It is also true that some people of color make a particular effort to excel in athletics, where they perceive greater opportunity than in other careers (Steele, 1990). In recent years, in fact, African American athletes have earned higher salaries, on average, than white players. But racial discrimination still taints professional sports in the United States: African Americans figure prominently in only five sports (basketball, football, baseball, boxing, and track), and, across the board, the vast majority of managers, head coaches, and owners of sports teams are white (Gnida, 1995).

Taking a wider view, who benefits most from professional sports? Individual players may get astronomical salaries, and millions of fans love to follow their teams, but the vast sums that teams take in are controlled by a small number of people (predominantly white men) for whom teams are income-generating property. In sum, sports in the United States are bound up with inequalities based on gender, race, and economic power.

Sports as Interaction

At a micro-level, a sporting event is a complex drama of face-to-face interaction. In part, play is guided by assigned positions and, of course, the rules of the game. But players are also spontaneous and unpredictable. Guided by the symbolic-interaction paradigm, then, we see sports less as a system than as an ongoing process.

From this point of view, too, we expect each player to understand the game a little differently. Some thrive in a setting of stiff competition while, for others, love[5] of the game may be greater than the need to win.

Team members also shape their particular realities according to the prejudices, jealousies, and ambitions they bring to the field. Then, too, the behavior of any single player changes over time. A rookie in professional baseball, for example, may feel very self-conscious during his first few games in the big leagues. In time, however, players begin to gain a comfortable sense of fitting in with the team. Coming to feel at home on the field was especially slow and

---

[5]The ancient Romans recognized this fact, evident in our word "amateur," literally, "lover," which designates someone who engages in an activity for the sheer love of it.

DISCUSS: Apply the theoretical paradigms to prostitution. Functions include sexual release and emotional support ("someone to tell my troubles to") for people who don't fulfill these needs elsewhere. Could prostitution function to keep some marriages together? A conflict analysis notes women's subordinate social position, restricted opportunities in many "legitimate" occupational spheres, and the social definition of women in terms of sexual attractiveness. Interactional analysis explores the gradual process by which most female (and male) prostitutes take on the role and identity of the streetwalker and the negotiations that take place between sex workers and clients (and also pimps).

CONTROVERSY & DEBATE

Is Sociology Nothing More Than Stereotypes?

"Protestants are the ones who kill themselves!"

"People in the United States? They're rich, they love to marry, and they love to divorce!"

"Everybody knows that you have to be black to play professional basketball!"

There is no question that sociologists make generalizations. But many beginning students of sociology may wonder if generalizations about categories of people amount to stereotypes. Are the three statements above sociological insights or simply stereotypes?

The short answer is that each of the statements at the top of this column is a **stereotype,** *an exaggerated description applied to all people in some category.* First, rather than describing averages, each statement paints every individual in a category with the same brush. Second, each ignores facts and distorts reality (though many stereotypes do contain some element of truth). Third, a stereotype sounds more like a "put down" than a fair-minded assertion.

Good sociology, in contrast, involves making generalizations, but with three important conditions. *First, sociologists do not indiscriminately apply any*

generalization to all individuals. Second, sociologists are careful that a generalization squares with available facts. Third, sociologists offer generalizations fair-mindedly, with an interest in getting at the truth.

Remember that the sociological perspective reveals "the general in the particular." Therefore, a sociological insight is a generalization about some category of people. For example, earlier in this chapter, we noted that the suicide rate among Protestants is higher than the rate for Catholics or Jews. However, the statement above— "Protestants are the ones who kill themselves"—is not a reasonable generalization because the vast majority of Protestants do no such thing. Furthermore, it would also be wrong to assume a particular friend, because he is a Protestant male, is on the verge of self-destruction. (Imagine refusing to lend some money to a roommate who happens to be a Baptist, explaining "Well, given your risk of suicide, I might never get paid back!")

Second, sociologists shape their generalizations to available facts. A more factual version of the second statement is that, on average and by world standards, the U.S. population has a very high standard of living. It is also true that our marriage rate is one

of the highest in the world. And so is our divorce rate (although few people take great pleasure in divorcing).

Third, sociologists strive to be fair-minded. That is, they are motivated by a passion for learning and for truth. The third statement, about African Americans and basketball, is not good sociology for two reasons. First, it is simply not true, and, second, it seems motivated by bias rather than truth-seeking.

Good sociology stands apart from harmful stereotyping, then. But a sociology course is an excellent setting for talking over common stereotypes. The classroom encourages discussion and the pursuit of truth, and offers the factual information you need to decide whether a popular belief is valid or just a stereotype.

Continue the debate . . .

1. *Are there stereotypes of sociologists? What are they? Are they valid?*

2. *Do you think taking a sociology course corrects people's stereotypes? Why or why not?*

3. *Can you name a stereotype of your own that sociology challenges?*

difficult for Jackie Robinson in 1947. At first he was painfully aware that many white players, and millions of white fans, resented his presence in Major League Baseball. Gradually, though, his outstanding ability and straightforward manner won him the respect of the entire nation.

The three theoretical paradigms—structural-functional, social-conflict, and symbolic-interaction—

provide different insights, but none is more correct than the others. Applied to any issue, each paradigm generates its own interpretations so that, to fully appreciate the power of the sociological perspective, you should become familiar with all three. Together, they stimulate fascinating debates and controversies. In the final box, we review many of the ideas presented in this chapter, asking how sociological generalizations differ from common stereotypes.

Q: "We shall not cease from exploration, and the end of all our exploring
Will be to arrive where we started, and know this place for the first time."
T. S. Eliot, *Four Quartets*

RESOURCE: Excerpts from Peter Berger's *Invitation to Sociology* and C. Wright Mills's *The Sociological Imagination* are found in the Macionis and Benokraitis reader, *Seeing Ourselves: Classic, Contemporary, and Cross-Cultural Readings in Sociology*, 4th ed., Prentice Hall, 1998.

SUMMARY

1. The sociological perspective shows "the general in the particular" or the power of society to shape our lives.

2. Because people in the United States tend to think in terms of individual choice, recognizing the impact of society on our lives may at first seem like "seeing the strange in the familiar."

3. Emile Durkheim's research on suicide rates among different categories of people shows that society affects even our most personal actions.

4. Global awareness is an important part of the sociological perspective because, first, societies of the world are becoming increasingly interconnected; second, many social problems are most serious beyond the borders of the United States; and, third, a global awareness also helps us better understand ourselves.

5. Socially marginal people are more likely than others to perceive the effects of society. For everyone, periods of social crisis foster sociological thinking.

6. There are four general benefits to using the sociological perspective. First, it challenges our familiar understandings of the world, helping us separate fact from fiction. Second, it helps us appreciate the opportunities and limits in our lives. Third, it encourages more active participation in society. Fourth, it increases our awareness of social diversity in the United States and in the world as a whole.

7. Auguste Comte gave sociology its name in 1838. Earlier social thinkers focused on what society ought to be, but Comte's new discipline of sociology used scientific methods to understand society *as it is*.

8. Sociology arose in reaction to vast changes in Europe during the eighteenth and nineteenth centuries. In particular, the rise of an industrial economy, the explosive growth of cities, and the emergence of new political ideas focused people's attention on how society operates.

9. A theory weaves observations into insight and understanding. Sociologists use theoretical paradigms to construct theories.

10. The structural-functional paradigm focuses on how social structures promote the stability and integration of society. This approach minimizes social inequality, conflict, and change.

11. The social-conflict paradigm highlights social inequality, conflict, and change. This approach downplays the extent of society's integration and stability.

12. In contrast to these broad, macro-level approaches, the symbolic-interaction paradigm is a micro-level framework that focuses on face-to-face interaction in specific settings.

13. Because each paradigm looks at different aspects of a social issue, the richest sociological understanding comes from applying all three.

14. Sociological thinking involves generalizations. But, unlike a stereotype, (1) a sociological statement is not applied indiscriminately to individuals, (2) it is supported by facts, and (3) it is put forward in the fair-minded pursuit of truth.

KEY CONCEPTS

sociology the systematic study of human society

global perspective the study of the larger world and our society's place in it

high-income countries industrial nations in which most people have an abundance of material goods

middle-income countries nations with limited industrialization and moderate personal income

low-income countries nations with little industrialization in which severe poverty is the rule

positivism an approach to understanding the world based on science

theory a statement of how and why specific facts are related

theoretical paradigm a basic image of society that guides sociological thinking and research

structural-functional paradigm a framework for building theory that sees society as a complex system whose parts work together to promote solidarity and stability

social structure relatively stable patterns of social behavior

social function the consequences of any social pattern for the operation of society

manifest functions the recognized and intended consequences of a social pattern

latent functions the unrecognized and unintended consequences of a social pattern

social dysfunction the undesirable consequences of any social pattern for the operation of society

social-conflict paradigm a framework for building theory that sees society as an arena of inequality that generates conflict and change

macro-level orientation a focus on broad social structures that shape society as a whole

micro-level orientation a focus on patterns of social interaction in specific situations

symbolic-interaction paradigm a framework for building theory that sees society as the product of the everyday interactions of individuals

stereotype an exaggerated generalization applied to every person in some category

CRITICAL-THINKING QUESTIONS

1. In what ways does using the sociological perspective make us seem less in control of our lives? In what ways does it give us greater power over our surroundings?

2. Do you agree or disagree with this statement: Sociology would not have arisen if human behavior were biologically programmed (as is the behavior of, say, ants); nor could sociology exist if our behavior were utterly random. Sociology thrives because human social life falls in a middle ground—as thinking people, we create social patterns but they are variable and changeable.

3. Can you give a sociological explanation of why sociology developed where and when it did?

4. Use the three major theoretical paradigms to develop a list of questions that a sociologist might ask about (a) television, (b) war, (c) humor, and (d) colleges and universities.

LEARNING EXERCISES

1. Spend a few hours walking or driving around your local community. Are there clear residential patterns? That is, does each neighborhood contain certain categories of people? As best you can, identify who lives where. What social forces explain such patterns?

2. Look ahead to Figure 17–3, which shows the U.S. divorce rate over the last century. Can you explain why the rate dropped after 1930, shot up rapidly after 1940, fell in the 1950s, and rose again after 1960?

3. As you sit in one of your classes, observe the behavior of the instructor and other students. What patterns do you see in their use of space? In who speaks? Are there patterns in the categories of people who attend college in the first place?

4. Go to a campus sporting event and observe it from a sociological perspective. What functions do sports serve for your college or university? What patterns of inequality do they reflect and reinforce?

5. Prentice Hall and John Macionis offer multimedia support for every chapter of this book. Check out the interactive study guide found at the following Web site: http://www.prenhall.com/macionis In addition, the CD-ROM provided with this text contains a wealth of information and activities, including chapter overviews by the author, supplemental reading, exercises using sociological data, suggestions for exploring the Internet, and media elements that illustrate important concepts and issues.

Harvey Dinnerstein, *Underground Together,* 1996

Oil on canvas, 90 × 107¼ in. © Harvey Dinnerstein. Photograph courtesy of Gerold Wunderlich & Co., New York, N.Y.

CHAPTER 2

SOCIOLOGICAL INVESTIGATION

While on a visit to Atlanta during the 1984 holiday season, sociologist Lois Benjamin (1991) paid a call to the mother of an old college friend. Benjamin was eager to learn what had become of her friend, Sheba, who had shared her own dream of earning a graduate degree, finding a teaching position, and writing books. Benjamin was proud that she had fulfilled her dream. But as she soon found out, Sheba had fallen disastrously short of her goal.

There had been early signs of trouble, Benjamin recalled. After college, Sheba began graduate work at a university in Canada. But in her letters to Benjamin, she was very critical of the world around her and seemed to be cutting herself off from others. Sheba attributed her bitterness to racism. As an African American woman, she felt she was the target of racial hostility. Before long, she flunked out of school, blaming her white professors for her failure. At this point, she left North America, finally earning a Ph.D. in England and then settling in Nigeria. Since then, Benjamin had not heard a word from her long-time friend.

Benjamin was happy to learn that Sheba had returned to Atlanta. But her delight dissolved into shock when she saw Sheba and realized that her friend had suffered a mental breakdown and was barely responsive to anyone.

Months later, Sheba's emotional collapse still troubled Benjamin. She knew that many factors combine to cause such a personal tragedy. But, having experienced the sting of racism herself, Benjamin was convinced that it had played a major role in Sheba's story. Partly as a tribute to her old friend, Benjamin set out to explore the effects of race in the lives of bright, well-educated people of color in the United States.

Benjamin was aware that she was challenging conventional wisdom, which said that race poses less of a barrier today than in previous generations, especially to talented African Americans (Wilson, 1978). But her own experiences—and, she believed, Sheba's too—seemed to contradict such thinking.

To test her ideas, Benjamin spent the next two years asking one hundred successful African Americans around the country how race affected their lives and shaped their work. In the words of these "Talented One Hundred"[1] men and women, she found evidence that, even among privileged African Americans, racism remains a heavy burden.

---

[1]Benjamin derived her concept from the term "Talented Tenth" used by W. E. B. Du Bois (1899) to describe African American leaders in his day.

SUPPLEMENTS: The *Data File* contains an annotated outline of Chapter 2, supplemental lecture material, and suggestions for class discussion.

GLOBAL: People in other times and places recognize different "truths." In the case of childhood sexuality, for example, the Melanesians of New Guinea typically shrug off sexual intercourse among children too young to reproduce as harmless.

Q: "Science is humankind pursuing truth with no holds barred." Harrison White

NOTE: *Empiricism* (the Greek root means "experience") is the philosophical doctrine that only the senses support claims of truth. The closely linked concept of *positivism* defines truth as "positive" facts based on sensory experience, while dismissing as speculation metaphysical or theological claims about ultimate causes of events.

Later in this chapter, we will take a closer look at Lois Benjamin's research. For the moment, though, notice how the sociological perspective helped her to spot broad social patterns operating in the lives of individuals. Just as important, Benjamin's work demonstrates the *doing* of sociology, the process of *sociological investigation*.

Many people think scientists work only in laboratories, carefully taking measurements using complex equipment. But, as this chapter explains, sociologists also conduct scientific research on neighborhood streets, in homes and workplaces, in schools and hospitals, in bars and prisons—in short, wherever people can be found.

This chapter discusses the methods that sociologists use to conduct research. Along the way, we shall see that research involves not just procedures for gathering information but controversies about values: Should research strive to be objective? Or should it offer prescriptions for change, however bold? Certainly, for example, Lois Benjamin did not undertake her study simply to document the existence of racism; she sought to bring racism out in the open as a strategy to challenge it. We shall tackle questions of values after addressing the basics of sociological investigation.

THE BASICS OF SOCIOLOGICAL INVESTIGATION

Sociological investigation begins with two simple requirements. The first was the focus of Chapter 1: *Look at the world using the sociological perspective.* This point of view reveals curious patterns of behavior all around us that call out for further study.

Lois Benjamin did exactly this as she wondered how race affects the lives of talented African Americans. This brings us to the second requirement for sociological investigation: *Be curious and ask questions.* Benjamin wanted to learn more about how race affects the lives of African Americans—even those with significant personal achievements. She asked questions: What effect does being part of a racial minority have on self-identity? On the way white people perceive individuals and their work? What patterns of education, occupation, and income characterize leaders in this country's black community?

These two requirements—seeing the world sociologically and asking questions—are fundamental to sociological investigation. Yet they are only the beginning. They draw us into the social world, stimulating our curiosity. But then we face the challenging task of

finding answers to our questions. To understand the insights sociology offers, we need to realize that there are various kinds of "truth."

SCIENCE AS ONE FORM OF "TRUTH"

When we say we "know" something, we can mean any number of things. Most members of our society, for instance, claim to believe in the existence of God. Few would assert that they have direct contact with God, but they say they believe all the same. We call this kind of knowing "belief" or "faith." A second kind of truth rests on the pronouncement of some recognized expert. Parents with questions about raising their children, for example, may consult a child psychologist or read books by experts. A third type of truth is based on simple agreement among ordinary people. We come to "know," for example, that sexual intercourse among young children is wrong because virtually everyone in our society says it is.

People's "truths" differ the world over, and we often encounter "facts" at odds with our own. Imagine being a Peace Corps volunteer who has just arrived in a small, remote village in Latin America. Your job is to help the local people to increase their crop yield. On your first day in the fields, you observe a curious practice: After planting the seeds, the farmers lay a dead fish on top of the soil. In response to your question, they reply that the fish are a gift to the god of the harvest. A local elder adds sternly that the harvest was poor one year when no fish were offered.

From that society's point of view, using fish as gifts to the harvest god makes sense. The people believe in it, their experts endorse it, and everyone seems to agree that the system works. But, with scientific training in agriculture, you have to shake your head and wonder. The scientific "truth" in this situation is something entirely different: The decomposing fish fertilize the ground, producing a better crop.

Science, then, represents a fourth way of knowing. **Science** is *a logical system that bases knowledge on direct, systematic observation.* Standing apart from faith, the wisdom of "experts," and general agreement, scientific knowledge rests on **empirical evidence**, meaning *information we can verify with our senses.*

Our Peace Corps example does not mean, of course, that people in traditional villages ignore what their senses tell them, or that members of technologically advanced societies reject nonscientific ways of knowing. A medical researcher using science to find a cure for cancer, for example, may still practice her

NOTE: Facts standing alone do not constitute compelling truth. Myth is a means of conveying broad cultural truths without relying on factual details. The success of the film *E.T.* was partly due to its mythic elements: (a) a main character who was born elsewhere, (b) who came to earth, (c) underwent a great testing, and (d) finally returned to his origins. The same four elements underlie the lives of Moses, Jesus, and Superman.

NOTE: Science and religion do not conflict but complement one another. Scientific truths involve proximate causes of events; religious truths deal with ultimate causes.
SOCIAL SURVEY: Members of our "scientific" society still cling to some metaphysics: 99% of General Social Survey respondents claim to know their astrological sign; a 1992 Roper survey found 18% of U.S. adults claim to have had direct experience with aliens.

Myths as well as scientific facts stand as an important part of human existence. In his painting,
Where Do We Come From?, *French artist Paul Gauguin (1848–1903) offers a mythic account of human origins. A myth (from the Greek* mythos, *meaning "story" or "word") may or may not be factual in the literal sense, but it conveys some basic truth about the meaning and purpose of life. It is science, rather than art, that is powerless to address such questions of meaning.*

Paul Gauguin (French, 1848–1903), *Where Do We Come From? What Are We? Where Are We Going?*, 1897, oil on canvas, 139.1 × 374.6 cm. (54¼ × 147½ in.). Tompkins Collection. Courtesy of Museum of Fine Arts, Boston.

religion as a matter of faith; she may turn to experts when making financial decisions; and she may develop political opinions through discussions with family and friends. In short, we all embrace various kinds of truths at the same time.

COMMON SENSE VERSUS SCIENTIFIC EVIDENCE

Scientific evidence sometimes challenges our common sense. Here are six statements that many North Americans assume are "true":

1. **Poor people are far more likely than rich people to break the law.** Watching a television show like "Cops," one might well conclude that police arrest only people from "bad" neighborhoods. And, as Chapter 8 ("Deviance") explains, poor people do stand out in the official arrest statistics. But research also reveals that police and prosecutors are more likely to respond leniently to apparent wrongdoing by well-to-do people. Furthermore, it may be that laws themselves are written in a way that criminalizes poor people more and affluent people less.

2. **The United States is a middle-class society where most people are more or less equal.**

Data presented in Chapter 10 ("Social Class in the United States") show that the richest 5 percent of our people control half the nation's total wealth. If people are equal, then, some are much "more equal" than others.

3. **Most poor people don't want to work.** Research described in Chapter 10 indicates that this statement is true of some but not most poor people. In fact, about half of poor individuals in the United States are children and elderly people whom no one would expect to work.

4. **Differences in the behavior of females and males reflect "human nature."** Much of what we call "human nature" is constructed by the society in which we are raised, as Chapter 3 ("Culture") explains. In fact, as Chapter 12 ("Sex and Gender") shows, some societies define "feminine" and "masculine" very differently from the way we do.

5. **People change as they grow old, losing many interests as they focus increasingly on their health.** Chapter 14 ("Aging and the Elderly") reports that aging actually changes our personalities very little. Problems of health increase in old age but, by and large, elderly people retain their distinctive personalities.

NOTE: Other examples of misleading common sense: The birth rate of "welfare mothers" is actually below that of all women; remarriages are more prone to divorce than first marriages.

Q: "The facts we see depend on where we are placed and the habits of our eyes." Walter Lippman

Q: "It is the pursuit of truth that gives us life, and it is to that pursuit that our loyalty is due." William Graham Sumner

NOTE: Precision and accuracy have an inverse relationship: The more precise our statements, the more likely they are wrong. Weather forecasters offer a case in point: When they predict that the high temperature five days from now will be, say, 73, they are almost always wrong.

Q: "It is the essence of the human mind to take apart what experience presents as a whole." Peter Berger

Common sense suggests that, in a world of possibilities, people fall in love with that "special someone." Sociological research reveals that the vast majority of people select partners who are very similar in social background to themselves.

6. **Most people marry because they are in love.** To members of our society, few statements are so self-evident. But as surprising as it may seem, research shows that in most societies, marriage has little to do with love. Chapter 17 ("Family") explains why.

These examples confirm the old saying that "It's not what we don't know that gets us into trouble as much as things we *do* know that just aren't so." We have all been brought up believing conventional truths, being bombarded by expert advice, and being pressured to accept the opinions of people around us. As adults, we must learn to evaluate critically what we see, read, and hear, and sociology can help us to do that. Like any way of knowing, sociology has limitations, as we shall see. But scientific sociology is a useful way to assess many kinds of information.

THE ELEMENTS OF SCIENCE

Sociologists apply science to the study of society in much the same way that natural scientists investigate the physical world. Whether they end up confirming a widely held opinion or revealing that it is way off base, sociologists scientifically gather empirical evidence. The following sections of this chapter introduce the major elements of scientific investigation.

CONCEPTS, VARIABLES, AND MEASUREMENT

A crucial element of science is the **concept**, *a mental construct that represents some part of the world, inevitably in a simplified form.* "Society" is itself a concept, as are the structural parts of societies, such as "the family" and "the economy." Sociologists also use concepts to describe individuals, as when we speak of their "gender," "race," or "social class."

A **variable** is *a concept whose value changes from case to case.* The familiar variable "price," for example, changes from item to item in a supermarket. Similarly, people use the concept "social class" to evaluate people as "upper class," "middle class," "working class," or "lower class."

The use of variables depends on **measurement,** *the process of determining the value of a variable in a specific case.* Some variables are easy to measure, as when the checkout clerk adds up the cost of our groceries. But measuring sociological variables can be far more difficult. For example, how would you measure a person's "social class"? You might be tempted to look at clothing, listen to patterns of speech, or note a home address. Or, trying to be more precise, you might ask about income, occupation, and education.

Because almost any variable can be measured in more than one way, sociologists sometimes have to make a judgment about which factors to consider. For example, having a very high income might qualify a person as "upper class." But what if the income comes from selling cars, an occupation most people think of as "middle class"? And, would having only an eighth-grade education make the person "lower class"? In this case, sociologists sensibly (but arbitrarily) combine these three measures—income, occupation, and education—to assign social class, as described in Chapter 9 ("Social Stratification") and Chapter 10 ("Social Class in the United States").

Sociologists face another interesting problem in measuring variables: dealing with vast numbers of

NOTE: Awards in medical malpractice cases illustrate wild variations in statistical measures. One recent study noted the modal settlement was zero (the most common award); median award was around $20,000, since most awards are small; yet the mean award was about $100,000 because the average is skewed upwards by a few high awards.

GLOBAL: The misleading character of averages is illustrated by the $21,875 per capita GDP of oil-rich Kuwait, which is close to the U.S. figure of $26,397. Yet Kuwait has one-and-one-half times the U.S. infant mortality rate and more than four times the adult illiteracy rate, indicating that most Kuwait residents have a low standard of living. Kuwait's considerable wealth is highly concentrated among a small elite.

SOCIOLOGY OF EVERYDAY LIFE

Three Useful (and Simple) Statistical Measures

We all talk about "averages": the average price of a gallon of gasoline, the average salary for new college graduates, or Tiger Woods's average on the golf course this season. Sociologists, too, are interested in averages, and they use three different statistical measures to describe what is typical.

Suppose we want to describe the salaries paid to seven members of a sociology department at a local college:

$35,000 $43,000 $41,700 $42,000
$35,000 $78,295 $35,000

The simplest statistical measure is the **mode,** defined as *the value that occurs often in a series of numbers.* In this example,

the mode is $35,000, since that value occurs three times, while each of the others occurs only once. If all the values were to occur only once, there would be no mode; if two values occurred three times (or twice), there would be two modes. Although easy to identify, sociologists rarely use a mode because it is a very crude measure of the "average."

A more common statistical measure, the **mean,** refers to *the arithmetic average of a series of numbers*, and is calculated by adding all the values together and dividing by the number of cases. The sum of the seven incomes is $309,995; dividing by seven yields a mean income of $44,285. But notice that the mean is actually higher than

the income of six of the seven sociologists. Because the mean is "pulled" up or down by an especially high or low value (in this case, the $78,295 paid to one sociologist who also serves as a dean), it gives a distorted picture of any distribution with extreme scores.

The **median** is *the value that occurs midway in a series of numbers arranged in order of magnitude or, simply, the middle case.* Here the median income for the seven people is $41,700, since three incomes are higher and three are lower. With an even number of cases, the median is halfway between the two middle cases. Since a median is unaffected by an extreme score, it gives a better picture of what is "average" than the mean does.

people. How, for instance, do you describe income for thousands or even millions of individuals? Reporting streams of numbers would carry little meaning and tell us nothing about the people as a whole. Thus sociologists use *statistical measures* to describe people efficiently and collectively. The box explains how.

Defining Concepts

Measurement is always a bit arbitrary since the value of a variable depends, in part, on how it is defined. And, deciding what abstract concepts such as "love," "family," or "intelligence" mean in real life could lead to lengthy debates before any attempt is made to measure them as variables.

But good sociological investigation requires that a researcher **operationalize a variable,** which means *specifying exactly what one is to measure in assigning a value to a variable.* Before measuring people's social class, for example, we would have to decide exactly what we were going to measure: say, income level, years of schooling, occupational prestige. Sometimes sociologists measure several of these things; in such cases, they need to specify exactly how they combine these variables into one overall score. When reading

about research, always look for how researchers operationalize each variable. How they define terms can have a big effect on the results.

When deciding how to operationalize a variable, sociologists may take people's opinions into account. Since 1977, for example, researchers at the U.S. Census Bureau have defined race and ethnicity as the following list of options: white, black, Hispanic, Asian or Pacific Islander, and American Indian or Alaskan Native. One problem with this list is that someone can be *both* Hispanic and white or black. On the other hand, someone of Arab ancestry might not identify with *any* of the choices. And, just as important, an increasing number of people in the United States are *multiracial.* As a result of such criticisms, the next national census in the year 2000 will allow people, if they wish, to describe their race and ethnicity by selecting more than one category.

Reliability and Validity

Useful measurement involves two further considerations. **Reliability** refers to *consistency in measurement.* For measurement to be reliable, in other words, the process must yield the same result if repeated time after time. But consistency is no guarantee of **validity,**

NOTE: Earl Babbie describes bad measurement as bullet holes scattered all around a target; reliable but not valid measurement as holes clustered together on a target but not in the bull's eye; reliable and valid measurement as holes clustered on the bull's eye. Note that validity implies reliability, but not vice versa.

NOTE: An independent variable in one situation may be a dependent variable in another; the designation is arbitrary and determined by the specific experiment.

SUPPLEMENTS: Use the *Student Social Survey*, available with this text, to demonstrate the use of control. This instructional package also lets students discover the relative strength of various factors working together; rarely does one independent variable generate more than a 20% change in the attitude or behavior under study.

Young people who live in the crowded inner city are more likely than those who live in the spacious suburbs to have trouble with the police. But does this mean that crowding causes delinquency? Researchers know that crowding and arrest rates do vary together, but they have demonstrated that the connection is spurious: Both factors rise in relation to a third factor—declining income.

which means *measuring precisely what one intends to measure.* Valid measurement, in other words, means more than hitting the same spot on a target again and again—it means hitting the bull's-eye.

Valid measurement is more difficult than it may at first seem. Say, for example, you want to study how religious people are. A reasonable strategy might be to ask how often respondents attend religious services. But, is going to a church or temple really the same thing as being religious? It may be that religious people do attend services more frequently, but people also join in religious rituals out of habit or because someone else wants them to. Moreover, some devout believers avoid organized religion altogether. Thus, even when a measurement yields consistent results (making it reliable), it can still miss the real, intended target (and lack validity). Later on in Chapter 18 ("Religion"), we suggest that measuring religiosity should probably take into account not only church attendance but a person's

beliefs and the degree to which a person lives by religious convictions. In sum, sociological research depends on careful measurement, which is always a challenge to the researcher.

Relationships Among Variables

Once sound measurement is completed, an investigator can pursue the real payoff, which is determining how variables are related. The scientific ideal is **cause and effect**, *a relationship in which we know that change in one variable causes change in another.* Cause-and-effect relationships occur all around us every day, as when studying for an exam results in a high grade. *The variable that causes the change* (in this case, studying) is called the **independent variable.** *The variable that changes* (the grade) is called the **dependent variable.** The value of one variable, in other words, depends on the value of another. Why is linking variables in terms of cause and effect important? Because doing so allows researchers (and sometimes students) to *predict* how one pattern of behavior will produce another.

But just because two variables change together does not mean that they are linked by a cause-and-effect relationship. Consider, for instance, that the marriage rate in the United States falls to its lowest point in January, exactly the same month as our national death rate peaks. This hardly means that people die because they fail to marry (or that they don't marry because they die). In fact, it is the dreary weather in much of the nation during January (and perhaps also the post-holiday blahs) that causes both a low marriage rate and a high death rate. The flip side holds as well: The warmer and sunnier summer months have the highest marriage rate as well as the lowest death rate. Thus researchers have to look below the surface to untangle cause-and-effect relationships.

To take a second case, sociologists have long recognized that juvenile delinquency is more common among young people who live in crowded housing. Say we operationalize the variable "juvenile delinquency" to mean the number of times (if any) a person under the age of eighteen has been arrested, and make the variable "crowded housing" mean a home's amount of square feet of living space per person. We would find the variables related. That is, delinquency rates are, indeed, high in densely populated neighborhoods. But should we conclude that crowding in the home (in this case, the independent variable) is what causes delinquency (the dependent variable)?

Not necessarily. **Correlation** is *a relationship in which two (or more) variables change together.* We know

GLOBAL: Illustrating spurious correlation, Sweden's National Bureau of Economic Research found that couples who cohabit before marriage are more likely to divorce than those who do not cohabit. Does cohabiting contribute to divorce? Researcher Neil Bennett describes the link as spurious: Cohabiters, he claims, are less religious and less committed to marriage to begin with; this "weak ties" pattern persists among cohabiters who marry.

DISCUSS: Another "spuriousness" example: Barney Beins (1993) notes the strong positive correlation between number of bars and number of churches in an area. Does booze drive people to religion? Does religion drive people to drink? Most likely, the casual factor is SES, since low SES areas have high numbers of both bars and churches.

that density and delinquency are correlated because they change together, as shown in Part (a) of Figure 2–1. This relationship *may* mean that crowding causes misconduct, but some third factor may be at work causing *both* variables to change. For example, think what kind of people live in crowded housing: people with little money, no power, and few choices—the poor. Poor children are also more likely to end up with police records. Thus, crowded housing and juvenile delinquency are found together because *both* are caused by a third factor—poverty—as shown in Part (b) of Figure 2–1. Put otherwise, the apparent connection between crowding and delinquency is "explained away" by a third variable—low income—that causes them both to change. So our original connection turns out to be a **spurious correlation,** *an apparent, although false, relationship between two (or more) variables caused by some other variable.*

Unmasking a correlation as spurious requires a bit of detective work, using a technique called **control,** *holding constant all variables except one in order to clearly see the effect of that variable.* In the example above, we suspect that income level may be causing a spurious link between housing density and delinquency. To check, we control for income (that is, we hold income constant by looking only at young people of one income level) and see if a correlation between density and delinquency remains. If the correlation between density and delinquency is still there despite the control (that is, if young people living in more crowded housing show higher rates of delinquency than young people in less crowded housing, all with the same family income), we have more reason to think that crowding does, in fact, cause delinquency. But if the relationship disappears when we control for income, as shown in Part (c) of the figure, we know we have a spurious correlation. In fact, research has shown that the correlation between crowding and delinquency just about disappears if income is controlled (Fischer, 1984). So we have now sorted out the relationship among the three variables, as illustrated in Part (d) of the figure. Housing density and juvenile delinquency have a spurious correlation; evidence shows that both variables rise or fall according to people's income.

To sum up, correlation means only that two (or more) variables change together. Cause and effect involves something more and rests on three conditions: (1) there is a demonstrated correlation, (2) the independent (or causal) variable precedes the dependent variable in time, and (3) no evidence suggests a third variable is responsible for a spurious correlation between the two.

Natural scientists have an easier time than social scientists identifying cause-and-effect relationships

FIGURE 2–1 Correlation and Cause: An Example

(a)

If two variables vary together, they are said to be correlated. In this example, density of living conditions and juvenile delinquency increase and decrease together.

(b)

Here we consider the effect of a third variable: income level. Low income level may cause *both* high-density living conditions *and* a high delinquency rate. In other words, as income level decreases, both density of living conditions and the delinquency rate increase.

(c)

If we control income level — that is, examine only cases with the same income level — do those with higher-density living conditions still have a higher delinquency rate? The answer is *no.* There is no longer a correlation between these two variables.

(d)

This finding leads us to conclude that income level is a cause of both density of living conditions and delinquency rate. The original two variables (density of living conditions and delinquency rate) are thus correlated, but neither one causes the other. Their correlation is therefore *spurious.*

RESOURCE: Max Weber's statement on value-free research is among the classics in the Macionis and Benokraitis reader *Seeing Ourselves: Classic, Contemporary, and Cross-Cultural Readings in Sociology*, 4th ed.

Q: "Instructors who feel called upon to intervene in the struggles of world views and party opinions . . . may do so outside, in the market place, in the press, in meetings . . . But after all it is somewhat too convenient to demonstrate one's courage in taking a stand where the audience and possible opponents are condemned to silence." Max Weber, "Science as a Vocation"

Q: "The direction of our scientific exertions . . . is conditioned by the society in which we live, and most directly by the political climate. . . . [S]tudents turn to research on issues that have obtained political importance." Gunnar Myrdal

because they can control many variables in a laboratory. The sociologist, however, carrying out research in a workplace or on the streets, must often be satisfied with demonstrating only correlation. Moreover, human behavior is highly complex, involving dozens of causal variables at any one time, so establishing all cause-and-effect relationships at work in a particular situation can be exceedingly difficult.

THE IDEAL OF OBJECTIVITY

Assume that ten reporters who work for a magazine in San Diego, California, are collaborating on a story about that city's best restaurants. With the magazine picking up the tab, they head out on the town for a week of fine dining. Later, they get together to compare notes. Do you think one restaurant would be everyone's clear favorite? That hardly seems likely.

In scientific terms, each of the ten probably operationalizes the concept "best restaurant" differently. For one, it might be a place that serves delicious steaks at reasonable prices; for another, "best" might mean a menu keyed to nutrition and health; to another, stunning decor and attentive service might be the deciding factor. Like so many other things in life, the best restaurant turns out to be mostly a matter of individual taste.

Personal values are fine when it comes to restaurants, but they pose a challenge to scientific research. On the one hand, every scientist has personal opinions about the world. On the other hand, science aims for **objectivity**, *a state of personal neutrality in conducting research*. Researchers must therefore hold to scientific procedures while reining in their own attitudes and beliefs in order not to bias the results. Of course, scientific objectivity is an ideal rather than a reality, because no one can be completely neutral about anything. After all, the subject anyone chooses to study reflects a personal interest of one sort or another, as Lois Benjamin's research on race attests. But scientists try to maintain a professional sense of detachment from how their results will turn out. Holding to scientific procedures is the best way to lessen the chance that conscious or unconscious biases will distort research. As an extra precaution, researchers should try to inform their readers about their personal leanings to help others evaluate their conclusions in the proper context.

Max Weber: Value-Free Research

The influential German sociologist Max Weber expected that people would choose their research topics according to their personal beliefs and interests. Why else would one person study world hunger, another the effects of racism, and still another how children fare in one-parent families? Knowing this, and realizing that topics are *value-relevant*, Weber admonished researchers to be *value-free* in their investigations. Only by being dispassionate (as we expect any professionals to be) can researchers study the world *as it is* and not lapse into telling others how they think *it should be*. This detachment, for Weber, is the crucial element in science that sets it apart from politics. Politicians, in other words, are committed to a particular outcome; scientists must maintain an open-minded readiness to accept the results of their investigations, whatever they may be.

Weber's argument still carries much weight in sociology, although most concede that we can never be completely value-free or even aware of all our biases (Demerath, 1996). Moreover, sociologists are not "average" people: Most are white people who are highly educated and more politically liberal than the population as a whole (Wilson, 1979). Sociologists need to remember that they, too, are influenced by their own social backgrounds.

One way to limit distortion caused by personal values is **replication,** *repetition of research by other investigators*. If other researchers repeat a study using the same procedures and obtain the same results, we gain confidence that the results are accurate. The need for replication in scientific investigation is probably the reason that the search for knowledge is called *research* in the first place.

In any case, keep in mind that the logic of science does not guarantee objective, absolute truth. What science offers is an approach to knowledge that is *self-correcting* so that, in the long run, researchers stand the best chance to overcome their own biases. Objectivity and truth lie, then, not in any particular research, but in the scientific process itself.

SOME LIMITATIONS OF SCIENTIFIC SOCIOLOGY

As early scientists explored the natural world, so do today's sociologists use science to study the social world. All social science, however, has several important limitations:

1. **Human behavior is too complex to allow sociologists to predict precisely any individual's actions.** Astronomers calculate the movement of heavenly bodies with remarkable precision, but comets and planets are unthinking

NOTE: Only a small proportion of social science research is actually subjected to replication (far less than in the natural sciences).
Q: "We may remind ourselves that disinterestedness is not disinterest. The passionate commitment to scholarly detachment and free inquiry . . . needs all the self-restraint we can muster to support it precisely because self-restraint goes against our natural preference for our own, including our own views." Pamela Jensen

Q: "As in all sciences, in sociology interpretation is all. A science may be loaded down with too many facts, its vision blurred by peering too intently at the machinery for collecting them. The collected facts can be brought to life, as the statisticians themselves agree, only by a compelling vision of their meaning. Untouched by the magic of a sufficiently powerful and trained imagination, data play dead." Philip Rieff

A basic lesson of social research is that being observed affects how people behave. Researchers can never be certain precisely how this will occur; while some people resent public attention, others become highly animated when they think they have an audience.

objects. Humans, by contrast, have minds of their own. Because no two people react to any event in exactly the same way, sociologists must be satisfied with showing that *categories* of people typically act in one way or another. This is not a failing of sociology. It is simply consistent with the nature of our mission: studying creative, spontaneous people.

2. **Because humans respond to their surroundings, the mere presence of a researcher may affect the behavior being studied.** An astronomer gazing at a comet has no effect whatever on it. But most people react to being observed. Some may become anxious, angry, or defensive; others may try to "help" by doing what they think the researcher expects of them.

3. **Social patterns change constantly; what is true in one time or place may not hold true in another.** The laws of physics apply tomorrow as well as today, and they hold true all around the world. But because human behavior is so variable, there are no unchanging sociological laws. In fact, some of the most interesting sociological research focuses on how some people take for granted what others can barely imagine.

4. **Because sociologists are part of the social world they study, being value-free when** conducting social research is difficult. Barring a laboratory mishap, chemists are rarely personally affected by what goes on in test tubes. But sociologists live in their "test tube"—the society they study. Therefore, social scientists face a greater challenge in controlling—or even recognizing—personal values that may distort their work.

THE IMPORTANCE OF SUBJECTIVE INTERPRETATION

Scientists condemn "subjectivity" and "bias" as sources of error to be avoided as much as possible. But there is also a good side to subjectivity, since subjective—or creative—thinking is vital to sociological investigation for three reasons.

First, science is basically a series of rules that guide research, rather like a recipe for cooking. But just as more than a recipe is required to make a great chef, so scientific procedure does not, by itself, produce a great sociologist. Also needed is an inspired human imagination. In truth, insight comes not from science itself but from the lively thinking of creative human beings (Nisbet, 1970). The genius of physicist Albert Einstein or sociologist Max Weber lay not only in their use of the scientific method but in their curiosity and ingenuity.

NOTE: "Facts" rarely speak for themselves. Surveys show that, among people over the age of eighty, men are much more sexually active than women. Does this suggest a biological difference allowing older men to continue to be sexually active? Or is it the fact that, given the difference in longevity, most older men live with wives, while older women live alone?

SUPPLEMENTS: The *Data File* includes an account of how

recently celebrated research by the late James Coleman was initially condemned as "politically incorrect."

NOTE: In principle, the issue can be cast as a choice between "scientific correctness" (based on empirical data) and "political correctness" (based on political priorities).

Q: "There is no position from which sociological research is not biased in one way or another." Howard S. Becker

Second, science cannot embrace the vast and complex range of human motivations and feelings. Science can help us gather facts about how people act, but it can never fully explain greed, love, pride, despair, or other complex meanings people attach to behavior (Berger & Kellner, 1981).

Third, we also do well to remember that scientific data never speak for themselves. After sociologists and other scientists "collect the numbers," they face the ultimate task of *interpretation*—constructing meaning from their observations. For this reason, good sociological investigation is as much art as science.

POLITICS AND RESEARCH

As Max Weber observed long ago, a fine line separates politics from science. Most sociologists endorse Weber's goal of value-free research. But a growing number of researchers are challenging the notion that politics and science can—or should—be distinct.

Alvin Gouldner (1970a, 1970b) was among the first to claim that the notion of "value-free" research paints a "storybook picture" of sociology. Every element of social life, he argues, is political in that it probably benefits some people more than others. If so, Gouldner reasons, the topics sociologists choose to study and the conclusions they reach also have political consequences.

If sociologists have no choice about their work being political, Gouldner continues, they do have a choice about *which* positions are worthy of support. Moreover, as he sees it, sociologists are obligated to endorse political objectives that will improve society. Although this viewpoint is not limited to sociologists of any one political orientation, it is most common among those with left-leaning politics, including those influenced by the ideas of Karl Marx. Recall that Marx (1972:109; orig. 1845) did not think the point of studying the world was simply to understand it but to change it.

Thus, supporters of Weber's value-free approach are pitted against proponents of Marx's endorsement of social activism. This controversy carries over into the classroom and has sparked spirited debates among sociologists over "political correctness": Should teaching and research be value-free? Or should sociologists try to promote positive social change?

GENDER AND RESEARCH

One political dimension of research involves **gender**, *the significance that members of a society attach to being*

female or male. Sociologists have come to realize that gender often plays an important role in their work; Margrit Eichler (1988) identifies five ways that gender can jeopardize good research:

1. **Androcentricity.** Androcentricity (*andro* is the Greek word for "male"; *centricity* means "being centered on") refers to approaching an issue from a male perspective. Sometimes researchers act as if only the activities of men are important, ignoring what women do. For years researchers studying occupations focused on the paid work of men while overlooking the housework and child care traditionally performed by women (Counts, 1925; Hodge, Treiman, & Rossi, 1966). Clearly, research that seeks to understand human behavior cannot ignore half of humanity.

   Of course, *gynocentricity*—seeing the world from a female perspective—is equally limiting to sociological investigation. However, in our male-dominated society, this problem arises less frequently.

2. **Overgeneralizing.** This problem occurs when researchers use data drawn from only one sex to support conclusions about both sexes. Historically, sociologists have studied men and then made sweeping claims about "humanity" or "society." For example, gathering information from a handful of public officials (typically, men) and then drawing conclusions about the entire community illustrates the problem of overgeneralizing.

   Here, again, the bias can occur in reverse. For example, collecting data on child-rearing practices only from women would allow researchers to draw conclusions about "motherhood" but not about the more general issue of "parenthood."

3. **Gender blindness.** Failing to consider the variable of gender at all is termed "gender blindness." As is evident throughout this book, the lives of men and women typically differ in countless ways. A study of growing old in the United States would be weakened by gender blindness if it overlooked the fact that most elderly men live with spouses while elderly women typically live alone.

4. **Double standards.** Researchers must be careful not to distort what they study by judging men and women differently. For example, a family researcher who labels a couple "man and wife" may define the man as the "head of household"

NOTE: Subtle gender biases are evident even in our tendency to speak of "males and females," despite the alphabetical convention that would reverse them.

NOTE: Eichler's gender issues noted here are both threats to sound research and also barriers to gender equality.

Q: "Researchers must examine their assumptions about gender . . . Of all the beliefs that anthropologists bring to the field, [these] may be the most difficult to put aside, [operating] on an unconscious level." Maureen Giovannini (1992)

Q: "Advocacy research often justifies playing fast and loose with the facts in service to a noble cause." Neil Gilbert

Q: ". . . every social theory is a tacit theory of politics [and] also a personal theory inevitably representing . . . the personal experience of the individuals who author it." Alvin Gouldner (1970b)

Feminist research is concerned not simply with studying the social standing of women. It also transforms research, putting the investigator on a more equal footing with subjects so that they can work together to solve their common problems.

and treat him accordingly, while assuming that the woman simply engages in family "support work."

5. **Interference.** In this case, gender distorts a study as a subject reacts to the sex of the researcher, thereby interfering with the research operation. While studying a small community in Sicily, for instance, Maureen Giovannini (1992) found many men responding to her as a woman rather than as a researcher. Gender dynamics kept her from certain activities such as private conversations with men, which were deemed inappropriate for a single woman. Local residents also denied Giovannini access to places considered off-limits to women.

There is nothing wrong with focusing research on one sex or the other. But all sociologists, as well as people who read their work, should be mindful of how gender can affect sociological investigation.

FEMINIST RESEARCH

Because sociology has focused on the lives of men in the past, some of today's researchers make special efforts to study the lives of women. The focus of feminist research is the condition of women in society, and research is guided by the assumption that women generally experience subordination. Thus feminist research rejects Weber's value-free orientation in favor of being overtly political—doing research in pursuit of gender equality.

There is no single feminist research strategy. On the contrary, feminists employ any and all conventional scientific techniques, including all those described in this chapter. But some go further, claiming that feminist research must transform science itself, which they see as a masculine form of knowledge. Whereas traditional science requires detachment, feminists seek connections: a sympathetic understanding between investigator and subject. Moreover, while conventional scientists set the research agenda, deciding in advance which issues to raise and how to study them, feminist researchers favor a more egalitarian approach. They allow participants in a study to voice their needs and interests in their own words (Stanley & Wise, 1983; Nielsen, 1990; Stanley, 1990; Reinharz, 1992; Wolf, 1996).

Conventional sociologists charge that feminist research is less science than simple political activism. Feminists respond that research and politics should not—indeed cannot—ever be distinct. Therefore, traditional notions that rigidly separate politics and science must give way to new thinking that merges the two.

RESEARCH ETHICS

Like all scientific investigators, sociologists must remember that research can be harmful as well as helpful to subjects or communities. For this reason, the American Sociological Association (ASA)—the major professional association of sociologists in North America—has established formal guidelines for conducting research (1997).

Sociologists must strive to be both technically competent and fair-minded in their work. Sociologists

DISCUSS: In the past, investigators (especially psychologists) readily employed deception in research; a well-known example is Asch's experiment (see Chapter 5). If the research depends on deception, is it ethical? When does deception move from benign to dangerous?

Q: "Unfettered thought is the essence of research methods." Stanislav Andreski

NOTE: The word "experiment" contains the Latin root *per*, "to try out." This is also the root of the word "peril"—a link demonstrated by the Zimbardo research.

Q: "All human errors are impatience, a premature breaking off of methodological procedure, an apparent fencing in of what is apparently at issue." Franz Kafka

must disclose all research findings, without omitting significant data. They are ethically bound to make their results available to other sociologists, especially those who wish to replicate the study.

Sociologists must also strive to ensure the safety of subjects taking part in a research project. Should their research begin to threaten the well-being of participants, investigators must stop their work immediately. Researchers must also protect the privacy of anyone involved in a research project. Yet this is a promise that may be difficult to keep, since researchers sometimes come under pressure (say, from the police or courts) to disclose information. Therefore, researchers must think carefully about their responsibility to protect subjects, and they should discuss this issue with participants. In fact, ethical research requires the *informed consent* of participants, which means that subjects understand their responsibilities and risks and agree—before the work begins—to take part.

Should researchers employ deception in their work? Obviously, if researchers tell people exactly what they are looking for, they will not observe natural behavior. Yet, misleading subjects can generate understandable resentment. Researchers decide how to proceed on a case-by-case basis, but they must avoid deception if it threatens to bring any harm to subjects.

Another important guideline concerns funding. Sociologists must include in their published results the sources of all financial support. Also, they must avoid any conflict of interest (or even the appearance of such conflict) that can compromise the integrity of their work. For example, a researcher must never accept funding from an organization that seeks to influence the research results for its own purposes.

We have raised only some of the ethical concerns that sociologists face as teachers, college administrators, and in clinical practice. Readers can review the current code of ethics by visiting the American Sociological Association home page on the Internet at http:www.asanet.org

There are also global dimensions to research ethics. Before beginning research in other countries, investigators must become familiar enough with that society to understand what people *there* are likely to perceive as a violation of privacy or a source of personal danger. In a multicultural society such as our own, of course, the same rule applies to studying people whose cultural background differs from one's own. The box offers some tips about how outsiders can effectively and sensitively study Hispanic communities.

THE METHODS OF SOCIOLOGICAL RESEARCH

A **research method** is *a systematic plan for conducting research*. The remainder of this chapter introduces four commonly used methods of sociological investigation. None is inherently better or worse than any other. Rather, in the same way that a carpenter selects a particular tool for a specific task, researchers choose a method according to who they wish to study and what they wish to learn.

TESTING A HYPOTHESIS: THE EXPERIMENT

The logic of science is most clearly expressed in the **experiment,** *a research method for investigating cause and effect under highly controlled conditions*. Experimental research is *explanatory*, meaning that it not only asks what happens but why. Researchers usually use the experimental method to test a **hypothesis,** *an unverified statement of a relationship between variables*.

The ideal experiment consists of three steps. First, the experimenter measures the dependent variable (the "effect"). Second, the investigator exposes the dependent variable to the independent variable (the "cause" or "treatment"). Third, the researcher again measures the dependent variable to see if the predicted change took place. If the expected change occurred, the experiment supports the hypothesis; if not, the hypothesis is incorrect.

But a change in the dependent variable can be due to something other than the supposed cause. To be certain that they identify the correct cause, researchers carefully control other factors that might intrude into the experiment and affect the outcome. Such control is most easily accomplished in a laboratory, a setting specially constructed for research purposes. Another strategy for controlling outside influences is dividing subjects into an *experimental group* and a *control group*. The researcher then measures the dependent variable for subjects in both groups but exposes only the experimental group to the independent variable or treatment (the control group typically gets a "placebo," a treatment that seems to be the same but really has no effect on the experiment). Then the investigator measures the subjects in both groups again. Any factor (such as some news event) occurring during the course of the research that influences people in the experimental group would do the same to those in the control group, thus "washing out" the factor. By comparing

NOTE: David Hume (1711–1776) argued that science can empirically determine (1) correlation and (2) temporal ordering of variables, but not (3) an actual causal connection, which defies observation. Perhaps with Hume's thought in mind, the National Cancer Institute acknowledged higher cancer rates among people living near nuclear power plants but argued that research "can neither confirm nor deny a link . . . because statistical studies, by their very nature, cannot prove cause and effect."

Q: "In science as in love, a concentration on technique is likely to lead to impotence." Peter Berger (1963)

Q: "To know is nothing at all. To imagine is everything." Anatole France

Q: "We have an obligation to tell the truth no matter how good the news may be." Jeanne Kirkpatrick

SOCIAL DIVERSITY

Conducting Research With Hispanics

In a society as racially, ethnically, and religiously diverse as our own, sociologists are always studying people who differ from themselves. Learning—in advance—some of the distinctive traits of any category of people can both ease the research process and ensure that no hard feelings are left when the work is finished.

Gerardo Marín and Barbara VanOss Marín have identified five areas of concern in conducting research with Hispanics:

1. **Terminology.** The Maríns point out that the term "Hispanic" is a label of convenience used by the Census Bureau. Few people of Spanish descent think of themselves as "Hispanic" or "Latino." Most identify with a particular country (generally, with a Latin American nation such as Mexico or Argentina, or with Spain).

2. **Cultural values.** By and large, the United States is a nation of individualistic, competitive people. Many Hispanics, however, have a more collective orientation. An outsider may therefore judge the behavior of a Hispanic subject as conforming or overly trusting when, in fact, the person is simply trying to be courteous. Researchers should realize that

Hispanic respondents might agree with a particular statement out of politeness rather than conviction.

3. **Family dynamics.** Generally speaking, Hispanic cultures have strong family loyalties. Asking subjects to reveal information about another family member may make them uncomfortable, and they may even refuse to do so. The Maríns add that, in the home, a researcher's request to speak privately with a Hispanic woman may be met with suspicion or outright disapproval from her husband or father.

4. **Time and efficiency.** Spanish cultures, the Maríns explain, tend to be more concerned with the

quality of relationships than with simply getting a job done. A non-Hispanic researcher who tries to hurry an interview with a Hispanic family, perhaps wishing not to delay the family's dinner, may be thought rude for not proceeding at a more sociable and relaxed pace.

5. **Personal space.** Finally, as the Maríns point out, people of Spanish descent typically maintain closer physical contact with others than many non-Hispanics do. Therefore, researchers who seat themselves across the room from their subjects may come across as "stand-offish." Conversely, researchers may inaccurately label Hispanics "pushy" when they move closer than the non-Hispanic researcher may find comfortable.

Of course, Hispanics differ among themselves just like people in every other category do, and these generalizations apply to some more than to others. But investigators should be aware of cultural dynamics when carrying out research. The challenge is especially great in the United States, where hundreds of distinctive categories of people make up our multicultural society.

Source: Marín and Marín (1991).

the before and after measurements of the two groups, a researcher can assess how much of the change is due to the independent variable.

The Hawthorne Effect

Another concern of experimenters is that subjects may change their behavior simply because they are getting special attention, as one classic experiment revealed. In the late 1930s, the Western Electric Company hired researchers to study worker productivity in its Hawthorne factory near Chicago (Roethlisberger & Dickson, 1939). One experiment tested the hypothesis that increasing the lighting would raise worker output. First, researchers measured workers' productivity (the dependent variable). Then they increased the lighting

Q: "Science is meaningless because it gives no answer to the question, the only question of importance for us: 'What shall we do and how shall we live?'" Leo Tolstoy

SOCIAL SURVEY: *Student Social Survey Software*, using the new Student CHIP program, is available with this text. It provides 1972 through 1996 NORC General Social Survey data, and now has graphing capability. Each GSS involves about 1,500 subjects, selected from a multistage survey in which researchers first randomly select geographical areas and then randomly select adults over age 18 from each area. Excluded are individuals who are in any way "institutionalized" (including college students).

RESOURCE: Harry O'Neill's article "Our Attitudes About Survey Research" appears in the new edition of the Macionis and Benokraitis reader, *Seeing Ourselves*.

Philip Zimbardo's research helps to explain why violence is a common element in our society's prisons. At the same time, his work demonstrates the dangers that sociological investigation poses for subjects and the need for investigators to observe ethical standards that protect the welfare of people who participate in research.

(the independent variable) and measured output a second time. Productivity increased, supporting the hypothesis. But when the research team later turned the lighting back down, productivity increased again. What was going on? In time, the researchers realized that the employees were working harder (even if they could not see as well) simply because people were paying attention to them. From this research, social scientists coined the term **Hawthorne effect** to refer to *a change in a subject's behavior caused simply by the awareness of being studied.*

An Illustration: The Stanford County Prison

Prisons are often violent settings, but is this due to the "bad" people who end up there? Or, as Philip Zimbardo suspected, does the prison itself somehow lead to violent behavior? This question led Zimbardo to devise a fascinating experiment (Zimbardo, 1972; Haney, Banks, & Zimbardo, 1973).

Zimbardo contends that, once inside a prison, even emotionally healthy people become prone to violence. Thus Zimbardo treated the *prison setting* as the independent variable capable of causing *violence*, the dependent variable.

To test this hypothesis, Zimbardo's research team first constructed a realistic-looking "prison" in the basement of the psychology building at Stanford University. Then they placed an ad in a Palo Alto newspaper offering to pay young men to help with a two-week research project. To each of the seventy who responded they administered a series of physical and psychological tests, and then selected the healthiest twenty-four for their experiment.

The next step was to select, randomly, half the men as "prisoners" and half as "guards." The plan called for the guards and prisoners to spend the next two weeks in the "Stanford County Prison." The "prisoners" began their part of the experiment soon afterward when the Palo Alto police "arrested" them at their homes. After searching and handcuffing the men, the police took them to the local police station to be fingerprinted. Then they transported their captives to the Stanford "prison" where the "guards" put them behind bars. Zimbardo then sat back with a video camera to see what would happen.

The experiment soon turned into more than anyone had bargained for. Guards and prisoners became hostile toward one another. Guards humiliated the prisoners by assigning them tasks such as cleaning out toilets with their bare hands. The prisoners, for their part, resisted and insulted the guards. Within four days, the researchers removed five prisoners who displayed "extreme emotional depression, crying, rage and acute anxiety" (1973:81). Before the end of the first week, the situation had become so bad that the researchers had to cancel the experiment. Zimbardo explains (1972:4): "The ugliest, most base, pathological side of human nature surfaced. We were horrified because we saw some boys (guards) treat others as if they were despicable animals, taking pleasure in cruelty, while other boys (prisoners) became servile, dehumanized robots who thought only of escape, of their own individual survival and of their mounting hatred for the guards."

The events that unfolded at the "Stanford County Prison" supported Zimbardo's hypothesis that prison violence is rooted in the social character of jails themselves, not in the personalities of guards and prisoners. This finding raises questions about how and why our society operates prisons and suggests the need for basic reform. But also note that this experiment shows how research can threaten the physical and mental well-being of subjects. Such danger is not always as obvious as it was in this case. Therefore, researchers must consider carefully the potential harm to subjects at all stages of their work and end any

SOCIAL SURVEY: "In general, do you feel that surveys usually serve a good purpose or do you feel that they are usually a waste of time and money?" (GSS 1982, N = 1,506; *Codebook*, 1996:256)
"Good purpose" 70.6%   "Waste of time/money" 14.2%
"Depends"   8.4%   DK/NR   6.8%
NOTE: Sometimes samples produce better results than populations, considering that the tedious work of contacting a whole population can lead to all sorts of nonsampling errors.

NOTE: In truth, polling for the 1996 presidential election was not as good as in earlier years, suggesting that Clinton would beat Dole by some 15 percentage points—he actually won by eight. This error reveals a weakness of pre-election polls: What people say they will do and what they do later may differ.

SOCIOLOGY OF EVERYDAY LIFE

National Political Surveys

One hundred million men and women voted in the presidential election in 1996. Yet, based on survey data, well before the first vote was cast almost everyone knew that Bill Clinton would defeat challenger Bob Dole.

Political surveys, or *polls*, are a familiar part of national life. But how can researchers use information drawn from several hundred subjects to predict what 100 million people will do? The key to accurate prediction lies in selecting a sample *representative* of the entire population.

The ability to do this was a long time coming. In 1936, the *Literary Digest* surveyed U.S. voters and predicted that Republican Alfred E. Landon would handily defeat Democrat Franklin Delano Roosevelt. They could hardly have been more wrong, as Roosevelt buried Landon in a historic landslide.

The reason for such an error was simply that the magazine's sample did not represent the voting population. The *Digest* mailed survey ballots to 20 million people (far more than would be included in a poll today) selected from telephone

listings and automobile registrations. But, back then, most people who owned a telephone or car were affluent and, therefore, likely to be Republicans.

This embarrassing prediction did nothing for the prestige of the *Literary Digest*, which soon closed up shop. But that same year a young researcher named George Gallup (1902–1984) not only correctly called the election but warned that the *Literary Digest* would be way off the mark. Gallup went on to become the best-known survey researcher in the United States. Today, the organization he founded carries out surveys around the world, providing not only accurate predictions about elections but offering information about a host of other issues as well.

Source: Adapted, in part, from Babbie (1995).

study, as Zimbardo responsibly did, if subjects can suffer harm of any kind.

ASKING QUESTIONS: SURVEY RESEARCH

A **survey** is *a research method in which subjects respond to a series of items in a questionnaire or an interview.* Surveys are the most widely used of all research methods. They are particularly well suited to studying attitudes—such as beliefs about politics, religion, or race—since there is no way to directly observe what people think. Sometimes surveys provide clues about cause and effect, but typically they yield *descriptive* findings. In other words, they paint a picture of people's views of some issue.

Population and Sample

A survey targets some **population**, *the people who are the focus of research.* In Lois Benjamin's study of racism, as

noted at the beginning of this chapter, the population was talented African Americans. At the broadest level, political pollsters seeking to predict election returns use surveys that treat every adult in the country as the population.

Obviously, however, contacting millions of people would overwhelm even the most well-funded and patient researcher. Fortunately there is an easier alternative that yields accurate results. Researchers collect data from a **sample**, *a part of a population that represents the whole.* The box describes the evolution of national political surveys, which now use a sample of some 1,500 people to gauge the political mood of the entire country.

Although the term may be new, you use the logic of sampling all the time. If you look around the classroom and notice five or six heads nodding off, you might conclude that the class finds the day's lecture dull. In reaching this conclusion, you are making a judgment about *all* the people (the "population") from

DIVERSITY: The 1990 census showed an unexpected rise from 49 million to 58 million in the number of people of German ancestry. The reason turned out to be that "German" was listed first on the 1990 survey and fourth back in 1980. Similarly, the 1990 form used "French Canadian" as an example in the ancestry section, apparently causing the number of people claiming such ancestry to triple from 780,000 in 1980 to 2.2 million in 1990.

NOTE: "Pop" research is often flawed because of poor surveys. For example, the last "Hite survey" of male-female relationships was based on a survey return rate of only 4.5 percent.

NOTE: Survey organizations have found that enclosing a small amount of money with a questionnaire (say, a dollar bill) greatly improves the response rate. Even with follow-up mailings, however, response rates rarely exceed 75%.

observing *some* of the people (the "sample"). But how can we know if a sample actually represents the entire population?

One way to do this is to use *random sampling,* in which researchers draw a sample from the population randomly so that every element in the population has the same chance of being selected. The mathematical laws of probability dictate that a random sample will, in the vast majority of cases, accurately represent the general population.

Beginning researchers sometimes make the mistake of assuming that "randomly" walking up to people on the street produces a sample representative of an entire city. Unfortunately, such a strategy does not give every person an equal chance to be included in the sample. For one thing, any street—whether in a rich neighborhood or a "college town"—contains more of some kinds of people than others. For another, the researcher is apt to find some people more approachable than others, again introducing a bias.

Although good sampling is no simple task, it saves considerable time and expense. We are spared the tedious—and often impossible—work of contacting everyone in a population, yet we can obtain essentially the same results.

Questionnaires and Interviews

Selecting subjects is only the first step in carrying out a survey. Also needed is a plan for asking questions and recording answers. Most surveys take the form of either questionnaires or interviews.

A **questionnaire** is *a series of written questions that a researcher presents to subjects.* One type of questionnaire provides not only the questions but also fixed responses (similar to a multiple-choice examination). This *closed-ended format* makes the task of analyzing the results relatively easy, yet narrows the range of responses in a way that might distort the findings. For example, Frederick Lorenz and Brent Bruton (1996) found that how many hours per week students report studying for a college course depends on the options researchers offered to them. When the researchers presented students with a scale ranging from one hour or less up to nine hours or more, 75 percent said they studied four hours or less per week. But when a comparable group was given choices ranging from four hours or less up to twelve hours or more (which suggests that they should be studying more), they suddenly became more studious, with only 34 percent reporting that they studied four hours or less each week.

A second type of questionnaire, using an *open-ended format,* allows subjects to respond freely, expressing various shades of opinion. The drawback of this approach is that the researcher has to make sense out of what can be a bewildering array of answers.

The researcher must also decide how to present questions to subjects. Most often, researchers use a *self-administered survey,* mailing questionnaires to respondents and asking that they complete the form and mail it back. Since no researcher is present when subjects read the questionnaire, it must be both inviting and clearly written. *Pretesting* a self-administered questionnaire with a small number of people before sending it to the entire sample can avoid the costly problem of finding out—too late—that instructions or questions were confusing.

Using the mail (or, more recently, electronic mail) has the advantage of allowing a researcher to contact a large number of people over a wide geographical area at minimal expense. But many people treat such questionnaires as "junk mail," so that typically no more than half are completed and returned. Researchers often send follow-up mailings to coax reluctant subjects to respond.

Finally, keep in mind that many people are not capable of completing a questionnaire on their own. Young children obviously cannot, nor can many hospital patients, or a surprising number of adults who simply lack the required reading and writing skills.

An **interview** is *a series of questions a researcher administers in person to respondents.* In a closed-format design, researchers read a question or statement and then ask the subject to select a response from several alternatives. Generally, however, interviews are open-ended so that subjects can respond as they choose and researchers can probe with follow-up questions. However, the researcher must guard against influencing a subject, which can be as subtle and unintentional as raising an eyebrow when a person begins to answer.

A subject is more likely to complete a survey if contacted personally by the researcher, yet interviews have some disadvantages. Tracking people down is costly and time consuming, especially if all subjects do not live in the same area. Telephone interviews allow far greater "reach," but the impersonality of "cold calls" by telephone can lower the response rate.

In both questionnaires and interviews, how a question is worded greatly affects the answer. When asked if they object to homosexuals serving in the military, for example, most adults in the United States say "yes." Yet, asked if the government should exempt

NOTE: The Census Bureau reports that 63% of people returned the 1990 census forms.
DISCUSS: Another example of wording affecting survey responses is found in a *Time*/CNN poll (May 18-19, 1994) in which 23% of respondents claimed "government is spending too much on assistance to the poor," yet 53% agreed that "government is spending too much on welfare" (*Time*, June 27, 1994:26).

Q: "Information is difference that makes a difference." Gregory Bateson
SUPPLEMENTS: W. S. Slater's "The Proper Study," an amusing poem about sociological research, is found in the *Data File*.
NOTE: Although widely used in survey research, "snowball sampling" is really a crude approach unlikely to represent a population accurately.

These African American women and men attending a Philadelphia convention all have master's of business administration degrees (MBAs) and are on their way to successful careers. But, according to Lois Benjamin, who conducted interviews with one hundred highly successful African Americans, "making it" in the business world does not eliminate the sting of racial prejudice. On the contrary, she found, even the highest achievers still have to contend with barriers based on skin color.

homosexuals from military service, most say "no" (NORC, 1991). Moreover, emotionally loaded language can easily sway subjects. For instance, the term "welfare mothers" rather than "women who receive public assistance" adds an emotional element that encourages respondents to answer more negatively.

In still other cases, the wording of a question may suggest what other people think and thereby steer subjects. For example, people are more likely to respond positively to the question "Do you *agree* that the police force is doing a good job?" than to the similar question "Do you *think* that the police force is doing a good job?" Similarly, respondents are more likely to endorse a statement to "*not allow*" something (say, public speeches against the government) than a statement to "*forbid*" the same activity (Rademacher, 1992).

Finally, researchers may confuse respondents by asking double questions like "Do you think that the government should cut spending and raise taxes to reduce the deficit?" The problem here is that a subject could very well agree with one part of the question but reject the other, so that saying *yes* or *no* distorts the opinion that the researcher is seeking.

An Illustration: Studying the African American Elite

We opened this chapter by recounting how Lois Benjamin came to investigate the effects of racism on talented African American men and women. Benjamin was convinced that, contrary to some published research, even high-achieving people of color contend with racial hostility. She based her belief on her own experiences as the only black professor in the history of the University of Tampa. But was she the exception or the rule? To answer this question, Benjamin set out to discover whether—and how—racism had plagued others like herself.

Opting to conduct a survey, Benjamin chose to conduct interviews rather than to distribute a questionnaire because, first, she wanted to enter into a conversation with her subjects, to ask follow-up questions and pursue topics that she could not have anticipated. A second reason to favor interviews over questionnaires is that racism is a sensitive topic. A supportive investigator can make it easier for subjects to respond to painful questions (Bergen, 1993).

Choosing to conduct interviews did make it necessary to limit the number of people in the study. Benjamin settled for one hundred men and women. Even this small number kept Benjamin busy for more than two years scheduling, traveling, and meeting with respondents. She spent two more years transcribing the tapes of her interviews, sorting out what the hours and hours of talk told her about racism, and writing up her results.

In selecting a sample, Benjamin first considered contacting, at random, people listed in *Who's Who in Black America*. But she rejected this idea in favor of starting out with people she knew and asking them to suggest others. This strategy is called *snowball sampling* because the number of individuals included grows rapidly over time.

NOTE: Conducting interviews, as Lois Benjamin did, is something like traveling abroad. We have some idea of our direction and destination, but the unexpected always arises along the way. Imaginative improvisation is needed to make the most of an interview opportunity and sometimes even to "save a situation."

NOTE: Lois Benjamin did not clearly operationalize "talented African Americans," so that the population her sample represents remains only vaguely defined.

RESOURCE: John Brewer's article "Sensitivity in Field Research: A Study of Policing in Northern Ireland" is included in the Macionis and Benokraitis reader.

TABLE 2–1 The Talented One Hundred: Lois Benjamin's African American Elite

Sex	Age	Childhood Racial Setting	Childhood Region	Highest Educational Degree	Occupational Sector	Income	Political Orientation
Male 63%	35 or Younger 6%	Mostly Black 71%	West 6%	Doctorate 32%	College/ University 35%	More than $50,000 64%	Radical 13%
Female 37%	36 to 54 68%	Mostly White 15%	North/ Central 32%	Medical/ Law 17%	Private, Profit 17%	$35,000 to $50,000 18%	Liberal 38%
	55 or Older 26%	Racially Mixed 14%	South 38%	Master's 27%	Private, Nonprofit 9%	$20,000 to $34,999 12%	Moderate 28%
			Northeast 12%	Bachelor's 13%	Government 22%	Less than $20,000 6%	Conservative 5%
			Other 12%	Less 11%	Self-Employed 14%		Depends on Issue 14%
					Retired 3%		Unknown 2%
100%	100%	100%	100%	100%	100%	100%	100%

Source: Adapted from Lois Benjamin, *The Black Elite: Facing the Color Line in the Twilight of the Twentieth Century* (Chicago: Nelson-Hall, 1991), p. 276.

The appeal of snowball sampling is that it is easy to do—we begin with familiar people who provide easy introductions to their friends and colleagues. The drawback, however, is that snowball sampling rarely produces a sample that is representative of the larger population. Benjamin's sample probably contained many like-minded individuals, and it was certainly biased toward people willing to talk openly about race. She understood these problems, and did try to make her sample as varied as she could in terms of sex, age, and region of the country. Table 2–1 gives a statistical profile of the people in Benjamin's investigation.

Benjamin based all her interviews on a series of questions, but used an open-ended format so her subjects could pursue whatever issues they wished. Like many interviewers, Benjamin found her interviews took place in a wide range of settings. She met subjects in offices (hers or theirs), in hotel rooms, and in cars. In each case, Benjamin tape-recorded the conversation—which lasted from two-and-one-half to three hours—so she would not be distracted by taking notes.

As research ethics demand, Benjamin offered full anonymity to any individual who wanted it. Even so, many of her respondents—including such notables as Vernon E. Jordan, Jr. (former president of the National Urban League) and Yvonne Walker-Taylor (first woman president of Wilberforce University)—were accustomed to being in the public eye and permitted Benjamin to use their names.

What surprised Benjamin the most about her research was how eagerly many people responded to her request for an interview. These busy men and women appeared to go out of their way to contribute to this project. Furthermore, during the interviews, many displayed a high degree of emotion. At some point in the conversation, about forty of the one hundred subjects shed tears. For many, apparently, the research provided an opportunity to release feelings and share experiences never revealed before. How did Benjamin, herself, respond to such sentiments? She reports that she laughed, reflected, or cried along with her respondents. In light of this close rapport, we might wonder whether someone more formal and aloof (or any white investigator, for that matter) could have done this research successfully.

Though some researchers have shown that African Americans have gained social standing in recent decades, Benjamin's interviews caution us that

NOTE: Among the first systematic participant observers of U.S. society was Alexis de Tocqueville who, along with his companion Gustave Beaumont, traveled some 7,000 miles across the United States and Canada between May 11, 1831, and February 20, 1832, before writing *Democracy in America*.

Q: "We can no longer view the world as Descartes and Laplace would have us do, as 'rational onlookers,' from outside. Our place is within the same world that we are studying, and whatever scientific understanding we achieve must be a kind of understanding that is available to participants within the process of nature, i.e., from inside." Stephen Toulmin

 CRITICAL THINKING

Reading Tables: An Important Skill

A table provides a great deal of information in a small amount of space, so learning to read tables can increase your reading efficiency. When you spot a table, look first at the title to see what information it contains. In Table 2–1, the title tells us that the table provides a profile of the one hundred subjects participating in Lois Benjamin's research. Across the top of the table, you will see eight variables that define these men and women. Reading down under each one are various categories, each with a percentage; the percentages in each column add to one hundred.

Starting at the top left, we see that Benjamin's sample was mostly men (63 percent versus 37 percent women). In terms of age, most of the respondents (68 percent) were in the middle stage of life, and most grew up in a predominantly black community either in the South or in the North-Central region of the United States.

These individuals are, indeed, a professional elite. Notice that half have earned either a doctorate (32 percent) or a medical or law degree (17 percent). Given their extensive education (and Benjamin's own position as a professor), we should not be surprised that the

largest share (35 percent) work in academic institutions. In terms of income, these are well-off individuals, with most (64 percent) earning more than $50,000 annually (a salary that only 20 percent of all workers in the United States currently make).

Finally, we see that these one hundred individuals generally identify themselves as left-of-center politically. In part, this reflects their extensive schooling (which encourages progressive thinking) and the tendency of academics to lean toward the liberal end of the political spectrum.

---

race continues to shape the daily lives of talented people of color. Many reported fears that their racial identity would at some point undermine their success. Others worried that a race-based "glass ceiling" stood between them and the highest positions in our society. Summing up her respondents' thoughts and feelings, Benjamin states that, despite the improving social standing of African Americans, black people in the United States continue to feel the sting of racial hostility. Just as important, Benjamin shows that being a member of this nation's professional elite is no protection from racism.

Finding a persistent "color line" in U.S. society, Benjamin ends her study by expressing her commitment to change. Following the lead of W. E. B. Du Bois, she states that research is not merely a source of knowledge but a way of helping the people we study and, perhaps, ourselves.

IN THE FIELD: PARTICIPANT OBSERVATION

Lois Benjamin's research demonstrates that sociological investigation takes place not only in laboratories but "in the field," that is, where people carry on their everyday lives. The most widely used strategy for field study is **participant observation,** *a method by which*

researchers systematically observe people while joining in their routine activities.

Participant observation allows researchers to gain an inside look at social life in settings ranging from night clubs to religious seminaries. Cultural anthropologists commonly use participant observation (which they call *fieldwork*) to study other societies. They term their studies of unfamiliar cultures *ethnographies*. Sociologists prefer to call their accounts of people in particular settings *case studies*.

At the outset of a field study, social scientists typically have just a vague idea of what they are likely to find. Thus, most field research is *exploratory* and *descriptive*. Researchers might have a hypothesis in mind, but, just as likely, they may not yet realize what the important questions will turn out to be.

As its name suggests, participant observation has two sides. On the one hand, gaining an "insider's" look depends on becoming a participant by "hanging out" with others, trying to act, think, and even feel the way they do. Compared to experiments and survey research, then, participant observation has fewer hard-and-fast rules. But it is precisely this flexibility that allows investigators to explore the unfamiliar and adapt to the unexpected.

Unlike other research methods, participant observation requires a researcher to become immersed in

GLOBAL: Cultural differences may significantly impede research in unfamiliar settings. Language problems, for example, may slow interviewing as well as generate errors of understanding. A researcher abroad may also unintentionally "steer" subjects, perhaps even coercing agreement to participate in the study.
NOTE: Other well-known examples of participant-observation studies include Robert and Helen Lynd's *Middletown* and *Middletown* *in Transition* (Muncie, Ind.), W. Lloyd Warner's Yankee City series (Newburyport, Mass.), Herbert Gans's *The Levittowners* (Willingboro, N.J.), and Elliot Liebow's *Tally's Corner* (Washington, D.C.).
RESOURCE: In the methodological appendix to *Street Corner Society* (1981; orig. 1943), William Foote Whyte candidly assesses how his own values influenced his work.

Anthropologists and photographers Angela Fisher and Carol Beckwith have documented fascinating rituals around the world. As part of their fieldwork, they lived for months with the Himba in Namibia, in order to gain their acceptance and trust. During this time, a village man was killed by a lion. Later, his wives fell under the control of a lion spirit, apparently sent by the husband to bring these women to him in the afterlife. In the ritual shown above, photographed by Fisher and Beckwith, the women seek to rid themselves of the curse.

the setting, not for a week or two, but for months or even years. At the same time, and for the duration of the study, the researcher must maintain some distance as an "observer," mentally stepping back to record field notes and, eventually, interpret them. There is great tension in this method, as the investigator wears two faces: "Playing the participant" helps win acceptance and provides access to people's lives, while "playing the observer" affords the distance and perspective needed for analysis. Obviously, carrying out the twin roles of "insider" participant and "outsider" observer often comes down to a series of careful compromises.

Most sociologists carry out participant observation alone, so they—and we—must remember that the results depend on the interpretations of a single individual. Participant observation is typically **qualitative research,** meaning *investigation in which a researcher gathers impressionistic, not numerical, data.* Unlike experiments or surveys, participant observation usually involves little **quantitative research,** *investigation in which a researcher collects numerical data.* Some scientists think a method that relies on personal impressions is "soft," or lacking in scientific rigor. Yet the personal approach of participant observation is also a strength. While a team of sociologists administering formal surveys would disrupt many social settings, a sensitive participant-observer can often gain considerable insight into people's natural behavior.

An Illustration: *Street Corner Society*

In the late 1930s, a young graduate student at Harvard University named William Foote Whyte was fascinated by the lively street life of a nearby, rather run-down section of Boston. His curiosity eventually led him to carry out four years of participant observation in this neighborhood, which he called "Cornerville," producing a sociological classic in the process.

At the time, Cornerville was home to first- and second-generation Italian immigrants. Many were poor, and popular wisdom in Boston considered Cornerville a place to avoid: a poor, chaotic slum inhabited by racketeers. Unwilling to accept easy stereotypes, Whyte set out to discover for himself exactly what life was like inside this community. His celebrated book, *Street Corner Society* (1981; orig. 1943), describes Cornerville as a highly organized community with a distinct code of values, complex social patterns, and particular social conflicts.

In beginning his investigation, Whyte considered a range of research methods. He could have taken a pile of questionnaires to one of Cornerville's community

NOTE: The two Lynd studies of Muncie display significant changes in orientation: The first is basically a nontheoretical description, while the second is guided by a vaguely Marxist class analysis. After publishing the first study, Columbia University gave Robert Lynd a PhD and a faculty position; only then did he learn much about theory. Perhaps the second study might better have been titled "Lynd in Transition."

Q: "[Community studies are] the poor sociologist's substitute for the novel." Ruth Glass
Q: "The possibility of drawing inferences from what has been observed and described in London, as to what we might expect in New York or Chicago, rests on the assumption that the same forces create everywhere essentially the same conditions." Robert Park

centers and asked local people to fill them out. Or he could have asked members of the community to come to his Harvard office for interviews. But it is easy to see that such formal strategies would have prompted little cooperation and yielded few insights. Whyte decided, therefore, to ease in to Cornerville life and patiently seek out the keys to understanding this rather mysterious place.

Soon enough, Whyte discovered the challenges of field research. After all, an upper-middle-class WASPy graduate student from Harvard did not exactly "fit in" with Cornerville life. He soon found out, for example, that what he took to be a friendly overture could seem pushy and rude. Early on, Whyte dropped in at a local bar, hoping to buy a woman a drink and encourage her to talk about Cornerville. He looked around the room, but could find no woman alone. Presently, he thought he might have an opportunity when a fellow sat down with two women. He gamely asked, "Pardon me. Would you mind if I joined you?" Instantly, he realized his mistake:

> There was a moment of silence while the man stared at me. Then he offered to throw me down the stairs. I assured him that this would not be necessary, and demonstrated as much by walking right out of there without any assistance. (1981:289)

As this incident suggests, gaining entry to a community is the crucial (and sometimes hazardous) first step in participant-observation research. "Breaking in" requires patience, ingenuity, and a little luck. Whyte's big break came in the form of a young man named "Doc," whom he met in a local social service agency. Listening to Whyte's account of his bungled efforts to make friends in Cornerville, Doc sympathetically decided to take Whyte under his wing and introduce him to others in the community. With Doc's help, Whyte soon became a neighborhood "regular."

Whyte's friendship with Doc illustrates the importance of a *key informant* in field research, someone who introduces a researcher to a community and often remains a source of information and help. But using a key informant also has its risks. Because every person has a particular circle of friends, a key informant's guidance introduces bias into the study. Moreover, in the eyes of others, the reputation of the key informant usually rubs off—for better or worse—on the investigator. In sum, a key informant is helpful at the outset, but a participant-observer must soon seek a broad range of contacts.

Having entered the Cornerville world, Whyte began his work in earnest. But he soon learned that a good field researcher needs to know when to speak up and when to simply listen, look, and learn. One evening, he joined a group of Cornerville people talking about neighborhood gambling. Wanting to get the facts straight, Whyte asked naively, "I suppose the cops were all paid off?" In a heartbeat,

> The gambler's jaw dropped. He glared at me. Then he denied vehemently that any policeman had been paid off and immediately switched the conversation to another subject. For the rest of that evening I felt very uncomfortable.

The next day, Doc offered some sound advice:

> "Go easy on that 'who,' 'what,' 'why,' 'when,' 'where' stuff, Bill. You ask those questions and people will clam up on you. If people accept you, you can just hang around, and you'll learn the answers in the long run without even having to ask the questions." (1981:303)

In the months and years that followed, Whyte became familiar with life in Cornerville, and even married a local woman. In the process, he learned that this neighborhood was hardly the stereotypical slum. On the contrary, most immigrants worked hard, many were quite successful, and some could even boast of having sent children to college. In short, Whyte's book makes for fascinating reading about the deeds, dreams, and disappointments of one ethnic community, and it contains a richness of detail that can only come from long-term participant observation.

Whyte's work shows that participant observation is a method filled with tensions and contrasts. Its flexibility allows a researcher to respond quickly to an unfamiliar setting but makes replication difficult. Insight depends on getting close to people, even as scientific observation demands detachment. Little expense is involved since no elaborate equipment or laboratory is needed, but a study typically takes a year or more. Perhaps this long-term time commitment explains why participant observation is used less often than other methods. Yet the depth of understanding gained through research of this kind has greatly enriched our knowledge of many types of human communities.

USING AVAILABLE DATA: SECONDARY AND HISTORICAL ANALYSIS

Not all research requires investigators to collect their own data personally. Sociologists also engage in **secondary analysis,** *a research method in which a researcher uses data collected by others.*

THE MAP: Generally speaking, African Americans, Asian Americans, and Latinos are concentrated in different regions of the country (look ahead to National Map 13–3). The largest urban regions (surrounding New York and Los Angeles) are home to affluent minorities of all kinds (although they often live in distinctive neighborhoods). In most cases, however, a single county contains a disproportionate share of affluent people of only one minority category. In general, at all income levels, people of various racial and ethnic categories live in different regions of the country as well as in different communities.

NOTE: Historical research allows sociologists to discern the contours and impacts of social developments (such as industrialization or deindustrialization) that come to light only over long periods.

SEEING OURSELVES

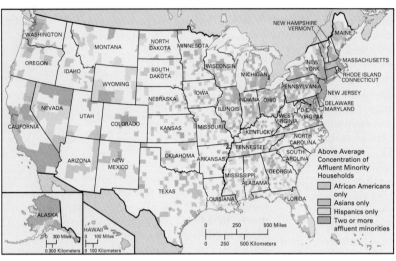

NATIONAL MAP 2–1
Affluent Minorities Across the United States

Based on 1990 census data, this map identifies the counties of the United States that contain an above-average share of affluent minority households—people earning at least $50,000 annually. (For the entire country, 23 percent of African American families, 23 percent of Hispanic families, and 35.0 percent of Asian families fall into this category.) Where in the United States do affluent members of each minority category live? Do members of one category tend to live where members of another category predominate? Can you explain this pattern?

Adapted from *American Demographics* magazine, Dec. 1992, pp. 34–35. Reprinted with permission. © 1992, *American Demographics* magazine, Ithaca, New York. Data from the 1990 decennial census.

The most widely used statistics in social science are gathered by government agencies. The Bureau of the Census continuously updates information about the U.S. population. Comparable data on Canada is available from Statistics Canada, a branch of that nation's government. In global investigations, researchers draw on publications from the United Nations and the World Bank. In short, a wide range of data about the whole world is as close as your library or the Internet.

Clearly, using available data—whether government statistics or the findings of individual researchers—saves time and money. This approach therefore holds special appeal for sociologists on low budgets. Perhaps even more important, though, government data are generally better than what even well-funded researchers could hope to obtain on their own.

Still, secondary analysis has its problems. For one thing, available data may not exist in precisely the form needed. Further, there are always questions about the meaning and accuracy of work done by others. For example, in his classic study of suicide, Emile Durkheim realized that he could not be sure that a death classified as a "suicide" was not, in reality, an "accident" and vice versa. He also knew that various agencies use different procedures and categories in collecting data, making comparisons difficult. In the end,

then, using secondhand data is a little like shopping for a used car: Bargains are plentiful, but you have to shop carefully to avoid ending up with a "lemon."

To illustrate, let's assume that reading about Lois Benjamin's account of African American elites sparks our interest in this country's affluent minorities. How many such people are there? Where do they live? National Map 2–1 displays Census Bureau data that address these questions. These statistics are the best available, and they are readily accessible at no cost. Yet to use them means accepting the Census Bureau's racial and ethnic categories (for example, as yet, no data on biracial people are available). It also means accepting people's self-reported income on government questionnaires as accurate. Finally, you must accept the given definitions of "affluent" and "above average," even though they may not exactly fit your purpose.

An Illustration: A Tale of Two Cities

Since we are all trapped in the present, secondary analysis provides a key to unlocking the secrets of the past. The award-winning study *Puritan Boston and Quaker Philadelphia*, carried out by E. Digby Baltzell (1979), exemplifies a researcher's power to analyze the past using data from historical sources.

RESOURCE: The *Statistical Abstract* is the single best source of statistical data about the population of the United States (order by telephone: 301-763-4100). For global data, see the World Bank's *World Development Report* (202-473-1155), and the United Nations's *Human Development Report* (212-963-8302).
NOTE: Interesting, although anecdotal, ways to describe the difference between the two cities: Puritan Boston named streets after great families, Quaker Philadelphia named streets after trees; a Boston accent often leads people to overestimate someone, a Philadelphia accent lends little prestige to the speaker. Boston's leading university (Harvard) was founded within a decade of the city's settlement and is at the top of the Ivy League; the founders of Philadelphia did not establish their university (University of Pennsylvania) for 60 years, and it is the least known Ivy.

It was a chance visit to Bowdoin College in Maine that prompted Baltzell to begin his investigation. Entering the college library, he was startled to see portraits of celebrated author Nathaniel Hawthorne, the eminent poet Henry Wadsworth Longfellow, and Franklin Pierce, our nation's fourteenth president. All three great men were members of a single class at Bowdoin, graduating in 1825. How could it be, Baltzell mused, that this small college had graduated more famous individuals in a single year than his own, much bigger University of Pennsylvania had done in its entire history? To answer this question, Baltzell was soon poring over historical documents to see if New England had indeed produced more famous individuals than his native Pennsylvania.

As his major source of data, Baltzell turned to the *Dictionary of American Biography*, twenty volumes profiling more than 13,000 men and women with records of greatness in fields such as politics, law, and the arts. Baltzell knew that relying on this source limited him to only those people who were deemed worthy by the *Dictionary*'s editors, but he also knew there was no better source.

The *Dictionary* told Baltzell *who* was great, but he also wanted to measure *how* great people were. He decided to base his ranking on the *Dictionary*'s claim that the more impressive the person's achievements, the longer the biography. So counting the number of lines in a biography yielded a crude "index of greatness." This strategy is certainly open to argument, but could Baltzell have done better entirely on his own?

By the time Baltzell had identified the seventy-five individuals with the longest biographies, he saw a striking pattern. Massachusetts had the most, with twenty-one of the seventy-five top achievers. The New England states, combined, claimed thirty-one of the entries. By contrast, Pennsylvania could boast of only two, and the entire Middle Atlantic region had just twelve. Looking more closely, Baltzell discovered that most of New England's great achievers had grown up in and around Boston. Again, in stark contrast, almost no one of comparable standing came from his own Philadelphia, a city with many more people than Boston.

What could explain this remarkable pattern? Baltzell drew inspiration from the German sociologist Max Weber (1958; orig. 1904–5), who believed that a region's record of achievement was largely a result of its predominant religious beliefs (see Chapter 4, "Society"). In the religious differences that set Boston apart from Philadelphia, Baltzell found the answer to his puzzle. Boston was a Puritan settlement, founded by people who pursued excellence and public achievement. Philadelphia, by contrast, was settled by Quakers, who were equally determined to shun any sort of public notice.

Both the Puritans and the Quakers were people fleeing religious persecution in England. But the two religious beliefs produced quite different cultural patterns. Convinced of humanity's innate sinfulness, Boston Puritans built a rigid society in which family, church, and school regulated people's behavior. They celebrated hard work as a way of glorifying God, and looked upon public success as a reassuring sign of God's blessing. In short, Puritanism fostered a disciplined life in which people vigorously sought and respected achievement.

Philadelphia's Quakers, on the other hand, built their way of life on the belief that all human beings are basically good. They saw little need for strong social institutions to "save" individuals from sinfulness. They believed in equality, so that even people who became rich considered everyone else a social equal. Thus rich and poor alike maintained a modest appearance and discouraged one another from standing out by seeking fame or pursuing public office.

In Baltzell's sociological imagination, Boston and Philadelphia took the form of two social "test tubes": Puritanism was poured into one, Quakerism into the other. Centuries later, we can see that different "chemical reactions" occurred in each case. The two belief systems apparently led to different attitudes toward personal achievement, which, in turn, shaped the history of each region and affect the lives of people who live there even today. For example, Boston's Kennedy family (despite being Catholic) still exemplifies the Puritan pursuit of fame and leadership, but there has *never* been a family with such public stature in the entire history of Philadelphia.

Baltzell's historical data do not *prove* his conclusions in any absolute sense. The best we can say is that his ideas make sense, his data support his theory, and his analysis squares with the work of major thinkers like Max Weber. But keep in mind that, especially when dealing with events far removed from the present, researchers use their interpretive talents. Baltzell's research reminds us that, in the end, sociological investigation is a complex weave of scientific skills, personal values, and a lively and practiced imagination.

Table 2–2 summarizes the four major methods of sociological investigation. We now turn to our final consideration: the link between research results and sociological theory.

NOTE: Inductive logical thought amounts to saying "If this is what happens, then what is true?" Deductive logical thought runs the other way: "If this is true, then what ought to happen?"

NOTE: Sherlock Holmes, celebrated for his great powers of deduction, actually engaged in *inductive reasoning*. On one occasion, while investigating a crime, Holmes was speaking with the woman of the house when he noticed the housekeeper searching for the cord to close the drapes. "Why did you dismiss your previous servant?" he asked. "How did you know!?" came her startled reply. "Elementary," he explained, "your present servant is obviously new to her duties."

TABLE 2–2 Four Research Methods: A Summary

Method	Application	Advantages	Limitations
Experiment	For explanatory research that specifies relationships among variables; generates quantitative data	Provides the greatest ability to specify cause-and-effect relationships; replication of research is relatively easy	Laboratory settings have an artificial quality; unless research environment is carefully controlled, results may be biased.
Survey	For gathering information about issues that cannot be directly observed, such as attitudes and values; useful for descriptive and explanatory research; generates quantitative or qualitative data	Sampling allows surveys of large populations using questionnaires; interviews provide in-depth responses	Questionnaires must be carefully prepared and may produce a low return rate; interviews are expensive and time consuming
Participant observation	For exploratory and descriptive study of people in a "natural" setting; generates qualitative data	Allows study of "natural" behavior; usually inexpensive	Time consuming; replication of research is difficult; researcher must balance roles of participant and observer
Use of available data	For exploratory, descriptive, or explanatory research whenever suitable data are available	Saves time and expense of data collection; makes historical research possible	Researcher has no control over possible biases in data; data may not be suitable for current research needs

THE INTERPLAY OF THEORY AND METHOD

No matter how they gather data, sociologists must ultimately transform facts into meaning by building theory. They do this in two ways.

Inductive logical thought is *reasoning that transforms specific observations into general theory.* In other words, the researcher's thinking moves from the specific to the general and goes something like this: "I have some interesting data here; I wonder what they mean? . . . ." E. Digby Baltzell's research illustrates the inductive model. His data show that one region of the country (the Boston area) produced many more high achievers than another (the Philadelphia region). He worked "upward" from ground-level observations to the high-flying theory that religious values were a key factor shaping people's attitude toward achievement.

A second type of logical thought works "downward" in the opposite direction. **Deductive logical thought** is *reasoning that transforms general theory into specific hypotheses suitable for scientific testing.* This time, the researcher's thinking moves from the general to the specific: "I have this hunch about human behavior; let's collect some data and put it to the test. . . ." Working deductively, the researcher first states the theory in the form of a hypothesis and then selects a method for testing it. To the extent that the data support the hypothesis, the theory is correct. Data that disprove the hypothesis tell us that the theory should be revised or even thrown out entirely.

Philip Zimbardo's Stanford County Prison experiment illustrates how deductive logic works. Zimbardo began with the general idea that prisons change human behavior. He then fashioned a specific, testable hypothesis: Placed in a prison setting, even emotionally well-balanced young men will behave violently. The violence that erupted soon after the experiment began supported Zimbardo's hypothesis. Had his experiment produced friendly behavior between "prisoners" and "guards," his original theory would have required revision.

Just as researchers commonly use several methods in one study, they typically make use of *both* types of logical thought. Figure 2–2 illustrates the two phases of scientific thinking: inductively building theory from observations and deductively making observations to test our theory.

Finally, the process of turning facts into meaning usually involves statistical data. And precisely how sociologists present their numbers affects the conclusions their readers draw. In other words, all research offers the chance to "spin" reality one way or another.

Often, we conclude that an argument must be true simply because there are statistics to back it up.

EXERCISE: Motivated students can learn a great deal from reading research reports. For example, Elliot Liebow's classic *Tally's Corner* (1967) or his last book *Tell Them Who I Am: The Lives of Homeless Women* both detail the research experience.

Q: "Truth must have one face, the same and universal." Michel de Montaigne

Q: "Plato is dear to me, but dearer still is truth." Aristotle
Q: "One unerring mark of the love of truth is not entertaining any proposition with greater assurance than the proofs it is built on will warrant." John Locke (1690)
Q: "The redeeming power of reflection cannot be supplanted by the extension of technically exploitable knowledge." Jürgen Habermas (1970:61)

However, we must look at statistics with a cautious eye. After all, researchers choose what data to present, they interpret their statistics, and they may use tables or graphs to steer readers toward particular conclusions. The final box, on pages 52–53, takes a closer look at this important issue.

PUTTING IT ALL TOGETHER: TEN STEPS IN SOCIOLOGICAL INVESTIGATION

We can draw together the material in this chapter by outlining ten steps in the process of carrying out research in sociology. Each step is represented by an important question:

1. **What is your topic?** Being curious and using the sociological perspective can generate ideas for social research anywhere. The issue you choose for study is likely to have some personal significance.

2. **What have others already learned?** You are probably not the first person with an interest in a particular issue. Visit the library to see what theories and methods other researchers have applied to your topic. In reviewing the existing research, note problems that may have come up before.

3. **What—exactly—are your questions?** Are you seeking to explore an unfamiliar social setting? To describe some category of people? Or to investigate cause and effect among variables? If your study is exploratory or descriptive, identify *who* you wish to study, *where* the research will take place, and *what* kinds of issues you want to explore. If it is explanatory, you also must formulate the hypothesis to be tested and carefully operationalize each variable.

4. **What will you need to carry out research?** How much time and money are available to you? Are special equipment or skills necessary? Can you do the work yourself? You should answer all these questions before beginning to plan the research project.

5. **Are there ethical concerns?** Not all research raises serious ethical questions, but you should be sensitive to this matter throughout your investigation. Can the research harm anyone? How can you minimize the chances for injury? Will you promise anonymity to the subjects?

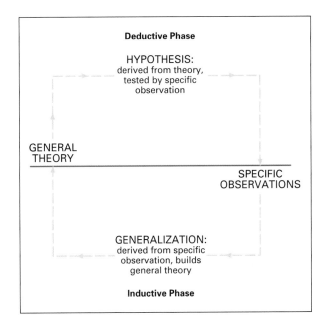

FIGURE 2–2 **Deductive and Inductive Logical Thought**

If so, how will you ensure that anonymity will be maintained?

6. **What method will you use?** Consider all major research strategies—as well as innovative combinations of approaches. Keep in mind that the appropriate method depends on the kinds of questions you are asking as well as the resources available to you.

7. **How will you record the data?** The research method you choose provides the system for data collection. Be sure to record information accurately and in a way that will make sense later (it may be some time before you actually write up the results of your work). Remain vigilant for any bias that may creep into the research.

8. **What do the data tell you?** Study the data in terms of your initial questions and decide what answers they suggest. If your study involves a specific hypothesis, you should be able to confirm, reject, or modify the hypothesis based on the data. Keep in mind that there may be several ways to interpret the results of your study, depending upon which theoretical paradigms you apply, and you should consider all the interpretations.

PART I
WELCOME TO THE INFORMATION REVOLUTION!

As we approach the new century—and the new millennium—we are witnessing astounding changes brought on by a new technology. For the last two centuries, the Industrial Revolution has shaped our society, dictating the kinds of work people do and how we think about the world. But now a transformation is under way—dubbed the Information Revolution—that is already redefining our world in novel ways.

At the end of each of the five parts of this text, we present a special section called "Cyber.Scope." These features look at important themes from the relevant chapters in terms of computers and other new information technology. In this first Cyber.Scope section, for example, we extend our discussions of the sociological perspective (Chapter 1) and sociological research (Chapter 2) to explain what the Information Revolution is all about.

The Age of Machines:
Industrial Society

The time line found inside the front cover of this book places the onset of the "modern era" about 250 years ago at the dawning of the Industrial Revolution. At that time— first in England and soon after in the United States—new sources of energy led imaginative people to create new products in new ways. First rivers and then steam generated by coal furnaces provided the power to operate large machines. Before long, the Industrial Revolution was changing all aspects of social life, drawing people away from home to work in the new factories and demanding that they learn the skills needed to operate large machines. As time went on, the increasing size and number of factories encouraged people to migrate from the countryside to the rapidly growing cities in eager search of jobs. There, most people experienced a faster-paced, more impersonal way of life and, in time, came to enjoy a higher material

Familiarity with computers is far more common among younger members of our society than with older generations. Today's young people, who will live out their lives during the twenty-first century, will find computers a natural and indispensable part of day-to-day living.

standard of living. These changes sparked an interest in studying society and played a major role in the birth of sociology.

The Age of Computers:
Information Society

The last half of this century has witnessed another technological transformation—the Information Revolution—which promises to change our world once again. The technology that will define the coming century is based on *information:* the computer and related technology, including the Internet, facsimile machines, cellular telephones, and satellite communications. The fact that we already use shorthand names for these devices—the "'Net," "fax," "cell phone," and "dish"—suggests how quickly they have become an established part of our lives.

The computer was invented in 1947 when U.S. engineers went "online" in a Philadelphia laboratory. They switched on a room-sized machine stuffed with wires and vacuum tubes. Despite its giant size, this "mother of all computers" could do no more than today's ten-dollar handheld calculator.

Since then, computers have become increasingly sophisticated and a basic element of our lives. We now find various devices using computer chips at work in virtually all new vehicles as well as the vast majority of our homes and businesses.

NOTE: The term "cyberspace" was coined by William Gibson in his 1984 novel, *Neuromancer*. Back in the 1940s, mathematician Norbert Weiner adapted the Greek *kybernan* (meaning "to steer") to coin "cybernetics," the science of automated systems (Wallis, 1996).

CYBER: In the Industrial Age, we thought of value in terms of material objects; in the Information Age, value lies in symbols. Thus, a new version of, say, Windows may have as much value as a new line of automobiles, but it exists only as a stored configuration of electrons.

Surveys show that in 1997, about 40 percent of U.S. households had at least one personal computer, with half of these connected to the Internet (FIND/SVP, 1997). As computers become more numerous—as well as more powerful, smaller, and more portable—they will write the rules of social life in the twenty-first century, just as monstrous machines defined social life in the industrial era now coming to a close.

What is different about new information technology? First, and most important, new information technology changes the kinds of work people do. Yesterday's industrial technology empowered people to create more and more *things*; information technology leads us to work with *ideas*, creating and manipulating symbols. The Industrial Age was represented by the factory assembly line, with workers toiling to make steel or to assemble cars. But the typical worker in the Information Age peers at a computer screen, entering data, writing, calculating, drawing, or designing.

A second key change brought about by the Information Revolution is the declining importance of distance and physical space. Industrial technology demands that people work in centralized factories (where the machinery and energy sources are located), but information technology allows people to work almost anywhere they can carry a computer or flip open a cell phone. Moreover, when we use this new technology to communicate with others, we often have no idea where they are. The term "cyberspace" even suggests that our emerging world is less and less bounded by physical dimensions. Interestingly, just as we gauged the output of industrial engines with a reference to the "horsepower" they made obsolete, so we now cling to older, physical images in describing new realities: We talk about the "information superhighway,"[1] read "bulletin boards," and enter "chat rooms." Yet these "places" are a "virtual reality," meaning that they are only computer simulations—they have no physical being at all. They exist only in the flow of electrons that illuminates our computers, electrons that circle the world at the speed of light.

As later chapters of the text explain, new information technology is changing nearly every dimension of our lives. It is reshaping culture and how we learn about the world, connecting us to people in new ways, generating new kinds of crime as well as new ways of pursuing criminals, and even altering patterns of social inequality. No doubt as we enter the new century we will see more changes that will spark people's sociological interest in the world around them.

New Information Technology: Thoughts on Theory

Chapter 1 ("The Sociological Perspective") discusses sociology's three major theoretical paradigms. What insights do these paradigms give us into new information technology?

A structural-functional analysis would point out that, because society is a system of countless interdependent elements, a new form of technology is likely to affect virtually all aspects of our lives. Since television was invented in 1939,

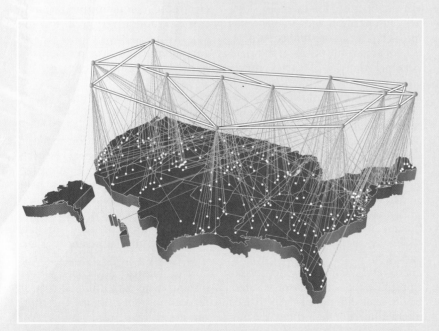

The Internet, an electronic superhighway that connects rapidly increasing numbers of people in the United States as well as around the world, will benefit researchers by improving our ability to communicate with one another and our access to sources of data.

---

[1]The rapidly increasing number of people logging onto the Internet has overwhelmed existing telephone lines and sometimes results in long delays in transmitting and receiving information. For a while, at least, the information "superhighway" may remain more of a "dirt road."

CYBER: In the 12 months from mid-1996 to mid-1997, the number of U.S. adults using the Internet doubled. Even if this rate slows, we should expect half of U.S. households to have logged on to the Internet by the end of this decade. The FIND/SVP survey found that, of all Internet users, 60% log on daily, and half do some "surfing" every day.

SOCIAL SURVEY: A survey in late 1995 found that 85% of respondents had heard of the Internet, although only 8% were current users (Katz, 1997).

SEEING OURSELVES

NATIONAL MAP I-1
Computer Users Across the United States

About 40 percent of U.S. households have a home computer, but computer literacy is not spread equally throughout the population. In general, personal computer (PC) ownership is high in major urban areas, where income and education levels are also high. Rural regions show below-average PC ownership. Also, more men than women own PCs, though this difference is fast disappearing.

Source: From Business Geographics. Copyright © 1994 GIS World, Inc., 155 E. Boardwalk Drive, Suite 250, Fort Collins, CO 80525, USA.

some 1 billion TV sets have been built. Television has altered what we know, how we learn, our patterns of recreation, and even the ways family members interact. The computer will almost certainly change our lives even more. Its manifest (that is, intended and expected) effects will range from decentralizing the workplace to encouraging entire cities to spread outward, since talking and working with others no longer requires being physically with them. The latent (that is, unintended) effects are harder to foresee, but they may well include new kinds of human communities, as people gradually pay less attention to their physical neighbors and spend more time online interacting with like-minded others.

A social-conflict analysis of the rise of new information technology offers some very different insights, especially regarding social inequality. We might note, for example, that new information technology has spread rapidly among affluent people, but not among the poor—as shown in National Map I-1. There is already evidence that the information age will be marked by two distinct classes: educated people with sophisticated symbolic skills (who are likely to prosper) and people without symbolic skills (who are likely to remain in low-income jobs). Statistics show that among workers in the same job, those able to use a computer earn 15 percent more than those who cannot (Ratan, 1995).

Finally, the symbolic-interaction paradigm asks questions at the micro-level of analysis. How, for example, does communication via electronic mail differ from face-to-face interaction? For one thing, lacking facial expression or tone of voice, electronic communication cannot convey emotion very well. For this reason, as shown in Figure I–1, computer users have developed a new cyber-language.

New Information Technology: What About Research?

How is new information technology changing sociological research, the focus of Chapter 2? A generation of sociologists has been trained to use computers to select random samples, perform complex statistical analysis, and prepare written reports efficiently. Electronic mail enables researchers to "travel" almost anywhere almost instantly and with minimal cost. In the coming years, more and more surveys will take place online. And

CYBER: Percent of homes with TV, 98%; personal computers, 40%; computers with CD-ROM, 19%; modems, 16%; fax machines, 8% (Electronic Industries Association survey, 1995).

NOTE: Microsoft, the leading software company, has sales rivaling industrial giant GM, but uses far fewer people in physical facilities a fraction of the size.

GLOBAL: The computer revolution may speed the use of English as a global language. Currently, almost all keyboards favor the Latin alphabet and, according to one study, 82.3% of home pages are in English. Other home page languages: German, 4.0%; Japanese, 1.6%; French, 1.5%; Spanish, 1.1% (Alis Technologies and the Internet Society; http://babel.alis.com:8080/palmares.html).

electronic surveys raise some interesting questions: Will this technology improve survey response rates or will people discard the surveys as electronic junk mail? Will cyber-surveys end up protecting respondents' anonymity or threatening their privacy?

What seems sure is that new information technology will greatly enhance communication among researchers throughout the world. The Internet—highlighted in the next Cyber.Scope on pages 232–33—now links at least 100 million people in 160 countries. It gives sociologists a powerful tool for building networks, sharing information, and conducting joint research. Just as important, faculty and students alike now have ready access to a vast amount of statistical information. For example, the U.S. Bureau of the Census (see their Web home page at http://www.census.gov) publishes reports of all kinds online, and will respond to questions from individuals doing research on their own.

Visit Us Online!

Please accept an invitation to visit the Web sites that accompany this text. To review our family of textbooks, and to find news and links of sociological interest, travel to http://www.macionis.com For interactive study resources, our Internet address is **http://www.prenhall.com/macionis** There, you will find learning objectives for each chapter, self-scoring practice tests, a chat room where you can share ideas with others, links to hundreds of other instructive and fascinating Web sites, and even a link that lets you send a note to the text author. Welcome, and enjoy!

FIGURE I–1 Cyber-Symbols: An Emerging Language

It all started with the "smiley" figure that shows someone is happy or telling a joke. Now a new language is developing as clever people use computer keystrokes to create emoticons, symbols that convey thoughts and emotions. Here's a sampling of the new cyber-language. (Rotate this page 90° to the right to fully appreciate the emoticon faces.)

: -)	I'm smiling at you.
: `-)	I'm so happy (laughing so hard) that I'm starting to cry.
: - O	Wow!
: - x	My lips are sealed!
: -||	I'm angry with you!
: - P	I'm sticking my tongue out at you!
: - (	I feel sad.
: - |	Things look grim . . . .
% -}	I think I've had too much to drink . . . .
-:(	Somebody cut my hair into a mohawk!
+O:-)	I've just been elected Pope!
@}——->———	Here's a rose for you!

Computers are as popular in Japan as they are in the United States. And the Japanese have their own emoticons:

(^_^)	I'm smiling at you.
(*^o^*)	This is exciting!
(^o^)	I am happy.
\(^o^)/	Banzai! This is wonderful!

How far will this new keyboard language go? If you're creative enough, anything is possible. Here's a routine that has been making the rounds on the Internet. It's called "Mr. Asciihead Learns the Macarena"! To see Mr. Asciihead in action, go to the link at http://www.macionis.com

```
o        o       o       o       o      <o      <o>      o>       o
.|.      \|.     \|/     //      X      \        |       <|      <|>
/\       >\      /<      >\      /<      >\      /<      >\      /<
```

Sources: Pollak (1996) and Krantz (1997). Mr. Asciihead is the creation of Leow Yee Ling.

Mike Larsen, *Generations*
Larsen & Larsen Studios, Inc.

CHAPTER 3

CULTURE

Patiently waiting outside a small building in Uncasville, Connecticut, about 9:00 A.M., a small group of people watch for ninety-eight-year-old Gladys Tantaquidgeon to begin the walk up the hill from the home she shares with her eighty-eight-year-old sister. She greets everyone as she opens the door to the museum her family founded back in 1931, which houses the heritage of the Mohegan tribe, a Native American people who have lived in this region for centuries.

To anyone familiar with James Fenimore Cooper's novel, *The Last of the Mohicans*, the fact that the Mohegans are flourishing in Connecticut may come as a surprise. But Gladys Tantaquidgeon knows better. Standing barely five feet tall, Tantaquidgeon serves as the Mohegan's tribal matriarch—a leader who keeps records of tribal members, collects and displays the artifacts of her people, and keeps alive the stories of centuries past.

For most of her life, Tantaquidgeon has also served as a medicine woman, turning forest herbs into healing tonics. But her greatest gift to her people has been helping them legally establish their tribal status.

Government officials did not doubt the historical reality of the Mohegans, but they demanded proof that Mohegans continue to live throughout the region today. Gladys Tantaquidgeon stepped forward, offering dozens of Tupperware containers containing her people's birth, marriage, and death certificates, as well as postcards from Mohegans living elsewhere. The officials nodded in agreement.

With the existence of the Mohegans no longer in question, the tribe has opened a gambling casino, and the proceeds provide a college education for every Mohegan youngster who completes high school. Thanks to Gladys Tantaquidgeon, the tribe is thriving, and no one in Uncasville is likely to become the last of the Mohegans. "No," Tantaquidgeon smiles shyly, adding "I've never even read the book" (Martin, 1997).

The 5.9 billion people living on earth are members of a single biological species: *Homo sapiens*. Even so, the differences among human beings can delight, puzzle, disturb, and sometimes overwhelm us. Many of the variations in lifestyles barely matter: Australians, for example, flip switches "down" to put lights "on," while North Americans flip them "up." The Australians, British, and Japanese all drive on the left side of the road, while we drive on the right. Other differences are quite charming. Take the practice of kissing: Most people in the United States kiss in public, but the Chinese kiss only in private; the French kiss publicly twice (once on each cheek), while Belgians kiss three times (starting on either cheek); the New Zealand Maoris rub noses and, for their part, most Nigerians don't kiss at all. At weddings, moreover, U.S. couples

SUPPLEMENTS: Chapter 3 of the *Data File* includes a detailed chapter outline, supplementary lecture material, and discussion questions.

GLOBAL: Another example of contrasting cultural conventions: The Chinese wear white at funerals while people in the United States prefer black; the Chinese people link the number four with bad luck, the way U.S. people view the number thirteen.

NOTE: To study formally her Mohegan culture, Gladys Tantaquidgeon spent 8 years in the anthropology department at the University of Pennsylvania; in 1970, she authored a book on herbal medicine, which led to an honorary degree from Yale University in 1994.

NOTE: Note that sociologists use "culture" in an all-inclusive way, not with highbrow connotations ("cul-chah").

Like so many elements of our lives, notions about kissing vary from place to place. People in the United States kiss in public; the Chinese do so only in private; moreover, while we touch lips, the French kiss on each cheek, and New Zealand's Maoris, shown above, rub noses.

kiss, Koreans bow, and a Cambodian groom touches his nose to the bride's cheek.

Some cultural differences, however, are more profound. The world over, people have many or few children, honor or push aside the elderly, are peaceful or warlike, embrace different religious beliefs, and enjoy different kinds of art and music. In short, although we are all the same creatures biologically, human beings have developed very different ideas about what is pleasant and repulsive, polite and rude, beautiful and ugly, right and wrong. Our species' capacity for startling difference is expressed through culture.

WHAT IS CULTURE?

Sociologists define **culture** as *the values, beliefs, behavior, and material objects that constitute a people's way of life.* Culture includes what we think, how we act, and what we own. By being a bridge to our past, culture is also a guide to the future (Soyinka, 1991).

To begin to understand all that culture involves, it helps to distinguish between thoughts and things. What sociologists call **nonmaterial culture** is *the intangible world of ideas created by members of a society,* ideas that range from altruism to zen. **Material culture,** on the other hand, refers to *the tangible things created by members of a society*, everything from armaments to zippers.

Not only does culture shape what we do, it also helps form our personalities—what we commonly (yet inaccurately) describe as "human nature." The warlike Yąnomamö of the Brazilian rain forest think aggression is natural in children, while, halfway around the world, the Semai of Malaysia expect their young to be peaceful and cooperative. The cultures of the United States and Japan both stress achievement and hard work; but members of our society value individualism more than the Japanese, who embrace tradition.

Given the cultural differences in the world and the tendency of all of us to view our own way of life as "natural," it is no wonder that travelers often feel **culture shock,** *personal disorientation that comes from experiencing an unfamiliar way of life.* The box on page 64 presents one researcher's encounter with culture shock.

`December 1, 1994, Istanbul, Turkey. Harbors everywhere, it seems, have two things in common: ships and cats. Istanbul, the tenth port on our voyage, is awash with felines, prowling about in search of an easy meal. People may change from place to place, but cats do not.`

No cultural trait is inherently "natural" to humanity, even though most people around the world view their own way of life that way. What is natural to our species is the capacity to create culture. Every other form of life—from ants to zebras—behaves in uniform, species-specific ways. To a world traveler, the enormous diversity of human life stands out in contrast to the behavior of, say, cats, which is the same everywhere. This uniformity follows from the fact that most living creatures are guided by *instincts,* biological programming over which animals have no control. A few animals—notably chimpanzees and related primates—have the capacity for limited culture; they can use tools and teach simple skills to their offspring. But the creative power of humans far exceeds that of any other form of life. In short, *only humans rely on culture rather than instinct to ensure the survival of their kind* (Harris, 1987).

To understand how human culture came to be, we must briefly review the history of our species on earth.

CULTURE AND HUMAN INTELLIGENCE

In a universe some 15 billion years old, our planet is a much younger 4.5 billion years of age (see the time

GLOBAL: In light of rapid technological advance, will people from various parts of the world, as shown here, appear so different a century from now?

NOTE: The Latin root of "culture," *cultur(a)*, means "a tilling." "Cultivate" and "agriculture" have the same root. In this sense, culture is the means by which humans cultivate the world.

Q: "Culture or civilization is that complex whole which includes knowledge, belief, art, morals, laws, customs, and any other capabilities and habits acquired by man as a member of society." Edward B. Tylor (1832–1917), writing perhaps the first formal definition of culture

Q: "The child that is born into any society finds that most of the problems . . . confronted in the course of . . . life have already been met and solved by those who have lived before." Ralph Linton

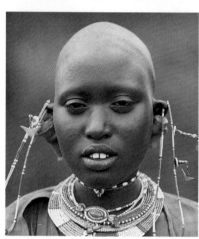

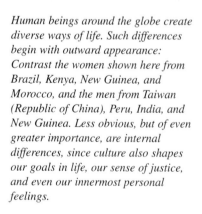

Human beings around the globe create diverse ways of life. Such differences begin with outward appearance: Contrast the women shown here from Brazil, Kenya, New Guinea, and Morocco, and the men from Taiwan (Republic of China), Peru, India, and New Guinea. Less obvious, but of even greater importance, are internal differences, since culture also shapes our goals in life, our sense of justice, and even our innermost personal feelings.

SUPPLEMENTS: How would we describe our own way of life to people from another country? See the "Culturegram" description of life in the U.S. found in the *Data File*.

NOTE: The early human ancestor Lucy, who lived about 3 million years ago, stood about 3 feet 6 inches tall and weighed 65 pounds; at that time, men might have reached 5 feet and 100 pounds. Sex differences have grown smaller with time: Today's global averages are 5 feet 6 inches tall for men, 5 feet 2 inches for women, 150 pounds for men, 125 for women.

Q: "Natives who beat drums to drive off evil spirits are objects of scorn to smart Americans who blow horns to break up traffic jams." Mary Ellen Kelly

Q: "Cultures are dramatic conversations about things that matter . . ." Robert Bellah

GLOBAL SOCIOLOGY

Confronting the Yąnomamö: The Experience of Culture Shock

A small aluminum motorboat chugged steadily along the muddy Orinoco River, deep within South America's vast tropical rain forest. Anthropologist Napoleon Chagnon was nearing the end of a three-day journey to the home territory of the Yąnomamö, one of the most technologically primitive societies on earth.

Some 12,000 Yąnomamö live in villages scattered along the border of Venezuela and Brazil. Their way of life could hardly be more different from our own. The Yąnomamö wear little clothing and live without electricity, cars, or other conveniences that people in the United States take for granted. Their traditional weapons, used for hunting and warfare, are the bow and arrow. Most Yąnomamö have had little contact with the outside world, so Chagnon would be as strange to them as they would be to him.

By 2:00 in the afternoon, Chagnon had almost reached his destination. The hot sun and humid air were almost unbearable. Chagnon's clothes were soaked with perspiration, and his face and hands were swollen from the bites of gnats swarming around him. But he scarcely noticed the discomfort,

so preoccupied was he with the prospect of meeting people unlike any he had ever known.

Chagnon's heart pounded as the boat slid onto the riverbank. Chagnon and his guide climbed from the boat and headed toward the Yąnomamö village, pushing their way through the dense undergrowth. Chagnon describes what happened next:

> I looked up and gasped when I saw a dozen burly, naked, sweaty, hideous men staring at us down the shafts of their drawn arrows! Immense wads of green tobacco were stuck between their lower teeth and lips making them look even more hideous, and strands of

dark green slime dripped or hung from their nostrils—strands so long that they clung to their [chests] or drizzled down their chins.

> My next discovery was that there were a dozen or so vicious, underfed dogs snapping at my legs, circling me as if I were to be their next meal. I just stood there holding my notebook, helpless and pathetic. Then the stench of the decaying vegetation and filth hit me and I almost got sick. I was horrified. What kind of welcome was this for the person who came here to live with you and learn your way of life, to become friends with you? (1992:11–12)

Fortunately for Chagnon, the Yąnomamö villagers recognized his guide and lowered their weapons. Chagnon knew he would survive at least the afternoon, but he was shaken by his inability to make any sense of these people. And this was to be his home for a year and a half! He wondered why he had forsaken physics to study human culture in the first place.

Source: Chagnon (1992).

lines inside the front cover of the text). Not until a billion years after the earth was formed did life appear. Several billion more years went by before dinosaurs ruled the planet and then disappeared. And then, some 65 million years ago, our history took a crucial turn with the appearance of creatures we call primates.

What sets primates apart is their intelligence: They have the largest brains (relative to body size) of all living creatures. About 12 million years ago, primates began to develop along two different lines, setting apart humans from the great apes, our closest relatives. But our common lineage is evident in the traits that we share with today's chimpanzees,

Q: "Man has no nature; what he has is history . . ." José Ortega y Gasset

NOTE: Light from the nearest galaxy (Andromeda) takes 2 million years to reach the earth; thus the light we see in the night sky was generated by the stars before humans existed on earth.

Q: "The problem with other cultures is that other people don't behave the way we expect them to, that is, like us." Craig Storti

NOTE: Illustrating the distinction between nation and society, French-speaking Canada (Quebec) is largely a separate society from the remainder of English-speaking Canada.

Q: "There can obviously be no culture without a society [and] no cultureless human society is known; it would even be hard to imagine. But it does not hold on the subhuman level . . . ants and bees do have genuine societies without culture . . ." A. L. Kroeber

gorillas, and orangutans: great sociability, affectionate and long-lasting bonds for child rearing and mutual protection, the ability to walk upright (normal in humans, less common among other primates), and hands that can manipulate objects with great precision.

Fossil records show that, about 3 million years ago, our distant ancestors grasped cultural fundamentals such as the use of fire, tools, and weapons, and were able to create simple shelters and basic clothing. These Stone Age achievements may seem modest, but they mark the point at which our ancestors embarked on a distinct evolutionary course, making culture the primary strategy for human survival.

To convey that human beings are wide-eyed infants in the larger scheme of things, Carl Sagan (1977) superimposed the 15-billion-year history of our universe on a single calendar year. The life-giving atmosphere of the earth did not develop until autumn, and the earliest beings who resembled humans did not appear until December 31—the last day of the year—at 10:30 at night. Only mere minutes before midnight (250,000 years ago) did our own species finally emerge. These *Homo sapiens* (Latin, meaning "thinking person") continued to evolve so that, about 40,000 years ago, humans who looked more or less like ourselves roamed the earth. With larger brains, these "modern" *Homo sapiens* developed culture at a rapid pace, as the wide range of tools and cave art from this period suggests.

The road to "civilization," based on permanent settlements and specialized occupations, became established in the Middle East (in what is today Iraq and Egypt) only about 12,000 years ago. In terms of Sagan's "year," this cultural flowering occurred during the final *seconds* before midnight on New Year's Eve. And what of our modern, industrial way of life? Begun only 300 years ago, in Sagan's scheme, it amounts to a mere millisecond flash.

Human culture, then, is very recent and was a long time in the making. As culture became a strategy for survival, our ancestors descended from the trees into the tall grasses of central Africa. There, walking upright, they learned the advantages of hunting in groups. From this point on, the human brain grew larger, allowing for greater human capacity to create a way of life—as opposed to simply acting out biological forces. Gradually, culture pushed aside instinct so that humans could *fashion the natural environment for themselves.* Ever since, people have made and remade their worlds in countless ways, which explains today's fascinating cultural diversity.

CULTURE, NATION, AND SOCIETY

At this point, we might well pause to clarify the proper use of several similar terms—"culture," "nation," and "society." *Culture* refers to a shared way of life. A *nation* is a political entity, that is, a territory within designated borders such as the United States, Canada, Argentina, or Zimbabwe. *Society*, the topic of the next chapter, is the organized interaction of people in a nation or within some other boundary.

We can correctly describe the United States, then, as both a nation and as a society. But many societies—including the United States—are *multicultural*, meaning that they include various ways of life that blend (and sometimes clash) in our everyday lives.

In the United States, how many cultures are there? One clue is that the 1990 census showed 130 Native American languages spoken in the United States, as well as hundreds of languages brought by immigrants from around the globe. Worldwide, experts have documented more than 5,000 languages, suggesting that at least this many cultures have existed on the earth (Durning, 1993; Crispell, 1997). Fewer cultures exist today because of high technology communication, greater international migration, and an expanding global economy. Even so, as the chapter-opening story of the Mohegans suggests, there is more cultural variety in our familiar surroundings than we often realize.

And what of world nations? The tally has risen and fallen throughout history as a result of political events. The breakup of the former Soviet Union and the former Yugoslavia, for example, added nineteen nations to the count. In 1997, there were 191 politically independent nations in the world.

THE COMPONENTS OF CULTURE

Although the cultures of the world's nations differ in many ways, they all are built on five components: symbols, language, values, norms, and material objects. We shall consider each in turn.

SYMBOLS

Like all creatures, human beings sense the surrounding world, but unlike others, we also create a reality of *meaning.* That is, humans transform elements of the world into **symbols,** *anything that carries a particular meaning recognized by people who share culture.* A whistle, a wall of graffiti, a flashing red light, and a fist raised

NOTE: Illustrate symbolic change by noting tattoos, once considered a mark of a person of low station, are now popular among affluent college students (if not always with their parents).
RESOURCE: Leslie White's article "Symbol: The Basic Element of Culture" and Robert Merton's "Manifest and Latent Functions" are two classics on culture found in the Macionis and Benokraitis reader, *Seeing Ourselves.*

GLOBAL: If one disturbs a woman in the bath, what body parts does she cover? According to Helen Colton (1983), an Islamic woman covers her face; a pre-revolutionary Chinese woman covered her feet; a Sumatran woman covers her knees; a Laotian woman covers her breasts; a Samoan woman covers her navel; a North American or European woman covers her breasts with one hand and her genital area with the other.

As shown by Alighierio e Boetti's artwork Map, *each of the world's 191 nations has created a symbol of itself in the form of a flag. Around the globe, people are expected to treat a flag with respect because, in any cultural system, the flag is the nation.*

Alighierio e Boetti, *Mappa* (Map), 1971–89, embroidery on canvas, 118 × 236¼ in. Collection Caterina Boetti, Rome. Photo courtesy of Cathy Carver/Dia Center for the Arts.

in the air are all symbols. We can see the human capacity to create symbols reflected in the different meanings associated with the simple act of winking the eye. In some settings, winking conveys interest; in others, understanding; in still others, insult.

Because we are surrounded by our culture's symbols, we take them for granted. We can, however, become keenly aware of the power of a symbol if someone uses it in an unconventional way, as, for example, when a person burns a U.S. flag in a political demonstration. We also realize the power of symbols when we visit another country. Culture shock is really the inability to "read" meaning in new surroundings. Not understanding the symbols of a culture leaves a person feeling lost and isolated, unsure of how to act, and sometimes frightened.

Culture shock is a two-way process. On the one hand, the traveler *experiences* culture shock when encountering people whose way of life is different. For example, North Americans who consider dogs beloved household pets might be put off by the Masai of eastern Africa, who ignore them and never feed them. These same travelers might well be horrified to find that in parts of Indonesia and in the northern regions of the People's Republic of China, people *roast* dogs for dinner.

On the other hand, a traveler *inflicts* culture shock on others by acting in ways that give offense. A North American who asks for a cheeseburger in an Indian restaurant offends Hindus, who hold cows to be sacred and not to be eaten.

Global travel provides almost endless opportunities for misunderstanding. In an unfamiliar setting, we need to remember that even behavior that seems innocent and normal to us may offend others, as the photos on page 67 suggest.

Then, too, symbolic meanings can vary within a single society. A fur coat may represent a luxurious symbol of success or the inhumane treatment of animals. Similarly, a Confederate flag, which for one individual embodies regional pride, may symbolize racial oppression to someone else.

Cultural symbols also change over time. Blue jeans were created more than a century ago as sturdy and inexpensive work clothes. In the liberal political climate of the 1960s, jeans became popular among affluent students, who wore them to look "different" or perhaps to identify with working people. A decade later, "designer jeans" appeared as high-priced status symbols. Today, jeans are as popular as ever, simply as comfortable apparel.

In sum, we use symbols to make sense of our lives. Shared symbols allow us to communicate with others in our own culture. In a world of cultural diversity, however, the careless use of symbols can cause embarrassment and even conflict.

LANGUAGE

In infancy, an illness left Helen Keller (1880–1968) blind and deaf. Without these two senses, she was cut off from the symbolic world, greatly limiting her social development. Only when her teacher, Anne Mansfield Sullivan, broke through Keller's isolation using sign language did Helen Keller begin to realize her human potential. This remarkable woman, who later became a renowned educator herself, recalls the moment she grasped the concept of language.

SUPPLEMENTS: A discussion of the development of human communication appears in the *Data File*.
DISCUSS: Introduce the concept of "collective memory," significant events that become part of a people's cultural heritage. Paul Revere's ride, Washington crossing the Delaware, M. L. King's "I have a dream" speech, and, recently, the O. J. Simpson trial and the Oklahoma City bombing are all part of our "collective memory."

NOTE: For decades, a "nurture versus nature" debate has surrounded language. Nurture advocates argue that language systems are distinctive and that language is learned along with other cultural elements. Nature advocates counter that all linguistic systems have similar internal structures, suggesting that language construction is "wired" into the human brain. Noam Chomsky is a well-known supporter of the latter view.

People throughout the world communicate not just with spoken words but also with bodily gestures, which vary from culture to culture. To most North Americans, there is nothing unusual about the young woman shown in the left-hand photo. But to people living in Muslim societies—who typically use the left hand for bathroom hygiene—eating this way is disturbing, to say the least! Similarly, the familiar "A-OK" gesture, by which we express approval and pleasure, is likely to insult a French person, who "reads" the message as "You're worth zero." Finally, even the commonplace "thumbs up" gesture we take to mean "Good job!" can get you into trouble in Australia, where people take it to mean "Up yours!"

We walked down the path to the well-house, attracted by the smell of honeysuckle with which it was covered. Someone was drawing water, and my teacher placed my hand under the spout. As the cool stream gushed over one hand, she spelled into the other the word *water*, first slowly, then rapidly. I stood still, my whole attention fixed upon the motions of her fingers. Suddenly I felt a misty consciousness as of something forgotten—a thrill of returning thought; and somehow the mystery of language was revealed to me. I knew then that "w-a-t-e-r" meant the wonderful cool something that was flowing over my hand. That living word awakened my soul; gave it light, hope, joy, set it free! (1903:21–24)

Language, the key to the world of culture, is *a system of symbols that allows members of a society to communicate with one another.* These symbols take the form of spoken and written words that vary from culture to culture. Not only do words differ, so do alphabets and conventions for writing. In general, people in Western societies write from left to right, people in northern Africa and western Asia write right to left, and people in eastern Asia write from top to bottom.

Global Map 3–1 on page 68 shows where in the world one finds the three most widely spoken languages.

Chinese is the official language of 20 percent of humanity (about 1.2 billion people). English is the mother tongue of about 10 percent (600 million) of the world's people, and Spanish is the official language of 6 percent (350 million). Notice, too, that you can travel almost anywhere in the world, except for western Africa, and "get by" speaking English. English is fast becoming the second tongue in most of the world and the international language of business and computer communication.

Language and Cultural Transmission

For people everywhere, language is the major means of **cultural transmission,** *the process by which one generation passes culture to the next.* Just as our bodies contain the genes of our ancestors, so our cultural heritage contains countless symbols of past generations. Language is the key that unlocks centuries of accumulated wisdom.

Throughout human history, people have transmitted culture through speech, a process sociologists call the *oral cultural tradition.* Only some 5,000 years ago did humans invent writing, and, even then, just a favored few learned to read and write. It was not until this century that nations (generally the industrial,

GLOBAL: Sanskrit is the oldest living language.

GLOBAL: Key reasons for the global reach of English are British colonialism, the worldwide U.S. presence in World War II, and the economic power of the U.S. since then. While younger Japanese people speak at least some English, most older people do not. The strength of the Japanese economy as well as that nation's historic monoculturalism account for this pattern.

GLOBAL: An illustration of global English: International regulations require all Boeing 747 pilots to be fluent in English.

GLOBAL: Another example of the diffusion of the English language and U.S. culture: The rising percentage of box office receipts abroad from U.S. films—France, 59%; Great Britain, 89%; Italy, 85%. English has become the universal language of entertainment, dominating television and pop music as well as film.

WINDOW ON THE WORLD

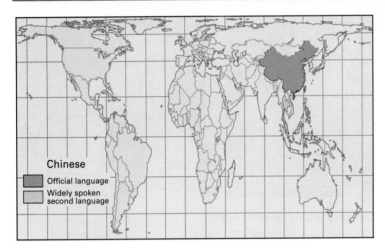

GLOBAL MAP 3–1
Language in Global Perspective

Chinese (including Mandarin, Cantonese, and dozens of other dialects) is the native tongue of one-fifth of the world's people, almost all of whom live in Asia. Although all Chinese people read and write with the same characters, they use several dozen dialects. The "official" dialect, taught in schools throughout the People's Republic of China and the Republic of Taiwan, is Mandarin (the dialect of Beijing, China's historic capital city). Cantonese, the language of Canton, is the second most common Chinese dialect; it differs in sound from Mandarin roughly the way French differs from Spanish.

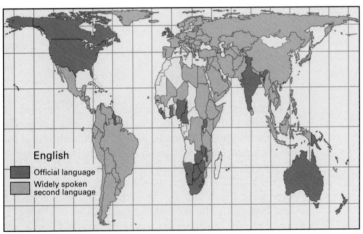

English is the native tongue or official language in several world regions and has become the preferred second language in most of the world.

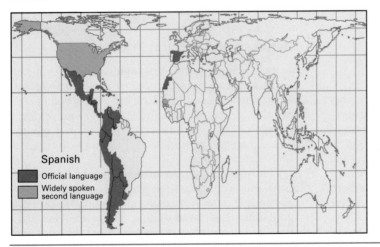

The largest concentration of Spanish speakers is in Latin America and, of course, Spain. Spanish is also the preferred second language of the United States.

Source: *Peters Atlas of the World* (1990).

NOTE: Although humans have been able to teach chimps to use symbols, evidence suggests that chimps are not capable of teaching each other to do so.
DISCUSS: The argument here contradicts the old adage "Sticks and stones can break my bones, but names can never hurt me." In what sense are symbols real?

GLOBAL: Illustrate the Sapir-Whorf thesis noting that the Greek language provides three words that represent variants of the English word "love": *philia*, referring to love between brothers or sisters; *agape*, a self-giving attitude of love toward others; and *eros*, a passionate, physical love.
DISCUSS: Even a slight change in symbols greatly changes meaning: Contrast a "person of color" with a "colored person."

high-income countries) could boast of nearly universal literacy. Still, 10 to 15 percent of U.S. adults (20 to 25 million people) cannot read and write, a barrier to opportunity in a society that demands symbolic skills. In low-income countries of the world, illiteracy rates range from 20 percent (People's Republic of China) to as high as 80 percent (Sierra Leone in Africa).

Language skills not only link us with others and with the past, they also set free the human imagination. Connecting symbols in new ways, we can imagine almost unlimited future possibilities. Language—both spoken and written—distinguishes human beings as the only creatures who are self-conscious, aware of our limitations and our ultimate mortality. Yet our symbolic power also enables us to dream and to bring that world into being.

Is Language Uniquely Human?

Creatures great and small direct sounds, smells, and gestures towards one another. In most cases, these signals are instinctive. But research shows that some animals have at least a rudimentary ability to use symbols to communicate with one another and with humans.

Consider the remarkable achievement of a twelve-year-old pygmy chimp named Kanzi. Chimpanzees lack the physical ability to mimic human speech. But researcher E. Sue Savage-Rumbaugh discovered that Kanzi could learn language by listening and observing people. Under Savage-Rumbaugh's supervision, Kanzi has developed a vocabulary of several hundred words and has learned to "speak" by pointing to pictures on a special keyboard. He can respond to requests like "Will you get a diaper for your sister?" and "Put the melon in the potty." Kanzi's abilities go beyond mere rote learning because he can respond to requests he has not heard before. In fact, Kanzi has the language ability of a human child of two-and-one-half years (Linden, 1993).

Still, the language skills of chimps, dolphins, and a few other animals are limited. And even specially trained animals cannot, on their own, teach language to others of their kind. But the achievement of Kanzi and others cautions us against assuming that humans alone can lay claim to culture.

Does Language Shape Reality?

Do the Chinese, who use one set of symbols to think, actually experience the world differently from North Americans who think in English or Spanish? The answer is yes, according to Edward Sapir (1929, 1949) and Benjamin Whorf (1956), two anthropologists who specialized in language. Many words and expressions in any language are unique, without counterparts in other tongues. In addition, all languages fuse symbols with distinctive emotions. Thus, as multilingual people can attest, an idea can "feel" different if spoken in, say, Spanish rather than in English or Chinese (Falk, 1987).

The **Sapir-Whorf thesis** states that *people perceive the world through the cultural lens of language.* Using different symbolic systems, a Filipino, a Turk, and a Brazilian actually experience "distinct worlds, not merely the same world with different labels attached" (Sapir, 1949:162).

Of course, the capacity to create and manipulate language also gives humans everywhere the power to alter how they experience the world. For example, many people hailed it as a step toward racial equality when the term "Negro" was replaced by the word "black," and, more recently, by "African American" or "person of color." In short, a system of language guides—but does not limit—how we understand the world.

VALUES AND BELIEFS

What accounts for the popularity of film characters such as James Bond, Shaft, Dirty Harry, Rambo, and Thelma and Louise? Each is ruggedly individualistic, relying on personal skill and savvy to challenge "the system." In applauding such characters, we are endorsing certain **values,** *culturally defined standards of desirability, goodness, and beauty that serve as broad guidelines for social living.* Values are statements, from the standpoint of a culture, of what ought to be.

Values are broad principles that underlie **beliefs,** *specific statements that people hold to be true.* In other words, values are abstract standards of goodness, while beliefs are particular matters that individuals consider to be true or false.

Cultural values and beliefs not only affect how we perceive our surroundings, they also form the core of our personalities. We learn from families, schools, and religious organizations to think and act according to approved principles, to pursue worthy goals, and to believe a host of cultural truths. Particular values and beliefs thus operate as a form of "cultural capital" that can give some people an optimistic determination to pursue success but leave others with a sense of hopelessness about the prospects of bettering their lives (Sowell, 1996).

GLOBAL: Regarding Williams's ten points for traditional societies—*Pts. 1 and 2:* Traditional societies generally embrace fate as a key value; *Pt. 3:* Spiritual comfort and well-being; *Pt. 4:* Greater reflectiveness (especially Eastern cultures); *Pt. 5:* Implies a rational world view; this value also suggests why we devalue academics as "eggheads"; *Pt. 6:* Members of most traditional societies are not optimistic (even the Japanese are less so); *Pt. 7:* Religion plays much more of a role than science; *Pt. 8:* Collective sentiment is higher, as is compliance to official authority; for example, Moroccans accept high-handed police direction with little evident complaint; *Pt. 9:* Most of the world is less individualistic than we are; *Pt. 10:* Most of the traditional world is much more group-oriented than we are.

Australian feminist artist Sally Swain alters a famous artist's painting to make fun of our culture's tendency to ignore the everyday lives of women. This spoof is entitled Mrs. Van Gogh Makes the Bed.

In a nation as large and diverse as the United States, few cultural values and beliefs are shared by everyone. In fact, with a long history of immigration from the rest of the world, the United States is a cultural mosaic, with contributions from many ways of life. In this regard, we stand apart from other nations (especially China and Japan), which have more homogeneous cultures. Even so, there is much agreement about our national life, leading sociologists to identify "key values."

Key Values of U.S. Culture

Sociologist Robin Williams (1970) has pointed to the following ten values as central to our way of life:

1. **Equal opportunity.** People in the United States endorse not equality of *condition* but equality of *opportunity*. This means that society should provide everyone with the chance to get ahead. At the same time, people's varying talents and efforts mean some of us will end up more successful than others.

2. **Achievement and success.** Our way of life encourages competition so that each person's rewards should reflect personal merit. Moreover, success confers worthiness on a person—the mantle of being a "winner."

3. **Material comfort.** Success in the United States generally means making money and enjoying what it will buy. People in the United States may quip that "money won't buy happiness," but most pursue wealth all the same.

4. **Activity and work.** U.S. heroes, from golf champion Tiger Woods to film's famed archaeologist Indiana Jones, are "action figures," people who get the job done. Members of our society prefer *action* to *reflection*. Through hard work, we try to control events rather than passively accept our fate. For this reason, many of us take a dim view of cultures that appear more easygoing or philosophical.

5. **Practicality and efficiency.** People in the United States value the practical over the theoretical—"doers" over "dreamers." Activity has value to the extent that it earns money. We also believe in solving problems with minimal effort. "Building a better mousetrap" is a cultural goal, especially when it's done in the most cost-effective way.

6. **Progress.** We are an optimistic people who, despite waves of nostalgia, believe that the present is better than the past. One way we embrace progress is by equating the "very latest" with the "very best."

7. **Science.** We readily turn to scientists to solve problems and improve our lives. We believe we are rational people, which probably explains our cultural tendency (especially among men) to devalue emotions and intuition as sources of knowledge.

8. **Democracy and free enterprise.** Members of our society recognize numerous individual rights that cannot be overridden by government. Our political system is based on free elections in which adults select their own leaders. In the

NOTE: Instant gratification is a value on the rise. Seventy percent of U.S. teen respondents agreed with this survey item: "I always try to have as much fun as I possibly can—I don't know what the future holds and I don't care what others think" (Teenage Research Unlimited).
DIVERSITY: Ann M. Beutel and Margaret Mooney Marini (1995) suggest that men's values are more oriented toward competition and materialism, while women's values emphasize compassion for others and finding meaning in life.
Q: "Our democracy is fraying. The populace as a whole is less ordered, less restrained . . ." Daniel Patrick Moynihan
DISCUSS: Does this country's cultural emphasis on independence help explain why three-fourths of workers drive to work alone?

same way, we believe that the U.S. economy responds to the needs of individual consumers.

9. **Freedom.** Our cultural value of freedom means that we favor individual initiative over collective conformity. Although we acknowledge that everyone has responsibilities to others, we believe that individuals should be free to pursue personal goals with minimal interference from anyone else.

10. **Racism and group superiority.** Despite strong notions about equality and freedom, most people in the United States still evaluate individuals according to gender, race, ethnicity, and social class. Our society values males above females, whites above people of color, people with northwestern European backgrounds above those whose ancestors came from other lands, and more privileged people above the disadvantaged. Although we like to describe ourselves as a nation of equals, there is little doubt that some of us are "more equal than others."

Values: Inconsistency and Conflict

As the list above suggests, cultural values can be inconsistent and even outright contradictory (Lynd, 1967; Bellah et al., 1985; Ray, 1997). Living in the United States, we sometimes find ourselves torn between the "me first" attitude of an individualistic, success-at-all-costs way of life and the opposing need to belong to some larger community. Similarly, we affirm our belief in equality of opportunity only to turn around and promote or degrade others because of their race or sex.

Inconsistent values reflect the cultural diversity of U.S. society and the process of cultural change by which new trends replace older traditions. Recently, for example, what some observers have tagged a new "culture of victimization" has arisen to challenge our society's long-time belief in individual responsibility (Best, 1997). The box on page 72 takes a closer look.

Whether due to the ethnic mix of U.S. society or changes in our way of life, value inconsistency leads to awkward balancing acts in how we view the world. Sometimes we pursue one value at the expense of another, supporting the principle of equal opportunity, say, yet opposing gays in the U.S. military. At other times, we simply ignore such contradictions. According to one recent national survey, the U.S. population may be losing a sense that it holds any key values at all. Asked whether "Americans are united or greatly divided when it comes to the most important values," 39 percent said united while 55 percent said divided (NORC, 1996:409).

Values in Action: The Games People Play

Cultural values affect every aspect of our lives. Children's games, for example, may seem like lighthearted fun, but they also serve to teach young people what our culture deems important.

Using the sociological perspective, James Spates (1976a) sees in the familiar game King of the Mountain our cultural emphasis on achievement and success.

> In this game, the King (winner) is the one who scrambles to the top of some designated area and holds it against all challengers (losers). This is a very gratifying game from the winner's point of view, for one learns what it is like (however brief is the tenure at the top before being thrown off) to be an unequivocal success, to be unquestionably better than the entire competition. (1976a:286)

Each player strives to become number one at the expense of all other players. But success has its price, and King of the Mountain teaches that as well.

> The King can never relax in such a pressurized position and constant vigilance is very difficult to endure, psychologically, for long. Additionally, the sole victor is likely to feel a certain alienation from others: Whom can one trust? Truly, "it is lonely at the top." (1976a:286)

Just as King of the Mountain teaches our cultural emphasis on winning, Tag, Keep Away, and Monkey in the Middle each convey the disadvantages of being a "loser." These sociological observations also help us understand the importance of competitive team sports in U.S. culture and why we celebrate star athletes as cultural heroes.

NORMS

Most people in the United States are eager to gossip about "who's hot and who's not." Members of the Native American Mohegans, however, condemn gossip, considering it rude and divisive. Both patterns illustrate the operation of **norms,** *rules and expectations by which a society guides the behavior of its members.* Some norms are *proscriptive,* mandating what we should *not* do, as when health officials warn us to avoid casual sex. *Prescriptive*

SOCIAL SURVEY: "There is a lot of discussion today about whether Americans are divided or united. Some say that Americans are united and in agreement about the most important values. Others think that Americans are greatly divided when it comes to the most important values. What is your view about this?" (GSS 1994, N = 1,474; *Codebook*, 1996:409)
"Americans are united and in agreement . . ." 39.4%

"Americans are greatly divided . . ." 55.0%
    DK/NR 5.6%
SOCIAL SURVEY: "People have to realize that they can only count on their own skills and abilities if they are going to win in this world." Percent agreeing: *1989*, 75%; *1994*, 86% (Yankelovich Monitor Perspective surveys).

SOCIOLOGY OF EVERYDAY LIFE

Don't Blame Me!
The New "Culture of Victimization"

A New York man recently leaped in front of a subway train. Lucky enough to survive, he sued the city because the train had failed to stop in time to prevent his serious injuries, and a court awarded him $650,000. In Washington, D.C., after realizing that he had been videotaped smoking crack cocaine in a hotel room, the city's mayor blamed his woman companion for "setting him up" and suggested that the police were racially motivated in arresting him. In Oregon, after more than a dozen women accused Senator Bob Packwood of sexual harassment, he tried to diffuse the scandal by checking into an alcohol treatment center. And in perhaps the most celebrated case, Dan White, who gunned down the mayor of San Francisco and a city council member, blamed his violence on insanity caused by eating too much junk food (the so-called "Twinkie defense").

In each of these cases, someone denied personal responsibility for an action and claimed instead to be a victim. More and more members of our society are pointing the finger elsewhere, which prompted sociologist Irving Horowitz (1993) to announce a developing "culture of victimization" in which "everyone is a victim" and "no one accepts responsibility for anything."

One indication of the cultural trend toward victimization is the proliferation of "addictions," a term that people once associated only with uncontrollable drug use. We now hear about gambling addicts, compulsive overeaters, sex addicts, and even people who

excuse runaway credit-card debt as a shopping addiction. Bookstores overflow with manuals to help people overcome "The Cinderella Complex," "The Casanova Complex," and even "Soap Opera Syndrome." And the U.S. courts are clogged by lawsuits that blame someone for misfortunes that we used to accept as part of life.

What's going on here? Is U.S. culture changing? Historically, our way of life has been based on a cultural ideal of "rugged individualism," the idea that people are responsible for whatever triumph or tragedy befalls them. But this value has been eroded in a number of ways. First, everyone is more aware (partly through the work of sociologists) of how society shapes our lives. Consequently, categories of people well beyond those who have suffered real historical disadvantages (such as Native Americans, African Americans, and women) now claim to be victims. The latest "victims" are, ironically, white males who claim that "everybody gets special treatment but us."

Second, since they began advertising their services in 1977, some lawyers

Since the 1980s, "tell-all" television programs have reinforced the emerging "culture of victimization."

encourage a sense of injustice in clients they hope to represent in court. The number of million-dollar lawsuit awards has risen more than twenty-five-fold in the last twenty-five years.

Third, there has been a proliferation of "rights groups," creating what sociologist Amitai Etzioni calls "rights inflation." Beyond the traditional constitutional liberties are many newly claimed rights, including the rights of hunters (as well as animals), the rights of smokers (and nonsmokers), the right of women to control their bodies (and the rights of the unborn), the right to own a gun (and the right to be safe from violence). Expanding and competing claims for unmet rights, then, generate victims (and victimizers) on all sides.

Does the shift from individualism to victimization signal a fundamental change in our culture? Perhaps, but the new popularity of being a victim also springs from some established cultural forces. For example, the claim to victimization depends on a long-standing belief that everyone has the right to life, liberty, and the pursuit of happiness. What is new, however, is that the explosion of "rights" now does more than alert us to injustice; it threatens to erode our sense of responsibility as members of a larger society.

Sources: Based on Etzioni (1991), Taylor (1991), and Hollander (1995).

NOTE: "Norm" is derived from Latin *norm(a)*, meaning "a carpenter square, a rule, or a pattern." The root of "moral" is *mor* or *mos*, meaning "custom." The rarely used singular form of mores is *mos*.

NOTE: Illustrate the changing norms of language on TV: In 1952, Lucy and Desi couldn't use "pregnant" to describe her condition.

GLOBAL: The way women dress is sometimes a matter of mores. Especially in Islamic societies, women must dress modestly, covering arms, shoulders, and sometimes even the head. U.S. military women serving in the 1991 Gulf War learned this when some stationed in Saudi Arabia innocently donned shorts, provoking outrage among the local population.

norms, on the other hand, state what we *should* do, as when U.S. schools teach practices of "safe sex."

Most important norms in a culture apply virtually anywhere and at any time. For example, parents expect obedience from young children regardless of the setting. Other norms depend on the situation. In the United States, we expect the audience to applaud after a musical performance; we may applaud (although it is not expected) at the end of a classroom lecture; we do not applaud when a priest or rabbi finishes a sermon.

Mores and Folkways

William Graham Sumner (1959; orig. 1906), an early U.S. sociologist, recognized that some norms are more important to our lives than others. Sumner used the term **mores** (pronounced MORE-ays) to refer to *a society's standards of proper moral conduct*. Sumner counted among the mores all norms essential to maintaining a way of life; due to their importance, he expected people to develop an emotional attachment to mores and to defend them publicly. Their importance also means that mores apply to everyone in a society all the time. Violation of mores—such as our culture's prohibition of sex between adults and children—brings a swift and strong reaction from others.

Sumner used the term **folkways** to designate *a society's customs for routine, casual interaction*. Folkways have less moral significance than mores and include notions about proper dress, appropriate greetings, and common courtesy. In short, while mores distinguish between right and wrong, folkways draw a line between right and *rude*. Because they are less important than mores, societies afford individuals greater personal discretion in observing folkways and punish infractions leniently. For example, a man who does not wear a tie to a formal dinner party is, at worst, guilty of a breach of etiquette. If, however, the man were to arrive at the dinner party wearing *only* a tie, he would challenge social mores and invite a more serious response.

Social Control

As participants in cultural systems, we learn to accept mores and folkways as the basic rules of everyday life, and we reinforce them in others through *sanctions*, which take the form of either reward or punishment. Conforming to norms brings praise and approval from others, while violating norms results in avoidance, contempt, or even the attention of police. Taken together, sanctions form the heart of a culture's system

Standards of beauty—including the color and design of everyday surroundings—vary significantly from one culture to another. Members of the Ndebele in South Africa lavishly paint their homes. Members of North American and European societies, by contrast, make far less use of bright colors and intricate detail so that their neighborhoods appear much more subdued.

Reprinted by permission of Margaret Courtney-Clarke, © 1990.

of **social control,** *various means by which members of society encourage conformity to norms.*

As we learn cultural norms, we develop the capacity to evaluate our own behavior. Doing wrong (say, downloading a term paper from the Internet) can cause not only *shame*—the painful sense that others disapprove of our actions—but also *guilt*, a negative judgment we make of ourselves. Only cultural creatures can experience shame and guilt: This is probably what Mark Twain had in mind when he quipped that human beings "are the only animals that blush . . . or need to."

"IDEAL" AND "REAL" CULTURE

Societies devise values and norms as "moral maps" for their members. As guidelines, they do not describe actual behavior as much as they suggest how we *should* behave. We must remember, then, that **ideal culture,** *social patterns mandated by cultural values and norms*, is not the same as **real culture,** *actual social patterns that only approximate cultural expectations.*

DISCUSS: Ideal culture often is revealed in legends; "legend" is derived from Latin meaning "things to be read." Thus the Greeks celebrated Homer; the Romans, Virgil; the Christians, saints and Joan of Arc; medieval nobles, King Arthur; and moderns, a list of rugged individualists, from Davy Crockett to James Bond, Rambo, and Thelma and Louise. Ask the class to characterize these figures.

NOTE: More complex technology empowers humanity to manipulate the natural world; members of industrial societies, therefore, risk losing sensitivity to the natural environment and the requirements of living in an ecological system. Look ahead to Chapter 22 ("Environment and Society").

GLOBAL SNAPSHOT

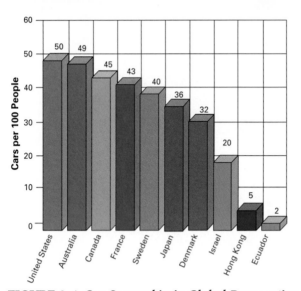

FIGURE 3–1 Car Ownership in Global Perspective

Source: Author's calculations based on data from U.S. Bureau of the Census (1997).

To illustrate, most women and men acknowledge the importance of fidelity in marriage. Even so, in a recent study, about 25 percent of married men and 10 percent of married women reported being sexually unfaithful to their spouses at some point in the marriage (Laumann et al., 1994). Such discrepancies occur in all societies, since no one lives up to ideal standards all the time. But a culture's moral prodding is important all the same, calling to mind the saying "Do as I say, not as I do."

MATERIAL CULTURE AND TECHNOLOGY

In addition to intangible elements such as values and norms, every culture includes a wide range of tangible (from Latin meaning "touchable") human creations that sociologists term *artifacts*. The Chinese eat with chopsticks rather than knives and forks, the Japanese put mats rather than rugs on the floor, and many men and women in India prefer flowing robes to the tighter clothing common in the United States. The material culture of a people can seem as strange to outsiders as their language, values, and norms.

The artifacts common to a society typically reflect cultural values. The fact that poison-tipped arrows are a prized possession of Yąnomamö males in the Amazon rain forest, for example, reflects the importance that society places on warfare and militaristic skills. Similarly, our own high regard for the automobile is rooted in cherished values of individuality and independence. Some 4 million miles of freeways criss-cross the United States (enough to reach the moon and back more than eight times), and our nation's people own 200 million vehicles—one for every licensed driver. Figure 3–1 shows that, even compared to other industrial societies, the United States stands out as a car-loving nation.

In addition to reflecting values, material culture also indicates a society's level of **technology,** *knowledge that a society applies to the task of living in a physical environment.* In short, technology ties the world of nature to the world of culture. The Yąnomamö are keenly aware of the cycles of rainfall and the movement of animals they hunt for food; but with only primitive technology, they have little ability to affect the natural environment. By contrast, technologically powerful societies (such as those of North America) are constantly reshaping the environment (for better or ill) according to their interests and priorities.

Because we attach great importance to science and praise the sophisticated technology it has produced, members of our society tend to judge cultures with simpler technology as less advanced. Some facts support such an assessment. For example, life expectancy for children born in the United States now exceeds seventy-five years; the lifespan of the Yąnomamö is only about forty years.

However, we must be careful not to make self-serving judgments about other cultures. Although many Yąnomamö are eager to acquire modern technology (such as steel tools and shotguns), they are generally well fed by world standards and most are quite satisfied with their lives (Chagnon, 1992). Remember, too, that while our complex technology has produced work-reducing devices and miraculous medical treatments, it has also contributed to unhealthy levels of stress, eroded the natural environment, and created weapons capable of destroying in a blinding flash everything humankind has achieved.

Finally, technology is another element of culture that varies greatly within the United States. Although some of us cannot imagine life without CD players, televisions, and personal computers, many members of our society cannot afford such items, and others reject them on principle. The Amish, for example, live in small farming communities across Pennsylvania, Ohio, and Indiana. These "Plain People" shun most modern conveniences on religious grounds. With their traditional

NOTE: As Donald Kraybill and Marc Olshan (1994) point out, the tension between the Amish and the surrounding society is increasing with the escalation of modern technology.

DISCUSS: Consider how modern communication and information technology mass-produce culture and direct it *at* people, rather than the earlier pattern by which culture emerged organically from people's own lives.

SUPPLEMENTS: The *Data File* details how the "Baby Bells" and the cable industry plan to bring high technology to U.S. households.

NOTE: The industrial era moved goods, first by ship, then by rail and truck. The postindustrial equivalent is information moving at the speed of light along the "information superhighway."

NOTE: One indicator that our society is moving into the postindustrial era: We now spend more on computers than on televisions.

EXPLORING CYBER-SOCIETY

Here Comes Virtual Culture!

The Information Revolution is now generating symbols—words, sounds, and images—at an unprecedented rate and rapidly spreading these symbols across the nation and around the world. What does this new information technology mean for our way of life?

One important trend is that more and more of our cultural symbols are intentionally *created*. In the past, sociologists viewed culture as a way of life transmitted over time from generation to generation. In this traditional view, culture is a deeply rooted heritage that is passed along over the centuries and is authentically our own because it belonged to our ancestors (Schwartz, 1996). But in the emerging cyber-society, more and more cultural symbols are new, intentionally generated by a small cultural elite of composers, writers, film makers, and others who work within the burgeoning information economy.

To illustrate this change, consider the changing character of cultural heroes, people who represent an ideal we strive to live up to. Earlier in this century, our heroes were real men and women who made a difference in the life of this nation—George Washington, Abigail Adams, Betsy Ross, Davy Crockett, Daniel Boone, Abraham Lincoln, and Harriet Tubman. Of course, when we make a hero of someone (almost always well after the person has died), we "clean

up" the person's biography, highlighting the successes and overlooking the shortcomings. But, although idealized, these people were authentic parts of our history.

Today's youngsters, by contrast, are fed a steady diet of *virtual culture*, images that spring from the minds of contemporary culture-makers and that reach us through a screen—on television, in the movies, or through computer cyberspace. Today's "heroes" include Power Rangers, Rugrats, Ninja Turtles, Barney, Batman, Barbie, and a continuous flow of Disney characters. No doubt these cultural heroes embody some of the key cultural values that have shaped our way of life. But none has any historical reality and almost all came into being for a single purpose: making money.

Source: Thanks to Roland Johnson (1996) for the basic idea for this box. His Web site address is http://personalwebs.myriad.net/Roland

black garb and horse-drawn buggies, the Amish may seem like a curious relic of the past. Yet their communities flourish, grounded in strong families and individuals who thrive on a sense of identity and purpose. And many of the outsiders who observe them each year come away with the suspicion that "local, enduring, and stable" Amish communities may well be "islands of sanity in a culture gripped by commercialism and technology run wild" (Hostetler, 1980:4; Kraybill, 1994:28).

NEW INFORMATION TECHNOLOGY AND CULTURE

Many industrial societies, including the United States, are now entering a postindustrial phase based on computers and new information technology. While industrial production depends on factories and machinery that generate material goods, postindustrial production relies on computers and other electronic devices that create, process, store, and apply information.

Thus, in an information economy, different skills become important. Mechanical abilities to make things are replaced by the symbolic abilities to speak, write, compute, design, and create images in art, advertising, and entertainment. This transformation is likely to bring, in turn, other major changes to our culture. In short, new information technology offers our society the capacity to *generate culture* on an unprecedented scale. The box takes a closer look.

NOTE: In *Highbrow, Lowbrow: The Emergence of Cultural Hierarchy in America*, Lawrence Levine claims that until the time of the Civil War, all classes were familiar with poetry and quoted Shakespeare. Then, as a new elite class emerged with the Industrial Revolution, "highbrow" culture emerged as a form of cultural capital.

Q: "Highbrow: a person who can listen to the William Tell Overture without thinking of 'The Lone Ranger'." Jack Perlis

Q: "If Hamlet is broadcast on network television, does it represent popular culture (since millions presumably see it) or elite culture, since it is a classic work of art?" Arthur Asa Berger

DIVERSITY: What is "popular culture" varies by age cohort: percentage who like or strongly like rap music by age: 18 and younger, 58%; 18–20, 59%; 21–24, 38%; 25–34, 25%; 35–44, 14%; 45 and older, 8% (SounData).

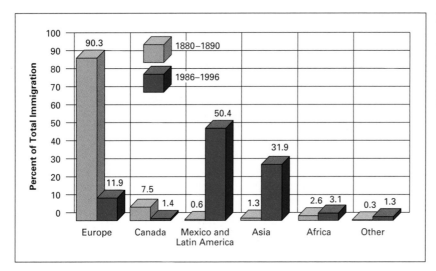

FIGURE 3–2
Recorded Immigration to the United States, by Region of Birth, 1880–1890 and 1986–1996

Source: U.S. Immigration and Naturalization Service (1996, 1997).

CULTURAL DIVERSITY: MANY WAYS OF LIFE IN ONE WORLD

As the chapter-opening story of the Mohegans in Connecticut suggests, our nation is becoming more aware of the cultural diversity within our borders. And that diversity continues to grow as, each year, almost 1 million people from other lands have come to our shores. In fact, centuries of heavy immigration make the United States the most *multicultural* of all industrial nations. By contrast, its historic isolation has marked Japan as the most *monocultural* of all industrial nations.

Between 1820 (when the government began keeping track of immigration) and 1997, more than 60 million people have added their ways of life to the U.S. cultural mix. A century ago, as shown in Figure 3–2, almost all immigrants came from Europe. By the 1980s, however, most newcomers were from Latin America and Asia.

We are aware of our cultural variety when we hear the distinctive accents of people from New England, the Midwest, or the South. Ours is also a nation of religious pluralism, a land of class differences, and a home to countless individualists who try to be like no one else.

Given the staggering extent of this diversity, sociologists sometimes call our "cloth of culture" a "patchwork quilt." To understand the reality of life in the United States, then, we must move beyond broad cultural patterns, such as the key values identified by Robin Williams (1970), to consider cultural diversity.

HIGH CULTURE AND POPULAR CULTURE

A great deal of our cultural diversity has its roots in social class. In fact, in everyday conversation, we usually reserve the term "culture" for art forms such as literature, music, dance, and painting. We describe people who regularly go to the opera or the theater as "cultured" because they presumably appreciate the "finer things in life." The term "culture" has the same Latin root as the word "cultivate," suggesting that the "cultured" individual has highly cultivated tastes.

We speak less generously of ordinary people, thinking that everyday culture is somehow less worthy. So we are tempted to judge the music of Beethoven as "more cultured" than the blues, couscous as better than cornbread, and polo as more polished than Ping-Pong.

But such judgments reflect the fact that many cultural patterns are readily accessible to only some members of a society (Hall & Neitz, 1993). Sociologists use the shorthand terms **high culture**[1] to refer to *cultural patterns that distinguish a society's elite* and **popular culture** to designate *cultural patterns that are widespread among a society's population.*

---

[1]The term "high culture" is derived from the term "highbrow." A century ago, people influenced by phrenology—the bogus nineteenth-century theory that personality was affected by the shape of the human skull—praised the tastes of those they termed "highbrows" while dismissing others' interests as "lowbrow."

NOTE: Most other texts offer technically incorrect definitions of subculture and counterculture as *groups of people* who embrace distinctive cultural patterns. Our approach is to use both terms to refer to culture, not people.

NOTE: Anthropologists have long conceptualized cultural diversity in terms of "big tradition" (dominant cultural patterns) and "little tradition" (folklife).

DIVERSITY: Subcultural communities such as the Amish are often seen by outsiders as internally homogeneous. John A. Hostetler (1980; see especially Chapter 13) makes clear that the Amish are in many respects internally diverse, divided over "the shape or color of a garment, the style of a house, carriage, or harness, the use of labor-saving farm machinery or the pace of singing."

Whether visual expression in lines and color is revered as "art" or dismissed as "graffiti" or even condemned as "vandalism" depends on the social standing of the creator. How would you characterize images such as this one, common to low-income neighborhoods of U.S. cities? Is this art? Why or why not?

Common sense may suggest that high culture is superior to popular culture. After all, history pays more attention to elites than to ordinary women and men. But sociologists are uneasy with such a sweeping evaluation and therefore use the term "culture" to refer to *all* elements of a society's way of life, including patterns of rich and poor alike (Gans, 1974).

We should resist quick judgments about the merits of high culture over popular culture for two reasons. First, neither elites nor ordinary people have uniform tastes and interests; people in both categories differ from one another in many ways. Second, do we praise high culture because it is inherently better than popular culture, or simply because its supporters have more money, power, and prestige? For example, there is no difference between a violin and a fiddle, yet we name the instrument one way when it is used to produce music typically enjoyed by someone of higher position, and the other way when it is used to play works appreciated by people with lower social standing.

National Map 3–1 on page 78 uses the popularity of two different forms of bread to show where in the United States the "cultural upper crust" lives.

SUBCULTURE

The term **subculture** refers to *cultural patterns that set apart some segment of a society's population.* Inner-city teens, elderly Polish Americans, frequent-flyer executives, "Yankee" New Englanders, Colorado cowboys, the southern California "beach crowd," jazz musicians, campus poets, and offshore powerboat racers—all display subcultural patterns.

It is easy—but often inaccurate—to put people in subcultural categories. At any time, we all fall within numerous subcultures, and we probably have little commitment to most of them.

In some cases, however, important cultural traits such as ethnicity or religion make commitments to subcultures strong and may even set people apart from one another—with tragic results. Consider the former nation of Yugoslavia in southeastern Europe. The ongoing turmoil there has been fueled by astounding cultural diversity. This *one* small country (which, before its breakup, was about the size of Wyoming with a population of 25 million) used *two* alphabets, professed *three* religions, spoke *four* languages, was home to *five* major nationalities, was divided into *six* political republics, and reflected the cultural influence of *seven* surrounding countries. The cultural conflict that plunged this nation into civil war shows that subcultures are a source not only of pleasing variety but also of tension and outright violence (cf. Sekulic, Massey, & Hodson, 1994).

Historically, we have taught our children to view the United States as a "melting pot" in which many nationalities blend into a single "American" culture. But, given the extent of our cultural diversity, how accurate is the "melting pot" image? For one thing, cultural diversity involves not just *variety* but also *hierarchy.* Too

THE MAP: Consumers of croissants (15% of the U.S. population) are higher-income, more educated people who live in urban areas. White bread households (44%) are largely in rural, lower-income regions.

DIVERSITY: The "What's in a Name?" box back in Chapter 1 suggested that the so-called "melting pot" in the United States actually involved Anglicizing immigrants' cultural backgrounds.

Q: "What the U.S. does best is understand itself. What it does worst is understand others." Carlos Fuentes, Mexican writer

GLOBAL: Compared to the United States, France is far less culturally diverse with standard times for many things. Notes Kenneth Jackson, there are almost no 24-hour restaurants or grocery stores in Paris, and most people vacation at the same time. France also imposed its way of life on colonies abroad.

SEEING OURSELVES

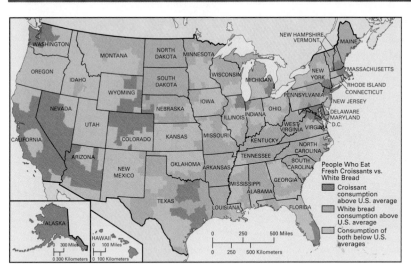

NATIONAL MAP 3–1
High Culture and Popular Culture Across the United States

Food patterns indicate a person's status as "highbrow" or "lowbrow." Enjoying croissants—the flaky, delicious pastries served fresh-baked at pricey coffee shops—is one indicator of highbrow standing. These generally well-to-do people drink water from bottles rather than the tap, prefer Grey Poupon to Gulden's mustard, and favor Häagen-Dazs over the local Tastee-Freeze. Eating white bread, on the other hand, marks a person as "lowbrow." Such a person has modest to low income, consumes above-average quantities of doughnuts, and frequents fast-food restaurants. Looking at the map, where have the "highbrows" and "lowbrows" created centers of either "high culture" or "popular culture"?

Source: Michael J. Weiss, *Latitudes & Attitudes: An Atlas of American Tastes, Trends, Politics and Passions.* Boston: Little, Brown, and Company, 1994.

often, what we view as "dominant" or "highbrow" culture are the patterns favored by powerful segments of the population, while we view the cultural patterns of the disadvantaged as "subculture." Some researchers, therefore, prefer to level the playing field of society by emphasizing multiculturalism.

MULTICULTURALISM

In recent years, the United States has been debating the policy of **multiculturalism,** *an educational program recognizing past and present cultural diversity in U.S. society and promoting the equality of all cultural traditions.* Multiculturalism represents a sharp turn from the past, when our society downplayed cultural diversity and defined itself primarily in terms of its European (and especially English) immigrants. Multiculturalism seeks to present a more accurate picture of U.S. cultural diversity and, more important, to include in our history *the point of view* of many marginalized categories of people, such as Native Americans and people of color.

In short, because multiculturalism seeks to redefine our culture, it is not surprising that it has generated

controversy. Many scholars and public officials clash over whether we should stress the common elements in our national experience or highlight our cultural differences (Schlesinger, Jr., 1991; Meyrowitz & Maguire, 1993; Orwin, 1996; Rabkin, 1996).

E Pluribus Unum, the Latin phrase that appears on each U.S. coin, means "out of many, one." This motto refers not only to our political framework, but also to the idea that the varied experiences of immigrants from around the world come together into a new and distinctive way of life. Even George Washington, the first U.S. president, confidently predicted that as future immigrants learned the nation's ways, they would become "one people" (Gray, 1991).

But, from the outset, the many cultures did not melt together as much as harden into a hierarchy. The early English majority established English as the dominant language and set up social institutions based on the British economy, legal system, and religions. For their part, the non-English minority had little choice but to stay on the sidelines or model themselves after "their betters." Thus, "melting" really amounted to a process of Anglicization—adopting English ways. As multiculturalists see it, early in our history, this society

THE MAP: The most culturally diverse regions of the United States are those with the greatest number of immigrants.
Q: "Every immigrant who comes here ought to learn English within five years or be forced to leave." Theodore Roosevelt
DISCUSS: Should Hispanic youngsters be taught in Spanish or English? Survey data suggest that about 80% of Hispanic parents favor instruction in English (Chavez, 1996).

DIVERSITY: In the United States, the need for multicultural skills is greatest among the young. Compare the age-based diversity (in 1996) among people ages 70 to 74 (8.0% African American, 4.8% Latino, 2.2% Asian and Pacific Islander) with the percentages among preschoolers (15.5% African American, 17.0% Latino, 4.4% Asian and Pacific Islander) (U.S. Bureau of the Census).

SEEING OURSELVES

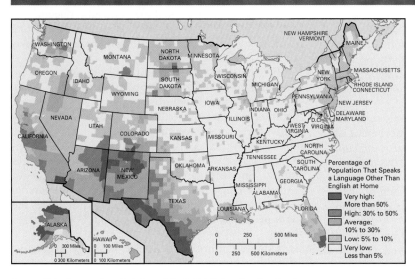

Source: *Time*, January 30, 1995. Copyright © 1995 *Time*, Inc. Reprinted by permission.

NATIONAL MAP 3–2
Language Diversity Across the United States

Of 230 million people over the age of five in the United States, the 1990 census reports that 32 million (14 percent) typically speak a language other than English at home. Of these people, for whom English is not the favored language, 54 percent speak Spanish, 14 percent use an Asian language, and the remaining 32 percent communicate with some other tongue (the Census Bureau lists twenty-five languages, each of which is favored by more than 100,000 people in the United States). The map shows that non-English speakers are concentrated in certain regions of the country. Which ones? What do you think accounts for this pattern?

---

set up the English way of life as an ideal to which all should aspire and by which all should be judged.

For more than two centuries, historians in the United States have chronicled events from the point of view of the English and others of European ancestry. Little attention has been paid to the perspectives and accomplishments of Native Americans, people of African descent, and immigrants from Asia. Multiculturalists call this approach **Eurocentrism,** *the dominance of European (particularly English) cultural patterns.* Molefi Kete Asante, a leading advocate of multiculturalism, draws this analogy: Like "the fifteenth-century Europeans who could not cease believing that the earth was the center of the universe, many today find it difficult to cease viewing European culture as the center of the social universe" (1988:7).

One reaction to multiculturalism is a movement to make English the official language of the United States. By 1997, legislatures in twenty-three states had enacted laws declaring English the official language, and Congress continues to debate such a law for the entire country. To some, "official English" may seem unnecessary, since a large majority of

people in this country are English-speakers. Even so, some 30 million men and women—roughly one in six—use a language other than English at home. Spanish is the second most commonly spoken U.S. language, and several hundred other tongues are heard across the nation, including Italian, German, French, Filipino, Japanese, Korean, Vietnamese and a host of Native American languages. National Map 3–2 shows where in the United States large numbers of people speak a language other than English at home.

A second controversy involves how our nation's schools—from the early grades through college—should teach about culture. Proponents of multiculturalism believe it presents a more accurate picture of our country's *past.* Multiculturalists, for example, point out that indigenous peoples inhabited the so-called "New World" for tens of thousands of years before Christopher Columbus and other European explorers arrived. Moreover, for the native peoples of this hemisphere, the European conquest was a catastrophe, unleashing domination and death from war and disease. In short, advocates claim multiculturalism recovers the history and achievements of non-European

Q: "As long as black people are viewed as 'them,' the burden falls on blacks to do all the cultural and moral work necessary for healthy race relations. The implication is that only certain Americans can define what it means to be an American—and the rest must simply 'fit in.'" Cornel West

GLOBAL: Problems of multiculturalism arise elsewhere: In Sri Lanka at mid-century, Sinhalese and Tamil (different languages using different alphabets) replaced English in an effort to end colonial influences. Within two decades, civil war broke out between the two populations. (Common language is no guarantee of peace: Speaking German did not save the Jews from the Holocaust.)

Q: "I was a student in the department of anthropology. They taught me that nobody was ridiculous or bad or disgusting." Kurt Vonnegut

women and men and offers a more balanced view of our nation's past.

Proponents also paint multiculturalism as a way of coming to terms with our country's even more diverse *present*. With the Asian and Hispanic populations of this country increasing rapidly, some analysts predict that children born in the 1990s will live to see people of African, Asian, and Hispanic ancestry become the *majority* of this country's population.

Finally, some proponents advance multiculturalism as a way to improve the academic achievement of African American children. To offset Eurocentrism, some multiculturalists are calling for **Afrocentrism,** *the dominance of African cultural patterns*, which they see as a corrective for centuries of minimizing or altogether ignoring the cultural achievements of African societies and African Americans.

Although multiculturalism has found widespread favor in the last several years, it has received its share of criticism as well. Opponents of multiculturalism say it encourages divisiveness rather than unity by urging individuals to identify with their own category rather than with the nation as a whole. Similarly, rather than recognizing common standards of truth, multiculturalism holds that we should evaluate ideas according to the race (and sex) of those who present them. Therefore, say critics, common humanity dissolves into an "African experience," an "Asian experience," and so on.

The bottom line, say the critics, is that multiculturalism may not end up helping minorities as its supporters claim. Some multiculturalist initiatives (from African American studies to all-black dorms) seem to endorse precisely the kind of racial segregation that our nation has struggled for decades to end. Then, too, an Afrocentric curriculum may well deny children a wide range of important knowledge and skills by forcing them to study only certain topics from a single point of view. Historian Arthur Schlesinger, Jr. (1991:21) puts the matter bluntly: "If a Kleagle of the Ku Klux Klan wanted to use the schools to handicap black Americans, he could hardly come up with anything more effective than the 'Afrocentric' curriculum."

Is there any common ground in this debate? Although sharp differences exist, the answer is yes. Virtually everyone agrees that all people in the United States need to better appreciate the extent of our cultural diversity. But precisely where the balance is to be struck—between the *pluribus* and the *unum*—is likely to remain a divisive issue for some time to come.

COUNTERCULTURE

Cultural diversity also includes outright rejection of conventional ideas or behavior. **Counterculture** refers to *cultural patterns that strongly oppose those widely accepted within a society*.

In many societies, counterculture is linked to youth (Spates, 1976b, 1983; Spates & Perkins, 1982). The youth-oriented counterculture of the 1960s, for example, rejected the cultural mainstream as overly competitive, self-centered, and materialistic. Instead, hippies and other counterculturalists favored a cooperative lifestyle in which "being" took precedence over "doing" and the capacity for personal growth—or "expanded consciousness"—was prized over material possessions like homes and cars. Such differences led some people at that time to "drop out" of the larger society.

Counterculture may involve not only distinctive values, but unconventional behavior (including dress and forms of greeting) as well as music. Many members of the 1960s counterculture, for instance, drew personal identity from wearing long hair, headbands, and blue jeans; from displaying a peace sign rather than offering a handshake; and from using drugs and listening to rock and roll music.

Countercultures are still flourishing. In the 1990s, militaristic bands of men and women, who are deeply suspicious of the federal government, advocate dropping out of the political system. Countercultural extremism of this kind led to the bombing of the Oklahoma City federal building in April of 1995, killing 168 people.

CULTURAL CHANGE

Perhaps the most basic truth of this world is that "All things shall pass." Even the dinosaurs, who thrived on this planet for some 160 million years (see the time line), exist today only as fossils (and movie villains). Will humanity survive for millions of years to come? All we can say with certainty is that—given our reliance on culture—for as long as we survive, the human record will be one of continuous change.

Table 3–1 shows changes in student attitudes between 1968 (the height of the sixties counterculture) and 1996. Some things have changed only slightly: Today, as a generation ago, most men and women look forward to raising a family. But a clear trend among today's students is the pursuit of money, with less interest in developing a philosophy of life.

NOTE: William Ogburn called nonmaterial culture "adaptive culture" since it helps us to adapt to technological change.
DISCUSS: Consider how some of the change each of us experiences over time is due to moving through the life course.
Q: "The atomic bomb was produced in two-and-one-half years . . . a decade later we have [not controlled] atomic energy [nor] banned the atomic bomb." William F. Ogburn

DISCUSS: Cultural lag involves folkways as well as mores. Is it rude to interrupt a lunchtime chat in a restaurant to take a call on a cell phone? Can the class think of other examples?
DIVERSITY: Regarding Table 3–1, changes in attitudes generally have been greater among women than among men. This differential can be traced to the women's movement, which intensified after 1968.

With change in one dimension of a culture, we usually find other transformations as well. For example, women's increased participation in the labor force is connected to changing family patterns, including first marriages at a later age, a rising divorce rate, and a growing share of children being raised in households without fathers. Such connections illustrate the principle of **cultural integration,** *the close relationship among various elements of a cultural system.*

Cultural Lag

But all elements of a cultural system do not change at the same speed. William Ogburn (1964) observed that technology moves quickly, generating new elements of material culture (like test-tube babies) faster than nonmaterial culture (such as ideas about parenthood) can keep up with them. Ogburn called this inconsistency **cultural lag,** *the fact that cultural elements change at different rates, which may disrupt a cultural system.* How are we to apply the traditional notions of motherhood and fatherhood in a culture where one woman can give birth to a child using another woman's egg, which has been fertilized in a laboratory with the sperm of a total stranger?

Causes of Cultural Change

Cultural changes are set in motion in three ways. The first is *invention,* the process of creating new cultural elements. Invention has given us the telephone (1876), the airplane (1903), and the aerosol spray can (1941), each of which has had a tremendous impact on our way of life. Invention goes on constantly, as indicated by the thousands of applications submitted annually to the United States Patent Office.

Discovery, a second cause of cultural change, involves recognizing and better understanding something already existing—from a distant star to the athletic prowess of U.S. women. Many discoveries result from scientific research. Yet discovery can also happen quite by accident, as when Marie Curie left a rock on a piece of photographic paper in 1898 and thus discovered radium.

The third cause of cultural change is *diffusion,* the spread of cultural traits from one society to another. The technological ability to send information around the globe in seconds—by means of radio, television, facsimile (fax), and computer—means that the level of cultural diffusion has never been greater than it is today.

TABLE 3–1 Attitudes Among Students Entering U.S. Colleges, 1968 and 1996

Life Objectives (Essential or Very Important)		1968*	1996	Change
Develop a philosophy of life	Men	79%	42%	–37%
	Women	87	42	–45
Keep up with political affairs	Men	52	33	–19
	Women	52	27	–25
Help others in difficulty	Men	50	53	+ 3
	Women	71	70	– 1
Raise a family	Men	64	72	+ 8
	Women	72	72	0
Be successful in my own business	Men	55	46	– 9
	Women	32	34	+ 2
Be well off financially	Men	51	76	+25
	Women	27	72	+45

*To allow comparisons, data from the early 1970s rather than 1968 are used for some items.

Sources: Richard G. Braungart and Margaret M. Braungart, "From Yippies to Yuppies: Twenty Years of Freshmen Attitudes," *Public Opinion,* vol. 11, no. 3 (September–October 1988): 53–56; Linda J. Sax, Alexander W. Astin, William S. Korn, and Kathryn M. Mahoney, *The American Freshman: National Norms for Fall 1996* (Los Angeles: UCLA Higher Education Research Institute, 1996).

Certainly our own society has contributed many significant cultural elements to the world, ranging from computers to jazz music. Sometimes, though, we forget that diffusion works the other way as well, so that much of what we assume is inherently "American" actually comes from other cultures. Ralph Linton (1937) explained that many elements of our way of life—from clothing, furniture, and clocks to newspapers, money, and even the English language—are derived from other cultures.

ETHNOCENTRISM AND CULTURAL RELATIVITY

December 10, 1994, a small village in rural Morocco. Watching our shipmates browse through this tiny ceramic factory, there is little doubt that North Americans are among the world's greatest shoppers. They delight in inspecting hand-woven carpets in China or India, fingering

SUPPLEMENTS: The excerpt from Ralph Linton's "One Hundred Percent American," found in the *Data File*, offers thought-provoking topics for a discussion of ethnocentrism.

NOTE: Dietary differences offer other illustrations of ethnocentrism. We find the drinking of goat's blood by the Masai of eastern Africa to be revolting; however, few Chinese drink milk, which we consider among the most healthful drinks.

DISCUSS: In 1997, two Iraqi brothers, aged 34 and 28, were charged under Nebraska law with the statutory rape of their wives, aged 13 and 14, whom they married according to Muslim law and the customs of their native southern Iraq. Were the charges appropriate or ethnocentric?

NOTE: One cultural-relativist friend has his first cocktail by 10 A.M., noting that "It must be 5 o'clock *somewhere*!"

Most people in the affluent United States take for granted that childhood should be a carefree time of life devoted to learning and play. In low-income societies of the world, however, poor families depend on the income earned by children, some of whom perform long days of heavy physical labor. We may not want to accept all cultural practices as "natural" just because they exist. But what universal standards can be used to judge social patterns as either right or wrong?

finely crafted metals in Turkey, and collecting the beautifully colored porcelain tiles we find here in Morocco. And, of course, all these items are wonderful bargains. But a major reason for the low prices is unsettling: Many products from the world's low- and middle-income countries are produced by children—some as young as five or six—who work long days for extremely low wages.

We think of childhood as a time of innocence and freedom from adult burdens like regular work. In poor countries throughout the world, however, families depend on income earned by children. So what people in one society think of as right and natural, people elsewhere find puzzling or even immoral. Perhaps the Chinese philosopher Confucius had it right when he noted that "All people are the same; it's only their habits that are different."

Just about every imaginable idea or behavior can be found somewhere in the world, and this cultural variation causes travelers equal measures of excitement and distress. The tradition in Japan is to name intersections rather than streets, a practice that confuses North Americans who do the opposite. Egyptians stand very close to others in conversation, which irritates North Americans used to maintaining several feet of "personal space." Bathrooms lack toilet paper in much of rural Morocco, causing great agitation among Westerners unaccustomed to using the left hand for bathroom hygiene.

Given that a particular culture is the basis for everyone's reality, it is not surprising that people everywhere exhibit **ethnocentrism,** *the practice of judging another culture by the standards of one's own culture.* On one level, some ethnocentrism seems inevitable if people are to be emotionally attached to their own way of life. On another level, however, ethnocentrism generates misunderstanding and sometimes conflict.

Even terminology is culturally biased. People in North America often refer to China as the "Far East." But this term, which has little meaning to the Chinese, is an ethnocentric expression for a region that is far east *of us.* For their part, the Chinese name their country using a word translated as "Central Kingdom," suggesting that they, too, see their society as the center of the world.

Is there an alternative to ethnocentrism? We could try to look at other people's cultural traits from *their* point of view rather than *ours.* When we see an Amish farmer tilling hundreds of acres with a team of horses rather than a tractor, instead of dismissing the practice as hopelessly backward and inefficient, consider the Amish point of view: Hard work is the foundation of religious discipline. The Amish are well aware of farm tractors; they simply believe that using such machinery would be their undoing.

This alternative approach is called **cultural relativism,** *the practice of judging a culture by its own standards.* Cultural relativism is a difficult attitude to adopt because it requires not only understanding the values and norms of another society but also suspending cultural standards we have known all our lives. But as people of the world come into increasing contact with

RESOURCE: Another jumping-off point for a discussion of eth-nocentrism and cultural relativity is Horace Miner's "Body Ritual Among the Nacirema" (*American Anthropologist* 58, 3 (1956):503–7), included in the Macionis and Benokraitis reader, *Seeing Ourselves*, 4th ed.

Q: "Father, mother, and me,
    Sister and Auntie say

All the people are like We,
And everyone else is They.
And They live over the sea
While We live over the way,
But—would you believe it?—they look upon We
As only a sort of They!?"
Rudyard Kipling, "We and They"

During this century, the culture of Japan has been strongly influenced by Western ways of life. Perhaps this explains the widespread use of Western-looking models in Japanese advertising for various products.

one another, there is an ever-greater need to better understand other cultures.

U.S. business is learning that success in the global economy depends on cultural sophistication. General Motors, for example, soon discovered that its Nova wasn't selling well in Spanish-speaking nations because its name in Spanish means "No Go." Coors' advertising slogan "Turn It Loose" startled Spanish-speaking customers by proclaiming that the beer would make you "Suffer From Diarrhea." Braniff Airlines turned "Fly in Leather" into clumsy Spanish reading "Fly Naked," and Eastern Airlines translated "We Earn Our Wings Every Day" into "We Fly Every Day to Heaven." Even Frank Purdue fell victim to poor marketing when his pitch "It Takes a Tough Man to Make a Tender Chicken" ended up in Spanish words reading "A Sexually Excited Man Will Make a Chicken Affectionate" (Helin, 1992).

The world may need greater cultural understanding, but cultural relativity introduces some problems of its own. If almost any kind of behavior is the norm *somewhere* in the world, does that mean that everything is equally right? Does the fact that Indian and Moroccan families benefit from having their children work long hours justify such child labor?

Since we all are members of a single species, surely there must be some universal standards of proper conduct. But what are they? And, in trying to identify them, how can we avoid imposing our own standards on others? There are no simple answers. But here are several general guidelines to keep in mind when dealing with other cultures.

First, while cultural differences fascinate us, they can also be deeply disturbing. Be prepared to experience an emotional reaction when encountering the unfamiliar. Second, resist making a snap judgment, so that you can observe unfamiliar cultural surroundings with an open mind. Third, try to imagine the issue from *their* point of view rather than *yours*. Fourth, after careful thought, try to evaluate an unfamiliar custom. There is no virtue in passively accepting every cultural practice. At the same time, bear in mind that—despite your efforts—you can never really experience the world as others do. Fifth, and finally, turn the argument around and think about your own way of life as others might see it. After all, what we gain most from studying others is insight into ourselves.

A GLOBAL CULTURE?

Today, more than ever before, we see many of the same cultural patterns the world over. Walking the streets of Seoul (South Korea), Kuala Lumpur (Malaysia), Madras (India), Cairo (Egypt), and

GLOBAL: The long-term consequences of the Industrial Revolution may be the emergence of a global culture, as suggested by modernization theory (Chapter 11, "Global Stratification"); see also Chapter 24 ("Social Change").

GLOBAL: According to Withlin Worldwide, a global opinion research company, Asian youth place honesty and accountability high on their list of virtues; U.S. youth place personal freedoms.

Q: ". . . we have failed to understand the relativity of cultural habits, and we remain debarred from much profit and enjoyment in our human relations with people of different cultural standards, and untrustworthy in our dealings with them." Ruth Benedict

GLOBAL: In general, Eastern and Western cultures differ in the following orientations: spiritual vs. material; feminine vs. masculine; community vs. individualism; connectedness vs. separateness.

The flow of immigrants around the world is generally from poor societies to rich nations. Despite vigorous efforts by U.S. authorities to control the border between Mexico and the United States, hundreds of people make their way into this country every day. Here a group of people aspiring to a better life look toward the border, waiting for dark before continuing their journey northward.

Casablanca (Morocco), we find blue jeans, hear well-known pop music, and see advertising for many of the same products we use at home. And, as suggested earlier by Global Map 3–1, English is rapidly emerging as the preferred second language of most of the world. Are local cultures the world over in decline? Are we witnessing the birth of a single global culture?

The world is still divided into 191 nation-states and thousands of different cultural systems. Further, as recent violence in the former Soviet Union, the former Yugoslavia, the Middle East, Sri Lanka, and elsewhere attests, many people are intolerant of others whose cultures differ from their own. Yet societies of the world now have more contact with one another and enjoy more cooperation than ever before. We are globally connected through the flow of goods, information, and people.

1. **The global economy: the flow of goods.** The extent of international trade has never been greater. The global economy has introduced many of the same consumer goods (from cars to TV shows to T-shirts) the world over.

2. **Global communications: the flow of information.** A century ago, communication around the world depended on written messages delivered by boat, train, horse and wagon, or, occasionally, telegraph wire. Today's satellite-based communication enables people to experience sights and sounds of events taking place thousands of miles away—often as they happen.

3. **Global migration: the flow of people.** Knowing about the rest of the world motivates people to move where they imagine life will be better. Moreover, today's transportation technology—especially air travel—makes relocating easier than ever before. As a result, in most countries, significant numbers of people have been born elsewhere (25 million people—about 9 percent of the U.S. population—were born abroad).

These global links have made the cultures of the world more similar in at least superficial respects. But there are three important limitations to the global culture thesis. First, the global flow of goods, information, and people is uneven. Generally speaking, urban areas (centers of commerce, communication, and people) have stronger ties to one another, while many rural villages remain isolated. Then, too, the greater economic and military power of North America and Western Europe means that these regions influence the rest of the world more than the other way around.

Second, for a global culture to exist, people everywhere would have to be able to *afford* various new goods and services. But as Chapter 11 ("Global Stratification") explains, the grinding poverty in much of

Q: "The function of any recurrent activity, such as the punishment of a crime, or a funeral ceremony, is the part it plays in the social life as a whole and therefore the contribution it makes to the maintenance of the structural continuity." A. R. Radcliffe-Brown, *American Anthropologist* 37 (1935):395–96.

DISCUSS: An interesting way to launch a functional analysis of culture is to analyze cultural heroes. What makes an act heroic?

NOTE: Ralph Linton (1937) first used the term "cultural universals" to refer to cultural traits found throughout a *single* society. The term has come to be used to designate a surprising number of cultural traits common to *all* societies.

NOTE: Anthropology has traditionally focused attention on traits common to all cultures and those unique to one.

the world deprives people of even the basic necessities of a safe and secure life.

Third, although many cultural traits are now found throughout the world, we should not conclude that people everywhere attach the same meanings to them. Do teenagers in Tokyo understand hip hop the way their counterparts in New York or Los Angeles do? Similarly, we enjoy foods from around the world while knowing little about the lives of people who first came up with them. In short, people everywhere look at the world through their own cultural "lenses" (Featherstone, 1990; Hall & Neitz, 1993).

THEORETICAL ANALYSIS OF CULTURE

Through culture, we make sense of ourselves and the surrounding world. Sociologists and anthropologists, however, have the special task of making sense of culture. They use various theoretical paradigms.

STRUCTURAL-FUNCTIONAL ANALYSIS

Recall from Chapter 1 ("The Sociological Perspective") that structural-functional analysis presents society as a relatively stable system of integrated parts that meets human needs. From this point of view, then, the significance of cultural traits lies in how they function to maintain the overall operation of society.

As functionalists see it, core values, like the U.S. values noted earlier, anchor a society's way of life (Parsons, 1964; Williams, 1970). This assertion—that ideas (rather than, say, the system of material production) form the basis of human reality—links structural-functionalism to the philosophical doctrine of *idealism*. Core values give shape to most everyday activities, in the process binding together members of a society. New arrivals, of course, do not necessarily share a society's core values. But, according to the functionalist vision of the melting-pot, with time, most immigrants learn to embrace them.

Thinking functionally helps us make sense of an unfamiliar way of life. Take, for example, the Amish farmer plowing hundreds of acres with a team of horses. His farming methods may violate the cultural value of efficiency, but from the Amish point of view, hard work functions to develop the discipline necessary for a deeply religious way of life. Long days of teamwork, along with family meals and recreation at home, not only make the Amish self-sufficient but unify families and local communities.

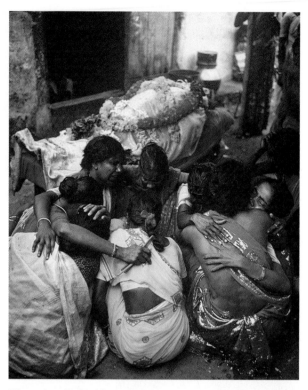

We tend to think of funerals as an expression of respect for the deceased. The social function of funerals, however, has much more to do with the living. For survivors, funerals reaffirm their sense of unity and continuity in the face of separation and disruption.

Of course, Amish practices have dysfunctions as well. The hard work of farming the Amish way and the strict religious discipline is too confining for some, and they ultimately leave the community. Then, too, different interpretations of religious principles can create tension and sometimes lasting divisions within the Amish world (Hostetler, 1980; Kraybill, 1989; Kraybill & Olshan, 1994).

Because cultures are strategies to meet human needs, we would expect that societies the world over would have some common cultural elements. The term **cultural universals** refers to *traits that are part of every known culture*. Comparing hundreds of cultures, George Murdock (1945) found dozens of cultural universals. One common element is the family, which functions everywhere to control sexual reproduction and to organize the upbringing of children. Funeral rites, too, are found everywhere, because all human

NOTE: More detailed analysis of the social-conflict approach to society is found in the section of Chapter 4 ("Society") dealing with the work of Karl Marx.

RESOURCE: Dianne Herman's gender conflict article "The Rape Culture" is one of the culture selections in the *Seeing Ourselves* reader.

Q: "We don't expect dreamers to explain their dreams; no more would we expect lifestyle participants to explain their lifestyles." Marvin Harris

NOTE: Sociobiology rejects the "tabula rasa" (blank slate) notion in favor of the alternative that humans are predisposed toward devising particular cultural patterns.

Q: "Between God and ourselves stands nature." Pope Pius XII

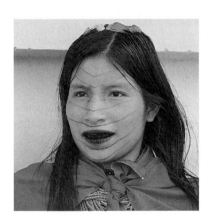

We claim that beauty is in the eye of the beholder, which suggests the importance of culture in setting standards of attractiveness. All of the people pictured here—from Morocco, South Africa, Nigeria, Myanmar (Burma), Japan, and Ecuador—are beautiful to members of their own society. At the same time, sociobiologists point out that, in every society on earth, people are attracted to youthfulness. The reason is that, as sociobiologists see it, attractiveness underlies our choices about reproduction, which is most readily accomplished in early adulthood.

communities cope with the reality of death. Jokes are another cultural universal, serving as a safe means of releasing social tensions.

Critical evaluation. The strength of the structural-functional paradigm is in showing how culture operates as an integrated system for meeting human needs. Yet, by emphasizing cultural stability, this approach downplays the extent to which societies change. Similarly, the idea that cultural values are embraced by every member of a society overlooks the range of cultural diversity. Finally, the cultural patterns favored by powerful people often dominate a society, while other ways of life are pushed to the margins. Thus, cultures typically generate more conflict than structural-functional analysis leads us to believe.

SOCIAL-CONFLICT ANALYSIS

According to the social-conflict paradigm, a society is a dynamic arena filled with cultural controversy. Conflict analysis draws attention to links between culture and inequality and highlights the ways in which any cultural trait benefits some members of society at the expense of others.

NOTE: From the point of view of sociobiology, genes use bodies (and societies) to create more genes. Thus, the chicken and egg dilemma is solved in the following way: Eggs come first; eggs use chickens to create more eggs.
RESOURCE: David Barash's *The Whisperings Within* (Harper & Row, 1981) is a good read that highlights the politics of sociobiology (see Chapter 8).

NOTE: Scientists discovered 50 years ago that DNA (deoxyribonucleic acid) is analogous to a 3-billion-bit-long computer program, shaped like a double helix, that generates protein and transmits human heredity. Scientists expect to complete the "mapping" of human DNA early in the next century. As this work proceeds, we will learn much more about how genetics affects human culture.

We might well begin a conflict analysis by asking why certain values dominate a society in the first place. Karl Marx's response was that values are shaped by a society's system of economic production. "It is not the consciousness of men that determines their being," Marx proclaimed, "it is their social being that determines their consciousness" (Marx & Engels, 1978:4; orig. 1859). Social-conflict theory, then, is rooted in the philosophical doctrine of *materialism*, the assertion that how people meet their material needs (in the United States, through a capitalist economy) has a powerful effect on the rest of their culture. The materialist approach contrasts with the idealist leanings of structural-functionalism.

Social-conflict analysis ties the competitive values of U.S. society to our capitalist economy, which serves the interests of people who own factories and other businesses. Furthermore, the individualistic culture of capitalism teaches that rich and powerful people are more energetic and talented than others and therefore deserving of their wealth and privileges. Viewing capitalism as somehow "natural," then, leads people to distrust any effort to help the economically disadvantaged.

Eventually, however, the strains of social inequality erupt into movements for social change. Two recent examples in the United States are the civil rights movement and the women's movement. Both continue to encounter opposition from defenders of the status quo.

Critical evaluation. The social-conflict paradigm shows that cultural systems do not address human needs equally, allowing some people to dominate others. This inequity, in turn, generates pressure toward change. Yet by stressing the divisiveness of culture, this paradigm understates the ways in which cultural patterns integrate members of society. Thus we should consider both the social-conflict and structural-functional paradigms for a fuller understanding of culture.

SOCIOBIOLOGY

We know culture is a human creation, but does our biological humanity influence how this process unfolds? A third paradigm, standing with one leg in biology and one in sociology, attempts to answer this question. **Sociobiology** is *a theoretical paradigm that explores ways in which biology affects how humans create culture.*

Sociobiology is based on the theory of evolution. In his treatise, *On the Origin of Species*, Charles Darwin (1859) asserts that living organisms change over long

periods of time as a result of *natural selection*, a matter of four simple principles. First, all living things seek to reproduce themselves. Second, the blueprint for reproduction is in genes, the basic units of life that carry traits of one generation into the next. Genes vary randomly in each species, which, in effect, means that a species can "try out" new ways of living in a particular environment. Third, due to genetic variation, some organisms are more likely than others to survive and pass on their advantageous genes to their offspring. Fourth, and finally, over thousands of generations, the genes that promote reproduction and survival become dominant. In this way, as biologists say, a species *adapts* to its environment, and dominant traits emerge as the "nature" of the organism.

In the case of humans, culture itself emerged as human nature. That is, rather than being biologically "wired" for specific behavior, humans developed the intelligence and sociability to devise life patterns for themselves. Such flexibility has allowed our species to flourish all over the planet. Even so, sociobiologists point out, we are all one species—a fact evident in the large number of cultural universals.

Consider, for example, the fact that, as sex researcher Alfred Kinsey put it, "Among all people everywhere in the world, the male is more likely than the female to desire sex with a variety of partners" (quoted in Barash, 1981:49). What insights does sociobiology offer into the so-called "double standard"?

To begin, we all know that a child results when an egg and sperm unite. But the biological significance of a single sperm and a single egg differ dramatically. For healthy men, sperm represent a "renewable resource" produced by the testes throughout most of the life course. A man releases hundreds of millions of sperm in a single ejaculation—technically, enough to fertilize every woman in North America (Barash, 1981:47). A newborn female's ovaries, however, contain her entire lifetime allotment of eggs. A woman releases a single egg cell from her ovaries each month. So, while a man is biologically capable of fathering thousands of offspring, a woman is able to bear only a relatively small number of children.

Given this biologically based difference, each sex is well served by a distinctive reproductive strategy. From a strictly biological perspective, a man reproduces his genes most efficiently by being promiscuous—readily engaging in sex. This scheme, however, is totally contrary to a woman's reproductive interests. Pregnancy requires that she carry the child for nine months, give birth, and provide care for long afterward. Thus, efficient reproduction for a woman

Q: "Although the genes have given away most of their sovereignty, they maintain a certain amount of influence in at least the behavioral qualities that underlie the variations between cultures." Edward O. Wilson

Q: "Absolute truth can belong to only one class of humans . . . the class of absolute fools." Ashley Montagu

NOTE: The final section of Chapter 5 ("Socialization") explores the "constraint versus freedom" controversy.

Q: "Society is indeed a contract between those who are living, those who are dead, and those who are yet to be born." Edmund Burke

Q: "Don't be so open minded that your brains fall out." Richard Rorty

depends on choosing a mate whose qualities (beginning with the likelihood that he will simply stay around) will contribute to their child's survival and, in turn, successful reproduction (Remoff, 1984).

The "double standard" certainly involves more than biology and is tangled up with the historical domination of women by men (Barry, 1983). But sociobiology suggests that this cultural pattern, like many others, has an underlying bio-logic. Simply put, the "double standard" exists around the world because women and men everywhere tend toward distinctive reproductive strategies.

Critical evaluation. Sociobiology has generated some intriguing theories about the biological roots of cultural patterns, especially cultural universals. But it remains controversial for several reasons.

First, some critics fear that sociobiology may revive the biological arguments of a century ago that claimed the superiority of one race or sex. But defenders counter that sociobiology rejects the past pseudo-science of racial superiority. In fact, sociobiology unites all of humanity because all people share a single evolutionary history. With regard to sex, sociobiology does assume that men and women differ biologically in some ways that culture cannot overcome—if, in fact, any society intended to. But, far from asserting that males are somehow more important than females, sociobiology emphasizes that both sexes are vital to human reproduction.

Second, say the critics, sociobiologists have little evidence to support their theories. A generation ago, Edward O. Wilson (1975, 1978), generally credited as the founder of sociobiology, optimistically claimed that this approach would reveal the biological roots of human culture. But research to date does not show that biology determines human behavior in any rigid sense. Rather, abundant evidence shows the opposite—that human behavior is *learned* within a cultural system. The contribution of sociobiology, then, lies in its explanation of why some cultural patterns seem "easier to learn" than others (Barash, 1981).

CULTURE AND HUMAN FREEDOM

An important issue throughout this chapter has been the extent to which cultural creatures are free. Does culture bind us to each other and to the past? Or does culture enhance our capacity for individual thought and independent choice?

CULTURE AS CONSTRAINT

Over the long course of human evolution, culture became the strategy for survival. Truly, we cannot live without culture. But culture does have its drawbacks. We may be the only animals who name ourselves, yet, as symbolic beings, we are also the only creatures who experience alienation. Moreover, culture is largely a matter of habit, which limits our choices and drives us to repeat troubling patterns, such as racial prejudice, in each new generation. And, in this age of new information technology, we may wonder about the extent to which business-dominated media manipulate our culture in pursuit of profits.

Moreover, our society's insistence on competitive achievement urges us toward excellence, yet this same pattern also isolates us from one another. Material comforts improve our lives in many ways, yet our preoccupation with things diverts us from the security and satisfaction of close relationships and spiritual pursuits. Our emphasis on personal freedom affords us privacy and independence, but at the cost of a human community in which to share life's problems (Slater, 1976; Bellah et al., 1985).

CULTURE AS FREEDOM

Just as other animals are prisoners of biology, so it appears that human beings are prisoners of culture. But there is a crucial difference, as this chapter suggests. Biological instinct creates a ready-made world, but culture gives to us the opportunity and responsibility to make and remake a world for ourselves.

Therefore, although culture seems at times to circumscribe our lives, it also embodies hope, creativity, and choice. There is no better evidence in support of this conclusion than the fascinating cultural diversity of our own society and the far greater human variety of the larger world. Furthermore, culture is ever-changing as the result of human imagination and inventiveness. And the more we discover about our culture, the greater our ability to use the freedom it offers us.

NOTE: In his book, *Culture Wars*, Hunter explains that today's political battles have much the same character as religious conflict between Catholics and Protestants during the last century: The issues are set in moral terms, raise powerful passions, and are resistant to compromise.

DISCUSS: Hunter concludes that the liberals currently have the upper hand in the culture wars, since they control the symbolic industries, including universities, the press, and Hollywood. Does the class agree? Why or why not?

DISCUSS: To what extent do the media—often seeking out the extremists in order to generate a good story—serve to polarize cultural conflict?

NOTE: "Culture wars" is derived from *kulturkampf*, a divisive debate in 1870s Germany over papal infallibility (Rabkin, 1996).

 ## CONTROVERSY & DEBATE

What Are the "Culture Wars"?

"Hi, there, this is WOSU's 'Open Line' talk show. This afternoon, we are debating the question 'Should gay people have the opportunity to marry under the law?' I have Rhonda from the East Side on the line; Rhonda, what do you think . . . ?"

The easy rhythm of radio talk shows is familiar to just about everyone all across the country. But there is nothing easy about the questions being asked and, more often than not, little agreement on the answers. Indeed, on a host of issues—including gay rights, gender equality, welfare, abortion, single parenting, prayer in schools, multiculturalism, government funding to the arts, and more—there now seems to be a wide and angry gulf in U.S. society. And, on both sides, people are thoughtful, committed to their principles, and concerned about the future of their country. They are fighting the "culture wars."

Today's "culture wars" represent our nation's latest round of **cultural conflict,** *political opposition, often accompanied by social hostility, rooted in different cultural values.* There is nothing novel about cultural conflict. Throughout much of the nineteenth century, for example, Protestants and Catholics clashed over the direction of U.S. society. Today the issues in the "culture wars" are new, of course, but as sociologist James Davison Hunter explains, the conflict remains a struggle to define our way of life.

Hunter offers several insights into the current cultural conflict. First, he points out that peoples' positions on many issues are consistent. That is, knowing an individual's views on one issue helps to predict that person's views on another. This connection stems from the fact that most individuals fall into one of two major camps—"traditionalists" and "progressives"—that have different cultural orientations.

Traditionalists, explains Hunter, see the world as a moral system; that is, they recognize "an external, definable, and transcendent authority" that clearly defines right and wrong and to whom everyone is responsible. For many—whether they are Christians, Jews, or Muslims—God is this authority. For others, the authority is a cultural heritage of self-reliance and strong families that has guided this country for centuries. Traditionalists, then, are conservatives who tend to be patriotic, religious, and believe in "old-fashioned family values." Thus traditionalists oppose lawful marriage for gay people, oppose abortion as morally wrong, and think that today's public schools have abandoned moral teaching in favor of tolerance for virtually every imaginable "lifestyle." From this point of view, the growing tide of violence, divorce, and "illegitimate" births comes from too little moral responsibility and too much personal freedom.

To progressives, on the other hand, a just world is composed of thoughtful people free to act according to their own principles. Progressives recognize no simple distinction between right and wrong. Indeed, they point out that our country deliberately removed religion from public life, making beliefs a matter of individual conscience. Certainly, some progressives are religious, but they tend to see the Bible and other religious texts as sources of historical wisdom that people must interpret for themselves in light of today's circumstances. Thus, progressives seek to overcome historic prejudices against gay people, they recognize a woman's right to abortion, and they support the law that bans religious observance from public schools. From this point of view, social problems like poverty and racial discrimination are best remedied not by greater moral discipline, but by making disadvantaged people equal and creating a just society.

One reason this country's "culture wars" generate so much heated discussion, claims Hunter, is that media coverage focuses on groups with extreme positions on one side or the other. But whatever role the media play in the culture wars, there is a solid wall of disagreement between traditionalists and progressives: What one side sees as the "solution," the other considers to be the "problem."

Continue the debate . . .

1. *Why do you think people find it hard to compromise on culture war issues, such as access to abortion or gay rights?*

2. *Are the culture wars evident on your campus? If so, cite examples.*

3. *Which side of the culture wars has the upper hand? Why?*

Sources: Adapted, in part, from Hunter (1991); see also Davis & Robinson (1996), DiMaggio, Evans, & Bryson (1996), and Nolan (1996).

EXERCISE: Consider ways in which humans, as cultural creatures, differ from other animals. List pairs of terms that fit the following sentence: While all forms of life have ____, only human beings have ____. Examples: Consciousness; self-consciousness; violence; prejudice; self-preservation; awareness of mortality.

EXERCISE: Museums are statements of what about a way of life (or *who* within a society) is virtuous. Visit a museum and analyze what is displayed, who is celebrated, and, as much as you can, determine what and who are left out. Try to find out who decides what is and is not included in museum displays.

SUMMARY

1. Culture refers to a way of life shared by members of a society. Several species display limited capacity for culture, but only human beings rely on culture for survival.

2. As the human brain evolved, the first elements of culture appeared some 2 million years ago; the development of culture accelerated toward the "rise of civilization" some 12,000 years ago.

3. Humans build culture on symbols by attaching meaning to objects and action. Language is the symbolic system by which one generation transmits culture to the next.

4. Values are culturally defined standards of what ought to be; beliefs are statements that people who share a culture hold to be true.

5. Cultural norms guide human behavior. Mores consist of norms of great moral significance; folkways are norms that guide everyday life and afford greater individual choice.

6. High culture refers to patterns that distinguish a society's elites; popular culture includes patterns widespread in a society.

7. The United States stands among the most culturally diverse societies in the world. Subculture refers to distinctive cultural patterns adopted by a segment of a population; counterculture refers to patterns strongly at odds with a conventional way of life. Multiculturalism represents educational efforts to enhance awareness and appreciation of cultural diversity.

8. Invention, discovery, and diffusion all generate cultural change. Cultural lag is the condition in which parts of a cultural system change at different rates.

9. Because we learn the standards of one culture, we evaluate other cultures ethnocentrically. An alternative to ethnocentrism is cultural relativism, judging another culture according to its own standards.

10. The structural-functional paradigm views culture as a relatively stable system built on core values. Cultural traits function to maintain the overall system.

11. The social-conflict paradigm envisions culture as a dynamic arena of inequality and conflict. Cultural patterns benefit some categories of people more than others.

12. Sociobiology studies how evolution shapes the human creation of culture.

13. Culture can constrain human needs and ambitions; yet, as cultural creatures, we have the capacity to shape and reshape the world to meet our needs and pursue our dreams.

14. The concept of cultural conflict refers to both political debate ("culture wars") on a host of specific issues and to disagreement about the general direction of cultural change in the United States.

KEY CONCEPTS

culture the values, beliefs, behavior, and material objects that constitute a people's way of life

nonmaterial culture the intangible world of ideas created by members of a society

material culture the tangible things created by members of a society

culture shock personal disorientation that comes from experiencing an unfamiliar way of life

symbols anything that carries a particular meaning recognized by people who share culture

language a system of symbols that allows members of a society to communicate with one another

cultural transmission the process by which one generation passes culture to the next

Sapir-Whorf thesis the thesis that people perceive the world through the cultural lens of language

values culturally defined standards of desirability, goodness, and beauty that serve as broad guidelines for social living

beliefs specific statements that people hold to be true

norms rules and expectations by which a society guides the behavior of its members

mores a society's standards of proper moral conduct

folkways a society's customs for routine, casual interaction

social control various means by which members of a society encourage conformity to norms

ideal culture (as opposed to real culture) social patterns mandated by cultural values and norms

real culture (as opposed to ideal culture) actual social patterns that only approximate cultural expectations

technology knowledge that a society applies to the task of living in a physical environment

high culture cultural patterns that distinguish a society's elite

popular culture cultural patterns that are widespread among a society's population

subculture cultural patterns that set apart some segment of a society's population

multiculturalism an educational program recognizing past and present cultural diversity in U.S. society and promoting the equality of all cultural traditions

Eurocentrism the dominance of European (particularly English) cultural patterns

Afrocentrism the dominance of African cultural patterns

counterculture cultural patterns that strongly oppose those widely accepted within a society

cultural integration the close relationship among various elements of a cultural system

cultural lag the fact that cultural elements change at different rates, which may disrupt a cultural system

ethnocentrism the practice of judging another culture by the standards of one's own culture

cultural relativism the practice of judging a culture by its own standards

cultural universals traits that are part of every known culture

sociobiology a theoretical paradigm that explores ways in which biology affects how humans create culture

cultural conflict political opposition, often accompanied by social hostility, rooted in different cultural values

CRITICAL-THINKING QUESTIONS

1. Many people in the United States pay careful attention to their lawns. What is the cultural significance of a carefully manicured lawn in a highly mobile and largely anonymous society? What does a well-tended (or untended) front yard say about a person?

2. How does a schoolroom activity such as a "spelling bee" embody U.S. cultural values? What cultural values are expressed by children's stories such as *The Little Engine That Could* and board games such as "Chutes and Ladders," "Monopoly," and "Risk"?

3. Do you think U.S. cultural values are changing? If so, how and why?

4. Do you identify with one or more subcultures? If so, which? How do they differ from "mainstream" U.S. values?

LEARNING EXERCISES

1. Try to find someone on campus who has lived in another country. Ask for a chance to discuss how the culture of that other society differs from the way of life here. Try to identify ways in which the other person sees U.S. culture differently than most people.

2. Step back from your everyday thinking and look at several of your favorite television shows as you imagine someone from another country would. What cultural values do the shows reflect?

3. Play a game of "Monopoly" with several friends. As you play, discuss what this popular game suggests about our way of life.

4. Approach someone in one of your classes who is of a different race or ethnicity than you are. Explain that you are doing an assignment for your sociology course, and see if you can strike up a discussion of the extent to which the two of you may experience campus life differently. To what extent do race and ethnicity give people a different "window" on your campus's culture?

5. If you have computer access, install the CD-ROM packaged inside the back cover of your text and complete the activities designed to accompany this chapter.

William Greaves, *Hammersmith Bridge on Boat Race Day,* 1862
Tate Gallery, London/Art Resource, NY.

CHAPTER 4

SOCIETY

Sididi Ag Inaka has never used a computer, sent a fax, or spoken on a cell phone. In today's high-technology world, this may seem strange enough, but how about this: Neither Inaka nor anyone in his family has ever seen a television or even read a newspaper.

Are these people visitors from another planet? Prisoners on some remote island? Not at all. They are Tuareg nomads of western Africa. They wander the vastness of the Sahara Desert, north of the city of Timbuktu in the nation we know as Mali. As unusual as Inaka's life may seem to us, it is perfectly natural to him: "My father was a nomad, his father was a nomad, I am a nomad, my children will be nomads."

Thousands of people live the same life—raising camels, donkeys, goats, and sheep—in this desolate corner of the world. Tuaregs wear tattered clothes, sleep in camel-hide tents, and cook with charcoal. There are no schools for the children, and even toilets are unknown. Inaka and his family regularly endure unforgiving heat and push their way through blinding sandstorms to find water and grass for their herd of about thirty-five animals. At an inviting oasis, they may find others, with whom they sell or trade animals and cheese.

The Tuaregs are among the poorest people of the world, living a simple and difficult existence. When the rains fail to come, they and their animals may lose their lives. Inaka and his people are a society set apart, largely isolated from the rest of humanity and virtually untouched by modern ideas and advanced technology. To many, no doubt, they seem a curious throwback to the past. But Inaka does not complain. "This is the life of my ancestors. This is the life that we know" (Buckley, 1996).

Human societies have taken many forms throughout history, and remarkable diversity is still evident in the world today. But what is a society, in the first place? What makes society "hang together"? How have societies changed over the course of human history? Why have they changed?

Society refers to *people who interact in a defined territory and share culture*. In this chapter, we shall examine this deceptively simple term from four different angles. We begin with **Gerhard Lenski** and **Jean Lenski,** who describe the changing character of human society over the last 10,000 years. They explain the importance of *technology*, and how a new technology can have revolutionary consequences for social life. Then we turn to three of sociology's founders. **Karl Marx,** like the Lenskis, understood human history as a long and complex process of social change. For Marx, however, the story of society spins around *social conflict* that arises from how people produce material goods. **Max Weber** added another twist, demonstrating the power of *ideas* to shape society. Weber contrasted the traditional thinking of simple societies with the rational thought that dominates our modern way of life. Finally, **Emile Durkheim** helps us to see how societies

SUPPLEMENTS: The *Data File* provides an outline of Chapter 4 along with discussion questions and supplementary lecture material.

NOTE: Use this chapter in any number of ways. Assign all of it to give students a detailed introduction to important historical material and key theorists whose ideas inform later chapters. Or assign sections separately along with later chapters: Use the Weber section to preface the discussion of bureaucracy in Chapter 7; the Durkheim section before the structural-functional analysis of deviance in Chapter 8; the Marx section before discussion of social inequality in Chapter 9. Instructors may also omit the chapter entirely without breaking the flow of the text.

NOTE: In effect, hunting and gathering societies have only one social institution: the family.

In technologically simple societies, successful hunting wins men great praise. However, the gathering of vegetation by women is a more dependable and easily available source of nutrition.

"hang together." He discovered that traditional and modern societies are cohesive for quite different reasons.

All four visions answer basic questions about society: What makes simple people such as the Tuareg of the Sahara Desert so different from the society familiar to us? How and why do all societies change? What forces divide a society? What forces hold it together? And, after looking at the trends over time, we ask whether societies seem to be getting better or worse.

GERHARD LENSKI AND JEAN LENSKI: SOCIETY AND TECHNOLOGY

As people who take for granted schooling and medical care, and who enjoy the rapid transportation and instant global communication of our way of life, we must wonder at the nomads of the Sahara. The work of Gerhard Lenski and Jean Lenski (Lenski, Nolan, & Lenski, 1995) helps us to understand the great differences among societies that have flourished and declined throughout human history. Just as important, their work helps us better understand how we live today.

The Lenskis study what they call **sociocultural evolution,** *the changes that occur as a society gains new technology.* Like a biologist examining how a living species has evolved over thousands of years, the Lenskis observe how societies change over centuries as they gain greater ability to manipulate their physical environments. Societies with simple technology (such as the Tuareg nomads) can provide for only a small number of people and offer few choices about how to live. Technologically complex societies—while not necessarily "better" in any absolute sense—support large populations who live diverse, highly specialized lives.

The Lenskis also explain that the more technological information a society has, the faster it changes. Technologically simple societies, then, change very slowly; as Sididi Ag Inaka says, he "lives the life of his ancestors." Modern, high-technology societies, on the other hand, change so quickly that dramatic transformations can occur during a single lifetime. Imagine how someone who lived just a few generations ago would react to beepers, phone sex, artificial hearts, the information superhighway, laser surgery, test-tube babies, genetic engineering, e-mail, fiber optics, smart bombs, the threat of nuclear holocaust, space shuttles, transsexualism, and "tell-all" talk shows.

In short, new technology sends ripples of change throughout a society's way of life. When our ancestors first discovered how to harness the power of the wind using a sail, they set the stage for building sailing ships, which took them to new lands, stimulated trade, and increased their military might. Consider, as a more recent example, in how many ways our lives are being changed by the spread of computer technology.

Drawing on the Lenskis' work, we will describe five general types of societies distinguished by their technology: hunting and gathering societies, horticultural and pastoral societies, agrarian societies, industrial societies, and postindustrial societies.

HUNTING AND GATHERING SOCIETIES

The most basic human societies live by **hunting and gathering,** *simple technology for hunting animals and gathering vegetation.* From the emergence of our species back several million years until just 10,000 years ago, *all* humans were hunters and gatherers. Even several centuries ago, numerous hunting and gathering societies existed in the world. Today, however, only a few remain, including the Aka and Pygmies of central Africa, the Bushmen of southwestern Africa, the Aborigines of Australia, the Kaska Indians of northwest

NOTE: Simple societies have yielded information about the medicinal properties of plants and are a general model for living in balance with nature (see Chapter 22, "Environment and Society").

NOTE: One might express the transition from hunting and gathering to pastoralism and horticulture as moving from *seeking food* to *growing one's own.*

NOTE: The Lenskis explain that hunters and gatherers limited property rights to personal tools and weapons. Natural resources, including fields and forests, were available to all, but ownership is claimed by the group. Thus, members of such societies expected outsiders to seek permission before entering an area. Horticulturalists, by contrast, typically (but not always) define land as private property.

Pastoralism historically has flourished in regions of the world where arid soil does not support crops. Pastoral people still thrive in northern Africa, living today much as they did a thousand years ago.

Canada, and the Batek and Semai of Malaysia (Endicott, 1992; Hewlett, 1992).

With little control over their environment, hunters and gatherers continually search for game and collect edible plants. Only in lush areas where food is plentiful do hunters and gatherers have any leisure time. Moreover, it takes a lot of land to support even a small number of people, so hunting and gathering societies remain small bands of just a few dozen people, and they are nomadic, moving on as they consume vegetation in one area or as they pursue migratory animals. Although they periodically return to favored sites, they rarely form permanent settlements.

The key organizing principle of hunting and gathering societies is kinship. The family obtains and distributes food, protects its members, and teaches the children. Everyone's life is much the same and focused on getting the next meal. There is some specialization related to age and sex. The very young and the very old contribute only what they can, while healthy adults secure most of the food. Women gather vegetation—the more reliable food source—while men take on the less certain task of hunting. The two sexes have somewhat different responsibilities, then, but most hunters and gatherers probably see men and women as having about the same social importance (Leacock, 1978).

Hunting and gathering societies have few formal leaders. Most recognize a *shaman*, or spiritual leader, who enjoys high prestige but receives no greater material rewards and must pitch in to find food like everyone else. In short, hunting and gathering societies are relatively simple and egalitarian.

Hunters and gatherers use simple weapons—the spear, the bow and arrow, and the stone knife—but rarely to wage war. Yet they often fall victim to the forces of nature. Storms and droughts can easily destroy their food supply, and there is little they can do in the event of accident and disease. Such vulnerability encourages cooperation and sharing, a strategy that increases everyone's odds of survival. Nonetheless, many die in childhood, and about half never reach the age of twenty (Lenski, Nolan, & Lenski, 1995:104).

During this century, technologically complex societies have slowly closed in on the few remaining hunters and gatherers, reducing their landholdings and depleting game and vegetation. The Lenskis predict that, by the year 2000, we may well witness the end of hunting and gathering societies on earth. Fortunately, study of this way of life has already produced valuable information about human history and our fundamental ties to the natural world.

HORTICULTURAL AND PASTORAL SOCIETIES

Ten to twelve thousand years ago, a new technology changed the lives of human beings (see the time line inside the front cover). People discovered **horticulture,** *the technology of using hand tools to cultivate plants.* Using a hoe to work the soil and a digging stick to punch holes in the ground for seeds may seem simple and obvious, but horticulture allowed people to give up gathering in favor of "growing their own." Humans first planted gardens in fertile regions of the Middle East and, soon after, in Latin America and Asia. Within some 5,000

NOTE: *Hort* is a Latin root meaning "garden." Latin *horti cultura* thus means "cultivation of a garden"; *agri cultura* means "cultivation of a field." *Pastoral* is derived from Latin meaning "shepherd" or, literally, "feeder."

NOTE: Horticulturalists practice *slash and burn* or *swidden* horticulture. This practice involves regular clearing of new land as land in use suffers depleted nutrients. Trees and other growth are killed, dried, and burned.

NOTE: The reason that warfare is common among horticulturalists and rare among hunting and gathering people probably involves increasing population density that limits both available land and game.

Q: "You can lead a horticulture, but you can't make her think." Dorothy Parker

Of Egypt's 130 pyramids, the Great Pyramids at Giza are the largest. Each of the three major structures stands more than forty stories high and is composed of 3 million massive stone blocks. Some 4,500 years ago, tens of thousands of people labored to construct these pyramids so that one man, the pharaoh, might have a godlike monument for his tomb. Clearly social inequality in this agrarian society was striking.

Then, too, people living in arid regions (such as the Sahara region of western Africa or the Middle East) or mountainous areas found horticulture to be of little value. Such people (including the Tuareg) turned to a different strategy for survival, **pastoralism,** which is *technology that supports the domestication of animals.* Still others mixed horticulture and pastoralism. Today, numerous horticultural-pastoral societies thrive in South America, Africa, and Asia.

Domesticating plants and animals greatly increased food production, enabling societies to support not dozens but hundreds of people. Pastoralists remained nomadic, leading their herds to fresh grazing lands. Horticulturalists, by contrast, formed settlements, moving only when they depleted the soil. As these settlements became joined by trade, they made up multicentered societies with overall populations reaching the thousands.

Now capable of producing a *material surplus*—more resources than needed to support day-to-day living—not everyone has to secure food. Some make crafts, trade, cut hair, apply tattoos, or serve as priests. Compared to hunting and gathering societies, then, horticultural and pastoral societies display more specialized and complex social arrangements.

Hunters and gatherers believe many spirits inhabit the world. Horticulturalists, however, practice ancestor worship and conceive of God as Creator. Pastoral societies carry this belief further, viewing God as directly involved in the well-being of the entire world. This view of God ("The Lord is my shepherd . . . ," Psalm 23) is widespread in our own society because Christianity, Islam, and Judaism were originally Middle Eastern, pastoral religions.

Expanding productive technology creates social inequality. As some families produce more food than others, they assume positions of relative power and privilege. Forging alliances with other elite families ensures that their social advantages endure over generations, and a formal system of social inequality emerges. Along with social hierarchy, a simple government—backed by military force—emerges to shore up the dominance of elites. However, without the ability to communicate or to travel over large distances, a ruler can control only a limited number of people, so there is little empire building.

The domestication of plants and animals surely made simpler societies more productive. But advancing technology is never entirely beneficial. The Lenskis point out that, compared to hunters and gatherers, horticulturalists and pastoralists exhibit more

years, cultural diffusion spread knowledge of horticulture throughout most of the world.

Not all societies abandoned hunting and gathering in favor of horticulture. Hunters and gatherers living amid plentiful vegetation and game probably ignored the new technology (Fisher, 1979). Others, like the Yąnomamö, described in Chapter 3 ("Culture"), incorporated some horticulture into traditional hunting and gathering (Chagnon, 1992).

GLOBAL: For most of our history, humans lived in hunting and gathering societies; during the last 2,000 years, however, agrarian societies have predominated, and they still contain about two-thirds of the world's people.

NOTE: Peter Berger (1986:99) points out that even average people today live better than agrarian elites. As late as World War I, for example, Schoenbrunn, the fabulous summer palace of the

Habsburgs (monarchs of Austria), had not a single indoor toilet.

NOTE: Worth repeating is the link between agrarian "cultivation" and the flowering of human "culture"—these words share a single root.

NOTE: Chapter 9 ("Social Stratification") examines the relative degree of social inequality in the types of societies described by the Lenskis. See, especially, Figure 9–2, the Kuznets curve.

SOCIAL DIVERSITY

Technology and the Changing Status of Women

In technologically simple societies of the past, women produced more food than men did. Hunters and gatherers valued meat highly, but hunting was not a dependable source of nourishment. Thus vegetation gathered by women was the primary means of ensuring survival. Similarly, it was women who took charge of the tools and seeds used in horticulture. For their part, men traded and tended herds of animals. Only at harvest time did men and women work side by side.

About 5,000 years ago, humans discovered how to mold metals. This technology spread by cultural diffusion, primarily along male trade networks. Thus it was men who developed the metal plow and, since they already managed animals, thought to hitch it to a cow.

The metal plow marked the beginning of agriculture, and, for the first time, men took over the dominant role in food production. Elise Boulding explains how this technological breakthrough undermined the social standing of women:

The shift of the status of the woman farmer may have happened quite rapidly, once there were two

male specializations relating to agriculture: plowing and the care of cattle. This situation left women with all the subsidiary tasks, including weeding and carrying water to the fields. The new fields were larger, so women had to work just as many hours as they did before, but now they worked at more secondary tasks. . . . This would contribute further to the erosion of the status of women.

Sources: Based on Boulding (1976) and Fisher (1979).

---

social inequality and, in many cases, engage in slavery, ongoing warfare, and even cannibalism.

AGRARIAN SOCIETIES

About 5,000 years ago, another technological revolution was under way in the Middle East that would eventually transform most of the world. This was the discovery of **agriculture**, *the technology of large-scale farming using plows harnessed to animals or, eventually, mechanical tractors.* So great was the social significance of the animal-drawn plow and other technological innovations of the period—including irrigation, the wheel, writing, numbers, and the expanding use of metals—that this era is commonly called "the dawn of civilization" (Lenski, Nolan, & Lenski, 1995:177).

Farmers with animal-drawn plows can cultivate fields vastly larger than the garden-sized plots worked by horticulturalists. Plows have the additional advantage of turning, and thereby aerating, the soil to increase fertility. As a result, farmers work the same land for generations, which, in turn, encourages permanent settlements. Large food surpluses, transported on animal-powered wagons, allow agrarian societies to expand their land area

and population. About 100 C.E., for example, the agrarian Roman Empire boasted a population of 70 million spread over some 2 million square miles (Stavrianos, 1983; Lenski, Nolan, & Lenski, 1995).

As always, increasing production means greater specialization. Tasks once performed by everyone, such as clearing land and securing food, become distinct occupations. Specialization also made the early barter system obsolete, and money became the standard of exchange. Money made trade easier, sparking the growth of cities as economic centers with populations soaring into the millions.

Agrarian societies exhibit dramatic social inequality. In many cases—including the United States early in its history—peasants or slaves make up a large share of the population. Freed from manual work, elites study philosophy, art, and literature. This explains the historical link between "high culture" and social privilege, discussed in Chapter 3 ("Culture").

Among hunters and gatherers, and also among horticulturalists, women are the primary providers of food. Agriculture, however, propels men into a position of social dominance (Boulding, 1976; Fisher, 1979). The box looks more closely at the declining

GLOBAL: The Lenskis report the following typical densities in persons per square mile: hunting and gathering societies, less than one; horticultural societies, 10 to 40; agrarian societies, over 100. Industrial societies have densities that range from about 70 (U.S.) to several hundred (most European nations), to about 1,000 (such as Japan and the Netherlands).

NOTE: At its height, the Roman Empire surrounded most of the

Mediterranean Sea (including Europe, the Middle East, and northern Africa).

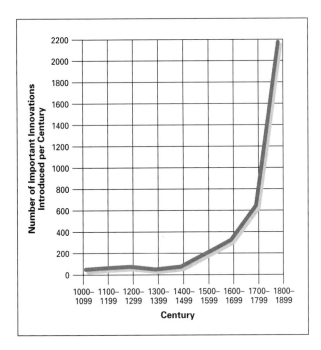

FIGURE 4–1 The Increasing Number of Technological Innovations

This figure illustrates the dramatic change in the number of technological innovations in Western Europe after the beginning of the Industrial Revolution in the mid-eighteenth century. Technological innovation occurs at an accelerating rate because each innovation combines with existing cultural elements to produce many additional innovations.

Source: Lenski, Nolan, & Lenski (1995).

position of women at this point in the course of sociocultural evolution.

Religion reinforces the power of agricultural elites. According to religious doctrine, people are morally obligated to perform their work. Many of the "Wonders of the Ancient World," such as the Great Wall of China and the Great Pyramids of Egypt, were possible only because emperors and pharaohs wielded absolute power, commanding their people to a lifetime of labor without wages.

In agrarian societies, then, elites gain unparalleled power. To maintain control of large empires, leaders require the services of a wide range of administrators. Along with the growing economy, then, the political system becomes established as a distinct sphere of life.

Of the societies described so far, agrarian societies have the greatest specialization and the most social

inequality. Agrarian technology also affords a greater range of possibilities as to how to live, which is why agrarian societies differ more from one another than horticultural and pastoral societies do.

INDUSTRIAL SOCIETIES

Industrialism, as found in the United States, Canada, and other rich nations of the world, is *technology that powers sophisticated machinery with advanced sources of energy.* Until the industrial era, the major source of energy was the muscles of humans and other animals. But around 1750, mills and factories began to use flowing water and then steam boilers to power ever-larger and more efficient machinery.

With industrial technology, societies began to change faster, as shown in Figure 4–1. Industrial societies transformed themselves more in a century than they had in thousands of years before. As explained in Chapter 1 ("The Sociological Perspective"), this stunning change stimulated the birth of sociology itself. During the nineteenth century, railroads and steamships revolutionized transportation, and steel-framed skyscrapers dwarfed the cathedrals that symbolized an earlier age.

In the twentieth century, automobiles further reshaped Western societies, and electricity powered "modern conveniences" such as lighting, refrigerators, and washing machines. Electronic communication, including the telephone, radio, and television, soon followed, extending our lives outward to make a large world seem smaller and smaller. And during the last generation, computers have ushered in the Information Revolution, dramatically increasing our capacity to process words and numbers.

Work, too, has changed. In agrarian societies, most men and women work in the home. Industrialization, however, creates factories near centralized machinery and energy sources. Lost in the process are close working relationships, strong kinship ties, and also many of the traditional values, beliefs, and customs that guide agrarian life.

Occupational specialization, which expanded over the long course of sociocultural evolution, has become more pronounced than ever. In fact, industrial people often size up one another in terms of their jobs rather than (as nonindustrial people do) according to their kinship ties. Rapid change and movement from place to place also generate anonymity and cultural diversity, creating numerous subcultures and countercultures, as described in Chapter 3 ("Culture").

NOTE: The Lenskis note that the term "Industrial Revolution" did not enter common usage until the final decades of the 19th century; at that point, it described events that had begun almost two centuries before.

GLOBAL: Marion Levy suggests a good index of modernization is the ratio of inanimate to animate sources of energy (that is, fuel to muscle power).

NOTE: Chapter 15 ("The Economy and Work") details the facets of the Industrial Revolution: (1) new forms of energy, (2) factories, (3) mass production, (4) productive specialization, and (5) wage labor.

NOTE: Further discussion of postindustrial society is found in Chapter 15 ("The Economy and Work").

A century ago, industrial workers (most of whom were men) used their skills to manipulate things, often using massive machinery. Today, the postindustrial economy demands that workers (now as likely to be women as men) manipulate symbols in the form of words, images, or music, often using computers.

Industrial technology recasts the family, too, diminishing its traditional significance as the center of social life. No longer does the family serve as the primary setting for economic production, learning, and religious worship. And, as Chapter 17 ("Family") explains, technological change also underlies the trend away from traditional families to greater numbers of single people, divorced people, single-parent families, and step-families.

The Lenskis point out that, early in the industrialization process, only a small segment of the population enjoys the benefits of technology. In time, however, the material benefits of industrial productivity spread more widely so that people live longer and more comfortably than ever before. Poverty remains a serious problem in industrial societies, but compared to a century ago, the standard of living has risen fivefold, and economic, social, and political inequality has declined. Some social leveling, discussed in Chapter 9 ("Social Stratification"), occurs because industrial societies require an educated and skilled labor force. While most people in nonindustrial societies are illiterate, industrial societies provide state-funded schooling and confer numerous political rights on virtually everyone. Industrialization, in fact, intensifies demands for political participation, as seen most recently in South Korea, Taiwan, the People's Republic of China, the nations of Eastern Europe, and the former Soviet Union.

POSTINDUSTRIAL SOCIETIES

Many industrial societies, including the United States, have now entered yet another phase of technological development, and we can briefly extend the Lenskis' analysis to take account of recent trends. A generation ago sociologist Daniel Bell (1973) coined the term **postindustrialism** to refer to *technology that supports an information-based economy.* While production in industrial societies centers on factories and machinery used to generate material goods, postindustrial production is based on computers and other electronic technologies that create, process, store, and apply information. Thus, while members of industrial societies develop and apply mechanical skills in the creation of physical objects, people in postindustrial societies develop information-based skills that enable them to work with computers and various forms of symbolic communication.

With this shift in key skills, postindustrialism dramatically changes society's occupational structure. Chapter 15 ("The Economy and Work") examines this process in detail, explaining that a postindustrial society uses less and less of its labor force for industrial production. At the same time, the ranks of clerical workers, managers, and other people who process information (in fields ranging from academia and advertising to marketing and public relations) swell.

RESOURCE: John Macionis's article "Welcome to Cyber-Society!" is included in the 4th edition of the *Seeing Ourselves* reader.

NOTE: In the industrial era, "setting the clocks" used to mean adjusting the bedroom clock and kitchen wall clock. Now it involves dozens of electronic devices—TVs, computers, VCRs, faxes, cellular phones, and so on.

NOTE: An indicator of the uneven pace of rationalization in the world is that half the world's scientific output is generated by six nations—the United States, United Kingdom, Japan, the former Soviet Union, France, and Germany.

NOTE: Roughly 5 to 10% of all people who have ever lived are alive now. However, about 90% of all *scientists* who have ever lived are living today.

TABLE 4–1 Sociocultural Evolution: A Summary

Type of Society	Historical Period	Productive Technology	Population Size
Hunting and Gathering Societies	Only type of society until about 12,000 years ago; still common several centuries ago; the few examples remaining today are threatened with extinction	Primitive weapons	25–40 people
Horticultural and Pastoral Societies	From about 12,000 years ago, with decreasing numbers after about 3000 B.C.E.	Horticultural societies use hand tools for cultivating plants; pastoral societies are based on the domestication of animals	Settlements of several hundred people, connected through trading ties to form societies of several thousand people
Agrarian Societies	From about 5,000 years ago, with large but decreasing numbers today	Animal-drawn plow	Millions of people
Industrial Societies	From about 1750 to the present	Advanced sources of energy; mechanized production	Millions of people
Postindustrial Societies	Emerging in recent decades	Computers that support an information-based economy	Millions of people

The Information Revolution is, of course, most pronounced in industrial societies, yet the reach of this new technology is so great that it affects almost the entire world. As explained in Chapter 3 ("Culture"), the unprecedented, worldwide flow of information ties societies together and fosters a more global culture.

Another key idea from Chapter 3—cultural lag—also applies to postindustrial societies. Recall that cultural lag refers to the process by which some cultural elements (especially technology) change faster than others (such as values and norms). So, for example, even though information is fast replacing objects as the center of our economy, our legal notions about property are still based on tangible things.

Consider the process by which the government tracks the flow of property in and out of the United States. Customs officers require that travelers declare all the property they are carrying with them when they arrive, and their baggage is subject to search. Curiously, though, while people are declaring liquor, antiques, jewelry, and oriental rugs, an individual in possession of valuable ideas or new software on a computer disk can legally walk past customs officials announcing "Nothing to declare!" because our legal system does not yet attach the same importance to nontangible property. In short, while recent decades have witnessed rapid technological change, many of our ways of thinking about our surroundings remain rooted in an earlier era.

NOTE: One indicator of our society moving into the postindustrial era is that we now spend more money on computers than on televisions.

GLOBAL: James Williams Gibson (*The Perfect War: Technowar in Vietnam*, Boston: Atlantic Monthly, 1986) argues that the U.S. defeat in Vietnam was caused by an ethnocentric view that military power involves only technology.

NOTE: Nuclear power was used for destruction (1945) ten years before it first generated electricity.

Q: "We have too many men of science, too few of God. We have grasped the mystery of the atom and rejected the Sermon on the Mount . . . Ours is a world of nuclear giants and ethical infants. We know more about war than we do about peace, more about killing than about living." General Omar N. Bradley (1948)

Type of Society	Settlement Pattern	Social Organization	Examples
Hunting and Gathering Societies	Nomadic	Family centered; specialization limited to age and sex; little social inequality	Pygmies of central Africa Bushmen of southwestern Africa Aborigines of Australia Semai of Malaysia Kaska Indians of Canada
Horticultural and Pastoral Societies	Horticulturalists form relatively small permanent settlements; pastoralists are nomadic	Family centered; religious system begins to develop; moderate specialization; increased social inequality	Middle Eastern societies about 5000 B.C.E. Various societies today in New Guinea and other Pacific islands Yąnomamö today in South America
Agrarian Societies	Cities become common, though they generally contain only a small proportion of the population	Family loses significance as distinct religious, political, and economic systems emerge; extensive specialization; increased social inequality	Egypt during construction of the Great Pyramids Medieval Europe Numerous nonindustrial societies of the world today
Industrial Societies	Cities contain most of the population	Distinct religious, political, economic, educational, and family systems; highly specialized; marked social inequality persists, diminishing somewhat over time	Most societies today in Europe and North America, Australia, and Japan generate most of the world's industrial production
Postindustrial Societies	Population remains concentrated in cities	Similar to industrial societies with information processing and other service work gradually replacing industrial production	Industrial societies noted above are now entering postindustrial stage

Table 4–1 summarizes how technology shapes societies at different stages of sociocultural evolution.

THE LIMITS OF TECHNOLOGY

While technology remedies many human problems by increasing productivity, reducing infectious disease, and sometimes simply relieving boredom, it provides no "quick fix" for social problems. Poverty, for example, remains the plight of millions of women and men in this country (detailed in Chapter 10, "Social Class in the United States") and of 1 billion people worldwide (see Chapter 11, "Global Stratification"). Moreover, technology has created new social problems that our ancestors (and people like Sididi Ag Inaka today) hardly could imagine. Industrial societies provide more personal freedom, but often at the cost of the sense of community that characterized preindustrial life. Further, although the most powerful societies in the world today rarely engage in all-out warfare, they have stockpiles of nuclear weapons that could return us to a technologically primitive state if, indeed, we survived at all.

Advancing technology has also led to a major social problem involving the environment. Each stage in sociocultural evolution has introduced more powerful sources of energy and increased our appetite for the earth's resources. An issue of vital concern—and the focus of Chapter 22 ("Environment and Society")—is whether humanity can continue to pursue material prosperity without damaging the planet to the point from which it will never recover.

NOTE: Marx was born in Trier, Germany, earned a doctorate in 1841, and went to work as a newspaper editor. He became controversial and moved to Paris; he soon resettled in London. Marxism played a very minor role in sociology until the 1960s.

Q: "The truth is that we are all caught in a great economic system which is heartless." Woodrow Wilson

NOTE: "Capitalism" is derived from the Latin word *caput*, meaning "head." The term was first used in 12th-century Europe at a time of expanding commerce. "Conflict" is derived from the Latin meaning "a striking together."

NOTE: In opposing capitalism, Marx encouraged workers to cease to be merely a social class *in* themselves and become a social class acting *for* themselves.

Karl Marx, shown here with his daughter Jenny, is surely the pioneering sociologist who had the greatest influence on the world as a whole. Only several decades ago, 1 billion people (one-fifth of humanity) lived in societies organized on Marxist principles.

In some respects, then, technological advances have improved life and brought the world's people closer, creating a "global village." But the technology alone can never establish peace, ensure justice, or sustain a safe environment.

KARL MARX: SOCIETY AND CONFLICT

The first of our classic visions of society comes from Karl Marx (1818–1883), one of the early giants of sociology. Few observed the industrial transformation of Europe as keenly as he did. Marx spent most of his adult life in London, then the capital of the vast British Empire. He was awed by the power of the new factories. All European societies were producing more goods than ever before, with resources from around the world funneling into British factories at a dizzying rate.

What astounded and disturbed Marx most was that industry's riches were concentrated in the hands of a few. A walk around London revealed striking contrasts of splendid affluence and wretched squalor. A handful of aristocrats and industrialists lived in fabulous mansions staffed by servants, where they enjoyed luxury and privilege. Most people, though, labored long hours for low wages, and lived in slums or slept in the streets, where many eventually died from disease or poor nutrition.

Throughout his life, Marx wrestled with a basic contradiction: In a society so rich, how could so many be so poor? Just as important, Marx asked, how can this situation be changed? Many people think Karl Marx set out to tear society apart. But he was motivated by compassion for humanity and wanted to help a badly divided society forge a new and just social order.

The key to understanding Marx's thinking is the idea of **social conflict**, *struggle between segments of society over valued resources.* Social conflict can, of course, take many forms: Individuals may quarrel, some colleges have long-standing rivalries, and nations sometimes go to war. For Marx, however, the most significant form of social conflict was between classes that arise from the way a society produces material goods.

SOCIETY AND PRODUCTION

Living in the nineteenth century, Marx observed the early stage of industrial capitalism in Europe. This economic system, Marx noted, transformed a small part of the population into **capitalists,** *people who own factories and other productive enterprises.* A capitalist's goal is profit, which results from selling a product for more than it costs to produce. Capitalism transforms most of the population into industrial workers, whom Marx called the **proletariat,** *people who provide the labor necessary to operate factories and other productive enterprises.* Workers sell their labor for the wages they need to live. To Marx, conflict between owners and workers is inevitable under the system of capitalist production. To maximize profits, capitalists must minimize wages, generally their single greatest expense. Workers, however, want wages to be as high as possible. Since profits and wages come from the same pool of funds, conflict occurs. Marx argued that this conflict could end only when people fundamentally changed the capitalist system.

All societies are composed of **social institutions,** defined as *the major spheres of social life, or society's subsystems, organized to meet basic human needs.* In his analysis of society, Marx argued that one institution—the economy—dominates all the others and sets the direction of a society. Drawing on the philosophical doctrine of *materialism*, which says that how humans produce material goods shapes their experiences, Marx believed the political system, family, religion, and education generally operated to support a society's economy. In other words, just as the Lenskis argue that technology molds a society, Marx argued that the economy is "the real foundation . . . The mode of production in material life determines the general character of the social, political, and spiritual processes of life" (1959:43; orig. 1859).

Marx therefore viewed the economic system as the social *infrastructure* (*infra* is Latin, meaning "below"). Other social institutions, including the family, the political system, education, and religion, which are built on this foundation, form society's *superstructure*. These institutions extend economic principles into other areas of life, as illustrated in Figure 4–2. In practical terms, social institutions maintain capitalists' dominant position by legally protecting their wealth, for example, and transmitting property from one generation to the next through the family.

Generally speaking, members of industrial-capitalist societies do not view their legal or family systems as hotbeds of social conflict. On the contrary, individuals come to see their right to private property as "natural." People in the United States find it easy to think that affluent people have earned their wealth, while those who are poor or out of work lack skills or motivation. Marx rejected this kind of reasoning as rooted in a capitalist belief that human well-being is less important than the "bottom line." Poverty and unemployment are not inevitable. As Marx saw it, grand wealth clashing with grinding poverty represents merely one possibility generated by capitalism (Cuff & Payne, 1979).

Marx rejected capitalist common sense, therefore, as **false consciousness,** *explanations of social problems in terms of the shortcomings of individuals rather than the flaws of society.* Instead, he thought industrial capitalism itself was responsible for the social problems he saw all around him. False consciousness, he maintained, victimizes people by hiding the real cause of their problems.

CONFLICT AND HISTORY

Marx studied how societies changed throughout history and found that they usually evolve gradually, but

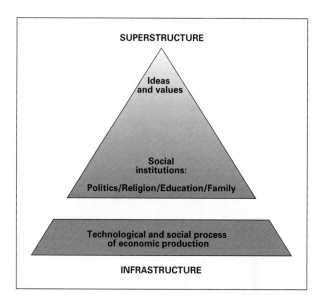

FIGURE 4–2 Karl Marx's Model of Society

This diagram illustrates Marx's materialist view that economic production underlies and shapes the entire society. Economic production involves both technology (industry, in the case of capitalism) and social relationships (for capitalism, the relationship between the capitalists, who control economic production, and the workers, who are simply a source of labor). Upon this infrastructure, or foundation, rests society's superstructure, which includes its major social institutions as well as core cultural values and ideas. Marx maintained that every part of a society supports the economic system.

sometimes they erupt, resulting in rapid, revolutionary reorganization. Marx also observed (as do the Lenskis) that change is partly prompted by technological advance. But he steadfastly held that the major engine of change is conflict rooted in a society's system of production.

To put the Lenskis' analysis in Marxist terms, early hunters and gatherers formed primitive communist societies. *Communism* refers to a system by which people share more or less equally in the production of food and other material goods. Because the resources of nature (although meager by our standards) were equally available to all hunters and gatherers (rather than privately owned), and because everyone performed similar work (rather than dividing work into specialized tasks), there was little possibility for social conflict.

Horticulture, Marx noted, introduced social inequality. Among horticultural, pastoral, and early

NOTE: The Protestant Ethic and the spirit of capitalism are not synonymous. Weber explained that the former becomes the latter only as it is *disenchanted*. The disenchanted spirit of Calvinism is then evident in three impersonal modern "types," all of which are highly disciplined but devoid of piety: (1) the *capitalist* (devotion to profits), (2) the *scientist* (devotion to knowledge), and (3) the *bureaucrat* (devotion to duty). Drawings in Chapter 24 illustrate these three types.

Q: "It is, of course, not my aim to substitute for a one-sided materialistic an equally one-sided spiritualistic causal explanation of culture and history." Max Weber

Q: Victor Hugo observed that nothing is as powerful as "an idea whose time has come."

A key element of U.S. culture has long been a "work ethic," with its roots in the Calvinist thinking that fascinated Max Weber. This Currier and Ives lithograph from 1875 makes a statement that people should shun the stock market, race track, lotteries, and even labor strikes as ways to improve their lives in favor of climbing the "Ladder of Fortune" based on personal virtue and individual effort.

divine favor in *this* world? Such reasoning led Calvinists to interpret worldly prosperity as a sign of God's grace. Eager to acquire this reassurance, Calvinists threw themselves into a quest for success, bringing rationality, discipline, and hard work to their tasks. Their pursuit of wealth was not for its own sake, of course, since self-indulgently spending money was clearly sinful. But neither were Calvinists moved to share their wealth with the poor, since poverty was a sign of God's rejection. Their duty was to carry forward what they considered their personal *calling* from God: reinvesting their profits for still greater success. Calvinists thus built the foundation of capitalism. They piously used wealth to generate more wealth, saved their money, and eagerly adopted whatever technological advances would aid their efforts.

These traits, Weber explained, distinguished Calvinism from other world religions. Catholicism, the traditional religion in most of Europe, gave rise to a passive, "otherworldly" view: Good deeds performed humbly on earth would be rewarded in the next world. For Catholics, material wealth had none of the spiritual significance that motivated Calvinists. And so it was, Weber concluded, that industrial capitalism became established primarily in areas of Europe where Calvinism was strong.

Weber's study of Calvinism provides striking evidence of the power of ideas to shape society (versus Marx's contention that ideas merely reflect the process of economic production). But Weber was not one to accept simple explanations; he knew that industrial capitalism had many causes. In fact, one reason for his research was to counter Marx's narrow, strictly economic explanation of modern society.

Although later generations of Calvinists were less religious, their success-seeking and personal discipline remained, and a *religious* ethic became simply a "*work* ethic." In other words, industrial capitalism could be viewed as "disenchanted" religion, with wealth now valued for its own sake. Before long, even the practice of "accounting," which to early Calvinists meant keeping a daily record of moral deeds, came to mean nothing more than keeping track of money.

RATIONAL SOCIAL ORGANIZATION

According to Weber, then, rationality gave rise to the Industrial Revolution and capitalism, and thereby defined modern society. Weber went on to identify seven characteristics of rational social organization:

1. **Distinctive social institutions.** Among hunters and gatherers, the family is the center of all activity. Gradually, however, other social institutions, including religious, political, and economic systems, become separate from family life. In modern societies, institutions of education and health care also appear. The separation of social institutions—each detailed in a later chapter—is a rational strategy to address human needs more efficiently.

2. **Large-scale organizations.** Modern rationality is clearly evident in the spread of large-scale organizations. As early as the horticultural era, political officials oversaw religious observances, public works, and warfare. In medieval Europe, the Catholic church grew into a huge organization with thousands of officials. In our modern,

Q: "The decisive reason for the advance of bureaucratic organization has always been its purely technical superiority over any other form of organization. The fully developed bureaucratic apparatus compares with other organizations exactly as does the machine with the nonmechanical modes of production." Max Weber (1978:973; orig. 1921)

GLOBAL: Socialist societies are more centralized and rationalized

than capitalist societies; the People's Republic of China, for example, has but a single time zone, although it spans roughly the same longitude as the United States, which has four time zones.

Q: "Capitalism, as an institutional arrangement, has been singularly devoid of plausible myths; by contrast, socialism, its major alternative under modern conditions, has been singularly blessed with myth-generating potency." Peter Berger

Max Weber agreed with Karl Marx that modern society is alienating to the individual, but the two thinkers identified different causes of this estrangement. For Marx, economic inequality is the culprit; for Weber, the issue is pervasive and dehumanizing bureaucracy. George Tooker's painting Landscape With Figures *echoes Weber's sentiments.*

George Tooker, *Landscape With Figures*, 1963, egg tempera on gesso panel, 26 x 30 in. Private collection.

rational society, the federal government employs millions, and most people work for large organizations.

3. **Specialized tasks.** Unlike members of traditional societies, individuals in modern societies perform a wide range of specialized jobs. Flipping through any city's "Yellow Pages" telephone directory gives some indication of the enormous number of occupations today.

4. **Personal discipline.** Modern society puts a premium on self-discipline. For early Calvinists, of course, such an approach to life was rooted in religious belief. Although now distanced from its religious origins, discipline is still encouraged by cultural values such as achievement, success, and efficiency.

5. **Awareness of time.** In traditional societies, people measure time according to the rhythm of the sun and seasons. Modern people, by contrast, schedule events precisely by the hour and even the minute. Interestingly, clocks began appearing in European cities some 500 years ago, about the time commerce began to expand. Soon, people began to think that (to borrow Benjamin Franklin's phrase) "time is money."

6. **Technical competence.** Members of traditional societies evaluate one another largely on the basis of *who* they are—how they are joined to others in the web of kinship. Modern rationality, by contrast, prompts us to judge people according to *what* they are—that is, with an eye toward their skills and abilities.

7. **Impersonality.** Finally, in a rational society technical competence takes priority over close relationships, rendering the world impersonal. People interact as specialists concerned with particular tasks, rather than as individuals broadly concerned with one another. Weber explained that we tend to devalue personal feelings and emotions as "irrational" because they often are difficult to control.

Rationality and Bureaucracy

Although the medieval church grew large, Weber thought that it remained largely traditional. Truly rational organizations, focused on efficiency, appeared only in the last few centuries. The kind of organization Weber termed *bureaucracy* arose along with capitalism and science as an expression of the rationality that shapes modern society.

RESOURCE: Ferdinand Tönnies's "Gemeinschaft and Gesellschaft" is one classic included in the *Seeing Ourselves* reader. Also find four selections by Weber: "The Case for Value-Free Sociology," "The Characteristics of Bureaucracy," "The Protestant Ethic and the Spirit of Capitalism," and "The Disenchantment of Modern Life."

Q: "When I fulfill my obligations as a brother, husband, or citizen, when I execute contracts, I perform duties that are defined externally to myself . . . Even if I conform in my own sentiments and feel their reality subjectively, such reality is still objective, for I did not create them; I merely inherited them." Emile Durkheim

NOTE: Durkheim claimed that society must be studied as an entity, *sui generis*, Latin meaning "of its own kind, a thing unto itself."

Chapter 7 ("Groups and Organizations") explains that bureaucracy is the model for modern businesses, government agencies, labor unions, and universities. For now, note that Weber considered a bureaucracy the clearest expression of a rational world view because all its parts—offices, duties, and policies—are intended to achieve specific goals as efficiently as possible. The inefficiency of traditional organization, on the other hand, is evident in its resistance to change. In short, just as industrialization had changed the economy, Weber asserted that bureaucracy had changed all of society.

Further, Weber noted, rational bureaucracy and capitalism have much in common. He wrote:

> Today, it is primarily the capitalist market economy which demands that the official business of public administration be discharged precisely, unambiguously, continuously, and with as much speed as possible. Normally, the very large capitalist enterprises are themselves unequaled models of strict bureaucratic organization. (1978:974; orig. 1921)

Rationality and Alienation

Max Weber joined Karl Marx in recognizing the efficiency of industrial capitalism. Weber also agreed that modern society generates widespread alienation, although he offered different reasons. While Marx thought alienation was caused by economic inequality, Weber blamed the stifling effect of bureaucracy's rules and regulations.

Bureaucracies, Weber warned, treat people as a series of cases rather than as unique individuals. In addition, working for large organizations demands highly specialized and often tedious routines. In the end, Weber envisioned modern society as a vast and growing system of rules seeking to regulate everything and threatening to crush the human spirit.

Like Marx too, Weber found it ironic that modern society—meant to serve humanity—turns on its creators and enslaves them. Just as Marx described the human toll of industrial capitalism, Weber portrayed the modern individual as "only a small cog in a ceaselessly moving mechanism that prescribes to him an endlessly fixed routine of march" (1978:988; orig. 1921). Although Weber could see the advantages of modern society, he ended his life deeply pessimistic about the future. He feared that, in the end, the rationalization of society would reduce human beings to robots.

EMILE DURKHEIM: SOCIETY AND FUNCTION

"To love society is to love something beyond us and something in ourselves." These are the words of Emile Durkheim (1858–1917), another founding architect of sociology. In this curious statement (1974:55; orig. 1924) we find one more influential vision of human society.

STRUCTURE: SOCIETY BEYOND OURSELVES

Emile Durkheim's great contribution lies in recognizing that society exists beyond ourselves. Society is more than the individuals who compose it; society has a life of its own that stretches beyond our personal experiences. It was here long before we were born, it shapes us while we live, and it will remain long after we are gone. Patterns of human behavior, Durkheim explained, exist as established structures. They are *social facts* that have an objective reality beyond the lives of individuals. Cultural norms, values, religious beliefs—all endure as social facts.

And because society looms larger than any one of us, it has the *power* to guide our thoughts and actions. This is why studying individuals alone (as psychologists or biologists do) can never capture the essence of the human experience. Society is more than the sum of its parts; it exists as a complex organism rooted in our collective life. A classroom of third graders, a family sharing a meal, people milling about a country auction—all are examples of the social situations that exist apart from any particular individual who has ever participated in them.

Once created by people, then, society takes on a life of its own and demands a measure of obedience from its creators. We experience the reality of society as we recognize that there is an order to our lives, or when we face temptation and feel the tug of morality.

FUNCTION: SOCIETY AS SYSTEM

Having established that society has structure, Durkheim turned to the concept of *function*. The significance of any social fact, he explained, extends beyond what it means to any of us as individuals; social facts help society itself to function as a complex system.

To illustrate, consider crime. Of course, individuals experience pain and loss as a result of crime. But, taking a broader view, Durkheim saw that crime is

Q: The term "tyranny of the tribe" suggests the power of the collective conscience in traditional societies.

Q: "In a word, we must discover the rational substitutes for those religious notions that for a long time have served as the vehicle for the most essential moral ideas." Emile Durkheim, *Moral Education*, (1961:9). (This is the idea behind the concept of "civil religion." See Chapter 17, "Religion.")

THEN AND NOW: U.S. suicide rates: *1950*, 11.4 per 100,000 people; *1960*, 10.6; *1970*, 11.6; *1980*, 11.9; *1990*, 12.4; *1995*, 11.8 (U.S. Bureau of the Census).

NOTE: By arguing society to have an objective existence, Durkheim (following Comte) may well have been attempting to establish a natural social order as a moral authority to replace declining tradition.

Durkheim's observation that people with weak social bonds are prone to self-destructive behavior stands as stark evidence of the power of society to shape individual lives. When rock-and-roll singers become famous, they are wrenched out of familiar life patterns and existing relationships, sometimes with tragic results. The history of rock and roll contains many tragic stories of this kind, including (from left) Janis Joplin's and Jimi Hendrix's deaths by drug overdose (both 1970) and Jim Morrison's (1971) and Kurt Cobain's (1994) suicides.

vital to the ongoing life of society itself. As Chapter 8 ("Deviance") explains, only by defining acts as criminal and responding to them do people construct and defend morality, giving purpose and meaning to our collective life. For this reason, Durkheim rejected the common view of crime as "pathological." On the contrary, he concluded, crime is quite "normal" for the most basic of reasons: A society could not exist without it (1964a, orig. 1895; 1964b, orig. 1893).

PERSONALITY: SOCIETY IN OURSELVES

Durkheim contended that society is not only "beyond ourselves"; it is also "in ourselves." In other words, every person builds a personality by internalizing social facts. How we act, think, and feel—our essential humanity—is drawn from the society that nurtures us. Moreover, Durkheim explained, society regulates our behavior through moral discipline. Durkheim believed that human beings are naturally insatiable, and in constant danger of being overpowered by their own desires. That is, "the more one has, the more one wants, since satisfactions received only stimulate instead of filling needs" (1966:248; orig. 1897). Having given us life, then, society must also rein us in.

Nowhere is the need for societal regulation better illustrated than in Durkheim's study of suicide (1966; orig. 1897), described in Chapter 1 ("The Sociological Perspective"). Why is it that rock stars—from Janice Joplin in the 1960s to Kurt Cobain in the 1990s—have been so prone to self-destruction? Using the sociological perspective, Durkheim had the answer long before anyone made electric music: A century ago as today, it is the *least* regulated categories of people who suffer the *highest* rates of suicide. The enormous freedom of the young, rich, and famous exacts a high price in terms of the risk of suicide.

MODERNITY AND ANOMIE

Compared to traditional societies, modern societies impose fewer restrictions on everyone. Durkheim acknowledged the advantages of modern-day freedom, but he warned of increased **anomie**, *a condition in which society provides little moral guidance to individuals.* What so many celebrities describe as "almost being destroyed by fame" is a good example of the destructive effects of anomie. Sudden fame tears people from their families and familiar routines; it disrupts society's support and regulation of an individual, sometimes with fatal results. Durkheim instructs,

RESOURCE: An example of a small society that approximates Durkheim's concept of mechanical solidarity is the Amish, described in John Hostetler's article in the Macionis and Benokraitis reader, *Seeing Ourselves*, 4th ed. The Amish practice of shunning illustrates the operation of collective conscience in today's U.S. society.

Q: "For Durkheim, the sacredness of the person could become one of the few cultural ideals capable of providing a crucial point of unification for an increasingly differentiated, yet interdependent, world." Mike Featherstone (1990:4)

Q: "The nail that stands up gets hit down." Japanese proverb that might describe social control in a traditional society

Historically, most members of human societies engaged in a narrow range of activities: searching out food and building shelters. Modern societies, explained Durkheim, display a rapidly expanding division of labor. Increasing specialization is evident on the streets of societies beginning to industrialize: Providing people with their weight is the livelihood of this man in Istanbul, Turkey; on a Bombay street in India, another earns a small fee for cleaning ears.

therefore, that an individual's desires must be balanced by the moral guidance of society—a balance that is precarious in the modern world.

EVOLVING SOCIETIES: THE DIVISION OF LABOR

Like Marx and Weber, Durkheim witnessed firsthand the rapid social transformation of Europe during the nineteenth century. But Durkheim offered his own interpretation of this change as a sweeping evolution in social organization.

In preindustrial societies, explained Durkheim, tradition operates as the social cement that binds people together. In fact, what he termed the *collective conscience* is so strong that the community moves quickly to punish anyone who dares to challenge conventional ways of life. Durkheim called this system **mechanical solidarity,** meaning *social bonds, based on shared morality, that unite members of preindustrial societies*. In practice, then, mechanical solidarity springs from *likeness*. Durkheim described these bonds as "mechanical"

because people feel a more or less automatic sense of belonging together.

With industrialization, though, mechanical solidarity becomes weaker and weaker and people cease to be bound by tradition. But this does not mean that society dissolves. Modern life generates a new kind of solidarity that fills the void left by discarded traditions. Durkheim called this new social integration **organic solidarity,** *social bonds, based on specialization, that unite members of industrial societies*. Where solidarity was once rooted in likeness, it is now based on *difference* among people who find that their specialized pursuits—as plumbers, consultants, midwives, or sociology instructors—make them rely on one another for many of their daily needs.

For Durkheim, then, the key to change in a society is the expanding **division of labor,** or *specialized economic activity*. Max Weber said that modern societies specialize in order to become more efficient, and Durkheim filled out the picture by showing that members of modern societies count on tens of thousands of others—most of them complete strangers—for the goods and services of everyday life. Put otherwise, as

GLOBAL: As Edward A. Tiryakian (1994) points out, neither Durkheim nor other social theorists predicted the reemergence of mechanical solidarity in the form of religious, ethnic, racial, and gender conflict around the world and on the U.S. campus.

NOTE: Durkheim linked mechanical solidarity to the extent of repressive (criminal) law and organic solidarity to the extent of restitutive (civil) law.

Q: "Computers are useless; they only give you answers." Pablo Picasso

Q: "Computers make it easier to do a lot of things, but most of the things they make it easier to do don't need to be done." Andy Rooney

Q: "The optimist proclaims that we live in the best of all possible worlds, and the pessimist fears that this is true." James Cabell

EXPLORING CYBER-SOCIETY

The Information Revolution:
What Would Durkheim (and Others) Have Thought?

Who can doubt that technological change is now reshaping society? If they were alive today, the founding sociologists discussed in this chapter would be eager observers of the current scene. Let's imagine for a moment the kind of questions Emile Durkheim, Max Weber, and Karl Marx might ask about the effects of computer technology on society.

Emile Durkheim, who emphasized the increasing division of labor in modern society, would probably be quick to wonder if new information technology is pushing specialization even further. There is good reason to think that it is. Because electronic communication (say, a Web site home page) gives any individual a vast market (there are already more than 100 million computers that can access the Internet), people can specialize far more than if they were confined to a limited geographical area. For example, while most small-town lawyers must have a general practice to survive, an information-age attorney (living anywhere) can become a specialist in, say,

prenuptial agreements or electronic copyright law. Indeed, as the electronic age unfolds, the number of highly specialized "micro-businesses" in all fields—some of which end up becoming quite large—is rapidly increasing.

Max Weber believed that modern societies are distinctive because their members share a rational world view, and, of course, nothing captured this way of thinking better than bureaucracy. But will bureaucracy continue to dominate the social scene in the next century? Here is one reason to think it may not: While it may make sense for organizations to regulate workers performing the kinds of routine tasks that were common in the industrial era, more and more work in the postindustrial era involves imagination. Think, for instance, of such "new age" work as designing homes, composing music, or writing software. The creativity involved cannot be regulated in the same way as, say, assembling automobiles on an assembly line. Perhaps this is why many high-technology companies have done away with the dress codes and

time clocks found in factories. The character of "rational organization" may well be changing along with the nature of work.

Finally, what might Karl Marx make of the Information Revolution? Since Marx considered the earlier Industrial Revolution a *class* revolution that allowed the owners of industry to dominate society, he would probably wonder whether a new symbolic elite is gaining dominance. Some analysts point out, for example, that film and television writers, producers, and performers now enjoy vast wealth, international prestige, and enormous power (Lichter, Rothman, & Lichter, 1990). Similarly, just as people without industrial skills stayed at the bottom of the class system in past decades, so people without symbolic skills are likely to become the "underclass" of the next century.

Durkheim, Weber, and Marx greatly improved our understanding of industrial societies. As we move into the postindustrial age, there is plenty of room for new generations of sociologists to carry on.

---

members of modern societies, we depend more and more on people we trust less and less. Why, though, do we put our faith in people we hardly know and whose beliefs may well differ from our own? Durkheim's answer is, "Because we can't live without them."

So modernity rests far less on *moral consensus* and far more on *functional interdependence*. And herein lies what might be called "Durkheim's dilemma": The technological power and greater personal freedom of modern society comes at the cost of a decreasing morality and the rising risk of anomie.

Like Marx and Weber, Durkheim had misgivings about the direction society was taking. But, of the three, Durkheim was the most optimistic. Confidence in the future sprang from his hope that we could create the laws and other restraints that had once been forced on us by tradition, without losing our modern freedom and privacy.

Finally, how might Durkheim respond to today's new information technology? As the box shows, Durkheim—and the other theorists we have considered in this chapter—would probably have had a great deal to say about the Information Revolution.

9. Industrial capitalism alienates workers in four ways: from the act of working, from the products of work, from other workers, and from human potential.

10. Marx believed that once workers overcame their false consciousness, they could overthrow capitalists and the industrial-capitalist system.

Max Weber

11. The idealist approach of Weber reveals that ideas have a powerful effect on society.

12. Weber contrasted the tradition of preindustrial societies to the rationality of modern, industrial societies.

13. Weber feared that rationality, especially in efficiency-conscious bureaucratic organizations, would stifle human creativity.

Emile Durkheim

14. Durkheim explained that society has an objective existence apart from individuals.

15. Durkheim relates social elements to the larger society through their functions.

16. Societies require solidarity. Traditional societies are fused by mechanical solidarity, which is based on moral likeness; modern societies depend on organic solidarity, which is based on the division of labor.

KEY CONCEPTS

society people who interact in a defined territory and share culture

sociocultural evolution the Lenskis' term for the changes that occur as a society gains new technology

hunting and gathering simple technology for hunting animals and gathering vegetation

horticulture technology based on using hand tools to cultivate plants

pastoralism technology that supports the domestication of animals

agriculture the technology of large-scale farming using plows harnessed to animals or more powerful sources of energy

industrialism technology that powers sophisticated machinery with advanced sources of energy

postindustrialism technology that supports an information-based economy

social conflict struggle between segments of society over valued resources

capitalists people who own factories and other productive enterprises

proletariat people who provide the labor necessary to operate factories and other productive enterprises

social institution a major sphere of social life, or societal subsystem, organized to meet a basic human need

false consciousness Marx's term for explanations of social problems in terms of the shortcomings of individuals rather than the flaws of society

class conflict antagonism between entire classes over the distribution of wealth and power in society

class consciousness Marx's term for the recognition by workers of their unity as a social class in opposition to capitalists and to capitalism itself

alienation the experience of isolation and misery resulting from powerlessness

ideal type an abstract statement of the essential characteristics of any social phenomenon

tradition sentiments and beliefs passed from generation to generation

rationality deliberate, matter-of-fact calculation of the most efficient means to accomplish a particular goal

rationalization of society Weber's term for the historical change from tradition to rationality as the dominant mode of human thought

anomie Durkheim's term for a condition in which society provides little moral guidance to individuals

mechanical solidarity Durkheim's term for social bonds, based on shared morality, that unite members of preindustrial societies

organic solidarity Durkheim's term for social bonds, based on specialization, that unite members of industrial societies

division of labor specialized economic activity

CRITICAL-THINKING QUESTIONS

1. Present evidence that supports and contradicts the assertion that technological advance amounts to "progress."

2. Explain how Marx, as a materialist, took a different view of society than Weber, an idealist.

3. Both Marx and Weber were concerned with modern society's ability to alienate people. How are their approaches different? How do their notions of alienation compare with Durkheim's concept of anomie?

4. What might each theorist discussed in this chapter say about the changing social standing of women? What issues might a feminist critique of these theories raise?

LEARNING EXERCISES

1. Hunting and gathering people mused over stars, and we still know the constellations in terms that were relevant to them—mostly animals and hunters. As a way of revealing what's important to *our* way of life, write a short paper imagining what meaning we would impose on the stars if we were beginning from scratch.

2. Spend an hour going around your home, trying to identify every device that has a computer chip in it. How many did you find? Were you surprised by the number?

3. Rent or watch the television schedule for an old "Tarzan" movie or another film that portrays technologically simpler people. How are they portrayed in the film?

4. Over the next few days, ask a dozen people over the age of twenty-five whether they think our society is getting better or worse, and why they hold their opinion. See how much agreement you find.

5. If you have computer access, install the CD-ROM packaged inside the back cover of your text and complete the activities designed to accompany this chapter.

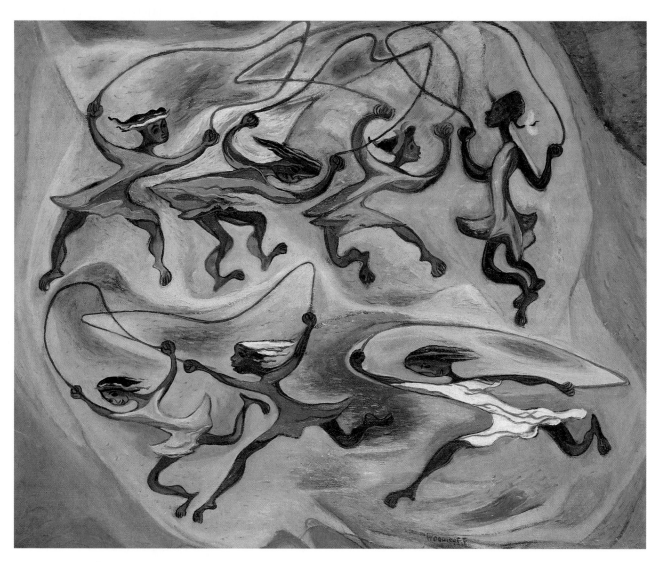

Hale Woodruff, *Girls Skipping*, 1949

Oil on canvas, 24 × 32 inches. Courtesy of Michael Rosenfeld Gallery, New York.

SOCIALIZATION

On a cold winter day in 1938, an anxious social worker walked quickly toward the door of a rural Pennsylvania farmhouse. Investigating a case of possible child abuse, the social worker soon discovered a five-year-old girl hidden in a second-floor storage room. The child, whose name was Anna, was wedged into an old chair with her arms tied above her head so that she could not move. Her clothes were filthy, and her arms and legs looked like matchsticks. She was so weak she could barely move.

Anna's situation can only be described as tragic. She was born in 1932 to an unmarried and mentally impaired woman of twenty-six who lived with her strict father. Enraged by his daughter's "illegitimate" motherhood, the grandfather did not even want the child in his house. For her first six months, therefore, Anna was shuttled among various institutions. But when her mother was no longer able to pay for care, Anna was returned to the hostile home of her grandfather.

To lessen the grandfather's anger, Anna's mother put the child in the storage room, where she received little attention and just enough milk to keep her alive. There she stayed—day after day, month after month, with essentially no human contact—for five long years.

Upon learning of Anna, sociologist Kingsley Davis (1940) immediately went to see the child. He found her at a county home, where local authorities had taken her. Davis was appalled by Anna's condition. She was emaciated and feeble. Unable to laugh, smile, speak, or even show anger, she was completely unresponsive, as if alone in an empty world.

SOCIAL EXPERIENCE: THE KEY TO OUR HUMANITY

Here is a deplorable case of a human being deprived of virtually all social contact, but Anna's ordeal teaches us something very important. Although physically alive, Anna hardly seemed human. Isolated as Anna was, an individual develops scarcely any capacity for thought, emotion, and meaningful behavior. In fact, without social experience, an individual is more an *object* than a *person*.

This chapter explores what Anna was deprived of—the means by which we become fully human. This process is **socialization,** *the lifelong social experience by which individuals develop human potential and learn patterns of their culture.* Unlike other species whose behavior is biologically set, human beings need social experience in order to learn their culture and survive.

Social experience is also the basis of **personality,** *a person's fairly consistent patterns of thinking, feeling, and acting.* We build a personality by internalizing—or taking in—our social surroundings. As personality develops, we participate in a culture while remaining, in some respects, distinct individuals. But in the absence of social experience, as Anna's case shows, personality does not emerge at all.

SUPPLEMENTS: An outline of Chapter 5, along with supplementary lecture material and discussion questions, are found in the *Data File*.

NOTE: "Nature" has the Latin root *nat(us)*, meaning "born"; "nurture" has the Latin root *nutrit(us)*, meaning "nourished."

NOTE: An interesting twist on the nature-nurture debate: Throughout history naturalists believed an untaught child would speak, but wondered what language. The naturalist Holy Roman Emperor Frederick II thought it would be Latin or Greek; James I of Scotland opined it would be Hebrew.

 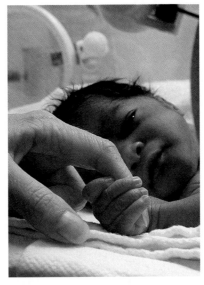 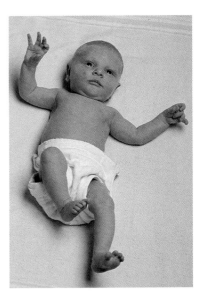

Human infants display various reflexes—biologically based behavior patterns that enhance survival. The sucking reflex, which actually begins before birth, enables the infant to obtain nourishment. The grasping reflex, triggered by placing a finger on the infant's palm causing the hand to close, helps the infant to maintain contact with a parent and, later on, to grasp objects. The Moro reflex, activated by startling the infant, has the infant swinging both arms outward and then bringing them together across the chest. This action, which disappears after several months of life, probably developed among our evolutionary ancestors so that a falling infant could grasp the body hair of a parent.

Because a society exists beyond the life span of any person, each generation must teach its way of life to the next. Socialization, then, also amounts to an ongoing process of cultural transmission. In short, social experience is the foundation of our lives—individually and collectively.

HUMAN DEVELOPMENT: NATURE AND NURTURE

Virtually helpless at birth, the human infant depends on others for care and nourishment as well as learning. Although Anna's short life makes these facts very clear, a century ago most people mistakenly believed that human behavior was the product of our biology.

Charles Darwin: The Role of Nature

Charles Darwin, whose groundbreaking theory is summarized in Chapter 3 ("Culture"), held that species evolve over thousands of generations as the genes that enhance reproduction and survival become dominant. The specific biologically rooted traits that enhance survival appear as a species' "nature." As Darwin's fame grew, people assumed that human beings, like other forms of life, also had a fixed, or instinctive, "nature."

Such notions are still with us. People sometimes say, for example, that our economic system reflects "instinctive human competitiveness," that some people are "born criminals," or that women are more "naturally" emotional while men are "inherently" more rational. We often describe personality traits as *human nature*, as if people were born with them as we are born with five senses. More accurately, our human nature leads us to create and learn culture, as we shall see.

People using Darwin's ideas to explain cultural diversity also misunderstood his thinking. Western Europeans knew from centuries of exploration and empire building that people around the world behaved quite differently. They attributed such differences to biology rather than to culture. It was a simple—although terribly damaging—step, therefore, to conclude that members of technologically simple societies were biologically less evolved and, therefore, less human. Such an ethnocentric view helped justify colonialism; it is easier to seize people's land and enslave them if you do not think they are human in the same sense you are.

NOTE: The term *tabula rasa* (Latin, meaning "clean slate") was introduced by English philosopher John Locke (1632–1704). An empiricist, Locke believed that human personalities were "written on" by experience.

DISCUSS: What does the class make of the fact that a substantial majority of people incarcerated for violent crimes had poor family lives as children?

GLOBAL: The diversity of economic systems through the years and throughout the world renders claims of "innate competitiveness" suspect.

Q: "Asking how people grew up may make all men equal yet." Clarence Darrow

DISCUSS: Is it simply a coincidence that all the isolated children of record are females?

The Social Sciences: The Role of Nurture

In the twentieth century, social scientists began to question biological explanations of human behavior. One of the first was John B. Watson (1878–1958), whose theory of *behaviorism* held that behavior patterns are not instinctive but learned. Thus, people the world over have the same claim to humanity; humans differ only in their cultural environment. For Watson, "human nature" was infinitely changeable:

> Give me a dozen healthy infants . . . and my own specified world to bring them up in, and I will guarantee to take any one at random and train him [or her] to become any type of specialist that I might select—doctor, lawyer, artist, merchant, chief, and yes, even beggar-man and thief— regardless of his [or her] talents, penchants, tendencies, abilities, vocations, and race of his [or her] ancestors. (1930:104)

Anthropologists entered the debate by showing how variable the world's cultures are. One outspoken supporter of the "nurture" view, Margaret Mead, summed up the evidence this way: "The differences between individuals who are members of different cultures, like the differences between individuals within a culture, are almost entirely to be laid to differences in conditioning, especially during early childhood, and this conditioning is culturally determined" (1963:280; orig. 1935).

Today, social scientists are cautious about describing any type of behavior as instinctive. Even sociobiology, discussed in Chapter 3 ("Culture"), states that human behavior is primarily guided by culture. Of course, we are not saying that biology plays *no* part in human behavior. Human life, after all, depends on the functioning of the body. We also know that children share many biological traits with their parents, especially physical characteristics such as height, weight, hair and eye color, and facial features. Intelligence and various personality characteristics (such as how one reacts to frustration) probably have some basis in heredity, as do artistic and musical talent. But whether a person realizes an inherited potential depends on the opportunities to develop it. Indeed, biologists point out that, unless children *use* their brains early in life, the brain itself will not fully develop (Herrnstein, 1973; Plomin & Foch, 1980; Goldsmith, 1983; Begley, 1995).

In sum, without denying the importance of nature, evidence shows that nurture is far more important in shaping human behavior. Indeed, rather than thinking of nature and nurture as opposites, it is more correct to say that nurture—social experience and the creation of culture—*is* our nature. For humans, nature and nurture are inseparable.

SOCIAL ISOLATION

For obvious ethical reasons, researchers cannot conduct social isolation experiments on human beings. Consequently, much of what we know about the effects of social isolation on humans comes from rare cases like Anna. Researchers have, however, experimented with animals.

Effects of Social Isolation on Nonhuman Primates

Psychologists Harry Harlow and Margaret Harlow (1962) conducted a classic investigation of the effects of social isolation on nonhuman primates. They used rhesus monkeys, whose behavior is in some ways surprisingly similar to that of humans.

In their first study, the Harlows found that complete social isolation for six months (despite adequate nutrition) seriously disturbed the monkeys' development. When these monkeys were returned to their group, they were passive, anxious, and fearful.

The Harlows then isolated infant rhesus monkeys, providing an artificial "mother" made of wire mesh with a wooden head and the nipple of a feeding tube where the breast would be. These monkeys survived, but they, too, showed emotional damage.

But when the Harlows covered the artificial "mother" with soft terry cloth, the infant monkeys would cling to it, apparently benefiting from the closeness. These monkeys later showed less emotional distress. The Harlows thus concluded that normal emotional development requires that adults cradle their infants affectionately.

The Harlows made two other discoveries. First, so long as they were surrounded by other infants, monkeys were not adversely affected by the absence of a mother. In other words, it was a lack of social experience, rather than the absence of a specific parent, that was emotionally damaging. Second, the Harlows found that lesser periods of social isolation—up to about three months—caused emotional distress, but only temporarily. The damage of short-term isolation, then, can be overcome; longer-term isolation, however, appears to cause irreversible emotional and behavioral damage.

DIVERSITY: Children of deaf parents sometimes learn sign language first and attempt spoken/written language only later when they enter school. Such children often have difficulty because, as researchers now recognize, the brain loses capacity for language if these skills are not learned within the first few years of life.

NOTE: The violence in Genie's family stemmed from a father who wanted no children. The first child in the family died from exposure at 2½ months; the second child died at 2 years; the third child survived, but only after the paternal grandmother took him into her own home; Genie was the family's fourth child. Genie's mother was almost blind; she isolated Genie to protect her. When Genie came to the attention of social workers, the father shot himself.

The personalities we develop depend largely on the environment in which we live. When a child's world is shredded by violence, the damage can be profound and lasting. This drawing, titled Memories From L.A. Riot, *was made by nine-year-old Abdullah Abbas. What are the likely effects of such experiences on a young person's self-confidence and capacity to form trusting ties with others?*

Effects of Social Isolation on Children

Unusual and tragic cases of isolated children show the catastrophic effects of depriving human beings of social experience. We will review three such cases.

Anna: the rest of the story. Anna, described earlier, is the best-known case of extended social isolation of a human infant. After her discovery, Anna benefited from intense social contact and soon showed improvement. In only ten days after his first visit to the county home, Kingsley Davis (1940) noted that Anna was more alert and even smiled with obvious pleasure. During the next year, Anna made slow but steady progress, showing greater interest in other people and gradually learning to walk. After a year and a half, she could feed herself and play with toys.

Consistent with the observations of the Harlows, however, it was becoming apparent that Anna's five years of social isolation had left her permanently damaged. At age eight, her mental and social development was still less than that of a two-year-old. Not until she was almost ten did she begin to use words. Of course, since Anna's mother was mentally retarded, perhaps Anna was similarly disadvantaged. Was it nature, or (lack of) nurture, that was responsible for her exceptionally slow development? The riddle was never solved, because Anna died at age ten from a blood disorder, possibly related to long years of abuse (Davis, 1940, 1947).

Another case: Isabelle. A second, quite similar case involves another girl found at about the same time as Anna and under strikingly similar circumstances. After more than six years of virtual isolation, this child—known as Isabelle—displayed the same lack of human responsiveness as Anna. Unlike Anna, though, Isabelle benefited from a special program directed by psychologists. Within a week, Isabelle was attempting to speak, and a year and a half later, she had a vocabulary of nearly 2,000 words. The psychologists concluded that intensive effort propelled Isabelle through six years of normal development in only two years. By the time she was fourteen, Isabelle was in sixth grade and apparently on her way to at least an approximately normal life (Davis, 1947).

A third case: Genie. Yet another case of childhood isolation involves a thirteen-year-old California girl. From the time she was two years old, Genie was tied naked to a potty chair and locked in a dark garage (Curtiss, 1977; Pines, 1981; Rymer, 1994). Sometimes at night she was put in a straitjacket. When she was discovered in 1970, Genie was emaciated (weighing only fifty-nine pounds), looked half her age, and had the mental development of a one-year-old. She could not walk, chew food, speak, or even control her bladder. She received intensive treatment by specialists and gradually improved physically. But even after years of care, she has the language ability of only a

NOTE: Another way to present the theorists is to pose the question "How do we learn?" Freud emphasizes *internalization* of culture; Piaget underscores internal *cognitive development;* behaviorists Watson and Skinner highlighted *environmental stimulation;* Mead advances a *social behaviorist* approach based on developing the capacity for symbolic interaction.

Q: "Anatomy is destiny." Sigmund Freud

Q: "The principal task of civilization, its actual *raison d'être*, is to defend us against nature." Sigmund Freud

RESOURCE: The most sociological of Freud's twenty-four books is *Civilization and Its Discontents*. The sociological implications of Freud's work are explored in Philip Rieff's *Freud: The Mind of the Moralist* (Doubleday, 1961).

young child. She lives today in a home for developmentally disabled adults.

Conclusion. All the evidence points to the crucial role of social experience in personality development. Human beings can sometimes recover from even the worst abuse and isolation. But there is a point—precisely when is unclear from the limited number of cases—when social isolation or other abuse in infancy causes irreparable developmental damage.

UNDERSTANDING THE SOCIALIZATION PROCESS

Socialization is a complex, lifelong process. The following sections highlight the work of six men and women who have made lasting contributions to our understanding of human development.

SIGMUND FREUD: THE ELEMENTS OF PERSONALITY

Sigmund Freud (1856–1939) lived in Vienna at a time when most Europeans thought human behavior was biologically fixed. Trained as a physician, Freud gradually turned to the study of personality and eventually developed his celebrated theory of psychodynamics. His work bears directly on our understanding of socialization.

Basic Human Needs

Freud contended that biology plays a major role in human development, although not in the form of simple instincts like those that guide other species. Humans, Freud theorized, respond to two general needs or drives. First, humans have a basic need for bonding, which Freud called the life instinct, or *eros* (from the Greek god of love). Second, we share an aggressive drive, which Freud termed the death instinct, or *thanatos* (from the Greek meaning "death"). Freud claimed that these opposing forces, operating at an unconscious level, generate deep inner tensions.

Freud's Model of Personality

Freud combined basic drives and the influence of society into a model of personality with three parts: id, ego, and superego. The **id** represents *the human being's basic drives*, which are unconscious and demand immediate satisfaction. (The word *id* is simply Latin for "it,"

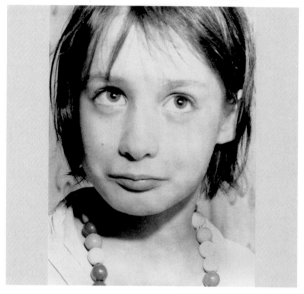

Like other children subjected to prolonged isolation, Genie never did develop a normal facility with language. Many researchers conclude that, unless a child learns language at an early age, this ability is permanently hindered. But others counter that children may well be mentally retarded by such abuse. Thus, cases such as Genie do not settle "nature-nurture" debates about human development.

suggesting the tentative way in which Freud explored the unconscious mind.) Rooted in our biology, the id is present at birth, making a newborn a bundle of demands for attention, touching, and food. But society opposes the self-centered id, which is why one of the first words a child learns is "no."

To avoid frustration, a child must learn to approach the world realistically. The second component of the personality, therefore, is the **ego** (Latin for "I"), which is *a person's conscious efforts to balance innate pleasure-seeking drives with the demands of society.* The ego arises as we gain awareness of our distinct existence; it develops as we face up to the fact that we cannot have everything we want.

Finally, the human personality develops a **superego** (Latin meaning "above" or "beyond" the ego), which is *the operation of culture within the individual.* Once we develop a superego, we understand *why* we cannot have everything we want. The superego consists of cultural values and norms—internalized to form our conscience—that define moral limits. The superego begins to develop when a child recognizes parental control, and it matures as the child comes to

NOTE: Champions of psychoanalysis included Franz Boas, Margaret Mead, and Ruth Benedict, all of whom thought it favored nurture over nature.

NOTE: A revealing example of Freud's influence on popular culture: the characterization of anything unintended as "Freudian."

Q: "The mind, of course, is just what the brain does for a living." Sharon Begley

RESOURCE: William Golding's *Lord of the Flies* is built on a Freudian model of personality. Jack (and his hunters) represent the power of the id; Piggy consistently opposes them as the superego; Ralph stands between the two as the ego, the voice of reason. Golding wrote the book after participating in the carnage of the D-Day landing in France; he traces the human proclivity for violence (as well as our capacity for learned restraint) to our basic nature.

Society, as Freud explained, is a compromise struck between our desire to satisfy our own individual needs and the necessity that we conform to others. The tapestry, Act Out Your Id, *is Lee Malerich's expression of our quest for freedom and release from life's trials and burdens. This particular art was inspired by her own experience with illness and chemotherapy.*

understand that everyone's behavior reflects the demands of culture.

Personality Development

To the id-centered infant, the world is a bewildering array of physical sensations that are either pleasurable or painful. As the superego gradually develops, however, the child learns the moral concepts of right and wrong. Initially, in other words, children feel good only in the physical sense, but, after three or four years, they feel good or bad as they evaluate their own behavior according to cultural standards.

Conflict between the id and the superego is ongoing, but, in a well-adjusted person, these opposing forces are managed by the ego. When conflicts are not resolved during childhood, they may surface as personality disorders later on.

As the source of the superego, culture controls human drives. Freud called this process *repression*. All culture involves repression, since any society must force people to look beyond their own needs and desires. Often the competing demands of self and society are resolved through compromise. This process, which Freud named *sublimation*, transforms selfish drives into socially acceptable activities. Sexual urges, for example, may lead to marriage, just as aggression gives rise to competitive sports.

Critical evaluation. Freud's work sparked controversy in his own lifetime, and some controversy still smolders

today. The world he knew repressed human sexuality, so that few of his contemporaries were prepared to accept sex as a basic human need. More recently, Freud has been criticized for presenting his theory in male terms and thereby devaluing women (Donovan & Littenberg, 1982). But Freud influenced virtually everyone who later studied the human personality. Of special importance to sociology is his idea that we internalize social norms and that childhood experiences have lasting impact on our personalities.

JEAN PIAGET: COGNITIVE DEVELOPMENT

Jean Piaget (1896–1980) studied human *cognition*—how people think and understand. As Piaget watched his own children, he wondered not just *what* they knew but *how* they made sense of the world. Careful observations revealed that, as children mature biologically and gain social experience, they pass through four stages of cognitive development.

The Sensorimotor Stage

Stage one is the **sensorimotor stage**, *the level of human development in which individuals experience the world only through sensory contact.* During this stage, roughly the first two years of life, the infant explores the world with the five senses—touching, tasting, smelling, looking, and listening. "Knowing" to infants amounts to direct, sensory experience.

NOTE: Stress that Piaget's stages of development are *maturational*; in this, he stands apart from George Herbert Mead, for whom biology played virtually no role in social development. (Piaget was trained as a biologist.)

NOTE: An example of preoperational thinking: Young children prefer nickels to dimes because nickels are bigger.

Q: "If we examine the intellectual development of the individual . . . we shall find that the human spirit goes through a certain number of stages, each different from the other . . ." Jean Piaget

NOTE: Because of their egocentric world view, young children may consider themselves responsible for family conflict and divorce.

The Preoperational Stage

At about age two, children enter the **preoperational stage,** *the level of human development in which individuals first use language and other symbols.* Now children begin to engage the world mentally, or *think,* and reality moves beyond the senses. Children develop imagination and appreciate the element of fantasy in fairy tales. But "pre-op" children between the ages of two and six still attach meaning only to specific experiences or objects. That is, they can identify a favorite toy, but not explain what kind of toy appeals to them.

Without abstract concepts, a child also cannot judge size, weight, or volume. In one of his best-known experiments, Piaget placed two identical glasses containing equal amounts of water on a table. He asked several children aged five and six if the amount in each glass was the same. They nodded that it was. The children then watched Piaget take one of the glasses and pour its contents into a taller, narrower glass, raising the level of the water. He asked again if each glass held the same amount. The typical five- and six-year-old now insisted that the taller glass held more water. But children of seven or eight, able to think abstractly, could comprehend that the amount of water remained the same.

We have all seen young children put their hands in front of their faces and cry, "You can't see me!" They assume that if they cannot see you, then you cannot see them. According to Piaget, this behavior reveals preoperational children's egocentric view of the world. They do not understand that the world could appear different to someone else.

The Concrete Operational Stage

Next comes the **concrete operational stage,** *the level of human development at which individuals first perceive causal connections in their surroundings.* Children typically enter this stage between seven and eleven. They begin to grasp how and why things happen and are therefore much better at manipulating their environment.

In addition, children can now attach more than one symbol to a particular event or object. For instance, if you say to a girl of five, "Today is Wednesday," she might respond, "No, it's my birthday!" indicating that she can use only one symbol at a time. But an older child at the concrete operational stage would be able to respond, "Yes, and this Wednesday is my birthday!"

Also at about this time, children move beyond their earlier egocentrism so that they can imagine themselves as others see them. This ability to "stand in

In a well-known experiment, Jean Piaget demonstrated that children over the age of seven had entered the concrete operational stage of development because they could recognize that the quantity of liquid remained the same when poured from a wide beaker into a tall one.

another's shoes" is the key to participating in complex social activities, such as games.

The Formal Operational Stage

The last step in Piaget's model is the **formal operational stage,** *the level of human development at which individuals think abstractly and critically.* By about the age of twelve, young people begin to reason in abstract terms rather than thinking only of concrete situations. If, for example, you ask a child of seven or eight, "What would you like to be when you grow up?" you would probably get a concrete response, such as "A teacher." But a teenager might well respond abstractly, saying "I would like a job that pays well." At this point, young people's energy is matched by their creativity and imagination, perhaps evident in a passion for science fiction or poetry.

Young people entering this stage are able to comprehend metaphors. Hearing the expression "A penny for your thoughts" might lead a child to ask for a coin, but the adolescent will recognize a gentle invitation to intimacy. Then, too, young adults begin to evaluate themselves, the people around them, and the world, which can lead to intense idealism.

Critical evaluation. While Freud envisioned personality as an ongoing battle between the opposing forces of biology and culture, Piaget viewed the human mind as active and creative. Piaget's contribution to

GLOBAL: Kohlberg claims, in essence, that good and evil span a continuum from selflessness at one end to selfishness at the other. This is a virtually universal theme of world religions.

SOCIAL SURVEY: One of Gilligan's interview items asked girls "How often do you feel happy the way you are?" Sixty percent of elementary school girls, but only 29% of high school girls, answered "always." Corresponding figures for boys were 67% and 46%.

Q: "In Gilligan's studies females moved from an early 'selfish' stage to an overly altruistic stage. The developmental task for the women in Gilligan's study was to achieve a position where they could take their own interests into account . . . A mature person, according to the ethic of care, recognizes her connection to others . . . and at the same time can articulate her own wants and needs." John R. Hall and Mary Jo Neitz (1993:37)

understanding socialization is showing that the capacity to engage the world unfolds predictably as the result of biological maturation and the gaining of social experience.

Whether people in every society progress through all four of the stages that Piaget identified is open to question. For instance, living in a traditional society that changes very slowly is likely to inhibit the capacity for abstract and critical thought. Finally, even in our own society, roughly 30 percent of thirty-year-olds never reach the formal operational stage at all (Kohlberg & Gilligan, 1971:1065). Thus, people exposed to little creative and imaginative thinking do not generally develop this capacity in themselves.

LAWRENCE KOHLBERG: MORAL DEVELOPMENT

Lawrence Kohlberg (1981) used Piaget's work as a springboard for studying moral reasoning—that is, how individuals come to judge situations as right or wrong. Following Piaget's lead, Kohlberg argues that moral development occurs in stages.

Young children who experience the world in terms of pain and pleasure (Piaget's sensorimotor stage) are at the *preconventional* level of moral development. At this early stage, in other words, "rightness" amounts to "what serves my needs" or, more simply, "what feels good to me."

The *conventional* level of moral development, Kohlberg's second stage, begins to appear during the teens (corresponding to Piaget's last, formal operational stage). At this point, young people shed some of their selfishness as they learn to define right and wrong in terms of what pleases parents and what fits with cultural norms. Individuals at this stage also try to infer people's intention in reaching moral judgments instead of taking behavior at face value.

In the final stage of moral development, the *postconventional* level, individuals move beyond the specific norms of their society to consider abstract ethical principles. They may philosophically reflect on the meaning of liberty, freedom, or justice, or criticize their society, arguing, for instance, that what is traditional or legal still may not be right.

Critical evaluation. Like the work of Piaget, Kohlberg's model explains that moral development occurs in more or less definable stages. Thus, some criticisms made of Piaget's ideas apply to Kohlberg's work, too. Whether this model applies to people in all societies, for example, remains unclear. Then, too, many people in the United States apparently never reach the postconventional level of moral reasoning, although exactly why is still an open question.

Another problem with Kohlberg's research is that his subjects were all boys. Kohlberg commits the research error, described in Chapter 2 ("Sociological Investigation"), of generalizing the results of male subjects to all people. This problem led a colleague, Carol Gilligan, to investigate how gender affects moral reasoning.

CAROL GILLIGAN: BRINGING IN GENDER

Carol Gilligan, whose approach is discussed in the box, was disturbed that Kohlberg's research involved only boys. This narrow focus, as she sees it, is typical of much social science, which uses male behavior as the norm for how everyone should act.

Therefore, Gilligan (1982, 1990) set out systematically to compare the moral development of girls and boys. She soon discovered that the two sexes make moral judgments in different ways. Males, she contends, have a *justice perspective*, relying on formal rules and abstract principles to define right and wrong. Girls, on the other hand, have a *care and responsibility perspective*, defining right and wrong with an eye toward personal relationships and loyalties. For example, as boys see it, stealing is wrong because it breaks the law and goes against common morality. Girls, however, are more likely to wonder why an individual would steal, and look sympathetically on someone who felt forced to steal in order to, say, feed a hungry child.

Kohlberg considers the abstract male perspective superior to the person-based female perspective. Gilligan notes that impersonal rules have long governed men's lives in the workplace, while personal attachments are more relevant to women's lives as wives, mothers, and caregivers. Why, then, Gilligan asks, should we set up male standards as the norms by which we evaluate everyone?

Critical evaluation. Gilligan's work sharpens our understanding of both human development and gender issues in research. Yet what accounts for the differences she documents between females and males? Is it nature or nurture? Although it is impossible to rule out biological differences between the sexes, Gilligan maintains that the difference reflects cultural conditioning. Thus, we might predict that as more women organize their lives around the workplace, the moral reasoning of women and men will become more similar.

RESOURCE: Mead's statement "The Self" is among the classics included in the *Seeing Ourselves* reader.

RESOURCE: Besides believing in the plasticity of human personality, George Herbert Mead also believed in people's ability to reform society. For a discussion of his views on social reform, see Dmitri N. Shalin, *American Journal of Sociology* 93, 4 (January 1988):913–51.

NOTE: Piaget argued that social behavior is shaped by maturational stages; by contrast, Mead implied that stages of life are defined and structured by society.

RESOURCE: George Herbert Mead also wrote about teaching; see "The Psychology of Social Consciousness Implied in Instruction" (*Science* XXXI, 1910:688–93) and "The Teaching of Science in College" (*Science* XXIV, 1906:390–97).

CRITICAL THINKING

The Importance of Gender in Research

Carol Gilligan, an educational psychologist at Harvard University, has demonstrated the importance of gender in our ideas about social behavior. Her early work was devoted to exposing the research bias present in the studies by Kohlberg and others, who had used only male subjects. But as her research progressed, Gilligan made a major discovery: Boys and girls actually employ different strategies in making moral decisions. Thus, by ignoring gender, we are left with an incomplete and distorted view of human behavior.

More recently, Gilligan has looked at the effect of gender on self-esteem. Her research team interviewed more than 2,000 girls, from age six to eighteen, over a five-year period. She found a clear pattern: Young girls start out eager and confident, but their self-esteem slips away as they pass through adolescence.

Why? Gilligan claims that the answer lies in the way our culture defines females. In our society, the ideal woman

is calm, controlled, and eager to please. Then, too, as girls move from the elementary grades to secondary school, they encounter fewer women teachers and find that most authority figures are men. The overall result is that, by their late teens, girls are struggling to regain the personal strength they had a decade before.

Ironically, when Gilligan and her colleagues returned to a girls' school— one site of their research—to present their findings, they found further evidence of their theory. Most younger girls who had been interviewed were eager to have their names appear in the forthcoming book, but the older girls were hesitant: Many were fearful that they would be talked about.

Sources: Gilligan (1990) and Winkler (1990).

GEORGE HERBERT MEAD: THE SOCIAL SELF

A major contribution to our understanding of socialization comes from George Herbert Mead (1863–1931). Mead's theory of *social behaviorism* (1962; orig. 1934) calls to mind the behaviorism of psychologist John B. Watson, described earlier. Both recognized the power of the environment to shape human behavior. But Watson focused on outward behavior, while Mead studied inward *thinking*, which he considered humanity's defining trait.

The Self

Mead's central concept is the **self,** *a dimension of personality composed of an individual's self-awareness and self-image.* Mead's genius lay in seeing that the self is inseparable from social experience, a connection explained in a series of steps.

First, Mead asserted, *the self develops over time.* The self is not part of the body, and it does not exist at birth. Mead rejected the idea that personality is guided by biological drives (as asserted by Freud) or biological maturation (as Piaget claimed). For Mead, self develops *only* through social experience. In the absence of interaction, as we see from the cases of isolated children, the body may grow but no self will emerge.

Second, Mead explained, *social experience is the exchange of symbols.* Using words, a wave of the hand, or a smile, people create meaning, which is a distinctively human experience. We can train a dog using reward and punishment, but the dog attaches no meaning to its actions. Human beings, by contrast, make sense of action by imagining people's underlying intentions. In short, a dog responds to *what you do;* a human responds to *what you have in mind* as you do it.

Return, for a moment, to our friendly dog. You can train a dog to walk to the corner and return carrying an umbrella. But the dog grasps no meaning in the act, no intention behind the command. Thus, if the dog cannot find the umbrella, it is incapable of the *human* response: to look for a raincoat instead.

NOTE: Mead's taking the role of the other is the basis of human morality, the ability to imagine the situation of other people. Thus, the Golden Rule: "Do unto others as you would have them do unto you."
RESOURCE: Italian playwright Luigi Pirandello (1867–1936) made use of the sociological perspective in his work. Many of his plays reveal a striking similarity to the ideas of George Herbert Mead (and also Erving Goffman). See, especially, *The Pleasure of Honesty*.
DISCUSS: We know that children vary with regard to innate talents and temperaments; moreover, biological maturation does affect behavior more than Mead allowed. Would it be more accurate to say that social experience is *necessary but not sufficient* to explain the development of personality?

George Herbert Mead wrote: "No hard-and-fast line can be drawn between our own selves and the selves of others." The painting Manyness *by Rimma Gerlovina and Valeriy Gerlovin conveys this important truth. Although we tend to think of ourselves as unique individuals, each person's characteristics develop in an ongoing process of interaction with others.*

Rimma Gerlovina & Valeriy Gerlovin, *Manyness*, 1990. © the artists, Pomona, N.Y.

Third, says Mead, *to understand intention, you must imagine the situation from another person's point of view.* Using symbols, we can imaginatively place ourselves in another person's shoes and thus see ourselves as that person does. This capacity allows us to anticipate how others will respond to us even before we act. A simple toss of a ball requires stepping outside ourselves to imagine how another will respond to our throw. Social interaction, then, involves seeing ourselves as others see us—a process that Mead termed *taking the role of the other.*

The Looking-Glass Self

How do we take the role of the other? Imagine that others represent a mirror (which people used to call a "looking glass") in which we can see ourselves. What we think of ourselves, then, depends in large measure on what we think others think of us. In other words, if we think others see us as clever, we will think of ourselves as clever. If we think others believe we are clumsy and worthless, we will imagine ourselves in the same way. Charles Horton Cooley (1864–1929), one of Mead's colleagues, used the phrase **looking-glass self** to designate *the self-image we have based on how we suppose others perceive us* (1964; orig. 1902). The concept of the looking-glass self goes a long way to explaining Carol Gilligan's finding that young women lose self-confidence as they come of age in a society that discourages assertiveness in women.

The I and the Me

Our capacity to see ourselves through others suggests that the self has two parts. First, as we initiate social action, *the self operates as a subject.* Humans are innately active and spontaneous, according to Mead. He called this subjective element of the self the *I* (the subjective form of the personal pronoun).

Second, as we take the role of the other, *the self operates as an object.* In interaction, in other words, we look at others and see ourselves. Mead called this objective element of the self the *me* (the objective form of the personal pronoun). All social experience has both components: We initiate an action (the I-phase of self), and then we continue the action based on how others respond (the me-phase of self). Taking the role of the other is, then, the interplay of the I and the me.

Mead stressed that thinking as well as action is social. Our thoughts are partly creative (representing the I), but in thought we also become objects to ourselves (representing the me), as we imagine how others will respond to us.

Development of the Self

According to Mead, we develop a self as we learn to take the role of the other. Like Freud and Piaget, he thought the process began in early childhood, but he emphasized that it goes on as long as we continue to have social experience.

Infants, said Mead, respond to others only through *imitation.* They mimic behavior without understanding underlying intentions. Unable to use symbols (thus, unable to take the role of the other), infants have no self.

Children first learn to use language and other symbols in the form of *play*, especially, role playing. Initially, they model themselves on important people in their lives—such as parents—we call *significant others.* Playing "mommy and daddy," for example, helps children imagine the world from their parents' point of view.

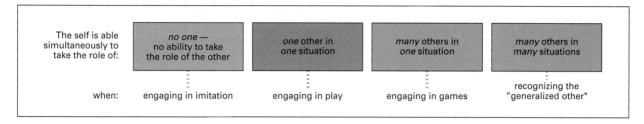

FIGURE 5–1 Building on Social Experience

George Herbert Mead described the development of the self as a process of gaining social experience. This is largely a matter of taking the role of the other with increasing sophistication.

Gradually, children learn to take the roles of several others at once. This skill allows them to move from simple play (say, playing catch) involving one other person to complex *games* (like baseball) involving many others. Only by the age of seven or eight have most children acquired enough social experience to engage in team sports that require taking the role of numerous others simultaneously.

Figure 5–1 shows the progression from imitation to play to games. But a final stage in the development of self remains. A game involves taking the role of others in just one situation. But members of a society also need to see themselves in terms of cultural norms, as *anyone* else might. In other words, as we learn a way of life, we begin to incorporate norms and values into the self. Mead used the term **generalized other** to refer to *the general cultural norms and values shared by us and others that we use as a point of reference in evaluating ourselves.*

As life goes on, the self continues to change along with our social experiences. The self may change, for example, with divorce, serious illness, or unexpected wealth. But no matter how much events and circumstances affect us, we always remain creative beings. Thus, Mead concluded, we play a key role in our own socialization.

Critical evaluation. Mead's work is valuable for explaining the character of social experience itself. In particular, he shows how our use of symbols makes possible both self and society.

Some critics say Mead's view is too radically social in not acknowledging any biological element whatsoever. In this position, he does stand apart from Freud (who saw general drives within the organism) and Piaget (whose stages of development are tied to biological maturity).

Mead's concepts of the I and the me are often confused with Freud's concepts of the id and the superego, but there are important differences. First, Freud rooted the id in the biological organism, while Mead rejected any link between the self and biology (although he never specified the origin of the I). Also, though the superego and me both reflect the power of society to shape personality, the superego and id are locked in continual combat, while the I and me work closely and cooperatively together (Meltzer, 1978).

ERIK H. ERIKSON: EIGHT STAGES OF DEVELOPMENT

All the thinkers we have discussed thus far point to childhood as the crucial period during which personality emerges. Erik H. Erikson (1902–1994) offered a broader view of socialization, believing that personality changes throughout the life course as we face challenges at different stages of life. In Erikson's theory (1959), life holds eight critical challenges:

Stage 1—Infancy: the challenge of trust (versus mistrust). Between birth and about 18 months, infants face the first of life's challenges: to gain a sense of trust that their world is a safe place. Family members play a key role in how well the infant meets this challenge.

Stage 2—Toddlerhood: the challenge of autonomy (versus doubt and shame). The challenge between eighteen months and age three is to acquire the skills to cope with the world in a confident way. Failure to gain self-control leads children to doubt their abilities.

Stage 3—Pre-school: the challenge of initiative (versus guilt). Four- and five-year-olds must learn to engage their surroundings—

Q: "Middle-class parents seem to regard child rearing as more problematic than do working-class parents." Melvin Kohn (1977:6)

SUPPLEMENTS: *Student CHIP Social Survey Software* allows students to analyze the effects of a family's class position on the socialization of children.

NOTE: An illustration of the significance of the family: Four of the five most powerful "social readjustment" experiences involve family members: death of spouse (100), divorce (73), marital separation (65), death of close family member (63), and jail term (63) (Holmes & Rahe, 1967).

Q: "For most [children of divorce], divorce was the most important cause of enduring pain and anomie in their lives." Judith S. Wallerstein and Sandra Blakeslee (1989)

including with people outside the family—or experience guilt at having failed to meet the expectations of parents and others.

Stage 4—Pre-adolescence: the challenge of industriousness (versus inferiority). Between ages six and thirteen, children enter school, establish peer groups, and strike out on their own more and more. They feel proud of their accomplishments or fear that they do not measure up.

Stage 5—Adolescence: the challenge of gaining identity (versus confusion). During the teenage years, young people struggle to establish their own identity. In part, teens identify with others close to them, but they also define themselves as unique. Almost all teens experience some confusion as they struggle to establish their identity.

Stage 6—Young adulthood: the challenge of intimacy (versus isolation). The challenge for young adults is to establish and maintain intimate relationships with others. Falling in love (as well as developing friendships and working relationships) involves balancing the need to bond with the need to maintain a separate identity.

Stage 7—Middle adulthood: the challenge of making a difference (versus self-absorption). The challenge of middle age is to contribute to the lives of others, in the family, at work, and in the larger world or to become stagnant and caught up in our own limited concerns.

Stage 8—Old age: the challenge of integrity (versus despair). As we near the end of our lives, we hope to look back on what we have accomplished with a sense of integrity and satisfaction. If we have been self-absorbed (think of Scrooge in Dickens's classic *A Christmas Carol*), old age brings a sense of despair at missed opportunities.

Critical evaluation. Erikson's theory states that personality formation is an ongoing process, beginning in childhood and continuing until the end of life. Further, success at one stage (say, an infant gaining trust) sets the stage for happily resolving the challenge of the next stage of life.

One problem with a model of set stages is that not everyone confronts these challenges in the exact order noted by Erikson. Nor is it clear that failing to meet a challenge at one stage of life means failing all future challenges. For example, a person may not form intimate relationships in young adulthood, but in middle adulthood may make a real difference in the lives of others. A broader question, raised earlier in our discussion of Piaget's ideas, is whether people in other cultures and in other times in history would define a successful life in the same terms as Erikson.

In sum, then, Erikson's model helps us make sense of the socialization process, but it may not actually describe how any single individual experiences the world. His model is valuable for stressing how the family, the school, and other settings shape us, and how we change over the life course. We turn now to take a closer look at these issues.

AGENTS OF SOCIALIZATION

Every social experience we have affects us in at least some small way. In modern industrial societies, however, several familiar settings are especially important to the socialization process.

THE FAMILY

The family is the most important agent of socialization because it stands at the center of children's lives. Because infants are almost totally dependent on others, the responsibility to meet their needs almost always falls on parents and other family members. And, at least until children begin school, the family also teaches children skills, cultural values, and attitudes about themselves and others.

Not all family-based socialization is intentional. Children learn continuously from the kind of environment that adults create. Whether children learn to think of themselves as strong or weak, smart or stupid, loved or simply tolerated, and, as Erik Erikson suggests, whether they believe the world is trustworthy or dangerous largely depends on their early environment.

Although parenting styles differ, research points to the importance of *paying attention* to children. Physical contact, verbal stimulation, and responsiveness from parents and others all foster intellectual growth (Belsky, Lerner, & Spanier, 1984).

The family also passes to children a social position. That is, parents not only bring children into the physical world, they also place them in society in terms of race, ethnicity, religion, and class. In time, all these elements become part of a child's self-concept. Of course, some aspects of social position may change

SOCIAL SURVEY: "How important is it that a child obey parents well?" (*CHIP1 Social Survey Software*, OBEYS1; GSS 1973–83, N = 7,253)

SES	"Very important"	Other
High	17.1%	82.9%
Middle	30.6%	69.4%
Low	41.1%	58.9%

Q: "Home is the place that, if you have to go there, they have to take you in." Robert Frost
Q: "I am always ready to learn, although I do not always like being taught." Winston Churchill
NOTE: Schooling emerged only with the declining economic value of children. "School" is derived from the Greek word *schole*, meaning "leisure employed in learning."

later on, but social standing at birth affects us throughout our lives.

Research shows that the class position of parents affects how they raise their children (Ellison, Bartkowski, & Segal, 1996). Perhaps most important, class position affects parents' expectations for their children. In survey research, when asked to pick from a list the traits that are most desirable in a child, lower-class people in the United States typically choose obedience and conformity. Well-to-do people, by contrast, tend to select good judgment and creativity (*Student CHIP Social Survey Software*, 1992). Why? Melvin Kohn (1977), who discovered the same pattern in his own research, explains that people of lower social standing usually have limited education and often perform routine jobs under close supervision. Expecting that their children eventually will hold similar positions, they cultivate obedience and conformity and make more use of physical punishment like spanking. Well-off parents, with more schooling, typically have jobs that allow more personal freedom and require good communication skills and imagination. These parents, therefore, try to inspire the same qualities in their children.

We know children are born both to rich and poor parents. What is less evident—and probably just as important—is that parents in different social classes give their children different hopes and dreams. In many ways, then, parents teach their children to follow in their footsteps.

SCHOOLING

Schooling enlarges children's social world to include people with social backgrounds different from their own. As children confront social diversity, they learn the significance society attaches to people's race and sex: Studies document that children tend to cluster in play groups composed of one race and gender (Lever, 1978; Finkelstein & Haskins, 1983).

Formal schooling teaches children a wide range of knowledge and skills. But schools informally convey a host of other lessons through what sociologists call the *hidden curriculum*. Activities such as spelling bees and sports teach children cultural values such as competitive achievement and success. In general, children receive countless formal and informal messages that their society's way of life is morally good.

Children entering school soon find their skills in areas such as reading and arithmetic evaluated by means of impersonal, standardized tests. That is, the

Sociological research indicates that affluent parents tend to encourage creativity in their children while poor parents tend to foster conformity. While this general difference may be valid, parents at all class levels can and do provide loving support and guidance by simply involving themselves in their children's lives. Henry Ossawa Tanner's painting The Banjo Lesson *stands as a lasting testament to this process.*

Henry Ossawa Tanner, *The Banjo Lesson*, 1893. Oil on canvas. Hampton University Museum, Hampton, Virginia.

emphasis shifts from *who* they are to *how* they perform. Of course, the confidence or anxiety that children develop at home can significantly affect how well they perform in school (Belsky, Lerner, & Spanier, 1984).

School is also most children's first experience with bureaucracy. The school day takes the form of a strict time schedule, teaching children to follow impersonal rules and to be punctual. Not surprisingly, these are the same traits expected by the large organizations that will employ them later in life.

NOTE: The word "peer" is derived from the Latin *par,* meaning "equal."
RESOURCE: George Gerbner's "Socialization and Television Violence" is included in the companion reader, *Seeing Ourselves.*
SOCIAL SURVEY: A 1996 study by Dale Kunkel (UC Santa Barbara, and sponsored by National Cable Television Association) reported that 57% of all shows sampled contained violence, including 85% of premium cable shows, 44% of network shows, and 18% of public television shows. Of violent shows, 73% presented violence with no negative consequences to perpetrators.
DIVERSITY: By the early 1990s, one-third of all television reporters were women, almost double the proportion a generation ago; 8 percent were African Americans, an increase from less than 1 percent in 1970 (Hess, 1991).

GLOBAL SNAPSHOT

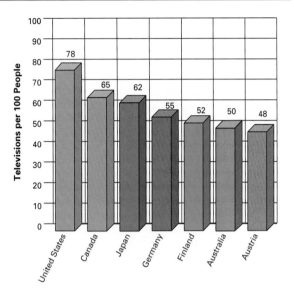

FIGURE 5–2 Television Ownership in Global Perspective

Source: U.S. Bureau of the Census (1997).

Finally, schools socialize children into gender roles. Raphaela Best (1983) points out that in primary school, boys engage in more physical activities and spend more time outdoors, while girls tend to be more sedentary, sometimes even helping the teacher with various housekeeping chores. Gender differences continue in higher grades and persist right through college. College women, for example, encounter pressure to major in the arts or humanities, while men are steered toward the physical sciences.

THE PEER GROUP

By the time they enter school, children have also discovered the **peer group,** *a social group whose members have interests, social position, and age in common.* A young child's peer group usually consists of neighborhood playmates; later, peer groups are composed of friends from school or elsewhere.

The peer group differs from the family and the school because it offers young people an escape from adult supervision. Members of peer groups thus gain valuable experience in developing social relationships on their own and establishing an identity apart from their families. Peer groups also furnish the opportunity to discuss interests that may not be shared by adults (such as styles of dress and popular music) or tolerated comfortably by parents (such as drugs and sex).

For the young, the appeal of the peer group lies in the ever-present possibility of activity not condoned by adults. For the same reason, parents express concern about who their children's friends are. In a rapidly changing society, peer groups can rival parents in influence, as parents' and children's attitudes diverge and a "generation gap" develops. The importance of peer groups peaks during adolescence. At this stage of life, young people often display conformity to peers because this sense of belonging eases some of the anxiety caused by breaking away from the family.

The conflict between parents and peers may be more apparent than real, however, for even during adolescence children remain strongly influenced by their families. Peers may guide short-term interests such as style of dress and musical taste, but parents have greater sway over their children's long-term aspirations. One study, for example, found that parents had more influence than even best friends on young people's educational aspirations (Davies & Kandel, 1981).

Finally, any neighborhood or school operates as a social mosaic composed of numerous peer groups. As we shall see in Chapter 7 ("Groups and Organizations"), individuals tend to perceive their own peer group in positive terms and discredit others. Moreover, individuals are also influenced by peer groups they would like to join, a process sociologists call **anticipatory socialization,** *social learning directed toward gaining a desired position.* In school, for example, young people may mimic the styles and banter of the group they hope to join. Or, later in life, a young lawyer who hopes to become a partner in her law firm may conform to the attitudes and behavior of the firm's partners in order to be accepted.

THE MASS MEDIA

September 29, 1994, the Pacific Ocean nearing Japan. We have been out of sight of land for two weeks now, which makes this ship our entire social world. But more than land, many of the students miss television! Tapes of "Beverly Hills 90210" are a hot item. . . .

The **mass media** are *impersonal communications directed to a vast audience.* The term "media" comes from

THE MAP: Generally, older, poorer, less educated, and unemployed people are the most avid television watchers; our society's primary newspaper readers also include older people, as well as the more affluent and better educated.

THEN AND NOW: U.S. spending on books: *1970*, $10.5 billion; *1992*, $16.5 billion (constant 1987 dollars). Spending on newspapers and magazines rose from $13.2 billion to $20.5 billion during the same period. Apparently, the growing presence of TV isn't wiping out other media. Yet, spending on TV and video gear rose over the same period from $8.8 billion to $70.3 billion.

SOCIAL DIVERSITY: Nielsen Media Research reports the following daily TV viewing for 1995: adult women, 5 hrs. 1 min.; adult men, 4 hrs. 17 min.; teens, 3 hrs. 14 min.; children 2–11, 3 hrs. 26 min.

SEEING OURSELVES

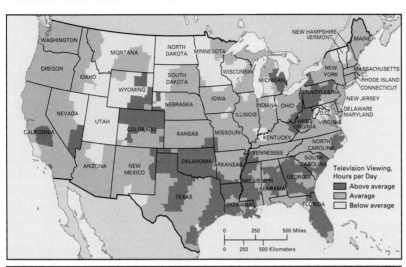

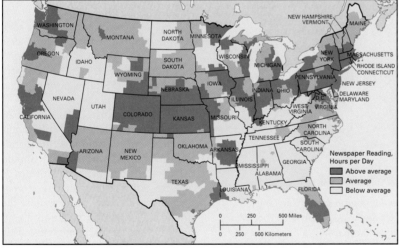

NATIONAL MAP 5–1
Television Viewing and Newspaper Reading Across the United States

The map on the left identifies U.S. counties in which television watching is above average, average, and below average. The map below provides comparable information for time devoted to reading newspapers. What do you think accounts for the high level of television viewing across much of the South and in rural West Virginia? Does your theory also account for patterns of newspaper reading?

Source: *American Demographics* magazine, August 1993, p. 64. Reprinted with permission. © 1993, *American Demographics* magazine, Ithaca, New York.

Latin meaning "middle," suggesting that media function to connect people. *Mass* media occur as communications technology (first newspapers and, more recently, radio and television) spread information on a *mass* scale.

In the United States today, the mass media have an enormous effect on our attitudes and behavior. They are, therefore, an important part of the socialization process. Television, introduced in 1939, has rapidly become the dominant medium in the United States. In 1950, according to the Census Bureau, only 9 percent of U.S. households had one or more television sets. By 1997, this share had soared to 98 percent (while only 94 percent had telephones). Videocassette recorders (VCRs) are now the fastest growing appliance in history and are found in three-fourths of homes (up from 1 percent in 1980). Two of three households also have cable television. In fact, as Figure 5–2 indicates, the United States has a higher rate of television ownership than any nation in the world.

Just how "glued to the tube" are we? Government statistics show that the average household turns on a television for seven hours each day (U.S. Bureau of the Census, 1995). Years before children learn to read, watching television is a regular routine. And as they grow, children spend as many hours in front of a television as they do in school; indeed, television consumes

DIVERSITY: Concern about the portrayal of African Americans in the mass media began with "Amos 'n' Andy" in the 1950s, as critics compared this show to old minstrel shows of the 19th century. During the 1970s, J. J. on "Good Times" used a similar shtick, punctuated by the trademark expression "dy-no-myte"; today, "Martin" isn't much better, showing African Americans as libido-driven. Generally, say critics, black people appear in too many sitcoms and too often as buffoons (cf. Hammer, 1992).

DIVERSITY: The inclusion of minorities in media advertising largely stems from advertisers' recognition of minorities' growing financial power—a market worth half a trillion dollars a year.

NOTE: Rothman and Lichter (1994) report that two-thirds of the people they count as "Hollywood elites" characterize their films or other works as efforts at social reform.

SOCIAL DIVERSITY

How Do the Media Portray Minorities?

On an old "Saturday Night Live" sketch, Ron Howard tells comedian Eddie Murphy about a new film, *Night Shift*, in which two mortuary workers decide to open their own sideline business—a prostitution ring. Murphy asks whether any black actors are in the film; Howard shakes his head "no." Murphy then thunders, "A story about two pimps and there wasn't no brothers in it? I don't know whether to thank you or punch you in the mouth, man!"

Murphy's response suggests twin criticisms of the U.S. mass media: Films and television either portray minorities as stereotypes or they exclude them altogether (Press, 1993:219). At the beginning of the television age in the 1950s, minorities were all but absent from television and films. Even the wildly successful 1950s comedy "I Love Lucy" was turned down by every major television studio because it featured Desi Arnaz—a Cuban—in a starring role. Since then, however, the media have steadily included more minorities, so that *visibility* is no longer the issue it once was.

But a second issue is just as important: *How* do the media portray minorities? The few African Americans who managed to break into television in the 1950s

(for example, "Amos 'n Andy" or Jack Benny's butler "Rochester") were strictly confined to stereotyped roles portraying uneducated, low-status people. Today, although many television shows feature African American stars, most are situation comedies ("sitcoms") filled with crude humor and bumbling characters.

Perhaps the major exception to this pattern has been "The Cosby Show,"

Should programs like "The Gregory Hines Show" depict African American families more as they are or more as we wish they all could be?

among the most popular television programs of the past decade. Although Cliff and Clair Huxtable were originally supposed to hold blue-collar occupations (chauffeur and plumber were one combination), TV producers decided to make them affluent professionals—a doctor and a lawyer. Many people praise the show for shattering the stereotype and placing minorities squarely within the middle class. But critics charge that the show unrealistically portrays African Americans, sending a false message that anyone can "make it." This, say the critics, is doubtful given the barriers of race and class in the United States.

Looking behind the camera, we see a growing number of minority producers and directors. Yet, African Americans and other minorities remain unrepresented in the executive positions that control the mass media.

Certainly, the mass media can boast of improvement in the portrayal of minorities. But troublesome questions remain (cf. MacDonald, 1992). Should the mass media portray minorities *as they are* and risk perpetuating stereotypes? Or—and this has been more the rule—should they portray minorities *as they should be* and risk being unrealistic about racial and ethnic inequality?

as much of their time as interacting with parents. The amount of time children spend watching television is a concern because researchers have found that television makes children more passive and less likely to use their imagination (Singer & Singer, 1983; APA, 1993; Fellman, 1995).

Virtually everyone in the United States reports watching television, but not to an equal degree. National Map 5–1 identifies the regions of the country in which television viewing is greatest and the regions where people spend the most time reading newspapers.

Comedian Fred Allen once quipped that we call television a "medium" because it is rarely well done. For a variety of reasons, television (as well as other mass media) have provoked plenty of criticism. Some liberal critics allege that television programs portray people in biased ways. That is, television shows (as well as newspapers) mirror our society's patterns of inequality and rarely challenge the status quo. For example, TV shows typically portray men and women according to cultural stereotypes, presenting men in positions of power and women as mothers or subordinates. Television also

NOTE: Why are Hollywood elites so nontraditional? Mary Ann Glendon, of Harvard Law School, claims that "In order to get where they are, they have to give up strong ties to people, places, and traditions. They are geographically mobile technocrats who get their prestige, power, and satisfaction from work."
Q: "Television is chewing gum for the eyes." Frank Lloyd Wright
SOCIAL SURVEY: "How many hours a day do you watch TV?"

(*Student CHIP Social Survey Software*, TVHRS2; GSS 1975–91, N = 14,073)

EDUC YRS	0–1	2–3	4+
13–20	34.2%	47.9%	18.0%
12	19.5%	47.7%	32.8%
0–11	17.2%	43.3%	39.4%
All	24.5%	46.6%	29.0%

tends to portray well-to-do people favorably and less affluent individuals (Archie Bunker is the classic example) as ignorant and wrongheaded. Moreover, although racial and ethnic minorities watch more television than white people, until recent decades minorities have been all but absent from programming (Gans, 1980; Cantor & Pingree, 1983; Ang, 1985; Parenti, 1986; Brown, 1990). The box provides a broader look at how the U.S. entertainment industry has characterized minorities.

On the other side of the fence, conservative critics charge that the television and film industries are dominated by a "cultural elite" who are far more liberal than the population as a whole. Especially in recent years, they maintain, the media have become "politically correct," advancing various politically liberal causes including feminism and gay rights (Lichter, Rothman, & Rothman, 1986; Woodward, 1992; Prindle, 1993; Prindle & Endersby, 1993; Rothman, Powers, & Rothman, 1993).

A final issue concerns violence and the mass media. In 1996, the American Medical Association (AMA) expressed concern that violence portrayed through the mass media—especially television and films—is a hazard to the well-being of this country's people. An AMA survey (1996) found that three-fourths of U.S. adults have either walked out of a movie or turned off a television program because of objectionable levels of violence. A majority of parents also express concern about the sexual and violent content of popular music, video games, and the Internet.

Such concerns led to the rating system adopted by the television industry in 1997. But larger questions remain: Does viewing sexual or violent programming harm people as much as critics say it does? And, why do the mass media contain so much sex and violence in the first place?

In sum, television and the other mass media have enriched our lives through entertaining and educational programming. The media also increase our understanding of diverse cultures and provoke discussion of current issues. At the same time, the power of the media—especially television—to shape how we think is highly controversial.

Finally, other spheres of life beyond family, school, and the media also play a part in social learning. For most people in the United States, these include religious organizations, the workplace, the military, and social clubs. As a result, socialization inevitably involves inconsistencies as we absorb information from different sources. In the end, socialization is not a simple learning process, but a complex balancing act. As we sort and weigh all the ideas we encounter, we form our own distinctive personalities and world views.

SOCIALIZATION AND THE LIFE COURSE

Although childhood has special importance in the socialization process, learning continues throughout life. Our society organizes human experience according to age, so we think of the life course as four distinct stages: childhood, adolescence, adulthood, and, finally, old age.

CHILDHOOD

Michael Jordan recently came under fire for endorsing Nike athletic shoes, because they are made in Taiwan and Indonesia by children who do not go to school but work full time for roughly fifty cents an hour. Such wages are typical for workers in poor countries, which include perhaps 200 million of the world's children (Gibbs, 1996). Global Map 5–1 shows that child labor is most common in nations of Africa and Asia.

Michael Jordan was criticized because North Americans think of *childhood*—the first twelve years of life—as a time for learning and carefree play. Many people might be surprised to learn, however, that, even a century ago, children in North America and Europe had much the same life as children in poor countries today: They worked long hours, often under hazardous conditions, for little pay.

In fact, according to historian Philippe Ariès (1965), the whole idea of "childhood" is a fairly recent invention. During the Middle Ages, Ariès explains, children of four or five were treated like adults and expected to fend for themselves.

Today, our notion of childhood is grounded in biological differences that set youngsters apart from adults. But, as historical and global comparisons show us, the concept of "childhood" is also rooted in culture. In rich countries, not everyone has to work. In addition, societies such as our own stretch out childhood to allow time for young people to learn the skills they will need in a high-technology workplace.

Recently, some social scientists think, our conception of childhood may be changing yet again. In an age of high divorce rates, with both mothers and fathers in the work force, and an increasing level of "adult" programming on television, children are no longer "protected" from grown-up concerns as in past generations.

NOTE: The International Save the Children Alliance reports that some 250,000 children under 18 fought in 33 armed conflicts during 1995. Children are easy to recruit and often deemed expendable. Girls are sometimes recruited for sex.

RESOURCE: D. Terri Heath's article about childhood socialization in global perspective is one of the cross-cultural selections in the *Seeing Ourselves* reader.

NOTE: Ariès is an art historian; his interest in the changing conceptions of childhood began when he noted that medieval artists portrayed children as miniature adults. This did not reflect a lack of technical sophistication, he concluded, but rather a different view of childhood.

RESOURCE: See Ruth Benedict's (1938) classic article on the social construction of childhood.

There is no better example of how parents can "hurry" their children into adulthood than beauty pageants for young girls. In this scene from a Georgia "baby beauty pageant," we see a girl, not even old enough for school, straining to embody traits usually associated with grown-up women. What are these traits? Would you want your daughter to compete in such pageants? Why or why not?

Rather, we are seeing a "hurried child" syndrome: Children have to grapple with sex, drugs, and violence as well as fend more and more for themselves (Elkind, 1981; Winn, 1983). Critics, however, counter that there is not yet convincing evidence of any dramatic shift in our society's conception of childhood. Further, they note, the "hurried child" thesis overlooks the fact that children in the lower class have always assumed adult responsibilities sooner than their middle- and upper-class counterparts (Lynott & Logue, 1993).

ADOLESCENCE

As industrialization gradually turned childhood into a distinct stage of life, adolescence emerged as a buffer between childhood and adulthood. Adolescence, or the teenage years, is the stage of life for establishing some independence and learning specialized skills required for adult life.

We generally associate adolescence with emotional and social turmoil—young people in conflict with their parents as they struggle to develop their own, separate identities. We may be tempted to attribute teenage turbulence to the physiological changes of puberty. But comparative research suggests that, like childhood, adolescence depends on culture. Studying the Samoan Islanders in the 1920s, Margaret Mead (1961; orig. 1928) found little evidence of stress among teenagers; there, children appeared to move easily to adult standing. Our society, however, defines childhood and adulthood in somewhat opposing terms, making the transition from one stage to the other more difficult.

Our society also seems to have mixed feelings about when exactly young people become adults. Eighteen-year-olds may vote and go to war; yet they cannot drink alcohol and they have a hard time getting a bank loan. We send the same mixed messages when it comes to adolescent sexuality. The mass media often encourage sexual activity, while parents urge restraint, and for their part, schools discourage casual sex even as they hand out condoms to students.

As is true of all stages of life, the experience of adolescence varies according to social background. Most young people from working-class families move directly from high school into the adult world of work and parenting. Wealthier teens, however, with the resources to attend college and perhaps graduate school, may extend adolescence into the late twenties and even the thirties. For different reasons, of course, poverty also can extend adolescence. Especially in the inner cities, many young minorities cannot attain full adult standing because jobs are not available.

ADULTHOOD

At the age of thirty-five, Eleanor Roosevelt, one of the most widely admired women in the United States, wrote in her diary: "I do not think I have ever felt so strangely as in the past year . . . all my self-confidence is gone and I am on the edge, though I never was better physically I feel sure" (quoted in Sheehy, 1976:260). Perhaps Eleanor Roosevelt was troubled by the attention her husband was paying to another, younger woman; perhaps as she looked to the future, she could not see what challenges or accomplishments might bring satisfaction to her life.

But as Eleanor Roosevelt struggled with what today we might call a "midlife crisis," there was much that she could not foresee. Her husband, Franklin Delano Roosevelt, was shortly to become disabled by polio, although his rising political career ultimately would lead to the White House. And Eleanor herself was to become one of the most active and influential of all First Ladies. Even after her husband's death, she remained in public life, serving as a delegate to the United Nations.

GLOBAL: Ruth Benedict found that childhood sexuality, which so disturbs our society, posed little problem for the Melanesian cultures of southwest New Guinea.

Q: "When I was fourteen my father was so ignorant I could hardly stand to have the old man around. But when I got to be twenty-one, I was astonished at how much he had learned in seven years." Mark Twain

Q: "Youth is wholly experimental." Robert Louis Stevenson

Q: "Only a moment, a moment of strength, of romance, of glamour . . . a flick of sunshine upon a strange shore." Joseph Conrad

DISCUSS: Is adolescence expanding? Primarily because of uncertainty, 60% of 20- to 24-year-olds now live at home with their parents. Ask the class (especially 18- to 22-year-olds) whether or not they consider themselves adults. Why?

WINDOW ON THE WORLD

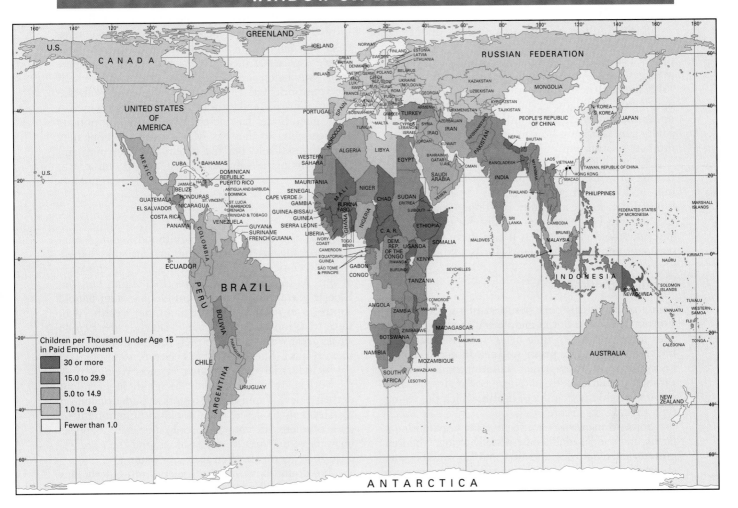

GLOBAL MAP 5–1 Child Labor in Global Perspective

Industrialization prolongs childhood and discourages children from work and other activities deemed suitable only for adults. Thus, child labor is relatively uncommon in the United States and other industrial societies. In less industrialized nations of the world, however, children serve as a vital economic asset, and they typically begin working as soon as they are able.

Source: *Peters Atlas of the World* (1990).

Eleanor Roosevelt's life illustrates two major characteristics of *adulthood*, which our culture defines as beginning during the twenties. First, adulthood is a time of accomplishment, when we pursue careers and raise families. Second, in later adulthood, as Erik Erikson explained, people reflect upon what they have achieved, perhaps with great satisfaction or with the sobering realization that the dreams of their youth will never come true.

Early Adulthood

By the onset of adulthood, personalities are largely formed. Even so, a marked shift in an individual's life

Q: "From birth to age 18, a girl needs good parents; from 18 to 35, she needs good looks; from 35 to 55, she needs a good personality; from 55 on she needs cash." Sophie Tucker
SOCIAL SURVEY: Income peaks between ages 45 and 54. Median income for full-time workers (1992): 25–34, $26,533; 35–44, $34,945; 45–54, $38,219; 55–64, $35,351; 65 and older, $35,256 (U.S. Bureau of the Census).

Q: "He was a bold man that first ate an oyster." Jonathan Swift
GLOBAL: The social standing of the elderly in industrial societies is lower than in agrarian societies, a pattern explained by more rapid change. Hoyt Alverson reports that, for the Tswana in southern Africa, the word "aging" means "seeing with one's own eyes." Similarly, "knowledge" is defined as "remembering things past," so that elders are the wisest of all the Tswana.

situation—brought on by unemployment, divorce, or serious illness—can cause significant change in the self (Dannefer, 1984).

Early adulthood—from twenty to about age forty—is generally a time of pursuing goals set earlier in life. Young adults break free of parents and learn to manage day-to-day responsibilities for themselves. With the birth of children, parents draw on their own upbringing, although, as children, they may not have understood much about adult life. In addition, young adults must work out how to live with a partner in an intimate relationship.

Early adulthood is also a period of juggling conflicting priorities: parents, partner, children, schooling, and work (Levinson et al., 1978). Women, especially, face the difficulty of "doing it all," since they still have primary responsibility for child rearing and household chores, even if they have demanding occupations outside the home (Hochschild, 1989).

Middle Adulthood

Young adults usually cope optimistically with the tensions in their lives. But in middle adulthood—roughly ages forty to sixty—people begin to sense that their life circumstances are pretty well set. In middle adulthood, then, we assess actual achievement in light of earlier expectations. At midlife, people also become more aware of the fragility of health, which the young typically take for granted.

Some women who have spent many years raising a family find middle adulthood especially trying. Children grow up and require less attention, and husbands become absorbed in their careers, leaving these women with spaces in their lives that they find difficult to fill. Women who divorce during middle adulthood also may experience serious financial problems (Weitzman, 1985, 1996). For all these reasons, an increasing number of women in middle adulthood return to school and seek new careers.

For both men and women, growing older means facing physical decline, but in our society, this prospect is more painful for women. Because good looks are considered more important for women, wrinkles, added weight, and hair loss can be traumatic. Men, of course, have their own particular difficulties. Some must admit that they are never going to reach their career goals. Others, now realizing that the price of career success has been neglect of family or personal health, harbor uncertainties about their self-worth even as they bask in the praise of others (Farrell & Rosenberg, 1981). Women, too, who devote themselves single-mindedly to careers in early adulthood,

may regret what they gave up in relationships, health, or personal goals.

Eleanor Roosevelt's midlife crisis may well have involved some of the personal transitions we have described. But her story also illustrates the fact that most people experience their greatest productivity and personal satisfaction after midlife—in later adulthood. In our youth-oriented culture, many people (especially the young) think life ends at forty. But as life expectancy in the United States has increased, such limiting notions are beginning to dissolve. Major transformations may become less likely, but the potential for learning and new beginnings fills this stage of life with promise.

OLD AGE

Old age—the later years of adulthood and the final stage of life itself—begins about the mid-sixties. Again, societies attach different meanings to this time of life. As explained in Chapter 14 ("Aging and the Elderly"), traditional societies often give older people control over most of the land and other wealth. Also, since traditional societies change slowly, older people amass great wisdom during their lifetime, which earns them respect (Sheehan, 1976; Hareven, 1982).

In industrial societies, however, most younger people work apart from the family, becoming independent of their elders. Rapid change fosters a youth orientation that leads us to define what is old as unimportant or even obsolete. To younger people, the elderly appear unaware of new trends and fashions, and their knowledge and experience often seem irrelevant.

No doubt, however, our society's anti-elderly bias will diminish as the proportion of older people steadily increases. The share of our population over sixty-five has almost tripled since the beginning of this century, so that today there are more elderly men and women than there are teenagers. Moreover, life expectancy is still increasing, so that most men and women in their mid-sixties (the "young elderly") can look forward to decades more of life. In fact, the Census Bureau (1997) predicts that the fastest-growing segment of our population in the next century will be people over eighty-five, whose numbers will soar sixfold.

Old age differs in an important way from earlier stages of the life course. Growing up means entering new roles and assuming new responsibilities; growing old is the opposite experience of leaving roles that provided both satisfaction and social identity. Retirement, for example, may be a period of restful activity, or it can mean the loss of valued routines and sometimes outright boredom. Like any life transition, retirement demands learning new, different patterns while simultaneously *un*learning familiar habits from the past. A nonworking wife or husband who must accommodate a partner spending more time at home has an equally difficult transition to make.

DYING

Through most of human history, low living standards and primitive medical technology meant that death, caused by disease or accident, came at any stage of life. Today, however, almost 85 percent of people in the United States die after the age of fifty-five (U.S. National Center for Health Statistics, 1997).

After observing many dying people, Elisabeth Kübler-Ross (1969) described death as an orderly transition involving five distinct responses. A person's first reaction to the prospect of dying is usually *denial*, since our culture tends to ignore the reality of death. The second phase is *anger* by which a person begins to face the prospect of dying but views it as a gross injustice. Third, anger gives way to *negotiation*, as the person imagines that death may not be inevitable and tries to strike a bargain with God in order to continue living. The fourth response, *resignation*, is often accompanied by psychological depression. Finally, adjustment to death is completed in the fifth stage, *acceptance*. At this point, rather than being paralyzed by fear and anxiety, the person whose life is ending sets out to make the most of whatever time remains.

As the proportion of women and men in old age increases, we can expect our culture to become more comfortable with the idea of death. In recent years, for example, people in the United States and elsewhere are discussing death more than in decades past, and the trend is to view dying as preferable to painful or prolonged suffering. Moreover, more married couples now anticipate their own deaths with legal and financial planning. This openness may ease somewhat the pain of the surviving spouse—a consideration for women, who usually outlive their husbands.

THE LIFE COURSE: AN OVERVIEW

This brief examination of the life course points to two major conclusions. First and more important, although each stage of life is linked to the biological process of aging, the life course is largely a social construction. For this reason, people in other societies may experience a stage of life quite differently, or not at all. Second, in

In this photograph, photographer Constance Stuart Larrabee suggests how the lives of young people—like this South African girl—are shaped for better or worse by the structures of society linked to color, gender, and social class.

Constance Stuart Larrabee (American, b.1914) *Witwatersand Goldminer Watching Sunday Mine Dance,* Johannesburg, South Africa, 1946. The National Museum of Women in the Arts. Gift of the artist.

any society, the stages in the life course present characteristic problems and transitions that require learning something new and unlearning familiar routines.

Note, too, that societies may organize the life course according to age, but other forces, such as class, race, ethnicity, and gender, also affect human experience. Thus, the general patterns we have described apply somewhat differently to various categories of people.

Finally, people's life experiences also vary depending on when, in the history of the society, they are born. A **cohort** is *a category of people with a common characteristic, usually their age.* Age-cohorts are likely to be influenced by the same economic and cultural trends, so that members have similar attitudes and values (Riley, Foner, & Waring, 1988). Women and men born in the 1940s and 1950s, for example, grew up during a time of economic expansion that gave them a sense of optimism that is less common among today's college students, who have grown up in an age of economic uncertainty.

Q: "A basic social arrangement in modern society is that the individual tends to sleep, play, and work in different places, with different co-participants, under different authorities, and without an overall rational plan. The central feature of total institutions can be described as the breakdown of the barriers ordinarily separating these three spheres of life." Erving Goffman (1961:6)
Q: "Humility is the final achievement." Anonymous

Q: "Are you going to let the system eat you up and relieve you of your humanity? Or are you going to use the system to human purposes?" Joseph Campbell
Q: "For of all sad words, of tongue or pen;
    The saddest are these: 'It might have been'!"
    John Greenleaf Whittier
Q: "Kites fly highest against the wind." Winston Churchill

The demand by guards that new prisoners publicly disrobe is more than a matter of issuing new clothing; such a degrading ritual is also the first stage in the process by which the staff in a total institution attempts to break down an individual's established social identity.

RESOCIALIZATION: TOTAL INSTITUTIONS

A final type of socialization, experienced by more than 1 million people in the United States at any one time, involves being confined—often against their will—in prisons or mental hospitals. This is the special world of the **total institution,** *a setting in which people are isolated from the rest of society and manipulated by an administrative staff.*

According to Erving Goffman (1961), total institutions have three distinctive characteristics. First, staff members supervise all spheres of daily life, including where residents (often called "inmates") eat, sleep, and work. Second, the environment of a total institution is highly standardized, with mass-produced food, uniform sleeping quarters, and one set of activities for everyone. Third, rules and schedules dictate when, where, and how inmates perform virtually every part of their daily routines.

The purpose of such regimentation is **resocialization,** *radically altering an inmate's personality through deliberate manipulation of the environment.* A great deal

of a total institution's power to resocialize comes from forcibly segregating inmates from the "outside." Cut off by locked doors, barred windows, and walls and fences topped with barbed wire and guard towers, the inmate's entire world can be manipulated by the administrative staff to produce lasting change—or at least immediate compliance—in the inmate.

Resocialization is a two-part process. First, the staff erodes the new inmate's autonomy and identity through what Goffman describes as "abasements, degradations, humiliations, and profanations of self" (1961:14). For example, an inmate must surrender personal possessions, including the clothing and grooming articles that could be used to maintain a distinctive appearance. Instead, the staff provides standard-issue clothes so everyone looks alike. Inmates also receive standard haircuts, so that, once again, what was personalized becomes uniform. The staff subjects new inmates to "mortifications of self," including searches, medical examinations, fingerprinting, and then assigns each a serial number. Once inside the walls, individuals surrender the right to privacy; guards may demand that inmates undress publicly as part of the admission procedure, and they routinely monitor the living quarters.

In the second part of the resocialization process, the staff systematically tries to build a different self in the inmate. The staff manipulates inmate behavior through a system of rewards and punishments. Having a book to read, watching television, or making a telephone call may seem trivial to outsiders, but, in the rigid environment of the total institution, winning these simple privileges can be a powerful motivation to conform. Bucking the system, on the other hand, means that privileges will be withdrawn or, in more serious cases, that the inmate will suffer further isolation or other punishment. The period of confinement in a prison or mental hospital depends on how well an inmate obeys official rules and regulations. But Goffman also emphasizes that the staff seeks to win the hearts and minds of inmates, punishing those who toe the line but have "an attitude problem."

In principle, total institutions can bring about considerable change in inmates. Yet the resocialization process is extremely complex, and no two people respond in precisely the same way. Moreover, while some inmates are considered "rehabilitated" or "recovered," others change very little, and still others become more confused, hostile, or bitter. Furthermore, over a long period of time, a rigidly controlled environment can destroy a person's capacity for independent living, so that *institutionalized* personalities end up unable to live in the outside world.

Q: "O wad some Power the giftie gie us,
    To see oursels as ithers see us!
    It wad frae monie a blunder free us,
    An' foolish notion."
    Scottish poet Robert Burns
EXERCISE: A fun exercise to suggest to the class: renting the video *Trading Places* with Eddie Murphy and Dan Aykroyd and

discussing the plot in terms of John B. Watson's ideas of nurture.
Q: "After all is said and done, more is said than done." Anonymous
EXERCISE: For motivated students, assign a special report on George Herbert Mead's ideas about teaching. Sources include "The Psychology of Social Consciousness Implied in Instruction" (*Science* XXXI, 1910:688–93) and "The Teaching of Science in College" (*Science* XXIV, 1906:390–97).

CONTROVERSY & DEBATE

Are We Free Within Society?

Throughout this chapter, we have returned to one key theme: Society shapes how we think, feel, and act. But, if this is so, in what sense are we free? To answer this important question, consider the Muppets, puppet stars of television and film. Watching the antics of Kermit the Frog, Miss Piggy, and the rest of the troupe, one almost believes that these creatures are real, not objects being animated from backstage. The sociological perspective points out that human beings are like puppets in that we, too, respond to backstage forces. Society, after all, gives us a culture, places us in a class position, and takes account of our race and sex. In the face of such social constraints, can we really claim to be free?

Sociologists speak with many voices when addressing this question. One response, with politically liberal overtones, is that individuals are *not* free of society—in fact, as social creatures, we never can be. But if we are to live in a society with power over us, we must do what we can to make our environment as just as possible. That is, we should

work to lessen class differences and other barriers that limit the opportunities of minorities, including women. Another approach, this time with conservative overtones, is that we *are* free because society can never control the aspirations or break the will of someone committed to a dream, whatever it may be. Our history as a nation—right from the revolutionary act that led to its founding—is the story of one individual after another who pursued personal goals, often overcoming great odds.

We find both of these attitudes in the work of George Herbert Mead, who made a crucial contribution to our understanding of socialization. Mead recognized that society makes demands on us, sometimes even setting itself before us as a barrier. But he also reminded us that human beings are spontaneous and creative, capable of continually acting back—individually or collectively— on society. Thus Mead acknowledged the power of society while still affirming the human capacity to evaluate, criticize, and, ultimately, to choose and to change.

In the end, then, we may resemble puppets, but only superficially. A crucial difference—one that allows us to claim a significant measure of freedom—is that we have the power to stop and look at the "strings" that animate much of our action, and perhaps even to jerk down on them defiantly (Berger, 1963:176). If our pull is persistent and powerful enough, we can accomplish more than we might imagine. As Margaret Mead once said, "Do not make the mistake of thinking that concerned people cannot change the world; it's the only thing that ever has."

Continue the debate . . .

1. *Do you think our society affords more freedom to males than to females? Why or why not?*

2. *What about members of modern, industrial countries compared to people living in traditional, agrarian nations: Are some of the world's people more free than others?*

3. *How does an understanding of sociology enhance personal freedom?*

SUMMARY

1. For individuals, socialization is the process of developing our humanity and particular identity through social experience. For society as a whole, socialization is the means by which one generation transmits culture to the next.

2. A century ago, people thought most human behavior was guided by biological instinct. Today, the nature-nurture debate has tipped the other way as we understand human behavior to be primarily a product of a social environment. But the two concepts are not entirely opposed since it is part of human nature to nurture.

3. The permanently damaging effects of social isolation reveal the importance of social experience to human development.

4. Sigmund Freud envisioned the human personality as composed of three parts. The id represents general human drives (the life and death instincts), which Freud claimed were innate. The superego embodies cultural values and norms internalized by individuals. The ego resolves competition between the demands of the id and the restraints of the superego.

5. Jean Piaget believed that human development reflects both biological maturation and increasing social experience. He asserted that socialization involves four major stages of cognitive development: sensorimotor, preoperational, concrete operational, and formal operational.

6. Lawrence Kohlberg applies Piaget's approach to the issue of moral development. Individuals, he claims, first judge rightness in preconventional terms, according to their individual needs. Next, conventional moral reasoning takes account of the attitudes of parents and the norms of the larger society. Finally, postconventional moral reasoning provides for a philosophical critique of society itself.

7. Beginning with a critique of Kohlberg's reliance on male subjects, Carol Gilligan discovered that gender affects moral reasoning. Females, she claims, look to the effect of decisions on relationships; males rely more on abstract standards of rightness.

8. To George Herbert Mead, socialization is based on the emergence of the self, which he viewed as partly autonomous (the I) and partly guided by society (the me). Mead claimed that, beginning with imitation, the self develops through play and games and eventually recognizes the "generalized other."

9. Charles Horton Cooley used the term "looking-glass self" to underscore that the self is influenced by how we think others respond to us.

10. Erik H. Erikson identified characteristic challenges that individuals face at each stage of life from childhood to old age.

11. Commonly the first setting of socialization, the family has the greatest influence on a child's attitudes and behavior.

12. School exposes children to social diversity and introduces the experience of impersonal evaluation. In addition to formal lessons, schools informally teach a wide range of cultural ideas, including attitudes about competitiveness and achievement.

13. Members of youthful peer groups can escape the adult supervision they experience in the family and in school. Peer groups take on great significance among adolescents.

14. The mass media have a considerable impact on the socialization process. The average U.S. child now spends as much time watching television as attending school or interacting with parents.

15. As with each phase of the life course, the characteristics of childhood are socially constructed. Medieval Europeans scarcely recognized childhood as a stage of life. In rich industrial nations such as the United States, people define childhood as being much different from adulthood.

16. Adolescence, the transition between childhood and adulthood, is considered a difficult period in our society. This is not the case in all societies.

17. During early adulthood, socialization involves settling into careers and raising families. Later adulthood is marked by reflecting on earlier goals in light of actual achievements.

18. In old age, people make many transitions, including retirement. While the elderly in preindustrial societies typically enjoy high prestige, industrial societies are more youth oriented, relegating old people to the sidelines of life.

19. Members of rich societies typically fend off death until old age. Adjustment to the death of a spouse (an experience more common to women) and acceptance of one's own death are part of socialization for the elderly.

20. Total institutions such as prisons and mental hospitals have the goal of resocialization— radically changing the inmate's personality.

21. Socialization demonstrates the power of society to shape our thoughts, feelings, and actions. Yet, as free humans, we also have the capacity to act back on society and, in so doing, shape ourselves and our world.

KEY CONCEPTS

socialization the lifelong social experience by which individuals develop human potential and learn patterns of their culture

personality a person's fairly consistent patterns of thinking, feeling, and acting

id Freud's designation of the human being's basic drives

ego Freud's designation of a person's conscious efforts to balance innate pleasure-seeking drives with the demands of society

superego Freud's designation of the operation of culture within the individual in the form of internalized values and norms

sensorimotor stage Piaget's term for the level of human development in which individuals experience the world only through sensory contact

preoperational stage Piaget's term for the level of human development in which individuals first use language and other symbols

concrete operational stage Piaget's term for the level of human development at which individuals first perceive causal connections in their surroundings

formal operational stage Piaget's term for the level of human development at which individuals think abstractly and critically

self George Herbert Mead's term for a dimension of personality composed of an individual's self-awareness and self-image

looking-glass self Cooley's term for the image people have of themselves based on how they suppose others perceive them

generalized other George Herbert Mead's term for the general cultural norms and values shared by us and others that we use as a point of reference in evaluating ourselves

peer group a social group whose members have interests, social position, and age in common

anticipatory socialization social learning directed toward gaining a desired position

mass media impersonal communications directed toward a vast audience

cohort a category of people with a common characteristic, usually their age

total institution a setting in which people are isolated from the rest of society and manipulated by an administrative staff

resocialization radically altering an inmate's personality through deliberate manipulation of the environment

CRITICAL-THINKING QUESTIONS

1. What do cases of social isolation teach us about the importance of social experience to human development?

2. Present the two sides of the nature-nurture debate. In what sense are human nature and nurture not opposed to one another?

3. What common ideas are found in the theories of Freud, Piaget, Kohlberg, Gilligan, Mead, and Erikson? On what key points do they differ?

4. Proportionately, television features far more good-looking people than exist in the population as a whole. Develop arguments for and against this practice. How does it affect the way we think about others—and ourselves?

LEARNING EXERCISES

1. Along with several members of your sociology class, gather some data: Each person should ask a variety of classmates to identify traits they think are "human nature." Get together later to compare notes and assess the extent to which the traits noted are the product of "nature" or "nurture."

2. Find a copy of the book (or video) *Lord of the Flies*, William Golding's tale based on a Freudian model of personality. Jack (and his hunters) represent the power of the id; Piggy opposes them as the superego; Ralph stands between the two as the ego, the voice of reason. Golding wrote the book after participating in the bloody D-Day landing during World War II. Do you agree with his belief that violence (as well as our capacity for cultural restraint) is basic to human nature?

3. Think about your own personality traits and, if you have the courage, ask others who know you well what they think. To what extent did you learn these traits?

4. Watch several hours of prime-time television. Note every time any kind of violence is shown. For fun, assign each program a "YIP rating," for the number of Years In Prison one would serve for committing the violent acts you witness (Fobes, 1996). What are your conclusions?

5. If you have computer access, install the CD-ROM packaged inside the back cover of your text and complete the activities designed to accompany this chapter.

Paul Cadmus, *Mask With False Noses,* 1955
© Christie's Images.

SOCIAL INTERACTION
IN EVERYDAY LIFE

Harold and Sybil are on their way to another couple's home in an unfamiliar section of Rochester, New York. They are late because, for the last twenty minutes, they have been driving in circles looking for Creek View Drive. Harold, gripping the wheel ever more tightly, is doing a slow burn. Sybil, sitting next to him, looks straight ahead, afraid to utter a word. Both realize the evening is off to a bad start (Tannen, 1990:62).

Here we have what appears to be a simple case of two people unable to find their friends' home. But Harold and Sybil are also lost in another way: They fail to grasp why they are growing more and more upset with their situation and with each other.

Consider the predicament from Harold's point of view. Like most men, Harold cannot tolerate getting lost, so the longer he drives around, the more incompetent he feels. Sybil, on the other hand, cannot understand why Harold does not pull over and ask someone where Creek View Drive is. If she were driving, she fumes to herself, they already would have arrived and would now be comfortably settled with drink in hand.

Why don't men ask for directions? Because men value their independence, they are uncomfortable asking for help (and also reluctant to accept it). To men, asking for assistance is an admission of inadequacy, a sure sign that others know something they don't. If it takes Harold a few more minutes to find Creek View Drive on his own—and to keep his self-respect in the process—he thinks it's a good bargain.

If men pursue self-sufficiency and are sensitive to hierarchy, women are more attuned to others and strive for connectedness. From Sybil's point of view, sharing information reinforces social bonds. Asking for directions seems as natural to her as searching on his own is to Harold. Obviously, getting lost is sure to generate conflict as long as neither one understands the other's point of view.

Such examples of everyday life are the focus of this chapter. We begin by presenting the building blocks of common experience and then explore the almost magical way in which face-to-face interaction generates reality. The central concept is **social interaction,** *the process by which people act and react in relation to others.* Through social interaction, we create the reality we perceive. And we interact according to particular social guidelines.

SOCIAL STRUCTURE:
A GUIDE TO EVERYDAY LIVING

October 21, 1994, Ho Chi Minh City, Vietnam. This morning we leave the ship and make our way along the docks toward the center of Ho Chi Minh City—known to an earlier generation as Saigon. The government security

SUPPLEMENTS: An outline of Chapter 6, as well as supplemental lecture material and topics for class discussion, appear in the *Data File*.
Q: "When I use a word, it means just what I choose it to mean—nothing more nor less." Humpty Dumpty
Q: "A status, as distinct from the individual who may occupy it, is simply a collection of rights and duties." Ralph Linton (1937:113)

GLOBAL: Typically, members of rich societies have a larger status set than people in traditional countries for whom kinship represents the core of social organization.
NOTE: In reality, ascribed status and achieved status operate as two endpoints on a continuum.
Q: "Status and role serve to reduce the ideal patterns for social life to individual terms." Ralph Linton (1937:114)

In any rigidly ranked setting, no interaction can proceed until people assess each other's social standing. Thus, military personnel wear clear insignia to designate their level of authority. Don't we size up one another in much the same way in routine interactions, noting a person's rough age, quality of clothing, and manner for clues about social position?

Members of every society rely on social structure to make sense out of everyday situations. As one family's introduction to the streets of Vietnam suggests, the world can be disorienting—even frightening—when cultural norms are unclear. So what, then, are the building blocks of our daily lives?

STATUS

One basic element of social structure is **status,** *a recognized social position that an individual occupies.* Notice that the sociological meaning of the term "status" differs from its everyday meaning of "prestige." In common usage, a college president has more "status" than a professor. Sociologically, however, both "president" and "professor" are statuses because they represent socially defined positions, even though one confers more power and prestige than the other.

Every status involves particular duties, rights, and expectations. The statuses people occupy thus guide their behavior in any setting. In the college classroom, for example, professors and students have distinctive, well-defined responsibilities. Similarly, family interaction turns on the interplay of mother, father, daughters, sons, and others. In all these situations, statuses connect us to others, which is why, in the case of families, we commonly call others "relations." In short, a status defines who and what we are *in relation to* others.

Status is also a key component of social identity. Occupation, for example, is such a major part of most people's self-concept that it is often part of a social introduction. Similarly, long after retirement, many people still present themselves in terms of their life's work.

officers wave us through the heavy iron gates. Pressed against the fence surrounding the port are dozens of men with nearby cyclos (bicycles with a small carriage attached to the front), the Vietnamese equivalent of taxicabs. We decline the offers of rides but still spend the next twenty minutes fending off several persistent drivers, who cruise alongside us pleading for our business. The pressure is uncomfortable. We decide to cross the street but realize suddenly that there are no stop signs or signal lights—and the steet is an unbroken stream of bicycles, cyclos, motorbikes, and small trucks. What to do? We observe that the locals just walk at a steady pace across the street, parting waves of vehicles that close in again immediately behind them. Walk right into traffic? With our small children on our backs? Yup, we did it; that's the way it works in Saigon.

STATUS SET

Everyone occupies many statuses simultaneously. The term **status set** refers to *all the statuses a person holds at a given time.* A girl may be a *daughter* to her parents, a *sister* to her siblings, a *friend* to members of her social circle, and a *goalie* to others on her hockey team. Just as status sets branch out in many directions, they also change over the life course. A child grows into an adult, a student becomes a lawyer, people marry to become husbands and wives, and some become single again as a result of divorce or death. Joining an organization or finding a job enlarges our status set; withdrawing from activities makes it smaller. Over a lifetime, individuals gain and lose dozens of statuses.

Q: "It is crucial that responsibilities, resources, and rights be assigned to statuses, not to particular individuals. For only by doing so can societies establish general and uniform rules or norms that will apply to many and diverse individuals who are to occupy the statuses . . ." Melvin Tumin (1985:21)
NOTE: Statuses sometimes have differing consequences for social identity. Consider introducing the concept of *status consistency*—the

degree of consistency in social ranking—discussed in Chapter 10 ("Social Class in the United States").
NOTE: "Status" has two Latin roots: *Sta* is derived from *stare*, meaning "to stand"; *tus* means "the use of." Thus, status is literally "the use of standing." The term "role" appears to be derived from the French word *rôle*, meaning a roll (of paper) that contains an actor's part.

Role models teach young people that any one person can truly make a difference in our world. Forty years to the day after she was arrested for refusing to give up her seat on a Montgomery, Alabama, bus to a white person, Rosa Parks attended this celebration in that city's Carver High School. The children who attend Carver High today have far greater opportunities than did their parents and grandparents, thanks to the courage of people like Rosa Parks.

ASCRIBED AND ACHIEVED STATUS

Sociologists classify statuses in terms of how people obtain them. An **ascribed status** is *a social position that someone receives at birth or assumes involuntarily later in life.* Examples of ascribed statuses include being a daughter, a Cuban, a teenager, or a widower. Ascribed statuses are matters about which people have little or no choice.

By contrast, an **achieved status** refers to *a social position that someone assumes voluntarily and that reflects personal ability and effort.* Achieved statuses in the United States include being an honors student, an Olympic athlete, a spouse, a computer programmer, a member of Phi Beta Kappa, or a thief. In each case, the individual has at least some choice in the matter.

In practice, of course, most statuses reflect some combination of ascription and achievement. That is, people's ascribed statuses influence the statuses they achieve. People who achieve the status of lawyer, for example, are likely to share the ascribed trait of being born into relatively privileged families. In general, someone of a privileged sex, race, ethnicity, or age has far more opportunity to achieve desirable statuses than someone without such advantages. By contrast, many less desirable statuses, such as criminal, drug addict, or being unemployed, are more easily "achieved" by people born into poverty.

MASTER STATUS

Some statuses matter more than others. A **master status** is *a status that has exceptional importance for social identity, often shaping a person's entire life.* For most people, occupation is a master status because it conveys a great deal about social background, education, and income.

In a negative sense, serious disease can also operates as a master status. Sometimes even lifelong friends avoid cancer patients or people with acquired immune deficiency syndrome (AIDS) simply because of their illness. Most societies of the world also limit the opportunities of women, whatever their abilities, making gender, too, a master status.

Sometimes a physical disability serves as a master status to the point that we dehumanize people by perceiving them only in terms of their impairment. In the box, two people with physical disabilities describe this problem.

ROLE

A second major component of social interaction is **role,** *behavior expected of someone who holds a particular status.* Think of a role as the dynamic expression of a status: Individuals *hold* a status and *perform* a role (Linton, 1937). Holding the status of student, for example,

NOTE: Barbara Laslett (1978) points out that role conflict and role strain were probably more pronounced in the Middle Ages than they are today, because parents not only raised children but produced their food, schooled them, guided their worship, and saw to their health.

NOTE: Evidence of role conflict: The Families and Work Institute found that 25% of respondents (employees of Fortune 1000 companies) had refused overtime for family reasons; 24% refused travel for the same reason; 19% refused relocations; 10% refused promotions (*Wall Street Journal*, July 22, 1991:B1).

SOCIAL DIVERSITY

Physical Disability as Master Status

In the following interviews, two women explain how a physical disability can become a master status, defining an individual. The first voice is twenty-nine-year-old Donna Finch, who holds a master's degree in social work and lives with her husband and son in Muskogee, Oklahoma. She is also blind.

Most people don't expect handicapped people to grow up, they are always supposed to be children. . . . You aren't supposed to date, you aren't supposed to have a job, somehow you're just supposed to disappear. I'm not saying this is true of anyone else, but in my own case I think I was more intellectually mature than most children, and more emotionally immature. I'd say that not until the last four or five years have I felt really whole.

Rose Helman is an elderly woman living near New York City. She suffers from spinal meningitis and is also blind.

You ask me if people are really different today than in the '20s and

'30s. Not too much. They are still fearful of the handicapped. I don't know if fearful is the right word, but uncomfortable at least. But I can understand it somewhat; it happened to me. I once asked a man to tell me which staircase to use to get from the subway out to the street. He started giving me directions that were confusing, and I said, "Do you mind taking me?" He said, "Not at all." He grabbed me on the side with my dog on it, so I asked him to take my other arm. And he said, "I'm sorry, I have no other arm." And I said, "That's all right, I'll hold onto the jacket." It felt funny hanging onto the sleeve without the arm in it.

Source: Orlansky and Heward (1981).

leads one to attend classes and complete assignments and, more broadly, to devote much of one's time to personal enrichment through academic study.

Both statuses and roles vary by culture. In the United States, the status "uncle" refers to a sibling of either mother or father. In Vietnam, however, the word for "uncle" is different on the mother's and father's sides of the family, and uncles on each side have different responsibilities. In every society, too, actual role performance varies according to an individual's unique personality, although some societies permit more individual freedom than others.

ROLE SET

Because we occupy many statuses simultaneously, we perform multiple roles. Robert Merton (1968) introduced the term **role set** to identify *a number of roles attached to a single status.*

Figure 6–1 illustrates a status set and corresponding role sets for one individual. This woman occupies four statuses, and each has a different role set. First, she occupies the status of "wife," with a "conjugal role" toward her husband (such as confidante and sexual partner) and a "domestic role" toward the household, which she shares with her husband. Second, she holds the status of "mother," with responsibilities toward her children (the "maternal role") as well as their school and other organizations (the "civic role"). Third, as a professor, she interacts with students (the "teacher role") and other academics (the "colleague role"). Fourth, in her work as a researcher, she gathers data (the "laboratory role") that she then publishes (the "author role"). Of course, Figure 6–1 lists only some of this person's status and role sets, since an individual generally occupies several dozen statuses at one time, each linked to a role set. This woman might also be

Q: "For some types of role exit, society has coined a term to denote exiters: divorcé(e), retiree, recovered alcoholic, widow, alumnus. This is usually the case for exits that are common and have been occurring for a long time . . . In addition to these institutionalized exits, however, there are numerous exits that are simply referred to with the prefix "ex": ex-doctor, ex-executive, ex-nun, ex-convict . . ." Helen Rose Fuchs Ebaugh (1988:1)

Q: "We do not first see, then define; we define first, then see . . ." Walter Lippman

a daughter caring for aging parents, an avid gardener, and a member of the city council.

ROLE CONFLICT AND ROLE STRAIN

Since members of industrial societies hold various statuses and roles, they must juggle numerous responsibilities. And, as most mothers can testify, the dual roles of parenting as well as working outside the home are both physically and emotionally draining. Sociologists thus recognize **role conflict** as *incompatibility among roles corresponding to two or more statuses*.

We experience role conflict when we find ourselves pulled in various directions as we try to respond to the many statuses we hold. Sometimes we decide "something has to go." A governor, for example, may decide not to run for national office because the demands of a campaign would interfere with family life. In other cases, ambitious people wait to have children or choose to remain childless in order to stay on the "fast track" for career success.

Even the roles linked to a single status can make competing demands on us. **Role strain** refers to *incompatibility among roles corresponding to a single status*. A plant supervisor may enjoy being friendly with workers. But at the same time, the supervisor has production goals and must maintain the personal distance necessary to evaluate employees. In short, although not all cases of role strain present serious problems, performing the various roles attached to even one status can be something of a balancing act (Gigliotti & Huff, 1995).

One strategy for minimizing role conflict is "compartmentalizing" our lives so that we perform roles for one status at one time and place and carry out roles for another status in a completely different setting. A familiar example of this scheme is deciding to "leave the job at work" before heading home to one's family.

ROLE EXIT

After she herself left the life of a Catholic nun to become a university sociologist, Helen Rose Fuchs Ebaugh (1988) began to study *role exit*, the process by which people disengage from important social roles. In studying a range of "exes," including ex-nuns, ex-doctors, ex-husbands, and ex-alcoholics, Ebaugh saw a pattern in the process of "becoming an ex."

According to Ebaugh, people begin the process of role exit by reflecting on their lives and coming to doubt their ability to continue in a certain role. As

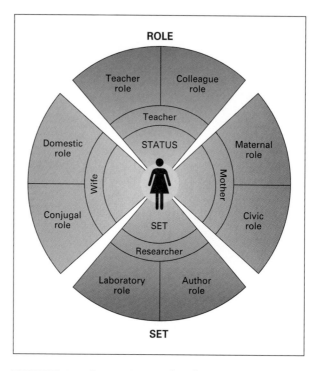

FIGURE 6–1 Status Set and Role Set

they imagine alternative roles, they ultimately reach a tipping point when they decide it is time to pursue a new life.

Even at this point, however, a past role can continue to influence our lives. "Exes" carry on a self-image shaped by an earlier role, which can interfere with building a new sense of self. An ex-nun, for example, may be reluctant to wear stylish clothing and makeup.

"Exes" must also rebuild relationships with people who knew them in their "earlier life." Learning new social skills is another challenge. For example, Ebaugh reports, nuns who begin dating after decades in the church are often startled to learn that sexual norms are very different from what they knew as teenagers.

THE SOCIAL CONSTRUCTION OF REALITY

More than fifty years ago, the Italian playwright Luigi Pirandello applied the sociological perspective to social interaction. In *The Pleasure of Honesty*, Angelo Baldovino—a brilliant man with a checkered past—

NOTE: Garfinkel's approach runs most directly counter to that of Talcott Parsons.

NOTE: Ethnomethodology has roots not only in symbolic interaction, but also in Alfred Schutz's phenomenology. Moreover, it shares with Berger and Luckmann's work an interest in the everyday round of life, not just a society's grand values or political ideologies.

NOTE: A curious fact about Erving Goffman is that, throughout his life, he permitted few people to photograph him. Thus, he remained essentially anonymous in public settings.

NOTE: In Goffman's sense, interior designers are professional "impression managers."

Around the world, culture frames the reality people experience. Most people living in rich countries such as the United States confront death only rarely. By contrast, these refugees in Rwanda—a poor nation shaken by violence and bloodshed—have been forced to accept death as a part of everyday life.

"methodology" designates a set of methods or principles. Combining them makes **ethnomethodology,** *the study of the way people make sense of their everyday lives.*

Ethnomethodology is largely the creation of Harold Garfinkel (1967), who sought to challenge the then-dominant view of society as a broad, abstract "system" (recall the approach of Emile Durkheim, described in Chapter 4, "Society"). Garfinkel wanted to explore how we make sense of countless familiar situations. Our talk and behavior, explained Garfinkel, rest on deeper assumptions about the world that, typically, we take quite for granted.

Think, for a moment, about what we assume in asking someone the simple question, "How are you?"

Do we mean physically? Mentally? Spiritually? Financially? Do we even want an answer, or are we "just being polite"?

Ethnomethodology, then, explores the process of making sense in social encounters. Because so much of the process is ingrained, Garfinkel argues that the only way to discover how we make sense of events is to purposefully *break the rules.* Deliberately ignoring conventional rules and observing how people respond, he suggests, allows us to tease out how people build a reality. Thus, Garfinkel (1967) directed his students to refuse to "play the game" in a wide range of situations. Some students living with their parents started acting as if they were boarders rather than children; others went to stores and insisted on bargaining for items; others invited people to play simple games (like tic-tac-toe) only to ignore the rules; still others began conversations while slowly moving closer and closer to the other person.

The students then reported on people's reactions to these rule violations. Typically, the "victims" became agitated, suggesting that even if reality is only something taken for granted, it is still very important to us. Trying to identify exactly *why* people were disturbed led students to consider the unspoken agreements that underlie family life, shopping, fair play, and the like.

Some sociologists view ethnomethodology as less-than-serious research because it focuses on commonplace experiences and employs unusual—even bizarre—methods. Still, ethnomethodology has heightened our awareness of many unnoticed patterns of everyday life.

REALITY BUILDING: SOME BROADER CONSIDERATIONS

People do not build everyday experience "out of thin air." In part, how we act or what we see in our surroundings depends on our interests. Scanning the night sky, for example, lovers discover romance, while scientists perceive the same stars as hydrogen atoms fusing into helium. Social background also directs our perceptions, since we build reality using elements in the surrounding culture. For this reason, residents of, say, Chicago's South Side encounter the world somewhat differently from people living along the city's affluent Gold Coast.

In truth, there are few common elements to the reality construction that goes on across the United States. Take baseball, long described as our "national pastime." Only about one-third of U.S. adults call

THE MAP: Areas of the United States in which minorities (and immigrants) predominate have relatively few baseball fans. In addition, baseball teams are located in large population centers, so that low-density states such as the Dakotas have relatively few fans.

DIVERSITY: Chinese American novelist Bette Bao Lord explains that, as an Asian American child in Brooklyn, she reconstructed the Pledge of Allegiance in the following way:

"I pledge allegiance to the frog
of the United States of America.
And to the wee puppet
for witch's hands.
One Asian, in the vestibule,
with little tea and just rice for all."
(quoted in *Newsweek*, July 6, 1992)

SEEING OURSELVES

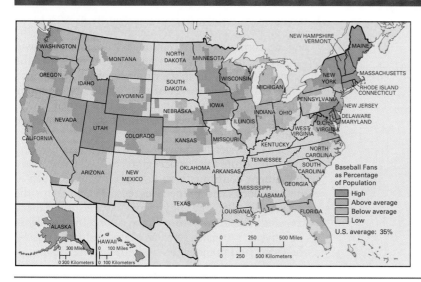

NATIONAL MAP 6–1
Baseball Fans
Across the United States

One in three U.S. adults claims to follow baseball. The map shows that fans are concentrated in the northern states from New England to the Pacific Northwest. Why? What categories of people have a world view that celebrates this kind of activity? (Hint: Baseball is more likely to appeal to white males over forty years of age who were born in the United States.)

Source: From Michael J. Weiss, *Latitudes & Attitudes: An Atlas of American Tastes, Trends, Politics, and Passions.* Copyright © 1994 by Michael J. Weiss. Reprinted by permission of the author.

themselves "fans" and, as National Map 6–1 indicates, they are concentrated in particular regions of the country.

In global perspective, reality construction is even more variable. Consider these everyday situations: People waiting for a bus in London typically "queue up" in a straight line; people in New York rarely are so orderly. The law forbids women in Saudi Arabia from driving a car, an unheard of idea in the United States. Fear of crime in our big cities is much greater than it is elsewhere—including London, Paris, Rome, Calcutta, and Hong Kong—and this sense of public danger shapes the daily realities of tens of millions of our citizens.

The general conclusion is that people build reality from the surrounding culture. Chapter 3 ("Culture") explained how people the world over see different meanings in specific gestures, so that travelers can find themselves building a most unexpected reality. Similarly, what we "see" in a book or a film also depends on the assumptions we make about the world. JoEllen Shively (1992) screened "western" films to men of European descent and Native American men. Both categories enjoyed the films but for different reasons. White men thought the films praised rugged people striking out for the West to impose their will on nature. Native American men, by contrast, saw a celebration of land and nature apart from any human ambitions.

If people the world over inhabit different realities, what about their chances for happiness? People living in high-income nations like the United States have reason to feel fortunate. And, as Figure 6–2 indicates, global survey data suggest that members of our society are happier than most.

Finally, what about the full range of human emotions? Are emotions generic and, therefore, much the same everywhere? Or is what we feel derived from our culture? Cross-cultural research, described in the box on pages 158–59, indicates that emotions are rooted in biology—and culture.

DRAMATURGICAL ANALYSIS: "THE PRESENTATION OF SELF"

Erving Goffman (1922–1982) contributed to our understanding of everyday life by comparing the way people interact to actors performing on a stage. If we imagine ourselves as directors observing what goes on in some situational "theater," we engage in what Goffman called **dramaturgical analysis,** *the investigation of social interaction in terms of theatrical performance.*

Dramaturgical analysis offers a fresh look at two now-familiar concepts, status and role. A status is like a part in a play, and a role serves as a script, supplying dialogue and action for the characters. Moreover, in any setting, a person is both the actor and audience.

RESOURCE: Erving Goffman's "The Presentation of Self" is among the classic selections included in the Macionis and Benokraitis reader, *Seeing Ourselves*.
GLOBAL: Figure 6–2 suggests that economic standard of living is one predictor of general happiness. But note the low percentage for Japan, suggesting that happiness is also a cultural phenomenon.

GLOBAL: Members of modern societies are more attuned to performances since our lives are divided into many spheres, each with different expectations. People in traditional societies, by contrast, have a more coherent identity.
Q: "Charm is the way of getting the answer yes without asking a clear question." Albert Camus

GLOBAL SNAPSHOT

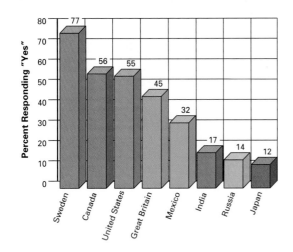

FIGURE 6–2 Happiness: A Global Survey

Survey Question: "We are interested in the way people are feeling these days. During the past few weeks, did you ever 'feel on top of the world,' feeling that life is wonderful?"
Source: *World Values Survey* (1994).

Goffman described an individual's "performance" as the **presentation of self,** *an individual's effort to create specific impressions in the minds of others.* Presentation of self, or *impression management,* has several distinctive elements (Goffman, 1959, 1967).

PERFORMANCES

As we present ourselves in everyday situations, we convey information—consciously and unconsciously—to others. One's performance includes dress (costume), objects carried along (props), and tone of voice and gestures (manner). In addition, people craft their performance according to the setting (stage). We may joke loudly in a bar, for example, but assume a reverent manner entering a church. Individuals may also design settings, such as a home or office, to enhance their performance and bring about desired reactions in others.

An Illustration: The Doctor's Office

Consider how a physician's office conveys information to an audience of patients. Physicians enjoy considerable prestige and power in the United States, which is immediately evident on entering a doctor's office. First, the physician is nowhere to be seen. Instead, in what Goffman describes as the "front region" of the setting, the patient encounters a receptionist who functions as a gatekeeper, deciding if and when the patient can see the physician. Who waits to see whom is, of course, a power game. And a simple survey of the doctor's waiting room, with patients (often impatiently) awaiting their call to the inner sanctum, leaves little doubt that the physician controls events.

The physician's private office and examination room constitute the "back region" of the setting. Here the patient confronts a wide range of props, such as medical books and framed degrees, that reinforce the impression that the physician has the specialized knowledge necessary to call the shots. In the office, the physician usually remains seated behind a desk—the larger and grander the desk, the greater the statement of power—while the patient is provided with only a chair.

The physician's appearance and manner convey still more information. The usual costume is a white lab coat, which may have the practical function of protecting clothes, but the social function is to let others know at a glance the physician's status. A stethoscope around the neck or a black medical bag in hand has the same purpose. A doctor's highly technical terminology—often mystifying to the patient—also emphasizes the hierarchy in the situation. Finally, patients use the title "doctor," but they are frequently addressed only by their first names, which further underscores the physician's dominant position. The overall message of a doctor's performance is clear: "I will help you only if you allow me to take charge."

NONVERBAL COMMUNICATION

Novelist William Sansom describes a fictional Mr. Preedy—an English vacationer on a beach in Spain:

He took care to avoid catching anyone's eye. First, he had to make it clear to those potential companions of his holiday that they were of no concern to him whatsoever. He stared through them, round them, over them—eyes lost in space. The beach might have been empty. If by chance a ball was thrown his way, he looked surprised; then let a smile of amusement light his face (Kindly Preedy), looked around dazed to see that there were people on the beach, tossed it back with a smile to himself and not a smile *at* the people. . . .

NOTE: Encountering others, interaction usually proceeds with "small talk," meaning that little is at stake. Only when sufficient information has been exchanged to guide more substantial discussion does "big talk" begin.

Q: "Male nonverbal communication has certain elements and effects that distinguish it from its female counterpart." Henley, Hamilton, and Thorne (1992:10)

NOTE: The words "person" and "mask" are derived from a single root: the Latin word *persona*. Perhaps the ancients well understood Goffman's insights.

NOTE: The fact that the slip of the tongue ("Freudian slip") is a clue to the unconscious is surely why Freud considered such clues to be so significant.

. . . [He] then gathered together his beach-wrap and bag into a neat sand-resistant pile (Methodical and Sensible Preedy), rose slowly to stretch his huge frame (Big-Cat Preedy), and tossed aside his sandals (Carefree Preedy, after all). (1956; quoted in Goffman, 1959:4–5)

Mr. Preedy offers a great deal of information about himself to anyone caring to observe him—without uttering a single word. His actions illustrate the process of **nonverbal communication,** *communication using, not speech, but body movements, gestures, and facial expressions.*

Virtually any part of the body can be used to transmit nonverbal communication. Facial expressions are the most significant form of "body language." As noted earlier, in the Global Sociology box, smiling and other facial gestures express basic emotions like pleasure, surprise, and anger the world over. People also express shades of meaning with their faces. We can distinguish, for example, between the deliberate smile of Kindly Preedy on the beach, a spontaneous smile of joy at seeing a friend, a pained smile of embarrassment, and a full, unrestrained smile of self-satisfaction that we associate with the "cat who ate the canary."

Eye contact is another important element of nonverbal communication. Generally, we use eye contact to invite social interaction. Someone across the room "catches our eye," for example, sparking a conversation. Avoiding eye contact, on the other hand, discourages communication. Hands, too, speak for us. Common hand gestures in our culture convey, among other things, an insult, a request for a ride, an invitation for someone to join us, or a demand that others stop in their tracks. Gestures also supplement spoken words. Pointing in a menacing way at someone, for example, intensifies a word of warning, as shrugging the shoulders adds an air of indifference to the phrase "I don't know," and rapidly waving the arms lends urgency to the single word "Hurry!"

Body Language and Deception

But, as any actor knows, the "perfect performance" is an elusive goal, not easily pulled off in front of a careful observer. In everyday performances, unintended body language can contradict our planned meaning. A teenage boy explains why he is getting home so late, for example, but his mother doubts his words because he avoids looking her in the eye. The movie star on a television talk show claims that her recent flop at the

When we enter the presence of others, we "construct" ourselves and begin a "presentation of self" that has much in common with a dramatic performance. Such a presentation involves clothing (costume), other objects (props), certain typical behavior (script), and it takes place in a particular setting (stage). No wonder the ancient Greeks, who understood the element of acting in everyday life, used the same word for "person" and "mask."

box office is "no big deal," but the nervous swing of her leg suggests otherwise. Nonverbal communication (most of which is not easily controlled) thus provides clues to deception, in much the same way that a lie detector records telltale changes in breathing, pulse rate, perspiration, and blood pressure.

Detecting lies is difficult, because no bodily gesture directly indicates deceit the way, say, a smile indicates pleasure. Even so, because a performance involves so many expressions, few people can lie without letting some piece of contradictory information slip by, arousing the suspicions of a careful observer. Therefore, the key to detecting deceit is to scan the whole performance with an eye for inconsistencies and discrepancies.

Specifically, Paul Ekman (1985) suggests scrutinizing four elements of a performance—words, voice, body language, and facial expression.

1. **Words.** Good liars can mentally rehearse their lines and manipulate words with ease. But they may not be able to avoid a simple slip of the

Q: "Emotions are shown primarily in the face, not in the body . . . there are facial patterns specific to each emotion." Paul Ekman
NOTE: Michael G. Flaherty (1988:25) describes the structural and emergent qualities of everyday life as situational "elasticity."

DIVERSITY: Research by Simon LeVay shows that women better recognize emotions in facial expressions than men do (cf. Begley, 1995).
DISCUSS: Ask students who have lived in other countries to comment on the three global variables described in this box.

GLOBAL SOCIOLOGY

Emotions in Global Perspective: Do We All Feel the Same?

On a New York sidewalk, a woman reacts angrily to a roller-blader who hurtles past her. Apart from a few choice words, her facial expression broadcasts a strong emotion that North Americans easily recognize. But would an observer from Nigeria, Nicaragua, or New Guinea interpret her emotion as anger? In other words, do all people share similar feelings, and do they express them in the same way?

Paul Ekman (1980) and his colleagues studied emotional life in a number of countries—even among members of a small society in New Guinea. From this research, they concluded that people the world over share six basic emotions: anger, fear, disgust, happiness, surprise, and sadness. Moreover, people everywhere express these feelings using the same distinctive facial gestures. To Ekman, this commonality is evidence that much of our emotional life is universal—rather than culturally variable—and that how we display emotion is biologically programmed in our facial features, muscles, and central nervous system.

But Ekman notes three ways in which emotional life does differ from culture to culture. First, *what triggers an emotion varies from one society to another*. Whether people define a particular situation as an insult (causing anger), a loss (calling out sadness), or a mystical event (bringing surprise and awe) depends on culture. In other words, people in various societies might react quite differently to the same event.

Second, *people display emotions according to the norms of their culture*. Every society has rules about when, where, and to whom an individual may exhibit certain emotions. People in the United States typically express emotions more freely among family members at home than among colleagues in the workplace. Similarly, we expect children to express emotions to parents, although parents are taught to guard their emotions in front of children.

Third, *societies differ in terms of how people cope with emotions*. Some societies encourage the expression of feelings, but others play down emotion and expect members to hide their feelings. Gender plays a part here, too. In the

United States, most people regard emotional expression as feminine, expected of women but a sign of weakness among men. In other societies, however, sex typing of emotions is less pronounced or even reversed.

In sum, emotional life in global perspective has both common and variable elements. People the world over experience the same basic emotions. Witnessing our angry New Yorker who opened this box, an individual from New Guinea would comprehend her expression right away. But what sparks a particular emotion, how and where a person expresses it, and how people define emotions in general all vary as matters of culture. In global perspective, therefore, everyday life differs not only in terms of how people think and act, but how they infuse their lives with feeling.

Sources: Ekman (1980a; 1980b), Lutz & White (1986), and Lutz (1988).

---

tongue. For example, a young man trying to deceive his parents by claiming that his roommate is a male friend rather than a female lover might inadvertently refer to "her" rather than "him." The more complicated the deception, the more likely a performer is to make a revealing mistake.

2. **Voice.** Tone and patterns of speech contain clues to deception because they are hard to

control. Someone trying to hide a powerful emotion, for example, cannot easily prevent the voice from trembling or breaking. On different occasions the same person may speak more quickly (suggesting anger) or slowly (indicating sadness) than usual. Nervous laughter, inappropriate pauses between words, or nonwords, such as "ah" and "ummm," also hint at discomfort.

To most people in the United States, these expressions convey anger, fear, disgust, happiness, surprise, and sadness. But do people elsewhere in the world define them in the same way? Research suggests that all human beings experience the same basic emotions and display them to others in the same basic ways. But culture plays a part by specifying the situations that trigger one emotion or another.

3. **Body language.** A "leak" of body language may tip off an observer to deception as well. Subtle body movements, for example, give the impression of nervousness, as does sudden swallowing or rapid breathing. These are especially good clues to deception because few people can control them. Sometimes, *not* using the body in the expected way to enhance words—as when a person tries to fake excitement—also suggests deception.

4. **Facial expressions.** Because facial expressions are hard to control, they give away many phony performances, as indicated by Figure 6–3. A sad person feigning happiness, for example, "flashes" momentary frowns through a crooked smile. Raising and drawing together the eyebrows signals genuine fear or worry, since this expression is virtually impossible to make willfully.

DISCUSS: Ask members of the class to identify other social situations that are "gendered." Can they identify any that are *not* "gendered"?

Q: "A woman's sex is treated as the most salient characteristic of her being; this is not the case for males." Henley, Hamilton, & Thorne

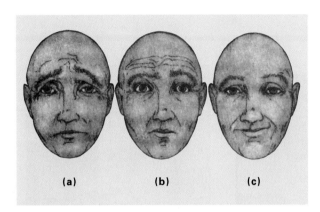

(a)   (b)   (c)

FIGURE 6–3 Which Is an "Honest Face"?

Telling lies is no easy task because most people cannot manipulate all their facial muscles. Looking at the three faces above, the expression of grief in sketch (a) is probably genuine, since few people can deliberately lift the upper eyelids and inner corners of the eyebrows in this way. Likewise, the apprehension displayed in (b) also appears authentic, since intentionally raising the eyebrows and pulling them together is nearly impossible. People who fake emotions usually do a poor job of it, as illustrated by the phony expression of pleasure shown in (c). Genuine delight, for most people, would produce a balanced smile.

In sum, lies are detectable, but training is the key to noticing relevant clues. Also important is knowing the person well, which is why parents can usually spot deceit in their children. Finally, almost anyone can unmask deception when the liar is trying to cover up strong emotions.

GENDER AND PERSONAL PERFORMANCES

Because women are socialized to be less assertive than men, they tend to be especially sensitive to nonverbal communication. In fact, gender is a central element in personal performances. Using the work of Nancy Henley, Mykol Hamilton, and Barrie Thorne (1992), we can extend our discussion of personal performances to spotlight the importance of gender.

Demeanor

Demeanor—that is, general conduct or deportment—reflects a person's level of social power. Simply put, powerful people enjoy far greater freedom in how they act; subordinates act more formally and self-consciously.

Off-color remarks, swearing, or casually removing shoes and putting feet up on the desk may be acceptable for the boss, but rarely for employees. Similarly, people in positions of dominance can interrupt others whenever they wish, while subordinates are expected to display deference by remaining silent (Smith-Lovin & Brody, 1989; Henley, Hamilton, & Thorne, 1992; Johnson, 1994).

Since women generally occupy positions of lesser power, demeanor is a gender issue as well. As Chapter 12 ("Sex and Gender") explains, about half of all working women in the United States hold clerical or service jobs that put them under the control of supervisors, who are usually men. Women, then, craft their personal performances more carefully than men and defer more often in everyday interaction.

Use of Space

How much space does a personal performance require? Here again, power plays a key role, since using more space conveys a nonverbal message of personal importance. According to Henley, Hamilton, and Thorne (1992), men typically command more space than women, whether pacing back and forth before an audience or casually lounging on a beach. Why? Our culture traditionally has measured femininity by how *little* space women occupy (the standard of "daintiness") and masculinity by how *much* territory a man controls (the standard of "turf").

The concept of **personal space** refers to *the surrounding area to which an individual makes some claim to privacy*. In the United States, people typically position themselves several feet apart when speaking; throughout the Middle East, by contrast, people stand much closer.

Throughout the world, gender further modifies patterns of personal space. In daily life, men often intrude on the personal space of women. A woman's movement into a man's personal space, however, is likely to be construed as a sexual overture. Here again, women have less power in everyday interaction than men do.

Staring, Smiling, and Touching

Eye contact encourages interaction. Typically, women employ eye contact to sustain conversation more than men do. Men have their own distinctive brand of eye contact: staring. When men stare at women, they are claiming social dominance and defining women as sexual objects.

NOTE: Use of space is another pattern subject to cultural interpretation (or misinterpretation). Across North Africa, from Cairo to Casablanca, people routinely move to within a foot or two when speaking in public. The U.S. traveler may consider such "in your face" behavior provocative, which it is not necessarily.

Q: "If we never tried to seem a little better than we are, how could we improve or 'train ourselves from the outside inward'?" Charles Horton Cooley (1964:352; orig. 1902)

Near the end of his life, Erving Goffman (1979) studied the place of gender in advertising—that is, how advertising portrays the relative social position of men and women. Look at this Pepsi ad from an earlier era: What messages does it convey about women and men? Do you think today's advertising is different in this regard? (See a recent ad for Diet Coke on page 326.)

Although frequently conveying pleasure, smiling has a host of other meanings, as well. In a male-dominated world, women often smile to make peace or indicate submission. For this reason, Henley, Hamilton, and Thorne maintain, women smile more than men; in extreme cases, smiling may become a nervous habit.

Finally, touching offers another gender-linked pattern. Mutual touching usually conveys intimacy and caring. Apart from close relationships, however, touching is generally something men do to women (although rarely, in our culture, to other men). A male physician touches the shoulder of his female nurse as they examine a report, a young man touches the back of his woman friend as he guides her across the street, or a male skiing instructor looks for opportunities to touch his female students. In these examples—and many others—touching may evoke little response, so common is it in everyday life. But it amounts to a subtle ritual by which men claim dominance over women.

IDEALIZATION

Complex motives underlie human behavior. Even so, Goffman suggests, we construct performances to *idealize* our intentions. That is, we try to convince others (and perhaps ourselves) that what we do reflects ideal cultural standards rather than more selfish motives.

Idealization is easily illustrated by returning to the world of physicians and patients. In a hospital, physicians engage in a performance known as "making rounds." Entering the patient's room, the physician often stops at the foot of the bed and silently examines the patient's chart. Afterward, physician and patient talk briefly. In ideal terms, the physician is making a personal visit to inquire about a patient's condition.

In reality, the picture is not so perfect. A physician who sees several dozen patients a day may remember little about most of them, so reading the chart is an opportunity to rediscover the patient's identity and medical problems. Revealing the impersonality of much medical care would undermine the culturally ideal perception of the physician as deeply concerned about the welfare of others.

Idealization is woven into the fabric of everyday life in countless ways. Physicians, college professors, and other professionals typically idealize their motives for entering their chosen careers. They describe their work as "making a contribution to science," "helping others," "answering a calling from God," or perhaps "serving the community." Rarely do people admit the

NOTE: "Embarrass" is derived from words meaning "to block or obstruct." "Tact" is derived from the Latin *tact(us)* meaning "sense of touch."

GLOBAL: There is little comparative data regarding tact. But, logically, one imagines that traditional societies engage in less of it, since reality is more well established.

GLOBAL: Worth noting is the fact that English does not follow the pattern of romance languages of designating all nouns as either female or male.

DISCUSS: Why are boys—but not girls—designated as Jr., II, III, etc.?

NOTE: "Androcentrism" is a masculine bias—in this case, of language. (*Andro* is Greek, meaning "male.")

Hand gestures vary widely from one culture to another. Yet people everywhere define a chuckle, grin, or smirk in response to someone's performance as an indication that one does not take another person seriously. Therefore, the world over, people who cannot restrain their mirth tactfully cover their faces.

less honorable, although common, motives of seeking the income, power, prestige, and leisure that these occupations confer.

More generally, idealization is the basis of social civility, since we smile and make polite remarks to people we do not like. Such little lies ease our way through social interactions. Even when we suspect that others are putting on an act, we are unlikely to challenge openly their performances, for reasons that we shall explain next.

EMBARRASSMENT AND TACT

The eminent professor consistently mispronounces the dean's name; the visiting dignitary rises from the table to speak, unaware of the napkin that still hangs from her neck; the president becomes ill at a state dinner. As carefully as individuals may craft their performances, slipups of all kinds frequently occur. The result is *embarrassment*, which, in dramaturgical terms, means the discomfort that follows a spoiled performance. Goffman describes embarrassment as "losing face."

Embarrassment is an ever-present danger because, first, all performances typically contain some deception. Second, most performances involve a complex array of elements, any one of which, in a thoughtless moment, can shatter the intended impression.

A curious fact is that an audience often overlooks flaws in a performance, thereby allowing an actor to avoid embarrassment. If we do point out a misstep ("Excuse me, but did you know your fly is open?"), we do it discretely and only to help someone avoid even

greater loss of face. In Hans Christian Andersen's classic fable "The Emperor's New Clothes," the child who blurts out that the emperor is parading about naked tells the truth but is scolded for being rude.

Even more often, according to Goffman, members of an audience help the performer recover from flaws in a performance. *Tact*, then, amounts to helping another person "save face." After hearing a supposed expert make an embarrassingly inaccurate remark, for example, people may tactfully ignore the comment as if it was never spoken at all. Or, mild laughter may indicate they wish to treat what they have heard as a joke. Or a listener may simply respond, "I'm sure you didn't mean that," acknowledging the statement but not allowing it to damage the actor's performance.

Why is tact such a common response? Because embarrassment provokes discomfort not simply for one person but for *everyone*. Just as the entire audience feels uneasy when an actor forgets a line, people who observe awkward behavior are reminded of how fragile their own performances are. Socially constructed reality thus functions like a dam holding back a sea of chaos. Should one person's performance spring a leak, others tactfully help make repairs. Everyone, after all, jointly engages in building reality, and no one wants it to be suddenly swept away.

In sum, Goffman's research shows that, while behavior is spontaneous in some respects, it is more patterned than we like to think. Almost 400 years ago, William Shakespeare captured this idea in lines that still ring true:

NOTE: The value function of language is also evident in terms such as "lady doctor," which suggest an exceptional case.

DISCUSS: What is the symbolism of a married woman choosing to use her husband's last name or to keep her own last name? A 1994 survey found 10% of married women use their own names. Those who do are typically highly educated, young, and relatively affluent.

GLOBAL: In Japan, reports Ellen Rudolph (1991), women display their greater subservience to men by speaking more quietly, looking down, and employing more deferential language.

DIVERSITY: "Widower" is the derivative term (from "widow") suggesting that marital standing is a master status for women more than for men.

All the world's a stage,
And all the men and women merely players:
They have their exits and their entrances;
And one man in his time plays many parts. . . .
(*As You Like It*, II)

INTERACTION IN EVERYDAY LIFE: TWO ILLUSTRATIONS

We have now examined the major elements of social interaction. The final sections of this chapter focus on two important elements of everyday life: language and humor.

LANGUAGE: THE GENDER ISSUE

As Chapter 3 ("Culture") explains, language is the thread that joins members of a society in the symbolic web we call culture. In everyday life, language conveys meaning on more than one level. Besides the obvious message in what people say, a host of additional meanings are embedded in our system of language. One such message involves gender. Language defines men and women differently in at least three ways—in terms of control, value, and attention.[1]

Language and Control

A young man astride his new motorcycle rolls proudly into the gas station and eagerly asks, "Isn't she a beauty?" On the surface, the question has little to do with gender. Yet, it is curious that a common linguistic pattern confers the female "she," and never the male "he," on a man's prized possession.

As we suggested at the beginning of this chapter, the language men use often reveals their concern with competence and control. In this case, a man attaches a female pronoun to a motorcycle (car, boat, or other object) because it reflects *ownership*.

A more obvious control function of language relates to people's names. Traditionally in the United States and in many other parts of the world, a woman takes the family name of the man she marries. While few people consider this an explicit statement of a

man's ownership of a woman, many believe that it reflects male dominance. For this reason, an increasing share of married women (currently 10 percent) have kept their own names or merged two family names (Brightman, 1994).

Language and Value

Language usually treats as masculine whatever has greater value, force, or significance. Although we may not think much about it, this pattern is deeply rooted in the English language. For instance, the adjective "virtuous," meaning "morally worthy" or "excellent," is derived from the Latin word *vir* meaning "man." By contrast, the adjective "hysterical," meaning excessive or uncontrollable emotion, is derived from the Greek word *hyster*, meaning "uterus."

In numerous, more familiar ways, language also confers different value on the two sexes. Traditional masculine terms such as "king" or "lord" have kept their positive meaning, while comparable terms, such as "queen," "madam," or "dame" have acquired negative connotations. Thus, language both mirrors social attitudes and helps to perpetuate them.

Similarly, the suffixes "ette" and "ess" to indicate femininity generally devalue the words to which they are added. For example, a "major" has higher standing than a "majorette," as does a "host" in relation to a "hostess." And, certainly, men's groups with names like the St. Louis Rams carry more stature than women's groups with names like the Radio City Music Hall Rockettes.

Language and Attention

Language also shapes reality by directing greater attention to masculine endeavors. The most obvious example is our use of personal pronouns. In the English language, the plural pronoun "they" is neutral as it refers to both sexes. But the corresponding singular pronouns "he" and "she" specify gender. Traditional grammar uses "he" along with the possessive "his" and objective "him" to refer to all people. Thus, we assume that the bit of wisdom "He who hesitates is lost" refers to women as well as to men. But choosing the masculine to represent all people reflects a larger cultural pattern of neglecting the lives of women.

The English language has no gender-neutral, third-person singular pronoun. In recent years, however, the plural pronouns "they" and "them" are increasingly used

---

[1] The following sections draw primarily from Henley, Hamilton, & Thorne (1992). Additional material comes from Thorne, Kramarae, & Henley (1983), and others as noted.

NOTE: Laughter also accompanies tickling. This is a disruption of what is conventional in a physical sense; tickling is also an ambiguous situation in which one does not know if the other's motives are loving or aggressive.

NOTE: Example of the audience having to "finish a joke" is the line Woody Allen directed to some guy who backed into his car: "Be fruitful and multiply—but not in those words."

NOTE: The link between humor and contrasting realities is inherent in the Monty Python troupe's signature line, "And now for something completely different."

NOTE: Humor can also be generated by leading an audience to expect two incongruent realities, one of which fails to materialize. Groucho Marx once quipped: "I worked myself up from nothing to a state of extreme poverty . . ."

of voice. In one of his films, for example, Groucho swaggers up to a young woman and brags, "This morning I shot a lion in my pajamas!" Then, dropping his voice and turning to the camera, he adds, "What the lion was doing in my pajamas *I'll never know . . .*" Such "changing channels" underscores the incongruity of the two parts. Following the same logic, many stand-up comics also "reset" the audience to conventional expectations by interjecting "But, seriously, folks . . ." after one joke and before the next one.

To construct the strongest contrast in meaning, comedians pay careful attention to their performances—the precise words they use and the timing of their delivery. A joke is "well told" if the comic creates the sharpest possible opposition between the realities, just as humor falls flat in a careless performance. Since the key to humor lies in the opposition of realities, it is not surprising that the climax of a joke is termed the "*punch* line."

The Dynamics of Humor: "Getting It"

Failing to understand both the conventional and unconventional realities embedded in a joke, the listener often complains, "I don't get it." To "get" humor, the audience must understand the two realities involved well enough to see why they are incompatible.

But getting a joke can be more challenging still, because comics may deliberately omit important information. The audience, therefore, must pay attention to the stated elements of the joke, and then fill in the missing pieces on their own. As a simple case, consider movie producer Hal Roach's comment on his one hundredth birthday:

> "If I had known I would live to be one hundred, I would have taken better care of myself!"

Here, "getting" the joke depends on realizing that Roach must have taken pretty good care of himself since he lived to be one hundred in the first place. Or take one of W. C. Fields's lines "Some weasel took the cork out of my lunch." "Some lunch!" we think to ourselves to "finish" the joke.

Of course, some jokes demand more mental effort than others. The following example was written on the wall of a college restroom:

> "Dyslexics of the World, Untie!"

To get this one, you must know, first, that people with dyslexia routinely reverse letters; second, you must identify the line as an adaptation of Karl Marx's

call to the world's workers to unite; third, you must recognize "untie" as an anagram of "unite," written as a disgruntled dyslexic person might write it.

Why would an audience want to make this sort of effort in order to understand a joke? Simply because our enjoyment of a joke is heightened by the pleasure of having completed the puzzle necessary to "get it." In addition, understanding a complex joke confers a favored status as an "insider" in the larger audience. These insights also explain the frustration of *not* getting a joke: the fear of mental inadequacy coupled with a sense of being socially excluded from a pleasure shared by others. Not surprisingly, "outsiders" in such a situation may fake "getting" the joke, or someone may tactfully explain a joke to end another's sense of being left out.

But, as the old saying goes, if a joke has to be explained, it won't be very funny. Besides taking the edge off the language and timing on which the *punch* depends, an explanation removes the mental involvement, and greatly reduces the listener's pleasure.

The Topics of Humor

People throughout the world smile and laugh, which makes humor a universal human trait. But the world's people differ in what they find funny, so humor does not travel well.

```
October 1, 1994, Kobe, Japan. Can you
share a joke with people who live halfway
around the world? At dinner, I ask two
Japanese college women to tell me a joke.
"You know 'crayon'?" Asako asks. I nod.
"How do you ask for a crayon in Japanese?"
I respond that I have no idea. She laughs
out loud as she says what sounds like
"crayon crayon." Her companion Mayumi
laughs, too. My wife and I sit awkwardly
straight-faced. Asako relieves some of
our embarrassment by explaining that the
Japanese word for "give me" is kureyo,
which sounds like "crayon." I force a
smile. . . .
```

What is humorous to the Japanese, then, may be lost on the Chinese, Iraqis, or people in the United States. To some degree, too, the social diversity of our own country means that people will find humor in different situations. New Englanders, southerners, and westerners have their own unique brands of humor, as

Q: "Most weight lifters are biceptual." John Rostoni
NOTE: Examples for eliciting the pleasure of "getting" jokes: What campus departments or offices would use these call letters for their radio station? WIXL (honors program); WSOS (security office); WURU (counseling service); WYMI (philosophy department); WYYY (religion department); WYRU (sociology department). (Barry Glassner and John Western)

NOTE: Some topics, in other words, are "off limits," because people expect them to be understood in only one way. The death of Princess Diana was such a case. No "sick" jokes have yet circulated since the tragedy.
NOTE: Here's an example of a one-line joke bordering on "sick": "Hey, do you know if, when you shoot a mime, you're supposed to use a silencer?"

do Latinos and Anglos, fifteen- and forty-year-olds, Wall Street bankers and hard-hat construction workers.

But, for everyone, humor deals with topics that lend themselves to double meanings or generate *controversy*. For example, the first jokes many of us learned when we were children concerned the great cultural taboo, sex. The mere mention of "unmentionable acts" or even certain parts of the body can dissolve young faces in laughter. Are there jokes that break through the culture barrier? Yes, but they must touch upon universal human experiences such as, say, turning on a friend.

```
 . . . I think of a number of jokes, but
none seems likely to work. So many of
our jokes are ethnic, and the two Japan-
ese women, not grasping much about the
U.S. cultural mix, would never connect.
Inspiration: "Two fellows are walking
in the woods and come upon a huge bear.
One guy leans over and tightens up the
laces on his running shoes. 'Jake,'
says the other, 'what are you doing? You
can't outrun this bear!' 'I don't have
to outrun the bear,' responds Jake, 'I
just have to outrun you!' Smiles all
around.
```

The controversy found in humor often walks a fine line between what is funny and what is considered "sick." During the Middle Ages, the word *humors* (derived from the Latin *humidus*, meaning "moist") referred to a balance of bodily fluids that regulated a person's health. Today's researchers have provided scientific evidence that "Laughter is the best medicine," because maintaining a sense of humor reduces a person's level of unhealthy stress (Robinson, 1983; Haig, 1988). At the extreme, however, people who always take conventional reality lightly risk being defined as deviant or even mentally ill (a common stereotype depicts insane people laughing uncontrollably, and we have long dubbed mental hospitals "funny farms").

And then there are certain topics that every social group considers too sensitive for humorous treatment. Of course, one can joke about such things, but doing so courts criticism for telling a "sick" joke (and, therefore, *being* sick). People's religious beliefs, tragic accidents, or appalling crimes are the stuff of "sick" jokes.

Because humor involves challenging established social conventions, most U.S. comedians—including the comic Sinbad—have been social "outsiders," members of racial and ethnic minorities.

The Functions of Humor

If humor is a cultural universal, it must make some serious contribution to social life. From a structural-functional perspective, humor operates as a social "safety valve," allowing people to release disruptive sentiments safely. Put another way, humor provides a way of discussing cultural taboos, from sex to prejudice to hostility toward parents.

Having strayed into controversy, an individual also can use humor to diffuse the situation. If an audience considers a remark offensive, a speaker can simply say, "I didn't mean anything by what I said; it was just a joke!" Likewise, an audience can use humor as a form of tact, smiling, as if to say, "We could take offense at what you said, but we'll assume you were only kidding."

Like theater and art, humor allows a society to challenge established ideas and to explore alternatives to the status quo. Sometimes, in fact, humor can actually promote social change because, by "taking things lightly," we loosen the hold of convention.

GLOBAL: Illustrating the use of humor to critique society, Soviets used to joke "We pretend to work, and they pretend to pay us . . ."

NOTE: Two simple examples to illustrate the elements of humor:

   #1: "What do you get when you cross the Atlantic with the *Titanic?*"

   #2: "I dunno, what?"

   #1: "About halfway . . ."

An elderly Jewish woman in a Miami park sees a new face sitting on a bench. "I haven't seen you before," she says by way of an overture. "I just finished forty years in jail," he replies. "What did you do?" "I killed my wife." "So," she concludes hopefully, "you're *single* . . ."

NOTE: Laughing at one's own joke is rather rude or odd, because there is no punch at all.

Humor and Conflict

If humor holds the potential to liberate those who laugh, it can also be used to oppress others. Men who tell jokes about women, for example, typically are expressing hostility towards them (Powell & Paton, 1988; Benokraitis & Feagin, 1995). Similarly, jokes at the expense of gay people reveal the tensions surrounding sexual orientation in the United States. Humor is often a sign of conflict in situations where one or both parties choose not to bring the discord out into the open (Primeggia & Varacalli, 1990).

"Put-down" jokes may make one category of people feel good, but at the expense of another. After analyzing jokes from many societies, Christie Davies (1990) concluded that conflict between ethnic groups is one force behind humor virtually everywhere. The typical ethnic joke makes fun of some disadvantaged category of people, thereby making the jokester and audience feel superior. Given the Anglo-Saxon traditions of U.S. society, Poles and other ethnic and racial minorities have long been the butt of jokes, as have

Newfoundlanders in eastern Canada, the Irish in Scotland, Sikhs in India, Turks in Germany, Hausas in Nigeria, Tasmanians in Australia, and Kurds in Iraq.

Disadvantaged people, of course, also make fun of the powerful, though usually more discreetly. Women in the United States joke about men, just as African Americans find humor in white people's ways, and poor people poke fun at the rich. Throughout the world, people target their leaders with humor, and officials often take such jokes seriously enough to suppress them.

In sum, the significance of humor is much greater than we may think. Humor amounts to a means of mental escape from a conventional world that is never entirely to our liking (Flaherty, 1984, 1990; Yoels & Clair, 1995). Indeed, this idea would explain why so many of our nation's comedians come from the ranks of historically oppressed peoples, including Jews and African Americans. As long as we maintain a sense of humor, we assert our freedom and are not prisoners of reality. And, by putting a smile on our faces, we change the world and ourselves just a little.

SUMMARY

1. Social structure provides guidelines for behavior, making everyday life understandable and predictable.

2. A major component of social structure is status. Within an entire status set, a master status has particular significance.

3. Ascribed statuses are essentially involuntary, while achieved statuses are largely earned. In practice, however, many statuses incorporate elements of both ascription and achievement.

4. Role is the dynamic expression of a status. The incompatibility of roles corresponding to two or more statuses generates role conflict; likewise, incompatible roles linked to a single status produce role strain.

5. The phrase "social construction of reality" refers to the idea that we build the social world through our interaction.

6. The Thomas theorem states, "Situations defined as real become real in their consequences."

7. Ethnomethodology seeks to reveal the assumptions and understandings people have of their social world.

8. Dramaturgical analysis studies how people construct their personal behavior. This approach casts everyday life in terms of theatrical performances, noting how people try to create particular impressions in the minds of others, the settings of interaction, and how performers often idealize their intentions.

9. Social power affects performances; our society's general subordination of women causes them to craft their behavior differently than men do.

10. Social behavior carries the constant risk of embarrassment. Tact is a common response to a "loss of face" by others.

11. Language is vital to the process of socially constructing reality. In various ways, language defines females and males differently, generally to the advantage of males.

12. Humor stems from the contrast between conventional and unconventional definitions of a situation. Because humor exists within specific cultures, people throughout the world find different situations funny.

EXERCISE: For better students, an interesting task is to read Luigi Pirandello's play *The Pleasure of Honesty* as a study of reality construction. Have students write a short essay, based on the play, in which they analyze what "honesty" in social interaction really means.

KEY CONCEPTS

social interaction the process by which people act and react in relation to others

status a recognized social position that an individual occupies

status set all the statuses a person holds at a given time

ascribed status a social position that someone receives at birth or assumes involuntarily later in life

achieved status a social position that someone assumes voluntarily and that reflects personal ability and effort

master status a status that has exceptional importance for social identity, often shaping a person's entire life

role behavior expected of someone who holds a particular status

role set a number of roles attached to a single status

role conflict incompatibility among roles corresponding to two or more statuses

role strain incompatibility among roles corresponding to a single status

social construction of reality the process by which people creatively shape reality through social interaction

Thomas theorem W. I. Thomas's assertion that situations we define as real become real in their consequences

ethnomethodology Harold Garfinkel's term for the study of the way people make sense of their everyday lives

dramaturgical analysis Erving Goffman's term for the investigation of social interaction in terms of theatrical performance

presentation of self an individual's effort to create specific impressions in the minds of others

nonverbal communication communication using body movements, gestures, and facial expressions as opposed to speech

personal space the surrounding area to which an individual makes some claim to privacy

CRITICAL-THINKING QUESTIONS

1. Consider ways in which a physical disability can serve as a master status. How do people commonly characterize, say, a person with cerebral palsy with regard to mental ability? With regard to sexuality?

2. How do people on a first date commonly present themselves and construct reality?

3. George Jean Nathan once quipped, "I only drink to make other people interesting." What does this mean in terms of reality construction? Can you identify the elements of humor in his comment?

4. Here is a joke about sociologists: "Question— How many sociologists does it take to change a light bulb? Answer—None, because there is nothing wrong with the light bulb; it's *the system* that needs to be changed!" What makes this joke funny? What sort of people are likely to "get it"? What kind of people probably won't? Why?

LEARNING EXERCISES

1. Write down as many of your own statuses as you can. Do you consider any a master status? To what extent is each of your statuses ascribed and achieved?

2. During the next twenty-four hours, every time someone asks "How are you?" stop and actually give an honest answer. What happens when you respond to a "polite" question in an unexpected way?

3. This chapter illustrates Erving Goffman's ideas by describing a physician's office. Analyze the offices of several professors in the same way. What furniture is there and how is it arranged? What "props"

do professors use? How are the offices of physicians and professors different? Why?

4. Spend an hour or two walking around the business district of your town or a local mall. Observe the presence (or absence) of women and men in each business. Based on your observations, would you conclude that physical space is "gendered"?

5. If you have computer access, install the CD-ROM packaged inside the back cover of your text and complete the activities designed to accompany this chapter.

Ed McGowin, *Society Telephone Society,* 1989
Oil on canvas with carved and painted wood frame, 54" × 54". © Ed McGowin 1997.

CHAPTER 7

GROUPS AND ORGANIZATIONS

Sixty years ago, the opening of a new restaurant in Pasadena, California, attracted little attention from the local community and went unnoticed by the nation as a whole. Yet this seemingly insignificant enterprise, owned and operated by Mac and Dick McDonald, would eventually revolutionize the restaurant industry and provide an organizational model copied by countless other businesses of all kinds.

The basic concept of the McDonald brothers—which we now call "fast-food"—amounted to serving food quickly and inexpensively to large numbers of people. The McDonalds trained employees to perform highly specialized jobs, so that one person grilled hamburgers, while others "dressed" them, made French fries, whipped up milkshakes, and presented the food to the customers in assembly-line fashion.

As the years went by, the McDonald brothers prospered, and they moved their restaurant from Pasadena to San Bernardino. It was there, in 1954, that events took an unexpected turn when Ray Kroc, a traveling blender and mixer merchant, paid a visit to the McDonalds.

Kroc was fascinated by the efficiency of the brothers' system, and he saw the potential for a greatly expanded chain of fast-food restaurants. Initially, Kroc launched his plans in partnership with the McDonald brothers. Soon, however, he bought their share of the business and set out on his own to become one of the greatest success stories of all time. Today, 20,000 McDonald's restaurants serve people throughout the United States and around the world.

From a sociological point of view, the success of McDonald's reveals much more than the popularity of hamburgers. As sociologist George Ritzer (1993) explains, the larger importance of McDonald's lies in the extent to which the principles that guide the operation of this company are coming to dominate social life in the United States and elsewhere.

We begin with an examination of *social groups*, the clusters of people with whom we interact in much of our daily lives. As we shall see, the scope of group life has expanded greatly during this century. From a world built on the family, the local neighborhood, and the small business, our society now turns on the operation of vast businesses and other bureaucracies that sociologists describe as *formal organizations*. Understanding how this expanding scale of life came to dominate our society, and what it means for us as individuals, are this chapter's key objectives.

SOCIAL GROUPS

Virtually everyone moves through life with a sense of belonging; this is the experience of group life. A **social group** refers to *two or more people who identify and interact with one another*. Human beings continually come together to form couples, families, circles of friends, neighborhoods, churches, businesses, clubs, and numerous large organizations. Whatever the form, groups are made up of people with shared experiences, loyalties,

SUPPLEMENTS: An outline and supplementary lecture material for Chapter 7 are included in the *Data File.*
NOTE: Cooley used only the term *primary group;* others introduced the term *secondary group* into sociological terminology, inferring the concept from Cooley's writings.
RESOURCE: An excerpt of Cooley's analysis of primary groups appears in the companion reader, *Seeing Ourselves.*

GLOBAL: The importance of traditional solidarities—of race, ethnicity, religion, or clan—typically surprise the U.S. traveler in less economically developed countries.
NOTE: One indicator of the character of social organization is the share of unlisted telephone numbers. In Albany, N.Y., and Minneapolis, about 12% are unlisted; in Los Angeles, 60% are unlisted.

As human beings, we live our lives as members of groups. Such groups may be large or small, temporary or long-lasting, and can be based on kinship, heritage, or some shared interest.

and interests. In short, while maintaining their individuality, the members of social groups also think of themselves as a special "we."

GROUPS, CATEGORIES, AND CROWDS

People often use the term "group" imprecisely. Its meaning becomes clearer when we distinguish the group from the similar concepts of category and crowd.

Category

A *category* refers to people who have some status in common. Women, single fathers, military recruits, millionaires, homeowners, and Roman Catholics are all examples of categories.

Why are categories not considered groups? Simply because, while the individuals involved are aware that they are not the only ones to hold that particular status, the vast majority are strangers to one another.

Crowd

A *crowd* refers to a temporary cluster of individuals who may or may not interact at all. Students sitting in a lecture hall interact and share a common identity as college classmates, so such a crowd might be termed a loosely formed group. By contrast, riders hurtling along on a subway train or bathers enjoying a summer day at the beach pay little mind to one another and amount to an anonymous collection of people. In general, then,

crowds are too transitory and too impersonal to qualify as social groups.

The right circumstances, however, could turn a crowd into a group. People riding in subway trains that collide under the city streets become keenly aware of their common plight and begin to help each other. Sometimes such extraordinary experiences become the basis for lasting relationships.

PRIMARY AND SECONDARY GROUPS

Acquaintances commonly greet one another with a smile and a "Hi! How are you?" The response is usually "Just fine, thanks. How about you?" This answer, of course, is often more scripted than truthful. Telling how you are *really* doing would make most people feel so awkward they would beat a hasty retreat.

Sociologists classify social groups by measuring them against two ideal types that are based on the level of concern members show for one another. This variation is the key to distinguishing *primary* from *secondary* groups.

According to Charles Horton Cooley (1864–1929), a **primary group** is *a small social group whose members share personal and enduring relationships.* Bound together by *primary relationships,* people typically spend a great deal of time together, engage in a wide range of activities, and feel that they know one another well. Although not without periodic conflict, members of primary groups show sincere concern for one another's welfare. The family is any society's most important primary group.

SOCIAL SURVEY: "How often do you spend an evening with relatives?" (*Student CHIP Social Survey Software*, SOCREL1; GSS 1974–91, N = 14,061) [Note strong correlation with SES.]

SES	Weekly	Less often
High	26.3%	73.7%
Middle	36.4%	63.6%
Low	42.5%	57.5%

Cooley called these personal and tightly integrated groups *primary* because they are among the first groups we experience in life. In addition, the family and early play groups also hold primary importance in the socialization process, shaping attitudes, behavior, and social identity.

The strength of primary relationships gives people a comforting sense of security. In the familiar social circles of family or friends, people feel they can "be themselves" without constantly worrying about the impression they are making.

Members of primary groups generally provide one another with economic and other forms of assistance as well. But, as important as primary ties are, most people think of a primary group as an end in itself rather than as a means to other ends. In other words, we prefer to think that kinship or friendship links people who "belong together," rather than people who expect to benefit from contact with each other. For this reason, we readily call on family members or close friends to help us move into a new apartment, without expecting to pay for their services. And we would do the same for them. A friend who never returns a favor, by contrast, is likely to leave us feeling "used" and wondering about the friendship.

Moreover, the personal orientation of a primary group means members view one another as unique and irreplaceable. We typically do not care who cashes our check at the bank or takes our money at the supermarket check-out. Yet in the primary group—especially the family—we are bound to specific others by emotion and loyalty. Although brothers and sisters do not always get along, they always remain siblings.

In contrast to the primary group, the **secondary group** is *a large and impersonal social group whose members pursue a specific interest or activity*. In most respects, secondary groups have precisely the opposite characteristics of primary groups. *Secondary relationships* usually involve weak emotional ties and little personal knowledge of one another. Secondary groups vary in duration, but they are frequently short term, beginning and ending without particular significance. Students in a college course, for instance, who may not see one another after the semester ends, exemplify the secondary group.

Weaker social ties permit secondary groups to include many more people than primary groups. For example, dozens or even hundreds of people may work together in the same office, yet most of them pay only passing attention to one another. Sometimes time transforms a group from secondary to primary, as with co-workers who share an office for many years. Generally,

TABLE 7–1 Primary Groups and Secondary Groups: A Summary

	Primary Group ⟷	Secondary Group
Quality of Relationships	Personal orientation	Goal orientation
Duration of Relationships	Usually long term	Variable; often short term
Breadth of Relationships	Broad; usually involving many activities	Narrow; usually involving few activities
Subjective Perception of Relationships	As ends in themselves	As means to an end
Typical Examples	Families; circles of friends	Co-workers; political organizations

however, people in a secondary group only occasionally think of themselves as "we," and the boundary distinguishing members from nonmembers is usually far less clear than in primary groups.

Secondary groups lack strong loyalties and emotions because members look to one another only to achieve limited ends. So, while members of primary groups display a *personal orientation*, people in secondary groups have a *goal orientation*. Secondary ties need not be aloof or cold, of course. Social interaction among students, co-workers, and business associates is often quite pleasant even if rather impersonal.

In primary groups, members define each other according to *who* they are, that is, in terms of kinship or unique personal qualities. Members of secondary groups, by contrast, look to one another for *what* they are or what they can do for each other. In secondary groups, in other words, we are always aware of what we offer others and what we receive in return. This "scorekeeping" comes through most clearly in business relationships. Likewise, the people next door typically expect that a neighborly favor will be returned.

The goal orientation of secondary groups encourages individuals to craft their behavior carefully. In these roles, we remain characteristically impersonal and polite. In a secondary relationship, therefore, we ask the question "How are you?" without really expecting a truthful answer.

Table 7–1 summarizes the characteristics of primary and secondary groups. Keep in mind that these

THE MAP: In general, New England is a high litigation region, while the Midwest and Rocky Mountain states have the lowest rates. Significant correlates are degree of urban population, affluence, and levels of migration (see National Map 24–1). This litigation index reflects percent of auto accidents that end up in court, extent of malpractice litigation, number of trial lawyers, extent of municipal litigation, and campaign spending by state's chief justice.

THEN AND NOW: Percentage of judges and lawyers who are women; *1960,* 3.3%; *1990,* 20.8%. (All public officials: *1960,* 19.1%; *1990,* 42.4%.)

GLOBAL: The United States has the most lawyers of any world nation, 780,000 in 1994. Based on 71 countries offering data, the world average is 5.3 lawyers per 10,000 people. The highest ratio is for Iceland (38.6); the U.S. is close behind with 33.0.

SEEING OURSELVES

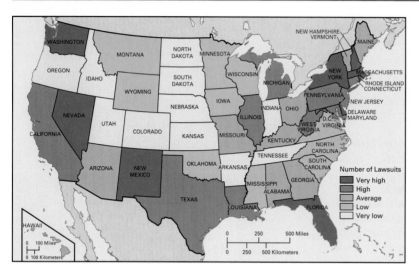

NATIONAL MAP 7–1
The Quality of Relationships: Lawsuits Across the United States

Social conflicts are found everywhere, but whether people tend to resolve them informally or resort to legal action varies from state to state. It stands to reason that, in regions of the country where litigation is least common, people's social ties are typically more primary. By contrast, where people are most likely to turn to lawyers, social ties would seem to be more secondary. Looking at the map, what do the states with high levels of litigation have in common? What traits mark the states in which people are reluctant to sue each other?

Source: Prepared by the author using data from Frum & Wolfe (1994).

traits define two types of social groups in ideal terms; actual groups may well contain elements of both. Nevertheless, putting these concepts at opposite ends of a continuum helps us describe and analyze group life.

Do some kinds of settlements have a more primary orientation than others? A longstanding sociological assertion holds that rural areas and small towns tend to emphasize primary relationships while large cities are characterized by more secondary relationships. While this generalization holds much truth, some urban neighborhoods—especially those populated by people of a single ethnic or religious category—are quite tightly knit. The state-by-state survey shown in National Map 7–1 measures one indicator of the primary or secondary character of social ties: namely, how likely people are to resolve disputes personally or to seek redress formally in court.

Finally, what about the world as a whole? In general, primary relationships dominate low-income, preindustrial societies throughout Latin America, Africa, and Asia where people's lives revolve around families and local villages. In these countries, especially in rural areas, strangers stand out in the social landscape. By contrast, secondary ties dominate in high-income, industrial societies where people assume highly specialized social roles. Most people in the United States, especially in cities, routinely engage in impersonal, secondary contacts with virtual

strangers—people about whom we know very little and may never meet again (Wirth, 1938).

GROUP LEADERSHIP

How do groups operate? One important dimension of group dynamics is the extent to which members recognize leaders. Large, secondary groups generally place leaders in a formal chain of command; a small circle of friends may have no leader at all. Parents assume leadership roles in families, although husband and wife may disagree about who is really in charge.

Two Leadership Roles

Groups typically benefit from two kinds of leadership (Bales, 1953; Bales & Slater, 1955). **Instrumental leadership** refers to *group direction that emphasizes the completion of tasks.* Members look to instrumental leaders to "get things done." **Expressive leadership,** on the other hand, *focuses on collective well-being.* Expressive leaders take less of an interest in achieving goals than in maintaining group morale and minimizing tension and conflict among members.

Because they concentrate on performance, instrumental leaders usually have formal, secondary relations with other group members. Instrumental leaders give orders and reward or punish people according to

NOTE: Emphasizing the expressive component while discounting the instrumental element of primary relationships is an example of Goffman's concept of idealization.
Q: "I was only following orders." Adolph Eichmann, Nazi death-camp officer
Q: "Why doth one man's yawning make another yawn?" Robert Burton

Q: "A little doubt came into my mind . . . Even though you know you are right, you wonder why everybody thinks differently. I was doubting myself and was puzzled." One of Solomon Asch's subjects
NOTE: Asch conducted control sessions to test the ability of subjects to make correct comparisons in the absence of group pressure; overall, 99% of such judgments were correct (compared to 66% in the conformity condition).

their contribution to the group's efforts. Expressive leaders, however, cultivate more personal, primary ties. They offer sympathy to a member having a tough time, keep the group united, and lighten serious moments with humor. While successful instrumental leaders enjoy more *respect* from members, expressive leaders generally receive more *affection*.

In the traditional North American family, the two types of leadership are linked to gender. Historically, cultural norms bestowed instrumental leadership on men so that, as fathers and husbands, they assumed primary responsibility for providing income, making decisions, and disciplining children. By contrast, expressive leadership traditionally belongs to women. Historically, mothers and wives have encouraged supportive and peaceful relationships among family members. This division of labor partly explains why many children have greater respect for their fathers but closer personal ties with their mothers (Parsons & Bales, 1955; Macionis, 1978).

Of course, increasing equality between men and women has blurred the gender-based distinction between instrumental and expressive leadership. In most group settings, women and men now assume both leadership roles.

Three Leadership Styles

Sociologists also characterize group leadership in terms of its orientation to power. *Authoritarian leadership* focuses on instrumental concerns, takes personal charge of decision making, and demands strict compliance from subordinates. Although this leadership style may win little affection from group members, a fast-acting authoritarian leader is appreciated in a crisis.

Democratic leadership has a more expressive focus and seeks to include everyone in the decision-making process. Although less successful when a crisis affords little time for discussion, democratic leaders generally draw on the ideas of all members to forge creative solutions to the tasks at hand.

Laissez-faire leadership (a French phrase roughly meaning "to leave alone") allows the group to function more or less on its own. This style typically is the least effective in promoting group goals (White & Lippitt, 1953; Ridgeway, 1983).

GROUP CONFORMITY

Okiki, a thirteen-year-old honors student at a Lorain, Ohio, middle school, sat in class, her arms and legs shaking nervously. In her book bag she concealed a

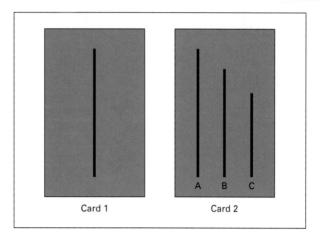

FIGURE 7–1 Cards Used in Asch's Experiment in Group Conformity

Source: Asch (1952).

twelve-inch kitchen knife. Her plan was to wait for the bell to ring and then rush to the front of the classroom and, with the help of another student, stab her teacher to death. Why? To settle a grudge against the teacher and to show her classmates (at least a dozen of whom placed bets on whether or not she would "chicken out") that she was worthy of their respect. Hearing about the plot only minutes before it was to be carried out, an assistant principal rushed in to avert a tragedy (Gregory, 1993).

The fact that young teens are anxious about fitting in surprises no one, although many people might be amazed at the lengths to which some will go to gain acceptance. Social scientists confirm the power of group pressure to shape human behavior and report that it remains strong into adulthood.

Asch's Research

Solomon Asch (1952) conducted a classic investigation that revealed the power of group conformity. Asch recruited students allegedly for a study of visual perception. Before the experiment began, however, he revealed to all but one person in each group that their real purpose was to put group pressure on the remaining person; the topic being studied was not visual perception at all, but group conformity.

Seating all the students around a table, Asch asked each, in turn, to match a "standard" line, as shown on Card 1 in Figure 7–1, to one of three lines on Card 2. Anyone with normal vision could easily see that the

NOTE: Many studies in social psychology rest on subject deception, a controversial practice included in Chapter 2's discussion of
research ethics. The Milgram experiment is the most troublesome
in this regard because it also subjected people to high stress.
NOTE: Milgram found the physical presence of the experimenter
generated the highest level of subject compliance. When com-
mands were issued by telephone, compliance dropped by 20%.

DISCUSS: Consider how pressure to conform comes from many
sources other than groups, including media presentations, pronouncements of experts, opinions of significant others, and so on.
Q: "Whatever crushes individuality is despotism, by whatever
name it may be called." John Stuart Mill
Q: "It is our nature to conform; it is a force not many can successfully resist." Mark Twain

line marked "A" on Card 2 was the correct choice. Initially, as planned, everyone made the correct matches.
But then Asch's secret accomplices began answering
incorrectly, so that the naive subject (seated to answer
next to last) became bewildered and uncomfortable.

What happened? Asch found that one-third of all
subjects in this situation chose to conform to the others by answering incorrectly. His investigation suggests that many of us are willing to compromise our
own judgment to avoid the discomfort of being different from others, even from people we do not know.

Milgram's Research

Stanley Milgram—a former student of Solomon
Asch—conducted far more controversial conformity
experiments of his own. In Milgram's initial study
(1963, 1965; Miller, 1986), a researcher explained to
male recruits that they would be participating in a
study of how punishment affects learning. One by one,
he assigned them the role of "teacher" and placed
another individual—actually, an accomplice of Milgram's—in a connecting room as the "learner."

The teacher watched the learner sit down in what
appeared to be an electric chair. As the teacher looked
on, the researcher applied electrode paste to the learner's
wrist, explaining that this would "prevent blisters and
burns," and then attached the electrode. The researcher
explained to the teacher that the leather straps holding
the learner were "to prevent excessive movement while
the learner was being shocked," and that, although the
shocks would be painful, they would cause "no permanent tissue damage."

The researcher then led the teacher back into an
adjoining room, explaining that the "electric chair"
was connected to a "shock generator," actually a bogus
but forbidding piece of equipment (a realistic-looking
label read "Shock Generator, Type ZLB, Dyson
Instrument Company, Waltham, Mass."). On the
front was a dial that supposedly regulated electric current, beginning with 15 volts (labeled "slight shock"),
escalating gradually to 300 volts (marked "intense
shock"), and peaking at 450 volts (marked "Danger:
Severe Shock" and "XXX").

Seated in front of the "shock generator," the
teacher was told to read aloud pairs of words. Then,
the teacher was to repeat the first word of each pair
and wait for the learner to recall the second word.
Whenever the learner failed to respond correctly, the
teacher was instructed to apply an electric shock from
the "shock generator."

The researcher directed the teacher to begin at
the lowest level (15 volts) and to increase the shock by
15 volts every time the learner made a mistake. And so
they did. At 75, 90, and 105 volts, the teacher heard
audible moans from the learner; at 120 volts, shouts of
pain; at 270 volts, screams; at 315 volts, pounding on
the wall; after that, deadly silence. None of forty subjects assigned to the role of teacher during the initial
research even questioned the procedure before reaching 300 volts, and twenty-six of the subjects—almost
two-thirds—went all the way to 450 volts. These startling results show just how readily ordinary people
obey authority figures.

Milgram (1964) then modified his research to see
if Solomon Asch had documented such a high degree
of group conformity only because the task of matching
lines seemed trivial. What if groups pressured people
to administer electrical shocks?

This time, Milgram used a group of three teachers,
two of whom were his accomplices. Each of the three
teachers was to suggest a shock level when the learner
made an error; it was understood that the group would
then administer the lowest of the three suggestions.
This arrangement gave the naive subject the power to
deliver a lesser shock regardless of what the others
proposed.

The accomplices called for increasing the shock
level with each error, putting group pressure on the
subject to do the same. And, in fact, they succeeded:
The subjects applied voltages three to four times
higher than other subjects in control conditions who
acted alone. Thus Milgram's research suggests that
people are likely to follow the directions of not only
"legitimate authority figures," but also of ordinary
individuals, even when the directions involve inflicting
harm on another person.

Janis's Research

The experts, too, cave in to group pressure, according
to Irving L. Janis (1972, 1989), sometimes with serious
consequences. Janis contends that a number of U.S.
foreign policy errors, including our failure to foresee
Japan's attack on Pearl Harbor during World War II
and our ill-fated military involvement in Vietnam,
may have been the result of group conformity among
our highest-ranking political leaders.

Common sense tells us that group discussion
improves decision making. Janis counters, however,
that group members often seek consensus, closing
off alternative points of view. Having settled on one

In many traditional societies, children of the same age forge strong loyalties, generally with members of their own sex. These young men, members of the Masai in Kenya, sit with shaved heads listening to a blessing by the elders, knowing they are about to pass together into adulthood.

"reality," members come to regard anyone with another opinion as the "opposition." Janis calls this process **groupthink,** *the tendency of group members to conform by adopting a narrow view of some issue.*

A classic example of groupthink resulted in the disastrous 1961 invasion of the Bay of Pigs in Cuba. Looking back, Arthur Schlesinger, Jr., an advisor to President Kennedy, confessed his guilt over "having kept so quiet during those crucial discussions in the Cabinet Room," adding that the group discouraged anyone from challenging what, in hindsight, Schlesinger considered "nonsense" (quoted in Janis, 1972:30, 40).

REFERENCE GROUPS

How do we assess our own attitudes and behavior? Frequently, we use a **reference group,** *a social group that serves as a point of reference in making evaluations or decisions.*

A young man who imagines his family's response to a woman he is dating is using his family as a reference group. Similarly, a supervisor who tries to gauge her employees' reactions to a new vacation policy is using her co-workers as a standard of reference. As these examples suggest, reference groups can be primary or secondary. In either case, our need to

conform means that the attitudes of others can greatly affect us.

We also use groups that we do *not* belong to for reference. Being well-prepared for a job interview means showing up dressed the way people in that company dress for work. Conforming to groups we do not belong to illustrates the process of *anticipatory socialization*, described in Chapter 5 ("Socialization"). In other words, we conform as a strategy to win acceptance to the group.

Stouffer's Research

Samuel A. Stouffer (1949) and his associates conducted a classic study of reference groups during World War II. Researchers asked soldiers to evaluate their own, or any competent soldier's, chances of promotion in their branch of the Army. One might guess that soldiers serving in outfits with a high promotion rate would be optimistic about their own advancement. Yet Stouffer's research pointed to the opposite conclusion: Soldiers in branches of the Army with low promotion rates were actually more optimistic about their own chances to move ahead.

The key to understanding Stouffer's results lies in the groups against which the soldiers measured themselves. Those in branches with low promotion rates

DISCUSS: Expand reference group dynamics with a discussion of relative deprivation (see Chapter 23). A *Times-Mirror* poll found that a growing share of older people in the United States have expressed dissatisfaction with their financial situation, while young people are more positive. Actual earnings data, however, show the opposite, with the incomes of the elderly rising through the 1980s, while income of people in their twenties actually fell.

NOTE: Ethnocentrism is one expression of valuing one's own ingroup while undervaluing those who differ as an outgroup.
NOTE: In the dyad, there can be no "social loafing."
Q: "A dyad . . . depends on each of its two elements alone—in its death, though not in its life: For its life, it needs both, but for its death, only one." Georg Simmel (1950:124)

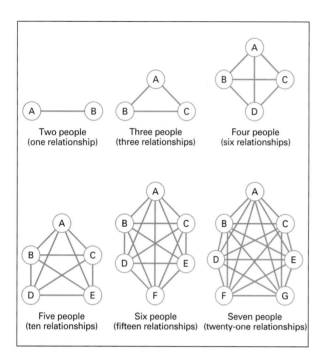

FIGURE 7–2 Group Size and Relationships

looked around and saw people making no more headway than they were. That is, they had not been promoted, but neither had most others, so they did not feel deprived.

Soldiers in branches with high promotion rates, however, could easily think of people who had been promoted sooner or more often than they had. With such people in mind, even competent soldiers who had been promoted themselves were likely to feel shortchanged.

Stouffer's research demonstrates that we do not make judgments about ourselves in isolation, nor do we compare ourselves with just anyone. Instead, we use specific social groups as standards in developing our attitudes. Whatever our situation in *absolute* terms, then, we assess our well-being subjectively, *relative* to some specific reference group (Merton, 1968; Mirowsky, 1987).

INGROUPS AND OUTGROUPS

Everyone favors some groups over others, whether due to political outlook, social prestige, or simply manner of dress. On the college campus, for example, left-leaning student activists may look down on fraternity members, whom they view as conservative; the Greeks, in turn, may snub the computer "nerds" as well as the "grinds" who work too hard. Virtually every social landscape has a mix of positive and negative evaluations.

Such judgments illustrate another important element of group dynamics: the opposition of ingroups and outgroups. An **ingroup** is *a social group commanding a member's esteem and loyalty.* An ingroup exists in relation to an **outgroup,** *a social group toward which one feels competition or opposition.*

Social life is the interplay of both kinds of groups. A college football team, for example, is an ingroup to its members and an outgroup for students uninterested in sports. A town's Democrats think of themselves as an ingroup in relation to the local Republicans. All ingroups and outgroups work on the principle that "we" have valued characteristics that "they" lack.

Tensions among groups often sharpen their boundaries and give people a clearer social identity. At the same time, these tensions also promote self-serving distortions of reality. Specifically, research shows that members of ingroups hold overly positive views of themselves and unfairly negative views of outgroups (Tajfel, 1982).

Power also shapes group relations. A powerful ingroup can define others as a lower-status outgroup; for their part, members of an outgroup may feel alienated from a system they feel victimizes them. For example, white people have historically viewed people of color in negative terms and subordinated them socially, politically, and economically. Internalizing these negative attitudes, minorities often struggle to overcome negative self-images. In this way, ingroups and outgroups foster loyalty as well as generate conflict (Bobo & Hutchings, 1996).

GROUP SIZE

If you are the first person to arrive at a party, you are in a position to observe some fascinating group dynamics. Until about six people enter the room, everyone generally shares a single conversation. But as more people arrive, the group divides into two or more clusters. Size obviously plays a crucial role in how group members interact.

To understand why this is so, consider the mathematical connection between the number of people in a social group and the number of possible relationships among them. As Figure 7–2 shows, two people

GLOBAL: Marriage in our society is dyadic; ideally, powerful emotional ties unite husbands and wives. However, marriage in other societies may involve more than two people. In that case, the household usually is more stable, although many of the marital relationships are weaker.

Q: "Among three elements [of a triad], each one operates as an intermediary between the other two, exhibiting the twofold function of such an organ, which is to unite and to separate." Georg Simmel (1950:135)
NOTE: Because of Simmel's focus on the intricate details of situational social life, Everett Hughes dubbed him "the Freud of sociology."

form a single relationship; adding a third person generates three relationships; adding a fourth person yields six. Increasing the number of people one at a time, then, increases the number of possible relationships much more rapidly because the new individual can interact with each person already there. Thus, five people define ten relationships, but, by the time seven people join in one conversation, twenty-one "channels" connect them. This leaves too many people unable to speak, which is why the group usually divides at this point.

The Dyad

German sociologist Georg Simmel (1858–1918) explored the social dynamics in the smallest social groups. Simmel (1950; orig. 1902) used the term **dyad** to designate *a social group with two members*. Throughout the world, most love affairs, marriages, and the closest friendships are dyadic.

What makes the dyad a special relationship? First, explained Simmel, social interaction in a dyad is typically more intense than in larger groups because, in a one-to-one relationship, neither member shares the other's attention with anyone else. Thus dyads have the potential to be the most meaningful social bonds we ever experience.

Second, Simmel explains, like a stool with only two legs, dyads are unstable. Both members of a dyad must actively sustain the relationship; if either one withdraws, the group collapses. Because the stability of marriage is important to society, the marital dyad is supported with legal, economic, and often religious ties. By contrast, a large group such as a symphony orchestra or a volunteer fire company is much more stable; it can survive the loss of many members without dissolving.

The Triad

Simmel also studied the **triad,** *a social group with three members*. A triad encompasses three relationships, each uniting two of the three people. A triad is more stable than a dyad because one member can act as a mediator if relations between the other two become strained. Such group dynamics help explain why members of a dyad (say, a married couple) often seek out a third person (a counselor) to air tensions between them.

On the other hand, two members of a triad can pair up to press their views on the third, or two may

Throughout the world, the most intense social bonds join two people. Even so, the dyad is also characteristically unstable, since withdrawal of either party causes the group to collapse.

intensify their relationship, leaving the other feeling like a "third wheel." For example, when two of the three develop a romantic interest in each other, they are likely to understand the old saying "Two's company, three's a crowd."

As groups grow beyond three members, they become progressively more stable because the loss of even several members does not threaten the group's existence. At the same time, increases in group size typically reduce the intense personal interaction possible only in the smallest groups. Larger groups are thus based less on personal attachment and more on formal rules and regulations. Such formality helps a large group persist over time, though the group is not immune to change. After all, their numerous members give large groups more contact with the outside world, opening the door to new attitudes and behavior (Carley, 1991).

DIVERSITY: Illustrating Blau's analysis, members of small racial and ethnic communities are more likely to marry out of their category than members of larger categories (cf. Gurak & Fitzpatrick, 1982).

SUPPLEMENTS: Supplementary material for this chapter includes an account of using small groups to combat racism.

NOTE: Networks are a characteristic feature of modern societies in which social ties are not built around localized kinship and neighborhood but a wide range of individual experiences and interests as well as high-technology means of communication.

NOTE: As a network increases in size, its value to members also increases since it offers more social resources. Moreover, key individuals may well be sought out by various networks. The end result is a fusion of numerous small networks into one larger one.

Today's college campuses value social diversity. One of the challenges of this movement is ensuring that all categories of students are fully integrated into campus life. This is not always easy. Following Blau's theory of group dynamics, as the number of minority students increases, these men and women are able to form a group unto themselves, perhaps interacting less with others.

Does a social group have an ideal size? The answer depends on the group's purpose. A dyad offers unsurpassed emotional intensity, while a group of several dozen members is more stable, capable of accomplishing larger, more complex tasks, and better able to assimilate new members or ideas. People typically find more *personal pleasure* in smaller groups, while deriving greater *task satisfaction* from larger organizations (Slater, 1958; Ridgeway, 1983; Carley, 1991).

SOCIAL DIVERSITY

Social diversity affects group dynamics, especially the likelihood that members will interact with someone from another group. Peter Blau (1977; Blau, Blum, & Schwartz, 1982; South & Messner, 1986) points out four ways in which the composition of social groups affects intergroup association:

1. **Large groups turn inward.** Extending Simmel's analysis of group size, Blau explains that the larger a group, the more likely members are to maintain relationships exclusively among themselves. The smaller the group, by contrast, the more members will reach beyond their immediate social circle.

    To illustrate, consider the efforts of many colleges to enhance social diversity. Increasing the number of, say, international students may add a dimension of difference to a campus, but eventually, as their numbers rise, these students are more likely to form their own social group. Thus, intentional efforts to promote social diversity may well have the unintended effect of promoting separatism.

2. **Heterogeneous groups turn outward.** The more internally heterogeneous a group is, the more likely its members are to interact with members of other groups. For example, campus groups that recruit members of both sexes and various ethnic and geographic backgrounds promote more intergroup contact than groups that choose members of one social type.

3. **Social equality promotes contact.** In an environment in which all groups have roughly equal standing, people of all social backgrounds tend to mingle and form social ties. Thus, whether groups insulate their members or not depends on whether the groups themselves form a social hierarchy.

4. **Physical boundaries promote social boundaries.** Blau contends that physical space affects the chance of contact among groups. To the extent that a social group is physically segregated from others (by having its own dorm or dining area, for example), its members are less apt to associate with other people.

SES	All/most	Few/none
High	55.6%	44.4%
Medium	61.4%	38.6%
Low	64.1%	35.9%

NETWORKS

A **network** is *a web of social ties that links people who identify and interact little with one another.* Think of a network as a "fuzzy" group: People come into occasional contact with one another but lack a group's sense of boundaries and belonging. Computer networks and other high-technology links now routinely connect people living all over the world. If we think of a group as a "circle of friends," then, we might describe a network as a "social web" expanding outward, often reaching great distances and including large numbers of people.

Some networks come close to being groups, as is the case with college friends who years after graduation stay in touch by e-mail and telephone. More commonly, however, a network includes people we *know of*—or who *know of us*—but with whom we interact infrequently, if at all. As one woman with a widespread reputation as a community organizer explains, "I get calls at home, someone says, 'Are you Roseann Navarro? Somebody told me to call you. I have this problem . . .'" (quoted in Kaminer, 1984:94). For this reason, social networks amount to "clusters of weak ties" (Granovetter, 1973).

Network ties may be weak, but they can be very important. For example, many people rely on their networks to find jobs. Even the scientific genius Albert Einstein needed a hand in landing his first job. After a year of unsuccessful interviewing, the father of one of his classmates put him in touch with an office manager who hired him (Clark, 1971; cited in Fischer, 1977:19). This use of networks suggests that, as the saying goes, *who you know* is often just as important as *what you know*.

Networks are based on people's colleges, clubs, neighborhoods, political parties, and personal interests. Obviously, some networks are made up of people with considerably more wealth, power, and prestige than others, which is what the expression "well connected" means. And some people have denser networks than others—that is, they are connected to more people—which is also a valuable social resource. Typically, the most extensive social networks are maintained by people who are young, well educated, and living in urban areas. Finally, size of community also affects who falls within social networks: People who live in small communities have more kin in their networks than people who live in large cities (Marsden, 1987; Markovsky et al., 1993; Kadushin, 1995; O'Brien, Hassinger, & Dersham, 1996).

Gender, too, shapes networks. Although the networks of men and women are typically the same size, women include more relatives (and women) in their networks, while men include more co-workers (and men). Women's networks, therefore, may not carry quite the same clout that the "old-boy" networks do. Even so, research suggests that, as gender inequality lessens in the United States, the networks of men and women are becoming more alike (Moore, 1991, 1992; Wright, 1995).

Finally, new information technology has generated a global network of unprecedented size in the form of the Internet. The box on page 182 takes a closer look at this twenty-first century form of communication, while Global Map 7–1 on page 183 shows access to the Internet around the world.

FORMAL ORGANIZATIONS

Throughout human history, most people lived in small groups of family members and neighbors; this pattern was still widespread in the United States a century ago. Today, families and neighborhoods persist, of course, but our lives revolve far more around **formal organizations,** *large, secondary groups that are organized to achieve their goals efficiently.*

Formal organizations, such as business corporations or government agencies, differ from families and neighborhoods: Their greater size makes social relationships less personal and fosters a formal, planned atmosphere. In other words, formal organizations operate in a deliberate way, not to meet personal needs, but to accomplish complex jobs.

When you think about it, organizing a society with some 265 million members is a remarkable feat. Countless tasks are involved, from collecting taxes to delivering the mail. To carry out most of these tasks, we rely upon large, formal organizations. The U.S. government, the nation's largest formal organization, employs more than 5 million people in various agencies and the armed forces. Large formal organizations develop lives and cultures of their own, so that as members come and go, the statuses they fill and the roles they perform remain unchanged over the years.

TYPES OF FORMAL ORGANIZATIONS

Amitai Etzioni (1975) has identified three types of formal organizations, distinguished by why people participate—utilitarian organizations, normative organizations, and coercive organizations.

CYBER: In 1997, some 2.6 trillion e-mail messages passed through the U.S. Internet system. By the year 2000, estimates place the number at 6.6 trillion. In 1997, about 40% of households had a personal computer, 20% of households had a PC with a modem, 10% of households had an Internet account (although about 25% of adults claim to use the Internet); 40% of the work force uses the Internet on the job.

NOTE: The section in Chapter 4, "Max Weber: The Rationalization of Society," provides general background for this discussion of bureaucracy. It introduces Weber's thesis of increasing rationalization; this section focuses more narrowly on bureaucracy as a major manifestation of that process.

Q: "Bureaucracy, the rule of no one, has become the modern form of despotism." Mary McCarthy

EXPLORING CYBER-SOCIETY

The Internet: Welcome to Cyberspace!

Its origins seem right out of the 1960s cold war film *Dr. Strangelove.* Three decades ago, government officials and scientists were trying to figure out how to run the country after an atomic attack, which, they assumed, would instantaneously knock out telephones and television. Their solution was brilliant: Devise a communication system with no central headquarters, no one in charge, and no main power switch—in short, an electronic web that would link the whole country in one vast network.

By 1985, the federal government was installing high-speed data lines around the country, and the Internet was about to be born. Today, tens of thousands of government offices, as well as colleges and universities across the United States, are joined by the Internet and share in the cost of its operation. Millions of other individuals connect their home computers to this "information superhighway" using a telephone-line modem and a subscription to a commercial "gateway" to the Internet.

No one knows precisely how many people use the Internet. But a rough estimate is that, by 1998, at least 100 million individuals in 175 (of 191) countries around the world were connected by the largest network in history. And the numbers are almost doubling each year.

What is available on the Internet? There are now millions of sites—far more than anyone could ever list in a single directory. But popular "search engines" such as YAHOO! (http://www.yahoo.com) provide site listings for just about any topic you can imagine. The Internet also allows you to send electronic mail: You can start a cyber-romance with a pen-pal, write to your textbook author (macionis@kenyon.edu), or even send a message to the president of the United States (president@whitehouse.gov). Through the Internet, you can also participate in discussion groups, visit museums for "virtual tours," locate data from a host of government agencies (a good starting point is http://www.census.gov), check out sociological resources through our Web sites (http://www.prenhall.com/macionis and http://www.macionis.com/), and search libraries across the campus

or around the world for books or other information. The excitement of the Internet lies in the fact that, given no formal rules for its use,* its potential defies the imagination.

Ironically, perhaps, it is precisely this unregulated quality that has many people up in arms. Pundits warn that "electronic democracy" will undermine established political practices, parents fear that their technologically sophisticated children will access "adult sites" that offer sexually explicit content, and purists bristle at the thought that the Internet may soon be flooded with advertising and other commercial ventures.

The "anything goes" character of the Internet only makes it more of a virtual image of the real world. Not surprisingly, therefore, a recent trend is that more and more users now employ passwords, fees, and other "gates" to create subnetworks limited to people like themselves. From one vast network, then, is emerging a host of social groups.

---

*In 1997, the U.S. Supreme Court declared that Constitutional guarantees of free speech apply to the Internet. This decision overturned the 1996 Communications Decency Act by which Congress attempted to restrict what critics claimed was indecent material easily accessible to children.

Sources: Based, in part, on Elmer-DeWitt (1993, 1994), Hafner (1994), and O'Connor (1997).

Utilitarian Organizations

Just about everyone who works for income is a member of a *utilitarian organization*, which pays its members to perform the jobs for which they were hired. Large business enterprises, for example, generate profits for their owners and salaries and wages for their employees. Joining a utilitarian organization is usually a matter of individual choice, although, obviously, most people must join one or another utilitarian organization to make a living.

Normative Organizations

People join *normative organizations* not for income but to pursue goals they consider morally worthwhile. Sometimes called *voluntary associations*, these include community service groups (such as the PTA, the Lions Club, the League of Women Voters, the Red Cross, and Kiwanis), political parties, religious organizations, and numerous others concerned with specific social issues.

In global perspective, people in the United States are especially likely to be members of voluntary

NOTE: From one individual's viewpoint, there are combinations of Etzioni's organizational types: Being drafted into an army is partly coercive (restricting freedoms) and partly utilitarian (offering pay), and partly normative (doing one's duty).

RESOURCE: An excerpt from Max Weber's analysis of bureaucracy is among the classic selections found in the companion reader, *Seeing Ourselves*.

NOTE: Note the rapid growth of the membership of the American Sociological Association: *1910,* 256; *1920,* 1,021; *1930,* 1,530; *1940,* 1,034; *1950,* 3,241; *1960,* 6,875; *1970,* 14,156; *1980,* 13,304; *1995,* 13,000. In the 1960s, the ASA had 2 employees; today, it has 25. The ASA did not respond to my requests for data about rising level of dues over time.

WINDOW ON THE WORLD

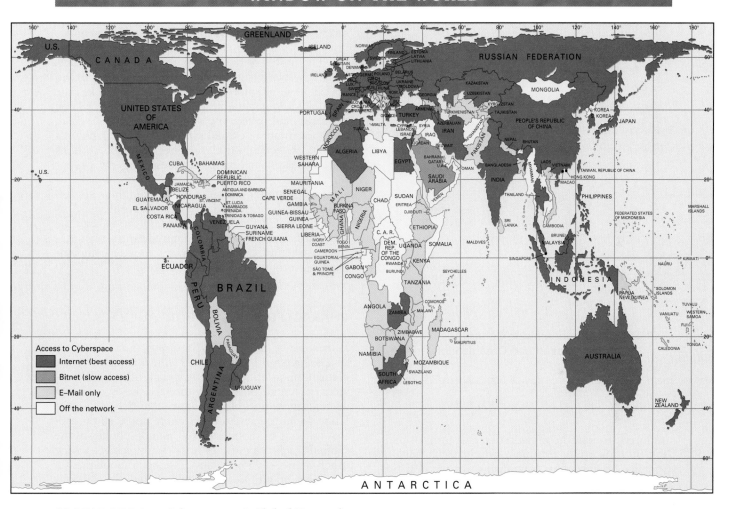

GLOBAL MAP 7–1 Cyberspace: A Global Network

While 175 of 191 world nations are connected to the Internet, a majority of the world's people have no access to this valuable resource. For one thing, computers are expensive, well out of reach of ordinary people in low-income countries, especially in Africa. Thus, the vast majority of Internet sites are in the United States, Canada, Western Europe, and Australia. But another barrier to global communication is language: Born in the U.S., the Internet's available software demands that users read and write in the Latin alphabet using English. But experts around the world are at work developing keyboards and interface programs that will link people using various languages. Perhaps, in the near future, the Internet may be as multicultural as the world it connects.

Source: Copyright © 1997 by The New York Times Co. Reprinted by permission.

associations (Curtis, Grabb, & Baer, 1992). Figure 7–3 on page 184 provides a comparative glance at membership in cultural or educational organizations for selected countries.

Coercive Organizations

In Etzioni's typology, *coercive organizations* are distinguished by involuntary membership. That is, people

NOTE: Throughout history, people favored "their own kind" (especially kin). A bureaucratic culture erodes ascription in favor of achievement. Favoring kin is transformed into "conflict of interest" and "nepotism."

NOTE: Exemplifying the inefficiency of a pre-bureaucratic world: Two weeks after the United States and Great Britain signed the Treaty of Ghent ending the War of 1812, 5,000 British troops,

unaware of the peace agreement, attacked U.S. forces at New Orleans, resulting in the loss of 2,000 soldiers.

NOTE: Specialization can also be a strategy. Mahnaz Kousha (1994) explains that domestic workers specialize in order to resist domination by employers (a more elaborate form of the venerable "I don't do windows . . .").

Q: "Punctuality is the virtue of the bored." Evelyn Waugh

GLOBAL SNAPSHOT

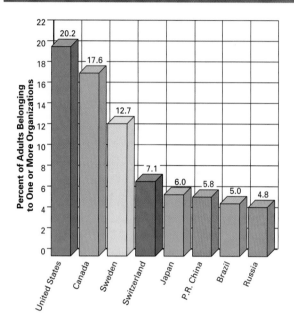

FIGURE 7–3   Membership in Cultural or Educational Organizations

Source: *World Values Survey* (1994).

are forced to join the organization as a form of punishment (prisons) or treatment (psychiatric hospitals). Coercive organizations have distinctive physical features, such as locked doors and barred windows, and are supervised by security personnel (Goffman, 1961). These are settings that segregate people as "inmates" or "patients" for a period of time and sometimes radically alter their attitudes and behavior. Recall from Chapter 5 ("Socialization") the power of *total institutions* to transform a human being's overall sense of self.

From differing vantage points, many organizations may fall into *all* these categories. A psychiatric hospital, for example, serves as a coercive organization for a patient, a utilitarian organization for a psychiatrist, and a normative organization to a hospital volunteer.

ORIGINS OF BUREAUCRACY

Formal organizations date back thousands of years. Elites who governed early empires relied on government officials to extend their power over millions of

people and vast geographical regions. Formal organization allowed these rulers to collect taxes, undertake military campaigns, and construct monumental structures, from the Great Wall of China to the pyramids of Egypt.

The power of these early organizations was limited, however. This was not because elites lacked grandiose ambition, but, first, because they lacked the technology to communicate quickly, travel over large distances, and collect and store information. Second, early organizations existed within a basically traditional setting. In preindustrial societies, cultural patterns placed greater importance on preserving the past or carrying out "God's will" than on organizational efficiency. Only in the last few centuries did there emerge what Max Weber called a "rational world view," as described in Chapter 4 ("Society"). In the wake of the Industrial Revolution, the nontraditional organizational structure called *bureaucracy* became commonplace in Europe and North America.

CHARACTERISTICS OF BUREAUCRACY

Bureaucracy is *an organizational model rationally designed to perform complex tasks efficiently.* In a bureaucratic business or government agency, officials deliberately enact and revise policy to make the organization as efficient as possible. To appreciate the power and scope of bureaucratic organization, consider the fact that any one of more than 160 million phones in the United States can connect you, within seconds, to any other phone—in homes, businesses, automobiles, even to a hiker on an Oregon mountain trail. Such instant communication was beyond the imagination of those who lived in the ancient world.

Of course, the telephone system depends on technological developments such as electricity, fiber optics, and computers. But neither could the system exist without the organizational capacity to keep track of every telephone call—recording which phone called which other phone, when, and for how long—and presenting all this information to tens of millions of telephone users in the form of monthly bills.

What specific traits promote organizational efficiency? Max Weber (1978; orig. 1921) identified six key elements of the ideal bureaucratic organization:

1. **Specialization.** Through most of human history, everyone pursued the basic goals of securing food and shelter. Bureaucracy, by contrast, assigns to individuals highly specialized duties.

NOTE: Photocopier machines, now essential to bureaucratic organizations, first appeared in the 1950s. Many people were skeptical that they would catch on.

NOTE: "Paperwork" is closely related to the negative connotation of bureaucracy. Some indicators of the sheer volume of paperwork in the U.S.: We mail more than 160 billion items per year, and the consumption of writing and printing paper has risen faster than the gross national product (Edward Tenner); *Federal Tax Regulations 1994* is 6,500 pages; the annual Chrysler Corp. tax return is a paper pile 6 feet tall—the work of 55 accountants.

Q: "The impersonal treatment of affairs which are at times of great personal significance to the client gives rise to the charge of 'arrogance' and 'haughtiness' of the bureaucrat." Robert K. Merton (1968:256)

Although formal organization is vital to modern, industrial societies, it is far from new. Twenty-five centuries ago, the Chinese philosopher and teacher K'ung Fu-Tzu (known to Westerners as Confucius) endorsed the idea that government offices should be filled by the most talented young men. This led to what was probably the world's first system of civil service examinations. Here, would-be bureaucrats compose essays to demonstrate their knowledge of Confucian texts.

2. **Hierarchy of offices.** Bureaucracies arrange personnel in a vertical ranking. Each person is supervised by "higher-ups" in the organization while, in turn, supervising others in lower positions. Usually, with fewer people in higher positions, the structure takes the form of a bureaucratic "pyramid."

3. **Rules and regulations.** Cultural tradition counts for little in a bureaucracy. Instead, rationally enacted rules and regulations control not only the organization's own functioning but, as much as possible, its larger environment. Ideally, a bureaucracy seeks to operate in a completely predictable fashion.

4. **Technical competence.** A bureaucratic organization expects officials and staff to have the technical competence to carry out their duties, and regularly monitors worker performance. Such impersonal evaluation based on performance contrasts sharply with the custom, followed through most of human history, of favoring relatives—whatever their talents—over strangers.

5. **Impersonality.** In bureaucratic organizations, rules take precedence over personal whim. This impersonality ensures that clients as well as workers are all treated uniformly. From this

TABLE 7–2 Small Groups and Formal Organizations: A Comparison

	Small Groups	Formal Organizations
Activities	Members typically engage in many of the same activities	Members typically engage in distinct, highly specialized activities
Hierarchy	Often informal or nonexistent	Clearly defined, corresponding to offices
Norms	Informal application of general norms	Clearly defined rules and regulations
Criteria for Membership	Variable, often based on personal affection or kinship	Technical competence to carry out assigned tasks
Relationships	Variable; typically primary	Typically secondary, with selective primary ties
Communications	Typically casual and face to face	Typically formal and in writing
Focus	Person-oriented	Task-oriented

detached approach stems the notion of the "faceless bureaucrat."

6. **Formal, written communications.** According to an old saying, the heart of bureaucracy is not people but paperwork. Rather than casual, verbal communication, bureaucracy relies on formal, written memos and reports. Over time, this correspondence accumulates into vast *files*. The files come to guide the operation of an organization in roughly the same way that social background shapes the life of an individual.

These traits stand in clear contrast to the more personal character of small groups. Bureaucratic organization promotes efficiency by carefully recruiting personnel and limiting the unpredictable effects of personal taste and opinion. In smaller, informal groups, members allow one another considerable discretion in their behavior; they respond to each other personally and consider everyone more or less equal in rank. Table 7–2 summarizes the differences between small social groups and large formal organizations.

ORGANIZATIONAL SIZE

Just as the character of social groups differs according to their size, so does the nature of formal organizations. Analyzing organizations of various sizes, Arne L. Kalleberg and Mark E. Van Buren (1996) found that "bigger is better" when it comes to many employee rewards. Large organizations typically provide their workers with higher salaries, more fringe benefits, and greater opportunities for promotion.

On the other hand, the researchers also concluded that "small is beautiful" when it comes to autonomy. That is small organizations usually allow their employees more discretion in how they perform their jobs.

THE INFORMAL SIDE OF BUREAUCRACY

Weber's ideal bureaucracy deliberately regulates every activity. In actual organizations, however, human beings have the creativity (or the stubbornness) to resist conforming to bureaucratic blueprints. Sometimes informality meets a legitimate need overlooked by formal regulations. In other situations informality may amount to simply cutting corners in one's job (Scott, 1981).

In principle, power in a bureaucracy resides in offices, not with the people who occupy them. Nonetheless, the personalities of officials greatly affect patterns of leadership. For example, studies of U.S. corporations document that the qualities and quirks of individuals—including personal charisma and interpersonal skills—have a tremendous impact on organizational outcomes (Halberstam, 1986).

Authoritarian, democratic, and laissez-faire types of leadership—described earlier in this chapter—reflect individual personality as much as any organizational plan. Then, too, in the "real world" of organizations, leaders and their cronies sometimes seek to benefit personally through abuse of organizational power. And perhaps even more commonly, leaders take credit for the efforts of their subordinates. Many secretaries, for example, have far more authority and responsibility than their official job titles and salaries suggest.

Communication offers another example of how informality creeps into large organizations. Memos and other written communications are the formal means of disseminating information through the hierarchy. Typically, however, individuals cultivate informal networks or "grapevines" that spread information much faster, if not always accurately. Grapevines—

CYBER: Will electronic communication, which gives almost anyone access to anyone else, let employees skip over levels to make bureaucratic pyramids flatter? Probably, although electronic "screens" may soon reinforce hierarchy online.

Q: "Specialists without spirit, sensualists without heart; this nullity imagines that it has attained a level of civilization never before achieved." Max Weber (1958:182; orig. 1904–5)

Q: "With increasing bureaucratization, it becomes plain to all who would see that man is to a very important degree controlled by his social relations to the instruments of production. This can no longer seem only a tenet of Marxism, but a stubborn fact to be acknowledged by all . . ." Robert K. Merton (1968:251

NOTE: "Pedantry," slavish attention to rules, has the Latin root *ped*, meaning "foot," implying a servile follower.

carried by both informal social networks as well as e-mail—are particularly important to subordinates because high officials often attempt to conceal information from them.

Electronic mail is inherently democratic, allowing even the lowest-ranking employee to bypass immediate superiors in order to communicate directly with the organization's president. Of course, some leaders may not welcome such "open-channel" communication. For this reason, Microsoft Corporation (whose leader, Bill Gates, has an "unlisted" address yet still receives hundreds of e-mail messages a day) is developing "screens" that will allow messages from only approved people to reach a particular computer terminal (Gwynne & Dickerson, 1997).

Using new information technology as well as age-old human ingenuity, members of organizations tend to personalize their procedures and surroundings. Such efforts suggest that we now take a closer look at some of the problems of bureaucracy.

PROBLEMS OF BUREAUCRACY

We rely on bureaucracy to manage countless details of everyday life, but many members of our society are, at best, ambivalent about bureaucratic organizations. Bureaucracy can dehumanize and manipulate individuals, and some say it poses a threat to personal privacy and political democracy.

Bureaucratic Alienation

Max Weber touted bureaucracy as a model of productivity. Nonetheless, Weber was keenly aware of bureaucracy's potential to *dehumanize* the people it is supposed to serve. The very same impersonality that fosters efficiency keeps officials and clients from responding to each other's unique, personal needs. On the contrary, officials must treat each client impersonally, as a standard "case." Perhaps the greatest challenge to a large, formal organization is responding to special requests or circumstances. Anyone who has ever tried to replace a lost driver's license, return defective merchandise to a discount store, or change an address on a magazine subscription knows that bureaucracies are sometimes maddeningly unresponsive.

The impersonal bureaucratic environment, then, gives rise to *alienation*. All too often, Weber contended, formal organizations reduce the human being to "a small cog in a ceaselessly moving mechanism"

According to Max Weber, bureaucracy is an organizational strategy that promotes efficiency. Impersonality, however, also fosters alienation among employees, who may become indifferent to the formal goals of the organization. The behavior of this municipal employee in Bombay, India, is understandable to members of formal organizations almost anywhere in the world.

(1978:988; orig. 1921). The historical trend toward more and more formal organization left Weber deeply pessimistic about the future of humankind. Although formal organizations are intended to benefit humanity, he feared that humanity could well end up serving formal organizations.

Bureaucratic Inefficiency and Ritualism

Then there is the familiar problem of inefficiency, the failure of a bureaucratic organization to carry out the work that it exists to perform. According to one recent report, the General Services Administration, the government agency that buys equipment for federal workers, takes up to three years to process a request for a new computer. Given the rapid development of

Q: "The only thing that saves us from bureaucracy is its inefficiency." Eugene McCarthy

Q: "The bureaucratic structure exerts a constant pressure upon the official to be methodical, prudent, disciplined . . . This may be exaggerated to the point where primary concern with conformity to the rules interferes with the achievement of the purposes of the organization." Robert K. Merton (1968:252–53)

NOTE: To illustrate the difficulty of disrupting bureaucracy: Early in the 1980s, the IRS issued a statement that, even in the event of nuclear war, they expected people to pay their taxes on time.

GLOBAL: As an example of successful opposition to entrenched leaders, Brazilian President Fernando Collor de Mello was impeached in 1993 on corruption charges.

George Tooker's painting Government Bureau *is a powerful statement about the human costs of bureaucracy. The artist depicts members of the public in monotonous similitude—reduced from human beings to mere "cases" to be disposed of as quickly as possible. Set apart from others by their positions, officials are "faceless bureaucrats" concerned more with numbers than with providing genuine assistance (notice that the artist places the fingers of the officials on calculators).*

George Tooker, *Government Bureau*, 1956. Egg tempera on gesso panel, 19⅝ x 29⅝ inches. The Metropolitan Museum of Art, George A. Hearn Fund, 1956 (56.78). Photograph © 1984 The Metropolitan Museum of Art.

computer technology, by the time the computer arrives, it is out of date (Gwynne & Dickerson, 1997).

The problem of inefficiency is captured in the concept of *red tape* (a term derived from the red tape used by eighteenth-century English administrators to wrap official parcels and records; Shipley, 1985). Red tape refers to a tedious preoccupation with organizational routine and procedures. Sociologist Robert Merton (1968) points out that red tape amounts to a new twist to the already-familiar concept of group conformity. He coined the term **bureaucratic ritualism** to describe *a preoccupation with rules and regulations to the point of thwarting an organization's goals.*

Ritualism stifles individual creativity and strangles organizational performance. In part, ritualism arises from the fact that organizations, which pay modest, fixed salaries, give officials little or no financial stake in performing efficiently. Then, too, bureaucratic ritualism stands as another expression of the alienation that Weber feared would arise from bureaucratic rigidity (Whyte, 1957; Merton, 1968; Coleman, 1990; Kiser & Schneider, 1994).

Bureaucratic Inertia

If bureaucrats sometimes have little motivation to be efficient, they certainly have every reason to protect their jobs. Thus, officials typically strive to perpetuate

their organization even when its purpose has been fulfilled. As Weber put it, "once fully established, bureaucracy is among the social structures which are hardest to destroy" (1978:987; orig. 1921).

Bureaucratic inertia refers to *the tendency of bureaucratic organizations to perpetuate themselves.* Formal organizations, in other words, tend to take on a life of their own beyond their formal objectives. For example, the Agriculture Department of the federal government maintains offices in 94 percent of the counties of the United States, even though, these days, only 16 percent of them contain working farms (Littman, 1992).

Members of an organization usually stay in business by redefining their agency's goals. The Agriculture Department, for example, now performs a broad range of work not directly related to farming, including nutritional and environmental research.

OLIGARCHY

Early in this century, Robert Michels (1876–1936) pointed out the link between bureaucracy and political **oligarchy,** *the rule of the many by the few* (1949; orig. 1911). According to what Michels called "the iron law of oligarchy," the pyramidlike structure of bureaucracy puts a few leaders in charge of vast and powerful government organizations.

NOTE: Evidence of bureaucracy's expansion: In 1950, 10 million farmers were served by 84,373 employees in the Department of Agriculture (ratio of 118:1); by 1990, the numbers were 2.9 million farmers but 129,000 DOA employees (22:1). Based on rates of growth and decline, by 2060 there will be more bureaucrats than farmers. Put otherwise, between 1950 and 1990, the number of farms fell 60 percent, the number of farmers dropped 70 percent, but the number of farm bureaucrats rose 53 percent (Littmann, 1992).

NOTE: "Peter's Corollary" is that, eventually, all positions in a large organization will be filled with incompetents.

SUPPLEMENTS: The *Data File* includes a discussion of women's management styles and the future of U.S. business.

Preindustrial societies did not possess the organizational means for even the most power-hungry ruler to control everyone. But the power of elites increased over the centuries with the development of new technology and the steady expansion of formal organizations.

Max Weber credited bureaucracy's strict hierarchy of responsibility with increasing organizational efficiency. By applying Weber's thesis to the organization of government, Michels shows how the hierarchical structure concentrates power and thus endangers democracy. While the public expects organizational officials to subordinate personal interests to organizational goals, people who occupy powerful positions can—and often do—use their access to information and the media and numerous other advantages to promote their personal interests.

Furthermore, bureaucracy insulates officials from the public and lets them avoid accountability. Take, for instance, the corporate president who is "unavailable for comment" to the local press, or the national president who withholds documents from Congress, claiming "executive privilege." Oligarchy, then, thrives in the hierarchical structure of bureaucracy and undermines people's control over their elected leaders (Tolson, 1995).

Political competition, term limits, and a system of checks and balances prevent the U.S. government from becoming an oligarchy. In 1974, for example, Richard Nixon was forced to resign as president of the United States, and, over the past twenty years, three presidents have been defeated in their bids for reelection. Even so, incumbents enjoy a significant advantage in U.S. politics: In the 1996 Congressional elections only 21 of 397 congressional office holders running for reelection were defeated by their challengers.

Parkinson's Law and the Peter Principle

Finally, and on a somewhat lighter note, we look at two other limitations of bureaucratic organizations. Parkinson's Law and the Peter Principle are familiar to anyone who has ever been a part of a formal organization.

C. Northcote Parkinson (1957) summed up bureaucratic inefficiency this way: *"Work expands to fill the time available for its completion."* Enough truth underlies this tongue-in-cheek assertion that it is known today as Parkinson's Law. To illustrate, suppose a bureaucrat working at the Division of Motor Vehicles processes fifty driver's license applications in an average day. If one day this worker has only twenty-five applications to process, how much time will the task require? The logical answer is half a day.

But according to Parkinson's Law, if a full day is available to complete the work, a full day is how long it will take.

Because organizational employees have little personal involvement in their jobs, few seek extra work to fill their spare time. Bureaucrats do strive to *appear* busy, however, and their apparent activity often prompts organizations to take on more employees. The added time and expense required to hire, train, supervise, and evaluate a larger staff make everyone busier still, setting in motion a vicious cycle that results in *bureaucratic bloat*. Ironically, the larger organization may accomplish no more real work than it did before.

In the same light-hearted spirit as Parkinson, Laurence J. Peter (Peter & Hull, 1969) proposed the Peter Principle: *"Bureaucrats are promoted to their level of incompetence."* The logic here is simple: Employees competent at one level of the organizational hierarchy are usually promoted to higher positions. Eventually, however, they reach a level where they are in over their heads; there they remain, performing poorly and no longer eligible for promotions.

Reaching their level of incompetence dooms officials to a future of inefficiency. After years in the office, though, they have almost certainly learned how to avoid demotion by hiding behind rules and regulations and taking credit for work actually performed by their more competent subordinates.

GENDER AND RACE IN ORGANIZATIONS

Rosabeth Moss Kanter began her career in the 1960s studying communes and other utopian settlements; today, she helps shape the real-world decisions of the most successful U.S. corporations. Kanter, a professor of business administration at Harvard University, works with business leaders to make their organizations more efficient and productive.

How? Kanter claims that a productive organizational environment depends on all categories of people having the opportunity to move up. This is not the case in many U.S. companies today. As Figure 7–4 shows, white men represent 42 percent of the U.S. population between the ages of twenty and sixty-four but hold 61 percent of management jobs. White women, a category of comparable size, trail with about 27 percent of managerial positions (U.S. Equal Employment Opportunity Commission, 1997). The members of various minorities lag further behind, even taking account of their smaller populations.

DIVERSITY: A growing number of women are trying to resolve role conflicts by leaving organizational jobs ("cashing out") and starting their own small businesses; 400,000 women did so in 1990.
DISCUSS: An interesting question is whether women need to learn about organizations or organizations need to learn about women.
RESOURCE: An excerpt from Arlie Hochschild's "The Managed Heart," discussing the manipulation of emotions by organizations,

is among the contemporary selections found in the Macionis and Benokraitis reader, *Seeing Ourselves.*
EXERCISE: Suggest that students who work try to personalize themselves more. Marketing researcher Michael Linn (1996) reports that waiters/waitresses who named themselves boosted their tips by 53%; a casual touch on the shoulder or hand by servers boosted tips 42%.

DIVERSITY SNAPSHOT

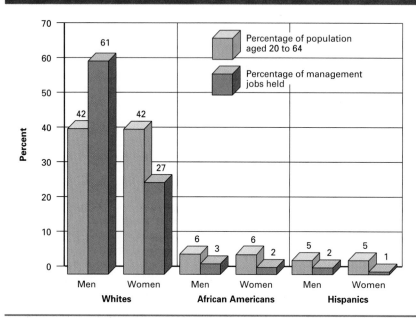

FIGURE 7–4
U.S. Managers by Race, Sex, and Ethnicity, 1996
Source: U.S. Equal Employment Opportunity Commission (1997).

Being underrepresented in the workplace, argues Kanter, leaves women, people of color, and those from economically disadvantaged backgrounds feeling like socially isolated outgroups. They are often uncomfortably visible, taken less seriously, and given fewer chances for promotion. Understandably, minorities themselves often end up thinking that they must work twice as hard as those in dominant categories just to maintain their present position, let alone advance to a higher position (Kanter, 1977; Kanter & Stein, 1979).

A structure with equal opportunities, Kanter continues, improves everyone's on-the-job performance. Widespread opportunity motivates employees, turning them into "fast-trackers" with higher aspirations, more self-esteem, and stronger commitment to the organization. A company with many "dead-end" jobs, on the other hand, turns workers into "zombies" with little aspiration, poor self-concept, and little loyalty to the organization.

Finally, Kanter claims that a flexible organizational structure encourages leaders to seek out the input of subordinates, which works toward everyone's benefit. It is officials in rigid organizations—those who, themselves, have little reason to be creative—

who jealously protect their own privileges and ride herd over their subordinates.

Other organizational researchers have focused on differences in management styles linked to gender. Deborah Tannen (1994) claims, for example, that women have a greater "information focus," and more readily ask questions in order to understand an issue. Men, however, have an "image focus" that makes them first consider how asking questions in a particular situation will affect their reputation.

In another study of women executives, Sally Helgesen (1990) found three additional gender-linked patterns. First, claims Helgesen, women tend to place greater value on communication skills and share information more than men do. Second, women are more flexible leaders who typically allow subordinates greater autonomy. Third, Helgesen notes, women tend to emphasize the interconnectedness of all organizational operations over narrow specialization. Because many business organizations must be more democratic and flexible to compete in today's complex, global environment, Helgesen concludes that women bring a "female advantage" to the workplace.

In sum, recent research shows that organizations that are open and adaptable bring out the best in their employees. The flip side of this trend—in which women are playing a major part—is that, when given a more flexible environment, employees contribute the most to the organization.

BEYOND BUREAUCRACY: HUMANIZING ORGANIZATIONS

Humanizing organizations means *fostering a more democratic organizational atmosphere that recognizes and encourages the contributions of everyone.* Research by Kanter (1977, 1983, 1989; Kanter & Stein, 1980) and others (Peters & Waterman, Jr., 1982) suggests that "humanizing" bureaucracy produces both happier employees and healthier profits. In the postindustrial era, in other words, organizations need to nurture the initiative and creativity of their employees. Based on the discussion so far, we can identify three paths to a more open and humane organizational structure:

1. **Social inclusiveness.** The social composition of the organization should, ideally, make no one feel out of place because of gender, race, or ethnicity. The performance of all employees will improve to the extent that no one is subject to social exclusion.

2. **Sharing responsibilities.** Humanizing bureaucracy means reducing rigid, oligarchical structures by spreading power and responsibility more widely. Managers cannot benefit from the ideas of employees who have no channels for expressing their opinions. Knowing that superiors are open to suggestions encourages all employees to think creatively, increasing organizational effectiveness.

3. **Expanding opportunities for advancement.** Expanded opportunity reduces the number of employees stuck in routine, dead-end jobs with little motivation to perform well. The organization should encourage employees at all levels to share ideas and try new approaches, and define everyone's job as the start of an upward career path.

Kanter's work takes a fresh look at bureaucracy in business organizations. Rigid formality may have made sense in the past, when organizations hired unschooled workers primarily to perform physical labor. But today's educated work force can contribute a wealth of ideas to bolster organizational efficiency—if the organization encourages and rewards innovation.

The recent trend is toward breaking down the rigid structure of conventional bureaucracy. One example of more flexible organizational form is the self-managed work team, whose members have the skills to carry out their tasks creatively and with minimal supervision.

There is broad support for the idea that loosening up rigid organizations improves performance. Moreover, companies that treat employees as a resource to be developed rather than as a group to be controlled stand out as more profitable. But some critics challenge Kanter's claim that social heterogeneity necessarily yields greater productivity. In controlled comparisons, they maintain, homogeneous work groups typically produce more, but heterogeneous groups are better at generating new ideas and approaches. The optimal working groups appear to be those that strike a balance: Team members should bring a variety of backgrounds and perspectives to the task yet be similar enough in outlook and goals that they can coordinate their efforts (Hackman, 1988; Yeatts, 1994).

NOTE: Self-managed work teams are an outgrowth of so-called "quality circles" in which employees provide critical analysis of operations.

NOTE: An interesting question involving organizational environment is whether the proper responsibility of company directors to shareholders is limited to pursuit of profit or taking account of broad cause-and-effect patterns involving the company. Lee Preston (1995) argues that the distinction is bogus, doing the latter (at least in the long term) should serve the former.

NOTE: Illustrating the effects of an organization's environment, Theodore Caplow (1992) argues that an organizational trend is toward bigger human resources divisions, which is a response to the increasing number of government regulations that affect business operations.

SELF-MANAGED WORK TEAMS

At mid-century, most formal organizations in the United States were conventional bureaucracies, run from the top down according to a stern chain of command. Today, especially as U.S. businesses face growing global competition, rigid structures are breaking down. This trend can be seen in the increasing use of *self-managed work teams.* Members of these small groups have the skills necessary to carry out tasks with minimal supervision. By allowing employees to operate within autonomous groups, organizations increase worker involvement in the job, provide a broader understanding of operations, and raise employee morale.

A few U.S. corporations (such as Procter & Gamble) have had autonomous work units in place since the 1960s. In recent years, many more (including Ford, General Motors, Caterpillar, and Digital Equipment) are following suit.

Comparing the performance of different organizations is difficult, given the many variables involved. But research suggests that self-managed work teams do boost productivity and, in the process, overcome some of the problems—including alienation—of the traditional bureaucratic model. Many businesses have also found that decentralizing responsibility in this way raises product quality and lowers rates of employee absenteeism and turnover (Yeatts, 1991, 1994; Maddox, 1994).

ORGANIZATIONAL ENVIRONMENT

How any organization performs depends not only on its internal structure but also on the **organizational environment,** *a range of factors external to an organization that affects its operation.* Such factors include technology, politics, population patterns, and the economy, as well as other organizations.

For example, modern organizations are shaped by the *technology* of computers, telephone systems, and copiers. Computers give employees access to more information and people than ever before. At the same time, computer technology allows executives to monitor closely the activities of workers (Markoff, 1991).

A second dimension of the organizational environment is *political and economic trends.* All organizations are helped or hindered by economic growth or recession, and no organization today can afford to overlook increasing competition from abroad. Similarly, changes in law—such as environmental regulations—can dramatically alter the way an organization operates.

Third, *population patterns*—such as the size and composition of the surrounding populace—also affect organizations. The average age, typical education, and social diversity of a local community shapes the available work force and sometimes the market for an organization's products or services.

Fourth, *other organizations* also contribute to the organizational environment. A hospital, for example, must be responsive to the insurance industry and organizations representing doctors, nurses, and other workers. And to remain competitive, the hospital must keep aware of the kinds of equipment and procedures available at other, nearby facilities.

In sum, no organization operates in a social vacuum. But, just as formal organizations are shaped by their environment, so do organizations act on the entire society, as we shall now explain.

THE McDONALDIZATION OF SOCIETY [1]

October 9, 1994, Macau. Here we are halfway around the world in the Portuguese colony of Macau—a little nub jutting from the Chinese coast. Few people here speak English, and life on the streets seems a world apart from the urban rhythms of New York, Chicago, or Los Angeles. Then I turn the corner and stand face to face with (who else?) Ronald McDonald! After eating who-knows-what for so long, forgive my failure to resist the lure of the Big Mac. But the most amazing thing is that the food—the burger, fries, and drink—looks, smells, and tastes exactly the same as it does back home 10,000 miles away!

As noted in the opening to this chapter, McDonald's has enjoyed enormous success. From a single store in the mid-1950s, McDonald's now operates more than 20,000 restaurants in the United States and throughout much of the world. There are more than

---

[1] Much of the material in this section is based on George Ritzer's (1993) book of the same name.

NOTE: The McDonaldization of society extends even to McFunerals. Service Corporation International currently operates 662 funeral homes in 39 states and is aggressively buying operations overseas. SCI now handles about 10 percent of all U.S. funerals in the United States (Myerson, 1993).

NOTE: McDonald's menu varies slightly in Japan, Hong Kong, and Singapore to meet local tastes. In New Delhi, India, McDonald's now serves 100% beef- and pork-free burgers (the "Maharaja Mac") in their trademark sesame seed buns.

DISCUSS: There are weak countertrends to McDonaldization. For example, people in their twenties are the most likely ever to drink micro-brewed beers—perhaps because they involve local companies with distinctive tastes versus the national giants. Can students identify other examples?

Is McDonaldization becoming a global trend? Yes and no. The spread of McDonald's around the world has been dramatic, and the company now earns most of its revenues from operations outside the United States. But, in some nations, McDonald's has altered its menu to take account of local cultural norms. When McDonald's opened a restaurant in New Delhi, India, Hindu people were not about to begin eating beef. Thus, this restaurant company promotes "vegetable burgers" (with fries, of course).

850 pairs of golden arches in Japan, for example, and the world's largest McDonald's recently opened in China's capital city of Beijing.

McDonald's has become a symbol of our way of life; in fact, one poll found that 98 percent of U.S. schoolchildren could identify Ronald McDonald, making the trademark clown as familiar as Santa Claus. Even more important, the organizational principles that underlie McDonald's are steadily coming to dominate our entire society. Our culture is becoming "McDonaldized"—an awkward way of saying that we model many aspects of life on the famous restaurant chain. Parents buy toys at worldwide chain stores like Toys 'Я' Us; we drive to Jiffy Lube for a ten-minute oil change; face-to-face communication is sliding more and more toward voice mail, e-mail, and junk mail; more vacations take the form of resort and tour packages; television presents news in the form of ten-second sound bites; college admission officers size up students they have never met by glancing at their GPA and SAT scores; and professors assign ghost-written textbooks[2] and evaluate students with tests mass-produced for them by publishing companies. The list goes on and on.

---

[2] Half a dozen popular sociology texts were not authored by the person or persons whose names appear on the cover. This book is not one of them.

McDonaldization: Four Principles

What do all these developments have in common? According to George Ritzer, the "McDonaldization of society" involves four basic organizational principles:

1. **Efficiency.** Ray Kroc, the marketing genius behind McDonald's, set out with one goal: to serve a hamburger, French fries, and a milkshake to a customer in fifty seconds or less. Today, one of the company's most popular items is the Egg McMuffin, an entire breakfast in a single sandwich. In the restaurant, customers bus their own trays or, better still, drive away from the pickup window, taking whatever mess they make with them.

    Efficiency is now a value virtually without critics in our society. We tend to think that anything that can be done quickly is, for that reason alone, good.

2. **Calculability.** The first McDonald's operating manual decreed that a regular raw hamburger must weigh 1.6 ounces, be 3.875 inches across, and have a fat content of 19 percent. A slice of cheese weighs exactly half an ounce. Fries are cut precisely 9/32 of an inch thick.

    Think about how many objects around the home, the workplace, or the campus are designed and mass-produced uniformly

NOTE: An example of the effects of organizational environment is a study by Linda Stearns and Kenneth Allan (1996) showing that waves of corporate mergers rise during eras of permissive government and available capital.

GLOBAL: Terry Besser (1993) argues that lower rates of absenteeism and turnover among Japanese workers do not necessarily indicate higher organizational commitment. Self-reported levels of commitment to organizations for workers in the United States and Japan are, in fact, similar.

GLOBAL: Boye de Mente argues that a crucial difference between Japanese and U.S. companies is that, in principle, the Japanese emphasize the worker more than the job; in the United States, we do the converse.

according to a standard plan. Not just our environment but our life experiences—from traveling the nation's interstates to sitting at home viewing television—are now more deliberately planned than ever before.

3. **Uniformity and predictability.** An individual can walk into a McDonald's restaurant almost anywhere and buy the same sandwiches, drinks, and desserts prepared in precisely the same way. Predictability, of course, is the result of a highly rational system that specifies every course of action and leaves nothing to chance.

4. **Control through automation.** The most unreliable element in the McDonald's system is human beings. People, after all, have good and bad days, sometimes let their minds wander, or simply decide to try something a different way. To eliminate, as much as possible, the unpredictable human element, McDonald's has automated its equipment to cook food at fixed temperatures for set lengths of time. Even the cash register at a McDonald's is keyed to pictures of the items, to minimize the responsibility of the human being taking the customer's order.

McDonaldization is expanding in the United States. Automatic teller machines are replacing banks, highly automated bakeries now produce bread with scarcely any human intervention, and chickens and eggs (or is it eggs and chickens?) emerge from automated hatcheries. In supermarkets, laser scanners are phasing out (less reliable) human checkers. Most of this country's shopping now occurs in malls, where everything from temperature and humidity to the kinds of stores and products are continuously controlled and supervised (Idle & Cordell, 1994).

Can Rationality Be Irrational?

There can be no argument about the popularity or the efficiency of McDonald's and similar organizations. But there is another side to the story.

Max Weber viewed the increasing rationalization of the world with alarm, fearing that formal organizations would cage our imagination and crush the human spirit. As he saw it, rational systems were efficient but dehumanizing. Each of the four principles just discussed reins in human creativity, discretion, and autonomy. Moreover, as George Ritzer points out, McDonald's products are not particularly good for people or the natural environment. Echoing Weber, Ritzer states that "the ultimate irrationality of McDonaldization is that people could lose control over the system and it would come to control us" (1993:145).

FORMAL ORGANIZATIONS IN JAPAN

We have described efforts to "humanize" U.S. formal organizations. Interestingly, however, organizations in some countries have long been more personal than those in the United States. Organizations in Japan, a small nation that has had remarkable economic success, exist within a culture of strong collective identity and solidarity. While most members of our society prize rugged individualism, the Japanese value cooperation.

Because of Japan's social cohesiveness, formal organizations in that society resemble very large primary groups. According to William Ouchi (1981), formal organizations in Japan and their counterparts in industrial societies of the West differ in five basic ways. In each case, the Japanese organization reflects that society's more collective orientation. The box considers how these five basic principles of Japanese organizations might be applied in the United States.

1. **Hiring and advancement.** Organizations in the United States hold out promotions and raises as prizes to be won through individual competition. In Japanese organizations, however, companies hire new school graduates together, and all employees in the group receive the same salary and responsibilities. Only after several years is anyone likely to be singled out for special advancement.

2. **Lifetime security.** Employees in the United States expect to move from one company to another to advance their careers. U.S. companies are also quick to lay off employees during an economic setback. By contrast, most Japanese firms hire employees for life, fostering strong, mutual loyalties. As jobs become obsolete, Japanese companies avoid layoffs by retraining workers for new jobs in the organization.

3. **Holistic involvement.** U.S. workers tend to see the home and the workplace as distinct spheres. Japanese organizations play a broad role in their employees' lives by providing home mortgages, sponsoring recreational activities, and scheduling social events. Such interaction beyond the workplace strengthens collective

RESOURCE: Boye de Mente's excerpt "Japanese Etiquette and Ethics in Business" is one of the cross-cultural selections included in the reader *Seeing Ourselves*.

GLOBAL: William Ouchi argues that their respective organizational contexts mean that business leaders in the United States can make quick decisions, but often struggle to achieve implementation. In contrast, Japanese leaders (who involve many others early on) are slow to make decisions, but implementation is subsequently rapid.

GLOBAL: A final difference between the two countries is that most U.S. executives have a secretary; relatively few Japanese business people do. In part, this difference reflects the more directly personal style of doing business in Japan.

GLOBAL SOCIOLOGY

The Japanese Model: Will It Work in the United States?

What the company wants is for us to work like the Japanese. Everybody go out and do jumping jacks in the morning and kiss each other when they go home at night. You work as a team, rat on each other, and lose control of your destiny. That's not going to work in this country.

John Brodie
President, United Paperworkers
Local 448
Chester, Pennsylvania

Who can argue with the economic success of the Japanese? Economic competition from Asia (and, increasingly, from Europe) is forcing U.S. companies to reconsider how corporate organizations should operate to be competitive in a global marketplace.

Business leaders are looking, for example, at the Japanese manufacturing plants built here in the United States. These "transplant-organizations" operated in the United States by Honda, Nissan, and Toyota have adapted well to a new environment, achieving the same high level of efficiency and quality that have won these companies praise in Japan. And, they have provided more than 250,000 jobs for U.S. workers.

Yet, some voices in this country—from the ranks of workers, union leaders, and managers—speak as bitterly about transplanting Japanese organizational techniques as they do about imported Japanese cars. Our corporate culture favors rigid hierarchy, praises individualism, and remembers its long history of labor-management conflict. As a result, workers and managers are wary of traditional Japanese practices, such as worker participation.

Some employees in the United States consider worker participation a thinly veiled strategy to increase their workload. While still responsible for building cars, for instance, workers would also have to worry about quality control, unit costs, and overall efficiency—concerns usually shouldered by management. Moreover, some employees see the broad training favored by the Japanese as endlessly moving

from job to job, always having to learn new skills. Many union leaders fear that any alliance of workers and managers could undermine union strength. Some managers, too, look warily on worker participation programs. Sharing the power to set production goals or schedule vacations does not come easily in light of past practices. Finally, U.S. corporations have a short-term outlook on profits, which discourages investing time and money in organizational restructuring.

Primarily due to rising global competition, however, worker participation programs are slowly changing the character of the U.S. workplace. A recent government survey found that 70 percent of large businesses had initiated at least some reforms of this kind. The advantages go right to the bottom line: Productivity and profits are usually higher when workers have a say in decision making. And most employees in worker participation programs—eventhose who may not want to sign up for morning jumping jacks—seem happier about their jobs. Workers who have used only their bodies in the past are now enjoying the opportunity to use their minds as well.

To a large extent, organizational life reflects the surrounding culture. But, stirred by the economic power of Japanese corporations, more and more workers in the United States are employing some of Japan's organizational techniques, such as quality control groups. However, few experts think that organizational patterns can be easily transplanted from one society to another.

Sources: Hoerr (1989) and Florida & Kenney (1991).

GLOBAL: As noted in Chapter 4, worker alienation has been linked to rigid bureaucracy (Weber) and rigid class structure (Marx). Japan has a favorable position in both respects. Japanese workers enjoy greater involvement in a more personalized organizational environment. Additionally, the compensation ratio (management/workers) in Japan is roughly half that in the United States.

DISCUSS: What about implanting computer chips in individuals that give identity, medical history, insurance information, and credit card numbers? This might help, say, Alzheimer's patients, but is it a boon or threat to everyone else?

SUPPLEMENTS: The *Data File* contains a new discussion of computers and the threat to personal privacy.

SEEING OURSELVES

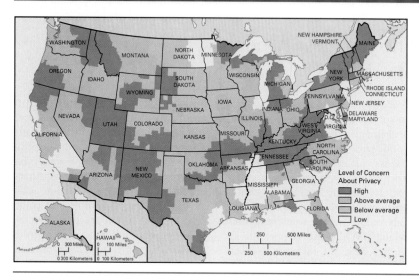

NATIONAL MAP 7–2
Concerns About Privacy Across the United States

At least one in three U.S. adults is concerned about the erosion of privacy. Looking at the map, which shows privacy concerns by county, what can you say about people who are most disturbed by this trend? Surprisingly, perhaps, the critics are not big-city residents who avoid eye contact and take refuge in unlisted telephone numbers. Who are they?

Source: *Business Geographics* © 1994 GIS World, Inc., 2101 S. Arlington Heights Boulevard, Arlington Heights, Ill., 60005–4185.

identity and offers the respectful Japanese worker an opportunity to voice suggestions and criticisms informally.

4. **Broad-based training.** Bureaucratic organization in the United States is based on specialization; many people spend an entire career at a single task. From the outset, a Japanese organization trains employees in all phases of its operation, again with the idea that employees will remain with the organization for life.

5. **Collective decision making.** In the United States, important decisions fall to key executives. Although Japanese leaders also take responsibility for their organization's performance, they involve workers in "quality circles" that discuss any decision that affects them. A closer working relationship is also encouraged by greater economic equality between management and workers. The salary differential between executives and lower-ranking employees is about half that in the United States.

These characteristics give the Japanese a strong sense of organizational loyalty. The cultural emphasis on *individual* achievement in our society finds its parallel in Japanese *groupism*. By tying their personal interests to those of their company, workers fulfill their ambitions through the organization.

GROUPS AND ORGANIZATIONS IN GLOBAL PERSPECTIVE

As this chapter has explained, formal organizations and their surrounding society interact, each influencing the other. This interaction explains why bureaucracy does not take a single organizational form; formal organizations in the United States and Japan, for example, differ in a number of ways.

Organizations also change over time. Several centuries ago, most businesses in Europe and the United States were small, family enterprises. But the Industrial Revolution created large, impersonal organizations. In this context, officials in Europe and the United States came to disparage primary relationships as a barrier to organizational efficiency. Favoritism shown to a family member, for example, is now branded as *nepotism*.

The development of formal organizations in Japan followed a different route. Historically, Japanese society was even more socially cohesive, organized according to family-based loyalties. As Japan rapidly industrialized, people there did not discard primary relationships as inefficient, as Westerners did. Rather, the Japanese modeled their large businesses on the family, transferring traditional kinship loyalties to corporations.

Japan, then, seems to be simultaneously modern and traditional, promoting organizational efficiency by cultivating personal ties. There are indications that

SOCIAL SURVEY: "How concerned are you about threats to your personal privacy in America today?" (GSS 1982, N = 1,506; *Codebook*, 1996:255)

"Very concerned"   44.6%   "Not concerned at all" 10.9%
"Somewhat concerned"   28.6%   DK/NR   1.5%
"Only a little concerned" 14.4%

SOCIAL SURVEY: "Should employers be allowed or not allowed to:" (*Time* poll, 1991)

"listen in on employee telephone conversations" (*Yes*, 6%; *No*, 93%)

"scan the work area with video cameras" (*Yes*, 38%; *No*, 56%)

"require employees to take drug tests" (*Yes*, 76%; *No*, 19%)

Q: "Mind your own business." Phrase appearing on the first coin minted in the United States in 1778

CONTROVERSY & DEBATE

Are Large Organizations a Threat to Personal Privacy?

Joe finishes dressing and calls an 800 number to check the pollen count. As he listens to a recorded message, a Caller ID computer identifies Joe, records the call, and pulls up Joe's profile from a public records database. The profile, which now includes the fact that Joe suffers from allergies, is later sold to a drug company, which sends Joe a free sample of a new allergy medication.

At a local department store, Nina uses her American Express card to buy an expensive new watch and some sleepwear. The store's computer adds Nina's name to their database of "buyers of expensive jewelry" and "buyers of sexy lingerie." The store trades their database with other companies. Within a month, Nina's mail includes four jewelry catalogues and an adult video brochure (Bernstein, 1997).

Are these organizations providing consumers with interesting products or violating people's privacy? The answer, of course, is both: The same systems that help organizations operate predictably and efficiently also allow them to invade our lives and manipulate us. So, as bureaucracy has expanded in the United States, privacy has declined.

The problem reflects the enormous power of large organizations, their tendency to treat people impersonally, and their appetite for information. In recent decades, the danger to privacy has increased as organizations have acquired more and more computers and other new information technology to store and share information.

Consider some of the obvious ways in which organizations compile personal information. As they issue driver's licenses, for example, state agencies generate files that they can dispatch at the touch of a button to officials, including the police. Similarly, the Internal Revenue Service, the Social Security Administration, regulatory agencies of all kinds, and government programs that benefit veterans, students, the poor, and unemployed people all collect extensive, personal information.

Businesses in the private sector now do much the same thing although, as the opening examples suggest, people may not be aware that their choices and activities end up in someone's database. Most people find the use of credit cards a great convenience (the U.S. population now holds more than 1 billion of them—averaging more than five per adult). But few people stop to think that credit card purchases automatically generate electronic records that can end up almost anywhere.

We also experience the erosion of privacy in the surveillance cameras that monitor more and more public places, along main street, in the shopping malls, and even across college campuses. And then there is the escalating amount of junk mail—now half of all material the post office delivers. Mailing lists proliferate as one company sells our names and addresses to others. Bought a new car recently? If so, you probably have found yourself receiving mail about all kinds of automotive products. Have you ever rented an X-rated video? Many video stores keep records of the movie preferences of customers and pass them along to other businesses whose advertising soon arrives in the mailbox.

Concern about the erosion of privacy in the United States runs high. In response, many states have enacted laws giving citizens the right to examine records about themselves kept by employers, banks, and credit bureaus. The U.S. Privacy Act of 1974 also limits the exchange of personal information between government agencies and permits citizens to examine and correct most government files. But the fact is that so many organizations now have information about us—experts estimate that 90 percent of U.S. households are profiled in databases somewhere—that current laws simply cannot address the full scope of the problem.

Across the United States, who is most concerned about the growing assault on privacy? National Map 7–2 provides some insights.

Continue the debate . . .

1. *Look at National Map 7–2. Where are people most concerned about losing their privacy? Can you explain this pattern?*

2. *Internet search engines such as YAHOO! [http://www.yahoo.com] have "people search" programs that let you locate almost anyone. Do you think such programs are, on balance, helpful or threatening to the public?*

3. *In our current age of large organizations and expanding computer technology, do you think the privacy problem will get worse or will it get better? Why?*

Sources: Dunn (1991), Miller (1991), and Bernstein (1997).

NOTE: With regard to social change: Durkheim characterized modernity as a gradual loss of moral bonds (collective conscience) with a concomitant rise of individualism and economic cooperation. But he recognized that modern culture generates limited social cohesion and argued that group memberships could enhance social solidarity. But do modern groups exert much moral pull on us?

Japanese workers are becoming more individualistic. Yet the Japanese model demonstrates that organizational life need not be so dehumanizing.

Economically challenged as never before, U.S. businesses are taking a closer look at organizational patterns elsewhere, especially in Japan. In fact, many efforts to "humanize" bureaucracy in the United States are clear attempts to do things the Japanese way.

Beyond the benefits for U.S. business organizations, there is another reason to study the Japanese approach. Our society is less socially cohesive now than the more family-based society Weber knew. A rigidly bureaucratic form of organization only further atomizes our social fabric. Perhaps by following the lead of the Japanese, our own formal organizations can promote—rather than diminish—a sense of collective identity and responsibility.

As some analysts point out, U.S. organizations are still the envy of the world for their productive efficiency; in fact, there are few places on earth where the mail arrives as quickly and dependably as in the United States (Wilson, 1991). But the extent of global diversity and change demands that we remain open-minded and curious about the possibilities for reorganizing our future.

SUMMARY

1. Social groups—important building blocks of societies—foster personal development and common identity as well as perform various tasks.

2. Primary groups tend to be small and person-oriented; secondary groups are typically large and goal-oriented.

3. Instrumental leadership is concerned with realizing a group's goals; expressive leadership focuses on members' morale and well-being.

4. The process of group conformity is well documented by researchers. Because members often seek consensus, work groups do not necessarily generate a wider range of ideas than individuals working alone.

5. Individuals use reference groups—both ingroups and outgroups—to form attitudes and make decisions.

6. Georg Simmel characterized the dyad relationship as intense but unstable; a triad, he added, can easily dissolve into a dyad by excluding one member.

7. Peter Blau explored how the size, homogeneity, social standing, and physical segregation of groups all affect members' behavior.

8. Social networks are relational webs that link people who typically have little common identity and limited interaction. The Internet is a vast electronic network linking millions of computers worldwide.

9. Formal organizations are large, secondary groups that seek to perform complex tasks efficiently. According to their members' reasons for joining, formal organizations are classified as utilitarian, normative, or coercive.

10. Bureaucratic organization expands in modern societies to perform many complex tasks efficiently. Bureaucracy is based on specialization, hierarchy, rules and regulations, technical competence, impersonal interaction, and formal, written communications.

11. Ideal bureaucracy may promote efficiency, but bureaucracy also generates alienation and inefficiency, tends to perpetuate itself beyond the achievement of its goals, and contributes to the contemporary erosion of privacy.

12. Formal organizations often mirror oligarchies. Rosabeth Moss Kanter's research has shown that the concentration of power and opportunity in U.S. corporations can compromise organizational effectiveness.

13. Humanizing bureaucracy means recognizing people as an organization's greatest resource. To develop human resources, organizations should spread responsibility and opportunity widely. One way to put this ideal into operation is through self-managed work teams.

14. Technology, political and economic trends, population patterns, and other organizations all combine to form the environment in which a particular business or agency must operate.

15. The trend dubbed "the McDonaldization of society" involves increasing automation and impersonality.

16. Reflecting the collective spirit of Japanese culture, formal organizations in Japan are based more on personal ties than their counterparts in the United States.

KEY CONCEPTS

social group two or more people who identify and interact with one another

primary group a small social group in which relationships are both personal and enduring

secondary group a large and impersonal social group devoted to some specific interest or activity

instrumental leadership group leadership that emphasizes the completion of tasks

expressive leadership group leadership that emphasizes collective well-being

groupthink the tendency of group members to conform by adopting a narrow view of some issue

reference group a social group that serves as a point of reference in making evaluations or decisions

ingroup a social group commanding a member's esteem and loyalty

outgroup a social group toward which one feels competition or opposition

dyad a social group with two members

triad a social group with three members

network a web of social ties that links people who identify and interact little with one another

formal organization a large secondary group organized to achieve its goals efficiently

bureaucracy an organizational model rationally designed to perform complex tasks efficiently

bureaucratic ritualism a preoccupation with rules and regulations to the point of thwarting an organization's goals

bureaucratic inertia the tendency of bureaucratic organizations to perpetuate themselves

oligarchy the rule of the many by the few

humanizing bureaucracy fostering a more democratic organizational atmosphere that recognizes and encourages the contributions of everyone

organizational environment a range of factors external to an organization that affects its operation

CRITICAL-THINKING QUESTIONS

1. What are the key differences between primary and secondary groups? Identify examples of each in the daily round of life.

2. What are some of the positive functions of group conformity (for example, fostering team spirit)? Note several dysfunctions.

3. According to Max Weber, what are the six characteristics of bureaucracy? How do Japanese organizations differ from organizations in the United States?

4. What does the "McDonaldization of society" mean? Cite examples of this trend beyond those discussed in this chapter.

LEARNING EXERCISES

1. Visit a large, public building with an elevator. Observe groups of people as they approach the elevator and, entering the elevator with them, watch what occurs next. What happens to the conversations? Where do people fix their eyes? Can you account for these patterns?

2. Write out a list of ingroups and outgroups on your campus. What traits account for groups falling into each category? Ask several other people to comment on your list to see if they agree with your classifications.

3. The next time you arrive early to a social gathering, observe how many people share the conversation.

What happens to the single group as more people arrive? What seems to be the maximum size for a group in one conversation?

4. Using available publications (and some assistance from an instructor), try to draw an "organizational pyramid" for your college or university showing the key offices and how they supervise and report to other offices.

5. If you have computer access, install the CD-ROM packaged inside the back cover of your text and complete the activities designed to accompany this chapter.

Christian Pierre, *Pool Hall Glow,* 1962

CHAPTER 8

DEVIANCE

A few years ago, crack cocaine transformed the area around 145th Street and Eighth Avenue in New York's Harlem into a war zone. Nine-year-old Rahmel Miller can recall lying in bed hearing gunshots echo through his neighborhood. And when Rahmel watched his mother kiss his brother goodbye every day, he knew the pained look on her face was fear—that this might be the last time she would ever see him alive.

Rahmel's neighborhood was convulsed by crime, and the reality of violence has forced young boys and girls to grow up quickly. Rahmel's older brother wondered whether he should carry a gun to protect himself going to school.

But in recent years, the violence has lessened, and Rahmel does not know the terror his brother did. "People are getting smarter," explains twenty-year-old Salahadeen Betts, one of Rahmel's neighbors. "Before people would sell drugs because it was the cool thing to do. Now people are getting smarter about guns and drugs" (Butterfield, 1997:1).

Across the country, official statistics confirm what Rahmel and his neighbors already know: The rising wave of crime that has paralyzed many urban communities seems—for the present, at least—to be turning around. But we continue to face a serious crime problem, one that is much worse than in other industrial countries like Japan or England.

This chapter explores the problem of crime, identifying kinds of crime, profiling offenders, and offering some ideas about why crime trends are currently down. But, first, we tackle a broader issue: why societies construct standards of right and wrong in the first place. As we shall see, the law is simply one element of a complex system of social control that teaches us to conform, at least most of the time, to countless social rules. We begin our investigation by defining several basic concepts.

WHAT IS DEVIANCE?

Deviance is *the recognized violation of cultural norms.* Norms guide virtually all human activities, so the concept of deviance covers a correspondingly broad spectrum. One category of deviance is **crime,** *the violation of norms a society formally enacts into criminal law.* Even

criminal deviance is extensive, ranging from minor traffic violations to serious offenses such as murder. A subcategory of crime, **juvenile delinquency,** refers to *the violation of legal standards by the young.*

Some instances of deviance barely raise eyebrows; other cases command a swift and severe response. Members of our society pay little notice to mild nonconformity like left-handedness or boastfulness; we take a dimmer view of reckless driving or dropping out of school, and we call the police in response to a violent crime like armed robbery.

Not all deviance involves action or even choice. The simple *existence* of some categories of individuals can be troublesome to others. To the young, elderly people can seem hopelessly "out of it"; and to whites, who are in the majority, the mere presence of people of color may cause discomfort. Able-bodied people often view those with disabilities as an outgroup. And affluent people may shun the poor for falling short of middle-class standards.

Most examples of nonconformity that come readily to mind are negative instances of rule breaking, such as stealing from a convenience store, abusing a child, or driving while intoxicated. But we also define especially righteous people—students who speak up

SUPPLEMENTS: An outline of Chapter 8 and supplementary lecture material are found in the *Data File*.
RESOURCE: Nathaniel Hawthorne's *The Scarlet Letter* is a wonderfully sociological tale of deviance and social control, and of the human spirit courageously emerging from a cloak of conformity.
Q: "Conscience is that inner voice that warns us that someone may be watching." H. L. Mencken

NOTE: "Glueck" rhymes with "book."
NOTE: The Gluecks' idea that treating boys as if they were bullies may bring on delinquency nicely illustrates the Thomas theorem, "Situations we define as real become real in their consequences."
NOTE: Phrenology, the 19th-century pseudoscience, contended that personality traits and behavioral dispositions could be determined by the shape of a person's skull.

The kind of deviance people create reflects the moral values they embrace. The Berkeley campus of the University of California has long celebrated its open-minded tolerance of sexual diversity. Thus, in 1992, when Andrew Martinez decided to attend classes wearing virtually nothing, people were reluctant to accuse "The Naked Guy" of immoral conduct. However, in Berkeley's politically correct atmosphere, it was not long before school officials banned Martinez from campus—charging that his nudity constituted a form of sexual harassment.

too much in class or people who are overly enthusiastic about new computer technology—as deviant, even if we accord them a measure of respect (Huls, 1987). What deviant actions or attitudes—whether negative or positive—have in common is some element of *difference* that causes us to regard another person as an "outsider" (Becker, 1966).

SOCIAL CONTROL

Members of a society try to influence each other's behavior through various kinds of *social control*. Much of the time, this process is informal, as when parents praise or criticize their children or friends playfully comment on someone's latest romantic interest. Cases of serious deviance, however, may provoke a response from the **criminal justice system,** *a formal response to alleged violations of law on the part of police, courts, and prison officials.*

In sum, deviance is much more than a matter of individual choice or personal failing. *How* a society defines deviance, *whom* individuals brand as deviant, and *what* people decide to do about nonconformity are all issues of social organization. Only gradually, however, have people recognized this essential truth, as we shall now explain.

THE BIOLOGICAL CONTEXT

Chapter 5 ("Socialization") explained that people a century ago understood—or, more correctly, misunderstood—human behavior as an expression of biological instincts. Early interest in criminality therefore emphasized biological causes. In 1876 Cesare Lombroso (1836–1909), an Italian physician who worked in prisons, proposed that criminals had distinctive physical features—low foreheads, prominent jaws and cheekbones, protruding ears, excessive hairiness, and unusually long arms—that, taken together, made them resemble the apelike ancestors of human beings.

But Lombroso's work was flawed, since the physical features he attributed to prisoners actually existed throughout the entire population. We now know that no physical attributes of the kind described by Lombroso distinguish criminals from noncriminals (Goring, 1972; orig. 1913).

At mid-century, William Sheldon (1949) took a different tack, suggesting that body type might predict criminality. He cross-checked hundreds of young men for body type and criminal history, and concluded that delinquency was most likely to occur among boys with muscular, athletic builds. Sheldon Glueck and Eleanor Glueck (1950) confirmed Sheldon's findings, but cautioned that a powerful build does not necessarily cause or even predict criminality. The Gluecks suggested that parents tend to be more distant from powerfully built sons so that they, in turn, grow up to display less sensitivity toward others. Moreover, in a self-fulfilling prophecy, people who expect muscular boys to act like bullies may provoke such aggressive behavior.

Today, genetic research seeks possible links between biology and crime. To date, though, no conclusive evidence connects criminality to any specific

NOTE: Psychology's more individualistic orientation is evident in the tendency to speak of *personal disorders* rather than *social deviance*.
DISCUSS: To illustrate changing conceptions of deviance, consider the falling rate of traditionally moral offenses concerned with decorum and honesty and the rising rate of offenses concerned with sexual or racial harassment or other "insensitivity."
Q: "I try to avoid temptation, unless I can't resist it." Mae West

DIVERSITY: Look ahead to Chapter 23 to the five photos showing changing hair styles in the United States over recent decades; fashion is a matter of changing conceptions of conformity and deviance. Students can attach considerable significance to small fashion details: Recall how baseball caps became popular one year, and then were worn backwards the next.
Q: "I can resist everything except temptation." Oscar Wilde

genetic trait. Yet, people's overall genetic composition, in combination with social influences, probably accounts for some variation in criminality. In other words, biological factors may have a real, but modest, effect on whether or not individuals engage in criminal activity (Rowe, 1983; Rowe & Osgood, 1984; Wilson & Herrnstein, 1985; Jencks, 1987).

Critical evaluation. At best, biological theories that try to explain crime in terms of rare physical traits explain only a small proportion of all crimes. Recent sociobiological research—noting, for example, that violent crime is overwhelmingly committed by males and that adults are more likely to abuse foster children than natural children—is promising, but we know too little about the links between genes and human behavior to draw firm conclusions (Daly & Wilson, 1988).

Then, too, because a biological approach looks just at the individual, it offers no insight as to how some kinds of behaviors come to be defined as deviant in the first place. Therefore, although there is much to be learned about how human biology may affect behavior, research currently places far greater emphasis on social influences (Gibbons & Krohn, 1986; Liska, 1991).

PERSONALITY FACTORS

Like biological theories, psychological explanations of deviance focus on cases of individual abnormality, this time involving personality. Some personality traits are hereditary, but most psychologists believe that temperament is shaped primarily by social experience. Deviance, then, is viewed as the product of "unsuccessful" socialization.

The work of Walter Reckless and Simon Dinitz (1967) illustrates the psychological approach. These researchers began by asking a number of teachers to categorize their twelve-year-old male students as either likely or unlikely to commit acts of juvenile delinquency. They then interviewed the boys and their mothers to assess each boy's self-concept and how he related to others. Analyzing their results, Reckless and Dinitz found that the "good boys" displayed a strong conscience (or superego, in Sigmund Freud's terminology), coped well with frustration, and identified with cultural norms and values. The "bad boys," by contrast, had a weaker conscience, displayed little tolerance for frustration, and sympathized less with conventional culture.

Furthermore, the researchers found that the "good boys" went on to have fewer run-ins with the police

than the "bad boys." Since all the boys lived in an area where delinquency was widespread, the investigators attributed staying out of trouble to a personality that reined in impulses toward deviance. Based on this conclusion, Reckless and Dinitz call their analysis *containment theory*.

Critical evaluation. Psychologists have demonstrated that personality patterns have some connection to delinquency and other types of deviance. Nevertheless, containment theory suffers from a serious limitation: The vast majority of serious crimes are committed by people whose psychological profiles are *normal*.

In sum, both biological and psychological approaches view deviance as an individual attribute without exploring how conceptions of right and wrong initially arise, why people define some rule breakers, but not others, as deviant, or what role power plays in shaping a society's system of social control. To explore these issues, we now turn to a sociological analysis of deviance.

THE SOCIAL FOUNDATIONS OF DEVIANCE

Although we tend to view deviance in terms of the free choice or personal failings of individuals, all behavior—deviance as well as conformity—is shaped by society. Three social foundations of deviance are identified below and explained in later sections of the chapter:

1. **Deviance varies according to cultural norms.** No thought or action is inherently deviant; it becomes deviant only in relation to particular norms. The life patterns of rural Vermonters, small-town Texans, and Southern Californians differ in significant ways; for this reason, what people in each area prize or scorn varies also. Laws, too, differ from place to place. In Texas, for example, you can legally consume alcohol in a car, a practice that draws the attention of police in most other states. Casino gambling is legal at least somewhere in twenty-three states, but illegal in twenty-seven others. Legal prostitution is found only in Nevada. Further, most cities and towns have at least one unique statute: Only in Seattle, for example, is a person suffering from the flu subject to arrest simply for appearing in public.

    Around the world, deviance is even more wide-ranging. Albania outlaws any public display

RESOURCE: The implications of art and the role of the artist in culture and deviance are explored in Philip Rieff's introductory essay "The Impossible Culture: Wilde as a Modern Prophet" in Oscar Wilde, *The Soul of Man Under Socialism and Other Essays* (New York: Harper & Row, 1970).

DISCUSS: Andres Serrano, who created "Piss Christ," a photograph of a crucifix submerged in Serrano's own urine, maintains that art reaches its greatest power when it is most provocative. Is such work art or obscenity?

Q: "Crime, then, is necessary; it is bound up with the fundamental conditions of all social life and by that very fact it is useful, because these conditions of which it is a part are themselves indispensable to the normal evolution of morality and law." Emile Durkheim (1964:70)

Artists have an important function in any society: to explore alternatives to conventional notions about how to live. For this reason, while we celebrate artists' creativity, we also accord them a mildly deviant identity. In today's more conservative political climate, some government officials have objected to art that seems to challenge traditional morality. For their part, some artists have found expressive ways to show their displeasure with such thinking.

of religious faith, such as "crossing" oneself, and Cuba can prosecute its citizens for "consorting with foreigners." Police can arrest people in Singapore for selling chewing gum, in Manila, the Philippines, for using a cell phone in a car, in the Malaysian state of Kaelantan for patronizing a unisex hair salon, and—anywhere in Iran—police can arrest a woman for wearing make-up.

2. **People become deviant as others define them that way.** Everyone violates cultural norms regularly, occasionally to the extent of breaking the law. For example, most of us have talked out loud to ourselves or "borrowed" a pen from our workplace. Whether such activities are sufficient to define us as mentally ill or criminal depends on how others perceive, define, and respond to our behavior.

3. **Both rule making and rule breaking involve social power.** The law, claimed Karl Marx, amounts to little more than the means by which powerful people protect their interests. For example, the owners of an unprofitable factory have a legal right to shut down their business, even if doing so puts thousands of people out of work. But a worker who commits an act of vandalism that closes the same factory for a single day is subject to criminal prosecution.

Similarly, a homeless person who stands on a street corner denouncing the city government risks arrest for disturbing the peace; a mayoral candidate during an election campaign does exactly the same thing and gets extensive police protection. In short, norms and how we apply them are linked to social inequality.

STRUCTURAL-FUNCTIONAL ANALYSIS

The structural-functional paradigm focuses on how deviance contributes to the operation of society.

EMILE DURKHEIM: THE FUNCTIONS OF DEVIANCE

In his pioneering study of deviance, Emile Durkheim (1964a, orig. 1895; 1964b, orig. 1893) made the astonishing statement that there is nothing abnormal about deviance; in fact, it contributes to the operation of society in four ways:

1. **Deviance affirms cultural values and norms.** Living demands that we make moral choices. To prevent our culture from dissolving into chaos, people must show preference for some attitudes

RESOURCE: Good illustrations of how crime functions to reaffirm norms and increase social unity are found in Truman Capote's *In Cold Blood* (Signet, 1965); see especially pages 279–80.
NOTE: A new functional issue is the pattern of "defining deviance upward," the pattern of refocusing a prosecution from a "lesser" issue to a more important one. The O. J. Simpson case was about a murder, but it was defined "up" to the issue of whether the criminal justice system is free of bias.
DISCUSS: Erikson found that 3–4% of the Puritans were defined as deviant at any time. What would Durkheim say about the fact that, in the U.S. today, about 3% of adults are in prison, on parole, or on probation?
Q: "Puritanism is the lurking fear that someone, somewhere, may be happy." H. L. Mencken

Emile Durkheim's important insight is that no society can exist without deviance. Thus, after arriving in New England in the early seventeenth century, the very religious Puritans soon found themselves accusing some of their members of serious wrongdoing. The best-known Puritan "crime wave" climaxed in the Salem "witch trials" of 1692, which led to two dozen executions of women and men thought to be doing the work of the devil. Following Durkheim's approach to deviance, what sense can you make of this startling episode?

and behaviors over others. But any conception of virtue rests upon an opposing notion of vice. And just as there can be no good without evil, there can be no justice without crime. Deviance, in short, is indispensable to creating and sustaining morality.

2. **Responding to deviance clarifies moral boundaries.** By defining some individuals as deviant, people draw a social boundary between right and wrong. For example, a college marks the line between academic honesty and cheating by punishing students who commit plagiarism.

3. **Responding to deviance promotes social unity.** People typically react to serious deviance with collective outrage. This, Durkheim explained, reaffirms the moral ties that bind them. For example, in response to the Oklahoma City bombing in 1995, our society joined together in a chorus of condemnation.

4. **Deviance encourages social change.** Deviant people, Durkheim claimed, push a society's moral boundaries, pointing out alternatives to the status quo and encouraging change. Moreover, he declared, today's deviance can become tomorrow's morality (1964a:71). In the 1950s, for example, many people thought rock-and-roll music threatened the morals of youth. Now, however, rock-and-roll is in the musical mainstream and a multibillion-dollar industry, perhaps more "all-American" than apple pie.

An Illustration:
The Puritans of Massachusetts Bay

Kai Erikson's (1966) historical investigation of the early Puritans of Massachusetts Bay is a good illustration of Durkheim's theory. Erikson shows that even the Puritans—a disciplined and highly religious group—created deviance to clarify their moral boundaries. In fact, Durkheim might well have had the Puritans in mind when he wrote:

> Imagine a society of saints, a perfect cloister of exemplary individuals. Crimes, properly so called, will there be unknown; but faults which appear [insignificant] to the layman will create there the same scandal that the ordinary offense does in ordinary consciousness. . . . For the same reason, the perfect and upright man judges his smallest failings with a severity that the majority reserve for acts more truly in the nature of an offense. (1964a:68–69)

Deviance, in short, is not a matter of having a few "bad apples" around; it is a necessary condition of "good" social living.

If deviance is universal, the *kind* of deviance people generate depends on the moral issues they seek to clarify. Over time, the Puritans faced a number of "crime waves." With each response, the Puritans sharpened their views on crucial moral issues. They answered questions about how much dissent to allow and what their religious goals should be by celebrating

NOTE: Another illustration of shifting moral boundaries: Is it any wonder, during the 1980s, a decade during which U.S. families tried to come to terms with the increased use of child care, that there were numerous child abuse cases against operators of child-care facilities (the McMartin case being the best known)?

Q: "Although I am not naturally honest, I am sometimes so by chance." William Shakespeare

NOTE: Thomas Szasz (1995) suggests that, economically speaking, people fall into one of three categories: producers (Merton's conformists); predators (innovators); or parasites (retreatists).

Q: "... differential pressures for deviant behavior will continue to be exerted upon certain groups and strata as long as the structure of opportunity and the cultural goals remain substantially unchanged." Robert K. Merton (1968:246)

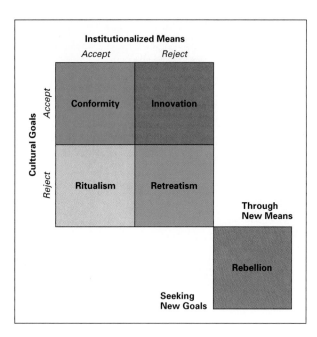

FIGURE 8–1 Merton's Strain Theory of Deviance
Source: Merton (1968).

some of their members while condemning others as deviant.

Perhaps most fascinating of all, Erikson discovered that, even though the offenses changed, the proportion of deviant Puritans remained steady over time. This stability, concludes Erikson, confirms Durkheim's contention that deviants serve as ethical markers, outlining a society's changing moral boundaries. In other words, by constantly defining a small number of people as deviant, the Puritans maintained a certain "shape" to their society.

MERTON'S STRAIN THEORY

Some deviance may be necessary for a society to function, but Robert Merton (1938, 1968) argues that *excessive* violations arise from particular social arrangements. Specifically, the scope and character of deviance depends on how well a society provides the institutionalized *means* (such as schooling and job opportunities) to achieve cultural *goals* (such as financial success).

Conformity, Merton begins, lies in pursuing conventional goals through approved means. Thus, the U.S. "success story" is someone who gains wealth and

prestige through talent and hard work. But not everyone who desires conventional success has the opportunity to attain it. Children raised in poverty, for example, may see little hope of becoming successful if they "play by the rules." As a result, they may seek wealth through crime—say, by dealing cocaine. Merton called this type of deviance *innovation*—using unconventional means (drug sales) to achieve a culturally approved goal (wealth). Figure 8–1 shows innovation as accepting the goal of success while rejecting the conventional means of becoming rich.

According to Merton, the "strain" between our culture's emphasis on wealth and the limited opportunity to get rich gives rise, especially among the poor, to theft and selling illegal drugs or other forms of street hustling. In some respects, at least, a "notorious gangster" like Al Capone was quite conventional—he pursued the fame and fortune at the heart of the "American Dream." But, like many minorities who find the doors to "legitimate" success all but closed, Capone blazed his own trail to the top. As one analyst put it (Allsop, 1961:236):

> The typical criminal of the Capone era was a boy who had . . . seen what was rated as success in the society he had been thrust into—the Cadillac, the big bankroll, the elegant apartment. How could he acquire that kind of recognizable status? He was almost always a boy of outstanding initiative, imagination, and ability; he was the kind of boy who, under different conditions, would have been a captain of industry or a key political figure of his time. But he hadn't the opportunity of going to Yale and becoming a banker or broker; there was no passage for him to a law degree from Harvard. There was, however, a relatively easy way of acquiring these goods that he was incessantly told were available to him as an American citizen, and without which he had begun to feel he could not properly count himself as an American citizen. He could become a gangster.

Perhaps we should not be surprised at the fact that Capone, denied the chance to attend Yale or Harvard, landed his first job with a gangster who called himself Mr. Frankie Yale and his nightclub, the "Harvard Inn."

The inability to become successful by normative means may also lead to another type of deviance that Merton calls *ritualism* (see Figure 8–1). Ritualists resolve the strain of limited success by abandoning cultural goals in favor of almost compulsive efforts to live "respectably." In essence, they espouse the rules to

NOTE: Becoming successful through illegitimate means explains the gangster's preoccupation with being respected and the desire, eventually, to "go legit." Capone often demanded that others address him as "Anthony Brown" and, in time, was delighted to enroll his son at Yale.

Q: "You don't want to be too moral; you miss too much living." Ruth Gordon in *Harold and Maude*

NOTE: Students may be surprised to learn that Prohibition was the law of the land between 1920 and 1933, a product of the 18th Amendment to the Constitution.

Q: "In this life one frequently finds greater rewards for vice than for virtue." René Descartes (1641)

Q: "The inescapable conclusion is that society secretly wants crime and needs crime . . ." Karl Menninger, *The Crime of Punishment*

In the Kosovo region of Serbia, as in the United States, young people (especially males) cut off from legitimate opportunity may form deviant subcultures as a strategy to gain the prestige denied them by the larger society.

the point that they lose sight of their larger goals. Low-level bureaucrats, for example, often succumb to ritualism as a way of gaining respectability.

A third response to the inability to succeed is *retreatism*—the rejection of both cultural goals and means, so that one, in effect, "drops out." Retreatists include some alcoholics and drug addicts, and some of the street people found in U.S. cities. The deviance of retreatists lies in unconventional living and, perhaps more seriously, in choosing to live that way.

The fourth response to failure is *rebellion*. Like retreatists, rebels reject both the cultural definition of success and the normative means of achieving it. Rebels, however, go one step further by advocating radical alternatives to the existing social order. Typically, they advocate the political or religious transformation of society, and often join a counterculture.

DEVIANT SUBCULTURES

Richard Cloward and Lloyd Ohlin (1966) extended Merton's theory in their investigation of delinquent youth. They maintain that criminal deviance results not simply from limited legitimate (legal) opportunity but also from the availability of illegitimate (illegal) opportunity. In short, deviance or conformity depends upon the *relative opportunity structure* that frames young people's lives.

The life of Al Capone shows how an ambitious person denied legitimate opportunity could organize a criminal empire to take advantage of the country's demand for alcohol during Prohibition (1920–1933). In other words, illegal opportunities foster the development of *criminal subcultures* that offer the knowledge, skills, and other resources people need to succeed in unconventional ways. Indeed, gangs may specialize in one or another form of criminality according to available opportunities and resources (Sheley et al., 1995).

But what happens when people are unable to identify *any* kinds of opportunities, legal or illegal? Then, delinquency often surfaces in the form of *conflict subcultures*, where violence is ignited by frustration and a desire for fame or respect. Alternatively, those who fail to achieve success, even through criminal means, may fall into *retreatist subcultures*, dropping out through abuse of alcohol or other drugs.

Albert Cohen (1971) suggests that delinquency is most pronounced among lower-class youths because they have the least opportunity to achieve success in conventional ways. Neglected by society, they seek self-respect by creating a delinquent subculture that "defines as meritorious the characteristics they *do* possess, the kinds of conduct of which they *are* capable" (1971:66). Having a notorious street reputation, for example, may win no points with society as a whole, but it may satisfy a youth's desire to "be somebody."

Q: "There is so much good in the worst of us, and so much bad in the best of us." Anonymous
GLOBAL: The labeling approach casts doubt on the old saying, "Sticks and stones can break my bones, but names can never hurt me." Members of our society recognize the power of labels in libel law; some other societies (Islamic, for instance) treat labels even more seriously than we do, as suggested by the Salman Rushdie case.

NOTE: People must sometimes contend with deviant labels when they have done nothing at all. Victims of violent rape may be subjected to labeling as deviants based on the misguided assumption that they encouraged the offender. Similarly, individuals with acquired immune deficiency syndrome (AIDS) sometimes find that they are shunned by employers, friends, and even family members.

The world is full of people who are unusual in one way or another. This Indian man grew the fingernails on one hand for more than thirty years just to do something that no one else had ever done. Should we define such behavior as harmless eccentricity or as evidence of mental illness?

Walter Miller (1970) agrees that delinquent subcultures typically develop among lower-class youths, who have the least opportunity to achieve success legitimately. He describes six "focal concerns" of delinquent subcultures: (1) *trouble*, arising from frequent conflict with teachers and police; (2) *toughness*, the value placed on physical size, strength, and athletic skills, especially among males; (3) *smartness* (or "street smarts"), the ability to succeed on the streets, to outthink or "con" others, and to avoid being similarly taken advantage of; (4) *excitement*, the search for thrills, risk, or danger as a release from a daily routine that is predictable and unsatisfying; (5) a preoccupation with *fate*, derived from the lack of control these youths feel over their own lives; and (6) *autonomy*, a desire for freedom often expressed as resentment toward figures of authority.

Critical evaluation. Durkheim's pioneering work in the functions of deviance remains central to sociological

thinking. Even so, critics point out that a community does not always come together in reaction to crime; sometimes fear of crime causes people to withdraw from public life (Liska & Warner, 1991).

Merton's strain theory, which is based on Durkheim's work, has also come under criticism for explaining some kinds of deviance (theft, for example) far better than others (such as crimes of passion or mental illness). In addition, not everyone seeks success in conventional terms of wealth, as strain theory implies. As explained in Chapter 3 ("Culture"), members of our society embrace many different cultural values and are motivated by various ideas of personal success.

The general argument of Cloward and Ohlin, Cohen, and Miller—that deviance reflects the opportunity structure of society—has been confirmed by subsequent research (Allan & Steffensmeier, 1989). However, these theories, too, fall short in assuming that everyone shares the same cultural standards for judging right and wrong. Moreover, we must be careful not to define deviance in ways that unfairly target poor people. If crime is defined to include stock fraud as well as street theft, then more affluent individuals are likely to be defined as criminals. Finally, all structural-functional theories imply that everyone who violates conventional cultural standards will be branded deviant. Becoming deviant, however, is actually a highly complex process, as the next section explains.

SYMBOLIC-INTERACTION ANALYSIS

The symbolic-interaction paradigm sees the creation of deviance as a social process. From this point of view, definitions of deviance and conformity are surprisingly flexible.

LABELING THEORY

The central contribution of symbolic-interaction analysis is **labeling theory,** *the assertion that deviance and conformity result, not only from what people do, but from how others respond to those actions.* Labeling theory stresses the relativity of deviance, arguing that all reality is socially constructed so that the same behavior may be defined in any number of ways. Howard S. Becker claims that deviance is, therefore, nothing more than "behavior that people so label" (1966:9).

Consider these situations: A woman takes an article of clothing from a roommate; a married man at a convention has sex with a prostitute; a mayor gives a

DISCUSS: The psychosexual dimensions of the cockfighting rituals described below are fairly obvious.

Q: "From this point of view, deviance is not a quality of the act a person commits, but rather a consequence of the application by others of rules and sanctions to an 'offender.' The deviant is one to whom the label has successfully been applied; deviant behavior is behavior that people so label." Howard S. Becker (1966:9)

SOCIAL SURVEY: "Morality is a personal matter and society should not force everyone to follow one standard." (GSS 1988, N = 1,481; *Codebook*, 1996:338)

"Agree strongly"	31.7%	"Disagree strongly"	7.6%
"Agree somewhat"	38.8%	DK/NR	4.4%
"Disagree somewhat"	17.5%		

GLOBAL SOCIOLOGY

Cockfighting: Cultural Ritual or Abuse of Animals?

You won't see it on television, but one of the most popular sports of the world—from North America to Europe and to Asia—is cockfighting. Legal in parts of Louisiana, Texas, New Mexico, and Arizona, cockfighting is big business in Mexico, and approaches something of a national pastime in the Philippines. There, the local cock pit is as important as the town square in the U.S. Midwest: Every village has one, and it draws a crowd on weekends and fiesta days.

On the surface, cockfights are about gambling. An afternoon or evening event might include ten fights. A fight begins with the cock owners displaying their birds to one another, calling out for bets as to the stronger bird. Members of the audience weigh in with cash. Taking the money and confirming the bets is the "cristo," by which Filipinos mean that he is expected to be as honest as Christ.

With the odds of winning set and the money on the table, the actual combat begins. Each rooster is outfitted with a small, sharp blade strapped to the rear of the left leg. The cocks need little encouragement to fight, but the owners do a bit of strutting themselves, swinging their birds in front of each other before dropping them on lines drawn in the pit sand. Immediately upon hitting the ground, the hackles rise and the birds fly at one another, merging in a blur of legs and feathers.

Within a few minutes, one bird may collapse from exhaustion; the owner steps in to revive his cock and the process is repeated. Before long, however, a blade finds its mark. The victor,

the bird who will live to fight another day, perches on the vanquished, who will not.

In many parts of the world, cockfighting is an important male ritual. Many men give their birds the kind of attention they otherwise reserve for their sons. They raise their roosters for about two years, often at considerable expense, before their fighting careers begin. At that point, cocks take on a crucial cultural function. Through the ritual of the cockfight, men test their own claims to manhood, establish their own standing in the community pecking order, and pass on to their sons lessons about honor, competition, and masculinity.

Many outside observers are repulsed by the spectacle. But cockfighting is obviously deeply important to insiders. Should one, therefore, condemn it as brutality or respect it as ceremony?

Sources: Based on *The Economist* (1994), Harris (1994), and the author's research in the Philippines.

big city contract to a major campaign contributor. In each case, "reality" depends on the response of others. Is the first situation a matter of borrowing or theft? The consequences of the second case depend largely on whether news of the man's behavior follows him back home. In the third situation, is the official choosing the best contractor or paying off a political debt?

The social construction of reality, then, is a highly variable process of detection, definition, and response.

Given that "reality" is relative to time and place, it is no surprise that one society's conventions may be another's deviance. The box describes cockfighting: Is this popular sport a meaningful cultural ritual or simply a vicious abuse of animals?

RESOURCE: Initial insights into the importance of audience reaction to an episode of deviance in fostering a deviant career were made by Frank Tannenbaum, *Crime and the Community* (Columbia University Press, 1938).
NOTE: The term "stigma" is derived from a Greek root meaning "tattoo."
Q: "The Greeks, who were apparently strong on visual aids, originated

the term *stigma* to refer to bodily signs designed to expose something unusual and bad about the moral status of the signifier." Erving Goffman, *Stigma* (1963)
NOTE: In the late 1950s, Thomas Szasz prepared a short article on the myth of mental illness and submitted it to every major U.S. psychiatric journal—every one rejected it. The article finally appeared in *The American Psychologist* (1960).

Primary and Secondary Deviance

Edwin Lemert (1951, 1972) notes that many episodes of norm violation—say, skipping school or underage drinking—provoke only slight reaction from others and have little effect on a person's self-concept. Lemert calls such passing episodes *primary deviance*.

But what happens if other people notice someone's deviance and make something of it? If, for example, people begin to describe a young man as a "boozer," and push him out of their social circle, he may become embittered, drink even more, and seek the company of others who approve of his behavior. So the response to initial deviance can set in motion *secondary deviance*, by which an individual repeatedly violates a norm and begins to take on a deviant identity. The development of secondary deviance is another example of the Thomas theorem (discussed in Chapter 6, "Social Interaction in Everyday Life"), which states that "Situations we define as real become real in their consequences."

Stigma

Secondary deviance also marks the emergence of what Erving Goffman (1963) calls a *deviant career*. As individuals develop a stronger commitment to deviant behavior, they typically acquire a **stigma,** *a powerfully negative social label that radically changes a person's self-concept and social identity.*

Stigma operates as a master status (see Chapter 6), overpowering other aspects of social identity so that an individual is diminished in the minds of others and, consequently, becomes socially isolated. Sometimes an entire community formally stigmatizes an individual through what Harold Garfinkel (1956) calls a *degradation ceremony.* A criminal prosecution is one example, operating much like a college award ceremony except that people stand before the community to be labeled in a negative rather than a positive way.

Labeling: Past and Future

Once people stigmatize an individual, they may engage in *retrospective labeling*, the interpretation of someone's past consistent with present deviance (Scheff, 1984). For example, after discovering that a priest has sexually molested a child, others rethink his past, perhaps musing, "He always did want to be around young children." Retrospective labeling distorts a person's biography by being selective and prejudicial, guided more by the present stigma than by any

attempt to be fair. It also helps deepen the person's deviant identity.

Similarly, people may engage in *projective labeling* of a stigmatized person. That is, others keep an individual's deviant identity in mind when assessing any future action. The result, of course, is that people find evidence of deviance in almost anything a stigmatized individual does.

Labeling and Mental Illness

Is a woman who believes that Jesus rides the bus to work with her every day seriously deluded or merely expressing a strong religious faith? Is a homeless man who refuses to allow police to take him to a city shelter on a cold night mentally ill or simply trying to live independently?

Psychiatrist Thomas Szasz charges that people apply the label of "insanity" to what is only "difference." Such reasoning has led Szasz to the controversial conclusion that the whole idea of mental illness should be abandoned (1961, 1970, 1994, 1995). Illness, Szasz argues, is physical and afflicts only the body; mental illness, then, is a myth. The world is full of people whose "differences" in thought or action may irritate us, but such differences are no grounds on which to define others as sick—suffering from "mood disorders" or other "personality disorders." Such labeling, Szasz claims, simply enforces conformity to the standards of people powerful enough to impose their will on others.

Many of Szasz's colleagues reject the notion that all mental illness is a fiction. But some hail his work for pointing out the danger of using medicine to promote conformity. Most of us, after all, experience periods of extreme stress or other mental disability from time to time. Such episodes, although upsetting, are usually of passing importance. If, however, others respond with labeling that forms the basis of a social stigma, the long-term result may be further deviance as a self-fulfilling prophecy (Scheff, 1984).

THE MEDICALIZATION OF DEVIANCE

Labeling theory, particularly the ideas of Szasz and Goffman, helps to explain an important shift in the way our society understands deviance. Over the last fifty years, the growing influence of psychiatry and medicine in the United States has encouraged the **medicalization of deviance,** *the transformation of moral and legal issues into medical matters.* National Map 8–1 suggests

THE MAP: Psychiatrists (and physicians, in general) are most likely to practice where personal income is high. The national distribution of psychiatrists resembles the distribution of high-income counties found in National Map 10–3.

Q: "Anyone who does what is forbidden, that is, who violates a taboo, becomes taboo himself." Sigmund Freud, *Totem and Taboo* (1950:32)

NOTE: The medicalization of deviance is one dimension of the cultural trend of victimization described in Chapter 3, "Culture."

NOTE: Colleges have expanded their medical and counseling staffs in recent decades. One likely result is that what people used to describe as student shortcomings now are described in terms of various disorders.

SEEING OURSELVES

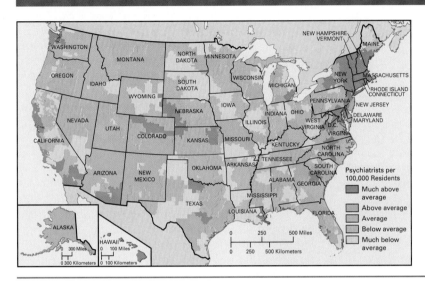

NATIONAL MAP 8–1
Where Psychiatrists Practice Across the United States

In general, psychiatrists are found in cities and are heavily concentrated along the East and West Coasts of the United States. By contrast, few psychiatrists work in the Plains States in the central region of the country. To some extent, these doctors work where the people are. But what other factors may explain this pattern?

Source: From *The Dartmouth Atlas of Health Care.* Copyright ©1996 by the Trustees of Dartmouth College. Reprinted with permission.

Psychiatrists per 100,000 Residents
- Much above average
- Above average
- Average
- Below average
- Much below average

where in this country this transformation is most pronounced.

Medicalization amounts to swapping one set of labels for another. In moral terms, we evaluate people or their behavior as "bad" or "good." However, the scientific objectivity of modern medicine passes no moral judgment, instead using clinical diagnoses such as "sick" and "well."

To illustrate, until the middle of this century, people generally viewed alcoholics as morally weak people easily tempted by the pleasure of drink. Gradually, however, medical specialists redefined alcoholism so that most people now consider alcoholism a disease, making individuals "sick" rather than "bad." Similarly, obesity, drug addiction, child abuse, sexual promiscuity, and other behaviors that used to be purely moral matters are widely defined today as illnesses for which people need help rather than punishment.

The Significance of Labels

Whether we define deviance as a moral or medical issue has three consequences. First, it affects *who responds* to deviance. An offense against common morality typically provokes a reaction by ordinary people or police. A medical label, however, places the situation under the control of clinical specialists, including counselors, psychiatrists, and physicians.

A second difference is *how people respond* to deviance. A moral approach defines the deviant as an "offender" subject to punishment. Medically, however, "patients" need treatment (for their own good, of course). Therefore, while punishment is designed to fit the crime, treatment programs are tailored to the patient and may involve virtually any therapy that a specialist thinks will prevent future illness (von Hirsh, 1986).

Third, and most important, the two labels differ on *the personal competence of the deviant person.* Morally speaking, whether we are right or wrong, at least we take responsibility for our own behavior. Once defined as sick, however, we are seen as lacking the capacity to control or (as with the label of "mentally ill") even to comprehend our actions. And people who are incompetent are, in turn, subject to treatment, often against their will. For this reason alone, attempts to define deviance in medical terms should be made only with extreme caution.

SUTHERLAND'S DIFFERENTIAL ASSOCIATION THEORY

Learning any social patterns—whether conventional or deviant—is a social process that takes place in groups. Therefore, according to Edwin Sutherland (1940), a person's tendency toward conformity or deviance

Artist Frank Romero was one of the founders of the Chicano movement in the late 1960s. Drawing on his own childhood in East Los Angeles, his art depicts the importance of cars, gangs, and violence in young people's efforts to gain a sense of importance and belonging in a society that has pushed them to its margins.

Frank Romero, *Freeway Wars*, 1990, Serigraph (edition of 99), 31½ × 38 inches. Frank Romero. © Serigraph. Nicolas and Cristina Hernandez Trust Collection, Pasadena, California.

depends upon relative contact with others who encourage conventional behavior versus those who do not. This is Sutherland's theory of *differential association*.

Sutherland's theory is illustrated by a study of drug and alcohol use among young adults in the United States (Akers et al., 1979). Questionnaires completed by junior and senior high school students showed a close connection between the extent of alcohol and drug use and the degree to which peer groups encouraged such activity. The researchers concluded that young people embrace delinquent patterns insofar as they receive praise and other rewards for defining deviance—rather than conformity—in positive terms.

HIRSCHI'S CONTROL THEORY

In his *control theory*, Travis Hirschi (1969; Gottfredson & Hirschi, 1995) claims that the essence of social control lies in anticipating the consequences of one's behavior. Hirschi assumes that everyone finds at least some deviance tempting. But imagining the reactions of family or friends is sufficient to deter most people; for others, the thought of a ruined career is enough. By contrast, individuals who think that they have little to lose from deviance are likely to become rule-breakers.

Specifically, Hirschi links conformity to four types of social control:

1. **Attachment.** Strong social attachments encourage conformity; weak relationships in the family, peer group, and school leave people freer to engage in deviance.

2. **Commitment.** The greater a person's commitment to legitimate opportunity, the greater the advantages of conformity. A young person bound for college, with good career prospects, has a high stake in conformity. By contrast, someone with little confidence in future success is freer to drift toward deviance.

3. **Involvement.** Extensive involvement in legitimate activities—such as holding a job, going to school, playing sports, or pursuing hobbies—inhibits deviance. People with few such activities—who simply "hang out" waiting for something to happen—have time and energy for deviant activity.

4. **Belief.** Strong beliefs in conventional morality and respect for authority figures restrain tendencies toward deviance. By contrast, people with a weak conscience (and those who spend a great

Q: "Research amply demonstrates that offenders are relatively unable to sustain a course of action directed at some distant goal, whether that goal be education, friendship, employment, or criminal gain. In fact the defining characteristic of offenders appears to be *low self-control.*" Travis Hirschi

Q: "Morality is simply the attitude that we adopt towards people whom we personally dislike." Oscar Wilde

Q: "In this century, America's only permanent growth industry has been organized crime." Selwyn Raab

NOTE: Power affects how labels are applied. An audience may discredit a privileged person for acting foolishly; observing a less-privileged person (say, a woman or person of color) acting foolishly, they are more likely to discredit the individual's entire category.

deal of time without an authority figure's supervision) are more vulnerable to temptation (Osgood et al., 1996).

Hirschi's analysis draws together a number of earlier ideas about the causes of deviant behavior. Note that relative social privilege and strength of moral character are both crucial in generating a stake in conformity to conventional norms (Wiatrowski, Griswold, & Roberts, 1981; Sampson & Laub, 1990; Free, 1992).

Critical evaluation. All the various symbolic-interaction theories see deviance as process. Labeling theory links deviance not to *action* but to the *reaction* of others. Thus some people come to be defined as deviant while others who think or behave in the same way are not. The concepts of secondary deviance, deviant careers, and stigma demonstrate how people can incorporate the label of deviance into a lasting self-concept.

Yet labeling theory has several limitations. First, because this theory takes a highly relative view of deviance, it glosses over how some kinds of behavior, such as murder, are condemned virtually everywhere (Wellford, 1980). Labeling theory is thus most usefully applied to less serious deviance, such as sexual promiscuity or mental illness.

Second, the consequences of deviant labeling are unclear. Research is inconclusive as to whether deviant labeling produces subsequent deviance or discourages further violations (Smith & Gartin, 1989; Shermin & Smith, 1992).

Third, not everyone resists the label of deviance; some people may actually relish being defined as deviant (Vold & Bernard, 1986). For example, individuals may participate in civil disobedience leading to arrest to call attention to social injustice.

Both Sutherland's differential association theory and Hirschi's control theory have had considerable influence in sociology. But they provide little insight into why a society's norms and laws define certain kinds of activities as deviant in the first place. This important question is addressed by social-conflict analysis, described in the next section.

SOCIAL-CONFLICT ANALYSIS

The social-conflict paradigm demonstrates how deviance reflects social inequality. This approach holds that who or what is labeled "deviant" depends on which categories of people hold power in a society.

Laws regulate the operation of businesses just as they direct the actions of individuals. But, as social-conflict analysis points out, powerful corporate leaders who face allegations of wrongdoing are rarely thought of as "criminals," and rarely are they subject to the punishment accorded to ordinary people.

DEVIANCE AND POWER

Alexander Liazos (1972) points out that the people who fit our everyday conceptions of deviants—"nuts, sluts, and 'preverts'"—all share the trait of powerlessness. Bag ladies (not corporate polluters) and unemployed men on street corners (not arms dealers) carry the stigma of deviance.

Social-conflict theory links deviance to power in three ways. First, the norms—and especially laws—of any society generally reflect the interests of the rich and powerful. People who threaten the wealthy, either by taking their property or by advocating a more egalitarian society, are often defined as "common thieves" or "political radicals." As noted in Chapter 4 ("Society"), Karl Marx argued that the law (and all social institutions) tends to support the interests of the rich. Or, as Richard Quinney puts it: "Capitalist justice is by the capitalist class, for the capitalist class, and against the working class" (1977:3).

Second, even if their behavior is called into question, the powerful have the resources to resist deviant

NOTE: With 12 on the record for 1996, "hate-crime" homicides account for only a tiny fraction of the 16,000 killings annually in the United States.

NOTE: Of 1996 hate crimes recorded by police, 63% were racial, 14% religious, 12% involved sexual orientation, and 11% ethnicity or national origin.

NOTE: A year of fighting between two Los Angeles street gangs—the Bloods and the Crips—left more dead bodies than Bonnie and Clyde or the Hatfields and McCoys ever did (Courtright, 1996).

Q: "There is no distinctly American criminal class except for Congress." Mark Twain

Q: "The fundamental sociological problem is not crime but the law . . ." Peter Berger (1963:37)

CRITICAL THINKING

Hate Crimes: Punishing Actions or Attitudes?

On an October evening in 1989, Todd Mitchell, an African American teenager, and a group of friends were standing in front of their apartment complex in Kenosha, Wisconsin, talking. They had just seen the film *Mississippi Burning* and were fuming over a scene in which a white man beats a young black boy kneeling in prayer.

"Do you feel hyped up to move on some white people?" asked Mitchell. Minutes later, they saw a young white boy walking toward them on the other side of the street. Mitchell commanded: "There goes a white boy; go get him!" The group swarmed around the white boy, beating him to the ground and leaving him bloody and in a coma. Mitchell and his friends took the boy's tennis shoes as a trophy.

Police soon arrested the black boys and charged them with the beating. Todd Mitchell went to trial as the ringleader, where the jury found him guilty of aggravated battery *motivated by racial hatred*. Instead of the usual two-year prison sentence, Mitchell went to jail for four years.

Three-fourths of the states have now adopted laws increasing sentences for crimes motivated by categorical bias. Supporters make three arguments in favor of hate-crime legislation. First, determining an offender's intentions has always been part of criminal cases, so considering hatred as an intention is nothing new. Second, crimes motivated by racial or other bias inflame the public mood more than those crimes carried out for more common reasons like monetary gain. Third, victims of hate

Many neighborhoods of U.S. cities seethe with racial hatred. In 1989, a gang of young Italians killed an African American man who ventured into their Bensonhurst section of Brooklyn in search of a used car. In the weeks that followed, African Americans led marches through the area claiming the right to move freely throughout the city; counterprotestors, too, made their feelings known.

crimes typically suffer greater injury than victims of crimes with other motives.

Critics counter that most hate-crime cases involve, not hard-core racism, but impulsive and situational behavior, often involving juveniles. Even more important, critics maintain, hate-crime law is a direct threat to First Amendment guarantees of free speech. Hate-crime laws allow courts to sentence offenders not just for actions but for underlying attitudes. As Harvard law professor Alan Dershowitz cautions, "As much as I hate bigotry, I fear much more the Court attempting to control the minds of its citizens." In short, according to the critics, hate-crime statutes open the door to punishing beliefs rather than behavior.

In 1993, the Supreme Court upheld the sentence handed down to Todd Mitchell. In a unanimous decision, the justices stated that the government did not intend to punish an individual's beliefs. But, they reasoned, an abstract belief is no longer protected when it becomes the motive for a crime.

Sources: Greenhouse (1993), Jacobs (1993), and Terry (1993).

toward the victim on the basis of race, religion, ancestry, sexual orientation, or physical disability.

Although hate crimes are nothing new, the federal government has tracked them only since 1990. While still a small share of all crime (almost 11,000 incidents in 1996), their numbers are rising. A survey conducted by the National Gay and Lesbian Task Force in eight U.S. cities found that one in five lesbians and gay men had been physically assaulted and more than 90 percent had been verbally abused because of their sexual orientation (cited in Berrill, 1992:19–20). Research indicates that victims of hate-motivated violence are especially likely to be people who contend with multiple stigmas, such as gay men of color.

As of 1997, thirty-six states had enacted hate-crime legislation. Supporters are gratified, but opponents say

NOTE: Changes in our view of violence are suggested by how common violence among officials was two centuries ago. For example, Vice President Aaron Burr shot and killed Alexander Hamilton (first U.S. Secretary of the Treasury) in a duel in 1804 in Weehawken, New Jersey.

NOTE: Technically, the *corpus delicti* ("body of a crime") is composed of (1) *actus reus* ("guilty act"), which is the physical act (or omission) in violation of criminal law; (2) *mens rea* ("guilty mind") or mental resolve to commit the crime; (3) causal order, by which the criminal intent precedes and is related to the criminal act; (4) all legal elements, the factors attached to the specific crime in a particular jurisdiction according to the wording of the criminal statute.

Q: "I am as pure as the driven slush." Tallulah Bankhead

such laws punish thoughts, not actions. The box examines a recent case, which led to a Supreme Court ruling upholding stiffer sentences for crimes motivated by hate.

CRIME

Crime is the violation of statutes enacted into criminal law by a locality, state, or the federal government. Thus, some criminal laws apply everywhere in the United States; others vary state by state, and some apply only within a local jurisdiction.

THE COMPONENTS OF CRIME

Technically, crime is composed of two elements: the *act* itself (or, in some cases, the failure to do what the law requires) and *criminal intent* (in legal terminology, *mens rea*, or "guilty mind"). Intent is a matter of degree, ranging from willful conduct to negligence in which a person does not deliberately set out to hurt anyone but acts (or fails to act) in a manner that may reasonably be expected to cause harm. Prosecutors weigh the degree of intent in charging an alleged offender with a crime at one of several possible levels of seriousness: In the case of a killing, for example, the charge might specify first-degree murder, second-degree murder, or negligent manslaughter. Alternatively, there may be no prosecution if prosecutors consider the killing justifiable, as in the case of self-defense.

TYPES OF CRIME

In the United States, the Federal Bureau of Investigation gathers information on criminal offenses and regularly reports the results in a publication called *Crime in the United States.* Two major types of offenses contribute to the FBI "crime index."

Crimes against the person constitute *crimes that direct violence or the threat of violence against others.* Such "violent crimes" include murder and manslaughter (legally defined as "the willful killing of one human being by another"), aggravated assault ("an unlawful attack by one person upon another for the purpose of inflicting severe or aggravated bodily injury"), forcible rape ("the carnal knowledge of a female forcibly and against her will"), and robbery ("taking or attempting to take anything of value from the care, custody, or control of a person or persons by force or threat of force or violence and/or putting the victim in fear").

Common sense suggests that the people we define as "criminal" are simply those who have broken the law. But the sociological perspective reveals that some categories of people are more likely than others to become entangled in the criminal justice system. As you read the remainder of this chapter, consider how our society places men, young people, and minorities at greater risk of becoming both offenders and victims of crime.

Crimes against property encompass *crimes that involve theft of property belonging to others.* "Property crimes" range from burglary ("the unlawful entry of a structure to commit a [serious crime] or a theft") to larceny-theft ("the unlawful taking, carrying, leading, or riding away of property from the possession of another"), auto theft ("the theft or attempted theft of a motor vehicle"), and arson ("any willful or malicious burning or attempt to burn the personal property of another").

A third category of offenses, not included in major crime indexes, is **victimless crimes,** *violations of law in which there are no readily apparent victims.* So-called "crimes without complaint" include illegal drug use, prostitution, and gambling. "Victimless crime" is often a misnomer, however. How victimless is a crime when young people abusing drugs may have to steal to support a drug habit? How victimless is a crime if a young pregnant woman smoking crack causes the death or

CYBER: The most recent stories and statistics concerning crime and law enforcement are found at the Bureau of Justice Statistics Web site (http://www.ojp.usdoj.gov/bjs/).
NOTE: Police reports versus victimization survey data (1996; cases or victims per 100,000 population): personal crimes: 634/4,350; violent rape: 36/40; robbery: 202/592; aggravated assault: 388/880; all property crime: 4,435/26,630; burglary: 1,943/4,720; larceny: 2,976/2,060; motor-vehicle theft: 526/1,350 (U.S. Federal Bureau of Investigation, 1997).
NOTE: Some critics point out that, despite more talk about "community policing," departments across the U.S. are increasing the number of paramilitary police units (Kraska & Kappeler, 1997).
SOCIAL DIVERSITY: Juveniles represent one-fourth of victims of violent crime.

Since the early 1990s, crime in the United States has shown a significant decline. Many factors are involved, including a strong economy, more vigorous law enforcement, and also the strategy of "community policing," by which law enforcement officials become involved in local communities, trying to prevent crime before it occurs.

permanent injury of her baby? How victimless is a crime when a young runaway lives a desperate life of prostitution on the streets? Often, the people who commit such crimes are themselves both offenders and victims.

Because public views of victimless crimes vary so much, laws differ from place to place. In the United States, gambling is legal only in certain locations within twenty-three states; prostitution is lawful only in one (part of Nevada). Yet both activities are commonplace across the country. Homosexual (and some heterosexual) behavior among consenting adults is legally restricted in about half of the states. Where such laws exist, enforcement is light and selective.

CRIMINAL STATISTICS

Statistics gathered by the Federal Bureau of Investigation show that crime rates have generally risen since 1960, although, as noted in the opening to this chapter, the trend has been downward in recent years. Even so, during the 1990s, police have tallied some 8 million serious crimes each year. Figure 8–2 illustrates the trends for various serious crimes.

Always read crime statistics with caution, however, since they include only crimes known to the police. The police learn about almost all homicides, but assaults—especially among acquaintances—are far less likely to be reported. The police learn about an even lower proportion of property crimes, especially when losses are small. Some victims may not realize that a crime has occurred, or they may assume they have little chance of recovering their property even if they notify the police. And reports of rape, although rising over time, still grossly understate the extent of this crime.

One way to evaluate official crime statistics is through a *victimization survey*, asking a representative sample of people about their experience with crime. Granted, people do not always respond fully or truthfully, but the data suggest that actual criminality is two to four times higher than what official reports indicate (Russell, 1995).

THE "STREET" CRIMINAL: A PROFILE

Government statistics paint a broad-brush picture of people arrested for violent and property crimes. We now examine the breakdown of these arrest statistics by age, gender, social class, race, and ethnicity.

Age

Official crime rates rise sharply during adolescence and peak in the late teens, falling thereafter. People between the ages of fifteen and twenty-four represent just 14 percent of the U.S. population, but they

RESOURCE: Drug abuse is closely linked to serious crime. See *Sourcebook of Criminal Justice Statistics 1996* (U.S. Bureau of Justice Statistics, 1997) for a study of the percentages of men and women arrested in major U.S. cities who tested positive for drug use.

NOTE: Of 5.1 million U.S. adults in the criminal justice system, 58% are on probation, 19% are in prison, 13% are on parole, and 9% are in local jails (U.S. Bureau of Justice Statistics).

NOTE: Violence is also linked to urbanization. Gerhard Falk (1990) calculates that the state of New York has a murder rate of 12.5 per 100,000 inhabitants; without New York City (which has 48% of the state's people but 87% of its murders) the state rate would be 3.1 per 100,000. This pattern is more or less true across the country.

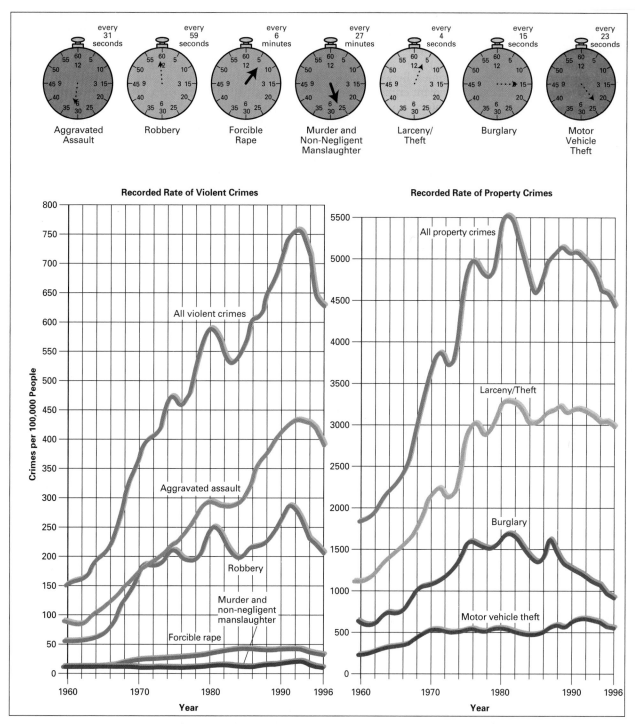

FIGURE 8–2 **Crime Rates in the United States, 1960–1996**

The graphs represent crime rates for various violent crimes and property crimes during recent decades. "Crime clocks" are another way of describing the frequency of crimes.

Source: U.S. Federal Bureau of Investigation (1997).

NOTE: A significant percentage of violent and property crimes are committed by young people. Under 21: 32.3% of arrests for violent crime; 49.5% of arrests for property crime. Under 18: 18.7% of arrests for violent crime; 35.2% for property crime (U.S. Federal Bureau of Investigation, 1997).

NOTE: About 70% of violent criminals grew up without fathers in the home (Kristol, 1994).

DIVERSITY: Our readiness to link color to criminality was illustrated in the Susan Smith case in which this white woman who murdered her children initially convinced investigators and the public that the crime was the work of an African American male.

DIVERSITY: By age 25, 15.9% of African American males will have served some time in federal or state prison; by age 30, 21.4%; by 35, 24.6%; by 40, 26.6% (Bonczar & Beck, 1997).

accounted for 40.6 percent of all arrests for violent crimes and 45.5 percent for property crimes in 1996 (U.S. Federal Bureau of Investigation, 1997).

A disturbing trend is that young people are responsible for more and more serious crimes. Between 1987 and 1996, arrests of juveniles for violent crime shot up by 60 percent (U.S. Federal Bureau of Investigation, 1997).

Gender

Although each sex constitutes roughly half of the population, police collared males in 72.1 percent of all property crime arrests in 1996. In other words, men are arrested three times as often as women for property crimes. In the case of violent crimes, the disparity is even greater: 84.9 percent of arrests were of males and just 15.1 percent were of females (a six-to-one ratio).

Some of this difference reflects the reluctance of law enforcement officials to define women as criminals—even when they do break the law. Even so, the difference in arrest rates for women and men has been narrowing, which probably indicates increasing sexual equality in our society. Between 1987 and 1996, the *increase* in arrests of women was greater (35.9 percent) than that for men (12.1 percent) (U.S. Federal Bureau of Investigation, 1997). In global perspective, this pattern holds, with the greatest gender difference in crime rates in societies that most limit women's social opportunities.

Social Class

The FBI does not assess the social class of arrested persons; thus, no statistical data of the kind given above are available. But research has long indicated that criminality is more widespread among people of lower social position. We also know that the connection between class and crime is more complicated than it appears on the surface (Wolfgang, Figlio, & Sellin, 1972; Clinard & Abbott, 1973; Braithwaite, 1981; Thornberry & Farnsworth, 1982; Wolfgang, Thornberry, & Figlio, 1987).

In part, this pattern reflects the historical tendency to view poor people as less worthy than those whose wealth and power confer "respectability" (Tittle & Villemez, 1977; Tittle, Villemez, & Smith, 1978; Elias, 1986). But it is a mistake to assume that being socially disadvantaged means being criminal. While crime—especially violence—is a serious problem in the poorest inner-city neighborhoods, most people who live in these communities have no criminal records, and most

crimes are committed by a relatively few hard-core offenders (Wolfgang, Figlio, & Sellin, 1972; Elliott & Ageton, 1980; Harries, 1990).

Moreover, the connection between social standing and criminality depends on what kind of crime one is talking about (Braithwaite, 1981). If we expand our definition of crime beyond street offenses to include white-collar crime, the "common criminal" suddenly looks much more affluent.

Race and Ethnicity

Both race and ethnicity are strongly correlated to crime rates, although the reasons are many and complex. Official statistics show that 66.9 percent of arrests for index crimes in 1996 involved white people. However, arrests of African Americans were higher than for whites in proportion to their numbers. African Americans represent 12.5 percent of the population and 32.4 percent of arrests for property crimes (versus 64.7 percent for whites) and 43.2 percent of arrests for violent crimes (54.6 percent for whites) (U.S. Federal Bureau of Investigation, 1997).

Clearly, our society faces a serious crime problem involving young African American men. In fact, a recent study found that one in three black men between the ages of twenty and twenty-nine is in jail, on probation, or on parole (The Sentencing Project, 1995). African Americans are also at high risk as victims of crime (Clarke, 1996).

What accounts for the link between race and crime? Several factors are important. To the degree that prejudice related to color or class prompts white police to arrest black people more readily, and leads citizens more willingly to report African Americans to police as suspected offenders, people of color are overly criminalized (Liska & Tausig, 1979; Unnever, Frazier, & Henretta, 1980; Smith & Visher, 1981; Holmes et al., 1993; Covington, 1995).

Second, race in the United States closely relates to social standing, which, as we have already explained, affects one's likelihood of engaging in street crimes. Judith Blau and Peter Blau (1982) suggest that poor people living in the midst of affluence come to perceive society as unjust and, thus, are more likely to turn to crime.

Third, black and white family patterns differ: Two-thirds of black children (compared to one-fifth of white children) are born to single mothers. In general, single-parenting means children grow up with less supervision and at a high risk for being poor. With almost half of black children growing up in poverty

DISCUSS: Consider the divergent reactions to the O. J. Simpson acquittal—most whites were stunned, most blacks were elated. How and why does race shape our views of the criminal justice system?
NOTE: For the first time, the Los Angeles-Long Beach, California, metropolitan area surpassed the New York metropolitan area in number of murders during 1996, with 1,401 recorded.
Q: "Good laws derive from evil habits." Macrobius

SOCIAL SURVEY: "Do you happen to have in your home (house or garage) any guns or revolvers?" (GSS 1996, N = 1,923; Codebook, 1996:227)
"Yes" 40.1%   "No" 59.4%   DK/NR 0.5%
NOTE: Gun control advocates believe that the presence of guns encourages deadly behavior; critics call this the "trigger pulls the finger" hypothesis.

(compared to one in six white children), no one should be surprised at proportionately higher crime rates for African Americans (Sampson, 1987; Courtwright, 1996; Jacobs & Helms, 1996).

Fourth, remember that the official crime index excludes arrests for offenses ranging from drunk driving to white-collar violations. This omission contributes to the view of the typical criminal as a person of color. If we broaden our definition of crime to include driving while intoxicated, insider stock trading, embezzlement, and cheating on income tax returns, the proportion of white criminals rises dramatically.

Finally, some categories of the population have unusually low rates of arrest. People of Asian descent, who account for about 3 percent of the population, figure in only 1 percent of all arrests. As Chapter 13 ("Race and Ethnicity") documents, Asian Americans enjoy higher-than-average educational achievement, good jobs, and above-average income. Moreover, Asian American culture emphasizes family solidarity and discipline, both of which inhibit criminality.

CRIME IN GLOBAL PERSPECTIVE

By world standards, the crime rate in the United States is high. Although recent crime trends are downward, the New York metropolitan area still recorded 1,030 murders during 1996. Rarely does a day pass without a murder in New York; annually, more New Yorkers are hit with stray bullets than the total number of people gunned down deliberately in large cities elsewhere in the world.

The violent crime rate in the United States stands at about five times that of Europe; the rate of property crime is twice as high. The contrast is even greater between our society and the nations of Asia, including India and Japan, where rates of violent and property crime are among the lowest in the world.

Elliott Currie (1985) suggests that crime in the United States stems from our culture's emphasis on individual economic success, frequently at the expense of family and community. The United States also has extraordinary cultural diversity, the legacy of centuries of immigration. Moreover, economic inequality is higher in this country than in most other industrial nations. Thus, our society's relatively weak social fabric, combined with considerable frustration among the have-nots, generates widespread criminal behavior.

Another contributing factor to violence in the United States is extensive private ownership of guns. Of 15,848 murder victims in the United States in

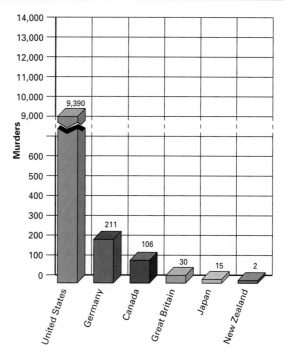

GLOBAL SNAPSHOT

FIGURE 8–3 **Number of Murders by Handguns, 1996**

Source: Handgun Control, Inc. (1998).

1996, 68 percent died from shootings. By the early 1990s, in Texas and several other southern states, deaths from gunshots were running ahead of automobile-related fatalities. And, as Figure 8–3 shows, the United States is the runaway leader in murders by handguns among industrial nations.

Surveys suggest that almost half of U.S. households own at least one gun (Gallup, 1993; Wright, 1995; NORC, 1996). Put differently, there are as many guns as there are adults in this country, and one-third of these weapons are handguns that figure in violent crime. In large part, gun ownership reflects people's fear of crime; yet, easy availability of guns in this country also makes crime more deadly.

But, as critics of gun control point out, waiting periods and background checks at retail gun stores (mandated by the 1993 Brady Bill) do not keep guns out of the hands of criminals, who almost always obtain

GLOBAL: A new form of crime, both high-tech and global in character, is pirating copyrighted software. The Internet now allows anyone with a computer and modem to send or receive materials globally. Software piracy is especially pronounced in low-income countries such as Mexico, Brazil, Pakistan, and Malaysia, where perhaps 85% of all software is procured illegally.
RESOURCE: Elliott Currie's global analysis of crime is included in the Macionis and Benokraitis reader, *Seeing Ourselves*.
GLOBAL: The People's Republic of China is much more efficient than the United States in disposing of prisoners. In the final days before the Chinese New Year in 1993, courts closed their books on 55 people convicted of crimes ranging from fraud to murder; all were quickly sentenced and shot in the back of the head with no delay and little fanfare.

guns illegally (Wright, 1995). Moreover, we should be cautious about assuming gun control is a magic bullet in the war on crime. Elliott Currie (1985) notes, for example, that the number of Californians killed each year by knives alone has exceeded the number of Canadians killed by weapons of all kinds. Most experts do think, however, that stricter gun control laws would lower the level of deadly violence.

Crime rates are soaring in some of the largest cities of the world like Manila, the Philippines, and São Paulo, Brazil, which have rapid population growth and millions of desperately poor people. Outside of such cities, however, the traditional character of less economically developed societies and their strong family structure allow local communities to control crime informally (Clinard & Abbott, 1973; *Der Spiegel*, 1989).

One exception to this pattern is crimes against women. Rape is surging throughout the world, especially in poor societies. Traditional social patterns that limit economic opportunities available to women also promote prostitution. Global Map 8–1 shows the extent of prostitution around the world.

Some kinds of crime have always been multinational, such as terrorism, espionage, and arms dealing (Martin & Romero, 1992). But, today, the "globalization" we are experiencing on many fronts also extends to crime. A recent case in point is the illegal drug trade. In part, the problem of illegal drugs in the United States is a "demand" issue. That is, there is a high demand for cocaine and other drugs in this country, and legions of young people have been willing to risk arrest or even violent death by entering the lucrative drug trade. But the "supply" side of the issue is just as important. In the South American nation of Colombia, at least 20 percent of the people depend on cocaine production for their livelihood. Furthermore, not only is cocaine Colombia's most profitable export, but it outsells all other exports combined (including coffee). Clearly, then, understanding global crime such as drug dealing means understanding social and economic conditions both in this country and elsewhere.

THE CRIMINAL JUSTICE SYSTEM

December 10, 1994, Casablanca, Morocco. Casablanca! An exciting mix of African, European, and Middle Eastern cultures. Returning from a stroll through the medina, the medieval section of this coastal, North African city, we confront lines of police along a boulevard, standing between us and our ship in the harbor. The police are providing security for many important leaders attending an Islamic conference in a nearby hotel. Are the streets closed? No one asks; people seem to observe an invisible line some fifty feet from the police officers. I play the brash urbanite and start across the street to inquire (in broken French) if we can pass by, but I stop cold as several officers draw a bead on me with their eyes. Their fingers nervously tap at the grips on their automatic weapons. This is no time to strike up a conversation.

The criminal justice system is a society's formal response to crime. In some of the world's countries, military police keep a tight rein on people's behavior; in others, including the United States, police have more limited powers to respond to specific violations of criminal law. We shall briefly introduce the major components of the criminal justice system: police, the courts, and the punishment of convicted offenders.

POLICE

The police serve as the primary point of contact between the population and the criminal justice system. In principle, the police maintain public order by uniformly enforcing the law. In reality, 595,170 full-time police officers in the United States (in 1996) cannot effectively monitor the activities of 265 million people. As a result, the police exercise considerable discretion about which situations warrant their attention and how to handle them.

How, then, do police carry out their duties? In a study of police behavior in five cities, Douglas Smith and Christy Visher (1981; Smith, 1987) concluded that, because they must respond swiftly, police quickly size up a situation in terms of six factors. First, *how serious is the alleged crime?* The more serious police perceive a situation to be, the more likely they are to make an arrest. Second, *what is the victim's preference?* Generally, if a victim demands that police make an arrest, they are likely to do so. Third, *is the suspect cooperative or not?* Resisting police efforts increases a suspect's chances of arrest. Fourth, *have they arrested the suspect before?* Police are more likely to take into custody

Q: "The entire [criminal justice] system . . . is charged with enforcing the law and maintaining order. What is distinctive about the responsibility of the police is that they are charged with performing these functions where all eyes are upon them and where the going is roughest, on the street." The President's Commission on Law Enforcement and the Administration of Justice (1966)

DIVERSITY: Although varying by jurisdiction, women make up

about 16% of U.S. police officers and detectives; African Americans (men and women) represent about 16%, and Latinos about 8% (U.S. Bureau of the Census, 1997).

Q: "They are sure to have something on me . . ." Josef K in Kafka's *The Trial*

NOTE: Prostitution was legal throughout the U.S. until 1909. Iowa was first to ban it; by 1920, all states followed suit.

WINDOW ON THE WORLD

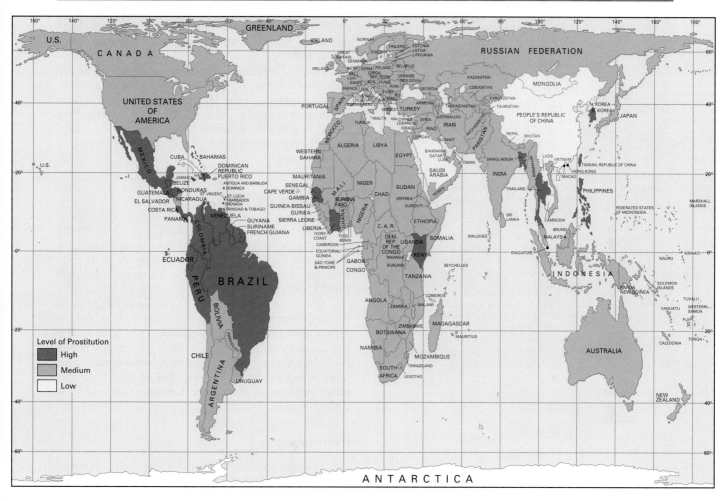

GLOBAL MAP 8–1 Prostitution in Global Perspective

Generally speaking, prostitution is widespread in societies of the world where women have low standing in relation to men. Officially, at least, the now-defunct socialist regimes in Eastern Europe and the former Soviet Union, as well as the People's Republic of China, boast of gender equality, including the elimination of "vice," such as prostitution, which oppresses women. By contrast, in much of Latin America, a region of pronounced patriarchy, prostitution is commonplace. In many Islamic societies patriarchy is also strong, but religion is a counterbalance so prostitution is limited. Western, industrial societies display a moderate amount of prostitution.

Source: *Peters Atlas of the World* (1990); updated by the author.

someone they have arrested before, presumably because previous arrest suggests guilt. Fifth, *are bystanders present?* According to Smith and Visher, the presence of observers prompts police to take stronger control of a situation; arrests also move the encounter from the street (the suspect's turf) to the police department (where law officers have the edge). Sixth, *what is the suspect's race?* All else being equal, Smith and Visher contend, police are more likely to arrest people of color than whites, perceiving suspects of African or

THEN AND NOW: Retribution is evident in virtually all ancient codes of law. The Latin concept, *lex talionis*, refers to the "law of retaliation" by which an offender's punishment fits the crime.

NOTE: Political pressure to jail offenders leads to prison over-crowding, which, in turn tends to produce shorter sentences, generating little or none of the initially expected results (cf. Clark & Lee, 1996).

NOTE: Mark A. Cohen estimates that crime costs U.S. society $500 billion annually. In California, the state spends more on crime than on colleges (Butterfield, 1996).

DIVERSITY: The oft-cited high proportion of African Americans in prison is of males: About 500,000 black men (7% of adult black men versus 1% of white men) are locked up, but only 30,000 black women (U.S. Bureau of Justice Statistics).

TABLE 8–2 Four Justifications for Punishment: A Summary

Retribution	The oldest justification for punishment that still holds sway today. Punishment is atonement for a moral wrong by an individual; in principle, punishment should be comparable in severity to the deviance itself.
Deterrence	An early modern approach. Deviance is considered social disruption, which society acts to control. People are viewed as rational and self-interested; deterrence works because the pains of punishment outweigh the pleasures of deviance.
Rehabilitation	A modern strategy linked to the development of social sciences. Deviance is viewed as the product of social problems (such as poverty) or personal problems (such as mental illness). Social conditions are improved and offenders subjected to intervention appropriate to their condition.
Societal protection	A modern approach easier to implement than rehabilitation. If society is unable or unwilling to rehabilitate offenders or reform social conditions, people are protected from further deviance by incarceration or execution of the offender.

Hispanic descent as either more dangerous or more likely to be guilty.

COURTS

After arrest, a court determines a suspect's guilt or innocence. In principle, our courts rely on an adversarial process involving attorneys—one team representing the defendant and another the state—in the presence of a judge who monitors legal procedures.

In practice, however, about 90 percent of criminal cases are resolved prior to court appearance through **plea bargaining,** *a negotiation in which the state reduces a defendant's charge in exchange for a guilty plea.* For example, the state may offer a defendant charged with burglary a lesser charge of possessing burglary tools in exchange for a guilty plea.

Plea bargaining is widespread because it spares the state the time and expense of court trials. In addition, since the number of cases entering the system has doubled during the last decade, government officials could not possibly bring every case to trial. Moreover, a trial is unnecessary if there is little disagreement as to the facts of the case. By selectively trying only a small proportion of the cases, then, the courts channel their resources into the most important cases (Reid, 1991).

But plea bargaining pressures defendants (who are presumed innocent) to plead guilty. A person can exercise the right to a trial, but only at the risk of receiving a more severe sentence if found guilty. Plea bargaining may be efficient but, say critics, it circumvents the adversarial process and undercuts the rights of defendants.

PUNISHMENT

In 1997, a jury found Timothy McVeigh guilty of murder in the 1995 bombing of the federal building in Oklahoma City that killed 168 people. A short time later, the jury declared that, for his crime, McVeigh should be put to death.

The jury's decisions offered a measure of justice to the nation as a whole and, especially, to hundreds of people who had lost family members and friends. But the decision also provoked a fresh debate about *how* and *why* a society should punish its wrongdoers. This leads us to consider four basic justifications for punishment: retribution, deterrence, rehabilitation, and societal protection.

Retribution

"It's revenge for me," declared thirty-seven-year-old Roy Sells, whose wife died in the Oklahoma City bombing. "Look at what he's done. Could anyone deserve to die more?" (Pooley, 1997:31) Observing people's passion for revenge when they suffer due to crime, Supreme Court justice Oliver Wendell Holmes stated that "the law has no choice but to satisfy [that] craving" (quoted in Carlson, 1976).

One key reason to punish, then, is to satisfy a society's need for **retribution,** *moral vengeance by which society inflicts suffering on the offender comparable to that caused by the offense.* Retribution rests on a view of society as a moral balance. When criminality upsets this balance, punishment exacted in comparable measure restores the moral order, as suggested in the biblical dictum "An eye for an eye."

Retribution is the oldest justification for punishment. During the Middle Ages, most people viewed crime as sin—an offense against God as well as society—

DISCUSS: California's 1994 "three strikes" law for any criminal with a prior serious or violent felony conviction doubled sentences for second felony convictions and imposed a 25-year-to-life sentence for a third felony conviction. Consequences included a clogged court system, prison overcrowding, and successful legal challenges (1996) that argued that the law pre-empted judicial discretion.

DIVERSITY: The U.S. incarcerated population was 1,078,545 people

(1995). Rates by race (per 100,000 people): African Americans: 700; white people: 122 (U.S. Bureau of Justice Statistics, 1997).

GLOBAL: The U.S. incarceration rate is the world's highest except for Russia's.

EXERCISE: Ask the college security office for data about crime on your campus. How well does security's view of campus crime square with your own?

that warranted a harsh response. Today, although critics point out that retribution does little to reform the offender, many people consider vengeance reason enough for punishment.

Deterrence

A second justification for punishment, **deterrence,** refers to *the attempt to discourage criminality through punishment.* Deterrence is based on the eighteenth-century Enlightenment notion that, as calculating and rational creatures, humans will not break the law if they think the pain of punishment will outweigh the pleasure of crime.

Deterrence emerged as reform in response to the harsh punishments based on retribution. Why put someone to death for stealing, critics asked, if theft can be discouraged with a prison sentence? As the concept of deterrence gained acceptance, execution and physical mutilation of criminals in most industrial societies were replaced by milder forms of punishment such as incarceration.

Punishment can deter in two ways. *Specific deterrence* convinces an individual offender that crime does not pay. Through *general deterrence*, the punishment of one person serves as an example to others.

Rehabilitation

The third justification for punishment is **rehabilitation,** *a program for reforming the offender to prevent subsequent offenses.* The concept of rehabilitation paralleled the development of the social sciences in the nineteenth century. According to sociologists of that time (and also since), crime and other deviance spring from an unfavorable environment marked by poverty or a lack of parental supervision. Logically, then, if offenders learn to be deviant, they can also learn to obey the rules; the key is controlling the environment. *Reformatories* or *houses of correction* provided controlled settings where people could learn proper behavior (recall the description of total institutions in Chapter 5, "Socialization").

Rehabilitation resembles deterrence in that both motivate the offender toward conformity. But rehabilitation emphasizes constructive improvement, while deterrence (like retribution) makes the offender suffer. In addition, while retribution demands that the punishment fit the crime, rehabilitation tailors treatment to the offender. Thus, identical crimes would prompt similar acts of retribution but might call for different programs of rehabilitation.

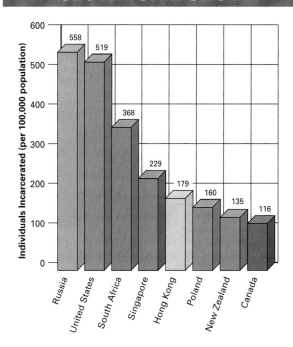

GLOBAL SNAPSHOT

FIGURE 8–4 Incarceration Rates, 1993
Source: Mauer (1994).

Societal Protection

A final justification for punishment is **societal protection,** *a means by which societ renders an offender incapable of further offenses temporarily through incarceration or permanently by execution.* Like deterrence, societal protection is a rational approach to punishment and seeks to protect society from crime.

Table 8–2 summarizes these four justifications of punishment. Currently, 1.6 million people are incarcerated in the United States (and another 4 million are on parole or probation). In response to tougher public attitudes and an increasing number of arrests for drug offenses, the U.S. prison population has tripled since 1980. Note, too, Figure 8–4, showing that the United States incarcerates a larger share of its population than most other countries in the world.

Critical evaluation. We have identified four purposes of punishment. Assessing the actual consequences of punishment, however, is no simple task.

SUMMARY

1. Deviance refers to normative violations ranging from mild breaches of etiquette to serious violence.

2. Biological investigation, from Cesare Lombroso's nineteenth-century observations of convicts to recent research in human genetics, offers little insight into the causes of crime.

3. Psychological study links deviance to abnormal personality resulting from either biological or environmental causes. Psychological theories help to explain some kinds of deviance.

4. Deviance has societal rather than individual roots because it is related to (1) cultural norms, (2) situational processes of social definition, and (3) patterns of social power.

5. Using the structural-functional paradigm, Durkheim claimed that, by responding to deviance, we affirm values and norms, clarify moral boundaries, heighten social unity, and encourage social change.

6. The symbolic-interaction paradigm is the basis of labeling theory, which holds that deviance arises in the reaction of others to a person's behavior. Acquiring a stigma of deviance can lead to secondary deviance and the onset of a deviant career.

7. Following the approach of Karl Marx, social-conflict theory holds that laws and other norms reflect the interests of powerful members of society. Social-conflict theory also spotlights white-collar crimes that cause extensive social harm, although the offenders are rarely branded as criminals.

8. Official statistics indicate that arrest rates peak in late adolescence, then drop steadily with advancing age. Three-fourths of those arrested for property crimes are males, as are almost nine of ten of those arrested for violent crimes.

9. People of lower social position commit more street crime than those with greater social privilege. When white-collar crimes are included among criminal offenses, however, the disparity in overall criminal activity diminishes.

10. More whites than African Americans are arrested for street crimes. However, African Americans are arrested more often than whites in proportion to their respective populations. Asian Americans have lower-than-average rates of arrest.

11. The police exercise considerable discretion in their work. Research suggests that factors such as the seriousness of the offense, the presence of bystanders, and the accused being African American make arrest more likely.

12. Although ideally an adversarial system, U.S. courts resolve most cases through plea bargaining. While efficient, this method puts less powerful people at a disadvantage.

13. Justifications of punishment include retribution, deterrence, rehabilitation, and societal protection. Because its consequences are difficult to evaluate scientifically, punishment—like deviance itself—sparks controversy among sociologists and the public as a whole.

KEY CONCEPTS

deviance the recognized violation of cultural norms

crime the violation of norms a society formally enacts into criminal law

juvenile delinquency the violation of legal standards by the young

criminal justice system a formal response to alleged violations of the law on the part of police, courts, and prison officials

labeling theory the assertion that deviance and conformity result, not only from what people do, but from how others respond to those actions

stigma a powerfully negative social label that radically changes a person's self-concept and social identity

medicalization of deviance the transformation of moral and legal issues into medical matters

white-collar crime crimes committed by persons of high social position in the course of their occupations

hate crime a criminal act against a person or person's property by an offender motivated by racial or other bias

crimes against the person (violent crimes) crimes that direct violence or the threat of violence against others

crimes against property (property crimes) crimes that involve theft of property belonging to others

victimless crimes violations of law in which there are no readily apparent victims

plea bargaining a legal negotiation in which the state reduces a defendant's charge in exchange for a guilty plea

retribution an act of moral vengeance by which society inflicts suffering on an offender comparable to that caused by the offense

deterrence the attempt to discourage criminality through punishment

rehabilitation a program for reforming the offender to prevent subsequent offenses

societal protection a means by which society renders an offender incapable of further offenses temporarily through incarceration or permanently by execution

criminal recidivism subsequent offenses by people previously convicted of crimes

CRITICAL-THINKING QUESTIONS

1. How does a sociological view of deviance differ from the common-sense notion that bad people do bad things?

2. Identify Durkheim's functions of deviance. From his point of view, could people create a society free from deviance? Why or why not?

3. How does social power affect deviant labeling? How do gender, race, and class enter into the process?

4. Why do you think crime rates have risen in the United States over the course of the last fifty years? Do you support or oppose efforts toward "community policing" as described in the chapter's final box?

LEARNING EXERCISES

1. Research computer crime. What new kinds of crime are emerging in the Information Age? Is computer technology also generating new ways of tracking down lawbreakers?

2. Rent a wheelchair (check with a local pharmacy or medical supply store) and try to use it as much as possible for a day or two. Not only will you gain a firsthand understanding of the accessibility issue, but you will discover people respond to you in many new ways.

3. Watch an episode of the real-action police show "Cops." As shown on this program, what kinds of people commit crimes?

4. If you have access to the Internet, stay abreast of the latest crime and law enforcement statistics by visiting the Web site (http://www.ojp.usdoj. gov/bjs/) for the Bureau of Justice Statistics, an agency of the U.S. Department of Justice.

5. Install the CD-ROM packaged inside the back cover of your text and complete the activities designed to accompany this chapter.

PART II
HOW NEW TECHNOLOGY IS CHANGING OUR WAY OF LIFE

cyber.scope

Marshall McLuhan (1969) summed up his pioneering research in the study of communications this way: "Any new technology tends to create a new human environment." In other words, technology affects not just how we work, but it shapes and colors our entire way of life. In this second Cyber.Scope, we pause to reflect on some of the ways the Information Revolution is changing our culture and society.

The Information Revolution and Cultural Values

Chapter 3 ("Culture") noted that members of our society attach great importance to material comfort. In fact, throughout our history, many people have defined "success" to mean earning a good income and enjoying the things money will buy, including a home, car, and fashionable clothing.

But some analysts wonder if, as we enter the next century, our values may shift from a single-minded focus on the accumulation of things (the products of industrial technology) to an appreciation of ideas (the products of information technology). "New age" ideas range from experiences (including both travel and virtual reality[1]) to well-being (including the self-actualization that has become popular in recent decades) (Newman, 1991).

---

[1] For example, "travel" to an Adirondack mountaintop and enjoy the view (http://www.adirondack.net/adnet/bluemt/bluemt4.html) or wander through a Shaker settlement in Massachusetts (http://www.hancockshaker village.org).

Socialization in the Computer Age

Half a century ago, television rewrote the rules for socialization in the United States and, as Chapter 5 ("Socialization") explained, young people now spend more time watching TV than talking to their parents. Today, in the emerging Information Society, screens are not just for television; they are our windows into a cyber-world where computers link, entertain, and educate us. But this trend toward "cyber-socialization" raises several important questions.

First, will the spread of computer-based information erode the regional diversity that distinguishes this country? Will New England no longer be set off from the Deep South, and the Midwest from the

West Coast? We know that new information technology is linking our nation with the world, so we might well expect to see a more national culture emerge and, with time, a more global culture as well.

Second, how will this "cyber-culture" affect our children? Will having computers at the center of their lives be good for them? For many children, computer-based images and information already play a significant role in the socialization process. Will this trend lessen the importance of parents in children's lives, as television did? Cyber-socialization can certainly entertain and instruct, but can it meet the emotional needs of children? Will it contribute to their moral development?

Almost unlimited access to information can be a mixed blessing, as parents can well understand. How can we prevent children from gaining access to pornography or other objectionable material on the Internet? Or, should we?

Third, who will control cyber-socialization? Just as parents have long expressed concern about what their children watch on television, they now worry about what kids encounter as they "surf the 'Net." To date, the federal courts have taken the position that the Internet should operate with minimal governmental interference. Do we—as citizens and as parents—have expectations for the content of "virtual culture"? Should the information industry operate for profit? With standards to ensure some measure of educational content? Who should decide?

The Cyber-Self

A person using the name "VegDiet" enters one of thousands of "chat rooms" found on the Internet, the vast global network described in Chapter 7 ("Groups and Organizations"). Within a few seconds, "VegDiet" is hammering the keyboard, actively debating the state of the world with three other people: "MrMaine," "Ferret," and "RedWine."

Computer-chat, which is growing increasingly popular, highlights how online interaction differs from conventional modes of interaction. After studying online interaction, Dennis Waskul (1997) concluded that the self transmitted via computer is "disembodied." Using Erving Goffman's dramaturgical approach (see Chapter 6), Waskul notes that computer technology screens out a host of "cues" about people's identities—where they are, what they look like, how they dress, and their

age and sex—and conveys only the identities they choose to present.

Cyberspace thus affords us great freedom to "try on" identities, in most cases with few, if any, lasting consequences. As one chat room participant explained, "Online is a game . . . Only here, I play with who I am" (1997:21).

But Wait A Minute . . .
The Neo-Luddites

Back in the eighteenth century, English weavers who opposed the Industrial Revolution traveled around the country demolishing the new machinery whenever they could gain access to a factory. The Luddites (named after Ned Ludd, their leader) were convinced that the new technology of their day would eliminate jobs and, in general, make life worse (Zachary, 1997).

"On the Internet, nobody knows you're a dog."

Although the Luddites lost their battle to stem the tide of change, their spirit lives on in people opposed to the Information Revolution today. These neo-Luddites, as they are called, speak with many voices. But they agree that we should not race headlong into a cyber-future without thinking critically about how new technology is likely to make our lives better and worse.

The neo-Luddites remind us, first, that technology is never socially neutral. That is, technology does not simply exist *in* the world, it *changes* the world, pushing human lives in one direction while closing off other alternatives. As a people, we tend to venerate technology as good in and of itself, Theodore Roszak (1986) points out, but, in the process, we give up the power to decide for ourselves how we should live. Putting computers in the classroom is no substitute for good teaching, Roszak declares. We would also do well to remember that no computer ever created a painting, penned a poem, or composed a symphony. And, perhaps most important, computers have no capacity to address ethical questions about what is right and wrong.

Living in a forward-looking culture, we easily see the benefits of new technology. But we need to remember that, just as technology can serve us, it also can diminish us and even destroy us. After all, the Luddites were not anti-technology; they simply wanted to be sure that technology responded to human needs—and not the other way around.

Antonio Ruiz, *Verano*, 1937
Oil on wood, 29 × 35 cm. Collection of Acervo Patrimonial, SHCP, Mexico.

CHAPTER 9

SOCIAL STRATIFICATION

On April 10, 1912, the ocean liner *Titanic* slipped away from the docks of Southampton, England, on its maiden voyage across the North Atlantic to New York. A proud symbol of the new industrial age, the towering ship carried twenty-three hundred passengers, some enjoying more luxury than most travelers today could imagine. Poor immigrants, however, crowded the lower decks, journeying to what they hoped would be a better life in the United States.

Two days out, the crew received radio warnings of icebergs in the area but paid little notice. Then, near midnight, as the ship steamed swiftly and silently westward, a lookout was stunned to see a massive shape rising out of the dark ocean directly ahead. Moments later, the *Titanic* collided with a huge iceberg, almost as tall as the ship itself, which split open its side as if the grand vessel were just a giant tin can.

Seawater exploded into the ship's lower levels, and within twenty-five minutes people were rushing for the lifeboats. By 2:00 A.M. the bow of the *Titanic* was submerged and the stern reared high above the water. Clinging to the deck, and quietly observed by those in the lifeboats, hundreds of helpless passengers solemnly passed their final minutes before the ship disappeared into the frigid Atlantic (Lord, 1976).

The tragic loss of more than 1,600 lives made news around the world. Looking back dispassionately at this terrible accident with a sociological eye, however, we see that some categories of passengers had much better odds of survival than others. In an age of conventional gallantry, women and children boarded the lifeboats first, so that 80 percent of the casualties were men. Class, too, was at work. More than 60 percent of people holding first-class tickets were saved, primarily because they were on the upper decks where warnings were sounded first and lifeboats were accessible. Only 36 percent of the second-class passengers survived, and of the third-class passengers on the lower decks, only 24 percent escaped drowning. On board the *Titanic*, class turned out to mean much more than the quality of accommodations: It was truly a matter of life or death.

The fate of the *Titanic* dramatically illustrates the consequences of social inequality for the ways people live—and sometimes whether they live at all. This chapter explores the important concept of social stratification. Chapter 10 continues the story by examining social inequality in the United States, and Chapter 11 examines how our country fits into a global system of wealth and poverty.

WHAT IS SOCIAL STRATIFICATION?

For tens of thousands of years the world over, humans lived in small hunting and gathering societies. Although members of these bands might single out one person as being swifter, stronger, or particularly skillful in collecting food, everyone had more or less the same social standing. As societies became more complex—a process detailed in Chapter 4 ("Society")—a monumental change came about. The social system elevated entire categories of people above others, providing one segment of the population with a disproportionate share of money, power, and schooling.

SUPPLEMENTS: The *Data File* contains a detailed outline of Chapter 9, along with supplementary lecture material and additional discussion topics.
Q: "All the animals are equal, but some are more equal than others." George Orwell, *Animal Farm*
Q: "You can do business with anyone, but only sail with a gentleman." J. P. Morgan

DIVERSITY: Regarding Point 4 below, Joan Huber Rytina, William H. Form, and John Pease found that people of higher social position saw the United States as a more "open" society. Moreover, they found that whites perceived more opportunity than blacks did. [See *American Journal of Sociology* 75, 4 (January 1970):703–16.]

The personal experience of poverty is captured in Sebastiao Salgado's haunting photograph, which stands as a universal portrait of human suffering. The essential sociological insight is that, however strongly individuals feel its effects, our social standing is largely a consequence of the way in which a society (or a world of societies) structures opportunity and reward. To the core of our being, then, we are all the products of social stratification.

Sociologists use the concept **social stratification** to refer to *a system by which a society ranks categories of people in a hierarchy*. Social stratification is a matter of four basic principles:

1. **Social stratification is a characteristic of society, not simply a reflection of individual differences.** Members of industrial societies think social standing is based on personal talent and effort, which is typical of our tendency to exaggerate the extent to which we control our destinies. Did a higher percentage of the first-class passengers survive the sinking of the *Titanic* because they were smarter or better swimmers than second- and third-class passengers? Hardly. They fared better because of their privileged position on the ship. Similarly, children born into wealthy families are more likely than children born into poverty to enjoy good health, achieve academically, succeed in their life's work, and live well into old age. Neither rich nor poor people are responsible for creating social stratification, yet this system shapes the lives of them all.

2. **Social stratification persists over generations.** To understand that stratification stems from society rather than individual differences, we need only look at how inequality persists over time. In all societies, parents pass their social position along to their children, so that patterns of inequality stay much the same from generation to generation.

Especially in industrial societies, however, some individuals do experience **social mobility,** *change in one's position in a social hierarchy*. Social mobility may be upward or downward. Our society celebrates the achievements of a Roseanne or a Bill Cosby, both of whom rose from modest beginnings to fame and fortune. But we also acknowledge that people move downward as a result of business setbacks, unemployment, or illness. More often, people move *horizontally*, that is, they exchange one occupation for another that is comparable. For most people, social standing remains much the same over a lifetime.

3. **Social stratification is universal but variable.** Social stratification is found everywhere. At the same time, *what* is unequal and *how* unequal people are vary from one type of society to another. Among the members of technologically simple societies, social differentiation is minimal and based mostly on age and sex. With the development of sophisticated technology for growing food, societies also forge complex and more rigid systems for distributing what people produce. As we shall see, the Industrial Revolution increased social mobility and reduced at least some kinds of social inequality. On the other hand, there is evidence that, for the short term at least, new information technology has had the opposite effect, increasing social inequality.

4. **Social stratification involves not just inequality but beliefs.** Any system of inequality not only gives some people more resources than others but defines certain arrangements as fair. Just as *what* is unequal differs from society to society, then, so does the explanation of *why* people should be unequal. Virtually everywhere, however, people with the greatest social privilege express the strongest support for their society's social stratification, while those with fewer social resources are more likely to seek change.

CASTE AND CLASS SYSTEMS

In describing social stratification in particular societies, sociologists often use two opposing standards: "closed" systems, which allow little change in social position, and "open" systems, which permit considerable social mobility (Tumin, 1985).

NOTE: The Latin root of "caste," *cast(us)*, means "chaste" or "pure"; its later use (for example, the Portuguese word *casta*) means "race" or "blood".
GLOBAL: The relatively weak performance of India's agrarian economy is evident in the fact that this vast country of 968 million people (1997) is outproduced by tiny, industrial Belgium with 10 million people.

GLOBAL: According to India's system of affirmative action, "backward castes" are guaranteed 27% of government jobs and college positions; such castes include 70% of India's people.
GLOBAL: Hope for India's economic development rests on three key elements that should attract foreign investment: (1) widespread use of the English language, (2) a democratic political system, and (3) a legal system suitable for modern business.

THE CASTE SYSTEM

A **caste system** amounts to *social stratification based on ascription*. A pure caste system, in other words, is "closed" so that birth alone determines one's social destiny with no opportunity for social mobility based on individual effort. In caste systems, then, categories of people are ranked in a rigid hierarchy and everyone is born, lives, and dies at the same social level.

Two Illustrations: India and South Africa

Many of the world's societies—most of them agrarian—approximate caste systems. One example is India, or at least India's traditional villages, where most of the people still live. The Indian system of castes (or *varna*, a Sanskrit word that means "color") is composed of four major categories: Brahmin, Kshatriya, Vaishya, and Shudra. On the local level, however, each of these is composed of hundreds of subcaste (or *jati*) groups.

Caste has also played a key role in the history of South Africa. Until recently, this nation's policy of *apartheid* gave the 5 million South Africans of European ancestry a commanding share of wealth and power, dominating some 30 million black South Africans. In a middle position were another 3 million mixed-race people, known as "coloreds," and about 1 million Asians. The box on page 238 describes the current state of South Africa's racial caste system.

In a caste system, birth determines the fundamental shape of people's lives in four crucial respects. First, traditional caste groups are linked to occupation, so that generations of a family perform the same type of work. In rural India, although some occupations (such as farming) are open to all, castes are identified by the work their members do (as priests, barbers, leather workers, sweepers, and so on). In South Africa, whites still hold almost all the desirable jobs, while most blacks perform manual labor and other low-level service work.

Second, no rigid social hierarchy can persist if people marry outside their own categories; if they did, what rank would their children hold? Consequently, caste systems mandate that people marry others of the same ranking. Sociologists call this pattern *endogamous* marriage (*endo* stems from Greek, meaning "within"). Traditionally, Indian parents select their children's marriage partners, often before the children reach their teens. Until 1985, South Africa banned marriage and even outlawed sex between the races; today, interracial couples still are rare since blacks and whites continue to live in separate areas.

A desire to better one's social position fuels immigration the world over, creating a flow of humanity from poorer countries to richer ones. The mix of fear and hope in the hearts of people seeking a better life is captured in the painting Los Emigrantes, *by Argentine artist Antonio Berni.*

Antonio Berni (1905–1981), *Los Emigrantes.* © Christie's Images.

Third, caste guides everyday life so that people remain in the company of "their own kind." Hindus in India enforce this segregation with the belief that a ritually "pure" person of a higher caste will be "polluted" by contact with someone of lower standing. Apartheid in South Africa operated much the same way.

Fourth, caste systems rest on powerful cultural beliefs. Indian culture is built on Hindu traditions of accepting one's life work, whatever it may be, as a moral duty. And, although apartheid is no longer law, South Africans still distinguish "white jobs" from "black jobs."

DIVERSITY: Leftists criticized capitalism for supporting the apartheid regime; defenders of capitalism claimed this economic system is a progressive force indifferent to all castelike factors (J. P. Morgan claimed he might "only sail with a gentleman," but he was happy to do business with anyone).

GLOBAL: The average black South African consumes about 10% of what the typical white person does; life expectancy for blacks is 58 years, compared to 70 years for whites.
RESOURCE: Daphne Topouzis's article, "Women's Poverty in Africa," is included in the new edition of the Macionis and Benokraitis reader, *Seeing Ourselves.*

GLOBAL SOCIOLOGY

Race as Caste: A Report From South Africa

At the southern tip of the African continent lies South Africa, a territory about the size of Alaska, with a 1997 population of some 46 million. Long inhabited by people of African descent, the region attracted Dutch traders and farmers in the mid-seventeenth century. Early in the nineteenth century, a second wave of colonization saw British immigrants push the Dutch inland. By the early 1900s, the British had taken over the country, proclaiming it the Union of South Africa. In 1961, the United Kingdom relinquished control and recognized the independence of the Republic of South Africa.

But freedom was a reality only for the white minority. To ensure their political control over the black majority, whites relied on a policy of *apartheid*, or racial separation. A common practice for many years, apartheid was enshrined in law in 1948, denying blacks national citizenship, ownership of land, and any formal voice in the government. In effect, black South Africans became a subordinate caste, receiving little schooling and performing menial, low-paying jobs. Under this system, even "middle class" white housewives became accustomed to having a black household servant.

The prosperous white minority defended apartheid, claiming that blacks threatened their cultural traditions or, more fundamentally, were inferior beings. But resistance to apartheid rose steadily, prompting whites to resort to brutal military repression to maintain their power.

Persistent resistance—primarily from younger blacks, impatient for a political voice and economic opportunity—gradually forced change. Adding to the pressure was criticism from most other industrial nations, including the United States. A decade ago, the tide began to turn as the South African government granted limited political rights to people of mixed race and Asian ancestry. Then came the right for all people to form labor unions, to enter occupations once restricted to whites, and to own property. Additionally, officials began to dismantle the system of "petty apartheid" regulations that segregated the races in all public places.

The process of change accelerated in 1990, with the release from prison of Nelson Mandela. In 1992, a majority of white voters endorsed the principle of bringing apartheid to an end and, in 1994, the first national election open to all races elevated Mandela to the presidency, ending centuries of white minority rule.

But, despite this dramatic political change, social stratification in South Africa is still based on race. Even with the right to own property, about one-third of black South Africans have no work, and the majority remain dirt poor. The worst off are those called *ukuhleleleka*, which means "marginal people" in the Xhosa language. Some 7 million blacks fall into this disadvantaged category. In Soweto-by-the-Sea, an idyllic-sounding community, thousands of people live crammed into shacks built of packing cases, corrugated metal, cardboard, and other discarded materials. There is no electricity for lights or refrigeration. Without plumbing, people use buckets to haul sewage; women line up awaiting their turn at a single water tap that serves more than 1,000 people. Jobs are hard to come by, partly because Ford and General Motors have closed their factories in nearby Port Elizabeth, and partly because people keep migrating to the town from regions where life is even worse. Those who can find work are lucky to earn $200 a month.

South Africa has ended white minority rule and, most analysts agree, there is no turning back. Yet, undoing centuries of racial caste cannot be accomplished simply by legal mandate. This still-divided society faces the long-term challenge of providing real opportunity to the majority of people who comprise a national underclass.

Although imprisoned for twenty-seven years for opposing apartheid, Nelson Mandela went on to become president of South Africa and has taken major steps to reduce racial inequality.

Sources: Fredrickson (1981), Wren (1991), and various news reports.

NOTE: Conceptions of "place" abound in any sort of caste system; for centuries, members of the U.S. upper class discouraged social contact with social inferiors through notions about remaining with "our kind" and exclusive rituals such as debutante parties.

NOTE: In the estate system, the terms "gentleman" and "lady" designated people of noble birth. In more democratic North America, the words have come to refer indiscriminately to males and females. Note, too, the link between military officers and noble birth, a pattern that persists today so that college ROTC graduates enter the military services as officers.

DISCUSS: The moral tone of medieval culture is evident in the seven deadly sins: covetousness, lust, anger, envy, pride, gluttony, and sloth. Only the last is much of a sin in today's more materialistic world.

Caste and Agrarian Life

Caste systems are typical of agrarian societies, because the lifelong routines of agriculture depend on a rigid sense of duty and discipline. Thus, caste hangs on in rural India, more than half a century after being formally outlawed and even as its grip is easing in industrial cities, where people exercise greater choice in their work and marriage partners. Similarly, the rapid industrialization of South Africa made personal choice and individual rights more important and the abolition of apartheid only a matter of time. In the United States, although elements of caste survive, treating people categorically on the basis of race or sex now invites charges of racism and sexism.

Note, however, that the erosion of caste does not signal the end of social stratification. On the contrary, it simply marks a change in its character, as the next sections explain.

THE CLASS SYSTEM

Agrarian life relies on the discipline generated by caste systems; industrial societies, however, depend on developing specialized talents. Industrialization thus erodes caste in favor of a **class system,** *social stratification based largely on individual achievement.*

A class system is more "open" so that people who gain schooling and skills may experience some social mobility in relation to their parents and siblings. Mobility, in turn, blurs class distinctions. Social boundaries also break down as people immigrate from abroad or move from the countryside to the city, lured by greater opportunity for schooling and work (Lipset & Bendix, 1967; Cutright, 1968; Treiman, 1970). Typically, newcomers take low-paying jobs; in the process they help push others up the social ladder (Tyree, Semyonov, & Hodge, 1979).

People in industrial societies come to think everyone—not just the rich—has certain "rights." The principle of equal standing before the law steadily assumes a central place in the political culture of industrial class systems. But class systems are no different from caste systems in a basic respect: People remain unequal. The difference is that social stratification in a class system rests more on personal talent and effort and less on the accident of birth. Careers become not a matter of moral duty but of individual choice; likewise, class systems allow more individual freedom in selecting marriage partners.

Status Consistency

Status consistency refers to *the degree of consistency in a person's social standing across various dimensions of social inequality.* In a caste system, limited social mobility generates high status consistency, so that the typical person has the same relative ranking with regard to wealth, power, and prestige. By contrast, the greater mobility of class systems means that they generate lower status consistency. In industrial nations such as the United States, then, a college professor with an advanced degree might enjoy high social prestige but rank lower in income. Low status consistency is the key reason that *classes* are less well defined than *castes*.

CASTE AND CLASS TOGETHER: THE UNITED KINGDOM

There are no pure caste or class systems; social stratification everywhere involves some combination of these two forms. This mix is particularly evident in the United Kingdom, an industrial nation with a long agrarian history.

The Estate System

In the Middle Ages, social stratification in England was a castelike system of three estates. (England, Wales, Scotland, and Northern Ireland constitute today's United Kingdom of Great Britain and Northern Ireland.) The first estate, a hereditary nobility, was composed of 150 families or barely 5 percent of the population (Laslett, 1984). These nobles exercised power and controlled wealth in the form of land. Typically, nobles had no formal occupation at all; to be "engaged in trade" or any other type of work for income was "beneath" the aristocracy. Well tended by servants, many nobles used their leisure time to cultivate refined tastes in art, music, and literature.

The estate system depended on keeping vast landholdings intact. To avoid division by heirs, the law of *primogeniture* (from Latin meaning "first born") mandated that all land pass to the eldest son or other male relation. Primogeniture maintained the great estates, but it forced younger sons to find other sources of support. One possibility was to enter the clergy—the second estate—where spiritual power was supplemented by the church's extensive landholdings. Other young men of high birth became military officers, lawyers, or took up other "honorable" professions set aside for "gentlemen."

And what of women? In an age when no woman could inherit her father's property and few women had the opportunity to earn a living on their own, the daughter of a noble family depended for her security on marrying well.

GLOBAL: Social hierarchy in the former Soviet Union was based more on power than on wealth. For example, Mikhail Gorbachev earned perhaps $40,000 per year as head of the USSR George Bush, his counterpart, earned $200,000 and was a millionaire many times over.

Q: "Soviet society follows the lead of Lenin towards becoming a classless, communist society." USSR secondary school textbook

GLOBAL: The Soviet empire in Eastern Europe included the Baltic nations of Estonia, Latvia, and Lithuania, Poland, East Germany, Czechoslovakia, Romania, Hungary, and Bulgaria. Between 1989 and 1991 all established their political independence from what is now the Russian Federation.

NOTE: Estimates placed the fortune of the Soviet Communist party, dissolved in August 1991, at roughly $175 billion.

During the 1990s, the former Soviet Union has moved towards a market economy. This process has made some people quite wealthy, while othes have lost their jobs as old, inefficient factories have closed. These residents of Moscow have been reduced to selling household goods in order to buy food.

A Classless Society?

This transformation of Russian society was guided by the ideas of Karl Marx, who asserted that private ownership of productive property is the basis of social classes (see Chapter 4, "Society"). When the state gained control of the economy, Soviet officials boasted that they had engineered the first classless society.

Outside of the Soviet Union, however, analysts were skeptical of the claim to classlessness (Lane, 1984). They pointed out that the jobs people held in the former Soviet Union actually fell into four levels. At the top were high government officials, or *apparatchiks*. Next came the Soviet intelligentsia, which included lower government officials, college professors, scientists, physicians, and engineers. Below them stood the manual workers and, in the lowest level, the rural peasantry.

The fact that these categories enjoyed very different living standards indicates that the former Soviet Union was never truly classless in the sense of having no social inequality. But one could say, more modestly, that putting factories, farms, colleges, and hospitals under state control did limit economic inequality (although doing so might have also expanded differences of power) compared to capitalist societies such as the United States.

The Second Russian Revolution

November 24, 1994, Odessa, Ukraine. The first snow of our voyage flies over the decks as our ship puts in at Odessa, the former Soviet Union's southernmost port on the Black Sea. A short distance from the dock, we gaze up the Potemkin Steps—the steep stairway leading to the city proper where the first shots of the Russian Revolution rang out. It has been six years since our last visit and much has changed; indeed, the Soviet Union itself has collapsed. Has life improved? Obviously, for some people: There are now chic boutiques where well-dressed shoppers pay cash for fine wines, designer labels, and imported perfumes. Outside, shiny new Volvos, Mercedes, and even a few Cadillacs stand next to the small Ladas from the "old days." But for most, life seems unmistakably worse. Flea markets line the curbs as families hawk home furnishings. Many are desperate in this town where meat sells for $4 a pound and the average person earns about $30 a

NOTE: In 1996, Vimpel Communications (a mobile telephone company) became the first Russian company listed on the New York Stock Exchange.

DIVERSITY: Socialism has done relatively little for incorporating women into positions of power; the ruling elites of both the former Soviet Union and the People's Republic of China, for instance, historically have been almost entirely male.

NOTE: Figure 9–1 is consistent with Figure 9–2, the Kuznets curve. Preindustrial societies typically have greater economic inequality than industrial nations do. Note, however, that income inequality also reflects intentional policies.

DIVERSITY: In every society, income inequality ratios are greater for men than for women, who are underrepresented at the highest income levels (cf. Hout, Brooks, & Manza, 1993).

month. Even the city government has to save money by shutting off street lights after eight o'clock. The spirits of most people seem as dim as Odessa's city streets.

After steady efforts to structure Soviet society according to the ideas of Karl Marx (and revolutionary Russian leader Vladimir Lenin), the Soviet Union shook with change throughout the 1980s. Economic reforms accelerated when Mikhail Gorbachev became president in 1985. His program, popularly known as *perestroika*, meaning "restructuring," sought to solve a dire economic problem: While the Soviet system had reduced economic inequality, everyone was relatively poor, and living standards lagged far behind those of other industrial nations. Simply put, Gorbachev hoped to stimulate economic expansion by ending inefficient government control of the economy.

Gorbachev's reforms soon escalated into one of the most dramatic social movements in history, as popular uprisings toppled one socialist government after another throughout Eastern Europe and, ultimately, brought down the Soviet system itself. In essence, people blamed their economic problems as well as their lack of basic freedoms on a repressive ruling class of Communist party officials.

From the founding of the Soviet Union in 1917 until its demise in 1991, the Communist party held a monopoly of power, often brutally putting down any opposition. Near the end, 18 million party members (6 percent of the Soviet people) still made all the decisions about Soviet life while enjoying privileges such as vacation homes, chauffeured automobiles, prized consumer goods, and an elite education for their children (Zaslavsky, 1982; Shipler, 1984; Theen, 1984). The second Soviet revolution, then, mirrors the first in that it was nothing less than the overthrow of the ruling class.

The rise and fall of the Soviet Union demonstrates that social inequality involves more than economic resources. As Figure 9–1 shows, Soviet society lacked the extremes of wealth and poverty found in Great Britain, Japan, and the United States. But an elite class existed all the same, one based on power rather than wealth. Thus, despite the fact that both Mikhail Gorbachev and his successor Boris Yeltsin earned far less than a U.S. president, they wielded awesome power.

And what about social mobility in the Soviet Union? Evidence suggests that during this century there was more upward social mobility in the Soviet Union than in Great Britain, Japan, or even the United

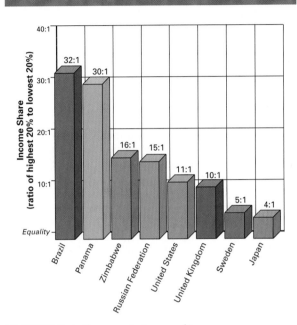

GLOBAL SNAPSHOT

FIGURE 9–1 Economic Inequality in Selected Countries, 1980–1996*

*These data are the most recent available, representing income share for various years between 1980 and 1996.

Source: The World Bank (1997).

States. One reason was that Soviet society lacked the concentrated wealth that families elsewhere pass from one generation to the next. Even more important, industrialization and rapid bureaucratization have helped a large proportion of the working class and rural peasantry rise to positions in industry and government (Dobson, 1977; Lane, 1984; Shipler, 1984).

In the last decade, however, the people of the Russian Federation have experienced downward social mobility. One staggering indicator of this slide is the fact that, between 1990 and 1997, the average lifespan for Soviet men declined by eight years (two years in the case of women). Many factors are involved—including Russia's poor system of health care—but, most important, the Russian people are suffering from a turbulent period of economic change (Róna-Tas, 1994; Specter, 1997). Sociologists describe such upward and downward trends as **structural social mobility,** *a shift in the social position of large numbers of*

NOTE: Since every society has some kind of social stratification, ideology may be described as the assertion that specific kinds of *inequality* should not be defined as *injustice*.

DIVERSITY: Justifications for inequality are embedded in gender. Among men, inequality is viewed more in terms of (classlike) individual merit; the subordination of women has been defended on the basis of (castelike) duty and natural order.

NOTE: Andrew G. Walder (1995) argues that communist organizations allocate rewards to members to promote conformity to the party line, a case of stratification enhancing political correctness rather than market productivity.

Q: "The ruling ideas of each age have ever been the ideas of its ruling class." Karl Marx, *Manifesto of the Communist Party*

people due more to changes in society itself than to individual efforts. As we shall see in Chapter 10 ("Social Class in the United States"), much of the mobility in our society, too, follows from broad economic changes that have taken place over the course of this century.

IDEOLOGY: STRATIFICATION'S "STAYING POWER"

Looking at the extent of social inequality around the world, we might wonder how societies persist without distributing their resources more equally. Castelike systems in Great Britain and Japan lasted for centuries, concentrating land and power in the hands of several hundred families. And, for 2,000 years, people in India have accepted the idea that they should be privileged or poor because of the accident of birth.

A key reason for the remarkable persistence of social hierarchies is that they are built on **ideology,** *cultural beliefs that serve to justify social stratification.* Any beliefs—for example, the idea that the rich are smart while the poor are lazy—are ideological to the extent that they support the dominance of wealthy elites and suggest that poor people deserve their plight.

Plato and Marx on Ideology

The ancient Greek philosopher Plato (427–347 B.C.E.) defined *justice* as agreement about who should have what. Every society, Plato explained, teaches its members to view some stratification system as "fair." Karl Marx, too, understood this process, although he was far more critical of inequality than Plato was. Marx took capitalist societies to task for channeling wealth and power into the hands of a few, and calling the process "a law of the marketplace." Capitalist law, Marx continued, makes the right to own property a bedrock principle. Then, laws of inheritance channel money and privileges from one generation to the next within the same families. In short, Marx concluded, ideas as well as resources come under the control of a society's elite, which helps to explain why established hierarchies are so difficult to change.

Both Plato and Marx recognized that ideology is rarely a simple matter of privileged people conspiring to generate self-serving ideas about social inequality. Rather, ideology usually takes the form of cultural patterns that evolve over a long period of time. As people learn to embrace their society's conception of fairness, they may question the rightness of their own position, but they are unlikely to challenge the system itself.

Historical Patterns of Ideology

The ideas that shore up social stratification change along with a society's economy and technology. Early agrarian societies depended on slaves to perform burdensome manual labor. Aristotle (384–322 B.C.E.) defended the practice of slavery among the ancient Greeks on the basis that some people with little intelligence deserve nothing better than life under the direction of their natural "betters."

Agrarian societies in Europe during the Middle Ages also required the daily labor of most people to support the small aristocracy. Thus, noble and serf learned to view occupation as rightfully determined by birth, and a person's work as a matter of moral responsibility. In short, caste systems always rest on the belief that social ranking is the product of a "natural" order.

Industrial capitalism transformed wealth and power into prizes to be won by those who display the greatest talent and effort. Class systems celebrate individualism and achievement, so that social standing serves as a measure of personal worthiness. Thus, poverty, which was the object of charity under feudalism, is scorned in industrial capitalism as a badge of personal failure. Nowhere has this harsh view been more clearly stated than by Herbert Spencer, whose ideas are described in the box.

Throughout human history, most people probably have regarded social stratification as unshakable. Especially as traditions weaken, however, people begin to question cultural "truths" and unmask their political foundations and consequences.

For example, historic notions of a "woman's place" today seem far from natural and are losing their power to deprive women of opportunities. Nevertheless, our contemporary class system still subjects women to castelike expectations: They should perform traditional tasks altruistically, while men are financially rewarded for their efforts. To illustrate, most chefs are men who work for income while most household cooks are women who perform this role as a household duty.

Yet, while gender differences persist in the United States, there is little doubt that women and men are steadily becoming more equal in important respects. Similarly, the continuing struggle for racial equality in South Africa is now dismantling apartheid, which for decades shaped economic, political, and educational life in that nation. Apartheid, never widely accepted by blacks, has now lost its support as a "natural" system among whites who reject ideological racism (Friedrich, 1987; Contreras, 1992).

NOTE: While Auguste Comte thought we should understand the laws of society in order to be more effective in our interventions, Herbert Spencer contended that once we understood society we would conclude that such intervention was pointless and most often destructive.

RESOURCE: Davis and Moore's analysis is one of the classics in the companion reader, *Seeing Ourselves.*

NOTE: In light of the Davis-Moore thesis, seniority is not a uniformly positive principle. Most brain surgeons, for example, get better with time. Science professors, by contrast, do their best work early in their careers and then slow down. The term limits debate suggests that legislators are more like the latter than the former (Pitney, Jr., 1995).

 ## CRITICAL THINKING

Is Getting Rich "The Survival of the Fittest"?

"The survival of the fittest"—we have all heard these words as a way of describing society as a competitive jungle. Actually, the phrase was coined by one of sociology's pioneers, Herbert Spencer (1820–1903), who expressed a view of social stratification that is still widespread today.

Spencer, who lived in England, was fascinated by the work of the natural scientist Charles Darwin (1809–1882). According to Darwin's theory of biological evolution, species change physically over many generations as they adapt to a particular natural environment. Spencer, however, distorted Darwin's evolutionary model by applying it to the operation of society. That is, Spencer argued that society operates like a jungle, with the "fittest" people rising to wealth and power and the deficient gradually sinking into miserable poverty.

It is no surprise that Spencer's thinking was extremely popular among the rising U.S. industrialists a century ago. John D. Rockefeller (1839–1937), who made a vast fortune building the modern oil industry, often recited Spencer's "social gospel" to young children in Sunday school. As Rockefeller saw it, the growth of giant corporations—and the astounding wealth of their owners—was merely the "survival of the fittest," a simple fact of nature. Neither Spencer nor Rockefeller had any sympathy for the poor, viewing their plight as clear evidence of inability or unwillingness to measure up in a competitive world. Indeed, social Darwinism actually condemned social welfare programs as an evil because they penalized society's "best" members (through taxes) and rewarded society's "worst" members (through welfare benefits).

Almost a century has passed since Spencer spread his message. Today, sociologists are quick to point out that social standing is not simply a matter of personal effort, as Spencer contended. And it is simply not the case that what produces the most wealth is necessarily the most beneficial to society. Yet, given our individualistic culture, Spencer's basic view that people get more or less what they deserve in life remains very much with us today.

THE FUNCTIONS OF SOCIAL STRATIFICATION

Why are societies stratified at all? One answer, consistent with the structural-functional paradigm, is that social inequality plays a vital part in the operation of society. This influential—and controversial—argument was set forth some fifty years ago by Kingsley Davis and Wilbert Moore (1945).

THE DAVIS-MOORE THESIS

The **Davis-Moore thesis** is *the assertion that social stratification has beneficial consequences for the operation of a society.* How else, ask Davis and Moore, can we explain the fact that some form of social stratification has been found everywhere?

Davis and Moore describe our society as a complex system involving hundreds of occupational positions of varying importance. Certain jobs—say, washing windows or changing spark plugs in a car—are fairly easy and can be performed by almost anyone. Other jobs—such as designing new generations of computers or transplanting human organs—are quite difficult and demand the scarce talents of people with extensive (and expensive) education. Positions of high day-to-day responsibility that demand special abilities are the most functionally significant.

In general, Davis and Moore explain, the greater the functional importance of a position, the more rewards a society attaches to it. This strategy pays off, since rewarding important work with income, prestige, power, and leisure encourages people to do these things. In effect, by distributing resources unequally, a society motivates each person to aspire to the most significant work possible, and to work better, harder, and longer. The overall result of a system of unequal rewards—which is what social stratification amounts to—is a more productive society.

Davis and Moore concede that any society can be egalitarian, but only to the extent that people are willing to let *anyone* perform *any* job. Equality also demands that someone who carries out a job poorly be rewarded on a par with someone who performs well. Logic dictates that such a system offers little incentive for people to try their best, and thereby reduces a society's efficiency and productivity.

SOCIAL SURVEY: "How important for getting ahead is natural ability?" (*CHIP1 Social Survey Software*, OPABLE2; GSS 1987, N = 1,486)

INCOME	"Very important"	"Less important"
Above average	53.0%	47.0%
Average	61.3%	38.7%
Below average	63.6%	36.4%

SOCIAL SURVEY: "How important for getting ahead in life is ambition?" (GSS 1987, N = 1,285; *Codebook*, 1996:705)

"Essential"	41.6%	"Not very important"	0.7%
"Very important"	44.9%	"Not important at all"	0.2%
"Fairly important"	10.4%	DK/NR	2.2%

Q: "I have no respect for the passion for equality, which seems to me to be merely idealizing envy." Oliver Wendell Holmes

MERITOCRACY

The Davis-Moore thesis implies that a productive society is a **meritocracy,** *a system of social stratification based on personal merit.* Such societies hold out rewards to develop the talents and encourage the efforts of everyone. In pursuit of meritocracy, a society promotes equality of opportunity while, at the same time, demanding unequal rewards. In other words, a pure class system would be a meritocracy since it rewards everyone based on ability and effort. In addition, a class-based meritocracy would have great social mobility, blurring social categories as individuals continuously move up or down in the system depending on their performance.

For their part, caste societies can speak of "merit" (from Latin, meaning "worthy of praise") only in terms of persistence in low-skill labor such as farming. Caste systems, in short, offer honor to those who remain dutifully "in their place."

Caste systems waste human potential, but they are quite orderly. And herein lies the answer to an important question: Why do modern industrial societies resist becoming complete meritocracies by retaining many castelike qualities? Simply because, left unchecked, meritocracy erodes social structure, including kinship. No one, for example, evaluates family members solely on the basis of performance. Class systems in industrial societies, therefore, retain some caste elements to promote order and social cohesion.

Critical evaluation. By investigating the functions of social stratification, Davis and Moore made a lasting contribution to sociological analysis. Even so, critics point to several flaws in their thesis. Melvin Tumin (1953) wonders, first, if functional importance really explains the high rewards that some people enjoy. In fact, can one even measure functional importance? Perhaps, he suggests, the high rewards our society accords to physicians partly result from deliberate efforts by medical schools to limit the supply of physicians and push up the demand for their services.

If so, income and other rewards may have little to do with an individual's functional contribution to society. With an income approaching $100 million per year, television personality Oprah Winfrey earns more in two days than the President earns all year. Would anyone argue that hosting a talk show is more important than leading the United States of America? The box takes a critical look at the link between pay and societal importance.

A second charge made by Tumin is that the Davis-Moore thesis exaggerates the role of social stratification in developing individual talent. Our society rewards individual

Medieval Europeans accepted rigid social differences as part of a divine plan for the world. This fifteenth-century painting by the Limbourg brothers shows a noble—the Duke of Berry—setting off on a hunt along with a group of his peers, while, in the background, serfs farm the land outside his castle.

The Davis-Moore thesis suggests why *some* form of stratification exists everywhere; it does not endorse any *particular* system of inequality. Nor do Davis and Moore specify precisely what reward should be attached to any occupational position. They merely point out that positions a society considers crucial must yield sufficient rewards to draw talent away from less important work.

NOTE: From a conservative, meritocratic point of view, social welfare systems penalize activity both on the part of poor people (by providing benefits for idleness) and rich people (by imposing taxes on earnings); they also foster immorality by encouraging the poor to cheat on qualifications for benefits and encouraging the rich to cheat on taxes.

DISCUSS: Ask the class what they make of the fact that a Pulitzer

Prize winner receives $3,000, while a "playmate of the year" earns $100,000 plus a new car.

NOTE: In July, 1997, Gilbert Amelio left Apple Computer with a severance package estimated at $7 million (Lohr, 1997).

NOTE: Denouncing a high executive salary, an AFL-CIO official pointed out that the $40 million in question exceeds what a minimum-wage worker would have earned, toiling since the birth of Christ.

CRITICAL THINKING

Big Bucks:
Are the Rich Worth What They Earn?

For an hour of work, a Los Angeles priest earns about $5, a hotel maid in New Orleans earns about $7, a bus driver in San Francisco makes about $15, a Phoenix bartender earns about $20, and a Detroit auto worker collects roughly $25. These wages shrink in comparison to the $40,000 that Barry Bonds earns per hour playing baseball for the San Francisco Giants. And what about the $100,000 actor Jim Carrey takes home for every hour he spends making movies? Or the $200,000 paid to Oprah Winfrey for each hour she chats with guests before the television cameras? Or the $1 million Tim Allen earns for filming a single episode of the sitcom "Home Improvement"?

The Davis-Moore thesis suggests that rewards reflect an occupation's value to society. But are the talents of Julia Louis-Dreyfus, who earned about $13 million a year as a sidekick on the "Seinfeld" television show, equal to the efforts of all 100 U.S. senators? With $100 million a year in earnings, is Oprah worth as much as, say, 3,000 police officers? In short, do earnings really reflect people's social importance?

Salaries in industrial-capitalist societies such as the United States are a product of the market forces of supply and demand. In simple terms, if you can do something better than others, and

people value it, you can command more reward. According to this view, movie and television stars, top athletes, skilled professionals, and many business executives have rare talents that are much in demand; thus, they may earn many times more than the typical worker in the United States.

But critics of the Davis-Moore thesis claim that the market is really a poor evaluator of occupational importance. First, they say, the U.S. economy is dominated by a small proportion of people who manipulate the system for their

own benefit. Corporate executives, for example, pay themselves multimillion-dollar salaries and bonuses whether their companies do well or not. Gilbert Amelio, CEO of Apple Computer, laid off more than 4,000 employees during 1996, and his company's stock price tumbled by almost 40 percent; yet he still paid himself more than $23 million (Quick, 1997).

There is another problem with the idea that the market measures people's contributions to society: Many people who make clear and significant contributions receive surprisingly little money. Hundreds of thousands of teachers, counselors, and health-care workers contribute daily to the welfare of others for very low salaries. The average teacher would have to work almost 700 years to earn as much as Mr. Amelio received in one year, and 22,500 years to equal the roughly $750 million received in 1997 by Michael Eisner, head of the Disney Corporation.

Using social worth to justify income, then, is hazardous. Those who defend the market as the most accurate measure of occupational worth ask, what would be better? But what is lucrative may or may not be socially valuable. From another standpoint, a market system amounts to a closed game in which only a handful of people have the money to play.

achievement, but we also allow families to transfer wealth and power from generation to generation in castelike fashion. Additionally, for women, people of color, and others with limited opportunities, caste elements of stratification still raise barriers to personal accomplishment. Overall, says Tumin, social stratification functions to develop some

people's abilities to the fullest while ensuring that others never reach their potential.

Third, by suggesting that social stratification benefits all of society, the Davis-Moore thesis ignores how social inequality promotes conflict and even outright revolution. This criticism leads us to the social-conflict

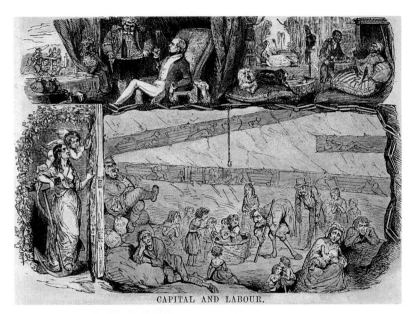

CAPITAL AND LABOUR.

This cartoon, titled "Capital and Labour," appeared in the English press in 1843, when the ideas of Karl Marx were first gaining attention. It links the plight of that country's coal miners to the privileges enjoyed by those who owned coal-fired factories.

paradigm, which provides a very different explanation for the persistence of social hierarchy.

STRATIFICATION AND CONFLICT

Social-conflict analysis argues that, rather than benefiting society as a whole, social stratification benefits some people at the expense of others. This analysis draws heavily on the ideas of Karl Marx, with contributions from Max Weber.

KARL MARX: CLASS AND CONFLICT

Karl Marx, whose approach to understanding social inequality is detailed in Chapter 4 ("Society"), identified two major social classes corresponding to the two basic relationships to the means of production: Individuals either (1) own productive property or (2) labor for others. In medieval Europe, the nobility and the church owned the productive land; peasants toiled as farmers. Similarly, in industrial class systems, the capitalists (or the bourgeoisie) control factories, which use the labor of workers (the proletariat).

Marx saw great disparities in wealth and power arising from this productive system, which, he contended, made class conflict inevitable. In time, he believed, oppression and misery would drive the working majority to organize and ultimately overthrow capitalism.

Marx's analysis drew on his observations of capitalism in the nineteenth century, when great industrialists dominated the scene. Andrew Carnegie, J. P. Morgan, John D. Rockefeller, and John Jacob Astor (one of the few very rich passengers to perish on the *Titanic*) lived in fabulous mansions adorned with priceless art and staffed by dozens of servants. Their fortunes were staggering: Andrew Carnegie, founder of U.S. Steel, reportedly earned some $20 million a year as this century began (about $100 million in today's dollars), at a time when the average worker earned roughly $500 a year (Baltzell, 1964; Pessen, 1990).

But, according to Marx, the capitalist elite draws its strength from more than the operation of the economy. Through the family, opportunity and wealth are passed down from generation to generation. Moreover, the legal system defends this practice through inheritance law. Similarly, exclusive schools bring children of the elite together, encouraging informal social ties that will benefit them throughout their lives. In short, from Marx's point of view, capitalist society *reproduces the class structure in each new generation.*

Critical evaluation. In analyzing how the capitalist economic system generates conflict between classes, Marx has had enormous influence on sociological thinking. But, because it is revolutionary—calling for the overthrow of capitalist society—Marxism is also highly controversial.

One of the strongest criticisms of the Marxist approach is that it denies a central tenet of the Davis-Moore thesis: that motivating people to perform various social roles requires some system of unequal rewards.

Q: "The alliance of the working class, the rural peasantry, and the intelligentsia . . . has been strengthened. The social, political, and ideological unity of Soviet society, with the working class its leading force, has formed . . . The supreme goal of the Soviet state is the building of a classless communist society . . ." The USSR Constitution (1977)

NOTE: Peter Berger (1986) suggests a flaw of Marxism is the empirical failure of the polarization thesis. Berger suggests that neo-Marxists have attempted to resolve this problem through global dependency theory (discussed in Chapter 11). Polarization, in short, has not occurred *within* industrial societies as much as it has among the world's nations as a whole.

Marx separated reward from performance, endorsing an egalitarian system based on the principle of "from each according to ability; to each according to need" (Marx & Engels, 1972:388). Critics argue that severing rewards from performance is precisely what generated the low productivity in the former Soviet Union and other socialist economies around the world.

Defenders of Marx rebut this line of attack by pointing to considerable evidence supporting Marx's view of humanity as inherently social rather than selfish (Clark, 1991; Fiske, 1991). We should not assume, therefore, that individual rewards (much less monetary compensation alone) are the only way to motivate people to perform their social roles.

A second problem is that the revolutionary developments Marx considered inevitable within capitalist societies have, by and large, failed to materialize. The next section explores why the socialist revolution Marx predicted and promoted has not occurred, at least in advanced capitalist societies.

WHY NO MARXIST REVOLUTION?

Despite Marx's prediction, capitalism is still thriving. Why have workers in the United States and other industrial societies not overthrown capitalism? Ralf Dahrendorf (1959) pointed to four reasons:

1. **The fragmentation of the capitalist class.** First, in the century since Marx's death, the capitalist class in the United States has greatly fragmented. Instead of *single families* owning large companies, today, *numerous stockholders* fill that position. Moreover, day-to-day operation of large corporations is now in the hands of a large managerial class, whose members may or may not be major stockholders. With stock widely held, an increasing number of people have a direct stake in preserving the capitalist system (Wright, 1985; Wright, Levine, & Sober, 1992).

2. **A higher standard of living.** As Chapter 15 ("The Economy and Work") explains, a century ago most workers were in factories or on farms performing **blue-collar occupations,** *lower-prestige work involving mostly manual labor.* Today, most workers hold **white-collar occupations,** *higher-prestige work involving mostly mental activity.* These jobs are in sales, management, and other service fields. Thus, many of today's white-collar workers do not think of themselves as an "industrial proletariat." Just as important, the average income in the United States has risen almost tenfold over the course of this century in dollars controlled for inflation, even as the workweek has decreased. Is it any wonder, then, that workers typically perceive themselves as better off than their parents and grandparents? This structural mobility has certainly cooled revolutionary aspirations among working people (Edwards, 1979; Gagliani, 1981; Wright & Martin, 1987).

3. **More extensive worker organization.** Employees have organizational strength that they lacked a century ago. Workers have won the right to organize into labor unions that, backed by threats of work slowdowns and strikes, can and do make demands of management. If not always peaceful, then, worker-management disputes are now institutionalized.

4. **More extensive legal protections.** During this century, the government has passed laws to make the workplace safer, and developed programs, such as unemployment insurance, disability protection, and Social Security, to provide workers with greater financial security.

A Counterpoint

Taken together, these four developments suggest that, despite persistent stratification, our society has smoothed many of capitalism's rough edges. Advocates of social-conflict analysis, however, believe that Marx's analysis of capitalism is still largely valid (Miliband, 1969; Edwards, 1979; Giddens, 1982; Domhoff, 1983; Stephens, 1986; Boswell & Dixon, 1993; Hout, Brooks, & Manza, 1993). They offer these counterarguments:

1. **Wealth remains highly concentrated.** As Marx contended, wealth remains in the hands of the few. In the United States, about half of all privately controlled corporate stock is owned by just 1 percent of individuals, who persist as a capitalist class.

2. **White-collar work offers little to workers.** As defenders of Marx's thinking see it, the white-collar revolution has delivered little in the way of higher income or better working conditions compared to the factory jobs of a century ago. On the contrary, although many of today's white-collar workers—especially women—sit in front of computer screens, their work remains monotonous and routine.

3. **Progress requires struggle.** Labor organizations may have advanced the interests of workers over the last half century, but regular negotiation

TABLE 9–1 Two Explanations of Social Stratification: A Summary

Structural-Functional Paradigm	Social-Conflict Paradigm
Social stratification keeps society operating. Linking greater rewards to more important social positions benefits society as a whole.	Social stratification is the result of social conflict. Differences in social resources serve the interests of some and harm the interests of others.
Social stratification matches talents and abilities to appropriate occupational positions.	Social stratification ensures that much talent and ability in society will not be developed at all.
Social stratification is both useful and inevitable.	Social stratification is useful only to some people; it is not inevitable.
The values and beliefs that legitimize social inequality are widely shared throughout society.	Values and beliefs tend to be ideological; they reflect the interests of the more powerful members of society.
Because systems of social stratification are useful to society as a whole and are supported by cultural values and beliefs, they are usually stable over time.	Because systems of social stratification reflect the interests of only part of society, they are unlikely to remain stable over time.

Source: Adapted, in part, from Arthur L. Stinchcombe, "Some Empirical Consequences of the Davis-Moore Theory of Stratification," *American Sociological Review*, Vol. 28, No. 5 (October 1963):808.

between workers and management hardly signals the end of social conflict. In fact, many of the concessions won by workers came about precisely through the class conflict Marx described. Moreover, workers still strive to gain concessions from capitalists and, in the 1990s, they struggle to hold on to advances already achieved. Even today, for instance, half of all people in the labor force have no company-sponsored pension program.

4. **The law still favors the rich.** Workers have gained some legal protection over the course of this century. Even so, the law still defends the overall distribution of wealth in the United States. Just as important, "average" people cannot use the legal system to the same advantage as the rich do.

In sum, according to social-conflict theory, the fact that no socialist revolution has taken place in the United States hardly invalidates Marx's analysis of capitalism. As we shall see in Chapter 10 ("Social Class in the United States"), pronounced social inequality persists, as does social conflict—albeit less overtly and violently than in the nineteenth century.

Finally, some defenders of capitalism point to the collapse of communist regimes in Eastern Europe and the former Soviet Union as proof of the superiority of capitalism to socialism. Most analysts agree that socialism failed to meet the needs of the people it was supposed to serve, either in terms of raising living standards or ensuring personal freedoms. But, to be fair, socialism's failings do not excuse flaws in capitalism. Capitalism in the United States has yet to demonstrate its ability to address problems of public education and

desperate poverty, especially among the urban underclass (Uchitelle, 1991). Table 9–1 summarizes the contributions of the two contrasting sociological approaches to understanding social stratification.

MAX WEBER: CLASS, STATUS, AND POWER

Max Weber, whose approach to social analysis is described in Chapter 4 ("Society"), agreed with Karl Marx that social stratification sparks social conflict, but he thought Marx's two-class model was simplistic. Instead, Weber viewed social stratification as a complex interplay of three distinct dimensions.

The first dimension is economic inequality—the crucial issue to Marx—which Weber termed *class* position. Weber did not think of "classes" as crude categories but as a continuum ranging from high to low. Weber's second dimension of social stratification is *status*, or social prestige, and the third is *power*.

The Socioeconomic Status Hierarchy

Marx regarded social prestige and power as simple reflections of economic position, and saw no reason to treat them as distinct dimensions of social inequality. But Weber observed that status consistency in modern societies is often quite low: A local government official, say, might wield considerable power yet have little wealth or social prestige.

Weber's contribution, then, lies in showing that social stratification in industrial societies is a multidimensional ranking rather than a simple hierarchy of clearly defined classes. In line with Weber's thinking, sociologists often use the term **socioeconomic status**

NOTE: The shrinking stature of the U.S. rich is suggested by this comparison: When William Henry Vanderbilt died in 1885, his obituary covered the entire front page of *The New York Times.* When Sam Walton died in 1992, his death was reported on 1/20th of a page.

SOCIAL SURVEY: "Is it government's responsibility to reduce income differences between the rich and the poor?" (*CHIP1 Social*

Survey Software, REDISTR; ISSP 1985)

	"Yes"	"No"
U.S.	34.6%	65.4%
Australia	52.6%	47.4%
Germany	66.9%	33.1%
U.K.	71.5%	28.5%
Austria	77.4%	22.6%

(SES) to refer to *a composite ranking based on various dimensions of social inequality.*

A population that varies greatly in class, status, and power—Weber's three dimensions of difference—displays a virtually infinite array of self-interested social categories. Thus, unlike Marx, who saw social conflict between two distinct classes, Weber considered social conflict highly variable and complex.

Inequality in History

Weber also made an important historical observation, noting that each of his three dimensions of social inequality stands out at different points in the evolution of human societies. Agrarian societies emphasize status or social prestige, typically in the form of honor. Members of these societies gain such status by conforming to the cultural norms that correspond to their rank.

Industrialization and the development of capitalism level traditional rankings based on birth but generate striking material differences in the population. Thus, Weber argued, the crucial difference among people in industrial societies lies in the economic dimension of class.

With time, industrial societies witness the growth of the bureaucratic state. This expansion of government and other types of formal organizations means that power gains importance in the stratification system. Especially in socialist societies, the government comes to regulate most aspects of life. The elite members of socialist societies are likely to be high-ranking and powerful officials rather than rich people.

This historical analysis underscores a final disagreement between Weber and Marx. Looking to the future, Marx believed that societies could largely eliminate social stratification by abolishing private ownership of productive property. Weber doubted that overthrowing capitalism would significantly diminish social stratification. It might lessen economic disparity, he reasoned, but socialism would simultaneously increase inequality by expanding government and concentrating power in the hands of a political elite. Recent popular uprisings against entrenched bureaucracies in Eastern Europe and the former Soviet Union support Weber's position.

Critical evaluation. Weber's multidimensional analysis of social stratification retains enormous influence among sociologists, especially in the United States. But some analysts (particularly those influenced by Marx's ideas) argue that while social class boundaries may have blurred, the United States and other industrial nations still show striking patterns of social inequality.

In this stone carving created in Egypt some 5,000 years ago, we see King Narmer about to slay his enemies with a mace, his sandals carried behind him and other fallen enemies below. Next to the king, the falcon represents the god Horus, who holds a rope attached to a head that grows from the soil like other plants. The message is that the king and Horus are one and the same, with the power of life and death over others.

Moreover, as we shall see in Chapter 10 ("Social Class in the United States"), income inequality has increased in recent years. In light of this trend, while some people continue to look at social stratification in terms of Weber's "multidimensional hierarchy," others think Marx's view of "the rich versus the poor" is closer to the mark.

STRATIFICATION AND TECHNOLOGY IN GLOBAL PERSPECTIVE

We can weave together a number of observations made in this chapter by considering the relationship between a society's technology and its type of social

NOTE: The Lenskis's analysis of historical changes in human societies—including the types noted here—is found in the first section of Chapter 4, "Society."

Q: "There is probably less economic injustice and class conflict now than at any time since the Industrial Revolution began." E. Digby Baltzell (1964)

SOCIAL SURVEY: "If someone has a high economic or social position, that indicates the person has special abilities or great accomplishments." (GSS 1984, N = 1,317; *Codebook*, 1996:97)
"Strongly agree"   11.7%   "Strongly disagree"   17.3%
"Somewhat agree"   36.2%   DK/NR   4.1%
"Somewhat disagree" 30.7%

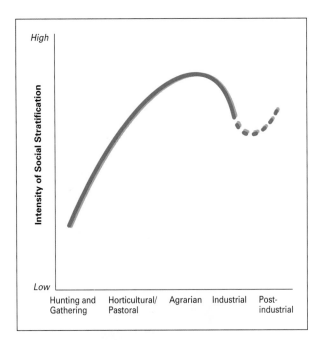

FIGURE 9–2 Social Stratification and Technological Development: The Kuznets Curve

The Kuznets curve reveals that greater technological sophistication is generally accompanied by more pronounced social stratification. The trend reverses itself, however, as industrial societies gradually become more egalitarian. Rigid castelike distinctions are relaxed in favor of greater opportunity and equality under the law. Political rights are more widely extended, and there is even some leveling of economic differences. The Kuznets curve may also be usefully applied to the relative social standing of the two sexes. The emergence of postindustrial society may signal greater social inequality, as indicated by the broken line.

Source: Created by the author, based on Kuznets (1955).

stratification. This analysis draws on Gerhard Lenski and Jean Lenski's model of sociocultural evolution, detailed in Chapter 4 ("Society").

HUNTING AND GATHERING SOCIETIES

Simple technology limits the production of hunting and gathering societies to only what is necessary for day-to-day living. Although some individuals produce more than others, the group's survival depends on all

sharing what they have. Thus, no categories of people emerge as better off than others.

HORTICULTURAL, PASTORAL, AND AGRARIAN SOCIETIES

As technological advances generate surplus production, social inequality increases. In horticultural and pastoral societies, a small elite controls most of the surplus. Large-scale agriculture generates even greater abundance, but marked inequality—as great as any time in human history—means that various categories of people lead strikingly different lives. Agrarian nobility typically exercise godlike power over the masses.

INDUSTRIAL SOCIETIES

Industrialization turns the tide, nudging inequality downward. Prompted by the need to develop individual talents, democratic thinking takes hold in these societies, eroding the power of traditional elites. The increasing productivity of industrial technology steadily raises the living standards of the historically poor majority. Specialized work also demands expanded schooling, which sharply reduces illiteracy. A literate population, in turn, tends to press for a greater voice in political decision making, further diminishing social inequality (and reducing the domination of women by men).

The net effect is that, over time, even wealth becomes somewhat less concentrated (countering the trend predicted by Marx). The proportion of all wealth controlled by the richest 1 percent of U.S. families peaked at about 36 percent just before the stock market crash in 1929, falling to about 30 percent by 1990 (Williamson & Lindert, 1980; Beeghley, 1989; *1991 Green Book*). Such trends help explain why Marxist revolutions occurred in agrarian societies—such as the former Soviet Union (1917), Cuba (1959), and Nicaragua (1979)—where social inequality is most pronounced, rather than in industrial societies, as Marx predicted.

THE KUZNETS CURVE

We can summarize the general pattern described above in this way: *In human history, technological progress first increases but then moderates the intensity of social stratification.* This pattern would suggest that, if greater inequality is functional for agrarian societies, then industrial societies benefit from a more egalitarian climate. This historical trend, recognized by Nobel Prize–winning economist Simon Kuznets (1955, 1966), is illustrated by the Kuznets curve, shown in Figure 9–2.

Q: "Nobody chooses his parents, but anyone, in principle, can accumulate capital." Peter Berger

Q: "Chiefly, the mold of a man's future is in his own hands." Francis Bacon

Q: "The chief vice of every egalitarian society is envy . . . Such constant comparing is really the quintessence of vulgarity." Hannah Arendt

GLOBAL: Figure 11–1 on page 290 shows the distribution of the world's income by fifths of humanity:

Richest 20%: 80% of income
Second 20%: 10% of income
Middle 20%: 6% of income
Fourth 20%: 3% of income
Poorest 20%: 1% of income

WINDOW ON THE WORLD

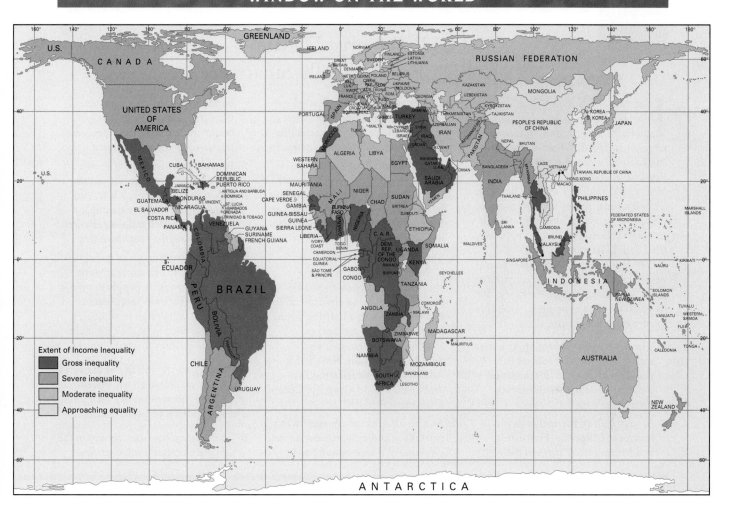

GLOBAL MAP 9–1 Income Disparity in Global Perspective

Societies throughout the world differ in the rigidity and intensity of social stratification as well as in overall standard of living. This map highlights income inequality. Generally speaking, countries that have had centralized, socialist economies (including the People's Republic of China, the former Soviet Union, and Cuba) display the least income inequality, although their standard of living is relatively low. Industrial societies with predominantly capitalist economies, including the United States and most of Western Europe, have higher overall living standards, accompanied by severe income disparity. The low-income countries of Latin America and Africa (including Mexico, Brazil, and the Democratic Republic of Congo) exhibit the most pronounced inequality of income.

Source: *Peters Atlas of the World* (1990).

Patterns of social inequality around the world today generally square with the Kuznets curve. As shown in Global Map 9–1, industrial societies have somewhat less income inequality—one important measure of social stratification—than nations that are predominantly agrarian. Specifically, mature industrial societies such as the United States and the nations of Western Europe exhibit less income inequality than the less-industrialized societies of Latin America, Africa, and Asia.

Q: "Our thesis is that . . . the twenty-first [century] will open on a world in which cognitive ability is the decisive dividing force." Richard Herrnstein and Charles Murray

Q: "The more complex a society becomes, the more valuable are the people who are especially good at dealing with complexity." Richard Herrnstein and Charles Murray

Q: "The very same people who scream freedom of expression for Snoop Doggy Dogg or Robert Mapplethorpe . . . would be only too happy to silence—or academically lynch—Charles Murray or his late partner, Richard Herrnstein . . ." Leon R. Kass

NOTE: Two comprehensive critiques of the "bell curve thesis" are the *New Yorker* article "Curveball" by Stephen Jay Gould (November 28, 1994:139–49) and Melvin Cohn's (1996) essay.

CONTROVERSY & DEBATE

The Bell Curve Debate: Are Rich People Really Smarter?

It is rare when the publication of a new book in the social sciences captures the attention of the public at large. But *The Bell Curve: Intelligence and Class Structure in American Life* by Richard J. Herrnstein and Charles Murray did that and more. The book ignited a firestorm of controversy over why pronounced social stratification divides our society and, just as important, what should be done about it.

The Bell Curve is a long (800 pages) book that addresses many important issues and resists simple summary. But its basic thesis is contained in the following eight propositions:

1. There exists something we can describe as "general intelligence"; people with more of it tend to be more successful in their careers than those with less.

2. At least half of the variation in human intelligence (Herrnstein and Murray use figures of 60

and 70 percent) is transmitted genetically from one generation to another; the remaining variability is due to environmental factors.

3. Over the course of this century—and especially since the "Information Revolution"—intelligence has become more necessary to the performance of our society's top occupational positions.

4. Simultaneously, the best U.S. colleges and universities have shifted their admissions policies away from favoring children of inherited wealth to admitting young people who perform best on standardized tests (such as the Scholastic Aptitude Test [SAT], American College Testing Program [ACT], and Graduate Record Examination [GRE]).

5. As a result of these changes in the workplace and in higher education, our society is now coming to be

dominated by a "cognitive elite," who are, on average, not only better trained than most people but actually more intelligent.

6. Because more intelligent people are socially segregated on the campus and in the workplace, it is no surprise that they tend to pair up, marry, and have intelligent children, perpetuating the "cognitive elite."

7. Near the bottom of the social ladder, a similar process is at work: Increasingly, poor people are individuals with lower intelligence, who live segregated from others, and who tend to pass along their modest abilities to their children.

Resting on the validity of the seven assertions presented above, Herrnstein and Murray then offer, as a final point, a basic approach to public policy:

8. To the extent that membership in the affluent elite or the impoverished

---

Yet income disparity reflects a host of factors beyond technology, especially political and economic factors. Societies that have had socialist economic systems (including the People's Republic of China, the former Soviet Union, and the nations of Eastern Europe) display relatively less income inequality. Keep in mind, however, that an egalitarian society like the People's Republic of China has an average income level that is quite low by world standards. Further, on noneconomic dimensions such as political power, China's society displays pronounced inequality.

And what of the future? Notice that we have extended the trend described by Kuznets (the broken line) to show an upturn in social inequality corresponding to the postindustrial era. That is, as the Information Revolution has begun transforming the United States,

we are experiencing some economic polarization (discussed in the next chapter). In sum, the long-term pattern may differ from what Kuznets observed almost half a century ago (Nielsen & Alderson, 1997).

SOCIAL STRATIFICATION: FACTS AND VALUES

The year was 2081 and everybody was finally equal. They weren't only equal before God and the law. They were equal every which way. Nobody was smarter than anybody else. Nobody was better looking than anybody else. Nobody was stronger or quicker than anybody else. All this equality was due to the 211th, 212th, and 213th Amendments

GLOBAL: In 1994, and intriguing in light of the "bell curve" debate, the People's Republic of China adopted a policy to ban marriages between people deemed likely to produce physically or mentally defective children that would undermine the "quality of the population."

Q: "All wealth and power are like clouds passing by." Chinese poet Li Bi (Bye)

Q: "Suppose a man, having plowed and cultivated his farm, should take in his hand a bag of mixed seeds . . . and walk straight across his land, sowing as he went. All pieces on his path would be sown alike: the rocks, the sandy ground, the good upland soil . . . but there would be great variety in the result when harvest time came around. . . . Something like this, I think, is the case with a stock of men passing through history." Charles Horton Cooley (1897)

underclass is rooted in intelligence and determined mostly by genetic inheritance, programs to help under-privileged people (from Head Start to Affirmative Action) will have few practical benefits.

Within weeks of its publication, analysts pro and con were squaring off on television shows and trading charges across the pages of practically every news magazine in the country. Critics of *The Bell Curve*—including most social scientists—question exactly what the concept "intelligence" means. They also argue that innate abilities can hardly be separated from the effects of socialization. Intelligence tests, they claim, don't measure cognitive *ability*, they measure certain kinds of cognitive *performance*. And we might well expect rich children to perform better on such tests because they have had the best schooling. At the very least, we should not think of "intelligence" as the cause of achievement because research shows that mental abilities and life experiences are *interactive*, each affecting the other.

Moreover, while most researchers who study intelligence agree that genetics does play a part in transmitting intelligence, the consensus is that no more than 25 to 40 percent is inherited—only about half what Herrnstein and Murray claim. Therefore, critics conclude, *The Bell Curve* misleads readers into thinking that social stratification is both natural and inevitable. In its assumptions and conclusions, *The Bell Curve* amounts to little more than a rehash of the social Darwinism popular a century ago, which heralded the success of industrial tycoons as "the survival of the fittest."

Perhaps, as one commentator suggested, the more society seems like a jungle, the more people think of stratification as a matter of blood rather than upbringing. But, despite its flaws and exaggerations, *The Bell Curve* raises many issues we cannot easily ignore. Can our democratic system tolerate the "dangerous knowledge" that elites (including not only rich people but our political leaders) are at least *somewhat* more intelligent than the rest of us? What of *The Bell Curve*'s description—which few challenge—that our society's elites are

increasingly insulating themselves from problems, including crime, homelessness, and poor schools? How do we face up to the fact that such problems have become worse in recent years while resisting the easy explanation that poor people themselves are hobbled by limited ability? And, perhaps above all, what should be done to ensure that all people have the opportunity to develop their abilities as fully as possible?

Continue the debate . . .

1. *Do you think there is such a thing as "general intelligence"? Why or why not?*

2. *In general, do you think that people of high social position are more intelligent than those of low social position? If you think intelligence differs by social standing, which factor is cause and which is effect?*

3. *Do you think sociologists should study controversial issues such as differences in human intelligence? Why or why not?*

Sources: Herrnstein & Murray (1994), Jacoby & Glauberman (1995), and Kohn (1996).

to the Constitution and the unceasing vigilance of agents of the Handicapper General.

With these words, novelist Kurt Vonnegut, Jr. (1961) begins the story of "Harrison Bergeron," a futuristic account of a United States in which social inequality has been totally abolished. Vonnegut warns that, although appealing in principle, this can be a dangerous concept in practice. His story describes a nightmare of social engineering in which every individual talent that makes one person different from another is systematically neutralized by the government.

To eradicate differences that make one person "better" than another, Vonnegut's state requires that physically attractive people wear masks that make them average looking, that intelligent people wear earphones

that generate distracting noise, and that the best athletes and dancers be fitted with weights to make them like everyone else. In short, although we may imagine that social equality would liberate people to make the most of their talents, Vonnegut warns that an egalitarian society could exist only by reducing everyone to a lowest common denominator.

Like Vonnegut's story, all of this chapter's explanations of social stratification involve value judgments. The Davis-Moore thesis states not only that social stratification is universal, but claims inequality is a helpful element of social organization. Class differences in U.S. society, then, reflect both variation in human abilities and the relative importance of different occupational roles. From this point of view, equality would be a threat to a society of diverse people, since uniformity could be achieved only through the relentless efforts of officials like Vonnegut's fictitious "Handicapper General."

Social-conflict analysis, advocated by Karl Marx, is based on egalitarian values. Rejecting the idea that inequality is at all necessary, Marx condemned social hierarchy as a product of greed, and advocated everyone sharing resources equally. He believed that equality would enhance, not diminish, human well-being.

Our concluding Controversy and Debate discussion addresses the link between intelligence and social class. This issue—also a mix of fact and value—is among the most troublesome in social science, partly because of the difficulty in defining and measuring "intelligence," but also because the idea that elites are inherently "better" than others challenges our democratic culture.

The next chapter ("Social Class in the United States") examines inequality in our own nation and reveals that, here again, even people who agree on the basic facts often interpret them quite differently. This lesson is repeated in Chapter 11 ("Global Stratification"), which examines inequality among the world's nations and explains why it exists. At all levels, then, the study of social stratification involves a complex, ongoing debate that yields no single or simple truth.

SUMMARY

1. Social stratification refers to categories of people ranked in a hierarchy. Stratification is (1) a characteristic of society, not something that merely arises from individual differences; (2) persistent over many generations; (3) universal, yet variable in form; and (4) supported by cultural beliefs.

2. Caste systems, typical of agrarian societies, are based on ascription and permit little or no social mobility. Caste hierarchy, which is supported by strong moral beliefs, shapes a person's entire life, including occupation and marriage.

3. Class systems, common to industrial societies, reflect a greater measure of individual achievement. Because the emphasis on achievement allows for social mobility, classes are less clearly defined than castes.

4. Socialist societies, with public ownership of productive property, have claimed to be classless. While such societies may exhibit far less economic inequality than their capitalist counterparts, they are notably stratified with regard to power.

5. Social stratification persists because it is supported by various social institutions and because the power of ideology defines certain kinds of inequality as both natural and just.

6. The Davis-Moore thesis states that social stratification is universal because it contributes to the operation of society. In class systems, unequal rewards motivate people to aspire to occupational roles most important to the operation of society.

7. Critics of the Davis-Moore thesis note that (1) it is difficult to assess objectively the functional importance of any occupational position; (2) stratification prevents many people from developing their abilities; and (3) social stratification often generates social conflict, benefiting some at the expense of others.

8. Karl Marx, a key architect of social-conflict analysis, recognized two major social classes in industrial societies. The capitalists, or bourgeoisie, own the means of production and pursue profits; the proletariat, by contrast, offer their labor in exchange for wages.

9. The socialist revolution that Marx predicted has not occurred in industrial societies such as the United States. Some sociologists see this fact as evidence that Marx's analysis was flawed; others, however, point out that our society is still marked by pronounced social inequality and substantial class conflict.

10. Max Weber identified three distinct dimensions of social inequality: economic class, social status or prestige, and power. Taken together, these three dimensions form a complex hierarchy of socioeconomic standing.

11. Gerhard Lenski and Jean Lenski explained that, historically, technological advances have been associated with more pronounced social stratification. A limited reversal of this trend occurs in advanced, industrial societies, as represented by the Kuznets curve. Recently, however, the emergence of a postindustrial economy in the United States has increased economic inequality.

12. Social stratification is a complex and controversial area of research because it deals not only with facts but with various values that suggest how society should be organized.

KEY CONCEPTS

social stratification a system by which a society ranks categories of people in a hierarchy

social mobility change in people's position in a social hierarchy

caste system a system of social stratification based on ascription

class system a system of social stratification based largely on individual achievement

status consistency the degree of consistency of a person's social standing across various dimensions of social inequality

structural social mobility a shift in the social position of large numbers of people due more to changes in society itself than to individual efforts

ideology cultural beliefs that serve to justify social stratification

Davis-Moore thesis the assertion that social stratification is a universal pattern that has beneficial consequences for the operation of a society

meritocracy a system of social stratification based on personal merit

blue-collar occupations lower-prestige work involving mostly manual labor

white-collar occupations higher-prestige work involving mostly mental activity

socioeconomic status (SES) a composite ranking based on various dimensions of social inequality

CRITICAL-THINKING QUESTIONS

1. How is social stratification evident on the college campus? What categories of people are there? In what respects are they unequal?

2. Why do agrarian societies have caste systems? Why does industrialization replace castes with classes?

3. According to the Davis-Moore thesis, why should a college president be paid more than a professor? Do you agree with this analysis?

4. In what respects have Karl Marx's predictions failed? In what respects are they correct?

LEARNING EXERCISES

1. If you have computer access, visit the Web site http://www.paywatch.org on the Internet to discover how much chief executive officers of various large corporations are paid. To see how their companies performed during the period, check the corporate stock price for that period (available from YAHOO!; click on the financial news link). What conclusions do you reach?

2. Read Kurt Vonnegut's short story "Harrison Bergeron" (in his collection of stories titled *Welcome to the Monkey House*). What are Vonnegut's views of social stratification and the prospect of an egalitarian society? Do you agree with him or not? Why?

3. Sit down with parents, grandparents, or other relatives and try to assess the social class position of your own family over the last three generations. Have changes taken place? If so, what caused this mobility?

4. Identify the "seven deadly sins," human failings according to the medieval church. These may be deadly to the agrarian caste system, but what about the modern, capitalist class system?

5. Install the CD-ROM packaged inside the back cover of your text and complete the activities designed to accompany this chapter.

William Gropper, *Sweat Shop*
© Christie's Images.

CHAPTER 10

SOCIAL CLASS
IN THE UNITED STATES

Elizabeth Jones reaches for the railing and steps aboard the Route 97 bus that winds through the far northeast corner of Washington, D.C. She turns quickly to extend a helping hand to each of her three children. As the bus jerks back into traffic, they collapse into the nearest seats and catch their breath. Twenty minutes later, after seeing her children safely enter Nalle Elementary School, Jones is again moving through the city on two more bus lines. She then briskly walks a final ten blocks to report—on time—to her job as a receptionist at the D.C. Private Industry Council.

After hanging up her coat, Jones straightens her neat, secondhand suit, sits down, and slides her chair under a large, wooden desk. She pauses and closes her eyes, just long enough to remind herself of what she calls "the receptionist's first rule": "Smile," she thinks (with no smile on her face) "got to remember to smile. . . ."

Elizabeth Jones, twenty-seven, is determined to climb the slippery ladder to the middle class.

When she had her first child at seventeen, she left school and went on welfare. But, a year ago, Congress enacted a new welfare law, which says, in effect, you have to find a job or lose your benefits. Ready for change, Jones saw an ad for a sixteen-week computer training course and immediately signed up. She completed the program successfully, which left her feeling new strength and independence and, best of all, led to her current job. She looks you straight in the eye and says, "No more; my kids are going to break the chain. Or I'll die trying. . . ."

Jones is determined, but she knows it won't be easy. Every month, she brings home $1,374 after taxes. But soon after she landed her job, the rent for her public housing apartment jumped from $103 per month to $497. She also gave up $325 per month in food stamps, and now must pay $380 a month for child care. Her new position provides health insurance for her, but not for her children. Last night she mailed half a dozen résumés in the hope of finding another job on the weekends. "It's the only way," she explains, "that I will ever make ends meet" (Boo, 1996).

Elizabeth Jones's story offers stark evidence of the power of social stratification to shape people's lives throughout the United States. Whether individuals easily achieve great success, struggle just to get by, or collapse with broken spirits is not a simple matter of talent and personal ambition. For all of us, social standing reflects the distribution of wealth, power, and opportunity in our society.

SUPPLEMENTS: An outline of Chapter 10, along with supplementary lecture material and discussion topics, is found in the *Data File*.

THEN AND NOW: 1970 income data for comparison with Figure 10–1 for each quintile: 40.9%, 23.8%, 17.6%, 12.2%, 5.5%.

DIVERSITY: Government estimates of before-tax mean income, 1996, for households and families:

Highest 5 percent: $201,220; $217,355
Highest fifth: $115,514; $125,627
Second fifth: $54,922; $62,052
Middle fifth: $35,486; $42,467
Fourth fifth: $21,097; $26,847
Lowest fifth: $8,596; $11,388

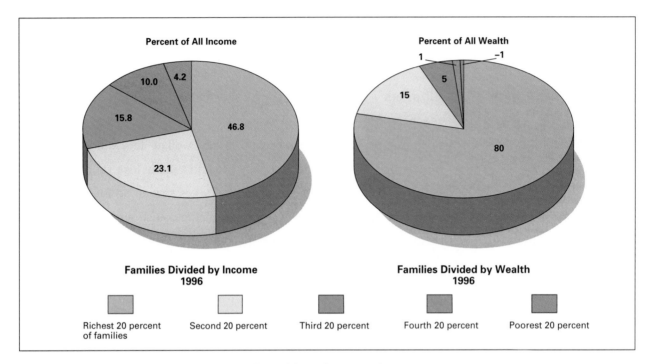

FIGURE 10–1 Distribution of Income and Wealth in the United States

Sources: Income data from U. S. Bureau of the Census (1997); wealth data are author estimates based on the Joint Economic Committee (1986) and Kennickell & Shack-Marquez (1992).

DIMENSIONS OF SOCIAL INEQUALITY

Many people think of the United States as a more-or-less equal society. After all, we do stand apart from most countries of the world in never having had a titled aristocracy. With the significant exception of our racial history, this nation has never known a caste system that rigidly ranks categories of people.

Even so, U.S. society is highly stratified. Not only do the rich control most of the money, they also receive the most schooling, enjoy the best health, and consume the greatest share of goods and services. Such privileges contrast sharply with the plight of millions of women and men who, like Elizabeth Jones, worry about paying next month's rent and fear that they cannot afford the medical costs if a child becomes ill.

So why do we think of the United States as a "middle-class" society? We underestimate the extent of stratification in our society for four reasons:

1. **In principle, the law gives equal standing to all.** Because our legal system accords equal

rights to everyone, we tend to think that all people have basically the same social standing.

2. **Our culture celebrates individual autonomy and achievement.** Our belief that people forge their own destinies through talent and hard work leads us to downplay the significance of birth as a factor influencing social position.

3. **We tend to interact with people like ourselves.** Throughout the United States, primary groups—including family, neighbors, and friends—typically are composed of people with similar social standing (Kelley & Evans, 1995). While we may speak of "how the other half lives," most of us have only brief and impersonal encounters with people very different from ourselves.

4. **The United States is an affluent society.** As noted back in Chapter 1 ("The Sociological Perspective"), the overall standard of living in the United States is among the highest in the world. Such affluence lulls us into believing that everyone in our country is relatively well off.

THEN AND NOW: Median income earned by top 20% and bottom 20% of U.S. households using constant 1996 dollars: *1968,* $78,084 and $7,624; *1996,* $115,514 (48% increase) and $8,596 (3% increase).

NOTE: In 1994, the IRS reported that 1,109,000 households reported incomes over $200,000; 66,000 reported incomes of more than $1 million. The Census Bureau indicates that the average

physician netted $218,000; the typical partner in a law firm earned $168,000.

NOTE: Below, we say "privately held wealth," since public property (lands, forests, roads, transportation systems, and the military) are excluded from such considerations. According to the World Bank, if all public and private wealth in the U.S. were divided equally, each person would have about $425,000.

When people do acknowledge social inequality, they often speak of a "ladder of social class" as if inequality were a matter of a single factor such as money. More accurately, however, social class in the United States has several, more subtle dimensions. Socioeconomic status (SES), as discussed in Chapter 9 ("Social Stratification"), is a composite measure of social position that includes not just money (income and wealth and the power they provide), but occupational prestige and schooling.

INCOME

One important dimension of inequality is **income,** *wages or salaries from work and earnings from investments.* The Bureau of the Census reports that the median U.S. family income in 1996 was $42,300. The first part of Figure 10–1 illustrates the distribution of income among all families[1] in the country. The richest 20 percent of families (earning at least $75,316 annually, with a mean of $125,627) received 46.8 percent of all income, while the bottom 20 percent (earning less than $19,680, with a mean of $11,388) received only about 4.2 percent.

Table 10–1 provides a closer look at income distribution. In 1996, the highest-paid 5 percent of U.S. families earned six-figure incomes (averaging $217,355), or 20.3 percent of all income, which surpassed the earnings of the lowest-paid 40 percent. In short, while a small number of people have very high incomes, the majority make do with far less. As discussed later in this chapter, income disparity in the United States has been increasing as a result of changes in the economy, new tax policies, more two-earner couples, and cuts in social programs that assist low-income people (Levy, 1987; Reich, 1989; Cutler & Katz, 1992; Holmes, 1996).

Chapter 9 ("Social Stratification") explained that social inequality declines as industrialization proceeds (according to the Kuznets curve shown in Figure 9–2 on page 252). Thus, the United States has less income inequality than Venezuela (South America), Kenya

TABLE 10–1 U.S. Family Income, 1996

Highest paid . . .	Annually earns at least . . .
0.5%	$1,200,000
1	250,000
5	130,000
10	90,000
20	75,000
30	60,000
40	50,000
50	42,000
60	35,000
70	26,000
80	20,000
90	10,000

Sources: U.S. Bureau of the Census (1997) and author calculations.

(Africa), or Sri Lanka (Asia). However, as Figure 10–2 on page 262 indicates, U.S. society has more income inequality than is found in many other industrial societies.

WEALTH

Income is only one component of a person's or family's **wealth,** *the total value of money and other assets, minus outstanding debts.* Wealth—including stocks, bonds, real estate, and other privately owned property—is distributed much less equally than income.

The second part of Figure 10–1 shows the approximate distribution of privately owned wealth in the United States. The richest 20 percent of U.S. families own approximately 80 percent of the country's entire wealth. High up in this privileged category are the wealthiest 5 percent of families—the "very-rich"—who control more than half of all private property. Richer still, with wealth into the tens of millions of dollars—are the 1 percent of U.S. households who qualify as the "super-rich" and possess one-third of our nation's privately held resources. And capping the wealth pyramid, the one dozen richest U.S. families have a combined net worth approaching $150 billion, which equals the total wealth of 1 million average families, including enough people to fill the cities of Alexandria, Virginia; Akron, Ohio; Anchorage, Alaska; and Albuquerque, New Mexico (Millman et al., 1993; Rogers, 1993; Weicher, 1995).

Recent government calculations place the wealth of the average U.S. household at about $40,000. This figure reflects the value of homes, cars, investments,

---

[1]The Census Bureau reports both mean and median income for families ("two or more persons related by blood, marriage or adoption") and households ("two or more persons sharing a living unit"). In 1996, mean family income was $53,676, higher than the median since high-income families pull the mean (but not the median) upward. Reported for households, the figures are somewhat lower— a mean of $47,123 and a median of $35,492—largely because families average 3.2 persons while households average 2.6.

GLOBAL: Additional data for share of income (%) received by top and bottom 20 percent, by country: Lesotho, 60.1, 2.8; Dominican Republic, 55.7, 4.2; Costa Rica, 50.7, 4.0; India, 42.6, 8.5; Australia, 42.2, 4.4; Sweden, 36.9, 8.0; Canada, 40.2, 5.7; U.K., 44.3, 4.6; Spain, 36.6, 8.3; Japan, 37.5, 8.7 (The World Bank, 1997).

GLOBAL: Top ten nations in per capita gross domestic product (using purchasing power parities) for 1994: Luxembourg, $34,155; Brunei Darussalam, $30,447; U.S., $26,397; Switzerland, $24,967; Hong Kong, $22,310; Kuwait, $21,875; Japan, $21,581; Canada, $21,459; Norway, $21,346; Denmark, $21,341 (United Nations Development Programme, 1997).

DISCUSS: Consider the extent to which jobs shown in Table 10–2 are gender-linked. What is the pattern?

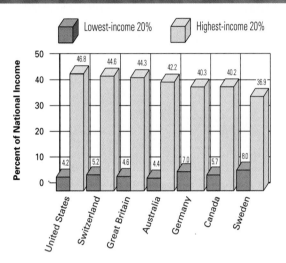

GLOBAL SNAPSHOT

FIGURE 10–2 Income Disparities for Selected Industrial Countries

Source: The World Bank (1997).

insurance policies, retirement pensions, furniture, clothing, and all other personal property, minus a home mortgage and other debts. The wealth of average people is not only less than that of the rich, however, it is also different in kind. While "ordinary" wealth usually centers on a home and a car or two—that is, property that generates no income—the wealth of the rich is mostly in the form of stocks and other investments that typically increase in value and generate income.

When financial assets are balanced against debits, the lowest-ranking 40 percent of U.S. families have virtually no wealth at all. The negative percentage shown in Figure 10–1 for the poorest 20 percent of the population means that these people actually live in debt.

POWER

In the United States, as elsewhere, wealth stands as an important source of power. Major stockholders, for example, make company decisions that create jobs for ordinary people or throw men and women out of work.

Even more important, the "super-rich" families who own most of the nation's wealth have a great deal of influence on the national political agenda. Thomas Jefferson (1953; orig. 1785), the third U.S. president and a wealthy man himself, cautioned that the vitality of a democratic system depends on "subdividing property" so that the many, not just the few, have a voice in political affairs.

Chapter 16 ("Politics and Government") delves into the debate surrounding wealth and power. Some analysts concede that the rich have certain advantages but maintain that they hardly dominate the political process. Others, however, believe that the political agenda largely represents the interests of the wealthy.

OCCUPATIONAL PRESTIGE

Occupation, too, is an important dimension of social standing, since one's job affects all the factors discussed thus far: income, wealth, and power. In addition, occupation is an important source of social prestige since we commonly evaluate each other according to the kind of work we do, respecting some while looking down on others.

For more than half a century, sociologists have assessed the social prestige of various occupations (Counts, 1925; Hodge, Treiman, & Rossi, 1966; NORC, 1996). Table 10–2 presents the results of a recent survey involving a random sample of U.S. adults. In general, people attach high prestige to occupations—such as physicians, lawyers, and engineers—that generate high income.

Prestige reflects more than just pay, however, since high-ranking occupations typically require considerable ability and demand extensive education and training. By contrast, less prestigious work—as a waitress or janitor, for example—not only pays less but usually requires less ability and schooling.

In global perspective, occupational prestige rankings are much the same in all industrial societies (Ma, 1987; Lin & Xie, 1988). Almost everywhere, white-collar work that involves mental activity with little supervision confers greater prestige than blue-collar occupations that require supervised, manual labor. There are exceptions to this pattern, however. In the United States, for example, a blue-collar aircraft mechanic enjoys greater social prestige than a white-collar filing clerk.

In any society, high-prestige occupations go to privileged categories of people. In Table 10–2, for example, the highest-ranking occupations are male-dominated. Only after passing a dozen jobs do we find "registered nurse," an occupation in which *most*

CYBER: As we move into a postindustrial society, will prestige be less a matter of owning things and more a matter of developing personal creative potential?

SOCIAL SURVEY: A 1992 Roper poll asked people how much income they would need "to fulfill all your dreams." The median response was $82,100, a good reason to treat this level as beginning to designate the "rich."

DIVERSITY: Median 1996 household income by age of householder: 15–25, $21,438; 25–34, $35,888; 35–44, $44,420; 45–54, $50,472; 55–64, $39,815; 65+, $19,449 (U.S. Bureau of the Census).

DIVERSITY: Median 1990 household wealth by age: under 35, $6,000; 35–44, $33,200; 45–54, $57,500; 55–64, $80,000; 65–69, $83,500; 70–74, $82,100; 75 and older, $61,500 (Longina & Crown, 1991).

TABLE 10–2 The Relative Social Prestige of Selected Occupations in the United States

White-collar Occupations	Prestige Score	Blue-collar Occupations	White-collar Occupations	Prestige Score	Blue-collar Occupations
Physician	86		Funeral director	49	
Lawyer	75		Realtor	49	
College/university professor	74		Bookkeeper	47	
Architect	73			47	Machinist
Chemist	73			47	Mail carrier
Physicist/astronomer	73		Musician/composer	47	
Aerospace engineer	72			46	Secretary
Dentist	72		Photographer	45	
Member of the clergy	69		Bank teller	43	
Psychologist	69			42	Tailor
Pharmacist	68			42	Welder
Optometrist	67			40	Farmer
Registered nurse	66			40	Telephone operator
Secondary-school teacher	66			39	Carpenter
Accountant	65			36	Brick/stone mason
Athlete	65			36	Child-care worker
Electrical engineer	64		File clerk	36	
Elementary-school teacher	64			36	Hairdresser
Economist	63			35	Baker
Veterinarian	62			34	Bulldozer operator
Airplane pilot	61			31	Auto body repairperson
Computer programmer	61		Retail apparel salesperson	30	
Sociologist	61			30	Truck driver
Editor/reporter	60		Cashier	29	
	60	Police officer		28	Elevator operator
Actor	58			28	Garbage collector
Radio/TV announcer	55			28	Taxi driver
Librarian	54			28	Waiter/waitress
	53	Aircraft mechanic		27	Bellhop
	53	Firefighter		25	Bartender
Dental hygienist	52			23	Farm laborer
Painter/sculptor	52			23	Household laborer
Social worker	52			22	Door-to-door salesperson
	51	Electrician		22	Janitor
Computer operator	50			09	Shoe shiner

Source: Adapted from *General Social Surveys 1972–1996: Cumulative Codebook* (Chicago: National Opinion Research Center, 1996), pp. 1077–85.

workers are women. Most women, in fact, are concentrated in *pink-collar* occupations—service and clerical positions such as secretaries, waitresses, and beauticians—that provide little income and fall near the bottom of the prestige hierarchy. Similarly, reading the table in reverse order shows many of the least prestigious and lowest-income jobs are commonly performed by people of color. The important point here is that social stratification involves various dimensions of inequality (based on income and prestige as well as sex and race) *that are superimposed on each other*, forming a complex, and often steep, hierarchy.

SCHOOLING

In industrial societies, schooling is necessary for adults to perform their work; thus, primary, secondary, and some college education is available at public expense. Like other dimensions of inequality, however, more schooling is available to some than to others.

Table 10–3 shows the level of formal education reached by U.S. men and women. In 1996, more than three-fourths of adults had completed high school, and just over 20 percent were college graduates.

Here, again, we see how dimensions of inequality are linked. Schooling affects both occupation and

TABLE 10–3 Schooling of U.S. Adults, 1996 (aged 25 and over)

	Women	Men
Not a high school graduate	**18.4%**	**18.1%**
8 years or less	8.0	8.2
9–11 years	10.4	9.9
High school graduate	**81.6**	**81.9**
High school only	35.1	31.9
1–3 years college	25.1	24.0
College graduate or more	21.4	26.0

Source: U.S. Bureau of the Census (1997).

income, since most (but not all) of the better-paying, white-collar jobs shown in Table 10–2 require a college degree or other advanced study. On the other hand, most blue-collar occupations, which offer lower income and social prestige, require less schooling.

ASCRIPTION AND SOCIAL STRATIFICATION

To a considerable degree, the class system in the United States rewards individual talent and effort. But, our class system also retains elements of caste. Ascription—who we are at birth—greatly influences what we become later in life.

ANCESTRY

Nothing affects social standing in the United States as much as our birth into a particular family, something over which we have no control. Ancestry determines our point of entry into the system of social inequality. Some families in the United States, including the duPonts, Rockefellers, Roosevelts, and Kennedys, are renowned around the world. And almost every city and town has families who have amassed wealth and power on a more modest scale.

Being born to privilege or poverty sets the stage for our future schooling, occupation, and income. Research suggests that at least half of the richest individuals—those with hundreds of millions of dollars in wealth—derived their fortunes primarily from inheritance (Thurow, 1987; Queenan, 1989). By the same token, the "inheritance" of poverty and the lack of opportunity that goes with it just as surely shape the future for those in need. The family, in short, transmits

property, power, and possibilities from one generation to the next, contributing to the persistence of social stratification.

GENDER

People of both sexes are born into families at every social level. Yet, on average, women earn lower income, accumulate less wealth, enjoy lower occupational prestige, and place lower in some areas of educational achievement than men do.

Perhaps the most dramatic difference, however, is that households headed by women are ten times more likely to be poor than those headed by men. A full picture of the connection between gender and social stratification is found in Chapter 12 ("Sex and Gender").

RACE AND ETHNICITY

Race is strongly connected to social position in the United States. Overall, white people have higher occupational standing than African Americans, and they receive more schooling, especially at the college level and beyond. These differences are evident in median income: African American families earned $26,522 in 1996, which is just 59 percent of the $44,756 earned by white families. Higher income is a key reason that white families are more likely to own their homes (77 percent) than black families (49 percent) (U.S. Bureau of the Census, 1997).

Another reason for this racial disparity involves family patterns: African American families with children are three times more likely than their white counterparts to have only one parent in the home. Single-parenthood, in turn, is a strong predictor of low family income. If we compare only families headed by married couples, about half the racial disparity disappears, with African Americans earning 84 percent of what whites earn.

Over time, income differential builds into a considerable "wealth gap." Figure 10–3 shows that the typical white household has a net worth of at least $46,000; the comparable figure for Hispanics and African Americans is barely one-tenth as much. Moreover, race is significant even among affluent families, as the box on page 266 explains.

Ethnicity, as well as race, shapes social stratification in the United States. Throughout our nation's history, people of English ancestry controlled the most wealth and wielded the greatest power. The rapidly growing Latino population in the United States, by

NOTE: The "Forbes Four Hundred"—a listing of the richest 400 people in the United States—contains interesting facts and patterns about U.S. wealth. This special issue of *Forbes* appears in late October each year. To make the 1993 list, wealth of at least $300 million was needed, with average (mean) wealth more than twice that figure. In 1980, the list began with individuals worth $230 million. Fewer than half of the people listed in 1996 were there a decade before. Such listings are skewed toward the new-rich corporate elite, whose wealth is mostly in the form of stocks (rather than, say, art) and whose compensation is a matter of public record.

THEN AND NOW: Back in 1993, the comparable *Forbes* figure for the richest 400 individuals was "only" $324 billion.

contrast, has long been relatively disadvantaged. In 1996, median income among Hispanic families was $26,179, which is 58 percent of the comparable figure for all white families. A detailed examination of how race and ethnicity affect social standing is presented in Chapter 13 ("Race and Ethnicity").

RELIGION

Finally, religion has a bearing on social standing in the United States. Among Protestant denominations, with which almost two-thirds of individuals identify, Episcopalians and Presbyterians have significantly higher social standing, on average, than Lutherans and Baptists. Jews, too, have high social standing, while Roman Catholics hold a more modest position (Roof, 1979; Davidson, Pyle, & Reyes, 1995).

Even John Fitzgerald Kennedy—a member of one of this country's wealthiest and most powerful families—had to overcome religious opposition to become our first Catholic president in 1960. Understandably, then, throughout our history, upward mobility has sometimes meant converting to a higher-ranking religion (Baltzell, 1979).

SOCIAL CLASSES IN THE UNITED STATES

As Chapter 9 ("Social Stratification") explained, people living in rigid caste systems can discern anyone's social rank at a glance. Assessing social position in a more fluid class system, however, is not so easy.

Consider the joke about a couple who order a pizza, asking that it be cut into six slices because they aren't hungry enough to eat eight. While all sociologists acknowledge extensive social inequality in the United States, they debate precisely how to divide up this social hierarchy. Some follow Karl Marx and recognize two major classes; others propose as many as six categories (Warner & Lunt, 1941) or even seven (Coleman & Rainwater, 1978). Still others align themselves with Max Weber, believing that people form a multidimensional status hierarchy, rather than clear-cut classes.

Defining classes in U.S. society is difficult due to the relatively low level of status consistency. Especially toward the middle of the hierarchy, standing on one dimension often contradicts standing on another. A government official, for example, may have the power to administer a multimillion-dollar budget yet he may earn a modest personal income. Similarly, members of

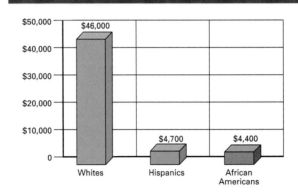

FIGURE 10–3 Average Wealth, by Race and Ethnicity, of the U.S. Population, 1996

Source: U.S. Bureau of the Census (1997).

the clergy enjoy ample prestige but only moderate power and low pay. Or consider a lucky professional gambler, who may win little respect but accumulates considerable wealth.

Finally, the social mobility of class systems—again, most pronounced near the middle—means that social position may change during a person's lifetime. In other words, mobility further blurs the lines between social classes.

With these reservations in mind, we now proceed to identify four general social classes in the United States: the upper class, the middle class, the working class, and the lower class. To these, we add a few further distinctions.

THE UPPER CLASS

Families in the upper class—5 percent of the U.S. population—earn more than $100,000 annually and may earn ten times that much. As a general rule, the more a family's income is derived from inherited wealth in the form of stocks and bonds, real estate, and other investments, the stronger a family's claim to being upper-class.

In 1997, *Forbes* magazine profiled the richest 400 people in the United States, estimating their combined wealth at $621 billion. These richest individuals had a *minimum* net worth of $475 million and included 170 billionaires. The upper class thus comprises Karl

GLOBAL: Edward N. Wolff calculates that Great Britain has become more equal in terms of wealth across this century, from the top 1 percent owning about two-thirds of all wealth in 1920 to about 18% in 1990. The comparable U.S. data are a high of 45% in 1929 dropping to about 20% in 1975 (as the stock market fell), then rising to about 38% in 1990. During the 1960s, the British and U.S. were the same in wealth inequality; since then the U.S. has been

more unequal, a curious fact since Reagan and Thatcher essentially followed the same economic policies. Perhaps rapidly rising U.K. housing costs inflated the middle-class wealth levels there.

NOTE: As income goes up, the share spent on necessities declines, and the share allocated to discretionary spending rises. Thus, while the typical U.S. household spends 12% of income for food, rich families with incomes above $200,000 spend just 2%.

SOCIAL DIVERSITY

The Color of Money:
Being Rich in Black and White

African American families earn 59 cents for every dollar a white family earns, a fact that underlies the greater risk of poverty among people of color. But there is another side to black America—an affluent side—that has expanded dramatically in recent decades.

The number of affluent families—those with annual incomes over $50,000—is increasing faster among African Americans than among whites. In 1996, almost 2 million African American families were financially privileged; adjusted for inflation, this represents a threefold increase since 1970. Today, 23 percent of African American families—more than 6 million adults and their children—are affluent. About 23 percent of Latino families rank as well-off, too, while 40 percent of non-Hispanic white families and 35 percent of Asian families rank as affluent.

The color of money is the same for everyone, but black and white affluence differs in several respects. First, well-off people of African descent are not *as rich* as their white counterparts. About half of affluent white families (22 percent of all white families) earn more than

$75,000 a year, compared to only 38 percent of affluent African American families (9 percent of all black families).

Second, African Americans are more likely than white people to achieve affluence through multiple incomes.

Rich people come in all colors. But are they all the same?

Families typically contain two employed spouses, perhaps with working children.

Third, affluent African Americans are more likely to derive their income from salaries rather than from investments. Three-fourths of affluent white families have investment income, compared to just half of affluent African American families.

Beyond differences in income, affluent people of color contend with social barriers that do not restrict whites. Even African Americans with the money to purchase a home, for example, may find they are unwelcome as neighbors. This is one reason that a smaller proportion of affluent African American families (40 percent) live in the suburbs (the richest areas of the country) than do affluent white families (61 percent).

Affluent Americans come in all colors. Yet race has a powerful effect on the lives of affluent people, just as it does on the lives of us all.

Sources: O'Hare (1989), Weicher (1995), and U.S. Bureau of the Census (1997).

Marx's "capitalists"—those who own much of the nation's private wealth.

Many members of the upper class work as top corporate executives or senior government officials. Typically, upper-class people attend the most expensive and highly regarded schools and colleges. Historically, though less so today, the upper class has been composed of white Anglo-Saxon Protestants (WASPs) (Baltzell, 1964, 1976, 1988).

Upper-Uppers

The *upper-upper class,* often described as "society" or "blue bloods," includes less than 1 percent of the U.S. population (Warner & Lunt, 1941; Coleman & Neugarten, 1971; Baltzell, 1995). Membership is almost always the result of ascription or birth, as suggested by the quip that the easiest way to become an upper-upper is to be born one. These families possess enormous

NOTE: A statistical profile of the average U.S. millionaire: a 57-year-old self-employed man, married with 3 children, who works about 50 hours a week, earns $130,000 annually, owns a home worth $320,000, is worth about $3.7 million, and is the first generation in his family to be rich. There are perhaps 3.5 million millionaires today (Sharpe, 1996).

NOTE: Often members of the "new rich" marry the "old rich" in order to gain the social prestige that cannot be achieved by the mere accumulation of money. For instance, bodybuilder and actor Arnold Schwarzenegger married Maria Shriver, member of the Kennedy clan. (*People* magazine described the match as "impeccable pedigree meets impeccable pectorals.")

NOTE: The average compensation for a Fortune 500 CEO in 1996 was about $7.5 million.

People often distinguish between the "new rich" and those with "old money." Men and women who suddenly begin to earn high incomes tend to spend their money on "status symbols" because they enjoy the new thrill of high-roller living and they want others to know of their success. Those who grow up surrounded by wealth, on the other hand, are used to a privileged way of life and are more quiet about it. Thus, the "conspicuous consumption" of the lower-upper class (left) can differ dramatically from the more private pursuits and understatement of the upper-upper class (right).

wealth, primarily inherited rather than earned. For this reason, we sometimes say that members of the upper-upper class have *old money*.

Set apart by their wealth, members of the upper-upper class live in a world of exclusive neighborhoods, such as Beacon Hill in Boston, Rittenhouse Square or the Main Line in Philadelphia, the Gold Coast of Chicago, and Nob Hill in San Francisco. Their children typically attend elite, private secondary schools with others of similar background and high-prestige colleges and universities. In the tradition of European aristocrats, they study liberal arts rather than vocationally directed subjects.

Women of the upper-upper class often maintain a full schedule of volunteer work for charitable organizations. While helping the larger community, such charitable activities also build networks that put these families at the center of this nation's power elite (Ostrander, 1980, 1984).

Lower-Uppers

Most upper class people actually fall into the *lower-upper class*. To most of us, these people seem every bit as privileged as the upper-upper class. The major difference, however, is that lower-uppers are the "working rich" who depend on earnings rather than inherited wealth as the primary source of their income.

To members of "society," the lower-upper class are the "new rich" who can never savor the prestige enjoyed by those with rich and famous grandparents. Thus, while the new rich typically live in the biggest homes, they rarely gain entry to the clubs and associations maintained by old-money families.

Historically, the American Dream has been to be successful enough to join the ranks of not the upper-upper class (difficult except, perhaps, through marriage) but the lower-upper class. The young author whose novel becomes a popular Hollywood movie; the athlete who signs a million-dollar contract to play in the big leagues; the computer whiz who designs a program that sets a standard for the industry—these are the lucky and talented achievers who reach the lower-upper class. The box sharpens the distinction between "society" and high achievers, people who seem like the rest of us—except that they make a lot of money.

THE MIDDLE CLASS

Encompassing 40 to 45 percent of the U.S. population, the large middle class exerts a tremendous influence on U.S. culture. Television and other mass media usually depict middle-class people, and most commercial advertising is directed toward these "average"

NOTE: Regional editions of the *Social Register* were published for Newport, Rhode Island (1887; discontinued), New York (beginning in 1888), Philadelphia and Boston (1890), Baltimore (1892), Chicago (1893), Washington, D.C. (1906), and Cleveland-Cincinnati-Dayton (1910). In 1976, these listings were merged into a single, national edition of the book (Baltzell, 1995).
NOTE: The 945-page winter edition of the 1996 *Social Register* contains 26,402 names, or about 1/10 of 1 percent of the U.S. population. There is also a summer edition for vacation homes and boats.
NOTE: The importance of a college education to middle-class standing is suggested by the practice, common in the United States, of placing college decals on the windows of automobiles.

CRITICAL THINKING

Caste and Class:
The *Social Register* and *Who's Who*

Small and exclusive, the upper-upper class comes closest to being a true social group. There is even a listing of these privileged families: the *Social Register*, first published in 1887 as fortunes grew along with the industrial economy. A century later, some 40,000 conjugal families are included in this inventory of our society's "blue bloods."

Because membership is typically based on birth, the upper-upper class operates much like a caste: You are either "in" or "out." Traditional upper-upper parents urge their children to seek out partners of their own kind, sustaining the class into another generation. Family is thus crucial to the upper-upper class, as it is to all caste groups. In fact, *Social Register* listings are of *families*, not *individuals*.

The listing for David Rockefeller, a member of one of the most socially prominent families in the United States, indicates (1) his family's address and home telephone number; (2) Mrs. Rockefeller's maiden name; (3) the names of the Rockefeller children, and the boarding schools and colleges they are attending; and (4) exclusive social clubs to which the family belongs. Since achievement is not the issue, entries in the *Social Register* omit any mention of occupation or place of business.

The lower-upper class, by contrast, is an achievement elite. This larger category of "new rich" individuals has no clear boundaries, and its members do not engage in formal rituals (like debutante parties) the way many old-money families do.

There is a listing—roughly speaking—of people at this class level: the

Two books: One lists "upper-uppers," the other, "lower-uppers."

national edition of *Who's Who in America*. Here, instead of "established" families, we find individuals distinguished for excellence: outstanding athletes, highly successful business people, college presidents, Nobel Prize winners, and famous entertainers.

Who's Who contains a few people, including David Rockefeller, who are also listed in the *Social Register*, but the information provided is quite different. David Rockefeller's entry in *Who's Who* includes a brief biography (date of birth, schooling, and honorary degrees), a list of accomplishments (military decorations, government service, books authored), and—most important—his position as board chair of Chase Manhattan Bank. The address provided in *Who's Who* is his place of business.

Comparing the two listings reveals that there are two kinds of elites in the United States. The castelike *Social Register* lists high-prestige families according to *who they are*. The more classlike *Who's Who* lists individuals on the basis of *what they have done*. But, as the dual listings for David Rockefeller suggest, social privilege and personal achievement sometimes overlap.

---

consumers. The middle class contains far more racial and ethnic diversity than the upper class.

Upper-Middles

The top half of this category is often termed the *upper-middle class*, based on above-average income in the range of $50,000 to $100,000 a year. Such income allows upper-middle-class families to accumulate considerable property—a comfortable house in a fairly expensive area, several automobiles, and investments. Two-thirds of upper-middle-class children receive college educations, and postgraduate degrees are common. Many go on to high-prestige occupations (physicians, engineers, lawyers, accountants, or business executives). Lacking the power of the upper class to influence national or international events, the upper-middle class often plays an important role in local political affairs.

Q: "The prosperity of the middle and lower classes depends on the good fortune of and light taxes on the rich." Andrew Mellon

Q: "The first and most intense passion that is produced by equality of condition is, I need hardly say, the love of that equality . . . Among democratic nations, men easily attain a certain equality of condition, but they can never attain as much as they desire." Alexis de Tocqueville

RESOURCE: Erik Olin Wright (1993) has argued that classes are discrete categories because (1) they correspond to different mechanisms for generating income, and (2) they are useful for explaining class conflict. An interesting debate on this issue is found in *American Sociological Review*, Vol. 58, No. 1, February 1993.

Q: ". . . *underclass* has become the code word for lower-income blacks and Puerto Ricans." Leslie Dunbar (1988:16)

Sometimes whole neighborhoods rise or fall due to a changing economy. The photo on the left, taken in 1979, shows Fern Street in Camden, New Jersey, as a stable though modest urban neighborhood. A decade later after several major industries closed their doors, the same neighborhood has the look of a ghost town.

Average-Middles

The rest of the middle class falls close to the center of the U.S. class structure. People in the *middle class* typically work in less prestigious white-collar occupations (bank tellers, middle managers, or sales clerks) or in highly skilled blue-collar jobs (including electrical work and carpentry). Household income is between $35,000 and $50,000 a year, which roughly equals the median household income for the United States as a whole.

Income at this level provides a secure, if modest, standard of living. Middle-class people generally accumulate some wealth over the course of their working lives, most in the form of a house. Middle-class men and women are likely to be high school graduates, but just four in ten young people at this class level attend college, usually enrolling in less expensive state-supported schools.

THE WORKING CLASS

About one-third of the population is working class (sometimes called the "lower-middle class"), people who have still less income and little or no accumulated wealth. In Marxist terms, the working class forms the core of the industrial proletariat. The blue-collar occupations of the working class produce a household income of between $15,000 and $35,000 a year, somewhat below the national average. Working-class families

thus find themselves vulnerable to financial problems, especially when faced by unemployment or illness.

Many working-class jobs provide little personal satisfaction—requiring discipline but rarely imagination—and subject workers to continual supervision. These jobs also provide fewer benefits, like medical insurance and pension plans. About half of working-class families own their homes, usually in less sought-after neighborhoods. College is a goal that only about one-third of working-class children realize. Still, many working-class families express a great deal of pride in what they do have, especially compared to people who are not working at all.

THE LOWER CLASS

The remaining 20 percent of our population make up the lower class. A lack of work and little income makes their lives unstable and insecure. In 1996, the federal government classified 36.5 million people (13.7 percent of the population) as poor. Millions more—the so-called working poor—are just barely better off, working at low-prestige jobs that provide little intrinsic satisfaction and minimal income. Elizabeth Jones, profiled at the beginning of this chapter, is included in the ranks of the working poor. Barely half of people at this class level manage to complete high school, and only one in four ever reaches college.

DIVERSITY: Attention to the term "underclass" has been considerable, although this category includes only about 5% of the poor. The term is used to designate those who are (1) chronically poor, (2) in inner-city areas, and (3) dependent on welfare.

DIVERSITY: High costs deter the poor from seeking health care. Nonetheless, low-income people have more medical care contacts (especially emergency room visits) than more affluent people. The

National Health Interview Survey reported 7.8 visits per person for persons in households with under $10,000 in annual income compared to 5.7 for those supported by $35,000 or more of household income.

NOTE: Herrnstein and Murray's controversial book, *The Bell Curve*, states that a 30-point IQ difference separates members of the lower and upper class.

Society segregates the lower class, especially when the poor are racial or ethnic minorities. About 40 percent of lower-class families own their own home, typically in the least desirable neighborhoods. Poor districts generally are found in inner cities, but lower-class families also live in rural communities, especially across the South.

THE DIFFERENCE CLASS MAKES

```
September 2, 1995, Mount Vernon, Ohio. My
bike leans right, leaving the trail for
the rest station that offers a chance for
a stretch and a drink of water. Here I
encounter Linda, a thirty-something woman
having trouble with her roller blades.
Eye contact and a perplexed look are a
call for help, so I walk over to see what
I might offer. Several of her boot buck-
les require adjustment. Close up, she
doesn't look well. "Are you OK?" I gently
ask. "Very tired," Linda responds, and
goes on to explain why. Now divorced, she
cannot pay off her debts with one low-
income job. So she works an 11 A.M. to 7
P.M. shift as a computer clerk at a bank
in town, catches four hours of sleep, and
then drives an hour to Columbus, where she
sits at another computer processing cat-
alog orders from 2 A.M. until 10 A.M. That
leaves just enough time to drive back to
Mount Vernon to start all over again at
the bank. . . .
```

Social stratification affects nearly every dimension of our lives. We will briefly examine some of the ways social standing is linked to our health, values, politics, and family life.

CLASS AND HEALTH

Health is one of the most important correlates of social standing. The lives of those we sometimes describe as the "beautiful people" are enhanced by almost every advantage imaginable. Then there are others (including Linda described above) whose lives are frayed by long hours of work and the stress of trying to make ends meet.

Among adults with annual income above $35,000, half describe their health as "excellent," a claim made by only one-fourth of people earning under $10,000. Conversely, only 4 percent of better-paid people complain of fair or poor health, compared to 22 percent of low-income individuals (U.S. National Center for Health Statistics, 1995).

Nutritious food, a safe environment, and regular medical care all promote well-being for those who can afford them. Medical costs have risen sharply in recent years, averaging more than $3,500 annually per person in the United States, which is clearly out of reach for people with low incomes. As a result, poor children are three times more likely to die in the first year of life, and those who reach adulthood will die some seven years sooner than affluent adults (U.S. Bureau of the Census, 1997).

Men and women in the lower social classes also live and work in more dangerous environments. Factories, mines, and construction sites represent greater threats to health than office buildings, just as poor neighborhoods are all too often plagued by drug use and crime. Over the long term, such stressful conditions place poor people at higher risk of mental health problems (Link, Dohrenwend, & Skodol, 1986; Mirowsky & Ross, 1989).

CLASS AND VALUES

Cultural values, too, vary from class to class. The "old rich" have an unusually strong sense of family history since their social position is based on wealth and social prestige passed down from generation to generation (Baltzell, 1979). With their birthright privileges, upper-uppers also favor understated manners and tastes, as if to say, "I know who I am, and I don't have to prove anything to anyone else."

Below the upper class, consumption takes on greater importance to social standing. Thorstein Veblen (1857–1929) coined the term *conspicuous consumption* to refer to the practice of buying fancy clothes, expensive cars, designer sunglasses, or even imported bottled water to "make a statement."

Tolerance is another class-linked value. Because of their greater education and sense of confidence, well-to-do people express greater tolerance toward controversial behavior such as homosexuality. Less tolerant are working-class people, who grow up in an atmosphere of greater supervision and discipline and are less likely to attend college (Kohn, 1977; NORC, 1996).

Q: "Class is for European democracies or something else; it isn't for the United States of America. We're not going to be divided by class." Former President George Bush

SOCIAL SURVEY: Unit Five of the Student Social Survey manual allows students to investigate the effects of class on how parents envision the traits of an ideal child.

RESOURCE: Lillian Rubin's *Worlds of Pain* (Basic, 1976) effectively shows the influence of class on the family life of women. While middle-class women seek personal qualities such as sensitivity and sharing in a spouse, working-class women have greater concern for basic traits such as holding a steady job and refraining from excessive drinking and domestic violence. In short, until economic standing is secure, women and men have little ability to consider other relational issues.

Even the way we think about time varies according to social class. Generations of wealth give upper-class families a keen awareness of the past. Middle-class people, especially those who are upwardly mobile, look optimistically to the future. The drive for daily survival focuses the attention of lower-class people more on the present; their present-time orientation is often a realistic assessment of the limited opportunities they have for advancement (Liebow, 1967; Lamar, Jr., 1985; Jacob, 1986).

CLASS AND POLITICS

Political affiliations tend to follow class lines. By and large, more privileged people in the United States support the Republican party, while those with fewer advantages favor the Democrats.

But, issue by issue, the pattern is more complex. A desire to protect wealth prompts well-off people to take a more conservative approach to *economic* issues, backing lower taxes and less government regulation of the economy. But on *social* matters, such as abortion and women's issues, highly educated, affluent people are more liberal. People of lower social standing, on the other hand, tend to be economic liberals, favoring expanded government social programs, while endorsing a more conservative social agenda (Erikson, Luttbeg, & Tedin, 1980; Syzmanski, 1983; Humphries, 1984).

Another clear pattern emerges when it comes to political involvement: Individuals with higher incomes, more schooling, and high-prestige white-collar jobs are more likely than those in the lower class to vote and to support various political organizations (Hyman & Wright, 1971; Wolfinger & Rosenstone, 1980). This difference is both cause and effect of the fact that privileged people are better served by the political system.

CLASS, FAMILY, AND GENDER

Finally, family life is closely related to social class. Because the typical individual marries someone of comparable social position, distinctive family patterns exist at each class level. For example, because lower-class people marry earlier in life and make less use of birth control, they have more children than middle-class parents do.

Working-class parents encourage children to conform to conventional norms and obey and respect authority figures. Parents of higher social standing,

Class position influences a host of individual values and attitudes. President John F. Kennedy was born to a family of established power and prestige; his privileged upbringing conferred on him the gentle manner of the upper class. Lyndon Baines Johnson, Kennedy's vice president, was a man of humble origins. Here we see Johnson displaying the spirited style that helped him fight his way to the top; Kennedy tries to restrain what he views as an inappropriate outburst.

Pipes, Richard, *Campaign 1960*, Gelatin-silver print, 14 × 11 (35.6 × 28 cm). The Museum of Modern Art, New York. Gift of the photographer. Copy Print © 1997 The Museum of Modern Art, New York.

however, transmit a different "cultural capital" to their children, teaching them to express their individuality and use their imaginations more freely. This difference reflects parents' expectations about their children's future: The odds are that less-privileged children will take jobs demanding close adherence to rules, while most advantaged children will enter fields that require more creativity (Kohn, 1977; McLeod, 1985).

Of course, it stands to reason that the more social resources a family has, the more parents can develop their children's talents and abilities. According to one recent study, an affluent family earning $87,300 a year will spend $218,400 raising a child born in 1996 to the age of eighteen. Middle-class people with income of $46,100 a year will spend $149,820, while families earning less than $34,700 will spend about $110,000 (Lino, 1997). Privilege, then, tends to beget privilege

NOTE: Mark Western and Erik Olin Wright (1994) argue that *authority boundaries* (separating managers from nonmanagers) are more permeable than *expertise boundaries* (separating experts from nonexperts); least permeable are *property boundaries* (dividing capitalists from wage laborers).

NOTE: To help students keep the terms straight, note that *intra* is Latin for "within" and *inter* means "between."

NOTE: Our society's belief in opportunity—and even the personal obligation to be upwardly mobile—is suggested by admonitions such as "pull yourself up by your own boot straps," which, curiously, is a physical impossibility.

NOTE: Joan Rodgers (1995) estimates that the children of poor parents in the United States have a 16–28% chance (with 95% confidence) of becoming poor as adults.

U.S. culture has long held the idea that, through talent and hard work, people can make their dreams come true. Do you think that social position is more a matter of individual effort or more a matter of the social class into which we are born? Why?

as family life reproduces the class structure in each generation.

Class also shapes our world of relationships. Elizabeth Bott (1971) found that most working-class couples divide their responsibilities according to gender; middle-class couples, by contrast, are more egalitarian, sharing more activities and expressing greater intimacy. More recently, Karen Walker (1995) discovered that working-class friendships typically provide material assistance; middle-class friendships, however, are likely to involve shared interests and leisure pursuits.

SOCIAL MOBILITY

Ours is a dynamic society in which many individuals move socially upward or downward over time. Earning a college degree, landing a higher-paying job, or marrying someone who earns a high income contributes to *upward social mobility;* dropping out of school, losing a job, or becoming the single, female head of a household may signal *downward social mobility.*

Over the long term, most social mobility is not a matter of individual decision as much as changes in society itself. During the first half of this century, for example, industrialization expanded the U.S. economy, dramatically raising living standards. Even without being very good swimmers, so to speak, people were able to "ride a rising tide of prosperity." More recently, *structural social mobility* in a downward direction has dealt many people economic setbacks.

Sociologists also distinguish between shorter- and longer-term changes in social position. **Intragenerational social mobility** refers to *a change in social position occurring within a person's lifetime.* **Intergenerational social mobility,** *upward or downward social mobility of children in relation to their parents,* has special significance because it usually indicates long-term changes in society that affect virtually everyone.

MYTH VERSUS REALITY

In few societies do people dwell on social mobility as much as in the United States. Moving up has always been central to the American Dream. But is there as much social mobility as we like to think?

Studies of intergenerational mobility (which, unfortunately, have focused almost exclusively on men) show that almost 40 percent of the sons of blue-collar workers attain white-collar jobs and almost 30 percent of sons born into white-collar families end up doing blue-collar work. Horizontal mobility—a change of occupation at one class level—is even more common, so that about 80 percent of sons show at least some type of social mobility in relation to their fathers (Blau & Duncan, 1967; Featherman & Hauser, 1978).

Research points to four general conclusions about social mobility in the United States:

1. **Social mobility, at least among men, has been fairly high.** The widespread notion that the United States has considerable social mobility is basically true. Mobility is what we would expect in an industrial class system.

2. **The long-term trend in social mobility has been upward.** Industrialization, which greatly

NOTE: To some extent, getting ahead economically today depends on limiting or entirely avoiding the expenses of child rearing. "Yuppies" (young-upwardly-mobile-professionals) are often "Dinks" (double-income-no-kids).

NOTE: During the recession that opened the 1990s, the process of "scaling back" threatened to transform the "Yuppies" of the 1980s into the "Dumpies" (downwardly-mobile-professionals) of the 1990s.

DISCUSS: What has caused the rise in income disparity? Factors include a rising stock market (which boosted income and wealth to the richest 20% of the population), also more two-income households (since higher-earning women tend to marry higher-earning men); some argue new technology fosters a "winner takes most" climate.

expanded the U.S. economy, and the growth of white-collar work over the course of this century have greatly boosted average incomes and living standards.

3. **Within a single generation, social mobility is usually incremental, not dramatic.** Only a very few people move "from rags to riches." While sharp rises or falls in individual fortunes may command public attention, social mobility usually involves subtle shadings *within* one class level rather than striking changes *between* classes.

4. **The short-term trend has been stagnation, with some income polarization.** As we shall explain presently, the rise in living standards that carried through most of this century hit a plateau in the early 1970s. Real income (that is, adjusted for inflation) for the U.S. population as a whole also changed little during the 1980s, then began rising slowly in the early 1990s (Veum, 1992).

Mobility by Income Level

General trends often mask the different experiences of various categories of people. Figure 10–4, shows how families in the United States fared between 1980 and 1996, according to their income level. Well-to-do families (the highest 20 percent) saw their incomes jump 34 percent, from an average $93,888 in 1980 to $125,627 in 1996, while people in the middle of the population held about even, and the lowest-income 20 percent suffered a 6.8 percent loss in earnings.

For families at the very top of the income scale (the highest 1 percent), the last fifteen years have been a windfall. High-income families, with an average income of $132,451 in 1980, were earning more than $250,000 in 1996, a 50 percent increase (Edmondson, 1995; Nielsen & Alderson, 1997; U.S. Bureau of the Census, 1997).

Mobility by Race, Ethnicity, and Gender

White people, generally in a more privileged position to begin with, have been more upwardly mobile than people of African or Hispanic ancestry in recent decades. Through the economic expansion of the 1980s and 1990s, more African Americans entered the ranks of the wealthy, but, overall, the real income of African Americans has changed little in two decades. Even so, African American families earned a slightly smaller percentage

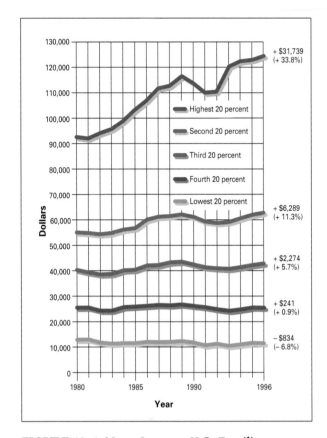

FIGURE 10–4 Mean Income, U.S. Families, 1980–1996 (in 1996 dollars, adjusted for inflation)

Source: U.S. Bureau of the Census (1997).

of white family income in 1996 (59 percent) than in 1970 (61 percent). For Latino families, the pattern is much the same. Compared to non-Hispanic white families, Latinos' earnings dropped between 1975 (67 percent) and 1996 (58 percent) (Featherman & Hauser, 1978; Pomer, 1986; U.S. Bureau of the Census, 1997).

Historically, women have had less opportunity for upward mobility than men, since the majority of working women hold clerical jobs (such as secretary) and service positions (like waitress) that offer little chance for advancement. And when marriages end in divorce (as almost half do), women (and less often men) commonly experience downward social mobility, since they may lose not only income but a host of benefits, including health care and insurance coverage (Weitzman, 1996).

THE MAP: Generally speaking, lower-income counties are those in which pessimism about the future is widespread. One interesting exception is counties containing large college campuses where many people, although fairly affluent, are doomsayers.

THEN AND NOW: Percent of a young couple's annual income need to purchase a new home: *1970*, 200%; *1995*, 400% (new car, 40% to 50%).

Q: "When some learn that all the American Dream does not fit all that is true about the realities of our life, they denounce the Dream and deny the truth of any of it. Fortunately, most of us are wiser and better adjusted to social reality; we recognize that, though it is called a Dream and some of it is false, by virtue of our firm belief in it we have made some of it true." W. Lloyd Warner, *Social Class in America*

SEEING OURSELVES

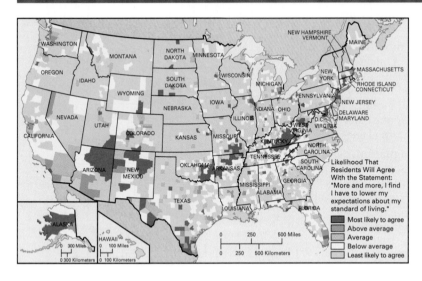

NATIONAL MAP 10–1
"Fear of Falling" Across the United States

This map shows, by county, how likely people are to agree with the statement "More and more, I find I have to lower my expectations about my standard of living." What characterizes regions (including Appalachia in Kentucky and West Virginia) where pessimism is high? But pessimism is pronounced not only in poor rural areas. In rich cities, including New York, Chicago, and Los Angeles, people are also afraid of losing their jobs.

Source: *American Demographics* magazine, February 1994, p. 60. Reprinted with permission. ©1994 *American Demographics* magazine, Ithaca, New York. Data from Yankelovich *Monitor* and Clarita's *Prizm* system.

Over time, however, the earnings gap between women and men has been closing. Women working full time in 1980 earned 60 percent as much as men working full time; by 1996, women earned 74 percent as much as men did. Unfortunately, much of the change was due to a *drop* in men's earnings through the 1980s, while women's income remained about the same (U.S. Bureau of the Census, 1997).

THE "AMERICAN DREAM": STILL A REALITY?

The expectation of upward social mobility is deeply rooted in our national culture. Through most of our history, in fact, economic expansion fulfilled the promise of prosperity by raising living standards. Beginning about 1970, however, this upward trend ended, ushering in a period of "income stagnation" that has shaken our national confidence (Pampel, Land, & Felson, 1977; Blumberg, 1981; Levy, 1987). Note these disturbing trends:

1. **For many workers, earnings have stalled.** The annual income of a fifty-year-old man working full time climbed by 50 percent between 1958 and 1973 (from $21,000 to $32,000 in constant 1990 dollars). Between 1973 and 1996, however, this worker's income remained flat, even as the number of hours worked increased and the cost of necessities like housing, education, and medical care went up (DeParle, 1991; Russell, 1995).

2. **Multiple job-holding is up.** According to the Bureau of Labor Statistics, 4.7 percent of the U.S. labor force worked at two or more jobs in 1975; by 1997, the proportion had risen to 6.1 percent.

3. **More jobs offer little income.** In 1979, the Census Bureau classified 12 percent of full-time workers as "low-income earners" because they earned less than $6,905; by 1996, this segment had increased to 15 percent, earning less than the comparable figure of $14,640.

4. **Young people are remaining at home.** Fully 53 percent of young people, aged eighteen to twenty-four, are now living with their parents. And the average age at marriage has moved upward three years since 1975 (to 24.5 years for women and 26.9 years for men).

Over the last generation, then, the rich have become richer. Moreover, the number of rich people has also increased: Estimates place the tally of U.S. millionaires at 3.5 million, perhaps twice the number of a decade ago (Sharpe, 1996). So for some, at least, the "American Dream" is alive and well. But most

DIVERSITY: During the last decade, some economic polarization has occurred in the United States (gini coefficients rose from .366 in 1980 to .455 in 1996). At the middle of the class structure, a "middle-class slide" accounts for about two-thirds of this change. Another one-third improved their economic standing, participating in what could be termed a "middle-class rise."

THEN AND NOW: The number of earners per family has increased in recent decades, one reason families are working harder to hold their economic position. Labor department figures show that, in 1950, 66% of families had one earner; by 1996, this dropped to 27%. During this period, two- (or more) earner families increased from 26% to 56%.

Q: "If a free society cannot help the many who are poor, it cannot help the few who are rich." John F. Kennedy

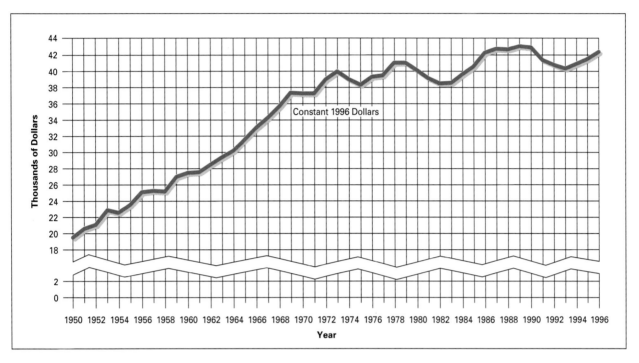

FIGURE 10–5 Median Income, U.S. Families, 1950–1996

Source: U.S. Bureau of the Census (1997).

people are decidedly less optimistic about the future, and a significant share feel the dream of a middle-class life slipping away (Kerckhoff, Campbell, & Winfield-Laird, 1985; Newman, 1993). National Map 10–1 shows where in the United States pessimism about the future is most widespread.

Dubbed the *middle-class slide*, this downward structural mobility is rooted in economic transformation. The brisk pace of economic expansion, long taken for granted, has now slowed for a generation as more new jobs offer low or modest pay. Figure 10–5 shows median U.S. family income between 1950 and 1996 in constant 1996 dollars. Between 1950 and 1973, median family income swelled by 65 percent, but it has moved up only slightly since then (U.S. Bureau of the Census, 1997).

THE GLOBAL ECONOMY AND THE U.S. CLASS STRUCTURE

Underlying the changes in U.S. class structure is a global economic transformation. Much of the industrial production that provided U.S. workers with high-paying jobs a generation ago has moved overseas, a trend termed "industrial migration" (Rosen, 1987; Thurow, 1987). With less industry at home, the United States now serves as a vast market for industrial goods such as cars, and popular items like stereos, cameras, and computers produced in Japan, Korea, and elsewhere.

High-paying jobs in manufacturing, held by 26 percent of the U.S. labor force in 1960, support 16 percent of workers today. In their place, the economy now offers "service work," which typically pays far less. For example, USX (formerly United States Steel) employs fewer people than McDonald's, which continues to expand, and fast-food clerks make only a fraction of what steel workers earn.

The global reorganization of work is not bad news for everyone. On the contrary, the growing global economy is driving the upward social mobility of a highly educated managerial class who specialize in areas such as law, finance, marketing, and computer technology. Moreover, the global economy has helped push up the stock market eightfold between 1980 and 1997, producing substantial profits for those families with money to invest.

NOTE: A 1988 media story began by describing Lyndon Johnson standing on Tom Fletcher's porch in Inez, Kentucky, two decades ago to launch the War on Poverty (*U.S. News and World Report*, January 11, 1988:18–24). Tom Fletcher lived in the same house a generation later, and his life is about the same as it was then. Perhaps Ronald Reagan was right when he quipped, "We had a war on poverty, and poverty won."

NOTE: In 1904, Robert Hunter (*Poverty*) estimated the U.S. poverty rate at 13% (defining poverty as annual income under $460 in the North and $300 in the South). Living standards rose sharply thereafter; but, in 1963, Michael Harrington (*The Other America*) claimed that at least 20% of the U.S. population was poor. Poverty definitions are thus historically specific (cf. Gilbert, 1994).

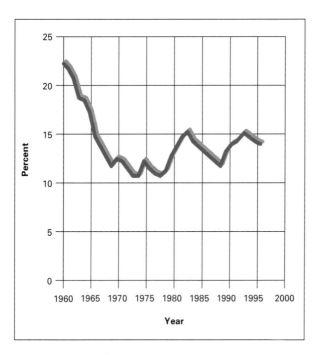

FIGURE 10–6 The Poverty Rate in the United States, 1960–1996

Source: U.S. Bureau of the Census (1997).

Industrialization spawned prosperity a century ago, but today's deindustrialization has tarnished the American Dream. Many "average" workers have seen their factory jobs relocated overseas. In addition, many companies are "downsizing"—cutting the ranks of their work force, blue-collar and white-collar alike—to become competitive in world markets (Reich, 1989, 1991). As a result, although half of all households contain two or more workers—double the share in 1950—many people are working harder simply to hold on to what they have.

POVERTY IN THE UNITED STATES

Social stratification simultaneously creates "haves" and "have-nots." Poverty is therefore an inevitable product of all systems of social inequality. Sociologists employ the concept of poverty in two different ways, however. **Relative poverty,** which is by definition universal and inevitable, refers to *the deprivation of some people in relation to those who have more.* Everyone, in other words, is rich or poor in comparison with someone else. Much more serious is **absolute poverty,** or *a deprivation of resources that is life-threatening.* Defined in this way, poverty is a pressing, but solvable, human problem.

As the next chapter ("Global Stratification") explains, the global dimensions of absolute poverty put the lives of about 800 million human beings—one in seven of the earth's people—at risk. Yet, even in the affluent United States, families go hungry, live in inadequate housing, and endure poor health because of wrenching poverty.

THE EXTENT OF U.S. POVERTY

In 1964, the federal government established an official *poverty line,* and began counting the poor and offering them certain benefits. The idea was to count as "poor" people living close to absolute poverty. Mollie Orshansky (1969:38), the architect of the poverty line, described it as the income needed "to purchase a nutritionally adequate diet on the assumption that no more than a third of the family income is used for food." In other words, the poverty threshold is three times what the government estimates people must spend to eat. The government sets the exact dollar amount according to family size with annual adjustments to reflect the changing cost of living.

Figure 10–6 shows the official poverty rate as calculated annually since 1960. During the 1960s, the poverty rate fell sharply, but there has been little overall change during the decades since. In 1996, some 36.5 million men, women, and children—13.7 percent of the U.S. population—were officially counted among the poor. Another 13 million people—the *marginally poor*—lived on income no greater than 125 percent of the poverty threshold.

For two adults and two children living in an urban area in 1996, the poverty threshold was $16,036. The income of the typical poor family, however, is some $5,000 *below* the poverty threshold. And, estimates suggest that almost 40 percent of the poor—those we might term *the poorest of the poor*—struggle to get by with no more than half the poverty line income (U.S. Bureau of the Census, 1997).

People like Elizabeth Jones, described at the beginning of this chapter, know very well the consequences of living on the edge—not being able to afford the expensive sneakers her son wants so badly, and, worse, worrying about what will happen if one of her children becomes injured or ill. In short,

NOTE: In 1996, the "poverty gap" was $6,252, meaning the average poor family would need this much more income to reach the poverty line.

SOCIAL DIVERSITY: Chance of poverty by household type (1996): married couple, 7%; single-woman householder, 36% (U.S. Bureau of the Census).

NOTE: The 1996 median income for families with a married couple was $49,707; for male heads of household with no wife present, $31,600; for female heads of household with no husband present, $19,911.

NOTE: About 2.5 million U.S. workers earn the minimum wage. The real value of the minimum wage has dropped about 50 cents since 1991 and currently stands at an all-time-low.

poverty means a daily life of stress, insecurity, and—for about half the poor adults and children in the United States—daily hunger (Schwartz-Nobel, 1981; Physicians' Task Force on Hunger in America, 1987).

WHO ARE THE POOR?

Although no single description covers all poor people, poverty is pronounced among certain categories of our population. Where these categories overlap, the problem of poverty is especially serious.

Age

A generation ago, the elderly were at greatest risk for poverty, but no longer. From 30 percent in 1967, the poverty rate for seniors over the age of sixty-five plummeted to 10.8 percent in 1996, or 3.4 million elderly poor. The elderly now have a poverty rate below the national average. This dramatic decline was due to expanding financial support from private employers and government. Even so, with the number of older people increasing, 9.4 percent of the poor are still elderly people.

Today, the burden of poverty falls most heavily on children. In 1996, 20.5 percent of people under age eighteen (14.5 million children) were officially classified as poor. Tallied another way, four in ten of the U.S. poor are children under the age of eighteen. International comparisons of infant mortality rates suggest that the poverty problem is greater in the United States than in other industrial nations. In fact, despite having the highest economic standard of living in the world, the United States ranks twentieth in global child mortality rates. The box on page 278 offers a closer look at child poverty in the United States.

Race and Ethnicity

Two-thirds of all poor people are white; about 27 percent are African Americans. But in relation to their overall numbers, African Americans are about three times as likely as white people to be poor. In 1996, 28.4 percent of African Americans (9.7 million people) lived in poverty, compared to 29.4 percent of Latinos (8.7 million), 14.5 percent of Asians and Pacific Islanders (1.5 million), and 8.6 percent of non-Latino white people (16.5 million). The "poverty gap" between whites and minorities has remained essentially unchanged since 1975 (U.S. Bureau of the Census, 1997).

A widespread stereotype links poverty to people of color in the inner cities of the United States. Although minorities are more likely to be disadvantaged, most of the U.S. poor are white people. Furthermore, although inner cities have the greatest concentration of poverty, rural residents are at higher risk of poverty than their urban counterparts.

Gender and Family Patterns

Of the U.S. poor over age eighteen, 62.7 percent are women and 37.3 percent are men. This disparity reflects the fact that women who head households bear the brunt of poverty. Of all poor families, 54 percent are headed by women with no husband present, while just 7 percent of poor families are headed by single men.

The link between single-parent families and poverty also means that divorce threatens even middle-class women and their children with poverty. Research by Andrew Cherlin (1990) shows that the income of single-parent families typically plummets by more

THE MAP: High child poverty rates are found across the South, which is also the region of high African American concentration.
THEN AND NOW: The child poverty rate stood at about 25% in 1960; it fell to 14% by 1969, and is now 20.5%.
Q: "No citizen should ever be wealthy enough to buy another, and none poor enough to be forced to sell himself." Jean Jacques Rousseau, *The Social Contract* (II, 46)

NOTE: Because women and children tend to suffer together from poverty, the feminization of poverty might also be termed the "juvenilization of poverty." Children are now the poorest of the U.S. poor.
Q: "In our society, it is murder, psychologically, to deprive a man of a job or an income. You are in effect saying to that man that he has no right to exist." Martin Luther King, Jr.

SOCIAL DIVERSITY

U.S. Children: Bearing the Burden of Poverty

We cringe at the sight of starving children in countries such as Somalia, the war-torn African nation where the average person struggles to live on less than $200 per year. But child poverty in the United States may be an even greater tragedy, since ours is such a rich nation with one hundred times Somalia's per capita income.

One in five U.S. children under the age of eighteen is poor—almost 15 million boys and girls. This is about the same number as thirty years ago when the government's "war on poverty" began. Since then, a national commitment has cut poverty among senior citizens by more than half, but child poverty is on the rise. National Map 10–2 reveals that the concentration of child poverty is greatest across the South.

Like poverty in general, the risk of child poverty varies within our population. In 1996, for the country as a whole, 20 percent of boys and girls under the age of eighteen were poor. But while 16 percent of white children were poor, 40 percent of Latino and African American youngsters were poor.

From another angle, 63 percent of poor children are white, while 31 percent are African American, and 5 percent are Asian; 25 percent of poor children are culturally Hispanic. But while poor children are a diverse lot, they share a key characteristic: They all live in households with low income. In fact, 44 percent of poor boys and girls live in households with incomes no more than half the poverty threshold (that is, less than $8,018 in 1996).

Researchers have found a strong link between rising rates of child poverty and the increasing share of single-parent households. Today, about eight in ten poor children live in a household with a single mother, and in the same proportion of cases this household contains no full-time worker.

The reasons for poverty, discussed shortly, are complex and controversial. But everyone agrees that no blame lies with the children. Tragically, however, this is precisely where the burden of poverty falls. Practically speaking, social intervention that eliminates the deforming experience of child poverty is much cheaper than dealing with the unemployment, drug use, crime, and violence that will come later on. So, whether we look at this issue from a practical or a moral standpoint, can we permit our society's most vulnerable members to suffer this way?

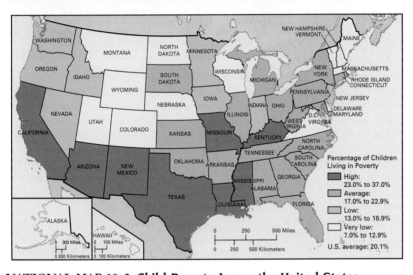

SEEING OURSELVES

Percentage of Children Living in Poverty

High: 23.0% to 37.0%
Average: 17.0% to 22.9%
Low: 13.0% to 16.9%
Very low: 7.0% to 12.9%
U.S. average: 20.1%

NATIONAL MAP 10–2 Child Poverty Across the United States
Source: U.S. Bureau of the Census (1998).

Sources: Eggebeen & Lichter (1991), Children's Defense Fund (1995), and U.S. Bureau of the Census (1997).

than one-third within several months of divorce or separation.

The term **feminization of poverty** describes *the trend by which women represent an increasing proportion of the poor.* In 1960, 25 percent of all poor households were headed by women; the majority of poor families had both wives and husbands in the home. By 1996, however, the proportion of poor households headed by a single woman had more than doubled to 54 percent.

THE MAP: The 20 highest-income counties in the United States are in metropolitan areas, 17 of them along the eastern seaboard (3 of the top 5 are in New Jersey). Poor counties are likely to be rural, and most are found in the South (11 of the poorest 20 are in Kentucky and Texas). Low-earning counties also have more single-parent families and more elderly people, while fewer people are in the high-earning age bracket from ages 45 to 54.

DIVERSITY: The importance of family patterns to poverty is indicated by the fact that, among two-parent families with children, the poverty rate is just 10.1 percent. Among all female heads of households, it was 35.8 percent in 1996 (U.S. Bureau of the Census, 1998).

DIVERSITY: The rural poverty rate paralleled the trend shown in Figure 10–4, rising from 16.6% in 1973 to 22.9% in 1990.

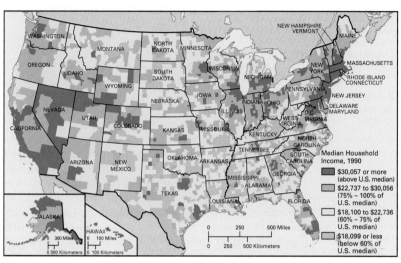

NATIONAL MAP 10–3
Median Household Income Across the United States

This map shows median household income for all 3,014 counties in the United States as recorded by the 1990 census. Surprisingly, just 15 percent of all counties can boast of a median household income greater than the median for the entire country. What do these counties (shown in dark green) have in common? Low-income counties (shown in red) with high rates of poverty also are not randomly spread throughout the nation. What do low-income counties have in common? Do the patterns found here square with our assertion linking affluence to urban areas and poverty to rural places?

Source: *American Demographics* magazine, Oct. 1992, p. 9. Reprinted with permission. ©1992 *American Demographics* magazine, Ithaca, New York. Data from the 1990 decennial census.

The feminization of poverty is thus part of a larger change: the rapidly increasing number of households—at all class levels—headed by single women. This trend, coupled with the fact that households headed by women are at high risk of poverty, is why women (and their children) make up an increasing share of the U.S. poor.

Urban and Rural Poverty

The greatest concentration of poverty is found in central cities, where the 1996 poverty rate stood at 19.6 percent. Suburbs, too, have destitute people, but because suburbanites are more affluent, their poverty rate is just 9.1 percent. Thus, the poverty rate for urban areas as a whole is 13.2 percent—lower than the 15.9 percent found in nonmetropolitan areas. National Map 10–3 presents income levels across the United States, and shows where poverty is most pronounced.

EXPLAINING POVERTY

For the richest nation on earth to have tens of millions of poor people raises serious questions. It is true, as some analysts remind us, that many of the people counted among the officially poor in the United States

are better off than the poor in other countries—40 percent of U.S. poor families own their home, for example, and 60 percent own a car (Jenkins, 1992). But it is also the case that persistent malnutrition and outright hunger are a widespread blight on this country.

Figure 10–7 on page 280 suggests that the public is divided over what to do about poverty. One-fourth of respondents to this national survey think government has the primary responsibility to raise living standards; slightly more think that people should take responsibility for themselves. The greatest number, however, straddle the fence, believing that both government and individuals bear some responsibility.

We now examine more closely the arguments underlying two basic approaches to the problem of poverty. Together, they frame a lively and pressing political debate.

One View: Blame the Poor

According to one view, *the poor are primarily responsible for their own poverty*. Historically, people in the United States have valued self-reliance, and believed that social standing is mostly a matter of individual talent and effort. This view sees society offering considerable opportunity to anyone able and willing to

Q: "No man suffers from poverty unless it be more than his fault—unless it be his *sin*." Preacher and social Darwinist Henry Ward Beecher

NOTE: Edward Banfield (1974) is another proponent of the social Darwinist view that the poor are largely responsible for their own poverty. Recently, Richard Herrnstein and Charles Murray (1994) echoed this logic, asserting that today's poor are largely people handicapped by low intelligence.

RESOURCE: Herrnstein and Murray's "bell curve thesis," along with a critical response, is included in the 4th edition of the Macionis and Benokraitis reader, *Seeing Ourselves.*

Q: "Dependent poverty ought to be held disgraceful." Thomas Robert Malthus (Malthus blamed the persistence of the poor in England on the Poor Laws.)

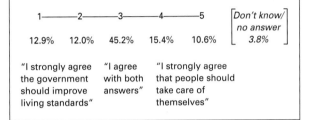

Survey Question: "Some people think that the government in Washington should do everything possible to improve the living standards of all poor Americans [they are at point 1 below]. Other people think it is not the government's responsibility, and that each person should take care of himself [they are at point 5 below]. Where would you place yourself on this scale, or haven't you made up your mind on this?"

1	2	3	4	5	Don't know/ no answer
12.9%	12.0%	45.2%	15.4%	10.6%	3.8%

"I strongly agree the government should improve living standards"

"I agree with both answers"

"I strongly agree that people should take care of themselves"

FIGURE 10–7 Government or Individuals: Who Is Responsible for Poverty?

Source: NORC (1996).

take advantage of it. Therefore, according to this line of reasoning, while some poor are "worthy" people who cannot fend for themselves (historically, widows and orphans), most are "unworthy" people with few skills, limited schooling, and little motivation. This view, which has much in common with the social Darwinist thinking discussed in the last chapter, is represented in responses on the right side of the continuum in Figure 10–7.

In a study of Latin American cities, anthropologist Oscar Lewis (1961) concluded that most poor people could do little about their plight. Yet, he did not blame them individually for their poverty. Rather, he contended that a *culture of poverty*—a lower-class subculture—inhibits personal achievement and fosters resignation. Socialized in poor families, children come to see little point in aspiring to a better life. The result is a self-perpetuating cycle of poverty.

With the hope of breaking the cycle of poverty in the United States, in 1996 Congress significantly altered the welfare system that has provided a federal guarantee of financial assistance to poor people since 1935. Now the federal government sends money to the states to distribute to needy people, but benefits carry strict time limits: in most cases, no more than two years at a stretch and a total of five years if an individual moves in and out of the welfare system. The objective of this welfare reform is to move people from depending on government to supporting themselves. The

implication, in short, is that people themselves can and should combat poverty through hard work, regular saving, and—most of all—the determination to get ahead.

Counterpoint: Blame Society

An alternative position, argued by William Julius Wilson (1996), holds that *society is primarily responsible for poverty.* Wilson points to the loss of jobs in our inner cities as the primary cause of poverty since there is simply not enough opportunity for people to support themselves and their families. Thus, Wilson sees any apparent lack of ambition on the part of poor people as a *consequence of insufficient opportunity* rather than a *cause of poverty.* From this point of view, then, Oscar Lewis's analysis amounts to "blaming the victims" for their own suffering (Ryan, 1976). The view that changes in society are needed to alleviate poverty is found on the left side of the continuum in Figure 10–7. The box provides a closer look at Wilson's argument and how it would shape public policy.

Weighing the Evidence

Each explanation of poverty has its share of public support and advocates among government policy makers. As the "blame the poor" side sees it, it is important that everyone have opportunity, but, beyond that, people should take responsibility for themselves.

The "blame society" side takes a more activist approach, holding that government policy should reduce poverty through more equitable redistribution of income. Programs like comprehensive child care, for example, would free poor mothers to learn job skills; indeed, the living standard of every poor person could be raised by a tax-funded, guaranteed minimum income for every U.S. family.

In the political arena, Republican policies reflect the first position, and Democratic policies support the second. But, based on research, what can sociologists contribute to the debate?

First, the fact that most poor adults in the United States do not hold full-time jobs seems to advance the "blame the poor" argument. Government statistics show that 44.8 percent of the heads of poor families did not work at all during 1996, and 38.1 percent of the heads of poor families had, at most, a part-time job (U.S. Bureau of the Census, 1997). So we can conclude that one major cause of poverty is *not holding a job.*

SOCIAL SURVEY: A U.S. Census Bureau survey of poor adults yielded these explanations for not working among those who did not work at all: Ill/disability, 18%; retired, 3%; home or family reasons, 44%; school/other, 23%; could not find work, 13%.

Q: ". . . it is a vicious cycle: You cannot get a job because you do not have an address, you do not have an address because you do not have any money, and you do not have any money because you do not have a job." Danny Cahill, *Forgotten Voices, Unforgettable Dreams*

NOTE: One critic of Wilson notes that the population of the Chicago neighborhoods in Wilson's research declined from 250,000 in 1950 to 86,000 in 1990. This drop, suggests Marvin Kosters (1996), seems to indicate that most people succeeded over time in moving on and up.

CRITICAL THINKING

When Work Disappears: The Result Is Poverty

The economy has churned out tens of millions of new jobs in the last two decades. In that same period, joblessness among inner-city blacks has reached catastrophic proportions. Yet in this Presidential election year [1996], the disappearance of work in the ghetto is not on either the Democratic or the Republican agenda. There is harsh talk about work instead of welfare but no talk about where to find it. (Wilson, 1996b:27)

According to William Julius Wilson, one of the best-known U.S. sociologists, some of the economic news about African Americans is good: The black middle class—and the ranks of affluent black families—have been expanding. But a minority of African Americans who live in the inner city face mounting economic barriers that, despite their best efforts, they cannot overcome.

Here is the problem: For the first time, a large majority of the adults in our inner cities are not working. Studying the Washington Park area of Chicago (near the University of Chicago where he works), Wilson found a troubling trend. In 1950, most of the adults in the African American community worked during a typical week but, by the 1990s, two-thirds did not. As one elderly woman who moved to the neighborhood in 1953 explains:

When I moved in, the neighborhood was intact. It was intact with homes, beautiful homes, mini-mansions, with stores, laundromats, with Chinese cleaners. We had drugstores. We had hotels. We had doctors over on 39th street. We had doctors' offices in the neighborhood. We had the middle class

and the upper-middle class. It has gone from affluent to where it is today . . . (1996b:28)

But *why* has this neighborhood declined? Wilson's eight years of research in the area point to one answer: There are barely any jobs. It is the disappearance of work, concludes Wilson, that has plunged people into desperate poverty, pushed up the crime rate, undermined families, and forced people to turn to welfare. In the nearby Woodlawn neighborhood, Wilson identified more than 800 businesses that operated in 1950; today, just 100 remain. Moreover, a number of major employers a generation ago—including the Western Electric's Hawthorne plant and an International Harvester plant—closed their doors in the late 1960s. We can trace this massive loss of jobs to the economic factors discussed earlier in this chapter, including downsizing and moving jobs overseas.

Wilson paints a grim picture. But he also believes there is a solution to the problems of the inner cities: Create jobs. Wilson proposes attacking the problem

in stages. First, the government can hire people to do all kinds of needed work, including clearing slums and putting up new housing. Such a program, modeled on the Works Progress Administration (WPA) enacted in 1935 during the Great Depression, can move people from welfare to work and, in the process, generate much-needed hope that people can improve their lives. In addition, federal and state governments must enact performance standards and provide the financing for schools in poor communities to teach children the language and computer skills needed to perform the jobs being created by the Information Revolution. Improved regional public transportation would connect cities (where people need jobs) and suburbs (where most jobs now are). In addition, more child-care programs would help single mothers and fathers balance the responsibilities of parenting and work.

Wilson claims that his proposals are well-grounded in research. But he knows politics revolves around other considerations as well. For one thing, to the extent that people *think* there are plenty of jobs, they will conclude that the poor are simply avoiding work, making any change unlikely. Moreover, he concedes that his proposals, at least in the short term, are more expensive than continuing to funnel welfare assistance to jobless communities.

But, for the long term, he asks, what are the costs of allowing our cities to decay while suburbs prosper? Of allowing a new generation of preschoolers to join the ranks of the restless and often angry people for whom there is no work? And what would be the benefits of affording everyone the hope and aspiration that are supposed to define our way of life?

Source: Based on Wilson (1996).

NOTE: Since 1959, poverty rates have declined; then, 18% of whites and 55% of African Americans were poor.

Q: "There is no way the 'real' numbers could reach the claims of millions of homeless persons advanced by the advocates for the homeless." Peter H. Rossi (1994:81)

NOTE: Some estimates suggest that half of homeless women are fleeing abusive partners.

SOCIAL SURVEY: "On the whole, do you think it should or should not be the government's responsibility to reduce income differences between the rich and the poor?" (GSS 1996, N = 1,324; *Codebook*, 1996:665)
"Definitely should be"   15.6% "Definitely should not be" 23.0%
"Probably should be"   27.4% DK/NR   10.3%
"Probably should not be" 23.7%

Mexican artist Diego Rivera captured the humility and humanity of poor people in his painting Our Bread. *This insight is important in a society like ours where many people tend to dismiss the poor as morally unworthy and deserving of their bitter plight.*

But the *reasons* that people do not work are more consistent with the "blame society" position. Middle-class women may be able to combine working and child rearing, but this is much harder for poor women who cannot afford child care. Few U.S. employers provide child-care programs for their employees, and many low-paid workers cannot afford child care on their own. Moreover, as William Julius Wilson explains, many people stand idle, not because they are avoiding work, but because there are not enough jobs to go around. In short, most poor people

in the United States find few options and alternatives (Popkin, 1990; Schiller, 1994; Edin & Lein, 1996; Wilson, 1996).

The Working Poor

But not all poor people are jobless, and the *working poor* command the sympathy and support of people on both sides of the poverty debate (Schwarz & Volgy, 1992). In 1996, 17.1 percent of the heads of poor families (1.2 million people) labored at least fifty weeks of the year and yet could not escape poverty. Another 38.1 percent of these families (2.7 million people) remained poor despite part-time employment by the head of the family. From another angle, 2.5 percent of full-time workers earn so little that they remain poor (U.S. Bureau of the Census, 1997). A key cause of "working poverty" is that, even with the recently enacted minimum wage level of $5.15 per hour, a full-time worker cannot lift a family above the poverty line.

To sum up, individual ability and personal initiative do play a part in shaping everyone's social position. However, the weight of sociological evidence points to society—not individual character traits—as the primary cause of poverty. Society must be at fault, because the poor are *categories* of people—women heads of families, people of color, people isolated from the larger society in inner-city areas—who contend with special barriers and limited opportunities.

HOMELESSNESS

Many low-income people in the United States cannot afford even basic housing. Despite enormous wealth and a commitment to providing opportunity for everyone, the United States has not effectively responded to homelessness, a scar on our society (Schutt, 1989).

Counting the Homeless

There is no precise count of homeless people. Fanning out across the cities of the United States on the night of March 20, 1991, Census Bureau officials tallied 178,828 people at shelters and 49,793 on the streets in neighborhoods where homeless people are known to congregate. But experts agree that a full count of the homeless would probably reach 500,000 *on any given night*, with as many as three times that number—1.5 million people—homeless *at some time during the course of a year* (Kozol, 1988; Wright 1989).

NOTE: As a case of mixed political attitudes, Jo Phelan et al. (1995) found more educated people to have greater tolerance for the homeless (liberal social attitude) but offer less support for economic assistance to the homeless (conservative economic attitude).

Q: "The most dangerous illusion of them all is the illusion that all is well." William Nicholson

DIVERSITY: The U.S. homeless profile is roughly: 75% unemployed; 35% substance abusers; 25% mentally ill; 25% prison records. The categories overlap somewhat, but estimates of those with drug, alcohol, or mental problems range up to two-thirds of all homeless (though some may be effect rather than cause). In any case, perhaps 400,000 U.S. adults have problems that make it impossible for them to work and live independently—one quarter of 1 percent of the total U.S. population.

Causes of Homelessness

The familiar stereotypes of homeless people—men sleeping in doorways and women carrying everything they own in a shopping bag—have been replaced by the reality of the "new homeless": people thrown out of work because of plant closings, those forced out of apartments by rent increases or condominium conversions, and others unable to meet mortgage or rent payments because they must work for low wages. Today, no stereotype paints a complete picture of the homeless.

But virtually all homeless people have one status in common: *poverty*. For that reason, the explanations of poverty already offered also apply to homelessness. One side of the debate places responsibility on the *personal* traits of the homeless themselves. One-third of homeless people are substance abusers, and one-fourth of homeless adults are mentally ill. More broadly, it should not be surprising that a fraction of 1 percent of our population, for one reason or another, is unable to cope with our complex and highly competitive society (Bassuk, 1984; Whitman, 1989).

The other side of the debate sees homelessness resulting from *societal factors*, including a lack of low-income housing and an increasing number of low-income jobs (Kozol, 1988; Schutt, 1989; Bohannan, 1991). Supporters of this position point out that one-third of all homeless people are entire families, and children are the fastest-growing category of the homeless. A minister living in a Pennsylvania town that has lost hundreds of industrial jobs due to plant closings describes the real-life effects of economic recession:

> Yes, there are new jobs. There's a new McDonald's and a Burger King. You can take home $450 in a month from jobs like that. That might barely pay the rent. What do you do if someone gets sick? What do you do for food and clothes? These may be good jobs for a teenager. Can you ask a thirty-year-old man who's worked for GM since he was eighteen to keep his wife and kids alive on jobs like that? There are jobs cleaning rooms in the hotel. . . . Can you expect a single mother with three kids to hold her life together with that kind of work? (Kozol, 1988:6)

No one disputes that a large proportion of homeless people are personally impaired to some degree, although how much is cause and how much is effect is difficult to untangle. But structural changes in the U.S. economy coupled with declining government aid

Social scientists debate the causes of poverty, some citing the failings of individuals such as lack of initiative or drug abuse and others pointing to flaws of society including a minimum wage that does not allow a full-time worker to support a family. Whatever side one takes in this controversy, it is impossible to turn away from the drama of children born into poor families. Noted photographer Mary Ellen Marks has followed this family for over a decade. She notes that the children have never known any life but poverty. Whatever their talents may be, are they destined to repeat the ordeal of their parents?

to low-income people have certainly contributed to homelessness.

This chapter's closing box examines "welfare," a topic that focuses our thinking about how to respond to issues such as poverty and homelessness.

Finally, social stratification extends far beyond the borders of the United States. In fact, the most striking social disparities are found not by looking inside one country but by comparing living standards in various parts of the world. In Chapter 11, we broaden our investigation of social stratification by looking at global inequality.

NOTE: Due to factors including the negative stigma attached to receiving welfare and highly variable eligibility standards, perhaps half of women and men eligible for welfare programs never apply for them.

RESOURCE: The key conservative criticisms of public assistance are found in Charles Murray's *Breaking Ground* (1984); his thesis is that the outlay for welfare must continue to grow because the system fails to alleviate the problems it set out to fix, actually making matters worse.

GLOBAL: In Japan, the law requires poor people to get help from kin before turning to the government for assistance; people physically able to work are not eligible for benefits in any case.

DISCUSS: What does the class think was William Julius Wilson's reaction to the 1996 welfare reform? (He was deeply disappointed.)

CONTROVERSY & DEBATE

The Welfare Dilemma

Elizabeth Jones, the young mother profiled in the opening to this chapter, is working as hard as she can to end ten years on public assistance, or, as she puts it, "to break the chain" and give her children a better chance than she had. Indeed, in 1996, Congress ended the federal public assistance that guaranteed some income to all poor people in favor of state-run programs that require people receiving aid to take training or find work—or have the benefits cut off.

Almost no one has a kind word to say about "welfare." Liberals criticize welfare as an inadequate response to poverty; conservatives charge it hurts the people it is supposed to help; and the poor themselves find welfare a complex, confusing, and often degrading program.

So what, exactly, *is* "welfare"? The term "welfare" refers to a host of policies and programs designed to improve the well-being of the U.S. population. Until the welfare reform of 1996, most people used the term to refer to one part of the overall system—Aid For Dependent Children (AFDC), a program of monthly financial support to parents (primarily single women) to care for themselves and their children. In 1996, some 5 million households received AFDC for some part of the year.

Did AFDC help or hurt the poor? There are two sides to the debate. Conservative critics charge that, rather than reducing child poverty, AFDC actually *made the problem worse* for two reasons. First, this form of "welfare" eroded the traditional family by subsidizing living single as an alternative to marriage. For years after the program began, public assistance regulations provided benefits to poor mothers *only if no husband lived in the home.* As conservatives see it, AFDC operated as an economic incentive to women to have children outside of marriage: one reason for the rapid rise in out-of-wedlock births among poor people. Conservatives highlight the connection between being poor and not being married: Fewer than one in ten married-couple families were poor; more than nine in ten AFDC families were headed by an unmarried woman.

Conservatives also believe that government assistance undermines self-reliance among the poor and fosters dependency. Depending on government "handouts," they claim, is the main reason that eight of ten heads of poor households do not have steady, full-time jobs. Furthermore, although more than half of non-poor, single mothers worked full-time, only 5 percent of single mothers receiving AFDC did. Clearly, conservatives continue, welfare strayed far from its original purpose of helping non-working women with children (typically, after the death or divorce of a husband) make the transition to self-sufficiency. On the contrary, "welfare" becomes a way of life. Once trapped in dependency, poor women are likely to raise children who will, themselves, remain poor as adults.

Liberals charge that their opponents use a double standard in evaluating government programs. Why, they ask, does our national dander rise at the thought of the government money going to poor mothers and children when most "welfare" actually goes to relatively rich people? The AFDC budget has been around $25 billion annually—no small sum, to be sure—but just half of the $50 billion in home mortgage deductions that homeowners pocket each year. And it pales in comparison to the $300 billion in annual Social Security benefits Uncle Sam provides to senior citizens, most of whom are quite well-off. And what about annual tax write-offs that corporations take, which can run into hundreds of billions? As liberals see it, "wealthfare" is far greater than "welfare."

Second, liberals claim that conservatives (and much public opinion) have a distorted picture of public assistance. The popular images of irresponsible "welfare queens" mask the fact that most poor families who turn to public assistance are truly needy. Moreover, the typical household receiving AFDC receives barely $400 per month, hardly enough to attract people to a "life of welfare dependency." And, in constant dollars, AFDC payments actually declined over recent decades. In fact, liberals fault public assistance as a band-aid approach to the serious social problems of too few jobs and too much income inequality in the United States.

As for the charge that public assistance undermines families, liberals concede that the proportion of single-parent families has risen, but they dispute that AFDC was to blame. Rather, they maintain, single-parenting is a broad cultural trend found at all class levels in most industrial societies.

NOTE: According to the Cato Institute, the hourly value of welfare benefits in 1995 ranged from $5.53 in Mississippi to $17.50 in Hawaii (Tanner & Moore, 1995).

NOTE: The $50-billion home-mortgage tax deduction (85% of which goes to top 20% income households) amounts to five times the $8 billion the government spends annually on low-income housing.

Q: ". . . A long time ago I concluded that the current welfare system undermines the basic values of work, responsibility, and family, trapping generation after generation in dependency . . . Welfare . . . was meant to be a second chance, not a way of life." President Bill Clinton

NOTE: The 1996 welfare reforms allow benefits beyond the cutoff point for "hardship cases."

Thus, liberals conclude, programs such as AFDC were not attacked because they have failed, but because they benefited a segment of the population considered "undeserving." Our cultural tradition of equating wealth with virtue and poverty with vice allows rich people to display privilege as a "badge of ability," while poverty is a sign of personal failure. According to Richard Sennett and Jonathan Cobb (1973), the negative stigma of poverty is the "hidden injury of class."

Indeed, as shown in Figure 10–8, more of the U.S. population attributes poverty to personal laziness than societal injustice. Such an attitude goes a long way toward explaining why the U.S. public is far less supportive of public assistance for the poor than people in other industrial nations are. It should not be surprising, then, that Congress and President Bill Clinton enacted reforms to replace the federal AFDC program with funding for new state-run programs called Temporary Assistance For Needy Families (TANF). States can set their own qualifications and benefits, but they must limit benefits to two consecutive years (with a lifetime limit of five years), and, by 2002, move half of single parents on welfare into jobs or job-training. By mid-1997, one year after the welfare reform bill took effect, President Clinton declared it a success because almost 1.5 million people had been dropped from the welfare rolls. But whether these people are in the work force (as supporters of these reforms hope) or worse off than ever (as opponents of these reforms fear) is not yet clear.

Continue the debate . . .

1. How does our cultural emphasis on self-reliance help explain the controversy surrounding public assistance? Why, then, do people not criticize benefits (like home mortgage deductions) for more well-to-do-people?

2. Do you think public assistance has become a "way of life" and eroded the family? Why or why not?

3. Do you approve of the benefit time limits built in to the new Temporary Assistance for Needy Families (TANF) program? Why or why not?

GLOBAL SNAPSHOT

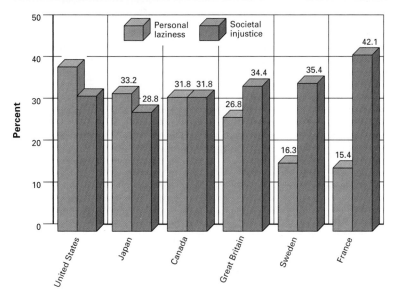

FIGURE 10–8 Assessing the Causes of Poverty

Survey Question: "Why are there people in this country who live in need?" Percentages reflect respondents' identification of either "personal laziness" or "societal injustice" as the primary cause of poverty.

Percentages for each country do not add up to 100 because less frequently identified causes of poverty were omitted from this figure.

Source: *World Values Survey* (1994).

Sources: Katz (1986), Mead (1989), Ehrenreich (1991), Weidenbaum (1991), Jensen, Eggebeen, & Lichter (1993), Shapiro (1995), Church (1996), Murray (1996), and Broder (1997).

SUMMARY

1. Social inequality in the United States involves disparities in several variables, including income, wealth, and power.

2. White-collar occupations generally confer higher incomes and more prestige than blue-collar work. The pink-collar occupations typically held by women offer little social prestige or income.

3. Schooling is also a resource that is distributed unequally. More than three-fourths of people over age twenty-five complete high school, but only one-fifth are college graduates.

4. Who we are at birth exerts a powerful effect on stratification in the United States; ancestry, race and ethnicity, sex, and religion are all related to social position.

5. The upper class, which is small (about 5 percent), includes the richest and most powerful families. Members of the upper-upper class, or the "old rich," derive their wealth through inheritance over several generations; those in the lower-upper class, or the "new rich," depend on earned income as their primary source of wealth.

6. The middle class includes 40 to 45 percent of the population. The upper-middle class may be distinguished from the rest of the middle class on the basis of higher income, higher-prestige occupations, and more schooling.

7. The working class, sometimes called the lower-middle class, includes about one-third of our population. With below-average income, working-class families have less financial security than middle-class families. Only one-third of working-class children reach college, and most eventually work in blue-collar or lower-prestige white-collar jobs.

8. About one-fifth of the U.S. population belongs to the lower class, which is defined as those living at or below the government's poverty threshold. People of African and Hispanic descent, as well as all women, are disproportionately represented in the lower class.

9. Social class affects nearly all aspects of life, beginning with health and survival in infancy and encompassing a wide range of attitudes and patterns of family living.

10. Social mobility is common in the United States as it is in other industrial societies; typically, however, there are only small changes from one generation to the next.

11. In the early 1970s, the historical rise in living standards for U.S. families ceased. A key reason for this stagnation is the expansion of the global economy that has reduced the number of (higher-paying) manufacturing jobs, replacing them with (lower-paying) service work.

12. The U.S. government classifies 36.5 million people as poor. About 40 percent of the poor are children under the age of eighteen. Two-thirds of the poor are white, but African Americans and Hispanics are disproportionately represented among people with low income. The "feminization of poverty" refers to the rising share of poor families headed by women.

13. Oscar Lewis advanced the *culture of poverty* thesis, suggesting that poverty is perpetuated by the social patterns of the poor themselves. Opposing this view, William Julius Wilson argues that poverty is caused by society's unequal distribution of jobs and wealth.

14. Homelessness may affect as many as 1.5 million people at some time during the course of a year.

KEY CONCEPTS

income wages or salaries from work and earnings from investments

wealth the total value of money and other assets, minus outstanding debts

intragenerational social mobility a change in social position occurring within a person's lifetime

intergenerational social mobility upward or downward social mobility of children in relation to their parents

relative poverty the deprivation of some people in relation to those who have more

absolute poverty a deprivation of resources that is life-threatening

feminization of poverty the trend by which women represent an increasing proportion of the poor

CRITICAL-THINKING QUESTIONS

1. Assess your own social class. Does your family have consistent standing on various dimensions of social stratification (such as income, education, and occupational prestige)? Why do most people find talking about their own social position awkward?

2. Identify some of the effects of U.S. social stratification on health, values, politics, and family patterns.

3. Would you be in favor of class-based affirmative action: that is, giving people born to lower-class families an edge in college admissions and company hiring? Why or why not?

4. Why is public assistance for the poor more controversial in the United States than in other industrial nations?

LEARNING EXERCISES

1. Develop several simple questions that, taken together, would let you measure someone's social class position. Try these on several adults—refine your questions as you proceed.

2. If you have access to the Internet, visit the site run by the government's Bureau of Economic Analysis: http://www.bea.doc.gov Here you will find income data by county as well as a host of other statistics about social inequality. See what you can learn about social standing in your part of the country.

3. During an evening of television viewing, assess the social class level of the characters you see in various shows. In each case, note precisely why you place someone in a particular social position. Do you discern any patterns?

4. Visit the social services office that oversees financial assistance to people with low incomes in your community. See what you can learn about how they are dealing with the 1996 welfare reform that limits poor people's benefits.

5. Install the CD-ROM packaged inside the back cover of your text and complete the activities designed to accompany this chapter.

Diego Rivera, *Formation of Revolutionary Leadership (Los Explotatores)*, 1926–27

GLOBAL STRATIFICATION

Standing against the burning sun at the edge of the North African desert, the two reporters nervously wait to meet their contacts. They have traveled thousands of miles in pursuit of a stunning story—that, in the 1990s, *slavery still exists*. To many people, slavery is a vestige of the 1800s, an evil that has been eradicated from the world. But this is not the case. And Gilbert Lewthwaite and Gregory Kane (1996) are about to prove it. They have traveled from Baltimore to the nation of Sudan with cash in hand to buy a human being.

Two men approach, carrying assault rifles. A few words pass between the men and the interpreter who accompanies the reporters. The interpreter then explains that the group will travel on foot to meet the slave trader. The sun climbs higher in the sky, and heat rises up from the ground. As they walk for one, two, three hours, the reporters drain their canteens, but the men with the rifles never drink at all.

Finally, up ahead stands a giant mango tree, where the group escapes from the pounding sun. Minutes later, seemingly out of nowhere, the slave trader appears, a small muscular figure with a close-fitting cap and a trimmed mustache. Calling himself Adam al Haj, he explains that he is in the business of trying to return to their families women and children seized by tribal raiders. Over the last five years, he claims, he has helped 473 slaves gain their freedom. His price is five cows or $500 per person. The reporters hand over $1,000 in cash. From around the tree, the trader's associates come forward with a dozen young boys, most showing signs of malnutrition. The trader motions to the reporters: Pick any two.

The boys are fearful, imagining that they are being resold and not knowing what their new owners will expect of them. For most such boys—seized by raiders in intertribal warfare—life as a slave means tending animals or doing menial labor for scraps of food and enduring periodic abuse. In the case of girls, sexual assault is commonplace.

The boys have no idea that the reporters mean to return them to their families, and so they stand expressionless, eyes fixed on the ground. The reporters are struck by the enormity of the moment, paralyzed by the thought of picking out two boys as if they were shirts on a rack. They settle on the boy who seems to be the oldest. Nearby stands a cluster of anxious parents who have heard that children are to be freed. The reporters ask if the boy's parents are there. The interpreter points and a man named Deng Kuot Mayen steps forward towards his son. The father points to a second boy—also his son. The deal is struck. The father is

SUPPLEMENTS: The *Data File* contains a detailed outline of Chapter 11 along with discussion topics and supplementary lecture material.

Q: "We now live in a global village . . ." Marshall McLuhan (1967)

Q: "Why is it that, according to the United Nations, almost 800 million people located in the so-called 'Third World' will be starving by the end of the century?" Andrew Webster

NOTE: We have revised the figures in Fig. 11–1 to reflect an emerging consensus that, in recent years, global income has become more concentrated.

NOTE: Peter Worsley (1990) claims that the term "third world" (and the three-worlds scheme) was first used in an August 14, 1952, article in *L'Observateur*, "Trois Mondes, Une Planète," by French demographer Alfred Sauvy.

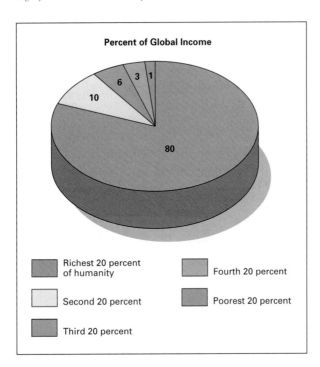

FIGURE 11–1 Distribution of World Income

Source: United Nations Development Programme (1997).

jubilant, dancing about and praising God for the return of his sons. Twelve-year-old Akok Deng Kuot and ten-year-old Garang Deng Kuot stand silently. It has been six years since they were seized: They do not recognize their father and it will be days before they fully comprehend that their ordeal is over.

While the details vary, this story is far from unique. In fact, experts estimate that tens of millions of children in poor countries across Latin America, Africa, and Asia have been seized by raiders or sold into bondage by their desperately poor families.

The fact that slavery still exists as we come to the end of this century is a powerful sign of the extent of social inequality in the world. As this chapter explains, poverty is a reality in the United States, but the problem is both more widespread and more severe in the poor countries of the world.

GLOBAL INEQUALITY: AN OVERVIEW

Chapter 10 described income inequality in the United States. In global perspective, however, social stratification is even more pronounced. Figure 11–1 divides the world's total income by fifths of the population. Recall that the richest 20 percent of the U.S. population earns almost 47 percent of the national income (see Figure 10–1); the richest 20 percent of global population, however, receives about 80 percent of all income. At the other end of the social scale, the poorest 20 percent of the U.S. population earns 4.2 percent of our national income; the poorest fifth of the world's people, by contrast, struggles to survive on just 1 percent of global income.

Because global income is so concentrated, even the average person living in a rich nation such as the United States lives extremely well by world standards. In fact, the living standard of most people below our government's poverty threshold far surpasses the living standard of the majority of the earth's people.

A WORD ABOUT TERMINOLOGY

Most people are familiar with the "Three Worlds" model for describing the unequal distribution of global income. Developed shortly after World War II, this model has been in wide use ever since. Rich, industrialized countries are "First World" nations, less-industrialized socialist countries are the "Second World," and the remaining nonindustrialized and poor countries are called the "Third World."

Recently, however, the "Three Worlds" model has lost validity. For one thing, it was a product of cold war politics by which the capitalist West (the First World) faced off against the socialist East (the Second World), while the rest of the world (the Third World) remained more or less on the sidelines. But the sweeping transformation of Eastern Europe and the former Soviet Union means that a distinctive Second World no longer exists. Even the superpower opposition that defined the cold war has faded in recent years.

A second problem is that the "Three Worlds" model lumped together as the Third World more than one hundred countries at different levels of development. Some relatively better-off nations of the Third World (such as Chile in South America) have ten times the per-person productivity of the poorest countries (including Ethiopia in eastern Africa).

Today's world calls for a modestly revised system of classification. We will, therefore, use the terms introduced in Chapter 1 ("The Sociological Perspective"): *High-income countries* are the richest forty

NOTE: A useful illustration here is to refer back to the "global village" box on page 6 in Chapter 1 ("The Sociological Perspective").
NOTE: By and large, poor countries have more internal stratification than the United States. Thus, the chasm separating the rich of the United States and the world's poorest people is truly immense. One manifestation of this is the pattern of wealthy U.S. households employing immigrant service workers.

GLOBAL: In 1995, the world's total wealth was about $500 trillion.
GLOBAL: A country's level of economic development reflects the distribution of the labor force by sectors of the economy. The relative percentages in agriculture, industry, and services: low-income countries, 62–15–22; middle-income countries, 32–28–40; high-income countries, 4–28–68 (author calculations from World Bank data).

When natural disasters strike rich societies, as in the 1993 floods in the midwest region of the United States, property loss is great but the loss of life is low. In poor societies, the converse is true, evident in the aftermath of this cyclone that devastated coastal Bangladesh, killing tens of thousands of poor people who lived on land prone to flooding.

nations with the most-developed economies and the highest overall standard of living. Next, the world's ninety *middle-income countries* are somewhat poorer nations whose economic development is more or less typical for the world as a whole. The remaining sixty *low-income countries* have the lowest productivity and the most severe and extensive poverty.

Compared to the older "Three Worlds" system, this new system has two advantages. First, it focuses on economic development rather than highlighting whether societies are capitalist or socialist. Second, this revision provides a more accurate picture of the relative economic development of the world's countries because it does not lump together all less-industrialized countries into a single "Third World."

Nonetheless, classifying the 191 nations on Earth into any three categories (or, even more crudely, to divide them into the "rich North" and the "poor South") ignores striking differences in their ways of life. The countries at each level of economic development have rich and varied histories, speak different languages, and encompass peoples proud of their cultural distinctiveness.

Keep in mind, too, that just as the world's nations form an economic hierarchy of very rich to very poor, so every country on earth is also internally stratified. In other words, the extent of global inequality is actually greater than national comparisons suggest, since

the most well-off people in rich countries (such as the United States) live worlds apart from the poorest people in low-income countries (such as Haiti, Sudan, and India). This striking contrast helps explain why, despite the affluence familiar to so many people in this nation, millions of the world's children fall victim to the horrors of slavery.

HIGH-INCOME COUNTRIES

High-income nations are rich because they were the first to be transformed by the Industrial Revolution more than two centuries ago, increasing their productive capacity one hundredfold. To understand the significance of the Industrial Revolution, consider that the small European nation of Holland is more productive than the vast continent of Africa below the Sahara Desert; likewise, tiny Belgium outproduces all of India.

Look back at Global Map 1–1 on page 7 to identify the forty high-income countries of the world. They include most of the nations of Western Europe, including England, where industrialization first began about 1750. Canada and the United States are also rich nations in which the Industrial Revolution was well under way by 1850. In Asia, high-income countries include Japan, as well as Singapore and Hong Kong (now part of the People's Republic of China). Finally, to the south of Asia, in the region known as

GLOBAL: The world's richest person is probably the Sultan of Brunei, worth $40 billion. In the U.S. Bill Gates is on top, with wealth of about $25 billion.

GLOBAL: The 1997 U.N. *Human Development Report* notes that the world's billionaires now number 447. The net wealth of the 10 richest exceeds the total national income of all the least-developed countries by more than 50 percent.

NOTE: Perhaps 5 percent of the U.S. population (13 million) are poor enough to experience the life of most residents of low-income nations. (That's roughly the population of Chile or Madagascar.)

GLOBAL: One indicator of economic development is the rate of passenger car ownership (persons per car). U.S., 1; Sweden, 2; Kuwait, 3; Panama, 12; Dominican Republic, 40; Paraguay, 44; Syria, 56 (U.S. Bureau of the Census, 1997).

Japan represents the world's high-income countries, in which industrial technology and economic expansion have produced material prosperity. The presence of market forces is evident in this view of downtown Tokyo (above, left). The Russian Federation represents the middle-income countries of the world. Industrial development has been slower in the former Soviet Union, as socialist economies have performed sluggishly. Residents of Moscow, for example, chafe at having to wait in long lines for their daily needs (above, right). The hope is that the introduction of a market system will raise living standards, although it probably will also increase economic disparity. Bangladesh (left) represents the low-income countries of the world. As the photograph suggests, these nations have limited economic development and rapidly increasing populations. The result is widespread poverty.

Oceania, Australia and New Zealand also rank as industrial, high-income nations.

Taken together, countries with the most-developed economies cover roughly 25 percent of the earth's land area, include parts of five continents, and lie mostly in the Northern Hemisphere. In mid-1998, the population of these nations was barely 900 million, or 15 percent of the earth's people. By global standards, rich nations are not densely populated; even so, some countries (such as Japan) are crowded while others (like Canada) are sparsely settled. Inside their borders, however, about three-fourths of the people in high-income countries live in or near cities.

High-income countries exhibit significant cultural differences—the nations of Europe, for example, recognize more than thirty official languages. But they all share an industrial capacity that generates, on average, a rich material life for their people. Per capita income in high-income societies ranges from about $10,000 annually (in Slovenia and South Korea) to more than $20,000 annually (in the United States and Switzerland).[1] In fact, members of the most-developed countries enjoy more than half the world's total income.

Finally, just as people in a single society perform specialized work, so is there a global division of labor. Generally speaking, high-income countries dominate in science and employ the most complex and productive technology. Production is capital-intensive, meaning high investments in factories and machinery. High-income countries also stand at the forefront of

[1]High-income countries have per capita annual income of at least $10,000. For middle- and low-income countries the comparable figures are $2,500 to $10,000, and below $2,500, respectively. All data reflect the United Nations' concept of "purchasing power parities," which avoids the distortion caused by exchange rates when converting all currencies to U.S. dollars. Instead, the data represent the local purchasing power of each nation's currency.

GLOBAL: The World Bank calculates that 100 million people in the Commonwealth of Independent States and the nations of Eastern Europe were poor (roughly 25%) prior to the recent reforms. They calculate that roughly the same number (but representing only 15%) of the people are poor in rich societies including the U.S., Canada, and the nations of Western Europe.
GLOBAL: The world's labor force numbers about 2.9 billion

people; about 30% (some 900 million people) are unemployed or underemployed, almost all living in poor nations.
GLOBAL: Refugees are on the rise, predominantly in the poorest regions of the world. Some 20 million people are displaced across international borders with another 25 million displaced within their own countries. As the numbers rise, rich countries are becoming more restrictive about admitting refugees.

the Information Revolution; most of the largest corporations that design and market computers, as well as most computer users, are found in rich nations. With the lion's share of wealth, high-income countries also control the world's financial markets; daily events in the financial exchanges of New York, London, and Tokyo affect people throughout the world.

MIDDLE-INCOME COUNTRIES

Middle-income countries have a per capita income ranging between $2,500 and $10,000, which is roughly the median for the world's *nations* (but above that for the world's *people* since most people live in low-income countries). Industrialization is limited and evident primarily in cities. About half of the people still live in rural areas and work in agriculture. Especially in the countryside, schooling, medical care, adequate housing and sometimes even safe water are hard to come by, which puts the standard of living far below what members of high-income societies take for granted.

Looking back at Global Map 1–1 (page 7), we see that about ninety of the world's nations fall into the middle-income category, and they are a very diverse lot. At the high end are Chile (Latin America), the Czech Republic (Europe), and Malaysia (Asia) with about $9,000 in annual income. At the low end are Guyana (Latin America), Albania (Europe), Swaziland (Africa), and China (Asia) with roughly $2,500 annually in per capita income.

One group of middle-income countries includes the former Soviet Union and the nations of Eastern Europe (in the past, known as the Second World). The former Soviet Union and its satellites in Eastern Europe—including Poland, the German Democratic Republic (East Germany), Czechoslovakia, Hungary, Romania, and Bulgaria—had predominantly socialist economies until popular revolts between 1989 and 1991 swept away their governments. Since then, these nations have begun to introduce market systems. This process, explained in Chapter 15 ("The Economy and Work"), has yet to solve serious economic woes; on the contrary, in the short term at least, nations of the former Eastern Bloc are battling high inflation, and many people enjoy fewer consumer goods than ever.

In the second category of middle-income countries are the oil-producing nations of the Middle East (or, less ethnocentrically, western Asia). These nations, including Saudi Arabia, Oman, and Iran, are very rich, but their wealth is so concentrated that most people receive little benefit and remain poor.

The third, and largest, category of middle-income countries is in Latin America and northern and western Africa. These nations (which might be termed the better-off countries of the Third World) include Argentina and Brazil in South America as well as Algeria and Botswana in Africa. Although South Africa's white minority lives as well as people in the United States, it too, must be considered middle income because its majority black population has far less income.

Together, middle-income countries cover roughly 40 percent of the earth's land area. About 2 billion people, or one-third of humanity, call these nations home. Some countries (like El Salvador) are far more crowded than others (such as Russia), but compared to high-income countries, these nations are densely populated.

LOW-INCOME COUNTRIES

Low-income countries of the world are primarily agrarian societies with little industry and very poor populations. These sixty nations, identified in Global Map 1–1 on page 7, are found primarily in central and eastern Africa as well as Asia. Low-income countries cover about 35 percent of the planet's land area but are home to half its people. The population density for poor countries is therefore high, although it is much higher in Asian countries (such as Bangladesh and India) than in more sparsely settled central African nations (like Chad and the Democratic Republic of Congo).

In poor countries, barely 25 percent of the people live in cities; most inhabit villages and farm as their families have for centuries. In fact, half the world's people are peasants, and most of them live in the low-income countries. By and large, peasants are staunchly traditional, following the folkways of their ancestors. And because they live without industrial technology, peasants are not very productive, one reason many endure severe poverty. Hunger, minimal housing, and frequent disease frame the lives of the world's poorest people.

This broad overview of global economic development is the foundation for understanding global inequality. People living in affluent nations such as the United States find it difficult to grasp the scope of human want in much of the world. From time to time, televised scenes of famine in very poor countries such as Ethiopia and Bangladesh give us a shocking glimpse of the absolute poverty that makes every day a life-and-death struggle. Behind these images lie cultural, historical, and economic forces that we shall explore in the remainder of this chapter.

Q: "While we may want to keep the term 'Third World' to describe a number of societies that are relatively poor, it would be wrong to see this poverty as being unconnected with the relative wealth of the 'First World'. In short, we need a global perspective if we are to make sense of the pattern of affluence and disadvantage in the world." Andrew Webster (1984:6)

NOTE: The upscale districts of Manila have U.S.-inspired names such as "Harvard Road," "Bel Air," and "Forbes."

GLOBAL: Starvation has been caused by social policies more than by natural forces such as droughts. Examples: 1846–50 Irish potato famine as food is diverted to England; 1932–34, some 5 million Soviet people die during Stalin's farm collectivization; 1958–61, perhaps 25 million starve during China's failed "Great Leap Forward."

By and large, rich nations such as the United States wrestle with the problem of relative poverty, meaning that poor people get by with less than we think they should have. In poor countries such as Ethiopia, absolute poverty means that people lack what they need to survive. What kind of diet, medical care, and access to clean water do you think families like these have?

GLOBAL WEALTH AND POVERTY

To classify a country as "low-income" does not mean that only poor people live there. On the contrary, the rich neighborhoods of Manila (the Philippines) and Madras (India) testify to some very high living standards. Indeed, given the low wages in most of these countries, the typical well-to-do household is staffed by several servants, a gardener, and a chauffeur. The following journal notes provide a sense of the dramatic inequality that marks poor nations.

October 14, 1994, Smokey Mountain, on the northern side of Manila, the Philippines. What caught my eye was how clean she was— a girl no more than seven or eight years old, hair carefully combed and wearing a freshly laundered dress. Her eyes followed us as we walked past; camera-toting Americans stand out in this, one of the poorest places in the entire world.

Fed by methane from the decomposing garbage, the fires never go out on Smokey Mountain, Manila's vast garbage dump. Smoke envelops the hills of refuse like a thick fog. But Smokey Mountain is more than a dump; it is a neighborhood that is home to thousands of people. The residents of Smokey Mountain are the poorest of the

poor, and one is hard pressed to imagine a setting more hostile to human life. Amidst the smoke and squalor, men and women do what they can to survive, picking plastic bags from the garbage and washing them in the river, stacking flattened cardboard boxes outside a family's plywood shack. And all over Smokey Mountain are children who must already sense the enormous odds against them. What chance do they have, living in families that earn scarcely a few hundred dollars a year? With barely any opportunity for schooling? Year after year, breathing this air?

And, against this backdrop of human tragedy, one lovely little girl has put on a fresh dress and gone out to play. . . .

With Smokey Mountain behind us, our taxi driver threads his way through heavy traffic towards the other side of Manila. The change is amazing: The forbidding smoke and smells of the dump give way to the polished neighborhoods that look like Miami or Los Angeles. In the distance, a cluster of yachts is visible on the bay. No more rutted streets; now we glide quietly along wide tree-lined boulevards filled with expensive Japanese cars. We

GLOBAL: Daily caloric consumption for some of the world's poorest countries (1992): Haiti, 1,707; Central African Republic, 1,691; Ethiopia, 1,610; Afghanistan, 1,523; Somalia, 1,505 (United Nations Development Programme, 1997).

Q: "In China, we waste nothing but time; in America, you waste everything but time." Comment made to the author by a student in the People's Republic of China

NOTE: The loss of life due to poor nutrition every 5 years surpasses the death toll from war, revolution, and murder during the last 150 years (Burch, 1983).

GLOBAL: The U.N. quality-of-life aggregate figures are: high-income countries, .907, middle-income countries, .667, and low-income countries, .403. Sudan, the nation featured in the chapter-opening vignette, has an index score of .333.

pass shopping plazas, upscale hotels, and high-rise office buildings. Every block or so stands the entrance to an exclusive residential enclave set off by gates and protected by armed guards. Here, in large, air-conditioned homes, the rich of Manila live and many of the poor work.

Poor nations are home to both rich and poor people, but hardly in equal numbers. Indeed, for most people in the world's poor countries, poverty is the rule. Moreover, with incomes of only several hundred dollars a year, the burden of poverty is greater than among the poor of the United States. This does not mean that deprivation here at home is a minor problem. Especially in a rich society, the lack of food, housing, and health care for tens of millions of people—almost half of them children—amounts to a national tragedy. Yet, poverty in poor countries is both *more severe* and *more extensive* than in the United States.

THE SEVERITY OF POVERTY

Poverty in poor countries is more severe than it is in rich nations such as the United States. The data in Table 11–1 give a statistical picture of global stratification. The first column of figures shows, for countries at each level of economic development, the gross domestic product (GDP).[2] Industrial societies have a high economic output mainly because of their industrial technology. A large, industrial nation like the United States had a 1994 GDP of about $7 trillion; Japan's GDP stood at about $4.6 trillion. Comparing GDP figures shows that the world's richest nations are thousands of times more productive than the poorest countries on earth.

The second column of figures in Table 11–1 indicates per capita GDP in terms of what the United Nations (1995) calls "purchasing power parities," the value of people's income in terms of what it can buy in

[2]Gross domestic product refers to all the goods and services on record as produced by a country's economy in a given year. Income earned outside the country by individuals or corporations is excluded; this is the key difference between GDP and gross national product (GNP), which includes foreign earnings. For countries that invest heavily abroad (Kuwait, for example), GDP is considerably less than GNP; in places where other nations invest heavily (Hong Kong), GDP is much higher than GNP. For countries that both invest heavily abroad and have considerable foreign investment at home (including the United States), the two measures are roughly comparable. For the present purpose, simply note the striking differences in productivity among various world economies.

TABLE 11–1 Wealth and Well-Being in Global Perspective, 1994

Country	Gross Domestic Product ($ billion)	GDP Per Capita (PPP$)*	Quality of Life Index
High Income			
Canada	543	21,459	.960
United States	6,648	26,397	.942
Japan	4,591	21,581	.940
Sweden	169	18,540	.936
Australia	332	19,285	.931
United Kingdom	1,017	18,621	.931
Switzerland	260	24,967	.930
Germany	2,046	19,675	.924
South Korea	377	10,656	.890
Middle Income			
Eastern Europe			
Hungary	41	5,884	.857
Poland	93	5,002	.834
Russian Federation	377	4,828	.792
Lithuania	5	4,011	.762
Latin America			
Argentina	282	8,937	.884
Mexico	377	7,384	.853
Brazil	555	5,362	.783
Asia			
Thailand	143	7,104	.833
Malaysia	71	8,865	.832
Middle East			
Iran, Islamic Republic of	64	5,766	.780
Saudi Arabia	117	9,338	.774
Africa			
Algeria	42	5,442	.737
Botswana	4	5,367	.673
Low Income			
Latin America			
Honduras	3	2,050	.575
Haiti	2	896	.338
Asia			
China, P.R.	522	2,604	.626
India	294	1,348	.446
Africa			
Zaire (now, Democratic Republic of Congo)	...	429	.381
Guinea	3	1,103	.271
Ethiopia	5	427	.244
Sierra Leone	1	643	.176

* These data are the United Nations' new "purchasing power parity" calculations that avoid currency rate distortion by showing the local purchasing power of each domestic currency.

Source: United Nations Development Programme, *Human Development Report, 1997* (New York: Oxford University Press, 1997).

GLOBAL: The share of the world's GNP by fifths of the global population resembles the distribution of wealth in the United States (compare Figures 10–1 and 11–1).
NOTE: Global production statistics also exclude the value of housework.
GLOBAL: According to calculations by various international agencies, the poorest nation in the world is probably Ethiopia, with annual per capita consumption below $100. As a result of war and drought, the lives of some 4 million people are currently at risk.
GLOBAL: Asia has the largest absolute number of poor (some 750 million people; between 20 and 25 percent); Africa has the highest proportion of poor people (35 percent).
NOTE: Life expectancy in poor countries is strongly depressed by high infant mortality.

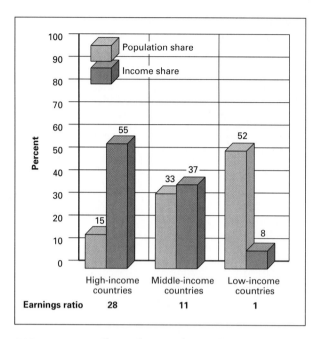

FIGURE 11–2 The Relative Share of Income and Population by Level of Economic Development

a local economy. The per capita GDP for rich countries like the United States, Switzerland, and Canada is very high—exceeding $20,000. Per capita GDP for middle-income countries, such as Brazil and Poland, is much lower—in the $5,000 range. And in the world's low-income countries, per capita annual income is no more than just a few hundred dollars. In the Republic of Congo or Ethiopia, for example, a typical person labors all year to make what the average worker in the United States earns in several days.

The last column in Table 11–1 indicates quality of life in the various nations. This index, calculated by the United Nations, combines income, education (extent of adult literacy and average years of schooling), and longevity (how long people typically live). Index values are decimals that fall between hypothetical extremes of 1 (highest) and zero (lowest). By this calculation, Canadians enjoy the highest quality of life (.960), with residents of the United States close behind (.942). At the other extreme, people in the African nation of Sierra Leone have the world's lowest quality of life (.176).

A key reason for marked disparities in quality of life is that economic productivity is lowest in precisely the regions of the globe where population growth is

highest. Figure 11–2 shows the current share of population and income for countries at each level of economic development. High-income countries are by far the most advantaged with 55 percent of global income supporting just 15 percent of the world's people. In middle-income nations, about 33 percent of the global population earn 37 percent of global income. This leaves half of the planet's population with just 8 percent of global income. Factoring together income and population, for every dollar earned in the low-income countries, someone in the high-income nations takes home twenty-eight dollars.

Relative Versus Absolute Poverty

The distinction made in the last chapter between relative and absolute poverty has an important application to global inequality. People living in rich countries typically focus on *relative poverty*, meaning that some people lack resources others take for granted. Relative poverty, by definition, cuts across every society, rich or poor.

Especially important in a global context is the concept of *absolute poverty*, a lack of resources that is life threatening. Human beings in absolute poverty lack the nutrition necessary for health and long-term survival. To be sure, some absolute poverty exists in the United States: Inadequate nutrition leaves children and elderly people vulnerable to illness and even outright starvation. But such immediately life-threatening poverty strikes only a small proportion of the U.S. population; in low-income countries, by contrast, one-third or more of the people are in desperate need.

Since absolute poverty threatens people with death, one indicator of the extent of the problem around the world is the median age at death. Global Map 11–1 identifies the age by which half of all people born in a society die. In rich societies, most people die after reaching the age of seventy-five; in poor countries, however, half of all deaths occur among children who have not yet reached the age of ten.

THE EXTENT OF POVERTY

Poverty in poor countries is more extensive than in rich nations such as the United States. Chapter 10 ("Social Class in the United States") indicated that the U.S. government officially classifies 13.7 percent of the population as poor. In low-income countries, however, *most* people live no better than the poor in our society, and many people are at the edge of survival. As Global Map 11–1 shows, the high death rates among children

THE MAP: The high mortality in low-income societies is all the more striking in light of the fact that infant mortality has actually dropped by half since 1965, from about 125 (per 1,000 live births) to about 65 today.

THEN AND NOW: Life expectancy in sub-Saharan Africa has risen from about 37 in 1960 to 51 today; but that's still about 25 years off the U.S. level.

GLOBAL: Life expectancy at birth is a major indicator of quality of life: Hong Kong, 82.4; Japan, 79.7; Canada, 79.3; U.K., 76.6; Taiwan, ROC, 76.3; Germany, 76.1; U.S., 76.0; Poland, 72.2; P.R. China, 70.0; Romania, 69.6; Russia, 63.8; Nigeria, 54.7; Angola, 47.3; Ethiopia, 46.6; Uganda, 39.7 (U.S. Bureau of the Census, 1997).

WINDOW ON THE WORLD

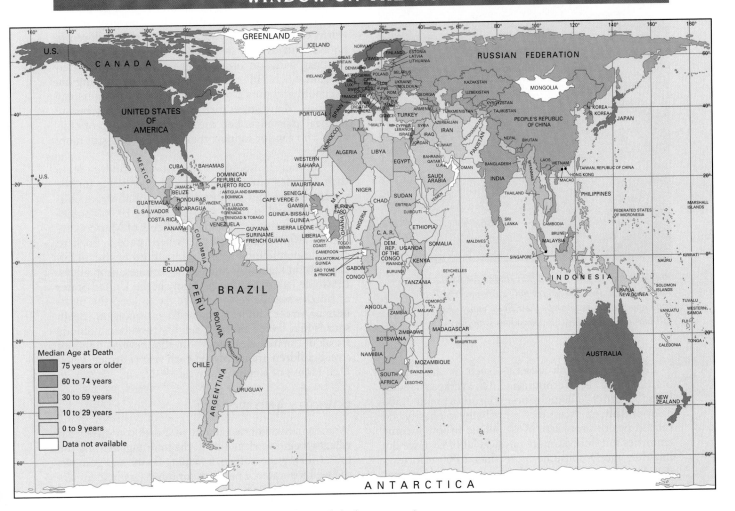

GLOBAL MAP 11–1 Median Age at Death in Global Perspective

This map identifies the age below which half of all deaths occur in any year. In the high-income countries of the world, including the United States, it is the elderly who face death—that is, people age seventy-five or older. In middle-income countries, including most of Latin America, most people die years or even decades earlier. In low-income countries, especially in Africa and parts of Asia, it is children who die, half of them never reaching their tenth birthday.

Sources: The World Bank (1993); map projection from *Peters Atlas of the World* (1990).

in Africa indicate that absolute poverty is greatest there: Half the population is malnourished. Worldwide, at any given time, 20 percent of the people (about 1 billion) suffer from chronic hunger. Periodic famine receives a great deal of press attention around the world, and each year hundreds of thousands of people die outright because they have no food. But the broader problems are undernutrition (too little food) and malnutrition (an unbalanced diet), which weaken people so that they can't work and leave them vulnerable to disease (Kates, 1996; United Nations Development Programme, 1996).

CHAPTER 11 Global Stratification   **297**

GLOBAL: One indicator of patterns of child poverty is the U.N.'s calculation of seriously underweight children below the age of five. In high-income countries, the figure is about 14%. The ten worst rates are in these low-income countries: Yemen, 39%; Cambodia, 40%; Eritrea, 41%; Myanmar, 43%; Lao People's Dem. Rep., 44%; Viet Nam, 45%; Ethiopia, 48%; Nepal, 49%; India, 53%; Bangladesh, 67%.

CYBER: UNICEF's annual State of the World's Children report is available online (http://www.unicef.org).
RESOURCE: Daphne Topouzis's article "Women's Poverty in Africa" is one of the cross-cultural selections in the Macionis and Benokraitis reader.

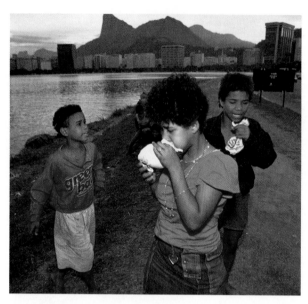

Rio de Janeiro is known as a playground for wealthy tourists. But many who live there know only stark poverty. Faced with little opportunity to improve their lives, many young people fall into despair and numb themselves with drugs.

Members of rich societies, such as the United States, tend to be overnourished. On average, an adult living in a high-income nation consumes about 3,500 calories daily, an excess that contributes to obesity and related health problems. Most people in low-income countries not only do more physical labor than we do, but they rarely consume more than 2,000 calories a day. In short, they lack sufficient food or, more precisely, enough of the right kinds of food.

Lack of necessary nutrition makes death a way of life in poor societies. In the ten minutes it takes to read this section of the chapter, about three hundred people in the world will die from disease because they have been weakened by an inadequate diet. This amounts to about 40,000 people a day, or 15 million people each year. Worldwide, the annual loss of life due to poverty is ten times greater than the number of lives lost in all the world's armed conflicts. Clearly, easing world hunger is one of the most serious responsibilities facing humanity today.

POVERTY AND CHILDREN

Death often comes early in poor societies, where families lack adequate food, safe water, secure housing, and access to medical care. In fact, many children in poor countries leave their families because their chances of surviving are better on the streets.

Organizations combating child poverty in the world estimate that some 75 million city children in poor countries beg, steal, sell sex, or serve as couriers for drug gangs in order to provide income for their families. Such a life almost always means dropping out of school and puts children at high risk of illness and violence. Many street girls, with little or no access to medical assistance, become pregnant—a case of children who cannot support themselves having still more children.

Another 25 million of the world's children leave their families altogether, sleeping and living on the streets as best they can. Perhaps half of all street children are found in Latin America. Some 10,000 homeless children move through the streets of Mexico City (Ross, 1996). And in Brazil, where people flock to cities desperate for a better life, millions of street children live in makeshift huts, under bridges, or in alleys. In Rio de Janeiro, known to many in the United States as Brazil's seaside resort, police try to keep the numbers of street children in check; on occasion, death squads may sweep through neighborhoods in a bloody ritual of "urban cleansing." In Rio, several hundred street children are murdered each year (Larmer, 1992; U.S. House of Representatives, 1992).

POVERTY AND WOMEN

Women in Sikandernagar, one of India's countless rural villages, begin work at 4:00 in the morning, lighting the fires, milking the buffalo, sweeping floors, and going to the well for water. They care for other family members as they rise. By 8:00, when many people in the United States are just beginning their day, these women move on to their "second shift," working under the hot sun in the fields until 5:00. Returning home, the women gather wood for their fires, all the time searching for whatever plants they can find to enrich the evening meal. The buffalo, too, are ready to eat, and the women tend to them. It is well past dark before their eighteen-hour day comes to an end (Jacobson, 1993:61).

In rich societies, the work women do is typically unrecognized, undervalued, and underpaid. In poor countries, this is even more the case. Furthermore, although women do most of the work in poor nations, they are disproportionately the poorest of the poor.

Families in poor societies depend on women's work to provide income. At the same time, tradition bars many women from school as it gives them primary responsibility for child rearing and maintaining

DIVERSITY: Of every 100 ministerial-level positions worldwide, four are held by women. By global region: Africa, 2.5; Asia and Pacific Islands, 1.6; Latin America, 4.0; socialist nations, 4.6; industrialized nations, 8.9 (Dr. Nafis Sadik, "Success in Developing Nations Depends on Women," *Popline*, Vol. 13, March–April, 1991, p. 4).

NOTE: The intensity of the problems of poor societies is most clearly evident in cities. Most of the largest cities of the world are now in poor countries, including Mexico City with some 25 million people.

NOTE: Points 1–3 below are incorporated into modernization theory; points 4–5 are elements of dependency theory. Both theories are discussed later in this chapter.

the household. The United Nations estimates that, in poor societies, men own 90 percent of the land, a far greater gender disparity in wealth than in industrial nations. Multilayered systems of tradition and law subordinate women in poor societies so that about 70 percent of the world's roughly 1 billion people near absolute poverty are women (Hymowitz, 1995).

Women in poor countries have limited access to birth control (which raises the birth rate), and they typically give birth without the help of trained health personnel. Figure 11–3 draws a stark contrast between high- and low-income countries in this regard.

Overall, gender inequality is strongest in low-income societies, especially in Asia where cultural traditions favor males. As the box on page 300 explains, the cultural preference for males is evident in virtually every dimension of life, and has produced a stunning lack of females in some regions (Kishor, 1993).

SLAVERY

Poor societies are vulnerable to a host of related problems: hunger, illiteracy, warfare, and slavery. Anti-Slavery International (ASI) is an organization that helped bring an end to slavery in the British Empire in 1833; the United States banned slavery in 1865. According to ASI, as many as 400 million men, women, and children (almost 7 percent of humanity) currently live in conditions that amount to slavery (Janus, 1996).

ASI distinguishes four types of slavery. First is *chattel slavery*, in which one person owns another. The number of chattel slaves is difficult to estimate because slavery violates laws almost everywhere. But slave trading—as portrayed in the opening to this chapter—takes place in many countries, mostly in Africa, the Middle East, and Asia. Second, *child slavery* refers to children abandoned by their families or boys and girls so poor that they take to the streets in an effort to survive. Perhaps 100 million children—many in poor countries of Latin America—fall into this category. Third, *debt bondage* refers to the practice, found in dozens of countries around the world, of paying people to work (sometimes as prostitutes), but charging them more than they earn for food and shelter. Never able to pay their debts, these workers are, for practical purposes, enslaved. Fourth, *servile forms of marriage* also amount to slavery. In India, Thailand, and some African nations, families marry off women against their will. Many end up as slaves to their husband's family; some are forced into prostitution.

In 1948, the United Nations issued the Universal Declaration of Human Rights, which states: "No one

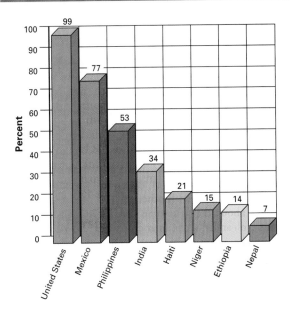

GLOBAL SNAPSHOT

FIGURE 11–3 Percentage of Births Attended by Trained Health Personnel

Source: United Nations Development Programme (1997).

shall be held in slavery or servitude; slavery and the slave trade shall be prohibited in all their forms." Unfortunately, fifty years later, this social evil persists.

CORRELATES OF GLOBAL POVERTY

What accounts for severe and extensive poverty throughout much of the world? The rest of this chapter weaves together explanations from the following facts about poor societies.

1. **Technology.** Almost two-thirds of people in low-income countries farm the land; the productive power of industrial technology is all but absent. Since energy from human muscle or beasts of burden falls far short of the force of steam, oil, or nuclear power, the use of complex machinery is greatly limited. Moreover, the focus on farming, rather than on specialized production, inhibits development of human skills and abilities.

2. **Population growth.** As Chapter 21 ("Population and Urbanization") explains, countries with the least-developed economies have the world's

THE MAP: An apparent inconsistency is that, while the economic gap between rich and poor countries has remained stable, the two categories of nations are closing on many social indicators. This is because rising income produces greater improvement in living standards for lower-income countries.

Q: "I am convinced that the global economy makes it more difficult to devise and enact redistributive policies." Robert A. Dahl

NOTE: Many products from rich countries—electricity, technology, communications equipment—are getting cheaper, which helps raise living standards abroad. The manufactured goods-raw goods exchange, in other words, has improved over time.

GLOBAL: Generally speaking, striking political and economic transformations in recent years have been centered in nations of the global semiperiphery (Korzeniewicz & Awbrey, 1992).

WINDOW ON THE WORLD

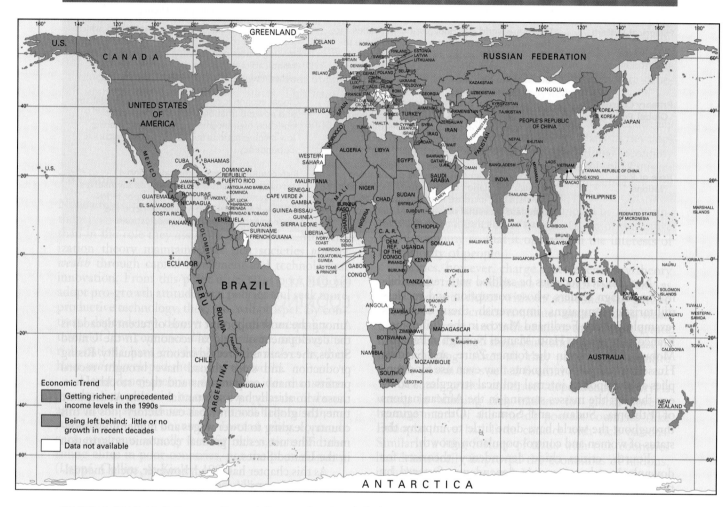

GLOBAL MAP 11–2 Prosperity and Stagnation in Global Perspective

In about sixty nations of the world, people are enjoying a higher standard of living than ever before. These prospering countries include some rich nations (such as the United States) and some poor nations (especially in Asia). For most countries, however, living standards have remained steady or even slipped in recent decades. Especially in Eastern Europe and the Middle East, some nations have experienced economic setbacks since the 1980s. And in sub-Saharan Africa, some nations are no better off than they were in 1960. The overall pattern is economic polarization, with an increasing gap between rich and poor nations.

Source: United Nations Development Programme (1996); updates by the author.

high-income countries but also dozens of poorer countries, especially in Asia. These developing nations stand as evidence that the market forces endorsed by modernization theory can raise living standards.

In about one-third of the world's countries, however, living standards are actually lower today than they were in 1980. A rising wave of poverty, especially in the nations of sub-Saharan Africa, supports the dependency theory assertion that current economic arrangements are leaving hundreds of millions of people behind.

The picture now emerging from this evidence thus calls into question arguments put forward by both

Q: "One billion more people are being fed today than in the early 1970s, but the number of hungry people continues to increase."
John W. Helmuth

GLOBAL: Types of foods change with rising income. People in low-income countries eat basic cereals; middle-income nations provide basic packaged foods; the availability of frozen foods marks high-income countries. In the highest-income countries, prepared foods are popular, with fresh foods and health foods enjoyed by the richest of the world's people.

NOTE: Crudely, at least, the "optimists" in the world hunger debate are friendly toward modernization theory; the "pessimists" typically favor dependency theory.

DISCUSS: Do you think there needs to be a universal "right to food"?

CONTROVERSY & DEBATE

Will the World Starve?

The animals' feet leave their prints
on the desert's face.
Hunger is so real, so very real,
that it can make you walk around
a barren tree looking for
nourishment.
Not once,
Not twice,
Not thrice . . .

These lines, by Indian poet Amit Jayaram, describe the appalling hunger found in Rajasthan, in northwest India. Hunger casts its menacing shadow not only in Asia, but also over much of Latin America, most of Africa, and even parts of North America. Throughout the world, hundreds of millions of adults do not eat enough food to enable them to work. And, most tragically, some 10 million of the world's children die each year because of hunger. As we near the end of this century, what are the prospects for eradicating the wretched misery of human beings who endure daily hunger?

It is easy to be pessimistic. The population of poor countries is increasing by 70 million people annually—equivalent to adding another Egypt to the world every year. Poor countries cannot feed the people they have now; how will they feed *twice* as many people just one generation from now?

In addition, hunger forces poor people to exploit the earth's resources by using short-term strategies for food production that lead to long-term disaster. For example, farmers are cutting rain forests in order to increase their farmland. But, without the protective canopy of trees, much of this land will turn to desert. Taken together, rising populations that borrow against the future raise the specter of unprecedented hunger, human misery, and political calamity.

But there are also grounds for optimism. Thanks to the Green Revolution, worldwide food production is up sharply over the last fifty years, well outpacing the growth in population. The world's economic productivity has risen steadily, so that the average person on the planet now has more food and other necessities than ever before.

This economic growth also has increased life expectancy, access to safe water, and adult literacy, while, around the world, infant mortality is half of what it was in 1960.

So what are the prospects for eradicating world hunger—especially in low-income nations? Overall, we see less hunger in both rich and poor countries, and a smaller *share* of the world's people hungry now than, say, in 1960. But as global population increases, with 90 percent of children born in middle- and low-income countries, the *number* of lives at risk is as great today as ever before. Moreover, as noted earlier, although many low-income countries have made solid gains, many more are stagnating or even losing ground.

Also bear in mind that aggregate data mask trends in various world regions. The "best-case" region of the world is eastern Asia, where incomes (controlled for inflation) have tripled over the last generation. It is to Asia that the "optimists" in the global hunger debate typically turn for evidence that poor countries can and do raise living standards and reduce hunger. The "worst-case" region of the world is sub-Saharan Africa, where living standards have actually fallen over the last decade and more and more people are pushed to the brink of starvation. It is here that technology is least evident and birth rates are highest. Pessimists typically look to Africa when they argue that poor countries are losing ground in the struggle to keep their people well nourished.

Television brings home the tragedy of hunger when news cameras focus on starving people in places like Ethiopia and Somalia. But hunger—and early death from illness—is the plight of millions all year round. The world has the technical means to feed everyone; the question is, do we have the moral determination to do so?

Continue the debate . . .

1. *In your opinion, what are the primary causes of global hunger?*

2. *Do you place more responsibility for solving this problem on poor countries or rich ones? Why?*

3. *Do you consider yourself an "optimist" or a "pessimist" about the problem of global hunger? Why?*

Sources: United Nations Development Programme (1994, 1995, 1996, 1997).

theories, and both camps are revising their views on the major "paths to development." On the one hand, few societies seeking economic growth now favor a market economy completely free of government control, which challenges orthodox modernization theory and its free-market approach to development. On the other hand, recent upheavals in the former Soviet Union and Eastern Europe demonstrate that a global re-evaluation of

EXERCISE: Ask students to look over past issues of *National Geographic*. How does this popular magazine portray life in poor nations? In light of facts noted in this chapter, is the portrayal realistic or not?

GLOBAL: The World Bank claims that, during the 1990s, the population of poor countries will increase by about 2% annually versus 0.5% for rich nations; economic growth in poor countries will be negative, against positive growth for the rich societies.

Q: "Current leftist journals are full of tortured attempts to interpret the developments of the last few years in Europe and elsewhere, most of them attempts to deny the obvious. I have every expectation that sociologists will be whole-hearted participants in this enterprise, bravely led by the old cohorts of dependency theory." Peter Berger (1992).

socialism is underway. Since these uprisings follow decades of poor economic performance and political repression, many poor societies are reluctant to consider a socialist path to development. Because dependency theory has historically supported socialist economic systems, changes in world socialism will surely generate new thinking here as well.

Perhaps the most basic problem caused by poverty is hunger. As the box on page 311 explains, many analysts wonder if we have the means and determination to rid the planet of hunger before it overtakes more of the world.

Although the world's future is uncertain, we have learned a great deal about global stratification. One key insight, offered by modernization theory, is that poverty is partly a *problem of technology*. A higher standard of living depends on raising agricultural and industrial productivity. A second insight, derived from dependency theory, is that global inequality is also a *political issue*. Even with higher productivity, we must address crucial questions concerning how resources are distributed—both within societies and around the globe.

Note, too, that while economic development increases living standards, it also strains the natural environment. Imagine, for example, if almost 1 billion people in India were suddenly to become "middle class," with automobiles guzzling gasoline and spewing hydrocarbons into the atmosphere.

Finally, the vast gulf that separates the world's richest and poorest people puts everyone at greater risk of war, as the most impoverished people challenge the social arrangements that threaten their very lives. In the long run, we can achieve peace on this planet only by ensuring that all people enjoy a significant measure of dignity and security.

SUMMARY

1. In the world as a whole, social stratification is more pronounced than in the United States. About 15 percent of the world's people live in industrialized, high-income countries such as the United States and earn 55 percent of the earth's total income. Another one-third live in middle-income countries with limited industrialization and earn about 37 percent of all income. Half the world's population live in low-income countries that have yet to industrialize; they earn only 8 percent of global income.

2. While relative poverty is found everywhere, poor societies contend with widespread, absolute poverty. Worldwide, the lives of some 1 billion people are at risk due to poor nutrition. About 15 million people, most of them children, die every year from various causes because they lack proper nourishment.

3. Women are more likely than men to be poor nearly everywhere in the world. Male domination of females is much more pronounced in poor, agrarian societies than it is in industrial societies such as the United States.

4. The poverty found in much of the world is a complex problem reflecting limited industrial technology, rapid population growth, traditional cultural patterns, internal social stratification, male domination, and global power relationships.

5. Modernization theory maintains that successful development hinges on acquiring advanced productive technology. This approach views traditional cultural patterns as the major barrier to modernization.

6. Modernization theorist W. W. Rostow identifies four stages of development: traditional, take-off, drive to technological maturity, and high mass consumption.

7. Arguing that rich societies have the keys to creating wealth, modernization theory shows how rich nations can assist poor nations: by bolstering population control strategies, providing crop-enhancing and industrial technologies, and providing investment capital and other foreign aid.

8. Critics of modernization theory say this approach has produced limited economic development in the world, while ethnocentrically assuming that poor societies can follow the path to development taken by rich nations centuries ago.

9. Dependency theory claims global wealth and poverty are directly linked to the historical operation of the capitalist world economy.

10. The dependency of poor countries on rich ones began five centuries ago with colonialism. Even though most poor countries have since won political independence, dependency theorists point to neocolonialism as a form of exploitation carried out by multinational corporations.

11. Immanuel Wallerstein views the high-income countries as the privileged "core" of the capitalist

world economy; middle-income nations are the "semiperiphery," and poor nations form the global "periphery."

12. Three factors—export-oriented economies, a lack of industrial capacity, and foreign debt—perpetuate poor countries' dependency on rich nations.

13. Critics of dependency theory argue that this approach overlooks the success of many nations in creating new wealth. Total global wealth, they point out, has increased fivefold since 1950. Furthermore, the world's poorest societies are not those with the strongest ties to rich countries.

14. Both modernization theory and dependency theory offer useful insights into global inequality. Some evidence supports each view. Less controversial is the urgent need to address the various problems caused by worldwide poverty.

KEY CONCEPTS

colonialism the process by which some nations enrich themselves through political and economic control of other countries

neocolonialism a new form of global power relationships that involves not direct political control but economic exploitation by multinational corporations

multinational corporation a large corporation that operates in many countries

modernization theory a model of economic and social development that explains global inequality in terms of technological and cultural differences among societies

dependency theory a model of economic and social development that explains global inequality in terms of the historical exploitation of poor societies by rich societies

CRITICAL-THINKING QUESTIONS

1. Distinguish between relative and absolute poverty. How do the two concepts describe social stratification in the United States and the world as a whole?

2. Why do many analysts argue that economic development in low-income countries depends on raising the social standing of women?

3. State the basic tenets of modernization theory and dependency theory. What are several criticisms of each approach?

4. Based on what you have read here and elsewhere, what is your prediction about the extent of global hunger fifty years from now? Will the problem be more or less serious? Why?

LEARNING EXERCISES

1. Keep a log book noting any advertising involving low-income countries (for coffee from Colombia or exotic vacations to Egypt or India) that you see on television or in other media. What image of life in low-income countries does the advertising present? In light of this chapter, do you think these images are accurate?

2. On most campuses, there are students who have come to the United States from poor countries. Approach one such woman and one such man. Explain that you have been studying global stratification, and ask if they would be willing to share their views of life in their countries. You may be able to learn quite a bit from them.

3. If you have access to the Internet, visit the Web site of an organization opposing African slavery: the Coalition Against Slavery in Mauritania and Sudan. Their address is http://www.columbia. edu/~slc11/ This site provides information about the problem of slavery as well as links to other organizations fighting this problem.

4. Look over all the global maps in this text. As you examine them, identify the various social traits associated with the world's richest and poorest nations. Try to use both modernization theory and dependency theory to build theoretical explanations of the patterns you find.

5. Install the CD-ROM packaged inside the back cover of your text and complete the activities designed to accompany this chapter.

Romare Bearden, *SHE-BA*, 1970

Romare Bearden (American, 1914–1988) *SHE-BA*, 1970, collage on composition board, 48 × 35⅞ in.
Ella Gallup Sumner and Mary Catlin Sumner Collection Fund. © Wadsworth Atheneum, Hartford.
© Romare Bearden Foundation/Licensed by VAGA, New York, NY.

CHAPTER 12

SEX AND GENDER

The little girl, just eighteen months old, huddled in the corner of the room, fighting back tears. Meserak Ramsey eyed her with concern. Ramsey, a friend of the child's mother, was there visiting. Both women had immigrated from Nigeria to the United States. The child was obviously in pain, and Ramsey crouched down to see what was wrong.

At that moment, the girl's mother entered the room. She explained that her daughter had just had a clitoridectomy, or female circumcision, whereby the clitoris is surgically removed. In Nigeria, Togo, Somalia, Egypt, and three dozen other nations in Africa and the Middle East, this painful procedure is commonly performed on young girls by midwives, tribal practitioners, or, sometimes, doctors, and typically without anesthesia. Meserak Ramsey swallowed hard. She, too, had suffered a genital mutilation as a child.

Why would anyone want to subject young girls to pain and the risk of infection and other complications? Because, according to the cultural tradition in some societies, women must be virgins at marriage and remain sexually faithful to their husbands. Genital mutilation eliminates sexual sensation so, the thinking goes, a female is less likely to violate sexual mores. Experts estimate that at least 100 million women in the world have suffered genital mutilation, and perhaps thousands of these procedures take place each year in the United States.

In most cases, immigrant mothers and grandmothers who have themselves been mutilated expect young girls in their family to follow suit. Indeed, many immigrant families subject their daughters to genital mutilation because they believe social mores in the United States are lax. "I don't have to worry about her now," explains Ramsey's friend, looking at her daughter. "She'll be a good girl" (Crossette, 1995).

Many people think there is something "natural" about sexuality, and that sexual behavior is simply an expression of the same biology that animates "the birds and the bees." But as we shall see, sex is bound up with culture, so that sexual practices—and our response to them—vary significantly from time to time and from place to place. Ideas about sexuality are also closely tied to the ways that societies expect girls to be "feminine" and boys to be "masculine." We can begin, then, by distinguishing between the key concepts of sex and gender.

SEX: A BIOLOGICAL DISTINCTION

Sex refers to *the biological distinction between females and males.* Sex is closely related to reproduction, in which both females and males play a part. A female ovum and a male sperm, each containing twenty-three pairs of chromosomes (biological codes that guide physical development), combine to form a fertilized embryo. One of these chromosome pairs determines the child's sex. The mother always contributes an X chromosome; the father contributes either an X or a Y. A second X

SUPPLEMENTS: An outline of this chapter, along with supplementary lecture material, is included in the *Data File*.
NOTE: The ratio of male to female fetuses is actually higher than 105/100, since male embryos are more likely to abort spontaneously than female embryos are. This further complicates the issue of which is the "weaker" sex.
Q: "To be born a woman means to inhabit, from early infancy to the last day of life, a psychological world which differs from the world of man." Mirra Komarovsky
NOTE: Students may confuse transsexuals (individuals feeling they are the other sex) with transvestism (wearing clothing appropriate to the other sex). Similarly, bisexuality (attraction to people of either sex) is sometimes confused with androgyny (having physical characteristics of both sexes).

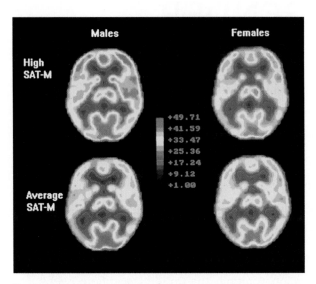

Do women and men differ in mental abilities? That is, do the two sexes think differently? Using high technology equipment that creates images such as these, physical scientists note slightly dissimilar patterns of brain activity in women and men when they are performing mathematical calculations. Sociologists link these small differences in mathematical aptitude (as well as other differences in interests and attitudes) to the social environment, which, right from birth, sets down different expectations for girls and boys.

from the father produces a female (XX) embryo; a Y from the father produces a male (XY) embryo. A child's sex, then, is determined at conception.

Within weeks, the sex of an embryo starts to guide its development. If the embryo is male, testicular tissues begin producing testosterone, a hormone that stimulates the development of the male genitals. In the absence of testosterone, the embryo develops female genitals. In the United States, about 105 boys are born for every 100 girls, but a higher death rate among males makes females a slight majority by the time people reach their mid-thirties (U.S. Bureau of the Census, 1997).

SEX AND THE BODY

At birth, females and males are distinguished by **primary sex characteristics,** namely, *the genitals, organs used to reproduce the human species.* Further sex differentiation occurs during puberty when reproductive systems become fully operational. At this point, humans exhibit **secondary sex characteristics,** *bodily development, apart from the genitals, that distinguishes biologically*

mature females and males. To accommodate pregnancy, giving birth, and nurturing infants, adolescent females develop wider hips, breasts, and soft fatty tissue, thereby providing a reserve supply of nutrition for pregnancy and breast-feeding. Adolescent males, usually slightly taller and heavier than females from birth, typically develop more muscle in the upper body, more extensive body hair, and deeper voices. These are general differences, however: Some males are smaller, have less body hair, and have higher voices than some females.

Hermaphrodites

Sex is not always a clear-cut matter. In rare cases, a hormone imbalance before birth produces a **hermaphrodite** (a word derived from Hermaphroditus, the offspring of the mythological Greek gods Hermes and Aphrodite, who embodied both sexes), *a human being with some combination of female and male genitalia.*

Because our culture is uneasy about sexual ambiguity, some people respond to hermaphrodites with confusion and even disgust. But such need not be the case: The Pokot of eastern Africa are indifferent to what they define as a simple biological error, and the Navaho regard hermaphrodites with awe, believing they embody the full potential of both the female and the male (Geertz, 1975).

Transsexuals

Hermaphrodites may undergo genital surgery to gain the appearance (and occasionally the function) of a sexually normal female or male. Other people deliberately change their sex: **Transsexuals** are *people who feel they are one sex though biologically they are the other.* Tens of thousands of transsexuals in the United States have surgically altered their genitals because they feel "trapped in the wrong body" (Restak, 1979, cited in Offir, 1982:146).

SEXUAL ORIENTATION

Sexual orientation refers to *an individual's preference in terms of sexual partners: same sex, other sex, either sex, neither sex* (Lips, 1993). For most living things, sexuality is biologically programmed, and, of course, biology is at work in humans, too. But, for humans, sexual orientation also is bound up in a complex web of cultural norms and attitudes. The norm in all industrial societies is *heterosexuality* (*hetero* is a Greek word meaning "the other of two"), meaning a person is sexually attracted to someone of the other sex. However,

SOCIAL SURVEY: "What about sexual relations between two adults of the same sex?" (GSS 1996, N = 1,923; *Codebook*, 1996:216)

"Always wrong"   56.1%   "Not wrong at all"   26.2%
"Almost always wrong"   4.8%   DK/NR   7.2%
"Wrong only sometimes"   5.7%

NOTE: Homosexuality presents an interesting case of shifting

labels. In the wake of decades of moral condemnation, in 1952 the American Psychological Association (APA) declared being gay or lesbian a "sociopathic personality disturbance," and public opinion reflected this new notion of homosexuality as a "sickness." Then, in 1974, the APA changed its stance once again, redefining homosexuality as simply "a form of sexual behavior" (Conrad & Schneider, 1980:193–209).

homosexuality (*homo* is the Greek word for "the same"), being attracted to people of the same sex, is not uncommon. Other sexual orientations are *bisexuality* (attraction to either sex) and *asexuality* (attraction to neither sex).

Although all societies endorse heterosexuality, many tolerate—and some have even encouraged—homosexuality. Among the ancient Greeks, for instance, upper-class men considered homosexuality the highest form of relationship, shunning women as their intellectual inferiors. As they saw it, heterosexuality was little more than a reproductive necessity, and men who did not have homosexual relations were viewed as deviant. But because homosexual relations do not permit reproduction, no record exists of a society that favored homosexuality to the exclusion of heterosexuality (Kluckhohn, 1948; Ford & Beach, 1951; Greenberg, 1988).

The Origin of Sexual Orientation

How does a person develop a particular sexual orientation? There is no definitive answer to this question, but mounting evidence suggests that homosexuality and heterosexuality are rooted in biological factors present at birth and reinforced by hormone balance as well as social experiences (Gladue, Green, & Hellman, 1984; Weinrich, 1987; Troiden, 1988; Isay, 1989; Puterbaugh, 1990; Angier, 1992; Gelman, 1992). Noting that most adults who describe themselves as homosexuals have had some heterosexual experiences (and many nominal heterosexuals have had at least homosexual feelings), researchers conclude that sexual orientation is a highly complex human trait affected by both nature and nurture.

Moreover, there is no reason to think that sexual orientation is established in precisely the same way for everyone. Though physical and social scientists have discovered a great deal about sexual orientation, we still have much to learn.

The Gay Rights Movement

In the 1960s, homosexuals became more visible and outspoken. They adopted the term *gay* to affirm their satisfaction with their sexual orientation. Gays also began to challenge stereotypes—pointing out that gay people vary as much as "straights"—and to organize in opposition to pervasive discrimination.

In recent years, gay men have had to contend with acquired immune deficiency syndrome, or AIDS. Not only has this deadly disease killed more than 200,000

More than 1 million gay and lesbian couples in the United States are currently raising children. This trend suggests that people of all sexual orientations support "traditional family values."

gay men (and almost as many nongay people) in the United States; it has provoked a renewed outburst of prejudice, discrimination, and outright violence against gays. But the longer-term picture shows a gradual softening of public attitudes. Although just over half of U.S. adults define homosexuality as morally wrong (down from three-fourths in the 1970s), the same majority thinks gays and straights deserve equal workplace opportunities (Salholz, 1990; NORC, 1996:216).

Until our society becomes more accepting of homosexuality, some gay people will choose to remain "in the closet," not disclosing their sexual orientation. Heterosexuals can begin to understand what this secrecy means by imagining what it would be like never to talk about their romances with parents, roommates, or colleagues (Offir, 1982).

For their part, many gay men and many gay women (commonly called *lesbians*) describe their critics as *homophobic* (with Greek roots meaning "fearing sameness"). Homophobia, first used in the late 1960s,

NOTE: The gay rights movement has long maintained that 10% of our society's members are gay, which lends moral urgency to their pursuit of social acceptance and equal standing (Kirk & Madsen, 1989). But a considerable number of recent studies in the United States and abroad have challenged this assertion, suggesting that it is simply too high (Crispell, 1992; Cole & Gorman, 1993; Horowitz et al., 1993).

NOTE: The 1992 NORC sex survey also painted a surprisingly moderate level of overall sexuality. Men reported a median of six sex partners (since age 18), women two; only 8% of men and 7% of women reported having sex four or more times per week during the past year; 10% of women and 14% of men reported no sex during the past year. Fifty-four percent of men but only 19% of women claimed to think about sex daily.

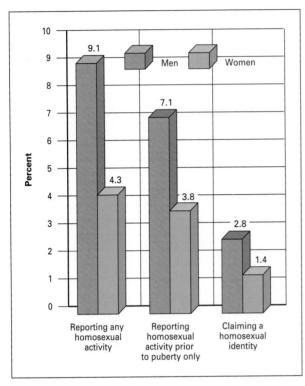

FIGURE 12–1 Measuring Sexual Orientation

Source: Laumann et al. (1994).

refers to an irrational fear of gay people (Weinberg, 1973). The concept of homophobia turns the table on society: Instead of asking "What's wrong with gay people?" the question becomes "What's wrong with people who can't accept a different sexual orientation?"

How Many Gay People?

What share of our population is gay? Answering this question is difficult because, for one thing, people are not always willing to reveal their sexuality to strangers (or even family members); for another, sexual orientation is not a matter of neat, mutually exclusive categories. Pioneering sex researcher Alfred Kinsey (1948, 1953) described sexual orientation as a continuum, from exclusively homosexual at one end to equally homosexual and heterosexual in the middle, to exclusively heterosexual at the other end. Kinsey suggested that about 4 percent of males and 2 percent of females have an exclusively same-sex orientation, although he also estimated that at least one-third of men and

one-eighth of women have at least one homosexual experience leading to orgasm.

In light of the Kinsey studies, most social scientists placed the gay share of the population at 10 percent. But a comprehensive 1992 survey[1] of sexuality in the United States indicates that precisely how one operationalizes "homosexuality" makes a big difference in the results (Laumann et al., 1994). As Figure 12–1 shows, about 9 percent of U.S. men and about 4 percent of women reported homosexual activity at some time in their lives. The second set of numbers suggests that a significant share of men (less so women) have a childhood homosexual experience that is not repeated after puberty. Finally, 2.8 percent of men and 1.4 percent of women define themselves as partly or entirely homosexual.

Bisexuality

Alfred Kinsey and his colleagues treated sexual orientation as an "either/or" trait: To be more homosexual is, by definition, to be less heterosexual. But the evidence suggests that same-sex and other-sex attractions operate independently. At one extreme, *asexual* people experience little sexual attraction to people of either sex; at the other, *bisexual* people feel strong attraction to people of both sexes.

In a recent national sexuality survey, less than 1 percent of adults described themselves as bisexual. But bisexuality is far more popular (at least as a phase) among younger people (especially on college campuses) who reject rigid conceptions of proper relationships (Laumann et al., 1994; Leland, 1995). Many bisexuals, then, do not think of themselves as either gay or straight, and their behavior reflects elements of both gay and straight living.

GENDER: A CULTURAL DISTINCTION

Gender refers to *the significance a society attaches to biological categories of female and male.* Gender is a basic organizing principle of society that shapes how we think about ourselves and guides how we interact with others. But while gender concerns difference, it also involves *hierarchy*, because it affects the opportunities

---

[1]This national survey involved 3,432 adults, aged eighteen to fifty-nine. Individuals responded to the first two items using a self-administered, anonymous questionnaire that they sealed in an envelope before giving it to the interviewer; subjects responded verbally to the third item in an interview.

Q: "At the bottom of it all, man's job is to protect woman, and woman's job is to protect her infant; all else is luxury." Steven Goldberg

RESOURCE: By and large, sociologists accept the view that biology plays no significant role in gender formation. Steven Goldberg's quote is therefore likely to elicit strong disapproval from most sociologists. Goldberg presents his evidence in "Reaffirming the Obvious" and "Utopian Yearning Versus Scientific Curiosity," *Society*, Vol. 23, No. 6 (September/October 1986):4–7 and 29–39.

Q: "Differences between the male and female endocrine/central nervous system are such that—statistically speaking—males have a greater tendency to exhibit whatever behavior is necessary in any environment to attain dominance in hierarchies . . ." Steven Goldberg

and constraints we face throughout our lives (Ferree & Hall, 1996; Riley, 1997).

The inequality inherent in gender is no simple matter of biological difference between the two sexes. Females and males do differ biologically, of course, but, as Figure 12–2 suggests, the physical abilities of men and women are more alike than we may think.

What are the main biological differences between the sexes? Beyond the primary and secondary sex characteristics already noted, males around the world average 150 pounds, compared to about 120 pounds for females. In addition, males have more muscle in the arms and shoulders, so the average man can lift more weight than the average woman can. Yet women outperform men in some tests of long-term endurance because they can draw on the energy contained in greater body fat. Females also outperform males in the ultimate game of life itself: The life expectancy for men is now 73.0 years, while women can expect to live 79.0 years (U.S. National Center for Health Statistics, 1997).

Adolescent males exhibit greater mathematical ability, while adolescent females excel in verbal skills, differences that researchers attribute to both biology and patterns of socialization (Maccoby & Jacklin, 1974; Baker et al., 1980; Lengermann & Wallace, 1985). But research shows no overall differences in intelligence between males and females.

Biologically, then, the sexes differ in limited ways with neither one naturally superior. Nevertheless, the deeply rooted *cultural* notion of male superiority may seem so natural that many assume it is the inevitable consequence of sex itself. But society, much more than biology, is at work here, as the global variability of gender attests.

GENDER IN GLOBAL PERSPECTIVE

The best way to see how gender is grounded in culture is through global comparisons. Here, we briefly review three studies that highlight the global variability of gender.

The Israeli Kibbutzim

Some researchers investigating gender have focused on collective settlements in Israel called *kibbutzim*. The *kibbutz* (the singular form) is important for gender research because its members historically have embraced social equality, with men and women sharing in both work and decision making.

DIVERSITY SNAPSHOT

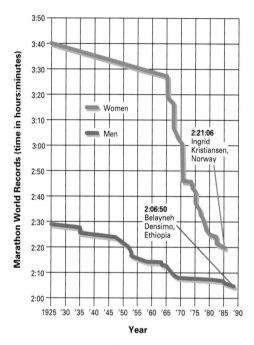

FIGURE 12–2 Men's and Women's Athletic Performance

Do men naturally outperform women in athletic competition? The answer is not obvious. Early in this century, men outdistanced women by many miles in marathon races. But, as opportunities for women in athletics increased, women have been closing the performance gap. Less than fifteen minutes separates the current world marathon records for women (set in 1985) and for men (set in 1988).

Source: *The Christian Science Monitor* (1995). © The Christian Science Publishing Society.

In the kibbutzim, both sexes typically take care of children, cook, clean, maintain the buildings, and make decisions about the operation of the kibbutz. Boys and girls are raised in the same way, and, from the first weeks of life, children live together in dormitories. Members of kibbutzim, then, do not consider sex relevant to most aspects of everyday life.

There is evidence that women and men in the kibbutzim have never achieved complete social equality (Tiger & Shepher, 1975). But, even so, the kibbutzim stand as evidence of wide cultural latitude in defining what is feminine and masculine.

RESOURCE: An excerpt from Margaret Mead's *Sex and Temperament in Three Primitive Societies* is one of the classic selections in the Macionis and Benokraitis reader.

Q: "In every known society, the male's need for achievement can be recognized. Men may cook, weave, or dress dolls . . . but if such occupations are appropriate occupations of men, the whole society . . . votes them as important. When the same occupations are performed by women, they are regarded as less important." Margaret Mead

Q: "To consider such traits as aggressiveness or passivity to be sex-linked is not possible in light of the facts." Margaret Mead

Q: "The whole trend in the United States is away from every sort of biological limitation on human activity and achievement." Margaret Mead

In every society, people assume certain jobs, patterns of behavior, and ways of dressing are "naturally" feminine while others are just as obviously masculine. But, in global perspective, we see remarkable variety in such social definitions. These men, Wodaabe pastoral nomads who live in the African nation of Niger, are proud to engage in a display of beauty most people in our society would consider feminine.

Margaret Mead's Research

Anthropologist Margaret Mead also carried out groundbreaking research on gender. To the extent that gender reflects biological facts of sex, she reasoned, people everywhere should define the same traits as feminine and masculine; if gender is cultural, these conceptions should vary.

Mead studied three societies of New Guinea (1963; orig. 1935). In the high mountainous home of the Arapesh, Mead observed men and women with remarkably similar attitudes and behavior. Both sexes, she reported, were cooperative and sensitive to others—in short, what our culture would label "feminine."

Moving south, Mead then studied the Mundugumor, whose culture of head-hunting and cannibalism stood in striking contrast to the gentle ways of the Arapesh. Both sexes were typically selfish and aggressive, traits we define as more "masculine."

Finally, traveling west to the Tchambuli, Mead discovered a culture that, like our own, defined females and males differently. But, Mead reported, the Tchambuli *reversed* many of our notions of gender: Females tended to be dominant and rational, while males were submissive, emotional, and nurturing toward children. Based on her observations, Mead concluded that culture is the key to gender, since what one culture defines as masculine another may consider feminine.

Some critics consider Mead's findings "too neat," as if she saw in these three societies precisely the patterns she was looking for. Moreover, Deborah Gewertz (1981) challenged Mead's "reversal hypothesis," claiming that, in fact, Tchambuli males tend to be more aggressive and Tchambuli females more submissive. Gewertz explains that Mead visited the Tchambuli (who actually call themselves the Chambri) during the 1930s, after they had lost much of their property due to war, and observed men working in the home. But she maintains that this "domestic role" for Chambri men was just temporary.

George Murdock's Research

In a broader study of more than 200 preindustrial societies, George Murdock (1937) found some global agreement about defining certain tasks as feminine and others as masculine. Hunting and warfare, Murdock found, generally fall to men, while home-centered responsibilities such as cooking and child care tend to be female work. With their simple technology, preindustrial societies apparently assign roles to take advantage of men's and women's physical attributes: Because of their greater size and short-term strength, men hunt game and protect the group; because women bear children, they assume domestic duties.

But beyond this general pattern, Murdock found significant variation. Consider agriculture: Women did the farming in about the same number of societies as men did; but, in most societies, the two sexes divided this work. When it came to other tasks—from building

Q: "The male is by nature fitter for command than the female, just as the elder and full-grown is fitter than the younger and immature . . . The courage of a man is shown in commanding, of a woman in obeying." Aristotle, *Politics*

Q: "Gender is what gender means. It has no basis in anything other than the social reality its hegemony constructs." Catharine MacKinnon

Q: "[Men] think themselves superior to women, but they mingle that with the notion of equality between men and women. It's very odd." Jean-Paul Sartre

NOTE: While scholars continue to debate the connection between biology and gender, the larger point is that any innate differences that do exist are certainly inadequate as an explanation of gender.

GLOBAL SOCIOLOGY

Patriarchy Breaking Down: A Report From Botswana

The judge handed down the decision and Unity Dow beamed, as people around her joined together in hugs and handshakes. Dow, then a thirty-two-year-old lawyer and citizen of the south African nation of Botswana, had won the first round in her effort to overturn laws that, she maintains, define women as second-class citizens.

The law that sparked Dow's suit against her government had to do with children's citizenship rights. Botswana is traditionally patrilineal, meaning that people trace family membership through males, making children part of their father's—but not their mother's—family line. Citizenship law reflects this tradition, very important for anyone who marries a citizen of another country, as Dow did. Under the law, a child of a Botswanan man and a woman of another nationality is a citizen of Botswana, since legal standing passes through the father. But the child of a Botswanan woman and a man from another nation has no citizenship rights. Thus, because she married a man from the United States, Unity Dow's children had no

citizen's rights in the country where they were born.

Ruling in Dow's favor, High Court Judge Martin Horwitz declared, "The time that women were treated as chattels [property] or were there to obey the whims and wishes of males is long past." In support of his decision, Horwitz pointed to the constitution of Botswana, which guarantees fundamental rights and freedoms to both women and men. Arguing for the government against Dow, Ian Kirby, a deputy attorney general, conceded that the constitution confers equal rights on the two sexes, but he claimed the law can and should take account of sex where such patterns are

Around the world, patriarchy is most pronounced in the economically poorest societies.

deeply rooted in Botswanan culture. To challenge national traditions in the name of Western feminism, he continued, amounts to cultural imperialism by foreign influences.

Women from many African nations attended the Dow court case, suggesting that support for sexual equality is widespread. Many analysts on both sides of the issue agree that Dow's victory probably signals the beginning of historic change. Indeed, as a result of the Dow ruling, the government of Botswana amended its constitution to move women and men toward social equality.

To many people in the United States, the Dow case may seem strange, since the notion that men and women are entitled to equal rights and privileges is widely accepted here. But, worth noting is the fact Botswana now has what the United States lacks: a constitutional guarantee of equal standing under the law for women and men.

Sources: Author's personal communication with Unity Dow, and Shapiro (1991).

shelters to tattooing the body—Murdock found societies of the world were as likely to turn to one sex as the other.

In Sum: Gender and Culture

Global comparisons show us that, by and large, societies do not consistently define most tasks as either

feminine or masculine. As societies industrialize, which gives people more choices and decreases the significance of muscle power, gender distinctions become smaller and smaller (Lenski, Nolan, & Lenski, 1995). Gender, then, is simply too variable across cultures to be considered a simple expression of biology. Instead, as with many other elements of culture, what it means to be female and male is mostly a creation of society.

Q: "There is in fact no true 'matriarchal,' as distinct from 'matri-lineal,' society in existence or known from literature, and the chances are there never has been." Kathleen Gough

NOTE: Sandra Bem (1993) uses the term "androcentrism" to refer to the belief in male superiority.

RESOURCE: An excerpt from *Subtle Sexism* by Nijole Benokraitis is included in the Macionis and Benokraitis reader.

NOTE: Patriarchy implies that paternity is the central social rela-tionship. Note the Old Testament emphasis on "begats," one man begetting a son (Rothman, 1995).

Q: "Women who seek to be equal with me lack ambition." Timothy O'Leary

Q: "Suffer women once to arrive at equality with you, and they will from that moment on become your superiors." Cato the Elder

Among the most striking consequences of patriarchy in China is the ancient practice of "foot-binding," by which young girls' feet are tightly wrapped as they grow, with predictable results. Although this practice—now rare—produces what people deem "dainty" proportions, what effect would you imagine this deformity has on the physical mobility of women?

The cultural variability of gender also means that, anywhere in the world, women's and men's lives change over time. Looking to the African nation of Botswana, the box on page 321 points up how and why gender is often controversial.

PATRIARCHY AND SEXISM

Although conceptions of gender vary from culture to culture, some degree of patriarchy is universal among world societies. **Patriarchy** (literally, "the rule of fathers"), is *a form of social organization in which males dominate females.* Despite mythical tales of societies dominated by female "Amazons," **matri-archy,** *a form of social organization in which females dominate males,* has never been documented in human history (Gough, 1971; Harris, 1977; Lengermann & Wallace, 1985).

But while some degree of patriarchy may be universal, Global Map 12–1 shows significant variation in the relative power and privilege of females and males worldwide. According to the United Nations, the Nordic nations (Norway, Sweden, and Finland) afford women the highest social standing; by contrast, women in the Asian nations of Pakistan and Afghanistan and the east African nation of Djibouti have the lowest social standing relative to men anywhere in the world.

Out of 116 countries in the U.N. study, the United States ranked eighth in terms of gender equality (*The Christian Science Monitor,* 1995).

Sexism, *the belief that one sex is innately superior to the other,* is the ideological basis of patriarchy. In effect, sexism justifies men dominating women in much the same way that racism legitimizes whites dominating people of color. Also like racism, sexism is more than a matter of individual attitudes. The idea that one sex is superior to the other is built into various institutions of our society. For example, *institutional sexism* per-vades the economy, with women highly concentrated in low-paying jobs. Similarly, the legal system has his-torically winked at violence against women, especially when committed by boyfriends, husbands, and fathers (Landers, 1990).

The Costs of Sexism

Sexism is a burden for all of society. It stunts the tal-ents and limits the ambitions of women, who are half the population. And even though men benefit in some respects from sexism, their privilege comes at a high price. Masculinity in our culture calls for men to engage in all sorts of high-risk behaviors, including using tobacco and alcohol, participating in physically dangerous sports, and even driving recklessly, so that motor-vehicle accidents are the leading cause of death among young males. Moreover, as Marilyn French (1985) argues, patriarchy compels men relentlessly to seek control—not only of women but of themselves and their world. Thus, masculinity is closely linked not only to accidents but also to suicide and violence as well as to diseases related to stress. The Type A per-sonality—characterized by chronic impatience, dri-ving ambition, competitiveness, and free-floating hostility—is a recipe for heart disease and almost per-fectly matches the behavior that our culture considers masculine (Ehrenreich, 1983).

Finally, insofar as men seek control over others, they lose opportunities for intimacy and trust. As one analyst put it, competition is supposed to separate "the men from the boys." In practice, however, it separates men from men, and from everyone else (Raphael, 1988).

Overall, when feelings, thoughts, and actions are rigidly scripted according to a culture's conceptions of gender, people cannot develop and express the full range of their humanity. Society saddles males with the burden of being assertive, competitive, and in con-trol; simultaneously, society requires females to be submissive, dependent, and self-effacing, regardless of their talents and inclinations.

WINDOW ON THE WORLD

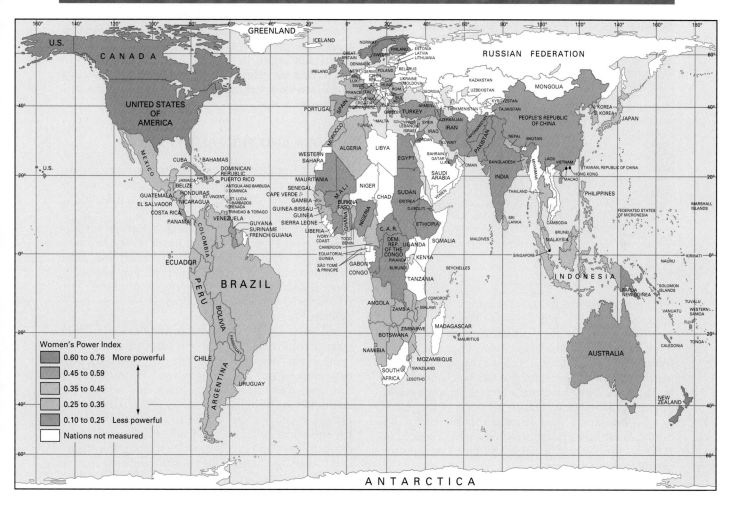

GLOBAL MAP 12–1 Women's Power in Global Perspective

A recent United Nations study ranked 116 nations on a scale of 0 (women have no power) to 1 (women have as much power as men). In general, women fare better in rich nations than they do in poor countries. Yet, some countries stand out: Scandinavian societies lead the world in promoting women's power.

Source: *The Christian Science Monitor* (1995). © The Christian Science Publishing Society.

Is Patriarchy Inevitable?

In preindustrial societies, women have little control over pregnancy and childbirth, which limits the scope of their lives. Similarly, men's greater height and physical strength are highly valued resources. But industrialization—including birth control technology—gives people choices about how to live. Today, then, in societies like our own, biological differences provide little justification for patriarchy.

But, legitimate or not, male dominance still holds sway in the United States and elsewhere. Does this mean that patriarchy is inevitable? Some sociologists claim that biological factors "wire" the sexes with

NOTE: The phrase "the opposite sex" clearly conveys the idea that gender is a matter of opposition.
SOCIAL SURVEY: "If the husband in a family wants children, but the wife decides that she does not want any children, is it all right for the wife to refuse to have children?" (GSS 1996, N = 755; Codebook, 1996:237)
"Yes" 76.3%   "No" 16.3%   DK/NR 7.4%

TABLE 12–1 Traditional Notions of Gender Identity

Feminine Traits	Masculine Traits
Submissive	Dominant
Dependent	Independent
Unintelligent and incapable	Intelligent and competent
Emotional	Rational
Receptive	Assertive
Intuitive	Analytical
Weak	Strong
Timid	Brave
Content	Ambitious
Passive	Active
Cooperative	Competitive
Sensitive	Insensitive
Sex object	Sexually aggressive
Attractive because of physical appearance	Attractive because of achievement

different motivations and behaviors—specifically, more aggressiveness in males—that make the eradication of patriarchy difficult, perhaps even impossible (Goldberg, 1974, 1987; Rossi, 1985; Popenoe, 1993). Most sociologists, however, believe that gender is primarily a social construction that *can* be changed. Just because no society has yet eliminated patriarchy does not mean that we must remain prisoners of the past.

To understand the persistence of patriarchy, we now examine how gender is rooted and reproduced in society, a process that begins in childhood and continues throughout our lives.

GENDER SOCIALIZATION

From birth until death, human feelings, thoughts, and actions reflect the social definitions that we attach to gender. Children quickly learn that their society defines females and males as different kinds of human beings; by about age three, they incorporate gender into their identities by applying society's standards to themselves (Kohlberg, 1966, cited in Lengermann & Wallace, 1985:37; Bem, 1981).

Table 12–1 presents the traits that people in the United States traditionally associate with "feminine" and "masculine" behavior. Such oppositional thinking remains part of our way of life even though research suggests that most young people do not develop consistently feminine or masculine personalities (L. Bernard, 1980; Bem, 1993).

Just as gender affects how we think of ourselves, so it teaches us to *act* in normative ways. **Gender roles** (or sex roles) are *attitudes and activities that a society links to each sex.* Insofar as our culture defines males as ambitious and competitive, we expect them to play team sports and aspire to positions of leadership. To the extent that we define females as deferential and emotional, we expect them to be good listeners and supportive observers.

GENDER AND THE FAMILY

The first question people usually ask about a newborn—"Is it a boy or a girl?"—looms large because the answer involves not just sex but the likely direction of the child's entire life.

In fact, gender is at work even before the birth of a child, since most parents in the world hope to have a boy rather than a girl. In China, India, and other strongly patriarchal societies, parents may choose to abort female embryos hoping later to produce a boy, whose social value is greater (United Nations Development Programme, 1991).

According to sociologist Jessie Bernard (1981), soon after birth, family members usher infants into the "pink world" of girls or the "blue world" of boys. Parents even convey gender messages unconsciously in the way they handle daughters and sons. One researcher at an English university presented an infant dressed as either a boy or a girl to a number of women; her subjects handled the "female" child tenderly, with frequent hugs and caresses, while treating the "male" child more aggressively, often lifting him up high in the air or bouncing him on the knee (Bonner, 1984). The lesson is clear: The female world revolves around passivity and emotion, while the male world puts a premium on independence and action.

GENDER AND THE PEER GROUP

As they approach school age, children move outside the family, making friends with others of the same age. Peer groups further socialize their members according to normative conceptions of gender. The box explains how play groups shaped one young boy's sense of himself as masculine.

Janet Lever (1978) spent a year observing children at play. She concluded that boys favor team sports—such as baseball and football—that involve many roles, complex rules, and clear objectives such as scoring a run or a touchdown. These games are nearly always

GLOBAL: About 85% of U.S. parents desire that their children (regardless of sex) attend college. In Japan, 75% of parents want their sons to go to college, but only 30% desire this for daughters.

NOTE: Historically, few men were literate; even fewer women were. So that their works would be read, 19th-century women authors often used male pseudonyms. The Brontë sisters all assumed gender-neutral pseudonyms: Charlotte Brontë (*Jane* *Eyre*) used the name Currer Bell; Anne Brontë (*Agnes Grey*) used Acton Bell; Emily Brontë (*Wuthering Heights*) used Ellis Bell.

NOTE: Another literary pattern that reflects on the power of gender: Heroines are often orphans (from *Jane Eyre* to *The Unsinkable Molly Brown*). Only when freed from men (as fathers or husbands) are such characters able to command the attention their central role demands.

SOCIOLOGY OF EVERYDAY LIFE

Masculinity as Contest

By the time I was ten, the central fact in my life was the demand that I become a man. By then, the most important relationships by which I was taught to define myself were those I had with other boys. I already knew that I must see every encounter with another boy as a contest in which I must win or at least hold my own. . . . The same lesson continued (in school), after school, even in Sunday School. My parents, relatives, teachers, the books I read, movies I saw, all taught me that my self-worth depended on my manliness, my willingness to stand up to the other boys. This usually didn't mean a physical fight, though the willingness to stand up and "fight like a man" always remained a final test. But the relationships between us usually had the character of an armed truce. Girls weren't part of this social world at all yet, just because they weren't part of this contest. They didn't have to be bluffed, no credit was gained by cowing them, so they were more or less ignored. Sometimes when there were no grownups around we would let each other know that we liked each other, but most of the time we did as we were taught.

Source: Silverstein (1977).

competitive, separating winners from losers. Male peer activities thus reinforce masculine traits of aggression and control.

Girls, on the other hand, play hopscotch or jump rope, or simply talk, sing, or dance together. Such spontaneous activities have few rules and rarely is "victory" the goal. Instead of teaching girls to be competitive, Lever explains, female peer groups promote interpersonal skills of communication and cooperation—presumably the basis for family life.

To explain Lever's observations, recall Carol Gilligan's (1982) gender-based theory of moral reasoning in Chapter 5 ("Socialization"). Boys, Gilligan contends, reason according to abstract principles. For them, "rightness" amounts to "playing by the rules." Girls, by contrast, consider morality a matter of moral responsibility to others. Thus, the games we play have serious implications for our larger lives.

GENDER AND SCHOOLING

School curricula encourage children to embrace appropriate gender patterns. For example, schools have long offered young women instruction in secretarial skills and home-centered know-how involving nutrition and sewing. Classes in woodworking and auto mechanics, conversely, attract mostly young men.

In college, the pattern continues, with men and women tending toward different majors. Men are disproportionately represented in mathematics and the sciences, including physics, chemistry, and biology. Women cluster in the humanities (such as English), the fine arts (painting, music, dance, and drama), education courses, and the social sciences (including anthropology and sociology). New areas of study are also likely to be gender-typed. Computer science, for example, enrolls mostly men, while courses in gender studies tend to enroll women.

GENDER AND THE MASS MEDIA

Since television first captured the public imagination in the 1950s, white males have held center stage. Racial and ethnic minorities were all but absent from television until the early 1970s, and only in the last decade have programs featured women in prominent roles.

Even when both sexes appear on camera, men generally play the brilliant detectives, fearless explorers, and skilled surgeons. Women, by contrast, play the less-capable characters, and are often important primarily for their sexual attractiveness. Historically, ads have presented women in the home, happily using cleaning products, serving food, trying out appliances, and modeling clothes. Men, on the other hand, predominate in

DIVERSITY: Historically, the labor-force participation of women of color was higher than that of white women. In 1940, for example, 40% of African American women worked for wages, compared to less than 30% of white women.
NOTE: The trend toward lower male participation in the labor force is due mostly to earlier retirement.
NOTE: Half of women working for pay work full time.

THEN AND NOW: Share of U.S. labor force represented by women: *1893*, 17%; *1945*, 36%; *1997*, 46%.
DIVERSITY: Women working full time typically contribute 38% of family income; those working part time contribute 14%, on average. Overall, 34 million working wives contribute 31% of family income. Of these 34 million, 9 million earn more than their husbands (Dunn, 1994).

Some recent advertising, typified by this television commercial for Diet Coke, reverses traditional gender definitions by portraying men as the objects of women's sexual attention. Although the reversal is new, the use of gender stereotypes to sell products has long been an element of our way of life.

ads for cars, travel, banking services, industrial companies, and alcoholic beverages. The authoritative "voiceover"—the faceless voice that describes a product on television and radio—is almost always male (Busby, 1975; Courtney & Whipple, 1983; Davis, 1993).

In a systematic study of magazine and newspaper ads, Erving Goffman (1979) found other, more subtle biases. Men, he concluded, are photographed to appear taller than women, implying male superiority. Women were more frequently presented lying down (on sofas and beds) or, like children, seated on the floor. The expressions and gestures of men exude competence and authority, whereas women more often appear in child-like poses. While men focus on the products being advertised, women focus on the men, playing a supportive and submissive role.

Advertising also actively perpetuates what Naomi Wolf called the "beauty myth." The box takes a closer look.

GENDER STRATIFICATION

Gender implies more than how people think and act. The concept of **gender stratification** refers to *a society's unequal distribution of wealth, power, and privilege between men and women.* In the United States, the lower social standing of women can be seen, first, in the world of work.

WORKING MEN AND WOMEN

In 1997, almost 70 percent of people in the United States aged sixteen and over were working for income: 75.0 percent of men and 59.8 percent of women, as shown in Figure 12–3 on page 328 (U.S. Department of Labor, 1998). This represents a dramatic change from 1900, when only about one-fifth of women were in the labor force (and these were typically poor women, who have always needed to work). Moreover, three-fourths of women in the labor force now work full time. So, the traditional view that earning an income is exclusively a "man's role" no longer holds true.

Several factors are at work in changing the look of the U.S. labor force, including the declining importance of farming, the growth of cities, a shrinking family size, a rising divorce rate, and the fact that 60 percent of married couples now depend on two incomes. Thus, the United States and other industrial societies today consider women working for income to be the rule rather than the exception. As Global Map 12–2 on page 329 shows, however, this

DISCUSS: Consider a recent survey that found the following percent of adult women used these products within one hour of getting up in the morning: lipstick/gloss, 56%; hair spray, 49%; mascara, 45%; foundation, 36%; eyeliner, 32% (Roper Starch Worldwide, 1995).

NOTE: About 85% of all cosmetic surgery is performed on women.

NOTE: The first Miss America beauty pageant was held in 1920, the same year that women gained the right to vote.

Q: "Rage grows when girls . . . perceive that their parents always expect them to be perfect. It is fertilized by a culture that constantly tells women how they should look, act, feel, and eat . . . [B]odies that are not skinny become indictments of poor character. These circumstances underlie 'angerexia.'" Margo Maine

CRITICAL THINKING

Pretty Is as Pretty Does: The Beauty Myth

The Duchess of Windsor once quipped, "A woman cannot be too rich or too thin." Perhaps the first half of this observation might apply to men as well, but certainly not the second. It is no surprise that the vast majority of ads placed by the $20-billion-a-year cosmetics industry and the $40-billion diet industry target women.

Indeed, Naomi Wolf (1990) argues, U.S. women are victimized by cultural patterns she terms the "beauty myth." The beauty myth arises, first, because society teaches women to measure themselves in terms of physical appearance (Backman & Adams, 1991). Yet, the standards of beauty (such as the *Playboy* centerfold or the one-hundred-pound New York fashion model) are unattainable for most women.

The beauty myth also derives from the way society teaches women to prize relationships with men, whom they

presumably attract with their beauty. Relentless pursuit of beauty not only

drives women toward being highly disciplined, but it also forces them to be highly attuned and responsive to men. Beauty-minded women, in short, try to please men and avoid challenging male power.

The beauty myth affects males as well: Men should want to possess beautiful women. In short, the concept of beauty reduces women to objects and motivates men to possess them as if they were dolls rather than human beings.

As Wolf explains, beauty is really more about behavior than appearance. It should not be surprising, therefore, that the beauty myth surfaced in our culture during the 1890s, the 1920s, and the 1980s—all decades of heightened debate about the social standing of women.

Source: Based on Wolf (1990).

is not the case in many of the poorer nations around the world.

A common misconception (especially among middle-class people) holds that working women are childless. But, today, 63 percent of married women with children under six work for income, and 77 percent of married women with children between six and seventeen years of age are employed. For divorced women with children, the comparable figures are 69 percent of women with younger children and 81 percent of women with older children (U.S. Bureau of the Census, 1997).

Gender and Occupations

While the proportions of men and women in the labor force have been converging, the work they do remains

different. According to the U.S. Department of Labor (1998), nearly half of working women hold just two types of jobs. Administrative support work draws 24 percent of working women, most of whom are secretaries, typists, or stenographers. From another angle, these are called "pink-collar" jobs because 79 percent are filled by women.

Another 17 percent of employed women perform service work. These jobs include waitressing and other food service work as well as health care. Both categories of jobs lie at the low end of the pay scale, offer limited opportunities for advancement, and are subject to supervision—most often by men.

Table 12–2 on page 330 identifies the ten occupations with the highest concentrations of women. The bottom line is that, although increasing numbers of women work for pay, they remain highly segregated in

DIVERSITY SNAPSHOT

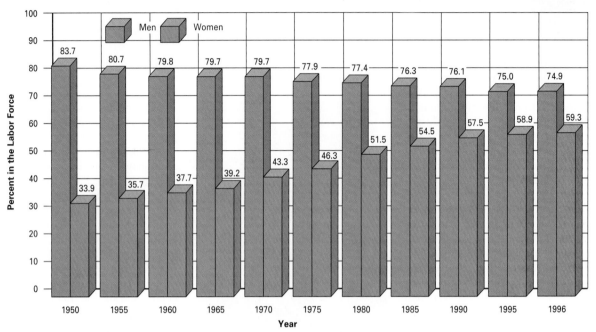

FIGURE 12–3 Men and Women in the U.S. Labor Force

Source: U.S. Department of Labor (1998).

the labor force because our society continues to view work through the lens of gender (Kemp & Coverman, 1989; Charles, 1992; Bianchi & Spain, 1996; U.S. Department of Labor, 1998).

Men dominate most other job categories. Men overwhelmingly control the building trades: 99 percent of brick and stone masons, structural metalworkers, and heavy equipment mechanics are men. Men also hold the lion's share of positions with the most income, prestige, and power. For example, 90 percent of engineers, 74 percent of physicians, 73 percent of judges and lawyers, and 56 percent of corporate managers are men. In the business world, men hold 95 percent of senior management jobs in this country's 1,000 largest companies, and 998 of these corporations have men as chief executive officers (Thomas, 1995; Townsend, 1996).

An important exception to the pattern of male domination of the business world is that women now own 8 million small businesses in the United States. This represents more than one-third of the total, and the share is rapidly rising. Although 86 percent of these businesses are sole proprietorships with a single employee, the success of tens of thousands of women demonstrates that women have the power to create opportunities for themselves outside of larger, male-dominated companies (Ando, 1990; O'Hare & Larson, 1991; Mergenhagen, 1996; U.S. Bureau of the Census, 1996).

Overall, then, gender stratification permeates the workplace, and the hierarchy is easy to spot: Female nurses assist male physicians, female secretaries serve male executives, and female flight attendants are under the command of male airplane pilots. Moreover, in any field, the greater the income and prestige associated with a job, the more likely it is held by a man. For example, women represent 98 percent of kindergarten teachers, 84 percent of elementary school teachers, 58 percent of secondary school teachers, 43 percent of college and university professors, and 16 percent of college and university presidents (U.S. Department of Labor, 1998).

NOTE: Housework (unpaid work within the home) has its complement in volunteer work (unpaid work outside the home).

NOTE: Lennon & Rosenfeld (1994) report that women evaluate their responsibilities for housework according to a social exchange model: Women without jobs find doing most domestic labor to be fair; those in the labor force do not.

NOTE: South & Spitze (1994) examine household division of labor for various types of households. In married-couple households (versus, say, cohabitants, widowed persons, and divorced persons), women spend the most time doing housework.

Q: "Everything Fred Astaire did, Ginger Rogers did backwards and in high heels." Bob Thaves

WINDOW ON THE WORLD

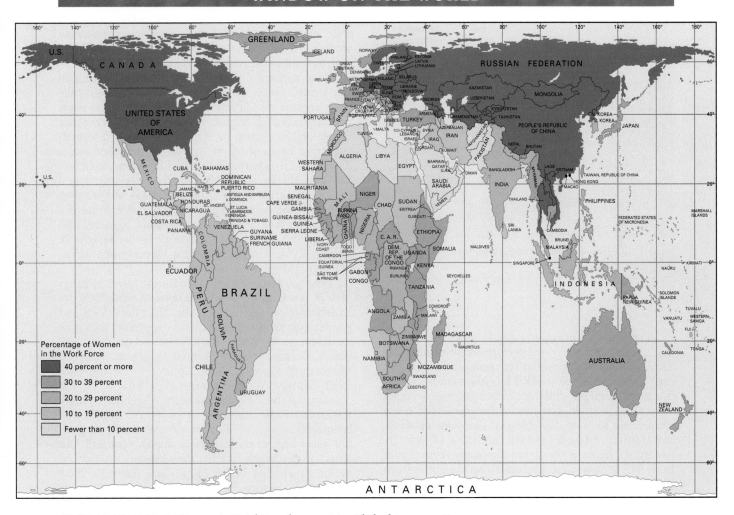

GLOBAL MAP 12–2 Women's Paid Employment in Global Perspective

In 1996, women comprised 46 percent of the labor force in the United States—up almost 10 percent over the last generation. Throughout the industrialized world, at least one-third of the labor force is made up of women. In poor societies, however, women work even harder than they do in this country, but they are less likely to be paid for their efforts. In Latin America, for example, women represent only about 15 percent of the paid labor force; in Islamic societies of northern Africa and the Middle East, the figure is even lower.

Source: *Peters Atlas of the World* (1990).

HOUSEWORK: WOMEN'S "SECOND SHIFT"

One indicator of the global pattern of patriarchy, shown in Global Map 12–3 on page 331, is the extent to which housework—cleaning, cooking, and caring for children—is the province of women. In the United States, housework has always embodied a cultural contradiction: It is touted as essential for family life on the one hand, but it carries little prestige or reward on the other (J. Bernard, 1981).

GLOBAL: The nation closest to earnings parity is Sweden, 89%. Other countries: France, 81%; Germany, 74%; Japan, 51%.
NOTE: Extending the current trend, gender parity at top management positions will take another 75 years. Congressional parity, however, would take 500 years.
NOTE: In two specific occupational categories, says the Bureau of Labor Statistics, women outearn men: psychological therapists and waiters/waitresses.
SOCIAL SURVEY: Gallup poll, 1942: "If women replace men in industry, should they be paid the same wages as men?" *Yes*, 78%; *No*, 14%; *Undecided*, 8%.
DIVERSITY: The earnings ratio between men and women working full time increases with age: 15–24, 90%; 25–34, 82%; 35–44, 72%; 45–54, 64%; 55–64, 63% (U.S. Bureau of the Census, 1997).

TABLE 12–2 **Jobs With the Highest Concentrations of Women, 1997**

Occupation	Number of Women Employed	Percent in Occupation Who Are Women
1. Secretary	3,033,000	98.6%
2. Dental hygienist	107,000	98.2
3. Family child-care provider	513,000	98.2
4. Prekindergarten and kindergarten teachers	574,000	97.8
5. Child-care worker/ private household	260,000	96.8
6. Dental assistant	231,000	96.7
7. Receptionist	1,005,000	96.5
8. Early childhood teacher's assistant	432,000	95.6
9. Stenographer	104,000	95.5
10. Speech therapist	102,000	95.0

Source: U.S. Department of Labor, Bureau of Labor Statistics, *Employment and Earnings*, vol. 45, no. 1, January 1998, pp. 174–79.

Despite women's rapid entry into the labor force, the amount of housework performed by women has declined only slightly (and the proportion done by men has not changed at all). The typical couple shares in disciplining the children and managing finances; otherwise, men do the repairs and yardwork while women see to most daily tasks of shopping, cooking, and cleaning. Since housework consumes, on average, twenty-six hours a week, most women return from their jobs to face a "second shift" on the home front (Schooler et al., 1984; Fuchs, 1986; Hochschild, 1989; Presser, 1993; Keith & Schafer, 1994; Benokraitis & Feagin, 1995).

In sum, men support the idea of women entering the labor force, and most count on the money women earn. But men nonetheless resist modifying their own behavior to help their partners establish and maintain their careers by making their home lives more manageable (Komarovsky, 1973; Cowan, 1992; Robinson & Spitze, 1992; Lennon & Rosenfeld, 1994; Heath & Bourne, 1995).

GENDER, INCOME, AND WEALTH

In 1996, women working full time earned a median $23,710, while men working full time earned $32,144. For every dollar earned by men, then, women earned about 74 cents.

Among full-time workers, 50 percent of women earned less than $25,000 in 1996, compared to 32 percent of comparable men. At the upper end of the income scale, men were more than three times more likely than women (10.7 percent versus 3.2 percent) to earn more than $75,000 (U.S. Bureau of the Census, 1997).

The earning differential has been narrowing in the United States (as recently as 1980, women full-time workers earned just 60 percent as much as comparable men). Key reasons for this convergence include more women in managerial jobs and women earning a larger share of college degrees, but also a decline in men's earnings due to a loss of manufacturing jobs. From a global perspective, gender-based income disparity in the United States is smaller than in Japan but higher than in most other industrial nations, including Australia, Canada, Norway, and Sweden (Rosenfeld & Kalleberg, 1990; Bianchi & Spain, 1997; United Nations Development Programme, 1997).

The most important reason for the lower earnings of U.S. working women is the *kind* of work they do: largely clerical and service jobs. In effect, jobs and gender interact. People still tend to perceive jobs with less clout as "women's work," and we devalue work simply because it is performed by women (Parcel, Mueller, & Cuvelier, 1986; Blum, 1991; England, 1992; Bellas, 1994; Huffman, et al., 1996).

During the 1980s, proponents of gender equality responded to this mindset by proposing a policy of "comparable worth." That is, people should be paid, not according to the historical double standard, but based on the worth of what they actually do. Several nations, including Great Britain and Australia, have adopted this policy, but it has found limited acceptance in the United States. In the absence of such a policy, critics argue, women in this country are losing as much as $1 billion annually.

A second reason for gender-based income disparity has to do with the family. Both men and women have children, of course, but our culture defines parenting as more a woman's responsibility than a man's. Pregnancy and raising small children keep many younger women out of the labor force at a time when their male peers are making significant occupational gains. As a result, women workers have less job seniority than their male counterparts (Fuchs, 1986; Stier, 1996; Waldfogel, 1997).

Moreover, women who choose to have children may be reluctant or unable to maintain fast-paced jobs that tie up their evenings and weekends. To avoid role strain, they may take jobs that offer a shorter

SOCIAL SURVEY: "Do you approve or disapprove of a married woman earning money in business or industry if she has a husband capable of supporting her?" (GSS 1996, N = 1,960; *Codebook*, 1996:204)
"Approve" 81.4%   "Disapprove" 16.3%   DK/NR 2.3%
SOCIAL SURVEY: The same item appears on *Student CHIP Social Survey Software* (GSS 1972–91, N = 17,547).

	"Approve"	"Disapprove"
Women	75.7%	24.3%
Men	74.3%	25.7%
Afri Amer	72.7%	27.3%
Latino	65.5%	34.5%
Whites	75.8%	24.2%

WINDOW ON THE WORLD

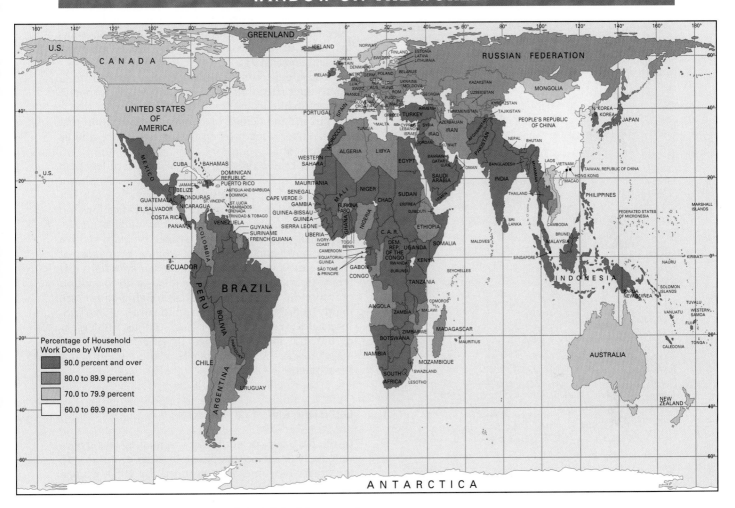

GLOBAL MAP 12–3 Housework in Global Perspective

Throughout the world, housework is a major component of women's routines and identities. This is especially true in poor societies of Latin America, Africa, and Asia, where women are not generally in the paid labor force. But our society also defines housework and child care as "feminine" activities, even though a majority of U.S. women work outside the home.

Source: *Peters Atlas of the World* (1990); updated by the author.

commuting distance, more flexible hours, and employer child-care services. Women pursuing both a career and a family are torn between their dual responsibilities in ways that men are not. Consider this: At age forty, 90 percent of men—but only 35 percent of women—in executive positions have had a child.

Felice Schwartz (1989) points out that corporate women risk their careers by having children. Rather than helping to meet the needs of a working mother, the typical corporation interprets a woman's decision to have a child as evidence that she may leave the company, taking with her a substantial investment in time

Q: "The cost of employing women in management is greater than the cost of employing men. This is a jarring statement, partly because it is true, but mostly because it is something people are reluctant to talk about. . . . We have become so sensitive to charges of sexism and so afraid of confrontation, even litigation, that we rarely say what we know to be true." Felice Schwartz (1989:65)

DISCUSS: In the corporate world, a secretary's pay is usually linked to that of her boss, regardless of the actual work she performs. Is this sex-based bias?

GLOBAL: Women represent about 54% of higher-education enrollments in the U.S., Canada, Finland, and France; about 40% in most other industrial societies; below 40% in Japan, Luxembourg, Switzerland, and Turkey (Organization for Economic Cooperation and Development).

TABLE 12–3 Earnings of Full-Time U.S. Workers, by Sex, 1996*

Selected Occupational Categories	Median Income		Women's Income as a Percentage of Men's
	Men	Women	
Executives, administrators, and managers	$46,654	$31,208	67%
Professional specialties	50,012	34,537	69
Technical workers	36,775	27,239	74
Sales	35,104	21,350	61
Clerical and other administrative support workers	30,381	21,758	72
Precision production, craft, and repair workers	30,421	21,165	70
Machine operators, assemblers, and inspectors	25,625	17,456	68
Transportation and material movers	27,723	17,681	64
Handlers, equipment cleaners, helpers, and laborers	20,793	16,856	81
Service workers	21,028	14,976	71
Farming, forestry, and fishing workers	18,127	17,251	95
All occupations listed above	32,144	23,710	74

*Workers aged 15 and over.

Source: U.S. Bureau of the Census, *Money Income in the United States: 1996*, Current Population Reports, ser. P-60, no. 197 (Washington, D.C.: U.S. Government Printing Office, 1997).

The two factors noted so far—type of work and family responsibilities—account for about two-thirds of the earnings disparity between women and men. A third factor—discrimination against women—accounts for most of the remainder (Pear, 1987; Fuller & Schoenberger, 1991).

Because discrimination is illegal, it is practiced in subtle ways (Benokraitis & Feagin, 1995). Corporate women often encounter a *glass ceiling*, a barrier that is hard to see and denied by company officials, but that effectively prevents women from rising above middle management.

For all these reasons, then, women earn less than men in all major occupational categories. As shown in Table 12–3, this disparity varies from job to job, but in only two of these major job classifications do women earn more than 75 percent as much as men.

Finally, perhaps because women typically outlive men, many people think that women own most of this country's wealth. Government statistics tell a different story: 53 percent of individuals with $1 million or more in assets are men, although widows are highly represented in this millionaire's club (U.S. Internal Revenue Service, 1993). And just 16 percent of the individuals identified in *Forbes* and *Fortune* magazines as the richest people in the United States are women.

GENDER AND EDUCATION

In the past, our society thought schooling was irrelevant for women because their lives revolved around the home. But times have changed. By 1980, women earned a majority of all associate's and bachelor's degrees; in 1995, their share stood at 56 percent (U.S. National Center for Education Statistics, 1997).

College doors have opened to women, and historic differences in men's and women's majors are becoming smaller. In 1970, for example, women earned just 17 percent of bachelor's degrees in natural sciences, computer science, and engineering; by 1995, that proportion had increased to 31 percent.

In 1993, women for the first time also earned a majority of postgraduate degrees, often a springboard to high-prestige jobs. For all areas of study in 1995, women earned 55 percent of master's degrees, although only 39 percent of all doctorates (53 percent of all Ph.D.s in sociology, however, went to women). Women now have a visible presence in many graduate fields that used to be almost all male. For example, in 1970 only a few hundred women received a master's of

and training. Instead, Schwartz calls on corporations to develop "mommy tracks" that allow women to meet family responsibilities while continuing their careers, with less intensity, for specified periods. This proposal has won praise, but it has also provoked strong criticism. Opponents of the "mommy track" say that it plays into the hands of corporate men who have long stereotyped women as being less attached to careers in the first place. Further, critics add, since companies are unlikely to apply such a plan to men, it can only hurt rather than help the career aspirations of corporate women.

SOCIAL SURVEY: "Women should take care of running their homes and leave running the country up to men." (GSS 1996, N = 1,960; *Codebook*, 1996:204)
"Agree"   15.7%   "Disagree"   80.4%   DK/NR   3.9%
SOCIAL SURVEY: "If your party nominated a woman for president, would you vote for her if she were qualified for the job?" (GSS 1996, N = 1,960; *Codebook*, 1996:204) [In a 1937 Gallup poll, 37% endorsed a qualified woman for president.]
"Yes"   90.4%   "No"   6.7%   DK/NR   2.9%
GLOBAL: Women have the greatest relative political power in Norway, in which leaders of both major parties and half the members of the cabinet and parliament are women. A constitutional provision requires parties to ensure that 40% of their candidates are women.

business administration (M.B.A.) degree; by 1995, more than 34,000 received M.B.A.s (37 percent of all such degrees) (U.S. National Center for Education Statistics, 1997).

Some professional fields, however, remain predominantly male. In 1995, men received 57 percent of law degrees (LL.B. and J.D.), 61 percent of medical degrees (M.D.), and 64 percent of dental degrees (D.D.S. and D.M.D.) (U.S. National Center for Education Statistics, 1997). Our society still defines high-paying professions (and the drive and competitiveness needed to succeed in them) as masculine; this fact helps to explain why an equal number of women and men begin most professional graduate programs, but women are less likely to complete their degrees (Fiorentine, 1987; Fiorentine & Cole, 1992). Nonetheless, the proportion of women in all these professions is steadily rising.

GENDER AND POLITICS

A century ago, virtually no women held elected office in the United States. In fact, women were legally barred from voting in national elections until the passage of the Nineteenth Amendment to the Constitution in 1920. A few women, however, were candidates for political office even before they could vote. The Equal Rights party supported Victoria Woodhull for the U.S. presidency in 1872; perhaps it was a sign of the times that she spent election day in a New York City jail. Table 12–4 cites subsequent milestones in women's gradual movement into political life.

Today, thousands of women serve as mayors of cities and towns across the United States, and tens of thousands more hold responsible administrative posts in the federal government. At the state level, 22 percent of legislators in 1997 were women (compared to just 6 percent in 1970). National Map 12–1 on page 334 shows where in the United States women have made the greatest political gains.

Less change has occurred at the highest levels of politics, although a majority of U.S. adults claim they would support a qualified woman for any office, including the presidency. After the 1996 national elections, 2 of the 50 state governors were women (2 percent), and, in Congress, women held 51 of 435 seats in the House of Representatives (12 percent), and 9 of 100 seats (9 percent) in the Senate.

A recent global survey found that, while women are half the earth's population, they hold just 11.7 percent of seats in the world's 179 parliaments. While this

TABLE 12–4 Significant "Firsts" for Women in U.S. Politics

1869	Law allows women to vote in Wyoming territory; Utah follows suit in 1870.
1872	First woman to run for the presidency (Victoria Woodhull) represents the Equal Rights party.
1917	First woman elected to the House of Representatives (Jeannette Rankin of Montana).
1924	First women elected state governors (Nellie Taylor Ross of Wyoming and Miriam ["Ma"] Ferguson of Texas); both followed their husbands into office. First woman to have her name placed in nomination for vice-presidency at the convention of a major political party (Lena Jones Springs).
1931	First woman to serve in the Senate (Hattie Caraway of Arkansas); completed the term of her husband upon his death and won reelection in 1932.
1932	First woman appointed to the presidential cabinet (Frances Perkins, secretary of labor in the cabinet of President Franklin D. Roosevelt).
1964	First woman to have her name placed in nomination for the presidency at the convention of a major political party (Margaret Chase Smith, a Republican).
1972	First African American woman to have her name placed in nomination for the presidency at the convention of a major political party (Shirley Chisholm, a Democrat).
1981	First woman appointed to the U.S. Supreme Court (Sandra Day O'Connor).
1984	First woman to be successfully nominated for the vice-presidency (Geraldine Ferraro, a Democrat).
1988	First woman chief executive to be elected to a consecutive third term (Madeleine Kunin, governor of Vermont).
1992	Political "Year of the Woman" yields record number of women in the Senate (six) and the House (forty-eight), as well as (1) first African American woman to win election to U.S. Senate (Carol Moseley-Braun of Illinois); (2) first state (California) to be served by two women senators (Barbara Boxer and Dianne Feinstein); (3) first woman of Puerto Rican descent elected to the House (Nydia Valasquez of New York).
1996	First woman appointed secretary of state (Madeleine Albright). Record number of women in the Senate (nine) and the House (fifty-one).

Sources: Based on data compiled from Sandra Salmans, "Women Ran for Office Before They Could Vote," *New York Times*, July 13, 1984, p. A11, and news reports.

represents a rise from 3 percent fifty years ago, only in the Nordic nations (Norway, Sweden, Finland, and Denmark) and the Netherlands does the share of parliamentary seats held by women (36.4 percent) even approach their share of the population (Inter-Parliamentary Union, 1997).

THE MAP: Roughly speaking, women hold the most power in state government in the western states (the region in which women first became state governors). By contrast, the South remains the region in which women are least likely to be in the labor force and where the political clout of women is lowest.
Q: "We can no longer go to war without women." Lt. Gen. Colin Powell

Q: "Pregnancy and warfare test the limits of equality." Wendy Kaminer
DIVERSITY: Of all families living below poverty level, 54% were headed by women in 1996. Of all poor African American families, 78.2% were headed by women; for Hispanics, the figure was 47.1%, and for all whites, 45.0% (U.S. Bureau of the Census, 1997).

SEEING OURSELVES

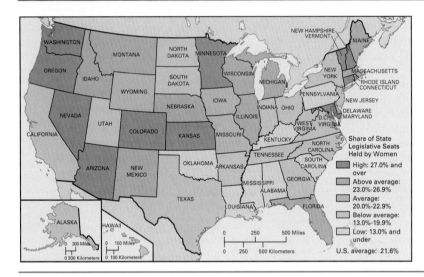

NATIONAL MAP 12–1
Women in State Government Across the United States

Although women represent half of U.S. adults, just 22 percent of seats in state legislatures are held by women. Look at the state-by-state variation in the map. In which regions of the country have women gained the greatest political power? What factors do you think account for this pattern?

Source: Center for the American Woman and Politics, "Women in State Legislatures 1997." [Online] Available http://www-rci.rutgers.edu/~cawp/stleg97.htm, January 4, 1998.

GENDER AND THE MILITARY

A small number of women served in the armed forces even before this country's Revolutionary War. In 1940, at the outset of World War II, only 2 percent of armed forces personnel were women. By 1990, this figure had increased to 12 percent. In the 1991 Persian Gulf war, 35,000 women represented 6.5 percent of a total deployment of 540,000 U.S. troops. Five of the 148 Gulf War casualties were women. In 1998, women represented 15 percent of all armed forces personnel.

Only the Coast Guard makes all assignments available to women; at the other extreme, the Marine Corps limits women to about one-third of all jobs. Gender explains the historically low representation of women in the military as well as the prohibition against women in combat roles. The argument is that, on average, women lack the physical strength of men. Critics counter that military women are better educated and score higher on intelligence tests than their male counterparts. At the heart of the issue, however, is our society's deeply held view of women as *nurturers*—people who give life and help others—which clashes intolerably with the image of women as professional killers.

In recent years, the armed forces have been awash in scandal over the treatment of women. Mounting evidence suggests that Army personnel—from recruiters to drill sergeants—target women recruits (20 percent of the total) with sexual advances and, sometimes, outright attacks (Thompson, 1997).

Although incorporating women into military culture has been difficult, women in all branches of the armed forces are taking on more and more military assignments. One reason is that high technology blurs the distinction between combat and noncombat personnel. A combat pilot can fire missiles at a radar-screen target miles away, while nonfighting medical evacuation teams often enter the immediate heat of battle (Moskos, 1985; Stiehm, 1989; McNeil, Jr., 1991; May, 1991; Segal & Hansen, 1992; Wilcox, 1992; Kaminer, 1997).

ARE WOMEN A MINORITY?

A **minority**[2] is *any category of people, set apart by physical or cultural difference, that is socially disadvantaged.* Given the clear economic disadvantage of being a woman in our society, it seems reasonable to say U.S. women are a minority.

---

[2]We use the term "minority" rather than "minority group" because, as explained in Chapter 7 ("Groups and Organizations"), a minority is a category, not a group.

Q: "A woman's brain evolves emotion rather than intellect; and whilst this feature fits her admirably as a creature burdened with the preservation and happiness of the human species, it painfully disqualifies her for the sterner duties to be performed by the intellectual facilities. The best wife and mother and sister would make the worst legislator, judge, and police officer." Nineteenth-century politician opposed to women's suffrage

SUPPLEMENTS: Use the cross-cultural *Data File* article on women in the military for class discussion.
NOTE: In 1996, 3,631 women died as a result of violence; 30% of them were victims of violence perpetrated by a spouse or intimate partner.
DISCUSS: To draw out the link between aggression and masculinity, ask the class what makes a man a "wimp"? A "real man"?

Subjectively speaking, however, most white women do *not* think of themselves this way (Hacker, 1951; Lengermann & Wallace, 1985). This is partly because, unlike racial minorities (including African Americans) and ethnic minorities (say, Hispanics), white women are well represented at all levels of the class structure, including the very top.

Bear in mind, however, that women at every class level typically have less income, wealth, education, and power than men do. In fact, patriarchy makes women dependent for much of their social standing on men—first their fathers and later their husbands (Bernard, 1981).

MINORITY WOMEN

If women are defined as a minority, what about minority women? Are they doubly handicapped? Generally speaking, the answer is yes, as we can show with some income comparisons. Looking first at race and ethnicity, the median income in 1996 for African American women working full time was $21,990, which is 87 percent as much as the $25,358 earned by white women; Hispanic women earned $19,272—just 76 percent as much as their white, Anglo counterparts.

Second, there is the obstacle associated with gender. Thus, African American women earned 85 percent as much as African American men, while Hispanic women earned 87 percent as much as Hispanic men.

Combining these disadvantages, African American women earned 63 percent as much as white men, and Hispanic women earned 55 percent as much (U.S. Bureau of the Census, 1997). These disparities reflect minority women's lower positions on the occupational and educational hierarchies compared to white women (Bonilla-Santiago, 1990). Further, whenever the economy sags, minority women are especially likely to suffer declining income and unemployment.

In short, gender has a powerful effect on our lives, but it never operates alone. Class position, race and ethnicity, and gender form a multilayered system of disadvantage for some and privilege for others (Ginsburg & Tsing, 1990).

VIOLENCE AGAINST WOMEN

The most wrenching kind of suffering endured by women is violence. As Chapter 8 ("Deviance") explains, criminal violence is overwhelmingly the actions of men—hardly surprising since aggressiveness

Many public organizations and private companies have adopted policies to discourage forms of behavior, conversation, or images that might create a "hostile or intimidating environment." In essence, such practices seek to remove sexuality from the workplace so that employees can do their jobs while steering clear of traditional notions about female and male relationships. Would a locker room "pinup" like this bother you? Why or why not?

is a trait our culture defines as masculine. Furthermore, a great deal of "manly" violence is directed at women, which we also might expect since we devalue what is culturally defined as feminine.

According to a recent Justice Department report, each year about 430,000 women are victims of sexual assault, including 316,000 rapes or attempted rapes. To this number can be added perhaps 1 million assaults (U.S. Bureau of Justice Statistics, 1996).

Most gender-linked violence occurs where men and women interact most—in the home. Richard Gelles (cited in Roesch, 1984) argues that, with the exception of the police and the military, the family is the most violent organization in the United States. Both sexes suffer from family violence, although, by and large, women sustain more serious injuries than men (Straus & Gelles, 1986; Schwartz, 1987; Shupe, Stacey, & Hazlewood, 1987; Gelles & Cornell, 1990; Smolowe, 1994).

Violence against women also occurs in casual relationships. As noted in Chapter 8 ("Deviance"), most

NOTE: The legal basis for charges of sexual harassment is Section 703 of Title VII of the 1964 Civil Rights Act that outlaws workplace discrimination based on sex; also Title IX of the Education Amendments of 1972.

GLOBAL: A clear case of ethnocentrism is that the Japanese child pornography industry—the biggest in the world—almost never uses Japanese girls; they "import" other Asian women.

rapes involve not strangers but men known (and often trusted) by women. Dianne Herman (1998) claims that abuse against women is built into our way of life. All forms of violence against women—from the wolf whistles that intimidate women on city streets to a pinch in a crowded subway to physical assaults that occur at home—express what she calls a "rape culture" by which men try to dominate women. Sexual violence, then, is fundamentally about *power* rather than sex, and therefore should be understood as a dimension of gender stratification.

Sexual Harassment

Sexual harassment refers to *comments, gestures, or physical contact of a sexual nature that are deliberate, repeated, and unwelcome.* During the 1990s, sexual harassment became an issue of national importance that rewrote the rules for workplace interaction between the sexes.

Most victims of sexual harassment are women. This is because, first, our culture encourages men to be sexually assertive and to perceive women in sexual terms; therefore, social interaction in the workplace, on campus, and elsewhere can readily take on sexual overtones. Second, most individuals in positions of power—including business executives, physicians, bureau chiefs, assembly line supervisors, professors, and military officers—are men who oversee the work of women. In surveys carried out in widely different work settings, half of women respondents report receiving unwanted sexual attention (Loy & Stewart, 1984; Paul, 1991).

Sexual harassment is sometimes blatant and direct: A supervisor solicits sexual favors from a subordinate and threatens reprisal if the advances are refused. Courts have declared such *quid pro quo* sexual harassment (the Latin phrase means "one thing in return for another") a violation of civil rights.

More often, however, sexual harassment involves subtle behavior—sexual teasing, off-color jokes, pin-ups displayed in the workplace—that may not even be *intended* to harass anyone. But, using the *effect* standard favored by many feminists, such actions create a *hostile environment* (Cohen, 1991; Paul, 1991). Incidents of this kind are far more complex because they involve different perceptions of the same behavior. For example, a man may think that complimenting a co-worker on her appearance is simply a friendly gesture; she, on the other hand, may find his behavior offensive and a hindrance to her job performance.

Pornography

A precise definition of *pornography* has long eluded scholars and lawmakers. Unable to set specific standards that distinguish what is—from what is not—pornographic, the Supreme Court has ruled that local communities should decide for themselves what violates "community standards" of decency and lacks any redeeming social value.

Definitions aside, pornography (loosely defined) is surely popular in the United States: X-rated videos, 1-900 telephone numbers for sexual conversations, and a host of sexually explicit movies and magazines together constitute a 7-billion-dollar-a-year industry. Recently, a high technology dimension has been added to the pornography debate. The box takes a closer look.

Traditionally, society has cast pornography as a *moral* issue. In fact, national survey data show that 60 percent of U.S. adults express concern that "sexual materials lead to a breakdown of morals" (NORC, 1996:217).

A more recent view focuses on how pornography demeans women. That is, pornography is really a *power* issue because it implies that men should control both sexuality and women. Catharine MacKinnon (1987) believes pornography is one foundation of male dominance in the United States because it dehumanizes women, presenting them as the subservient playthings of men. It is worth noting in this context that the word "pornography" is derived from the Greek word *porne*, which refers to a harlot who acts as a man's sexual slave.

Some critics also argue that pornography promotes violence against women. While demonstrating a scientific cause-and-effect relationship between what people view and how they act is difficult, research does show that pornography makes men think of women as objects rather than as people. The public at large also voices concern about the effects of pornography, with almost half of adults holding the opinion that pornography encourages people to commit rape (NORC, 1996:217).

Like sexual harassment, pornography raises complex and conflicting issues. While everyone objects to offensive material, many also think we must protect free speech and artistic expression. Nevertheless, pressure to restrict pornography is building because of an unlikely coalition of conservatives (who oppose pornography on moral grounds) and progressives (who condemn it as a type of subordination of women).

CYBER: What about the future of cyber-sex: "teledildonics," or virtual sex in sensory suits that "connect" individuals or simply provide sexual stimulation?
DISCUSS: Ask how the class distinguishes between "erotic" and "pornographic" material. Debate a proper balance among conservative moral concerns, liberal support for freedom of expression, and feminist opposition to the patriarchal dimensions of pornography.

NOTE: *Playboy*, which was founded in 1953, had a U.S. circulation of 110,000 in one year, and 1.4 million in ten years. Peak circulation was 6 million in the early 1970s; it has fallen to about half that now, although overseas circulation is up (Joseph E. Scott and J. Cuvelier, "Violence in *Playboy* Magazine: A Longitudinal Analysis," *Archives of Sexual Behavior*, Vol. 16 (1987):279–88).

EXPLORING CYBER-SOCIETY

Pornography: As Close as Your Computer

The days when customers passed quickly through the door of the adult bookstore—a windowless building near the airport or along the interstate—may be coming to an end. But that hardly means people are losing their appetite for pornography. Far from it: Pornography is readily available in the privacy of your home via the information superhighway, much of it "hard core," and lots of it for free.

No one knows exactly how much pornography there is on the Internet. Relatively speaking, only a small percentage of Web sites provide anything that might be construed as pornographic. In absolute terms, however, this worldwide communications network includes thousands of sites in dozens of countries that offer erotic stories, sexually explicit chat, and countless images for viewing and downloading.

There are some safeguards. Most pornographic sites require credit card payment before they provide full access. Moreover, software programs (such as Surf Watch and Net Nanny) can be installed to block access to certain sites. But critics of online sex point out that, in most families, young people are the computer experts and there is little

many parents can do to keep their children from finding sexually explicit material on the Web. Especially disturbing to critics is that the most objectionable material seems to be extremely popular: images of naked children and of people engaging in sexual acts with animals.

Defenders of Internet freedoms argue that censoring communication represents a greater threat to people's well-being than pornography does. And, to date, the courts have resisted imposing restrictions on Internet content. But critics—both conservatives seeking to uphold moral standards and progressives who condemn the sexual exploitation of women—say they will continue to speak out against cyber-porn. Perhaps continued attention to the problem of cyber-porn will also make us face up to another question: Why are men—who are overwhelmingly the greater consumers—drawn to pornography in the first place?

THEORETICAL ANALYSIS OF GENDER

Each of sociology's major theoretical paradigms addresses the significance of gender in social organization.

STRUCTURAL-FUNCTIONAL ANALYSIS

The structural-functional paradigm views society as a complex system of many separate but integrated parts. From this point of view, gender functions to organize social life.

As Chapter 4 ("Society") explained, members of hunting and gathering societies had little power over the forces of biology. Lacking effective birth control, women were frequently pregnant, and the responsibilities of child care kept them close to home. At the same time, men's greater strength made them more suited for warfare and hunting game. Over the centuries, this sexual division of labor became institutionalized and largely taken for granted (Lengermann & Wallace, 1985).

Industrial technology, however, opens up a vastly greater range of cultural possibilities. Since human muscle power is no longer the main energy source, so the physical strength of men becomes less significant. And the ability to control reproduction gives women greater choice in shaping their lives. Modern societies have come to see that traditional gender roles waste an enormous amount of human talent; yet change comes slowly, because gender is deeply embedded in social mores.

Q: "Presumably there is continuity from sub-human origins in one critical respect, namely the centering of the earliest child-care responsibilities on the mother. This fact, plus the disabilities of pregnancy and the fact that only recently has other than breast-feeding become widely feasible, lie at the basis of the differentiation of sex roles." Talcott Parsons (1951:155)

SOCIAL SURVEY: "Being born a man or a woman—how important is that for getting ahead in life?" (GSS 1987, N = 1,285; *Codebook*, 1996:707)

"Essential"	2.7%	"Not very important"	32.8%
"Very important"	11.4%	"Not important at all"	26.5%
"Fairly important"	22.7%	DK/NR	3.9%

Here four of the most successful women in Hollywood— Sharon Stone, Jodie Foster, Demi Moore, and Alicia Silverstone—celebrate their position as film industry tycoons. Yet, given our notions linking gender and power, it is little wonder that popular culture often portrays powerful women in masculine terms.

Talcott Parsons: Gender and Complementarity

As Talcott Parsons (1942, 1951, 1954) observed, gender helps to integrate society—at least in its traditional form. Gender, Parsons noted, forms a *complementary* set of roles that links men and women into family units, which, in turn, carry out various functions vital to the operation of society. Women take charge of family life, assuming primary responsibility for managing the household and raising children. Men connect the family to the larger world, primarily by participating in the labor force.

Parsons further argued that socialization teaches the two sexes appropriate gender identity and skills needed for adult life. Thus, society teaches boys—presumably destined for the labor force—to be rational, competitive, and self-assured. This complex of traits Parsons termed *instrumental*. To prepare girls for child rearing, their socialization stresses what Parsons called *expressive* qualities, such as emotional responsiveness and sensitivity to others.

Society, explains Parsons, promotes gender conformity by instilling in men and women a fear that straying too far from accepted standards of masculinity or femininity courts rejection by the opposite sex. In simple terms, women learn to view nonmasculine men as sexually unattractive, while men learn to shun unfeminine women.

Critical evaluation. Structural-functionalism puts forward a theory of complementarity by which gender integrates society both structurally (in terms of what people do) and morally (in terms of what they believe). Although influential at mid-century, this approach has lost much of its standing today.

For one thing, functionalism assumes a singular vision of society that is not shared by everyone. For example, many women have always worked outside the home because of economic necessity, a fact not reflected in Parsons's conventional, middle-class view of family life. Second, critics charge that Parsons's analysis minimizes the personal strains and social costs of rigid, traditional gender roles (Wallace & Wolf, 1995). Third, for those who seek sexual equality, what Parsons describes as gender "complementarity" amounts to little more than male domination.

SOCIAL-CONFLICT ANALYSIS

From a social-conflict point of view, gender involves not just differences in behavior but disparities in power. Historically, ideas about gender have benefited men and limited the lives of women, in a striking parallel to the ways whites have benefited from oppressing racial and ethnic minorities (Hacker, 1951, 1974; Collins, 1971; Lengermann & Wallace, 1985). Thus, conflict theorists claim, conventional ideas about gender promote not cohesion but division and tension, with men seeking to protect their privileges while women challenge the status quo.

As earlier chapters explain, the social-conflict paradigm draws heavily on the ideas of Karl Marx. Yet Marx was a product of his time insofar as his writings focused almost exclusively on men. His friend and collaborator Friedrich Engels, however, did develop a theory of gender stratification (1902; orig. 1884).

Friedrich Engels: Gender and Class

Looking back through history, Engels noted that in hunting and gathering societies the activities of women and men, although different, had comparable importance. A successful hunt brought men great prestige,

SOCIAL SURVEY: "Some people think that the best way for women to improve their position is through women's rights groups (point 1). Other people think that the best way for women to improve their position is for each individual woman to become better trained and more qualified (point 7). Where would you place yourself on this scale?" (GSS 1983, N = 825; *Codebook,* 1996:324)

1 (Women's rights groups), 4.7%   5, 13.7%
2, 2.5%   6, 14.1%
3, 3.6%   7 (Better trained), 43.3%
4, 16.5%   NR, 1.6%

NOTE: An early feminist was Amelia Bloomer, who opposed the hoop skirts of her day. In 1851, she wore a pants outfit designed by a friend, introducing "bloomers" into our language.

but the vegetation gathered by women provided most of a group's food supply. As technological advances led to a productive surplus, however, social equality and communal sharing gave way to private property and, ultimately, a class hierarchy. At about this time, men gained pronounced power over women. With surplus wealth on their hands, upper-class men wanted to be sure of paternity, so they would be able to pass on property to their heirs; they could do this only by controlling women's sexuality. The desire to control property, then, led to monogamous marriage and the family. Women were then taught to remain virgins until marriage, to stay faithful to their husbands thereafter, and to build their lives around bearing and raising children.

According to Engels, capitalism intensifies this male domination. First, capitalism creates more wealth, which confers greater power on men as owners of property and as primary wage earners. Second, an expanding capitalist economy depends on turning people—especially women—into consumers and encouraging them to seek personal fulfillment through buying and using products. Third, to support men in the factories, society assigns women the task of maintaining the home. The double exploitation of capitalism, as Engels saw it, lies in paying low wages for male labor and no wages at all for female work (Eisenstein, 1979; Barry, 1983; Jagger, 1983; Vogel, 1983).

Critical evaluation. Social-conflict analysis highlights how society places the two sexes in unequal positions of wealth, power, and privilege. It is, as a result, decidedly critical of conventional ideas about gender, claiming that society would be better off if we minimized or even eliminated this dimension of social structure.

But social-conflict analysis, too, has its critics. One problem is that this approach sees conventional families—defended by traditionalists as morally good—as a social evil. Second, from a more practical standpoint, social-conflict analysis minimizes the extent to which women and men live together cooperatively, and often quite happily, in families. A third problem with this approach lies in its assertion that capitalism stands as the basis of gender stratification. In fact, agrarian countries are typically more patriarchal than industrial-capitalist societies, and socialist nations—including the People's Republic of China and the former Soviet Union—are strongly patriarchal (Moore, 1992).

Margaret Higgins Sanger (1883–1966) was a pioneer activist in the crusade for women's reproductive rights, a cause that placed her in frequent conflict with the laws of her time. This 1916 photograph shows Sanger, on trial, sitting with her sister Ethel Byrne in a courtroom. Half a century later, at the time of her death, some birth control devices (including condoms) were still not sold over the counter in stores everywhere in the United States.

FEMINISM

Feminism is *the advocacy of social equality for men and women, in opposition to patriarchy and sexism.* The "first wave" of the feminist movement in the United States began in the 1840s as women who opposed slavery, including Elizabeth Cady Stanton and Lucretia Mott, drew parallels between the oppression of African Americans and the oppression of women (Randall, 1982). Their primary objective was to secure the right to vote, which was finally achieved in 1920. But other disadvantages persisted and a "second wave" of feminism arose in the 1960s and continues today.

SOCIAL SURVEY: "How important is the women's rights issue to you?" (GSS 1996, N = 1,460; *Codebook*, 1996:205)
"One of the most important" 11.2% "Not important at all" 9.9%
"Important" 52.1% DK/NR 1.8%
"Not very important" 25.1%
NOTE: In general, support for feminism is stronger on both coasts than in the Midwest and the South.

GLOBAL SNAPSHOT

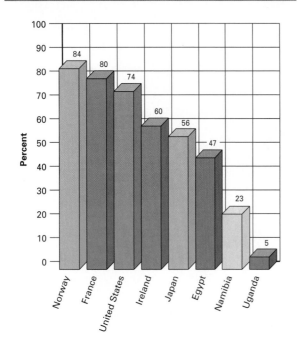

FIGURE 12–4 Use of Contraception by Married Women of Childbearing Age

Source: The World Bank (1995).

BASIC FEMINIST IDEAS

Feminism views the personal experiences of women and men through the lens of gender. How we think of ourselves (gender identity), how we act (gender roles), and our sex's social standing (gender stratification) are all rooted in the operation of our society.

Although people who consider themselves feminists disagree about many things, most support five general principles:

1. **The importance of change.** Feminist thinking is decidedly political, linking ideas to action. Feminism is critical of the status quo, advocating change toward social equality for women and men.

2. **Expanding human choice.** Feminists maintain that cultural conceptions of gender divide the full range of human qualities into two opposing and limited spheres: the female world of emotions and cooperation and the male world of

rationality and competition. As an alternative, feminists propose a "reintegration of humanity" by which each human can develop *all* human traits (French, 1985).

3. **Eliminating gender stratification.** Feminism opposes laws and cultural norms that limit the education, income, and job opportunities of women. For this reason, feminists advocate passage of the Equal Rights Amendment (ERA) to the U.S. Constitution, which states:

Equality of rights under the law shall not be denied or abridged by the United States or any State on account of sex.

The ERA, first proposed in Congress in 1923, has the support of two-thirds of U.S. adults (NORC, 1996:235). Even so, it has yet to become law, which probably reflects the opposition of men who dominate state legislatures around the country.

4. **Ending sexual violence.** Today's women's movement seeks to eliminate sexual violence. Feminists argue that patriarchy distorts the relationships between women and men, encouraging violence against women in the form of rape, domestic abuse, sexual harassment, and pornography (Millett, 1970; J. Bernard, 1973; Dworkin, 1987).

5. **Promoting sexual autonomy.** Finally, feminism advocates women's control of their sexuality and reproduction. Feminists support the free availability of birth control information. As Figure 12–4 shows, contraceptives are much less available in most of the world than they are in the United States. Most feminists also support a woman's right to choose whether to bear children or terminate a pregnancy, rather than allowing men—as husbands, physicians, and legislators—to control women's sexuality. Finally, many feminists support gay people's efforts to overcome the many barriers they face in a predominantly heterosexual culture (Deckard, 1979; Barry, 1983; Jagger, 1983).

VARIATIONS WITHIN FEMINISM

People pursue the goal of sexual equality in various ways, yielding three general types of feminism: liberal, socialist, and radical (Barry, 1983; Jagger, 1983; Stacey, 1983; Vogel, 1983).

Q: "We hold these truths to be self-evident: that all men and women are created equal; that they are endowed by their Creator with certain unalienable rights . . ." Declaration of Sentiments, Seneca Falls, New York (1848)

Q: "The early socialists often argued that problems associated with gender stratification would simply disappear under socialism. The leadership in socialist countries still gives lip service to the

ideal of gender equality and includes it among its long-term goals . . ." Charlotte G. O'Kelly and Larry S. Carney

NOTE: Socialist feminists also oppose the family because living in isolated units discourages the solidarity that leads to collective action by women and men.

NOTE: Radical feminism dovetails with the "children's rights" movement that aspires to free children from dependence on adults.

Violence against women is an important public issue of the 1990s. But, some analysts ask, isn't it men whose lives are built around the experience of violence? In pursuit of a less violent society, how would you change our culture's definitions of masculinity?

Liberal Feminism

Liberal feminism is based on classic liberal thinking that individuals should be free to develop their own talents and pursue their own interests. Liberal feminists accept the basic organization of our society but seek to expand the rights and opportunities of women. Liberal feminists support the Equal Rights Amendment as a means of ending many limitations on women's aspirations.

Liberal feminists also endorse reproductive freedom for all women. They respect the family as a social institution, but seek changes including widely available maternity leave and child care for women who wish to work. They applauded congressional passage of the Family Leave Act in 1992, by which the United States joined more than one hundred nations in guaranteeing maternity leave for all working women.

With their strong belief in the rights of individuals, liberal feminists do not think that all women need to move collectively toward any one political goal. Both women and men, through their individual achievement, are capable of improving their lives if society simply ends legal and cultural barriers rooted in gender.

Socialist Feminism

Socialist feminism evolved from the ideas of Karl Marx and Friedrich Engels, partly as a response to Marx's inattention to gender (Philipson & Hansen, 1992). From this point of view, capitalism increases patriarchy by concentrating wealth and power in the hands of a small number of men.

Socialist feminists reject the reforms sought by liberal feminism as inadequate. The bourgeois family fostered by capitalism must change, they argue, to replace "domestic slavery" with some collective means of carrying out housework and child care. This goal can only be realized through a socialist revolution that creates a state-centered economy to meet the needs of all. Such a basic transformation of society requires women and men to pursue their personal liberation together, rather than individually, as liberal feminists maintain.

Radical Feminism

Radical feminism, too, finds the reforms of liberal feminism inadequate. Moreover, radical feminists claim that even a socialist revolution would not end patriarchy. Instead, this variant of feminism holds that

GLOBAL: In 1990, 10% of the members of the Central Committee of the Communist party in the People's Republic of China were women; none of 19 Politburo members was a woman.
NOTE: Of all people arrested for drunk driving, 95% are men.
NOTE: Boys are 50% more likely to be held back a grade than girls are, twice as likely to be placed in special education classes, and twice as likely to drop out of school.

Q: "For a guy to walk into a bar and have every woman there be ready to jump into bed with him, he would have to be the world's richest, best looking, and bravest guy. For a woman to get the same response from men, she only has to do her hair." Bill Maher, "Politically Incorrect"
Q: "Why isn't 'man's best friend' woman?" Carol Tavris and Carole Offir

gender equality can be realized only by eliminating the cultural notion of gender itself.

The foundation of gender, say radical feminists, is the biological fact that only women bear children. Radical feminists, therefore, look toward new reproductive technology (see Chapter 17, "Family") to separate women's bodies from the process of childbearing. With the demise of motherhood, radical feminists reason, the entire family system could be left behind, liberating women, men, and children from the tyranny of family, gender, and sex itself (Dworkin, 1987). Thus, radical feminism envisions a revolution much more far-reaching than that sought by Marx. It seeks an egalitarian and gender-free society.

OPPOSITION TO FEMINISM

Feminism provokes criticism and resistance from both men and women who hold conventional ideas about gender. Some men oppose feminism for the same reasons that many white people have historically opposed social equality for people of color: They want to preserve their own privileges. Other men and women, including those who are neither rich nor powerful, distrust a social movement (especially its more radical expressions) that attacks the traditional family and rejects time-honored patterns that have guided male-female relationships for centuries.

Further, for some men, feminism threatens the basis of their status and self-respect: their masculinity. Men who have been socialized to value strength and dominance feel uneasy about feminist ideals of men as gentle and warm (Doyle, 1983). Similarly, women whose lives center on their husbands and children may see feminism as trying to deprive them of cherished roles that give meaning to their lives (Marshall, 1985).

Resistance to feminism also comes from academic circles. Some sociologists charge that feminism willfully ignores a growing body of evidence that men and women do think and act in somewhat different ways (which may make gender equality impossible). Furthermore, say critics, with its drive to enhance women's presence in the workplace, feminism denigrates the crucial and unique contribution women make to the development of children—especially in the first years of life (Baydar & Brooks-Gunn, 1991; Popenoe, 1993).

Finally, there is the question of *how* women should go about improving their social standing. A large majority of U.S. adults believe women should have

equal rights, but most also think that women should advance individually, according to their abilities. In a national survey, 70 percent of respondents claimed that women should expect to get ahead on the basis of their own training and qualifications; only 10 percent favor women's rights groups or collective action (NORC, 1996:324).

Thus, opposition to feminism is primarily directed at its socialist and radical variants; otherwise, there is widespread support for the principles of liberal feminism. Moreover, we are seeing an unmistakable trend toward greater gender equality. In 1977, 65 percent of all adults endorsed the statement, "It is much better for everyone involved if the man is the achiever outside the home and the woman takes care of the home and family." By 1996, however, support for this statement had dropped sharply, to 37 percent (NORC, 1996:234).

LOOKING AHEAD: GENDER IN THE TWENTY-FIRST CENTURY

Predictions about the future are always informed speculation. Just as economists disagree about the inflation rate a year from now, and political scientists can only guess at the outcome of next year's elections, so sociologists can offer only general observations about the likely future state of gender and society.

To begin, change has been remarkable. A century ago, women in the United States clearly occupied a subordinate position. Husbands controlled property in marriage, and laws barred women from most jobs, from holding office, and from voting. Although women today remain socially disadvantaged, the movement toward equality has surged ahead. Two-thirds of people entering the work force during the 1990s have been women, and today's economy *depends* on the earnings of women (Hewlett, 1990).

Many factors have contributed to this transformation. Perhaps most important, industrialization has both broadened the range of human activity and shifted the nature of work from physically demanding tasks that favored male strength to jobs that require human thought and imagination, putting the talents of women and men on an even footing. Additionally, medical technology gives us control over reproduction, so women's lives are less constrained by unwanted pregnancies.

Many women and men have also deliberately pursued social equality. Sexual harassment complaints, for example, now are taken much more seriously in the

Q: "Friends are generally of the same sex, for when men and women agree, it is only in their conclusions: Their reasons are always different." George Santayana

Q: "My father and he had one of those English friendships which began by avoiding intimacies and eventually eliminate speech altogether." Jorge Luis Borges

Q: "Conventionality is not morality." Charlotte Brontë

EXERCISE: An enlightening independent research project might focus on the U.S. "dream home." Surveys show that women are more likely than men to desire a "state-of-the-art kitchen" and "walk-in closets," both sexes agree on "in-ground pool," men ask for "game/billiard room," "workshop," and "high-tech entertainment center" (see Mogelonsky, 1997).

CONTROVERSY & DEBATE

Men's Rights! Are Men *Really* So Privileged?

"Anti-male discrimination has become far greater in scope, in degree, and in damage than any which may exist against women." Men's rights advocate Richard F. Doyle

It is men, this chapter argues, who dominate society. Men enjoy higher earnings, control more wealth, exercise more power, do less housework, and get more respect than women do. The quotation above, however, sums up an important counterpoint advanced by the "men's rights movement"—that the male world is not nearly as privileged as most people think.

If men are so privileged in our society, why do they turn to crime more often than women do? Moreover, the operation of the criminal justice system emphasizes the *lack* of special privileges accorded to men. Most people would not be surprised to learn that police are reluctant to arrest a woman (especially if she has children). This fact helps explain why, when police make an arrest for a serious crime, 80 percent of the time the handcuffs are slapped on a man. Moreover, it would seem that men get no break from the courts, since they make up 95 percent of the U.S. prison population. And, even though women can and do kill, all but two of the almost 400 offenders executed during the last several decades have been male.

Culture, too, is not always generous to men. Our way of life praises as "real men" those males who work and play hard, and who typically drink, smoke, and speed on the highways. Given this view of maleness, is it any wonder that men are twice as likely as women to suffer serious assault, three times more likely to fall victim to homicide, and four times more likely to commit suicide? In light of such statistics, even more curious is our national preoccupation with violence against *women*! Perhaps, say men's rights advocates, we are in the grip of a cultural double standard: We expect males to be self-destructive, but lament the far fewer cases in which brutality harms women. It is this same double standard, the argument continues, that moves women and children out of harm's way and expects men to "go down with the ship" or to die defending their country.

Child custody is another sore point from the perspective of many men. Despite decades of consciousness-raising for gender fairness, and clear evidence that men earn more than women, courts across the United States routinely award primary care of children to mothers. And, to make matters worse, men separated from their children by the courts are often stigmatized as "runaway fathers" or "dead-beat dads," even though government studies show that *women* are more likely to

refuse to pay court-ordered child support (in 37 percent of cases) than men are (24 percent of cases).

Moreover, the case against male privilege also notes expanding affirmative action laws, which now cover three-fourths of the population, notably excluding white males. In today's affirmative action climate, critics charge, women have the inside track to college (where they now outnumber men) as well as the work force (where businesses know they will be called to account for hiring practices that favor men).

Even nature seems to plot against men, as, on average, women live six years longer. But the controversial question is, when society plays favorites, who is favored?

Continue the debate . . .

1. *Do you think police are more likely to ticket men than women for traffic violations? If so, why?*

2. *On your campus, do male organizations (such as fraternities and athletic teams) enjoy special privileges? What about women's organizations?*

3. *On balance, do you agree or disagree with the "men's rights" perspective? Which specific points do you find convincing or objectionable? Why?*

Sources: Based on Doyle (1980) and Scanlon (1992).

workplace. And as more women assume positions of power in the corporate and political worlds, social changes in the twenty-first century may be as great as those we have already witnessed.

Gender is an important part of personal identity and family life, and it is deeply woven into the moral

fabric of our society. Therefore, efforts at change will continue to provoke opposition, as the final box illustrates. On balance, however, while changes may be incremental, the movement toward a society in which women and men enjoy equal rights and opportunities seems certain to gain strength.

SUMMARY

1. Sex is a biological concept; a human fetus is female or male from the moment of conception. Hermaphrodites represent rare cases of people who combine the biological traits of both sexes. Transsexuals are people who feel they are one sex when, biologically, they are the other.

2. Heterosexuality is our species' dominant sexual orientation, although people with a bisexual or exclusively homosexual orientation make up a small percentage of the population everywhere.

3. Gender involves how a culture links human traits and power to each sex. Gender varies historically and across cultures. Some degree of patriarchy, however, exists in every society.

4. Through the socialization process, people link gender with personality (gender identity) and their actions (gender roles). The major agents of socialization—family, peer groups, schools, and the mass media—reinforce cultural definitions of what is feminine and masculine.

5. Gender stratification entails numerous social disadvantages for women. Although most women are now in the paid labor force, a majority of them hold clerical or service jobs. Unpaid housework also remains a task performed mostly by women.

6. On average, women earn 74 percent as much as men do. This disparity stems from differences in jobs and family responsibilities as well as discrimination.

7. Women now earn a slight majority of all bachelor's and master's degrees. Men still receive a majority of all doctorates and professional degrees.

8. The number of women in politics has increased sharply in recent decades. Still, the vast majority of elected officials—especially at the national level—are men.

9. An increasing share of U.S. military personnel (currently 15 percent) are women.

10. On the basis of their distinctive identity and social disadvantages, women are a social minority, although many do not think of themselves that way.

11. Minority women encounter greater social disadvantages than white women. Overall, minority women earn about 60 percent as much as white men, which is one reason that half the households headed by African American women are poor.

12. Violence against women is a widespread problem in the United States. Our society is also grappling with the issues of sexual harassment and pornography.

13. Structural-functional analysis suggests preindustrial societies benefit from distinctive roles for males and females reflecting biological differences between the sexes. In industrial societies, marked gender inequality becomes dysfunctional and slowly decreases. Talcott Parsons claimed that complementary gender roles promote the social integration of families and society as a whole.

14. Social-conflict analysis views gender as a dimension of social inequality and conflict. Friedrich Engels tied gender stratification to the development of private property. He claimed that capitalism devalues women and housework.

15. Feminism endorses the social equality of the sexes and actively opposes patriarchy and sexism. Feminism also seeks to eliminate violence against women and give women control over their sexuality.

16. There are three variants of feminist thinking. Liberal feminism seeks equal opportunity for both sexes within current social arrangements; socialist feminism advocates abolishing private property as the means to social equality; radical feminism seeks to create a gender-free society.

17. Even though two-thirds of adults in the United States support the Equal Rights Amendment, this legislation—first proposed in Congress in 1923—has yet to become part of the U.S. Constitution.

KEY CONCEPTS

sex the biological distinction between females and males

primary sex characteristics the genitals, organs used to reproduce the human species

secondary sex characteristics bodily development, apart from the genitals, that distinguishes biologically mature females and males

hermaphrodite a human being with some combination of female and male genitalia

transsexuals people who feel they are one sex though biologically they are the other

sexual orientation an individual's preference in terms of sexual partners: same sex, other sex, either sex, neither sex

gender the significance (including power and privileges) a society attaches to the biological categories of female and male

patriarchy a form of social organization in which males dominate females

matriarchy a form of social organization in which females dominate males

sexism the belief that one sex is innately superior to the other

gender roles (sex roles) attitudes and activities that a society links to each sex

gender stratification a society's unequal distribution of wealth, power, and privilege between men and women

minority any category of people, set apart by physical or cultural difference, that is socially disadvantaged

sexual harassment comments, gestures, or physical contact of a sexual nature that are deliberate, repeated, and unwelcome

feminism the advocacy of social equality for men and women, in opposition to patriarchy and sexism

CRITICAL-THINKING QUESTIONS

1. In what ways are sex and gender related? In what respects are they distinct?
2. What techniques do the mass media employ in order to "sell" conventional ideas about gender to women and men?
3. Why is gender a dimension of social stratification? How does gender interact with inequality based on class, race, and ethnicity?
4. What do feminists mean by asserting that "the personal is political"? Explain how liberal, socialist, and radical feminism differ from one another.

LEARNING EXERCISES

1. If you have access to the Internet, visit the Web site for the National Organization of Women (http://www.now.org). What issues does N.O.W. find most important for women? How is this organization using a Web site to advance its political goals?
2. Take a walk through a business area of your local community. Which businesses are frequented almost entirely by women? By men? By both men and women?
3. Several of the research studies cited in this chapter would be easy to replicate on a small scale. Try spending several hours observing children at play. Do you find that boys and girls play different kinds of games, as Janet Lever's research suggests (see page 324)? Or, examine a sample of newspaper or magazine advertisements; does gender figure in them the way Erving Goffman claims (see page 326)?
4. Do some research on the history of women's issues in your state. When was the first woman sent to Congress? What laws have existed restricting the work of women? Did your state support the passage of the Equal Rights Amendment or not?
5. Install the CD-ROM packaged inside the back cover of your text and complete the activities designed to accompany this chapter.

Harry Roseland, *Beach Scene, Coney Island,* 1891

CHAPTER 13

RACE AND ETHNICITY

On a bright, fall day more than forty years ago, in the city of Topeka, Kansas, a minister walked hand-in-hand with his daughter to enroll her in an elementary school four blocks from their home. But the school refused to admit her. Instead, public school officials required Linda Brown to attend another school two miles away, which meant a daily six-block walk to a bus stop where she sometimes waited half an hour for the bus. In bad weather, the child could be soaking wet by the time the bus came; one day she was so cold that she walked back home. Why, she asked her parents, could she not attend the school only four blocks away?

The answer—difficult for loving parents to give their child—was Linda Brown's introduction to a harsh fact: Skin color made her a second-class citizen in the United States. The injustice of separate schools for black and white children led the Browns and others to file a lawsuit on behalf of Linda Brown and other children, and, in 1954, Linda Brown's question was put to the Supreme Court of the United States. In *Brown v. the Board of Education of Topeka*, the Supreme Court ruled unanimously that racially segregated schools inevitably provide African Americans with inferior schooling, thus striking down the historic doctrine of supposedly "separate but equal" education for the two races.

Many greeted the Supreme Court's decision as a turning point in U.S. public education. Yet, more than four decades later, most U.S. children still attend racially imbalanced schools. Indeed, in a society officially committed to the idea that all people are created equal, race and ethnicity continue to guide the lives of men, women, and children in all sorts of ways.

Globally, the pattern of inequality and conflict based on color and culture is even more pronounced. With the collapse of the former Soviet empire, Ukrainians, Moldavians, Azerbaijanis, and a host of other ethnic peoples in Eastern Europe are struggling to recover their cultural identity after decades of Soviet subjugation. In the Middle East, Arabs and Jews attempt to overcome deep-rooted tensions in much the same way that blacks and whites strive to establish a just society in South Africa. In the African nation of Rwanda, in the Asian countries of India and Sri Lanka, in the Balkans, and elsewhere in the world, racial and ethnic rifts often flare into violent conflict.

SUPPLEMENTS: The *Data File* includes an outline of this chapter, as well as lecture and discussion topics.
NOTE: "Race" is derived from Latin meaning "root"; "ethnic" is derived from the Greek, meaning "culture" or "people"; "minority" has a Latin root meaning "smaller" or "lesser."
DIVERSITY: Of the 133,000 interracial births in 1994, black/white couples account for 56,000; Asian/white, 42,000; Native

American/white, 22,000; Asian/black, 4,000; Native American/black, 1,500; Native American/Asian, 800; other or unknown, 6,700 (U.S. National Center for Health Statistics).
NOTE: Underlying the trend favoring interracial marriages is the rising affluence of African Americans: 1 of 4 black families earns more than $50,000 annually, compared to 1 in 17 who earned a comparable amount in 1970.

Surely one of the greatest ironies of the human condition is that color and culture—sources of our greatest pride—are also traits that so often foment hatred and propel us into war. This chapter examines the meaning of race and ethnicity, explains how these social constructs have shaped our history, and suggests why they continue to play such a central part—for better or worse—in the world today.

THE SOCIAL MEANING OF RACE AND ETHNICITY

People in the United States and elsewhere in the world frequently use the terms "race" and "ethnicity" imprecisely and interchangeably. For this reason, we begin with important definitions.

RACE

A **race** is *a category composed of people who share biologically transmitted traits that members of a society deem socially significant.* People may classify each other into races based on physical characteristics such as skin color, facial features, hair texture, and body shape.

Racial diversity appeared among our human ancestors as the result of living in different geographical regions of the world. In regions of intense heat, for example, humans developed darker skin (from the natural pigment, melanin) as protection from the sun; in regions with moderate climates, people have lighter skin. Such differences are—literally—only skin deep because *every* human being the world over is a member of a single biological species.

The striking variety of racial traits found today is also the product of migration and intermarriage over the course of human history, so that many genetic characteristics once common to a single place are now evident in many lands. Especially pronounced is the racial mix found in the Middle East (that is, western Asia), a region that has long served as a "crossroads" of human migration. Greater racial uniformity, by contrast, characterizes more isolated people such as the island-dwelling Japanese. But every population has some genetic mixture, and increasing contact among the world's people ensures that racial blending will accelerate in the future.

Racial Typology

Nineteenth-century biologists studying the world's racial diversity developed a three-part typology of racial classifications. They called people with relatively light skin and fine hair *Caucasian;* people with darker skin and coarser, curlier hair, *Negroid;* and people with yellow or brown skin and distinctive folds on the eyelids, *Mongoloid.*

Sociologists consider such categories misleading, at best, since we now know that no society is composed of biologically pure individuals. In fact, the traveler notices gradual and subtle racial variations around the world. The skin color of people we might call "Caucasian" (or "Indo-Europeans" or, more commonly, "white people") ranges from very light (typical in Scandinavia) to very dark (as in southern India). The same variation exists among so-called "Negroids" (Africans, or, more commonly, "black people") and "Mongoloids" (that is, "Asians"). In fact, many "white" people (say, in southern India) actually have darker skin than many "black" people (like the Negroid aborigines of Australia).

Although people in the United States distinguish "black" and "white" people, our population is actually genetically mixed. Over many generations and throughout the Americas, the biological traits of Negroid Africans, Caucasian Europeans, and Mongoloid Native Americans (whose ancestors came from Asia) have intermingled. Many "black" people, therefore, have a significant Caucasian ancestry, and many "white" people have some Negroid genes. In short, whatever people may think, race is no black-and-white issue.

Despite the reality of biological mixing, people are quick to classify and rank each other racially. People sometimes defend racial hierarchy, claiming that one category is inherently "better" or more intelligent than another, although no sound scientific research supports such assertions. But because so much is at stake, it is no wonder that societies focus on racial labeling more than facts permit. Earlier in this century, for example, many southern states legally defined as "colored" anyone with as little as one-thirty-second African ancestry (that is, one African American great-great-great grandparent). Today, with less caste distinction in the United States, the law allows parents to declare the race of a child as they may wish.

A Trend Toward Mixture

Indeed, some analysts point out that, in the United States, the concept of race has less and less meaning. For one thing, the number of officially recorded interracial births has doubled in the last fifteen years to 150,000, and now accounts for 4 percent of all births.

NOTE: The faces shown below are from Brazil, China, Sudan, Venezuela, Guatemala, and Egypt.
GLOBAL: People the world over differ not only in skin color but height. The Masai of eastern Africa are tall and thin (which helps to dissipate heat in that equatorial climate); the Eskimos and Aleuts of North America, by contrast, are short and stout, which serves to protect them in a far colder habitat.

GLOBAL: Morocco is a country with a high level of racial mix—southern African, European, and Middle Eastern. Brazil represents another highly varied case with a population descended from all continents.
GLOBAL: Of the world's 191 nations, 90% are ethnically heterogeneous. Among industrial countries, the United States is the most heterogeneous while Japan stands out as the most homogeneous.

The range of biological variation in human beings is far greater than any system of racial classification allows. This fact is made obvious by trying to place all of the people pictured here into simple racial categories.

Moreover, when completing their 1990 census forms, almost 10 million people described themselves by checking more than a single racial category. As time goes on, biologically speaking, race is becoming less of a reality in this society and elsewhere.

ETHNICITY

Ethnicity is *a shared cultural heritage.* Members of an *ethnic category* have common ancestors, language, or religion that, together, confer a distinctive social identity. The United States is a multiethnic society in which English is the favored language, but some 30 million people speak Spanish, French, German, Vietnamese, or some other tongue in their homes. Similarly, the United States is a predominantly Protestant nation, but most people of Spanish, Italian, and Polish ancestry are Roman Catholic, while others of Greek, Ukrainian, and Russian descent belong to the Eastern Orthodox church. More than 6 million Jewish Americans (with ancestral ties to various nations) share a religious history. And, several million men and women in the United States are Muslims.

Race and ethnicity, then, are quite different: One is biological, the other cultural. But the two may go hand in hand. Japanese Americans, for example, have distinctive physical traits and—for those who maintain a traditional way of life—distinctive cultural attributes as well. People can fairly easily modify their ethnicity as, for instance, Korean immigrants who discard their cultural traditions over time. Assuming that people mate with others like themselves, however, racial distinctiveness persists over generations.

Finally, ethnicity involves even more variability and mixture than race, because most people identify with more than one ethnic background. Golf star Tiger Woods, for example, describes himself as one-eighth white, one-eighth American Indian, one-fourth black, and one-half Asian—one-fourth Thai and one-fourth Chinese (White, 1997). Moreover, people intentionally modify their ethnicity. Some immigrants to the United States from India, for example, become

DISCUSS: Does "American" represent an ethnic identity?
DIVERSITY: Worth stressing is that race and ethnicity are categories that interact with class and gender.
SOCIAL SURVEY: As Chapter 19 ("Religion") details, 57% of U.S. adults identify themselves as Protestants, 24% as Catholics, 2% as Jews, and 12% claim no affiliation or preference. (GSS 1996, N = 2,904; *Codebook*, 1996:116)

DIVERSITY: The U.S. Census undercounts minorities. The Census Bureau estimates that, in 1990, roughly 98% of all adults were counted (based on estimates from a post-enumeration survey). Inclusion estimate for African American women is 95%; for African American men, 94%.
DISCUSS: Should gay people be counted as a minority? Why or why not?

TABLE 13–1 Racial and Ethnic Categories in the United States, 1990

Racial or Ethnic Classification	Approximate U.S. Population	Percent of Total Population
African descent	**29,986,060**	**12.1%**
Hispanic descent*	**22,354,059**	**9.0**
Mexican	13,495,938	5.4
Puerto Rican	2,727,754	1.1
Cuban	1,043,932	0.4
Other Hispanic	5,086,435	2.1
Native American descent	**1,959,234**	**0.8**
American Indian	1,878,285	0.8
Eskimo	57,152	<
Aleut	23,797	<
Asian or Pacific Islander descent	**7,273,662**	**2.9**
Chinese	1,645,472	0.7
Filipino	1,406,770	0.6
Japanese	847,562	0.3
Asian Indian	815,447	0.3
Korean	798,849	0.3
Vietnamese	614,547	0.2
Hawaiian	211,014	<
Samoan	62,964	<
Guamanian	49,345	<
Other Asian or Pacific Islander	821,692	0.3
European descent	**200,000,000**	**80.0**
German	57,947,000	23.3
Irish	38,736,000	15.6
English	32,652,000	13.1
Italian	14,665,000	5.9
French	10,321,000	4.1
Polish	9,366,000	3.8
Dutch	6,227,000	2.5
Scotch-Irish	5,618,000	2.3
Scottish	5,314,000	2.1
Swedish	4,681,000	1.9
Norwegian	3,869,000	1.6
Russian	2,953,000	1.2
Welsh	2,034,000	0.8
Danish	1,635,000	0.6
Hungarian	1,582,000	0.6

*People of Hispanic descent may be of any race. Many people also identify with more than one ethnic category. Thus, figures total more than 100 percent. White people represent 80 percent of the U.S. population.

< Indicates less than 1/10 of 1 percent.

Source: U.S. Bureau of the Census (1997).

less "Indian" by absorbing new ethnic traits from others. Sometimes this process goes the opposite way: Recently, many people with Native American ancestry have renewed interest in their cultural heritage (Nagel, 1994; Spencer, 1994).

MINORITIES

As Chapter 12 ("Sex and Gender") described, a racial or ethnic *minority* is a category of people, set apart by physical or cultural traits, that is socially disadvantaged. Distinct from the dominant "majority," in other words, minorities are set apart and subordinated. In recent years, the breadth of the term "minority" has expanded in meaning to include not only people with particular racial and ethnic traits but also people with physical disabilities, and, as the previous chapter explained, women as well.

Table 13–1 presents the broad sweep of racial and ethnic diversity in the United States as recorded by the 1990 census. White people of non-Hispanic background (80 percent of the total) continue to predominate numerically. But the absolute numbers and share of population for virtually every other category are growing rapidly so that, within a century, minorities, taken together, may form a majority of the U.S. population. The box takes a closer look.

Minorities have two major characteristics. First, they share a *distinctive identity*. Because race is highly visible (and virtually impossible for a person to change), most minority men and women are keenly aware of their physical differences. The significance of ethnicity (which people *can* change) is more variable. Throughout U.S. history, some people (such as Reform Jews) have downplayed their historic ethnicity, while others (including many Orthodox Jews) have worked to maintain their cultural traditions and even form their own neighborhoods.

A second characteristic of minorities is *subordination*. As the remainder of this chapter shows, U.S. minorities typically have lower income, lower occupational prestige, and limited schooling. These facts mean that class, race, and ethnicity, as well as gender, are not mutually exclusive but overlapping and reinforcing dimensions of social stratification.

Of course, not all members of any minority category are disadvantaged. Some Latinos, for example, are quite wealthy, certain Chinese Americans are celebrated business leaders, and African Americans are included among our nation's leading scholars. But even the greatest success rarely allows individuals to transcend their minority standing (Benjamin, 1991). That is, race or ethnicity often serves as a *master status* (described in Chapter 6, "Social Interaction in Everyday Life") that overshadows personal accomplishments.

The term "minority" suggests that these categories of people constitute a small proportion of a society's population. But this is not always the case.

Q: "Mentally the Negro is inferior to the white." *Encyclopedia Britannica* (1911)

DIVERSITY: The prospect of a minority-majority is fueling contemporary anti-immigration sentiment, as noted later in this chapter. Recent polls show that about 2 out of 3 U.S. adults want immigration curtailed.

DIVERSITY: Students can see the coming minority-majority in the differing minority composition of young and old in the United States. Among people over 35 years of age, one-fifth are racial or ethnic minorities; among those under 35, one-third are. Thus, young people will reach a minority-majority first (before 2050), while older people will remain mostly white. Similarly, during the next century, central cities will become minority-majority settings while suburbs will remain mostly white.

SOCIAL DIVERSITY

The Coming Minority-Majority?

About a decade ago, Manhattan, the central borough of New York City, achieved a *minority-majority*. This means that people of African, Asian, and Latino descent, together with other racial and ethnic minorities, became a majority of the population. As shown by National Map 13–1 on page 352, the same transformation has also taken place in 186 counties across the United States (about 6 percent of the total). According to some projections, by 2050 minorities will represent a majority of the country as a whole.

A look at Census Bureau data confirms the prospect of a minority-majority. Between 1990 and 1997, the "majority" white, non-Hispanic population increased a modest 6 percent. The number of Asians and Pacific Islanders, however, soared by 34 percent. The Hispanic population increased 30 percent, and the number of Native Americans, Eskimos, and Aleuts jumped by 12 percent. African Americans increased their numbers by 11 percent—almost twice the white rate. This population growth is highly concentrated, however, with more than half the increase taking place in just three states: California, Florida, and Texas.

Not everyone thinks that this country will have a minority-majority in the foreseeable future. Stephan Thernstrom (1990) points out, for example, that such a projection rests on two questionable assumptions. First, the immigration rate must remain at its current high level despite government projections of a coming downturn. Second, the high birth rates that characterize many immigrant minorities today must continue. But, Thernstrom notes, as the years pass, immigrants typically begin to behave more or less like everyone else.

But whatever the specific projections, few people doubt that a great change in the racial and ethnic profile of the United States is underway. It seems only a matter of time before people of European ancestry (other than Hispanics) will become minorities as others—those often termed *people of color*—emerge as the majority in the United States.

For example, black South Africans are a numerical majority in their society, although they are grossly deprived of economic and political power by whites. In the United States, women represent slightly more than half the population but are still struggling to gain opportunities and privileges enjoyed by men.

PREJUDICE

November 19, 1994, Jerusalem, Israel. We are driving along the outskirts of this historic city—a holy place to Jews, Christians, and Muslims—when Razi, our taxi driver, spots a small group of Ethiopians at a street corner. Their mere presence provokes an outburst: "Those people," he begins, "they are different. They don't drive cars. They don't want to improve themselves. Even when our country offers them schooling, they don't take it." He shakes his head and pronounces the Ethiopians "socially incorrigible."

Prejudice is *a rigid and irrational generalization about an entire category of people.* Prejudice is irrational insofar as people hold inflexible attitudes supported by little or no direct evidence. Further, prejudice leads people to characterize an entire category, the vast majority of whom they have never even met. Prejudice may target people with a particular social class, sex, sexual orientation, age, political affiliation, race, or ethnicity.

Prejudices are *prejudgments* that may be positive or negative. Our positive prejudices tend to exaggerate the virtues of people like ourselves, while our negative prejudices condemn those who differ from us. Negative prejudice runs along a continuum, ranging from mild aversion to outright hostility. Because attitudes are rooted in culture, everyone has at least some measure of prejudice.

Most people recognize that white people commonly hold prejudiced views of minorities. But

THE MAP: Minority-majority counties predominate in the South (where the proportion of African Americans historically has been high) and the Southwest (where immigration from Latin America and Asia has been pronounced).

DISCUSS: Consider how stereotypes figure in the following expressions: "Dutch treat," "French kiss," "Russian roulette," or "gypping" someone (derived from "Gypsy"). What traits make up stereotypes concerning the Irish? the Italians? the English?

DIVERSITY: Wood and Chesser (1994) reviewed data showing stereotypes of black people voiced by white university students from 1932 to 1993 and noted a shift toward images more threatening to whites. 1932 top adjectives applied to blacks: "superstitious" and "lazy"; 1993 top adjectives: "loud" and "aggressive."

SEEING OURSELVES

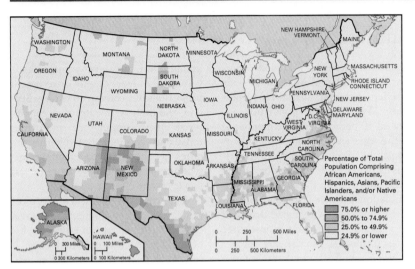

NATIONAL MAP 13–1
Where the Minority-Majority Already Exists

As recorded by the 1990 census, minorities predominate in 186 counties (out of 3,014). That is, the total number of African Americans, Asian Americans, Hispanics, and other minorities exceeds 50 percent of the population. The map also identifies some 40 counties in which minorities together exceed 75 percent of the population and more than 200 counties in which minority population surpasses the 25 percent mark. Why do you think most of these counties are in the South and Southwest?

Source: *Time*, July 12, 1993, p. 15. Copyright © 1993 Time Inc. Reprinted by permisson. Data from the 1990 decennial census.

minorities, too, harbor prejudices, sometimes against whites and often against other minorities. Some Koreans, for example, portray African Americans as dishonest. African Americans, in turn, sometimes express much the same attitude towards Jewish people (Smith, 1996).

STEREOTYPES

Prejudice supports **stereotypes** (*stereo* is derived from Greek meaning "hard" or "solid"), *prejudicial views or descriptions of some category of people.* Because many stereotypes involve emotions like love and loyalty (generally toward members of ingroups) or hate and fear (toward outgroups), they are hard to change even in the face of contradictory evidence. For example, some people have a stereotypical understanding of the poor as lazy, irresponsible freeloaders who would rather rely on welfare than support themselves (NORC, 1996). As Chapter 10 ("Social Class in the United States") explained, however, this stereotype distorts reality since most poor people in the United States are children, working adults, and elderly people.

Stereotypes exist for virtually every racial and ethnic minority, and such attitudes may become deeply rooted in a society's culture. In the United States, almost half of white people stereotype African Americans as lacking the motivation to improve their lives (NORC, 1996:241). Such stereotypes assume social disadvantage is largely a matter of personal deficiency, which, in most cases, it is not. Moreover, stereotypes of this kind ignore the fact that most poor people in the United States are white and that most African Americans work as hard as anyone else and are *not* poor. In this case the bit of truth in the stereotype is that black people are more likely than white people to be poor (and slightly more likely, if poor, to receive welfare assistance). But by constructing a rigid attitude out of a few selected facts, stereotypes grossly distort reality.

RACISM

A powerful and destructive form of prejudice, **racism** refers to *the belief that one racial category is innately superior or inferior to another.* Racism has pervaded world history. The ancient Greeks, the peoples of India, and the Chinese—despite their many notable achievements—were all quick to view people unlike themselves as inferior.

Racism has also been widespread in the United States, where, for centuries, notions about racial inferiority supported slavery. Today, overt racism in this country has subsided to some extent because our more egalitarian culture urges us to evaluate people,

NOTE: Illustrating the power of race, Charles Dryden, one of the Tuskegee airmen—the U.S. Army Air Corps's first unit of African American combat pilots—recalled being forced to give up his seat and move to Negro cars on trains so that white, German POWs could sit down and being barred from military cafeterias where Italian POWs ate (Farley, 1995).

DIVERSITY: Through most of human history, people identified and responded to one another in terms of social categories. The individualistic culture of industrial societies, however, has transformed such categorical responses into social problems. From a modern point of view, various "isms" (racism, ageism, sexism, etc.) are all problematic because they deny people their individuality and value as distinct persons.

in Dr. Martin Luther King's words, "not by the color of their skin, but by the content of their character."

Even so, racism—in thought and deed—remains a serious problem everywhere, and people still contend that some racial and ethnic categories are "better" than others. As the box on page 354 explains, however, racial differences in mental abilities are due to environment rather than biology.

THEORIES OF PREJUDICE

What are the origins of prejudice? Social scientists have provided various answers to this vexing question, citing the importance of frustration, personality, culture, and social conflict.

Scapegoat Theory

Scapegoat theory holds that prejudice springs from frustration. Such attitudes, therefore, are common among people who are themselves disadvantaged (Dollard, 1939). Take the case of a white woman frustrated by the low wages she earns working in a textile factory. Directing hostility at the powerful people who operate the factory carries obvious risk; therefore, she may well attribute her low pay to the presence of minority co-workers. Her prejudice may not go far towards improving her situation, but it serves as a relatively safe way to vent anger, and it may give her the comforting feeling that at least she is superior to someone.

A **scapegoat,** then, is *a person or category of people, typically with little power, whom people unfairly blame for their own troubles.* Because they are often "safe targets," minorities are easily used as scapegoats.

Authoritarian Personality Theory

According to T. W. Adorno (1950), extreme prejudice is a personality trait in certain individuals. This conclusion is supported by research showing that people who display strong prejudice toward one minority are usually intolerant of all minorities. These *authoritarian personalities* rigidly conform to conventional cultural values and see moral issues as clear-cut matters of right and wrong. People with authoritarian personalities also look upon society as naturally competitive and hierarchical, with "better" people (like themselves) inevitably dominating those who are weaker.

Adorno also found that people tolerant toward one minority are likely to be accepting of all. These people

In a legal effort to mitigate sharp patterns of social inequality, India reserves half of all government positions for members of castes deemed disadvantaged. Because the government is the largest employer, higher-caste college students fear that this policy will shut them out of the job market after graduation. So intense are these concerns that eleven students killed themselves recently—five by fire—in public protest over this controversial policy.

tend to be more flexible in their moral judgments and believe that all people should be more or less equal.

Adorno claimed that people with little education who are raised by cold and demanding parents tend to develop authoritarian personalities. Filled with anger and anxiety as children, they grow into hostile and aggressive adults, seeking scapegoats whom they consider inferior.

Cultural Theory

A third theory contends that, while extreme prejudice may be characteristic of certain people, some prejudice is found in everyone because it is embedded in culture. Emory Bogardus (1968) studied the effects of culturally rooted prejudices for more than forty years. He devised the concept of *social distance* to gauge how close or distant people feel in relation to various racial and ethnic categories. Bogardus found that most people feel closest to people of English, Canadian, and Scottish background, even welcoming marriage with them. Attitudes are less favorable toward the French,

NOTE: The success of nativists in restricting immigration after 1920 was fueled in part by "evidence" that southern and eastern Europeans had lower intelligence than northern and western Europeans.

Q: "Despite the emotionally charged philosophical and political issues involved, [the connection between race and intelligence] is ultimately an empirical question . . ." Thomas Sowell

Q: "After all, there is but one race—humanity." George Moore

DIVERSITY: While some researchers cite evidence of genetic differences in brain size and intelligence among various racial categories, social scientists have generally condemned such research as inherently racist. A review of some of this evidence and a discussion of research that has unacceptable political consequences is found in Joynson (1994).

CRITICAL THINKING

Does Race Affect Intelligence?

Are Asian Americans smarter than white people? Is the typical white person more intelligent than the average African American? Throughout the history of the United States, we have painted one category of people as more intellectually gifted than another. Moreover, people have used such thinking to justify the privileges of an allegedly superior category or even to bar supposedly inferior people from entering this country.

Scientists know that the distribution of human intelligence forms a "bell curve," as shown in the figure. By convention, average intelligence is defined as an IQ score of 100 (technically, an IQ score is mental age as measured by a test, divided by age in years, with the result multiplied by one hundred; thus, an eight-year-old who performs like a ten-year-old has an IQ of 10/8 = 1.2 × 100 = 120).

In a controversial study of intelligence and social inequality, Richard Herrnstein and Charles Murray (1994) claim that overwhelming research shows that race is related to intelligence. Specifically, they place the average intelligence quotient (IQ) of people with European ancestry at 100, people of East Asian ancestry at 103, and people of African descent at 90.

Of course, assertions of this kind are explosive because they fly in the face of our democratic and egalitarian sentiments, which say no racial type is inherently "better" than another. In response, some people charge that intelligence tests are not valid, while others question whether what we call "intelligence" has much real meaning.

Most social scientists acknowledge that IQ tests do measure something important that we think of as "intelligence," and they agree that some *individuals* have more intellectual aptitude than others. But they reject the notion that any *category* of people, on average, is "smarter" than any other. That is, categories of people may show small differences on intelligence tests, but the crucial question is *why.*

Thomas Sowell, an African American social scientist, has demonstrated that most of the documented racial differences in intelligence are not due to biology but to people's environment. In some skillful sociological detective work, Sowell tracked down IQ scores for various racial and ethnic categories from early in this century. He found that, on average, immigrants from European nations such as Poland, Lithuania, Italy, and Greece as well as Asian countries including China and Japan scored ten to fifteen points below the U.S. average. Sowell's critical discovery came next: People in these same categories *today* have IQ scores that are average or above average. Among Italian Americans, for example, average IQ jumped almost ten points in fifty years;

among Polish and Chinese Americans, the rise was almost twenty points.

Because genetic changes occur over thousands of years and these people largely intermarried among themselves, biological factors simply cannot explain such a rise in IQ scores. Rather, the evidence points to changing cultural patterns as the cause. As immigrants settled in the United States, their new surroundings affected them over the years, in ways that improved their intellectual performance as measured in intelligence tests.

Sowell found the same pattern applies to African Americans. Sowell explains that African Americans living in the North have historically outscored people living in the South on IQ tests by about ten points. And, among African Americans who migrated from the South to the North after 1940, IQ scores soon rose as they did among earlier immigrants. Thus, if environmental factors are the same for various categories of people, racial IQ differences largely disappear.

What IQ test score disparities do tell us, according to Sowell, is that *cultural patterns* matter. Asians who score high on tests are inherently no smarter than other people, but they have been raised to value learning and to pursue excellence. For their part, African Americans are no less intelligent than anyone else, but they carry a legacy of socioeconomic disadvantage that undermines self-confidence and discourages achievement.

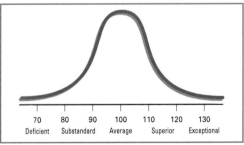

IQ: The Distribution of Intelligence

Sources: Herrnstein & Murray (1994) and Sowell (1994, 1995).

The efforts of these four women greatly advanced the social standing of African Americans in the United States. Pictured above, from left to right: Sojourner Truth (1797–1883), born a slave, became an influential preacher and outspoken abolitionist who was honored by President Lincoln at the White House. Harriet Tubman (1820–1913), after escaping from slavery herself, masterminded the flight from bondage of hundreds of African American men and women via the "Underground Railroad." Ida Wells-Barnett (1862–1931), born to slave parents, became a partner in a Memphis newspaper and served as a tireless crusader against the terror of lynching. Marian Anderson (1897–1993), an exceptional singer whose early career was restrained by racial prejudice, broke symbolic "color lines" by singing in the White House (1936) and on the steps of the Lincoln Memorial to a crowd of almost 100,000 people (1939).

Germans, Swedes, and Dutch, and the most negative prejudices target people of African and Asian descent.

According to Bogardus, then, prejudice is so widespread that we cannot explain it as merely a trait of a handful of people with authoritarian personalities, as Adorno suggests. Rather, Bogardus concludes, almost everyone expresses some bigotry because we live in a "culture of prejudice."

Conflict Theory

A fourth analysis views prejudice as the product of social conflict. According to this theory, powerful people use prejudice to justify their oppression of minorities. To the extent that Anglos look down on illegal Latino immigrants in the Southwest, for example, more well-off people are able to pay Latinos low wages for hard work. Similarly, all elites benefit when prejudice divides workers along racial and ethnic lines and discourages them from working together to advance their common interests (Geschwender, 1978; Olzak, 1989).

A different conflict-based argument, advanced by Shelby Steele (1990), is that minorities themselves cultivate a climate of *race consciousness* in order to win greater power and privileges. In raising race consciousness, Steele explains, minorities argue that they are victims and white people their victimizers. Because of their historic disadvantage, minorities claim that they are entitled to special considerations based on their race. While this strategy may yield short-term gains, Steele cautions that such policies are likely to spark a backlash from white people and others who condemn "special treatment" for anyone on the basis of race or ethnicity.

DISCRIMINATION

Closely related to prejudice is **discrimination,** *treating various categories of people unequally.* While prejudice refers to attitudes, discrimination is a matter of action. Like prejudice, discrimination can be either positive (providing special advantages) or negative (subjecting people to obstacles). Discrimination also varies in intensity, ranging from subtle to blatant.

Prejudice and discrimination often occur together: A prejudiced personnel manager, for example, may

DIVERSITY: In 1991, Supreme Court decisions recognized that, as long as residential segregation exists, desegregating local schools is a virtual impossibility.

NOTE: The most racially segregated U.S. cities in 1990: Gary, Ind.; Detroit, Mich.; and Chicago, Ill.; (all of the top ten were in the Midwest and Northeast); the least segregated: Honolulu, Hawaii; Anaheim, Calif.; and Cheyenne, Wyo. (Farley, 1997).

DIVERSITY: Massey & Denton found *hypersegregation* of African Americans in Baltimore, Chicago, Cleveland, Detroit, Milwaukee, Philadelphia, Gary, Ind., Los Angeles, and New York. Black people, they concluded, are subjected to segregation in the form of multidimensional "layering."

NOTE: The *Brown* decision struck down the "separate but equal" doctrine established in *Plessy* v. *Ferguson* in 1896.

"Star Trek" has been a television favorite for more than thirty years. Compare the cast of the original show, which first aired in 1966, to the crew of the most recent "Star Trek: Voyager." What does the difference in casting suggest about our society's changing view of women? Of racial and ethnic minorities?

and defining them (rather than elites) as the ones who need to do all the changing.

Another limitation of assimilation is that, as a cultural process, it involves changes in ethnicity but not in race. For example, many Americans of Japanese descent have discarded their traditional way of life but still have their racial identity. For racial traits to diminish over generations what is needed is **miscegenation**, *biological reproduction by partners of different racial categories.* Although the rate of interracial marriage is rising, it is still quite low: Only four in one hundred U.S. births are to parents of different races. Even so, miscegenation (often outside of marriage) has occurred throughout U.S. history.

SEGREGATION

Segregation refers to *the physical and social separation of categories of people.* Some minorities, especially religious orders like the Amish, voluntarily segregate themselves. Mostly, however, majorities segregate minorities involuntarily by excluding them. Segregation characterizes residential neighborhoods, schools, occupations, hospitals, and even cemeteries. While pluralism fosters distinctiveness without disadvantage, segregation enforces separation to the detriment of a minority.

South Africa's system of apartheid (described in Chapter 9, "Social Stratification") illustrates rigid and pervasive racial segregation. Apartheid was created by the European minority it served, and white South Africans brutally enforced this system for generations. South Africa has now ended official apartheid but, as yet, its basic racial structure has changed little. The nation remains essentially two different societies that touch only when blacks provide services for whites.

In the United States, too, racial segregation has a long history beginning with slavery and evolving into racially separated lodging, schooling, buses, and trains. Decisions such as the 1954 *Brown* case have reduced overt and *de jure* (Latin meaning "by law") discrimination in the United States. However, *de facto* ("in fact") segregation continues to this day in the form of countless neighborhoods that are home to people of a single race.

Research points to modest declines in racial segregation in the United States during recent decades (Farley, 1997). Yet Douglas Massey and Nancy Denton (1989) have documented the *hypersegregation* of African Americans in some inner cities. These people have little contact of any kind with people in the larger society. Hypersegregation affects about one-fifth of all African Americans but only a few percent of comparably poor whites (Jagarowsky & Bane, 1990).

Segregated minorities understandably resent their second-class citizenship, and sometimes the action of

Q: First they came for the Jews,
   but I did not speak out
   because I was not a Jew.
   Then they came for the Communists,
   and I did not speak out
   because I was not a Communist.

Then they came for the trade unionists,
and I did not speak out
because I was not trade unionist.
Then they came for me,
and no one was left
to speak out for me.
Pastor Martin Niemoeller, victim of the Nazis

even a single person can make a difference. On December 1, 1955, Rosa Parks boarded a bus in Montgomery, Alabama, and sat in the section designated by law for African Americans. When a crowd of white passengers boarded the bus, the driver asked four black people to give up their seats to white people. Three did so, but Rosa Parks refused. The driver left the bus and returned with police, who arrested her for violating the racial segregation laws. A court later convicted Parks and fined her $14. Her stand (or sitting) for justice led the African American community of Montgomery to boycott city buses and ultimately brought this form of segregation to an end (King, 1969).

GENOCIDE

Genocide is *the systematic annihilation of one category of people by another.* Though this deadly form of racism and ethnocentrism violates nearly every recognized moral standard, it has occurred time and again in human history.

Genocide figured prominently in contacts between Europeans and the original inhabitants of the Americas. From the sixteenth century on, as the Spanish, Portuguese, English, French, and Dutch forcefully colonized vast empires, they decimated the native populations of North and South America. Some native people fell victim to calculated killing sprees; most succumbed to diseases brought by Europeans, to which they had no natural immunities (Matthiessen, 1984; Sale, 1990).

Genocide has also occurred in the twentieth century. Unimaginable horror befell European Jews throughout the 1930s and 1940s, during Adolf Hitler's reign of terror known as the Holocaust. The Nazis exterminated more than 6 million Jewish men, women, and children. Soviet dictator Josef Stalin murdered his country's people on an even greater scale, killing perhaps 30 million real and imagined enemies during his violent rule. Between 1975 and 1980, Pol Pot's communist regime in Cambodia slaughtered anyone associated in any way with capitalist culture. Men and women able to speak a Western language and even individuals who wore eyeglasses, construed as a symbol of capitalist culture, were cut down. In all, some 2 million people (one-fourth of the population) perished in Cambodian "killing fields" (Shawcross, 1979).

These four patterns of minority-majority interaction have all been played out in the United States. We proudly point to patterns of pluralism and assimilation, and only reluctantly acknowledge the degree to which

A resurgence of Native American pride is evident in this celebration held in Window Rock, Arizona, in 1991 to honor Navajo soldiers returning from the Persian Gulf War. The older men shown here are World War II veterans—famous Navajo "code talkers"—who fought in the Pacific using their native language as a "code" that the opposing Japanese army could not understand.

our society has been built on segregation (of African Americans) and genocide (of Native Americans). The remainder of this chapter examines how these four patterns have shaped the history and present social standing of major racial and ethnic categories in the United States.

RACE AND ETHNICITY IN THE UNITED STATES

Give me your tired, your poor,
Your huddled masses yearning to breathe free,
The wretched refuse of your teeming shore,
Send these, the homeless, tempest-tossed to me:
I lift my lamp beside the golden door.

These words by Emma Lazarus, inscribed on the Statue of Liberty, express cultural ideals of human dignity, personal freedom, and opportunity. Indeed, the United States has provided more of the "good life" to

SOCIAL SURVEY: "Have we gone too far in pushing equal rights in this country?" "Yes," 51%; "No," 46% (white respondents, 54% and 43%; African Americans, 31% and 64%) (*Newsweek* poll, 2/1–3/95). 1987 responses to same question: "Yes," 42%; "No," 53%.

Q: "What happens to a dream deferred?
    Does it dry up like a raisin in the sun?

Or fester like a sore, and then run?
Does it stink like rotten meat?
Or crust and sugar over, like a syrupy sweet?
Maybe it just sags like a heavy load;
Or does it explode?"
Langston Hughes (*Harlem*, 1951)

Although sometimes portrayed as a highly successful "model minority," Asian Americans are highly diverse and, like other categories of people, include both rich and poor. These young people contend with many of the same patterns of prejudice and discrimination familiar to members of other minorities.

we can take pride in how far we have come in this pursuit. Overt discrimination is now illegal, and research documents a long-term decline in prejudice against African Americans (Firebaugh & Davis, 1988; J. Q. Wilson, 1992; NORC, 1996).

Assessing the state of African Americans in 1913—fifty years after the abolition of slavery—W. E. B. Du Bois pointed to the extent of black achievement. But Du Bois also cautioned that racial caste remained strong in the United States, and, eighty-five years later, racial hierarchy still persists.

ASIAN AMERICANS

Although Asian Americans share some racial traits, enormous cultural diversity marks this category of people with ancestors from dozens of nations. The 1990 census put their number at more than 7 million—approaching 3 percent of the population. The largest category of Asian Americans is people of Chinese ancestry (1.6 million), followed by those of Filipino (1.4 million), Japanese (850,000), Asian Indian (825,000), and Korean (800,000) descent. Most Asian Americans live in the western United States, with 40

percent in California (U.S. Bureau of the Census, 1997).

Young Asian Americans command respect as high achievers and are disproportionately represented at our country's best colleges and universities. Many of their elders, too, have made great economic and social gains; most Asian Americans now live in middle-class suburbs (O'Hare, Frey, & Fost, 1994). Yet, despite (and sometimes because of) their exceptional record of achievement, Asian Americans often find that others are aloof or outright hostile.

At the same time, the "model minority" image of Asian Americans obscures the poverty found within their ranks. We now focus on the history and current standing of Chinese Americans and Japanese Americans—the longest-established Asian American minorities—and conclude with a brief look at the most recent arrivals.

Chinese Americans

Chinese immigration to the United States began during the economic boom of the California Gold Rush of 1849. With new towns and businesses springing up virtually overnight, businesses in need of cheap labor employed some 100,000 Chinese immigrants. Most Chinese immigrants were young, hard-working men willing to take lower-status jobs shunned by whites. But the economy soured in the 1870s, and desperate whites began to compete with the Chinese for whatever work could be found. Suddenly the industriousness of the Chinese and their willingness to work for low wages posed a threat. In short, economic hard times sparked mounting prejudice and discrimination (Ling, 1971; Boswell, 1986).

Soon, whites acted to legally bar the Chinese from many occupations. Courts also withdrew legal protection, unleashing vicious campaigns against "the Yellow Peril." Everyone seemed to line up against the Chinese, as expressed in the popular phrase of the time that someone up against great odds didn't have "a Chinaman's chance" (Sung, 1967; Sowell, 1981).

In 1882, the U.S. government passed the first of several laws curtailing Chinese immigration. This action created great domestic hardship because, in the United States, Chinese men outnumbered women by almost twenty to one (Hsu, 1971; Lai, 1980). The sex imbalance limited marriages and sent the Chinese population plummeting to about 60,000 by 1920. Chinese women already in the United States, however, were in high demand and they soon became far less submissive to men (Sowell, 1981).

NOTE: In 1943, the U.S. government extended the right of citizenship to Chinese Americans born abroad partly in response to China's status as a military ally in the war against Japan (Japanese Americans born abroad could not become U.S. citizens until 1952).

Q: Chinese American novelist Bette Bao Lord recalls that, as an immigrant schoolgirl in Brooklyn, she devised her own version of the Pledge of Allegiance:

I pledge a lesson to the frog
of the United States of America.
And to the wee puppet
for witch's hands.
One Asian, in the vestibule,
with little tea and just rice for all.
(quoted in *Newsweek*, July 6, 1992)

TABLE 13–4 The Social Standing of Asian Americans, 1990

	All Asian Americans	Chinese Americans	Japanese Americans	Korean Americans	Filipino Americans	Entire United States
Median family income	$42,240	$41,316	$51,550	$33,909	$46,698	$35,225
Percent in poverty	14.0%	14.0%	7.0%	13.7%	6.4%	13.1%
Completion of four or more years of college (age 25 and over)	37.7%	40.7%	34.5%	34.5%	39.3%	20.3%

Source: U.S. Bureau of the Census (1997).

Responding to racial hostility, some Chinese moved eastward; many more sought the relative safety of urban Chinatowns. There Chinese traditions flourished, and kinship networks, called clans, provided financial assistance to individuals and represented the interests of all. At the same time, however, living in Chinatown often meant residents did not learn the English language and thus could not find work outside the local community (Wong, 1971).

A renewed need for labor during World War II prompted President Franklin Roosevelt in 1943 to end the ban on Chinese immigration and to extend the rights of citizenship to Chinese Americans born abroad. Many responded by moving out of Chinatowns and pursuing cultural assimilation. In turn-of-the-century Honolulu, for example, 70 percent of the Chinese people lived in Chinatown; today, the figure is down to below 20 percent.

By 1950, many Chinese Americans had experienced considerable upward social mobility. Today, people of Chinese ancestry are no longer restricted to self-employment in laundries and restaurants; they now work in various high-prestige occupations, especially in fields related to science and new information technology (Sowell, 1981).

As shown in Table 13–4, the median family income of Chinese Americans in 1990 ($41,316) stood above the national average ($35,225). The higher income of all Asian Americans reflects, on average, a larger number of family members in the labor force.[3] Chinese

Americans also have an enviable record of educational achievement, with twice the national average of college graduates.

Despite their success, many Chinese Americans still grapple with subtle (and sometimes overt) prejudice and discrimination. Such hostility is one reason that poverty among Chinese Americans stands above the national average. Poverty is higher still among those who remain in the restrictive circle of Chinatowns where many women and men work in restaurants or other low-paying jobs. In fact, sociologists debate whether racial and ethnic enclaves help their residents or exploit them (Portes & Jensen, 1989; Zhou & Logan, 1989; Kinkead, 1992; Gilbertson & Gurak, 1993).

Japanese Americans

Japanese immigration to the United States began slowly in the 1860s, reaching only 3,000 by 1890. Owners of sugar plantations welcomed Japanese immigrants to the Hawaiian Islands (annexed by the United States in 1898 and made a state in 1959) as a source of cheap labor. Early in this century, however, the number of entrants to California rose along with demands for better pay; white people responded by seeking limits to immigration (Daniels, 1971). In 1907 the United States signed an agreement with Japan curbing the entry of men, who were deemed the greater economic threat, while allowing Japanese women to immigrate to ease the sex-ratio imbalance. By the 1920s, state laws in California and elsewhere mandated segregation and banned interracial marriage, virtually ending further Japanese immigration. Not until 1952 did the United States extend citizenship to foreign-born Japanese.

Japanese and Chinese immigrants differed in three ways. First, there were fewer Japanese immigrants, so they escaped some of the hostility directed

---

[3]Data for 1994 place the median income for Chinese Americans at $44,456, above the national figure of $36,782. Median age for all Asian Americans is 30.8, somewhat below the national median age of 34.6 and the white median of 35.7. But specific categories vary considerably in median age: Japanese, 36.1; Chinese, 32.1; Filipino, 31.1; Korean, 29.1; Asian Indian, 28.9; Cambodian, 19.4; Hmong, 12.5 (U.S. Bureau of the Census, 1995).

NOTE: Social diversity was much greater in our history than most people realize, and also perhaps greater than it is today. Vincent Parrillo (1994) describes inaccurate comparisons between past and present diversity as the "Dillingham Flaw," named for Vermont's Senator William P. Dillingham who presided over the Congressional Commission on Immigration (1907–11).

NOTE: Before the Industrial Revolution, relatively few people moved from one country to another. The word "immigrant" entered the English language only around 1790.
SOCIAL SURVEY: "Should immigrants be encouraged to blend into American culture or maintain their own culture more?" (CNN/Gallup Poll, June, 1995)
Blend, 59%   Maintain, 32%   DK/NR, 9%

The strength of family bonds and neighborhood ties is evident in this painting of street life in old San Juan, La Vida en Broma, *by Puerto Rican artist Nick Quijano (1988).*

© Nick Quijano 1997. *La Vida en Broma, 1988: Streetlife in Old San Juan.*

family income for Mexican Americans was $23,240, about two-thirds of the national standard. One-fourth of Chicano families are poor—almost twice the national average. And, despite gains since 1980, Mexican Americans still acquire less schooling than U.S. adults as a whole and have a high dropout rate.

Puerto Ricans

Puerto Rico (like the Philippines) came under U.S. control when the Spanish-American War ended in 1898. In 1917, Puerto Ricans (but not Filipinos) became U.S. citizens.

New York City is the center of Puerto Rican life in the continental United States. Today, this city is home to about 1 million Puerto Ricans. However, one-third of this Puerto Rican community is severely disadvantaged. Adjusting to cultural patterns on the mainland—including, for many, learning English—is one major challenge; also, Puerto Ricans with darker skin encounter especially strong prejudice and discrimination. As a result, about as many people return to Puerto Rico each year as arrive.

This "revolving door" pattern hampers assimilation. Three-fourths of Puerto Rican families in the United States speak Spanish at home, compared with about half of Mexican American families (Sowell, 1981; Stevens & Swicegood, 1987). Speaking only Spanish maintains a strong ethnic identity, but it also limits economic opportunity. Puerto Ricans also have a higher incidence of women-headed households than

other Hispanics, a pattern that places families at greater risk of poverty.

Table 13–5 shows that the 1990 median family income for Puerto Ricans was $18,008, about half the national average. Although long-term mainland residents have made economic gains, more recent immigrants from Puerto Rico continue to struggle to find work. Averaging out the differences, Puerto Ricans remain the most socially disadvantaged Hispanic minority (Rivera-Batiz & Santiago, 1994; Holmes, 1996b).

Cuban Americans

In the decade after the 1959 Marxist revolution led by Fidel Castro, 400,000 Cubans immigrated to the United States. Most settled in Miami. Those who fled Castro's Cuba were generally not the "huddled masses" described on the Statue of Liberty but highly educated business and professional people. They wasted little time becoming as successful in the United States as in their homeland (Fallows, 1983; Kraft, 1993).

Table 13–5 shows that the median household income for Cuban Americans in 1990 was $31,439— well above that of other Hispanics yet still below the national average. The 1 million Cuban Americans living in the United States have managed a delicate balancing act—achieving in the larger society while retaining much of their traditional culture. Of all Hispanics, Cubans are the most likely to speak Spanish in their homes; eight out of ten families do (Sowell,

SOC
Polit
achie
"It w
"Nev
NOT
actio

THEN AND NOW: In 1890, 15% of the U.S. population was foreign born; today, the figure is about 9%.
DISCUSS: Ask students to comment on California's Proposition 187, passed in November, 1994, but not yet put into practice, prohibiting illegal immigrants from using state public services. Also, Californians passed Proposition 209 in 1996, mandating that governments treat people in a racially and ethnically blind manner.

NOTE: The current wave of immigration began in 1965 with liberalization of the old quota system dating from 1924. In essence, "country of origin" ceased to be a key criterion for admission to the United States in favor of special skills and family ties. This sparked a shift from Europe to Latin America and Asia as the source of immigrants, and also allowed many families to join earlier immigrants.

hirin
first
tion.
port
Afric
B
tract
court
ics ar
out
fair c
tem
In ot
main
color
Civil
had
favor
perfo
ethni
Se
mativ
prefe
they
shou
whon
nalize

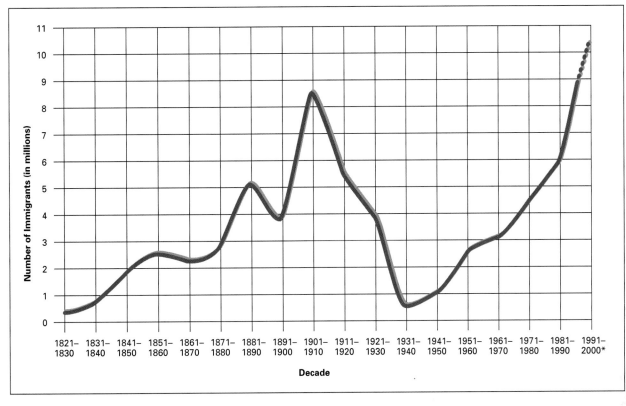

FIGURE 13-3 Immigration to the United States, by Decade

Source: U.S. Immigration and Naturalization Service (1997).
*Projection based on 1991–1996 data.

1981). However, cultural distinctiveness and living in highly visible communities, like Miami's Little Havana, provoke hostility from some people.

WHITE ETHNIC AMERICANS

The term *white ethnics* recognizes the ethnic heritage—and social disadvantages—of many white people. White ethnics are non-WASPs whose ancestors lived in Ireland, Poland, Germany, Italy, or other European countries. More than half the U.S. population falls into one or another white ethnic category (Alba, 1990).

Unprecedented emigration from Europe during the nineteenth century (see Figure 13–3) first brought Germans and Irish and then Italians and Jews to our shores. Despite cultural differences, all shared the hope that the United States would offer greater political freedom and economic opportunity than they had known in their homelands. The belief that "the streets of America were paved with gold" turned out to be a

far cry from the reality, though. Many immigrants found only hard labor for low wages.

White ethnics also endured their share of prejudice and discrimination. Nativist organizations in the mid-nineteenth century opposed the entry of non-WASP Europeans to the United States, and many newspaper ads seeking workers warned new arrivals, "None need apply but Americans" (Handlin, 1941:67).

Some of this prejudice and discrimination was based on class rather than ethnicity, since immigrants with little command of English were typically poor as well. But even distinguished achievers faced hostility. Fiorello La Guardia, the son of immigrants, half Italian and half Jewish, served as mayor of New York between 1933 and 1945. Yet President Herbert Hoover addressed La Guardia with unambiguous ethnic hatred:

You should go back where you belong and advise
Mussolini how to make good honest citizens in
Italy. The Italians are preponderantly our
murderers and bootleggers. . . . Like a lot of

assim
ship
(1942
cans
A
wave
swell
in the
1 mil
year,
the '
newc
many
from
Mexi
the la
N
and

SUMMARY

1. Race involves a cluster of biological traits. Although a century ago scientists identified three broad overarching categories—Caucasians, Mongoloids, and Negroids—there are no pure races. Ethnicity is based not on biology but on shared cultural heritage. Minorities—including people of certain races and ethnicities—are categories of people both socially distinct and socially disadvantaged.

2. Prejudice is an inflexible and distorted generalization about a category of people. Racism, a destructive type of prejudice, asserts that one race is innately superior or inferior to another.

3. Discrimination is a pattern of action by which a person treats various categories of people unequally.

4. Pluralism refers to a state in which racial and ethnic categories, although distinct, have equal social standing. Assimilation is a process by which minorities gradually adopt the patterns of the dominant culture. Segregation means the physical and social separation of categories of people. Genocide is the extermination of a category of people.

5. Native Americans—the original inhabitants of the Americas—have endured genocide, segregation, and forced assimilation. Today the social standing of Native Americans is well below the national average.

6. WASPs predominated among the original European settlers of the United States, and they continue to enjoy high social position today.

7. African Americans endured two centuries of slavery. Emancipation in 1865 gave way to rigid segregation prescribed by law. Today, despite legal equality, African Americans are still relatively disadvantaged.

8. Chinese and Japanese Americans have suffered both racial and ethnic hostility. Although some prejudice and discrimination continues, both categories now have above-average income and schooling. Recent immigration—especially of Koreans and Filipinos—has made Asian Americans the fastest-growing racial category of the U.S. population.

9. Hispanics include many ethnicities sharing a Spanish heritage. Mexican Americans, the largest Hispanic minority, are concentrated in the Southwest. Puerto Ricans, one-third of whom live in New York, are poorer. Cubans, concentrated in Miami, are the most affluent category of Hispanics.

10. White ethnics are non-WASPs of European ancestry. While making gains during this century, many white ethnics still struggle for economic security.

11. Immigration has increased in recent years. No longer primarily from Europe, most newcomers now arrive from Latin America and Asia.

KEY CONCEPTS

race a category composed of people who share biologically transmitted traits that members of a society deem socially significant

ethnicity a shared cultural heritage

prejudice a rigid and irrational generalization about an entire category of people

stereotype a prejudiced view or description of some category of people

racism the belief that one racial category is innately superior or inferior to another

scapegoat a person or category of people, typically with little power, whom people unfairly blame for their own troubles

discrimination treating various categories of people unequally

institutional prejudice or discrimination bias in attitudes or action inherent in the operation of society's institutions

pluralism a state in which racial and ethnic minorities are distinct but have social parity

assimilation the process by which minorities gradually adopt patterns of the dominant culture

miscegenation biological reproduction by partners of different racial categories

segregation the physical and social separation of categories of people

genocide the systematic annihilation of one category of people by another

CRITICAL-THINKING QUESTIONS

1. Differentiate between race and ethnicity. Do you think all non-white people should be considered minorities, even if they have above-average incomes?

2. In what ways do prejudice and discrimination reinforce each other?

3. Are *all* generalizations about minorities wrong? What distinguishes a fair generalization from an unfair stereotype?

4. Do you think U.S. society is becoming more or less color-blind? Is color-blindness a goal worth striving for? Why or why not?

LEARNING EXERCISES

1. Does your college or university take account of race and ethnicity in their admissions policies? Ask to speak with an admissions officer, and see what you can learn about your school's policies and the reasons for them. Ask, too, if there is a "legacy" policy that favors applicants with a parent who attended the school.

2. Give several of your friends or family members a quick quiz, asking them what share of the U.S. population is white, Hispanic, African American, and Asian (see Table 13–1). If they are like most people, they will exaggerate the share of all minorities and understate the white proportion (Labovitz, 1996). What do you make of the results?

3. There are probably immigrants on your campus or in your local community. Have you ever thought about asking them to tell you about their homeland and their experiences since arriving in the United States? Most immigrants would be pleased to be asked and can provide a wonderful learning experience.

4. If you have computer access, visit the Web site of an organization working to improve the social standing of a U.S. minority: the National Association for the Advancement of Colored People (http://www.naacp.org); the Jewish Defense League (http://www.jdl.org); or the Institute for Puerto Rican Policy (http://www.iprnet.org/IPR/). What are the organization's strategies and goals?

5. Install the CD-ROM packaged inside the back cover of your text and complete the activities designed to accompany this chapter.

Deidre Scherer, *Gifts,* 1996
From the collection of St. Mary's Foundation, Rochester, N.Y.

CHAPTER 14

AGING AND THE ELDERLY

Almost as soon as it was released, the book *Final Exit* shot to the top of the best-seller list. This is a book about dying—not about the death of a famous person or a philosophical treatise, but a "how-to" manual explaining how to commit suicide. *Final Exit* gives specific instructions for killing yourself in a host of ways, from swallowing sleeping pills to self-starvation to suffocation with a plastic bag.

The author of *Final Exit*, Derek Humphrey, is a founder and executive director of the Hemlock Society, an organization that offers support and practical assistance to people who wish to die. Humphrey argues that the time has come for people in the United States to have straightforward information about how to end their own lives. The immediate and remarkable popularity of *Final Exit*—especially among the elderly—suggests that millions of people agree with him.

Not surprisingly, *Final Exit* sparked controversy. While supporters view the work as a humane effort to assist people who are painfully and terminally ill, critics worry that it encourages suicide by people who, perhaps, are temporarily depressed (Angelo, 1991). The legal debate went all the way to the U.S. Supreme Court, which, in 1997, declared that terminally ill people have no legal "right to die" with a doctor's help.

Final Exit also raises broader questions that are no less disturbing and controversial than the "right to die." As this chapter explains, the ranks of the elderly are swelling rapidly as more and more men and women live longer and longer. As a result, many younger people are uneasy about their responsibilities toward aging parents. For their part, many older people are, on the one hand, fearful of not being able to afford the medical care they may need and, on the other hand, alarmed at the prospect of losing control of their lives to a hospital staff driven to prolong life at any cost. And people of all ages worry whether the health-care system must shortchange the young in order to meet the escalating demands of seniors.

Today, issues relating to aging and the elderly command the attention of policymakers as never before. In some respects, growing old in the United States has never been better: People live longer, have better health care, and enjoy a higher standard of living than they did a generation ago. But stubborn problems persist. Older people, for example, continue to face prejudice and discrimination. And, because an unprecedented number of women and men are now entering old age, new problems loom on the horizon.

THE GRAYING OF THE UNITED STATES

A quiet but powerful revolution is reshaping the United States: The number of elderly people—women and men aged sixty-five and over—is increasing more than twice as fast as the population as a whole. Between 1970 and 1996, while the overall U.S. population rose 31 percent, the number of seniors climbed by 69 percent and the number over age

SUPPLEMENTS: An outline of this chapter, along with supplementary lecture material and discussion topics, is found in the *Data File.*

NOTE: As the ranks of the elderly swell, our society's share of people under eighteen will drop dramatically. From 36 percent in 1960, and 26 percent in 1990, young people will account for just over 20 percent of the U.S. population by 2030.

NOTE: If today's longevity were the same as it was in 1900, half of the U.S. population would not be here at all; half would have already died, and half would never have been born (White & Preston, cited in Crispell, 1997b).

GLOBAL: Japan has the world's greatest life expectancy. In 1947, figures were: men, 50.1 years, women, 54.0 years; by 1994, comparable data were 76.6 and 82.8 years.

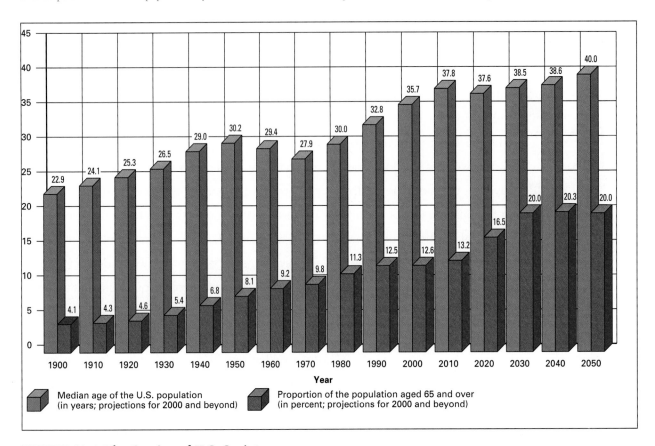

FIGURE 14–1 The Graying of U.S. Society

Source: U.S. Bureau of the Census (1996).

eighty-five soared by 167 percent. This "graying" of the United States promises profound effects.

A few statistical comparisons bring this population shift into sharper focus. In 1900, half the U.S. population was under age twenty-three and only 4 percent had reached sixty-five. By the year 2000, as Figure 14–1 shows, the median age will climb to almost thirty-six, with the elderly accounting for close to 13 percent of the population. Looking at absolute numbers, the elderly population jumped tenfold during this century, surpassing the 34 million mark in 1996. Looking ahead to the year 2050—within the lifetimes of many readers of this book—the number of "seniors" will have tripled, and people over sixty-five will represent fully one-fifth of the population, while *half* the U.S. population will be over forty (U.S. Bureau of the Census, 1997).

Global Map 14–1 shows that it is in the rich nations, including the United States, where the share

of elderly people is rapidly increasing. Typically, two factors combine to drive up the elderly population: low birth rates (so there are fewer children) and increasing longevity (so people typically live well into old age).

In the United States, another factor will soon further swell the ranks of the elderly: the aging of the "baby boomers," some 75 million people born soon after the end of World War II. Moreover, after 1965, the birth rate took a sharp turn downward (the so-called "baby bust" era), so that, early in the next century, the U.S. population will become increasingly "top-heavy."

LIFE EXPECTANCY: GOING UP

This century has witnessed a remarkable thirty-year increase in life expectancy. Females born in 1900 lived, on average, only about forty-eight years, and males,

THE MAP: By 2020, almost all high-income nations will have high proportions of elderly people. Poor countries are those with high birthrates and limited longevity.

GLOBAL: Share of the population aged 65 and older, 1997: Italy, 17.0%; France, 15.6%; Germany, 15.4%; Japan, 15.4%; Canada, 12.5%; Argentina, 10.0%; Ethiopia, 2.7% (U.S. Bureau of the Census, 1997).

GLOBAL: In terms of size of the elderly population, P.R. China leads the world—due to its population size—with nearly 200 million elderly people (about 16 percent of its total population).

THEN AND NOW: Most of the increase in life expectancy occurred during the first half of this century: *1900,* 47.3 years; *1950,* 68.2; *1960,* 69.7; *1970,* 70.8; *1980,* 73.7; *1990,* 75.4; *1996,* 76.1 (U.S. National Center for Health Statistics, 1997).

WINDOW ON THE WORLD

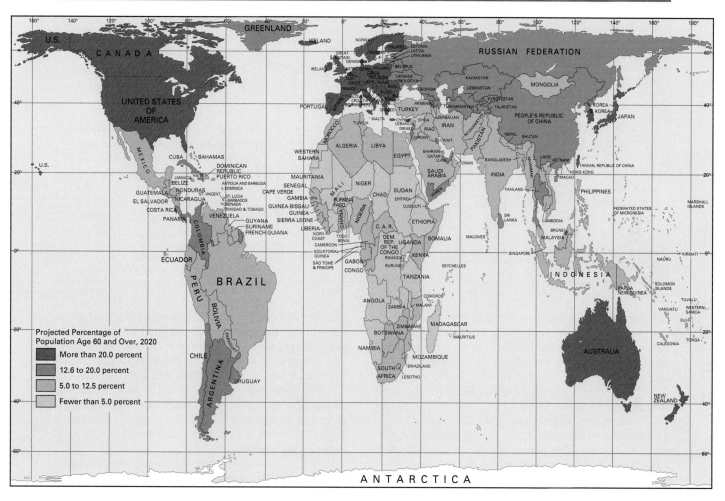

GLOBAL MAP 14–1 The Elderly in Global Perspective, 2020

Here we see projections for the share of population aged sixty-five and older in the year 2020, one generation from now. What relationship do you see between a country's income level and the size of its elderly population?

Source: U.S. Bureau of the Census (1992).

forty-six years. By contrast, females born in 1996 can look forward to seventy-nine years, and men, to seventy-three years (U.S. National Center for Health Statistics, 1997).

Our longer life spans are mainly due to medical advances that virtually eliminated the infectious diseases such as smallpox, diphtheria, and measles that killed many infants and young people a century ago. More recent medical strides fend off cancer and heart disease, afflictions common to the elderly. And, of course, a rising standard of living over the course of this century has promoted the health of people of all ages.

As life becomes longer, the fastest-growing segment of the U.S. population is people over eighty-five, who

THE MAP: Young people migrate to regions of the country where jobs are plentiful; thus, counties with high proportions of elderly people are those that are economically contracting (especially rural counties in the middle of the country).

NOTE: Between 1960 and 1990, overall U.S. population grew 48%; the over-65 population increased 104%, and the 85 and older population soared 305%.

DISCUSS: Pointing ahead to Figure 21–2, an age-sex pyramid for the United States, illustrates the effect of the baby boom and the baby bust.

Q: "Life is one long process of getting tired." Robert Butler

Q: "Our society is getting older, but the old are getting younger. The 70-year-old of today is more like a person of 50 twenty years ago." Robert B. Maxwell, American Association of Retired Persons

SEEING OURSELVES

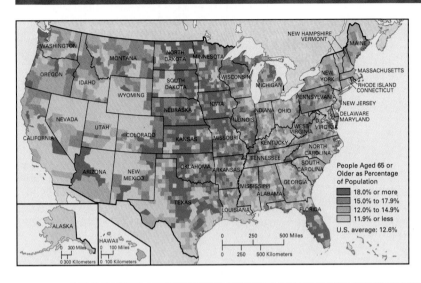

NATIONAL MAP 14–1
The Elderly Population of the United States

Common sense suggests that elderly people live in the Sunbelt, savoring the warmer climate of the South and Southwest. While it is true that Florida has a disproportionate share of people over age sixty-five, it turns out that most counties with high percentages of older people are in the Midwest. What do you think accounts for this pattern? (Hint: Which regions of the United States do *younger* people leave in search of jobs?)

Sources: *American Demographics* magazine, March 1993, p. 34. Reprinted with permission. ©1994, *American Demographics* magazine, Ithaca, New York. Data from the 1990 decennial census.

are already more than twenty times more numerous than they were at the turn of the century. These men and women now number 4 million (about 1.5 percent of the total population). Projections put their number at 18 million (about 5 percent of the total) by the year 2050 (Kaufman, 1990; Harbert & Ginsberg, 1991; U.S. Bureau of the Census, 1996).

We can only begin to imagine the consequences of this massive increase in the elderly population. As more and more older people steadily retire from the labor force, the proportion of nonworking adults—already about ten times greater than in 1900—will generate ever-greater demands for health care and other social resources. Thus, the ratio of elderly people to working-age adults, which analysts term the *old-age dependency ratio*, will almost double in the next fifty years (rising from twenty to thirty-seven elderly people per one hundred people aged eighteen to sixty-four). So far this century, federal spending to support people over sixty-five has tripled. With yet more elderly people needing support from fewer workers, what security can today's babies expect in their old age? (Treas, 1995; Edmondson, 1996)

AN AGING SOCIETY: CULTURAL CHANGE

As the number of people and the share of the population over sixty-five push upward, our way of life will change. In coming decades, interacting with elderly people will become commonplace. Through much of this century, the young rarely mingled with the old, so that most people know little about aging. In the twenty-first century, as the elderly population of the United States increases, age segregation will likely decline.

But, tomorrow as well as today, how frequently younger people interact with the elderly depends a great deal upon where in the country they live. National Map 14–1 looks at residential patterns of people aged sixty-five and older.

Will a "culture of aging" ever emerge? Probably not, for one key reason: the elderly are too diverse. After all, the elderly is an open category in which all of us, if we are lucky, end up. Thus, elderly people in the United States represent not just the two sexes but all cultures, classes, and races.

THE "YOUNG OLD" AND THE "OLD OLD"

Analysts sometimes distinguish two cohorts of the elderly. The younger elderly, who are between sixty-five and seventy-five years, are typically autonomous with good health and financial security; they are likely to be living as couples. The older elderly, who have passed age seventy-five, are more likely to be dependent on others because of health and money problems. Women outnumber men in the elderly population (due to their greater longevity), a discrepancy that increases with advancing age: Among the "oldest

RESOURCE: An excerpt from Betty Friedan's book, *The Fountain of Age*, is included in the 4th edition of the Macionis and Benokraitis reader, *Seeing Ourselves*.
NOTE: Of the hundreds of films released in 1996, 18 had a lead role played by an actor aged 65 or older; of these, 1 (Jeanne Moreau) was a woman (Bandon, 1997).

NOTE: The world's oldest person (at the time of her death in 1997) was Jeanne Calment of Arles, France, age 122. Although suffering poor hearing and lost vision, her mind was sharp: Asked what kind of future she expected, she responded "A very short one" (Wallis, 1995).
Q: "The older I grow, the more I distrust the common notion that age brings wisdom." H. L. Mencken

old"—those over age eighty-five—about two-thirds are women.

GROWING OLD: BIOLOGY AND CULTURE

Studying the graying of the United States is the focus of **gerontology** (derived from the Greek word *geron*, meaning "an old person"), *the study of aging and the elderly*. Gerontologists not only explore how people change as they grow old, they also investigate the different ways societies around the world view the aging process.

BIOLOGICAL CHANGES

Aging consists of a series of gradual, ongoing changes. How we think about life's transitions—whether we welcome our maturity or bemoan our physical decline—depends largely on whether our culture labels aging as positive or negative. The youth-oriented way of life in the United States views biological changes that occur early in life as positive. Through childhood and adolescence, we gain responsibility and look forward to expanded legal rights.

But our culture takes a dimmer view of biological changes that unfold later in life. Few people receive congratulations for getting old. Rather, we commiserate with friends as they turn fifty or sixty, and make jokes to avoid acknowledging that the elderly are on a slippery slope of physical and mental decline. We assume, in short, that at about age fifty, people cease growing *up* and begin growing *down*.

Growing old does bring on certain physical problems. Gray hair, wrinkles, loss of height and weight, and an overall decline in strength and vitality are part of growing old. After age fifty, bones become more brittle so that injuries take longer to heal, and the odds of contracting chronic illnesses (such as arthritis and diabetes) and life-threatening conditions (like heart disease and cancer) rise steadily. The sensory abilities—taste, sight, touch, smell, and especially hearing—also become less keen with age (Colloway & Dollevoet, 1977; Treas, 1995).

Though health becomes more fragile with advancing age, the vast majority of older people are neither discouraged nor disabled by their physical condition. Only about one in ten seniors reports trouble walking, and fewer than one in twenty requires intensive care in a hospital or nursing home. No more than 1 percent of the elderly are bedridden. Overall, while 30 percent

of people over age sixty-five characterize their health as "fair" or "poor," about 70 percent consider their overall condition "good" or "excellent" (U.S. National Center for Health Statistics, 1994).

Bear in mind, however, that patterns of well-being vary greatly within the elderly population. More health problems beset the "older elderly" past the age of seventy-five. Moreover, because women typically live longer than men, women spend more of their lives suffering from chronic disabilities like arthritis. In addition, well-to-do people are likely to live and work in healthful and safe environments, a fact that pays benefits well into old age. And, of course, richer people can afford much more preventive medical care. About 85 percent of elderly people with incomes exceeding $35,000 assess their own health as "excellent" or "good," compared to less than 60 percent of people with incomes under $10,000. Lower income as well as stress linked to prejudice and discrimination also explain why just half of older African Americans assess their health in positive terms, in contrast to three-fourths of elderly white people (U.S. National Center for Health Statistics, 1994; Feagin, 1997).

PSYCHOLOGICAL CHANGES

Just as we tend to overstate the physical problems of aging, it is easy to exaggerate the psychological changes that accompany growing old. The conventional wisdom, in terms of intelligence over the life course, can be summed up as "What goes up, must come down" (Baltes & Schaie, 1974).

If we operationalize intelligence to refer to skills like sensorimotor coordination—the ability to arrange objects to match a drawing—we do find a steady decline as people grow old. The ability to learn new material and think quickly also appears to diminish, although not until around age seventy. But the ability to apply familiar ideas holds steady with advancing age, and some studies actually show improvement in verbal and mathematical skills (Baltes & Schaie, 1974; Schaie, 1980).

We all wonder if we will think or feel differently as we get older. Gerontologists assure us that, for better or worse, the answer is usually no. The only common personality change with advancing age is becoming more introspective. That is, people become more engaged with their own thoughts and emotions and less materialistic. Generally, therefore, two elderly people who were childhood friends would recognize

Q: "How can anyone deny that parents who have toiled for their children in their youth, have lost many a good night's sleep when they were ill, have washed their diapers long before they could talk, and have spent about a quarter of a century bringing them up and fitting them for life, have the right to be fed by them and respected when they are old?" Chinese writer Lin Yutang

NOTE: The social clout of the baby boomer generation is evident in the fact that they defined the 1960s, bringing an end to the Vietnam War, got the vote by the time many of them were eighteen, initiated the second wave of feminism, celebrated the first Earth Day, and then raised the drinking age before their own children turned eighteen (Longino, Jr., 1994).

The reality of growing old is as much a matter of culture as it is of biology. In the United States, being elderly is often synonymous with being inactive; yet, in the Alps mountain region of France and in other more traditional countries, old people commonly continue many familiar routines.

in each other the same personality traits that brought them together as youngsters (Neugarten, 1971, 1972, 1977; Wolfe, 1994).

AGING AND CULTURE

November 1, 1994, approaching Kandy, Sri Lanka. Our little van struggles up the steep mountain incline. Breaks in the lush vegetation offer spectacular views that interrupt our conversation about growing old. "Then there are no old-age homes in your country?" I ask. "In Colombo and other cities, I am sure," our driver responds, "but not many. We are not like you Americans." "And how is that?" I counter, stiffening a bit. His eyes remain fixed on the road: "We would not leave our fathers and mothers to live alone."

When do people grow old? How do younger people regard society's oldest members? The different answers to these questions demonstrate that, while aging is universal, the significance of growing old varies from culture to culture.

At one level, how well—and, more basically, how long—people live is closely linked to a society's technology and overall standard of living. Through most

of human history, as English philosopher Thomas Hobbes (1588–1679) put it, people's lives have been "nasty, poor, brutish, and short" (although Hobbes himself lasted to the ripe old age of ninety-one). In his day, most people married and had children while in their teens, became middle-aged in their twenties, and began to succumb to various illnesses in their thirties and forties. In today's rich nations, it took several more centuries for a rising standard of living and advancing medical technology to curb deadly infectious diseases, so that living to age fifty became common only at the beginning of the twentieth century. Since then, a rising standard of living coupled with medical advances have added almost thirty years to people's longevity.

But living into what we consider "old age" is not yet the rule in much of the world. Global Map 14–2 shows that in the poorest countries the average life span is still just fifty years.

Just as important as longevity is the importance societies attach to their senior members. As Chapter 9 ("Social Stratification") explains, all societies distribute basic resources unequally. We now turn to the importance of age in this process.

AGE STRATIFICATION: A GLOBAL ASSESSMENT

Like race, ethnicity, and gender, age is a basis for ranking individuals socially. **Age stratification,** then, is *the*

THE MAP: Life expectancy closely parallels level of economic development; compare this map to Global Map 1–1 on page 7.

DIVERSITY: Currently, about 54,000 people in the U.S. are centenarians; the Census Bureau projects about 72,000 by the year 2000, and 834,000 by the year 2050. Of today's oldest-of-the-old, 82 percent are women, and 82 percent are white. (African Americans are slightly overrepresented among centenarians.)

NOTE: Life expectancy is affected by changes in infant mortality and tends to exaggerate the change in life span for those who reach old age. In 1900, Americans reaching age 65 typically lived to age 77; by 1990, they could expect to reach 83.

GLOBAL: Japan is graying faster than any other country in the world. This is largely due to a falling birthrate: Japanese women now have a median 1.47 children contrasted to 4.54 in 1949.

WINDOW ON THE WORLD

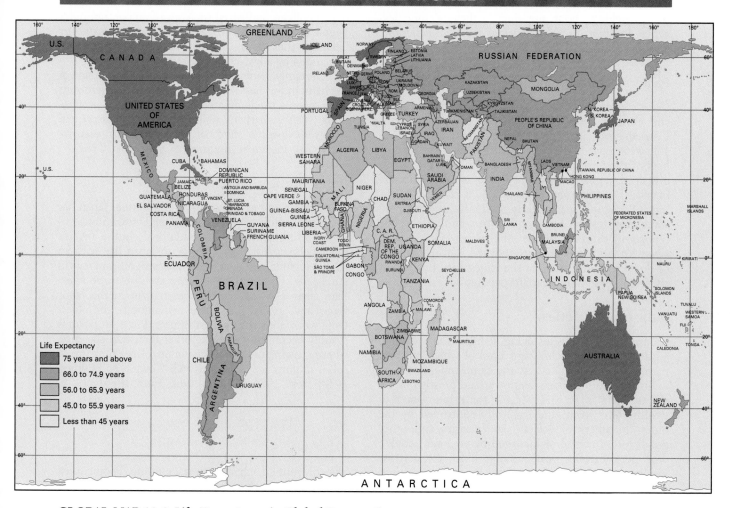

GLOBAL MAP 14–2 Life Expectancy in Global Perspective

Life expectancy has shot upward over the course of this century in industrial countries, including Canada, the United States, Western Europe, Japan, and Australia. A newborn in the United States can expect to live about seventy-six years, and our life expectancy would be greater still were it not for the high risk of death among infants born into poverty. Since poverty is the rule in much of the world, lives are correspondingly shorter, especially in parts of Africa where life expectancy may be as low as forty years.

Source: *Peters Atlas of the World* (1990).

unequal distribution of wealth, power, and privilege among people at different stages of the life course. As is true of other dimensions of social hierarchy, age stratification varies according to a society's level of technological development.

Hunting and Gathering Societies

As Chapter 4 ("Society") explains, without the technology to produce a surplus of food, hunters and gatherers must be nomadic. Moving about as they do,

Q: "While much of the world thinks Japan is a society where the children look after their elderly parents, that is simply no longer the case." Tsuneo Iida, Nagoya University

RESOURCE: Changes in the traditional care structures in Japan are examined in the film, "Aging in Japan: When Traditional Mechanisms Vanish," available from Films for the Humanities and Sciences, Box 2053, Princeton, N.J. 08543.

GLOBAL: Hoyt Alverson reports that, for the Tswana of southern Africa, the concept of aging is synonymous with the notion of "seeing with one's own eyes." For this traditional society, knowledge is "remembering things past," making the elderly the wisest of all (*Mind in the Heart of Darkness*, Yale University Press, 1978:171).

survival depends on physical strength and stamina. Thus, as members of these societies grow old (in this case, reaching about age thirty), they become less active, leading others to consider them an economic burden (Sheehan, 1976).

Pastoral, Horticultural, and Agrarian Societies

Once societies control food supplies by raising crops and animals, they can produce a material surplus. Consequently, individuals can accumulate considerable wealth over a lifetime. The most privileged members of these societies are typically the elderly, which gives rise to **gerontocracy,** *a form of social organization in which the elderly have the most wealth, power, and prestige.* Old people, particularly men, are honored (and sometimes feared) by their families, and, as the box reports in the case of the Abkhasians, they remain active leaders of society until they die. This veneration of the elderly also explains the widespread practice of ancestor worship in agrarian societies.

Industrial Societies

Industrialization pushes living standards upward and advances medical technology, both of which, in turn, increase life expectancy. At the same time, however, industrialization erodes the power and prestige of the elderly. This is, in part, because the prime source of wealth shifts from land (typically controlled by the oldest members of society) to factories and other goods (often owned or managed by younger people). The peak earning years among U.S. workers, for instance, occur around age fifty; after that, earnings generally decline.

Modern living also physically separates the generations as younger people move away to pursue their careers; therefore, they depend less on their parents and more on their own earning power. Furthermore, because industrial, urban societies change rapidly, the skills, traditions, and life experiences that served the old seem less relevant to the young. Finally, the tremendous productivity of industrial nations means that some members of a society do not need to work, so most of the very old and the very young play nonproductive roles (Cohn, 1982).

The long-term effect of all these factors transforms *elders* (a term with positive connotations) into the *elderly* (commanding far less prestige). In mature, industrial societies such as the United States and Canada, economic and political leaders are usually middle-aged people who combine seasoned experience and up-to-date skills. In rapidly changing sectors of the economy—especially high-tech fields—many key executives are quite young, and sometimes barely out of college. Industrial societies often consign older people to marginal participation in the economy because they lack the knowledge and training demanded by a fast-changing marketplace.

Certainly some elderly men and women remain at the helm of businesses they own, but, more commonly, older people predominate only in traditional occupations (such as barbers, tailors, and seamstresses) and jobs that involve minimal activity (night security guards, for instance) (Kaufman & Spilerman, 1982).

Japan: An Exceptional Case

Japan stands out as an exception to the rule. Japan has about the same share of seniors as the United States (14 versus 13 percent), but its traditional culture reveres older people. Most aged people in Japan live with an adult daughter or son, and they play a significant role in family life. Elderly men in Japan are also more likely than their U.S. counterparts to remain in the labor force, and, in many Japanese corporations, the oldest employees enjoy the greatest respect. But even Japan is steadily becoming more like other industrial societies, where growing old means giving up a large measure of social importance (Harlan, 1968; Cowgill & Holmes, 1972; Treas, 1979; Palmore, 1982; Yates, 1986).

TRANSITIONS AND PROBLEMS OF AGING

We confront change at each stage of life. People must unlearn self-concepts and social patterns that no longer apply to their lives and simultaneously learn to cope with new circumstances. Of all stages of the life course, however, old age presents the greatest challenges.

Physical decline in old age is less serious than most younger people think, but even small changes can cause emotional stress. Older people endure more pain, become resigned to limiting their activities, adjust to greater dependence on others, lose dear friends and relatives, and face up to their own mortality. Moreover, because our culture places such a high value on youth, aging in the United States often means added frustration, fear, and self-doubt (Hamel, 1990). As one retired psychologist commented about entering old age: "Don't let the current hype about the joys of retirement fool you. They are not the best of times. It's just that the alternative is even worse" (Rubenstein, 1991:13).

RESOURCE: Another global perspective on aging is Helena Znaniecka Lopata's "Widowhood in Israel" in the Macionis and Benokraitis reader, *Seeing Ourselves.*

NOTE: The age distribution for the American Sociological Association: 34 and below, 19.9%; 35–39, 12.7%; 40–44, 16.9%; 45–49, 17.9%; 50–54, 11.3%; 55 and older, 21.3%.

NOTE: Academics are aging far faster than the population as a whole. According to the National Center for Education Statistics, by the year 2000, a majority of full-time college faculty members will be aged 60 or older. In every discipline except mathematics, at least one-third of faculty members will be 65 or older by 2002. With increasing college enrollments and many coming retirements, our colleagues should be in rising demand.

GLOBAL SOCIOLOGY

Growing (Very) Old: A Report From Abkhasia

Anthropologist Sula Benet was sharing wine and conversation with a man in Tamish, a small village in the Republic of Abkhasia, once part of the Soviet Union. Judging the man to be about 70, she raised her glass and offered a toast to his long life. "May you live as long as Moses," she exclaimed, sipping her wine. Her gesture of goodwill fell flat: Moses lived to 120, but Benet's companion was already 119.

Most outsiders are skeptical about Abkhasians' claims of longevity. In one village of 1,200 visited by Benet, for example, 200 people declared they were over 80. But government statistics confirm that, even if some Abkhasians exaggerate, most handily outlive the average North American.

What accounts for the Abkhasians' remarkable life span? The answer certainly is not advanced medical technology, so important to people in the United States. In fact, many Abkhasians have never even seen a physician or entered a hospital.

The probable explanation for many Abkhasians living so long is cultural, including diet and physical activity. Abkhasians eat little saturated fat (which is linked to heart disease), they use no sugar, and they drink no coffee or tea. Few Abkhasians smoke or chew tobacco. On the other hand, they consume large amounts of healthful fruits and vegetables, and young and old alike drink lots of buttermilk and low-alcohol wine. Abkhasians of all ages also lead active lives built around regular physical work.

Moreover, Abkhasians live according to traditional values that give everyone a strong feeling of belonging and clear sense of purpose. The elderly are active and valued members of the community, in marked contrast to our own practice of pushing old people to the margins of social life. As Benet explains: "The old [in the United States], when they do not simply vegetate, out of view and out of mind, keep themselves 'busy' with bingo and shuffleboard." The Abkhasians, however, do not even have a

word for old people and have no concept of retirement. Furthermore, younger people accord senior members great prestige and respect since, in their slowly changing society, advanced age confers great wisdom. Elders are indispensable guardians of a cultural heritage, and the senior members of the community preside at important ceremonial occasions where they transmit their knowledge to the young. In Abkhasia, in short, people look to the old, rather than the young, for decisions and guidance in everyday life.

Given their positive approach to growing old, Abkhasians expect to enjoy a long and useful life. They feel needed because—in their own minds and everyone else's—they are. Far from being a burden, elders stand at the center of society.

Source: Based on Benet (1971).

SOCIAL SURVEY: "As you know, many older people share a home with their grown children. Do you think this is generally a good idea or a bad idea?" (GSS 1996, N = 1,925; *Codebook*, 1996:187)

"A good idea"	45.9%	"Depends"	19.3%
"A bad idea"	32.8%	DK/NR	2.0%

NOTE: In the 1970s, companies began the practice of providing early retirement benefits or offering other inducements to workers who agreed to retire early, which doubled the rate of early retirement and pulled down the average age at retirement from 67 years in 1950 to 63 years in 1994.

TABLE 14–1 Living Arrangements of the Elderly, 1996

	Men	Women
Living alone	17%	41%
Living with spouse	73%	40%
Living with other relatives or nonrelatives	9%	18%
Living in nursing home	1%	1%

Source: U.S. Bureau of the Census (1997).

FINDING MEANING

Recall from Chapter 5 ("Socialization") Erik Erikson's (1963, 1980) theory that elderly people must resolve a tension of "integrity versus despair." No matter how much they still may be learning and achieving, older people recognize that their lives are nearing an end. Thus the elderly spend much time reflecting on their past accomplishments and disappointments. To shore up their personal integrity, Erikson explains, older women and men must live with past mistakes as well as savor their successes. Without such honesty, this stage of life may turn into a time of despair—a dead end with little positive meaning.

In a classic study of people in their seventies, Bernice Neugarten (1971) found that some people cope with growing older better than others. Worst off are those who fail to come to terms with aging, developing *disintegrated and disorganized personalities* marked by despair. Many of these people end up as passive residents of hospitals or nursing homes.

A second segment of Neugarten's subjects, with *passive-dependent personalities*, were only slightly better off. They have little confidence in their abilities to cope with daily events, sometimes seeking help even if they do not actually need it. Always in danger of social withdrawal, their level of life satisfaction is relatively low.

A third category of people had *defended personalities*, living independently but fearful of aging. They try to shield themselves from the reality of old age by fighting to stay youthful and physically fit. While concerns about health are certainly positive, setting unrealistic standards breeds stress and disappointment.

Most of Neugarten's subjects, however, displayed what she termed *integrated personalities*: They coped well with the challenges of growing old. As Neugarten sees it, the key to successful aging lies in maintaining one's dignity and self-confidence and accepting the inevitability of growing old.

SOCIAL ISOLATION

Being alone can provoke anxiety at any age; isolation, however, is most common among elderly people. Retirement closes off one source of social interaction, physical problems may limit mobility, and negative stereotypes of the elderly as "over the hill" may discourage younger people from close social contact with them.

The greatest cause of social isolation, however, is the inevitable death of significant others. Few human experiences affect people as profoundly as the death of a spouse. One study found that almost three-fourths of widows and widowers cited loneliness as their most serious problem (Lund, 1989). In such cases, people must rebuild their lives in the glaring absence of others with whom, in many instances, they spent most of their adult lives. Some survivors choose not to live at all. One study of widowers found a sharp increase in mortality, sometimes by suicide, in the months following the death of their wives (Benjamin & Wallis, 1963).

The problem of social isolation falls most heavily on women because they typically outlive their husbands. Table 14–1 shows that three-fourths of men aged sixty-five and over live with spouses compared to only four in ten elderly women. On the other hand, 41 percent of older women (especially the "older elderly") live alone, compared to 17 percent of older men. Greater isolation among elderly women in the United States may account for the research finding that their mental health is not as sound as that of elderly men (Chappell & Havens, 1980). Keep in mind, too, that living alone—which many older people value as a sign of independence—presumes the financial means to do so (Mutchler, 1992).

For most older people, families are the primary source of social support. The majority of older people have at least one adult child living no more than ten miles away. About half of these nearby children visit their parents at least once a week, although much research confirms that daughters are more likely than sons to visit regularly (Stone, Cafferata, & Sangl, 1987; Lin & Rogerson, 1994).

RETIREMENT

Work not only provides us with earnings, it also figures prominently in our personal identity. It follows that retirement entails not only a reduction in income but also diminished social prestige and some loss of purpose in life.

Some organizations strive to ease this transition. Colleges and universities, for example, confer the title

DIVERSITY: Historically, retirement has been more a transition for men than for women; today, however, men and women are more equal in this regard.

NOTE: Evidence that people are retiring earlier includes the fact that, in 1956, 2% of Social Security beneficiaries received payments before 65; now more than two-thirds do.

NOTE: Despite the present trend toward greater affluence for the elderly, several factors may undermine their future financial security: (1) the shift toward lower-income jobs noted in Chapter 10; (2) more people reaching 65 will have living parents who require support; (3) an increasingly minority work force that has been historically underpaid will support the retirement system.

SUPPLEMENTS: The *Data File* includes a closer look at hunger among the U.S. elderly.

"professor emeritus" (from Latin, meaning "fully earned") on retired faculty members, who are permitted to maintain their library privileges, parking spaces, and e-mail accounts.

For many older people, new activities and interests minimize the personal disruption and loss of prestige brought on by retirement. Volunteer work can be very rewarding, allowing individuals to apply their career skills to new challenges and opportunities. The American Association of Retired People (AARP), with more than 15 million members over the age of fifty, supports a wide range of volunteer opportunities. Surveys of the oldest baby-boomers—those now reaching fifty—suggest that most expect to work at least part-time after they retire (Mergenhagen, 1996b).

Although the idea of retirement is familiar to everyone today, it emerged only within the last century and only in industrial societies (Atchley, 1982). Advancing technology reduces the need for everyone to work, and it places a premium on up-to-date skills. Retirement permits younger workers, who presumably have the most current knowledge and training, to predominate in the labor force. Then, too, the start of private and public pension programs makes it financially possible for older people to retire. In poor societies, no pension programs exist, so most people work until they can work no more.

Given how varied the elderly population is, we might wonder exactly when (or even if) we should expect people to retire. In our own history, Congress began phasing out mandatory retirement policies in the 1970s and virtually ended the practice by 1987. Even so, as the economic security of the elderly rises, the median age at retirement has been going down: dropping from sixty-eight in 1950 to about sixty-three today. By age sixty-five, then, 83 percent of men and 91 percent of women are not in the paid labor force (Mergenbagen, 1994; U.S. Bureau of the Census, 1997).

AGING AND POVERTY

For many elderly people, the cost of homes and children's college tuitions have been paid; even so, costs for medical care, household help, and home utilities typically go up. And, for most people, retirement means a significant decline in income. Moreover, while some elderly people are affluent, many lack sufficient savings or pension benefits to be self-supporting: Social Security is the major source of income for people over sixty-five. Thus, the risk of poverty rises after midlife, as shown in Figure 14–2.

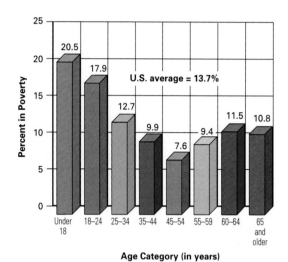

DIVERSITY SNAPSHOT

FIGURE 14–2 U.S. Poverty Rates, by Age, 1996
Source: U.S. Bureau of the Census (1997).

Historically, the rate of poverty among the elderly has fallen sharply. From about 35 percent in 1960, the official poverty rate for elderly people in the United States stood at 10.8 percent in 1996—below the rate (13.7 percent) for the population as a whole. Moreover, since about 1980, seniors have posted a 23 percent increase in average income (in constant dollars), while income of people under thirty-five has actually declined (U.S. Bureau of the Census, 1998).

Several factors have caused this financial windfall: Better health now allows people who want to work to remain employed, employer pension programs are more generous, and more couples now enjoy double incomes. Government policy, too, has played a part, with programs benefiting the elderly (including Social Security) swelling to almost half of all government spending, even as spending on children has remained more or less flat.

But the effects of race and ethnicity are not blunted by growing old. In fact, income inequality among the elderly is greater than among younger adults. In 1996, the poverty rate among elderly Hispanics (24.4 percent) and among elderly African Americans (25.3 percent) was two-and-a-half times the rate for their white, non-Hispanic counterparts (9.4 percent).

Gender, too, continues to shape the lives of people as they age. Among full-time workers, women over

NOTE: Looking at a cross-section of the U.S. population, income is highest about age 50 and wealth is greatest about age 67 (median wealth of $84,000, up from about $57,000 at age 40).
DIVERSITY: The earning disparity between men and women rises with age, since older women have less education relative to their male peers than their younger counterparts do. But even among college graduates, due to different work patterns, women aged 25–34 earn 82% of what comparable men do, while women aged 65 and over earned 38% as much as comparable men.
SOCIAL SURVEY: The National Aging Center on Elder Abuse reports that in about one-third of cases seniors are abused by adult children at home; abuse from spouses comes next, with self-abuse through neglect third.

sixty-five had median earnings of $27,070 in 1996, compared to $42,836 for men over sixty-five. A quick calculation shows that these older full-time working women earn just 63 percent as much as comparable men; thus, the income gap linked to gender is greater among older than younger people (recall that *all* working women earn 74 percent as much as *all* working men). This is because older women typically have much less schooling than men their age and, thus, hold lower-paying jobs.

But, of course, the majority of elderly people have retired from the labor force. Thus, a more realistic financial assessment must take account of the entire elderly population—nonworking as well as working. From this point of view, median individual income is far lower: $9,626 for women, which is 58 percent of the $16,684 earned by men.

In the United States, then, although the elderly are faring better than ever before, growing old (especially among women and other minorities) still means a rising risk of poverty. One recent study, for example, found that poor elderly households typically spend three-fourths of income on basic necessities, which means that these people are just getting by (Koelln, Rubin, & Picard, 1995).

Note, too, that poverty among the elderly is often hidden from view. Due to personal pride and a desire to maintain the dignity of independent living, many elderly people conceal financial problems even from their own families. People who have supported their children for years find it difficult to admit that they can no longer provide for themselves, even though it may be no fault of their own.

ABUSE OF THE ELDERLY

In the United States, we seem to awaken to social problems in stages: We became aware of child abuse during the 1960s, spouse abuse in the 1970s, and, finally, elderly abuse in the 1980s. Abuse of older people takes many forms, from passive neglect to active torment, and includes verbal, emotional, financial, and physical harm. Research suggests that 1 million elderly people (3 percent) suffer serious maltreatment each year, and three times as many (about one in ten) suffer abuse at some point. Like other forms of family violence, abuse of the elderly often goes unreported because victims are reluctant to talk about their plight. But as the proportion of elderly people rises, so does the incidence of abuse (Bruno, 1985; Clark, 1986; Pillemer, 1988; Holmstrom, 1994).

What motivates people to abuse the elderly? Often the cause lies in the stress—both financial and emotional—of caregiving. Today's middle-aged adults are a "sandwich generation" who may well spend as much time caring for their aging parents as for their own children. This stress is especially pronounced among adult women who not only look after parents and children but often hold down a job as well.

Even in Japan—where tradition demands that adult children care for aging parents at home—more and more people find themselves unable to cope. Abuse appears to occur most often when the stress is greatest: in families with a very old person suffering from serious health problems. Family life becomes grossly distorted by demands and tensions that people—even with good intentions—simply cannot endure (Douglass, 1983; Gelman, 1985; Yates, 1986).

AGEISM

In earlier chapters, we explained how ideology—including racism and sexism—serves to justify the social disadvantages of minorities. Sociologists use the parallel term **ageism** for *prejudice and discrimination against the elderly.*

Like racism and sexism, ageism can be blatant (as when a college decides not to hire a sixty-year-old professor because of her age) or subtle (as when a nurse speaks to elderly patients in a condescending tone, as if they were children). Also like racism and sexism, ageism builds physical traits into stereotypes; in the case of the elderly, people view graying hair, wrinkled skin, and stooped posture as signs of personal incompetence. Negative stereotypes portray the aged as helpless, confused, resistant to change, and generally unhappy (Butler, 1975). Even sentimental views of sweet little old ladies and eccentric old gentlemen gloss over people's individuality and ignore years of experience and accomplishment.

Sometimes, like other expressions of prejudice, ageism has some foundation in reality. Statistically speaking, old people are more likely than young people to be mentally and physically impaired. But we slip into ageism when we make unwarranted generalizations about an entire category of people, most of whom do not conform to the stereotypes.

Betty Friedan (1993), a pioneer of the contemporary feminist movement, believes ageism is central to our culture. Friedan points out that elderly people are still conspicuously absent in the mass media; only a small percentage of television shows, for example,

NOTE: Robert Butler coined the term "ageism" in 1969.
RESOURCE: Robert Butler's statement "The Tragedy of Old Age in America," which challenges various myths about old age, is included among the classics in the Macionis and Benokraitis reader, *Seeing Ourselves*.
DIVERSITY: A crucial difference between ageism and racism or sexism that being old is an *open* category that intersects all others.

SUPPLEMENTS: Making use of the *Student CHIP Social Survey Software* reveals that age corresponds to a relatively large difference in most attitudes; much more, typically, than one finds between the sexes.
Q: "Let us recognize ourselves in this old man or in that old woman." Simone de Beauvoir

include main characters over sixty. More generally, when most of us *do* think about older people, it is often in negative terms: This older man *lacks* a job, that older woman has *lost* her vitality, and seniors *look back* to their youth. In short, we tend to think about being old as if it were a disease—marked by decline and deterioration—for which there is no cure.

Rejecting such pessimism, Friedan points out that, all over the United States, older women and men are discovering that they have far more to contribute than others give them credit for. Playing in orchestras, advising small business owners, designing housing for the poor, teaching children to read—there are countless ways in which older people can enhance their own lives and help others.

THE ELDERLY: A MINORITY?

No one doubts that, as a category of people in this country, the elderly face social disadvantages. But sociologists disagree as to whether the aged form a minority in the same way as, say, African Americans or women.

According to Leonard Breen (1960), the elderly are a minority because they have a clear social identity based on their age, and they are subject to prejudice and discrimination. But Gordon Streib (1968) counters that minority status is usually both permanent and exclusive. That is, a person is an African American or woman *for life* and cannot become part of the dominant category of whites or males. Being elderly, says Streib, is an *open* status because, first, people are elderly for only part of their lives and, second, everyone who has the good fortune to live long enough grows old.

Streib further points out that social disadvantages faced by the elderly are less substantial than those experienced by true minorities. For example, old people have never been deprived of the right to own property, to vote, or to hold office, as African Americans and women have. Some elderly people, of course, do suffer economic disadvantages, but these do not stem primarily from old age. Instead, most of the aged poor fall into categories of people likely to be poor at any age. To Streib, it is less true that "the old grow poor" than it is that "the poor grow old."

In light of Streib's arguments and the rising economic fortunes of the elderly in recent decades, it seems reasonable to conclude that old people are not a minority in the same sense as other categories are. Instead, perhaps we should describe the elderly as a distinctive segment of our population with characteristic pleasures and challenges.

Women and men experience stages of the life course in different ways. Most men, for example, pass through old age with the support of a partner. Women, who typically outlive men, endure much of their old age alone.

In sum, growing old involves problems and transitions. Some are brought on by physical decline. But others—including social isolation, adjustment to retirement, and risk of poverty, abuse, and ageism—are social problems. In the next section, we delve into various theoretical perspectives on how society shapes the lives of the elderly.

THEORETICAL ANALYSIS OF AGING

Each of sociology's major theoretical paradigms sheds light on the process of aging in the United States. We examine each in turn.

STRUCTURAL-FUNCTIONAL ANALYSIS: AGING AND DISENGAGEMENT

Drawing on the ideas of Talcott Parsons—an architect of the structural-functional paradigm—Elaine Cumming

NOTE: The cultural value of individualism encourages elderly people to fend for themselves in order to be self-reliant. This kind of social disengagement is vividly evident in the single-room occupancy (SRO) hotels inhabited by many poor, elderly men (Cowgill, 1986:49).

NOTE: Another limitation of activity theory is putting too much emphasis on physical activity (Dale Lund).

NOTE: In 1995, 81,000 people (.2%) aged 65 or older were enrolled in U.S. colleges and universities.

DIVERSITY: The elderly are politically active: 61% of seniors claim to have voted in the 1994 national elections, compared to 32% of people 25 to 34 years of age.

Q: "We must wait until the evening to see how splendid the day has been." Sophocles

and William Henry (1961) point out that aging threatens to disrupt society as physical decline and death take their toll. In response, society *disengages* the elderly—gradually transferring statuses and roles from the old to the young so that tasks are performed with minimal interruption.

Disengagement is thus a strategy to ensure the orderly operation of society by removing aging people from productive roles while they are still able to perform them. Disengagement has an added benefit in a rapidly changing society, since young workers typically bring the most up-to-date skills and training to their work. Formally, then, **disengagement theory** is *the proposition that society enhances its orderly operation by disengaging people from positions of responsibility as they reach old age.*

Disengagement also benefits elderly people as well. People with diminishing capacities presumably look forward to relinquishing the pressures of a job in favor of new pursuits of their own choosing (Palmore, 1979b). Finally, we all tend to grant the elderly greater freedom, viewing any unusual behavior on their part as harmless eccentricity rather than dangerous deviance.

Critical evaluation. Disengagement theory explains why rapidly changing industrial societies typically define their oldest members as socially marginal. But there are several limitations to this approach.

First, many workers cannot disengage from paid work because they do not have the financial resources to fall back on. Second, many elderly people—regardless of their financial circumstances—do not wish to disengage from their productive roles. Disengagement, after all, comes at a high price, including loss of social prestige and social isolation. Third, it is far from clear that the benefits of disengagement outweigh its social costs. There is the loss of human resources on the one hand, and, on the other, the costs of increased care for people who might otherwise be able to fend for themselves. Indeed, as the numbers of elderly people swell, finding ways to help seniors remain independent will be a high priority. Fourth, a rigid system of disengagement does not allow for widely differing abilities among the elderly.

SYMBOLIC-INTERACTION ANALYSIS: AGING AND ACTIVITY

One rebuttal to disengagement theory draws heavily on the symbolic-interaction paradigm. **Activity theory** is *the proposition that a high level of activity enhances personal satisfaction in old age.* Because individuals build their social identities from statuses and roles, disengagement is bound to reduce satisfaction and meaning in elderly people's lives. What seniors need, in short, is not to be yanked out of roles, but a wider range of productive and recreational activities.

Activity theory does not reject the notion of disengagement; rather, it proposes that people substitute new roles and responsibilities for those they leave behind. After all, as members of a society that celebrates productivity, the elderly enjoy active lives as much as younger people do. Research confirms that elderly people who maintain high activity levels derive the most satisfaction from their lives.

Activity theory also recognizes that the elderly are no monolithic category. Older people have highly variable needs, interests, and physical abilities that guide their activities. Therefore, the activities people pursue and how vigorously they pursue them is always an individual matter (Havighurst, Neugarten, & Tobin, 1968; Neugarten, 1977; Palmore, 1979a; Moen, Dempster-McClain, & Williams, 1992).

Critical evaluation. Activity theory shifts the focus of analysis from the needs of society (as stated in disengagement theory) to the needs of the elderly themselves. It emphasizes the social diversity among elderly people, an important consideration in formulating any government policy.

A limitation of this approach, from a structural-functionalist point of view, is the tendency to exaggerate the well-being and competence of the elderly. Functionalist critics ask if we really want elderly people serving in crucial roles, say, as physicians or airline pilots. In 1996, for example, Senator Bob Dole's presidential candidacy was weakened by the fact that he was seventy-seven. From another perspective, activity theory falls short by overlooking the fact that many problems besetting older people have more to do with how society, not any individual, operates. We turn now to that point of view, social-conflict theory.

SOCIAL-CONFLICT ANALYSIS: AGING AND INEQUALITY

A social-conflict analysis is based on the idea that different age categories have different opportunities and different access to social resources, creating a system of age stratification. By and large, middle-aged people in the United States enjoy the greatest power and the most opportunities and privileges, while the elderly (as well as children) contend with less power and prestige

DIVERSITY: The Age Discrimination in Employment Act, 1967, prohibits age discrimination against workers or job applicants aged 40 to 65. As amended in 1975, it outlaws discrimination in federally funded job programs; in 1986 an additional change banned mandatory retirement in almost all types of jobs.

Q: "Let us endeavor to live so that when we come to die even the undertaker will be sorry." Mark Twain

NOTE: Today death is associated with old age; in contrast, a century ago death was common at any age. For instance, none of the Brontë sisters of literary fame lived to the age of 40; Anne (*Agnes Grey*) died at age 29, Emily (*Wuthering Heights*) at 30, and Charlotte (*Jane Eyre*) at 39.

NOTE: A grim demographic fact is that, after age 30, an individual's chance of death doubles every eight years (Waldrop, 1992).

The world's cultures display strikingly different attitudes toward death. Chinese families in Manila, capital city of the Philippines, build tombs big enough to allow the living to gather for meals in the presence of the dead.

and a higher risk of poverty. Employers often replace elderly workers with younger men and women as a way of keeping down wages. Consequently, as conflict theorists see it, older people may well become second-class citizens (Atchley, 1982; Phillipson, 1982).

To conflict theorists, age-based hierarchy is inherent in an industrial-capitalist society. In line with the ideas of Karl Marx, Steven Spitzer (1980) points out that, because our society has an overriding concern with profit, we devalue those categories of people who are economically unproductive. Viewed as mildly deviant because they are less efficient than their younger counterparts, Spitzer explains, the elderly are destined to be marginal members of a society consumed by material gain.

Social-conflict analysis also draws attention to social diversity in the elderly population. Differences of class, race, ethnicity, and gender divide older people as they do everyone else. Thus the fortunate seniors in higher social classes have far more economic security, greater access to top-flight medical care, and more options for personal satisfaction in old age than others do. Likewise, elderly WASPs typically enjoy a host of advantages denied to older minorities. And women—an increasing majority as people age—suffer the social and economic disadvantages of both sexism and ageism.

Critical evaluation. Social-conflict theory adds to our understanding of the aging process by underscoring age-based inequality and explaining how capitalism devalues elderly people who are less productive. The implication is that the aged fare better in noncapitalist societies, a view that has support in research (Treas, 1979).

One problem goes right to the core of the social-conflict approach: Capitalism is not to blame for the lower social standing of elderly people, say critics; *industrialization* is the culprit. Thus, socialism might not lessen age stratification. Furthermore, the notion that either industrialization or capitalism dooms the elderly to economic distress is challenged by the steady rise in income and well being among the U.S. elderly in recent decades.

DEATH AND DYING

To every thing there is a season,
And a time for every matter under heaven:
A time to be born and a time to die . . .

These well-known lines from the Book of Ecclesiastes in the Bible state two basic truths about human existence: the fact of birth and the inevitability of death. Just as life varies in striking ways throughout history and around the world, so death, too, has many faces. We conclude this chapter with a brief look at the changing character of death—the final stage in the process of growing old.

NOTE: Jenny Hockey and Alison James (1993) claim that, as people transit the life course, they move from margins to center and back to the margins.
DIVERSITY: Rates of wearing glasses, by age: under 35: men, 28.8%; women, 39.9%; 35–54: 44.4%, 53.4%; 55 and older: 60.7%, 65.6% (Crispell, 1995).
Q: "Death itself is clearly among the biologically normal phenomena, and the changes which are inseparably connected with the passage of time are equally so . . . [Even so,] it has sometimes been said that we Americans do our best to deny the reality of death . . . The most important point seems to be that we (as Americans) cannot glorify death simply because we value achievement in this life, and death necessarily puts an end to that achievement." Talcott Parsons

HISTORICAL PATTERNS OF DEATH

In the past, confronting death was commonplace. No one assumed that a newborn child would live for long, a fact that led many parents to delay naming children until they survived for a year or two. For those fortunate enough to survive infancy, illness, accident, and natural catastrophe combined to make life uncertain, at best.

Sometimes, in fact, societies facing food shortages have protected the majority by sacrificing the least productive members. *Infanticide* is the killing of newborn infants and *geronticide* is the killing of the elderly.

If death was routine, it was also readily accepted. Medieval Christianity assured Europeans, for example, that death fit into the divine plan for human existence. Historian Philippe Ariès describes Sir Lancelot, one of King Arthur's Knights of the Round Table, preparing for death when he thinks he is mortally wounded:

> His gestures were fixed by old customs, ritual gestures which must be carried out when one is about to die. He removed his weapons and lay quietly upon the ground. . . . He spread his arms out, his body forming a cross . . . in such a way that his head faced east toward Jerusalem. (1974:7–8)

As societies gradually gained more knowledge about health, death became less of an everyday experience. Fewer children died at birth, and accidents and disease took a smaller toll among adults. Except in times of war or catastrophe, people came to view dying as quite *extra*ordinary, except among the very old. In 1900, about one-third of all deaths in the United States occurred before the age of five, and fully two-thirds occurred before the age of fifty-five. Today, by contrast, 85 percent of our population dies *after* the age of fifty-five. Thus death and old age have become fused in our culture.

THE MODERN SEPARATION OF LIFE AND DEATH

Now removed from everyday experience, death seems rather unnatural. If social conditions prepared our ancestors to accept their deaths, modern society, with its youth culture and aggressive medical technology, fosters a desire for eternal youth and immortality. Death has become separated from life.

Death is also *physically* removed from everyday activities. The clearest evidence of this is that many of us have never seen a person die. While our ancestors typically died at home in the presence of family and friends, most deaths today occur in impersonal settings such as hospitals and nursing homes. Even in hospitals, dying patients occupy a special part of the building, and hospital morgues are located well out of sight of patients and visitors alike (Sudnow, 1967; Ariès, 1974).

ETHICAL ISSUES: CONFRONTING DEATH

Moral questions are more pressing than ever now that technological advances give humans the power to prolong life and, therefore, to draw the line separating life and death. We now grapple with how to use these new powers, or whether to use them at all.

When Does Death Occur?

Perhaps the most basic question is one of the most difficult: Precisely how do we define death? Common sense suggests that life ceases when breathing and heartbeat stop. But the ability to revive or replace a heart and artificially sustain breathing renders such notions of death obsolete. Medical and legal experts in the United States now define death as an *irreversible* state involving no response to stimulation, no movement or breathing, no reflexes, and no indication of brain activity (Ladd, 1979; Wall, 1980).

The "Right to Die" Debate

The popularity of the book *Final Exit*, described in the opening to this chapter, suggests that many aging people are less terrified of death than the prospect of being kept alive at all costs. In other words, medical technology now threatens personal autonomy by letting doctors rather than the dying person decide when life is to end. In response, many people now seek control over their deaths just as they seek control over their lives.

Individuals are now taking the initiative and choosing not to employ medical technology to prolong life. After long deliberation, patients, families, and doctors may decide to forgo "heroic measures" to resuscitate a person who is dying. *Living wills*—statements of which medical procedures an individual wants and does not want under specific conditions—are now widespread.

A more difficult issue involves mercy killing or **euthanasia,** *assisting in the death of a person suffering from an incurable disease.* Euthanasia (from the Greek, meaning "a good death") poses an ethical dilemma

NOTE: In Oregon, according to a 1996 study, 21% of physicians reported being asked to assist in a suicide and 7% said they had done so.

NOTE: Philosophically, the "right to die" debate breaks down this way: Those who categorically view life—even with suffering—as preferable to death reject euthanasia. Those who recognize circumstances under which death is preferable to life endorse euthanasia, but they face the practical problem of determining just when life should be ended.

NOTE: People with one year or less to live consume 30% of all Medicare funds; the average person in the United States receives more than one-third of all medical care in the last six months of life.

Q: "I'm not afraid to die; I just don't want to be there when it happens." Woody Allen

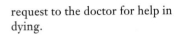

GLOBAL SOCIOLOGY

Death on Demand: A Report From the Netherlands

Marcus Erich picked up the telephone and dialed his brother Arjen's number. In a quiet voice thirty-two-year-old Marcus announced, "It's Friday at 5 o'clock." When the time came, Arjen was there, having driven to his brother's farmhouse an hour south of Amsterdam. They said their final goodbyes. Soon afterward, Marcus's physician arrived. Marcus and the doctor spoke for a few moments, and the doctor then prepared a "cocktail" of barbiturates and other drugs. As Marcus drank the mixture, he made a face, joking "Can't you make this sweeter?"

As the minutes passed, Marcus lay back and his eyes closed. But, after half an hour, he was still breathing. At that point, according to their earlier agreement, the doctor administered a lethal injection. In a few minutes, Marcus's life came to an end.

Events like this take us to the heart of the belief that people should have a "right to die." Marcus Erich was dying from the virus that causes AIDS. For five years, his body wasted away so that he was suffering greatly and had no hope for recovery. It was then that he asked his doctor to end his life.

The Netherlands, a small nation in northwestern Europe, has gone further than any nation in the world in allowing mercy killing or euthanasia. A Dutch law, enacted in 1981, allows a physician to assist in a suicide if the following five conditions are met:

1. The patient must make a voluntary, well-considered, and repeated request to the doctor for help in dying.

2. The patient's suffering must be unbearable and without prospect of improvement.

3. The doctor and the patient must discuss alternatives.

4. The doctor must consult with at least one colleague who has access to the patient and the patient's medical records.

5. The assisted suicide must be performed in accordance with sound medical practice.

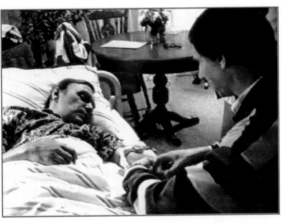

In 1995, according to official records, doctors ended the lives of 3,600 people in the Netherlands. Since many such cases are never reported, the actual number is probably at least twice that many. A rough estimate is that, today, about 5 percent of the Dutch people die with the assistance of a physician.

Sources: Based on della Cava (1997) and Mauro (1997).

since it involves not just refusing life-extending treatment but actively taking steps to end life. In euthanasia, some see an act of kindness, while others find just a form of killing.

Currently, the weight of legal opinion in the United States opposes euthanasia. As of 1998, in almost every state it is a crime for a doctor to help someone die (in five states, the law is unclear). Moreover, in 1997, the U.S. Supreme Court ruled that the Constitution provides no "right to die," further setting back the cause of euthanasia. The Netherlands, however, has the most permissive euthanasia law in the world. The box takes a closer look.

Should the United States hold the line on euthanasia or follow the lead of the Dutch? Supporters of a "right to die" maintain that, faced with unbearable suffering, an individual should be able to choose to live or to die. And, if death is the choice, medical assistance can help people achieve a "good death." Supporters point to public opinion surveys

NOTE: In 1963, Jessica Mitford's *The American Way of Death* pointed out this culture's extravagant funeral rites. Today, we spend half as much on funerals, largely because of the increasing popularity of cremation—up to about 20% of deaths from about 3% in 1960 (Gill, 1996).

Q: "Do not go gentle into that good night; Rage, rage against the dying of the light." Dylan Thomas

CYBER: The first cyber-funeral service has begun operation: For about $6,500, Cybermourn will set up a camera at a funeral and post the live video to a home page site for anyone invited to "participate."

Q: "There may be some good in coming to death at least as well prepared as we go on our vacations, our driving tests, or our weddings." Pico Iyer

Our society has long been concerned with the "good life"; more recently, attention has turned to the idea of a good death. The hospice movement is an important part of this trend. In some cases, terminally ill patients move to a hospice facility, where a professional staff provides medical support and emotional comfort. In other cases, hospice workers provide care in the familiar surroundings of a person's home.

that show about two-thirds of U.S. adults think doctors should be allowed to end the life of a dying person if both the patient and the family request it (NORC, 1996:220).

On the other side of the debate, opponents fear that opening the door to physician-assisted suicide invites abuse. Some point to the Netherlands: In about one-third of all cases, critics estimate, the five conditions noted in the box are not strictly met. In 1991, moreover, a Dutch doctor assisted in the death of a woman who was not dying at all, but was simply depressed over the death of her two sons. (The doctor was prosecuted, but not punished.) More generally, opponents fear that legalization will put society on a "slippery slope" toward more and more euthanasia. Can anyone deny, they ask, that ill people may be pushed into accepting death by doctors who consider suicide the "right" choice for the terminally ill or by family members who are weary of caring for them or who want to avoid the expenses of medical care?

However the debate over the "right to die" turns out in the future, our society has now entered a new era when it comes to dying. Individuals, family members, and medical personnel often must face death not as a medical fact but as a negotiated outcome (Flynn, 1991; Humphrey, 1991; Markson, 1992).

BEREAVEMENT

Elisabeth Kübler-Ross (1969) found that people usually confront their own death in stages (see Chapter 5, "Socialization"). Initially, individuals react with *denial*, followed by *anger*; then they try to *negotiate* a divine intervention. Gradually, they fall into *resignation* and, finally, reach *acceptance*.

According to some researchers, bereavement follows the same pattern of stages. Those close to a dying person, for instance, may initially deny the reality of impending death, and, with time, gradually reach a point of acceptance. Other investigators, however, question any linear "stage theory," arguing that bereavement is an unpredictable process (Lund, Caserta, & Dimond, 1986; Lund, 1989). But all experts agree that how family and friends view an impending death affects the person who is dying. Specifically, if others accept approaching death, the dying person can do the same. By contrast, denying death can isolate the dying person, who is unable to share feelings and experiences with others.

Many dying people find support in the *hospice movement*. Unlike a hospital that is designed to cure disease, a hospice helps people have a good death. These care centers for dying people work to minimize pain and suffering—either there or at home—and encourage family members to remain close by (Stoddard, 1978).

Even under the most favorable circumstances, though, bereavement may involve profound grief and social disorientation that persist for some time. Research documents that bereavement is less intense for someone who accepts the death of a loved one and feels the relationship with the dying person has reached a satisfactory resolution. By taking the opportunity to put appropriate closure on the relationship with a dying person, in other words, family and friends are better able to comfort one another after death occurs (Atchley, 1983).

LOOKING AHEAD: AGING IN THE TWENTY-FIRST CENTURY

This chapter has explored the "graying" of the United States and other industrial nations. We can predict with confidence that the ranks of the elderly will swell dramatically in the century to come: By 2050, our elderly population will exceed the population of the entire country back in 1900. Moreover, one in five of these seniors will be over eighty-five. Within the next fifty years, then, society's oldest members will gain a

DISCUSS: Daniel Callahan's analysis raises important questions: Is getting older *good* for everyone? Is it even *possible* for everyone?
DISCUSS: How will the rising responsibility to care for aging parents affect today's younger people? What are the financial and emotional concerns? Will this speed or delay their own retirement?
NOTE: Deaths in the U.S. are most numerous in winter and about 25% lower in the summer months (Edmondson, 1997).

Q: Daniel Callahan advocates "an understanding of the process of aging and death that looks to our obligations to the young and to the future, that sees old age as a source of knowledge and insight of value to other age groups, that recognizes the necessity of limits and the acceptance of decline and death, and that values the old for their age and not their continuing youthful vitality." (1987:223)

CONTROVERSY & DEBATE

Setting Limits:
Must We "Pull the Plug" on Old Age?

Because death struck at any time, often without warning, our ancestors would have found the question, "Can people live *too long*?" absurd. In recent decades, however, an increasing U.S. elderly population, widespread support for using technology to prolong life, and a dizzying increase in the cost of life-extending medical technology have prompted people to wonder how much old age we can afford.

Currently, about half an individual's lifetime expenditure for medical care falls during the final years of life, and this share is projected to increase. Against the spiraling costs of prolonging life, then, we well may ask if what is technically possible is necessarily desirable. As we enter the next century, warns gerontologist Daniel Callahan, a surging elderly population ready and eager to extend their lives will eventually force us either to "pull the plug" on old age or to shortchange everyone else.

Even to raise this issue, Callahan concedes, smacks of a lack of caring. But consider that the bill for the elderly's health care will top $200 billion by the year 2000—more than twice what it cost in 1980. This dramatic increase reflects our current policy of directing more and more medical resources toward studying

and treating the diseases and disabilities of old age.

So Callahan makes a bold case for limits. He reasons, first, that to spend more on behalf of the elderly we must spend less on others. But with a growing problem of poverty among children, can we continue to spend more and more on the oldest members of our society?

Second, Callahan reminds us, a *longer* life does not necessarily make for a *better* life. Cost aside, does heart surgery that may prolong the life of an eighty-four-year-old woman a year or two truly improve the quality of her life? Cost considered, would those resources yield more "quality of life" if used, say, to transplant a kidney into a ten-year-old boy?

Third, Callahan urges us to reconsider our idea of death. Today, many people rage against death as an enemy to be conquered at all costs. Yet, he suggests, a sensible health-care program for an aging society must acknowledge death as a natural end to the life course. If we cannot make peace with death for our own well-being, limited financial resources demand that we do so for the benefit of others.

A compelling counterpoint, of course, is that people who have worked

all their lives to make our society what it is should enjoy society's generosity in their final years. Moreover, in light of our tradition of personal independence and responsibility, can we ethically deny medical care to an aging person able and willing to pay for it?

What is clear from everyone's point of view is that, in the next century, we will face questions that few would have imagined even fifty years ago: Is peak longevity good for everyone? Is it even *possible* for everyone?

Continue the debate . . .

1. *Should doctors and hospitals use a double standard, offering more complete care to the youngest people and more limited care to society's oldest members?*

2. *Do you think that a goal of the medical establishment should be to extend life at all costs?*

3. *Is the idea of rationing medical care really new? Hasn't our society historically done exactly this by allowing some people to amass more wealth than others?*

Source: Callahan (1987).

---

far greater voice in everyday life. Gerontology—the study of the elderly—is also sure to gain in stature.

The reshaping of the age structure of our society raises many serious concerns. With more people in their old age (and living longer once they enter old age), will we have the support services to sustain them? Remember that, as the elderly make demands, proportionately fewer younger people will be there to respond. And what about

the spiraling medical-care costs of an aging society? As the baby boomers enter old age, some analysts paint a doomsday picture of the United States as a "twenty-first century Calcutta," with desperate and dying elderly people everywhere (Longino, Jr., 1994:13).

But not all the signs are ominous. For one thing, the health of tomorrow's elderly people (that is, today's young and middle-aged adults) is better than ever:

Smoking is way down and the consumption of heathy foods, way up. Such trends probably mean that the elderly of the next century will be more vigorous and independent than their counterparts are today. Moreover, tomorrow's seniors will enjoy the benefits of steadily advancing medical technology although, as the closing box explains, the claim of the old on our nation's resources is already hotly debated.

Another positive sign is the financial strength of the elderly. Though the cost of living is sure to rise, tomorrow's elderly will draw on greater affluence than ever before. Note, too, that the baby-boomers will be the first generation of U.S. seniors in which most women have been in the labor force, a fact reflected in their substantial savings and pensions.

One concern, as we look ahead, is that younger adults will face a mounting responsibility to care for aging parents. Indeed, a falling birthrate coupled with a growing elderly population means caregiving in our society will be redirected from the very young to the very old.

Finally, an aging population will almost certainly change the way we view death. In all likelihood, death will become less of a social taboo and reestablish itself as a natural part of the life course. Should this come to pass, both young and old alike will benefit.

SUMMARY

1. The proportion of elderly people in the U.S. population has risen from 4 percent in 1900 to almost 13 percent today; by the middle of the next century, 20 percent of our people will be elderly.

2. Gerontology, the study of aging and the elderly, focuses on how people change in old age, and how various cultures define aging.

3. Growing old is accompanied by a rising incidence of disease and disability. Most seniors, however, are healthy. Younger people, moreover, commonly exaggerate the extent of disability among the elderly.

4. Psychological research confirms that growing old does not result in overall loss of intelligence or great personality change.

5. The age at which people are defined as old varies historically: Until several centuries ago, old age began as early as thirty. In poor societies today, where life expectancy is substantially lower than in North America, people become old at fifty or even forty.

6. In global perspective, industrialization fosters a decline in the social standing of elderly people.

7. As people age, they face social isolation brought on by retirement, physical disability, and the death of friends or spouse. Even so, most elderly people enjoy the support of family members.

8. Since 1960, poverty among the elderly has dropped sharply. The aged poor are categories of people—including single women and people of color—who are at high risk of poverty throughout the life course.

9. Ageism—prejudice and discrimination against old people—is used to justify age stratification.

10. Although many seniors are socially disadvantaged, the elderly are men and women of all races, ethnicities, and social classes. Thus, older people do not qualify as a minority.

11. Disengagement theory, based on structural-functional analysis, suggests that society helps the elderly disengage from positions of social responsibility before the onset of disability or death. This process provides for the orderly transfer of statuses and roles from the older to the younger generation.

12. Activity theory, based on symbolic-interaction analysis, claims that a high level of activity affords people personal satisfaction in old age.

13. Age stratification is one focus of social-conflict analysis. Capitalist society's emphasis on economic efficiency leads to devaluing those who are less productive, including the elderly.

14. Modern society has set death apart from everyday life, prompting a cultural denial of human mortality. In part, this attitude is related to the fact that most people now die after reaching old age. The "right to die" debate suggests that people are confronting death more directly and seeking control over the process of dying.

KEY CONCEPTS

gerontology the study of aging and the elderly

age stratification the unequal distribution of wealth, power, and privilege among people at different stages of the life course

gerontocracy a form of social organization in which the elderly have the most wealth, power, and prestige

ageism prejudice and discrimination against the elderly

disengagement theory the proposition that society enhances its orderly operation by disengaging people from positions of responsibility as they reach old age

activity theory the proposition that a high level of activity enhances personal satisfaction in old age

euthanasia (mercy killing) assisting in the death of a person suffering from an incurable disease

CRITICAL-THINKING QUESTIONS

1. Why are the populations of industrial societies getting older? What are some of the likely consequences of "the graying of rich societies"?

2. Consider common phrases such as "little old lady" and "dirty old man." Identify other ways that our culture devalues old people.

3. Why does industrialization reduce the social standing of the elderly?

4. Political analyst Irving Kristol (1996) praised the elderly as "our most exemplary citizens" because, compared to younger people, they do not kill, steal, use illegal drugs, fall deep into debt, or speak badly of their country. Do you think the elderly receive the respect and social support they deserve? Why or why not?

LEARNING EXERCISES

1. What practices and policies does your college or university have for helping older faculty pass through the transition of retirement? Ask several faculty nearing retirement—and several already retired—for their views. In what ways does retiring from an academic career seem harder or easier than ending other kinds of work?

2. Look through an issue of any popular magazine—say, *Time*, *Newsweek*, or *Life*—and note images of men and women featured in stories and pictured in advertising. Are elderly people fairly represented in such publications?

3. Obtain a copy of a living will and try to respond to all the questions it asks. Does filling out such a form help clarify your own thinking about confronting death?

4. If you have computer access, learn about hospices by visiting the Web site (http://www.nho.org) for the National Hospice Organization. Or, check your local telephone book to contact people who operate a hospice in your community.

5. Install the CD-ROM packaged inside the back cover of your text and complete the activities designed to accompany this chapter.

PART III
NEW INFORMATION TECHNOLOGY AND SOCIAL STRATIFICATION

Change in technology transforms the nature of work. Just as important, such shifts alter the reward structure, reshaping patterns of social inequality. This third Cyber.Scope considers several ways in which the spread of computer technology is linked to social stratification.

The Information Revolution and U.S. Stratification

Most analysts agree that recent decades have witnessed economic polarization in the United States, with economic growth primarily enriching families that already had high incomes (Persell, 1997). At the outset, at least, technological revolution typically concentrates income and wealth as a small number of people make key discoveries and, with the resulting products and services, establish and expand new markets. Just as John D. Rockefeller and Andrew Carnegie amassed great fortunes a century ago as captains of the Industrial Revolution, the Information Revolution has created a new elite today. For several years, the richest person in the country has been Bill Gates, founder and head of Microsoft Corporation that produces, not oil or steel, but the operating systems found on most of today's personal computers. More broadly, it is those with money to invest (the upper-middle and upper classes or, according to Karl Marx, the capitalist class) who reap the profits from

successful new industries. During the 1990s, key stock market indicators leaped fivefold, with new technology companies such as Microsoft (software), Intel (computer chips), Compaq (personal computers), and Dell (computer sales) making even more spectacular gains.

But the wave of technological change does not benefit everyone. As companies adopt new technology in their efforts to become more efficient and profitable, some people lose out. In recent decades, for example, tens of millions of jobs in the United States have simply disappeared. For each job lost, of course, a worker—and usually an entire family—suffers.

Another key link between new information technology and social

inequality concerns the unequal spread of computing skills. In mid-1997, one-fourth of the U.S. population aged sixteen or older were users of the Internet. Yet, these users are not "average" people; they represent an information-elite, privileged in more ways than one. About 95 percent are white (compared to 85 percent of the population), 60 percent are men (versus half the population), and 40 percent are professionals or managers (versus 18 percent of the population). Computer users are, in short, people with above-average incomes. Research suggests that, over time, computer users will come to mirror more closely the population as a whole. But there can be little doubt that, at least in the foreseeable future, new information technology is playing a role in rising levels of economic inequality as it creates a cyber-elite and generates a new underclass made up of those without crucial symbolic skills (Wynter, 1995; Edmondson, 1997b).

The Information Revolution: Gender, Race, and Age

The Industrial Revolution ushered in a trend by which women and men are becoming more socially equal. Machinery eroded the link between work and physical strength, and more women entered the labor force as birth control technology helped lower the birthrate by making motherhood a matter of individual choice. The

CYBER: Explore the following site about new information technology for women and girls: http://www.cybergrrl.com
NOTE: Analysts estimate that, early in the new century, one in six new jobs will directly involve computing.

GLOBAL: One possible solution to the problem of keyboards using Latin script is the development of a digital code, known as Unicode, that would allow any script or alphabet to be input into a computer.

Information Revolution promises to continue this trend. Work in the computer age involves not making or moving *things* but manipulating *ideas*—activity that favors neither men nor women.

Note, too, that communication via computers obscures a person's sex—obvious in face-to-face interaction—placing men and women on an ever-more-equal footing. The same holds for race and ethnicity, so that the coming cyber-society may well be marked by greater contact among people of all colors and cultural backgrounds.

But an important counterpoint involves *access* to computer technology. To date, cultural biases within the new cyber-society have favored males: Most games that introduce children to computers are designed for boys, just as computer science courses in colleges enroll mostly men. Similarly, to the extent that racial and ethnic minorities are economically disadvantaged and

Both blind and deaf, Georgia Griffith was able to communicate only through conversations traced out on her palms, until specially equipped computers opened up her life. Do you think that, in general, advances in information technology will improve the lives of all persons with disabilities? Or will these people be left behind by the Information Revolution?

Is computer software aimed more at males than females? Visit a local store and see for yourself.

are confined to inferior schools, this segment of our population will be cut off from owning and operating computers—the key to success in the labor force of the coming century.

Finally, the effects of computing on age stratification are likely to be mixed. On the one hand, the fact that computing demands mental more than physical vitality—and allows work to be performed almost anywhere—should expand opportunities for people to continue to work well past the standard of "retirement" that emerged during the industrial era. On the other hand, new technology is almost always age-biased: readily adopted by the young, but regarded more cautiously by the old whose life experiences have been shaped by earlier ways. Unless our society expands programs of adult education, then, younger people are likely to predominate in, and benefit from, work and other activities involving new information technology.

The Information Revolution and Global Stratification

Worldwide, the elite pattern we have described holds even more:

The Information Revolution directly involves only a tiny share of the planet's people. A look back at Global Map 7–1, on page 183, shows that it is the rich regions of the world where Internet access is readily available, at least to those who can afford it. But, in most of Africa, by contrast, nations have, at best, only slow e-mail connections, and a dozen African countries have no network access at all. Moreover, the large number of African languages and alphabets will slow the spread of computing there.

While Internet access is found throughout most of Asia, at present, a cultural and technical problem limits the spread of computing there: Almost all computer keyboards use the Latin alphabet. In China and other Asian societies, while the technical elite is likely to speak and write English, most people speak languages that utilize complex character sets that have yet to be incorporated into computer technology. Overall, then, the Information Revolution has come to that part of the world already benefiting from industrial technology: yet another case of the rich getting richer.

Neale Osborne, *Money Maze,* 1996

CHAPTER 15

THE ECONOMY AND WORK

Norman and Sharolyn Gagnon were proud of the remodeling they had done to their modest home in Biddeford, Maine, about twenty miles south of Portland. They paid for the work with a $75,000 bank loan, a lot of money for a couple earning just $900 a week. But the Gagnons were confident that they could make the payments to the bank because they had "good" jobs at the local Sunbeam plant, which makes electric blankets: Norman earned $10.44 an hour, Sharolyn made $11.99.

But then they heard that Sunbeam had a new president, who pledged to make the company more profitable. Albert J. Dunlap, nicknamed "Chainsaw Al," was known as a tough and determined chief executive who had pushed up the stock prices of other corporations by cutting them up—keeping the most efficient plants and selling off the others. In the process, however, many workers had lost their jobs.

Nevertheless, the Gagnons and the other 350 workers at the Biddeford plant felt secure. Sunbeam is the only U.S. company making electric blankets, a popular and profitable product selling in department stores for as much as $179. Besides, Norman was no newcomer to Sunbeam—he had worked there since 1974. "We'll be fine," he assured Sharolyn.

Then came the announcement: The Biddeford plant would either be sold or shut down as part of Dunlap's plan to cut Sunbeam's work force to half its present size. Two days before Christmas Norman received his termination notice and joined the ranks of other victims of what corporations call "downsizing." For Sharolyn and those who remained, it was only a matter of time (Nordheimer, 1997).

This chapter explores the economy, widely considered the most influential of all social institutions. (The other major social institutions are examined in subsequent chapters: Chapter 16, "Politics and Government"; Chapter 17, "Family"; Chapter 18, "Religion"; Chapter 19, "Education"; and Chapter 20, "Health and Medicine.") As the chapter-opening story suggests, the economy does not always operate to the advantage of everyone. Indeed, as we shall see, sociologists debate how the economy ought to work, whose interests it ought to serve, and what companies and workers owe each other.

THE ECONOMY: HISTORICAL OVERVIEW

To begin, the **economy** is *the social institution that organizes the production, distribution, and consumption of goods and services.* As an "institution," the economy operates in an established, predictable manner, at least in its general outlines. This is not to say the economy operates to everyone's liking, and, as we shall see, societies the world over organize their economies in various ways with various consequences.

SUPPLEMENTS: An outline of this chapter, supplementary mini-lectures, and suggested topics for discussion are found in the *Data File*.
DISCUSS: The Industrial Revolution involved not only technological upheaval but much more. What was it for Marx? (A capitalist revolution.) For Weber? (The triumph of rationality.) For Durkheim? (A process of expanding specialization.)

SOCIAL SURVEY: "How much confidence do you have in the people running banks and financial institutions?" (GSS 1996, N = 1,925; *Codebook*, 1996:165)
"A great deal"   24.7%   "Hardly any"   16.5%
"Only some"   56.1%   DK/NR   2.7%
Q: "Economics is the study of money and why it is good." Woody Allen

Goods are commodities ranging from necessities (such as food, clothing, and shelter) to luxury items (such as automobiles, swimming pools, and yachts). *Services* refer to activities that benefit others (for example, the work of priests, physicians, police officers, or software specialists).

We value goods and services because they ensure survival or because they make life easier, more interesting, or more aesthetically pleasing. The things we produce and consume are also important to our self-image and social identity. How goods and services are distributed, then, shapes the lives of everyone in a number of basic ways.

The economies of modern industrial societies are the result of centuries of social change. The following sections highlight three technological revolutions that reorganized the means of production and, in the process, transformed many other dimensions of social life.

THE AGRICULTURAL REVOLUTION

Members of the earliest human societies relied on hunting and gathering to live off the land. In these technologically simple societies, there was no distinct economy; rather, production, distribution, and consumption of goods were all a part of family life.

As Chapter 4 ("Society") explained, the development of agriculture about 5,000 years ago greatly expanded economic productivity. When people harnessed animals to plows, they produced ten times the yield of hunting and gathering. The resulting surplus meant that not everyone had to be engaged in food production. Some people began to adopt specialized economic roles: creating handicrafts, designing tools, raising animals, and constructing dwellings.

Once agriculture was under way, towns arose, and they were soon linked by traders dealing in food, animals, and other goods (Jacobs, 1970). These four factors—agricultural technology, job specialization, permanent settlements, and trade—transformed and greatly expanded the economy.

In the process, the world of work became distinct from family life, although most people still worked close to home. In medieval Europe, for instance, most people farmed nearby fields. And many country and city dwellers labored in their homes—a pattern called *cottage industry*—producing a wide range of goods sold in frequent outdoor "flea markets" (a term suggesting that not everything in these village sales was of high quality).

THE INDUSTRIAL REVOLUTION

By the mid-eighteenth century, a second technological revolution was under way, first in England and, soon afterward, elsewhere in Europe and North America. The development of industry was to transform societies even more radically than agriculture had done thousands of years before. Industrialization introduced five fundamental changes in the economies of Western societies:

1. **New forms of energy.** Throughout history, people derived energy from their own muscles or from animals. Then, in 1765, English inventor James Watt introduced the steam engine. Surpassing muscle power a hundred times over, steam engines could operate large, heavy machinery.

2. **The centralization of work in factories.** Steam-powered machines soon rendered cottage industries all but obsolete. Factories—centralized and impersonal workplaces apart from the home—became the new work sites.

3. **Manufacturing and mass production.** Before the Industrial Revolution, most work involved growing and gathering raw materials, such as grain, wood, and wool. The industrial economy shifted that focus so that most people worked in factories to turn raw materials into a wide range of salable products. For example, factory workers mass-produced lumber into furniture and transformed wool into clothing.

4. **Specialization.** Most cottage industries relied on a single skilled worker to fashion a product from beginning to end. In the factory, by contrast, a laborer repeated a single task over and over, making only a small contribution to the finished product. Thus, specialization in factories raised productivity but lowered the skill level of the average worker (Warner & Low, 1947).

5. **Wage labor.** Instead of working for themselves or joining together as households, industrial workers in factories became wage laborers. They sold their labor to strangers who often cared less for them than for the machines they operated. Supervision became intense.

The impact of the Industrial Revolution gradually rippled outward from the factories to transform all of society. Greater productivity steadily raised the standard of living as countless new products and services

Q: "Women have always worked in factories. Indeed it was women's labor that was initially responsible for the very beginnings of the Industrial Revolution." Ellen Israel Rosen (1987:18)

Q: "Despite the toil, we all agree, Or out of mills or in;
Dependent on others we ne'er will be, So long as we're able to spin."
"Song of the Spinners" from *The Lowell Offering* (1842)

NOTE: The effects of technological advancement are summarized in Chapter 4's opening section, which examines "Society and Technology." Marvin Harris estimates the rising productive capacity linked to societies at various stages of technological development in terms of the ratio of calories expended to calories produced: hunting and gathering, 1:3; horticultural and pastoral, 1:5; agrarian, 1:50; industrial, 1:5,000.

SOCIAL DIVERSITY

Women in the Mills of Lowell, Massachusetts

Few people paid much attention to Francis Cabot Lowell, ancestor of two prominent Boston families, the Cabots and the Lowells, when he returned from England in 1822. But Lowell carried with him documents that would change the course of the U.S. economy: plans, based on mills operating in England, for this country's first textile factory.

Lowell built his factory beside a waterfall on the Merrimack River in Massachusetts, transforming the farming village into a thriving town. From the outset, 90 percent of the mill workers were women. The factory owners preferred women because they could be paid $2 to $3 a week, half the wages men required. Many immigrant men were willing to work for low wages, but prejudice disqualified "foreigners" from any job at all.

Recruiters, driving wagons from one small town to another in New England, urged parents to send their daughters to the mill where, they promised, the young women would be properly supervised as they learned skills and discipline. The offer

appealed to many families who could barely provide for their children, and the prospect of getting out on her own surely excited many young women. After all, there were few occupations open to women at that time, and those that were—including teaching and household service—paid even less than factory work.

At the Lowell factory, young women lived in dormitories, paying one-third of their wages for room and board. They were subject to a curfew and, as a condition of employment, regularly attended church. Any morally questionable conduct (such as bringing men to their rooms) brought firm disciplinary action.

Besides fulfilling their promise to parents, factory owners had another motive for their strict rules: They knew that closely supervised women could not organize among themselves. Working almost thirteen hours a day, six days a week, the Lowell employees had good reason to seek improvements in their working conditions. Yet any public criticism of the factory, or even possessing "radical" literature, could cost a worker her job.

Sources: Based on Eisler (1977) and Wertheimer (1982).

filled an expanding marketplace. Yet, the benefits of industrial technology were spread very unequally, especially at the beginning. Some factory owners made vast fortunes, while the majority of industrial workers hovered perilously close to poverty. Children worked in factories or deep in coal mines for pennies a day. Women factory workers, among the lowest paid, endured special problems, as the box explains.

THE INFORMATION REVOLUTION AND THE POSTINDUSTRIAL SOCIETY

By the middle of this century, the nature of production itself was changing once again. The United States was becoming a **postindustrial economy,** *a productive system based on service work and extensive use of information technology.* Automated machinery (and, more recently,

Q: "[The preindustrial economy] was limited to what could be organized within a family, and within the lifetime of its head." Peter Laslett (1984)

Q: "A fundamental characteristic of the world we have lost was the scene of labor, which was universally supposed to be the home." Peter Laslett (1984)

DISCUSS: Chapter 4 defined a social institution as a major sphere of social life organized to meet a basic human need. How well do people think the economy meets the needs of society's members?

Q: "Banks are more dangerous than standing armies." Thomas Jefferson

The postindustrial economy allows people to perform work almost anywhere, and many more people now choose to work at home. As the line between "the office" and "home" blurs, many children will see more of their parents, even if they don't always command their parents' attention.

robotics) reduced the role of human labor in factory production, while simultaneously expanding the ranks of clerical workers and managers. Today, service industries—such as public relations, health care, advertising, banking, and sales—employ most working people in this country. Distinguishing the postindustrial era, then, is a shift from industrial work to service jobs.

Driving this economic change is a third technological transformation: the development of the computer. The Information Revolution is generating new kinds of information, new means of communication, and changing the character of work just as factories did two centuries ago. The Information Revolution has unleashed three major trends:

1. **From tangible products to ideas.** As we have discussed in earlier chapters, the industrial era was defined by the production of goods; in the postindustrial era, work involves creating and manipulating symbols. Computer programmers, writers, financial analysts, advertising executives, architects, editors, and all sorts of consultants make up the labor force of the Information Age.

2. **From mechanical skills to literacy skills.** Just as the Industrial Revolution required mechanical skills, the Information Revolution requires literacy skills—speaking and writing well, and, of course, using computers. People able to communicate effectively enjoy new opportunities; people with limited skills face declining prospects.

3. **The decentralization of work away from factories.** Industrial technology drew workers into factories containing the machines and energy sources, but computer technology allows workers to be virtually anywhere. Indeed, laptop computers, cell phones, and portable facsimile (fax) machines now turn the home, car, or even an airplane into a "virtual office." New information technology, in short, blurs the line between work and home life, bringing about a return of cottage industries in the form of home-based offices and small businesses.

The need for face-to-face communication as well as the availability of supplies and information still keep most workers in the office. But the trend is clear, and many of today's more educated and skilled workers no longer require—and often resist—the close supervision of yesterday's factories.

SECTORS OF THE ECONOMY

The three revolutions we have just described reflect a shifting balance among the three sectors of a society's economy. The **primary sector** is *the part of the economy that generates raw materials directly from the natural environment.* The primary sector, which includes agriculture, animal husbandry, fishing, forestry, and mining, predominates in preindustrial societies. Figure 15–1 shows that 63 percent of the economic output of low-income countries is from the primary sector. As a society develops economically, the primary sector becomes less important. Thus, this sector represents 32 percent of economic activity in middle-income nations and just 4 percent in high-income countries like the United States.

The **secondary sector** is *the part of the economy that transforms raw materials into manufactured goods.* This

NOTE: The shift from an industrial to a service economy can be seen in the falling number of U.S. homes with a workshop and the rising number with a home office equipped with a computer.

DISCUSS: Is there a link between the rise of a service economy and the increasing number of overly committed two-career couples who utilize services ranging from housecleaning to take-out food?

Q: "The business of the United States is business." President Warren G. Harding

NOTE: Figure 15–1 shows the share of the economy each sector represents by level of income. Even though industrial output constitutes the same 28% relative share in high-income countries and middle-income nations, the former category greatly outproduces the latter.

sector grows quickly as societies industrialize, just as manufacturing grew rapidly in the United States during the first half of this century. Secondary sector production includes the refining of petroleum into gasoline and turning metals into tools and automobiles.

The **tertiary sector** is *the part of the economy that generates services rather than goods.* Accounting for just 22 percent of economic output in low-income countries, the tertiary sector grows with industrialization, and dominates the economies of high-income nations as they enter the postindustrial era. Today, about 70 percent of the U.S. labor force does some form of service work, including secretarial and clerical work and positions in food service, sales, law, accounting, advertising, and teaching.

THE GLOBAL ECONOMY

As technology draws people around the world closer together, a worldwide economic transformation is under way. Recent decades have witnessed the emergence of a **global economy,** *economic activity spanning many nations of the world with little regard for national borders.*

The new global economy has four major consequences. First, we see a global division of labor so that different regions of the world specialize in one sector of economic activity. As Global Map 15–1 on page 406 shows, agriculture occupies more than 70 percent of the work force in many low-income countries. Global Map 15–2 indicates that industrial production is concentrated in the middle- and high-income nations of the world. The richest nations, including the United States, now specialize in service-sector activity.

Second, an increasing number of products pass through the economies of more than one nation. For instance, workers in Taiwan may manufacture shoes, which a Hong Kong distributor sends to Italy to receive the stamp of an Italian designer; then another distributor in Rome forwards the shoes to New York, where they are sold in a department store owned by a firm with headquarters in Tokyo.

A third consequence of the global economy is that national governments no longer control the economic activity that takes place within their borders. In fact, governments cannot even regulate the value of their national currencies, since money is now traded around the clock in the financial centers of Tokyo, Hong Kong, London, and New York. Global markets are the result of satellite communications that instantaneously link the world's major cities.

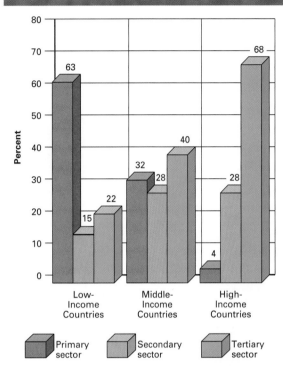

GLOBAL SNAPSHOT

FIGURE 15–1 The Size of Economic Sectors by Income Level of Country

Source: Author estimates based on The World Bank (1995).

The fourth consequence of the global economy is that a small number of businesses, operating internationally, now control a vast share of the world's economic activity. According to one estimate, the 600 largest multinational companies account for fully half the earth's entire economic output (Kidron & Segal, 1991).

The world is still divided into 191 politically distinct nations. But increasing international economic activity makes "nationhood" less significant.

ECONOMIC SYSTEMS: PATHS TO JUSTICE

October 20, 1995, Saigon, Vietnam. Sailing up the narrow Saigon River is an unsettling experience for anyone who came

THE MAP: The two maps show that the economies of low-income nations such as India and the People's Republic of China are dominated by the primary sector. Middle-income countries, like Russia and Mexico, have a secondary economic sector that is roughly the same size as their primary sector. The second global map is virtually a negative image of the first.

Q: "The greatest distinction between one government and another is in the degree to which market replaces government or government replaces market. Both Adam Smith and Karl Marx knew this." Charles Lindblom

GLOBAL: Worldwide, 2.5 billion (of 5.9 billion) people are employed: 1.4 billion in low-income countries, 660 million in middle-income countries, and 380 million in high-income nations (United Nations Development Programme, 1995).

WINDOW ON THE WORLD

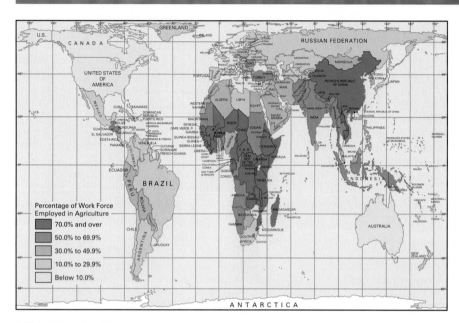

GLOBAL MAP 15–1
Agricultural Employment in Global Perspective

The primary sector of the economy predominates in societies that are least developed. Thus, in the poor countries of Africa and Asia, half, or even three-fourths, of all workers are farmers. This picture is altogether different in the world's most economically developed countries—including the United States, Canada, Great Britain, and Australia—which have less than 10 percent of their work force in agriculture.

Source: *Peters Atlas of the World* (1990).

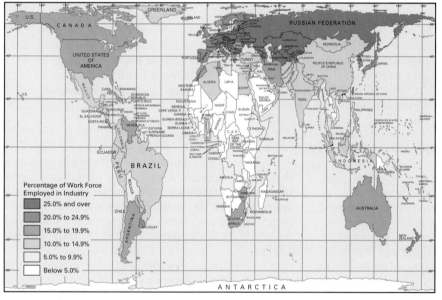

GLOBAL MAP 15–2
Industrial Employment in Global Perspective

Because the world's poor societies, by and large, have yet to industrialize, only a small proportion of their labor force engages in industrial work. The nations of Eastern Europe and the Russian Federation have far more of their workers in industry. In the world's richest societies, we see workers moving from industrial jobs to service work. Thus, the postindustrial economy of the United States now has about the same share of workers in industrial jobs as the much poorer nation of Argentina.

Source: *Peters Atlas of the World* (1990).

of age in the United States during the 1960s. We need to remember that Vietnam is a country not a war, and that twenty years have passed since the last military helicopter lifted off from the rooftop of

the U.S. embassy in Saigon, bringing an end to the hostilities.

Saigon (Ho Chi Minh City—in honor of the revolutionary leader—is now falling out of use) is on the brink of becoming a

406 CHAPTER 15 The Economy and Work

NOTE: The *Oxford English Dictionary* explains that the word "capitalism" entered the English language in the late 18th century. (Apparently, Adam Smith never used the term.) The etymology of the word reveals a Latin root, *caput*, meaning "of the head."

Q: "It is not from the benevolence of the butcher, the brewer, or the baker that we expect our dinner, but from their regard to their own interest." Adam Smith

SOCIAL SURVEY: International data regarding whether or not the government should reduce income disparity. (*CHIP1 Social Survey Software*, REDISTR; ISSP 1985, N = 3,795)

	"Yes"	"No"
Australia	52.6%	47.4%
United Kingdom	71.5%	28.5%
Austria	77.4%	22.6%

boom town. Neon signs bathe the city's waterfront in color; hotels, bankrolled by Western corporations, push skyward from a dozen construction sites; taxi meters record fares in U.S. dollars, not Vietnamese dong; Visa and American Express stickers decorate the doors of fashionable shops that cater to shoppers from Japan, France, and (since the U.S. embargo on visiting Vietnam was lifted in 1994) the United States.

There is a heavy irony here: After decades of fighting, the loss of millions of lives on both sides, and the victory of Communist forces, the Vietnamese are doing an about-face and turning toward capitalism. What we see today is what might well have happened had the U.S. forces won the war . . .

Every society's economic system makes a statement about justice, since the economy broadly determines who gets what. Two general economic models are capitalism and socialism. No society has an economy that is completely capitalist or entirely socialist; these models represent two ends of a spectrum along which all actual economies can be located. We shall consider each pure type in turn.

CAPITALISM

Capitalism refers to *an economic system in which natural resources and the means of producing goods and services are privately owned.* Ideally, a capitalist economy has three distinctive features:

1. **Private ownership of property.** In a capitalist economy, individuals can own almost anything. The more capitalist an economy is, the more private ownership there is of wealth-producing property such as factories, real estate, and natural resources.

2. **Pursuit of personal profit.** A capitalist society encourages the accumulation of private property and considers the profit motive natural, simply a matter of "doing business." Further, claimed the Scottish economist Adam Smith (1723–1790), the individual pursuit of self-interest helps the entire society prosper (1937:508; orig. 1776).

3. **Free competition and consumer sovereignty.** A purely capitalist economy operates as a free-market system with no government interference (sometimes called a *laissez-faire* economy, from the French words meaning "to leave alone"). Adam Smith contended that a freely competitive economy regulates itself by the "invisible hand" of the laws of supply and demand.

Smith maintained that a free-market system is dominated by consumers, who select goods and services that offer the greatest value. As producers compete with one another for the business of consumers, they provide the highest-quality goods and services at the lowest possible price. Thus, while entrepreneurs and consumers are motivated by personal gain, everyone benefits from more efficient production and ever-increasing value. This is what Smith had in mind when he declared that narrow self-interest produces the "greatest good for the greatest number of people." Any government control of an economy, he claimed, distorts market forces, reduces producer motivation, diminishes the quantity and quality of goods produced, and shortchanges consumers.

"Justice," in a capitalist context, amounts to "market freedoms" that allow people to produce, invest, and buy according to their self-interest. The "worth" of products—or workers—is determined by the dynamic process of supply and demand. From a capitalist point of view, closing the Sunbeam plant in Biddeford, Maine, described in the opening to this chapter, is "just" if it is profitable to the stockholders who own the company. The company's workers can either buy the plant themselves or find other jobs where they can be more "competitive."

The United States is a capitalist nation in that the vast majority of businesses are privately owned. Even so, government plays an extensive role in economic affairs. The government itself owns and operates a number of businesses that are considered too vital to be left to the uncertainties of the marketplace, including almost all of this country's schools, roads, parks, and museums, the U.S. Postal Service, the Amtrak railroad system, the Tennessee Valley Authority (a large electrical utility company), and the Nuclear Regulatory Commission (which conducts atomic research and produces nuclear materials). In addition, the entire U.S. military is government operated. In all these cases, meeting public needs is deemed more important than "making a profit."

NOTE: For Adam Smith, the architect of capitalism, there is no explicit category of the social; social good springs from individual interests. By contrast, for Karl Marx, the architect of socialism, there is no explicit category of the individual; individual satisfaction springs from collective action.
NOTE: The taxation system of the United States (and, even more so, of European countries) reveals that the government controls much of the "market" economy through taxation. A household earning $60,000 pays 35%–40% in federal, state, and local income taxes, plus another 5%–7% in sales tax on every expenditure, as well as property taxes and other taxes. At a person's death, the government taxes estates worth more than about $1,200,000 at half their value. The richest one-third of the U.S. population, in short, surrender more than half their lifetime earnings to taxes.

Capitalism still thrives in Hong Kong (left), evident in streets choked with advertising and shoppers. Socialism is more the rule in China's capital of Beijing (right), a city dominated by government buildings rather than a downtown business district.

The government also uses taxation and other forms of regulation to affect what companies produce, to control the quality and cost of merchandise, to influence what businesses import and export, and to motivate consumers to conserve natural resources.

Furthermore, government policies mandate minimum wage levels, enforce workplace safety standards, regulate corporate mergers, provide farm price supports, and funnel income in the form of Social Security, public assistance, student loans, and veterans' benefits to a majority of the people in the United States. In fact, local, state, and federal governments together are the country's biggest employer, with 16 percent of the labor force on their payrolls (U.S. Bureau of the Census, 1997).

SOCIALISM

Socialism is *an economic system in which natural resources and the means of producing goods and services are collectively owned.* In its ideal form, a socialist economy is the exact opposite of capitalism.

1. **Collective ownership of property.** An economy is socialist to the extent that it limits the right to private property, especially property used to produce goods and services. Laws establish government ownership of property and make housing and other goods available to all, not just to people with the most money.

Karl Marx claimed that private ownership of productive property generates social classes by which an economic elite serves its own interest at the expense of everyone else. Socialism, then, seeks to lessen economic inequality and create a classless society.

2. **Pursuit of collective goals.** The individualistic pursuit of profit is also at odds with the collective orientation of socialism. Socialist values and norms condemn the capitalist entrepreneurial spirit as simple "greed." For this reason, socialist nations outlaw trading as "black market" activity.

3. **Government control of the economy.** Socialism also rejects the idea that a free-market economy regulates itself. Instead of a laissez-faire approach, socialist governments oversee a *centrally controlled* or *command* economy.

Socialism also rejects the idea that consumers guide capitalist production. From this point of view, consumers lack the information necessary to evaluate products and are manipulated by advertising to buy what is profitable for factory owners rather than what the consumers genuinely need. Commercial advertising thus plays little role in socialist economies.

"Justice," in a socialist context, refers not to letting people compete for whatever they can accumulate, but ensuring that the society meets everyone's basic needs. Thus, a "just" economy does not concentrate income

THEN AND NOW: U.S. GNP: *1947,* $1.75 trillion; *1996,* $6.9 trillion (in constant 1992 dollars).
DISCUSS: Measures of economic output do not include unpaid work (volunteer work and housework), which are historically the responsibilities of women. Should they? How does one measure the value of unpaid work?
NOTE: Welfare capitalism is also called democratic socialism;

state capitalism might also be called market socialism.
Q: "Socialism, in addition to being a set of political programs and the source of social-scientific interpretations, is also one of the most powerful myths of the contemporary era; to the extent that socialism retains this mythic quality, it cannot be disconfirmed by empirical evidence in the minds of its adherents." Peter Berger (1986:204)

and wealth in the hands of a few. From a socialist point of view, closing the Biddeford plant in order to raise Sunbeam's stock price and benefit investors is unjust because it threatens the well-being of people who depend on the income they earn there.

The People's Republic of China and a number of societies in Asia, Africa, and Latin America—some two dozen in all—model their economies on socialism, placing almost all wealth-generating property under state control (McColm et al., 1991). The extent of world socialism has declined in recent years, however, as societies in Eastern Europe and the former Soviet Union have restructured their economic systems to increase the role of market forces.

Socialism and Communism

Most people equate the terms *socialism* and *communism.* More precisely, **communism** is *a hypothetical economic and political system in which all members of a society are socially equal.* Karl Marx viewed socialism as a transitory stage on the path toward the ideal of a communist society that had abolished all class divisions. In many socialist societies today, the dominant political party describes itself as communist, but nowhere has the communist goal been achieved.

Why? For one thing, social stratification involves differences of power as well as wealth. In general, socialist societies have succeeded in reducing disparities in wealth only by expanding government bureaucracies and extensively regulating daily life. In the process, government did not "wither away" as Karl Marx imagined. On the contrary, socialist political elites have enormous power and privilege.

Probably Marx would have agreed that a communist society is a *utopia* (from Greek words meaning "not a place"). Yet Marx considered communism a worthy goal and might well have disparaged reputedly "Marxist" societies such as North Korea, the former Soviet Union, the People's Republic of China, and Cuba for not fulfilling what he saw as the promise of communism.

WELFARE CAPITALISM
AND STATE CAPITALISM

Some of the nations of Western Europe—including Sweden and Italy—have combined a market-based economy with extensive social welfare programs. Analysts call this "third way" **welfare capitalism,** *an economic and political system that combines a mostly market-based economy with government programs to provide for people's basic needs.*

Under welfare capitalism, the government owns some of the largest industries and services, such as transportation, the mass media, and health care. In Sweden and Italy, about 12 percent of economic production is "nationalized," or state controlled. That leaves most industry in private hands, although subject to extensive government regulation in the public interest. High taxation (aimed especially at the rich) funds a wide range of social welfare programs, including universal health care and child care (Olsen, 1996).

Yet another blend of capitalism and socialism is **state capitalism,** *an economic and political system in which companies are privately owned although they cooperate closely with the government.* Systems of state capitalism are common in the rapidly developing Asian countries along the Pacific Rim. Japan, South Korea, and Singapore, for example, are all capitalist nations, but their governments work in partnership with large companies, supplying financial assistance and controlling imports of foreign products to help their businesses compete in world markets. Countries in East Asia and Western Europe demonstrate that governments and private companies can work cooperatively in many ways (Gerlach, 1992).

RELATIVE ADVANTAGES OF CAPITALISM AND SOCIALISM

In practice, which economic system works best? Comparing economic models is difficult because all countries mix capitalism and socialism to varying degrees. Moreover, nations differ in cultural attitudes toward work, available natural resources, level of technological development, and patterns of trade. Some also carry the burdens of war more than others (Gregory & Stuart, 1985).

Despite these complicating factors, some crude comparisons are revealing. The following sections contrast two categories of countries—those with predominantly capitalist economies and those with predominantly socialist economies. The supporting data reflect economic patterns prior to recent changes in the former Soviet Union and Eastern Europe.

Economic Productivity

One key dimension of economic performance is productivity. A common measure of economic output is gross domestic product (GDP), the total value of all

GLOBAL: The South Korean system of state capitalism has concentrated more than half of all GNP in just four major corporations, including Hyundai.
DISCUSS: Does socialism's lower productivity result from Marx's separation of reward from effort (implied in his famous call: "From each according to ability; to each according to need")?
Q: "Communism is like one big phone company." Lenny Bruce

Q: "Market capitalism has not been abolished in any democratic country. Yet the market capitalism that Marx knew has been peacefully transformed by democratic means into a far more humane and decent economic order than perhaps even he envisioned." Robert A. Dahl
Q: "The function of socialism is to raise suffering to a higher level." Norman Mailer

Economic Equality

How resources are distributed within a society is a second test of an economy. A comparative study completed in the mid-1970s looked at income ratios based on the earnings of the richest and poorest 5 percent of the population (Wiles, 1977). This research found that societies with predominantly capitalist economies had an income ratio of about 10 to 1; the figure for socialist countries was 5 to 1.

This comparison of economic performance shows that *capitalist economies support a higher overall standard of living but generate greater income disparity*. Or, put otherwise, *socialist economies create less income disparity but offer a lower overall standard of living*.

Overall Well-Being

Can we conclude that one economic system provides better for a society's population than the other? To date, capitalist systems are more productive and generate higher overall living standards; but capitalist systems also produce striking economic inequality. Thus, a more capitalist nation such as the United States produces a larger number of very rich families than a more socialist nation like Sweden. But it is also true that economically disadvantaged people in this country receive poorer schooling and less medical care and contend with greater problems of drugs and violence than their counterparts in Sweden do.

In short, an assessment of capitalism and socialism must go beyond simple statistics. Also involved are complex moral and political judgments about how people ought to live.

Personal Freedom

One final consideration in evaluating capitalism and socialism involves the personal freedoms a society accords its people. The capitalist conception of liberty is the *freedom to* act in pursuit of one's self-interest. A capitalist economy, after all, depends on the freedom of producers and consumers to interact without extensive interference from the state.

On the other hand, a socialist conception of liberty is *freedom from* basic want. Providing for the basic needs of everyone means promoting economic equality. This goal requires considerable state intervention in the economy, which limits the personal choices of citizens for the benefit of the public as a whole.

People have yet to devise a social system that both expands political freedoms and creates economic

Global comparisons indicate that socialist economies generate the greatest economic equality although living standards remain relatively low. Capitalist economies, by contrast, engender more income disparity although living standards are typically higher. As the former Soviet Union has moved towards a market system, however, the majority of people have suffered a decline in living standards, while some people have become quite rich.

goods and services produced annually by a nation's economy. "Per capita" (or per person) GDP divides total production by number of people and thus allows us to compare the economic performance of nations of different population size.

Averaging out the economic output of the United States, Canada, and the nations of Western Europe at the end of the last decade yields a per capita GDP of about $13,500. The comparable figure for the former Soviet Union and the nations of Eastern Europe is about $5,000. In other words, capitalist countries outproduced socialist nations by a ratio of 2.7 to 1 (United Nations Development Programme, 1990).

SOCIAL SURVEY: "Should the government in Washington reduce income differences between the rich and the poor?" (1–7 Likert scale; GSS 1996, N = 1,925; *Codebook*, 1996:100)
(1) "Gov't should" 17.2%   (5) 12.3%
(2) 10.4%   (6) 8.2%
(3) 15.7%   (7) "Gov't should not" 12.2%
(4) 21.2%   DK/NR 2.8%

SOCIAL SURVEY: Same question, responses by SES (*Student CHIP Social Survey Software*, EQWLTH; GSS 1978–91, N = 10,464)

SES	1, 2	3, 4, 5	6, 7
High	33.6%	19.0%	47.5%
Middle	48.8%	20.4%	30.8%
Low	60.8%	19.9%	19.3%

equality. In the capitalist United States, our political system guarantees many personal freedoms, but are these freedoms worth as much to a poor person as a rich one? On the other side of the coin, formerly socialist nations of Eastern Europe, while more economically equal, restricted the rights of their people to express themselves and move freely inside and outside their borders.

CHANGES IN SOCIALIST COUNTRIES

During the last decade, a profound transformation took place in many socialist countries of the world. It began in the shipyards of Poland's port city of Gdansk in 1980, where workers organized in opposition to their repressive government. Despite setbacks, the Solidarity movement eventually dislodged the Soviet-backed party officials and elected its leader, Lech Walesa, national president. Poland is now in the process of introducing market principles into its economy.

Other countries of Eastern Europe that had fallen under the political control of the former Soviet Union at the end of World War II also shook off repressive socialist regimes during 1989 and 1990. These nations—including the German Democratic Republic, Czechoslovakia, Hungary, Romania, and Bulgaria—have likewise introduced capitalist elements into what were centrally controlled economies. In 1992, the Soviet Union itself formally dissolved, liberating the Baltic states of Estonia, Latvia, and Lithuania, as well as Georgia and Azerbaijan. Russia and the other remaining republics became the Commonwealth of Independent States (now named the Russian Federation).

The reasons for these sweeping changes are many and complex. In light of the preceding discussion, however, two factors stand out. First, these predominantly socialist economies grossly underproduced their capitalist counterparts. Though they achieved remarkable economic equality, living standards were low by Western European standards. Second, the Soviet brand of socialism created heavy-handed and unresponsive government that rigidly controlled the media and people's ability to move about, even within their own countries.

In short, socialism did away with economic elites, as Karl Marx predicted. But, as Max Weber might have foreseen, socialism *increased* the clout of political elites to gargantuan proportions.

At this stage, the market reforms are proceeding unevenly. Some nations (Czech Republic, Slovakia,

TABLE 15–1 Participation in the Labor Force by Sex, Race, and Ethnicity, 1997

Category of the Population	In the Labor Force	
	Number (in millions)	Percentage
Men (aged 16 and over)	**73.3**	**75.0%**
White	62.6	75.9
African American	7.4	68.3
Hispanic	8.3	80.1
Women (aged 16 and over)	**63.0**	**59.8**
White	52.1	59.5
African American	8.2	61.7
Hispanic	5.5	55.1

Source: U.S. Department of Labor, *Employment and Earnings*, vol. 45, no. 1 (January 1998), pp. 164–66.

Poland, and the Baltic states of Latvia, Estonia, and Lithuania) are faring well and many people are prospering, but other countries (Romania, Bulgaria, and the former Soviet republics) are buffeted by price increases and falling living standards. Officials hope that in the longer term an expanding market will raise living standards through greater productivity. However, there is already evidence that if this happens, a rising standard of living will be accompanied by increasing economic disparity (Pohl, 1996; Buraway, 1997; Specter, 1997b).

WORK IN THE POSTINDUSTRIAL ECONOMY

Change is not restricted to the socialist world; the last century has also transformed the economy of the United States. In 1997, 136 million people were in the labor force, representing two-thirds of the population age sixteen and over. As shown in Table 15–1, a larger proportion of men (75.0 percent) than women (59.8 percent) are in the labor force, although the gap between the sexes is steadily diminishing in recent decades. Among men, the proportion of people of African descent in the labor force (68.3 percent) is somewhat less than the proportions of white people (75.9 percent) and Hispanics (80.1 percent); among women, 61.7 percent of African Americans are employed, compared to 59.5 percent of white people and 55.1 percent of Hispanics.

THE MAP: Counties with low rates of labor force participation not only lack jobs but also are culturally conservative, with high percentages of women who remain at home.

DISCUSS: How many of your students work? The University of Michigan's Institute for Social Research estimates that three-fourths of high school seniors worked for income; 40% of all seniors work more than 20 hours a week.

SUPPLEMENTS: The *Data File* examines the rising number of men who fail to reenter the work force after being laid off.

GLOBAL: A decline of agricultural employment characterizes all mature industrial societies, as Figure 15–1 suggests.

THEN AND NOW: The decline of farming can be seen in the falling number of farms owned by African Americans: 926,000 in 1920 compared to 19,000 in 1992.

SEEING OURSELVES

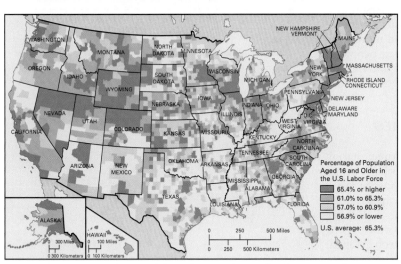

Sources: *American Demographics Desk Reference Series # 4.* Reprinted with permission. ©1992 *American Demographics* magazine, Ithaca, New York. Data from the 1990 decennial census.

NATIONAL MAP 15–1
Labor Force Participation Across the United States

Counties with high levels of labor force participation have steady sources of employment, including military bases, recreation areas, and large cities. By contrast, counties with low employment rates generally include a high proportion of elderly people (as well as students). Another important consideration revolves around gender: What do you think is the typical level of employment in regions of the country (stretching from the South up into coal-mining districts of Kentucky and West Virginia) where traditional cultural norms encourage women to remain at home?

National Map 15–1 shows labor force participation by county for the United States. Since work and income go hand in hand, regions of the country with above average labor force participation typically are more affluent.

THE DECLINE OF AGRICULTURAL WORK

When this century began, almost 40 percent of the U.S. labor force engaged in farming. By the time it ends, a mere 2 percent will work in agriculture. Figure 15–2 illustrates this rapid decline, which, in turn, reflects the shrinking role of the primary sector in the U.S. economy.

Although it involves fewer people, farming is more productive than ever. A century ago, a typical farmer grew food for five people; today, one farmer feeds seventy-five. This dramatic rise in productivity reflects new varieties of crops, pesticides that raise yields, and more efficient farm machinery and farming techniques. The average U.S. farm has also doubled in size since 1950, to about 491 acres today.

The "family farms" of yesterday have been replaced by *corporate agribusinesses.* Agriculture may be more productive today, but the transformation has

required painful adjustments in farming communities across the country, as a way of life is lost.

FROM FACTORY WORK TO SERVICE WORK

Industrialization swelled the ranks of blue-collar workers early in this century. As shown in Figure 15–2, back in 1900 more than 40 percent of working people in this country had industrial jobs—surpassing the share employed in agriculture. By 1950, however, a white-collar revolution had moved a majority of workers into service occupations. By 1997, 90 percent of new jobs were in the service sector, and 70 percent of the entire labor force held service-sector jobs. Meanwhile, industrial-sector work had slipped to about 28 percent of the labor force.

The growth of service occupations is one reason that many people characterize the United States as a middle-class society. As explained in Chapter 10 ("Social Class in the United States"), however, much service work—including sales positions, secretarial work, and jobs in fast-food restaurants—provides little of the income and prestige of professional white-collar occupations and, often, fewer rewards than factory work. In short, many jobs in this postindustrial era provide only a modest standard of living.

RESOURCE: Work in the secondary labor market is the focus of Mary Romero's article "Maid in the U.S.A." in the *Seeing Ourselves* reader.

NOTE: The number of strikes has fallen steadily since the 1970s, paralleling not only the decline of unions but also the fading strength of U.S. industries that historically have been most unionized (such as the steel and auto industries).

SOCIAL SURVEY: "How much confidence do you have in people running organized labor?" (GSS 1996, N = 1,925; *Codebook*, 1996:166)

"A great deal"	11.2%	"Hardly any"	29.5%
"Only some"	50.9%	DK/NR	8.5%

NOTE: Only about 10% of U.S. service workers are unionized.

THE DUAL LABOR MARKET

Sociologists divide the jobs in today's economy into two categories. The **primary labor market** includes *occupations that provide extensive benefits to workers.* This segment of the labor market includes the traditional white-collar professions and upper management positions. These are jobs that people think of as *careers*. Work in the primary labor market provides high income, better job security, and is usually challenging and satisfying. Such occupations require a broad education rather than specialized training and offer solid opportunity for advancement.

But few of these advantages apply to work in the **secondary labor market,** *jobs that provide minimal benefits to workers.* This segment of the labor force is employed in low-skill, blue-collar assembly-line operations and low-level service-sector jobs, including clerical positions. Workers in the secondary labor market receive lower income, have less job security, and find fewer chances to advance. Not surprisingly, then, these workers are more likely to feel alienated and dissatisfied with their jobs. These problems most commonly beset women and other minorities, who are overly represented in the secondary labor market (Edwards, 1979; Kohn & Schooler, 1982; Kemp & Coverman, 1989; Hunnicutt, 1990; Greenwald, 1994; Nelson, 1994).

Most new jobs in our postindustrial economy fall within the secondary labor market, and they involve the same kind of unchallenging tasks, low wages, and poor working conditions characteristic of factory work a century ago (Gruenberg, 1980). Moreover, as the box on page 414 explains, in the current age of "downsizing," many companies are turning to temporary workers who receive lower pay and minimal benefits.

LABOR UNIONS

In the summer of 1997, workers at United Parcel Service went on strike. About a month later, the workers claimed a major victory as UPS agreed to many of their demands. Organized labor took heart because recent decades have not been good to U.S. labor unions.

Labor unions are *worker organizations that seek to improve wages and working conditions through various strategies, including negotiations and strikes.* During the Great Depression of the 1930s, membership in labor unions increased rapidly, and, by 1950, one in three nonfarm workers was in a union. In absolute numbers, union membership peaked during the 1970s at almost

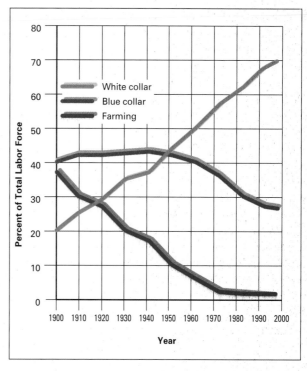

FIGURE 15–2 The Changing Pattern of Work in the United States, 1900–1997

Source: Author estimates based on U.S. Department of Labor (1998).

25 million people. Since then, however, the union rolls have steadily declined to about 14 percent of nonfarm workers, or about 16 million men and women.

Unions have also declined in other high-income countries, but fewer workers in the United States join unions than elsewhere. In the Scandinavian countries, at least 80 percent of workers belong to unions; in Europe as a whole, about 40 percent do; and in Canada and Japan, it's about 33 percent (Western, 1993, 1995).

Unions have declined as work once done in highly unionized factories has been "exported" to lower-income nations. Furthermore, most of the new service-sector jobs being created today are not unionized, and hardly any temporary workers belong to a labor union.

Yet, as some analysts see it, falling job security may well make union membership important again in the years to come. But unions will also have to adapt to the new global economy. Union members in the United States used to thinking of foreign workers as "the enemy" will have to build new international alliances (Mabry, 1992; Church, 1994).

DIVERSITY: The percentage of workers who are actively seeking to change jobs is highest among teens (8%), falls quickly with age to about 5% of men and women aged 35–44, and bottoms out at about 1% among workers over age 65. Over a lifetime, says the Bureau of Labor Statistics, the average U.S. worker has held 10 jobs (U.S. Department of Labor, 1994, 1997).

NOTE: The *Yellow Pages* periodically updates its listing categories to reflect new consumer trends: Recently dropped, for example, were "go-carts" and "razor sharpening," while "espresso," "karaoke," "foreign-exchange brokers," "videoconferencing services," and even "scholarships and financial aid" have been added (Brightman, 1995).

NOTE: For young people, at least one of the jobs they will hold has yet to be invented!

EXPLORING CYBER-SOCIETY

The New Information Economy: The "Temping" of the United States

Three hundred years ago, Scottish landlords evicted thousands of farmers in order to put the land to more profitable use, raising sheep to supply wool to the burgeoning textile factories. Almost overnight, the security of an established way of life vanished. The lucky farmers emigrated to North America and started over; the least fortunate starved to death.

Today, for many workers, the Information Revolution is, once again, undermining job security. A generation ago, workers confidently assumed that hard work and playing by the rules all but guaranteed that their jobs would be there until they were ready to retire. No longer. As one analyst puts it:

The rise of the knowledge economy means a change, in less than twenty years, from an overbuilt system of large, slow-moving economic units to an array of small, widely dispersed economic centers, some as small as an individual boss. In the new economy,

geography dissolves, the highways are electronic. Even Wall Street no longer has a reason to be on Wall Street. Companies become concepts . . . and jobs are almost as susceptible as electrons to vanishing into thin air. (Morrow, 1993:41)

In the short run, at least, the dislocation for U.S. workers is tremendous. Companies scrambling to "remain competitive" in the global economy are decentralizing and "downsizing." Gaining corporate "flexibility" in this way

may be good for profits, but it means reducing the payroll and replacing long-term employees with temporary workers. By hiring "temps," companies no longer have to provide training programs, health insurance, paid vacations, or pensions. And, if next month workers are no longer needed, they can be released without further cost or fear of lawsuits.

"Temping" is entrenched in the U.S. economy: Suppliers of temporary workers—including Manpower and Kelly Services—now dispatch 2 million employees daily. In all, "temps," part-timers, and contract workers in government and corporate jobs number 35 million and account for 30 percent of the U.S. labor force—a share that continues to rise. Most analysts agree that, in the Information Age, there is probably no going back to the traditional notion of lifetime employment with one company.

Sources: Castro (1993) and Morrow (1993).

PROFESSIONS

A **profession** is *a prestigious white-collar occupation that requires extensive formal education.* As distinct from *amateur* (from Latin meaning "lover," one who acts simply out of love for the activity itself), a professional pursues some task for a living. The term "profession" also suggests a public declaration to abide by certain principles. Traditional professions include the ministry, medicine, law, and academia and, more recently, architecture, accountancy, and social work. People describe their occupations as professions to the extent that they demonstrate the following four characteristics (W. Goode, 1960; Ritzer & Walczak, 1990):

1. **Theoretical knowledge.** Professionals have a theoretical understanding of their field rather than mere technical training. Anyone can master

Q: "A profession is a conspiracy against the layman." George Bernard Shaw

SOCIAL SURVEY: Percentage of U.S. adults claiming to trust people in various occupations: pharmacists, 61%; clergy, 54%; public opinion pollsters, 27%; journalists, 20%; lawyers, 17%; advertisers, 12%; car salesmen, 6% (Fulkerson, 1995).

CYBER: Data on small-business ownership by women can be found at the Small Business Administration Web site: www.sbaonline.sba.gov

DIVERSITY: The number of African American businesses increased by 50% between 1987 and 1992, to 625,000; blacks are still underrepresented in such businesses, however, with 12% of the population and 3.6% of all U.S. businesses (Mergenhagen, 1996a).

first-aid skills, for example, but physicians claim a theoretical understanding of human health and illness.

2. **Self-regulating practice.** The typical professional is self-employed, "in practice" rather than working for a company. Professionals oversee their own work and observe a code of ethics.

3. **Authority over clients.** Many jobs—sales, for example—require people to respond directly to the desires of customers. Based on their extensive training, however, professionals expect their clients to follow their direction and advice.

4. **Orientation to community rather than to self-interest.** The traditional "professing" of faith or duty is a professional's vow to serve the community rather than merely seek income. Some professional associations, including the American Medical Association, even forbid their members from advertising their services.

Many new service occupations in the postindustrial economy have sought to *professionalize* their work. A claim to professional standing often begins by renaming the work to imply special, theoretical knowledge, which also distances the field from its previously less-distinguished reputation. Stockroom workers, for example, become "inventory supply officials," and dog-catchers are reborn as "animal control specialists."

Interested parties may also form a professional association to formally attest to their specialized skills. This organization then licenses people who perform the work and develops a code of ethics that emphasizes the occupation's contribution to the community. In its effort to win public acceptance, a professional association may also establish schools or other training facilities and perhaps start a professional journal (Abbott, 1988).

Not all occupations claim full professional status. Some *paraprofessionals*, including paralegals and medical technicians, possess specialized skills but lack the extensive theoretical education required of full professionals.

SELF-EMPLOYMENT

Self-employment—earning a living without working for a large organization—was once commonplace in the United States. In the early 1800s, about 80 percent of the labor force was self-employed. Today, self-employment accounts for only 8 percent of workers (9 percent of men and 7 percent of women) (U.S. Department of Labor, 1998).

Jose Clemente Orozco's painting The Unemployed *is a powerful statement of the personal collapse and private despair that afflict men and women who are out of work. How does a sociological perspective help us to understand being out of work as more than a personal problem?*

Jose Clemente Orozco, *The Unemployed.* © Christie's Images. © Estate of Jose Clemente Orozco/Licensed by VAGA, New York, N.Y.

Lawyers, physicians, and some other professionals are well represented among the ranks of the self-employed. But most self-employed workers are small-business owners, plumbers, carpenters, free-lance writers, editors, artists, house cleaners, child-care providers, and long-distance truck drivers. Overall, the self-employed are more likely to have blue-collar jobs than white-collar jobs.

Our society has always painted an appealing picture of working independently: no time clocks to punch and no one looking over your shoulder. But the potential of earning a great deal of money is rarely realized. In fact, just one-fifth of small businesses survive for ten years.

Finally, a notable trend is that women now own about 30 percent of this country's 15 million small businesses, and the share is rising. Moreover, the 5 million

NOTE: Leslie Dunbar (1988) estimates that a 1% drop in unemployment saves the U.S. government $36 million in assistance payments.
GLOBAL: Unemployment rates (1996): Japan, 3.4%; U.S., 5.4%; Netherlands, 6.3%; U.K., 8.2%; Germany, 9.0%; Canada, 9.7%; Sweden, 10.0%; France, 12.4% (U.S. Bureau of the Census, 1997).
THEN AND NOW: African American unemployment, 1930: about 4% vs. 11% today. Richard Vedder and Lowell Gallaway (1993) link this rise to black people's movement out of low-unemployment farming and into urban manufacturing jobs (where lay-offs are common) but also to expanding entitlement programs, which have undermined employment.
SUPPLEMENTS: The *Data File* includes an overview of African American entrepreneurs.

DIVERSITY SNAPSHOT

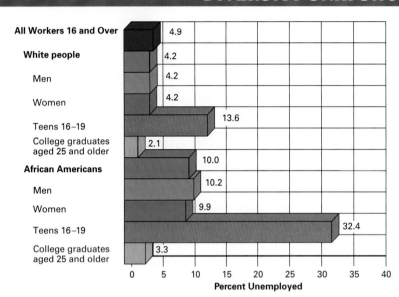

FIGURE 15–3
Official U.S. Unemployment Rate Among Various Categories of Adults, 1997

Sources: U.S. Bureau of the Census (1997) and U.S. Department of Labor (1998).

firms owned by U.S. women now employ more people than all the Fortune 500 corporations combined (Small Business Administration, 1996).

UNEMPLOYMENT

Every society has some unemployment. Few young people entering the labor force find a job right away; workers may temporarily leave their jobs to seek a new job or have children, or because of a labor strike; others suffer from long-term illnesses; and still others are illiterate or without the skills to perform useful work.

But unemployment is also caused by the economy itself. Jobs disappear as occupations become obsolete, as businesses close in the face of foreign competition or economic recession, and, as noted at the beginning of this chapter, sometimes companies cut their work force in an effort to become more profitable. Since 1980, the "downsizing" of U.S. businesses has eliminated some 5 million jobs—one-fourth of the total—in the 500 largest corporations.

In 1997, 6.7 million people over the age of sixteen were unemployed—about 4.9 percent of the civilian labor force. As a glance back at National Map 15–1 shows, some regions of the country, including parts of West Virginia and New Mexico, contend with unemployment at twice the national rate.

Figure 15–3 shows the official unemployment rate for various categories of U.S. workers in 1997. Unemployment among African Americans was more than twice the rate (10.0 percent) among white people (4.2 percent). For both races, men and women have roughly the same rates of unemployment.

THE UNDERGROUND ECONOMY

The U.S. government requires all businesses and individual workers to periodically report on their economic activity, especially earnings. Not reporting income received makes a transaction part of the **underground economy,** *economic activity involving income that is not reported to the government as required by law.*

On a small scale, most people participate in the underground economy from time to time: A family makes extra money by holding a garage sale, or a teenager babysits for the neighbors without reporting the income. Of course, far more of the underground economy is attributable to criminal activity such as the sale of illegal drugs, prostitution, bribery, theft, illegal gambling, and loan-sharking.

NOTE: The historic trend that linked a high risk of unemployment to blue-collar work shifted in the late 1980s as white-collar executives faced rising joblessness.

GLOBAL: Worldwide, some 120 million people are unemployed: one-third in low-income countries, 40% in middle-income nations, and one-fourth in high-income countries (United Nations Development Programme, 1995).

DISCUSS: Is the home-based "virtual office" a good thing? Pluses include more freedom, no commute, more flexibility; cons include isolation, harder to get help, and blurring between home and work life.

Q: "Among the purposes of a society should be to try to arrange for a continuous supply of work at all times and seasons." Pope Leo XIII

But the single largest segment of contributors to the underground economy is "honest" people who fail to report some or all of their legally obtained income. Self-employed persons such as carpenters, physicians, and owners of small businesses may understate their incomes on tax forms; waiters, waitresses, and other service workers may not report their entire earnings from tips. Individually, the omissions and misrepresentations may be small, but millions of individuals hedging on income tax returns add up to about $170 billion annually in lost revenues (Speer, 1995).

SOCIAL DIVERSITY IN THE WORKPLACE

Another major change in the U.S. economy involves the composition of the work force. Traditionally, white men have been the mainstay of the country's labor force. As explained in Chapter 13 ("Race and Ethnicity"), however, this nation's proportion of minorities is rapidly rising. Between 1990 and 1997, the African American population increased by 11 percent, almost twice the rate of increase for white people (6 percent). The jump was even greater in the Hispanic (30 percent) and Asian American (34 percent) populations. Should these trends continue, there will be a "minority-majority" in the United States toward the end of the next century. The prospect of this change is already having profound consequences. The box on page 418 takes a closer look at how the increasing social diversity of our society will affect the workplace of the next century.

NEW INFORMATION TECHNOLOGY AND WORK

Another key issue in the workplace of the twenty-first century is the central role of computers and other new information technology. The Information Revolution is changing the kind of work people do as well as where they do it. Computers are also altering the character of work in four additional ways (Zuboff, 1982; Rule & Brantley, 1992; Vallas & Beck, 1996):

1. **Computers are deskilling labor.** Just as industrial machinery "deskilled" the master crafts worker of an earlier era, so computers now threaten the skills of managers. More and more business decisions are based not on executive decision making but on computer modeling. In other words, a machine determines whether to buy or sell a product, make an investment, or approve or reject a loan.

2. **Computers are making work more abstract.** Industrial workers typically have a "hands-on" relationship with their product. Postindustrial workers manipulate symbols in pursuit of abstract goals such as making a Web site more attractive, a company more profitable, or software more "user friendly."

3. **Computers limit workplace interaction.** The Information Revolution forces employees to perform most of their work at computer terminals, which isolates workers from one another.

4. **Computers enhance employers' control of workers.** Computers allow supervisors to monitor each worker's output precisely and continuously, whether employees are working at computer terminals or on an assembly line.

The changes wrought by computers remind us that technology is not socially neutral. Rather, it shapes the way we work and alters the balance of power between employers and employees. Understandably, then, people are likely to welcome some aspects of the Information Revolution while opposing others.

CORPORATIONS

At the core of today's capitalist economy lies the **corporation,** *an organization with a legal existence, including rights and liabilities, apart from those of its members.* By incorporating, an organization becomes an entity unto itself, able to enter into contracts and own property. Of some 21 million businesses in the United States, 4 million are incorporated (U.S. Bureau of the Census, 1997). Incorporating protects the personal wealth of owners and top executives from lawsuits that might arise from business debts or harm to consumers; it also provides lower tax rates on profits for smaller businesses.

ECONOMIC CONCENTRATION

About half of U.S. corporations are small, with assets of less than $100,000. The largest corporations, however, dominate our country's economy. Corporations of record in 1995 included 445 with assets exceeding $1 billion, representing more than 72 percent of all corporate assets and profits (U.S. Bureau of the Census, 1997).

NOTE: Refer students to the box on page 351 of Chapter 13, "The Coming Minority-Majority?" for further details on the changing face of minority representation in the United States.

NOTE: National Maps 13–1 and 13–2, on pages 352 and 361, illustrate the areas of the country in which the character of the work force is most affected by racial and ethnic diversity.

NOTE: About 80% of U.S. employers have 15 or fewer employees.

NOTE: A significant portion of corporate stock is held by institutional investors (corporations investing in each other). In terms of individuals, about 20% of U.S. residents have such investments (exclusive of pension funds). Most stock is owned by a much smaller proportion of the population, as noted in Chapter 10. Perhaps 10% of Britons are stockholders (again, exclusive of pension funds).

SOCIAL DIVERSITY

Work Force 2000: The Trend Toward Diversity

The significant rise in the U.S. minority population has transformed the labor force in recent years. The figure shows a projection that the number of white men in the U.S. labor force will rise by a modest 5 percent between 1996 and 2005. The rate of increase among African American working men will be greater, at 8 percent. Among Hispanic men, the increase will be greater still, 25 percent.

Among women, projected increases are even larger. Although the projected rise of 13 percent among white women exceeds the 10 percent increase forecast for African American women, Hispanic women will show the greatest gains, estimated at 33 percent.

The overall result is that, by 2000, non-Hispanic white men will represent just 45 percent of all workers, a figure that will continue to drop. Therefore, companies that welcome social diversity will tap the largest talent pool and enjoy a competitive advantage in the twenty-first century.

Responding to this opportunity means more than recruiting talented workers of all colors and cultural backgrounds. Developing the potential of all employees will require several additional changes in the workplace environment.

First, companies must realize that the needs and concerns of women and other minorities may not be the same as those of white men. For example, corporations will be pressed to provide workplace child care in the future.

Second, businesses must develop strategies for defusing tensions that arise from social differences. They will have to work harder at treating all workers equally and respectfully, and no corporate culture can tolerate racial or sexual harassment.

Third, companies will have to rethink current promotion practices. At present, only 2 percent of Fortune 500 top executives are women, and just 1 percent are other minorities. In a broad survey of U.S. companies, the U.S. Equal Employment Opportunity Commission confirmed that white men (42 percent of adults aged twenty to sixty-four) hold 61 percent of management jobs; the comparable figures for white women are 42 and 27 percent; for African Americans, 12 and 6 percent; and, for Hispanics, 10 and 3 percent.

In sum, "glass ceilings" that prevent advancement by skilled workers not only discourage achievement, but beyond the year 2000, they will deprive companies of their largest source of talent—women and other minorities.

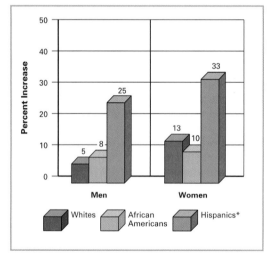

Projected Increase in the Numbers of People in the U.S. Labor Force, 1996–2005

*Hispanics can be of any race.

Source: U.S. Bureau of the Census (1997).

Sources: U.S. Bureau of the Census (1997, 1998) and U.S. Equal Employment Opportunity Commission (1997).

The largest U.S. corporation in terms of sales is automaker General Motors, with more than $222 billion in total assets. GM's annual sales ($168 billion in 1996) roughly equal the tax revenue of half the states combined. GM also employs more people than the state governments of California, Oregon, Washington, Alaska, and Hawaii.

CONGLOMERATES AND CORPORATE LINKAGES

The largest businesses are **conglomerates,** *giant corporations composed of many smaller corporations.* Conglomerates emerge as corporations enter new markets, spin off new companies, or take over other companies. Viacom

SOCIAL SURVEY: "How much confidence do you have in the people running major companies?" (GSS 1996, N = 1,925; *Codebook*, 1996:166)

| "A great deal" | 23.2% | "Hardly any" | 13.5% |
| "Only some" | 59.1% | DK/NR | 4.2% |

NOTE: Oligopoly does not preclude successful economic challenges, either in well-established industries like automaking (consider the success of the Japanese entering the U.S. auto market) or in new industries like software (note Microsoft's outdistancing of IBM and other rivals to set a world standard).

DISCUSS: In 1996 the federal government probed Frito Lay for their domination (55% of sales dollars) of the snack food industry. Is this against the public interest or simply evidence that some companies perform better than others?

is one giant corporate "umbrella"—with 1996 revenues of $12.1 billion—that encompasses many smaller corporations including Paramount (entertainment), Blockbuster (videos and theme parks), MTV, Nickelodeon, some two dozen television and radio stations, as well as Simon & Schuster publishing, which includes Prentice Hall, the publisher of this text (Fortune 500, 1998).

Corporations are not only linked in conglomerates, but also by owning each other's stock. For example, in today's global economy, many U.S.-based companies invest heavily in other corporations commonly regarded as their competitors. In the automobile industry, Ford owns a significant share of Mazda, General Motors is a major investor in Isuzu, and Chrysler is part owner of Mitsubishi.

In addition, corporations are linked through *interlocking directorates*, social networks of people serving simultaneously on the boards of directors of many corporations. A member of General Motors's board of directors may, for example, sit alongside a board member from Ford on the board of Exxon—giving all parties access to valuable information about each other's products and marketing strategies (Herman, 1981; Scott & Griff, 1985; Weidenbaum, 1995).

Beth Mintz and Michael Schwartz (1981) found General Motors is linked through board members to another 700 companies. Interlocking directorates do not necessarily run counter to the public interest, but they may encourage illegal activity and they certainly concentrate wealth and power.

CORPORATIONS: ARE THEY COMPETITIVE?

The capitalist model suggests that businesses operate independently in a competitive market. But large corporations are not truly competitive because, first, their extensive linkages mean that they do not operate independently. Second, a small number of corporations dominate many large markets.

Law forbids a large company from establishing a **monopoly,** *domination of a market by a single producer,* because such a company could simply dictate prices. But **oligopoly,** *domination of a market by a few producers,* is legal and a common pattern. Oligopoly arises because the investment needed to enter a major product market, such as the auto industry, is beyond the reach of all but the biggest companies. Moreover, true competition means risk, which big business tries to avoid.

Corporate power is now so great—and competition among corporations so limited—that government regulation may be the only way to protect the public

McDonald's, which now operates more than 15,000 restaurants around the world, illustrates the central role that large corporations play in an expanding global economy. Here, South African children enjoy familiar fare.

interest. Yet, the government is the corporate world's single biggest customer. Washington also frequently intervenes to support struggling corporations, as in the recent savings and loan bailout. In truth, U.S. corporations and the federal government often work together to make the entire economy more stable and profitable.

CORPORATIONS AND THE GLOBAL ECONOMY

Corporations have grown in size and power so fast that they account for most of the world's economic output. In the process, the largest corporations—based in the United States, Japan, and Western Europe—have spilled across national borders and consider the entire world one huge marketplace.

NOTE: In 1995 (for the first time in 40 years) *Fortune* added service industries to its Fortune 400—including life insurance companies and banks. Showing the growing significance of information technology, Microsoft now rivals General Motors in value.

NOTE: The trend toward a postindustrial economy is reflected by changes in the Dow's 30 stocks. In 1997, Texaco, Westinghouse Electric, and Bethlehem Steel were dropped in favor of Travelers Group, Hewlett-Packard, and Johnson & Johnson.

GLOBAL: In 1996, foreign interests invested an estimated $630 billion in the United States; by region, the largest investor is Europe ($410 billion), followed by Asia ($134 billion). The list of individual investor nations is topped by the United Kingdom ($143 billion), Japan ($118 billion), and the Netherlands ($74 billion) (U.S. Bureau of Economic Analysis, 1998).

GLOBAL SNAPSHOT

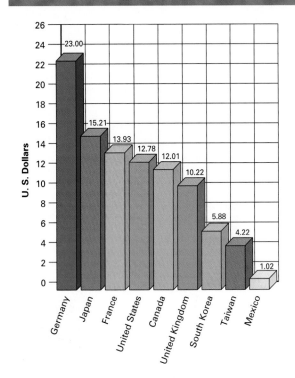

FIGURE 15–4 Average Hourly Wages for Workers in Manufacturing, 1996

Source: Calculations by the author based on U.S. Bureau of the Census (1997).

Multinational corporations produce and market products in many different nations. Beatrice Foods, for example, operates factories in thirty countries and sells products in more than one hundred. General Motors, Ford, Exxon, and the other huge multinationals earn much—and, in some cases, most—of their profits outside the United States.

Because most of the planet's resources and people are found in less-developed countries, multinational corporations spread their operations around the world in order to gain access to raw materials, inexpensive labor, and vast markets. As shown in Figure 15–4, labor costs are far lower in poor countries of the world: A manufacturing worker in Taiwan labors all week to earn what a German worker earns in a single day.

The impact of multinationals on poor societies is controversial, as Chapter 11 ("Global Inequality") explains in detail. On one side of the argument, modernization theorists claim that multinationals unleash the great productivity of the capitalist economic system, which will propel poor nations toward a higher standard of living. Specifically, corporations offer poor societies tax revenues, capital investment, new jobs, and advanced technology that act together to accelerate economic growth (Rostow, 1978; Madsen, 1980; Berger, 1986; Firebaugh & Beck, 1994).

On the other side, dependency theorists argue that multinationals intensify global inequality. Multinational investment, as they see it, actually creates few jobs in poor countries, inhibits the development of local industries, and pushes developing countries to produce goods for export rather than food and other products for local consumption. From this standpoint, multinationals make poor societies poorer and increasingly dependent on rich, capitalist societies (Vaughan, 1978; Wallerstein, 1979; Delacroix & Ragin, 1981; Bergesen, 1983; Walton & Ragin, 1990).

While modernization theory hails the market as the key to progress and affluence for all the world's people, dependency theory calls for replacing market systems with government-based economic policies. The final box on pages 422–23 takes a closer look at the issue of market versus governmental economies.

LOOKING AHEAD: THE ECONOMY OF THE TWENTY-FIRST CENTURY

Social institutions are organizational strategies by which societies meet various needs of their members. But, as we have seen, the U.S. economy only partly succeeds in this respect. Though highly productive, our economy distributes its products in a highly unequal fashion. Moreover, as we move into the new century, economic transformations in our society and the world present us with new opportunities and challenges.

As this chapter highlighted, the Information Revolution is driving much of this change. In the postindustrial era, the share of the U.S. labor force engaged in manufacturing has tumbled to half of what it was in 1960; service work—and especially computer-related jobs—have climbed just as quickly. For workers who depend on industrial skills to earn a living, this change has brought rising unemployment and declining wages. As we look to the coming century, our society must face up to the fact that millions of men

GLOBAL: In recent years, exports have accounted for most of the growth of the U.S. economy; and most of this is the output of multinationals.

Q: Pope John Paul II has charged that both capitalism and socialism have "a tendency toward imperialism" by seeking wealth and power at the expense of low-income nations. (*Sollicitudo Rei Socialis*—"The Social Concerns of the Church")

NOTE: Arguments about economic development on the political right tend to focus on productivity; those on the left tend to highlight distribution. This mirrors global theories of economic development—modernization theory and dependency (world systems) theory. See discussion of these approaches in Chapter 11, "Global Stratification."

The global expansion of multinational corporations centered in high-income countries has altered consumption patterns almost everywhere, encouraging a homogeneous "corporate culture" that is—for better or worse—undermining countless traditional ways of life.

and women lack the language and computer skills needed to participate in a postindustrial economy. Can we afford to consign these workers and their families to the margins of society? How can the government, schools, and families prepare young people to perform the kind of work their society makes available to them?

A second transformation that will define the next century is the emergence of a global economy. Two centuries ago, the ups and downs of a local economy reflected events and trends within a single town. One century ago, local communities throughout the country had become economically interconnected so that prosperity in one place depended on producing goods demanded by people elsewhere. We will enter the new century with powerful economic connections on the global level. In fact, it now makes little sense to speak of a national economy; what people in a Kansas farm town produce and consume may be affected more by what transpires in the wheat-growing region of Russia than by events in their own state capital. In short, U.S. workers and business owners are not only generating new products and services, but doing so in response to factors and forces that are distant and unseen.

Finally, change is causing analysts around the world to rethink conventional economic models. The emerging global economic system shows that socialist economies are less productive than their capitalist counterparts, one important reason for the recent collapse of socialist regimes in Eastern Europe and the former Soviet Union. At its peak, socialism claimed one-fourth of humanity; now only the People's Republic of China, North Korea, Cuba, and a few other nations hold steadfastly to government-operated economies.

But capitalism, too, has seen marked changes, especially an increasing involvement of government in the economy. Moreover, the largest U.S. corporations have expanded into most parts of the world, just as foreign-based corporations are increasing their investment in the United States.

We are nearing the end of what some analysts call "the American century." Ours is still the most productive economy in the world. But a turning point occurred in 1990 when, for the first time, foreign corporations owned more of the United States than U.S. corporations owned abroad. Foreign investors now have title to half of the commercial property in downtown Los Angeles, 40 percent in Houston, 35 percent in Minneapolis, and 25 percent in Manhattan (Selimuddin, 1989).

What will be the long-term effects of all these changes? Two conclusions seem inescapable. First, the economic future of the United States and other nations will be played out in a global arena. The emergence of the postindustrial economy in the United States is, after all, inseparable from the increasing industrial production of other nations, especially in Asia's rapidly developing Pacific Rim. Second, we must face up to the issue of global inequality. Whether the world economy ultimately reduces or deepens the disparity between rich and poor societies may well be what steers our planet toward peace or war.

DISCUSS: Advocates of government regulation argue that such supervision guards against monopoly. Defenders of the market claim that allowing free international trade forces large companies to be competitive (witness how the Japanese automakers successfully challenged the U.S. Big Three).

Q: "The market delivers rough justice; the welfare state takes the roughness out of justice." Columnist George Will

DISCUSS: True or false: The political left favors large government and condemns "big business," while the political right favors large business and condemns "big government."

RESOURCE: An excerpt from William Julius Wilson's book *When Work Disappears*, found in the companion reader *Seeing Ourselves*, explores the issue of inner-city poverty and offers suggestions for solving this problem.

CONTROVERSY & DEBATE

The Market: Does the "Invisible Hand" Serve Our Interests or Pick Our Pockets?

"The market" or "government planning"? Each is a means of economic decision making to determine what products and services companies will produce and what people will consume. So important is this process that the degree to which the market or government directs the economy largely determines how nations define themselves, choose their allies, and identify their enemies.

Historically, U.S. society has relied on the market—the "invisible hand" of supply and demand—for most economic decisions. According to market dynamics, a market moves prices for products upward or downward according to the supply of sellers and the demand of buyers. The market thus coordinates the efforts of countless people, each of whom—to return to

Adam Smith's insight—is motivated only by self-interest.

Defenders also praise the market for discouraging racial and ethnic prejudice. Industrialist J. P. Morgan once commented that he would only sail with a gentleman but he would do business with *anyone*—explicitly acknowledging that market transactions focus on value, not the social traits of traders. And, perhaps most important of all, as economists Milton and Rose Friedman remind us, a more-or-less freely operating market system has provided members of our society with an unprecedented economic standard of living.

But others point to the contributions government makes to the U.S. economy. First, government steps in to carry out tasks that no one would do for profit: Even Adam Smith, for example,

looked to government to defend the country against external enemies. Government also plays a key role in constructing and maintaining public projects such as roads, utilities, schools, libraries, and museums.

However, free market advocates like the Friedmans counter that virtually any task the government undertakes, it performs inefficiently. The least satisfying goods and services available today—including public schools, postal service, and passenger railroad service among them—are government-operated. The products we most enjoy—such as computers, household appliances, and the myriad offerings of supermarkets and shopping centers—are primarily products of the market. Thus, while some government presence in the economy is necessary, the Friedmans and other

SUMMARY

1. The economy is the major social institution by which a society produces, distributes, and consumes goods and services.

2. In technologically simple societies, the economy is part of the family. In agrarian societies, most economic activity takes place apart from the home. Industrialization sparks significant economic expansion built around new energy sources, large factories, mass production, and worker specialization.

3. The postindustrial economy is characterized by a shift from producing tangible goods to services. Just as the Industrial Revolution propelled the industrial economy of the past, the Information Revolution is now advancing the postindustrial economy.

4. The primary sector of the economy generates raw materials; the secondary sector manufactures

various goods; the tertiary sector produces services. In preindustrial societies, the primary sector predominates; in industrial societies, the secondary sector; and in postindustrial societies, the tertiary sector.

5. The emergence of a global economy means that nations no longer produce and consume products and services within national boundaries. Moreover, the 600 largest corporations, operating internationally, now account for most of humanity's economic output.

6. Social scientists describe the economies of today's industrial societies in terms of two models. The capitalist model rests on private ownership of productive property and the pursuit of personal profit in a competitive marketplace. Socialism is based on collective ownership of productive property

DISCUSS: How does morality figure in the market system? Some say there is no morality in a market economy, only profit; the political left describes the market as implicitly immoral, since it ignores social good; the political right says that self-seeking is inherently moral, because it represents people freely serving their own chosen ends. Also, a market system offers people freedoms as producers and consumers and bridges national, religious, racial, ethnic, and other historic divides.

EXERCISE: To help them become familiar with economic data, direct students to the *Statistical Abstract* (U.S. Bureau of the Census), *Human Development Report* (The United Nations), and *World Development Report* (The World Bank). These three annual publications provide extensive data about the economies of the United States and other world nations.

supporters of free markets believe that minimal state regulation serves the public interest best.

But supporters of government intervention in the economy do not concede the argument. Far from it: Many analysts all but view the market as a negative force. For one thing, they claim, the market has little incentive to produce anything that is not profitable. This is why few private companies set out to meet the needs of poor people since, by definition, they have little money to spend.

Second, critics look to government to curb what they see as the market system's self-destructive tendencies. In 1890, for example, the government passed the Sherman Antitrust Act to break up monopolies that controlled the nation's oil and steel production. Especially since President Franklin Roosevelt's "New Deal" of the 1930s, government has taken a strong regulatory role, intervening in the market to control inflation (by setting interest rates), protect the well-being of workers (by imposing workplace safety standards), and benefit consumers (by mandating standards for product quality). Even so, advocates of a stronger role for government point out that the power of corporations in U.S. society is so great that the government still cannot effectively challenge the capitalist elite.

Third, critics support government's role in curbing the market's tendency to magnify social stratification. Since capitalist economies concentrate income and wealth in the hands of a few, a government system of taxation that applies higher rates to the rich counters this tendency in the name of social justice.

Does the market's "invisible hand" feed us well or pick our pockets? While most people in the United States think the market is good, they also support some government intervention to benefit the public. Indeed, government assists not only citizens but business itself by providing investment capital, constructing roads and other infrastructure, and shielding companies from foreign competition. Yet, in the United States and around the world, people continue to debate the optimal balance of market forces and government decision making.

Continue the debate . . .

1. *Why do defenders of the free market assert that "the government that governs best is the government that governs least"? What do you think?*

2. *What difference does it make if a society's economy is more market-based system or government-centered?*

3. *What is your impression of the successes and failures of socialist economic systems? What about "welfare capitalism" as found in Sweden?*

Sources: Friedman (1980) and Erber (1990).

and the pursuit of collective well-being through government control of the economy.

7. Although the U.S. economy is predominantly capitalist, government is broadly involved in economic life. Government plays an even greater role in the "welfare capitalist" economies of some Western European nations such as Sweden and the "state capitalism" of many Asian nations, including Japan. The former Soviet Union and the nations of Eastern Europe are gradually introducing market elements into their formerly centralized economies.

8. Capitalism is very productive, providing a high overall standard of living. A capitalist system provides freedom to act according to one's self-interest. Socialism is less productive but generates greater economic equality. A socialist system offers freedom from basic want.

9. In the United States, agricultural work has declined over the course of this century to just 2 percent of the labor force. The share of blue-collar jobs has also diminished, now accounting for little more than one-fourth of the labor force. The share of white-collar service occupations, however, has been rising rapidly; about 70 percent of the labor force now performs white-collar work.

10. Work in the primary labor market provides greater rewards than work in the secondary labor market. Most new jobs in the United States are service positions in the secondary labor market, and about one-third of today's workers hold temporary jobs with no promise of job security.

11. A profession is a special category of white-collar work based on theoretical knowledge, occupational autonomy, authority over clients, and a claim to serving the community.

12. Today, 8 percent of U.S. workers are self-employed. Although many professionals fall into

this category, most self-employed workers have blue-collar occupations.

13. Unemployment has many causes, including the operation of the economy itself; in the United States at least 5 percent of the labor force is typically without work.

14. The underground economy, which includes criminal as well as legal activity, generates income that goes unreported on income tax forms.

15. Women and minorities represent an increasing share of the U.S. labor force. By the year 2000, white males, traditionally the backbone of the labor force, will account for less than half of all workers.

16. New information technology is transforming the kind of work people do, as well as subjecting workers to greater control by supervisors.

17. Corporations form the core of the U.S. economy. The largest corporations, which are conglomerates, account for most corporate assets and profits. Many large corporations operate as multinationals, producing and distributing products in most nations of the world.

KEY CONCEPTS

economy the social institution that organizes the production, distribution, and consumption of goods and services

postindustrial economy a productive system based on service work and extensive use of information technology

primary sector the part of the economy that generates raw materials directly from the natural environment

secondary sector the part of the economy that transforms raw materials into manufactured goods

tertiary sector the part of the economy that produces services rather than goods

global economy economic activity spanning many nations of the world with little regard for national borders

capitalism an economic system in which natural resources and the means of producing goods and services are privately owned

socialism an economic system in which natural resources and the means of producing goods and services are collectively owned

communism a hypothetical economic and political system in which all members of a society are socially equal

welfare capitalism an economic and political system that combines a mostly market-based economy with government programs to provide for people's basic needs

state capitalism an economic and political system in which companies are privately owned although they cooperate closely with the government

primary labor market occupations that provide extensive benefits to workers

secondary labor market jobs that provide minimal benefits to workers

labor unions worker organizations that seek to improve wages and working conditions through various strategies, including negotiation and strikes

profession a prestigious white-collar occupation that requires extensive formal education

underground economy economic activity involving income that is not reported to the government as required by law

corporation an organization with a legal existence, including rights and liabilities, apart from its members

conglomerate a giant corporation composed of many smaller corporations

monopoly domination of a market by a single producer

oligopoly domination of a market by a few producers

CRITICAL-THINKING QUESTIONS

1. What is a social institution? In principle, what is the economy supposed to do? How well do you think our economy does its job?

2. Identify several ways in which the Industrial Revolution reshaped the economy of the United States. How is the Information Revolution transforming the economy once again?

3. What key characteristics distinguish capitalism from socialism? Compare these two systems in terms of productivity, economic inequality, and their approach to personal freedoms.

4. In light of the growing power of multinationals, does it still make sense to speak of "national economies" as we have done in the past?

LEARNING EXERCISES

1. The profile of the overall U.S. economy—70 percent of output in the tertiary sector, 28 percent in the industrial sector, and 2 percent in the primary sector—obscures great variety within this country. A trip to the library will allow you to profile your local economy (a city, county, or state).

2. Here are two interesting exercises involving the Internet. The Bureau of Labor Statistics publishes a wide range of data and reports at its Web site. Visit them at http://stats.bls.gov/blshome.html As another possibility, see the results of student research into Ohio family farms at this student-created Web site: http://www.kenyon.edu/projects/famfarm/welcome/welcome.htm

3. How are computers changing the character of the college campus? Meet with your sociology instructor or an official in the computer center to find out the various ways computers are used on campus. Does the arrival of new information technology seem to be changing professional or personal relationships on the campus? How?

4. Visit a discount store such as Wal-Mart or K-Mart and select an area of the store of interest to you. Do a little "fieldwork," inspecting products to see where they are made. Does your research support the existence of a global economy?

5. Install the CD-ROM packaged inside the back cover of your text and complete the activities designed to accompany this chapter.

Terracotta Army, People's Republic of China

CHAPTER 16

POLITICS AND GOVERNMENT

Charlotte Williams sat straight up in the folding metal chair behind the ballot box, her eyes fixed on the door. It was Election Day, 1996, and she was four hours into her day-long shift overseeing the voting in Washington, D.C.'s, Precinct Number 15. To her left, a man of about sixty leaned over a table, completing his ballot. But, save the man and Williams herself, the large room was empty.

As the man deposited his ballot, he smiled and shrugged his shoulders. "Today, we are picking a president," he began, "yet nobody bothers to come out to vote." "Tell me about it," Charlotte Williams responded. "People ought to care, but— you know what—they don't. The welfare system is going to change. You *know* what's happening in our schools. There's way too much crime. I'm sorry, but I can't see it. I just can't see people not caring."

Across the country, in 1996, less than half the voting-age population cast ballots for President, the lowest rate since 1924. And no category of our population was less likely to vote than the poor. In fact, according to government surveys, 80 percent of people earning more than $50,000 a year reported voting in 1996, but only 35 percent of people earning under $10,000 said they went to the polls (Clymer, 1996).

What does this apathy mean? Is our political system failing to meet the needs of the people, especially the poor? Indeed, can we realistically call our nation a "democracy" when most people don't participate in politics—even as once-a-year voters?

This chapter investigates *politics*, the dynamics of power within societies and among nations. Formally, **politics** (or "the polity") is *the social institution that distributes power, sets a society's agenda, and makes decisions.* But, as the low turnout in many voting precincts suggests, politics may meet the concerns of some far better than others.

POWER AND AUTHORITY

Every society rests on **power,** which sociologist Max Weber (1978; orig. 1921) defined as *the ability to achieve desired ends despite resistance.* To a large degree, the exercise of power is the business of **government,** *a formal organization that directs the political life of a society.* Yet, as Weber explained, few governments obtain compliance by openly threatening their people. Most of the time, people respect (or, at least, accept) their political system.

Practically speaking, it would be difficult for any large, complex society to persist if power derived *only* from sheer force, and life in such a society would be a nightmare of terror. Social organization, by contrast, depends on some degree of consensus about proper goals (often in the form of cultural values) and suitable means of pursuing them (cultural norms).

Every society, then, seeks to establish its power as legitimate. Weber therefore focused on the concept of **authority,** *power that people perceive as legitimate rather than coercive.* How is sheer power transformed into stable authority? There are three ways, Weber explained, and the one a society relies on most depends on its level of economic development.

SUPPLEMENTS: Consult the *Data File* for an outline of this chapter, supplementary lecture material, and discussion topics.
NOTE: As Hannah Arendt explained, the concept of authority is Roman in origin with roots in the Latin verb *augere*, meaning "to augment." Thus authority involves steadily augmenting some past foundation.
NOTE: Ferdinand Tönnies, too, described the social roots of authority: He linked authority to (1) advanced age, (2) force, and (3) wisdom or spirit.
GLOBAL: The British have melded traditional and bureaucratic authority by their recent practice of elevating individuals to nobility based on distinguished accomplishment, but mandating that the rank not pass to any descendants.

TRADITIONAL AUTHORITY

Preindustrial societies, Weber explained, rely on **traditional authority,** *power legitimized through respect for long-established cultural patterns.* In ideal terms, traditional authority is power woven into a society's collective memory, so that people consider social arrangements almost sacred. Chinese emperors in antiquity were legitimized by tradition, as were nobles in medieval Europe. In both cases, the power of tradition was strong enough that—for better or worse—people typically viewed members of the hereditary ruling family as almost godlike.

But traditional authority declines as societies industrialize. Hannah Arendt (1963) pointed out that traditional authority is compelling only so long as everyone shares the same heritage and world view. This form of authority, then, is undermined by the specialization demanded by industrial production, by modern, scientific thinking, and by the social change and cultural diversity that accompany immigration. Thus, no president of today's United States, for example, could ever make the claim of ruling by grace of God. Even so, as E. Digby Baltzell (1964) points out, some well-established upper-class families such as the Kennedys, Roosevelts, and Rockefellers have occupied a privileged position for several generations, so that when one of them enters the political arena, it is with some measure of traditional authority.

If traditional authority plays a small part in U.S. national politics, it persists in other aspects of everyday life. Patriarchy, the domination of women by men, is a traditional form of power that remains widespread, even though it is increasingly challenged. Less controversial is the traditional authority parents exert over their children. The fact that traditional authority is linked to a person's status as parent is obvious every time a parent answers a doubting child with, "Because I said so!" There is no debating the parent's decision because that would defeat traditional authority by putting parent and child on an equal footing.

RATIONAL-LEGAL AUTHORITY

Weber defined **rational-legal authority** (sometimes called *bureaucratic authority*) as *power legitimized by legally enacted rules and regulations.* Rational-legal authority, then, is power legitimized in the operation of lawful government.

As Chapter 7 ("Groups and Organizations") explains, Weber viewed bureaucracy as the organizational backbone of rational-thinking, industrial societies.

Moreover, just as a rational world view promotes bureaucracy, so it erodes traditional customs and practices. Instead of venerating the past, members of modern societies look to formally enacted rules—especially law—for principles of justice.

Rationally enacted rules also underlie many power relationships in everyday life. The authority of classroom teachers and deans, for example, rests on the offices they hold in bureaucratic colleges and universities. The police, too, are officers, within the bureaucracy of local government. In contrast to traditional authority, rational-legal authority flows not from family background but from organizational position. Thus, while a traditional monarch rules for life, a modern president accepts and relinquishes power according to law; presidential authority is in the office, not the person.

CHARISMATIC AUTHORITY

Finally, Weber claimed power could be transformed into authority through charisma. **Charismatic authority** is *power legitimized through extraordinary personal abilities that inspire devotion and obedience.* Unlike tradition and rational law, then, charisma has less to do with social organization and is more a mark of an exceptionally forceful and magnetic personality.

Throughout history, some members of societies have been regarded as charismatic. Charisma can enhance the stature of an established leader or strengthen the appeal of an outside challenger. Charismatics turn an audience into followers, often making their own rules and challenging the status quo: Vladimir Lenin guided the overthrow of feudal monarchy in Russia in 1917; Mahatma Gandhi inspired the struggle to free India from British colonialism after World War II; Martin Luther King, Jr., galvanized the civil rights movement in the United States; and, through her work ministering to the poor in Calcutta, India, Mother Teresa asked the world to confront stunning poverty.

Because charismatic authority emanates from a single individual, any charismatic movement faces a crisis of survival when its leader dies. Thus, Weber explained, the persistence of a charismatic organization depends on the **routinization of charisma,** *the transformation of charismatic authority into some combination of traditional and bureaucratic authority.* Christianity, for example, began as a cult driven by the personal charisma of Jesus of Nazareth. After the death of Jesus, followers institutionalized his teachings in a church eventually centered in Rome and built on both tradition and bureaucracy. Routinized in this way, the Roman Catholic church has flourished for 2,000 years.

Q: "The essential problem of social order is the [legitimization] and not the elimination of social power." E. Digby Baltzell

DISCUSS: Is the controversial (and often revolutionary) character of charisma evident in the fact that charismatics rarely die of old age?

NOTE: Another reason for the routinization of charisma is to prevent the rise of new charismatics.

DIVERSITY: Most people recognized as charismatic have been men. But this century has seen the rise of many exceptional women, from Amelia Earhart to Princess Diana. In politics, charismatic women leaders have included Indira Gandhi of India, Golda Meir of Israel, Benazir Bhutto of Pakistan, and Margaret Thatcher of the United Kingdom.

The powers that be have often disparaged popular opposition as a "mob." Such an argument was used to justify police violence against strikers—including ten who died—in a bloody confrontation near Chicago's Republic Steel Mill in 1936. Philip Evergood commemorates the event in his painting American Tragedy.

Philip Evergood, *American Tragedy*, 1936, oil on canvas, 29½ x 39½", Terry Dintenfass Gallery, New York.

POLITICS IN GLOBAL PERSPECTIVE

Political systems have taken many forms throughout history. The technologically simple hunting and gathering societies that once were found all over the planet operated like one large family. Leadership generally fell to a male with unusual strength, hunting skill, or personal charisma. But these leaders exercised little power, since they lacked the resources to control their own people, much less extend their rule outward. In the simplest societies, then, leaders were barely discernible from everyone else, and government did not exist as a distinct sphere of life (Lenski, Nolan, & Lenski, 1995).

Larger and more complex agrarian societies are characterized by specialized activity and a material surplus. These societies become hierarchical, with a small elite gaining control of most wealth and power; politics moves outside the family to become a social institution in its own right. Leaders who manage to pass along their power over several generations may acquire traditional authority, perhaps even claiming divine right to govern. Such leaders also may benefit from Weber's rational-legal authority since they are served by a bureaucratic political administration and system of law.

As societies expand, politics eventually takes the form of a national government or *political state*. But the emergence of a political state depends on technology. Just a few centuries ago, armies moved slowly and communication over even short distances was uncertain. For this reason, the early political empires we learned about in school—such as Mesopotamia in the Middle East about 5,000 years ago—actually took the form of many small *city-states*.

More complex technology helped the modern world develop the larger-scale system of *nation-states*. Currently, the world has 191 independent nation-states, each with a somewhat distinctive political system. Generally speaking, however, the world's political systems can be analyzed in terms of four categories: monarchy, democracy, authoritarianism, and totalitarianism.

MONARCHY

Monarchy (with Latin and Greek roots meaning "one ruler") is *a political system in which a single family rules from generation to generation*. Monarchy is typical in the history of agrarian societies; the Bible, for example, tells of great kings such as David and Solomon. Today's British monarchy—the Windsor family—traces its lineage back roughly 1,000 years. In Weber's terms, then, monarchy is legitimized by tradition.

During the medieval era, *absolute monarchy*, in which hereditary rulers claimed a monopoly of power based on divine right, flourished from England to China and in parts of the Americas. Monarchs in some

NOTE: The word "democracy" has Greek roots meaning "rule of the people" or "popular authority."
Q: "Whether we like to admit it or not, a society which encourages the full flowering of individual liberty is, and can only be, a stratified society." Andrew Hacker
Q: "Democracy is a device that guarantees that we will be governed no better than we deserve." George Bernard Shaw

NOTE: Generally speaking, the political left (following Rousseau and Marx) seeks to lessen inequality, viewing inequality as equivalent to injustice. The political right (following Plato) defends dimensions of inequality as legitimate or just. Thus, the concept of "authority" has been of more interest to the right, while the left has critiqued legitimizing "ideologies."

nations, such as Saudi Arabia, still exercise virtually absolute control over their people.

During this more egalitarian century, however, monarchs have gradually passed from the scene in favor of elected officials. Europe's remaining monarchs—in Great Britain, Spain, Norway, Sweden, Belgium, Denmark, and the Netherlands—now preside over *constitutional monarchies*. They serve as symbolic heads of state, while elected politicians led by a prime minister govern according to political principles embodied in a constitution. In these nations, then, the nobility may formally reign, but elected officials actually rule.

DEMOCRACY

The historical trend in the modern world is toward **democracy,** *a political system in which power is exercised by the people as a whole.* But members of democratic societies rarely participate directly in decision making; numbers alone make this an impossibility. Instead, a system of *representative democracy* places authority in the hands of elected leaders who are accountable to the people.

Most rich countries of the world claim to be democratic. Economic development and democratic government go together because both depend on a literate populace. Moreover, the traditional legitimization of power in a monarchy gives way, with industrialization, to rational-legal authority. A rational election process puts leaders in offices regulated by law. Thus democracy and rational-legal authority are linked just as monarchy and traditional authority are.

But countries such as the United States are not truly democratic for two reasons. First, there is the problem of bureaucracy. All democratic political systems rely on the work of large numbers of bureaucratic officials. The federal government of the United States, for example, employs more than 3 million people (excluding the armed forces), and another 17 million people work in some 80,000 local governments across the country. The vast majority of these bureaucrats are never elected by anyone and are not directly accountable to the people (Scaff, 1981; Edwards, 1985; Etzioni-Halevy, 1985).

The second problem involves economic inequality. In a highly stratified society, the rich will have far more political clout than the poor. In the 1996 national elections, for example, magazine magnate Steve Forbes financed his own run for the White House, spending $25 million. He managed to win seventy-three electoral delegates (a cost of about $350,000 each), demonstrating that, in the game of politics, "money talks." Moreover, given the even greater resources of large

organizations (such as billion-dollar corporations), how can we think our "democratic" system responds to—or even hears—the voices of "average people"?

Democracy and Freedom: Capitalist and Socialist Approaches

Despite the problems we have just described, rich capitalist nations such as the United States claim to operate as democracies. Of course, socialist countries like Cuba and the People's Republic of China make the same claim. This curious fact suggests we need to look more closely at *political economy:* the interplay of politics and economics.

The political life of the United States, Canada, and the nations of Europe is largely shaped by the economic principles of capitalism. The pursuit of profit within a market system requires that "freedom" be defined in terms of people's rights to act in their own self-interest. Thus, the capitalist approach to political freedom translates into personal liberty—to act in whatever ways maximize profits or other forms of income. From this point of view, moreover, "democracy" means that individuals have the right to select their leaders from among those running for office.

However, as we noted earlier, capitalist societies are marked by a striking inequality of wealth. If everyone acts in a self-interested way, in other words, the inevitable result is that some people accumulate far more wealth and power than others. It is this elite, then, that dominates the economic and political life of the society.

Socialist systems, by contrast, claim they are democratic because their economies meet everyone's basic needs for housing, schooling, work, and medical care. Despite being a much poorer country than the United States, for example, Cuba provides basic medical care to all without regard for people's ability to pay.

But critics of socialism counter that the extensive government regulation of social life in these countries can become oppressive. The socialist governments of China and Cuba, for example, do not allow their people to move freely inside or outside of their borders and do not tolerate organized political opposition.

These contrasting approaches to democracy and freedom raise an important question: Are economic equality and political liberty compatible? To foster economic equality, socialism constrains the choices of individuals. Capitalism, on the other hand, provides broad political liberties, which, in practice, mean little to the poor. A look back at Global Map 9–1, on page 253, shows the extent of income inequality in the world's nations. Global Map 16–1 shows one organization's

RESOURCE: The classic analysis of monarchy, aristocracy, and democracy is found in Aristotle's *Politics*. He favors aristocracy—the rule of the most able—but warns of its corruption into self-serving class rule. His critique of democracy focuses on this system's granting of an equal voice in government to all people, learned and unlearned, virtuous and nonvirtuous alike.

THEN AND NOW: In 1985, according to Freedom House, 34.9% of the world's people were "free," 23.3% were "partly free," and 41.8% were "not free"; comparable figures for 1998; 22% "free," 39% "partly free," and 39% "not free."

GLOBAL: According to World Bank data, in 1974 39 countries—1 in 4—were considered democracies; in 1997, 117 nations—nearly 2 in 3—elected leaders through open elections (The World Bank, 1997).

WINDOW ON THE WORLD

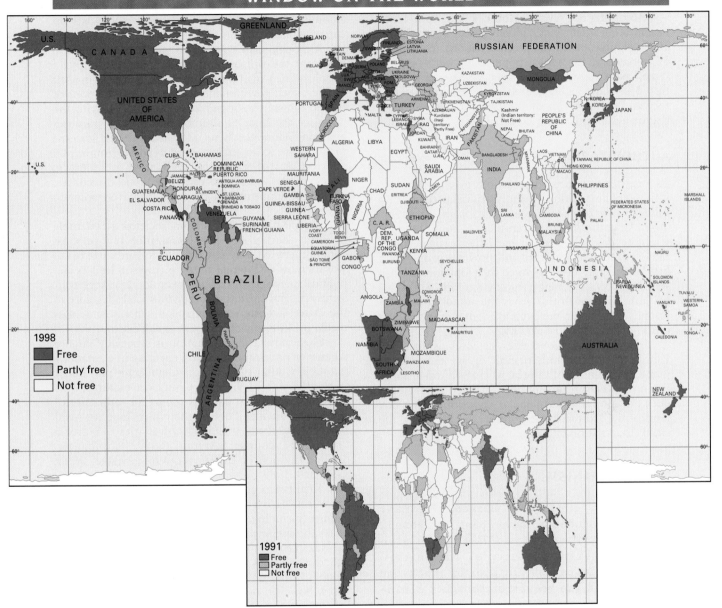

GLOBAL MAP 16–1 Political Freedom in Global Perspective

In 1998, 81 of the world's nations, containing 22 percent of all people, were politically "free"—that is, they offered their citizens extensive political rights and civil liberties. Another 57 countries that included 39 percent of the world's people were "partly free," with more limited rights and liberties. The remaining 53 nations, home to 39 percent of humanity, fall into the category of "not free." In these countries, government sharply restricts individual initiative. Between 1980 and 1998 democracy made significant gains, largely in Latin America and Eastern Europe, although, in Asia, India (containing nearly 1 billion people) slipped from "free" to "partly free" in 1992.

Source: Freedom House (1998).

NOTE: *Authoritarian* regimes are concerned mostly with overt compliance, while *totalitarian* regimes seek to win "the hearts and minds" of their people.

NOTE: Totalitarianism opposes all pluralism. As an example, anti-Semitism in the former Soviet Union probably was less about religion and more an attempt to quash all loyalties except those to the state.

GLOBAL: After the crackdown, the Chinese government required students at all 67 Beijing universities to take part in a one-month political "refresher" program; also, all college graduates were assigned to work one year in the countryside or in a factory.

CYBER: Will new information technology enhance democracy by expanding available information or promote totalitarianism by increasing the technical capacity for social control?

assessment of the extent of political freedoms around the world.

According to Freedom House, a New York–based organization that tracks global political trends, by 1998, eighty-one of the world's nations (containing 22 percent of the global population) were rated as "free," with considerable respect for basic civil liberties. This is the highest number of free nations in history and compares to only fifty-eight free nations a decade before (Freedom House, 1998).

AUTHORITARIANISM

As a matter of policy, some nations give their people little voice in politics. **Authoritarianism** refers to *a political system that denies popular participation in government.* An authoritarian government is not only indifferent to people's needs, it lacks the legal means to remove leaders from office and provides people with little or no way even to voice their opinions. Polish sociologist Wlodzimierz Wesolowski (1990:435) sums up authoritarianism this way: "the authoritarian philosophy argues for the supremacy of the state [over other] organized social activity."

The absolute monarchies in Saudi Arabia and Kuwait are highly authoritarian, as are the military juntas in Congo and Ethiopia, where political dissatisfaction is widespread. But heavy-handed government does not always breed popular opposition. The box looks at the "soft authoritarianism" that thrives in the small Asian nation of Singapore.

TOTALITARIANISM

```
October 22, 1994, near Saigon, Vietnam.
Six U.S. students have been arrested,
allegedly for talking to Vietnamese stu-
dents and taking pictures at the univer-
sity. The Vietnamese Minister of Education
has canceled the reception tonight, claim-
ing that our students meeting their stu-
dents threatens Vietnam's security . . .
```

The most controlling political form is **totalitarianism,** *a political system that extensively regulates people's lives.* Totalitarian governments emerged only during this century, with the development of the technological means for rigidly regulating a populace. The Vietnamese government closely monitors the activities of its citizens as well as visitors to the country. Similarly,

the government of North Korea uses surveillance equipment and sophisticated computers to store vast amounts of information and thereby manipulate an entire population.

Although some totalitarian governments claim to represent the will of the people, most seek to bend people to the will of the government. As the term itself implies, such governments are *total* concentrations of power, allowing no organized opposition. Denying the populace the right to assemble for political purposes and controlling access to information, these governments thrive in an environment of social atomization and fear. In the former Soviet Union, for example, most citizens could not own telephone directories, copying equipment, fax machines, or even accurate city maps.

Socialization in totalitarian societies is intensely political, seeking not just compliance but personal commitment to the system. In North Korea, one of the world's most totalitarian states, pictures of leaders and political messages broadcast over loudspeakers constantly remind citizens that they owe total allegiance to the state. Government-controlled schools and mass media present only official versions of events.

Government indoctrination is especially intense whenever political opposition surfaces in a totalitarian society. After the 1989 pro-democracy movement in the People's Republic of China, for example, officials demanded that citizens report all "unpatriotic" people—even members of their own families—and subjected students at Beijing universities to political "refresher" courses (Arendt, 1958; Kornhauser, 1959; Friedrich & Brzezinski, 1965; Nisbet, 1966; Goldfarb, 1989).

Totalitarian governments span the political spectrum from fascist (including Nazi Germany) to communist (including North Korea). In some totalitarian states, businesses are privately owned (as was the case in Nazi Germany and, more recently, in Chile); in others, businesses are government-owned (as in North Korea, Cuba, or the former Soviet Union). In all cases, however, one party claims total control of the society and permits no opposition.

A GLOBAL POLITICAL SYSTEM?

Chapter 15 ("The Economy and Work") described the emergence of a global economy, by which more and more companies operate with little regard to national boundaries. Is there a parallel development of a global political system?

GLOBAL: As of 1995, Singapore has enjoyed economic growth of 9% annually, with unemployment at 2.6%; just 1% of births are out of wedlock. Note that Freedom House characterizes Singapore as "partly free." Since 1965, this country has had only two leaders (of one party): Lee Kuan Yew and, after 1990, Goh Chok Tong.

Q: "Man is born free, and everywhere he is in chains." Jean-Jacques Rousseau, *The Social Contract* (1762)

Q: "Wherever two or three are gathered together, there the party-state desires to be." Timothy Garton Ash (1983:8), on totalitarianism

GLOBAL: Worldwide, many more nations describe themselves as "democratic" than really are. As examples, the People's Democratic Republic of Korea has one party and is rigidly ruled by dictator Kim Jon Il. Similarly, Somali Democratic Republic is an arena of warring factions and clans.

GLOBAL SOCIOLOGY

"Soft Authoritarianism" or Planned Prosperity? A Report From Singapore

To many, Singapore, a tiny nation on the tip of the Malay Peninsula with a population of 3.5 million, seems an Asian paradise. Surrounded by poor societies grappling with rapidly increasing populations, squalid, sprawling cities, and rising crime rates, Singapore's affluence, cleanliness, and safety make North American visitors think more of a theme park than a country.

In fact, since its independence from Malaysia in 1965, Singapore has startled the world with its economic development; its per capita income rivals that of the United States. But, unlike the United States, Singapore has scarcely any social problems such as crime, slums, unemployment, or children living in poverty. In fact, people in Singapore don't even contend with traffic jams, graffiti on subway cars, or litter in the streets.

The key to Singapore's orderly environment is the ever-present hand of government, which actively promotes traditional morality and regulates just about everything. The state owns and manages most of the country's housing and has a hand in many businesses. It provides tax incentives for proper family planning and completing additional years of schooling. To keep traffic under control, the government slaps hefty surcharges on cars, pushing the price of a basic sedan up around $40,000.

Singapore has tough anti-crime laws that mandate death by hanging for drug dealing and permit police to detain a person suspected of a crime without charge or trial. The government has outlawed some religious groups (including Jehovah's Witnesses) and bans pornography outright. To keep the city clean, the state forbids smoking in public, bans eating on the subway, imposes stiff fines for littering, and has even outlawed the sale of chewing gum.

In economic terms, Singapore defies familiar categories. Government control of scores of businesses, including television stations, telephone service, airlines, and taxis seems socialist. Yet, unlike most socialist enterprises, these businesses are operated efficiently and

very profitably. Moreover, Singapore's capitalist culture applauds economic growth (although the government cautions people against the evils of excessive materialism), and this nation is home to hundreds of multinational corporations.

Singapore's political climate is as unusual as its economy. Members of this society feel the presence of government far more than their counterparts in the United States. Just as important, one political organization—the People's Action party—has ruled Singapore without opposition since its independence thirty years ago.

Clearly, Singapore is not a democratic country in the conventional sense. But most people in this prospering nation wholeheartedly endorse their way of life. What Singapore's political system offers is a simple bargain: Government demands unflinching loyalty from the populace; in return, it provides security and prosperity. Critics charge that this system amounts to a "soft authoritarianism" that stifles dissent and controls people's lives. Most of the people of Singapore, however, know the struggles of living elsewhere and, for now at least, consider the trade-off a good one.

Source: Adapted from Branegan (1993).

On one level, the answer is no. Although most of the world's economic activity now involves more than one nation, the planet remains divided into nation-states, just as it has been for centuries. The United Nations (founded in 1945) might seem a step toward global government, but, to date, its political role has been limited.

On another level, however, politics has become a global process. In the minds of some analysts, multinational corporations represent a new political order,

NOTE: Where does government money come from? The IRS took in $590 billion in 1995, 39% of government revenue; corporate taxes, 10%; Social Security, retirement, and insurance premiums, 32%; excise, customs, gift, and estate taxes, 8%; borrowing to cover deficit, 11%. Where it goes: Social Security, Medicare, and other retirement programs, 36%; national defense and veterans benefits, 21%; social programs, 18%; interest on debt, 15%;

physical, human, and community development, 8%; law enforcement, 2% (Speer, 1997).

THEN AND NOW: The last federal balanced budget was in 1969 (a $3.2 million surplus); after 30 years of federal deficits, the proposed budget for 1999 is balanced.

NOTE: The growth of government is one dimension of the rise of a service economy.

GLOBAL SNAPSHOT

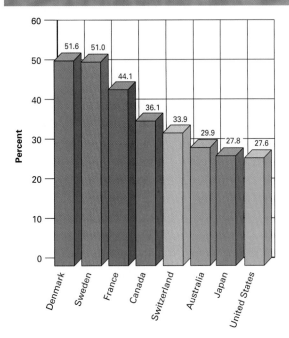

FIGURE 16–1 The Size of Government: Tax Revenues as Share of Gross Domestic Product, 1994

Source: U.S. Bureau of the Census (1997).

since they have enormous power to shape social life throughout the world. In other words, politics is dissolving into business as corporations grow larger than governments. As one multinational leader declared, "We are not without cunning. We shall not make Britain's mistake. Too wise to govern the world, we shall simply own it" (quoted in Vaughan, 1978:20).

Then, too, the Information Revolution has helped move national politics onto the world stage. Hours before the Chinese government sent troops to Tiananmen Square to crush the 1989 pro-democracy movement, officials "unplugged" the satellite transmitting systems of news agencies to keep the world from watching. Despite their efforts, news of the massacre flashed around the world in minutes via fax machines in universities and private homes.

Finally, several thousand non-governmental organizations (NGOs) are now in operation, most with global membership and focus. Typically, these organizations seek to advance universal principles, such as human rights (Amnesty International) or an ecologically sustainable world (Greenpeace). In the coming century, NGOs will almost certainly play a key part in forming a global political culture (Boli & Thomas, 1997).

In short, then, just as the economies of individual nations are linked globally, so are their politics. Today, no nation exists strictly within its own borders.

POLITICS IN THE UNITED STATES

After winning a war against Great Britain to gain political independence, the United States replaced the British monarchy with a democratic political system. Since then, our nation's political development reflects its distinctive history, capitalist economy, and cultural heritage.

U.S. CULTURE AND THE RISE OF THE WELFARE STATE

The political culture of the United States can be summed up in a word: individualism. This emphasis derives from the Bill of Rights, which guarantees freedom from undue government interference. It was this individualism that nineteenth-century poet and essayist Ralph Waldo Emerson had in mind when he said, "The government that governs best is the government that governs least."

But Emerson's assertion would find little support today among the vast majority of this nation's people, who recognize that government is necessary to maintain national defense, highway systems, schools, and law and order. Moreover, the government has grown into a vast and complex **welfare state,** *a range of government agencies and programs that provides benefits to the population.* Government benefits begin even before birth (through prenatal nutrition programs) and continue into old age (through Social Security and Medicare). Some programs are especially important to the poor, who are not well served by our capitalist economic system; but students, farmers, homeowners, small business operators, veterans, performing artists, and even the executives of giant corporations also get various subsidies and supports. In fact, a majority of U.S. adults now look to government for at least part of their income (Caplow et al., 1982; Devine, 1985).

Today's welfare state is the result of a gradual increase in the size and scope of government. Back in

THEN AND NOW: Federal spending: *1960*, $92.2 billion; *1997*, $1.63 trillion (controlled for inflation, a threefold increase). Federal debt: *1960*, $290.5 billion; *1997*, 5.5 trillion (also a threefold increase, controlled for inflation). Federal tax collections from individuals: *1960*, $40.7 billion; *1997*, $672.7 billion (a threefold rise controlled for inflation).

SOCIAL SURVEY: "Do you consider the amount of federal income tax which you have to pay as too high, about right, or too low?" (GSS 1996, N = 1,923; *Codebook*, 1996:102)

"Too high"	64.6%	"Too low"	0.8%
"About right"	30.6%	DK/NR	4.0%

Q: "Just be glad you're not getting all the government you're paying for." Will Rogers

TABLE 16–1 The Political Spectrum: A National Survey, 1996

Survey Question: "We hear a lot of talk these days about liberals and conservatives. I'm going to show you a seven-point scale on which the political views people might hold are arranged from extremely liberal—point 1—to extremely conservative—point 7. Where would you place yourself on this scale?"

1	2	3	4	5	6	7
Extremely liberal	Liberal	Slightly liberal	Middle of the road	Slightly conservative	Conservative	Extremely conservative
2.0 %	10.4 %	11.5 %	36.0 %	15.5 %	15.8 %	3.2 %

[*Don't know/no answer* 5.5%]

Source: *General Social Surveys, 1972–1996: Cumulative Codebook* (Chicago: National Opinion Research Center, 1996), p. 84.

1789, when the presence of the federal government amounted to little more than a flag in most communities, the entire federal budget was a mere $4.5 million ($1.50 for every person in the nation). Since then, it has steadily risen, reaching $1.5 trillion in 1997 (a per capita figure of $5,600).

Similarly, when our nation was founded, one government employee served every eighteen hundred citizens. Today, there is one official to serve every thirteen citizens for a total of 20 million government employees, more than are engaged in manufacturing (U.S. Bureau of the Census, 1997).

As much as government has expanded in this country, the U.S. welfare state is still smaller than in many other industrial nations. Figure 16–1 shows that government is larger in most of Europe, and especially in Scandinavian countries like Denmark and Sweden.

THE POLITICAL SPECTRUM

Who supports the welfare state? Who would like to see it grow larger? Who wants to cut back on the size of government? Such questions tap attitudes that form the *political spectrum*. Table 16–1 shows how adults in the United States describe their political orientation. Not quite one-fourth of the respondents fall on the liberal or "left" side, while more than one-third describe themselves as conservative to some degree, placing them on the political "right." But an even greater share (36.0 percent) claim to be moderates, in the political "middle" (NORC, 1996:84).

One reason so many people identify themselves as "moderates" is that most of us are conservative on some issues and liberal on others (Barone & Ujifusa, 1981; McBroom & Reed, 1990). In making sense of people's political attitudes, analysts distinguish two kinds of issues. *Economic issues* focus on economic inequality and the opportunities available for all categories of people.

Social issues refer to moral concerns about how people ought to live.

Economic Issues

In the second half of the last century, industrialization generated enormous wealth in the United States, but much of it ended up in the pockets of a small elite. By the time the stock market crashed in 1929, signalling the start of the Great Depression, mounting evidence suggested that a market system with minimal government regulation provided little financial security for much of the population. In response, President Franklin Delano Roosevelt initiated the New Deal programs, greatly expanding government efforts to promote well-being and building the foundation of our current welfare state.

Today, both the Democratic and Republican parties—the two major political organizations in the United States—support the basic outlines of the welfare state, although they disagree about what the government should and should not do. Generally, the Democratic party offers greater support to the role of government in U.S. society, including government regulation of the economy. The Republican party, however, has sought to trim the size and scope of government in recent years, especially in the marketplace.

Thus, economic liberals (mostly on the Democratic side of the fence) expect the government to maintain a healthy economy and an adequate supply of jobs. Economic conservatives (likely to be Republicans) counter that government intervention inhibits economic productivity.

Social Issues

Social issues are moral matters, ranging from abortion to the death penalty to gay rights and treatment of

NOTE: Generally speaking, Republicans seek to use the power of government to regulate the moral environment, while Democrats enlist government in regulating the economic environment.

SOCIAL SURVEY: These items show how SES is related to views on economic issues and social issues. (*Student CHIP Social Survey Software*, ABNOMOR1 [GSS 1972–91, N = 20,411] and EQWLTH1 [GSS 1978–91, N = 10,464]) Undecided Rs omitted.

SES	Pro-choice	Pro-life	Should gov't reduce income differences? "Yes"	"No"
High	58.5%	41.5%	41.4%	58.6%
Middle	44.5%	55.5%	61.3%	38.7%
Low	31.8%	68.2%	75.9%	24.1%

Lower-income people have more pressing financial needs and so they tend to focus on "economic issues" such as the level of the minimum wage. Higher-income people, by contrast, provide support for many "social issues" such as animal rights.

minorities. Social liberals are broadly tolerant of social diversity. They endorse equal rights and opportunities for all categories of people, view abortion as a matter of individual choice, and oppose the death penalty because, in their view, it does little to discourage crime and has been unfairly applied to minorities.

On the other side of the political spectrum are social conservatives, who advance a "family values" agenda. They support traditional gender roles and oppose public acceptance of gay families, affirmative action, and other "special programs" for minorities that, as they see it, recognize group membership rather than reward individual initiative. Social conservatives also condemn abortion and support the death penalty as a just response to heinous crime.

Overall, the Republican party is more conservative on both economic and social issues, while the Democratic party takes a more liberal stand. In practice, then, Republicans endorse traditional values and individual initiative, while Democrats think the government should take an active role in enhancing social well-being and reducing inequality. Yet each party has conservative and liberal wings so that the difference between a liberal Republican and a conservative Democrat may be insignificant. Furthermore, both

Republicans and Democrats favor big government—as long as it advances their aims. Conservative Republicans (like President Ronald Reagan) have sought to increase military strength, for example, while more liberal Democrats (like President Bill Clinton) have tried to expand the government's "social safety net," through programs that, for instance, extend health care coverage and subsidize housing for the poor.

Mixed Positions

Pegging the political views of individuals is difficult because most people do not maintain the same positions on economic and social issues. Well-to-do men and women tend to be conservative on economic issues (because they have wealth to protect) but liberal on social issues (due, in large part, to higher levels of education). Working-class people display the opposite pattern, combining economic liberalism with social conservatism (Nunn, Crocket, & Williams, 1978; Erikson, Luttbeg, & Tedin, 1980; Syzmanski, 1983).

Race and ethnicity modify these patterns slightly. With significantly less income than white people, African Americans are more liberal on economic issues and, since the New Deal era of the 1930s, have

Q: "A man who is not a liberal at sixteen has no heart; a man who is not a conservative at sixty has no head." Benjamin Disraeli

NOTE: The lobbying industry is Washington, D.C.'s, largest nongovernmental employer: 67,062 people as of 1996, making them a multibillion-dollar industry (Armey, 1996).

DISCUSS: Ask the class to comment on these data linking family income to how people voted in the 1996 presidential election.

Family income	Clinton	Dole	Perot
under $15,000	59%	28%	11%
$15,000–$29,999	51	35	13
$30,000–$49,999	48	40	18
over $50,000	44	48	7
over $75,000	41	51	7
over $100,000	38	54	6

overwhelmingly voted Democratic (in 1996, 84 percent of African American voters supported Democrat Bill Clinton over Republican Bob Dole). And on many social issues (including reproductive rights for women), disadvantaged African Americans, like poor white people, tend to be conservative. But when the topic involves race—say, busing schoolchildren or increasing government spending to assist minorities—people of African and Hispanic descent are decidedly liberal, even more so than affluent white people (NORC, 1996).

Party Identification

Because so many people hold mixed political attitudes—espousing liberal views on some issues and taking conservative stands on others—party identification is weak in the United States. In this way, our nation differs from European countries, where most people adhere strongly to one political party. Table 16–2 shows the results of a recent national survey of party identification among U.S. adults (NORC, 1996). Some 46 percent identified themselves—to some degree—as Democrats and about 37 percent as Republicans. Sixteen percent claimed to be independents, voicing no preference for either party. Even though a large majority declare a party preference, their allegiance is weak. Republicans scored a landslide victory in the 1994 Congressional elections, for example, while the Democrats gained ground in Congress and recaptured the White House just two years later in 1996.

SPECIAL-INTEREST GROUPS

When President Bill Clinton suggested at one point that the cost of a "business lunch" should no longer be tax-deductible, the National Restaurant Association, representing eating and drinking establishments nationwide, immediately mobilized in opposition.

The restaurant industry—which was ultimately successful in fending off reform—is an example of a **special-interest group,** *a political alliance of people interested in some economic or social issue.* Special-interest groups, which include associations of elderly people, tour bus operators, women's organizations, farmers, fireworks producers, and environmentalists, flourish in nations, including the United States, where political parties tend to be weak. Special-interest groups employ *lobbyists* (Washington, D.C., is home to more than 75,000 of them) as their professional advocates in political circles.

TABLE 16–2 Political Party Identification in the United States, 1996

Party Identification	Proportion of Respondents
Democrat	**46.0%**
Strong Democrat	13.8
Not very strong Democrat	19.9
Independent, close to Democrat	12.3
Republican	**36.7**
Strong Republican	10.6
Not very strong Republican	17.2
Independent, close to Republican	8.9
Independent	**15.7**
Other party, no response	**1.7**

Source: *General Social Surveys, 1972–1996: Cumulative Codebook* (Chicago: National Opinion Research Center, 1996), p. 77.

One example of a special-interest group concerned with economic issues is the American Federation of Labor–Congress of Industrial Organizations (AFL-CIO), this nation's largest labor union. Special-interest groups lobbying on social issues include the environmentalist Sierra Club, the American Civil Liberties Union, and the National Rifle Association.

Political action committees (PACs) are *organizations formed by a special-interest group, independent of political parties, to pursue political aims by raising and spending money.* Political action committees channel most of their funds directly to candidates likely to support their interests. Since the 1970s, legal reforms have limited direct contributions to candidates; consequently, the number of PACs has grown rapidly to nearly 4,000 (U.S. Federal Election Commission, 1998).

Because of the rising costs of campaigns, most candidates eagerly accept support from political action committees. In recent congressional elections, about one-fourth of all funding came from PACs, and two-thirds of all Senators seeking reelection received more than $1 million each in PAC contributions. Supporters maintain that PACs represent interests of a vast array of businesses, unions, and church groups, thereby increasing political participation. Critics counter that organizations supplying cash to politicians expect to be treated favorably in return so that, in effect, PACs try to buy political influence (Sabato, 1984; Allen & Broyles, 1991; Cook, 1993; Center for Responsive Politics, 1998).

Whether PACs are good or not, they certainly point up the importance of money in our political system. The rising costs of campaigns is a problem for all

SEEING OURSELVES

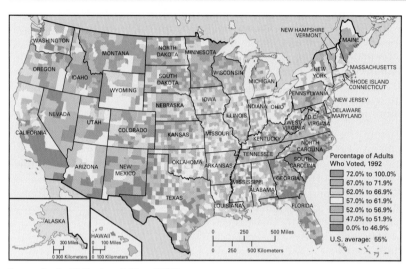

NATIONAL MAP 16–1
Voter Turnout
Across the United States

In the 1992 presidential race, just 55 percent of eligible voters went to the polls. The map shows that turnout was high in the North-Central region of the country: In Minnesota, the Dakotas, and Montana, for example, the turnout exceeded 75 percent. By contrast, turnout is low in South Carolina, Georgia, and much of the South. Age is one important correlate of voting, with older people much more likely to vote than young adults. Do you think age plays a part in the regional differences shown here? How?

Percentage of Adults Who Voted, 1992
- 72.0% to 100.0%
- 67.0% to 71.9%
- 62.0% to 66.9%
- 57.0% to 61.9%
- 52.0% to 56.9%
- 47.0% to 51.9%
- 0.0% to 46.9%
U.S. average: 55%

Source: Lewis, McCracken, & Hunt (1994).

candidates, but incumbents have an edge because they have better access to PACs. In the 1996 congressional elections, 66 percent of PAC funds went to those already in office, 94 percent of whom won reelection.

VOTER APATHY

It is a disturbing fact of U.S. political life that many people seem indifferent to their right to vote. The long-term trend has been toward greater *eligibility* to vote—the Fifteenth Amendment, ratified in 1870, enfranchised African American men; the Nineteenth Amendment extended voting rights to women in 1920; in 1971, the Twenty-Sixth Amendment lowered the voting age to eighteen years. However, a countertrend shows that, over the last century, a smaller and smaller share of eligible citizens *actually do vote*. In the 1996 presidential election, less than half the registered voters took the time and trouble to cast a vote, well below the comparable share in most other industrialized nations.

Who is and is not likely to vote? Women and men are equally likely to cast a ballot. People over sixty-five, however, are three times as likely to vote as young adults aged eighteen to twenty-four (U.S. Bureau of the Census, 1997). White people are more likely to vote (64 percent voted in 1996) than African Americans (58 percent), with Hispanics (30 percent) the least likely of all

to vote. Generally speaking, people with a bigger stake in society—homeowners, parents with children at home, people with good jobs, higher incomes, and extensive schooling—are most likely to vote (Bennett, 1991; Hackey, 1992; Lewis, McCracken, & Hunt, 1994). National Map 16–1 looks at the extent of voter apathy across the United States.

Some nonvoting, of course, is to be expected. At any given time, millions of people are sick or disabled; millions more are away from home having made no arrangement to submit an absentee ballot. Many more people forget to reregister after moving to a new neighborhood. And registration and voting depend on the ability to read and write, which discourages the tens of millions of U.S. adults who have limited literacy skills.

Conservatives suggest that apathy amounts to an *indifference* to politics. That is, most people who do not vote are reasonably content with their lives. But liberals (and especially political radicals) counter that most nonvoters are *alienated* from politics: Although dissatisfied with the way society operates, they doubt that elections will make any real difference. As Figure 16–2 shows, income is strongly related to whether or not people vote: Most high-income people *do* and most low-income people *don't*. The fact that it is the disadvantaged and powerless people who are least likely to vote suggests that the liberal explanation for apathy is probably closer to the truth.

NOTE: Speaking of apathy, in the 1997 American Sociological Association elections, just 23.4% of 11,179 voting members returned ballots, a steady decline from more than 60% in the 1950s.
SOCIAL SURVEY: In a 1997 *USA Today*/CNN/Gallup poll, 51% of respondents claimed Clinton is "not honest and trustworthy"; yet, in the same poll, 55% claimed he is "honest and trustworthy enough to be president" *(USA Today, March 28, 1998, page 3A).*

RESOURCE: An excerpt from C. Wright Mills's *The Power Elite* is among the classics included in the Macionis and Benokraitis reader, *Seeing Ourselves.*
Q: "The power elite is composed of men whose positions enable them to transcend the ordinary environments of ordinary men and women; they are in positions to make decisions having major consequences." C. Wright Mills (1956:3–4)

In the end, apathy probably signifies that people want more of a choice. The two major parties of our political system, after all, have much in common. Perhaps, if additional parties represented a wider spectrum of political opinion—as they do in European countries—people would have more reason to vote (Zipp & Smith, 1982; Zipp, 1985; Piven & Cloward, 1988; Lewis, McCracken, & Hunt, 1994; Phillips, 1994).

THEORETICAL ANALYSIS OF POWER IN SOCIETY

Sociologists have long debated how power is distributed in the United States. Power is one of the most difficult topics to study scientifically because decision making is complex and takes place behind closed doors. Moreover, it is difficult to separate a theory of power from the theorist's personal beliefs and interests. Nevertheless, three competing models of power in the United States have emerged.

THE PLURALIST MODEL: THE PEOPLE RULE

The **pluralist model** is *an analysis of politics that views power as dispersed among many competing interest groups.* This approach is closely tied to structural-functional theory.

Pluralists claim, first, that politics is an arena of negotiation. With limited resources, no organization can expect to realize all its goals. Organizations, therefore, operate as *veto groups*, realizing some success but mostly keeping opponents from achieving all their goals. The political process, then, relies heavily on negotiating alliances and compromises among numerous interest groups so that policies gain wide support. In short, pluralists see power as widely dispersed throughout society so that all people have a voice in the political system (Dahl, 1961, 1982).

THE POWER-ELITE MODEL: A FEW PEOPLE RULE

The **power-elite model** is *an analysis of politics that views power as concentrated among the rich.* This second approach is closely allied with the social-conflict paradigm.

The term *power elite* is a lasting contribution of C. Wright Mills (1956), who argued that a small number of people in the United States effectively control this

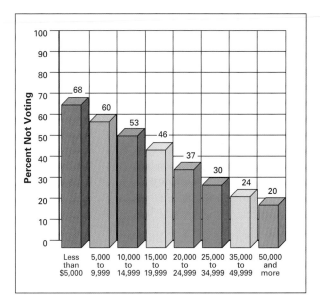

FIGURE 16–2 Political Apathy by Income Level

Percentage of adults who reported not voting in the 1992 presidential election presented according to their annual family income.

Source: U.S. Bureau of the Census (1997).

nation's political system. Mills claimed that the power elite stands atop each of the three major sectors of U.S. society—the economy, the government, and the military. Thus, the power elite is made up of the "super-rich" (executives and large stockholders of major corporations), top officials in government (the most powerful figures in Washington, D.C., and state capitals around the country), and the highest-ranking officers in the U.S. military (senior Pentagon officials).

Further, Mills explained, these elites move from one sector to another, consolidating their power as they go. Alexander Haig, for example, served as a top corporate executive, as a member of Ronald Reagan's cabinet (and 1988 presidential candidate), and as a general of the Army. Haig is far from the exception: A majority of national political leaders enter government from powerful and highly paid positions—when President Clinton took office and assembled his cabinet, ten of thirteen members were reputed to be millionaires—and most return to the corporate world later on.

Power-elite theorists challenge the claim that the United States is a political democracy. They maintain that the concentration of wealth and power is simply

DISCUSS: Is Congress a club for the rich? One in 6 members of Congress (99 of 535 members of Congress) is a millionaire, compared to 1 out of 200 people in the general population. The richest member in 1997 was Senator John Kerry (D-Mass.). The top six Congressional members in wealth include 5 Democrats and 1 Republican, five men and one woman (Dianne Feinstein, D-Calif.). In the 1996 elections, 149 Congressional candidates spent at least $100,000 of their own money to promote their reelection. The trend is for more rich people to enter Congress because of the rising costs of media campaigns.

SOCIAL SURVEY: "How much confidence do you have in Congress?" (GSS 1996, N = 1,925; *Codebook*, 1996:168)

| "A great deal" | 7.6% | "Hardly any" | 42.6% |
| "Only some" | 46.4% | DK/NR | 3.4% |

too great for the average person's voice to be heard. They reject the pluralist idea that various centers of power serve as checks and balances on one another. Instead, the power-elite model holds that people at the top encounter no real opposition.

THE MARXIST MODEL: BIAS IN THE SYSTEM ITSELF

A third approach to understanding U.S. politics is the **Marxist political-economy model,** *an analysis that explains politics in terms of the operation of a society's economic system.* Like the power-elite model, the Marxist model rejects the idea that the United States operates as a political democracy. But, while the power-elite model focuses on the disproportionate wealth and power of certain individuals, the Marxist model highlights bias rooted within this nation's institutions, especially its economy. As noted in Chapter 4 ("Society"), Karl Marx claimed that a society's economic system (capitalist or socialist) goes a long way toward shaping how the political system operates. Power elites, therefore, do not simply appear on the scene; they are creations of capitalism itself.

From this point of view, reforming the political system—say, by limiting the amount of money that rich people can contribute to political candidates—is unlikely to bring about true democracy. The problem does not lie in the *people* who exercise great power or the *people* who don't vote, the problem is rooted in the *system* itself, what Marxists term the "political-economy of capitalism." In other words, as long as the United States is a predominantly capitalist economy, the majority of people will be shut out of politics just as surely as they are exploited in the workplace.

Critical evaluation. Which of the three different models of the U.S. political system is correct? Over the years, research has provided support for each model, suggesting that a case can be made for all three. In the end, how one views this country's political system, and how one thinks it ought to operate, turn out to be as much a matter of political values as scientific fact.

Research by Nelson Polsby (1959) supports the pluralist model. Polsby studied the political scene in New Haven, Connecticut, and concluded that key decisions on various issues—including urban renewal, nominating political candidates, and operating the schools—were made by different groups. He also found that few of the upper-class families listed in New Haven's *Social Register* were also economic leaders. Thus, Polsby concluded, no one segment of society rules all the others.

Robert Dahl (1961) also investigated New Haven's history, finding that, over time, power had become more and more dispersed. Thus, Dahl's research also supports the pluralist model. As he put it, "no one, and certainly no group of more than a few individuals, is entirely lacking in [power]" (1961:228).

Supporting the power-elite position is research by Robert Lynd and Helen Lynd (1937) in Muncie, Indiana (which they called "Middletown," to suggest that it was a typical city). They documented the fortune amassed by a single family—the Balls—from their business manufacturing glass canning jars, and showed how the Ball family dominated the city's life. If anyone doubted the Balls' prominence, the Lynds explained, there was no need to look further than the local bank, a university, a hospital, and a department store, which all bear the family name. In Muncie, according to the Lynds, the power elite more or less boiled down to a single family.

In a study of Atlanta, Georgia, Floyd Hunter (1963) found further support for the power-elite model. No one family dominated Atlanta as was the case in Muncie. Yet, Hunter found that about forty people held all the top positions in the city's businesses and controlled the city's politics.

From the Marxist perspective, the point is not to look at which individuals make decisions at the local or even the national level. Rather, as Alexander Liazos (1982:13) explains, "The basic tenets of capitalist society shape everyone's life: the inequalities of social classes and the importance of profits over people." As long as the basic institutions of society are organized to meet the needs of the few rather than the many, Liazos concludes, a democratic society will elude us.

Table 16–3 summarizes the three political models. In the end, then, what are we to make of the U.S. political system? At one level, it affords almost everyone the right to participate in the political process through elections. This is an important opportunity, one that is not enjoyed by a majority of the world's people. At the same time, however, the power-elite and Marxist models point out that, at the very least, the U.S. political system is far less democratic than most people think it is. Most citizens may have the right to vote, but the major political parties and their candidates typically support only those positions acceptable to the most powerful segments of society and consistent with the operation of our capitalist economy (Bachrach & Baratz, 1970).

SOCIAL SURVEY: "How much influence do you think people like you have over local government decisions?" (GSS 1987, N = 1,466; *Codebook*, 1996:317)

"A lot"	14.0%	"None at all"	14.5%
"A moderate amount"	33.8%	DK/NR	2.1%
"A little"	35.7%		

NOTE: The word "radical" is derived from the Latin meaning "of the root" (a radish is also a root). Thus, radical politics seeks not reform but a change in the system itself.
Q: "Since all political systems were created by [people], it follows that [people] can also change them." Peter Berger (1963:128)
Q: "Prophets are followed by popes, revolutionaries by administrators." Peter Berger

TABLE 16–3 Three Models of U.S. Politics: A Summary

	Pluralist Model	Power-Elite Model	Marxist Model
How is power distributed in U.S. society?	Highly dispersed	Concentrated	Concentrated
Is the United States basically democratic?	Yes, because voting offers everyone a voice, and no one group or organization dominates society	No, because a small share of the people dominate the economy, government, and military	No, because the bias of the capitalist system is to concentrate both wealth and power
How should we understand voter apathy?	Apathy is indifference; after all, even poor people can organize for a greater voice if they wish	Apathy is understandable, given how difficult it is for ordinary people to oppose the rich and powerful	Apathy is alienation generated by a system that will always leave most people powerless

Whatever the reasons, many people in the United States are losing confidence in their leaders. Over the last decade, the share claiming to have a "great deal" of confidence in Congress and the Executive Branch has fallen below 10 percent, while about 45 percent report having "hardly any" confidence (NORC, 1997).

POWER BEYOND THE RULES

Politics always involves disagreement over a society's goals and the means to achieve them. Political systems, therefore, try to resolve controversy within a system of rules. But political activity sometimes exceeds—or tries to do away with—established practices.

REVOLUTION

Political revolution is *the overthrow of one political system in order to establish another.* In contrast to reform, which involves change *within* a system, revolution involves change *of the system itself.* Thus, even one leader deposing another—called a *coup d'état* (in French, literally, "stroke concerning the state")—falls short of revolution since it involves only a change at the top. And while reform rarely escalates into violence, revolution often does. The revolutions in Eastern Europe beginning in 1989 were surprisingly peaceful, with the exception of Romania, where violence claimed thousands of lives.

No type of political system is immune to revolution; nor does revolution invariably produce any one kind of government. Our country's Revolutionary War transformed colonial rule by the British monarchy into democratic government. French revolutionaries in 1789 also overthrew a monarch, only to set the stage for the return of monarchy in the person of Napoleon.

In 1917, the Russian Revolution replaced monarchy with a socialist government built on the ideas of Karl Marx. In 1992, the Soviet Union was reborn as the Russian Federation, moving toward a market system and a greater political voice for its people.

Despite their striking variety, analysts claim, revolutions share a number of traits (Tocqueville, 1955, orig. 1856; also Davies, 1962; Brinton, 1965; Skocpol, 1979; Lewis, 1984; Tilly, 1986):

1. **Rising expectations.** Although common sense suggests that revolution would be more likely when people are grossly deprived, history shows that most revolutions occur when people's lives are improving. Rising expectations, rather than bitter resignation, fuel revolutionary fervor.

2. **Unresponsive government.** Revolutionary zeal gains strength if a government is unwilling or unable to reform, especially when such demands are made by powerful segments of society.

3. **Radical leadership by intellectuals.** The English philosopher Thomas Hobbes (1588–1679) observed that intellectuals often provide the justification for revolution, and universities frequently are the center of sweeping political change. During the 1960s in the United States, students were at the forefront of much of the political unrest. Students also played a critical role in China's recent pro-democracy movement and in the Eastern European uprisings.

4. **Establishing a new legitimacy.** Overthrowing a political system is not easy, but more difficult still is ensuring a revolution's long-term success. Some revolutionary movements are unified mostly by hatred of the past regime and fall apart once new leaders are installed.

NOTE: The U.S. State Department's definition of terrorism: "Premeditated, politically motivated violence perpetrated against noncombatant targets by subnational groups or clandestine state agents, normally intended to influence an audience."
GLOBAL: There were 296 deaths worldwide from terrorist actions in 1996. Bombs were the most commonly used weapon. Iran, Libya, and Iraq are the countries most often implicated in terrorist incidents, according to the U.S. State Department (U.S. State Department, 1998).
NOTE: Stohl and Lopez (1984) differentiate among three related concepts. *Oppression* is denying some category of people social and economic rights and privileges. *Repression* is more pronounced, coercing one's perceived opponents in order to weaken them. *Terrorism* is more intense still, using violence to force compliance.

TERRORISM

Terrorism constitutes *random acts of violence or the threat of such violence employed by an individual or a group as a political strategy.* Like revolution, terrorism is a political act beyond the rules of established political systems. According to Paul Johnson (1981), terrorism has four distinguishing characteristics.

First, terrorists try to paint violence as a legitimate political tactic, despite the fact that such acts are condemned by virtually every nation. Terrorists also bypass (or are excluded from) established channels of political negotiation. Terror is therefore a weak organization's strategy to harm a stronger foe. Holding U.S. hostages in Iran between 1979 and 1981 may have been morally wrong, but the terrorists who did so succeeded in directing the world's attention to Iran's grievances against the United States.

Second, terrorism is employed not just by groups, but also by governments against their own people. *State terrorism* is the use of violence, generally without support of law, by government officials. State terrorism is lawful in some authoritarian and totalitarian states, which survive by inciting fear and intimidation. Saddam Hussein, for example, shores up his power in Iraq through state terrorism.

Third, democratic societies reject terrorism in principle, but they are especially vulnerable to terrorists because they afford extensive civil liberties to their people and have less extensive police networks. In contrast, totalitarian regimes make widespread use of state terrorism, although, at the same time, their extensive police power minimizes opportunities for individual acts of terror.

Hostage-taking and outright killing provoke popular anger, but responding to such acts is difficult. Before taking action, a government must identify those responsible. However, because most terrorist groups are shadowy organizations with no formal connection to any established state, a reprisal may be all but impossible. Yet, terrorism expert Brian Jenkins warns, the failure to respond "encourages other terrorist groups, who begin to realize that this can be a pretty cheap way to wage war" (quoted in Whitaker, 1985:29). At the same time, a forceful military reaction to terrorism may risk confrontation with other governments.

Fourth, and finally, terrorism is always a matter of definition. Governments claim the right to maintain order, even by force, and may brand opposition groups who use violence as "terrorists." Similarly, political differences may explain why one person's "terrorist" is another's "freedom fighter."

Because of highly publicized acts of violence against U.S. citizens by Middle Eastern people in recent years, some members of our society tend to link Islam with terrorism. More correctly, however, this religion (like Christianity) seeks harmony and justice. Officials in Egypt have countered a recent wave of terrorism by a few religious extremists by reminding citizens (and outsiders) of their religious responsibility to promote peace.

Revolutionaries must also guard against counter-revolutionary drives led by the deposed leaders. This explains the speed and ruthlessness with which victorious revolutionaries dispose of previous rulers.

Scientific analysis cannot declare that a revolution is good or bad. The full consequences of such an upheaval depend on one's values and, in any case, become evident only after many years. In the wake of recent revolution, for example, the future of the former Soviet Union remains unsettled.

GLOBAL: Among the most damaging elements of war are land mines—experts estimate that more than 100 million mines remain in the ground in 65 countries, killing or maiming some 30,000 people annually, most civilians (Fedarko, 1996).

Q: "In the Third World, where one child in ten dies before the age of five, there are six times as many soldiers as there are physicians." Ruth Leger Sivard (1993:6)

NOTE: As Figure 16–3 shows, in absolute terms the Civil War was the bloodiest of all for the United States; in proportion to population, it is even more so.

SOCIAL SURVEY: "How much confidence do you have in the U.S. military?" (GSS 1996, N = 1,925; *Codebook*, 1996:168)
"A great deal"   37.2%   "Hardly any"   11.1%
"Only some"   48.4%   DK/NR   3.3%

WAR AND PEACE

Perhaps the most critical political issue is **war,** *organized, armed conflict among the people of various societies.* War is as old as humanity, of course, but understanding it now takes on greater urgency. Because we have the technological capacity to destroy ourselves, war poses unprecedented danger to the entire planet. Most scholarly investigation of war aims to promote peace, meaning the absence of war (but not necessarily the end of all political conflict).

Many people think of war as an extraordinary occurrence; yet, for almost all of this century, nations somewhere on earth were in violent conflict. In our country's short history, we have participated in ten large-scale wars, resulting in the deaths of more than 1.3 million U.S. men and women, as shown in Figure 16–3, and injury to many times that number. Thousands more died in "undeclared wars" and limited military actions in the Dominican Republic, Lebanon, Grenada, Panama, and elsewhere.

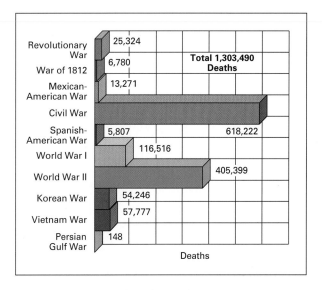

FIGURE 16–3 Deaths of Americans in Ten U.S. Wars

Sources: Compiled from various sources by Maris A. Vinovskis (1989) and the author.

THE CAUSES OF WAR

The frequency of war in human affairs might imply that there is something natural about armed confrontation. But while many animals are naturally aggressive, research provides no basis for concluding that human beings inevitably wage war under any particular circumstances. Indeed, as Ashley Montagu (1976) observes, governments around the world have to use considerable coercion in order to mobilize their people for war.

Like all forms of social behavior, warfare is a product of *society* that varies in purpose and intensity from place to place. The Semai of Malaysia, among the most peace-loving of the world's people, rarely resort to violence. In contrast, the Yąnomamö, described in Chapter 3 ("Culture"), are quick to wage war with others.

If society holds the key to war or peace, under what circumstances *do* humans go to battle? Quincy Wright (1987) identifies five factors that promote war:

1. **Perceived threats.** Societies mobilize in response to a perceived threat to their people, territory, or culture. The danger of armed conflict between the United States and the former Soviet Union, for example, has gone down as the two nations have become less fearful of each other.

2. **Social problems.** When internal problems generate widespread frustration at home, a society's leaders may divert attention by attacking an external "enemy" as a form of scapegoating. Some analysts see the lack of economic development in the People's Republic of China as underlying that nation's hostility toward Vietnam, Tibet, and the former Soviet Union.

3. **Political objectives.** Leaders sometimes use war as a political strategy. Poor societies, such as Vietnam, have fought wars to end foreign domination. For powerful societies such as the United States, a periodic "show of force" (such as the recent deployment of troops in Somalia, Haiti, and Bosnia) enhances their global political stature.

4. **Moral objectives.** Rarely do nations claim to fight merely to increase their wealth and power. Leaders infuse military campaigns with moral urgency, rallying their people around visions of "freedom" or the "fatherland." Although few doubted that the 1991 Persian Gulf War was largely about *oil,* U.S. strategists portrayed the mission as a drive to halt a Hitler-like Saddam Hussein.

GLOBAL: From data collected by the U.S. Arms Control and Disarmament Agency for 1995, Kuwait has the highest per capita spending on the military at $1,919. Other nations: Israel, $1,646; Singapore, $1,191; United States, $1,056; Saudi Arabia, $919; France, $826; Russia, $513; Mexico, $25 (U.S. Bureau of the Census, 1997).

GLOBAL: Nations around the world spend an average of 3.5% of GDP on the military; this percentage is about the same for industrial and nonindustrial nations, although the absolute amounts vary, of course.

GLOBAL: Global military spending has fallen from about 4% of GDP in 1990 to 2.4% in 1995. Reasons include the breakup of the Soviet Union and increasing democratization in the world (The World Bank, 1997).

GLOBAL SOCIOLOGY

Former
Yugoslavia

Violence Beyond the Rules:
A Report From the Former Yugoslavia

War is violent, but it also has rules. Many of our current rules of warfare were written at the end of World War II, when the victorious Allies, including the United States, charged German and Japanese military officials with war crimes. The United Nations, too, spells out the "right" way to wage war, in the "Geneva Conventions."

One of the most important rules of war is that, whatever violence soldiers inflict upon each other, they cannot imprison, torture, rape, or murder civilians; nor can they deliberately destroy civilian property or wantonly bomb or shell cities. Even so, a growing body of evidence suggests that the Serbs, Croats, and Muslims have committed all these war crimes in the former Yugoslavia. Tens of thousands of civilians were killed, raped, and seriously injured; the loss of property has been enormous.

In 1993, therefore, a United Nations tribunal convened in the Netherlands to consider possible responses.

Civil wars, such as the conflict in the former Yugoslavia, are among the most tragic forms of bloodshed because a large proportion of casualties are not soldiers but civilians who find themselves in harm's way. Dozens of people died on this street in Sarajevo as mortar rounds fired from the mountains surrounding the city rained down on men, women, and children who were going about their daily lives.

After World War II, the Allies successfully prosecuted (and, in several cases, executed) German officers for their crimes against humanity, based on evidence obtained from extensive Nazi records. This time around, however, the task of punishing offenders has turned out to be far more difficult. For one thing, there are few written records of the Balkan conflict; for another, United Nations officials fear that arrests may upset delicate diplomatic efforts to bring peace to the region.

Even so, since beginning their investigations, the United Nations has indicted fifty-seven military officers on all sides of the conflict. But only five have been taken into custody, and it seems more and more likely that—despite a staggering toll in civilian deaths—no one will ever be convicted.

Sources: Adapted from Nelan (1993), Sebastian (1996), and various news reports.

5. **The absence of alternatives.** A fifth factor promoting war is the absence of alternatives. Although the United Nations has the job of maintaining international peace, the U.N. has had limited success in resolving tensions among self-interested societies.

In short, war is rooted in social dynamics on both national and international levels. Moreover, even combat has rules, and breaking them can lead to charges of *war crimes*. The box takes a closer look.

THE COSTS AND CAUSES OF MILITARISM

The cost of armed conflicts extends far beyond battlefield casualties. Together, the world's nations spend some $5 trillion annually (almost $1,000 for every person on the planet) for military purposes. Such expenditures, of course, divert resources from the desperate struggle for survival by hundreds of millions of poor people. If the world's nations could muster the will and the political wisdom to redirect their military spending, they could greatly reduce global poverty.

Q: "It will be a great day when our schools get all the money they need and the Air Force has to hold a bake sale to buy a bomber." Women's International League for Peace and Freedom

NOTE: The concept of a "military-industrial complex" was used by President Dwight D. Eisenhower in his farewell speech in 1960.

Q: "The electron is the ultimate precision-guided weapon." CIA Director John M. Deutch

NOTE: The "doomsday clock," created in 1947 at the outset of the cold war, was initially set to 7½ minutes to midnight. In 1996, it stood, more optimistically, at 14 minutes to midnight (but was 17 minutes to midnight in 1991) (Moore, 1996).

Q: "One of the keys to our thinking in New Zealand is that the nuclear weapons of so-called allies are as dangerous as those of so-called enemies." Helen Clark, member of NZ parliament

Although the two nuclear superpowers— the United States and the Russian Federation—have reduced their arsenals in recent years, global security is threatened by the spread of nuclear weapons. In 1998, both India and Pakistan tested atomic bombs, raising fears that long-time tensions between these neighboring nations might in the future escalate into catastrophic warfare.

In recent years, defense has been the U.S. government's largest single expenditure, accounting for 19 percent of all federal spending, or $267 billion in 1997. This huge sum is the result of the *arms race,* a mutually reinforcing escalation of military power, between the United States and the former Soviet Union.

Yet, even after the collapse of the Soviet Union, military expenditures remain high. Thus, analysts who support power-elite theory say that the United States is dominated by a **military-industrial complex,** *the close association among the federal government, the military, and defense industries.* The roots of militarism, then, lie not just in external threats to our security, but also within the institutional structures of our own society (Marullo, 1987).

Another reason for persistent militarism in the post–cold war world is regional conflict. Since the collapse of the Soviet Union, for example, localized wars have broken out in Bosnia, Chechnya, and Zambia, and tensions remain high in a host of other countries, including Northern Ireland, Iraq, and a divided Korea. Even wars of limited scope have the potential to escalate and involve other countries, including the United States. In 1998, for example, India and Pakistan exploded atomic bombs, raising fears of nuclear confrontation in that region. And as more and more nations acquire nuclear weapons, the risk that regional conflicts will erupt into deadly wars goes up.

NUCLEAR WEAPONS

Despite the easing of superpower tensions, nations still hold almost 25,000 nuclear warheads, a destructive force equivalent to five tons of TNT for every person on the planet. Should even a small fraction of this stockpile be used in war, life as we know it might cease on much of the earth. Albert Einstein, whose genius contributed to the development of nuclear weapons, reflected: "The unleashed power of the atom has changed everything *save our modes of thinking,* and we thus drift toward unparalleled catastrophe." In short, nuclear weapons make unrestrained war unthinkable in a world not yet capable of peace.

Great Britain, France, and the People's Republic of China all have a substantial nuclear capability, but the vast majority of nuclear weapons are based in the United States and the Russian Federation. The two superpowers have agreed to reduce their stockpiles of nuclear warheads by 75 percent by the year 2003. But even as the superpower rivalry winds down, the danger of catastrophic war increases with **nuclear proliferation,** *the acquisition of nuclear-weapons technology by more and more nations.* Most experts agree that Israel, India, Pakistan, and South Africa already possess some nuclear weapons, and other nations (including Argentina, Brazil, Iraq, North Korea, and Libya) are in the process of developing them. Early in the next century, as many as fifty nations could have the ability

NOTE: Historically, does the emergence of the state reduce lethal conflict (war, rebellion, homicide, and execution)? Hobbes thought so. But research suggests that the relationship is U-shaped: high conflict in cases of no state authority, but also high conflict in cases of very centralized state authority (Cooney, 1997).

Q: "The arms race is not preordained and part of some inevitable course of history. We can make history." Ronald Reagan

RESOURCE: Jack Mendelsohn's article "Arms Control and the New World Order" is included in the Macionis and Benokraitis reader, *Seeing Ourselves.*

Q: "When we discuss national security, we tend too often to give it a military label. It is, in fact, much broader than military power and much more complex. There can be no security without social betterment." Hubert H. Humphrey

In recent years, the world has become aware of the death and mutilation caused by millions of land mines placed in the ground during wartime and left there afterward. Civilians—many of them children—maimed by land mines receive treatment in this Kabul, Afghanistan, clinic.

to fight a nuclear war, making any regional conflict much more dangerous (Spector, 1988).

THE PURSUIT OF PEACE

How can the world reduce the danger of war? Here are the most recent approaches to peace:

1. **Deterrence.** The logic of the arms race linked security to a "balance of terror" between the superpowers. Based on the principle of mutually assured destruction (MAD)—meaning that whichever side launched a first-strike nuclear attack against the other would sustain massive retaliation—deterrence has kept the peace for almost fifty years. But it has three flaws. First, it has fueled an exorbitantly expensive arms race. Second, as missiles become capable of delivering their warheads more and more quickly, computers are left with less and less time to react to an apparent attack, thereby increasing the risks of unintended war. Third, deterrence cannot control nuclear proliferation, which poses a growing threat to peace.

2. **High-technology defense.** If technology created the weapons, some maintain, it can also deliver us from the threat of war. This is the idea behind the *strategic defense initiative* (SDI) proposed by the Reagan administration in 1981. Under SDI, satellites and ground installations provide a protective shield or umbrella against enemy missiles. In principle, the system would detect enemy missiles soon after launch and destroy them with lasers and particle beams before they could reenter the atmosphere. If perfected, advocates argue, such a "star wars" defense would render nuclear weapons obsolete.

   But critics charge that even years of research costing trillions of dollars would yield at best a leaky umbrella. The collapse of the Soviet Union also calls into question the need for such an extensive and costly defense scheme.

   Worth noting, too, is that sophisticated technology raises not only new possibilities for defense, but also new strategies for waging war. The box takes a closer look at the possibilities for "information warfare."

3. **Diplomacy and disarmament.** Still other analysts point out that the best path to peace is diplomacy rather than technology (Dedrick & Yinger, 1990). Diplomacy can enhance security by reducing, rather than building, weapon stockpiles.

   But disarmament, too, has limitations. No nation wishes to become vulnerable by reducing its defenses. Successful diplomacy, then, depends not on "soft" concession making, or "hard"

EXPLORING CYBER-SOCIETY

Information Warfare:
Let Your Fingers Do the Fighting

For decades, scientists and military officials have studied how to use computers to defend against missiles and planes. More recently, however, the military has recognized that new information technology can fundamentally transform warfare itself, replacing rumbling tanks and screaming aircraft with electronic "smart bombs" that are capable of silently penetrating an enemy country's computer system and rendering it unable to transmit information.

In such "virtual wars," soldiers seated at workstation monitors would dispatch computer viruses to shut down the enemy's communication links, causing telephones to fall silent, air traffic control and railroad switching systems to fail, computer systems to feed phony orders to field officers, and televisions to broadcast "morphed" news bulletins urging people to turn against their leaders.

Like the venom of a poisonous snake, the weapons of "information warfare" might quickly paralyze an enemy prior to a conventional military attack. Another more hopeful possibility is that new information technology might not just precede conventional fighting but prevent it entirely. If the "victims" of computer warfare could be limited to a nation's communications links—rather than its citizens and cities—wouldn't we all be more secure?

Yet so-called "info-war" also poses new dangers, since, presumably, a few highly skilled operators with sophisticated electronic equipment could also wreak communications havoc on the United States. This country may be militarily without equal in the world, but, given our increasing reliance on high technology, we are also more vulnerable to cyber-attack than any nation on earth. As a result, in 1996, the Central Intelligence Agency (CIA) began work on a defensive "cyberwar center" that, it is hoped, would prevent what one official termed an "electronic Pearl Harbor."

Sources: Waller (1995) and Weiner (1996).

demands, but on everyone involved sharing responsibility for a common problem (Fisher & Ury, 1988).

While the United States and the former Soviet Union have managed to negotiate arms reduction agreements, the threat from other nations like Libya, North Korea, and Iraq—all of which desire to build a nuclear arsenal—remains great.

4. **Resolving underlying conflict.** Perhaps the best way to reduce the danger of nuclear war is to resolve underlying conflicts. Even in the post–cold war era, basic differences between the United States and Russia remain. Moreover, militarism also springs from nationalism, ethnic differences, and class inequality, which have fueled regional conflicts in Latin America, Africa, Asia, and the Middle East. If peace depends on solving international disputes, why do world nations currently spend 3,000 times as much money on militarism as they do on peacekeeping? (Sivard, 1988)

LOOKING AHEAD: POLITICS IN THE TWENTY-FIRST CENTURY

Just as economic systems—the focus of the last chapter—are changing, so are political systems. As we look ahead to the next century, several problems and trends will likely command widespread attention.

One vexing problem in the United States is the inconsistency between our democratic ideals and our low public participation in politics. Perhaps, as the pluralists contend, many people do not bother to vote because they are basically satisfied with their lives. But perhaps the power-elite theorists are right: People withdraw from a system that concentrates wealth and power in the hands of so few. Or, as Marxist critics contend, perhaps people find our political system

NOTE: As the Republicans see it, the Democrats have been "losing touch" with the people since the 1960s, which, they say, explains the steady erosion of public support for Congress from about 70% approval then to about 20% now. Democrats counter that this slide is due to the rise of big money in U.S. politics.

Q: "When I was a boy, I was told that anyone could become president. I'm beginning to believe it." Clarence Darrow

EXERCISE: Students may want to investigate various "gaps" in politics. The gender gap is real but smaller than many others: Percentage gap of men/women who voted for a Democratic House candidate in 1994: 11.1%; married/single gap: 12.5%; $50,000+ vs. under $15,000 annual income: 19.4%; urban/rural gap: 28.9%; Protestant/Jewish gap: 37.6%; white/black gap: 49.7% (data from Women's Political Caucus).

CONTROVERSY & DEBATE

"Online" Democracy:
Can Computers Increase Political Participation?

How about this as a way to get more people actively involved in politics: Give every home a computer and an Internet connection; allow anyone to propose new legislation; and, on the first Saturday of every month, every adult with a voting password gets to vote and make law. What could be easier? Or more truly democratic?

Is it possible, as some predict, that new information technology is about to reverse the trend toward apathy and lead our nation into a new age of democracy? High technology promises to make citizens better informed about the workings of government than ever before by broadcasting government debates live to every home and providing telephone, e-mail, and fax links to all government officials.

Moreover, using computer technology, citizens everywhere could participate in "electronic town meetings," pushing a button on a computer keyboard to help balance the budget, ban handguns, or, perhaps, close our borders to further immigration. In short, as some see it, we are entering the age of a "wired Congress" and "online democracy."

The push for high-tech politics began with the landslide victory in 1994 that gave the Republican party control of both houses of Congress for the first time in more than half a century. Republicans read the victory as evidence that people across the country are fed up with the liberal, big-government politics favored by people "inside the Beltway" (a reference to the interstate that circles our nation's capital). What better way to defeat the government establishment, they reasoned, than to open up debate to the "real" voice of the nation—the people in local towns and neighborhoods from Sarasota to Spokane? Moreover, the Republicans continued, Congress managed to pass a number of unpopular programs over the years only by shutting out the voice of "ordinary people." If the people had been asked in the first place, Republicans suggested, would we have today's high levels of immigration, rigid affirmative action programs, and a vast federal bureaucracy? As the Republicans see it, much of our law is the creation of

gives little real choice, limiting options and policies to those consistent with our capitalist economic system. In any case, it seems certain that we cannot endure a rising tide of apathy and a falling level of confidence in government without moving toward significant political reforms.

A major trend discussed in this chapter is the expansion of a global political process. The Information Revolution is changing politics just as it is reformulating the economy (although political change seems to be somewhat slower). Communications technology now allows news and political analysis to flow instantly from one point in the world to another. But will this global avalanche of information expand democracy by empowering individuals? Or will new information technology provide governments with new tools to manipulate their citizens? More basically, perhaps, some critics wonder if we really want to give the average person—who is, after all, no expert—the power to decide important issues. The final box takes a look at two sides of the recent "online democracy" debate.

Another major trend is the global rethinking of political models. The cold war between the United States and the Soviet Union cast political debate in the form of two rigid political alternatives based on capitalism, on the one hand, and socialism, on the other. Today, in the post–cold war era, analysts envision a broader range of political systems, linking government to economic production in various ways. "Welfare capitalism" as found in Sweden or "state capitalism" as found in Japan and South Korea are just two possibilities.

Fourth, and finally, we still face the danger of war in many parts of the world. Even as tensions between the United States and the former Soviet Union have eased, vast stockpiles of weapons remain, and nuclear technology continues to proliferate around the world. New superpowers may arise in the century ahead (the People's Republic of China seems a likely candidate), just as regional conflicts will surely continue to fester. One can only hope that, in the century to come, world leaders will devise nonviolent solutions to the age-old problems that provoke war.

Q: "Refine and enlarge the public views by passing them through the medium of a chosen body of citizens, whose wisdom may best discern the true interest of their country and whose patriotism and love of justice will be least likely to sacrifice it to temporary or partial considerations." James Madison, *Federalist Papers*

Q: "One cannot fully grasp the political world unless one understands it as a confidence game . . ." Peter Berger

GLOBAL: Asked which of the two is more important, 72% of a U.S. sample picked freedom (20% equality). Europeans, by contrast, assign roughly equal value to each (Wattenberg, 1989).

Q: "It is evident that the state is a creation of nature, and man is by nature a political animal. . . . He who is unable to live in society, or who has no need because he is sufficient for himself, must be either a beast or a god: He is no part of a state." Aristotle, *Politics*

liberal, self-righteous politicians who rarely venture outside the Beltway.

But not everyone is rushing out to "wire" Congress to public opinion. Many Democrats counter that using high technology to open up the political process amounts to "hyperdemocracy." Our system of government, they explain, was structured not as a *direct* democracy but a *representative* democracy. That is, we elect officials to lead, not to follow the whims of the voters. The British statesman Edmund Burke (1729–1797), himself a conservative, believed that government officials should do more than work hard for their constituents; leaders, he said, owe the people their judgment. In these days of media frenzy and passion-politics, when would-be leaders often seek to inflame public opinion, online democracy would result in the impulsive passing of questionable laws. In the

early 1960s, Democrats point out, the people of the United States were too racially prejudiced to support the civil rights legislation that Congress enacted. But would we have wanted them to do otherwise?

Like it or not, everyone agrees, new information technology will operate in two directions: It will give people a greater voice in government, and it will allow elected leaders to present and defend their own thinking to the public. But the question remains: Will this prescription for *more* democracy motivate a larger share of citizens to become politically active? And, more to the point, is a more direct democracy necessarily a *better* democracy?

Continue the debate . . .

1. *Do you think new information technology will give the public a greater voice in government? Why or why*

not? Could political leaders use new information technology to manipulate the public? How?

2. *Does technology that provides the means for a greater public voice necessarily mean that government will better reflect the public interest? Why or why not? Do you think our leaders should consult the people before making decisions, or should they rely mostly on their own judgment?*

3. *Some critics suggest that if we want more democracy, innovations in technology are no substitute for real change in the economic and power structures of this country. Do you agree? Why or why not?*

Sources: Toffler & Toffler (1993), McConnell (1995), Roberts, (1995), and Wright (1995).

SUMMARY

1. Politics is the major social institution by which a society distributes power and organizes decision making. Max Weber explained that three social contexts transform coercive power into legitimate authority: tradition, rationally enacted rules and regulations, and the personal charisma of a leader.

2. Traditional authority is common to preindustrial societies; industrial societies legitimize power mostly through bureaucratic organizations and law. Charismatic authority, which arises in every society, sustains itself through routinization into traditional or rational-legal authority.

3. Monarchy is based on traditional authority and is common in preindustrial societies. Although constitutional monarchies persist in some industrial nations, industrialization favors democracy based on rational-legal authority and extensive bureaucracy.

4. Authoritarian political regimes deny popular participation in government. Totalitarian political systems go even further, tightly regulating people's everyday lives.

5. The world is divided into 191 politically independent nation-states. One global political trend, however, is the growing wealth and power of multinational corporations. Additionally, new technology associated with the Information Revolution means that national governments can no longer control the flow of information across national boundaries.

6. Government has grown in the United States during the past two centuries and now acts in a wide range of ways to protect the public and regulate the economy. The welfare state in this country, however, is less extensive than in most other industrial nations.

7. Liberals and conservatives take different positions on economic and social issues. Liberals call for government regulation of the economy and action to ensure economic equality; conservatives believe the government should not interfere in these arenas. Conservatives, however, do support government regulation of moral issues such as abortion, while liberals argue that government should not interfere in matters of conscience.

8. Special-interest groups advance the political aims of specific segments of the population. These groups employ lobbyists and political action committees (PACs) to influence the political process.

9. Many people in the United States do not readily describe themselves in political terms, nor do they strongly identify with either the Democratic or the Republican parties. Furthermore, only 48 per-

cent of those eligible to vote actually voted in the 1996 national elections.

10. The pluralist model holds that political power is widely dispersed in the United States; the power-elite model takes an opposing view, arguing that power is concentrated in a small, wealthy segment of the population. The Marxist political-economy view claims political policies are limited by our capitalist economy.

11. Revolution radically transforms a political system. Terrorism, another unconventional political tactic, employs violence in the pursuit of political goals. States as well as individuals engage in terrorism.

12. War is armed conflict directed by governments. The development of nuclear weapons, and their proliferation, has increased the threat of global catastrophe. World peace ultimately depends on resolving the tensions and conflicts that fuel militarism.

KEY CONCEPTS

politics the social institution that distributes power, sets a society's agenda, and makes decisions

power the ability to achieve desired ends despite resistance

government a formal organization that directs the political life of a society

authority power that people perceive as legitimate rather than coercive

traditional authority power legitimized through respect for long-established cultural patterns

rational-legal authority (also **bureaucratic authority**) power legitimized by legally enacted rules and regulations

charismatic authority power legitimized through extraordinary personal abilities that inspire devotion and obedience

routinization of charisma the transformation of charismatic authority into some combination of traditional and bureaucratic authority

monarchy a political system in which a single family rules from generation to generation

democracy a political system in which power is exercised by the people as a whole

authoritarianism a political system that denies popular participation in government

totalitarianism a political system that extensively regulates people's lives

welfare state a range of government agencies and programs that provides benefits to the population

special-interest group a political alliance of people interested in some economic or social issue

political action committee (PAC) an organization formed by a special-interest group, independent of political parties, to pursue political aims by raising and spending money

pluralist model an analysis of politics that views power as dispersed among many competing interest groups

power-elite model an analysis of politics that views power as concentrated among the rich

Marxist political-economy model an analysis that explains politics in terms of the operation of a society's economic system

political revolution the overthrow of one political system in order to establish another

terrorism random acts of violence or the threat of such violence employed by an individual or group as a political strategy

war organized, armed conflict among the people of various societies

military-industrial complex the close association among the federal government, the military, and defense industries

nuclear proliferation the acquisition of nuclear-weapons technology by more and more nations

CRITICAL-THINKING QUESTIONS

1. What is the difference between authority and power? What forms of authority characterize preindustrial and industrial societies? Why does democracy gradually replace monarchy as societies industrialize?

2. How would you describe the attitudes of the U.S. population on the political spectrum? How is class position linked to political opinions?

3. Contrast the pluralist, power-elite, and Marxist political-economy models of societal power. Which do you find more convincing?

4. Do you think danger of war in the world is greater or less than in past generations? Why?

LEARNING EXERCISES

1. Immediately after every national election (held the first Tuesday in November), newspapers publish an analysis of who voted and for whom. Visit the library to obtain a "scorecard" for the last election (a good one for the 1996 election was in *The New York Times*, November 10, 1996, page 28). To what extent do men and women vote for different presidential candidates? What about people of various racial categories? Ages? Religions? Income levels? In short, what variables affect political attitudes the most?

2. The Internet provides enormous organizational potential, linking people who share an interest in some political issue. The goal of the Web site http://www.womenconnect.com is to increase the political clout of women. If you have computer access, visit the site: Do you think such sites will make a difference in U.S. politics?

3. Along with several other people, make a list of leaders you think are or were charismatic. Discuss why someone is on the list. Do you think personal charisma is something more than "being good on television"? If so, precisely what?

4. Do a little research to trace the increase in the size of the federal government over the last fifty years. Try to discover how organizations at different points along the political spectrum (from socialist organizations on the left through the Democratic and Republican parties to right-wing militia groups) view the size of the current welfare state.

5. Install the CD-ROM packaged inside the back cover of your text and complete the activities designed to accompany this chapter.

Frida Kahlo, *My Grandparents, My Parents, and I (Family Tree)*, 1936
Oil and tempera on metal panel, 12⅛ × 13⅝ in. (30.7 × 34.5 cm). The Museum of Modern Art, New York.
Gift of Allan Roos, MD, and B. Matthieu Roos. Photograph © 1996 The Museum of Modern Art.

CHAPTER 17

FAMILY

It started out in 1991 as a routine application for a marriage license: After being together twenty years, Joseph Melillo and Pat Lagon decided that they wanted to "tie the knot." But their request soon became anything but routine, because Melillo and Lagon are both men and, under Hawaiian law (as well as the laws of every other state), only man-woman couples can be joined in marriage.

Of course, both Melillo and Lagon knew the law. As they saw it, however, it was high time to change the rules. So, with two other same-sex couples, they went back to the courthouse to file a lawsuit challenging the marriage law. In 1993, the Supreme Court of Hawaii declared that denying marriage licenses to the three gay couples amounted to unconstitutional discrimination unless state officials could offer the court compelling evidence showing why they could not marry.

This decision set off a national debate as to exactly what marriage is and who is entitled to wed.

Within a year, the Hawaiian legislature enacted a statute declaring that marriage should be extended only to "man-woman units." Soon, legislators in every other state—recognizing that the U.S. Constitution would require every state to honor marriages performed in any other state—were taking up the same question. To date, a majority of states have either passed "man-woman" marriage laws or are considering such legislation. And, in 1996, the U.S. Congress weighed in with a "Defense of Marriage Act" that forbids gay couples from marrying (Dunlap, 1996).

In 1997, the original Hawaiian case came to a close with a compromise. For the time being, only heterosexual couples will be permitted to marry, but Hawaii will extend many of the benefits of marriage—including medical insurance, state pensions, and inheritance rights—to all couples. Said Joseph Melillo, "Something good did come out of this [lawsuit], albeit not the outcome we would have liked to have. But for some people this will benefit them in the interim until we get our marriage legalized."

Should the law permit gay couples to marry? What exactly is a "family"? Are families disappearing? Such questions are part of the "family values" debate going on across the United States. Indeed, to hear some people tell it, the family is fast becoming an endangered species. And some hard facts back up this

claim. The U.S. divorce rate has doubled over the past thirty years so that, if the trend holds, almost half of today's marriages will end in divorce. Marital breakdown, coupled with the fact that about one in three children is born to an unmarried woman, means that half the U.S. children born today will live with a

SUPPLEMENTS: An outline of this chapter, suggested discussion topics, and supplementary lecture material highlighting cross-cultural family patterns are found in the *Data File*.

Q: "Some kind of family exists in all known human societies, although it is not found in every segment or class of all stratified, state societies. Greek and American slaves, for example, were prevented from forming families." Kathleen Gough (1989:239)

NOTE: Of the 69.6 million U.S. families (1996), 41% were married couples without children; 36% were married couples with children; 11% were women heads of households with children; 2% were men heads of households with children; 10% were all other categories (U.S. Bureau of the Census, 1997).

Q: "The happiest moments of my life have been the few which I have passed at home in the bosom of my family." Thomas Jefferson

In modern industrial societies, the members of extended families usually pursue their careers independently and live apart from one another. However, various nuclear families may assemble periodically for rituals such as weddings, funerals, and family reunions.

as we shall also point out, changing family patterns are nothing new. A century ago, for example, concern over the decline of the family swept our nation as the Industrial Revolution moved men off farms and into factories. Today, of course, many of the same concerns are expressed about women leaving home for careers. In short, changes in other social institutions, especially the economy, are leaving their mark—for better or worse—on marriage and family life.

THE FAMILY: BASIC CONCEPTS

The **family** is *a social institution that unites individuals into cooperative groups that oversee the bearing and raising of children.* These social units are, in turn, built on **kinship,** *a social bond, based on blood, marriage, or adoption, that joins individuals into families.* Although all societies contain families, just who people call their kin has varied through history, and varies today from one culture to another.

During this century, most members of our society have regarded a **family unit** as *a social group of two or more people, related by blood, marriage, or adoption, who usually live together.* Initially, individuals are born into a family composed of parents and siblings; this is sometimes termed the *family of orientation* because it is central to socialization. In adulthood, people form a *family of procreation* in order to have or adopt children of their own.

Throughout the world, families form around **marriage,** *a legally sanctioned relationship, usually involving economic cooperation as well as normative sexual activity and childbearing, that people expect to be enduring.* Our cultural belief that marriage is the appropriate context for procreation is apparent in the historical use of the term *illegitimate* for children born out of wedlock. Moreover, *matrimony*, in Latin, means "the condition of motherhood." The link between childbearing and marriage has weakened, however, as the share of children born to single women (nearing one in three) has increased.

Today, some people object to defining only married couples and children as "families" because it implies that everyone should accept a single standard of moral conduct. Moreover, because many company and government programs extend health care and other benefits only to members of "families" as conventionally defined, unmarried, committed partners—whether heterosexual or homosexual—are excluded. As a result, an increasing number of businesses—as well as San Francisco and other cities—are recognizing

single parent at some time before reaching age eighteen. This trend is one key reason that the proportion of U.S. children living in poverty has been rising steadily.

Not everyone, of course, is worried that the family will disappear. But the fact is that the family has changed more during the last several decades than any other social institution (Bianchi & Spain, 1996). Not long ago, the cultural ideal of the family consisted of a working husband, a homemaker wife, and their young children. Today, fewer people embrace such a singular vision of the family, and, at any given time, only about one in four U.S. households fits that description.

This chapter highlights important changes in family life and offers some insights into these trends. Yet,

DIVERSITY: Although the extended family is not favored in the United States partly because of the association of kin and dependency, the poor often establish fictional kin out of need (as in Carol Stack's *All Our Kin*). During economic recessions, families become more extended with, for example, more men and women in their twenties and thirties continuing to live with their parents.

NOTE: Throughout the world, societies pressure people to marry someone of the same social background (endogamy) but of the other sex (exogamy).

NOTE: Illustrating exogamy is the legal prohibition against homosexual marriages; a case of endogamy is the historical prohibition against interracial marriage.

families of affinity, that is, people with or without legal or blood ties who feel they belong together and wish to define themselves as a family.

The U.S. Census Bureau, which uses the conventional definition of family, also plays a role in this debate: Sociologists who wish to use Census Bureau data describing "families" must accept this definition.[1] The trend in public opinion as well as in legal terms, however, favors a wider and more inclusive definition of the "family unit."

THE FAMILY: GLOBAL VARIETY

Members of preindustrial societies take a broad view of family ties, recognizing the **extended family** as *a family unit including parents and children, but also other kin.* Extended families are also called *consanguine families,* meaning that they include everyone with "shared blood." With industrialization, however, increasing geographic and social mobility gives rise to the **nuclear family,** *a family unit composed of one or two parents and their children.* Because it is based on marriage, the nuclear family is also known as the *conjugal family.* Although many members of our society live in extended families, the nuclear family is the predominant form in the United States.

Family change has been greatest in nations that have the most expansive welfare state (see Chapter 16, "Politics and Government"). In the box on pages 456–57, sociologist David Popenoe takes a look at Sweden, which, he claims, has the weakest families in the world.

MARRIAGE PATTERNS

Cultural norms, as well as laws, identify people as suitable or unsuitable marriage partners. Some marital norms promote **endogamy**, *marriage between people of the same social category.* Endogamy limits marriage prospects to others of the same age, race, religion, or social class. By contrast, **exogamy** mandates *marriage between people of different social categories.* In rural India, for example, people expect a person to marry someone of the same caste (endogamy), but from a different village (exogamy). The logic of endogamy is that people of similar social position pass along their standing to offspring, thereby maintaining traditional social patterns. Exogamy, on the other hand, builds alliances and encourages cultural diffusion.

In industrial societies, laws prescribe **monogamy** (from the Greek, meaning "one union"), *a form of marriage joining two partners.* Our high level of divorce and remarriage, however, suggests that *serial monogamy* is a more accurate description of this nation's marital practice.

Global Map 17–1 on page 458 shows that while monogamy is the rule throughout the Americas and in Europe, many lower-income societies—especially in Africa and southern Asia—permit **polygamy** (from the Greek, meaning "many unions"), *a form of marriage uniting three or more people.* Polygamy can be one of two types. By far the more common is **polygyny** (from the Greek, meaning "many women"), *a form of marriage uniting one male and two or more females.* Islamic nations in Africa and southern Asia, for example, permit men up to four wives. Even so, most families in these countries are monogamous because few men have the wealth needed to support several wives and even more children.

Polyandry (from the Greek, meaning "many men" or "many husbands") is *a form of marriage uniting one female with two or more males.* This pattern appears only rarely. One example is among people of Tibet, where agriculture is difficult. There, polyandry discourages the division of land into parcels too small to support a family and divides the work of farming among many men. Polyandry has also been linked to female infanticide—aborting female fetuses or killing female infants—because a decline in the female population forces men to share women.

Historically, most world societies have permitted more than one marital pattern, although, as noted already, most actual marriages have been monogamous (Murdock, 1965). This cultural preference for monogamy reflects two facts of life: Supporting multiple spouses is a heavy financial burden, and the number of men and women in most societies is roughly the same.

RESIDENTIAL PATTERNS

Just as societies regulate mate selection, so they designate where a couple resides. In preindustrial societies, most newlyweds live with one set of parents, gaining economic assistance and security in the process. Most

---

[1]According to the U.S. Census Bureau, there were 99.6 million U.S. households in 1996, of which 69.6 million (70 percent) were family households. The remaining living units contained single people or unrelated individuals living together. In 1960, 85 percent of all households were families.

DIVERSITY: Statistically speaking, the typical U.S. family is a married couple, both of whom are high school graduates and in the labor force, with one child (mean) or no children (mode), living in a (mortgaged) home that they own. At any given point in time, about 25% of all households have a wife, husband, and one or more children at home, although more than half take this form during the life course; at any given time, about one in ten households comprises a working man, homemaker woman, and one or more children although, again, about 25% take this form at some point.

NOTE: Some of the changes in our thinking about family life involve a shift from family *form* to family *function*. In other words, rather than defining the family as a single, traditional form, more people (especially sociologists) say "If it works like a family, it *is* a family." The Latin root *familia* means simply "a household."

GLOBAL SOCIOLOGY

The Weakest Families on Earth?
A Report From Sweden

The Swedes have few of the social problems that plague us here in the United States. Urban Sweden has little of the violent crime, drug abuse, and grinding poverty that blights whole districts of our own cities. Instead, this Scandinavian nation seems to fulfill the promise of the modern welfare state, with an extensive and professional government bureaucracy that sees to virtually all human needs.

But one drawback of an expanding welfare state, according to David Popenoe, is that Sweden has the weakest families on earth. Because people look to the government—not spouses—for economic assistance, Swedes are less likely to marry than members of any other industrialized society.

For the same reason, Sweden also has a high share of adults living alone (more than 20 percent, similar to the share in

In Sweden, unmarried women bear half of all children, twice the rate of births by single women in the United States.

the United States). Moreover, a large proportion of couples live outside of marriage (25 percent versus 4 in the United States), and half of all Swedish children (compared to about one in three in the United States) are born to unmarried parents. Average household size in Sweden is also the smallest in the world (2.2 persons versus 2.7 in the United States). Finally, Swedish couples (whether married or not) are more likely to break up than partners in any other country. According to Popenoe, the family "has probably become weaker in Sweden than anywhere else—certainly among advanced Western nations. Individual family members are the most autonomous and least bound by the group . . ." (1991:69).

---

societies observe a norm of **patrilocality** (Greek for "place of the father"), *a residential pattern in which a married couple lives with or near the husband's family.* But some societies (such as the North American Iroquois) favor **matrilocality** (meaning "place of the mother"), *a residential pattern in which a married couple lives with or near the wife's family.* Societies that engage in frequent, local warfare tend toward patrilocality since families want their sons close to home to offer protection. Societies that engage in distant warfare may be patrilocal or matrilocal, depending on whether sons or daughters have greater economic value (Ember & Ember, 1971, 1991).

Industrial societies show yet another pattern. When finances permit, they favor **neolocality** (from the Greek, meaning "new place"), *a residential pattern in which a married couple lives apart from the parents of both spouses.*

PATTERNS OF DESCENT

Descent refers to *the system by which members of a society trace kinship over generations.* Most preindustrial societies trace kinship through only one side of the family—the father or the mother. The more prevalent pattern is **patrilineal descent,** *a system tracing kinship through males.* In a patrilineal system, children are related to others only through their fathers, and fathers typically pass property on to their sons. Patrilineal descent characterizes most pastoral and agrarian societies, since men produce the most valued resources. Less common is **matrilineal descent,** *a system tracing kinship through women.* Matrilineal descent, through which mothers pass property to their daughters, is found more frequently in horticultural societies where women are the primary food producers.

GLOBAL: Along with the other Scandinavian countries, Sweden has the world's highest tax rates, which peak at an 85% marginal rate.

Q: "As the welfare state has advanced, the family has declined. The weakened family, in turn, has serious negative social consequences, especially for the children involved. . . . By weakening the family, the welfare state has undermined the very welfare it seeks to promote." David Popenoe

Q: "As long as the term 'family' is used to cover both the 'real' family and its antithesis—the single-parent version—the question of whether a society can do without families is hopelessly obfuscated. Moreover a challenging thesis is hidden: the thesis that it does not matter which social arrangements adults devise to bring up children." Amitai Etzioni

Popenoe contends that a growing culture of individualism and self-fulfillment, along with the declining influence of religion, began eroding Swedish families in the 1960s. The movement of women into the labor force also played a part. Today, Sweden has the lowest proportion of women who are housewives (10 percent versus about 25 in the United States) and the highest percentage of women in the labor force (77 percent versus 60 in the United States).

But, most important, according to Popenoe, is the expansion of the welfare state. The Swedish government offers its citizens a lifetime of services. Swedes can count on the government to deliver and school their children, provide comprehensive health care, support them when they are out of work, and, when the time comes, pay for their funeral.

Many Swedes supported the growth of welfare, thinking it would *strengthen* families. But with the benefit of hindsight, Popenoe explains, we can see that,

by expanding benefits, government actually has been *replacing* families. Take the case of child care: The Swedish government operates public child-care centers, staffed by professionals, and available regardless of parents' income. At the same time, however, the government offers no subsidy for parents who desire to care for children in their own home. In effect, then, government benefits operate as incentives for people to let the state do what family members used to do for themselves.

But if Sweden's system has solved so many social problems, why should anyone care about the erosion of family life? For two reasons, says Popenoe. First, it is very expensive for government to provide many "family" services; this is the main reason that Sweden has one of the highest rates of taxation in the world.

Second, can government employees in large child-care centers provide children with the level of love and emotional security available from two parents living

as a family? Unlikely, says Popenoe, noting that small, intimate groups can accomplish some human tasks much better than large organizations.

Popenoe concludes that the Swedes have gone too far in delegating family responsibilities to government. But, he wonders, have we in the United States gone far enough? With the birth of a child, a Swedish parent may apply for up to eighteen months' leave at 90 percent of regular salary. In the United States, the 1993 Family and Medical Leave Act guarantees workers only ninety days—without pay—to care for newborns or sick family members. Should our society follow Sweden's lead? And if we look to government to help working parents care for children, will it strengthen or weaken families?

Sources: Popenoe (1991, 1994); also Herrstrom (1990).

Industrial societies with greater gender equality recognize **bilateral descent** ("two-sided descent"), *a system tracing kinship through both men and women.* In this pattern, children recognize people on both their "father's side" and their "mother's side" as relatives.

PATTERNS OF AUTHORITY

The predominance of polygyny, patrilocality, and patrilineal descent in the world reflects the universal presence of patriarchy. Without denying that wives and mothers exercise considerable power in every society, as Chapter 12 ("Sex and Gender") explains, no truly matriarchal society has ever existed.

In industrial societies like the United States, more egalitarian family patterns are evolving, especially as increasing numbers of women enter the labor force. However, even here, men are typically heads of

households. Parents in the United States also still prefer boys to girls, and (usually) give children their father's last name.

THEORETICAL ANALYSIS OF THE FAMILY

As in earlier chapters, several theoretical approaches offer a range of insights about the family.

FUNCTIONS OF THE FAMILY: STRUCTURAL-FUNCTIONAL ANALYSIS

The structural-functional paradigm suggests that the family performs several vital tasks. This analysis explains why we sometimes think of the family as "the backbone of society."

NOTE: Signaling the personal significance of the family, four of the five most severe "social readjustment experiences" involve kinship: death of a spouse (100), divorce (73), marital separation (65), jail term (63), death of a close family member (63) (Holmes & Rahe, 1967).

Q: "Despite the profound changes in the nature of the family that have come with the industrialization and urbanization of the past century, today's family remains the basic unit for the protection and rearing of young children, and the center of emotional life. Indeed, its role as the major source of psychological support for its members has, if anything, increased. The family is a 'haven in a heartless world,' an oasis of stable, diffuse and largely unquestioned love and support." Lenore J. Weitzman (1982:2–3)

WINDOW ON THE WORLD

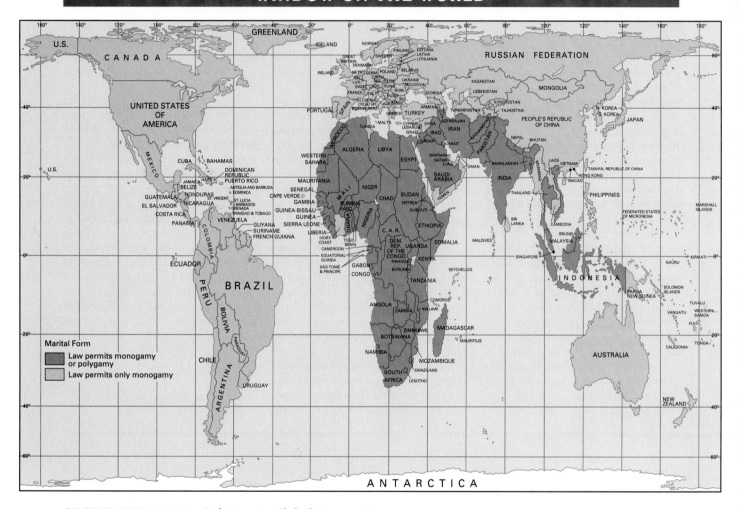

GLOBAL MAP 17–1 Marital Form in Global Perspective

Monogamy is the legally prescribed form of marriage in all industrial societies and throughout the Western Hemisphere. In most African nations, as well as in southern Asia, however, polygamy is permitted by law. In many cases, this practice reflects the historic influence of Islam, a religion that allows a man to have up to four wives. Even so, most marriages in these traditional societies are monogamous, primarily for financial reasons.
Source: *Peters Atlas of the World* (1990).

1. **Socialization.** As explained in Chapter 5 ("Socialization"), the family is the first and most influential setting for socialization. Ideally, parents teach children to be well-integrated and contributing members of society (Parsons & Bales, 1955). Of course, family socialization continues throughout the life cycle. Adults change within marriage, and, as any parent knows, mothers and fathers learn as much from raising their children as their children learn from them.

SOCIAL SURVEY: "It is better for all if the man is the achiever outside the home and the woman takes care of the home and the family." (*Student CHIP Social Survey Software*, FEFAM1; GSS 1977, 1985–91, N = 6,752)

	"Agree"	"Disagree"
Men	51.7%	48.3%
Women	44.9%	55.1%

2. **Regulation of sexual activity.** Every culture regulates sexual activity in the interest of maintaining kinship organization and property rights. One universal regulation is the **incest taboo,** *a cultural norm forbidding sexual relations or marriage between certain kin.* Precisely which kin fall within the incest taboo varies from one culture to another. The matrilineal Navajo, for example, forbid marrying any relative of one's mother. Our bilateral society applies the incest taboo to both sides of the family but limits it to close relatives, including parents, grandparents, siblings, aunts, and uncles. But even brother-sister marriages found approval among the ancient Egyptian, Incan, and Hawaiian nobility (Murdock, 1965).

Reproduction between close relatives of any species can mentally and physically impair offspring. Yet, only human beings observe an incest taboo, suggesting that the real reason to control incest is social. Why? First, the incest taboo minimizes sexual competition within families by restricting legitimate sexuality to spouses. Second, it forces people to marry outside of their immediate families, which serves to integrate the larger society. Third, since kinship defines people's rights and obligations toward each other, reproduction among close relatives would hopelessly confuse kinship ties and threaten social order.

3. **Social placement.** Families are hardly necessary for people to reproduce, but they do help maintain social organization. Parents confer their own social identity—in terms of race, ethnicity, religion, and social class—on children at birth. This fact explains the long-standing preference for birth to married parents.

4. **Material and emotional security.** People view the family as a "haven in a heartless world," looking to kin for physical protection, emotional support, and financial assistance. To a greater or lesser extent, most families do all these things, although not without periodic conflict. Not surprisingly, then, people living in families tend to be healthier than those living alone.

Critical evaluation. Structural-functional analysis explains why society, at least as we know it, could not exist without families. But this approach glosses over the great diversity of family life in the United States. Also, it ignores ways in which other social institutions

The family is a basic building block of society because it performs important functions such as conferring social position and regulating sexual activity. To most family members, however, the family (at least in ideal terms) is a "haven in a heartless world" in which individuals find a sense of belonging and emotional support, an idea conveyed in Marc Chagall's Scène Paysanne.

Marc Chagall, *Scène Paysanne*. © 1999 Artists Rights Society (ARS), New York/ADAGP, Paris.

(government, for instance) could meet some of the same human needs. Finally, structural-functional analysis overlooks negative aspects of family life, including its support of patriarchy and the alarming extent of family violence.

INEQUALITY AND THE FAMILY: SOCIAL-CONFLICT ANALYSIS

Like the structural-functional approach, the social-conflict paradigm considers the family central to the operation of society, but rather than focusing on societal benefits, conflict theorists investigate how the

Q: In *The Republic*, Plato advocates the abolition of the "private" family in the interests of justice: "All these women are to belong to all these men in common, and no woman is to live privately with any man. And the children, in their turn, will be in common, and neither will a parent know his own offspring, nor a child his parent." (Book V)

Q: "The bourgeoisie has torn away from the family its sentimental veil, and has reduced the family to a mere money relation." Karl Marx and Friedrich Engels, *The Communist Manifesto*

NOTE: Social-exchange analysis represents one kind of rational-choice theory.

NOTE: Social-exchange analysis also explains why people who perceive more potential new partners in their surroundings have higher divorce rates (cf. South & Lloyd, 1995).

family perpetuates social inequality. This process occurs in three major ways, with regard to class, gender, and race.

1. **Property and inheritance.** Friedrich Engels (1902; orig. 1884) traced the origin of the family to the need to identify heirs so that men (especially in the higher classes) could transmit property to their sons. Families thus support the concentration of wealth and reproduce the class structure in each succeeding generation (Mare, 1991).

2. **Patriarchy.** According to Engels, men determine their heirs by controlling the sexuality of women. Families therefore transform women into the sexual and economic property of men. A century ago in the United States, most wives' earnings belonged to their husbands. Today, despite striking economic gains, women still bear major responsibility for child rearing and housework (Fuchs, 1986; Hochschild, 1989; Presser, 1993; Keith & Schafer, 1994; Benokraitis & Feagin, 1995).

3. **Race and ethnicity.** Racial and ethnic categories will persist over generations only to the degree that people marry others like themselves. Thus endogamous marriage shores up the racial and ethnic hierarchy of a society.

Critical evaluation. Social-conflict analysis reveals another side of family life: its role in maintaining social inequality. Engels condemned the family as part and parcel of capitalism. Yet noncapitalist societies have families (and family problems) all the same. While kinship and social inequality are deeply intertwined, as Engels argued, the family carries out societal functions that are not easily accomplished by other means.

CONSTRUCTING FAMILY LIFE: MICRO-LEVEL ANALYSIS

Both structural-functional and social-conflict analyses are macro-level approaches that take a broad view of the family as a structural system. Micro-level approaches, by contrast, explore how individuals shape and experience family life day-to-day.

Symbolic-Interaction Analysis

People experience family life in terms of relationships, and these vary from person to person and change from day to day. In ideal terms, however, family living offers an opportunity for intimacy, a word with Latin roots mean "sharing fear." That is, as a result of sharing a wide range of activities over a long period of time, members of families forge emotional bonds. Of course, the fact that parents act as authority figures often inhibits their communication with younger children. But, as young people reach adulthood and are less subject to discipline by their parents, kinship ties typically "open up" to include confiding as well as turning to one another for emotional support and assistance with numerous tasks and responsibilities (Macionis, 1978).

Social-Exchange Analysis

Social-exchange analysis, another micro-level approach, depicts courtship and marriage as forms of negotiation (Blau, 1964). Dating allows each person to assess the advantages and disadvantages of taking the other as a spouse, always keeping in mind the value of what one has to offer in return. In essence, exchange analysts suggest, individuals "shop" in a marriage market, seeking to make the best "deal" they can for themselves in selecting a partner.

Physical attractiveness is one critical element of exchange. Throughout history, patriarchal societies have made beauty a commodity offered by women on the marriage market. The high value assigned to beauty explains women's traditional concern with physical appearance and their sensitivity about revealing their age. Men, in turn, have traditionally offered their financial resources. Recently, however, because women are joining the labor force, they are less dependent on men to support them and their children. Thus, the terms of exchange have been converging for men and women.

Critical evaluation. Micro-level analysis offers a counterpoint to structural-functional and social-conflict visions of the family as an institutional system. Both the interactional and exchange viewpoints give a better sense of the individual's experience of family life and how people shape this aspect of reality for themselves.

This approach, however, misses the bigger picture, namely, that family life is similar for people in the same social and economic categories. U.S. families vary in predictable ways, according to social class and ethnicity, and, as the next section explains, they typically evolve through distinct stages linked to the life course.

NOTE: The Latin root of "intimacy" is *timere*, meaning "to fear" (an etymology shared with the word "intimidate"). Intimacy, then, is a relationship of "sharing fears."

Q: "What does a woman do for herself and for her children by being fussy about her sexual partners? . . . if she focuses on male traits that are heritable, she sees to it that her kids start with a genetic edge. We aren't all created equal . . . [She also] makes it possible to pick males who will stick around and help raise the kids. A woman is not simply competing for quality sperm; she's competing for the man who goes with it." Heather Trexler Remoff (1984)

RESOURCE: Among the classics included in the Macionis and Benokraitis reader, *Seeing Ourselves*, is Jessie Bernard's "'His' and 'Her' Marriage."

People in every society recognize the reality of physical attraction. But the power of romantic love, captured in Christian Pierre's painting, I Do, *holds surprisingly little importance in traditional societies. In much of the world, it would be less correct to say that individuals marry individuals and more true to say that families marry families. In other words, parents arrange marriages for their children with an eye to the social position of the kin-groups involved.*

STAGES OF FAMILY LIFE

The family is dynamic, with marked changes across the life course. New families begin with courtship, and new partners then settle into the realities of married life. Next, for most couples at least, is raising children, leading to the later years of marriage after children have left home to form families of their own. We will look briefly at each of these stages.

COURTSHIP

November 2, 1994, Kandy, Sri Lanka. Winding our way through the rainforest of this beautiful island, the van driver Harry recounts to his audience how he met his wife. Actually, it was more of an arrangement: The two families were both Buddhist and of the same caste group. "But we got along well, right from the start," recalls Harry. "We had the same background. I suppose she or I could have said 'no'. But 'love marriages' happen in the city, not in the village where I grew up."

People in Sri Lanka, and in preindustrial societies throughout the world, generally consider courtship too important to be left to the young (Stone, 1977). Arranged marriages represent an alliance between two extended families of similar social standing and usually involve not just an exchange of children, but also wealth and favors. Romantic love has little to do with it, and parents may make such arrangements when their children are quite young. A century ago in Sri Lanka and India, for example, half of all girls married before reaching age fifteen (Mayo, 1927; Mace & Mace, 1960). And, as the box on page 462 explains, in some parts of the world, child marriage persists today.

Arranged marriages fit into Emile Durkheim's model of *mechanical solidarity* (see Chapter 4, "Society"). Because traditional societies are culturally homogeneous, almost any member of the opposite sex has been suitably socialized to perform the roles of spouse and parent. Thus parents can arrange marriages with little concern for whether the two individuals involved are *personally* compatible; they can be confident that virtually any couple will be *culturally* compatible.

Industrialization erodes the importance of extended families and weakens traditions while enhancing personal choice in courtship. Young people expect to choose their own mates, and usually delay doing so until they have financial security and the experience to select a suitable partner. Dating sharpens courtship skills and serves as a period of sexual experimentation.

RESOURCE: Check Bron B. Ingoldsby's article, "Mate Selection and Marriage Around the World," in the new edition of the Macionis and Benokraitis reader, *Seeing Ourselves*.

DIVERSITY: As people age, there are proportionately fewer males than females eligible for marriage. Regionally, this pattern is most pronounced in the Sunbelt; in San Diego, for example, there are three men aged 20–59 for every four women.

DISCUSS: Distinguish homogamy (marriage between partners of similar background) from endogamy (marriage within some specific category).

CYBER: In 1996, the world's first cyber–wedding chapel opened: GlamOrama Internet wedding chapel. They offer weddings for $49.95, including e-mail invitations. People "attend" by entering a chat room.

GLOBAL SOCIOLOGY

Early To Wed: A Report From Rural India

Sumitra Jogi was crying as her wedding was about to begin. Were they tears of joy? Not exactly: This "bride" is an eleven-month-old squirming in the arms of her mother. The groom? A boy of six.

In a remote, rural village in India's western state of Rajasthan, two families gather at midnight to celebrate a traditional wedding ritual. It is the second of May, an especially good day to marry according to Hindu tradition. Sumitra's father smiles as the ceremony begins; her mother cradles the infant, who, having just finished nursing, has now fallen asleep. The groom, dressed in a special costume with a red and gold turban on his head, gently reaches up and grasps the baby's hand. Then, as the ceremony reaches its conclusion, the young boy leads the child and mother three and one-half times around the wedding fire—while the audience beams—marking the couple's first steps together as husband and wife.

Child weddings of this kind are illegal in India, but in the rural regions, traditions are strong and marriage laws are difficult to enforce. In fact, experts estimate that thousands of young children

are married each year in ceremonies of this kind. "In rural Rajasthan," explains one social welfare worker, "all the girls are married by age fourteen. These are poor, illiterate families, and they don't

want to keep girls past their first menstrual cycle."

For the immediate future, Sumitra Jogi will remain with her parents. But, by the time she is eight or ten years old, a second ceremony will mark the time for her to move to the home of her husband's family, where her married life will begin.

If the responsibilities of marriage lie years in the future, why do families push their children to marry at such an early age? Parents of girls know that, the younger the bride, the smaller the dowry offered to the groom's parents. Then, too, when girls marry this young, there is no chance that they will lose their virginity, which would spoil their attractiveness on the marriage market. But, of course, the entire system rests on the assumption that love has nothing to do with it. Marriage is an alliance between families, so no one worries that the children are too young to understand what is taking place.

Source: Based on Anderson (1995).

Romantic Love

Our culture celebrates *romantic love*—the feeling of affection and sexual passion toward another person—as the basis for marriage. We find it hard to imagine marriage without love, and popular culture, from remakes of traditional fairy tales like "Cinderella" to today's paperback romance novels, portrays love as the key to a successful marriage. However, as Figure 17–1 shows, in many other countries, romantic love plays a much smaller role in marriage.

Our society's emphasis on romance has some useful consequences. Passionate love motivates individuals to "leave the nest" to form new families of their own, and it can help a new couple through the difficult adjustments of living together (Goode, 1959). On the other hand, because feelings wax and wane, romantic love is a less stable foundation for marriage than social and economic considerations—an assertion supported by the high divorce rate in this country compared to lower rates in nations that allow less choice in partners.

THEN AND NOW: Age at first marriage: *1955*, 20.1 yrs. for women, 22.5 yrs. for men; *1995*, 24.5 yrs. for women; 26.9 yrs. for men.
NOTE: According to the National Center for Health Statistics, 9% of U.S. births are unwanted; another 22% are "ill timed," meaning wanted but at a later date.

NOTE: Research confirms that delaying childbirth increases the income of both women and men (cf. Chandler, Kamo, & Werbel, 1994).
GLOBAL: Ideal family size is higher in poor societies. One recent survey in Honduras placed the ideal figure as 3.2 children. In rural areas (containing 60% of the people) the actual average family size is 6.9 children.

But even in a culture of more choice, sociologists know that Cupid's arrow is aimed by society more than we like to think. Most people fall in love with others of the same race, of comparable age, and similar social class. All societies, in fact, "arrange" marriages to the extent that they encourage **homogamy** (literally, "like marrying like"), *marriage between people with the same social characteristics.*

In short, "falling in love" may be a strong personal feeling, but it is guided by social forces. Perhaps we exaggerate the importance of romantic love to reassure ourselves that we—not society—steer our own lives.

SETTLING IN: IDEAL AND REAL MARRIAGE

Our culture presents marriage to the young in idealized, "happily-ever-after" terms. But such optimistic thinking can lead to disappointment, especially for women, who, more than men, are taught to see marriage as the key to future happiness.

Then, too, romantic love involves a good deal of fantasy. We fall in love with others, not necessarily as they are, but as we want them to be (Berscheid & Hatfield, 1983). Only after marriage do many spouses really get to know each other as they carry out the day-to-day routines of maintaining a household.

Sexuality can also be a source of disappointment. In the romantic haze of falling in love, people may anticipate marriage as an endless sexual honeymoon, only to face the sobering realization that sex becomes a less-than-all-consuming passion. About two in three married people report that they are satisfied with the sexual dimension of their relationship, though marital sex does decline over time.

Many experts agree that couples with the most fulfilling sexual relationships experience the greatest satisfaction in their marriages. This correlation does not mean that sex is the key to marital bliss, but more often than not, good sex and good relationships go together (Hunt, 1974; Tavris & Sadd, 1977; Blumstein & Schwartz, 1983).

Infidelity—sexual activity outside marriage—is another area where the reality of marriage does not coincide with our cultural ideal. We strongly support traditional marriage vows "to forsake all others." In a recent survey, for example, 90 percent of U.S. adults said sex outside of marriage is "always wrong" or "almost always wrong." Even so, 21 percent of men and 13 percent of women indicated on a private, written questionnaire that they had—at least once—been sexually unfaithful to their partners (NORC, 1994:679; 1996:218).

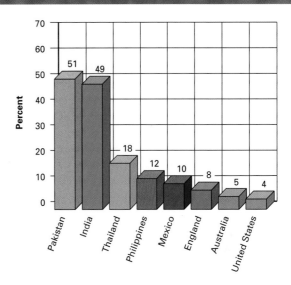

GLOBAL SNAPSHOT

FIGURE 17–1 Percentage of College Students Who Express a Willingness to Marry Without Romantic Love

Source: Levine (1993).

CHILD REARING

Adults in the United States overwhelmingly identify raising children as one of life's greatest joys (NORC, 1996:734). This is so despite the demands children make on the time and energy of parents, sometimes to the point of straining their marriage.

Not surprisingly, therefore, almost all adults in this society think the ideal family should have at least one child. Table 17–1 on page 464 indicates that most prefer two or three, with few wishing to have four or more children. Smaller families are a big change from two centuries ago, when *eight* children was the U.S. average.

Big families pay off in preindustrial societies because children perform needed labor. Indeed, people generally regard having children as a wife's duty, and without reliable birth control technology, childbearing is a regular event. Of course, a high death rate in preindustrial societies prevents many children from reaching adulthood; as late as 1900, one-third of children born in the United States died by age ten (Wall, 1980).

SOCIAL SURVEY: "How much satisfaction do you get from your family life?" (GSS 1994, N = 511; *Codebook*, 1996:164)

"A very great deal"	39.5%	"Some"	3.3%
"A great deal"	35.0%	"A little"	2.5%
"Quite a bit"	10.4%	"None"	2.0%
"A fair amount"	6.8%	DK/NR	0.4%

TABLE 17–1 The Ideal Number of Children for U.S. Adults, 1996

Number of Children	Proportion of Respondents
0	1.2%
1	2.8
2	54.7
3	20.9
4	8.3
5	1.1
6 or more	1.0
As many as you want	6.1
No response	4.0

Source: *General Social Surveys, 1972–1996: Cumulative Codebook* (Chicago: National Opinion Research Center, 1996), p. 212.

Economically speaking, industrialization transforms children from an asset to a liability. Today it costs more than $200,000, including the costs of a college education, to raise one child (Lino, 1997). This expense helps explain the steady drop in U.S. family size during the twentieth century to one child per family today.[2]

The trend toward smaller families also holds for other all-industrial societies. But the picture differs sharply in low-income countries in Latin America, Asia, and, especially, Africa, where many women have few alternatives to bearing and raising children. In such societies, four to six children is still the norm.

Parenting is not only expensive, it is a lifetime commitment. As our society has given people greater choice about family life, more U.S. adults have opted to delay childbirth or to remain childless. In 1960, almost 90 percent of women between twenty-five and twenty-nine who had ever married had at least one child; by 1995 this proportion had tumbled to 70 percent (U.S. Bureau of the Census, 1997). About two-thirds of parents in the United States say they would like to devote more of their time to child rearing (Snell, 1990). But unless we are willing to accept a lower standard of living, economic realities demand that most parents pursue careers outside the home.

[2]According to the U.S. Bureau of the Census (1997), the median number of children per family was 1.0 in 1996. Among only married couples with children, the medians were .90 for whites, 1.12 for African Americans, and 1.58 for Hispanics.

NOTE: The share of latchkey children rises with age, the number of hours a mother works, and parental income.

THEN AND NOW: Number of U.S. working mothers with preschool children: *1975*, 6 million; *1996*, 15 million. Number of U.S. children receiving daily care by someone other than mother; *1975*, 4 million; *1996*, more than 10 million.

Thus, people give less attention to their families partly because economic change demands it.

As Chapter 12 ("Sex and Gender") explained, most women with young children now work for income. In 1997, 60 percent of women over the age of fifteen—and 77 percent of mothers with children under eighteen—were in the work force (U.S. Bureau of the Census, 1997; U.S. Department of Labor, 1998). But while women and men share the burden of earning income, women continue to bear the traditional responsibility for raising children and doing housework. Many men in our society are eager parents, but most resist doing household tasks that our culture historically has defined as "women's work" (Hochschild, 1989; Presser, 1993; Keith & Schafer, 1994).

As more women join men in the labor force, parents have less time for parenting. Children of working parents spend most of the day at school. But after school, about 2 million youngsters (roughly 10 percent of the total) are *latchkey kids* who fend for themselves (U.S. Bureau of the Census, 1994). Traditionalists in the "family values" debate caution that mothers often work at the expense of children, who receive less parenting. Progressives counter that such criticism targets women for wanting the same opportunities men have long enjoyed.

Congress took a step toward easing the conflict between family and job responsibilities by passing the Family and Medical Leave Act in 1993. This law allows up to ninety days of unpaid leave from work because of a new child or a serious family emergency. On a day-to-day basis, however, most adults must juggle parental and occupational responsibilities. Understandably, then, child care is an urgent concern, as the box explains.

THE FAMILY IN LATER LIFE

Increasing life expectancy in the United States means that, barring divorce, couples are likely to remain married for a long time. By about age fifty, most have completed the task of raising children. The remaining years of marriage bring a return to living with only one's spouse.

Like the birth of children, their departure (the "empty nest") requires adjustments, although the marital relationship often becomes closer and more satisfying in midlife. Years of living together may diminish a couple's sexual passion for each other, but mutual understanding and companionship are likely to increase.

Q: "We think of ourselves as a nation that cherishes its children, but, in fact, America treats its children like excess baggage. Our tax code offers greater incentives for breeding horses than for raising children. We slash school budgets and deny working parents the right to spend even a few weeks with their newborns. We spend 23% of the federal budget on the elderly but less than 5% on children." Sylvia Ann Hewlett

DIVERSITY: Later family life differs by sex: See Table 14–1 on page 386 for the different living arrangements of elderly women and men.
RESOURCE: David Popenoe's article "The Decline of Marriage and Fatherhood" is one of the contemporary selections in the Macionis and Benokraitis reader, *Seeing Ourselves*, 4th ed.

CRITICAL THINKING

Who's Minding the Kids?

Traditionally, the task of providing daily care for young children fell to mothers. But with a majority of mothers and fathers now in the labor force, finding quality, affordable child care is a high priority for parents.

The figure shows how U.S. children under age five receive care while their mothers work. Most often—in 33 percent of all cases—the child remains at home with the father or another relative. An additional 31 percent of children receive care in another person's home, with relatives, neighbors, or friends looking after them. A small share of children accompany their mothers to work.

The remaining 29 percent of children with working mothers attend day-care or preschool. The proportion in day-care centers has doubled over the last decade because many parents cannot find in-home care for their children.

Some day-care centers are so big that they amount to "tot lots" in which parents "park" their children for the day to

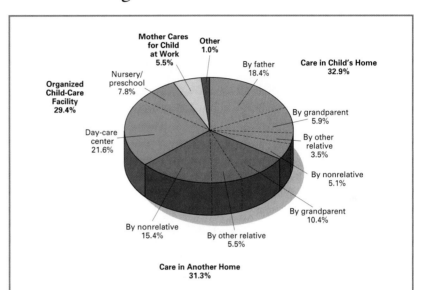

receive minimal attention. The impersonality of such settings and rapid turnover in staff prevent the warm and consistent nurturing that young children need in order to develop a sense of trust. Other child-care centers, however, offer

a secure and healthful environment. Research suggests that *good* care centers are good for children; *bad* facilities are not.

Source: U.S. Bureau of the Census (1997).

Personal contact with children usually continues, since most older adults live a short distance from at least one of their children. Moreover, one-third of all U. S. adults (more than 50 million) are grandparents, many of whom help with child care and other responsibilities. Among African Americans (who have a high rate of single parenting), many grandmothers assume a central position in family life (Cherlin & Furstenberg, 1986; Crispell, 1993; Jarrett, 1994).

The other side of the coin, explained in Chapter 14 ("Aging and the Elderly"), is that more adults in midlife must care for aging parents. The "empty nest" may not be filled by a parent coming to live in the home, but parents living to eighty and beyond require practical, emotional, and financial care that can be more taxing than raising young children. The oldest of the "baby

boomers"—now in their fifties—are often called the "sandwich generation" because they will spend as many years caring for their aging parents as they did for their offspring.

The final, and surely the most difficult, transition in married life comes with the death of a spouse. Wives typically outlive their husbands because of women's longer life expectancy and the fact that wives are usually younger than husbands to begin with. Wives can thus expect to spend a significant period of their lives as widows. The bereavement and loneliness accompanying the death of a spouse are extremely difficult, and the experience may be worse for widowers, who usually have fewer friends than widows and may be unskilled at cooking and housework (Berardo, 1970).

DIVERSITY: Among the poor, female-headed households are predominantly African American; among more affluent people, they are mostly white.

THEN AND NOW: African American households with female heads: *1940*, 18%; *1996*, 47%; dual-parent households: *1940*, 77%; *1996*, 50%. Percent of African American children residing with both parents: *1960*, 75%; *1996*, 37% (Allen, 1995).

NOTE: The Census Bureau reports that, in 1996, 63% of the 10.4 million African American children under 18 lived with only one parent (up 97% since 1970). Those families with a woman heading the household (almost all of them) had a median income of $16,256, 39% of the comparable figure for black married-couple families ($42,069).

Historically, Latinos have maintained strong kinship ties. Carmen Lomas Garza's painting Lala's and Tudi's Birthday Party *portrays the extended family that is a foundation of traditional Hispanic culture.*

© 1989 Carmen Lomas Garza. *Cumpleanos de Lala y Tudi*, oil on canvas, 17"x15". Collection of the artist. Photo: Wolfgang Dietze.

U.S. FAMILIES: CLASS, RACE, AND GENDER

Dimensions of inequality—social class, ethnicity and race, and gender—are powerful forces that shape marriage and family life. This discussion addresses each factor in turn, but bear in mind that they overlap in our lives.

SOCIAL CLASS

Social class frames a family's financial security and range of opportunities. Interviewing working-class women, Lillian Rubin (1976) found that wives thought a good husband was one who held a steady job and refrained from excessive drinking and violence. Rubin's middle-class informants, by contrast, never mentioned such things; these women simply *assumed* a husband would provide a safe and secure home. Their ideal husband was someone with whom they could communicate easily and share feelings and experiences.

This difference reflects the fact that people with higher social standing have more schooling, and most have jobs that emphasize verbal skills. In addition, middle-class couples share a wider range of activities, while working-class life is more divided along gender lines. As Rubin explains, many working-class men hold traditional ideas about masculinity and self-control, so they stifle emotional expressiveness. Women then turn to each other as confidants.

What women (and men) think they can hope for in marriage—and what they end up with—is linked to their social class. Much the same holds for children: Boys and girls lucky enough to be born into more affluent families enjoy better mental and physical health, develop higher self-confidence, and go on to greater achievement than children born to poor parents (Komarovsky, 1967; Bott, 1971; Rubin, 1976; Fitzpatrick, 1988; McLeod & Shanahan, 1993).

ETHNICITY AND RACE

As Chapter 13 ("Race and Ethnicity") discusses, ethnicity and race are powerful social forces, and the effects of both ripple through family life. Keep in mind, however, that like white families, Latino and African American families are diverse and conform to no single stereotype (Allen, 1995).

DIVERSITY: David Blankenhorn (1995) reports that 66% of children in single-mother homes are poor versus 13% in married-couple families. Among married-couple parents with children, 92% of whites are above the poverty line as are 82% of blacks and 82% of Hispanics.

DIVERSITY: About 70% of African American women ever marry, compared to 90% of white women.

NOTE: Steven Ruggles (1994) reports that the pattern by which African Americans are two to three times more likely than whites to live without one or both biological parents extends back at least to 1880.

DIVERSITY: The share of children under 18 years of age living with both parents (1996) was 68% overall; for whites, 75%; for African Americans, 33%; for Hispanics, 62%.

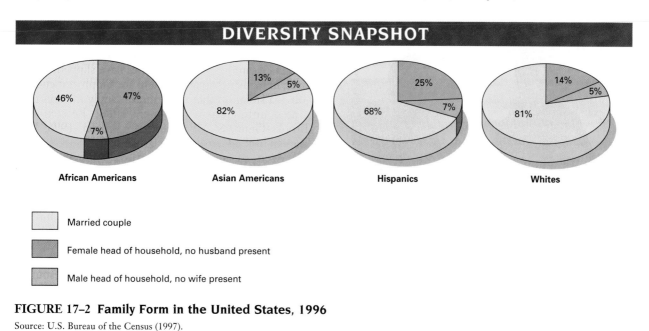

DIVERSITY SNAPSHOT

Married couple

Female head of household, no husband present

Male head of household, no wife present

FIGURE 17–2 Family Form in the United States, 1996
Source: U.S. Bureau of the Census (1997).

Latino Families

Latinos in the United States generally enjoy the loyalty and support of extended families. Traditionally, too, Latino parents exercise greater control over their children's courtship, considering marriage an alliance of families rather than a union based simply on romantic love. A third trait of Latino family life is adherence to conventional gender roles. Machismo—masculine strength, daring, and sexual prowess—is pronounced among some Latinos, while women are both honored and closely supervised.

Assimilation into the larger society is gradually changing these traditional patterns, however. Many Puerto Ricans who migrate to New York, for example, do not maintain the strong extended families they knew in Puerto Rico. Traditional male authority over women has also diminished, especially among affluent Hispanic families, whose number has tripled in the last twenty years (Staples & Mirande, 1980; Moore & Pachon, 1985; Nielsen, 1990; O'Hare, 1990).

Though some Latinos have become quite prosperous, the overall social standing of this segment of the U.S. population remains below average. The U.S. Bureau of the Census (1997) reports that, in 1996, the typical Hispanic family had an income of $26,179, about 62 percent of the mean annual income for all U.S. families. Consequently, many Hispanics suffer the stress of unemployment and other problems related to poverty.

African American Families

An analysis of African American families must begin with the stark reality of economic disadvantage: As noted in earlier chapters, the typical African American family earned $26,522 in 1996, only 63 percent of the national standard. People of African ancestry are also three times as likely as whites to be poor, and poverty means that families experience unemployment, underemployment, and, in some cases, a physical environment replete with crime and drug abuse.

Under these circumstances, maintaining stable family ties is difficult. For example, 25 percent of African American women in their forties have never married, compared to about 10 percent of white women of the same age (Bennett, Bloom, & Craig, 1989). This means that African American women—often with children—are more likely to be single heads of households. As Figure 17–2 shows, women headed 47 percent of all African American families in 1996, compared to 25 percent of Hispanic families, 13 percent of Asian or Pacific Islander families, and 14 percent of white families (U.S. Bureau of the Census, 1997).

Q: "Neither the pessimists who believe that the family is falling apart nor the unbridled optimists who claim that the family has never been in better shape provide an accurate picture of family life in the near future. But . . . what we have come to view as the 'traditional' family will no longer predominate." Andrew Cherlin and Frank F. Furstenberg, Jr.

NOTE: Almost 60% of U.S. children live in the Census Bureau's

"traditional nuclear family" made up of married biological parents and no one else (by race, 66% white, 28% black, 45% Hispanic). Using a broader definition of family, 77% of children live in two-parent families (not necessarily biological parents nor a married couple).

SUPPLEMENTS: The *Data File* includes a discussion of "pro-gay, pro-family" policy.

CONTROVERSY & DEBATE

Should We Save the Traditional Family?

What are "traditional families"? Are they vital to our way of life or a barrier to progress? To begin, people use the term "traditional family" to mean a married couple who, at some point in their lives, raise children. But the term is more than description; it is also a moral statement. That is, belief in traditional family implies putting a high value on becoming and remaining married, placing children ahead of careers, and favoring two-parent families over various "alternative lifestyles."

On one side of the debate, David Popenoe notes with alarm the rapid erosion of the traditional family since 1960. At that time, married couples with young children accounted for almost half of all households; today, the figure is a mere 27 percent. Singlehood is up, from 10 percent then to 25 percent of households now. And the divorce rate has doubled since 1960, so that half of today's marriages will end in permanent separation. Moreover, due

to both divorce and having children out of wedlock, the proportion of youngsters that will live with a single parent before age eighteen has quadrupled since 1960 to 50 percent. In other words, just one in four of today's children will grow up with two parents and go on to maintain a stable marriage as an adult.

In light of such data, Popenoe concludes, it may not be an exaggeration to say that the family is falling apart. He sees a fundamental shift from a "culture of marriage" to a "culture of divorce." Traditional vows of marital commitment—"till death us do part"—now amount to little more than "as long as I am happy." Daniel Yankelovich (1994:20) sums it up this way:

> The quest for greater individual choice clashed directly with the obligations and social norms that held families and communities together in earlier years. People came to feel that questions of how

to live and with whom to live were a matter of individual choice not to be governed by restrictive norms. As a nation, we came to experience the bonds to marriage, family, children, job, community, and country as constraints that were no longer necessary. Commitments have loosened.

The negative consequences of the cultural trend toward weaker families, Popenoe continues, are obvious everywhere: As we pay less and less attention to children, the crime rate goes up along with a host of other problematic behaviors, including underage smoking and drinking and premarital sex.

As Popenoe sees it, then, we must work hard and quickly to reverse current trends. Government cannot be the solution (and may even be part of the problem) because, since 1960, as families have grown weaker, government spending on social programs has soared five-fold. Instead, says Popenoe, we need a

LOOKING AHEAD: FAMILY IN THE TWENTY-FIRST CENTURY

Family life in the United States has changed in recent decades, and this change will continue. Change causes controversy, in this case pitting advocates of "traditional family values" against supporters of new family forms and greater personal choice: The closing box sketches some of the issues. Sociologists cannot predict the outcome of this debate, but we can posit five probable future trends.

First, divorce rates are likely to remain high, even in the face of evidence that marital dissolution harms children. Yet, today's marriages are about as durable as they were a century ago, when many were cut short by death (Kain, 1990). The difference is that more couples now

choose to end marriages that fail to live up to their expectations. Thus, although the divorce rate has recently stabilized, it is unlikely that marriage will ever again be as durable as in the 1950s. But perhaps we should view today's high divorce rates less as a threat to families than as a sign of change in family form. After all, most divorces still lead to remarriage, so marriage is hardly becoming obsolete.

Second, family life in the twenty-first century will be highly variable. Cohabiting couples, one-parent families, gay and lesbian families, and blended families are all increasing in number. Most families, of course, still are based on marriage, and most married couples still have children. But, taken together, the variety of family forms implies a growing belief that family life is a matter of choice.

NOTE: David Popenoe (1994) reports that one of his colleagues describes the consequences of fatherlessness as "too many little boys with guns and too many little girls with babies."
NOTE: Judith Stacey notes that Bill Clinton (like George Washington) was reared by a single parent.
THEN AND NOW: In 1960, 17% of children under 18 lived without their biological fathers; today, the figure is 25% and rising.

Q: Laumann et al. found that married people had more sex than singles, leading one commentator to quip: "In addition to having more sex, the married have more money. It hardly seems fair." Linda J. Waite
Q: ". . . [C]ommitment must be developed and nurtured in modern society if humanity is to survive." Edward L. Kain (1990:152)

cultural turnaround by which people turn away from a "me-first" view of life in favor of commitment to spouses and children. (We have seen such a turnaround in the case of cigarette smoking.) To save the traditional family, we must publicly affirm the value of staying married and endorse the two-parent family as best for the well-being of children.

Judith Stacey, who says "good riddance" to the traditional family, takes issue with this position. For Stacey, the traditional family is more problem than solution. Striking to the heart of the matter, Stacey writes (1990:269):

> The family is not here to stay. Nor should we wish it were. On the contrary, I believe that all democratic people, whatever their kinship preferences, should work to hasten its demise.

The main reason for rejecting the traditional family, Stacey explains, is that it perpetuates various kinds of social inequality. Families play a key role in maintaining the class hierarchy, transferring wealth as well as "cultural capital" from one generation to another. Moreover, feminists criticize the traditional family's patriarchal form, subjecting women to their husbands' authority and saddling them with most of the responsibility for housework and child care. And from a gay rights perspective, she adds, a society that values traditional families inevitably denies homosexual men and women equal participation in social life.

Stacey thus applauds the breakdown of the family as social progress. She does not see the family as a basic social institution, but as a political construction that elevates one category of people—affluent white males—at the expense of women, homosexuals, and poor people who lack the resources to maintain middle-class respectability.

Moreover, Stacey continues, the concept of "traditional family" is increasingly irrelevant in a diverse society where both men and women work for income. What our society needs, Stacey concludes, is not a return to some golden age of the family but political and economic change, including income parity for women, universal health care and child care, programs to reduce unemployment, and expanded sex education in the schools. Only with such programs can we support our children and ensure that people in diverse family forms receive the respect everyone deserves.

Continue the debate . . .

1. *To strengthen families, Popenoe suggests that parents put children ahead of their own careers by limiting their joint work week to sixty hours. Do you agree? Why or why not?*

2. *Judith Stacey thinks that marriage is weaker today because women are rejecting patriarchal relationships. Do you agree? Why or why not?*

3. *Do you think we need to change family patterns for the well-being of our children? As you see it, what specific changes are called for?*

Sources: Popenoe (1993), Stacey (1990, 1993), and Council on Families in America (1995).

Third, men are likely to continue to play a limited role in child rearing. In the 1950s, a decade many people see as the "golden age" of families, men began to withdraw from active parenting (Snell, 1990; Stacey, 1990). A counter-trend is now emerging as some fathers—older, on average, and more established in their careers—eagerly jump into the parenting role. But, on balance, the high U.S. divorce rate and the surge in single motherhood point to more children growing up with weak ties to fathers. At the same time, the evidence is building that the absence of fathers harms children, at the very least by putting the family at high risk of being poor.

Fourth, we will continue to feel the effects of economic changes in our families (Hochschild, 1989). In many families, both household partners now work, making marriage the interaction of weary men and women who try to squeeze in a little "quality time" for themselves and their children (Dizard & Gadlin, 1990). Two-career couples may advance the goal of gender equality, but the long-term effects on families as we have known them are likely to be mixed.

Fifth and finally, the importance of new reproductive technology will increase. Ethical concerns will slow these developments, but new forms of reproduction will continue to alter the traditional meanings of parenthood.

Despite the social changes buffeting the family in the United States, most people still report being happy as partners and parents. Marriage and family life today may be more controversial than in the past, but both will likely remain the foundation of our society for some time to come.

SUMMARY

1. All societies are built on kinship, although family forms vary considerably across cultures and over time.

2. In industrial societies such as the United States, marriage is monogamous. Many preindustrial societies, however, permit polygamy, of which there are two types: polygyny and polyandry.

3. In global perspective, patrilocality is most common, while industrial societies favor neolocality and a few societies have matrilocal residence. Industrial societies use bilateral descent, while preindustrial societies tend to be either patrilineal or matrilineal.

4. Structural-functional analysis identifies major family functions: socializing the young, regulating sexual activity, transmitting social placement, and providing material and emotional support.

5. Social-conflict theories explore how the family perpetuates social inequality by transmitting divisions based on class, ethnicity, race, and gender.

6. Micro-level analysis highlights the variable nature of family life both over time and as experienced by various family members.

7. Families originate in the process of courtship. Unlike the United States, few societies base the choice of a mate on romantic love. But even among members of our society, romantic love tends to join people with similar social backgrounds.

8. The vast majority of married couples have children, although family size has decreased over time. The key reason for this decline is industrialization, which transforms children into economic liabilities, encourages women to gain an education and join the labor force, and reduces infant mortality.

9. Married life changes as children leave home to form families of their own. Many middle-aged couples, however, care for aging parents and are active grandparents. The final stage of this life course begins with the death of one spouse, usually the husband.

10. Families differ according to class position, race, and ethnicity. Latino families, for example, are more likely than others to maintain extended kinship ties. African American families are more likely than others to be headed by women. Among all categories of people, well-to-do families enjoy the most options and greatest financial security.

11. Gender affects family dynamics since husbands dominate in most marriages. Research suggests that marriage provides more benefits to men than to women.

12. The divorce rate today is ten times what it was a century ago; more than four in ten current marriages will end in divorce. Most people who divorce—especially men—remarry, often forming blended families that include children from previous marriages.

13. Most family violence victimizes women and children and is far more common than official records indicate. Most adults who abuse family members were themselves abused as children.

14. Our society's family life is becoming more varied. One-parent families, cohabitation, gay and lesbian couples, and singlehood have proliferated in recent years. While the law does not recognize homosexual marriages, many gay men and lesbians form long-lasting relationships and, increasingly, are becoming parents.

15. Although ethically controversial, new reproductive technology is changing conventional notions of parenthood.

KEY CONCEPTS

family a social institution, found in all societies, that unites individuals into cooperative groups that oversee the bearing and raising of children

kinship a social bond, based on blood, marriage, or adoption, that joins individuals into families

family unit a social group of two or more people, related by blood, marriage, or adoption, who usually live together

marriage a legally sanctioned relationship, involving economic cooperation as well as normative sexual activity and childbearing, that people expect to be enduring

extended family (consanguine family) a family unit including parents and children, but also other kin

nuclear family (conjugal family) a family unit composed of one or two parents and their children

endogamy marriage between people of the same social category

exogamy marriage between people of different social categories

monogamy a form of marriage joining two partners

polygamy a form of marriage uniting three or more people

polygyny a form of marriage uniting one male with two or more females

polyandry a form of marriage uniting one female with two or more males

patrilocality a residential pattern in which a married couple lives with or near the husband's family

matrilocality a residential pattern in which a married couple lives with or near the wife's family

neolocality a residential pattern in which a married couple lives apart from the parents of both spouses

descent the system by which members of a society trace kinship over generations

patrilineal descent a system tracing kinship through men

matrilineal descent a system tracing kinship through women

bilateral descent a system tracing kinship through both men and women

incest taboo a cultural norm forbidding sexual relations or marriage between certain kin

homogamy marriage between people with the same social characteristics

family violence emotional, physical, or sexual abuse of one family member by another

cohabitation the sharing of a household by an unmarried couple

CRITICAL-THINKING QUESTIONS

1. How has the emerging postindustrial economy affected family life? What other factors are changing the family?

2. Why do some analysts describe the family as the "backbone of society"? Why do others stress that families perpetuate social inequality?

3. Do you think that single-parent households do as good a job as two-parent households in raising children? Why or why not?

4. On balance, are families in the United States becoming weaker or not? What evidence can you cite?

LEARNING EXERCISES

1. Parents and grandparents can be a wonderful source of information about changes in marriage and the family. Spend an hour or two with married people of two different generations and ask about when they married, what their married lives have been like, and what changes in today's world stand out to them.

2. Relationships with various family members differ. With which family member—mother, father, brother, sister—do you most readily and least readily share secrets? Why? Which family member would you turn to first in a crisis? Why?

3. The Family Research Council is a conservative organization supporting what they call "traditional family values." If you have computer access, visit their Web site (http://www.frc.org) and find out what they see as a "traditional family." Why do they defend "traditional families"? What problems of families do they ignore?

4. Organize a debate for one class period with one team arguing each side of the "family-values controversy." Present arguments for and against the statement: "Resolved: The traditional family is necessary for the survival of our country's way of life."

5. Install the CD-ROM packaged inside the back cover of your text and complete the activities designed to accompany this chapter.

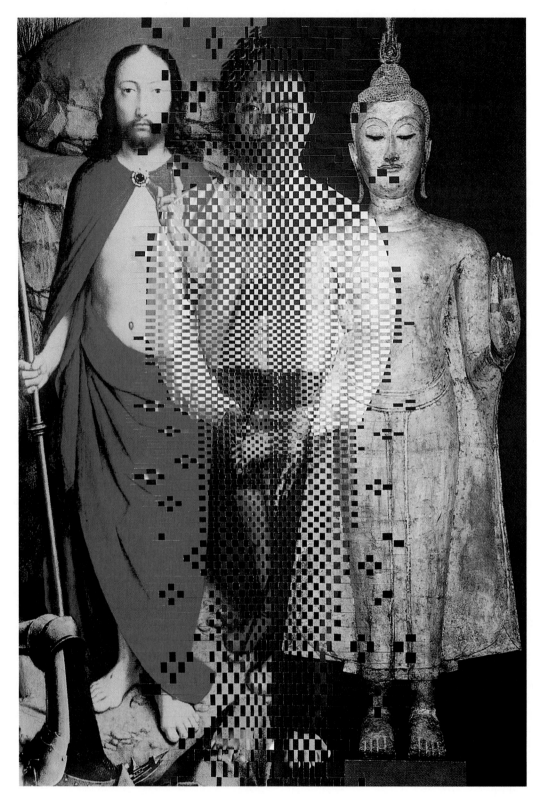

Dinh Le, *Interconfined,* 1994
© 1994 Dinh Le, c-print and linen tape, 55 × 39 in.

CHAPTER 18

RELIGION

Elisha Hack was elated at the news: Highly prestigious Yale University had accepted him for the Class of 2001. But when he arrived on campus in the fall of 1997, his excitement turned to disappointment and confusion. In his dorm, Hack—an Orthodox Jew—was stunned to find only a short staircase separating men's and women's rooms. Copies of the "Safer Sex Menu" were prominently displayed in the lounges alongside bowls of condoms, and orientation that evening was a "safe-sex" seminar complete with a demonstration of how to use dental dams.

Was college life—at least college life at Yale—consumed by sin like the biblical cities of Sodom and Gomorrah? Hack wanted an education, but not if the living arrangements violated his religious principles. So Hack proposed what he viewed as a reasonable solution: He would enroll at Yale, but live off campus in an environment more to his liking. Yale, however, stuck to its requirement that all first-year students live in dorms, where they learn to interact with others who are different from themselves. The case now seems likely to end up in court (Cloud, 1997).

Religion has always played a central part in U.S. society, and conflicts like the one between Elisha Hack and Yale University are nothing new. Indeed, this dispute is merely one example of the long-standing debate over the proper role of religion in social life. This chapter explains what religion is, explores the changing face of religious belief throughout history and around the world, and examines the vital—yet sometimes controversial—place of religion in today's modern, scientific culture.

RELIGION: BASIC CONCEPTS

For French sociologist Emile Durkheim, whose ideas are discussed in detail in Chapter 4 ("Society"), the focus of religion is "things that surpass the limits of our knowledge" (1965:62; orig. 1915). As human beings, we organize our surroundings by defining most objects, events, or experiences as **profane** (from Latin meaning "outside the temple"), *that which is an ordinary element of everyday life.* But we set some things apart, Durkheim continued, by designating them as **sacred,** *that which is defined as extraordinary, inspiring a sense of awe, reverence, and even fear.* Distinguishing the sacred from the profane is the essence of all religious belief. **Religion,** then, is *a social institution involving beliefs and practices based upon a conception of the sacred.*

A global perspective reveals great variety in matters of faith, with no one thing that is sacred to everyone on earth. Although people regard most books as profane, Jews believe the Torah (the first five books of the Hebrew Bible or Old Testament) is sacred, in the same way that Christians revere the Old and New Testaments of the Bible and Muslims exalt the Qur'an (Koran).

But no matter how a community of believers draws religious lines, Durkheim (1965:62) explained, people understand profane things in terms of their everyday usefulness: We log onto the Web with our computer or turn a key to start our car. What is sacred, however, we reverently set apart from everyday life and denote as "forbidden." Marking the boundary between the sacred and the profane, for example, Muslims remove their shoes before entering a mosque to avoid defiling a sacred place of worship with soles that have touched the profane ground outside.

The sacred is embodied in **ritual,** *formal, ceremonial behavior.* Holy communion is the central ritual of Christianity; the wafer and wine consumed during

SUPPLEMENTS: An outline for this chapter, supplementary lecture material, and suggested discussion topics are provided in the *Data File.*

Q: "Sociologists have a hard time coming to terms with the intensely religious character of the contemporary world. Whether politically on the left or not, they suffer from ideological blinders when it comes to religion, and the tendency is to explain away what cannot be explained. But, ideology apart, parochialism is an important factor here too. Sociologists live in truly secularized milieus—academia and the other institutions of the professional knowledge industry—and it appears that they are no more immune than the sociologically untrained to the common misconception that one can generalize about the world from one's own little corner." Peter Berger (1992:15–16)

Religion is founded on the concept of the sacred: that which is set apart as extraordinary and which demands our submission. Bowing, kneeling, or prostrating oneself—shown in Fred Ehrlich's painting Facing Mecca—*are common elements in religious life that symbolize this surrender to a higher power.*

communion are sacred symbols of the body and blood of Jesus Christ, and are never treated in a profane way as food.

RELIGION AND SOCIOLOGY

Because religion deals with ideas that transcend everyday experience, neither sociology nor any other scientific discipline can verify or disprove religious doctrine. Religion is a matter of **faith,** *belief anchored in conviction rather than scientific evidence.* The New Testament of the Bible, for instance, describes faith as "the assurance of things hoped for, the conviction of things not seen" (Heb. 11:1) and exhorts Christians to "walk by faith, not by sight" (2 Cor. 5:7).

Through most of our history, human beings lived in small societies and attributed birth, death, and whatever happened in between to the operation of supernatural forces. Over the last several hundred years, however, science has emerged as an alternative way of understanding the natural world, and scientific sociology has much to say about how and why societies operate the way they do.

Some people with strong faith may be disturbed by the thought of sociologists turning a scientific eye to what they hold as sacred. In truth, however, a sociological study of religion is no threat to anyone's faith. Sociologists recognize that religion is central to virtually every culture on earth, and they seek to understand how religious beliefs and practices guide human societies. As sociologists, they cannot comment on the meaning and purpose of human existence or pass judgment on any religion as right or wrong. Rather, scientific sociology takes a more "worldly" approach by delving into why religions take particular forms in one society or another and how religious activity affects society as a whole.

THEORETICAL ANALYSIS OF RELIGION

Although, as individuals, sociologists may hold any number of religious beliefs—or none at all—they agree that religion plays a major part in the operation of society. Each theoretical paradigm suggests ways in which religion shapes social life.

FUNCTIONS OF RELIGION: STRUCTURAL-FUNCTIONAL ANALYSIS

According to Emile Durkheim (1965; orig. 1915), people engage in religious life to celebrate the awesome power of their society. Doesn't society, he asked, *have* an awesome power and an existence of its own beyond the life of any individual? Thus, some form of religion is found everywhere because society itself is "godlike." No wonder, too, that people in all societies transform certain everyday objects into sacred symbols of their collective life. Members of technologically simple societies, Durkheim explained, do this with the **totem,** *an object in the natural world collectively defined as sacred.* The totem—perhaps an animal or an elaborate work of art—becomes the centerpiece of ritual, symbolizing the power of collective life over any individual. In our society, the flag is a quasi-sacred totem. It is not to be used in a profane manner (say, as clothing) or allowed to touch the ground. In addition, putting the inscription "In God We Trust" on all currency (a practice begun in

DISCUSS: Is the naming of sports teams an element of totemic symbolism in the United States? Honoring ancestors: Washington Redskins, Cleveland Indians, Atlanta Braves, Kansas City Chiefs, Pittsburgh Pirates, Dallas Cowboys, Philadelphia 76ers; honoring animals: Denver Broncos, Miami Dolphins, Detroit Tigers, Chicago Cubs, Baltimore Orioles.

Q: "In everyday life it is just as important that some things can be silently taken for granted as that some things are reaffirmed in so many words. Indeed, the most fundamental assumptions about the world . . . are so 'obvious' that there is no need to put them into words." Peter Berger
Q: "We are not human beings on a spiritual journey; we are spiritual beings on a human journey." Stephen Covey

the 1860s at the time of the Civil War) implies a national bond of religious belief. Local communities across the United States also gain a sense of unity through totemic symbolism attached to sports teams: from the New England "Patriots," to the Ohio State University "Buckeyes," to the Los Angeles "Rams."

Why is the religious dimension of social life so important? Durkheim pointed out three major functions of religion:

1. **Social cohesion.** The shared symbols, values, and norms of religion unite people. Religious doctrine and ritual establish rules of "fair play" that make organized social life possible. Religion also involves *love* and *commitment*, which underscore both our moral and emotional ties to others (Wright & D'Antonio, 1980).

2. **Social control.** Every society uses religious imagery and rhetoric to promote conformity. Societies give many cultural norms—especially mores that deal with marriage and reproduction—religious justification. Religion even legitimizes the political system. In medieval Europe, in fact, monarchs claimed to rule by divine right. Few of today's political leaders invoke religion so explicitly, but many publicly ask for God's blessing, implying to audiences that their efforts are right and just.

3. **Providing meaning and purpose.** Religious belief offers the comforting sense that the vulnerable human condition serves some greater purpose. Strengthened by such conviction, people are less likely to despair when confronted by life's calamities. For this reason, major life-course transitions—including birth, marriage, and death—are usually marked by religious observances that enhance our spiritual awareness.

Critical evaluation. In Durkheim's structural-functional analysis, religion represents the collective life of society. The major weakness of this approach, however, is that it downplays religion's dysfunctions—especially the fact that strongly held beliefs can generate social conflict. During the early Middle Ages, for example, religious faith was the driving force behind the Crusades, in which European Christians battled Muslims for the Holy Lands that both religions considered to be sacred. Conflict among Muslims, Jews, and Christians is still a source of political instability in the Middle East today. Similarly, tensions continue to divide Protestants and Catholics in Northern Ireland; Dutch Calvinism historically supported apartheid in South Africa; and religious conflict persists in Algeria, India,

Sri Lanka, and elsewhere. In short, many nations have marched to war under the banner of their god, and few analysts dispute that differences in faith have provoked more violence in the world than have differences of social class.

CONSTRUCTING THE SACRED: SYMBOLIC-INTERACTION ANALYSIS

"Society," says Peter Berger (1967:3) "is a human product and nothing but a human product, that yet continuously acts back upon its producer." In other words, from a symbolic-interaction point of view, religion (like all of society) is socially constructed (although perhaps with divine inspiration). Through various rituals—from daily prayers to annual religious observances like Easter or Passover—individuals sharpen the distinction between the sacred and profane. Further, Berger explains, by placing everyday events within a "cosmic frame of reference," people give their fallible, transitory creations "the semblance of ultimate security and permanence" (1967:35–36).

Marriage serves as a good example. If two people look on marriage as merely a legal contract between them, they can end the marriage whenever they want to. But defined as holy matrimony, their relationship makes far stronger claims on them. This fact, no doubt, explains why the divorce rate is lower among people who are more religious.

Especially when humans confront uncertainty and life-threatening situations—such as illness, war, and natural disaster—we turn to religion. Seeking sacred meaning helps people recover from life's setbacks and even have courage at the prospect of death.

Critical evaluation. The symbolic-interaction approach views religion as a social construction, placing everyday life under a "sacred canopy" of meaning (Berger, 1967). Of course, Berger adds, religion's ability to legitimize and stabilize society depends on its constructed character going unrecognized. After all, we would derive little strength from sacred beliefs that we saw as strategies for coping with tragedy. Then, too, this micro-level view ignores religion's part in maintaining social inequality, to which we now turn.

INEQUALITY AND RELIGION: SOCIAL-CONFLICT ANALYSIS

The social-conflict paradigm highlights religion's support of social hierarchy. Religion, claimed Karl Marx,

Q: "The more of himself man attributes to God, the less he has left in himself." Karl Marx

Q: "[Rationalization] means that principally there are no mysterious, incalculable forces that come into play, but rather that one can, in principle, master all things by calculation." Max Weber

RESOURCE: An excerpt from Max Weber's *The Protestant Ethic and the Spirit of Capitalism* is among the classics included in the Macionis and Benokraitis reader, *Seeing Ourselves*.

Q: ". . . Established religious institutions have generally had a stake in the status quo and hence have fostered conservatism. . . . On the other hand, as the source of both humanistic values and the strength that can come from believing one is carrying out God's will in political matters, religion has occasionally played a role in movements for radical social change." Gary T. Marx

The foundation of all religious life is ritual. Formal religious observances, such as this Buddhist ceremony in Seoul, South Korea, reveal the discipline needed in order to live out religious principles.

serves ruling elites by legitimizing the status quo and diverting people's attention from social inequities.

Even today, for example, the British monarch is the nominal head of the Church of England, illustrating the close alliance between religious and political elites. In practical terms, working for political change may mean opposing the church and, by implication, God. Religion also encourages people to look with hope to a "better world to come," minimizing the social problems of this world. In one of his best-known statements, Marx offered a stinging criticism of religion as "the sigh of the oppressed creature, the sentiment of a heartless world, and the soul of soulless conditions. It is the opium of the people" (1964:27; orig. 1848).

Religion and social inequality are also linked through gender. Virtually all the world's major religions reflect and encourage male dominance in social life, as the box explains.

During Marx's lifetime, powerful Christian nations of Western Europe justified the conquest of Africa, the Americas, and Asia by claiming that they were "converting heathens." In the United States, churches in the South viewed enslaving African Americans as consistent with God's will. Moreover, churches across the country remain segregated to this day. In the words of African American novelist Maya Angelou, "Sunday at 11:30 A.M., America is more segregated than at any time of the week."

Critical evaluation. Social-conflict analysis reveals the power of religion to legitimize social inequality. Yet critics of religion, Marx included, minimize the ways religion has promoted both change and equality. Nineteenth-century religious groups in the United States, for example, were at the forefront of the movement to abolish slavery. During the 1950s and 1960s, religious organizations and their leaders (including the Reverend Martin Luther King, Jr.) were at the core of the Civil Rights movement. During the 1960s and 1970s, many clergy actively opposed the Vietnam War, and, as explained presently, some have supported revolutionary change in Latin America and elsewhere.

RELIGION AND SOCIAL CHANGE

Religion is not just the conservative force portrayed by Karl Marx. At some points in history, as Max Weber (1958; orig. 1904–5) explained, religion has promoted dramatic social transformation.

MAX WEBER: PROTESTANTISM AND CAPITALISM

Max Weber contended that new ideas are often the engines of change. It was the religious doctrine of Calvinism, for example, that sparked the Industrial Revolution in Western Europe.

As Chapter 4 ("Society") explains in detail, John Calvin (1509–1564), a leader in the Protestant Reformation, preached the doctrine of predestination. According to Calvin, an all-powerful and all-knowing God predestined some people for salvation and condemned most to eternal damnation. With each individual's fate sealed

SOCIAL SURVEY: "Where would you place your image of God on the scale [between (1) Mother and (7) Father]?" (GSS 1996, N = 991; *Codebook*, 1996:129)

(1) 3.6%   (4) 23.3%   (7) 47.1%
(2) 1.4%   (5) 9.4%   DK/NR 4.6%
(3) 2.2%   (6) 8.3%

NOTE: The movement of women into the clergy has lagged behind their entry into law and medicine (Chaves, 1996).
DIVERSITY: The proportion of women serving as clergy in Protestant denominations ranges from 14% for Presbyterians to 35% for Unitarians.
Q: "Christianity might be a good thing if anyone ever tried it." George Bernard Shaw

SOCIAL DIVERSITY

Religion and Patriarchy: Does God Favor Males?

Why do two-thirds of U.S. adults envision God in primarily or exclusively male terms (NORC, 1996:129)? Probably because we link "godly" attributes such as wisdom and power to men. Thus, it is hardly surprising that organized religions tend to favor males, a fact evident in passages from many of the sacred writings of major world religions.

The Qur'an (Koran)—the sacred text of Islam—declares that men are to dominate women:

> Men are in charge of women. . . . Hence good women are obedient . . . As for those whose rebelliousness you fear, admonish them, banish them from your bed, and scourge them. (quoted in Kaufman, 1976:163)

Christianity—the major religion of the Western world—also supports patriarchy. While many Christians revere Mary, the mother of Jesus, the New Testament also includes the following passages:

> A man . . . is the image and glory of God; but woman is the glory of man. For man was not made from woman, but woman from man. Neither was man created for woman, but woman for man. (1 Cor. 11:7–9)

As in all the churches of the saints, the women should keep silence in the churches. For they are not permitted to speak, but should be subordinate, as even the law says. If there is anything they desire to know, let them ask their husbands at home. For it is shameful for a woman to speak in church. (1 Cor. 14:33–35)

> Wives, be subject to your husbands, as to the Lord. For the husband is the head of the wife as Christ is the head of the church. . . . As the church is subject to Christ, so let wives also be subject in everything to their husbands. (Eph. 5:22–24)

> Let a woman learn in silence with all submissiveness. I permit no woman to teach or to have authority over men; she is to keep silent. For Adam was formed first, then Eve; and Adam was not deceived, but the woman was deceived and became a transgressor. Yet woman will be saved through bearing children, if she continues in faith and love and holiness, with modesty. (1 Tm. 2:11–15)

Judaism, too, traditionally supports patriarchy. Male Orthodox Jews say the following words in daily prayer:

> Blessed art thou, O Lord our God, King of the Universe, that I was not born a gentile.

> Blessed art thou, O Lord our God, King of the Universe, that I was not born a slave.

> Blessed art thou, O Lord our God, King of the Universe, that I was not born a woman.

Major religions are also patriarchal in historically excluding women from the clergy. Even today, Islam and the Roman Catholic church ban women from the priesthood. But a growing number of Protestant denominations—including the Church of England—ordain women, who now represent 10 percent of U.S. clergy (Chaves, 1996). Orthodox Judaism upholds the traditional prohibition against women serving as rabbis, but Reform and Conservative Judaism look to both men and women as spiritual leaders. Across the United States, the proportion of women in seminaries has never been higher (now roughly one-third), further evidence that change is only a matter of time.

Challenges to the patriarchal structure of organized religion—from ordaining women to gender-neutral language in hymns and prayers—has sparked heated controversy, delighting progressives while outraging traditionalists. Propelling these developments is a lively feminism in many religious communities. According to feminist Christians, for example, patriarchy in the church stands in stark contrast to the largely feminine image of Jesus Christ in the Scriptures as "nonaggressive, noncompetitive, meek and humble of heart, a nurturer of the weak and a friend of the outcast" (Sandra Schneiders, quoted in Woodward, 1989:61).

Feminists argue that, unless traditional notions of gender are removed from our understanding of God, women will never be equal to men in the church. Theologian Mary Daly puts the matter bluntly: "If God is male, then male is God" (quoted in Woodward, 1989:58).

DISCUSS: Do the following two pronouncements of the Roman Catholic church favor Marxism or market capitalism?
Q: "The needs of the poor must take priority over the desires of the rich; and the rights of workers over the maximization of profits." John Paul II
Q: ". . . In today's world . . . the right of economic initiative is often suppressed. Yet it is a right which is important not only for the individual but for the common good. Experience shows that the denial of this right, or its limitation in the name of alleged 'equality' of everyone in society, diminishes, or in practice absolutely destroys the spirit of initiative . . ." John Paul II
NOTE: Churches, with formally ordained (rather than charismatic) leaders, exemplify the routinization of charisma that, as Simmel might have said, favors form over content.

even before birth and known only to God, the only certainty is what hangs in the balance: eternal glory or hellfire.

Understandably anxious about their fate, Calvinists sought signs of God's favor in *this* world and gradually came to regard prosperity as a symbol of divine blessing. This conviction, and a rigid sense of duty, led Calvinists to work all the time, and many amassed great riches. But wealth was never to fuel self-indulgent spending or for sharing with the poor, whose plight Calvinists saw as a mark of God's rejection.

As agents of God's work on earth, Calvinists believed that they best fulfilled their "calling" by reinvesting profits and reaping ever-greater success in the process. All the while, they were thrifty and eagerly embraced technological advances that would enhance their efforts. Driven by religious motives, then, they laid the groundwork for the rise of industrial capitalism. In time, the religious fervor that motivated early Calvinists evaporated, leaving a profane Protestant "work ethic." In this sense, concluded Weber, industrial capitalism amounts to a "disenchanted" religion. Weber's analysis clearly demonstrates the power of religious thinking to alter the basic shape of society.

LIBERATION THEOLOGY

Christianity has a long-standing concern for poor and oppressed people, urging all to strengthen their faith in a better life to come. In recent decades, however, some church leaders and theologians have embraced **liberation theology,** *a fusion of Christian principles with political activism, often Marxist in character.*

This social movement started in the late 1960s in Latin America's Roman Catholic church. Today, in addition to the church's spiritual work, Christian activists are helping people in the least-developed countries to liberate themselves from abysmal poverty. The message of liberation theology is simple: Social oppression runs counter to Christian morality and is also preventable. Therefore, as a matter of faith and social justice, Christians must promote greater social equality.

A growing number of Catholic men and women have taken up the cause of the poor in the liberation theology movement. The cost of opposing the status quo, however, has been high. Many church members—including Oscar Arnulfo Romero, the archbishop of San Salvador (the capital of El Salvador)—have been killed for seeking political change.

Liberation theology has also divided the Catholic community. Pope John Paul II condemns the movement for distorting traditional church doctrine with left-wing politics. But, despite the pontiff's objections, the liberation theology movement has become powerful in Latin America, where many people find their Christian faith drives them to improve conditions for the world's poor (Boff, 1984; Neuhouser, 1989).

TYPES OF RELIGIOUS ORGANIZATION

Sociologists categorize the hundreds of different religious organizations that exist in the United States along a continuum, with *churches* at one end and *sects* at the other. We can describe any actual religious organization, then, in relation to these two ideal types by locating it on the church-sect continuum.

CHURCH AND SECT

Drawing on the ideas of his teacher Max Weber, Ernst Troeltsch (1931) defined a **church** as *a type of religious organization well integrated into the larger society.* Churchlike organizations usually persist for centuries and include generations of the same family. Churches have well-established rules and regulations and expect their leaders to be formally trained and ordained.

While concerned with the sacred, a church accepts the ways of the profane world, which gives it broad appeal. Church doctrine conceives of God in highly intellectualized terms (say, as a force for good), and favors abstract moral standards ("Do unto others as you would have them do unto you") over specific rules for day-to-day living. By teaching morality in safely abstract terms, a church can avoid social controversy. For example, many churches that, in principle, celebrate the unity of all peoples have, in practice, all-white memberships. Such duality minimizes conflict between a church and political life (Troeltsch, 1931).

December 11, 1994, Casablanca, Morocco. The waves of the Atlantic crash along the walls of Casablanca's magnificent coastline mosque, reputedly the largest in the world. From the top of the towering structure, a green laser points eastward toward Mecca, the holy city of Islam, toward which the faithful bow in prayer. To pay for this monumental house of worship, King Hassam II, Morocco's head of state and religious leader, levied a tax on every citizen in his realm, all of whom

Q: "A permanent danger of an established church . . . is that a national church might become a nationalistic church." T. S. Eliot

GLOBAL: Some members of a society with an ecclesia see denominations as chaotic: "If Protestantism is a true religion," one Moroccan commented, "why do you Americans have hundreds of denominations?"

GLOBAL: Illustrating the operation of an ecclesia, the capital city

of Pakistan is Islamabad ("City of Islam").

GLOBAL: In Japan, the emperor has traditionally been the head priest of the Shinto religion.

GLOBAL: The Church of Sweden (the Lutheran Church) counts all Swedes among its members, unless they officially withdraw from it. The state owns and controls church property and pays clergy as state employees.

In global perspective, the range of human religious activity is truly astonishing. Members of this Christian cult in the Latin American nation of Guatemala observe Good Friday by vaulting over a roaring fire, an expression of their faith that God will protect them.

`are officially Muslim. Our notion of the separation of church and state sharply contrasts to this "government religion."`

A church generally takes one of two forms. Islam in Morocco represents an **ecclesia,** *a church formally allied with the state.* Ecclesias have been common in history; for centuries Roman Catholicism was the state religion of the Roman Empire, as was Confucianism in China until early in the twentieth century. Today, the Anglican Church is the official Church of England, as Islam is the official religion of Pakistan and Iran. State churches count everyone in a society as members; tolerance of religious difference, therefore, is severely limited.

A **denomination,** by contrast, is *a church, independent of the state, that accepts religious pluralism.* Denominations exist in nations that formally separate church and state, such as ours. The United States has dozens of Christian denominations—including Catholics, Baptists, Methodists, and Lutherans—as well as various categories of Judaism and other traditions. While members of a denomination hold to their own beliefs, they recognize the right of others to disagree.

The second general religious form is the **sect,** *a type of religious organization that stands apart from the larger society.* Sect members hold rigidly to their religious convictions and discount the beliefs of others. In extreme cases, members of a sect may withdraw completely from society in order to practice their religion without interference from outsiders. The Amish are one example of a

North American sect that isolates itself (Kraybill, 1994). Since our culture views religious tolerance as a virtue, members of sects are sometimes accused of being narrow-minded in their insistence that they alone follow the true religion (Stark & Bainbridge, 1979).

In organizational terms, sects are less formal than churches. Thus, sect members may be highly spontaneous and emotional in worship, while members of churches tend to listen passively to their leader. Sects also reject the intellectualized religion of churches, stressing instead the personal experience of divine power. Rodney Stark (1985:314) contrasts a church's vision of a distant God—"Our Father, who art in Heaven"—with a sect's more immediate God—"Lord, bless this poor sinner kneeling before you now."

A further distinction between church and sect turns on patterns of leadership. The more churchlike an organization, the more likely that its leaders are formally trained and ordained. Sectlike organizations, which celebrate the personal presence of God, expect their leaders to exhibit divine inspiration in the form of **charisma** (from Greek meaning "divine favor"), *extraordinary personal qualities that can turn an audience into followers,* infusing them with an emotional experience.

Sects generally form as breakaway groups from established churches or other religious organizations (Stark & Bainbridge, 1979). Their psychic intensity and informal structure render them less stable than churches, and many sects blossom only to disappear a short time later. The sects that do endure typically

DISCUSS: Are "Deadheads" a cult? Following the death of Jerry Garcia in 1995, the news media compared the musician to a priest or god and his band to a church.
Q: "In societies under stress, there is a strong tendency for new cults to arise." Felicitas Goodman
GLOBAL: Similar to the Heaven's Gate suicides, since 1994, 74 members of the Order of the Solar Temple have killed themselves in Canada, Switzerland, and France. Some analysts point out that the approach of the year 2000 has stimulated cult formation around the world.
NOTE: Because animistic peoples perceive the entire world as "enchanted," it may be said that they do not distinguish between the sacred and the secular.
Q: "No man has a body distinct from his soul." William Blake

become more like churches, losing fervor as they become more bureaucratic and established.

To sustain their membership, many sects actively recruit, or *proselytize*, new members. Sects highly value the experience of *conversion*, a personal transformation or religious rebirth. Jehovah's Witnesses, for example, eagerly share their faith with others in hopes of attracting new members.

Finally, churches and sects differ in their social composition. Because they are more closely tied to the world, well-established churches tend to include people of high social standing. Sects, by contrast, attract more disadvantaged people. A sect's openness to new members and promise of salvation and personal fulfillment appeal to people who may perceive themselves as social outsiders.

CULT

A **cult** is *a religious organization that is substantially outside a society's cultural traditions.* Whereas a sect breaks off from a conventional religious organization, a cult represents something mostly new. Cults typically form around a highly charismatic leader who offers a compelling message of a new way of life. As many as 5,000 cults now exist in the United States (Marquand & Wood, 1997).

Because some cult principles or practices may seem unconventional, the popular view is that they are deviant or even evil. The suicides of thirty-nine members of California's Heaven's Gate cult in 1997—people who claimed that dying was a doorway to a higher existence, perhaps in the company of aliens from outer space—confirmed the negative image the public holds of most cults. In short, according to some scholars, calling any religious community a "cult" amounts to dismissing its members as crazy (Richardson, 1990; Gleick, 1997).

This view of cults is unfortunate because there is nothing intrinsically wrong with this kind of religious organization. Many long-standing religions—Christianity, Islam, and Judaism included—began as cults. Of course, not all or even most cults exist for very long. One reason is that they are even more at odds with the larger society than sects. Many cults demand that members not only accept their doctrine but embrace a radically new lifestyle. Such lifestyle changes sometimes prompt others to accuse cults of brainwashing their members, although research suggests that most people who join cults experience no psychological harm (Barker, 1981; Kilbourne, 1983).

RELIGION IN HISTORY

Religion shapes every society of the world. And, like other social institutions, religion shows considerable variation both historically and cross-culturally.

RELIGION IN PREINDUSTRIAL SOCIETIES

Religion predates written history. Archaeological evidence indicates that our human ancestors performed religious rituals some 40,000 years ago.

Early hunters and gatherers embraced **animism** (from Latin meaning "the breath of life"), *the belief that elements of the natural world are conscious life forms that affect humanity.* Animistic people view forests, oceans, mountains, even the wind as spiritual forces. Many Native American societies are animistic, which accounts for their historical reverence for the natural environment. Hunters and gatherers conduct their religious life entirely within the family. Members of such societies may single out someone as a *shaman* with special religious skills, but there are no full-time, specialized religious leaders.

Belief in a single divine power responsible for creating the world arose with pastoral and horticultural societies. We can trace our society's conception of God as a "shepherd," directly involved in the world's well-being, to the roots of Christianity, Judaism, and Islam, whose original followers were all pastoral peoples.

As societies develop more productive capacity, religious life expands beyond the family, and priests take their place among other specialized workers. In agrarian societies, religion becomes more important, evident in the huge medieval cathedrals in town centers throughout Europe.

RELIGION IN INDUSTRIAL SOCIETIES

The Industrial Revolution ushered in science as a way of knowing. More and more, people looked to physicians and scientists for the knowledge and comfort they had sought from religious leaders.

Even so, religious thought persists simply because science is powerless to address issues of ultimate meaning in human life. In other words, learning *how* the world works is a matter for scientists; but *why* we and the rest of the universe exist is a question about which science has nothing to say. Science may improve our material lives, but religion is uniquely suited to address the spiritual dimension of human existence.

Q: "To be mistaken in believing that the Christian religion is true is no great loss to anyone; but how dreadful to be mistaken in believing it to be false!" Blaise Pascal (1623–1662)
GLOBAL: The fact that Christians and Jews live in so many societies reflects the missionary work of the former and the frequent expulsion of the latter.
NOTE: Although Judaism and Christianity are both monotheistic

religions, they may have polytheistic origins. In the original Hebrew, the accounts of creation in Genesis used plural pronouns ("Then God said, Let us make man in our image . . ." 1:26), leading scholars to speculate that the religion evolved from polytheistic roots.
GLOBAL: Singapore bans Jehovah's Witnesses as disruptive; in 1995, that government seized 66 of the sect's Bibles.

In this outstanding example of U.S. folk art, Anna Bell Lee Washington's Baptism 3 *(1924) depicts the life-changing experience by which many people enter the Christian faith.*

WORLD RELIGIONS

The diversity of religious expression in the world is almost as wide-ranging as the diversity of culture itself. Many of the thousands of different religions are highly localized with few followers. *World religions*, by contrast, are widely known and have millions of adherents. We shall briefly describe six world religions, which together claim some 4 billion believers—almost three-fourths of humanity.

CHRISTIANITY

Christianity is the most widespread religion, with 2 billion followers, roughly one-third of the world's people. Most Christians live in Europe or the Americas; more than 85 percent of people in the United States and Canada identify with Christianity. Moreover, as shown in Global Map 18–1 on page 490, people who are at least nominally Christian represent a large share of the population in many other regions, with the notable exceptions of northern Africa and Asia. European colonization spread Christianity throughout much of the world over the last 500 years. Its dominance in the West is shown by the fact that the calendar begins with the birth of Christ.

Christianity originated as a cult, incorporating elements of its much older predecessor, Judaism. Like

many cults, Christianity was propelled by the personal charisma of a leader, Jesus of Nazareth, who preached a message of personal salvation. Jesus did not directly challenge the political powers of his day, admonishing his followers to "Render therefore to Caesar the things that are Caesar's" (Matt. 22:21). But his message was revolutionary, nonetheless, promising that faith and love would triumph over sin and death.

Christianity is one example of **monotheism,** *belief in a single divine power,* and it thus broke with the Roman Empire's traditional **polytheism,** *belief in many gods.* Yet Christianity has a unique vision of the Supreme Being as a sacred Trinity: God the Creator; Jesus Christ, Son of God and Redeemer; and the Holy Spirit, a Christian's personal experience of God's presence.

The claim that Jesus was divine rests on accounts of his final days on earth. Tried and sentenced to death in Jerusalem on charges that he was a threat to established political leaders, Jesus was executed by crucifixion. The cross therefore became a sacred Christian symbol. According to Christian belief, three days later Jesus arose from the dead, showing that he was the Son of God.

Jesus's apostles spread Christianity throughout the Mediterranean region. Although the Roman Empire initially persecuted Christians, by the fourth century Christianity had become an ecclesia—the official

NOTE: Literal interpretation of the sacred texts of any religion sharply limits debate among adherents about religious truth, thereby fostering consensus. But literal readings may still reveal inconsistencies; there are, for example, *two* creation stories in Genesis.

SUPPLEMENTS: The *Data File* examines the traditional Muslim practice of women wearing veils in the context of the changing role of women in Saudi Arabian society.

DIVERSITY: Muslims hold the Qur'an (Koran) to be the *literal* words of God. For this reason, even translation from Arabic into other languages raises fears of distortion.

RESOURCE: The article by Jane I. Smith, "Women and Islam," is among the cross-cultural selections found in the *Seeing Ourselves* reader.

WINDOW ON THE WORLD

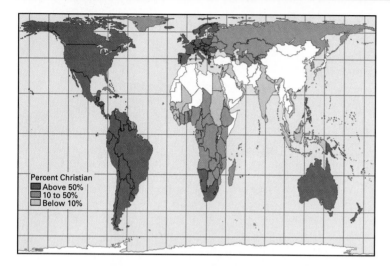

GLOBAL MAP 18–1
Christianity in Global Perspective

Source: *Peters Atlas of the World* (1990).

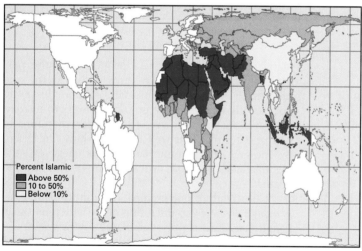

GLOBAL MAP 18–2
Islam in Global Perspective

Source: *Peters Atlas of the World* (1990).

religion of what then became known as the Holy Roman Empire. What had begun as a cult four centuries before was now an established church.

Christianity took various forms, including the Roman Catholic church and the Orthodox church, based in Constantinople (now Istanbul, Turkey). Toward the end of the Middle Ages, the Protestant Reformation in Europe created hundreds of new denominations. Dozens of these denominations—the Baptists and Methodists are the two largest—now command sizable followings in the United States (Smart, 1969; Kaufman, 1976; Jacquet & Jones, 1991).

ISLAM

Islam has some 1.1 billion followers (about 20 percent of humanity); followers of Islam are called Muslims. A majority of people in the Middle East are Muslims, which explains our tendency to associate Islam with Arabs in that region of the world. But most Muslims live elsewhere; Global Map 18–2 shows that most people in northern Africa and western Asia are also Muslims. Moreover, significant concentrations of Muslims are found in Pakistan, India, Bangladesh, Indonesia, and the southern republics of

GLOBAL: Note that religion is a less-pronounced element of U.S. culture than it is in an officially Islamic society such as Morocco. (The U.S. is more like Turkey, which has no official religion and, although 98% of the population is Muslim, many are not actively religious.)

SUPPLEMENTS: The *Data File* explores how economic success among Jews in the U.S. may be weakening Jewish ethnic identity

and religious cohesion.

GLOBAL: According to the Israeli Central Bureau of Statistics, Israeli Jews represent 27% of world Jewry. About 45% of all Jews live in North America.

NOTE: Jews also look to the Talmud [composed of the Mishnah (text) and Gemara (commentary)] for explicit guidance in everyday life.

the former Soviet Union. Although representing a small share of the population, Muslims in North America number between 5 and 10 million (Roudi, 1988; Weeks, 1988; University of Akron Research Center, 1993).

Islam is the word of God as revealed to the prophet Muhammad, who was born in the city of Mecca (now in Saudi Arabia) about the year 570. To Muslims, Muhammad is a prophet, not a divine being as Jesus is to Christians. The Qur'an (Koran), sacred to Muslims, is the word of God (in Arabic, "Allah") as transmitted through Muhammad, God's messenger. In Arabic, the word Islam means both "submission" and "peace," and the Qur'an urges submission to Allah as the path to inner peace. Muslims express this personal devotion in a daily ritual of five prayers.

Islam spread rapidly after the death of Muhammad, although divisions arose, as they did within Christianity. All Muslims, however, accept the Five Pillars of Islam: (1) recognizing Allah as the one, true God, and Muhammad as God's messenger; (2) ritual prayer; (3) giving alms to the poor; (4) fasting during the month of Ramadan; and (5) making a pilgrimage once to the Sacred House of Allah in Mecca (Weeks, 1988; El-Attar, 1991). Like Christianity, Islam holds people accountable to God for their deeds on earth. Those who live obediently will be rewarded in heaven, while evil-doers will suffer unending punishment.

Muslims are also obligated to defend their faith, which has led to holy wars against unbelievers (in roughly the same way that medieval Christians fought in the Crusades). Recently, in Algeria, Egypt, Iran, and elsewhere, some Muslims have sought to rid their society of Western influences that they regard as morally wrong (Martin, 1982; Arjomand, 1988).

To many Westerners, Muslim women are among the most socially oppressed people on earth. Muslim women do lack many of the personal freedoms enjoyed by Muslim men, yet many—and perhaps most—accept the mandates of their religion and find security in a rigid system that guides the behavior of both women and men (Peterson, 1996). Moreover, patriarchy was well established in the Middle East long before the birth of Muhammad. Some defenders argue that Islam actually improved the social position of women by demanding that husbands deal justly with their wives. Further, although Islam permits a man to have up to four wives, it admonishes men to have only one wife if having more would cause him to treat any woman unjustly (Qur'an, "The Women," v. 3).

Followers of Islam reverently remove their shoes—which touch the profane ground—before entering this sacred mosque in the Southeast Asian nation of Brunei.

JUDAISM

In terms of simple numbers, Judaism's 14 million followers worldwide makes it something less than a world religion. Moreover, only in Israel do Jews represent a national majority. But Judaism has special significance to the United States because the largest concentration of Jews (6 million people) is found in North America.

Jews look to the past as a source of guidance in the present and for the future. And Judaism has deep historical roots that extend some 4,000 years before the birth of Christ to the ancient cultures of Mesopotamia. At this time, Jews were animistic; but this belief changed after Jacob—grandson of Abraham, the earliest great ancestor—led his people to Egypt.

Jews endured centuries of slavery in Egypt. In the thirteenth century B.C.E., a turning point came as Moses, the adopted son of an Egyptian princess, was called by God to lead the Jews from bondage. This exodus (this word's Latin and Greek roots mean "a marching out") from Egypt is commemorated by Jews today in the annual ritual of Passover. Once liberated, Jews became monotheistic, recognizing a single, all-powerful God.

A distinctive concept of Judaism is the *covenant*, a special relationship with God by which Jews became

NOTE: As members of many religions have done, the ancient Hebrews distinguished between the sacred and the secular through practices such as keeping the Sabbath, dietary restrictions, and maintaining holy places.

Q: "There is only one religion, although there are a hundred versions of it." George Bernard Shaw

NOTE: Although people in the United States associate the word "ghetto" with people of color, the word was first used to describe a section of medieval Venice in which Jews were segregated.

NOTE: The precise meaning of *Semite* is a person with ancestral roots in southwest Asia, including both Arabs and Jews. In the United States, however, people commonly use the term to refer only to Jews.

When Western people perform religious rituals they typically do so collectively and formally as members of specific congregations. Eastern people, by contrast, visit shrines individually and informally, without joining a specific congregation. For this reason, Asian temples such as this one in Hong Kong, shown above, receive a steady flow of people—families praying, individuals engaged in business, and foreign tourists just watching—that seems somehow inappropriate to the Western visitor.

the "chosen people." The covenant also implies a duty to observe God's law, especially the Ten Commandments as revealed to Moses on Mount Sinai. Jews regard the Old Testament of the Bible as both a record of their history and a statement of the obligations of Jewish life. Of special importance are the Bible's first five books (Genesis, Exodus, Leviticus, Numbers, and Deuteronomy), designated as the *Torah* (a word roughly meaning "teaching" and "law"). In contrast to Christianity's central concern with personal salvation, therefore, Judaism emphasizes moral behavior in this world.

Judaism is composed of three main denominations. Orthodox Jews (including more than 1 million people in the United States) strictly observe traditional beliefs and practices, wear traditional dress, segregate men and women at religious services, and eat only kosher foods. Such traditional practices set off Orthodox Jews in the United States as the most sect-like. In the mid-nineteenth century, many Jews sought greater acceptance by the larger society, leading to the formation of more churchlike Reform Judaism (now including more than 1.3 million people in this country). A third segment, Conservative Judaism (with about 2 million adherents), has since established a middle ground between the other two denominations.

Whatever their denomination, Jews share a cultural history of prejudice and discrimination. A collective memory of centuries of slavery in Egypt, conquest by Rome, and persecution in Europe have shaped Jewish identity. It was Jews in Italy who first lived in an urban ghetto (derived from the Italian word *borghetto*, meaning "settlement outside of the city walls"), and this form of residential segregation soon spread to other parts of Europe.

Jewish immigration to the United States began in the mid-1600s. Many early immigrants prospered, and many were also assimilated into largely Christian communities. But as larger numbers entered the country towards the end of the nineteenth century, prejudice and discrimination against them—commonly termed *anti-Semitism*—increased. During World War II, anti-Semitism reached a vicious peak as the Nazi regime in Germany systematically annihilated 6 million Jews.

Today, many Jews are concerned about the future of their religion, but for a different reason: During the 1990s, more than 50 percent of Jews are marrying non-Jews. In only a few cases are non-Jewish spouses converting to Judaism. Just as significantly, about half the children raised in Jewish households are not learning Jewish culture and ritual. For the present, such patterns symbolize Jewish success and acceptance. At the same time, however, they cast some doubt on the future of Judaism in North America (Bedell, Sandon, & Wellborn, 1975; Holm, 1977; Schmidt, 1980; Seltzer, 1980; B. Wilson, 1982; Eisen, 1983; Dershowitz, 1997; Van Biema, 1997).

HINDUISM

Hinduism is the oldest of all the world religions, originating in the Indus River Valley about 4,500 years ago. Hindus number some 793 million (14 percent of humanity). Global Map 18–3 shows that Hinduism remains an Eastern religion, predominantly practiced in India and Pakistan, but with a significant presence in southern Africa and Indonesia.

Over the centuries, Hinduism and Indian culture have become intertwined, so that now one is not easily described apart from the other. This connection also explains why Hinduism, unlike Christianity, Islam, and Judaism, has not diffused widely to other

DIVERSITY: More than half of Jewish men and women who have married since 1985 have gentile spouses. What are the consequences of this trend for this religion's future?

NOTE: Jewish assimilation into U.S. society can be seen in the declining concentration of Jews in the Northeast: from 68% in 1930 to 44% in 1990. Another index of religious assimilation: About 55% of U.S. Jews now marry non-Jews.

GLOBAL: One could say that, to the Hindu, nothing is sacred or everything is sacred.

NOTE: The diffusion of religious elements is usually selective. For instance, in the 1960s, many young people in the United States adopted the Hindu concepts of *dharma* (fate) and *karma* (spiritual progression of souls), while scorning the caste system historically associated with Hinduism.

WINDOW ON THE WORLD

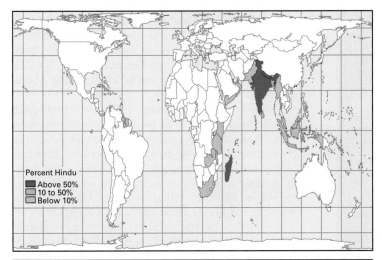

GLOBAL MAP 18–3
Hinduism in Global Perspective

Source: *Peters Atlas of the World* (1990).

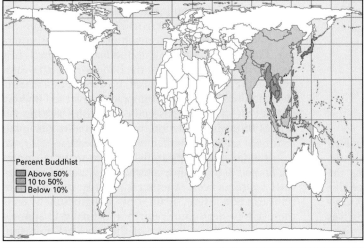

GLOBAL MAP 18–4
Buddhism in Global Perspective

Source: *Peters Atlas of the World* (1990).

nations. Nevertheless, with 1.4 million followers in the United States, Hinduism is a significant part of this country's cultural diversity.

Hinduism differs from most other religions by not being linked to the life of any single person. Hinduism also has no sacred writings comparable to the Bible or the Qur'an. Nor does Hinduism envision God as a specific entity. For this reason, Hinduism—like other Eastern religions, as we shall see—is sometimes described as an "ethical religion." Hindu beliefs and practices vary widely, but all Hindus recognize a moral force in the universe that presents everyone with responsibilities, termed *dharma*. Dharma, for example,

calls people to observe the traditional caste system, described in Chapter 9 ("Social Stratification").

Another Hindu principle, *karma*, is a belief in the spiritual progress of the human soul. To a Hindu, all actions have spiritual consequences, and proper living contributes to moral development. Karma works through *reincarnation*, a cycle of death and rebirth, by which the individual is reborn into a spiritual state corresponding to the moral quality of a previous life. Unlike Christianity and Islam, Hinduism proclaims no ultimate judgment at the hands of a supreme god, although in the cycle of rebirth, people reap exactly what they have sown. *Moksha* is the sublime state of

DIVERSITY: By 1990, chaplains in the U.S. armed forces represented 105 religious organizations, including one Buddhist chaplain (some 2,500 military personnel are adherents of this religion).
NOTE: Buddhism's "eightfold path" to enlightenment includes: proper views, resolve, speech, action, livelihood, effort, mindfulness, and concentration.

GLOBAL: Eastern religions—Buddhism, Hinduism, Confucianism, Shintoism—are sometimes termed "ethical religions" since they have no gods in the Western sense. Another difference is that Eastern religions use a cyclical framework of birth and rebirth; most Western religions use a linear sense of time.
Q: "All civilizations are based on religion." Arnold Toynbee

Buddhists believe that a preoccupation with material things inhibits spiritual development, an idea that is also central to most Western religions. Buddhist monks, therefore, live a simple life devoted to meditation, music, and righteousness in everyday behavior.

spiritual perfection: Only when a soul reaches this level is it no longer reborn.

Hinduism stands as evidence that not all religions can be neatly labeled monotheistic or polytheistic. Hinduism is monotheistic insofar as it envisions the universe as a single moral system; yet Hindus see this moral order at work in every element of nature. Moreover, many Hindus participate in public rituals, such as the *Kumbh Mela*, which, every twelve years, brings some 20 million pilgrims to the sacred Ganges River to bathe in its purifying waters. At the same time, Hindus practice private devotions, which vary from village to village across the vast nation of India.

While elements of Hindu thought have characterized some cults in the United States over the years, Hinduism is still unfamiliar to most Westerners. But, like religions better known to us, Hinduism is a powerful force offering both explanation and guidance in life (Pitt, 1955; Sen, 1961; Embree, 1972; Kaufman, 1976; Schmidt, 1980).

BUDDHISM

Some 2,500 years ago, the rich culture of India also gave rise to Buddhism. Today more than 325 million people

(6 percent of humanity) embrace Buddhism, and almost all are Asians. As shown in Global Map 18–4, Buddhists make up more than half the populations of Myanmar (Burma), Thailand, Cambodia, and Japan; Buddhism is also widespread in India and the People's Republic of China. Of the world religions considered so far, Buddhism most resembles Hinduism in doctrine, but, like Christianity, its inspiration stems from the life of one individual.

Siddhartha Gautama was born to a high-caste family in Nepal about 563 B.C.E. As a young man, he was preoccupied with spiritual matters. At the age of twenty-nine, he underwent a radical personal transformation, and set off for years of travel and meditation. His journey ended when he achieved what Buddhists describe as *bodhi*, or enlightenment. Understanding the essence of life, Gautama became a Buddha.

Energized by his personal charisma, followers spread Buddha's teachings—the *dhamma*—across India. In the third century B.C.E., the ruler of India became a Buddhist and sent missionaries throughout Asia, making Buddhism a world religion.

Buddhists believe that much of life involves suffering. This idea is rooted in the Buddha's own travels in a society rife with poverty. But the Buddha rejected wealth as a solution to suffering; in fact, he warned that materialism inhibits spiritual development. Instead, Buddha taught that we must transcend our selfish concerns and desires through meditation, with the goal of obtaining *nirvana*, a state of enlightenment and peace.

Buddhism closely parallels Hinduism in recognizing no god of judgment; yet, each daily action has spiritual consequences. Another similarity is a belief in reincarnation. Here, again, only enlightenment ends the cycle of death and rebirth and finally liberates a person from the suffering of the world (Schumann, 1974; Thomas, 1975; Van Biema, 1997b).

CONFUCIANISM

From about 200 B.C.E. until the beginning of this century, Confucianism was an ecclesia—the official religion of China. But after the 1949 Revolution, religion was suppressed by the communist government of the new People's Republic of China. Today, though officials provide no precise count, hundreds of millions of Chinese are still influenced by Confucianism. Almost all Confucianists live in China, although Chinese immigration has spread this religion to other nations in Southeast Asia. Perhaps 100,000 followers of Confucius live in North America.

GLOBAL: Many Marxist states have been intentionally nonreligious. When Mikhail Gorbachev was sworn in as the U.S.S.R.'s president in 1985, he placed his hand on a copy of that nation's constitution. Albania outlaws any religious gesture; "crossing oneself" can bring a prison sentence.

Q: "A myth is a religion in which no one any longer believes." James Feibleman

GLOBAL: Proportion describing the personal significance of religion as very important or quite important: U.S., 78.9%; Italy, 66.8%; Canada, 61.5%; U.K., 44.8%; France, 42.7%; W. Germany, 37.3%; Sweden, 27.2%; Japan, 20.3% (*World Values Survey,* 1994).

Q: "If you don't believe in something, you'll fall for anything." Anonymous

Confucius, or, properly, K'ung Fu-tzu, lived between 551 and 479 B.C.E. Like Buddha, Confucius was deeply concerned about people's suffering. The Buddha's response was a sectlike spiritual withdrawal from the world; Confucius, by contrast, instructed his followers to engage the world according to a strict code of moral conduct. Thus it was that Confucianism became fused with the traditional culture of China. Here we see a second example of what might be called a "national religion": As Hinduism has remained largely synonymous with Indian culture, Confucianism is enshrined in the Chinese way of life.

A central concept of Confucianism is *jen*, meaning humaneness. In practice, this means that we must always subordinate our self-interest to moral principle. In the family, the individual must be loyal and considerate. Likewise, families must remain mindful of their duties toward the larger community. In this way, layer upon layer of moral obligation integrates society as a whole.

Most of all, Confucianism stands out as lacking a clear sense of the sacred. Recalling Durkheim's analysis, we might view Confucianism as the celebration of the sacred character of society itself. Or, we might argue that Confucianism is less a religion than a model of disciplined living. Certainly the historical dominance of Confucianism helps explain why Chinese culture is skeptical toward the supernatural. But even as a disciplined way of life, Confucianism shares with religion a body of beliefs and practices that have as their goal goodness, concern for others, and the promotion of social harmony (Kaufman, 1976; Schmidt, 1980; McGuire, 1997).

RELIGION: EAST AND WEST

This overview of world religions points up two general differences between the belief systems of Eastern and Western societies. First, Western religions (Christianity, Islam, Judaism) are typically deity-based, with a clear focus on God. Eastern religions (Hinduism, Buddhism, Confucianism), however, tend to be ethical codes; therefore, they make a less clear-cut distinction between the sacred and secular.

Second, the operational unit of Western religious organization is the congregation. That is, people worship in formal groups at a specific time and place. Eastern religious organization, by contrast, is more informally fused with culture itself. For this reason, for example, a visitor finds a Japanese temple filled with tourists and worshipers alike, who come and go as they please and pay little attention to those around them.

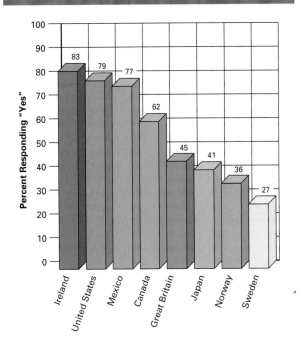

GLOBAL SNAPSHOT

FIGURE 18–1 Religiosity in Global Perspective

Survey Question: "Do you gain comfort and strength from religion?"

Source: *World Values Survey* (1994).

These two distinctions do not overshadow the common element of all religions: a conception of a higher moral force or purpose that transcends the concerns of everyday life. In their global variety, religious beliefs give people of the world guidance and a sense of purpose in their lives.

RELIGION IN THE UNITED STATES

In global perspective, the United States is a relatively religious nation. As Figure 18–1 shows, eight-in-ten members of our society say they gain "comfort and strength from religion," a substantially higher share than in most other industrial countries.

Although U.S. society is more religious than most, there is considerable debate about how religious it is. While some scholars find that religion remains central to our way of life, others wonder if the erosion of the traditional family and the advancing role of science and technology are steadily undermining religious commitment

SOCIAL SURVEY: "How close do you feel to God most of the time?" (GSS 1989, N = 1,006; *Codebook*, 1996:126)

"Extremely close"	28.9%	"Not close at all"	6.4%
"Somewhat close"	52.3%	"Does not believe in God"	2.1%
"Not very close"	8.8%	DK/NR	1.5%

Q: "Religious insanity is very common in the United States."
Alexis de Tocqueville

DIVERSITY: David Cone (Alabama State University) describes the black church itself as a variant of liberation theology.
SOCIAL SURVEY: "The United States Supreme Court has ruled that no state or local government may require the reading of the Lord's Prayer or Bible verses in public schools. What are your views on this?" (GSS 1996, N = 1,960; *Codebook*, 1996:138)
"Approve" 39.8%   "Disapprove" 56.1%   DK/NR 4.1%

TABLE 18–1 Religious Identification in the United States, 1996

Religion	Proportion Indicating Preference
Protestant denominations	**57.3%**
Baptist	21.6
Methodist	8.4
Lutheran	6.8
Presbyterian	3.6
Episcopalian	2.7
All others or no denomination	14.2
Catholic	**23.6**
Jewish	**2.3**
Other or no answer	**5.1**
No religious preference	**11.7**

Source: *General Social Surveys, 1972–1996: Cumulative Codebook* (Chicago: National Opinion Research Center, 1996), p. 117.

and faith (Collins, 1982; Greeley, 1989; Woodward, 1992; Hadaway, Marler, & Chaves, 1993).

RELIGIOUS AFFILIATION

The vast majority of people in the United States identify with a religion. On national surveys, nearly 90 percent of U.S. adults claim a religious preference (NORC, 1996:116). Table 18–1 shows that 57 percent of adults consider themselves Protestants; 24 percent, Catholics; and 2 percent, Jews. Eleven percent state no religious preference. While growing up, 68 percent of adults say they attended classes in religious instruction, and 60 percent consider themselves a member of some religious organization (NORC, 1996:334–35).

National Map 18–1 shows a strong regional pattern in religious affiliation. New England and the Southwest are predominantly Catholic, the South is overwhelmingly Baptist, and in the northern Plains states, Lutherans predominate. In and around Utah, there is a heavy concentration of members of the Church of Jesus Christ of Latter Day Saints (Mormons).

RELIGIOSITY

Religiosity refers to *the importance of religion in a person's life.* Identifying with a religion is only one measure of religiosity, of course, and a superficial one at that. How religious the U.S. turns out to be, therefore, depends on how we operationalize the concept.

Years ago, Charles Glock (1959, 1962) proposed five distinct dimensions of religiosity. *Experiential*

religiosity refers to the strength of a person's emotional ties to a religion. *Ritualistic* religiosity means the frequency of ritual activity such as prayer and church attendance. *Ideological* religiosity describes an individual's degree of belief in religious doctrine. *Consequential* religiosity has to do with how strongly religious beliefs figure in a person's daily behavior. Finally, *intellectual* religiosity refers to a person's knowledge of the history and doctrines of a religion. Any person is likely to be more religious on some dimensions and less on others so that assessing religiosity is a difficult task.

When asked directly, almost everyone in the United States (95 percent) claims to believe in a divine power of some kind, although in follow-up questions, only 62 percent are firm enough in their belief to say "I know that God exists and have no doubts about it" (NORC, 1996:336). Most people in the United States, then, seem to have high experiential religiosity.

Measures of ideological religiosity yield lower numbers. Seventy-three percent of U.S. adults report a belief in a life after death. And, the numbers of ritualistic religiosity drop further: Fifty-seven percent of adults say they pray at least once a day, and only 30 percent report attending religious services on a weekly or almost-weekly basis (NORC, 1996:118, 120, 124).

In short, the question "How religious are we?" yields no easy answers. Keep in mind, too, that many people probably claim to be more religious than they really are. For example, a team of researchers posted observers at every place of worship in Ashtabula County, Ohio, and counted people arriving for Sunday services; in a subsequent survey of county residents, twice as many people claimed that they attended church that Sunday than really did so. A more accurate estimate, then, may be that only about 20 percent of people attend church regularly (Hadaway, Marler, & Chaves, 1993).

Overall, then, while most people in the United States claim to be at least somewhat religious, probably no more than about one-third actually are. Moreover, religiosity varies among denominations. Members of sects are the most religious of all, followed by Catholics, and then "mainstream" Protestants (Stark & Glock, 1968; Hadaway, Marler, & Chaves, 1993).

RELIGION AND SOCIAL STRATIFICATION

Sociologists who study religion have found that religious affiliation is related to other familiar social patterns. We shall consider three: social class, race, and ethnicity.

THE MAP: Immigration (of Lutherans to the upper Midwest) and migration (of Mormons to Utah) shaped much of the religious diversity of the United States.
SOCIAL SURVEY: "Which of these statements comes closest to describing your feelings about the Bible?" (GSS 1996, N = 1,960; *Codebook*, 1996:139)

"The Bible is the actual word of God and is to be taken literally" 30.2%
"The Bible is the inspired word of God but not everything in it should be taken literally, word for word" 49.5%
"The Bible is an ancient book of fables, legends, history, and moral precepts recorded by men" 17.0%
Other/DK/NR 3.3%

SEEING OURSELVES

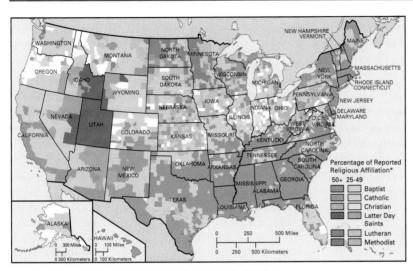

Source: The Glenmary Research Center, Atlanta, Georgia (1990).

NATIONAL MAP 18–1
Religious Diversity Across the United States

In the vast majority of counties, at least 25 percent of people who report having a religious affiliation are members of the same organization. Thus, although the United States is religiously diverse at the national level, most people live in communities where one denomination predominates. What historical facts might account for this pattern?

*When two or more churches have 25 to 49 percent of the membership in a county, the largest is shown. When no church has 25 percent of the membership that county is left blank. A few exceptions include Palm Beach County in southern Florida, which is primarily Jewish, and Holmes County in central Ohio, which is largely Amish.

Social Class

A recent study of *Who's Who in America*, which profiles U.S. high achievers, showed that 33 percent of the people who gave a religious affiliation were Episcopalians, Presbyterians, and United Church of Christ members, denominations that together account for less than 10 percent of the population. Jews, too, enjoy high social position, with this 2.3 percent of U.S. adults accounting for 12 percent of listings.

Moreover, research shows that other denominations—including Methodists and Catholics—have a moderate social position. Lower social standing is typical of Baptists, Lutherans, and members of sects. Within every denomination, of course, there is much variation (Roof, 1979; Davidson, Pyle, & Reyes, 1995; Waters, Heath, & Watson, 1995).

By and large, Protestants with high social standing are people of northern European background whose families came to the United States at least a century ago. They encountered little prejudice and discrimination and have had the longest time to establish themselves socially. Roman Catholics, more recent immigrants to the United States, have faced greater social barriers because of their religion.

Jews command unexpectedly high social standing considering that they often contend with anti-Semitism from the Christian majority. The reason for this achievement is mostly cultural, since Jewish tradition places great value on both education and hard work. Although a large proportion of Jews began life in the United States in poverty, many—although certainly not all—improved their social position in subsequent generations.

Ethnicity and Race

Throughout the world, religion is tied to ethnicity. Many religions predominate in a single nation or geographic region. Islam predominates in the Arab societies of the Middle East; Hinduism is fused with the culture of India, as is Confucianism with life in China. Christianity and Judaism, however, do not follow this pattern; while these religions are mostly Western, Christians and Jews are found all over the world.

Religion and national identity come together in the United States as well. We have, for example, *Anglo-Saxon* Protestants, *Irish* Catholics, *Russian* Jews, and people who are *Greek* Orthodox. This linking of nation and creed results from the influx of immigrants from nations with a single major religion. Still, nearly every ethnic category displays some religious diversity. People of English ancestry, for instance, may be Protestants, Roman Catholics, Jews, or followers of other religions.

Historically, the church has been central to the spiritual—and political—lives of African Americans.

NOTE: The secularization thesis can be linked to Max Weber's account of the "disenchantment" of the world, discussed in Chapter 4.

GLOBAL: Peter Berger argues that the secularization thesis applies best to European societies, and has less application to the United States.

NOTE: One index of secularization is cremations, which are replacing traditional burials as religious and ethnic traditions weaken. They are also most popular in regions of the country—including California and Florida—where the population is most geographically mobile. Four percent of people chose cremation in 1972, according to the Cremation Association of North America; the current figure is about 20%.

Transported to the Western Hemisphere in slave ships, most Africans were forced to embrace Christianity—the dominant religion of European Americans—but they blended Christian belief with elements of African religions. Guided by this religious mix, Christian people of color therefore have developed rituals that are—by European standards—quite spontaneous and emotional. These expressive qualities still characterize many African American religious organizations today (Frazier, 1965; Roberts, 1980).

When African Americans migrated from the rural South to the industrial cities of the North around 1940, the church played a major role in addressing problems of dislocation, poverty, and prejudice. Moreover, among people often cut off from the larger society, the church provided the opportunity for talented men and women to distinguish themselves as leaders. Ralph Abernathy, Martin Luther King, Jr., and Jesse Jackson each became internationally recognized for leadership while serving as ministers in primarily African American religious organizations.

RELIGION IN A CHANGING SOCIETY

All social institutions evolve over time. Just as the economy, politics, and family life have changed over the course of this century, so has our society's religious life.

SECULARIZATION

One of the most important patterns of social change is **secularization**, *the historical decline in the importance of the supernatural and the sacred.* For society as a whole, secularization points to a declining influence of religion in everyday life. For religious organizations, becoming more secular means that they focus less on otherworldly issues (such as life after death) and more on worldly affairs (such as sheltering the homeless and feeding the hungry). Secularization also means that functions once performed by the church (such as charity) are now primarily the responsibility of business and government.

With Latin roots meaning "the present age," secularization is associated with modern, technologically advanced societies (Cox, 1971; O'Dea & Aviad, 1983). Conventional wisdom holds that secularization results from the increasing role of science in understanding human affairs. Today, in other words, people perceive birth, illness, and death less as the work of a divine power than as natural stages in the life course. These events are now more likely to occur in the presence of

physicians (scientific specialists) than religious leaders (whose knowledge is based on faith). As Harvey Cox explains:

> The world looks less and less to religious rules and rituals for its morality or its meanings. For some, religion provides a hobby, for others a mark of national or ethnic identification, for still others an aesthetic delight. For fewer and fewer does it provide an inclusive and commanding system of personal and cosmic values and explanations. (1971:3)

If Cox is correct, should we expect that religion will disappear completely some day? The consensus among sociologists is "no." The vast majority of people in the United States still profess a belief in God, and more people claim to pray each day than vote in national elections. Note, too, that religious affiliation today is actually higher than it was in 1850 (Hammond, 1985; Hout & Greeley, 1987; McGuire, 1997).

Secularization does not, then, signal the death of religion. More correctly, some dimensions of religiosity (such as belief in life after death) may have declined, but others (such as religious affiliation) have increased. A global perspective shows the same mixed pattern: Religion is declining in importance in some regions (the Scandinavian countries, for example), but rising in others (such as Algeria) (Cox, 1990).

Our society is of two minds as to whether secularization is good or bad. Conservatives take any erosion of religion as a mark of moral decline. Progressives, however, think secularization liberates people from the all-encompassing beliefs of the past and allows them to choose what to believe. Secularization has also brought the practices of many religious organizations (for example, ordaining both men and women) in line with widespread social attitudes.

CIVIL RELIGION

One dimension of secularization is the rise of what Robert Bellah (1975) calls **civil religion**, *a quasi-religious loyalty binding individuals in a basically secular society.* In other words, although some dimensions of formal religion are weakening, our patriotism and citizenship retain many religious qualities.

Certainly, most people in the United States consider our way of life a force for moral good in the world. And most people find religious qualities in political movements, whether liberal or conservative (Williams & Demerath, 1991).

Q: "In a word, we must discover the rational substitutes for those religious notions that for a long time have served as the vehicle for the most essential moral ideas." Emile Durkheim, *Moral Education* (1961:9)

NOTE: Civil religion is evident in the writing of Jean-Jacques Rousseau, who hated the church but wanted to keep a spirit and

discipline in citizenship; curiously, secular conservatives, too, wish to maintain religion's capacity to legitimize public order and maintain the social fabric.

GLOBAL: One measure of the strength of civil religion is the number of national holidays each year: the United States, 32; Japan, 19; Germany, 13; Canada and France, 11; Sweden and Great Britain, 10 (Baker, 1997).

GLOBAL SOCIOLOGY

Great Britain

The Changing Face of Religion: A Report From Great Britain

Although the Church of England enjoys the elite status of being that nation's official religious organization, only one-fifth of regular worshipers in Great Britain today are Anglicans. As in the United States, Britain's established, mainstream churches have lost members. The figure shows that the membership in the Anglican, Roman Catholic, Presbyterian, and Baptist churches is down significantly in recent years.

Overall, however, religiosity in Great Britain is holding steady (although at a lower level than in the United States). Why? As the established churches lose members, newer religious organizations are showing surprising strength. Immigration is behind some of this religious revival,

adding large numbers of Muslims, Sikhs, and Hindus to the British population.

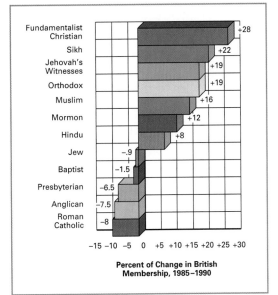

Percent of Change in British Membership, 1985–1990

Newly formed cults are also a factor. Experts estimate that as many as 600 cults may exist in Britain at any one time.

But the most significant rise in British religious affiliation is among fundamentalist Christian organizations that embrace highly energetic and musical forms of worship, often under the direction of charismatic leaders. Like their counterparts in the United States, these religious communities typically seek and express the experience of God's presence in a much more intense and spontaneous way than the more staid, mainstream churches.

Sources: Barker (1989) and *The Economist* (1993).

Civil religion also involves a range of rituals, from rising to sing the national anthem at sporting events to sitting down to watch public parades—the United States has more public holidays than any other industrial nation (Baker, 1997). At all such events, like the Christian cross or the Jewish Star of David, the U.S. flag serves as a sacred symbol of our national identity that we expect people to treat with reverence.

Civil religion is not a specific doctrine. It does, however, incorporate many elements of traditional religion into the political system of a secular society.

RELIGIOUS REVIVAL

We have argued that, all things considered, religiosity in the United States has been stable in recent decades.

But a great deal of change is going on within the world of organized religion. Membership in established, mainstream denominations like the Episcopal or Presbyterian churches has plummeted by almost 50 percent since 1960. During the same period, affiliation with other religious organizations (including the Mormons, Seventh-Day Adventists, and, especially, Christian sects) has risen just as dramatically.

Secularization itself may be self-limiting so that, as churchlike organizations become more worldly, many people abandon them in favor of more sectlike communities that offer a more intense religious experience (Stark & Bainbridge, 1981; Roof & McKinney, 1987; Jacquet & Jones, 1991; Warner, 1993; Iannaccone, 1994). Much the same pattern is found in other industrial societies. The box takes a look at changing religious affiliation in Great Britain.

SOCIAL SURVEY: Characterization of religion respondent was raised in. (GSS 1996, N = 2,904; *Codebook*, 1996:133)
"Fundamentalist" 31.1%   "Liberal"   24.8%
"Moderate"   40.1%   DK/NR   4.0%
NOTE: Fundamentalism is, in part, a product of our frontier history, when circuit preachers made dramatic presentations in hopes of prompting an immediate conversion by those attending.

Fundamentalism is less pronounced in Europe because European churches are more "established," and usually linked to the state.
SOCIAL SURVEY: "Would you say that you have been 'born again', or have had a 'born again' experience—that is, a turning point in your life when you committed yourself to Christ?" (GSS 1988, 1991, N = 2,840; *Codebook*, 1996:336)
"Yes"   35.7%   "No"   62.2%   DK/NR   2.1%

The painting Arts of the South, *by Thomas Hart Benton (1889–1975), suggests that religious fundamentalism is strongly integrated into the community life of rural people in the southern United States.*

Thomas Hart Benton, *Arts of the South*, tempera with oil glaze, 8 x 13 feet, Harriet Russell Stanley Fund/New Britain Museum of American Art, Connecticut.
© T. H. Benton and R. P. Benton Testamentary Trusts/Licensed by VAGA, New York, N.Y.

Religious Fundamentalism

One of the striking religious trends today is the growth of **fundamentalism,** *a conservative religious doctrine that opposes intellectualism and worldly accommodation in favor of restoring traditional, otherworldly spirituality.* In the United States, fundamentalism has made the greatest gains among Protestants. Southern Baptists, for example, are the largest religious community in the United States. But fundamentalist groups have also proliferated among Roman Catholics and Jews.

In response to what they see as the growing influence of science and the erosion of the conventional family, religious fundamentalists defend what they call "traditional values." As they see it, liberal churches are simply too tolerant of religious pluralism and too open to change. Religious fundamentalism is distinctive in five ways (Hunter, 1983, 1985, 1987):

1. **Fundamentalists interpret sacred texts literally.** Fundamentalists insist on a literal interpretation of the Bible and other sacred texts in order to counter what they consider excessive intellectualism among more liberal religious organizations. Fundamentalist Christians, for example, believe that God created the world precisely as described in Genesis.

2. **Fundamentalists reject religious pluralism.** Fundamentalists believe that tolerance and

relativism water down personal faith. They maintain, therefore, that their religious beliefs are true while those of others are not.

3. **Fundamentalists pursue the personal experience of God's presence.** In contrast to the worldliness and intellectualism of other religious organizations, fundamentalism seeks a return to "good old-time religion" and spiritual revival. To fundamentalist Christians, being "born again" and having a personal relationship with Jesus Christ should be evident in a person's daily life.

4. **Fundamentalism opposes "secular humanism."** Fundamentalists think that accommodation to the changing world undermines religious conviction. *Secular humanism* is a general term fundamentalists use to refer to our society's tendency to look to scientific experts (including sociologists) rather than God for guidance about how to live.

5. **Many fundamentalists endorse conservative political goals.** Although fundamentalism tends to back away from worldly concerns, some fundamentalist leaders (including Ralph Reed and Pat Robertson) have entered politics to oppose the "liberal agenda" of feminism and gay rights. Fundamentalists oppose abortion, gay marriages, and liberal bias in the media, while supporting the traditional two-parent family and seeking a return

SOCIAL SURVEY: "About how often do you pray?" (GSS 1983–89, N = 8,997; *Student CHIP Social Survey Software*, PRAY1)

	Daily	Weekly	Less often/Never
Women	65.3%	20.2%	14.5%
Men	42.8%	23.6%	33.6%
Afri Amer	72.8%	16.0%	11.2%
Latino	63.4%	21.0%	15.6%

Wh Anglo	52.5%	22.5%	24.9%
High SES	48.6%	25.4%	26.0%
Middle SES	55.4%	21.6%	23.0%
Low SES	63.4%	17.4%	19.2%
65 and older	74.6%	12.0%	13.3%
35–64	56.5%	21.7%	21.8%
18–34	43.8%	26.6%	29.6%

EXPLORING CYBER-SOCIETY

The Cyber-Church: Logging On to Religion

The bumpy red-clay road used to be the only link between the outside world and the Monastery of Christ in the Desert. The monastery, a brown adobe structure hidden away in a remote site in northwestern New Mexico, is twenty miles from the nearest power line and maybe fifty from the closest telephone. Those who make the two-hour auto trek from Albuquerque are greeted by an ancient-looking, hand-carved wooden sign that states simply "Ring this bell."

But, in the 1990s, the brothers of the monastery entered the Information Age. On the roof, a dozen solar panels supply power to a personal computer linked to a cellular phone, allowing the monks to spread their message throughout the world on the Benedictine home page.*

This is hardly the first time technological innovation has brought change to religion. Six hundred years ago in medieval Europe, face-to-face speaking was the major channel for transmitting religious ideas, as clerics gathered in the universities of the largest cities of the day, and people went to services in churches and other houses of worship across the land. At this time, Bibles and other sacred texts were few and far between; monks in monasteries took years

*Access their home page at http://www.christdesert.org

to complete the painstaking task of copying them by hand. But religion changed when Johann Gutenberg, a German inventor, built a movable-type press and published the first printed book—a Bible—in 1456. Within fifty years, millions of books were in print across Europe, and most of them were about religious matters. It is no coincidence that the spread of printed books was soon followed by a major religious transformation—the Protestant Reformation—as an expanding market of

religious ideas prompted people to rethink established principles and practices.

In this century, radio (beginning in the 1920s) and television (after 1950) have extended the reach of religious leaders, who founded "media congregations" no longer confined by the walls of a single building. During the 1990s, the Internet accelerated this trend, as hundreds of thousands of Web sites offer messages from established churches, obscure cults, and "New Age" organizations.

How will computer technology affect religious life? With more to learn than ever before, some analysts anticipate a new "post-denominational" age in which people's religious ideas are not bound by particular organizations, as in the past. New information technology may also usher in an age of "cyber-churches." Television has already shown it can transmit the personal charisma and spiritual message of religious leaders to ever-larger audiences. Perhaps the Internet will lead to "virtual congregations," both larger in number and broader in background than any before.

Source: Based on Ramo (1996).

of prayer in schools (Viguerie, 1981; Hunter, 1983; Speer, 1984; Ostling, 1985; Ellison & Sherkat, 1993; Green, 1993; Thomma, 1997).

Opponents regard fundamentalism as rigid and self-righteous. But many find in fundamentalism—

with its greater religious certainty and emphasis on the emotional experience of God's presence—an appealing alternative to the more intellectual, tolerant, and worldly mainstream denominations (Marquand, 1997).

Which religions are "fundamentalist"? The term is most correctly applied to conservative Christian

Q: "We have too many men of science, too few of God. We have grasped the mystery of the atom and rejected the Sermon on the Mount. . . . Ours is a world of nuclear giants and ethical infants. We know more about war than about peace, more about killing than about living." General Omar N. Bradley (1948)

Q: "Science without religion is lame; religion without science is blind." Albert Einstein

SOCIAL SURVEY: In a recent *Time*/CNN poll, 55% of U.S. adults thought religion would have a greater role in our society after the year 2000; 37% said a lesser role.

DISCUSS: Do colleges discriminate against religious people? A 1995 Supreme Court ruling (5–4) concluded that the University of Virginia violated free-speech guarantees when it failed to fund a Christian magazine along with other student groups.

 CONTROVERSY & DEBATE

Does Science Threaten Religion?

At the dawning of the modern age, the Italian physicist and astronomer Galileo (1564–1642) made a series of startling discoveries. Dropping objects from the Leaning Tower of Pisa, he discovered some of the laws of gravity; fashioning his own telescope, he surveyed the heavens and found that the earth orbited the sun, not the other way around.

For his discoveries, Galileo was denounced by the Roman Catholic church, which had preached for centuries that the earth stood motionless at the center of the universe. In response, Galileo only made matters worse by declaring that religious leaders and Biblical doctrine had no place in the growing wave of science. Before long, he found his work banned and himself condemned to house arrest.

From its beginnings, science has had an uneasy relationship with religion. Indeed, as Galileo's life makes clear, the claims of one sometimes infringe on the other's truth.

Through this century, too, science and religion have had their battles, mostly over the issue of creation. In the wake of Charles Darwin's masterwork, *On the Origin of Species*, scientists concluded that humanity evolved from lower forms of life over the course of a billion years. Yet the theory of evolution seems to fly in the face of the Biblical account of creation found in Genesis, which states that "God created the heavens and the earth," introducing life on the third day and, on the fifth and sixth days, creating animal life, including human beings, fashioned in God's own image.

Galileo would certainly have been an eager observer of the famous "Scopes monkey trial" of 1925, when the state of Tennessee prosecuted science teacher John Thomas Scopes. Scopes taught evolution in violation of a state law that forbade teaching "any theory that denies the story of the Divine Creation of man as taught in the Bible" and especially the idea that "man descended from a lower order of animals." Scopes was found guilty and fined $100. His conviction was reversed on appeal, perhaps to prevent the case from reaching the U.S. Supreme Court, and so the Tennessee law continued to ban the teaching of evolution until 1967. A year later, the U.S. Supreme Court (in the case of *Epperson* v. *Arkansas*) struck down all such laws as an unconstitutional case of government-supported religion.

Today—almost four centuries after Galileo was silenced—many people still ponder the apparently conflicting claims of science and religion. Nearly one-third of U.S. adults believe the Bible is the literal word of God, and many of them reject any scientific findings that run counter to Biblical scripture (NORC, 1996:139).

---

organizations in the evangelical tradition, including Pentecostals, Southern Baptists, Seventh-Day Adventists, and Assemblies of God. Several national social movements, including Promise Keepers for men and Chosen Women, have a fundamentalist orientation. In national surveys, 31 percent of U.S. adults describe their religious upbringing as "fundamentalist"; 40 percent claim a "moderate" religious tradition; and 25 percent call their religion "liberal" (NORC, 1996:133).

The Electronic Church

In contrast to small village congregations of years past, some religious organizations—especially fundamentalist ones—have become electronic churches featuring "prime-time preachers" (Hadden & Swain, 1981). Electronic religion, found only in the United States, has propelled Oral Roberts, Pat Robertson, Robert Schuller, and others to greater prominence than all but a few clergy in the past. About 5 percent of the national television audience (about 10 million people) regularly view religious television, while perhaps 20 percent (about 40 million) watch some religious program every week (Martin, 1981; Gallup, 1982; NORC, 1996).

Recently, an increasing number of religious organizations are using computer technology to spread their message via the Internet to people everywhere in the world. Pope John Paul II has termed this technological trend the "new evangelism." The box on page 501 takes a look at finding God online.

NOTE: In the 1987 *Edwards* v. *Aguillard* case, the Supreme Court declared as unconstitutional a 1981 Louisiana law that mandated the teaching of creation science alongside of evolution. In 1996, the Tennessee legislature debated (but did not pass) a law calling for the dismissal of any public school science instructor who did not teach evolution as a theory rather than as scientific fact. Similarly, Alabama recently required biology textbooks to include the disclaimer that evolution is a "controversial theory."

NOTE: In 1991, Arkansas, California, Indiana, Oregon, and West Virginia mandated that children should receive instruction about religions in school, reversing the earlier trend.

Q: "If we do discover a complete theory [of physics] . . . it would be the ultimate triumph of human reason—for then we would truly know the mind of God." Stephen Hawking

But a middle ground is emerging: Half of U.S. adults (and also many church leaders) say the Bible may be inspired by God and contain important philosophical truth without being literally correct in a scientific sense. That is, science and religion represent two levels of understanding that respond to different questions. Both Galileo and Darwin devoted their lives to investigating *how* the natural world operates. Yet only religion can address *why* humans and the natural world exist in the first place.

This basic difference between science and religion helps explain how our nation can be at once among the most actively scientific and devoutly religious in the world. Moreover, the more scientists discover about the origins of the universe, the more awesome creation seems. Indeed, as one scientist recently pointed out, the mathematical odds that some cosmic "Big Bang" 12 billion years ago created the universe and led to the development of life on earth as we know

it today are utterly infinitesimal—much smaller than the chance of one person winning a state lottery twenty weeks in a row. Doesn't such a scientific fact allow for an intelligent and purposeful power in our creation? Can't one be both a religious believer and scientific investigator?

There is another reason to acknowledge the importance of both scientific and religious thinking: The rapid advances of science continue to present society with troubling ethical dilemmas. Latter-day Galileos have unleashed the power of atomic energy, yet we still struggle to find its rightful use in the world. And, discovering secrets of human genetics has brought us to the threshold of being able to manipulate life itself, a power that few have the moral confidence to use.

In 1992, a Vatican commission created by Pope John Paul II conceded that the church had erred in silencing Galileo. Most scientific and religious leaders agree that science and religion

represent distinctive truths, and their teachings are complementary. And many believe that, in today's rush to scientific discovery, our world has never been more in need of the moral guidance afforded by religion.

Continue the debate . . .

1. *On what grounds do some scientists completely reject religious accounts of human creation? Why do some religious people reject scientific accounts?*

2. *Do you think the sociological study of religion challenges anyone's faith? Why or why not?*

3. *Does it surprise you that about half of U.S. adults think science is changing too much of our way of life? Do you agree or not?*

Sources: Based on Gould (1981), Huchingson (1994), and Applebome (1996).

LOOKING AHEAD: RELIGION IN THE TWENTY-FIRST CENTURY

The popularity of media ministries, the rapid growth of religious fundamentalism, and the continuing adherence of millions more people to mainstream churches lead us to conclude that religion will remain a major institution of modern society, especially in the United States. Moreover, high levels of immigration from many religious countries (in Latin America and elsewhere) will intensify and diversify the religious character of U.S. society over the course of the twenty-first century.

In addition, the pace of social change seems to be accelerating. As the world becomes more complex, rapid change seems to outstrip our capacity to make

sense of it all. But rather than undermining religion, this process fires the religious imagination of people who seek a sense of religious community and are looking for ultimate meaning in their lives. Tensions between the spiritual realm of religion and the secular world of science and technology will surely continue; the final box takes a closer look at this dynamic—and sometimes troubling—relationship.

But science is simply unable to provide answers to the most basic human questions about the purpose of our lives. Moreover, new technology that can begin life and sustain life confront us with vexing moral dilemmas as never before. Against this backdrop of uncertainty, it is little wonder that many people today—like people throughout history—rely on their faith for assurance and hope.

SUMMARY

1. Religion is a major social institution based on distinguishing the sacred from the profane. Religion is a matter of faith, not scientific evidence, which people express through various rituals.

2. Sociology analyzes the consequences of religion for social life, but no scientific research can assess the truth of any religious belief.

3. Emile Durkheim argued that, through religion, individuals experience the power of their society. His structural-functional analysis suggests that religion promotes social cohesion and conformity and confers meaning and purpose on life.

4. Using the symbolic-interaction paradigm, Peter Berger explains that religious beliefs are socially constructed as a means of responding to life's uncertainties and disruptions.

5. Using the social-conflict paradigm, Karl Marx charged that religion promotes social inequality and the status quo. On the other hand, Max Weber's analysis of Calvinism's contribution to the rise of industrial capitalism demonstrates religion's power to promote social change.

6. Churches, which are religious organizations well integrated into their society, fall into two categories—ecclesias and denominations.

7. Sects, the result of religious division, are marked by charismatic leadership and suspicion of the larger society.

8. Cults are religious organizations that embrace new and unconventional beliefs and practices.

9. Technologically simple human societies were generally animistic, with religion just one facet of family life; in more complex societies, religion emerges as a distinct social institution.

10. Followers of six world religions—Christianity, Islam, Judaism, Hinduism, Buddhism, and Confucianism—represent three-fourths of all humanity.

11. Almost all adults in the United States identify with a religion; more than 80 percent state a religious affiliation, with the largest number belonging to various Protestant denominations.

12. How religious we conclude our nation is depends on how we operationalize the concept of religiosity. The vast majority of people say they believe in God, but only about one-fifth of the U.S. population attends religious services regularly.

13. Secularization refers to the diminishing importance of the supernatural and the sacred. In the United States, while some indicators of religiosity (like membership in mainstream churches) have declined, others (such as membership in sects) are on the rise. Thus, it is doubtful that secularization will bring on the demise of religion.

14. Civil religion refers to the quasi-religious patriotism that ties people to their society.

15. Fundamentalism opposes religious accommodation to the world, favoring a more otherworldly focus. Fundamentalist Christianity also advocates literal interpretation of the Bible, rejects religious diversity, and pursues the personal experience of God's presence. Some fundamentalist Christian organizations actively support conservative political goals.

16. Some of the continuing appeal of religion lies in the inability of science (including sociology) to address timeless questions about the ultimate meaning of human existence.

KEY CONCEPTS

profane that which is defined as an ordinary element of everyday life

sacred that which is defined as extraordinary, inspiring a sense of awe, reverence, and even fear

religion a social institution involving beliefs and practices based upon a conception of the sacred

ritual formal, ceremonial behavior

faith belief anchored in conviction rather than scientific evidence

totem an object in the natural world collectively defined as sacred

liberation theology a fusion of Christian principles with political activism, often Marxist in character

church a type of religious organization well integrated into the larger society

ecclesia a church that is formally allied with the state

denomination a church, independent of the state, that accepts religious pluralism

sect a type of religious organization that stands apart from the larger society

charisma extraordinary personal qualities that can turn an audience into followers

cult a religious organization that is substantially outside a society's cultural traditions

animism the belief that elements of the natural world are conscious forms of life that affect humanity

monotheism belief in a single divine power

polytheism belief in many gods

religiosity the importance of religion in a person's life

secularization the historical decline in the importance of the supernatural and the sacred

civil religion a quasi-religious loyalty binding individuals in a basically secular society

fundamentalism a conservative religious doctrine that opposes intellectualism and worldly accommodation in favor of restoring a traditional, otherworldly spirituality

CRITICAL-THINKING QUESTIONS

1. Explain the basic distinction between the sacred and the profane that underlies all religious belief.

2. Explain Karl Marx's argument that religion supports the status quo. Based on Max Weber's analysis of Calvinism, develop a counter-argument that religion can be a major force for social change.

3. Distinguish between churches, sects, and cults. Is one type of religious organization inherently better than another? Why or why not?

4. What evidence suggests that religion is experiencing a decline in importance in the United States? In what ways does religion seem to be getting stronger?

LEARNING EXERCISES

1. Some colleges are decidedly religious; others are passionately secular. Investigate the place of religion on your campus. Is your school affiliated with a religious organization? Was it ever? Is there a chaplain or other religious official? See if you can learn from sources on campus what share of students regularly attend any religious service.

2. Assessing people's religious commitment is very difficult. Develop several questions measuring religiosity that might be asked on a questionnaire or in an interview. Present them to several people; how well do they seem to work?

3. At first, only cults used the Internet. But, today, many religious organizations are online, and even the Roman Catholic church has a Web page. If you

have computer access, try using Yahoo! or another search engine to locate sites by searching on a key word such as "religion," "Christ," "Judaism," "Hindu," or "cult." Visit several and see what you can learn about online religion.

4. Is religion getting weaker? To test the secularization thesis, go to the library or local newspaper office and obtain an issue of your local newspaper published fifty years ago and, if possible, one hundred years ago. Compare the attention to religious issues then and now.

5. Install the CD-ROM packaged inside the back cover of your text and complete the activities designed to accompany this chapter.

Romare Bearden, *The Piano Lesson,* 1983

Collage and watercolor, 29 × 22 in. © Romare Bearden Foundation/Licensed by VAGA, New York, N.Y.

CHAPTER 19

EDUCATION

Thirteen-year-old Naoko Matsuo returns from school to her home in suburban Yoko-hama, Japan. But instead of dropping off her books to begin an afternoon of fun, she settles in to do her homework. Several hours later, Naoko's mother reminds her that it is time to leave for the *juku*, a "cram school" that Naoko attends for three hours three evenings a week. Mother and daughter take the subway to an office building in downtown Yoko-hama where Naoko joins dozens of other girls and boys for intensive training in Japanese, English, math, and science.

Attending the *juku* costs the Matsuo family several hundred dollars a month. But the extra class-room hours are a good investment that will pay off when Naoko takes national examinations for high school placement. Later on, the challenge will be to gain admission to an exclusive national university, a prize earned by just one-third of Japanese students. Given the cutthroat competition for educational success in Japan, the Matsuos know that their daughter cannot work too hard or begin too early (Simons, 1989).

Why do the Japanese pay such attention to schooling? In this modern, industrial society, admission to an elite university all but ensures a high-paying, prestigious career. This chapter spotlights **education,** *the social institution guiding a society's transmission of knowledge—including basic facts, job skills, and also cultural norms and values—to its members.* In industrial societies, as we shall see, education is largely a matter of **schooling,** *formal instruction under the direction of specially trained teachers.*

EDUCATION: A GLOBAL SURVEY

Like people in Japan, we in the United States expect children to spend much of their first eighteen years of life in school. A century ago, however, only a small elite enjoyed the privilege of schooling. And, even today, in poor countries this pattern continues, with most young people receiving only a few years of formal schooling.

SCHOOLING AND ECONOMIC DEVELOPMENT

The extent of schooling in any society is closely tied to its level of economic development. Chapter 4 ("Society") explained that our hunting and gathering ancestors lived a simple life in families without governments, churches, or schools. For these people, "schooling" amounted to the knowledge and skills parents transmitted directly to their children (Lenski, Nolan, & Lenski, 1995).

In agrarian societies, which make up most of the world today, young people spend several years in school, but they learn mainly the practical knowledge they need to farm or perform other traditional tasks. The opportunity to study literature, art, history, and science is generally available only to the lucky few whose wealth frees them from the need to work. It is no surprise, then, that the word "school" has roots in the Greek word for "leisure." In ancient Greece, the students of renowned teachers such as Socrates, Plato, and Aristotle were almost all aristocratic young men. The same was true in ancient China, where the famous philosopher K'ung Fu-tzu (Confucius), for example, shared his wisdom with only a select few. And during the Middle Ages in Europe, the first colleges and universities founded by the Catholic church admitted only males from privileged families.

SUPPLEMENTS: An outline for this chapter, supplementary lecture material, and discussion topics are found in the *Data File*.

NOTE: The world's oldest university was founded in Paris early in the 12th century. In England, the oldest is Oxford, also founded early in the 12th century. By the 13th century, historical notes mention "university chests," benefactions for the assistance of poor students—the earliest form of financial aid.

GLOBAL: Since 1970, significant improvements in elementary school enrollment have been reported by most nations in sub-Saharan Africa. Still, many of these societies have a level of schooling that is comparable to that offered in the United States in 1850.

GLOBAL: A classic example of a foreign nation structuring an educational system is the U.S. remaking of Japanese schooling during the occupation after World War II.

WINDOW ON THE WORLD

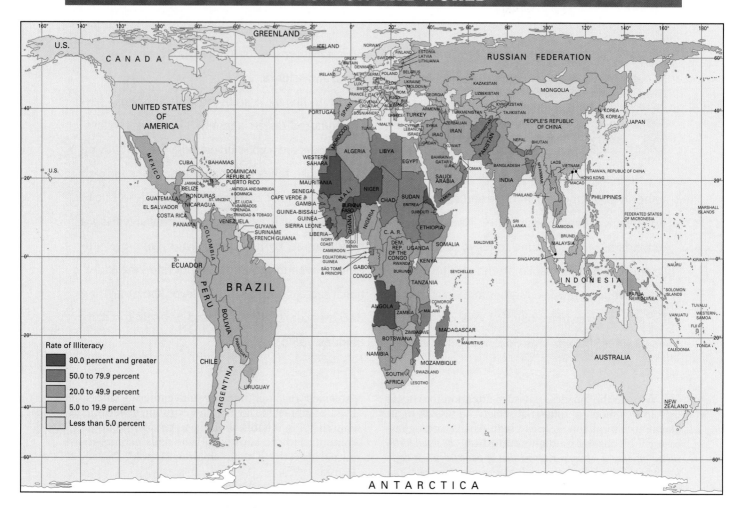

GLOBAL MAP 19–1 Illiteracy in Global Perspective

Reading and writing skills are widespread in every industrial society, with illiteracy rates generally below 5 percent. Throughout Latin America, however, illiteracy is more commonplace—one consequence of limited economic development. In about a dozen nations of the world—many of them in Africa—illiteracy is the rule rather than the exception. In such societies, people rely on what sociologists call "the oral tradition" of face-to-face communication rather than the written word.

Sources: The World Bank (1997); map projection from *Peters Atlas of the World* (1990).

Today, schooling in low-income nations is very diverse because it reflects the local culture. In Iran, for example, schooling is closely tied to Islam. Similarly, schooling in Bangladesh (Asia), Zimbabwe (Africa), and Nicaragua (Latin America) has been molded by a distinctive cultural tradition.

But all low-income countries have one trait in common when it comes to schooling—there is not very much of it. In the world's poorest nations (including several in central Africa), only half of all elementary-aged children ever get to school; in the world as a whole, just half of all children reach the secondary

GLOBAL: The share of people of all ages in Japan who never finish high school is about 10%, less than the comparable rate in the U.S. of 18%. However, almost 25% of U.S. young people are now gaining college degrees, twice the Japanese rate.
GLOBAL: One key to Japanese educational achievement is powerful cultural discipline. Such collective pressure generates collective distinction but produces fewer highly innovative individuals.

To illustrate, U.S. men and women have received proportionately more Nobel Prizes than have the Japanese, even allowing for differences in population size.
GLOBAL: Research explains the U.S.-Asian "math gap" in terms of parental attitudes: Most U.S. parents are satisfied with their children's learning and amount of homework; most Asian parents are not and are more demanding of their children.

grades (Najafizadeh & Mennerick, 1992). As a result, one-third of Latin Americans, almost half of Asians, and two-thirds of Africans are illiterate. Global Map 19–1 shows the extent of illiteracy around the world.

Industrial, high-income societies endorse the idea that everyone should go to school. For one thing, industrial workers need at least basic reading, writing, and arithmetic skills. For many industrial nations, literacy is also a necessary condition of political democracy.

The following national comparisons show how schooling is linked to economic development. Notice, too, how even industrial nations differ in their approach to educating their populations.

SCHOOLING IN INDIA

India is a low-income country: People earn about 5 percent of the income standard in the United States, and poor families often depend on the earnings of children. Thus, even though India has outlawed child labor, many Indian children work in factories—weaving rugs or making handicrafts—up to sixty hours per week, which greatly limits their opportunity for schooling.

In recent decades, schooling in India has increased. Most children now receive some primary education, typically in crowded schoolrooms where one teacher attends to perhaps sixty children (more than twice as many as in U.S. classrooms). This is all the schooling most people ever acquire, since less than half enter secondary school and very few go to college. The result is that about half of the people in this vast country are literate.

Patriarchy also significantly shapes Indian education. Indian parents are joyful at the birth of a boy, since he and his future wife both will contribute income to the family. Girls are a financial liability because parents must provide a dowry at the time of marriage, and a daughter's work then benefits her husband's family. Thus, many Indians see little reason to invest in the schooling of girls, so only 30 percent of girls reach the secondary grades compared to 45 percent of boys. The flip side of this pattern is that a large majority of the children working in Indian factories are girls—a family's way of benefiting from their daughters while they can (United Nations Development Programme, 1995).

SCHOOLING IN JAPAN

September 30, 1994, Kobe, Japan. Compared to people in the United States, the Japanese

Traditionally, the Japanese have placed a strong emphasis on fitting in with the group. This cultural value is evident in the widespread wearing of school uniforms—a practice that is also gaining favor in the United States as a means to improve school discipline.

are, above all, orderly. Young boys and girls on their way to school stand out with their uniforms, armloads of books, and a look of seriousness and purpose.

Schooling has not always been part of the Japanese way of life. Before industrialization brought mandatory education in 1872, only a privileged few attended school. Today, Japan's educational system is widely praised for producing some of the world's highest achievers.

The early grades concentrate on transmitting Japanese traditions, especially obligation to family. By their early teens, as illustrated by Naoko Matsuo's story at the beginning of this chapter, students encounter Japan's system of rigorous and competitive examinations. These written tests, which resemble the Scholastic Aptitude Tests (SATs) used for college admissions in the United States, make all the difference in the future of each Japanese student.

In Japan, schooling reflects personal ability more than it does in the United States, where family income plays a greater part in a student's college plans. In Japan, government pays much of the costs of higher

GLOBAL: British "public" schools number about 1,000 and cost roughly $20,000 a year. Their popularity has dropped in recent years, perhaps due to the high cost and growing opposition by parents to sending off their young children to fend for themselves.
DIVERSITY: College completion (in 1996, aged 25 and over), as in Table 19–1, by sex: 26.0% for men, 21.4% for women; African American men, 12.4%, African American women, 14.6%; Asian/Pacific Islander men, 43.2%, Asian/Pacific Islander women, 35.5%; Hispanic men, 10.3%, Hispanic women, 8.3%.
NOTE: A bit of sociological trivia: The legality of free, public-sponsored education was decided in 1874 by the Michigan Supreme Court, under the control of Justice Thomas Cooley, Charles Horton Cooley's father.

TABLE 19–1 Educational Achievement in the United States, 1910–1996*

Year	High School Graduates	College Graduates	Median Years of Schooling
1910	13.5%	2.7%	8.1
1920	16.4	3.3	8.2
1930	19.1	3.9	8.4
1940	24.1	4.6	8.6
1950	33.4	6.0	9.3
1960	41.1	7.7	10.5
1970	55.2	11.0	12.2
1980	68.7	17.0	12.5
1990	77.6	21.3	12.4
1996	81.7	23.6	12.7

*For persons twenty-five years of age and over. Percentage for high school graduates includes those who go on to college. Percentage of high school dropouts can be calculated by subtracting percentage of high school graduates from 100 percent.

Source: U.S. Bureau of the Census (1997).

education. But without high examination scores, even the richest families cannot get their children into a good university.

More men and women graduate from high school in Japan (90 percent) than in the United States (82 percent). But because of competitive examinations, only about 30 percent of high school graduates—compared to 65 percent in the United States—end up entering college. Understandably, then, Japanese students take entrance examinations very seriously, and about half attend cram schools to prepare for them. Japanese mothers, most of whom are not in the labor force, often devote themselves to their children's success in school.

Because of the pressure it places on students, Japanese schooling produces impressive results. In a number of fields, notably mathematics and science, young Japanese students outperform students in every other industrial society, including the United States (Benedict, 1974; Hayneman & Loxley, 1983; Rohlen, 1983; Brinton, 1988; Simons, 1989).

SCHOOLING IN GREAT BRITAIN

During the Middle Ages, schooling was a privilege of the British nobility, who studied classical subjects since they had little interest in the practical skills related to earning a living. But as the Industrial Revolution created a need for an educated labor force, and as working-class people demanded access to schools, a rising share of the population entered the classroom.

British law now requires every British child to attend school until age sixteen.

Traditional social distinctions, however, persist in British education. Most wealthy families send their children to what the British call *public schools*, the equivalent of U.S. private boarding schools. These elite schools not only teach academic subjects, they also convey to children from wealthy (especially newly rich) families the distinctive patterns of speech, mannerisms, and social graces of the British upper class. These academies are far too expensive for most students, however, who attend state-supported day schools.

Since 1960, the British have lessened the influence of social background on schooling by expanding their university system and using competitive entrance examinations. For those who score the highest, the government pays most of college costs. These exams are less important than those in Japan, however, since many well-to-do children who do not score well still manage to attend Oxford and Cambridge, the most prestigious British universities, on a par with Yale, Harvard, and Princeton in the United States. "Oxbridge" graduates go on to take their places at the core of the British power elite: More than two-thirds of the top members of the British government, for example, have "Oxbridge" degrees (Sampson, 1982; Gamble, Ludlam, & Baker, 1993).

These brief sketches of schooling in India, Japan, and Great Britain show the crucial importance of economic development. In poor countries, many children—especially girls—work rather than go to school. Rich nations adopt mandatory education laws to create an industrial work force as well as to satisfy demands for greater equality. But rich nations vary among themselves, as we see in the intense competition of Japanese schools, the traditional social stratification that shapes schools in Great Britain, and the practical emphasis found in the schools of the United States.

SCHOOLING IN THE UNITED STATES

The United States was among the first countries to set a goal of mass education. By 1850, about half the young people between the ages of five and nineteen were enrolled in school. In 1918, the last of the states passed a *mandatory education law* requiring children to attend school until the age of sixteen or completion of the eighth grade. Table 19–1 shows that a milestone was reached in the mid-1960s when, for the first time, a majority of U.S. adults had high school diplomas. Today,

NOTE: Mandatory education laws helped establish our conception of childhood, as young people left the world of work on farms and in factories to study in classrooms.

THEN AND NOW: One measure of U.S. educational pragmatism is the rapidly growing number of business degrees: *1948*, 38,371 BAs, 2,341 MAs, and 14 doctorates; in *1995*, 234,323 BAs, 93,809 MAs, and 1,394 doctorates.

DISCUSS: Discuss the cultural values implicit in the classroom spelling bee (including competition, individual performance, specific standards of achievement).

NOTE: The U.S. has 14.4 million college students, 22% of the world's total. About 50 very selective schools reject more students than they accept; 200 more reject 10% to 50%; the rest of 3,600 total accept almost all applicants.

more than four out of five have a high school education, and almost one in four a four-year college degree.

The educational system in the United States has been shaped by both our affluence and democratic principles. Thomas Jefferson thought the new nation could become democratic only if people "read and understand what is going on in the world" (quoted in Honeywell, 1931:13). As Figure 19–1 shows, the United States has an outstanding record of higher education for its people: It leads all other nations in the share of the adult population holding a university degree (U.S. Bureau of the Census, 1997).

Schooling in the United States also tries to promote *equal opportunity*. National surveys show that most people think schooling is crucial to success, and about 70 percent think that everyone has the chance to get an education consistent with personal ability and talent (NORC, 1996). In truth, this opinion better expresses our aspirations than our achievement. Earlier in this century, for example, women were all but excluded from higher education, and, even today, most people who attend college come from families with above-average incomes.

In the United States, the educational system stresses the value of *practical* learning, that is, knowledge that has a direct bearing on individuals' work and interests. The educational philosopher John Dewey (1859–1952) championed *progressive education*, constantly updating what our schools teach to make learning relevant to people's lives.

Reflecting this pragmatism, today's college students select their major area of study with an eye toward future jobs. The box on page 512 takes a closer look at the changing interests of college students.

THE FUNCTIONS OF SCHOOLING

Structural-functional analysis looks at how formal education contributes to the operation of society. One of the most important functions is socialization. Schooling provides a cultural lifeline that links the generations.

SOCIALIZATION

Technologically simple societies transmit their ways of life informally from parents to children. As societies develop complex technology, however, kin can no longer stay abreast of rapidly expanding information and skills. Thus, schooling gradually emerges as a distinctive social institution employing specially trained personnel to convey the knowledge needed for adult roles.

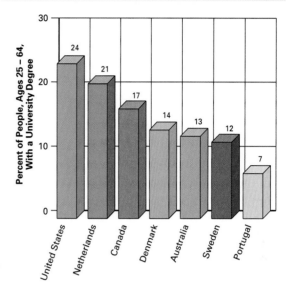

GLOBAL SNAPSHOT

FIGURE 19–1 **College Degrees in Global Perspective**

Source: U.S. Bureau of the Census (1997).

In primary school, children learn basic language and mathematical skills. Secondary school builds on this foundation, and, for many, college allows further specialization. In addition, schools transmit cultural values and norms. Civics classes, for example, explicitly instruct students in our political way of life. Sometimes the operation of the classroom itself serves to teach important cultural lessons. From the earliest grades, rituals such as saluting the flag and singing "The Star-Spangled Banner" foster patriotism. Likewise, spelling bees and classroom drills develop competitive individualism, respect for authority, and a sense of fair play.

CULTURAL INNOVATION

Education creates as well as transmits culture. Schools stimulate intellectual inquiry and critical thinking, sparking the development of new ideas.

Today, for example, college professors throughout the country are engaged in research to expand our knowledge in countless areas. Medical research conducted at major universities over the years has increased life expectancy, just as research by sociologists and psychologists helps us take advantage of our longevity.

DIVERSITY: Dovetailing with the social integration function of schooling is the multiculturalism debate, examined in Chapter 3 ("Culture").

DISCUSS: Discuss Herrnstein and Murray's contention in *The Bell Curve* that higher education has become more meritocratic across this century, with the effect of segregating an emerging "cognitive elite."

Q: "Education, then, beyond all other devices of human origin, is a great equalizer of conditions of men—the balance wheel of the social machinery." Horace Mann (1948)

DIVERSITY: In general, men outperform women on both verbal and math SATs. Verbal scores, *1967:* men, 540; women, 545. Math scores: men, 535; women, 495. Verbal scores, *1996:* men, 507; women, 503. Math: men, 527; women, 492.

SOCIOLOGY OF EVERYDAY LIFE

Following the Jobs:
Trends in Bachelor's Degrees

College attendance in the United States has never been higher, especially among women. Both sexes, however, see college education in *practical* terms, and pursue degrees in fields where they think jobs are plentiful.

In our postindustrial economy, the greatest surge in bachelor's degrees is in pre-law, as the figure shows. The number of degrees in the social sciences, communications, and education, all central to the postindustrial economy, are also up sharply. On the other hand, students shy away from majors in areas where the demand for workers is slipping. Library science heads the list of fields posting reductions, followed by engineering, philosophy and religion, and agriculture.

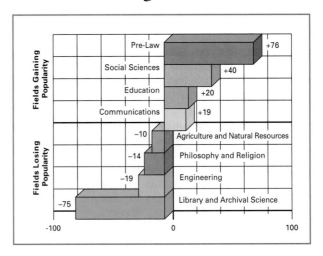

Percentage Changes in Bachelor's Degrees Earned, 1985–1995

Source: U.S. National Center for Education Statistics (1997).

SOCIAL INTEGRATION

Schooling helps forge a mass of people into a unified society. This integrative function is especially important in nations with pronounced social diversity, where various cultures know little about—or may even be hostile to—one another. In the past, the Soviet Union and Yugoslavia relied on schools to unite their disparate peoples—without ultimately succeeding.

Societies in the Americas, Africa, and Asia similarly strive to foster social integration through schooling. A basic way schools integrate culturally diverse people is by teaching a common language that encourages broad communication and builds a national identity. Of course, some ethnic minorities resist state-sponsored schooling for exactly this reason. In the former Soviet Union, for example, Lithuanians, Ukrainians, and Azerbaijanis objected to learning Russian because they saw it as a threat to their own traditions and emblematic of their domination by others. The Amish, a culturally distinctive people in the United States, historically fought to keep their children out of public schools in order to preserve their cultural traditions.

A century ago, mandatory education laws in the United States coincided with the arrival of millions of European immigrants and helped to integrate society. Today as well, formal education helps integrate large numbers of immigrants from Latin America and Asia, who, in turn, offer their traditions to our ever-changing cultural mix. At the same time, as racial and ethnic minorities have become a numerical majority in many of the largest school districts, the debate over multicultural education has grown (highlighted in Chapter 3, "Culture").

SOCIAL PLACEMENT

Formal education helps young people assume culturally approved statuses and perform roles that contribute to the ongoing life of society. Ideally, schools accomplish this by identifying and developing each individual's

DIVERSITY: Students of color are now 25% of those taking the SAT, up from about 15% in 1980.
DIVERSITY: The SAT, ACT, and GRE all show modest declines in black-white differences over the last 20 years. By category, 1996 SAT scores: white, 1049; African American, 856; Asian American, 1054; Hispanic, 931; Native American, 960.

RESOURCE: Among the classics in the Macionis and Benokraitis reader is "Education and Inequality," by Samuel Bowles and Herbert Gintis.
Q: "The SAT *is* a very biased test. It is biased against those who don't read." Christopher de Vinck, arguing that the bias issue is clear only with regard to reading ("Why I Read to My Children," *Wall Street Journal*, Nov. 22, 1993:A14)

aptitudes and abilities and then evaluating a student's performance in terms of achievement rather than social background.

In principle, teachers encourage the "best and the brightest" to pursue the most challenging and advanced studies, while guiding students with more ordinary ability into educational programs suited to their talents. Schooling, in short, enhances meritocracy by making personal merit a foundation of future social position (Hurn, 1978).

LATENT FUNCTIONS OF SCHOOLING

Besides these manifest functions of formal education, a number of latent functions are less widely recognized. One is child care. As the number of one-parent families and two-career couples rises, schools have become vital to relieving parents of some child-care responsibilities.

For teenagers, too, schooling consumes considerable time and energy, often fostering conformity at a time of life when the risk of unlawful behavior is high. Also, because many students attend school well into their twenties, education engages thousands for whom jobs might not be available.

Another latent function of schools is establishing relationships and networks. Many people form lifelong friendships—as well as meet their future spouses—in high school and college. Affiliation with a particular school also can create valuable career opportunities.

Critical evaluation. Structural-functional analysis of formal education identifies both manifest and latent contributions of this social institution to an industrial way of life. But it overlooks one core truth: The quality of schooling is far greater for some than for others. Indeed, critics of the U.S. educational system maintain that schooling actually reproduces the class structure in each generation. In the next section, social-conflict analysis takes up precisely this issue.

SCHOOLING AND SOCIAL INEQUALITY

Social-conflict analysis counters the functionalist view that schooling is a meritocratic strategy for developing people's talents and abilities. Rather, this approach argues that schools routinely provide learning according to students' social background, thereby perpetuating social inequality.

Many of the world's societies consider schooling more important for males than for females. Although the U.S. education gap between women and men has largely closed in recent decades, many women still study conventionally "feminine" subjects such as literature, while men pursue mathematics and engineering. And by stressing the experiences of some types of people (say, military generals) while ignoring the lives of others (such as farm women), schools reinforce the values and importance of dominant categories of people. Finally, as we shall see later in this chapter, affluent people have much more educational opportunity than poor people have.

SOCIAL CONTROL

Social-conflict analysis suggests that schooling acts as a means of social control, reinforcing acceptance of the status quo. In various—sometimes subtle—ways, schools reproduce the status hierarchy.

Samuel Bowles and Herbert Gintis (1976) point out that the clamor for public education in the late nineteenth century arose at precisely the time that capitalists were seeking a literate, docile, and disciplined work force. Mandatory education laws ensured that schools would teach immigrants not only English, but also cultural values that support capitalism. Compliance, punctuality, and discipline were—and still are—part of what conflict theorists call the **hidden curriculum,** *subtle presentations of political or cultural ideas in the classroom.*

STANDARDIZED TESTING

Here is a question of the kind historically used to measure academic ability of school-age children in the United States:

Painter is to painting as _____ is to sonnet.
Answers: (a) driver   (c) priest
(b) poet   (d) carpenter

The correct answer is (b) *poet:* A painter creates a painting just as a poet creates a sonnet. This question supposedly measures logical reasoning, but demonstrating this skill depends upon knowing what each term means. Unless students are familiar with sonnets as a Western European form of written verse, they are not likely to answer the question correctly.

Educational specialists claim that bias of this kind has been all but eliminated from standardized tests, since testing organizations carefully study response patterns and drop any question that favors one racial

Q: "And then in high school, they sorted us into college prep and vocational ed types, sorted us like apples, some mashed into cider and applesauce, others polished, wrapped in tissue paper, crated and marked for export . . ." P. F. Kluge
Q: "Children in one set of schools are trained to be governors; children in the other set are trained to be governed." Jonathan Kozol

SOCIAL SURVEY: "Does everyone in this country have an opportunity to obtain an education corresponding to their abilities and talents?" (GSS 1984, N = 1,473; *Codebook*, 1996:99)
"Yes"   69.8%   "No"   27.9%   DK/NR   2.3%
Q: "In education, there should be no class distinction." Confucius
NOTE: Of some 14,000 American Sociological Association members, only about 400 are sociology of education specialists.

From a functionalist point of view, schooling provides children with the knowledge and skills they will need as adults. A conflict analysis adds that schooling differs according to the resources of the local community. When some schools offer children much more than others do, education perpetuates the class structure rather than increasing equality of opportunity.

or ethnic category over another. Critics, however, maintain that some bias based on class, race, or ethnicity is inherent in any formal testing, because questions inevitably reflect our society's dominant culture and thereby put minorities at a disadvantage (Owen, 1985; Crouse & Trusheim, 1988; Putka, 1990).

SCHOOL TRACKING

Despite continuing controversy over standardized tests, most schools in the United States use them as the basis for **tracking,** *the assignment of students to different types of educational programs.* Tracking is also a common practice in many other industrial societies, including Great Britain, France, and Japan.

The official justification for tracking is to give students the kind of learning that fits their abilities and motivation. Young people have different interests, with some drawn to, say, the study of languages and others to art or physical education. Given disparate talents and goals, no single program for all students would serve any of them well.

Education critic Jonathan Kozol (1992) considers tracking part of the "savage inequalities" in our school

system by which our society defines some children as winners and others as losers. Research shows that social background has as much to do with tracking as personal aptitude. Students from affluent families generally do well on standardized, "scientific" tests and so are placed in college-bound tracks, while students from modest backgrounds (including a disproportionate share of the poor) end up in programs that curb their aspirations and teach technical trades. Tracking, therefore, effectively segregates students—academically and socially—into different worlds. As National Map 19–1 shows, it is in the affluent sections of the country where most young people go on to attend college.

Furthermore, most schools reserve their best teachers for students in the top tracks. These teachers put more effort into teaching, show more respect to students, and expect more from them. By contrast, teachers in lower tracks employ more memorization, classroom drill, and other unstimulating techniques. They also emphasize regimentation, punctuality, and respect for authority figures.

In light of these criticisms, schools across the United States are now cautious about making tracking assignments and allow more mobility between tracks. Some have even moved away from the practice

THE MAP: Relatively affluent regions of the United States have a higher share of young people enrolled in college; in addition, high-enrollment counties are those where people endorse greater opportunities for women (compare to National Map 12–1).

DIVERSITY: Of all U.S. public school teachers, 7.4% are African American and 4.2% are Hispanic. In New York City, the corresponding figures are 19% and 10%.

Q: "The [private] school—rather than the upper-class family—is the most important agency for transmitting the traditions of the upper classes, and regulating the admission of new wealth and talent. . . . It is by means of these schools more than by any other single agency that the older and the newer families . . . become members of a self-conscious upper class." C. Wright Mills (1959:64-65)

SEEING OURSELVES

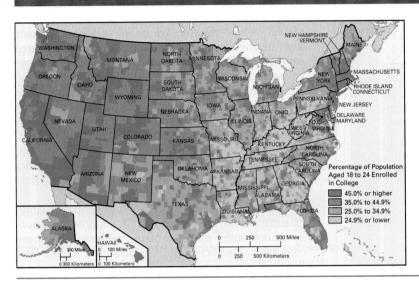

NATIONAL MAP 19–1
College Attendance Across the United States

Generally speaking, college attendance is highest among adults along the Northeast and West coasts. By contrast, adults in the Midwest and the South (especially the Appalachian region) are the least likely members of our society to attend college. How would you explain this pattern? (Income is one obvious consideration; would people's ideas about gender equality be another?)

Source: *American Demographics* magazine, April 1993, p. 60. Reprinted with permission. ©1993 *American Demographics* magazine, Ithaca, New York.

Percentage of Population Aged 18 to 24 Enrolled in College
- 45.0% or higher
- 35.0% to 44.9%
- 25.0% to 34.9%
- 24.9% or lower

ve
inc
wl
La
re
Fc
ha
Ui

int
inc

TA

Ec

Pr
Dc
Ma
Ba
1–
4 y
9–
0–

*Per
earn
leve
Sou

entirely. Some tracking seems to be necessary to match instruction with student abilities. But rigid tracking has a powerful impact on students' learning and self-concept. Young people who spend years in higher tracks tend to see themselves as bright and able, whereas students in lower tracks have less ambition and low self-esteem (Bowles & Gintis, 1976; Persell, 1977; Davis & Haller, 1981; Oakes, 1982, 1985; Hallinan & Williams, 1989; Kilgore, 1991; Gamoran, 1992).

INEQUALITY AMONG SCHOOLS

Just as students are treated differently within schools, schools themselves differ in fundamental ways. The biggest difference is between public and private schools.

Public and Private Schools

In 1996, 86 percent of the 55 million U.S. school-aged children attended state-funded public schools. The remainder were in private schools.

Most private school students attend one of the 8,000 *parochial schools* (from the Latin meaning "of the parish") operated by the Roman Catholic church. The Catholic school system grew rapidly a century ago as cities swelled with millions of Catholic immigrants and their children. These schools helped the new arrivals maintain their religious heritage in the midst of a predominantly Protestant society. Today, after decades

of flight from the city by white people, many parochial schools enroll non-Catholics, including a growing number of young African Americans whose families seek an alternative to the neighborhood public school.

Protestants, especially in fundamentalist denominations, also have private schools or Christian academies. These Christian schools are favored by parents who want their children to receive religious instruction or seek higher academic and disciplinary standards. Some white parents turn to Christian schools to provide a racially homogeneous environment for their children in the face of mandated school desegregation. In recent years, however, African Americans, too, have sought out Christian schools as an alternative to public education (James, 1989; Dent, 1996).

Some 1,500 nonreligious private schools in the United States also enroll students, mostly from well-to-do families. These prestigious and expensive preparatory schools are especially favored by "newly rich" parents eager for their daughters and sons to rub elbows with children from "old money." These institutions—many modeled on boarding schools in Great Britain—are academically outstanding and send many graduates to equally prestigious and expensive private universities. After learning the mannerisms, attitudes, and social graces of the socially prominent, "preppies" generally maintain lifelong school-based networks that provide numerous social advantages.

Are private schools better than public schools? Research indicates that, given similar backgrounds,

Q: "Should we produce competent bureaucrats and narrowly trained technicians, or should we develop creative, reflective individuals who will help to transform the world into more democratic forms?" Harvey Holtz (1989:193)

Q: "Instructors who want dialogue to return to the classroom must take it upon themselves to challenge students with a freer, more reflexive form of learning. Professors who rely solely on [lecture-oriented] teaching techniques—but then slouch on their podiums and lament that 'teaching is dead' when these techniques fail—are guilty of murder." Richard A. Wright, "Curing Doonesbury's Disease—A Prescription for Dialogue in the Classroom," *Quarterly Journal of Ideology* 9, 4 (1985):3–8

Q: "A college professor is someone who talks in other people's sleep." Bergen Evans

During the last few years, a rash of deadly shootings in U.S. schools—some by youngsters barely into their teens—has stunned the nation. The truth is that thousands of children come to school each day armed with deadly weapons. Why do you think this is the case? What can we do to put an end to this problem?

the United States, Theodore Sizer (1984) identified five ways in which large, bureaucratic schools undermine education (207–9):

1. **Rigid uniformity.** Bureaucratic schools, run by outsider specialists (such as state education officials), generally ignore the cultural character of local communities and the personal needs of their children.

2. **Numerical ratings.** School officials define success in terms of numerical attendance records, dropout rates, and achievement test scores. Therefore, they overlook dimensions of schooling that are difficult to quantify, such as the creativity of students and the energy and enthusiasm of teachers.

3. **Rigid expectations.** Officials expect fifteen-year-olds to be in the tenth grade, and eleventh-graders to score at a certain level on a standardized verbal achievement test. Rarely are exceptionally bright and motivated students permitted to graduate early. Likewise, the system pushes students from grade to grade whether they have learned anything or not.

4. **Specialization.** High school students learn Spanish from one teacher, receive guidance from another, and are coached in sports by still others. Although specialized teachers may know more about their subjects, no school employee comes to know and appreciate the "complete" student. Students experience this division of labor as a continual shuffling from one fifty-minute period to another throughout the school day.

5. **Little individual responsibility.** Highly bureaucratic schools do not empower students to learn on their own. Similarly, teachers have little latitude in what and how they teach their classes; they dare not accelerate instruction for fear of disrupting "the system."

Of course, some formal organization in schools is inevitable given the immense size of the task. The number of students in the New York City public schools alone now exceeds the student population of the entire country a century ago. But, Sizer maintains, we can humanize schools to make them more responsive to the students they claim to serve. He recommends eliminating rigid class schedules, reducing class size, and training teachers more broadly to help them become more involved in the lives of their students. Overall, as James Coleman (1993) recently suggested, schools need to be less "administratively driven" and more "output-driven." Perhaps this transformation

RESOURCE: The Karp and Yoels article, "Why Don't College Students Participate?" is included in the Macionis and Benokraitis reader, *Seeing Ourselves.*
NOTE: The blackboard, which may encourage passivity among college students, was first used at Bowdoin College in 1823.
NOTE: Dropout rates are extremely high for large, urban school systems in the U.S. Examples: Boston, 46%; Chicago, 45%; Los Angeles, 45%; New York, 34%; St. Louis, 30%.
DIVERSITY: Dropping out of college is a growing problem among African Americans. Despite efforts to recruit more minorities, fewer black students finish school. In 1965, of all students beginning college, the proportion of African Americans completing four years was 90% as high as for whites; it has now fallen to about 69%.

could begin by ensuring that graduation from high school depends on what a student has learned rather than simply on the number of years spent in the building.

College: The Silent Classroom

Here are the observations of a bright and highly motivated first-year student at a prestigious four-year college. Do they strike a familiar chord?

> I have been disappointed in my first year at college. Too many students do as little work as they can get away with, take courses that are recommended by other students as being "gut" classes, and never challenge themselves past what is absolutely necessary. It's almost like thinking that we don't watch professors but we watch television. (Forrest, 1984:10)

Passivity is also common in colleges and universities. Martha E. Gimenez (1989) describes college as the "silent classroom" because the only voice heard is usually the teacher's. Sociologists tend not to conduct research on the college classroom—a curious fact considering how much time they spend there. A fascinating exception is a study at a coeducational university where David Karp and William Yoels (1976) found that—even in small classes—only a handful of students said anything at all during the typical class period. Karp and Yoels concluded that passivity is a classroom norm, and that students even become irritated if one of their number is especially talkative.

Gender also affects classroom dynamics. Karp and Yoels found that in coeducational classes taught by a man, male students carried on most classroom discussion. With women as instructors, however, the two sexes were more equal in terms of participation. Why? Perhaps because women instructors directed questions to women students as frequently as to men, while male teachers favored their male students.

Students offered Karp and Yoels various explanations for classroom passivity, including not having done the assigned reading or fearing that they might sound unintelligent to teachers and other students. To them, passivity is mostly their own fault. Yet long before they reach college, Karp and Yoels point out, students learn to view instructors as "experts" who serve up "truth." Thus they find little value in classroom discussion and perceive that the student's proper role is to quietly listen and take notes. This perception squares with the finding of Karp and Yoels that only 10 percent of class time is devoted to discussion.

Students also realize that instructors generally come to class ready to deliver a prepared lecture. Lecturing allows teachers to present a great deal of material in each class, but only to the extent that they avoid being sidetracked by student questions or comments (Boyer, 1987). Early in each course, most instructors single out a few students who are willing and able to provide the occasional, limited comments they desire. Taken together, such patterns form a recipe for passivity on the part of most college students.

Yet faculty can bring students to life in their classrooms: The key is actively involving them in learning. One recent study of classroom dynamics, for example, linked higher levels of student participation to four teaching strategies: (1) calling on students by name when they volunteer, (2) positively reinforcing student participation, (3) asking analytical rather than factual questions and giving students time to answer, and (4) asking for students' opinions even when they do not volunteer (Auster & MacRone, 1994).

DROPPING OUT

If many students are passive in class, others are not there at all. The problem of *dropping out*—quitting school before earning a high school diploma—leaves young people (many of whom are disadvantaged to begin with) ill-equipped for the world of work and at high risk for poverty.

The dropout rate in the United States has declined slightly in recent decades; currently about 11 percent of people between the ages of sixteen and twenty-four have dropped out of school, a total of some 4.5 million young women and men. Dropping out is least pronounced among non-Hispanic whites (7.3 percent), slightly greater among African Americans (13 percent), and the most serious among Hispanics (29 percent) (U.S. National Center for Education Statistics, 1997).

Some students drop out because of problems with the English language or because of pregnancy; others, whose families are poor, must go to work to earn income. The dropout rate (23 percent) among children growing up in the bottom 20 percent of households is eight times higher than that (3 percent) for youngsters whose households fall in the top 20 percent by income (U.S. National Center for Education Statistics, 1997). These data point to the fact that many dropouts are young people whose parents also have little schooling, creating a multigenerational cycle of disadvantage.

DIVERSITY: In 1995, 36.9% of U.S. teens between 15 and 17 years of age were either one or more grade levels behind or had dropped out entirely—up from 29.1% in 1980. By race, 34.9% whites, 50.4% African Americans, 51.3% Hispanics (U.S. Bureau of the Census, 1997).

NOTE: Federal literacy programs enroll several million adults each year, a small proportion of those who are functionally illiterate.

NOTE: Recent research suggests that one-third of parents are "seriously disengaged" from their adolescent children's lives (Steinberg, 1996).

NOTE: One study of the mathematical skills of 12th graders concluded that 48.2% knew the basics, 35.6% were below "basics" level, 13.6% were "proficient," and 2.6% were "advanced" (National Assessment of Educational Progress).

GLOBAL SNAPSHOT

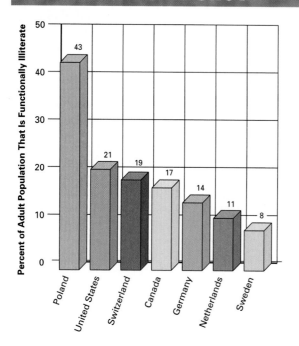

FIGURE 19–4 Functional Illiteracy in Global Perspective

Source: Fiske (1997).

Supporting this conclusion, the report noted that "nearly 40 percent of seventeen-year-olds cannot draw inferences from written material; only one-fifth can write a persuasive essay; and only one-third can solve mathematical problems requiring several steps" (1983:9). Furthermore, scores on the Scholastic Aptitude Test (SAT) have declined since the early 1960s. In 1967, median scores for students were 516 on the mathematical test and 543 on the verbal test; by 1996, the averages had slipped to 508 and 505. Some of this decline may be due to the greater number of students taking the SATs, not all of whom are well prepared (Owen, 1985). But few doubt that, in recent decades, schooling has suffered a setback.

A Nation at Risk also noted with alarm the extent of **functional illiteracy,** *reading and writing skills insufficient for everyday living.* Roughly one in eight children in the United States completes secondary school without learning to read or write very well. For older people, the problem is even worse, so that, overall, some 40 million adults (about 21 percent of the total) read and write at an eighth-grade level or below. As Figure 19–4 shows, the extent of functional illiteracy in the United States, while below that of middle-income nations (such as Poland), is higher than in other rich countries (such as Canada and Sweden).

To improve our educational system, *A Nation at Risk* calls for drastic measures. First, all schools should require students to complete several years of English, mathematics, social studies, general science, and computer science courses. Second, schools should not promote failing students from grade to grade; instead, students should remain in the classroom as long as necessary to learn basic skills. Third, teacher training must improve and teachers' salaries should rise to attract talent into the profession. *A Nation at Risk* concludes that educators must ensure that schools meet public expectations and that citizens must be prepared to bear the costs of good schools.

A final concern is the low performance of U.S. students in global context: Despite some recent improvement, U.S. eighth graders still place seventeenth in the world in science achievement and twenty-eighth in mathematics (Bennett, 1997). Cultural values play a big part in international comparisons. For example, U.S. students are generally less motivated than their counterparts in Japan and also do less homework. Moreover, Japanese young people spend sixty more days in school each year than U.S. students. Perhaps we might improve student performance simply by lengthening the school year.

For young people who drop out of school in a credential society such as our own, the risk of unemployment or becoming stuck in a low-paying job is very real. Faced with this reality, approximately one-third of those who leave school return to the classroom at a later time.

ACADEMIC STANDARDS

Perhaps the most serious educational issue confronting our society involves the quality of schooling. *A Nation at Risk*, a comprehensive report on the quality of U.S. schools made in 1983 by the National Commission on Excellence in Education, began with this alarming statement:

> If an unfriendly foreign power had attempted to impose on America the mediocre educational performance that exists today, we might well have viewed it as an act of war. As it stands, we have allowed this to happen to ourselves. (1983:5)

CYBER: By the end of 1997, fifteen western states and Guam were cooperating in the Western Governors' University. Throughout the United States, some online programs are now found at hundreds of colleges and universities.

THEN AND NOW: By-mail college courses date back to the 1890s; cyber-college is a new way to do something that has been around a while.

CYBER: Applying to college is now an online experience. Virtual campus tours are proliferating. And www.collegelink.com and other Web sites take applications to some 800 schools.

Q: "[The magnet school] is a blueprint for school desegregation in the future without relying on mandatory busing, which does not work in a very meaningful way." William Bradford Reynolds

EXPLORING CYBER-SOCIETY

Welcome to "Cyber-College"!

There was no crowd on hand to watch a ritual groundbreaking. But a new U.S. institution was born in mid-1996 when the governors of ten western states agreed to create the nation's first "virtual university."

What is a "cyber-college"? In the Information Age, "college" no longer means a grand campus of stone buildings, a library full of books, and classrooms filled with students and faculty. Going to college today can be a simple matter of logging on to a personal computer.

That's the way it is at the new Western Governors' University, where students enroll online, go to class using their keyboards, read assignments on the computer screen, and send in assignments by e-mail. And, instead of face-to-face class discussions, students gather in online "chat rooms."

What is the future of online learning? Certainly, many students will continue to opt for a conventional college experience with dorms, lecture halls, and playing fields. But the lower costs of a virtual college and the fact that learning can be done at home and according to a person's individual schedule are sure to attract a wave of new "cyber-students."

Source: Based on Cushman, Jr. (1996).

RECENT ISSUES IN U.S. EDUCATION

Our society's schools continuously confront new challenges. This final section explores several recent and important educational issues.

One of the forces reshaping the educational system is technology. The box takes a closer look at how new information technology is creating new possibilities for higher education.

SCHOOL CHOICE

Some analysts claim that the reason our schools do not teach very well is that they have no competition. Thus, giving parents options for schooling their children might force all schools to do a better job. This is the essence of a policy called *school choice*.

Proponents of school choice advocate creating a market for schooling, so that parents and students can shop for the best value. According to one proposal, the government would give vouchers to families with school-aged children and allow them to spend that money at public, private, or parochial schools. During the 1990s, Indianapolis, Minneapolis, Milwaukee, and Cleveland have experimented with choice plans in the hope that public schools would be forced to perform better and win the confidence of families. Supporters of school choice claim that the policy does improve schools. But critics (including teachers' unions) charge that school choice amounts to giving up our nation's commitment to public education and will do little to improve schools in the central cities where the need is greatest (Martinez et al., 1995).

A more modest form of school choice involves creating *magnet schools*, 1,000 of which now exist across the country. Magnet schools offer special facilities and programs to promote educational excellence in a particular area, such as computer science, foreign languages, science and mathematics, or the arts. In school districts with magnet schools, parents can choose the one best suited to a particular student's talents and interests.

Yet another recent development in the school choice movement is *schooling for profit*. Advocates of this proposal say school systems can be operated by private profit-making companies more efficiently than by local governments. Of course, private schooling is nothing new; more than 10,000 schools are currently run by private organizations and religious groups. What is new, however, is the idea that private companies can carry out *mass* education in the United States.

Research confirms that many public school systems suffer from bureaucratic bloat, spending too much and teaching too little. And our society has long

NOTE: The most powerful opponent of school choice programs is the National Education Association (NEA), with more than 2 million members, mostly teachers.
NOTE: Some charter schools "opt out" of local school board control; others are start-up schools. All have considerable autonomy and limited bureaucracy.
NOTE: A century ago, reformers praised school bureaucracies run by "specialists" as a way to keep schools out of the hand of urban political machines.
NOTE: About four in ten adults will take part in adult education at some point in their lives.
DISCUSS: Is grade inflation a problem? Since 1970, 93% of Stanford University's grades have been As and Bs—and no Fs. In 1995, Stanford reintroduced failing grades (NP for "not passed").

Currently, our society is debating many strategies for improving education. Proponents of Afrocentric schooling argue that teaching African languages and cultures (left) will heighten children's self-esteem and interest in learning. Some parents have kept their children out of formal education altogether (right), believing their youngsters can learn more at home, using information available not only in books, but also in cyberspace.

looked to competition as a strategy to improve quality. But the results of schooling for profit appear mixed. Several companies claim to have improved student learning; yet, some cities have cut back on business-run schools. In 1995, for example, Baltimore canceled the contract of the corporation that had taken over nine of its schools in 1992; school boards in Miami and Hartford, Connecticut, have also canceled contracts. In short, public school systems perform poorly in many cities; but whether or not private business can improve on this record remains unclear.

Finally, *charter schools* are another recent innovation. These are public schools that operate with less state regulation so teachers and administrators can try out new teaching strategies. One condition of a "charter" is that the school must promise to perform as well or better than other schools in the district. In 1998, some 700 charter schools were operating in about half the states (Toch, 1991; Putka & Stecklow, 1994; Kanamine, 1995; Ravitch & Viteritti, 1996; Bennett, 1997).

SCHOOLING PEOPLE WITH DISABILITIES

Bureaucratic schools do not readily meet the special needs of some people, including many of the 5 million U.S. children with physical impairments. Many children with disabilities have difficulty getting to and from school, and many with crutches or wheelchairs cannot negotiate stairs and other obstacles inside school buildings. Children with developmental disabilities like mental retardation require extensive personal attention from specially trained teachers. As a result, many children with mental and physical disabilities have received a public education only because of persistent efforts by parents and other concerned citizens.

About one-fourth of children with disabilities are schooled in special facilities; the rest attend public schools, many participating in regular classes. Thus, most schools avoid expensive "special education" in favor of **mainstreaming**, *integrating special students into the overall educational program*. Mainstreaming is a form of *inclusive education* that works best for physically impaired students who have no difficulty keeping up academically with the rest of the class. Moreover, putting children with and without disabilities in the same classroom allows everyone to learn more about interacting with people who differ from themselves.

ADULT EDUCATION

Most schooling involves young people. However, the share of U.S. students aged twenty-five and older has risen sharply in recent years and now accounts for 43 percent of people in the classroom.

By 1996, more than 25 million U.S. adults were enrolled in some type of schooling. These older students range in age from the middle-twenties to the seventies

DISCUSS: Assess Max Weber's contention, detailed in Chapter 2 ("Sociological Investigation"), that political advocacy necessarily clashes with science.
Q: "University politics are so vicious precisely because the stakes are so small." Henry Kissinger
Q: "An intellectual is a person who uses more words than necessary to tell you more than he knows." Dwight D. Eisenhower

NOTE: James Davison Hunter (1991) notes that the American Sociological Association has passed resolutions on a number of political issues, supporting the *Roe* v. *Wade* decision, gay rights, and calling for an end to aid to El Salvador as well as a boycott of Gallo wines. Moreover, he adds, ASA's policy is to locate its annual meeting with political considerations in mind, for instance, avoiding states that did not pass the ERA.

CONTROVERSY & DEBATE

Political Correctness:
Improving or Undermining Education?

Are you "p.c."? Is your teacher? What about this textbook? The last decade has seen a heightened level of political debate on the college campus. In about 1990, the term *political correctness* entered our language to refer to thinking and acting in accordance with liberal political principles. To be "politically correct," at least as opponents see it, implies that "truth" is less a matter of scientific evidence than having the "correct" politics. Surveying today's campus scene, James Davison Hunter (1991:211) concludes, "The cultural ethos of the modern university clearly favors a progressivist agenda," including support for feminism, gay rights, and various other movements toward social equality.

To some people, political correctness threatens the traditional open-mindedness of the university; at its worst, it turns professors into activists and teaching into indoctrination. Moreover, political correctness may have a chilling effect in the classroom, making students afraid to offer opinions on controversial issues (say, homosexuality or racial differences in measured intelligence) for fear of offending others who

might, in turn, charge them with "homophobia" or "racism." Professors, too, feel the pressure to be politically correct: Douglas Massey (1995) points out that a number of well-known researchers have been ostracized by their peers for conducting research that is scientifically solid but that advances "unpopular notions" about race and gender.

But not everyone thinks "p.c." is a problem. Many students and faculty defend a politically engaged campus on moral grounds. As they see it, there is a great deal of injustice in the world that should be addressed. Richard Rorty (1994), for example, applauds the fact that some academic departments have become "sanctuaries for left-wing political views" because activist colleagues do "a great deal of good for people who have gotten a raw deal in our society: women, African Americans, gay men, and lesbians." By focusing on marginalized people, he continues, the campus "will, in the long run, help to make our country much more decent, more tolerant, and more civilized."

Keep in mind, too, that "political correctness" can be easily exaggerated. While it is probably fair to characterize

academia (and sociologists, overall) as politically liberal, virtually every campus includes faculty, administrators, and students who espouse a wide range of political opinions. Furthermore, charges of political correctness in academia are nothing new. Just sixty years ago, for example, a majority of states sought to keep teachers in check by requiring that they sign loyalty oaths before permitting them to speak in the classroom (Hunter, 1991). Perhaps it is true that "the more things change . . . "

Continue the debate . . .

1. *Overall, do you agree that academia has a left-wing political bias? Why or why not?*

2. *Should teachers (or textbooks) take explicit political stands on controversial issues?*

3. *Have you or other students remained silent during class discussion for fear of sounding "politically incorrect"? Has a course ever led you to change attitudes you came to see as narrow-minded?*

and beyond. Adults in school are twice as likely to be women as men and generally have above-average incomes. Some are part-time students completing college degrees; others already have a college diploma and other advanced degrees (Speer, 1996; Miller, 1997b).

What draws adults back to school? The reasons are as varied as the students, but most return to enhance their careers, enrolling in business, health, or engineering courses. Others, who study everything from astronomy to Zen, simply enjoy learning.

LOOKING AHEAD: SCHOOLING IN THE TWENTY-FIRST CENTURY

Despite the fact that the United States leads the world in higher education, our public school system continues to struggle with serious problems, many of which have their roots in the larger society. Thus, as we approach the next century, we cannot expect schools—by themselves—to raise the quality of education. Schools will only improve to the extent to which students, teachers,

NOTE: Higher-education institutions offering the top average salaries for full professor include Harvard, number one at $104,000, to Rutgers, Newark, N.J.; Princeton; and Yale, ranging from $96,500 to $99,300. National averages: full, $63,450 (men, $64,560; women, $57,160); associate, $47,040; assistant, $39,050; instructor, $29,680; lecturer, $32,600; overall average, $49,500. Average at doctorate-granting institutions, $71,290; community colleges, $51,790; private colleges, $84,790; public colleges, $67,560. Forty percent of all faculty are part-timers who earn much less than these figures. Lawyers earn 70% more than professors, on average (AAUP).

NOTE: Comparing the top ten states in terms of teacher salaries and rates of student graduation from high school, there is only one overlap (New Jersey).

parents, and local communities commit to educational excellence. In short, educational dilemmas are *social* problems for which there is no "quick fix."

Another important factor reshaping schools is new information technology. Today, 97 percent of conventional primary and secondary schools have instructional computers. The promise of this new technology goes beyond helping students learn basic skills; computers actually can improve the overall quality of learning. Interacting with computers prompts students to be more active and allows them to progress at their own pace. For students with disabilities who cannot write using a pencil, computers permit easier self-expression. Using computers in schools—in some cases, as early as kindergarten—also appears to increase significantly learning speed and retention of information (Fantini, 1986).

The numerous benefits of computers should not blind us to their limitations, however. Computers will never bring to the educational process the personal insight or imagination of a motivated human teacher. Nor can computers tap what one teacher calls the "springs of human identity and creativity" we discover through exploring literature and language rather than simply manipulating mathematical codes. As to whether or not computers really improve teaching, then, the jury is still out (Golden, 1982:56; Skinner, 1997).

Indeed, despite their proliferation in the classroom, computers have yet to change teaching and learning in any fundamental sense or even to replace the traditional blackboard (Berger, 1991; Elmer-DeWitt, 1991). Thus, as our society enters the twenty-first century, we should not look to technology to solve many of the problems—including violence and rigid bureaucracy—that plague our schools. What we need is a broad plan for social change that refires this country's early ambition to provide quality universal schooling—a goal that has so far eluded us.

SUMMARY

1. Education is the major social institution for transmitting knowledge and skills, as well as teaching cultural norms and values. In preindustrial societies, education occurs informally within the family; industrial societies develop formal systems of schooling.

2. The United States was among the first countries to institute compulsory mass education, reflecting both democratic political ideals and the needs of the industrial-capitalist economy.

3. Structural-functional analysis highlights major functions of schooling, including socialization, cultural innovation, social integration, and placing people in the social hierarchy. Latent functions of schooling involve providing child care and building social networks.

4. Social-conflict analysis links schooling to hierarchy involving class, race, and gender. Formal education also serves as a means of generating conformity to produce compliant adult workers.

5. Standardized achievement tests are controversial: Some see them as a reasonable measure of academic aptitude and learning, while others say they are culturally biased tools used to label less-privileged students as personally deficient.

6. Tracking, too, is controversial: Some see tracking as the way schools provide instruction to students with different interests and aptitudes; others say tracking gives privileged youngsters a richer education.

7. The great majority of young people in the United States attend state-funded public schools. Most private schools offer a religious education. A small proportion of students—usually well-to-do—attend elite, private preparatory schools.

8. Almost one-fourth of U.S. adults over the age of twenty-five are now college graduates, marking the emergence of a "credential society." People with college degrees enjoy greatly increased lifetime earnings.

9. Most adults in the United States are critical of public schools. Violence permeates many schools, especially those in poor neighborhoods. The bureaucratic character of schools also fosters high dropout rates and student passivity.

10. Declining academic standards are reflected in today's lower average scores on achievement tests and the functional illiteracy of a significant proportion of high school graduates.

11. The school choice movement seeks to make schools more responsive to the public. Innovative

options include magnet schools, schools for profit, and charter schools, all of which are topics of continuing policy debate.

12. Children with mental or physical disabilities historically have been schooled in special classes or not at all. Mainstreaming affords them broader opportunities.

13. Adults represent a growing proportion of students in the United States. Most older learners are women and are engaged in job-related study.

14. The Information Revolution is changing schooling through the increasing use of computers. Although computers permit interactive, self-paced learning, they are not suitable for teaching every subject.

KEY CONCEPTS

education the social institution guiding a society's transmission of knowledge—including basic facts, job skills, and also cultural norms and values—to its members

schooling formal instruction under the direction of specially trained teachers

hidden curriculum subtle presentations of political or cultural ideas in the classroom

tracking the assignment of students to different types of educational programs

credentialism evaluating a person on the basis of educational degrees

functional illiteracy reading and writing skills insufficient for everyday living

mainstreaming integrating special students into the overall educational program

CRITICAL-THINKING QUESTIONS

1. Why does industrialization lead societies to expand their system of schooling?

2. Referring to the United States and other countries, describe ways in which schooling is shaped by economic, political, and cultural factors.

3. From a structural-functional perspective, why is schooling important to the operation of society?

From a social-conflict point of view, how does formal education operate to reproduce social inequality in each generation?

4. Do you agree with research findings presented in this chapter that, by and large, college students are passive in class? If so, what do you think colleges can do to make students more active participants in learning?

LEARNING EXERCISES

1. Arrange to visit a secondary school near your college or home. Does it have a "tracking" policy? If so, find out how it works. How much importance does a student's social background have in making a track assignment?

2. Most people agree that teaching our children is a vital task. Yet, most teachers earn relatively low salaries. Check the prestige ranking for teachers back in Table 10–2. What can you find out at the library about the average salaries of teachers compared to other workers? Can you explain this pattern?

3. If you have computer access, visit the Family Farm Project Web site at Kenyon College: http://www. Kenyon.edu/projects/famfarm/welcome/welcome.htm

This site was created by students to share what they had learned in a course investigating farms and rural life in central Ohio.

4. Since 1975, the federal government and every state have passed special-education laws providing for children with physical disabilities. But policies and available funding vary widely. Do some library research, or contact teachers or other officials, to determine the situation in your own state.

5. Install the CD-ROM packaged inside the back cover of your text and complete the activities designed to accompany this chapter.

Li T'ang, *Itinerant Physician in Village, China,* c. 1100

HEALTH AND MEDICINE

Nineteen-year-old Melody Barrett squirms restlessly on her chair in the waiting room of the medical clinic at her exclusive private college in Minnesota. She is annoyed and uneasy; her roommate pressured her to see the doctor, and she is afraid her parents will find out. There isn't anything wrong, she keeps telling herself. Her parents, both lawyers, live in Minneapolis forty miles away. They expect their daughter home for the weekend, but Melody is trying to think up an excuse to not go.

This young woman's problem is failing health from starvation. Far from thinking that she is starving, however, she feels fat. She knows that she weighs only eighty-seven pounds, and she expects the doctor to warn her that she weighs far too little for a woman five feet, three inches tall. But for over three years Melody has been preoccupied—her roommate would say obsessed—with being thin.

Melody Barrett's problem is anorexia nervosa, a disorder that doctors describe as "severe caloric restriction," and college students know as intense, compulsive dieting. Like most diseases, anorexia nervosa has social as well as biological causes: About 95 percent of its victims are females, most of them white and from affluent families. Many women who contend with eating disorders are pressured by their parents to be high achievers. Although Melody Barrett's case is severe, up to half of college-age women actively try to lose weight, even though most of them are not, medically speaking, obese. About one in seven diet so much that doctors would say that they have an eating disorder.

To appreciate the social foundation of eating disorders[1], consider a comment once made by the Duchess of Windsor: "A woman cannot be too rich or too thin." Women fall victim to eating disorders because our culture places such importance on physical appearance, making slenderness an ideal part of femininity (Parrott, 1987). As some researchers see it, our society teaches young women they are "never too thin to feel fat." Young women, therefore, engage in a form of "mass starvation," which some critics see as no different from the "foot-binding, lip-stretching, and other forms of woman mutilation" found in other cultures (Wooley, Wooley, & Dyrenforth, 1979; Levine, 1987; Robinson, 1987).

Obviously, health is a concern of physicians and other medical professionals. But sociologists, too, study health because, as Melody Barrett's case shows, social forces shape the well-being of everyone.

WHAT IS HEALTH?

The World Health Organization (1946:3) defines **health** as *a state of complete physical, mental, and social well-being.* This definition underscores the major theme of this chapter: *Health is as much a social as a biological issue.*

---

[1]This profile of victims of anorexia nervosa is based on Levine (1987). Young women with another eating disorder, *bulimia*, engage in binge-eating and then induce vomiting to keep from gaining weight.

SUPPLEMENTS: An outline of this chapter, supplementary lecture material, and suggested discussion topics are included in the *Data File*.

SOCIAL SURVEY: "If you had to pick one, which would you choose—to be 5 years younger or weigh 15 pounds less?" Men: years, 63%; pounds, 29%; women: years, 41%; pounds, 48% (remainder is dk/nr) (Crossen & Graham, 1996).

Q: ". . . [D]ifferences in attitudes toward pain in Jewish, Italian, and 'Old American' families are closely related to the role and image of the father in the respective cultures in terms of his authority and masculinity." Mark Zborowski (1953)

NOTE: Some 60% of U.S. adults report thinking they are at least 5 pounds overweight; 13% say 20 or more pounds overweight (Crossen & Graham, 1996).

Medieval medical practice was heavily influenced by astrology, so that physicians and lay people alike attributed disease to astral influence; this is the root of our word "influenza." In this woodcut by Swiss artist Jost Amman (1580), as midwives attend a childbirth astrologers cast a horoscope for the newborn.

HEALTH AND SOCIETY

Society shapes the health of people in five major ways.

1. **People judge their health in relation to others they know.** René Dubos (1980; orig. 1965) points out that early in this century yaws, a contagious skin disease, was so common in sub-Saharan Africa that people there considered it normal. In truth, health is sometimes a matter of having the same diseases as one's neighbors (Quentin Crisp, cited in Kirk & Madsen, 1989).

2. **People define as "healthy" what they think of as morally good.** Members of our society (especially men) think a competitive way of life is "healthy" because it fits our cultural mores. This is so even though stress contributes to heart disease and many other illnesses. On the other hand, some people who object to homosexuality on moral grounds call this sexual orientation "sick" even though it is quite natural from a biological point of view. Thus, ideas about good health amount to a form of social control that encourages conformity to cultural norms.

3. **Cultural standards of health change over time.** Early in this century, some physicians warned women not to go to college because higher education would strain the female brain. Others denounced masturbation as a danger to health. Today, on both counts, we know differently. Conversely, fifty years ago, few doctors understood the danger of cigarette smoking, a practice that almost everyone now sees as a threat to health.

4. **Health relates to a society's technology.** In poor societies, infectious diseases are rampant because of malnutrition and poor sanitation. As industrialization raises living standards, people become more healthy. But industrial technology also creates new threats to health. As Chapter 22 ("Environment and Society") explains, rich countries threaten human health by overtaxing the world's resources and creating pollution.

5. **Health relates to social inequality.** Every society on earth distributes important resources unequally, making some people healthier than others. This pattern starts at birth, with infant mortality highest among the poor. Poor people also live fewer years than rich people.

HEALTH: A GLOBAL SURVEY

Because health is closely linked to social life, we find human well-being has increased over the long course of history. Today, as well, we see striking differences in health around the world.

HEALTH IN HISTORY

With only simple technology, our ancestors could do little to improve health. Hunters and gatherers faced frequent food shortages, which sometimes forced mothers to abandon their children. Those lucky enough to survive infancy were still vulnerable to a host of injuries and illnesses for which there was no treatment. Thus, few people lived to the age of forty and about half never made it to twenty (Lenski, Nolan, & Lenski, 1995).

NOTE: The terms "healthful" and "wholesome" are used to refer to what is both medically and morally desirable.

NOTE: One sign of long-term improvement in nutrition: Lucy, the 3-million-year-old adult fossilized skeleton found in Ethiopia, stood only about 3 feet 6 inches tall; she would have weighed some 65 pounds.

Q: "Hunger may have been the human race's constant companion, and 'the poor may always be with us,' but in the twentieth century, one cannot take this fatalistic view of the destiny of millions of fellow creatures. Their condition is not inevitable but is caused by identifiable forces within the province of rational, human control." Susan George

GLOBAL SOCIOLOGY

Killer Poverty: A Report From Africa

The television images of famine in Africa bring home to people in the United States the horror of starving children. Some of the children we see appear bloated, while others seem to have shriveled to little more than skin drawn tightly over bones. Both of these deadly conditions, explains Susan George (1977), are direct results of poverty.

The bloated bodies of some children are caused by protein deficiency. In West Africa this condition is known as *kwashiorkor,* which means literally "one-two." The term comes from the common practice among mothers of abruptly weaning a first child upon the birth of a second. Deprived of mother's milk, a baby may receive no protein at all.

The shriveled bodies of other children come from a lack of both protein and calories. These children have too little food of any kind.

Strictly speaking, starvation is rarely what kills children. Hunger weakens children, leaving them vulnerable to stomach ailments such as gastroenteritis or diseases like measles. The death rate from measles, for example, is a thousand times greater in parts of Africa than in North America.

Eating just a single food also makes for poor nutrition, providing too little protein, vitamins, and minerals. Millions of people in low-income countries suffer from goiter, a debilitating, diet-related disease of the thyroid gland. Pellagra, common among people who consume mostly corn, is a serious disease that can lead to insanity. Similarly, people who eat only processed rice are prone to beriberi.

Health is obviously a social issue since diseases that are virtually unknown to the people in rich countries are a common experience of life in poor nations around the world.

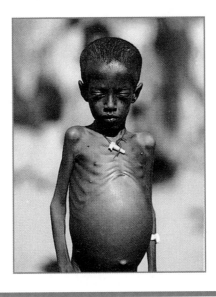

With the discovery of agriculture, food became more plentiful. Yet, social inequality, too, increased, so that elites enjoyed better health than peasants and slaves, who often lived in crowded, unsanitary shelters and went hungry. In the growing cities of medieval Europe, human waste and other refuse spread infectious diseases, and plagues periodically wiped out entire towns (Mumford, 1961).

HEALTH IN LOW-INCOME COUNTRIES

`November 1, 1988, central India.` Poverty is not just a matter of what you have; it shapes what you are. Probably most of the people we see in the villages here have never had the benefit of a doctor or a dentist. The result is easy to see: People look old before their time.

Abject poverty in much of the world cuts life expectancy far below the seventy or more years typical of rich societies. A look back at Global Map 14–2 on page 383 shows that people in most parts of Africa have a life expectancy of barely fifty, and in the world's poorest nations, such as Ethiopia and Somalia, the figure falls to forty.

GLOBAL: Only about one-third of the world's people tap into a safe water supply. Worldwide, more than 500,000 women, almost all in poor countries, die each year from pregnancy-related causes.

THEN AND NOW: Japan's diet is getting richer. Per capita calories consumed in *1946*, 1,448; *1993*, 2,618.

Q: "The ways in which the poor die reflect the conditions of their lives." Carol Stack (1975)

GLOBAL: Illustrating high mortality from infectious disease early in this century, a 1918 flu epidemic killed millions worldwide, including 500,000 in the United States.

NOTE: Until the end of the 19th century, Philadelphia drew water from the Delaware River at one point while discharging sewage at another. Such practices were common until the germ theory of disease led to programs to improve environmental quality.

WINDOW ON THE WORLD

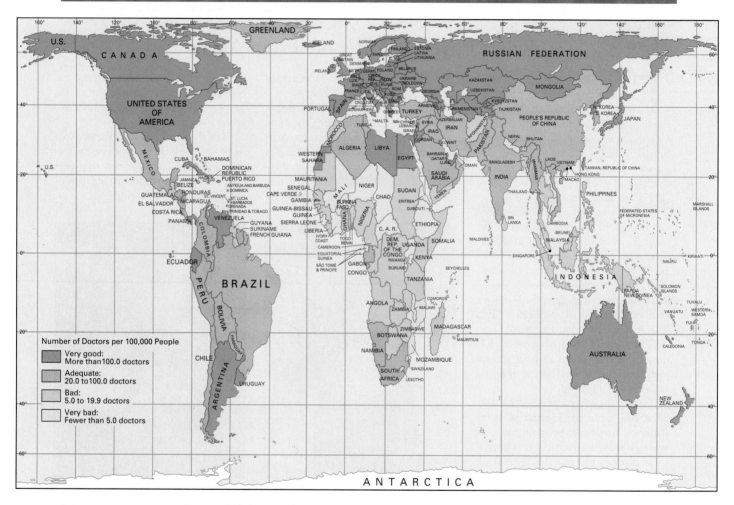

GLOBAL MAP 20–1 The Availability of Physicians in Global Perspective

Medical doctors, widely available to people in rich nations, are perilously scarce in poor societies. While traditional forms of healing do improve health, antibiotics and vaccines—vital for controlling infectious diseases—are often in short supply. In poor countries, therefore, death rates are high, especially among infants.

Source: *Peters Atlas of the World* (1990).

The World Health Organization reports that 1 billion people around the world—one in six—suffer from serious illness due to poverty. Poor sanitation and malnutrition kill people of all ages, especially children. Bad health results not just from having too little to eat, but also from consuming only one kind of food, as the box on page 531 explains.

In impoverished countries, sanitary drinking water is as hard to come by as a balanced diet. Unsafe water is a major cause of the infectious diseases that imperil both adults and children. The leading causes of death in the United States a century ago, including influenza, pneumonia, and tuberculosis, are widespread killers in poor societies today.

GLOBAL: The leading causes of death in the United States in 1900, as presented in Table 20–1, are leading causes of death in poor societies today.
NOTE: As noted in Chapter 17 ("Family"), U.S. children were more likely to live in a one-parent family a century ago than they are today. The reason? High mortality from infectious diseases.

THEN AND NOW: The U.S. diet is getting healthier. According to the U.S. Bureau of the Census, annual per capita consumption of red meat fell from 135 pounds in 1970 to 115 pounds in 1995. Gallons of whole milk fell even more, from 27 gallons to about 9. Eggs consumed dropped from 315 to 233. Per capita consumption of broccoli rose from .5 pounds in 1970 to 3.2 pounds in 1995.

To make matters worse, medical personnel are few and far between, so that the world's poorest people—many of whom live in central Africa—never see a physician. Global Map 20–1 shows the availability of doctors throughout the world.

In poor nations with minimal medical care, it is no wonder that 10 percent of children die within a year of their birth. In some countries, half the children never reach adulthood—a pattern that parallels the death rates seen in Europe two centuries ago (George, 1977; Harrison, 1984).

In much of the world, illness and poverty form a vicious circle: Poverty breeds disease, which, in turn, undermines people's ability to work. Moreover, when medical technology does curb infectious disease, the populations of poor nations soar. Without resources to ensure the well-being of the people they have now, poor societies can ill afford a larger population. Ultimately, programs to lower death rates in poor countries will succeed only if they can reduce birth rates as well.

HEALTH IN HIGH-INCOME COUNTRIES

Industrialization dramatically changed patterns of human health in Europe, although, at first, not for the better. By 1800, as the Industrial Revolution took hold, factories offered jobs that drew people from all over the countryside. Cities quickly became overcrowded, creating serious sanitation problems. Moreover, factories fouled the air with smoke, which few saw as a threat to health until well into this century. Accidents in the workplace were common.

But industrialization gradually improved health in Western Europe and North America as rising living standards translated into better nutrition and safer housing for most people. After 1850, medical advances also improved health, primarily by controlling infectious diseases. In 1854, for example, John Snow mapped the street addresses of London's cholera victims and found they all had drunk contaminated water from the well in Golden Square (Rockett, 1994). It was not long after that scientists linked cholera to a specific bacterium and developed a protective vaccine against the deadly disease. Armed with scientific knowledge, early environmentalists campaigned against age-old practices such as discharging raw sewage into rivers used for drinking water. By the early twentieth century, death rates from infectious diseases had fallen sharply.

Over the long term, then, industrialization has dramatically improved human health. In 1900, influenza

TABLE 20–1 The Leading Causes of Death in the United States, 1900 and 1996

1900	1996
1. Influenza and pneumonia	1. Heart disease
2. Tuberculosis	2. Cancer
3. Stomach/ intestinal diseases	3. Stroke
4. Heart disease	4. Lung disease (noncancerous)
5. Cerebral hemorrhage	5. Accidents
6. Kidney disease	6. Pneumonia and influenza
7. Accidents	7. Diabetes
8. Cancer	8. HIV/AIDS
9. Diseases in early infancy	9. Suicide
10. Diphtheria	10. Chronic liver disease and cirrhosis

Sources: Information for 1900 is from William C. Cockerham, *Medical Sociology*, 2d ed. (Englewood Cliffs, N.J.: Prentice-Hall, 1986), p. 24; information for 1996 is from U.S. National Center for Health Statistics, *Monthly Vital Statistics Report* (Hyattsville, Md.: The Center, 1997), vol. 46, no. 1, supplement 2 (Sept. 11, 1997).

and pneumonia caused one-fourth of all deaths in the United States. Today, these diseases cause fewer than 3 percent of deaths. As Table 20–1 indicates, other infectious diseases that were once major killers now rarely threaten our health.

With infectious diseases less of a threat, it is now chronic illnesses such as heart disease, cancer, and stroke that claim most people in the United States. Nothing alters the reality of death, but industrial societies at least manage to delay death until old age (Edmondson, 1997a).

HEALTH IN THE UNITED STATES

In the United States, well-off people are among the healthiest people in the world. The poorest, however, are no better off than the people living in low-income countries.

SOCIAL EPIDEMIOLOGY: THE DISTRIBUTION OF HEALTH

Social epidemiology is *the study of how health and disease are distributed throughout a society's population.* Just as early social epidemiologists traced the origin and spread of epidemic diseases, researchers today examine the connection between health and our physical

THE MAP: One component of health differences is income: People living in Fairfax County, Va. (a Washington, D.C., suburb) live about 15 years longer than people living in the downtown capital 12 miles away. Race, too, is at work, with African Americans and Native Americans worse off than whites, even controlling for income.

DIVERSITY: A quality-of-life scale, based on health, housing, education, public safety, the arts, and geography, places Vermont and Hawaii as the "best places to live" followed by Connecticut, Massachusetts, and New Hampshire. The worst five are Oklahoma, Arkansas, Alabama, Mississippi, and, in last place, Louisiana (Thomas, 1995).

SEEING OURSELVES

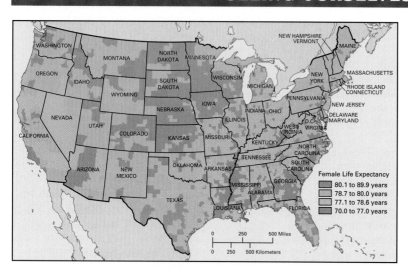

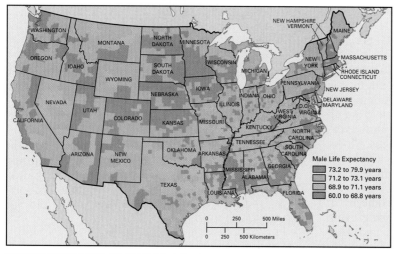

NATIONAL MAP 20-1
Life Expectancy Across the United States

These two maps show that, on average, women live longer than men. Yet a gap of roughly twenty years separates people in the healthiest counties of the United States and those in the least healthy counties. Looking over the maps, in which regions of the country is health the best and the worst? Compare these maps with the income distribution shown in National Map 10–3 on page 279 and racial distribution shown in National Map 13–3 on page 369. Can you offer an explanation for the differences in health found here?

Source: Harvard School of Public Health (1997).

and social environments. National Map 20–1 surveys the health of people across the United States, showing that there is as much as a twenty-year difference in average life expectancy between rich and poor communities. The following sections explain this difference in terms of age, sex, social class, and race.

Age and Sex

Death is now rare among young people, with two notable exceptions: a rise in mortality resulting from accidents and, more recently, from acquired immune deficiency syndrome (AIDS).

Across the life course, women fare better in terms of health than men. Females have a slight biological advantage that renders them less likely than males to die before or immediately after birth. Then, as socialization takes over, males become more aggressive and individualistic, which results in higher rates of accidents, violence, and suicide. Our cultural conception of masculinity also pressures adult men to be more competitive, to repress their emotions, and to take up

NOTE: Supporting the validity of self-assessments of health, one study found people who characterize their health as "poor" were 7 times more likely to die in the subsequent 12 years than those who described their health as "excellent" (Goleman, 1991).

DIVERSITY: Joe Feagin (1997) argues that African Americans suffer from work-related stress, which leads to health problems. He calls this pattern "death by discrimination."

DIVERSITY: Leading causes of death among 15-to-24-year-olds by sex and race (U.S. Nat. Ctr. for Health Statistics, 1997):
Af. Amer. females: homicide, accidents, AIDS, heart disease, cancer
Af. Amer. males: homicide, accidents, suicide, heart disease, AIDS
White females: accidents, homicide, suicide, cancer, heart disease
White males: accidents, suicide, homicide, cancer, heart disease

TABLE 20–2 Assessment of Personal Health by Income, 1994

Family Income	Excellent	Very Good	Good	Fair	Poor
$35,000 and over	47.9%	30.2%	17.5%	3.5%	0.9%
$20,000–$34,999	35.3	29.9	25.5	7.1	2.2
$10,000–$19,999	28.4	26.1	29.4	11.2	4.9
Under $10,000	25.5	23.6	29.0	14.1	7.8

Source: U.S. National Center for Health Statistics, *Current Estimates from the National Health Interview Survey United States, 1994,* series 10, no. 193 (Washington, D.C.: U.S. Government Printing Office, 1995).

hazardous behaviors like smoking cigarettes and drinking alcohol to excess. As the box on page 536 explains, what doctors call "coronary-prone behavior" is really a fairly accurate description of what our culture defines as masculinity.

Social Class and Race

Infant mortality—the death rate among newborns—is twice as high for disadvantaged children as for children born to privilege. While the health of the richest children in our nation is the best in the world, our poorest children are as vulnerable as those in many poor countries, including Sudan and Lebanon.

Table 20–2 shows that almost 80 percent of adults in families with incomes over $35,000 think their health is excellent or very good, but not quite half of adults in families earning less than $10,000 say the same. Conversely, while only about 4 percent of high-income people describe their health as fair or poor, almost one-fourth of low-income people respond this way.

Poverty among African Americans—at three times the rate of whites—helps explain why black people are more likely to die in infancy and, as adults, suffer the effects of violence, drug abuse, and illness. Table 20–3 presents life expectancy for U.S. children born in 1996. Whites can expect to live more than seventy-six years; African Americans, about seventy years.

Sex is an even stronger predictor of health than race, since African American females outlive males of either race. The table also shows that 76 percent of white men—but just 58 percent of African American men—will live to age sixty-five. The comparable figures for women are 86 percent for whites and 78 percent for African Americans.

Poverty condemns people to crowded, unsanitary living conditions that breed infectious diseases. With a higher risk of poverty, African Americans are four times as likely as whites to die from tuberculosis. Poor people of all races also suffer from nutritional deficiencies.

About 20 percent of the U.S. population—some 50 million people—cannot afford a healthful diet or adequate medical care. As a result, wealthy people can expect to die in old age of chronic illnesses such as heart disease and cancer, while poor people are likely to die younger from infectious diseases such as pneumonia.

Poverty also breeds stress and violence. The leading cause of death among African American men age fifteen to twenty-four—who figure prominently in the urban underclass—is homicide. In 1996 alone, 3,562 African Americans were killed by others of their race—one-third the number of black soldiers killed in the entire Vietnam War.

HEALTH AND SOCIETY: THREE EXAMPLES

Since we all make choices about how to live, we all have some control over our health. But as the following discussions indicate, dangerous behaviors such as cigarette smoking and compulsive dieting are pronounced among certain categories of people. Sexually transmitted diseases, too, reveal a distinctive social profile.

TABLE 20–3 Life Expectancy for U.S. Children Born in 1996

	Females	Males	Both Sexes
Whites	79.6 (86%)*	73.8 (76%)	76.8 (81%)
African Americans	74.2 (78%)	66.1 (58%)	70.3 (67%)
All races	**79.0 (85%)**	**73.0 (74%)**	**76.1 (80%)**

*Figures in parentheses indicate the chances of living to age sixty-five.
Source: U.S. National Center for Health Statistics, *Monthly Vital Statistics Report* (Hyattsville, Md.: The Center, 1997), vol. 46, no. 1, supplement 2 (Sept. 11, 1997).

DISCUSS: Do males engage in more risky behavior than females? Percent of high school students, grades 9–12, who report rarely or never using seat belts: national average, 19%; white males, 23%; white females, 12%; African American males, 35%; African American females, 26%; Latinos, 22%; Latinas, 17% (Kann et al., 1995).
NOTE: Another example: A *Time*/CNN poll (January 1995) asked, "Have you ever driven a car when you probably had too much alcohol to drink?" Men: yes, 63%; no, 36%; women: yes, 29%; no, 70% (unsure omitted).
DISCUSS: Is competition "natural," even though high levels of stress contribute to heart disease, which is the leading killer in the United States (see Table 20–1)? Heart disease kills about 1 million people annually: more than the total killed in all U.S. wars over the course of the 20th century.

SOCIOLOGY OF EVERYDAY LIFE

Masculinity: A Threat to Health?

What doctors call "coronary-prone behavior," and psychologists call the "Type-A personality," sociologists describe as our cultural conception of masculinity. It is a combination of attitudes and behavior—common among men in our society—that includes (1) chronic impatience ("C'mon! Go faster or get outta' my way!"), (2) uncontrolled ambition ("I've gotta have it . . . I need that!"), and (3) free-floating hostility ("Why are so many people *such idiots*!?").

This pattern, although quite normal from a cultural point of view, is one major reason that men who are driven to succeed are at high risk for heart disease. By acting out the "Type-A personality," we may get the job done, but we set in motion complex biochemical processes that are very hard on the human heart.

Here are a few questions to help you assess your own degree of risk (or that of someone important to you):

1. *Do you believe that a person has to be aggressive to succeed? Do you think that "nice guys finish last"?* For your heart's sake, try to remove hostility from your life. One starting point: How about eliminating profanity from your speech? Try replacing aggression with compassion, which can be surprisingly effective in dealing with other people. Medically speaking, compassion and humor—rather than irritation and aggravation—will enhance your life.

2. *How well do I handle uncertainty and opposition?* Do you have moments when you fume "Why won't the

waiter take my order?" or "Environmentalists are plain nuts!"? We all like to know what's going on and we like others to agree with us. But the world often doesn't work this way. Accepting uncertainty and opposition makes us more mature and certainly healthier.

3. *Am I uneasy showing positive emotion?* Many men think giving and accepting love— from women, from children, and from other men—is a sign of weakness. But the medical truth is that love supports health while hate damages it.

As human beings, we have a great deal of choice about how to live. Think about the choices you make, and reflect on how our society's idea of masculinity often makes us hard on others (including those we love) and, just as important, hard on ourselves.

Sources: Based on Friedman & Rosenman (1974) and Levine (1990).

Cigarette Smoking

Cigarette smoking, which tops the list of preventable hazards to health, has a definite cultural dimension. Only after World War I did smoking become popular in the United States, and despite growing evidence of its dangers, smoking remained fashionable even a generation ago. Since then, among adults—but not young people—smoking has been falling out of favor and is now considered a mild form of social deviance.

The popularity of cigarettes peaked in 1960, when almost 45 percent of U.S. adults smoked. By 1995, however, only 25 percent were still lighting up (U.S. Centers for Disease Control and Prevention, 1997). For smokers, quitting is difficult because cigarette smoke contains nicotine, which we now know to be a physically addictive drug. But people also smoke to cope with stress: Divorced and separated people are likely to smoke, as are the unemployed and people in the armed forces.

GLOBAL: Singapore is poised to become the world's first smoke-free city. This so-called "socially engineered ministate" (see the box in Chapter 16) forbids public smoking and cigarette vending machines, and prohibits tobacco companies from sponsoring public events.

DIVERSITY: The University of Michigan's Institute for Social Research reports that 4.1% of black high school seniors were regular smokers in 1993 (vs. 24.9% in 1977) (that is, they had smoked 20 or more cigarettes in the last 30 days); comparable figures for whites: 28.9% falling to 21.4%.

NOTE: Recall from Chapter 12 ("Sex and Gender") that our culture embraces a "beauty myth" that teaches women to exaggerate the importance of physical attractiveness and to orient themselves toward pleasing men (Wolf, 1990).

Generally speaking, among the U.S. population, the less schooling people have, the greater their chances of smoking. A slightly larger share of men (28 percent) than women (24 percent) smoke. But cigarettes—the only form of tobacco popular with women—have taken a toll on women's health. A decade ago, lung cancer surpassed breast cancer as a cause of death among U.S. women.

Some 450,000 men and women die prematurely each year as a direct result of cigarette smoking—a greater number than the combined death toll from alcohol, cocaine, heroin, homicide, suicide, automobile accidents, and AIDS (Mosley & Cowley, 1991). Smokers also suffer from more minor illnesses such as the flu, and pregnant women who smoke increase the likelihood of spontaneous abortion, prenatal death, and low birth-weight babies. Even nonsmokers exposed to cigarette smoke have a higher risk of smoking-related diseases.

Tobacco is a $30-billion industry in the United States. In 1997, the tobacco industry conceded that cigarette smoking is harmful to health, and agreed to end marketing strategies that targeted young people. But, despite the antismoking trend in the United States, the use of chewing tobacco—also a threat to health—is increasing, especially among the young. Moreover, the tobacco industry is selling more products abroad, especially in low-income societies where there is little legal regulation of tobacco sales and advertising (Scherer, 1996; Pollack, 1997). Figure 20–1 shows that in many countries, especially in Asia, a large majority of men smoke. Worldwide, more than 1 billion adults (about 30 percent) smoke, consuming some 6 trillion cigarettes annually, and tobacco use is on the rise. However, there remains a very good reason for smokers to kick the habit: About ten years after quitting, an ex-smoker's health is about as good as that of someone who never smoked at all.

Eating Disorders

An **eating disorder** is *an intense form of dieting or other kind of weight control in pursuit of being very thin.* As the vignette that opened this chapter suggests, eating disorders illustrate how cultural pressures shape human health.

Consider, first, that 95 percent of people who suffer from anorexia nervosa or bulimia are women, mostly from white, relatively affluent families. As Michael Levine (1987) explains, our culture equates slenderness with being successful and attractive to men. On the flip side, we tend to stereotype overweight

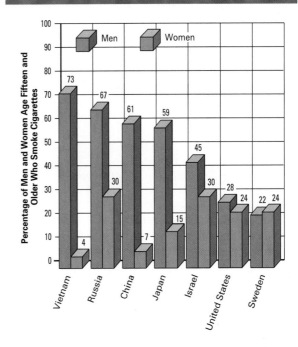

GLOBAL SNAPSHOT

FIGURE 20–1 Cigarette Smoking in Selected Countries

Sources: *Journal of the American Medical Association* (1996) and World Health Organization (1996).

women and men as "lazy," "ugly," "sloppy," and even "stupid."

Studies show that most college-age women (1) agree that "guys like thin girls," (2) think being thin is the most important dimension of physical attractiveness, and (3) believe that they are not as thin as men would like them to be. In fact, most college women want to be even thinner than college men say women should be. Most men, on the other hand, think their actual body shape is just about what they want it to be; thus, compared to women, men display little dissatisfaction over body shape (Fallon & Rozin, 1985).

Since few women approach our culture's unrealistic standards of beauty, many women develop a low self-image. Moreover, our idealized image of beauty leads many young women to diet compulsively to the point of risking their health.

NOTE: The most common STD, according to the Centers for Disease Control, is now chlamydia, with 490,000 cases reported annually.

NOTE: 1996 recorded the lowest syphilis rate since 1957: 4.4 new cases per 100,000 people. There were 11,624 new cases reported in 1996, half of them in just 37 counties mostly in the South; 73% of U.S. counties reported no new cases at all.

SUPPLEMENTS: Information on "The Face of AIDS in Asia" is included in the *Data File.*

NOTE: There are some 50 STDs overall; estimates suggest that one-fifth of the U.S. adult population has one STD other than AIDS. Roughly 7,000 American deaths annually are related to STDs other than AIDS.

Evidence of the health hazards of smoking cigarettes first appeared in the 1930s. But cigarettes continued to increase in popularity, helped, in part, by celebrity advertising that was, at best, misleading.

Sexually Transmitted Diseases

Sexual activity, though pleasurable and vital to the continuation of our species, can transmit more than fifty kinds of infections. Sometimes called *venereal diseases* (from Venus, the Roman goddess of love), these diseases date back to humanity's origins. Since our culture historically has linked sex to sin, some people regard venereal diseases not only as illness but also as marks of immorality.

Sexually transmitted diseases (STDs) grabbed national attention during the "sexual revolution" of the 1960s, when people began sexual activity earlier and had a greater number of partners. As a result, STDs are an exception to the general decline in infectious diseases during this century. Recently, however, the rising danger of STDs—and especially AIDS—has sparked a

sexual counterrevolution that discourages casual sex (Kain, 1987; Kain & Hart, 1987). The following sections briefly describe several common STDs.

Gonorrhea and syphilis. Gonorrhea and syphilis, among the oldest diseases, are caused by microscopic organisms that are almost always transmitted by sexual contact. Untreated, gonorrhea can cause sterility; syphilis damages major organs and can result in blindness, mental disorders, and death.

About 325,000 cases of gonorrhea and 53,000 cases of syphilis were recorded in 1996, although the actual numbers may be several times higher. Most cases are contracted by African Americans (83 percent), with lower numbers among white people (15 percent), Latinos (4 percent), and Asian Americans and Native Americans (less than 1 percent)[2] (Masters, Johnson, & Kolodny, 1988; Moran et al., 1989; U.S. Centers for Disease Control and Prevention, 1997).

Gonorrhea and syphilis can easily be cured with antibiotics, such as penicillin. Thus, neither disease is currently a major health problem in the United States.

Genital herpes. Genital herpes is a virus that infects an estimated 20 to 30 million adults in the United States (one in seven). While far less serious than gonorrhea and syphilis, herpes is incurable. People with genital herpes may exhibit no symptoms or they may experience periodic, painful blisters on the genitals accompanied by fever and headache. Although not fatal to adults, women with active genital herpes can transmit the disease during a vaginal delivery to infants, to whom it can be deadly. Infected women, therefore, usually give birth by Cesarean section.

AIDS. The most serious of all sexually transmitted diseases is acquired immune deficiency syndrome, or AIDS. Identified in 1981, this disease is incurable and fatal. AIDS is caused by the human immunodeficiency virus (HIV), which attacks white blood cells, the core of the immune system. AIDS thus renders a person vulnerable to a wide range of other diseases that eventually cause death.

AIDS is now the leading killer of young adults age twenty-five to forty-four in the United States. During the twelve-month period ending June, 1997, officials recorded some 63,000 new cases in the United States, raising the total number of people who have contracted

---

[2] Percentages do not add up to 100 because Latinos can be of any race.

DISCUSS: How should we combat STDs? Liberals accept that people engage in casual sexual activity and call for widespread availability of birth control devices and sex education; conservatives urge revival of an ethic of abstinence and marital fidelity.

GLOBAL: Heterosexual transmission of HIV is pronounced in poor societies partly because of the high incidence of genital lesions.

GLOBAL: In global perspective, the use of condoms is highest in Japan (the "pill" is not widely available there); lowest use is in sub-Saharan Africa (where the AIDS epidemic is worst).

GLOBAL: In 1997, Japan moved to end its longtime ban on oral contraceptives (the "pill"), a strategy praised for promoting use of condoms, which held down the rate of HIV and other sexually transmitted diseases.

WINDOW ON THE WORLD

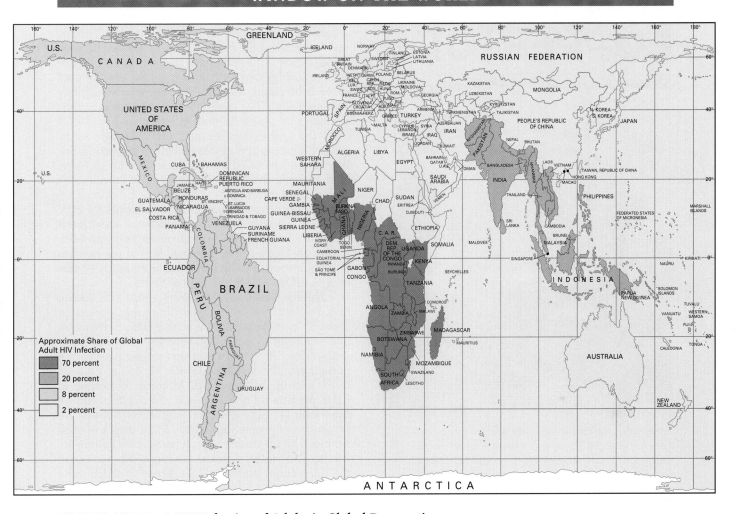

GLOBAL MAP 20–2 HIV Infection of Adults in Global Perspective

Approximately 70 percent of all global HIV cases are recorded in sub-Saharán Africa. This high infection rate reflects the prevalence of other sexually transmitted diseases and infrequent use of condoms, factors that promote heterosexual transmission of HIV. Southeast Asia, where HIV is spreading most rapidly, accounts for another 20 percent of infections. South and North America together account for another 8 percent of all cases. The incidence of infection is still low in the remaining regions of the world.

Sources: *AIDS* (1997); map projection from *Peters Atlas of the World* (1990).

AIDS to 592,000. Of these, more than 379,000 have already died (U.S. Centers for Disease Control and Prevention, 1997).

In global perspective, HIV infects some 30 million people—half under age twenty-five—and the number is rising rapidly. Global Map 20–2 shows that Africa (more specifically, countries south of the Sahara Desert) has the highest HIV infection rate and currently accounts for two-thirds of all world cases. In central African nations such as Burundi, Rwanda, Uganda, and Kenya, roughly

NOTE: There are about 8,000 children under 13 years of age with HIV in the United States; almost all were infected in the womb.

NOTE: A 1995 research report indicates that 22% of semen samples from men infected with HIV contained live virus. There are no indicators of when infected males will "shed" the virus in this way, underscoring the need for caution in all sexual encounters.

DISCUSS: Some proponents of euthanasia claim we are more humane to dying pets than to dying parents. Ask the class to consider why we should or should not treat dying people and pets in the same way.

GLOBAL: Has the spread of euthanasia led to higher general suicide in the Netherlands? No, according to a recent study by Marvin Zalman and Steven Stack (1996).

TAN...don't burn...use COPPERTONE

Get a faster, deeper tan plus GUARANTEED sunburn protection!

Sunbalanced Screening does it! With Coppertone, you get a faster, smoother, *deeper* tan, with maximum sunburn protection—than with any other leading product! That's because Coppertone's special screening agent, homomenthyl salicylate, lets *in* the ultraviolet tanning rays that activate coloring matter deep within your skin ... as it shuts *out* rays that burn and coarsen your skin.

Conditions Skin, too! The extra lanolin and other protectives in Coppertone keep it on the skin longer, protect you even after swimming. Coppertone prevents ugly drying and peeling, too.

America's Favorite! Originated in sunny Florida, Coppertone now far outsells all other suntan products. Use it whenever you're out in the sun—at beach, pool, fishing, or right in your own backyard. Available in Lotion, Oil, Cream, Spray, and new Coppertone Shade for children and those with sensitive skin. Also Noskote. Get a rich, long-lasting Coppertone tan! Get Coppertone in large size to save most.

COPPERTONE
Suntan Lotion

Also available in Canada. Another quality product of Plough, Inc.

Don't be a paleface!

For decades, the United States has been a nation of "sun-worshippers." Is sunshine always good for you, as generations of parents have told their children? There is nothing wrong with getting outdoors for some fresh air and exercise. But as people age, sun-damaged skin is prone to cancer, a fact that is starting to make us see sunshine in a whole new light.

one-fifth of all young adults are infected (Tofani, 1991; Scommegna, 1996). North Americans account for less than 5 percent of global HIV cases. In the United States, officials noted a decline in AIDS deaths in 1997, but the total number of people with HIV in this country still approaches 900,000.

Upon infection, people with HIV display no symptoms at all, so most are unaware of their condition. Not for a year or longer do symptoms of HIV infection appear. Within five years, one-third of infected people develop full-blown AIDS; half develop AIDS within ten years, and almost all become sick within twenty years. Even though the number of AIDS deaths began to decline in 1997, the 400,000 deaths so far make AIDS potentially the most serious epidemic of modern times.

HIV is infectious but not contagious. That is, HIV is transmitted from person to person through blood, semen, or breast milk but *not* through casual contact such as shaking hands, hugging, sharing towels or dishes, swimming together, or even by coughing and sneezing. The risk of transmitting the virus through saliva (as in kissing) is extremely low. Moreover, the risk of transmitting HIV through sexual activity is greatly reduced by the use of latex condoms. But in the age of AIDS, abstinence or an exclusive relationship with an uninfected person is the only sure way to avoid infection.

Specific behaviors put people at high risk for HIV infection. The first is *anal sex*, which can cause rectal bleeding, allowing easy transmission of HIV from one person to another. The practice of anal sex explains why homosexual and bisexual men account for 49 percent of AIDS cases in the United States.

Sharing needles used to inject drugs is a second high-risk behavior. Intravenous drug users account for about 25 percent of persons with AIDS. Sex with an intravenous drug user is also very risky. Because intravenous drug use is more common among poor people in the United States, AIDS is now becoming a disease of the socially disadvantaged. Although 47 percent of AIDS patients are non-Hispanic white people, African Americans (12 percent of the population) account for 36 percent of people with AIDS. More than half of all women with the disease and 58 percent of children are African Americans. Similarly, Latinos (11 percent of the population) represent 18 percent of AIDS cases (and 20 percent of women with AIDS). Asian Americans and Native Americans, however, together account for less than 1 percent of people with AIDS (Huber & Schneider, 1992; U.S. Centers for Disease Control and Prevention, 1997).

Using any drug, including alcohol, also increases the risk of HIV infection to the extent that it impairs judgment. In other words, even people who understand what places them at risk of infection may act less responsibly if they are under the influence of alcohol, marijuana, or some other drug.

As Figure 20–2 shows, only 9 percent of people with AIDS in the United States became infected through heterosexual contact (although heterosexuals, infected in various ways, account for more than 30 percent of AIDS cases). But heterosexual activity does transmit HIV, and the danger rises with the number of sexual partners, especially if they fall into high-risk categories. Worldwide,

NOTE: The term "a negotiated death" has emerged to indicate the decision by family members, medical-legal-religious-ethical specialists, and sometimes patients themselves about how and when death should occur. Such negotiation often results in a doctor issuing a "Do Not Resuscitate" order for a terminally ill patient.

NOTE: Oregon's physician-assisted suicide Proposal 16, the first of its kind in the U.S., passed narrowly in November, 1994. A patient wishing to die must obtain statements from two physicians confirming the terminal illness, and from two other witnesses stating that the patient really wants to die and rationally understands that decision. Then a physician may prescribe a lethal dose of medication, which the patient may decide to take. The proposal is currently undergoing court review.

heterosexual relations are the primary means of HIV transmission, accounting for two-thirds of all infections (Eckholm & Tierney, 1990).

Treating a single person with AIDS costs hundreds of thousands of dollars, and this figure may rise as new therapies appear. Government health programs, private insurance, and personal savings rarely cover more than a fraction of the cost of treatment. In addition, there is the mounting cost of caring for the children orphaned by AIDS, whose numbers, some analysts predict, could reach 80,000 by the year 2000. Overall, AIDS is both a medical and a social problem of monumental proportions.

Initially, the government responded slowly to the AIDS crisis, largely because gays and intravenous drug users are widely viewed as deviant. But funds allocated for AIDS research have increased rapidly (now totaling some $7 billion annually), and researchers have identified drugs, including recent "protease inhibitors," that dramatically suppress symptoms and prolong life in many patients. But educational programs remain the most effective weapon against AIDS, since prevention is the only way to stop a disease that currently has no cure.

ETHICAL ISSUES: CONFRONTING DEATH

Health issues involve ethical considerations, especially now that technological advances give human beings the power to draw the line separating life and death.

When does death occur? Common sense suggests that life ceases when breathing and heartbeat stop. But the ability to replace a heart and artificially sustain respiration makes such a definition of death obsolete. U.S. medical and legal experts now define death as an *irreversible* state involving no response to stimulation, no movement or breathing, no reflexes, and no indication of brain activity (Ladd, 1979; Wall, 1980).

Do people have a right to die? Today, medical personnel, family members, and patients themselves face the agonizing burden of deciding when a terminally ill person should die. Among the most difficult cases are the roughly 10,000 people in the United States who lie in a permanent vegetative state and cannot express their own desires. Generally speaking, the first responsibility of physicians and hospitals is to protect a patient's life. Even so, a mentally competent person in the process of dying may refuse medical treatment or even nutrition. Moreover, federal law requires hospitals, nursing homes, and other medical facilities to honor the desires of a patient made earlier in the form

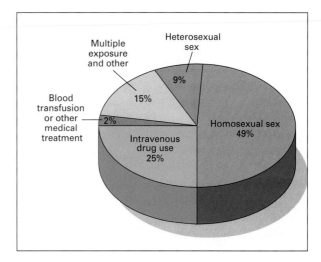

FIGURE 20–2 Types of Transmission for Reported U.S. AIDS Cases, 1997
Source: U.S. Centers for Disease Control and Prevention (1997).

of a living will. Thus, most cases of death in the United States now involve a human decision about when and how death will occur.

What about mercy killing? *Mercy killing* is the common term for **euthanasia,** *assisting in the death of a person suffering from an incurable disease.* Euthanasia (from Greek, meaning "a good death") poses an ethical dilemma, being both an act of kindness and a form of killing.

In 1997, the Supreme Court decided that, under the U.S. Constitution, there is no "right to die." Such a right would permit *active* euthanasia, allowing a dying person to enlist the services of a physician to bring on a quick death. Supporters of the right to die argue that there are circumstances (such as when a dying person suffers from great pain) that make death preferable to life. Critics, however, counter that permitting active euthanasia invites abuse. Can we really expect family members to ignore the skyrocketing costs of hospital care for a dying person when they are pressed to make a decision to withhold treatment?

By 1997, three states (Oregon, Washington, and New York) passed laws to allow physician-assisted suicide. So far, court challenges have prevented any of these laws from taking effect. Yet, a majority of U.S. adults express support for giving dying people the right to choose to die with a doctor's help (NORC, 1996; Rosenbaum, 1997). Therefore, the "right to die" debate is sure to continue.

Q: "Medicine, a synthesis of many disciplines, is essentially the practice of knowledge and skills and attitudes helpful in the care of the sick." Patricia L. Kendall and George G. Reader

NOTE: MD income varies significantly by specialty and level of experience. Doctors in training earn about $30,000 annually, says the AMA; physicians in general practice average $112,000, and radiologists top the list at $253,000 annually.

THEN AND NOW: Technology has rapidly changed the character of modern medicine. The first map of the circulatory system was made in 1628. The first heart transplant was done only in 1961; for several years thereafter, each transplant was a major media event. Today, such procedures are commonplace (about 1,500 performed annually), and are covered (with special provisions) by Medicare.

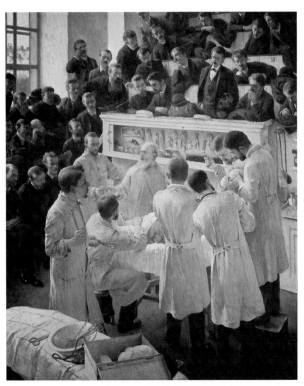

The rise of scientific medicine during the nineteenth century resulted in new skills and technology for treating many common ailments that had afflicted humanity for centuries. At the same time, however, scientific medicine pushed forms of health care involving women to the margins, and placed medicine under the control of men living in cities. We see this pattern in the A. F. Seligmann painting General Hospital, *showing an obviously all-male medical school class in Vienna in 1880.*

THE MEDICAL ESTABLISHMENT

Medicine is *a social institution concerned with combating disease and improving health.* Through most of human history, health care was the responsibility of individuals and their families. Medicine emerges as a social institution only as societies become more productive, assigning their members formal, specialized roles. Traditional medical practitioners use the healing properties of certain plants to address physical and emotional illness. From the point of view of some modern people, traditional healers such as herbalists

and acupuncturists may seem unscientific, but, in truth, they improve human health throughout the world (Ayensu, 1981).

As a society industrializes, health care becomes the responsibility of specially schooled and legally licensed healers, from anesthesiologists to X-ray technicians. Today's medical establishment in the United States took form over the last 150 years.

THE RISE OF SCIENTIFIC MEDICINE

In colonial times, doctors, herbalists, druggists, midwives, and ministers all engaged in various forms of healing arts. But not all were effective: Unsanitary instruments, lack of anesthesia, and simple ignorance made surgery a terrible ordeal, and doctors probably killed as many patients as they saved.

Medical specialists gradually learned more about human anatomy, physiology, and biochemistry. By about 1850, doctors had established themselves as self-regulating professionals with medical school degrees. The American Medical Association (AMA), founded in 1847, symbolized the growing acceptance of a scientific model of medicine. The AMA publicized the successes of its members in identifying bacteria as the cause of many life-threatening diseases and developing vaccines to combat them.

Still, other approaches to health care, such as regulating nutrition, also had defenders. The AMA responded boldly—some thought arrogantly—by criticizing these alternative ideas about health. By the early 1900s, state licensing boards agreed to certify only physicians trained in scientific programs approved by the AMA. With control of the certification process, the AMA began closing down schools teaching other healing skills, which limited the practice of medicine to those with an M.D. degree. In the process, both the prestige and income of physicians rose dramatically; today, men and women with M.D. degrees earn, on average, $182,000 annually.

Practitioners of other approaches, such as osteopathic physicians, concluded that they had no choice but to fall in line with medical doctors and follow AMA standards. Thus osteopaths (with D.O. degrees), who originally manipulated the skeleton and muscles, today treat illness with drugs in much the same way as medical doctors (with M.D. degrees). Other practitioners—such as chiropractors, herbal healers, and midwives—have held to traditional roles, but at the cost of being relegated to the fringe of the medical profession.

Q: "One must ask whether the medical intellect functions only or even best solely on a foundation of natural science." John H. Knowles

NOTE: There are some 724,000 physicians in the United States, about 74% of whom are men (94% of all nurses are women). Men now receive 61% of medical degrees, so that their representation in the profession is declining.

NOTE: A problem with the medical establishment has been research that focuses only on males. The famous 1981 study examining whether aspirin reduces heart attacks, for example, utilized 22,000 subjects, all men. In 1990, however, the National Institutes of Health opened an Office of Research on Women's Health.

THEN AND NOW: Share of U.S. physicians who are women: *1960, 7%; 1997, 26%.*

The People's Republic of China has a long history of folk medicine, an effective strategy to meet the health-care needs of more than 1 billion people in a largely rural society. Here a "barefoot doctor" displays herbal remedies at a Sunday market.

Scientific medicine, taught in expensive, urban medical schools, also changed the social profile of doctors. After the AMA standards were adopted, most physicians came from privileged backgrounds and practiced in cities. Furthermore, women, who had figured in many fields of healing, were scorned by the AMA. Some early medical schools did train women and African Americans but, faced with declining financial resources, most of these schools eventually closed. Only in recent decades has the social diversity of the medical profession increased, with women and African Americans accounting for 26 percent and 5 percent of all physicians, respectively (Gordon, 1980; Starr, 1982; Huet-Cox, 1984; U.S. Department of Labor, 1998).

HOLISTIC MEDICINE

The scientific model of medicine has recently been tempered by the more traditional model of **holistic medicine,** *an approach to health care that emphasizes prevention of illness by taking account of a person's entire physical and social environment.*

Holistic practitioners agree on the need for drugs, surgery, artificial organs, and high technology, but they don't want technological advances to turn medicine into narrow specialties concerned with symptoms rather than people, and with disease instead of health. Here are three foundations of holistic health care (Duhl, 1980; Ferguson, 1980; Gordon, 1980):

1. **Patients are people.** Holistic practitioners are concerned not only with symptoms but with how people's lifestyles and environment affect health. For example, stress caused by poverty or intense competition at work increases the risk of illness. In addition, holistic practitioners extend the bounds of conventional medicine by actively combating environmental pollution and other dangers to public health.

2. **Responsibility, not dependency.** In the scientific model, patients are dependent on physicians. Holistic medicine tries to shift some responsibility for health from physicians to people themselves by helping them engage in health-promoting behavior. Holistic medicine thus favors an *active* approach to *health*, rather than a *reactive* approach to *illness.*

3. **Personal treatment.** Conventional medicine locates medical care in impersonal offices and hospitals, which are disease-centered settings. By contrast, holistic practitioners favor, as much as possible, a personal and relaxed environment such as the home. Holistic medicine seeks to restore the personal ties that joined healers and patients before the era of specialists. The AMA currently recognizes more than fifty specialized areas of medical practice, and a growing proportion of M.D.s are entering these high-paying specialties rather than family practice. Therefore,

GLOBAL: Great Britain's National Health program has suffered severe financial problems in recent years, and delays in treatment are common. Liberals claim that privatization has meant disastrous cutbacks in government funding; conservatives counter that the system has become bloated with bureaucrats, with about three administrators for every medical practitioner.

GLOBAL: Costs for health care in Britain and other European countries are rising as their populations age.

GLOBAL: Physicians in most poor societies of the world do not share diagnostic information freely with patients.

THEN AND NOW: Medical care in the United States represented 5% of GNP in 1950 and 15% of GNP in 1995.

The United States is the only industrial nation to have no government-operated health care program that covers everyone. Critics of such a plan claim that government is unable to provide good care at a reasonable cost; proponents point out that more than 40 million people in this country have no coverage at all.

there is a need for practitioners who are concerned with the patient in the holistic sense.

In sum, holistic care does not oppose scientific medicine but shifts the emphasis away from narrowly treating disease towards achieving the highest possible level of well-being for everyone.

PAYING FOR HEALTH: A GLOBAL SURVEY

As medicine has come to rely on high technology, the costs of health care in industrial societies have skyrocketed. To meet these costs, countries have adopted various strategies.

Medicine in Socialist Societies

In societies with predominantly socialist economies, the government provides medical care directly to the people. These nations hold that all citizens have the right to basic medical care. In practice, then, people do not pay physicians and hospitals on their own; instead, the government uses public funds to pay medical costs. The state owns and operates medical facilities and pays salaries to practitioners, who are government employees.

People's Republic of China. As a poor, agrarian society in the process of industrializing, the People's Republic of China faces the daunting task of providing for the health of more than 1 billion people. China has experimented with private medicine, but the government controls most health care. China's famed barefoot doctors, roughly comparable to U.S. paramedics, bring some modern methods of medical care to millions of peasants in remote rural villages.

Traditional healing arts, including acupuncture and the use of medicinal herbs, are also still widely practiced in China. In general, a holistic concern for the well-being of both mind and body characterizes the Chinese approach to health (Sidel & Sidel, 1982b; Kaptchuk, 1985).

The former Soviet Union. The former Soviet Union is struggling to transform a state-dominated economy into more of a market system. For this reason, medical care is in transition. Nonetheless, the belief that everyone has a right to basic medical care remains widespread.

Currently, the government uses tax funds to provide medical care. And, as in China, people do not choose a physician but report to a local government health facility.

Physicians in the former Soviet Union have lower income than their counterparts in the United States, earning about the same salary as skilled industrial workers (compared to roughly a five-to-one ratio in this country). Worth noting, too, is that about 70 percent of physicians in the former Soviet Union are women, compared with about 26 percent in the United States. As in our society, occupations dominated by women yield fewer financial rewards.

In recent years, the new Russian Federation has suffered setbacks in health care, partly due to a falling standard of living. Rising demand for medical care has strained a bureaucratic system that, at best, provides highly standardized and impersonal care. The optimistic view is that, as market reforms proceed, both living standards and the quality of medical services will

SOCIAL SURVEY: "In general, some people think that it is the responsibility of the government in Washington to see to it that people have help in paying for doctors and hospital bills. Others think that these matters are not the responsibility of the federal government and that people should take care of these things themselves. Where do you place yourself on this scale?" (GSS 1996, N = 1,925; *Codebook*, 1996:275)

(1) "Government should help" 26.9%
(2) 20.9%
(3) "Agree with both views" 32.3%
(4) 10.3%
(5) "People should take care of themselves" 6.5%
DK/NR 3.0%

improve. In any case, what does seem certain is that disparities in medical care among various segments of the population will increase (Specter, 1995).

Medicine in Capitalist Societies

People living in nations with predominantly capitalist economies usually pay for their own health care. However, because high cost puts medical care beyond the reach of many people, government programs underwrite a considerable share of the expense.

Sweden. In 1891 Sweden instituted a compulsory, comprehensive system of government medical care. Citizens pay for this program with their taxes, which are among the highest in the world. Typically physicians receive salaries from the government rather than fees from patients, and government officials manage most hospitals. Because this medical system resembles that found in socialist societies, it is often described as **socialized medicine,** *a health-care system in which the government owns and operates most medical facilities and employs most physicians.*

Great Britain. In 1948 Great Britain, too, established socialized medicine. The British did not do away with private care, however; instead, they created a "dual system" of medical service. All British citizens are entitled to medical care provided by the National Health Service, but those who can afford to may purchase more extensive care from doctors and hospitals that operate privately.

Canada. Canada has a "single-payer" model of health care. Like a vast insurance company, the Canadian government pays doctors and hospitals according to a set schedule of fees. But Canada also has a two-tiered system like Great Britain's, with some physicians working outside the government-funded system and setting their own fees.

Canada boasts of providing care for everyone at a lower cost than the (nonuniversal) medical system in the United States. However, the Canadian system uses less state-of-the-art technology and responds slowly to people's needs, so that people may wait months to receive major surgery (Grant, 1984; Vayda & Deber, 1984; Rosenthal, 1991).

Japan. Physicians in Japan operate privately, but a combination of government programs and private insurance pays medical costs. As shown in Figure 20–3, the Japanese approach health care much like the

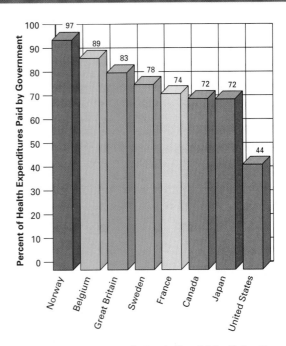

GLOBAL SNAPSHOT

FIGURE 20–3 Extent of "Socialized Medicine" in Selected Countries

Source: United Nations Development Programme (1997).

Europeans, with most medical expenses paid through government.

MEDICINE IN THE UNITED STATES

With our primarily private system of medical care, the United States stands alone among industrialized societies in having no government-sponsored medical system that provides care for every citizen. Called a **direct-fee system,** ours is a *medical-care system in which patients pay directly for the services of physicians and hospitals.* Thus while Europeans look to government to fund about 80 percent of their medical costs (paid for through taxation), the U.S. government pays less than half of this country's medical costs (Lohr, 1988; U.S. Bureau of the Census, 1997).

In the United States, rich people can purchase the best medical care in the world. Yet the poor fare worse than their counterparts in Europe. This disparity explains the relatively high death rates among both

DIVERSITY: About 16% of the U.S. population lacks any medical insurance; half of those uninsured are under the age of 25, making people between 18 and 25 the most likely to be without insurance. Among whites, 14% lack insurance; among African Americans, 22%; among Hispanics, 34%. Men are more likely than women to lack coverage, because of the larger numbers of elderly and poor women who participate in Medicaid and Medicare.

DIVERSITY: Of U.S. white males in the labor force, 75% are covered by health plans; only 58% of women and other minorities have such protection (Hersch & White-Means, 1993).
NOTE: Health costs are daunting, even to corporations. General Motors, for example, spends some $3 billion per year to provide health care to workers, retirees, and their families, adding hundreds of dollars to the price of the average car.

infants and adults in the United States compared to many European countries (United Nations Development Programme, 1995).

Why does the United States have no national health-care program? First, our society has historically limited government in the interest of greater personal liberty. Second, political support for a national medical program has not been strong, even among labor unions, which have concentrated on winning health-care benefits from employers. Third, the AMA and the health insurance industry have strongly and consistently opposed any such program (Starr, 1982).

Expenditures for medical care in the United States have increased dramatically since 1950, from just $12 billion to more than $1 trillion in 1996. This amounts to $3,300 per person, more than any other industrial society spends for medical care, and double the figure in Australia and Japan. Who pays the medical bills?

Private insurance programs. In 1996, 160 million people (60 percent) received some medical-care benefits from a family member's employer or labor union. Another 25 million people (9 percent) purchased private coverage on their own. Seventy percent of our population, then, has private insurance (such as Blue Cross and Blue Shield), although few such programs pay all medical costs (U.S. Bureau of the Census, 1997).

Public insurance programs. In 1965 Congress created Medicare and Medicaid. Medicare pays a portion of the medical costs of men and women over sixty-five; in 1995 it covered 38 million women and men, about 14 percent of the population. During the same year, Medicaid, a medical insurance program for the poor, provided benefits to more than 36 million people, about 14 percent of the population. An additional 26 million veterans (10 percent of the population) can obtain free care in government-operated hospitals. In all, 35 percent of this country's people enjoy some medical-care benefits from the government, but most also participate in a private insurance program.

Health maintenance organizations. An increasing number of people in the United States belong to a **health maintenance organization** (HMO), *an organization that provides comprehensive medical care to subscribers for a fixed fee.* In the United States today, HMOs enroll some 46 million individuals, about 17 percent of the population. HMOs vary in their costs and benefits, and none provides full coverage.

But fixed fees make these organizations profitable to the degree that their subscribers stay healthy; many, therefore, take a preventive approach to health.

In all, 84 percent of the U.S. population has some medical-care coverage, either private or public. But most plans do not provide full coverage, so serious illness threatens even middle-class people with financial hardship. Most programs also exclude certain medical services, such as dental care and treatment for mental health problems. Most seriously, 42 million people (about 16 percent of the population) have no medical insurance at all. Almost as many lose their medical coverage temporarily each year due to layoffs or job changes. Some of these people choose to forgo medical coverage (especially young people who take good health for granted), but most are part-time or full-time workers who receive no health-care benefits. Caught worst in the medical-care bind are low- and moderate-income people who cannot afford to become ill but cannot afford to pay for the medical care they need to remain healthy (Altman et al., 1989; Health Insurance Association of America, 1991; Hersch & White-Means, 1993; Smith, 1993; U.S. Bureau of the Census, 1997).

Recent debate. In 1994, the Clinton administration proposed a sweeping reform of health care called "managed competition." Under the "competition" element of this program, employees would collectively bargain with various medical providers in order to receive the greatest value. The "managed" dimension meant that government would oversee the entire process to ensure that everyone participated.

But after lengthy debate, Congress rejected the Clinton reforms. Therefore, at this point, the status quo continues. Still, public concern about health care runs high, so that debate over this issue is sure to persist.

THEORETICAL ANALYSIS OF HEALTH AND MEDICINE

Each of the major theoretical paradigms in sociology provides a means of organizing and interpreting the facts and issues presented in this chapter.

STRUCTURAL-FUNCTIONAL ANALYSIS

Talcott Parsons (1951) viewed medicine as society's strategy to keep its members healthy. In this scheme, illness is dysfunctional, because it undermines people's abilities to perform their roles.

DIVERSITY: One recent study found that 26% of whites, 38% of African Americans, and 52% of Hispanics lacked health insurance for at least a month during the year.

NOTE: Ten percent of the U.S. population accounts for 90% of all medical expenditures; 1% accounts for half of all expenditures.

NOTE: By 2005, perhaps half of the U.S. population will be served by an HMO, compared to 17% today.

Q: "In the USA—the richest country in the world—even the relatively affluent are now concerned about their ability to pay for medical care, while the poor have always been acutely aware of the gross deficiencies in the medical facilities available to them." Lesley Doyal

Q: "A great doctor kills more people than a great general." G. W. Leibniz

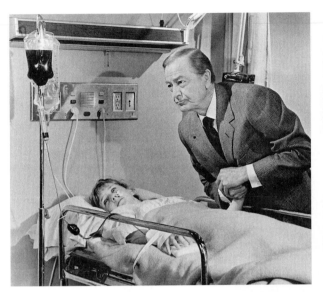
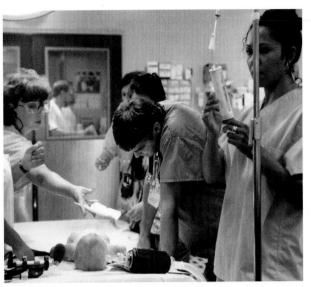

Our national view of medicine has changed during the last several decades. Television viewers in the 1970s watched doctors like Marcus Welby, M.D., confidently take charge of situations in a fatherly—and almost godlike—manner. By the 1990s, programs like "E.R." gave a more realistic view of the limitations of medicine to address illness, as well as the violence that wracks our society.

The Sick Role

Society responds to sickness, Parsons argued, by providing a **sick role,** *patterns of behavior defined as appropriate for people who are ill.* According to Parsons, the sick role has three characteristics:

1. **Illness suspends routine responsibilities.** Serious illness relaxes or suspends normal social obligations such as going to work or attending school. To prevent abuse of this privilege, however, people do not simply declare themselves ill; they must enlist the support of others—especially a recognized medical expert—before assuming the sick role.

2. **A sick person must want to be well.** We assume that no one wants to be sick. Thus people suspected of feigning illness to escape responsibility or receive special attention have no legitimate claim to a sick role.

3. **An ailing person must seek competent help.** People who are ill must seek competent assistance and cooperate with health-care practitioners. By failing to seek medical help or to follow the doctor's orders, a person gives up any claim on the sick role's exemption from routine responsibilities.

The Physician's Role

Society expects physicians to evaluate people's claims of sickness and help to restore the sick to normal routines. To do this, Parsons explained, physicians use their specialized knowledge. Physicians expect patients to provide whatever personal information may reasonably assist their efforts and to follow "doctor's orders" in completing treatment.

Although it is always hierarchical, the doctor-patient relationship varies from society to society. Japanese tradition, for example, gives physicians great authority over their patients. Japanese physicians even take it upon themselves to decide how much information about the seriousness of an illness they will share with the patient (Darnton & Hoshia, 1989).

Until about thirty years ago, physicians in the United States acted in much the same way. But the patient's rights movement demands that physicians readily share more and more medical information. A more equal relationship between doctor and patient is developing in Europe, too, and even in Japan.

RESOURCE: A discussion of the sick role by Talcott Parsons is included among the "classics" in the Macionis and Benokraitis reader, *Seeing Ourselves*.

CYBER: Given that social interaction helps prevent and heal illness, the cyber-world's potential to isolate us in self-designed virtual worlds could have negative effects on health, not to mention becoming couch-potatoes rather than getting outside and walking.

Q: "If you treat a sick child like an adult, and a sick adult like a child, everything usually works out pretty well." Ruth Carlisle

DISCUSS: Defining death is a good symbolic-interaction issue. Who participates in the definition of death? When may this definition be a negotiation among parties with various interests? What kinds of power are exercised by patients, family members, clergy, and physicians with scientific training?

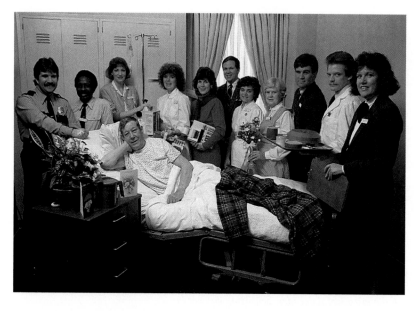

The cost of medical care in the United States has been rising at a dizzying rate. In part, this high rate of increase reflects the fact that hospitals are large, bureaucratic organizations that employ dozens of specialized workers in the treatment of any single patient. Here one man poses for a picture with just the medical staff who directly provide for him.

Critical evaluation. Parsons's analysis links illness and medicine to the broader organization of society. Others have extended the concept of the sick role to some nonillness situations such as pregnancy (Myers & Grasmick, 1989).

One limitation of the sick-role idea is that it applies to acute conditions (like the flu) better than to chronic illness (like heart disease), which may not be reversible. Moreover, a sick person's ability to regain health depends on available resources. Many poor people simply cannot afford either medical care or taking time off from work.

Finally, critics point out that Parsons's analysis implies that doctors—rather than people themselves—bear the primary responsibility for health. A more prevention-oriented approach makes physicians and patients equal partners in the pursuit of health.

SYMBOLIC-INTERACTION ANALYSIS

According to the symbolic-interaction paradigm, society is less a grand system than a series of complex and changing realities. Here we see health and medical care as social constructions within everyday interaction.

The Social Construction of Illness

If we socially construct our ideas of health and illness, it follows that members of a very poor society may view hunger and malnutrition as quite normal. Similarly, people in rich nations, such as our own, may give little thought to the harmful effects of spending leisure time passively watching television or consuming a rich diet.

How we respond to illness, too, is based on social definitions that may or may not square with medical facts. For instance, people with AIDS contend with fear and sometimes outright bigotry that has no medical basis.

Furthermore, whether we decide we are "sick" or "well" may rest on a host of nonmedical "contingencies." College students, for example, pay less attention to signs of illness on the eve of a vacation, but they dutifully report to the infirmary hours before a midterm examination. Health, in short, is less an objective commodity than a negotiated outcome.

Indeed, how people define a medical situation may actually affect how they feel. Medical experts marvel at *psychosomatic* disorders (a fusion of Greek words for "mind" and "body"), when state of mind guides physical sensations (Hamrick, Anspaugh, & Ezell, 1986). As sociologist W. I. Thomas (1931) might have said, when health or illness is defined as real, it becomes real in its consequences.

The Social Construction of Treatment

In Chapter 6 ("Social Interaction in Everyday Life"), we used Erving Goffman's dramaturgical approach to explain how physicians tailor their physical surroundings

Q: "Less access to the present health system would, contrary to popular rhetoric, *benefit* the poor." Ivan Illich

Q: "Since the 1960s, access to medical care for black Americans has improved significantly. In 1963, the proportion of blacks who saw a physician was 18% lower than for whites; by 1982, this gap had been almost eliminated . . . [But given a lower standard of living among blacks,] if there were real parity in access to medical

care between the two racial groups, there would be a substantially higher use of health services on the average among black Americans." Robert Blendon, Linda Aiken, Howard Freedman, and Christopher Corey

DIVERSITY: As late as 1969, some localities in the United States legally required blood products to be labeled with the race of the donor; recipients were able to refuse blood on these grounds.

("the office") and their behavior ("the presentation of self") so others see them as competent and in charge.

Sociologist Joan Emerson (1970) further illustrates this process of constructing reality in her analysis of the gynecological examination carried out by a male doctor. This situation is vulnerable to serious misinterpretation, since a man touching a woman's genitals is conventionally viewed as a sexual act and possibly even an assault.

To ensure that people define the situation as impersonal and professional, the medical staff wear uniforms and furnish the examination room with nothing but medical equipment. The doctor's manner and overall performance are designed to make the patient feel that, to him, examining the genital area is no different from treating any other part of the body. A female nurse is usually present during the examination not only to assist the physician but to dispel any impression that a man and woman are "alone in a room."

Managing situational definitions in this way is a topic long overlooked by medical schools. The oversight is unfortunate because, as Emerson's analysis shows, understanding how people construct reality in the examination room is as important as mastering the medical skills required for effective treatment.

Critical evaluation. One strength of the symbolic-interaction paradigm lies in revealing that what people view as healthful or harmful depends on numerous factors, many of which are not, strictly speaking, medical. This approach also shows that, in any medical procedure, both patient and medical staff engage in a subtle process of reality construction.

Critics fault this approach for implying that there are no objective standards of well-being. Certain physical conditions do indeed cause specific changes in people, whatever we may think about it. People who lack sufficient nutrition and safe water, for example, suffer from their unhealthy environment, whether they define their surroundings as normal or not.

SOCIAL-CONFLICT ANALYSIS

Social-conflict analysis draws a connection between health and social inequality and, taking a cue from Karl Marx, ties medicine to the operation of capitalism. Researchers have focused on three main issues: access to medical care, the effects of the profit motive, and the politics of medicine.

Scientists are learning more and more about the genetic factors that prompt the eventual development of serious diseases. If offered the opportunity, would you want to undergo a genetic screening that would predict the long-term future of your own health?

The Access Issue

Personal health is the foundation of social life. Yet, by making health a commodity, capitalist societies allow health to follow wealth. The access problem is more serious in the United States, for example, than in other industrialized societies because our country has no universal medical-care system.

Finally, conflict theorists concede that capitalism provides excellent health care for the rich, but it does not provide very well for the rest of the population. Most of the 42 million people who lack any health-care coverage at present have low incomes.

The Profit Motive

Some conflict analysts go further, arguing that the real problem is not access to medical care but the character of capitalist medicine itself. The profit motive turns physicians, hospitals, and the pharmaceutical industry into multibillion-dollar corporations. The quest for higher profits encourages unnecessary tests

Q: "Medicine and biology were of crucial importance, providing the basic concepts through which the class and sexual divisions of Victorian society were expressed and ultimately justified." Lesley Doyal (1981:141)

RESOURCE: Efua Dorkenoo and Scilla Elworthy's article, "Female Genital Mutilation," is included in the Macionis and Benokraitis reader, *Seeing Ourselves*, fourth edition.

NOTE: Settling the breast implant class-action suit, three companies—Dow Corning, Bristol-Myers Squibb, and Baxter Healthcare—agreed to pay $3.7 billion over 30 years to women claiming injuries. Dow subsequently filed for bankruptcy, raising doubts about eventual payments.

NOTE: The importance of the natural environment to health is addressed in Chapter 22 ("Environment and Society").

and surgery as well as an overreliance on drugs (Ehrenreich, 1978; Kaplan et al., 1985).

Of some 25 million surgical operations performed in the United States each year, three-fourths are "elective," meaning that they promote long-term health and are not prompted by a medical emergency. Social-conflict theorists contend that the decision to perform surgery reflects the financial interests of surgeons and hospitals as much as the medical needs of patients (Illich, 1976). And, of course, any medical procedure or use of drugs is risky and harms between 5 and 10 percent of patients (Sidel & Sidel, 1982a; Cowley, 1995).

Finally, say social-conflict analysts, our society is all too tolerant of physicians having a direct, financial interest in the tests and procedures they order for their patients (Pear & Eckholm, 1991). In short, health care should be motivated by a concern for people, not profits.

Medicine as Politics

Although science declares itself politically neutral, scientific medicine frequently takes sides on significant social issues. For example, the medical establishment has mounted a strong and sustained campaign against government health-care programs. Moreover, the history of medicine itself shows how racial and sexual discrimination have been supported by "scientific" opinions (Leavitt, 1984). Consider the diagnosis of "hysteria," a term that has its origins in the Greek word *hyster*, meaning "uterus." In choosing this word to describe a wild, emotional state, the medical profession suggested that being a woman is somehow the same as being irrational.

Even today, according to conflict theory, scientific medicine explains illness exclusively in terms of bacteria and viruses and ignores the damaging affects of social inequality. From a scientific perspective, in other words, a lack of sanitation and an unhealthy diet make poor people sick; but what about asking why people are poor in the first place? In this way, scientific medicine depoliticizes health by reducing social issues to simple biology.

Critical evaluation. Social-conflict analysis provides still another view of the relationships among health, medicine, and our society. According to this paradigm, social inequality is the reason some people have better health than others.

The most common objection to the conflict approach is that it minimizes the gains in U.S. health brought about by scientific medicine and higher living standards. Though there is plenty of room for improvement, health indicators for our population as a whole have risen steadily during this century and compare well with those of other industrial societies.

In sum, sociology's three major theoretical paradigms convincingly argue that health and medicine are social issues. Indeed, as the final box explains, advancing technology is making it more and more true as time goes on. The famous French scientist Louis Pasteur (1822–1895), who spent much of his life studying how bacteria cause disease, said just before he died that health depends much less on bacteria than on the social environment where bacteria operate (Gordon, 1980:7). Explaining Pasteur's insight is sociology's contribution to human health.

LOOKING AHEAD: HEALTH IN THE TWENTY-FIRST CENTURY

At the beginning of this century, deaths from infectious diseases like diphtheria and measles were widespread, and scientists had yet to develop penicillin and other antibiotics. Even a simple infection from a minor wound, therefore, could be life-threatening. Today, members of our society take for granted the good health and long life that was the exception, not the rule, a century ago. It seems reasonable to expect the positive trend in U.S. health to continue into the next century.

Another encouraging trend is that more people are taking responsibility for their own health (Caplow et al., 1991). Every one of us can live better and longer if we avoid tobacco, eat sensibly and in moderation, and exercise regularly.

Yet, health problems will continue to plague U.S. society in the decades to come. For one thing, with no cure in sight, it seems likely that the AIDS epidemic will persist. For the present, the only way to steer clear of HIV is to make a personal decision to avoid the risky behaviors described in this chapter.

But the changing social profile of people with AIDS—which increasingly afflicts the poor—reminds us that the United States needs to do more to improve the health of people at the margins of our society. How can a rich society afford to let millions of people live without the security of medical care?

NOTE: The National Council on Alcoholism estimates that, by age 18, young people in the U.S. have viewed 100,000 beer ads in the various media.

GLOBAL: Experts estimate that 14 million young U.S. children have high cholesterol (over 200) because of a diet of too much "junk food" and too little exercise. This problem is greater in the United States than in any other industrial country.

DISCUSS: Would you want to know what diseases lie in your future? Half of survey respondents indicate that they would not wish to be tested to learn what diseases they will suffer later in life.

EXERCISE: Read up on the Human Genome Project. What are its goals? How much progress has been made? What ethical debates does it raise?

CONTROVERSY & DEBATE

The Genetic Crystal Ball: Do We Really Want to Look?

The liquid in the laboratory test tube seems ordinary enough, rather like a syrupy form of water. But this liquid represents one of the greatest medical breakthroughs of all time; it may even be the key to life itself. The liquid is deoxyribonucleic acid, or DNA, the spiraling molecule found in cells of the human body that contains the blueprint for making each one of us human as well as different from every other person.

In medical terms, the human body is composed of some 100 trillion cells, most of which contain a nucleus of twenty-three pairs of chromosomes (one of each pair comes from each parent). Each chromosome is packed with DNA, in segments called genes. Genes guide the production of protein, the building blocks of the human body.

If genetics sounds complicated (and it is), the social implications of genetic knowledge are more complex still. Scientists discovered the structure of the DNA molecule in 1952, and now an aggressive program is underway to "map" our genetic landscape. The ultimate goal of the Human Genome Project is to understand how each bit of DNA shapes our being. But do we really want to turn the key to understand life itself?

In the Human Genome Project, many scientists see a completely new approach to medicine that discards treating symptoms and aims to stop illness before it begins. Research, they point out, already has identified genetic abnormalities that cause some forms of cancer, sickle cell anemia, muscular dystrophy, Huntington's disease, cystic fibrosis, and other crippling and deadly afflictions. In the next century, genetic screening—a scientific "crystal ball"—could let people know their medical destiny, and allow doctors to manipulate segments of DNA to prevent the diseases before they appear.

But some people, both in and out of the scientific community, urge caution in such research, warning that genetic information can easily be abused. At its worst, genetic mapping opens the door to Nazi-like efforts to breed a super-race. Indeed, in 1994, the People's Republic of China began to regulate marriage and childbirth with the purpose of avoiding "new births of inferior quality."

It seems inevitable that some parents will want to use genetic testing in order to predict the health (or even the eye and hair color) of their future child. Should people be permitted to abort a fetus that falls short of their standards? Or, further down the road when genetic manipulations become possible, should parents be able to create "designer children"?

Then there is the issue of "genetic privacy." Can a prospective spouse request a genetic evaluation of her fiancé before agreeing to marry? Can life insurance companies demand genetic testing before issuing policies? Can an employer screen job applicants to weed out those whose future illnesses might drain their health-care funds? Clearly, what is scientifically possible is not always morally desirable. Society is already grappling with questions about the proper use of our expanding knowledge about human genetics. These ethical dilemmas will only mount as genetic research moves forward in the years to come.

Continue the debate . . .

1. *Traditional wedding vows join couples "in sickness and health." Do you think individuals have a right to know the future health of a potential partner before tying the knot?*

2. *What about the desire of some parents to genetically design their children?*

3. *Where do we turn to develop standards for the proper use of genetic information?*

Sources: Elmer-DeWitt (1994), Thompson (1994), and Nash (1995).

Finally, repeating a pattern seen in earlier chapters, we find that health problems are far greater in low-income nations than in the United States. The good news is that life expectancy for the world as a whole has been rising—from forty-eight years in 1950 to sixty-five years today—and the biggest gains have been in poor countries (Mosley & Cowley, 1991). But in much of Latin America, Asia, and especially Africa, hundreds of millions of adults and children lack adequate food, safe water, and basic medical attention. Improving the health of the world's poorest people remains a critical challenge as we enter the next century.

SUMMARY

1. Health is a social as well as a biological issue, and well-being depends on the extent and distribution of a society's resources. Culture shapes both definitions of health and patterns of health care.

2. Through most of human history, health has been poor by today's standards. Health improved dramatically in Western Europe and North America in the nineteenth century, first as industrialization raised living standards and later as advances in medical technology helped control infectious diseases.

3. Infectious diseases were the major killers at the beginning of this century. Today most people in the United States die in old age of heart disease, cancer, or stroke.

4. Health in low-income countries is undermined by inadequate sanitation and hunger. Average life expectancy is about twenty years less than in the United States; in the poorest nations, half the children do not survive to adulthood.

5. In the United States, more than three-fourths of children born today will live to at least age sixty-five. Throughout the life course, however, people of high social position enjoy better health than the poor.

6. Cigarette smoking increased during this century to become the greatest preventable cause of death in the United States. Now that the health hazards of smoking are known, social tolerance for using tobacco products is declining.

7. The incidence of sexually transmitted diseases has risen since 1960, an exception to the general decline in infectious disease.

8. The ability to prolong the lives of terminally ill people is forcing us to confront a number of ethical issues surrounding death and the rights of the dying.

9. Historically a family concern, health care is now the responsibility of trained specialists. In the United States, the dominant model is scientific medicine.

10. Holistic healing encourages people to assume greater responsibility for their own health and well-being, and urges professional healers to get to know patients personally and become familiar with their environment.

11. Socialist societies define medical care as a right that governments offer equally to everyone. Capitalist societies view medical care as a commodity to be purchased, although most capitalist governments support medical care through socialized medicine or national health insurance.

12. The United States, with a direct-fee system, is the only industrialized society with no comprehensive medical-care program. Most people have private health insurance, government insurance, or belong to a health maintenance organization. One in six adults in the United States cannot afford to pay for medical care.

13. Structural-functional analysis links health and medicine to other social structures. Central to structural-functional analysis is the concept of the sick role, by which the ill person is excused from routine social responsibilities.

14. The symbolic-interaction paradigm investigates how health and medical treatments are largely matters of socially constructed definitions.

15. Social-conflict analysis focuses on the unequal distribution of health and medical care. It criticizes the U.S. medical establishment for overly relying on drugs and surgery, giving free rein to the profit motive in medicine, and overemphasizing the biological rather than the social causes of illness.

KEY CONCEPTS

health a state of complete physical, mental, and social well-being

social epidemiology the study of how health and disease are distributed throughout a society's population

eating disorder an intense form of dieting or other kind of weight control in pursuit of being very thin

euthanasia (mercy killing) assisting in the death of a person suffering from an incurable disease

medicine a social institution concerned with combating disease and improving health

holistic medicine an approach to health care that emphasizes prevention of illness by taking account of a person's entire physical and social environment

socialized medicine a health-care system in which the government owns and operates most medical facilities and employs most physicians

direct-fee system a medical-care system in which patients pay directly for the services of physicians and hospitals

health maintenance organization (HMO) an organization that provides comprehensive medical care to subscribers for a fixed fee

sick role patterns of behavior defined as appropriate for those who are ill

CRITICAL-THINKING QUESTIONS

1. Explain why health is as much a social as a biological issue.

2. In global context, what are the "diseases of poverty" that kill people in poor countries? What are the "diseases of affluence," the leading killers in rich nations?

3. Sexually transmitted diseases represent an exception to the historical decline in infectious illness. What social forces are reflected in the rise in STDs since 1960?

4. Should the United States follow the lead of other industrial countries and enact a government program of health care for everyone? Why or why not?

LEARNING EXERCISES

1. In most communities, a trip to the local courthouse or city hall is all it takes to find public records showing people's causes of death. Take a look at such records for people a century ago and recently. How do causes of death differ?

2. If you have access to the Internet, visit the Web site for the Centers for Disease Control and Prevention: http://www.cdc.gov Here you will find information about this organization, health news, statistical data, and even travelers' health advisories. This site offers considerable evidence of the social dimensions of health.

3. Is there a medical school on or near your campus? If so, obtain a course catalog and see how much (if any) of the medical curriculum involves the social dimensions of health care.

4. Arrange to speak with a midwife about her work helping women give birth. How do midwives differ from medical obstetricians in their approach?

5. Install the CD-ROM packaged inside the back cover of your text and complete the activities designed to accompany this chapter.

NEW INFORMATION TECHNOLOGY AND SOCIAL INSTITUTIONS

cyber.scope

Social institutions change over time for many reasons. One source of change, highlighted in Chapters 15 through 20, is societal conflict over how institutions ought to operate. We have highlighted debates, for example, about what kind of economy works best, how democratic our political system really is, the meaning of "the family," the role of religion in the modern world, the ways schools go about doing the job of teaching young people, and how nations provide health care to their people.

Another source of change is technology. In the Information Age, all social institutions are in transition as computers and other communications equipment play a greater role in our lives. This fourth Cyber.Scope briefly reviews ways in which computer technology is reshaping several of the major social institutions.

The Symbolic Economy

The computer is at the center of the new postindustrial economy. As Chapter 15 ("The Economy and Work") explained, work in the postindustrial economy is less likely to involve making *things* and more likely to involve manipulating *symbols*. Thus, gaining literacy skills is as crucial to success in the coming century as learning mechanical skills was to workers a century ago.

As the Industrial Age progressed, machines took over more and more of the manual skills performed by human workers. We might well wonder, then, if computers are destined to replace humans in performing many of the tasks that involve *thinking*. After all, the human brain is capable of only 100 calculations per second; the most powerful computers process information a billion times faster.

Then, too, the expanding array of information available through the Internet to people with computer access may make many traditional jobs obsolete. Will we need as many librarians when people can browse online catalogs of books? (Indeed, will we even need *libraries* as we have known them in the

As industrial production gives way to postindustrial work, fewer and fewer people are employed in factories. At the same time, new kinds of work are being invented by people clever at managing information. Tom and David Gardner started putting their views of stock market trends on the Internet and people paid attention. Soon they were in charge of a successful new business called "The Motley Fool." Of course, many new information companies don't succeed nearly this well. But the opportunities are bounded only by your imagination.

past?) Will there still be travel agents, when anyone can readily access flight schedules, shop for good fares, and purchase tickets as well as reserve hotel rooms and rental cars on the 'Net? Even the shopping mall may lose much of its popularity in the century to come as consumers purchase more products from online vendors.

Finally, computer technology seems sure to accelerate the expansion of a global economy as the Internet draws together businesses and consumers into a worldwide market. Perhaps, in the computer-based economy of the twenty-first century, we will have to invent a new "virtual currency" to replace the outmoded idea of paper money.

Politics in the Information Age

Cyberspace, by its very nature, is both global and lacking centralized control. In the emerging Information Age, it is likely that the current system of dividing humanity into almost 200 distinct nation-states will evolve into a new form. In other words, because the flow of information is unaffected by national boundaries, it makes less and less sense to think of people—who may work, shop, and communicate with others all over the world—as citizens of one geographically bounded nation.

And what effect will the global flow of information have on politics itself? By increasing the amount of available information and helping people to communicate more easily, it is reasonable

DISCUSS: Debate the idea of protecting material on the Web by extending copyright law. One side: Without regulation, people's ideas (writing, poetry, music, software) can be spread uncontrollably; another side: Everything will be sold, making the Internet a big vending machine. (In fact, sites presently can "read" surfers and dish up customized ads.)

CYBER: In the United States, medical training now makes extensive use of computers by having physicians-in-training treat "virtual patients."

DISCUSS: Will new information technology help make people healthier? Or will computer-based activities discourage physical activity and erode good health?

to imagine that cyber-technology will be a force for political democracy. As long as computer-based communication remains free of government control, at least, how can a totalitarian political order persist?

On the other hand, should governments gain control of computer-based communication, they will have a powerful new tool for spreading propaganda and manipulating their populations. Or, more modestly, governments bent on tyranny may not be able to control the global Internet, but they may try to control access to computer technology within their borders. Such regulation of information would be a blow to democracy, of course. At the same time, however, any nation would pay a high price for isolating itself from the expanding world of computer-based information and trade.

Families of the Future

Over the centuries, new technology has shaped and reshaped the family. The Industrial Revolution moved work from farm and home to factories, making "the job" and "the family" separate spheres of life.

More recently, the Information Revolution is creating the opposite effect as new communications technology allows people to work at home (or, with portable computers and telephones, to work virtually anywhere). The trend toward *decentralizing* work means that, for more and more people, the line between "the office" and "the home" is disappearing.

In some respects, this trend should strengthen families, allowing parents, for example, to create more flexible work schedules and placing both fathers and mothers closer to children. Yet, in the cyber-age, televisions and computers are playing a

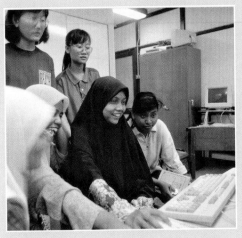

New information technology is spreading ideas and images around the world as never before. These young women live in Maylasia, a relatively traditional society. How do you think the spread of culture via the Internet from the United States and other rich countries will affect the labor force, family patterns, and the desire for education in societies like this one? Will changes be for the better or worse? Why?

larger role in socializing the young. In short, families may be able to spend more time together in the coming century, but whether they will choose to do so is less certain.

Medicine and the Pursuit of Health

Just as computer technology is decentralizing work, so it is making medical care more readily available. In the years to come, many routine health checks (pulse rate, blood pressure, heart function) will be performed at home by people with computer access who transmit data via modem to specialists at medical centers.

Around the world, too, new information technology is making better health care available to more and more people. In the United States, hospitals now rely on Internet sites to match patients and available organs, with the result of saving lives. In villages throughout poor

nations, practitioners in clinics now log on to computers to consult with specialists in medical centers in the world's largest cities, gaining the information they need to provide more effective treatments. In 1995, for example, computer links were vital in helping physicians in central Africa share news, skills, and equipment while fighting the outbreak of the deadly Ebola virus.

New information technology is also making an important contribution to the lives of people with mental and physical disabilities. On one level, new computer programs allow officials to determine whether or not plans for new public buildings and private homes will include access to people with disabilities. On another level, specialists at numerous universities and hospitals now use computer simulations to train children to operate wheelchairs and to teach mentally retarded adults to ride the train or bus. More broadly, computers now allow people with various physical and mental limitations to enjoy and learn from virtual experiences, including travel, skiing, and even hanggliding, that seemed impossible a generation ago (Biggs, 1996).

Institutions and Technology: Each Shaping the Other

New technology is bringing changes to all aspects of our lives. But although technology is a powerful agent of change, it does not determine the shape of society. On the contrary, technology alters the boundaries of what is possible. Therefore, *how* and even *if* we employ new information technology are important decisions that societies must make. And how we decide these questions comes back to our social institutions, which, after all, define *for whom* society should operate in the first place.

Ernest Fiene, *Nocturne*

CHAPTER 21

POPULATION AND URBANIZATION

"We don't want to have children," declares Naomi Hamada, a twenty-eight-year-old Tokyo housewife. "My husband just doesn't like annoying things. And, since he won't help out raising them, I don't want kids, either."

To hear his wife tell it, Mr. Hamada sounds like something of a grouch. But, in today's Japan, he has a lot of company. In the city of Tokyo, with its small apartments, congested streets, living-room-sized parks, and sky-high prices, people are choosing to have fewer and fewer children. The city's birth rate, in fact, has fallen to just one child per couple—half the level necessary to replace the people alive now.

For the nation as a whole, the birth rate is only slightly higher. Should this trend continue, Japan's population will be cut in half by the end of the twenty-first century. To allay fears that the Japanese may "disappear," government officials have proposed new policies, ranging from paying cash incentives so couples will have large families, to importing "mail-order" wives from the Philippines, and restricting access to college and careers. Not surprisingly, such proposals have provoked a firestorm of controversy. But few are happy at the prospect of their nation's population skidding downward (Kristof, 1996).

As this chapter explains, a low birth rate is found in other industrial nations as well. But the picture is quite different in poor countries, where population is rising rapidly and cities are reaching unprecedented size. This chapter examines both population changes and urbanization, powerful forces that, together, are changing the face of our world.

DEMOGRAPHY: THE STUDY OF POPULATION

From the time the human species appeared about 250,000 B.C.E. until about 250 years ago, the earth's population hovered around 500 million—less than the number of Europeans today. Life for our ancestors was brutal and often short; people fell victim to countless diseases, frequent injury, and periodic natural disasters. Looking back, one might well be amazed that our species has managed to survive for 10,000 generations.

About 1750, however, world population began to "spike" upward. We now add 80 million people to the planet each year, which put the global total in 1998 at almost 6 billion. Ironically, perhaps, human beings have become so successful at reproduction that the future well-being of our species is again in doubt.

The causes and consequences of this human drama are the basis of **demography,** *the study of human population.* Demography (from the Greek, meaning "description of people") is a specialty within sociology that analyzes the size and composition of a population and the flow of people from place to place. Although partly concerned with statistics, demography also poses important questions about the effects of population growth and how population might be controlled. The following sections present basic demographic concepts.

SUPPLEMENTS: An outline of this chapter, supplementary lecture material, and suggested discussion topics are found in the *Data File.*

GLOBAL: In Islamic nations high fertility rates and low use of contraception are the norm. Yet fertility is falling in these societies. Morocco is a case in point: It still has a 2.0% growth rate, but its fertility has fallen during recent decades from seven births per woman to less than four. Contraceptive use among women of childbearing age has risen from about 25% to about 50%.

DIVERSITY: African Americans have the highest infant mortality rate (16) in the United States. Mexican Americans, with even less income and education, on average, have a much lower infant mortality rate (9). This advantage probably reflects greater social support patterns as well as dietary and hereditary differences.

GLOBAL SNAPSHOT

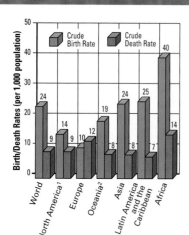
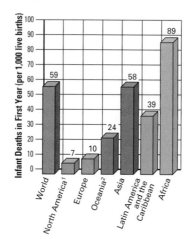
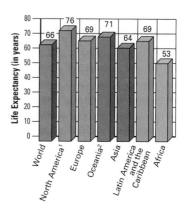

FIGURE 21–1 **Crude Birth Rates and Crude Death Rates, Infant Mortality Rates, and Life Expectancy, 1997**

[1] United States and Canadaz
[2] Australia, New Zealand, and South Pacific Islands
Source: Population Reference Bureau (1997).

FERTILITY

The study of human population begins with how many people are born. **Fertility** is *the incidence of childbearing in a country's population.* During a woman's childbearing years, from the onset of menstruation (typically in the early teens) to menopause (usually in the late forties), she is capable of bearing more than twenty children. But *fecundity,* or maximum possible childbearing, is sharply reduced in practice by cultural norms, finances, and personal choice.

Demographers measure fertility using the **crude birth rate,** *the number of live births in a given year for every thousand people in a population.* They calculate a crude birth rate by dividing the number of live births in a year by a society's total population and multiplying the result by 1,000. In the United States in 1996, there were 3.9 million live births in a population of 265 million (U.S. National Center for Health Statistics, 1997). According to the formula, then, the crude birth rate was 14.7.

This birth rate is "crude" because it is based on the entire population, not just women in their childbearing years. Comparing the crude birth rates of various countries can be misleading, then, if one society has a larger share of women of childbearing age than another. A crude birth rate also tells us nothing about how fertility differs among a society's racial and ethnic categories. But this measure is easy to calculate and serves as a good indicator of a society's overall fertility. Figure 21–1 shows that, in global perspective, the crude birth rate of North Americans is low.

MORTALITY

Population size is also affected by **mortality,** *the incidence of death in a country's population.* To measure mortality, demographers use a **crude death rate,** *the number of deaths in a given year for every thousand people in a population.* This time, we take the number of deaths in a year, divide by the total population, and multiply the result by 1,000. In 1996 there were 2.3 million deaths in the U.S. population of 265 million, yielding a crude death rate of 8.7. Figure 21–1 shows that, in global context, this rate is about average.

A third widely used demographic measure is the **infant mortality rate,** *the number of deaths among infants under one year of age for each thousand live births in a given year.* Infant mortality is computed by dividing the number of deaths of children under one year

THE MAP: The main reason for internal migration is the search for economic opportunity. People leave economically depressed areas for those that promise better jobs. Migrants tend to be younger people; those who remain are older, on average, and have less schooling.

GLOBAL: One key predictor of fertility is women's income. As wages and salaries rise, fertility falls, and vice versa.

NOTE: One dramatic illustration of mortality change: A greater proportion of U.S. babies born today will reach age 65 than survived a single year in 1900.

EXERCISE: Trace the regional migration of the U.S. population by looking at the shifting location of Major League Baseball teams. (In 1956, all but 2 of 16 teams were in the Northeast or Midwest; in 1997, the South and West had 12 of 26 teams; see Pollard, 1996.)

SEEING OURSELVES

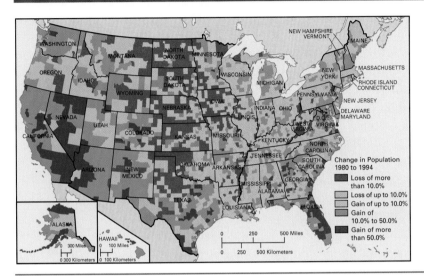

NATIONAL MAP 21–1
Population Change Across the United States

In general, population is moving from the heartland of the United States toward the coasts. What do you think is causing this internal migration? Can you offer a demographic profile of the people who remain in counties that are losing population?

Source: *Time*, January 30, 1995, pp. 54–55. Copyright © 1995 Time Inc. Reprinted by permission.

Change in Population 1980 to 1994

- Loss of more than 10.0%
- Loss of up to 10.0%
- Gain of up to 10.0%
- Gain of 10.0% to 50.0%
- Gain of more than 50.0%

---

of age by the number of live births during the same year and multiplying the result by 1,000. In 1996 there were 28,100 infant deaths and about 3.9 million live births in the United States. Dividing the first number by the second and multiplying the result by 1,000 yields an infant mortality rate of 7.2. The second part of Figure 21–1 indicates that, by world standards, North American infant mortality is low.

Here again, though, we must bear in mind variations among different categories of people. For example, African Americans, with three times the burden of poverty as whites, have an infant mortality rate of about 14—more than twice the rate of 6 for white Americans.

Low infant mortality greatly raises **life expectancy,** *the average life span of a society's population.* U.S. males born in 1996 can expect to live 73 years, while females can look toward 79 years. As the third part of Figure 21–1 shows, U.S. life expectancy exceeds that of low-income countries in Africa by more than twenty years.

MIGRATION

Population size is also affected by **migration,** *the movement of people into and out of a specified territory.* Migration is sometimes involuntary, such as the forcible transport of 10 million Africans to the Western Hemisphere as slaves (Sowell, 1981). Voluntary migration, however, is usually the result of complex "push-pull" factors. Dissatisfaction with life in poor countries may "push" people to move, while the opportunity for a better life may "pull" them to the city.

Movement into a territory—or *immigration*—is measured as an *in-migration rate,* calculated as the number of people entering an area for every thousand people in the population. Movement out of a territory—or *emigration*—is measured in terms of an *out-migration rate,* the number leaving for every thousand people. Since both types of migration usually occur simultaneously, the difference is called the *net migration rate.*

All nations also experience internal migration, that is, movement within their borders, from one region to another. National Map 21–1 shows where the U.S. population is moving, and the places left behind.

POPULATION GROWTH

Fertility, mortality, and migration all affect the size of a society's population. In general, rich nations (like the United States) grow almost as much from immigration as natural increase; less economically developed societies (like Mexico) grow almost entirely from natural increase.

To calculate a population's natural growth rate, demographers subtract the crude death rate from the crude birth rate. The natural growth rate of the U.S.

NOTE: The table in the end-of-chapter box sketches global birth, death, and natural increase rates over time.

GLOBAL: Median age in Europe has risen from 30 in 1950 to about 36 today, and will probably reach 40 by 2025. This suggests little overall growth due to natural increase. In Africa, by comparison, during the same period, median age has fallen from about 18 to 17, indicating high population growth.

GLOBAL: In 1997. there were 318 million Chinese under 15 years of age. Even with rigid regulation of births, China will certainly have a serious population problem for decades to come. Even success in controlling population will produce strains: Rapidly dropping fertility would eventually result in more than half of China's population being over the age of 65, greatly taxing social resources.

WINDOW ON THE WORLD

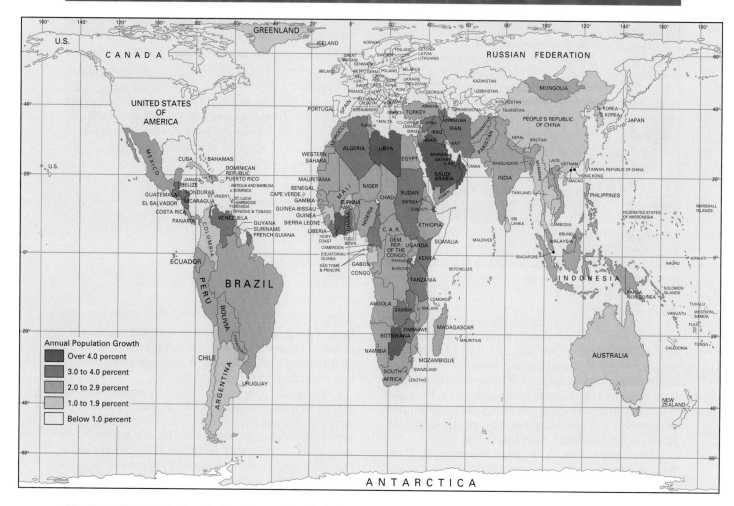

GLOBAL MAP 21–1 Population Growth in Global Perspective

The richest countries of the world—including the United States, Canada, and the nations of Europe—have growth rates below 1 percent. The nations of Latin America and Asia typically have growth rates approaching 2 percent, which double a population in thirty-five years. Africa has an overall growth rate of 2.6 percent, which cuts the doubling time to twenty-seven years. In global perspective, we see that a society's standard of living is closely related to its rate of population growth: Population is rising fastest in the world regions that can least afford to support more people.

Source: *Peters Atlas of the World* (1990), with statistics updated by the author.

population in 1996 was 6.0 per thousand (the crude birth rate of 14.7 minus the crude death rate of 8.7), or about 0.6 percent annual growth.

Global Map 21–1 shows that population growth in the United States and other industrialized nations is well below the world average of 1.5 percent. The earth's low-growth continents are Europe (currently posting a slight decline expressed as −0.1 percent annual growth), North America (0.6 percent), and Oceania (1.1 percent); Asia (1.6 percent) and Latin

THEN AND NOW: The U.S. age-sex pyramid in 1900 resembled that of Mexico today.

GLOBAL: Demographic profiles of the U.S. and Mexico: populations, 265 million and 98 million; population densities, 76 and 131 persons per square mile; growth 1980–97, 17.7% and 42.0%; persons per household, 2.6 and 4.9; households with five or more members, 14% and 51%.

DIVERSITY: Sex ratios differ by race: at birth, whites = 105, blacks = 102; at age 20, whites = 105, blacks = 97; at age 40, whites = 100, blacks = 86 (Schaub, 1997).

GLOBAL: Sex-ratio imbalance in Asia is especially high for second and third births. In South Korea, for example, 115 boys are born for every 100 girls as second children; for third children, the figure soars to 190 boys for every 100 girls.

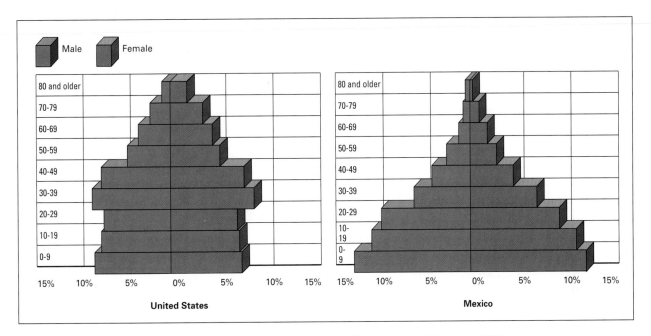

FIGURE 21–2 Age-Sex Population Pyramids for the United States and Mexico, 1997

Source: U.S. Bureau of the Census (1997).

America (1.8 percent) stand slightly above the global average; Africa (2.6 percent) is the highest-growth region of the world.

Demographers have a handy rule of thumb for estimating population growth: They divide a society's population growth rate into the number seventy to calculate the *doubling time* in years. Thus, an annual growth of 2 percent (common in Latin America) doubles a population in thirty-five years, and a 3 percent growth rate (found in some of Africa) drops the doubling time to just twenty-four years. The rapid population growth of the poorest countries is deeply troubling because they can barely support the populations they have now.

POPULATION COMPOSITION

Demographers also study the makeup of a society's population at a given point in time. One variable is the **sex ratio,** *the number of males for every hundred females in a given population.* In 1997 the sex ratio in the United States was 96, or 96 males for every 100 females. Sex ratios are usually below 100 because women typically outlive men. In India, however, the sex ratio is 107. There are more males than females in India because parents value sons more than daughters

and may either abort a female fetus or, after birth, give more care to a male infant, raising the odds that a girl child will die.

A more complex measure is the **age-sex pyramid,** *a graphic representation of the age and sex of a population.* Figure 21–2 presents two age-sex pyramids, showing the contrasting composition of the United States and Mexico. The rough pyramid shape of these figures results from higher mortality as people age. In the U.S. pyramid, the bulge corresponding to ages thirty through forty-nine reflects high birth rates during the *baby boom* from the mid-1940s to 1970. The contraction just below—that is, people under thirty—reflects the subsequent *baby bust* as the birth rate dipped from 25.3 in 1957 to a low of 14.7 in 1996.

Comparing the U.S. and Mexican age-sex pyramids, we can predict different demographic trends. The age-sex pyramid for Mexico, like that of other low-income nations, is wide at the bottom (reflecting higher birth rates) and narrows quickly by what we would term middle age (due to higher mortality rates). Mexico, in short, is a much younger society overall, with a median age of twenty as compared to thirty-four in the United States. With a larger share of females still in their childbearing years, Mexico's crude birth rate (26) is, not surprisingly, nearly twice

NOTE: Malthus made a personal contribution to population control by having only three children (about half the average for his day); typical for that time, only one of his children lived to adulthood.

NOTE: Malthus's thesis, first published anonymously, was a critical response to Rousseau's notion that social evils were due to social institutions; but abolish marriage, countered Malthus, and humanity's inherent selfishness will doom the species.

RESOURCE: David Berreby's analysis of "The Global Population Crisis" is included among the cross-cultural selections in the companion reader, *Seeing Ourselves.*

GLOBAL: With a current population growth rate of 2.9% annually, Nigeria's population of 111 million will double by 2018. Nigerian women bear, on the average, six children.

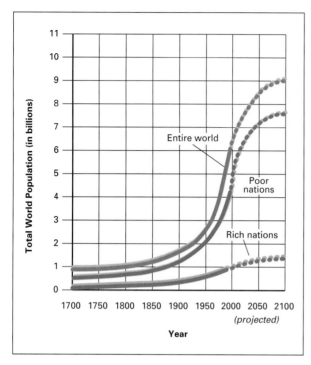

FIGURE 21–3 The Increase in World Population, 1700–2100

our own (15), and its annual rate of population growth (2.1 percent) is almost four times the rate of the United States (0.6 percent).

HISTORY AND THEORY OF POPULATION GROWTH

Through most of human history, people favored large families since human labor was the key to productivity. Moreover, until rubber condoms appeared 150 years ago, preventing pregnancy was an uncertain proposition at best. But high death rates, resulting from widespread infectious diseases, put a constant brake on population growth.

But, as shown in Figure 21–3, a major demographic shift began about 1750 as the world's population turned upward, reaching the 1 billion mark by 1800. This milestone (requiring all of human history up to this point) was repeated by 1930—barely a century later—when a second billion people were added to the planet. In other words, not only did population increase, but the *rate* of growth accelerated. Global population reached 3 billion by 1962 (just thirty-two

years later) and 4 billion by 1974 (a scant twelve years later). The rate of world population increase has recently slowed, but our planet passed the 5 billion mark in 1987 and will reach 6 billion before the year 2000. In no previous century did the world's population even double. In the twentieth century, it has increased *fourfold*.

Currently, the world is gaining 80 million people each year, with 90 percent of this increase in poor countries. Looking ahead, experts predict, the earth's population will reach between 8 and 9 billion by 2050 (Wattenberg, 1997). Given the world's troubles feeding its present population, such an increase has become a matter of urgent concern.

MALTHUSIAN THEORY

It was the sudden population growth two centuries ago that sparked the development of demography. Thomas Robert Malthus (1766–1834), an English clergyman and economist, warned that population increase would soon lead to social chaos.

Malthus (1926; orig. 1798) predicted that population would increase by what mathematicians call a *geometric progression*, illustrated by the series of numbers 2, 4, 8, 16, 32, and so on. At such a rate, Malthus concluded, world population would soon soar out of control.

Food production would also increase, Malthus explained, but only in *arithmetic progression* (as in the series 2, 3, 4, 5, 6) because, even with new agricultural technology, farmland is limited. Thus, Malthus presented a troubling vision of the future: people reproducing beyond what the planet could feed, leading ultimately to widespread starvation.

Malthus acknowledged that artificial birth control or abstinence might change the equation. But he considered them either morally wrong or practically impossible. Thus, famine and war stalked humanity in Malthus's scheme, and he was justly known as "the dismal parson."

Critical evaluation. Fortunately for us, Malthus's prediction was flawed. First, by 1850 the birth rate in Europe began to drop, partly because children were becoming more of an economic liability than an asset and partly because people *did* use artificial birth control. Second, Malthus underestimated human ingenuity: Irrigation, fertilizers, and pesticides have increased farm production far more than he ever imagined.

Some criticized Malthus for ignoring the role of social inequality in world abundance and famine. Karl

NOTE: Demographic transition theory is one element of modernization theory, discussed in Chapter 11, "Global Stratification."

GLOBAL: A population comparison of two comparably sized delta lands—Louisiana and Bangladesh—shows that Louisiana has a population of 4.4 million and a growth rate of 1.1%, while Bangladesh has 120 million people and a growth rate of 1.6%.

Q: "Ten thousand generations to reach 2 billion and then in one human lifetime—ours—we leap from 2 billion toward 10 billion." Vice President Al Gore

NOTE: Ronald Lee, University of California at Berkeley demographer, estimates that 110 billion people have ever lived on earth; the almost 6 billion people living now are 5.5% of the historical total.

FIGURE 21–4
Demographic Transition Theory

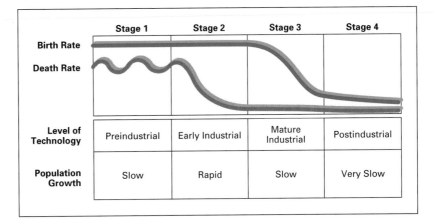

Marx (1967; orig. 1867) objected to viewing suffering as a "law of nature" rather than the curse of capitalism.

Still, we should not entirely dismiss Malthus. Habitable land, clean water, and fresh air are finite resources, and greater economic productivity has taken a toll on the natural environment. In addition, medical advances have lowered death rates, pushing up world population. Population growth is especially rapid in low-income countries, which are, in fact, experiencing much of the catastrophe Malthus envisioned.

In principle, of course, no level of population growth can go on indefinitely. Thus, people everywhere must become aware of the dangers of population increase.

DEMOGRAPHIC TRANSITION THEORY

Malthus's rather crude analysis has been superseded by **demographic transition theory,** *a thesis linking demographic changes to a society's level of technological development.* Figure 21–4 shows the demographic consequences at four levels of technological development. Preindustrial, agrarian societies—those at Stage 1—have high birth rates because of the economic value of children (many of whom will not survive until adulthood) and the lack of effective birth control. Death rates are also high, the result of low living standards and little medical technology, so that people fall victim to infectious diseases including periodic outbreaks of plague. Deaths thus neutralize births, so population rises and falls with only a modest overall increase. This was the case for thousands of years in Europe before the Industrial Revolution.

Stage 2—the onset of industrialization—brings a demographic transition as population surges. Technology expands food supplies and science combats disease.

Death rates fall sharply while birth rates remain high, resulting in rapid population growth. It was in a Stage 2 era that Malthus formulated his ideas, which explains his pessimistic view of the future. Most of the world's poorest countries today are in this high-growth stage.

In Stage 3—a mature industrial economy—the birth rate drops, curbing population growth once again. Fertility falls, first, because most children survive to adulthood and, second, because high living standards make raising children expensive. Affluence, in short, transforms children from economic assets into economic liabilities. Smaller families, made possible by effective birth control, are also favored by women working outside the home. As birth rates follow death rates downward, population growth slows further.

Stage 4 corresponds to a postindustrial economy. The birth rate continues to fall, partly because dual-income couples gradually become the norm and partly because the cost of raising children continues to rise. This trend, coupled with steady death rates, means that, at best, population grows only very slowly or even *decreases.* This is the case in Europe currently and, as noted in the opening to this chapter, may soon be true of Japan as well.

Critical evaluation. Demographic transition theory suggests that the key to population control lies in technology. Instead of the runaway population increase feared by Malthus, this theory sees technology reining in growth and ensuring material plenty.

Demographic transition theory dovetails with modernization theory, an approach to global development discussed in Chapter 11 ("Global Stratification"). Modernization theorists are optimistic that poor countries will solve their population problems as they industrialize. But critics—notably dependency

DISCUSS: The UN predicts that, between 1995 and 2025, rich societies will grow by 57 million people and poor societies by 1.7 billion people. What are the implications of this pattern?

GLOBAL: In rich societies, women average just under one child during their reproductive lifetimes (counting only those who have children, the median is just under two). In poor societies, virtually all women have children, averaging almost five.

NOTE: Voluntary sterilization has increased dramatically to become the most common form of birth control in the United States. Moreover, U.S. Catholics, whose religious doctrine prohibits artificial birth control, no longer differ from others in contraceptive practices.

NOTE: Abortion also contributes to low fertility. About 1.5 million pregnancies end in this way each year in the United States.

theorists—strongly disagree. Unless there is a significant redistribution of global resources, they maintain, our planet will become increasingly divided into industrialized "haves," enjoying low population growth, and nonindustrialized "have-nots," struggling in vain to feed soaring populations.

GLOBAL POPULATION TODAY: A BRIEF SURVEY

What can we say about population in today's world? Drawing on the discussion so far, we can highlight key patterns and reach a number of conclusions.

The Low-Growth North

When the Industrial Revolution began, population growth in Western Europe and North America peaked at 3 percent annually, which doubles a population in little more than one generation. But, in the centuries since, the growth rate steadily declined and, in 1970, dropped below 1 percent. As our postindustrial society enters Stage 4, the U.S. birth rate has dropped below the replacement level of 2.1 children per woman, a point demographers term **zero population growth,** *the level of reproduction that maintains population at a steady state.* Some fifty nations, almost all of them rich, have reached or passed the point of zero population growth (Wattenberg, 1997).

Factors holding down population in these postindustrial societies include a high proportion of men and women in the labor force, rising costs of raising children, trends toward singlehood or later marriage, and widespread use of contraceptives and abortion.

In industrial nations, therefore, population increase is not the pressing problem that it is in poor countries. Indeed, some analysts point to a future problem of *underpopulation* in countries such as Japan, Italy, and the United States, where the swelling ranks of the elderly have fewer and fewer young people to look to for support in old age (Chesnais, 1997).

The High-Growth South

Population is a critical problem in poor nations of the Southern Hemisphere. Only a few societies lack industrial technology altogether, placing them in demographic transition theory's Stage 1. But most of Latin America, Africa, and Asia are in Stage 2, with agrarian economies and some industry. At the same time, advanced medical technology, supplied by rich

societies, has sharply reduced death rates, while birth rates remain high. This is why poor societies now account for two-thirds of the earth's people and 90 percent of global population increase.

In poor countries throughout the world, birth rates have fallen from an average of about six children per woman in 1950 to around four today. But even this level of increase will intensify global poverty if it continues. At a 1994 global population conference in Cairo, delegates from 180 nations agreed on the need for vigorous action to contain population growth. They also pointed to the connection between population control and the status of women. The box on page 566 offers a closer look.

In the last decade, the world has made significant progress in lowering fertility. Yet the other half of the demographic equation—mortality—is also critical and, worldwide, death rates are falling. Although few would oppose medical programs that save lives—mostly of children—lower death rates mean population increase. In fact, population growth in most low-income regions of the world is due *primarily* to declining death rates. Around 1920, Europe and North America began to export advances in scientific medicine, nutrition, and sanitation around the world. Since then, inoculations against infectious diseases and the use of antibiotics and insecticides have pushed down death rates with stunning effectiveness. For example, in Sri Lanka, malaria caused half of all deaths in the 1930s; a decade later, use of insecticides to kill malaria-carrying mosquitoes cut the death toll from this disease in half. Although this is a great medical achievement, Sri Lanka's population began to soar. Similarly, India's infant mortality rate decreased from 130 in 1975 to 74 in 1997, boosting that nation's population to 1 billion.

In short, in much of the world, fertility is falling. But so is mortality, especially among children. Now we must control birth in poor countries as successfully as we fended off death in the past.

URBANIZATION: THE GROWTH OF CITIES

October 8, 1994, Hong Kong. The cable train grinds to the top of Victoria Peak where one of the world's most spectacular vistas awaits us: the Hong Kong harbor at night! A million bright, colorful lights ring the harbor as ships, ferries,

GLOBAL: Immunization throughout poor societies has increased dramatically in recent decades. In 1975, 5% of infants were immunized against diseases such as measles, polio, tetanus, and diphtheria. By 1995, 50–75% of all children were immunized against these diseases. One result: In Africa, not just infant mortality rates but the absolute number of infants dying has declined.

Q: "Earth is overpopulated today by a very simple standard: Humanity is able to support itself—often none too well, at that—only by consuming its capital." Paul and Anne Ehrlich

Q: "In the course of my own lifetime, the earth's population has increased two and a half times, and most of this increase is now to be found in the exploding urban centers, especially in the slums and shantytowns, of Africa, Asia, and Latin America." Isaac Asimov

The Natomo family, pictured in the top photo, lives in the western African nation of Mali. The Hodson family, shown below, lives in England. What relationship do you see between a society's level of material affluence and its typical family size? Can you explain this pattern?

and traditional Chinese "junks" churn by. Although, in the distance, the city seems almost asleep, few settings match Hong Kong for sheer energy. This small city is as productive as the state of Wisconsin or the nation of Finland. One could sit here for hours entranced by the spectacle of Hong Kong.

CRITICAL THINKING

Empowering Women:
The Key to Controlling Population Growth

Sohad Ahmad lives with her husband in a farming village fifty miles south of Cairo, Egypt's capital city. Ahmad lives a poor life, like hundreds of millions of other women in the world. Yet her situation differs in an important respect: She has had only two children and will have no more.

Why do Sohad and her husband reject the conventional wisdom that children are an economic asset? One part of the answer is that Egypt's growing population has already created such a demand for land that her family could not afford more even if they had the children to farm it. Another part of the answer is that the Ahmads recognize that a bigger family means more bodies to feed, clothe, and house. In other words, if growing more food requires more hungry workers, how is a family better off? But the main reason is that Sohad Ahmad does not want her life defined by childbearing.

Like Sohad Ahmad, more women in Egypt are taking control of their fertility and seeking more opportunities. Indeed, this country has made great progress in reducing its annual population growth from 3.0 percent just ten years ago to 2.3 percent today. This success in reducing fertility is why the International Conference on Population and Development selected Cairo for its historic 1994 meeting.

The 1994 Cairo conference broke new ground, linking global efforts to control population to raising the standing of women. In the past, population

Dr. Nafis Sadik is in charge of United Nations efforts to monitor and control the growth of world population. In her view, success in controlling population growth depends directly on our ability to expand the opportunities for education and paid employment for women—especially in poor countries.

control programs focused on making birth control technology available to women. This is certainly important, since only half of the world's married women use birth control. But the larger picture shows that even when birth control is readily available, population continues to increase in societies that define women's primary responsibility as raising children.

Dr. Nafis Sadik, an Egyptian woman who heads the United Nations' population control programs, sums up the new approach to lowering birth rates this way: *Give women more life choices and they will have fewer children.* In other words, women with access to schooling and jobs, who can decide when and if they wish to marry, and who bear children as a matter of choice, will limit their own fertility. Schooling must be available to older women too, Sadik adds, because they exercise great influence in local communities.

The lesson of Egypt and the Cairo conference—and mounting evidence from countries around the world—is that controlling population and raising the social standing of women are one and the same.

Sources: Linden (1994) and Ashford (1995).

For most of human history, the sights and sounds of great cities such as Hong Kong, New York, or Los Angeles were simply unimaginable. The world's people lived in small, nomadic groups, moving as they depleted vegetation or searched for migrating herds. The small settlements that marked the emergence of civilization in the Middle East some 12,000 years ago held only a small fraction of the earth's people. Today the largest three or four cities of the world together contain as many people as the entire planet did back then.

Urbanization is *the concentration of humanity into cities.* Urbanization both redistributes population within a society and transforms many patterns of

Mont St. Michel, a French town that rises against the Atlantic Ocean, is a wonderful example of a medieval settlement: small and walled, with narrow, irregular streets that, even today, make walking seem like a delightful stroll back in time.

social life. We will trace these changes in terms of three urban revolutions—the emergence of cities beginning 10,000 years ago, the development of industrial cities after 1750, and the explosive growth of cities in poor countries today.

THE EVOLUTION OF CITIES

Cities are a relatively new development in human history. Only about 12,000 years ago did our ancestors found a permanent settlement, setting the stage for the *first urban revolution*.

PRECONDITIONS OF CITIES

The first precondition of urban development is a *favorable ecology*. As glaciers receded at the end of the last ice age, people congregated in warm regions with fertile soil. The second precondition is *advanced technology*. At about the same time, humans discovered how to domesticate animals and cultivate crops. Whereas hunting and gathering demanded continual movement, raising food required people to remain in one place (Lenski, Nolan, & Lenski, 1995). Third, domesticating animals and plants provided a *material surplus*, a third precondition for urban development. A surplus of food freed some people from raising animals and crops, allowing them to build shelters, make tools, weave cloth, and take part in religious rituals. The emergence of cities was truly revolutionary, leading to increased specialization and raising living standards.

The First Cities

The first city, the historians tell us, is Jericho, which lies to the north of the Dead Sea in disputed land currently occupied by Israel. About 8000 B.C.E., Jericho contained some 600 people. By 4000 B.C.E., it was one of numerous cities flourishing in the Fertile Crescent between the Tigris and Euphrates rivers in present-day Iraq and, by 3000 B.C.E., along the Nile River in Egypt.

Some cities, with populations reaching 50,000, became centers of urban empires. Priest-kings wielded absolute power over lesser nobles, administrators, artisans, soldiers, and farmers. Slaves, captured in frequent military campaigns, built monumental structures like the pyramids of Egypt (Kenyon, 1957; Hamblin, 1973; Stavrianos, 1983; Lenski, Nolan, & Lenski, 1995).

In at least three other areas of the world, cities developed independently. Several large, complex settlements bordered the Indus River in present-day Pakistan starting about 2500 B.C.E. Scholars date Chinese cities from 2000 B.C.E. And in Central and South America, urban centers began about 1500 B.C.E. In North America, only a few Native American societies formed settlements; widespread urbanization had to await the arrival of European settlers in the seventeenth century (Lamberg-Karlovsky, 1973; Change, 1977; Coe & Diehl, 1980).

Preindustrial European Cities

Urbanization in Europe began about 1800 B.C.E. on the Mediterranean island of Crete. Soon Greece could boast of more than 100 city-states. The most famous was Athens. During this city's Golden Age, which

One of the earliest settlements made by Europeans in what they called "the New World" was St. Augustine, Florida. Begun in 1565, this engraving shows the city a century later in 1673. It was not until the industrial era two centuries after that that cities came to resemble those of today.

lasted barely a century after 500 B.C.E., some 300,000 people living within scarcely one square mile made lasting contributions to the Western way of life in philosophy, the arts, and politics. Unfortunately, Athenian society rested on the labor of slaves, who were one-third of the population. And democratic principles notwithstanding, Athenian men denied citizenship to women and foreigners (Mumford, 1961; Gouldner, 1965; Stavrianos, 1983).

As Greek civilization faded, the city of Rome grew to almost 1 million inhabitants and became the center of a vast empire. By the first century C.E., the militaristic Romans had subdued much of northern Africa, Europe, and the Middle East. In the process, Rome spread its language, arts, and technology. Four centuries later, the Roman Empire fell into disarray, a victim of its gargantuan size, internal corruption, and militaristic appetite. Yet, between them, the Greeks and Romans founded cities across Europe, including Vienna, Paris, and London.

The fall of the Roman Empire began an era of urban decline and stagnation lasting 600 years. Cities became smaller as people withdrew within defensive walled settlements and warlords battled for territory. In the eleventh century, the "Dark Ages" came to an end as a semblance of peace allowed trade to bring life to cities once again.

Medieval cities slowly removed their walls as trade expanded. Beneath the towering cathedrals, the narrow and winding streets of London, Brussels, and Florence soon teemed with merchants, artisans, priests, peddlers, jugglers, nobles, and servants. Typically, occupational groups such as bakers, keymakers, and carpenters clustered together in distinct sections or "quarters." Ethnic categories also inhabited their own neighborhoods, often because people kept them out of other districts. The term "ghetto" (from the Italian word *borghetto*, meaning "outside the city walls") first described the segregation of Jews in Venice.

Industrial European Cities

Throughout the Middle Ages, steadily increasing commerce enriched a new urban middle class or *bourgeoisie* (French, meaning "of the town"). By the fifteenth century, the power of the bourgeoisie rivaled that of the hereditary nobility.

By about 1750, industrialization was under way, triggering a *second urban revolution*, first in Europe and then in North America. Factories unleashed tremendous productive power, causing cities to grow to unprecedented size. London, the largest European city, swelled from 550,000 people in 1700 to 6.5 million by 1900 (A. Weber, 1963, orig. 1899; Chandler & Fox, 1974).

Cities not only grew but changed shape as well. Broad, straight boulevards replaced older irregular streets to accommodate the flow of commercial traffic and, eventually, motor vehicles. Steam and electric trolleys, too, crisscrossed the expanding cities. Historian Lewis Mumford (1961) points out that, because land was a commodity to be bought and sold, developers divided cities into regular-sized lots. Before long, city life no longer revolved around the cathedrals; instead, bustling central business districts arose,

SUPPLEMENTS: The condition of cities in sub-Saharan Africa is examined in the *Data File*.

Q: "In Europe, the modern European community emerged by gradual stages out of the simple town economy of the Middle Ages; by comparison, the American city leaped into being with breathtaking speed." Arthur M. Schlesinger, Jr.

NOTE: The importance of commerce explains the fact that almost every one of early U.S. cities was founded on a waterway (Atlanta, a railroad terminus, is the exception).

NOTE: Urban growth late in the nineteenth century was nothing less than staggering, contributing to the birth of urban sociology. Chicago, the first city of urban sociology, grew 12 times over between 1870 and 1920.

filled with banks, retail stores, and ever-taller office buildings.

As cities focused on business, they became increasingly crowded and impersonal. Crime rates rose. Especially at the outset, a small number of industrialists lived in grand style, but for most men, women, and children, factory work proved exhausting and provided bare subsistence.

Organized efforts by workers and other city dwellers to improve their plight led to legal regulation of the workplace, better housing, and the right to vote. Public services such as water, sewage, and electricity further enhanced urban living. Today some urbanites still live in poverty, but a rising standard of living has partly fulfilled the city's historical promise of a better life.

THE GROWTH OF U.S. CITIES

Most of the Native Americans who inhabited North America for thousands of years before the arrival of Europeans were migratory people, so there were few permanent settlements. Large numbers of villages and towns first sprang up, then, as a product of European colonization. In 1565, the Spanish built a settlement at St. Augustine, Florida, and, in 1607, the English founded Jamestown, Virginia. In 1624, the Dutch established New Amsterdam (later called New York), which soon overshadowed these smaller settlements. Today, the United States has 200 cities with more than 100,000 inhabitants. How we became an urban society is explained in the brief history that follows.

Colonial Settlement: 1624–1800

New York and Boston started out as tiny villages in a vast wilderness. Dutch New Amsterdam at the tip of Manhattan Island (1624) and English Boston (1630) developed along the lines of medieval towns in Europe, with narrow, winding streets that still curve through lower Manhattan and downtown Boston. New Amsterdam was walled on the north, the site of today's Wall Street. In 1700, Boston was the largest U.S. city, with just 7,000 people.

Capitalism would soon transform these and other quiet villages into thriving towns with wide streets, usually built on a grid pattern. But, when the United States won independence from Great Britain, this nation was still overwhelmingly rural. In 1790 the government's first census recorded barely 4 million people and, as Table 21–1 shows, just 5 percent of them lived in cities.

TABLE 21–1 The Urban Population of the United States, 1790–1994

Year	Population (in millions)	Percent Urban
1790	3.9	5.1%
1800	5.3	6.1
1820	9.6	7.3
1840	17.1	10.5
1860	31.4	19.7
1880	50.2	28.1
1900	76.0	39.7
1920	105.7	51.3
1940	131.7	56.5
1960	179.3	69.9
1980	226.5	73.7
1990	253.0	75.2
1994	260.4	79.8

Source: U.S. Bureau of the Census (1997).

Urban Expansion: 1800–1860

Early in the nineteenth century, towns began springing up along the transportation routes that opened the American West. In 1818 the National Road (now Route 40) funneled wagon trains of settlers from Baltimore to the Ohio Valley. A decade later the Baltimore and Ohio Railroad and the Erie Canal (1825) carried people from New York to build new cities along the banks of Great Lakes, including Buffalo, Cleveland, and Detroit.

By 1860, as a result of the Industrial Revolution, about one-fifth of the U.S. population lived in cities. Urban expansion was greatest in the northern states. In 1850, for example, New York City had ten times the population of Charleston, South Carolina. The division of the United States into the industrial-urban North and the agrarian-rural South was a major cause of the Civil War (Schlesinger, 1969).

The Great Metropolis: 1860–1950

The Civil War (1861–1865) gave an enormous boost to urbanization, as factories strained to produce the tools of combat. After the war, waves of people deserted the countryside for cities in hopes of obtaining better jobs. In the final decades of the century, tens of millions of immigrants—most from Europe—joined the surge to the cities to form a culturally diverse urban mix.

In 1900 New York soared past the 4 million mark, and Chicago—a city of scarcely 100,000 people in

NOTE: Cities grew upward, propelled by advances in building technology. In 1848, five-story iron frame buildings were big news; by 1884, a steel structure in Chicago reached 10 stories, and buildings began to utilize elevators (devised in the 1850s). By 1900, skylines reached 30 stories and, on the eve of World War I, New York had 61 buildings more than 20 stories tall. Today, Chicago's Sears Tower is the world tallest (110 stories and 1,454

feet). The technology exists to raise towers to a mile or more, restrained by high cost, the inability to control fire, and people's general reluctance to live that high above the ground.
NOTE: Houston exerts political control over another 1,500 square miles beyond its official borders.
NOTE: Just one-third of U.S. people live in central cities; about 55% live in suburban areas, and the remainder are rural residents.

1860—was closing in on 2 million. This growth marked the era of the **metropolis** (from Greek words meaning "mother city"), *a large city that socially and economically dominates an urban area.* Metropolises soon became the manufacturing, commercial, and residential centers of the United States. By 1920, the burgeoning cities contained a majority of the U.S. population.

Industrial technology not only expanded the population but, once again, changed the physical shape of cities. By the 1880s, steel girders and mechanical elevators raised structures over ten stories high. In 1930, New York's Empire State Building became an urban wonder, a true "skyscraper" stretching 102 stories into the clouds.

Urban Decentralization: 1950–Present

The industrial metropolis reached its peak about 1950. Since then, something of a turnaround—termed *urban decentralization*—has occurred as people have deserted downtown areas for outlying suburbs. Thus, the large cities of the Northeast and Midwest stopped growing—and some lost considerable population—in the decades after 1950. The 1990 census recorded half a million fewer New Yorkers, for example, than at mid-century. The urban landscape of densely packed central cities evolved into sprawling suburban regions.

SUBURBS AND URBAN DECLINE

Just as central cities flourished a century ago, we have recently witnessed the expansion of **suburbs,** *urban areas beyond the political boundaries of a city.* About a century ago, well-to-do people, imitating the European nobility who shuttled between their town houses and country estates, became the first suburbanites (Baltzell, 1979). The popularity of suburbs also reflected racial and ethnic prejudice, as urbanites fled central cities filled with immigrants for exclusive neighborhoods beyond the financial reach of the masses.

With the economic boom of the late 1940s, less wealthy people also came to view a single-family house on its own piece of leafy suburban ground as part of the American Dream. This was the era of the automobile, four-lane beltways, government-backed mortgages, and inexpensive tract homes, all of which put suburbia within the grasp of the average U.S. household. The baby boom, described earlier in this chapter, took hold in the suburbs. So popular was suburban living that, by 1970, more of our population lived in the suburbs than in the central cities.

Following the consumers, business, too, moved to the suburbs. Today, suburban malls have largely replaced the downtown stores of the metropolitan era. Many manufacturing companies have also relocated to industrial parks far from the high taxes, congested streets, and soaring crime rates of inner cities (Rosenthal, 1974; Tobin, 1976; Geist, 1985; Palen, 1995).

Decentralization was not good news for everyone, however. Rapid suburban growth threw many older cities of the Northeast and Midwest into financial chaos. Population decline meant falling tax revenues. Furthermore, cities that lost affluent taxpayers to the suburbs were left with the burden of funding expensive social programs for the poor who stayed behind. And so inner-city decay began after 1950 in major cities throughout the Northeast. Especially to white people, the deteriorating inner cities became synonymous with slum housing, crime, drugs, unemployment, the poor, and minorities. This perception fueled wave after wave of "white flight," pushing some cities (including New York) to the brink of bankruptcy (Clark, 1979; Gluck & Meister, 1979; Sternlieb & Hughes, 1983; Logan & Schneider, 1984; Stahura, 1986; Galster, 1991).

The official response to the plight of the central cities was *urban renewal.* Under this program, federal and local funds paid for rebuilding many inner cities. However, critics of urban renewal charge that these programs benefited business communities but did little to meet the housing needs of low-income residents (Jacobs, 1961; Greer, 1965; Gans, 1982).

POSTINDUSTRIAL SUNBELT CITIES

In the new postindustrial economy (see Chapter 15, "The Economy and Work"), people are not only moving beyond the boundaries of central cities, they are also migrating from the Snowbelt to the Sunbelt. The Snowbelt—the traditional industrial heartland of the United States—runs from the Northeast through the Midwest. In 1940, the Snowbelt was home to almost 60 percent of the U.S. population. By 1975, however, the Sunbelt—the South and the West—passed the Snowbelt in overall population and, by 1997, this region was home to 60 percent of our population.

This demographic shift is shown in Table 21–2, which compares the ten largest U.S. cities in 1950 and in 1996. In 1950, eight of the top ten were industrial cities of the Snowbelt, whereas, by 1996, six out of ten were postindustrial cities of the Sunbelt.

Why are Sunbelt cities so popular? Unlike their colder counterparts, these cities came of age *after*

Q: "The Northeastern seaboard of the United States is today the site of a remarkable development—an almost continuous stretch of urban and suburban areas from New Hampshire to northern Virginia and from the Atlantic shore to the Appalachian foothills." Jean Gottman (1961:3)
Q: "Cities have been *delocalized . . .*" Jean Gottman

RESOURCE: The Macionis and Benokraitis reader, *Seeing Ourselves*, includes three urban classics: Ferdinand Tönnies's "Gemeinschaft and Gesellschaft," Georg Simmel's "The Metropolis and Mental Life," and Louis Wirth's "Urbanism As a Way of Life."
GLOBAL: Edge cities now mark the fringes of Bangkok, Beijing, London, Paris, and Sydney.

urban decentralization began. Since Snowbelt cities have long been enclosed by a ring of politically independent suburbs, outward migration took place at the expense of central cities. Postindustrial Sunbelt cities, by contrast, simply expanded outward with the population flow. Chicago, for example, covers 227 square miles, compared to Houston's 540.

The great sprawl of Sunbelt cities does have drawbacks, however. Traveling across town is time consuming, making automobile ownership a virtual necessity. Lacking a dense center, Sunbelt cities also generate far less of the excitement and intensity that draw people to New York or Chicago. Critics have long described Los Angeles, for example, as a vast cluster of suburbs in search of a center.

MEGALOPOLIS: REGIONAL CITIES

Urban decentralization—the growth of suburbs around Snowbelt cities and the expansion of Sunbelt cities—has produced regional urban sprawl. The Bureau of the Census (1997) recognized 255 urban regions, which the Bureau calls *metropolitan statistical areas* (MSAs). Each MSA includes at least one city with 50,000 or more people plus densely populated surrounding counties. Almost all of the fifty fastest-growing MSAs are in the Sunbelt.

The biggest MSAs contain more than 1 million people and are called *consolidated metropolitan statistical areas* (CMSAs). In 1997, there were forty CMSAs. Heading the list is New York and adjacent urban areas in Long Island, western Connecticut, and northern New Jersey, with a total population of 20 million. Next in size is the CMSA in southern California that includes Los Angeles, Riverside, and Anaheim, with a population of over 15 million (U.S. Bureau of the Census, 1997).

Some regional cities have grown so large that they collide with one another. The East Coast now contains a 400-mile supercity extending from New England to Virginia. In the early 1960s, French geographer Jean Gottmann (1961) coined the term **megalopolis** to designate *a vast urban region containing a number of cities and their surrounding suburbs.* Although composed of hundreds of politically independent cities and suburbs, from an airplane at night, a megalopolis appears to be a single continuous city. Other supercities cover the eastern coast of Florida and stretch from Cleveland west to Chicago. More megalopolises will undoubtedly emerge, especially in the fast-growing Sunbelt.

TABLE 21–2 The Ten Largest Cities in the United States, 1950 and 1996

1950		
Rank	City	Population
1	New York	7,892,000
2	Chicago	3,621,000
3	Philadelphia	2,072,000
4	Los Angeles	1,970,000
5	Detroit	1,850,000
6	Baltimore	950,000
7	Cleveland	915,000
8	St. Louis	857,000
9	Boston	801,000
10	San Francisco	775,000

1996		
Rank	City	Population
1	New York	7,380,906
2	Los Angeles	3,553,638
3	Chicago	2,721,547
4	Houston	1,744,058
5	Philadelphia	1,478,002
6	San Diego	1,171,121
7	Phoenix	1,159,014
8	San Antonio	1,067,816
9	Dallas	1,053,292
10	Detroit	1,000,272

Source: U.S. Bureau of the Census (1997).

EDGE CITIES

Urban decentralization has also created *edge cities,* business centers that stand some distance away from the old downtowns. Edge cities are a mix of corporate office buildings, shopping malls, hotels, and entertainment complexes. Thus, they differ from suburbs, which contain mostly homes. Indeed, the population of suburbs peaks at night, while the population of edge cities peaks during the working day.

In the postindustrial economy, "the office" is the locus of most work, and most office buildings are now found in hundreds of edge cities across the United States. Because they are part of expanding urban regions, most edge cities have no clearly marked physical boundaries. Some do have names, including Los Colinas (near the Dallas-Fort Worth airport), Tyson's Corner (in Virginia, near Washington, D.C.), and King of Prussia (northwest of Philadelphia). Other edge cities are known only by the major highways that flow through them, including Route 1 in Princeton, New Jersey, and Route 128 near Boston (Garreau, 1991; Macionis & Parrillo, 1998).

A recent development in the United States is the "edge city," the product of the urban population spreading over a larger and larger area. This is King of Prussia, which lies on the northwestern edge of Philadelphia, about fifteen miles from the downtown center. King of Prussia is best known as a corporate and retail sales area, with one of the country's largest shopping malls.

URBANISM AS A WAY OF LIFE

Early sociologists in Europe and the United States focused a great deal of attention on the rise of cities. We will briefly present their accounts of urbanism as a way of life.

FERDINAND TÖNNIES: GEMEINSCHAFT AND GESELLSCHAFT

In the late nineteenth century, the German sociologist Ferdinand Tönnies (1855–1937) studied how life in the new industrial metropolis differed from life in traditional rural settings. From this contrast, he developed two concepts that have become a lasting part of sociology's terminology.

Tönnies (1963; orig. 1887) used the German word ***Gemeinschaft*** (meaning roughly "community") to refer to *a type of social organization by which people are bound closely together by kinship and tradition.* The *Gemeinschaft* of the rural village, Tönnies explained, joins people into what amounts to a single primary group.

By and large, argued Tönnies, *Gemeinschaft* is absent in the modern city. On the contrary, urbanization fosters ***Gesellschaft*** (a German word meaning roughly "association"), *a type of social organization by which people come together only on the basis of individual self-interest.* In the *Gesellschaft* way of life, individuals are motivated by their own needs rather than a drive to enhance the well-being of everyone. City dwellers display little sense of community or common identity and look to others mostly as a means of advancing their individual goals. Thus, Tönnies saw in urbanization the erosion of close, enduring social relations in favor of the fleeting and temporary ties typical of business.

EMILE DURKHEIM: MECHANICAL AND ORGANIC SOLIDARITY

The French sociologist Emile Durkheim (see Chapter 4, "Society"), agreed with much of Tönnies's thinking about cities. But Durkheim did not think urban people lacked social bonds; they simply organize social life differently than rural people do.

Durkheim described traditional, rural life as *mechanical solidarity*, social bonds based on common sentiments and shared moral values. With its emphasis on tradition, Durkheim's concept of mechanical solidarity bears a striking similarity to Tönnies's *Gemeinschaft.*

Urbanization erodes mechanical solidarity, Durkheim explained, but it also generates a new type of bonding, which he termed *organic solidarity*, social bonds based on specialization and interdependence. This concept parallels Tönnies's *Gesellschaft*, but there is an important difference between the two thinkers. Both thought the growth of industrial cities undermined tradition, but Durkheim took a more positive view of this change as creating a new kind of

Q: This late-medieval poem by Robert Crowley expressed the growing impersonality of city life:

And this is a city,
In name but in deed
It is a pack of people
That seek after meed [profit].
For officers and all

Do seek their own gain
But for the wealth of the commons
No one taketh pain.
And hell without order
I may it well call
Where every man is for himself
And no man is for all.

The painting Peasant Dance *(c.1565), by Pieter Breughel the Elder, conveys the essential unity of rural life forged by generations of kinship and neighborhood. By contrast, Fernand Léger's* The City *(1919) communicates the disparate images and discontinuity of experience that are commonplace in urban areas. Taken together, these paintings capture Tönnies's distinction between* Gemeinschaft *and* Gesellschaft.

Pieter Breughel the Elder (c. 1525/30–1569), *Peasant Dance*, c. 1565, Kunsthistorisches Museum, Vienna/Superstock.
Fernand Léger, *The City*, 1919, oil on canvas, 90¾ × 117¼, Philadelphia Museum of Art, A. E. Gallatin Collection.
© 1999 Artists Rights Society (ARS), New York/ADAGP, Paris.

solidarity. Where societies had been built on *likeness*, Durkheim observed, social organization was now based on *difference*.

For Durkheim, urban society offers more individual choice, moral tolerance, and personal privacy than people find in rural villages. In sum, Durkheim thought that something is lost in the process of urbanization, but much is gained.

GEORG SIMMEL: THE BLASÉ URBANITE

German sociologist Georg Simmel (1858–1918) offered a micro-analysis of cities, studying how urban life shapes people's attitudes and behavior. According to Simmel, individuals experience the city as an intense crush of people, objects, and events. To prevent being overwhelmed by all this stimulation of urban living, people develop a *blasé attitude*, tuning out much of what goes on around them. Such detachment does not mean that city dwellers lack compassion for others, although they may sometimes seem "cold and heartless." Rather, as Simmel saw it, a blasé attitude is simply a strategy for social survival by which people devote their time and energy to what really matters to them.

THE CHICAGO SCHOOL: ROBERT PARK AND LOUIS WIRTH

Sociologists in the United States soon joined the study of rapidly growing cities. Robert Park, a leader of the first U.S. sociology program at the University of Chicago, sought to give urban studies in this country a street-level perspective by getting out and studying real cities. In one of his most memorable comments, Park said of himself:

I suspect that I have actually covered more ground, tramping about in cities in different parts of the world, than any other living man. (1950:viii)

What did Park conclude from his lifetime of walking city streets? He found the city to be an organized mosaic of distinctive ethnic communities, commercial centers, and industrial districts. Over time, he observed, these "natural areas" develop and change in relation to each other. To Park, then, the city was a living organism—a human kaleidoscope.

Another major figure in the Chicago School of urban sociology was Louis Wirth (1897–1952). Wirth (1938) is best known for blending the ideas of Tönnies,

Q: "Characteristically, urbanites meet one another in highly segmental roles. They are, to be sure, dependent on more people for the satisfactions of their life needs than are rural people . . . but they are less dependent upon particular persons, and their dependence upon others is confined to a highly fractionalized aspect of the other's round of activity. This is essentially what is meant by saying that the city is characterized by secondary rather than primary contacts." Louis Wirth (1938)

Q: "The city, and particularly the great city, is . . . where human relationships are likely to be impersonal and rational, defined in terms of interest and in terms of cash . . ." Robert Park

NOTE: The criticism that urban ecology ignores the role of political and economic elites stands at the core of what has become known as the "new" urban sociology.

Durkheim, Simmel, and Park into a comprehensive theory of urban life.

Wirth began by defining the city as a setting with a large, dense, and socially diverse population. These characteristics interact to create an impersonal, superficial, and transitory way of life. Living among millions of others, urbanites come into contact with many more people than rural residents do. Thus, when city people notice others at all, they usually know them not in terms of *who they are* but *what they do:* bus driver, florist, or grocery store clerk, for instance.

Specialized, urban relationships are sometimes quite pleasant for all concerned. But, we should remember that self-interest rather than friendship is the main reason for the interaction. Finally, limited social involvement coupled with great social diversity make city dwellers more tolerant than rural villagers. Rural communities often jealously enforce their narrow traditions, but the heterogeneous population of a city rarely shares any single code of moral conduct (T. Wilson, 1985, 1995).

Critical evaluation. Both in Europe and in the United States, early sociologists presented a mixed view of urban living. On the one hand, rapid urbanization was troubling. Tönnies and Wirth, especially, saw the personal ties and traditional morality of rural life lost in the anonymous rush of the city. On the other hand, Durkheim and Park emphasized urbanism's positive face, including greater personal autonomy and a wider range of life choices.

What of Wirth's specific claims about urbanism as a way of life? Decades of research support only some of his conclusions. Wirth was correct in thinking that, compared to rural areas, cities have a weaker sense of local community. But conflict is found in the countryside as well in the city. Furthermore, while urbanites treat most people impersonally, they typically welcome such privacy, and, of course, they maintain close personal relationships with select others, often not their neighbors (Keller, 1968; Cox, 1971; Macionis, 1978; Wellman, 1979; Lee et al., 1984).

Another problem is that Wirth and others painted urbanism in broad strokes that overlook the effects of class, race, and gender. There are many kinds of urbanites—rich and poor, black and white, Anglo and Latino, women and men—all leading distinctive lives (Gans, 1968). And, in fact, cities can intensify these social differences. That is, we see the extent of social diversity most clearly in cities where different categories of people live in close proximity (Macionis & Parrillo, 1998).

URBAN ECOLOGY

Sociologists (especially members of the Chicago School) also developed **urban ecology,** *the study of the link between the physical and social dimensions of cities.* Consider, for example, why cities are located where they are. The first cities emerged in fertile regions where the ecology favored raising crops and, thus, settlement. Preindustrial societies, concerned with defense, built their cities on mountains (ancient Athens was perched on an outcropping of rock) or surrounded by water (Paris and Mexico City were founded on islands). With the Industrial Revolution, economic considerations situated all the major U.S. cities near rivers and natural harbors that facilitated trade.

Urban ecologists also study the physical design of cities. In 1925 Ernest W. Burgess, a student and colleague of Robert Park, described land use in Chicago in terms of *concentric zones.* City centers, Burgess observed, are business districts bordered by a ring of factories, followed by residential rings with housing that becomes more expensive the farther it is from the noise and pollution of the city's center.

Homer Hoyt (1939) refined Burgess's observations by noting that distinctive districts sometimes form *wedge-shaped sectors.* For example, one fashionable area may develop next to another, or an industrial district may extend outward from a city's center along a train or trolley line.

Chauncy Harris and Edward Ullman (1945) added yet another insight: As cities decentralize, they lose their single-center form in favor of a *multicentered model.* As cities grow, residential areas, industrial parks, and shopping districts typically push away from one another. Few people wish to live close to industrial areas, for example, so the city becomes a mosaic of distinct districts.

Social area analysis investigates what people in particular neighborhoods have in common. Three factors seem to explain most of the variation—family patterns, social class, and race and ethnicity (Shevky & Bell, 1955; Johnston, 1976). Families with children gravitate to areas with large apartments or single-family homes and good schools. The rich generally seek high-prestige neighborhoods, often in the central city near cultural attractions. People with a common social heritage tend to cluster in distinctive communities.

Finally, Brian Berry and Philip Rees (1969) tie together many of these insights. They explain that distinct family types tend to settle in the concentric zones described by Ernest Burgess. Specifically, households with few children tend to cluster toward

RESOURCE: Joe Feagin and Robert Parker take a critical look at the physical and social development of U.S. cities in their article, "The Urban Real Estate Game," included in the Macionis and Benokraitis reader.

SOCIAL SURVEY: "How much satisfaction do you get from the city or place you live in?" (*Student CHIP Social Survey Software*, SATCITY1; GSS 1973–91, N = 19,648)

	High	Middle	Low
High SES	51.2%	44.7%	4.1%
Middle SES	47.2%	46.1%	6.7%
Low SES	45.9%	45.2%	8.9%
Afri Amer	37.5%	51.2%	11.3%
Latino	41.8%	49.9%	8.3%
Whites	49.4%	44.7%	6.0%

the city's center, while those with more children live farther away. Social class differences are primarily responsible for the sector-shaped districts described by Homer Hoyt as, for instance, the rich occupy one "side of the tracks" and the poor, the other. And racial and ethnic neighborhoods are found at various points throughout the city, consistent with Harris and Ullman's multicentered model.

URBAN POLITICAL ECONOMY

Especially after the urban rioting of the 1960s, some analysts turned away from the ecological approach to a social-conflict understanding of city life. Urban political economy is influenced by the thinking of Karl Marx, although the scene of social conflict shifts from the workplace to the city (Lindstrom, 1995).

The Chicago School sociologists took an ecological approach that saw the city as a "natural" organism, with particular districts and neighborhoods developing according to an internal logic. Political economists disagree. They claim that city life is defined mostly by people with power: corporate leaders and political officials. Capitalism, which transforms the city into "real estate" that is to be traded for profit and concentrates wealth in the hands of the few, is the key to understanding city life. From this point of view, for example, the decline in industrial Snowbelt cities after 1950 was the result of deliberate decisions by the corporate elite to move their production facilities to the Sunbelt (where labor is cheaper and less likely to be unionized) or move them out of the country entirely to low-income nations (Harvey, 1976; Molotch, 1976; Castells, 1977, 1983; Feagin, 1983; Lefebvre, 1991).

Critical evaluation. The urban political economy paradigm has gained much attention in recent years. For one thing, compared to the older urban ecology approach, the political economy view seems better able to address a harsh reality: Many U.S. cities are in *crisis*, with widespread poverty, high crime, and barely functioning schools.

But one criticism applies to both approaches: They focus on U.S. cities during a limited period of history. Much of what we know about industrial cities does not apply to preindustrial towns in our own past or the rapidly growing cities in many poor nations today. Therefore, it is unlikely that any single model of cities can account for the full range of urban diversity that we find in the world today.

The fortunes of cities rise and fall along with economic conditions. Atlantic City was long a favorite seaside resort for people in New Jersey and neighboring Pennsylvania. By 1975, however, the city had suffered a dramatic decline, and lawmakers approved gambling casinos in the hope that this new industry would bring needed cash to Atlantic City. A generation later, however, towering casinos cast a long shadow over neighborhoods that remain poor. What does this turn of events suggest about the success of many "urban renewal" programs?

URBANIZATION IN POOR SOCIETIES

November 16, 1988, Cairo, Egypt. People call the vast Muslim cemetery in Old Cairo "The City of the Dead." In truth, it is very much alive: Tens of thousands of squatters have moved into the mausoleums, making this place an eerie mix of life and death. Children run across the stone floors, clotheslines stretch between the monuments, and an occasional television

GLOBAL: Selected population densities: Macau, 81,314; Hong Kong, 16,794; Lebanon, 977; India, 843; Japan, 825; Israel, 705; U.K., 628; Haiti, 621; China, 339; Mexico, 131; U.S., 76; Brazil, 50; Canada, 8 (U.S. Bureau of the Census, 1997)

GLOBAL: The location of the world's ten tallest buildings shows urban growth in poor nations: (Top Ten of Everything 1996): (1) Nina Tower, Hong Kong (1,535 feet) finished 1998; (2) Chonging Tower, Chonging, PRC (1,500) 1997; (3) Petronas Towers, Kuala Lumpur (1,475) 1996; (4) Sears Tower, Chicago (1,454) 1973; (5) Tours Sans Fin, Paris (1,377) 1998; (6) World Trade Center, NYC (1,362) 1973; (7) Jin Mao Building, Shanghai (1,255) 1997; (8) Empire State Building, NYC (1,250) 1931; (9) Amoco Building, Chicago (1,136) 1973; (10) John Hancock Center, Chicago (1,127) 1969.

WINDOW ON THE WORLD

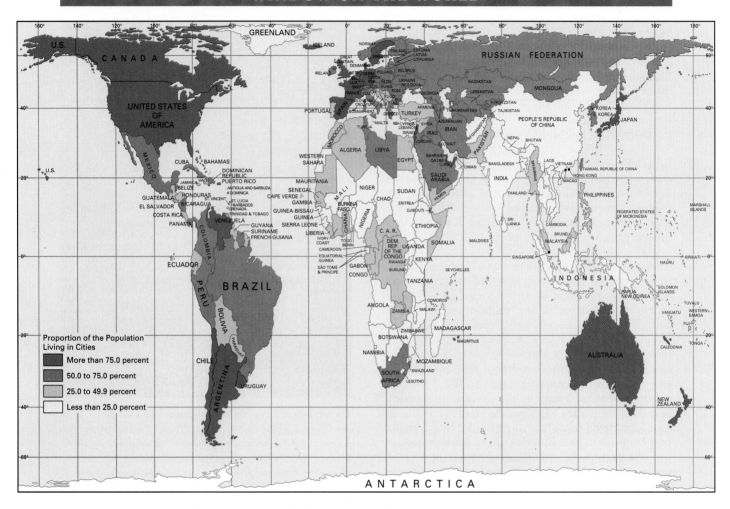

GLOBAL MAP 21–2 Urbanization in Global Perspective

Urbanization is closely linked to economic development. Thus, in rich nations—including the United States and Canada—more than three-fourths of the population cluster in cities, while in the poorest countries of the world—found in Africa and Asia—fewer than one-fourth of the people live in urban centers. Urbanization is now proceeding rapidly in poor countries, however, with emerging "supercities" of unprecedented size.

Source: *Peters Atlas of the World* (1990).

antenna protrudes from a tomb roof. With Cairo gaining 1,000 people a day, families live where they can . . .

Twice in human history the world has experienced a revolutionary expansion of cities. The first urban revolution began about 8000 B.C.E. with the first urban settlements and continued until permanent settlements were in place on the various continents. Then, about 1750, the second urban revolution took off and lasted for two centuries as the Industrial Revolution sparked rapid growth of cities in Europe and North America.

GLOBAL: One consequence of the rapid growth of Mexican cities is a desire to emigrate to the United States. In response to a recent *Los Angeles Times* survey, 22% of Mexicans in 42 urban centers in Mexico claimed that it was "very likely" or "fairly likely" that they would be living in the United States within one year. .

Q: "In a genuine community, the antithesis of living for oneself and living for others, selfishness and altruism, is transcended. The self and the others are incorporated in a venture that serves at once as the ground of their self-fulfillment and the focus of their duties . . . all live in a community which is *theirs*." Lawrence Hayworth

Q: "We must restore to the city the maternal, life-nurturing functions, the autonomous activities, the symbiotic associations that have been neglected or suppressed. For the city should be an organ of love . . ." Lewis Mumford (1961:575)

A third urban revolution is now under way. As Global Map 21–2 shows, 75 percent of people in industrial societies are already city dwellers. But extraordinary urban growth is occurring in poor societies. In 1950, about 25 percent of the people in low-income countries lived in cities; by 1995, the proportion had risen to 42 percent; by 2005, it will exceed 50 percent.

Moreover, in 1950, only seven cities in the world had populations over 5 million, and only two of these were in low-income countries. By 1995, thirty-three cities had passed this mark, and twenty-five of them were in less-developed nations (U.S. Bureau of the Census, 1996).

Table 21–3 looks back to 1980 and ahead to 2015, locating the world's ten largest urban areas (cities and surrounding suburbs). In 1980, six of the top ten were in industrialized nations, including three in the United States. By early in the next century, however, only two of the ten will be in industrialized countries—one in Japan—and one in the United States. The majority will be in less economically developed societies.

Not only will these urban areas be the world's largest; their populations will explode. Relatively rich countries such as Japan may have the resources to provide for cities with upwards of 30 million people, but for poor nations, such as Mexico and Brazil, supercities will tax resources that are already severely strained.

A third urban revolution is taking place because many poor nations have entered the high-growth Stage 2 of demographic transition theory. Falling death rates have fueled population increase in Latin America, Asia, and especially Africa. For urban areas, the rate of increase is *twice* as high because, in addition to natural increase, millions of people leave the countryside each year in search of jobs, health care, education, and conveniences like running water and electricity.

Cities do offer more opportunities than rural areas, but they do not provide a quick fix for the massive problems of escalating population and grinding poverty. Many cities in less-developed societies—Mexico City is one good example—are simply unable to meet the basic needs of much of their population. Thousands of rural people stream into Mexico City every day, even though more than 10 percent of the *current* 25 million residents have no running water in their homes, 15 percent lack sewerage facilities, and the city can process only half the trash and garbage it produces now. To make matters even worse, exhaust from factories and cars chokes everyone, rich and poor alike (Friedrich, 1984; Gorman, 1991).

TABLE 21–3 The World's Ten Largest Urban Areas, 1980 and 2015

1980	
Urban Area	**Population (in millions)**
New York, U.S.A.	16.5
Tokyo-Yokohama, Japan	14.4
Mexico City, Mexico	14.0
Los Angeles-Long Beach, U.S.A.	10.6
Shanghai, China	10.0
Buenos Aires, Argentina	9.7
Paris, France	8.5
Moscow, U.S.S.R.	8.0
Beijing, China	8.0
Chicago, U.S.A.	7.7

2015 (*projected*)	
Urban Area	**Population (in millions)**
Tokyo-Yokohama, Japan	28.8
Bombay, India	26.2
Lagos, Nigeria	24.6
São Paulo, Brazil	20.3
Mexico City, Mexico	19.2
Shanghai, China	18.0
New York, U.S.A.	17.6
Calcutta, India	17.3
Delhi, India	16.9
Beijing, China	15.6

Sources: U.S. Bureau of the Census (1997) and *The World Almanac and Book of Facts, 1998* (1998).

Like other major cities throughout Latin America, Africa, and Asia, Mexico City is surrounded by wretched shantytowns—settlements of makeshift homes built from discarded materials. As noted in Chapter 22 ("Environment and Society"), even city dumps are home to thousands of poor people, who pick through the waste hoping to find enough to survive for another day.

LOOKING AHEAD: POPULATION AND URBANIZATION IN THE TWENTY-FIRST CENTURY

The demographic analysis presented in this chapter points to some disturbing trends. We see, first of all, that the earth's population is unprecedented because birth rates remain high in poor nations and death rates

GLOBAL: A population control "success story" in Africa is Kenya, where lifetime average births dropped from 6.7 per woman in 1989 to 4.26 in 1997. Even so, population is still growing.

Q: "Although individual women [worldwide] are having fewer children, on average, than their mothers, there are simply more women having children, resulting in continuing increases in additions to world population." Population Reference Bureau

SOCIAL SURVEY: "Methods of birth control should be available to teenagers between the ages of 14 and 16 if their parents do not approve." (GSS 1996, N = 1,960; *Codebook*, 1996:214)

"Strongly agree"	28.8%	"Strongly disagree"	18.0%
"Agree"	29.9%	DK/NR	3.1%
"Disagree"	20.2%		

Q: "Children are poor men's riches." Old proverb

Every year, some 80 million people are added to the Earth's population. Do you think this rate of growth can be sustained? What are the likely consequences of continuing population increase for the future of our planet?

have fallen just about everywhere. The numbers lead us to the sobering conclusion—the focus of the final box—that controlling global population in the next century will be a monumental task. Some cause for optimism comes from recent reductions in birth rates that have at least slowed the rate of global population increase.

But population growth remains greatest in the poorest countries of the world, those that lack productive capacity to support their present populations, much less their future ones. Most of the privileged inhabitants of high-income nations are spared the trauma of poverty. But supporting about 80 million additional people on our planet each year—70 million of these in poor societies—will require a global commitment to provide not only food but housing, schools, and employment. The well-being of the entire world may ultimately depend on resolving the economic and social problems of poor, overly populated countries and bridging the widening gulf between "have" and "have-not" societies.

Great cities have always had the power to intensify the triumphs and tragedies of human existence. Thus the world's demographic, environmental, and social problems are most evident in urban places,

especially when the cities are in poor nations. In Mexico City, São Paulo (Brazil), Kinshasa (Democratic Republic of Congo), Bombay (India), and Manila (the Philippines), urban problems now seem to defy solution, as people stream into the city from rural areas where life is even worse.

Earlier chapters suggested different answers to the population problem. According to modernization theory, as poor societies industrialize, greater productivity will simultaneously raise living standards and reduce population growth (as happened in Western Europe and North America a century ago). Dependency theory, however, argues that progress will elude poor nations as long as they remain locked in dependent trading relationships with rich nations that dominate the world economy.

Throughout history, the city has improved people's living standards more than any other kind of settlement. The question facing humanity now is whether cities in poor countries will be able to meet the needs of larger populations in the coming century. The answer—which depends on issues of technology, international relations, global economic ties, and simple justice—will affect us all.

GLOBAL: Europe's population is projected to increase 2% to 743 million by 2025, while the world's population overall jumps by almost 50% to 8 billion.

NOTE: Population "conservatives" tend to argue that rising populations reflect *success* in combating death rates; population "liberals" claim that rising population results from *failure* to control births.

Q: "Over the last century, population predictions have been renamed population projections out of consideration for the reputations of people making the forecasts." Nicholas Eberstadt (1995)

NOTE: The neo-Malthusians fall within the environmental movement, arguing that growth is a social danger. The anti-Malthusians tend to be economists who follow Adam Smith in viewing growth as good.

CONTROVERSY & DEBATE

Apocalypse Soon?
Will People Overwhelm the Earth?

Are you worried about the world's increasing population? Think about this: By the time you finish reading this box, more than 1,000 people will be added to our planet. By this time tomorrow, global population will increase by 218,000. Currently, as the table below shows, there are about two-and-one-half births for every death on the planet, pushing the world's population upward by 80 million annually. Put another way, global population growth amounts to adding another Egypt to the world every year.

Global Population Increase

	Births	Deaths	Net Increase
Per Year	133,350,000	53,756,000	79,594,000
Per Month	11,112,500	4,479,667	6,632,833
Per Day	365,342	147,277	218,066
Per Hour	15,223	6,137	9,086
Per Minute	254	102	151
Per Second	4.2	1.7	2.5

It is no wonder that many population analysts are deeply concerned about the future. The earth now has an unprecedented population: The 2 billion people we have *added* since 1974 alone exceeds the planet's total in 1900. Might the pioneer demographer Thomas Robert Malthus—who predicted that population would one day outstrip the earth's resources and plunge humanity into war and suffering—be right after all?

Lester Brown, a *neo-Malthusian* population and environmental activist, sees no escape from a coming apocalypse if we do not change our ways. Brown concedes that Malthus failed to imagine how much technology (especially fertilizers and altering plant genetics) could boost the planet's agricultural output. But he maintains that the earth's rising population is nevertheless rapidly outstripping its finite resources. Families in many poor countries can find little firewood; members of rich societies consume our depleting oil reserves; everyone is draining our supply of clean water.

Just as important, according to the neo-Malthusians, humanity is steadily poisoning the planet with waste. There is a limit to the earth's capacity to absorb pollution, they warn, and as the number of people continues to increase, so will quality of life decline.

But another camp—the *anti-Malthusians*—sharply disagrees. Asks Julian Simon, "Why the doom and gloom?" Two centuries ago, he points out, Malthus predicted catastrophe. But today the earth supports almost six times as many people who, on average, live longer, healthier lives than ever before. As Simon sees it, the current state of the planet is cause for great celebration.

The neo-Malthusians err, Simon argues, in assuming the world has finite resources that are spread thinner and thinner as population increases. Rather, he maintains, human beings have the capacity to control population growth and also to improve their lives in numerous ways. Furthermore, we do not know what number of people the earth might be able to support in the future because humans keep rewriting the rules, in effect, by developing new fertilizers, new crops, and new forms of energy. Simon also notes that today's global economy makes available more resources than ever (including energy and consumer goods), at increasingly low prices. He looks optimistically to the future because technology, economic investment, and, above all, human ingenuity, have consistently proven the doomsayers wrong. And he is betting they will continue to do so.

Continue the debate . . .

1. *Where do you place your bet? Do you think the earth can support 8 or 10 billion people? Why or why not?*

2. *Ninety percent of current population growth is in poor countries. What does this mean for rich nations? For poor ones?*

3. *What should people in rich countries do to ensure our children's future?*

Sources: Based, in part, on Brown et al. (1993), Brown (1995), and Simon (1994).

Anatoly Shdanow, *Warning*, 1991

CHAPTER 22

ENVIRONMENT AND SOCIETY

The tiny island of Nauru (pronounced NAH-roo) is the world's smallest and most isolated country. Just eight square miles of windswept sand and coral reef, Nauru lies in the South Pacific, roughly 1,700 miles northeast of Australia and hundreds of miles from its nearest neighbor.

Yet Nauru's 7,500 people are among the richest on earth. Do they own oil wells? Diamond mines? Not quite: Their wealth comes from bird droppings. Over hundreds of thousands of years, the excrement from sea birds roosting here has fossilized into a rich phosphate fertilizer. Since Nauru's independence from Australia in 1968, the mining revenues have gone to the local people, who now have a trust fund of almost $1 billion.

But all is not well on Nauru. Ninety percent of the island has been strip-mined. This gives the island yet another distinction—as one of the most environmentally ravaged places on earth. Its lush vegetation is all but gone, leaving an eerie moonscape of bare rock canyons. The people, whose easy income from phosphate led them to abandon farming decades ago, now import their food—mostly high-fat canned meats they consume with potato chips and beer. As a result, most Nauruans are overweight and suffer from diabetes and high blood pressure. Few live past the age of sixty.

The Nauruans may have money in the bank, but they have lost their way of life and their island is no longer habitable. They now face the grim reality of abandoning their ancestral home (Shenon, 1995).

Nauru may seem far removed from life here in the United States. But the tragic lesson of this one-time island paradise holds for people everywhere: Humans must protect their natural environment. Or, as one analyst concluded, human beings have brought more change to the earth in the last two centuries than the planet endured over the last billion years (Milbrath, 1989).

Certainly, many of these changes have benefited humanity. Especially in rich nations, most people enjoy a level of material comfort that our ancestors scarcely could have imagined. However, as the Nauruans have learned, comfort often comes at a high cost. As this chapter explains, the way of life that has evolved in rich societies puts such great strain on the natural environment that it threatens the future of the entire planet. And, at least for the present, this planet is the only home we have.

ECOLOGY: THE STUDY OF THE NATURAL ENVIRONMENT

Ecology is *the study of the interaction of living organisms and the natural environment.* Ecology is necessarily interdisciplinary; it draws on the work of both social and natural scientists. Here, however, we focus on only those aspects of ecology that have to do with now familiar sociological concepts and issues.

The concept **natural environment** refers to *the earth's surface and atmosphere, including living organisms, air, water, soil, and other resources necessary to sustain life.*

SUPPLEMENTS: The *Data File* provides an outline for this chapter, supplementary lecture material, and discussion topics.
Q: "We all live downwind." Bumper sticker
Q: "The 'control of nature' is a phrase conceived in arrogance, born of the Neanderthal age of biology and philosophy, when it was supposed that nature exists for the convenience of man." Rachel Carson (1962):297

NOTE: Given global connections, argues Lester Milbrath, one principle of environmentalism is that "We can never do just one thing."
DIVERSITY: Cultures vary in how they view the environment. While most Western cultures are materialistic and aggressive toward the environment, some (the North American Hopi and the Hindu, as examples) see humans and the environment as linked.

Like every other living species, humans depend on the natural environment. Yet humans stand apart from other species in our capacity for culture; we alone take deliberate action to remake the world according to our own interests and desires. Thus our species is unique in its capacity to transform the world, for better and worse.

THE ROLE OF SOCIOLOGY

What are topics like solid waste, pollution, acid rain, global warming, and biodiversity doing in a sociology text? The answer is simple: None of these problems is a product of the "natural world" operating on its own. On the contrary; as we shall explain, each results from the specific actions of human beings and are, therefore, *social* issues (Marx, 1994).

Of course, there are limits to the role sociologists can play in ecological matters. Unless they have technical training in the natural sciences, sociologists cannot assess scientific evidence. They cannot say, for example, whether global warming is actually occurring or not, or, if it is, whether it will cause rainfall to go up or down. But sociologists can make three vital contributions to ecological debates. First, sociologists can explore what "the environment" means to people of varying social backgrounds. Images of "wild rivers" and "the frontier" are highly significant to people in the western United States, for example, while "gardens" and "the sea" take on special meaning to Caribbean Latinos (Lynch, 1993).

Second, sociologists can monitor the public pulse on many environmental issues, reporting people's thoughts, hopes, and fears. Moreover, sociologists also analyze why certain categories of people support one side or another on controversial issues (Roberts, 1993).

Third, and perhaps most important, sociologists can demonstrate how human social patterns put mounting stress on the natural environment. That is, sociologists are taking the lead in showing how particular cultural patterns and specific political and economic arrangements affect the natural environment (Cylke, 1993, 1995; Crenshaw & Jenkins, 1996).

THE GLOBAL DIMENSION

A comprehensive study of the natural environment is necessarily global in scope. The reason is that, regardless of national divisions, the planet constitutes a single **ecosystem**, a *system composed of the interaction of all living organisms and their natural environment.*

The Greek meaning of *eco* is "house," which reminds us that this planet is our home and that all living things and their natural environment are *interrelated.* In practice, this connectedness means that changes in any part of the natural environment ripple through the entire global ecosystem.

To illustrate, consider the effects of our use of chlorofluorocarbons (CFCs, which were marketed under the brand name "Freon") as a propellant in aerosol spray cans and as a gas in refrigerators, freezers, and air conditioners. Both producers and consumers have praised CFCs as cheap, easy to use, nontoxic, and effective. But, once released, CFCs accumulate in the upper atmosphere, where, reacting with sunlight, they form chlorine atoms. Chlorine destroys ozone, the layer in the atmosphere that restricts the entry of harmful ultraviolet radiation. Thus, recent evidence of a "hole" in the atmospheric ozone layer over Antarctica may signal an impending rise in human skin cancers and countless other effects on plants and animals (Clarke, 1984a). In response to the dangers of ozone depletion, the United States and many other nations began in the early 1980s to restrict the use of CFCs, and, by 1996, they were all but phased out in favor of safer alternatives.

Given the complexity of the global ecosystem, many threats to the environment go unrecognized. Probably few Australians who purchase fertilizer for their gardens realize that they are contributing to the destruction of the island of Nauru. Similarly, as the box explains, few people think of the global environmental effects of ordering a fast-food hamburger.

THE HISTORICAL DIMENSION

How have people gained the power to threaten the natural environment? The answer lies in the human capacity for culture. As humans have devised more powerful technology, we have been able to make and remake the world as we choose.

Members of societies with simple technology—the hunters and gatherers described in Chapter 4 ("Society")—have scarcely any ability to affect the environment, whether they want to or not. On the contrary, members of such societies are keenly dependent on nature, so that their lives are defined by the migration of game and the rhythm of the seasons. They are especially vulnerable to natural catastrophes, such as fires, floods, droughts, and storms.

Societies at intermediate stages of sociocultural evolution have a somewhat greater capacity to affect

GLOBAL: Even as Costa Rican beef production shot upward after 1960, the per capita consumption of beef in that country fell slightly. This is an example of how making products for export ignores the needs of the local people.

GLOBAL: The global connections that affect ecology are also evident in the case of the Nauru (see chapter opening): Australians buying fertilizer, the fertilizer company's investors, and even the Nauruans themselves all participated in the ecological destruction of that island.

DISCUSS: A widespread view is that only "modern" people are concerned about the environment. What do students think? The conventional view that environmental concerns rise along with affluence is challenged by Brechin & Kempton (1994), who argue that "folk societies" are typically environmentally aware.

GLOBAL SOCIOLOGY

The Global Ecosystem: The Environmental Consequences of Everyday Choices

People living in high-income societies such as the United States have the greatest power to affect the earth's ecosystem. Why? Because we consume so much of the planet's resources. Thus, small, everyday decisions about how we live can add up to big consequences for the planet as a whole.

Consider this country's favorite meal—the hamburger. McDonald's and dozens of other fast-food chains serve billions of hamburgers each year to eager customers not only across North America, but also in Europe and Asia. This worldwide appetite for beef creates a huge market for cattle, which has greatly expanded ranching in Latin America. As our consumption of hamburgers grows, ranchers in Brazil, Costa Rica, and other Latin American countries devote more and more land to cattle grazing.

Latin American cattle graze on grass (rather than being grain-fed, as is the practice in this country). A grass diet produces the lean meat demanded by the fast-food corporations, but it requires a great deal of land.

Where does the land come from? Ranchers in Latin America are solving their land problem by clearing forests at the rate of thousands of square miles each year. But these tropical forests, as we shall explain presently, are vital to maintaining the earth's atmosphere. Therefore, deforestation threatens the well-being of everyone—even the people

back in the United States who enjoy hamburgers without a thought to the environment.

Increasing global consciousness is thus a vital dimension of environmental awareness. Ecologically speaking, our choices and actions ripple throughout the world, even though most of us never realize it. People in the United States are looking for a quick hamburger. Fast-food companies want to make a profit by serving meals that people want. Ranchers are trying to make money by raising beef cattle. No one intends to harm the planet, but, taken together, these actions have serious consequences for everyone.

People on this planet inhabit a single ecosystem. In a world of countless environmental connections, we need to think critically about the effects of choices we make every day—like what to have for lunch!

Source: Based on Myers (1984a).

the environment. But the environmental impact of horticulture (small-scale farming), pastoralism (the herding of animals), and even agriculture (the use of animal-drawn plows) is limited because people still rely on muscle power for producing food and other goods.

The relationship between humans and the natural environment changed dramatically with the Industrial Revolution. Muscle power was replaced by combustion engines that burn fossil fuels: coal, at first, and then oil. Such machinery affects the environment in two ways: by consuming natural resources and by releasing pollutants into the atmosphere. But, even more important, humans armed with industrial technology become able to bend nature to their will far more than ever before, tunneling through mountains, damming rivers, irrigating deserts, and drilling for oil on the ocean floor.

Global Map 22–1 shows the global pattern of energy consumption: High-income, industrial societies consume the most energy. The typical adult in the United States consumes perhaps one hundred times more energy annually than the average member of the world's poorest societies. Globally, high-income nations account for just 15 percent of humanity but use fully 80 percent of all energy (Connett, 1991; Miller, 1992).

NOTE: The increase in productivity of industrial societies is not simply a matter of technology but also of greatly increased energy consumption.

NOTE: While the United States accounts for scarcely 5% of the planet's population, this nation consumes one-third of the world's energy.

GLOBAL: Poor nations are increasing their consumption of

energy rapidly (use has almost tripled since 1970), while in rich nations the use has risen a more modest 20% over the same period.

GLOBAL: More than 90% of nuclear power facilities are in rich nations. The costs and complex technology that have made these systems controversial there also render them unsuitable for poor societies.

WINDOW ON THE WORLD

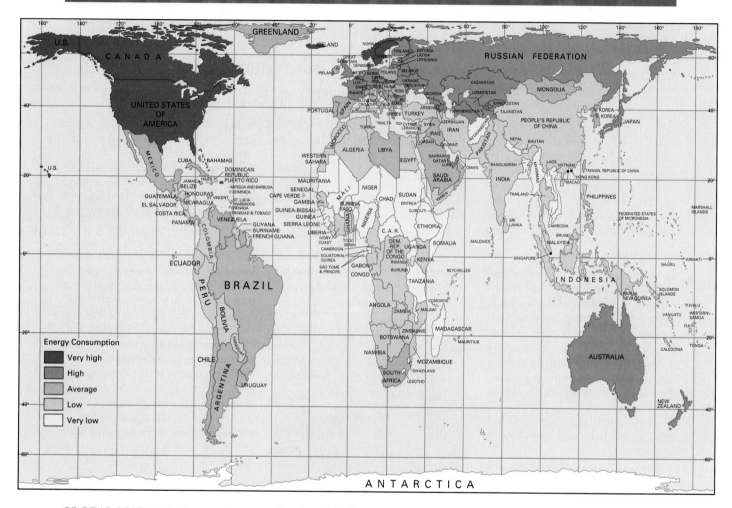

GLOBAL MAP 22–1 Energy Consumption in Global Perspective

Members of industrial societies consume far more energy than others on the planet. The typical U.S. resident uses the same amount of energy in a year as one hundred people in the Central African Republic. This means that the most economically productive societies also put the greatest burden on the natural environment.

Source: *Peters Atlas of the World* (1990).

The environmental impact of industrial technology goes beyond energy consumption. Just as important is the fact that members of industrial societies produce one hundred times more goods than people in agrarian societies do. Thus, raising the material standard of living greatly increases the problem of solid waste (since people ultimately throw away most of what they produce) and pollution (since industrial production generates smoke and other toxic substances).

Right from the start, people recognized the material benefits of industrial technology. But only a century later did they begin to see the long-term effects on the natural environment. Indeed, one trait of the recent postindustrial era is a growing concern for

GLOBAL: The U.S. uses twice the per capita energy that European societies do.
NOTE: The military, say some analysts, is our most environmentally destructive institution, producing far more toxic waste than the 5 largest chemical corporations combined. An F-16 jet uses as much fuel in 30 minutes as the average U.S. motorist consumes in a year.

NOTE: Environmentalists use the term "overshoot" to refer to exceeding the carrying capacity of an environment (intentionally or otherwise).
GLOBAL: As a personal solution to the myriad problems of poor nations, tens of millions of people are migrating toward richer, northern countries. Many rich societies, in response, are tightening restrictions on immigration.

Poor countries affect the natural environment primarily by the size of the populations; rich nations tax the environment because of their high standard of living. Today, most people in Vietnam and other low-income nations use muscle power rather than fossil fuels to move about. But what will happen to the environment if billions of poor people manage to improve their lives and become more "middle class"?

environmental quality (Abrahamson, 1997; Kidd & Lee, 1997).

From today's vantage point, we draw an ironic and sobering conclusion: As we have gained the greatest technological power to make our lives better, we have put the lives of future generations in jeopardy (Voight, cited in Bormann & Kellert, 1991:ix–x). The evidence is mounting that we are running up an **environmental deficit,** *profound and negative long-term harm to the natural environment caused by humanity's focus on short-term material affluence* (Bormann, 1990).

The concept of environmental deficit is important for three reasons. First, it reminds us that the state of the environment is a *social issue,* reflecting choices people make about how to live. Second, it suggests that environmental damage—to the air, land, or water—is often *unintended.* By focusing on the short-term benefits of, say, cutting down forests, strip mining, or using throwaway packaging, we fail to see their long-term environmental effects. Third, in some respects, the environmental deficit is *reversible.* Inasmuch as societies have created environmental problems, in other words, societies can undo many of them.

POPULATION INCREASE

After the development of more powerful technology, population increase is the second major threat to the natural environment. Twelve thousand years ago, at the dawn of civilization, the entire world's population barely reached 100 million, about the population of the eastern seaboard today.

But with the Industrial Revolution, higher living standards and improved medical technology sent death rates in Western Europe plummeting. The predictable result: a sharp upward spike in world population. By 1800, global population reached 1 billion.

But that was just the beginning. In the decades that followed, global population growth accelerated, reaching 2 billion by 1930, 3 billion in 1962, 4 billion in 1974, and 5 billion in 1987. In 1999, the world's population stands at about 6 billion, with 80 million people added to the total each year (218,000 every day).

Such population growth can quickly overwhelm available resources. A classic illustration conveys how runaway growth can wreak havoc on the natural environment (Milbrath, 1989:10):

> A pond has a single water lily growing on it. The lily doubles in size each day. In thirty days, it covers the entire pond. On which day does the lily cover half the pond?

The answer that first comes to mind—the fifteenth day—is wrong because the lily was not increasing in size by the same amount every day—it was *doubling.* The correct answer is that the lily covered half the pond on the twenty-ninth day. The lesson of the riddle is that, for a long time, the increasing lily seems manageable. On the twenty-ninth day, the lily covers half the pond—*now* it is easy to see the problem—but a day later (too little time to take corrective action) it chokes off the entire pond.

Today, the earth continues to gain population but at a slowing rate (Wattenberg, 1997). Even so, there

GLOBAL: About 90% of world population growth is currently taking place in poor nations.

GLOBAL: A study by the Pakistani government concludes that new technology and other innovations will allow that nation to support some 200 million people—up from the present 130 million. But the study foresees no way of supporting 400 million people, the population level Pakistan will reach (assuming today's trends continue) by 2040.

Q: "An indefinitely rising standard of living has nearly the same effect on the biosphere as an indefinitely rising population." Study of Critical Environmental Problems (1970)

Q: "Nothing would be more dangerous today to the human future than if the American standard were to be achieved in country after country." Norman Cousins

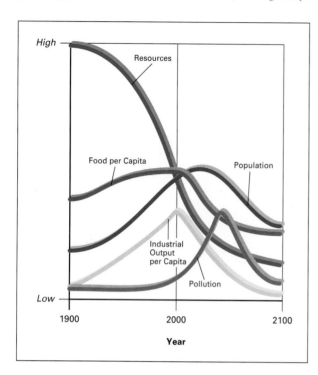

FIGURE 22–1 The Limits to Growth: Projections

Source: Based on Meadows et al. (1972).

seems little doubt that at least 8 billion people will inhabit the earth by 2050. And, as Chapter 21 ("Population and Urbanization") explained, the most rapid population growth is now occurring in the poorest regions of the world. A glance back at Global Map 21–1 on page 560 shows that the nations of Africa, taken together, are adding to their population at an annual rate of 2.6 percent. At this rate, Africa's population will double in twenty-seven years.

Rapid population growth goes hand in hand with poverty. For one thing, a surging population neutralizes any improvement in living standards. If a society's population doubles, doubling its productivity amounts to no gain at all.

And poverty itself strains the environment. Preoccupied with survival, poor people have no choice but to consume whatever resources are at hand, without thought to long-term consequences.

At the same time, imagine the environmental impact if poor societies suddenly industrialized. For example, what if a poor nation like India were suddenly transformed into a land of prosperity? Overnight, a "middle-class" India would put more than 1 billion additional cars on its streets. What would that mean for the world's oil reserves or for global air quality?

Simply put, if people around the world lived at the level of material abundance that many of us in the United States take for granted, the natural environment would soon collapse. Thus, our planet suffers not just from economic *under*development in some regions but also from economic *over*development in others.

CULTURAL PATTERNS: GROWTH AND LIMITS

Our cultural outlook—especially how we construct a vision of "the good life"—also has environmental consequences. Thus, along with technology and population growth, culture is a third factor underlying the environmental deficit.

The Logic of Growth

Why does our nation set aside specific areas as "parks" and "wildlife preserves"? Doing this seems to imply that, except for these special areas, people can freely use natural resources for their own purposes (Myers, 1991). Such an aggressive approach to the natural environment has long been a central element of our way of life.

Chapter 3 ("Culture") described the core values that underlie social life in the United States (Williams, 1970). One of these is *material comfort*, the belief that money and the things it buys enrich our lives. We also believe in the idea of *progress*, thinking that the future will be better than the present. Moreover, we rely on *science*, looking to experts and new technology to make our lives easier and more rewarding. Taken together, such cultural values form the foundation for *the logic of growth*.

The logic of growth is an optimistic view of the world. It holds, first, that we have improved our lives by devising more productive technology and, second, that we will continue to do so into the future. In simple terms, the logic of growth asserts that "people are clever," "having things is good," and "life will improve." A powerful force throughout the history of the United States and other Western industrial societies, the logic of growth has driven individuals to settle the wilderness, clear the land, build towns and roads, and pursue material affluence.

But even optimistic people realize that "progress" can lead to unexpected problems, environmental or otherwise. The logic of growth responds by arguing that people (especially scientists and other technology experts) are inventive and will find a way out of any

NOTE: The limits to growth authors called themselves the "club of Rome." Their arguments bring to mind the earlier contentions of Thomas Robert Malthus; thus, they are also known as the "neo-Malthusians."

NOTE: Members of our society have always tended to treat "growth" as more or less synonymous with "progress," with both viewed as "better" than the alternatives.

GLOBAL: The available basic resources per person for the world (1990) include (1) grain land, 0.33 acres; (2) irrigated land, 0.11 acres; (3) forest land, 1.95 hectares; and (4) grazing land, 1.5 acres. Projected figures for 2000 are 0.27, 0.1, 1.58, and 1.24 (U.S. Department of Agriculture).

Q: "Man has lost the capacity to foresee and to forestall. He will end by destroying the earth." Albert Schweitzer

problem that growth places in our path. If, say, present resources are inadequate for future needs, we will come up with new alternative resources that will do the job just as well.

For example, most people in the United States would probably agree that while automobiles provide swift and comfortable travel, they make us dependent on oil. According to the logic of growth, by the time the growing number of cars in the world threatens to deplete the planet's oil reserves, scientists will have come up with electric, solar, or nuclear engines or some as-yet-unknown technology to free us from dependence on oil.

The logic of growth is deeply rooted in U.S. culture, which worries environmentalists. Lester Milbrath (1989), for one, thinks that the logic of growth is flawed in assuming that natural resources such as oil, clean air, fresh water, and the earth's topsoil will always be plentiful. On the contrary, he warns, these are *finite* resources that we can and will exhaust if we continue to pursue growth at any cost.

And what of our faith in human ingenuity to resolve problems of scarcity? Milbrath claims that human resourcefulness, too, has its limits. Do we dare assume that we can come up with a solution to every crisis that confronts us, especially those wreaking serious damage on the life-giving environment? Moreover, the more powerful and complex the technology (nuclear reactors, say, compared to gasoline engines), the greater the dangers posed by miscalculation and the more significant the unintended consequences are likely to be. Thus, Milbrath reaches the troubling conclusion that if we call on the earth to support increasing numbers of people using finite resources, we will eventually destroy the environment and, in the process, ourselves.

The Limits to Growth

If we cannot invent our way out of the problems created by the logic of growth, perhaps we should come up with another way of thinking about the world. Environmentalists, therefore, propose the counterargument that growth must have limits. Stated simply, the *limits to growth thesis* is that humanity must implement policies to control the growth of population, production, and use of resources in order to avoid environmental collapse.

In *The Limits to Growth*, a controversial book that had a large hand in launching the environmental movement, Donella Meadows and her colleagues (1972) used a computer model to calculate the planet's

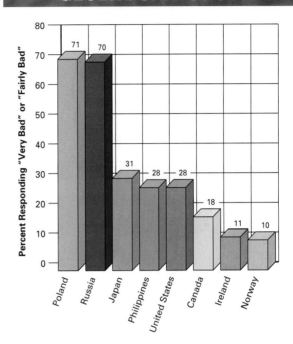

GLOBAL SNAPSHOT

FIGURE 22–2 Rating the Local Environment: A Global Survey

Survey Question: "When we say environment, we mean your surroundings—both the natural environment, namely, the air, water, land, plants, and animals—as well as buildings, streets, and the like. Overall, how would you rate the quality of the environment in your local community: very good, fairly good, fairly bad, or very bad?"

Source: Dunlap, Gallup, & Gallup (1992).

available resources, rates of population growth, amount of land available for cultivation, levels of industrial and food production, and amount of pollutants released into the atmosphere. The model reflects changes that have occurred since 1900, and then projects forward to the end of the twenty-first century. The authors concede that such long-range predictions are speculative, and some critics think they are plain wrong (Simon, 1981). But, right or wrong, the general conclusions of the study, shown in Figure 22–1, call for serious consideration.

According to limits to growth logic, we are quickly consuming the earth's finite resources. Supplies of oil, natural gas, and other sources of energy

GLOBAL: Heavy reliance on landfills is typical of some industrial nations (U.S., U.K., Australia, Canada) but not others, where incineration is the favored means of disposal (Japan, Sweden, Switzerland, Luxembourg).

NOTE: One sign of increasing public concern with solid waste is that, between 1980 and 1990, the weight of discarded grocery packaging dropped by about 10% even as the U.S. population rose

10%. This was accomplished through lighter and more efficient packaging.

DISCUSS: What do people think about junk mail? The U.S. Postal Service delivers about 65 billion pieces annually; 10 billion are thrown out without even being opened. The paper in a year's junk mail represents almost 10 million trees (a forest about twice the size of Manhattan island).

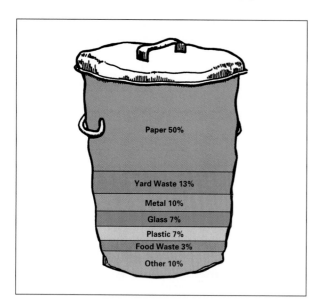

FIGURE 22–3 Composition of Household Trash

Sources: Based on Franklin Associates (1986) and Corley et al. (1993).

are already falling sharply and will continue to drop, a little faster or slower depending on conservation policies in rich nations and how fast other nations industrialize. While food production per person will continue to rise into the next century, world hunger will persist because existing food supplies are so unequally distributed. By 2050, the model predicts that hunger will reach a crisis level, first stabilizing population and then sending it back downward. Eventually, depletion of resources will cripple industrial output as well. Only then will pollution rates fall.

Limits to growth theorists are also known as neo-Malthusians because, like Thomas Robert Malthus (discussed in Chapter 21, "Population and Urbanization"), they are pessimistic about the future of humanity. They doubt, in fact, that current patterns of life are sustainable for even another century. This leaves us with a fundamental choice: Either we make deliberate changes in how we live, or widespread calamity will force change upon us.

ENVIRONMENTAL ISSUES

In the United States, technological development, population growth, and cultural outlook have put increasing demands on the natural environment, and

people are becoming concerned. In one national poll, two-thirds of respondents thought the natural environment had "gotten worse" over the last twenty years, and 80 percent described themselves as "environmentalists" (Gutfeld, 1991a).

Moreover, people in many other countries face even greater problems of overpopulation and poverty. As Figure 22–2 on page 589 shows, people in less affluent nations tend to be are most unhappy with their surroundings (Dunlap, Gallup, & Gallup, 1992).

What are the facts about the state of our environment? The following sections briefly examine several key environmental issues, with particular attention to the United States.

SOLID WASTE: THE "DISPOSABLE SOCIETY"

As an interesting exercise, carry a trash bag around for a single day and collect everything you throw away. Most people are surprised to find that the average person in the United States discards close to five pounds of paper, metal, plastic, and other disposable materials daily (over a lifetime, that's about fifty tons!). For the country as a whole, this amounts to about 1 billion pounds of solid waste *each and every day*. Figure 22–3 shows the composition of a normal household's trash.

It would be fair to describe the United States as a *disposable society*. Not only are we materially rich, but our culture values convenience. As a result, we consume more products than virtually any nation on earth, and much of them have throwaway packaging. The most familiar case is fast food, served in cardboard, plastic, and Styrofoam containers that we throw away within minutes. But countless other products—from film to fishhooks—are elaborately packaged to make the product more attractive to the customer (or harder to tamper with or steal).

Consider, too, that manufacturers market soft drinks, beer, and fruit juices in aluminum cans, glass jars, or plastic containers, which not only consume finite resources but also generate mountains of solid waste. Then there are countless items intentionally designed to be disposable: pens, razors, flashlights, batteries, even cameras. Other products—from light bulbs to automobiles—are designed to have a limited useful life, and then become unwanted junk. As Paul H. Connett (1991) points out, even the words we use to describe what we throw away—*waste, litter, trash, refuse, garbage, rubbish*—reveal how little we value what we cannot immediately use and how we quickly put it out of sight and out of mind. But this was not always the case, as the box explains.

NOTE: In 1993, the space shuttle *Endeavour* had to change course quickly to avoid a large piece of "space junk" (an old U.S.S.R. rocket). This near-collision raises the specter of future "space pollution." Currently, more than 1,000 pieces of space junk can be seen from earth; the oldest being tracked is the remains of the 1958 *Vanguard I* satellite.

NOTE: Projections of increased U.S. recycling to 30% of all waste in 2000 would just keep pace with the increase in our waste stream and would not reduce the flow of waste to landfills (cf. Starr, 1995). Note, too, that recycling is not a final solution to the problem of solid waste since most of what is recycled eventually becomes refuse.

THEN AND NOW: Urban waste recycled: *1973*, 7.9%; *1995*, 27.0%.

CRITICAL THINKING

Why Grandmother Had No Trash

Grandma Macionis, we always used to say, never threw away anything. She was born and raised in Lithuania—the "old country"—where life in a poor village shaped her in ways that never changed, even after she immigrated to the United States as a young woman.

After opening a birthday present, she would carefully save the box, wrapping paper, and ribbon, which meant as much to her as the gift they contained. Grandma never wore new clothes; her kitchen knives were worn narrow from decades of sharpening, and every piece of furniture she ever bought stayed with her to the end of her life.

As strange as Grandma seemed to her grandchildren, she was a product of her culture. A century ago, in fact, there was little "trash." If a pair of socks wore thin, Grandma mended them, probably

more than once. When they were beyond repair, she used them as a rag for cleaning, or sewed them (with other old clothing) into a quilt. For her, everything had value—if not in one way, then in another.

During this century, as women joined men working out of the home, family income went up and more and more "time-saving" products became available. Before long, few people cared about the home recycling that Grandma practiced. Soon, cities sent crews from block to block to pick up truckloads of discarded material. The era of "trash" began.

Living in a rich society, the average person in the United States consumes 50 times more steel, 170 times more newspaper, 250 times more gasoline, and 300 times more plastic each year than the typical individual in India (Miller, 1992). This high level of consumption means that we in the United States not only use a disproportionate share of the planet's natural resources, but also generate most of the world's refuse.

We like to say that we "throw things away." But 80 percent of our solid waste is not burned or recycled and never "goes away." Rather, it ends up in landfills. These dumping grounds pose several threats to the natural environment.

First, the sheer volume of discarded material is filling up landfills all across the country. Second, material in landfills contributes to water pollution. Although, in most places, laws now regulate what can be discarded in a landfill, the Environmental Protection Agency has identified 30,000 dump sites across the United States containing hazardous materials that are polluting water both above and below the ground. Third, what goes into landfills all too often stays there—sometimes for centuries. Tens of millions of

tires, diapers, and other items that we bury in landfills each year do not readily decompose and will be an unwelcome legacy for future generations.

Environmentalists argue that we should address the problem of solid waste by doing what many of our grandparents did: turn "waste" into a resource. One way to do this is through *recycling*, reusing resources we would otherwise discard. Recycling is an accepted practice in Japan and many other nations, where more than one-third of waste material is reused. In the United States, by contrast, we recycle just 10 percent of waste materials, mostly thanks to volunteer or government-run programs. But the share is increasing, in part due to laws now enacted in most states that mandate reuse of certain materials such as glass bottles and aluminum cans. In nations with market-based economies, recycling works to the extent that it becomes profitable. At present, the demand for most materials that can be recycled is soft. But as recycling processes become more efficient, industry should increasingly view waste as a useful resource (Corley et al., 1993). The box on pages 592–93 provides a look at one recycling "success story" in Egypt.

NOTE: Water is a renewable resource, since the hydrological cycle helps clean it, but water is also a finite resource. Keep in mind, too, that water supplies must remain far larger than what we use in order for the oceans to be able to absorb pollutants.

NOTE: Fresh water amounts to only about 1% of all global water.

THEN AND NOW: U.S. fresh water availability, per capita, *1955:* 17,000 cubic meters; *1990:* 6,000 cubic meters (Pollard, 1996b).

GLOBAL: About 85% of the world's cropland is not artificially irrigated, receiving water only from rainfall. The 15% that is irrigated consumes a greatly disproportionate share of water reserves.

GLOBAL: Israel has made remarkable strides toward curbing water use. This has been done largely through innovations in which "microirrigation" systems bring water directly to a plant's roots rather than spraying the water over a wide area.

GLOBAL SOCIOLOGY

Turning the Tide: A Report From Egypt

November 14, 1988, Cairo, Egypt. Half an hour from the center of Cairo, Egypt's capital city, the bus bumps along a dirt road and jerks to a stop. It is not quite dawn, and the Mo'edhdhins will soon climb the minarets of Cairo's many mosques to call the Islamic faithful to morning prayers. The driver turns, quite bewildered, to the busload of U.S. students and their instructor. "Why," he asks, mixing in a few Arabic words, "do you want to be here? And in the middle of the night?"

Why, indeed? No sooner had we left the bus than smoke and stench, the likes of which we had never before encountered, swirled around us. Eyes squinting, handkerchiefs pressed against noses and mouths, we moved slowly uphill, across mountains of trash and garbage that extended for miles. This was the Cairo dump, where the refuse generated by 15 million people in one of the world's largest cities ends up. We walked hunched over and with great care, guided by only a spattering of light from small fires smoldering around us. Up ahead, through clouds of smoke, we saw blazing piles of trash encircled by people seeking warmth and enjoying companionship.

Human beings actually live in this inhuman place, making the scene something like the aftermath of the next global war. As we approached, the fires cast an eerie light on their faces. We stopped some distance from them, separated by a vast chasm of culture and circumstances. But smiles eased the tension, and soon we were sharing the comfort of their fires. At that moment, the melodious call to prayer sounded across the city.

The people of the Cairo dump, called the Zebaleen, belong to a religious minority—Coptic Christians—in a mostly Muslim society. Barred by religious discrimination from many jobs, the Zebaleen drive donkey carts and small trucks to pick up Cairo's refuse and haul it here. For decades now, the routine culminates at dawn when hundreds of Zebaleen swarm over the new piles in search of anything of value.

Upon our visit in 1988, we observed men, women, and children picking through Cairo's refuse, filling baskets with bits of metal, strips of ribbon, even scraps of discarded food. Every now and then, someone gleefully displayed a "precious" find that would bring the equivalent of a few dollars in the city. Watching in silence, we became keenly

PRESERVING CLEAN WATER

Oceans, lakes, and streams supply the lifeblood of the global ecosystem. Humans depend on water for drinking, bathing, cooling, and cooking, for recreation, and for a host of other activities.

According to what scientists call the *hydrological cycle,* the earth naturally recycles water and refreshes the land. The process begins as heat from the sun causes the earth's water, 97 percent of which is in the oceans, to evaporate and form clouds. Water then returns to earth as rain, which drains into streams and rivers and rushes toward the sea. The hydrological cycle not only renews the supply of water but cleans it as well. Because water evaporates at lower temperatures than most pollutants, the water vapor that rises from the seas is relatively pure, leaving various contaminants behind. Although the hydrological cycle generates clean water in the form of rain, pollutants steadily build up in the oceans.

Two major concerns, then, dominate discussions of water and the natural environment. The first is supply; the second is pollution.

Water Supply

For thousands of years, since the ancient civilizations of China, Egypt, and Rome, water rights have figured prominently in codes of law. Today, as Global Map 22–2 on page 594 shows, some regions of the world, especially the tropics, enjoy a plentiful supply of water, although most of their annual rainfall occurs over a relatively brief season. High demand for fresh water, coupled with more modest reserves, makes water supply a matter of concern in much of North America and Asia, where people look to rivers—rather than rainfall—for their water. In the Middle East, water supply has already reached a critical level. In Egypt, for instance, an arid region of the world,

GLOBAL: Irrigation is not only the main source of water use, but a major source of energy consumption. In India, for example, some 8 million irrigation pumps consume one-fourth of that nation's power.

NOTE: Water use by industry in the United States has fallen by one-third since 1950 (as heavy industry has declined overall). This pattern holds true, more or less, for other industrial nations as well.

GLOBAL: In the former Soviet Union, the Aral Sea is disappearing because of shortsighted irrigation projects. It is now almost half its original size.

Q: "When the well is dry, we know the worth of water." Benjamin Franklin

NOTE: A 1993 EPA survey of U.S. drinking water found that systems serving 30 million people had too much lead.

aware of our sturdy shoes and warm clothing and self-conscious that our watches and cameras represented more money than most of the Zebaleen earn in an entire year.

A decade later, the Cairo Zebaleen still work the city's streets collecting trash. But much has changed, and they now represent one of the world's environmental success stories. The Zebaleen have won a legal contract to perform their work and, most important, they have established a large recycling center near the dump. There, dozens of workers operate machines that shred discarded cloth into stuffing to fill furniture, car seats, and pillows. Other workers separate plastic and metal into large bins for cleaning and sale. In short, the Zebaleen have become business people. With start-up loans from the World Bank, the Zebaleen have not only constructed a recycling center, they also have built an apartment

complex complete with electricity and running water.

The Zebaleen are still poor by U.S. standards. But they are prospering and now own the land on which they live and work. And many international environmental organizations hope their example will inspire others elsewhere. When the 1992 environmental summit meeting convened in Rio de Janeiro, officials presented the Cairo Zebaleen with the United Nations award for environmental protection.

The Zebaleen people of Cairo have amazed the world with their determination and ingenuity, turning one of the planet's foulest dumps into an efficient recycling center and providing new apartment units for themselves in the process.

Source: Based on author's visits to Egypt (1988, 1994).

people depend on the Nile River for most of their water. But, as the Egyptian population increases, shortages are becoming frequent. Egyptians today must make do with one-sixth the amount of water per person from the Nile compared to 1900, and experts project that the supply will shrink by half again in the next twenty years (Myers, 1984c; Postel, 1993).

Much of the rest of northern Africa and the Middle East faces an even more critical situation. Within thirty years, according to current predictions, 1 billion people in this region will lack necessary water. The world has recently witnessed the tragedy of hunger in Ethiopia and Somalia; these countries face an even more serious lack of water for irrigation and drinking.

Soaring population and complex technology—especially in manufacturing and power-generating facilities—have greatly increased societies' appetite for water. The global consumption of water (estimated at 5 billion cubic feet per year) has tripled since 1950 and is expanding even faster than the world's population (Postel, 1993).

As a result, even in parts of the world that receive significant rainfall, people are using groundwater faster than it can be naturally replenished. Take the Tamil Nadu region of southern India, for example. There, the rapidly growing population is drawing so much groundwater that the local water table has fallen 100 feet over the last several decades. In the United States, water is being pumped from the massive Ogallala aquifer, which lies below seven states from South Dakota to Texas, so rapidly that some experts fear it could be depleted several decades into the next century.

In light of such developments, we must face the reality that water is a valuable, finite resource. Greater conservation of water by individuals (the average person consumes 10 million gallons in a lifetime) is part of the answer. However, households

NOTE: The federal government's Clean Water Act of 1972 was a first step toward improving this country's water. Before then, many urban rivers were so polluted that the water was dangerous for drinking or even for bathing. In one of the most egregious examples, Cleveland's Cuyahoga River became so choked with oil and other toxic substances that it actually caught fire.

SOCIAL SURVEY: "Modern science will solve our environmental problems with little change to our way of life." (GSS 1994, N = 1,386; *Codebook*, 1996:791)
"Strongly agree"   2.0%   "Disagree"   41.6%
"Agree"   16.7%   "Strongly disagree" 11.5%
"Neither agree nor disagree" 21.5%   DK/NR   6.7%

WINDOW ON THE WORLD

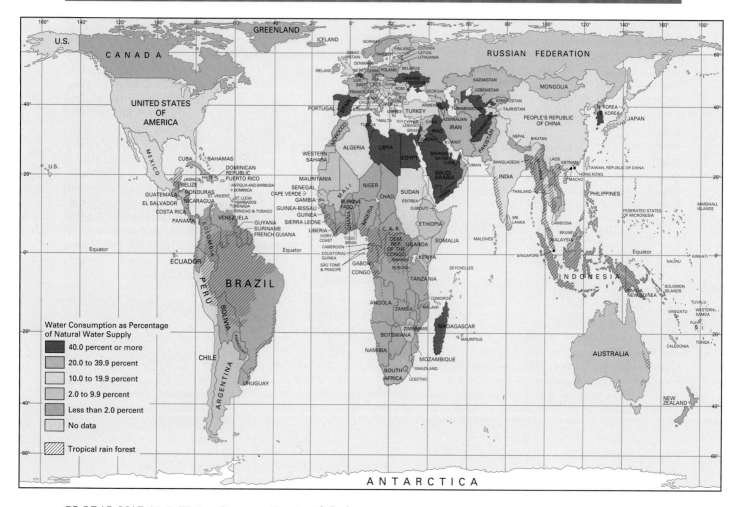

GLOBAL MAP 22–2 Water Consumption in Global Perspective

This map shows each country's water consumption as a percentage of its internal renewable water resources. Nations near the equator consume only a tiny share of their available resources; indeed, as the map shows, much of this region is covered with rain forest. Northern Africa and the Middle East are a different story, however, with dense populations drawing on very limited water resources. As a result, in Libya, Egypt, Saudi Arabia, and other countries, people (especially the poor) do not have as much water as they would like or, often, as they need.

Source: United Nations Development Programme (1995).

around the world account for no more than 10 percent of water use. We need to curb water consumption by industry, which uses 25 percent of the global total, and by farming, which consumes two-thirds of the total for irrigation.

New irrigation technology may reduce the demand for water in the future. But, here again, we see how population increase, as well as economic growth, strains our ecosystem (Myers, 1984a; Goldfarb, 1991; Falkenmark & Widstrand, 1992; Postel, 1993).

NOTE: All the major auto makers are developing alternative-energy cars, although only about 2% of research and development money is spent on such designs. The most promising alternative fuel at present is natural gas that would be compressed and stored in a "gas tank" similar to the one now used for gasoline. A push (or shove) to development of alternative-energy autos is a recent California law mandating that 2% of 1998 corporate auto sales be emission-free.

GLOBAL: Worldwide, bicycle production currently stands at three times the level of automobile production.

NOTE: Older cars are far "dirtier" than newer ones. Analysts have found that some new cars could actually run on the amount of hydrocarbons spewing from the exhaust pipe of some older models. The dirtiest 10% of cars emit more than half of all pollutants.

Water Pollution

In large cities—from Mexico City to Cairo to Shanghai—many people have little choice but to drink contaminated water. Infectious diseases like typhoid, cholera, and dysentery, all caused by water-borne microorganisms, spread rapidly through these populations (Clarke, 1984b; Falkenmark & Widstrand, 1992). Thus, besides ensuring ample *supplies* of water, we must protect the *quality* of water. In most areas of the world, the available water is not safe for drinking.

Water quality in the United States is generally good by global standards. However, even here the problem of water pollution is steadily growing. According to the Sierra Club, an environmental activist organization, rivers and streams across the United States absorb some 500 million pounds of toxic waste each year. This pollution results not just from intentional dumping, but also from the runoff of agricultural fertilizers and lawn chemicals.

CLEARING THE AIR

Most people in the United States are more aware of air pollution than contaminated water, in part because air is our constant and immediate environment. Then, too, many U.S. urbanites are familiar with the mix of smoke and fog (the origin of the word "smog") that hangs over our cities.

One of the unexpected consequences of industrial technology—especially the factory and the motor vehicle—has been a decline in air quality. The thick, black smoke belching from factory smokestacks, often twenty-four hours a day, alarmed residents of early industrial cities a century ago. By 1950, exhaust fumes from automobiles shrouded cities like Los Angeles that had escaped the earlier rush of industrial development. On a clear day, one can see across the city, but there are few clear days.

In London, factory discharge, automobile emissions, and smoke from coal fires used to heat households combined to create what was probably the worst urban air quality of the century. What some British jokingly called "pea soup" was, in reality, a deadly mix of pollution: During five days in 1952, an especially thick haze that hung over London killed 4,000 people (Clarke, 1984a).

Fortunately, great strides have been made in combating air pollution caused by our industrial way of life. Laws now prohibit high-pollution heating methods, including the coal fires that choked London in mid-century. Scientists have also developed new technologies to reduce the noxious output of factories and, even more

In the United States, most of us take safe water for granted. But people, and especially children, in poor countries around the world are at high risk from infectious diseases that are spread by unclean water used for bathing, cooking, and drinking.

important, to reduce the pollution caused by growing numbers of automobiles and trucks. The switch to unleaded gasoline in the early 1970s and changes in engine design and exhaust systems have softened the automobile's environmental impact. Still, with almost 200 million vehicles in the United States alone, keeping the air clean remains a challenge. National Map 22–1 identifies the states with the best and worst air quality.

If rich societies of the world can breathe a bit more easily than they once did, the problem of air pollution in poor societies is becoming more serious. One reason is that people in low-income countries still rely on wood, coal, peat, or other "dirty" fuels for cooking fires and to heat their homes. Moreover, many nations are so eager to encourage short-term industrial development that they pay little heed to the longer-term dangers of air pollution. As a result, many cities in Latin America, Eastern Europe, and Asia are plagued by air pollution as bad as London's fifty years ago.

THE MAP: A few states are home to the sources of most air pollution in the United States. High-pollution states contain a large share of this nation's industrial plants and are also home to much of the country's people.

THEN AND NOW: Annual U.S. emissions of sulfur dioxide (millions of tons): *1970,* 31; *1995,* 21; carbon dioxide emissions (millions of tons): *1970,* 128; *1995,* 98.

NOTE: Scientists estimate that three-fourths of Europe's remaining forests show damage from acid rain.

GLOBAL: Costa Rica leads the world's tropical countries in the rate at which it is cutting its rain forest—7% annually. Brazil, however, is cutting the most forest in absolute terms, about 8 million hectares (3.2 million acres) annually. Throughout the world, about 100 acres of rain forest disappear every minute.

SEEING OURSELVES

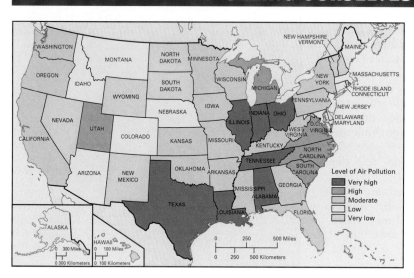

NATIONAL MAP 22–1
Air Pollution
Across the United States

The Environmental Protection Agency monitors the emission of 647 compounds into the atmosphere. In 1995, the five states that polluted the air the least were Hawaii, Vermont, Nevada, New Mexico, and South Dakota (although these states each emitted 400,000 pounds of toxins during that year). High-pollution states—including Texas, Tennessee, Alabama, Louisiana, and Ohio—each sent 100 times as much toxic material into the atmosphere. What traits distinguish high-pollution from low-pollution states?

Source: Prepared by the author using data from the Environmental Protection Agency.

ACID RAIN

Acid rain refers to *precipitation, made acidic by air pollution, that destroys plant and animal life.* Acid rain (or snow) begins with power plants burning fossil fuels (oil and coal) to generate electricity; this burning releases sulfuric and nitrous oxides into the air. As the wind sweeps these gases into the atmosphere, they react with the air to form sulfuric and nitric acids, which turn atmospheric moisture acidic. Figure 22–4 illustrates the process that creates acid rain.

Taking a closer look at this figure, we also see that one type of pollution can cause another. In this case, air pollution (from smokestacks) ends up contaminating water (in lakes and streams that collect acid rain). Notice, too, that acid rain is truly a global phenomenon because the regions that suffer the harmful effects may be thousands of miles from the original pollution. Acid rain from British power plants has devastated forests and fish as far away as Norway and Sweden. In the United States we see a similar pattern, as Midwestern smokestacks have poisoned the natural environment of New England (Clarke, 1984a).

THE RAIN FORESTS

Rain forests are *regions of dense forestation, most of which circle the globe close to the equator.* A glance back at

Global Map 22–2, on page 594, shows that the largest tropical rain forests are in South America (notably Brazil), but west central Africa and southeast Asia also have sizable rain forests. In all, the world's rain forests cover an area of some 2 billion acres, or 7 percent of the earth's total land surface.

Like the rest of the world's resources, rain forests are falling victim to the needs and appetites of the surging world population. As noted earlier in this chapter, to meet the demand for beef, ranchers in Latin America burn forested areas to increase their supply of grazing land. We are also losing rain forests to the hardwood trade. People in rich nations pay high prices for mahogany and other woods because, as environmentalist Norman Myers (1984b:88) puts it, they have "a penchant for parquet floors, fine furniture, fancy paneling, weekend yachts, and high-grade coffins." Under such economic pressure, the world's rain forests are now just half their original size, and they continue to shrink by about 1 percent (65,000 square miles) annually. At this rate of loss, the rain forests will vanish before the end of the next century, and, with them, protection for the earth's biodiversity and climate.

Global Warming

Rain forests play an important part in cleansing the atmosphere of carbon dioxide (CO_2). Since the

GLOBAL: In the Western Hemisphere, cutting of rain forest accelerated with the proliferation of sugar cane plantations. By the 1700s, sugar had become a staple in the European diet, and a heavy and steady demand for sugar fueled this process.
NOTE: Most of the nutrients in the rain forests' soil come from decaying vegetation. Thus cutting rain forests begins a process of turning the soil arid over a decade or so.

SOCIAL SURVEY: "Every time we use coal or oil or gas, we contribute to the greenhouse effect." (GSS 1994, N = 1,386; Codebook, 1996:798)

"Definitely true"	13.4%	"Definitely not true"	4.1%
"Probably true"	45.4%	DK/NR	16.5%
"Probably not true"	20.6%		

beginning of the Industrial Revolution about 250 years ago, the amount of carbon dioxide produced by humans (mostly from factories and automobiles) has risen tenfold. Much of this CO_2 is absorbed by the oceans. But plants take in carbon dioxide and expel oxygen. This is why the rain forests play a major part in maintaining the chemical balance of the atmosphere and why saving the remaining rain forests is so important to our planet's future.

The problem, then, is that production of carbon dioxide is rising while the amount of plant life on the earth is shrinking. To make matters worse, rain forests are being destroyed mostly by burning, which releases even more carbon dioxide into the atmosphere. Experts estimate the atmospheric concentration of carbon dioxide is now 20 to 30 percent higher than it was 150 years ago.

In the atmosphere, carbon dioxide behaves much like the glass roof of a greenhouse, letting heat from the sun pass through to the earth while preventing much of it from radiating back away from the planet. Ecologists therefore speculate about a possible **greenhouse effect,** *a rise in the earth's average temperature due to an increasing concentration of carbon dioxide in the atmosphere.*

A 1997 world environmental conference in Kyoto, Japan, focused on the problem of global warming. Scientists have noted a rise in global temperature (about 1.0 degree Fahrenheit) over the last century. Some also predict that the average temperature of our planet (58° F in recent years) will rise by five to ten degrees during the coming century, a warming trend that would melt vast areas of the polar icecaps and raise the sea level to cover low-lying land around the world. Were this to happen, water would cover all of Bangladesh, for example, and much of the coastal United States, including Washington, D.C., right up to the steps of the White House. On the other hand, the U.S. Midwest—currently one of the most productive agricultural regions in the world—would likely become arid.

Not all scientists share this vision of global warming in our future. Some point out that global temperature changes have been taking place throughout history, apparently having little or nothing to do with rain forests. Moreover, higher concentrations of carbon dioxide in the atmosphere might actually accelerate plant growth (since plants thrive on this gas), which would correct the imbalance and nudge the earth's temperature downward once again. Still other scientists think global warming might have its benefits, including longer growing seasons and lower food prices (Silverberg, 1991; Moore, 1995; Begley, 1997).

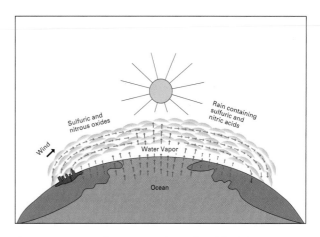

FIGURE 22–4 The Formation of Acid Rain

Declining Biodiversity

Whatever the effects on our climate, clearing rain forests undeniably lessens the earth's *biodiversity*. Simply put, while rain forests account for just 7 percent of the earth's surface, they are home to almost half of this planet's living species.

Estimates of the total number of species of animals, plants, and microorganisms range as high as 30 million. Researchers, in fact, have identified more than 1,000 species of ants alone (Wilson, 1991). Several dozen unique species of plants and animals cease to exist each day; but, given the vast number of species on the earth, why should we be concerned with declining biodiversity? Environmentalists give three reasons. First, our planet's biodiversity provides a vast and varied source of human food. Using agricultural high technology, scientists can "splice" familiar crops with more exotic plant life, making crops more bountiful as well as more resistant to insects and disease. Thus, biodiversity plays a major part in nourishing our planet's rapidly increasing population.

Second, the earth's biodiversity is a vital genetic resource. Medical and pharmaceutical research depends on animal and plant biodiversity to discover compounds that will cure disease and improve our lives. Children in the United States, for example, now have a good chance of surviving leukemia, a disease that was almost a sure killer two generations ago, because of a compound derived from a pretty tropical flower called the rosy periwinkle. The oral birth control pill, used by tens of millions of women in this country, is another product of plant research, this time involving the Mexican forest

DISCUSS: The biodiversity debate also involves the ethical question of whether all forms of life have a basic right to exist. Are actions by one species that threaten the existence of other species inherently unethical?
GLOBAL: Coastal reefs represent another localized ecosystem with considerable biological diversity, some of which is threatened at present.

NOTE: In historical perspective, 75% of all humans who have ever lived on earth have been hunters and gatherers.
RESOURCE: Alan Thein Durning's article, "Supporting Indigenous Peoples," is included in the *Seeing Ourselves* reader.
RESOURCE: Lester Brown's essay, "The State of the World's Natural Environment," is one of the contemporary selections in the companion reader, *Seeing Ourselves.*

The earth's rain forests—vital to the planet's ecology—are now half their original size and become smaller every year. Once the lush vegetation of such forests is lost, the soil is at risk of drying out and turning into a desert. Thus, environmental damage is often irreversible.

yam. Scientists have tested tens of thousands of plants for their medical properties, and they have developed hundreds of new medicines each year based on this research.

Third, with the loss of any species of life—whether it is one variety of ant, the spotted owl, the magnificent California condor, or the famed Chinese panda—the beauty and complexity of our natural environment is diminished. And there are clear warning signs: Three-fourths of the world's 9,000 species of birds are declining in number.

Finally, keep in mind that, unlike pollution and other environmental problems, the extinction of species is irreversible and final. An important ethical question, then, is whether we who live today have the right to impoverish the world for those who live tomorrow (Myers, 1984b; Myers, 1991; Wilson, 1991; Brown et al., 1993).

SOCIETY AND THE ENVIRONMENT: THEORETICAL ANALYSIS

We have introduced a number of key concepts and important environmental issues. Sociological theory can help us tie this material together to see how the operation of society affects the natural environment.

STRUCTURAL-FUNCTIONAL ANALYSIS

The structural-functional paradigm offers three significant insights about the natural environment. First, as earlier chapters have made clear, this approach

highlights the fundamental importance of *values* and *beliefs* to the operation of a social system. Thus, because values guide human actions, the state of the environment reflects our attitude toward the natural world.

Members of industrial societies generally consider nature a resource to serve our needs; this point of view (discussed earlier as the "logic of growth") justifies imposing our human will on the planet. Our ancestors therefore cleared forests for farmland, dammed rivers for irrigation and water power, covered vast areas with asphalt and concrete, and erected buildings to make cities.

Moreover, materialistic Western cultures historically have looked to *things* (sometimes more than, say, kinship or spirituality) as a source of comfort and happiness. At the same time, we tend to think that if owning *some* things is good, having *more* things is better. Our tendency toward "conspicuous consumption" leads us to purchase and display things as a way of indicating our social position to others. Such values, not surprisingly, set the stage for the kinds of environmental stress this chapter has described.

Second, structural-functional theory points up the interconnectedness of various dimensions of social life. Our ideas about efficient and private travel, for example, go a long way toward explaining the U.S. fascination with automobiles. Building and operating hundreds of millions of trucks and automobiles, in turn, puts great stress on natural resources (like oil) and the environment (especially the air).

Third, structural-functional analysis suggests that, given the connection between the natural environment

Q: "[Much public discussion] proceeds as if the issue is pollution versus no pollution, as if it were desirable and possible to have a world without pollution. That is clearly nonsense . . . We could have zero pollution from automobiles, for example, by simply abolishing all automobiles. That would also make the kind of agricultural and industrial productivity we now enjoy impossible, and so condemn most of us to a drastically lower standard of living,

perhaps even many to death." Milton and Rose Friedman

Q: "We don't expect dreamers to explain their dreams; no more would we expect lifestyle participants to explain their lifestyles." Marvin Harris

RESOURCE: Marvin Harris's article, "India's Sacred Cow," is included in the Macionis and Benokraitis reader, *Seeing Ourselves*.

and the operation of society, environmental problems demand far-reaching and complex solutions. How can we control the rate at which humanity consumes the earth's resources, for example, as long as we add 218,000 people to the global population each day? Limiting population growth, in turn, depends on expanding the range of occupational and educational opportunities for women so they have alternatives to staying home and having more children.

However difficult the task may be, structural-functionalism provides grounds for optimism that societies can respond to threats to the environment. Consider, once again, the case of air quality. Air pollution rose sharply with the onset of the Industrial Revolution. But gradually societies in Europe and North America recognized and responded to the problem, enacting new laws and employing new technology to clean the air. Similarly, just as companies once fouled the natural environment in the course of making money, new companies are profiting from cleaning up our physical surroundings. In short, because we need a livable natural environment, determined effort can cope with whatever environmental problems may arise.

CULTURAL ECOLOGY

Closely allied with structural-functional theory is **cultural ecology,** *a theoretical paradigm that explores the relationship of human culture and the natural environment.* This paradigm broadens our analysis by exploring not just how culture affects the environment, but also how the environment (say, climate or the availability of natural resources) shapes human culture.

First-time travelers to India might wonder why this nation, which contends with widespread hunger and malnutrition, forbids the killing of cows. But, according to Hindu cultural beliefs, cows are sacred animals. In fact, when Marvin Harris (1975) studied rural India's ecology, he concluded that the Hindu veneration of the cow makes excellent sense. The importance of cows extends well beyond their value as a food source.

Harris points out that cows cost little to raise, since they consume grasses of no interest to humans. Cows also produce two valuable resources: oxen (their neutered offspring) and manure. Unable to afford expensive farm machinery, Indian farmers rely on oxen to power their plows. For Indians, killing cows would be as silly as farmers in the United States destroying factories that build tractors. Furthermore, each year Indians process millions of tons of cow

Members of small, simple societies, such as the Tan't Batu, who thrive in the Philippines, live in harmony with nature; such people do not have the technological means to greatly affect the natural world. Although we in complex societies like to think of ourselves as superior to such people, the truth is that there is much we can—and must—learn from them.

manure into building material and burn "cow pies" as fuel (India has little oil, coal, or wood). Culture, in short, is shaped by local ecology: Killing cows for food would deprive Indians of needed help in the fields, materials to build homes, and a major source of heat.

Critical evaluation. Structural-functional analysis, including the cultural ecology approach, shows that the condition of the natural environment cannot be analyzed apart from the operation of society itself. To its credit, this paradigm reveals the extent to which the environment is a sociological concern.

But critics point out certain weaknesses. Cultural ecology applies more to some societies than others. The natural environment more directly shapes the culture of people with limited technology, but the connection is less apparent in industrial societies.

More generally, as we have seen before, structural functionalism overlooks issues of inequality. As we shall see presently, the burdens of environmental pollution are shouldered disproportionately by people with less social power—the poor and minorities. Furthermore, many environmentalists are skeptical of

NOTE: The kinds of environmental policies societies adopt are primarily shaped by the interests of elites. Consider the relatively small amount of national support for solar power (a decentralized form of energy) compared to coal, gas, oil, or nuclear power (which remain under the control of corporate and technical elites).

NOTE: California now generates enough solar and wind power to meet the needs of 2 million people.

NOTE: Conflict theorists point to the irony that, having contributed to the poor environment in low-income countries (by depleting their natural resources), the officials of rich nations then scold poor nations for promoting overpopulation and rapid industrialization that does not meet U.S. environmental standards.

Q: "None of us can evade the responsibility that comes with our high standard of living . . ." Paul W. Taylor

A challenge of the coming century lies in our moving beyond the notion of discarding "waste" toward the idea of recycling materials in new and creative ways. Perhaps this year's drink containers may become next year's fashion fabrics.

structural-functionalism's optimistic view that society can protect the natural world. For one thing, many people have vested interests in continuing past ways, even if they threaten the well-being of the general public. For another, many environmental problems—especially rapid population growth—are simply too far out of control at present to justify an optimistic outlook.

SOCIAL-CONFLICT ANALYSIS

Social-conflict theory highlights the very issues that structural-functionalism tends to overlook: power and inequality. Far from being inevitable, conflict theorists maintain, problems of the natural environment result from social arrangements favored by elites. In other words, elites directly or indirectly aggravate environmental problems as they advance their self-interest. Social-conflict analysis also reminds us that the global disparity of wealth and power has important environmental consequences.

First, there is the issue of elites. As conflict theorists see it, in the hierarchical organization of U.S. society, a small proportion of the population has the power to control events. The "power elite," described in Chapter 16 ("Politics and Government"), sets the national and global agenda by controlling the world's economy, law, and orientation to the natural environment.

Early capitalists led the United States into the industrial age, hungrily tapping the earth's resources and frantically turning out manufactured goods in pursuit of profits. By and large, they did not worry about environmental consequences, nor were they concerned about workers who toiled in dangerous factories and lived in neighborhoods soiled with smoke.

Furthermore, our society often winks at blatant environmental destruction, even when elite perpetrators run afoul of the law. Corporate pollution falls under the category of white-collar crime (discussed in Chapter 8, "Deviance"). Such offenses typically escape prosecution; when action is taken, it is usually in the form of fines levied on a company rather than criminal penalties imposed on individuals. Thus, corporate executives who have buried or dumped toxic waste have been subject to penalties no greater (and sometimes less) than ordinary citizens who throw litter from car windows.

Conflict theorists who embrace a Marxist view of society argue that capitalism itself poses a threat to the environment. As they see it, the logic of capitalism is the pursuit of profit, which demands continuous economic growth. But what is profitable does not necessarily advance the public welfare, nor is it likely to be good for the natural environment. Capitalist industries often shore up their profits by designing products to have a limited useful life (the concept of "planned obsolescence"). Such practices may improve the "bottom line" in the short term, but they raise the long-term risk of depleting natural resources as well as producing mountains of solid waste.

A second issue raised by social-conflict theory is inequality. Members of rich societies consume most of the earth's resources and generate most of the global pollution. That is, we maintain our affluent way of life by exploiting the poor of the less-developed countries and harming our planet in the process.

From this point of view, rich nations are actually *over*developed and consume too much. We should not expect that the majority of the earth's people, who live in poor societies, can ever match the living standard in this country. Nor, given the current environmental crisis, would that be desirable. Instead, social-conflict theorists

DIVERSITY: The term "environmental racism" was first used in a public speech by Benjamin Chavis, then with the United Church of Christ Commission for Racial Justice (later director of the NAACP) at a 1982 protest in Warren County, North Carolina, over siting of a toxic dump near an African American community.

DIVERSITY: The concept of "environmental racism" partly reflects the movement's concern over its largely white, middle-class membership. (One recent survey found that 43% of readers of the Sierra Club's magazine have postgraduate degrees, ten times the share of the U.S. adult population, with a median income of over $50,000.)

NOTE: In 1994, the Clinton administration ordered federal agencies to ensure that their policies and programs do not unfairly inflict environmental harm on poor people or minorities.

call for a more equitable distribution of resources among all people of the world as both a matter of social justice and a way of preserving the natural environment (Schnaiberg & Gould, 1994; Szasz, 1994).

ENVIRONMENTAL RACISM

Conflict theory has given birth to the concept of **environmental racism,** *the pattern by which environmental hazards are greatest in proximity to poor people, especially minorities.* Historically, factories that spew pollution stand near neighborhoods of the poor and people of color. Why? In part, because the poor themselves were drawn to factories in search of work and, once hired, their low incomes often meant they could afford housing only in undesirable neighborhoods. Sometimes the only housing that fit their budgets stood in the very shadow of the plants and mills where they worked.

Nobody wants a factory or dump nearby, of course, but the poor have little power to resist. Through the years, then, the most serious environmental hazards have been placed near Newark, New Jersey (not in upscale Bergen County), in southside Chicago (not wealthy Lake Forest), or on Native American reservations in the West (not in affluent suburbs of Denver or Phoenix) (Commission for Racial Justice, United Church of Christ, 1987; Perrolle, 1993; Szasz, 1994; Pollak & Vittas, 1995).

Critical evaluation. The social-conflict paradigm complements other analyses by raising the important questions of who sets a society's agenda and who benefits (and suffers) most from decisions that are made. Environmental problems, from this point of view, result from a society's class structure and, globally, the world's hierarchy of nations.

Like structural-functionalism, this approach comes in for its share of criticism. While it may be true that elites have always dominated U.S. society, the record shows a steady trend toward legal protection of the natural environment. We have seen significant improvements in our air and water quality. Moreover, some analysts find the evidence for environmental racism far from convincing (Boerner & Lambert, 1995; Yandle & Burton, 1996).

And what of the charge that capitalism is particularly hostile to the natural world? There is little doubt that capitalism's logic of growth stresses the environment. At the same time, however, capitalist societies in North America and, especially, in Europe have made notable strides toward environmental protection. By

No one wants to live or work in a dangerous environment. But, in a world of political competition, it is the poor who often end up with the hazards in their backyards. Here, residents of this urban neighborhood protest plans to construct a power plant in the area.

contrast, the environmental record of socialist societies has been strikingly poor. Surveys confirm that the strongest complaints about environmental quality (look back at Figure 22–2) come from citizens living in the socialist nations of Eastern Europe, such as Poland and Russia (Dunlap, Gallup, & Gallup, 1992; Olsen, Lodwick, & Dunlap, 1992).

Finally, there is little doubt that high-income countries place the greatest demands on the natural environment. However, this pattern is beginning to shift as global population swells in poor countries. Environmental problems are also likely to grow worse in poor societies as they develop economically, using more resources and producing more waste and pollutants in the process.

In the long run, all nations of the world share a vital interest in protecting the natural environment. This general concern leads us to the final topic of this chapter, the concept of a sustainable environment.

SOCIAL SURVEY: "In general do you think that [see below] is [extremely or very] dangerous to the environment?" (GSS 1994, N = 1,386; *Codebook*, 1996:799–801)
Pesticides and chemicals used in farming, 33.0%
A rise in the world's temperature caused by the 'greenhouse effect,' 34.1%
Nuclear power stations, 40.6%

Air pollution caused by industry, 53.2%
Pollution of U.S. rivers, lakes, and streams, 60.8%
GLOBAL: Debate over the North American Free Trade Agreement (NAFTA) cited environmental issues: Critics feared that open trade would lead to U.S. companies moving to Mexico where environmental laws are more lax, or U.S. states relaxing their laws to compete with Mexico for industry (cf. Lash, 1994).

LOOKING AHEAD: TOWARD A SUSTAINABLE SOCIETY AND WORLD

India's great leader Mahatma Gandhi once declared that societies must provide "for people's need, but not for their greed." From an environmental standpoint, this means that the earth will be able to sustain future generations only if people today refrain from rapidly consuming finite resources such as oil, hardwoods, and water. Nor can we persist in polluting the air, water, and soil at anything like the current levels. We must also stop cutting down our rain forests if we are to preserve the global climate. Finally, we cannot risk the future of the planet by adding people to the world at the rate of 80 million each year.

The planet's environmental deficit is growing. In effect, our present way of life is borrowing against the well-being of our children and their children. And, from a global perspective, members of rich societies, who currently consume so much of the earth's resources, are mortgaging the future security of the poor countries of the world.

In principle, the solution to the entire range of environmental problems described in this chapter is for all of us to live in a way that does not add to the environmental deficit. An **ecologically sustainable culture** refers to *a way of life that meets the needs of the present generation without threatening the environmental legacy of future generations.*

Sustainable living calls for three basic goals. The first is the *conservation of finite resources*, that is, satisfying our present wants with a responsible eye toward the future. Conservation involves using resources more efficiently, seeking alternative sources of energy, and, in some cases, learning to live with less.

The second goal is *reducing waste*. Whenever possible, simply using less is the most effective way to reduce waste. In addition, societies around the world need to expand recycling programs. Success depends on educating people to reduce waste and passing laws that require the recycling of certain materials. Looking down the road, as recycling programs become commercially profitable, they will be adopted more readily by free-market economies around the world.

The third goal in any plan for a sustainable ecosystem must be to bring world population growth under control. As we have explained, the current (1998) population of almost 6 billion is already straining the natural environment. Clearly, the higher world population climbs, the greater environmental problems will become. Even if the recent slowing of population growth continues, the world will have 8 billion people by 2050. Few analysts think that the earth can support this many people; most argue that we must hold the line at about 7 billion. Controlling population growth requires immediate action in poor regions of the world where growth rates are highest.

But even sweeping environmental strategies—put in place with the best intentions—will fail without some fundamental changes in how we think about ourselves and our world. Our *egocentric* outlook sets our own interests as standards for how to live; a sustainable environment demands an *ecocentric* outlook, one that makes three important connections.

First of all, we need to realize that *the present is tied to the future*. Simply put, today's actions shape tomorrow's world. Thus, we must learn to evaluate our short-term choices in terms of their long-range consequences for the natural environment.

Second, rather than viewing humans as "different" from other forms of life and assuming that we have the right to dominate the planet, we must acknowledge that *all forms of life are interdependent*. Ignoring this truth not only harms other life forms; it will eventually undermine our own well-being.

Third, and finally, achieving a sustainable ecosystem requires *global cooperation*. The planet's rich and poor nations differ greatly in terms of interests, cultures, and living standards. One reason is that most countries in the northern half of the world are overdeveloped, using more resources than the earth can sustain over time. At the same time, most nations in the southern half of the world are underdeveloped, unable to meet the basic needs of many of their people. A sustainable ecosystem depends on bold new programs of cooperation. And, while the cost of change will certainly be high, it pales before the eventual cost of not responding to the growing environmental deficit (Humphrey & Buttel, 1982; Burke, 1984; Kellert & Bormann, 1991; Brown et al., 1993).

Along with these changes, we must also critically reevaluate the logic of growth that has dominated our way of life for several centuries. The final box traces the growing support in the United States for environmentalism that could offer a blueprint for sustainable living.

In closing, we might consider that the great dinosaurs dominated this planet for some 160 million years and then perished forever. Humanity is far younger, having existed for a mere 250,000 years. Compared to

EXERCISE: What does the concept of "environmental justice" mean? As a starting point, read journal articles by Gary Alan Fine (1997) and Stella A. Čapek (1993). Presenting another side of the picture are Boerner & Lambert (1995).

Q: "It isn't much, really, in dispute—only the land we live on, the water we drink, the air we breathe, the food we eat, and the energy that supports us." Aaron Wildavsky

SOCIAL SURVEY: "It is just too difficult for someone like me to do much about the environment." (GSS 1994, N = 1,386; *Codebook*, 1996:795)

"Strongly agree"   4.5%   "Disagree"   45.4%
"Agree"   21.3%   "Strongly disagree"   7.9%
"Neither agree nor disagree" 16.7%   DK/NR   4.2%

CONTROVERSY & DEBATE

Reclaiming the Environment: What Are You Willing to Give Up?

Surveys tell us that most people in the United States describe themselves as concerned about their natural surroundings. But exactly what are we willing to give up in order to protect the environment?

At the outset, the environmental movement did not ask much of us. A century ago, the "first wave" of environmentalism was little more than a conservation movement to protect natural wilderness—especially in the western United States—in the face of rapid settlement. Conservationists lobbied Congress to create national parks and establish the U.S. Forest Service. Early activists also founded the Sierra Club and the National Audubon Society, both of which continue to work for environmental causes today.

During the 1960s, a "second wave" of environmentalism arose in the United States that soon became decidedly more critical of the status quo. In 1962 Rachel Carson's *Silent Spring* exposed the danger of spreading pesticides across the land; agricultural "business as usual," Carson warned, was courting disaster.

In 1970, with the celebration of the first "Earth Day," the environmental movement had come of age. It addressed a wide range of issues—including those discussed in this chapter—and increasingly called for radical changes in our way of life. During the pro-business 1980s, the Reagan administration was at odds with the environmental movement and tried to paint environmentalists as a special-interest group that was out of the political mainstream.

In the 1990s, environmentalism is more popular than ever, at least in theory. But how much are we really willing to change? As the figure shows, almost six people in ten think the government should spend more money on environmental issues. Yet a smaller share is willing to pay higher prices or more in taxes to protect the environment. And not even one in three respondents is willing to accept a lower standard of living in exchange for environmental protection.

Perhaps our society has come to accept the idea that environmentalism is good in principle. But most people seem unwilling to make the hard choices necessary to shift to a sustainable way of life.

Continue the debate . . .

1. *Do you think limiting economic growth is necessary to secure our environmental future? Would you be willing to accept a lower standard of living to protect the natural environment?*

2. *What action have you ever taken (signing a petition, participating in a demonstration, modifying your consumption patterns) to safeguard the environment?*

3. *Where do you think the major U.S. political parties stand on environmental issues?*

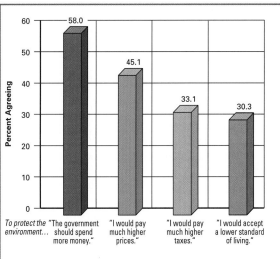

Concern for the Environment: A Survey

Sources: Based on Dunlap & Mertig (1992); survey data from Dunlap, Gallup, & Gallup (1992) and NORC (1996).

the rather dim-witted dinosaurs, our species has the gift of great intelligence. But how will we use this ability? What are the chances that our species will continue to flourish 160 million years—or even 1,000 years—from now? Our present civilization is not on the verge of collapse. But we would be foolish to ignore the warning signs (Burke, 1984). One certainty is that tomorrow's world depends on choices we make today.

SUMMARY

1. The most important factor affecting the state of the natural environment is how human beings organize social life. Thus, one important focus of sociology is ecology, the study of how living organisms interact with their environment.

2. Societies increase the environmental deficit by focusing on short-term benefits and ignoring the long-term consequences brought on by their way of life.

3. Studying the natural environment demands a global perspective. All parts of the ecosystem—including the air, soil, and water—are linked. Similarly, actions in one part of the globe affect the natural environment elsewhere.

4. Humanity's enormous influence on the natural environment springs from our capacity for culture. Our manipulation of the environment has expanded with the development of complex technology.

5. Increasing human population also affects the natural environment. The world population has soared over the last two centuries and now threatens to overwhelm available resources.

6. The "logic of growth" argument defends economic development and asserts that people can solve environmental problems as they arise. Countering this view, the "limits to growth" thesis states that societies have little choice but to curb development to head off eventual environmental collapse.

7. As a "disposable society," the United States generates 1 billion pounds of solid waste each day. Currently, our society recycles just 10 percent, and disposes of about 80 percent in landfills.

8. Water consumption is rapidly increasing everywhere. Much of the world—notably Africa and the Middle East—is approaching a crisis of water supply.

9. The hydrological cycle purifies rainwater, but water pollution from dumping and chemical contamination still poses a threat to water quality in the United States. Unsafe water is a common problem for people living in poor nations.

10. Since 1950, high-income countries have made significant progress in limiting air pollution. In poor nations—especially in cities—air pollution levels are dangerously high due to burning "dirty" fuels.

11. Acid rain, the product of pollutants entering the atmosphere, often contaminates land and water thousands of miles away.

12. Rain forests play a vital role in removing carbon dioxide from the atmosphere. Under pressure from commercial interests, the world's rain forests are now half their original size and are shrinking by about 1 percent annually.

13. Global warming refers to predictions that the average temperature of the earth will rise because of increasing levels of carbon dioxide in the atmosphere. Contributing to this problem are carbon emissions from factories and automobiles as well as the shrinking rain forests, which consume carbon dioxide.

14. Eliminating rain forests also reduces the planet's biodiversity, since these tropical regions are home to about half of all living species. Biodiversity is a source of natural beauty and is also critical to agricultural and medical research.

15. Structural-functional theory points out that cultural values have much to do with a society's orientation to the natural environment. Cultural ecology, one application of this approach, explains that a society's natural environment influences culture.

16. Social-conflict analysis highlights the importance of inequality in understanding environmental issues. This perspective blames environmental decay on the self-interest of elites. It also points to a pattern of environmental racism by which the poor—especially minorities—suffer most from environmental hazards.

17. A sustainable environment does not threaten the well-being of future generations. Achieving this goal requires that people today conserve finite resources, reduce waste and pollution, and control the size of the world's population.

KEY CONCEPTS

ecology the study of the interaction of living organisms and the natural environment

natural environment the earth's surface and atmosphere, including various living organisms, air, water, soil, and other resources necessary to sustain life

ecosystem a system composed of the interaction of all living organisms and their natural environment

environmental deficit profound and negative long-term harm to the natural environment caused by humanity's focus on short-term material affluence

acid rain precipitation, made acidic by air pollution, that destroys plant and animal life

rain forests regions of dense forestation, most of which circle the globe close to the equator

greenhouse effect a rise in the earth's average temperature (global warming) due to an increasing concentration of carbon dioxide in the atmosphere

cultural ecology a theoretical paradigm that explores the relationship of human culture and the natural environment

environmental racism the pattern by which environmental hazards are greatest in proximity to poor people, especially minorities

ecologically sustainable culture a way of life that meets the needs of the present generation without threatening the environmental legacy of future generations

CRITICAL-THINKING QUESTIONS

1. On one level, we dismiss chemical spills as mere "accidents." But what social patterns and cultural priorities make such occurrences regular events?

2. What special role can sociology play in understanding the natural environment?

3. What evidence supports the idea that humanity is running up an "environmental deficit"? What evidence suggests that environmental problems are subsiding?

4. Suggest ways in which your own life might change were we to establish an environmentally sustainable society.

LEARNING EXERCISES

1. Get a plastic trash bag and carry it around with you for one full day. Put everything you throw away in the bag. Afterward, weigh what you have; multiply this amount by 365 to estimate your yearly "trash factor." Multiply this amount by 265 million to estimate the annual waste of the entire U.S. population.

2. In the Bible, read Genesis, chapter 1, especially verses 28–31. According to this account of creation, are humans empowered to do what we wish to the earth? Or are we charged to care for the earth? (For more on this idea, see Wolkomir et al., 1997.)

3. Identify environmentally hazardous areas in or around your home or campus. What categories of people live near these hazards? Do your findings support the environmental racism hypothesis?

4. If you have access to the Internet, visit the Web sites of two organizations devoted to environmentalist causes: the Sierra Club (http://www.sierraclub.org) and Greenpeace (http://www.greenpeace.org). How do the two organizations differ in their goals and strategies?

5. Install the CD-ROM packaged inside the back cover of your text and complete the activities designed to accompany this chapter.

Harvey Dinnerstein, *Walking Together, Montgomery,* 1956
Collection of the Parrish Art Museum, Southampton, N.Y. Photograph courtesy of the artist.

CHAPTER 23

COLLECTIVE BEHAVIOR AND SOCIAL MOVEMENTS

On a bright October day in 1995, upwards of 1 million African American males, of all ages and all social classes, gathered in Washington, D.C. They had traveled from all corners of the United States—many from New York and Chicago, some from as far away as Los Angeles, San Francisco, and even the Hawaiian Islands—to form a sea of humanity that stretched from the Capitol Building to the Lincoln Memorial more than a mile and a half away.

This was the "Million Man March." To those assembled, it was a national display of pride, brotherhood, and determination to bring about change. The marchers gathered to rededicate themselves to core cultural values like self-reliance and strong families. Equally important, they wanted to call attention to the fact that U.S. society still withholds full membership from 30 million people based on their skin color.

Such demonstrations have been an important part of the civil rights movement since the 1950s. As this chapter explains, a **social movement** is *an organized activity that encourages or discourages social change.* Social movements are the most important type of **collective behavior,** *activity involving a large number of people, often spontaneous, and usually in violation of established norms.* Other forms of collective behavior—also controversial and sometimes provoking change—are crowds, mobs and riots, rumor and gossip, public opinion, panic and mass hysteria, and fashions and fads.

For most of this century, sociologists focused on established social patterns like the family and social stratification. They paid little attention to collective behavior, considering most of it unusual or deviant. But numerous social movements that burst on the scene during the tumultuous 1960s sparked sociological interest in all types of collective behavior (Weller & Quarantelli, 1973; G. Marx & Wood, 1975; Aguirre & Quarantelli, 1983; Turner & Killian, 1987; McAdam, McCarthy, & Zald, 1988).

STUDYING COLLECTIVE BEHAVIOR

Despite its importance, collective behavior is difficult for sociologists to study for three main reasons:

1. **Collective behavior is wide-ranging.** Collective behavior involves a bewildering array of human actions. The traits common to fads, rumors, and mob behavior, for example, are far from obvious.

2. **Collective behavior is complex.** A rumor seems to come out of nowhere and circulates in countless different settings. For no apparent reason, one new form of dress "catches on" while another does not. And, historically speaking, why would millions of African Americans patiently endure second-class standing for decades and then begin a modern civil rights movement in the mid–1950s?

3. **Much collective behavior is transitory.** Sociologists can readily study the family because it is a continuing element of social life. Fashions, rumors, and riots, however, arise and dissipate quickly, making them difficult to study.

Some researchers point out that these problems apply not just to collective behavior but to *most* forms of human behavior (Aguirre & Quarantelli, 1983). Moreover, collective behavior is not always so surprising; anyone can predict that crowds will form at sports events and music festivals, and sociologists can study these gatherings firsthand or later by using videotapes.

SUPPLEMENTS: An outline of this chapter, suggested discussion topics, and supplementary lecture material on topics such as disaster research are found in the *Data File*.
NOTE: Peter Dahlgren characterizes collective behavior as the breakdown of "the smooth rationality upon which the social order rests." Enrico Quarantelli, by contrast, counters that most collective behavior is both continuous and rational.

NOTE: The term "collective behavior" was coined by Robert E. Park; in fact, Park defined sociology as "the science of collective behavior," suggesting a focus on dynamic rather than stable social patterns. (See Ralph Turner's introduction to *Robert E. Park: On Social Control and Collective Behavior*, University of Chicago Press, 1967.)
Q: "Never confuse motion with action." Ernest Hemingway

Researchers can even anticipate natural disasters and study the human responses they provoke. Each year, for example, about sixty major tornadoes occur in particular regions of the United States; sociologists interested in how disasters affect behavior can be prepared to begin research on short notice (Miller, 1985). Researchers can also use historical documents to reconstruct details of a past natural disaster or riot.

Sociologists now know a great deal about collective behavior, but they still have much to learn. The most serious shortcoming, according to Benigno Aguirre and E. L. Quarantelli (1983), is that sociologists have no theory that ties together all the different actions termed "collective behavior."

At the least, all collective behavior involves the action of some **collectivity,** *a large number of people whose minimal interaction occurs in the absence of well-defined conventional norms.* Collectivities are of two kinds. A *localized collectivity* refers to people in physical proximity to one another; this first type is illustrated by crowds and riots. A *dispersed collectivity* or *mass behavior* involves people who influence one another even though they are separated by great distances; examples here include rumors, public opinion, and fashion (Turner & Killian, 1993).

It is important to distinguish collectivities from the already familiar concept of social groups (see Chapter 7, "Groups and Organizations"). Here are three key differences:

1. **Collectivities are based on limited social interaction.** Group members interact frequently and directly. People in mobs or other localized collectivities interact very little. Most people taking part in dispersed collectivities like a fad do not interact at all.

2. **Collectivities have no clear social boundaries.** Group members share a sense of identity that is usually missing among people engaged in collective behavior. Localized crowds may have a common object of attention (such as someone on a ledge threatening to jump), but they show little sense of unity. Individuals involved in dispersed collectivities, such as the "public" that turns out to vote in an election, have almost no awareness of shared membership. Of course, some issues divide the public into well-defined factions, but often it is difficult to tell who falls within the ranks of, say, the environmentalist or feminist movements.

3. **Collectivities generate weak and unconventional norms.** Conventional cultural norms usually regulate the behavior of group members. Some collectivities, such as people traveling on an airplane, observe conventional norms, but their interaction is usually limited to polite smalltalk, respectful of the privacy of people sitting nearby. Other collectivities—such as crazed soccer fans who destroy property as they leave a stadium—spontaneously develop very unconventional norms (Weller & Quarantelli, 1973; Turner & Killian, 1993).

LOCALIZED COLLECTIVITIES: CROWDS

One major form of collective behavior is the **crowd,** *a temporary gathering of people who share a common focus of attention and who influence one another.* Historian Peter Laslett (1984) points out that crowds are a modern development; in medieval Europe, about the only time large numbers of people gathered in one place was when armies faced off on the battlefield. Today, however, crowds of 25,000 or more are common at sporting events, rock concerts, and even the registration halls of large universities.

But all crowds are not alike. Herbert Blumer (1969) identified four categories of crowds. A *casual crowd* is a loose collection of people who interact little, if at all. People at the beach or at the scene of an automobile accident have only a passing awareness of one another.

A *conventional crowd* results from deliberate planning, as illustrated by a country auction, a college lecture, or a family funeral. In each case, interaction conforms to norms appropriate to the situation.

An *expressive crowd* forms around an event with emotional appeal, such as a religious revival, a wrestling match with Hulk Hogan, or a New Year's Eve celebration in New York's Times Square. Excitement is the main reason people join expressive crowds, which makes this experience rather spontaneous and exhilarating for those involved.

An *acting crowd* is a collectivity motivated by an intense, single-minded purpose, such as an audience rushing the doors of a concert hall or fleeing from a theater on fire. Acting crowds are ignited by very powerful emotions, which can reach a feverish intensity and sometimes erupt into mob violence.

Any crowd can change from one type to another. In 1985, for example, a conventional crowd of 60,000 fans filed into a soccer stadium to watch the European Cup Finals between Italy and Great Britain. But once the game started, some drunk British fans began taunting

GLOBAL: The 1998 visit of Pope John Paul II gave Cuba its first large crowd since the 1959 revolution to hear a speaker other than Fidel Castro.

NOTE: The term "mob" is derived from the Latin *mobile vulgus*, meaning the "movable or changeable common people." Note the historical association of mobs with common people.

Q: "Collective behavior is not merely identical with the study of groups. . . . Organizational behavior is the behavior of groups that are governed by established rules or procedures, which have the force of tradition behind them. . . . Collectivities, or the groups within which collective behavior takes place, are not guided in a straightforward fashion by the culture of the society . . ." Ralph H. Turner and Lewis N. Killian (1987:4)

the Italians sitting nearby. At this point, the crowd became expressive. The two sides began to throw bottles at each other; then, in a human wave, the British surged toward the Italians. Some 400 million television viewers watched in horror as what was now an acting crowd trampled hundreds of helpless spectators. In minutes, 38 people were dead and another 400 injured (Lacayo, 1985).

Deliberate action by a crowd is not simply the product of rising emotions. Participants in *protest crowds*—a fifth category we can add to Blumer's list— may stage strikes, boycotts, sit-ins, and marches for political purposes (McPhail & Wohlstein, 1983). For example, students in a protest crowd vary in emotional energy; some display the low-level energy characteristic of a conventional crowd, while others are emotional enough to be in an acting crowd. Sometimes, too, a protest begins peacefully, but people become aggressive when counterdemonstrators appear, as happens when pro-choice and pro-life activists clash.

MOBS AND RIOTS

When an acting crowd turns violent, we may witness the birth of a **mob,** *a highly emotional crowd that pursues a violent or destructive goal.* Despite, or perhaps because of, their intense emotions, mobs tend to dissipate quickly. How long a mob exists often depends on its precise goals and whether its leadership tries to inflame or stabilize the crowd.

Lynching is the most notorious example of mob behavior in the United States. The term is derived from Charles Lynch, a Virginia colonist who sought to maintain law and order in his own way before formal courts were established. The word soon became synonymous with violence and murder outside the law.

Lynching has always been colored by race. After the Civil War, lynch mobs became a terrorist form of social control over emancipated African Americans. African Americans who challenged white superiority risked being hanged or burned alive by hateful whites.

Lynch mobs—typically composed of poor whites threatened by competition from freed slaves—reached their peak between 1880 and 1930. Police recorded some 5,000 lynchings in that period, though, no doubt, many more occurred. Most of these killings were committed in the Deep South, where a farming economy depended on a cheap and docile labor force. On the western frontier, lynch mobs targeted people of Mexican and Asian descent. In only about 25 percent of the cases, whites lynched other whites. Lynchings of

Much of the exuberance of Beatlemania, which swept up millions of young fans in Europe and North America beginning in the early 1960s, can be traced to the music and personal charisma of the Beatles. But being "part of the crowd" is itself appealing, because collective life generates its own emotional intensity.

women were rare; only about a hundred such instances are known, almost all involving women of color (White, 1969, orig. 1929; Grant, 1975).

A frenzied crowd without any particular purpose is a **riot,** *a social eruption that is highly emotional, violent, and undirected.* Unlike the action of a mob, a riot usually has no clear goal. Underlying most riots is longstanding anger that is ignited by some minor incident, and participants then become violent, destroying property or harming other persons (Smelser, 1962). Whereas a mob action usually ends when a specific violent goal has been achieved (or decisively blocked), a riot tends to disperse only as participants run out of steam or police and community leaders gradually bring them under control.

Throughout our nation's history, riots have erupted as a reaction to social injustice. Industrial workers, for example, have rioted to vent rage about their working conditions. In 1886, a bitter struggle by Chicago factory workers demanding an eight-hour workday led to the explosive Haymarket Riot, which left eleven dead and scores injured. Rioting born of anger and despair also takes place frequently in prisons.

NOTE: The word "riot" was used in medieval Europe to refer to a dispute or quarrel; its likely Latin root is *rugire*, meaning "to roar."

DIVERSITY: Racial violence has a long history in the United States. Most common were white attacks on black people, Asians, and Native Americans. The pattern of African Americans rioting against whites emerged later, in the 1960s.

Q: "For freedom and justice and so the troopers can't hit us anymore." An African American school girl explaining why she was joining the Selma march (1965)

Q: "Interest in the field [of collective behavior and social movements] has hardly been constant, tending instead to wax and wane partly in response to the level of movement activity in society." Doug McAdam, John D. McCarthy, and Mayer N. Zald

The powers that be often disparage popular opposition as a "mob." Such an argument was used to justify the use of deadly force by Illinois National Guard against strikers at the Pullman railroad car company in Chicago on July 7, 1894.

In addition, race riots have occurred in this country with striking regularity. Early in this century, crowds of whites attacked African Americans in Chicago, Detroit, and other cities. In the 1960s, violent riots rocked numerous inner-city ghettos when seemingly trivial events sparked rage at continuing prejudice and discrimination. In Los Angeles in 1992, the acquittal of police officers involved in the beating of Rodney King set off an explosive riot. Violence and fires killed more than fifty people, injured thousands, and destroyed property worth hundreds of millions of dollars.

Riots are not always fired by hate. They can also result from positive feelings, such as the high spirits of young people who flock to resort areas during spring break from college. In March of 1986, for example, more than 100 young men were arrested in Palm Springs, California, when crowds began throwing rocks and bottles at passing cars and tearing the clothes off terrified women (DeMott, 1986).

CROWDS, MOBS, AND SOCIAL CHANGE

November 2, 1988, Delhi, India. The sidewalk in front of an office building is blocked by a crowd of people staging some kind of protest. The demonstrators chant slogans; anger swirls in the air. From a window several stories above, an older man dressed in a suit glances downward—perhaps he is the target of their attention? His expression of disgust leaves little doubt of what he thinks about his accusers.

Ordinary people typically gain power only by acting collectively. But, historically, because crowds have been able to effect social change, they have also provoked controversy. Defenders of the established social order fear "the mob." In countries around the world, elites know that the masses—when well organized—pose a threat to their power. However, the collective action that some people condemn, others support as rightful protest. In 1839, fifty-three Africans rose up and seized the ship *Amistad* off the coast of Cuba to prevent landing in the Americas and being sold into slavery. Were these men a vicious mob? Not according to the U.S. Supreme Court, which, after the ship put in to New York Harbor, ruled that the men were fighting for their freedom and entitled to be released.

Moreover, crowds share no single political cast: Some call for change and some resist it. Judeans rallying to the Sermon on the Mount by Jesus of Nazareth, traditional weavers destroying industrial machines that were threatening their jobs, masses of marchers carrying banners and shouting slogans for or against abortion—these and countless other cases across the centuries show that crowds can challenge their society or support it (Rudé, 1964; Canetti, 1978; Tarrow, 1994).

Q: "The age we are about to enter will in truth be the era of crowds." Gustave Le Bon
Q: Gustave Le Bon, himself an aristocrat, denounced crowds as "only powerful for destruction." (1960:18; orig. 1895)
Q: "What constituted a people, a unity, a whole, becomes in the end an agglomeration of individualities lacking cohesion." Gustave Le Bon (1895)

RESOURCE: The *Student CHIP Social Survey Software* program provides General Social Survey data sets for this chapter.
Q: "Usually the judgment that someone has acted irrationally is made in hindsight or by someone who is not in the situation of the actor and thus has a different perspective." Ralph H. Turner and Lewis N. Killian

EXPLAINING CROWD BEHAVIOR

What accounts for the behavior of crowds? Social scientists have developed several different explanations.

Contagion Theory

An early explanation of collective behavior was formulated by French sociologist Gustave Le Bon (1841–1931). According to Le Bon's *contagion theory* (1960; orig. 1895), crowds exert a hypnotic influence over their members. Shielded by the anonymity of a crowd, people abandon personal responsibility and surrender to the contagious emotions of the crowd. A crowd thus assumes a life of its own, stirring up emotions and driving people toward irrational, perhaps violent, action.

Critical evaluation. Le Bon's idea that crowds foster anonymity and sometimes generate emotion is surely true. Yet, as Clark McPhail (1991) points out, systematic research reveals that "the madding crowd" does not take on a life of its own, apart from the thoughts and intentions of members. For example, Norris Johnson (1987), investigating panic at a 1979 Who concert in Cincinnati, identified specific factors that led to the deaths of eleven people, including an inadequate number of entrance doors, an open-seating policy, and insufficient police supervision. Far from an episode of collective insanity, Johnson concluded, the crowd was composed of many small groups of people mostly trying to help each other.

Convergence Theory

Convergence theory holds that crowd behavior is not a product of the crowd itself, but is carried into the crowd by particular individuals. Thus, crowds amount to a convergence of like-minded individuals. In other words, while contagion theory states that crowds cause people to act in a certain way, convergence theory says the opposite: that people who wish to act in a certain way come together to form crowds.

We have all heard of white people banding together to threaten African Americans who try to move into their neighborhoods. In such cases, convergence theorists contend, the crowd itself does not generate racial hatred or violence; in all likelihood, hostility has been simmering for some time among many local people. A crowd then arises from a convergence of people who oppose the presence of black neighbors.

What explains the behavior of crowds? Although people once thought a crowd takes on a "a mind of its own," it is more correct to say that people are brought together by some shared interest. In the case of this protest crowd on the Berkeley campus of the University of California, the participants are demanding that the university maintain its affirmative action program. Exactly what happens next, however, depends on many factors that unfold as the protest proceeds.

Critical evaluation. By linking crowds to broader social forces, convergence theory claims that crowd behavior is not irrational, as Le Bon held. Rather, people in crowds express existing beliefs and values (Berk, 1974).

But, in fairness to Le Bon, people sometimes do things in a crowd that they would not have the courage to do alone, because crowds can diffuse responsibility. In addition, crowds can intensify a sentiment simply by creating a critical mass of like-minded people.

Emergent-Norm Theory

Ralph Turner and Lewis Killian (1993) developed the *emergent-norm theory* of crowd dynamics. These researchers concede that social behavior is never entirely predictable, but neither are crowds as irrational as Le Bon thought. If similar interests may draw people together, distinctive patterns of behavior may emerge in the crowd itself.

According to Turner and Killian, crowds begin as collectivities containing people with mixed interests and motives. Especially in the case of less stable crowds—expressive, acting, and protest crowds—norms may be

Q: "Public opinion in this country is everything." Abraham Lincoln
Q: "To regard gossip as 'idle chatter' is to underestimate its use-fulness. . . . By making some people 'insiders,' gossip may serve the social needs of other-directed people." Jack Levin and Arnold Arluke (Gossip: The Inside Scoop, Plenum, 1987)

CYBER: Many of the rumors about the TWA flight 800 explosion broke over the Internet; in 1998, the story of President Clinton's alleged affair with a White House intern also began on the Internet.
THEN AND NOW: Public opinion on any issue also changes over time: Support for women's right to abortion rose steadily from 1973 to 1992 (reaching about 50% of adults), and has fallen since (to about 35%).

vague and changing as when, say, one person at a rock concert holds up a lit cigarette lighter to signal praise for the performers, and others follow suit. In short, people in crowds make their own rules as they go along.

Critical evaluation. Emergent-norm theory represents a symbolic-interaction approach to crowd dynamics. Turner and Killian (1972:10) explain that crowd behavior is neither as irrational as contagion theory suggests, nor as deliberate as convergence theory implies. Certainly, crowd behavior reflects the desires of participants, but it is also guided by norms that emerge as the situation unfolds.

Decision making, then, plays a major role in crowd behavior, although casual observers of a crowd may not realize it. For example, frightened people clogging the exits of a burning theater may appear to be victims of irrational panic, but, from their point of view, fleeing a life-threatening situation is entirely sensible.

Further, emergent-norm theory points out that people in a crowd take on different roles. Some step forward as leaders, others become lieutenants, rank-and-file followers, inactive bystanders, or even opponents (Weller & Quarantelli, 1973; Zurcher & Snow, 1981).

DISPERSED COLLECTIVITES: MASS BEHAVIOR

It is not just people clustered together in crowds who participate in collective behavior. **Mass behavior** refers to *collective behavior among people dispersed over a wide geographical area.*

RUMOR AND GOSSIP

A common type of mass behavior is **rumor,** *unsubstantiated information spread informally, often by word of mouth.* People pass along rumors through face-to-face communication, of course, but today's technology—telephones, the mass media, and now the Internet—spreads rumors faster and farther than ever before.

Rumor has three essential characteristics:

1. **Rumor thrives in a climate of ambiguity.** Rumors arise when people lack definitive information about an important issue. When investigators could not determine the cause of the explosion that destroyed TWA flight 800 in 1996, for example, dozens of rumors arose.

2. **Rumor is unstable.** People change a rumor as they pass it along, usually giving it a "spin" that

serves their own interests. Before long, many competing versions exist.

3. **Rumor is difficult to stop.** The number of people aware of a rumor increases exponentially as each person spreads information to several others. Rumors dissipate with time; but, in general, the only way to control rumors is for a believable source to issue a clear and convincing statement of the facts.

Rumor can trigger the formation of crowds or other collective behavior. For this reason, officials establish rumor-control centers during a crisis in order to manage information. Yet some rumors persist for years, perhaps just because people enjoy them; the box gives one notable example.

Gossip is *rumor about people's personal affairs.* Charles Horton Cooley (1962; orig. 1909) explained that rumor involves an issue of concern to a large audience, but gossip interests only a small circle of people who know a particular person. Rumors, therefore, spread widely, while gossip tends to be more localized.

Communities use gossip as a means of social control, praising or scorning someone to encourage conformity to local norms. Moreover, people gossip about others to raise their own standing as social "insiders." Yet no community wants gossip to get out of control, which may be the reason people who gossip *too* much are criticized as "busybodies."

PUBLIC OPINION AND PROPAGANDA

Another form of dispersed collective behavior is *public opinion,* widespread attitudes about controversial issues. Exactly who is, or is not, included in any "public" depends on the issue. Over the years in the United States, "publics" have formed over numerous controversial issues, from water fluoridation, air pollution, and the social standing of women, to handguns and health care (Lang & Lang, 1961; Turner & Killian, 1993). More recently, the public has debated affirmative action, welfare reform, and government funding of public radio and television. National Map 23–1 on page 614 shows where supporters of public broadcasting reside.

On any given issue, anywhere from 2 to 10 percent of people offer no opinion at all because of ignorance or indifference. Moreover, over time, public interest in issues rises and falls. For example, interest in the social position of women in the United States ran high a century ago during the women's suffrage movement but declined after 1920 when women gained the right to vote. Since the 1960s, a second

NOTE: Delbert Miller claimed that, in 1945, only a small number of people on his campus learned of the death of President Roosevelt directly from radio reports. Within 30 minutes, however, about 90% of the people had been informed by word of mouth (*American Sociological Review* 10:691–94). Obviously, today's more powerful mass media reduce the significance of word of mouth in spreading national rumor.

NOTE: Levin and Arluke spread a rumor on their campus by widely distributing flyers announcing a fictitious wedding. The flyers were not circulated until a day before the supposed event. Still, the researchers found that, one week later, 52% of a campus sample had heard about the wedding, and 12% claimed to have actually attended it! (1987:14–15)

SOCIOLOGY OF EVERYDAY LIFE

The Rumor Mill: Paul Is Dead!

Everyone knows the Beatles. The music of John Lennon, Paul McCartney, George Harrison, and Ringo Starr caused a cultural revolution in the 1960s. Not everyone today, however, knows the rumor that circulated about Paul McCartney at the height of the group's popularity.

On October 12, 1969, a young man telephoned a Detroit disk jockey to say that he had discovered "evidence" that Paul McCartney was dead:

1. At the end of the song "Strawberry Fields Forever" on the *Magical Mystery Tour* album, filtering out background noise allows the listener to hear a voice saying, "I buried Paul!"

2. The phrase "Number 9, Number 9, Number 9" from the song "Revolution 9" on the *White Album*, when played backward, seems to intone, "Turn me on, dead man!"

Two days later, the University of Michigan student newspaper ran a story entitled "McCartney Is Dead: Further Clues Found." It sent millions of Beatles fans scurrying for their albums.

3. A picture inside the *Magical Mystery Tour* album shows John, George, and Ringo wearing red carnations, while Paul is wearing a black flower.

4. The cover of the *Sergeant Pepper's Lonely Hearts Club Band* album shows a grave with yellow flowers arranged in the shape of Paul's bass guitar.

5. On the inside of that album, McCartney wears an armpatch with the letters "OPD." Is this the insignia of some police department or confirmation that Paul had been "Officially Pronounced Dead"?

6. On the back cover of the same album, three Beatles are facing forward while McCartney has his back to the camera.

7. On the album cover of *Abbey Road*, John Lennon is clothed as a clergyman, Ringo Starr wears an undertaker's black tie, and George Harrison is clad in workman's attire as if ready to dig a grave. For his part, McCartney is

barefoot, which is how Tibetan ritual prepares a corpse for burial. Behind Paul, a Volkswagen nearby displays the license plate "28 IF," apparently stating that McCartney would be *28 if* he were alive.

The rumor explained that McCartney had died of head injuries suffered in an automobile accident in November, 1966. After the accident, record company executives had secretly replaced Paul with a double.

Of course, Paul McCartney is very much alive and still jokes about the episode. Few doubt that Paul himself dreamed up some of the details of his "death" with a little help from his friends to encourage the interest of their fans. But the incident has a serious side, showing how quickly rumors can arise and persist in a climate of distrust. In the late 1960s, many disaffected young people were quite ready to believe that the media and other powerful interests were concealing McCartney's death.

In 1969, McCartney himself denied the rumor in a *Life* magazine story. But thousands of suspicious readers noticed that on the other side of the page with McCartney's picture was an ad for an automobile: Holding this page up to the light, the car lay across McCartney's chest and blocked his head. Another clue!

Sources: Based on Rosnow & Fine (1976) and Kapferer (1992).

---

wave of feminism has again created a public with strong opinions on gender-related issues.

Also, keep in mind that on any issue, not everyone's opinion carries the same weight. Some categories of people have more clout because they are better educated, wealthier, or better connected. As

Chapter 16 ("Politics and Government") explained, many special-interest groups shape public policy in the United States even though they represent just a small fraction of the population. For example, physicians are a well-organized and well-funded interest group that greatly influences U.S. health-care policy.

THE MAP: Support for PBS is strong in urban areas with high numbers of affluent, well-educated (and generally liberal) people.
SOCIAL SURVEY: Scanning the General Social Survey data reveals that a significant proportion of respondents have no opinion about many issues: Should authorities prevent parents from showing pornographic films to their 10-year-old child? (17% express no opinion.) Does the average person influence

government decisions? (8% voice no opinion.) Is the world getting better? (19% express no opinion.) Is there life after death? (8% have no opinion.)

Q: "Perhaps there are situations such as a fire in a crowded theater in which people totally ignore others as they try to escape from danger. However, documented cases . . . are surprisingly rare in the literature." Norris Johnson

SEEING OURSELVES

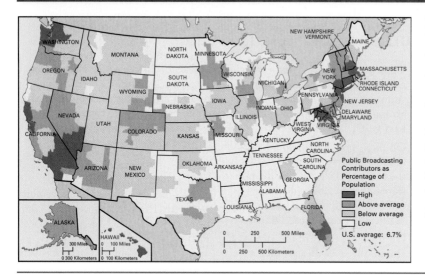

NATIONAL MAP 23–1
Support for Public Broadcasting Across the United States

About 7 percent of people in the United States pledge money to support the Public Broadcasting System (PBS). In 1994, they contributed $280 million to maintain public radio and television (one-seventh of the PBS budget). As the map shows, PBS supporters are concentrated in particular regions of the country. What do you think accounts for this pattern?

Source: *Time* (January 16, 1995). Copyright © 1995 Time, Inc. Reprinted by permission.

Special-interest groups and political leaders all try to shape public tastes and attitudes by using **propaganda,** *information presented with the intention of shaping public opinion.* Although the term has negative connotations, propaganda is not necessarily false. A thin line separates information from propaganda; the difference depends mostly on the presenter's intention. We offer *information* to enlighten others; we use *propaganda* to sway an audience toward some viewpoint. Political speeches, commercial advertising, and even some college lectures may disseminate propaganda in an effort to steer people toward thinking or acting in some specific way.

PANIC AND MASS HYSTERIA

A **panic** is *a form of localized collective behavior by which people react to a threat or other stimulus with irrational, frantic, and often self-destructive behavior.* The classic illustration of a panic is people streaming toward exits of a crowded theater after someone yells "Fire!" As they flee, however, they trample one another, blocking exits so that few actually escape.

Closely related to panic is **mass hysteria,** *a form of dispersed collective behavior by which people react to a real or imagined event with irrational, frantic, and often self-destructive behavior.* Whether the cause of the hysteria is real or not, a large number of people certainly take it

very seriously. Parents' fears that their children may become infected from a schoolmate who has AIDS may cause as much hysteria in a community as the very real danger of an approaching hurricane. Moreover, people in the grip of mass hysteria sometimes act to make matters worse. At the extreme, mass hysteria leads to chaotic flight and sends crowds into panic. People who see others overcome by fear may become more afraid themselves, as hysteria feeds on itself.

So it was on the night before Halloween in 1938, when CBS Radio broadcast a version of H. G. Wells's novel *War of the Worlds* (Cantril, Gaudet, & Herzog, 1947; Koch, 1970). It started with a typical program of dance music. Suddenly, a voice interrupted the music with a "special report" of explosions on the surface of the planet Mars and, soon after, the crash landing of a mysterious cylinder near a New Jersey farmhouse. The program then switched to an "on-the-scene reporter" who gave a graphic description of giant monsters equipped with death-ray weapons emerging from the spaceship. An "eminent astronomer" somberly informed the audience that Martians had begun a full-scale invasion of earth. Back then, most people relied on radio for factual news; thus, there was an announcement to clarify that the broadcast was fiction. But about 1 million of the 10 million listeners missed the announcement and actually believed the report.

Q: "The nearer the people are drawn to the common level of an equal and similar condition, the less prone does each man become to place implicit faith in a certain man or a certain class of men. But his readiness to believe the multitude increases, and opinion is more than ever the mistress of the world." Alexis de Tocqueville
Q: "Fashion . . . is a product of class distinction." Georg Simmel

NOTE: The Greek root of the word "hysteria" is *hystero*, meaning "uterus." This etymology reveals the historical association between irrational behavior and women. Moreover, in European and North American history, most witches were women, usually women who did not conform to conventional definitions of femininity.
RESOURCE: Worth reading is Georg Simmel's essay, "Fashion" (Levine, 1971; orig. 1904:294–323).

By the time the show was over, thousands of hysterical people were spilling into the streets with news of the "invasion" and flooding telephone switchboards with warnings to friends and relatives. One college senior and his roommate jumped into their cars and fled:

> My roommate was crying and praying. He was even more excited than I was—or more noisy about it anyway; I guess I took it out in pushing the accelerator to the floor. . . . After it was all over, I started to think about that ride, I was more jittery than when it was happening. The speed was never under 70. I thought I was racing against time. . . . I didn't have any idea exactly what I was fleeing from, and that made me all the more afraid. (Cantril, Gaudet, & Herzog, 1947:52)

FASHIONS AND FADS

Two more kinds of collective behavior—fashions and fads—involve people spread over a large area. A **fashion** is *a social pattern favored by a large number of people.* Some fashions last for years, while others change after just a few months. The arts (including painting, music, drama, and literature), the shape of buildings, automobiles, and clothes, our use of language, and public opinion all change as ideas go in and out of fashion.

Lyn Lofland (1973) explains that, in preindustrial societies, clothing and personal appearance reflect traditional *style,* which changes very little. Women and men, the rich and the poor, lawyers and carpenters wear distinctive clothes and hairstyles that indicate their social and occupational position.

In industrial societies, however, style gives way to changing fashion. For one thing, modern people care less about tradition and often eagerly embrace new ways of living. Then, too, high social mobility means that people use their "looks" to make a statement about themselves. German sociologist Georg Simmel (1971; orig. 1904) explained that affluent people are usually the trendsetters, since people look up to those who have the money to spend on luxuries. Or as U.S. sociologist Thorstein Veblen (1953; orig. 1899) put it, fashion involves *conspicuous consumption,* as people buy expensive products (whether well-made or not) simply to show off their wealth.

Ordinary people who want to appear wealthy often snap up less-expensive copies of what the rich make fashionable. In this way, a fashion trickles downward

In 1997, a wave of emotion surged not only across Great Britain, but all around the world as television carried live coverage of the funeral of Diana, Princess of Wales. The event demonstrated the power of the mass media to support collective behavior on a global scale.

through the class structure. But, before long, the fashion loses its prestige when too many average people now share "the look," so the rich move on to something new. In short, fashions are born along the Fifth Avenues and Rodeo Drives of the rich and rise to mass popularity in discount stores across the country.

A reversal of this pattern sometimes occurs when rich people mimic a fashion found among people of lower social position. In the 1960s, for example, affluent college students began buying blue jeans, or dungarees (from a Hindi word for a coarse fabric). For decades, manual laborers have worn blue jeans, but in the era of civil rights and antiwar movements, jeans became the uniform of political activists and were soon popular on college campuses across the country. Author Tom Wolfe (1970) coined the phrase "radical chic" to satirize the desire of the rich to look fashionably poor.

A **fad** is *an unconventional social pattern that people embrace briefly but enthusiastically.* Fads, sometimes called *crazes,* are commonplace in rich industrial societies where many people have the money to spend on amusing, if often frivolous, products. During the 1950s, two young entrepreneurs in California produced a brightly colored plastic version of a popular Australian toy, a three-foot-diameter hoop that could

DISCUSS: A rather long-lived fad is Rubik's cube, invented in 1974 by Erno Rubik, a Hungarian architect. Sales exceeded 30 million cubes (and 10 million books on how to solve it) by 1982; subsequently, it fizzled. Another example is the troll doll, devised by a Danish woodcutter as a gift for his daughter in 1959; it became a hit in 1964 and is still around. What other fads can students identify?

NOTE: Contrast transient *fads* with more lasting *trends*, which are rooted in a basic cultural pattern. A recent marketing trend is "value pricing" in fast food, automobiles, and even textbooks, which caught on as the economy sagged in the late 1980s. Another example is the McDonaldization trend, discussed in Chapter 7, involving fast food, fast oil changes, and packaged vacations, which responds to our need for quick products on the go (Letscher, 1994).

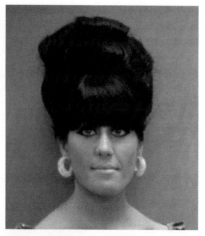

Because change in industrial societies is so rapid, we can see differences in personal appearance—one important kind of fashion—over short periods of time. The five photographs (beginning with the top left) show hair styles commonly worn by women in the 1950s, 1960s, 1970s, 1980s, and 1990s.

be swung around the waist by gyrating the hips. In no time, the "hula hoop" was a national craze. But in less than a year, hula hoops vanished from the scene.

Streaking—running naked in public—had an even briefer moment in the sun, lasting only a few months in early 1974. Their fleeting duration suggests that fads happen almost at random, although national fads are usually begun by high-prestige people (Aguirre, Quarantelli, & Mendoza, 1988).

How do fads differ from fashions? Fads are passing fancies that capture the mass imagination but quickly burn out and disappear. Fashions, by contrast, reflect basic cultural values like individuality and sexual attractiveness and tend to evolve over time. Therefore, a fashion—but rarely a fad—is incorporated into a society's culture. The fad of streaking, for instance, came out of nowhere and soon vanished; the fashion of wearing blue jeans, on the other hand, originated in

the rough mining camps of Gold Rush California more than a century ago and still influences clothing designs today. This staying power explains why we are happy to be called "fashionable" but put off by being called "faddish" (Blumer, 1968; Turner & Killian, 1987).

SOCIAL MOVEMENTS

Social movements are different from crowds, rumors, and other types of collective behavior we have examined so far in three ways: They are deliberately organized, they have lasting importance, and they seek to change or defend some social pattern.

Social movements occur more frequently in today's world than in the past. Preindustrial societies are tightly bound by tradition, making social

RESOURCE: Jo Freeman's article, "On the Origin of Social Movements," is among the "classics" included in the 4th edition of the Macionis and Benokraitis reader, *Seeing Ourselves*.

NOTE: Joan Fitzgerald and Louise Simmons (1991) point out that to evaluate the success of any social movement, we must look beyond *immediate* effects to assess the movement's contribution to *future* social change.

SOCIAL SURVEY: What are your personal feelings about people who organize protests against a government action they strongly oppose?" (GSS 1990, N = 1,217; *Codebook*, 1996:665)
"Extremely favorable"   8.8%   "Unfavorable"   14.2%
"Favorable"   26.5%   "Extremely unfavorable"   5.7%
"Neutral"   33.9%   DK/NR   11.0%

movements extremely rare. Industrial societies, however, foster diverse subcultures and countercultures so that social movements develop around a wide range of public issues. In recent decades, for example, the gay rights movement has won legal changes in numerous cities and several states, forbidding discrimination based on sexual orientation. Like any social movement that challenges conventional practice, the gay rights movement has prompted a countermovement made up of traditionalists who want to limit social acceptance of homosexuality. In today's society, almost every important public issue gives rise to a social movement favoring change and an opposing countermovement resisting it (Lo, 1982; Meyer & Staggenborg, 1996).

TYPES OF SOCIAL MOVEMENTS

Sociologists classify social movements according to several variables (Aberle, 1966; Cameron, 1966; Blumer, 1969). One variable asks *who is changed?*: Some movements target selected people, while others try to change everyone. A second variable asks *how much change?*: Some movements seek only limited change in our lives, while others are radical. Combining these variables results in four types of social movements, shown in Figure 23–1.

Alternative social movements are least threatening to the status quo because they seek limited change in only a part of the population. Promise Keepers, one example of an alternative social movement, encourages Christian men to be more spiritual and supportive of their families.

Redemptive social movements also have a selective focus, but they seek radical change in the individual they engage. For example, Alcoholics Anonymous is an organization that helps people with an alcohol addiction achieve a sober life.

Reformative social movements aim for only limited social change but target everyone. Multiculturalism, described in Chapter 3 ("Culture"), is an educational and political movement that advocates working toward social parity for people of all races and ethnicities. Reformative social movements generally work inside the existing political system. Some are *progressive* (promoting a new social pattern), while others are *reactionary* (countermovements trying to preserve the status quo or to revive past social patterns). Thus, just as multiculturalists push for greater racial equality, so white supremacist organizations try to maintain the historical dominance of white people.

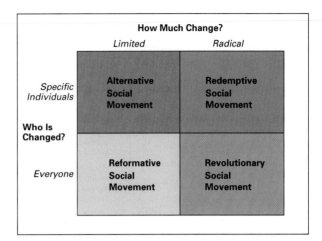

FIGURE 23–1 Four Types of Social Movements
Source: Based on Aberle (1966).

Revolutionary social movements are the most extreme of all, striving for basic transformation of an entire society. Sometimes pursuing specific goals, sometimes spinning utopian dreams, these social movements reject existing social institutions as flawed while promoting radically new alternatives. Both the left-wing Communist Party (pushing for government control of the economy) and right-wing militia groups (advocating the destruction of "big government") seek to radically change our way of life.

EXPLAINING SOCIAL MOVEMENTS

Because social movements are intentional and long-lasting, sociologists find this type of collective behavior easier to explain than fleeting incidents of mob behavior or mass hysteria. Several theories have come to the fore.

Deprivation Theory

Deprivation theory holds that social movements arise among people who feel deprived. People who feel they lack enough income, safe working conditions, basic political rights, or plain human dignity may organize a social movement to bring about a more just state of affairs (Morrison, 1978; Rose, 1982).

The rise of the Ku Klux Klan and passage of Jim Crow laws by whites intent on enforcing segregation in the South after the Civil War illustrate deprivation theory. With the end of slavery, white people lost a source

Q: "Psychological attributes of individuals, such as frustration and alienation, have minimal direct impact for explaining the occurrence of rebellion and revolution per se." Carol Mueller

RESOURCE: One of the cross-cultural selections in the Macionis and Benokraitis reader, *Seeing Ourselves*, is Brian Russo's "Tiananmen Square: A Personal Chronicle From China."

NOTE: The conservative character of mass-society theory stems from the implication that it is the loss of traditional social ties (and not social inequality) that leads to social movements. Kornhauser follows Tocqueville rather than Marx in focusing on mass movements rather than on class movements. The distinction between mass society and class society is developed further in Chapter 24 ("Social Change: Traditional, Modern, and Postmodern Societies").

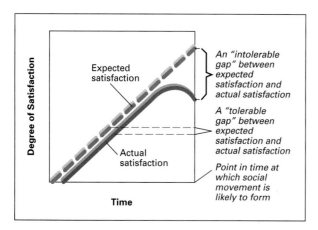

FIGURE 23–2 Relative Deprivation and Social Movements

In this diagram, the solid line represents a rising standard of living over time. The dotted line indicates the expected standard of living, which is typically somewhat higher. James C. Davies describes the difference between the two as "a tolerable gap between what people want and what they get." If the standard of living suddenly drops in the midst of rising expectations, however, the gap becomes intolerable. At this point, we can expect social movements to form.

Source: Davies (1962).

of free labor and the claim that they were socially superior to African Americans. Many whites reacted to "deprivation" by trying to keep all people of color "in their place" (Dollard et al., 1939). African Americans had experienced much greater deprivation, of course, but as slaves they had little opportunity to organize. During this century, however, African Americans have organized successfully in pursuit of racial equality.

As Chapter 7 ("Groups and Organizations") explained, deprivation is a relative concept. Regardless of anyone's absolute amount of money and power, people feel either better or worse off compared to some category of others. **Relative deprivation,** then, is *a perceived disadvantage arising from some specific comparison* (Stouffer et al., 1949; Merton, 1968).

More than a century ago, Alexis de Tocqueville (1955; orig. 1856) studied the French Revolution. Why, he asked, did rebellion occur in progressive France rather than in more traditional Germany, where peasants were, by any objective measure, worse off? Tocqueville's answer was that, as bad as their condition was, German peasants had known nothing but feudal servitude and thus had no basis for feeling deprived. French peasants, on the other hand, had seen improvements in their lives that whetted their appetites for more. Thus the French—not the Germans—felt a keen sense of relative deprivation. The irony, as Tocqueville saw it, was that increasing freedom and prosperity did not satisfy people as much as stimulating their desire for an even better life (1955:175; orig. 1856).

James C. Davies (1962) agrees that, as life gets better, people take their rising fortunes for granted and expect even more. But what happens if the standard of living suddenly stops improving or, worse, begins to drop? As Figure 23–2 illustrates, relative deprivation is the result, generating unrest and social movements aimed at change.

Critical evaluation. Deprivation theory challenges our common-sense assumption that the worst-off people are the most likely to organize for change. People do not organize simply because they suffer in an absolute sense; rather, they form social movements because of *relative* deprivation. Indeed, both Tocqueville and Marx—as different as they were in many ways—agreed on the importance of relative deprivation in the formation of social movements.

But most people experience some discontent all the time, so deprivation theory leaves us wondering why social movements arise among some categories of people and not others. A second problem is that deprivation theory suffers from circular reasoning: We assume that deprivation causes social movements, but often the only evidence of deprivation is the social movement itself (Jenkins & Perrow, 1977). A third limitation of this approach is that it focuses exclusively on the cause of a social movement and tells us little about movements themselves (McAdam, McCarthy, & Zald, 1988). Fourth, some researchers claim that relative deprivation has not turned out to be a very good predictor of social movements (Muller, 1979).

Mass-Society Theory

William Kornhauser's mass-society theory (1959) argues that social movements attract socially isolated people who feel personally insignificant. From this point of view, social movements occur in large *mass* societies. Social movements are also more *personal* than *political* in that they offer a sense of purpose and belonging to people otherwise adrift in society (Melucci, 1989).

NOTE: Mass-society theory has much in common with Hirschi's control theory of deviance (see Chapter 8, "Deviance"): Both suggest that the behavior in question arises among those with few social attachments.

Q: "[In every] revolutionary movement, the leadership, paradoxically, is likely to come from the least oppressed and marginal members of the population, or from people outside the group completely." Richard Farson

Q: "All previous historical movements were movements of minorities, or in the interests of minorities. The proletarian movement is the self-conscious, independent movement of the immense majority, in the interest of the immense majority." Karl Marx and Friedrich Engels

Kornhauser's theory holds that it is categories of people with weak social ties who most readily join a social movement. People who are well-integrated socially, by contrast, are unlikely to seek membership in a social movement.

Like Gustave Le Bon, discussed earlier, Kornhauser offers a conservative view of social movements. Activists tend to be psychologically vulnerable people who eagerly join groups and are often manipulated by group leaders. Social movements, in Kornhauser's view, are unlikely to be very democratic.

Critical evaluation. To Kornhauser's credit, his theory focuses on both the kind of society that produces social movements and the kinds of people who join them. But one criticism is that, if we try to test the idea that mass societies foster social movements, we end up having no simple standard against which to measure the extent to which we live in a "mass society."

A second criticism is that explaining social movements in terms of people hungry to belong belittles the social justice issues that movements address. Put otherwise, mass-society theory suggests that flawed people—rather than a flawed society—are responsible for social movements.

And what does research show about mass-society theory? The record is mixed. On the down side, some studies conclude that the Nazi movement in Germany did not draw heavily from socially isolated people (Lipset, 1963; Oberschall, 1973). Similarly, urban rioters during the 1960s typically had strong ties to their communities (Sears & McConahay, 1973). Evidence also suggests that young people who join religious cults do not have particularly weak family ties (Wright & Piper, 1986). Finally, researchers who have examined the biographies of 1960s political activists find evidence of deep and continuing commitment to political goals rather than isolation from society (McAdam, 1988, 1989; Whalen & Flacks, 1989).

On the up side, research by Frances Piven and Richard Cloward (1977) supports this approach. Piven and Cloward found that a breakdown of routine social patterns has encouraged poor people to form social movements. Also, in a study of the New Mexico State Penitentiary, Bert Useem (1985) found that when prison programs that promoted social ties among inmates were suspended, inmates displayed higher levels of protest.

Structural-Strain Theory

One of the most influential theories about social movements was developed by Neil Smelser (1962). *Structural-strain theory* identifies six factors that encourage the

These people in San Francisco's Marina Park are protesting the 1992 execution of convicted murderer Robert Alton Harris. Many of those shown here have engaged in similar protests at prison executions in other states. Mass-society theory suggests that people join social movements in order to gain a sense of meaning and purpose in their lives. How well do you think this theory explains the behavior of such people? Why?

development of social movements. Smelser's theory also suggests which kinds of situations lead to unorganized mobs or riots and which to highly organized social movements. We will use the prodemocracy movement that transformed Eastern Europe during the late 1980s to illustrate Smelser's theory:

1. **Structural conduciveness.** Social movements arise as people come to think their society has some serious problems. In Eastern Europe, these problems included low living standards and political repression by socialist governments.

2. **Structural strain.** People begin to experience relative deprivation when their society fails to meet their expectations. Eastern Europeans joined the prodemocracy movement because they knew their living standards were far lower than living standards in Western Europe and much below what years of propaganda about prosperous socialism had led them to expect.

3. **Growth and spread of an explanation.** Forming a well-organized social movement requires a clear statement of a problem, its causes, and its

DISCUSS: Use the women's movement to illustrate the stages of Smelser's theory. (1) Historical pattern of patriarchy; women organize in opposition. (2) Strain between U.S. ideal of equality and reality of patriarchy. (3) Early feminist scholarship and organization. (4) First wave of feminism—passage of 13th, 14th, and 15th Amendments extended rights to African American men but ignored women of both races; second wave of feminism—African American civil rights movement (predominantly led by men) and the increasing proportion of women in the labor force. (5) Mobilization spearheaded by organizations such as National Organization for Women (NOW); widespread publication of feminist ideas (e.g., *Ms.* magazine, founded in 1972). (6) Passage of the 19th Amendment slowed the women's movement; ERA remains unratified, but legislation has advanced women's social and economic rights.

How can we explain a change as monumental as the fall of Soviet-backed governments throughout Eastern Europe at the beginning of the 1990s? At the outset, this movement was simply a strike by shipyard workers, led by Lech Walesa, in the Polish city of Gdansk. But within a decade, discontent and collective action had toppled the Polish government, made Walesa the nation's new president, and spilled throughout the region, ultimately bringing an end to the Soviet Union itself.

solutions. If people are confused about their suffering, they are likely to express their dissatisfaction in an unorganized way such as rioting. In the case of Eastern Europe, intellectuals played a key role in the prodemocracy movement by pointing out economic and political flaws in the system and proposing strategies to increase democracy.

4. **Precipitating factors.** Discontent frequently festers for a long time, only to be transformed into collective action by a specific event. Such an event occurred in 1985 when Mikhail Gorbachev came to power in the Soviet Union and began his program of *perestroika* (restructuring). As Moscow relaxed its rigid control over Eastern Europe, people there saw a historic opportunity to reorganize political and economic life.

5. **Mobilization for action.** Once people share a concern about some public issue, they are ready to take action—to stage protest rallies, distribute leaflets, and build alliances with sympathetic organizations. The initial success of the Solidarity movement in Poland—covertly aided by the Reagan administration in the United States and by the Vatican—mobilized people throughout Eastern Europe to press for change. The rate of change accelerated as reform movements gained strength: What had taken a decade in Poland required only months in Hungary and only weeks in other Eastern European nations.

6. **Lack of social control.** The success of any social movement depends, in large part, on how political officials, police, and the military respond. Sometimes the state moves swiftly to crush a social movement, as happened with the prodemocracy forces in the People's Republic of China. But Gorbachev adopted a policy of nonintervention in Eastern Europe, thereby opening the door for change. Ironically, the movements that began in Eastern Europe soon spread to the Soviet Union itself, ending the historic domination of the Communist party and producing a new political confederation in 1992.

Critical evaluation. Smelser's analysis recognizes the complexity of social movements and suggests how various factors encourage or inhibit their development. Structural-strain theory also explains why people may respond to their problems either by forming organized social movements or through spontaneous mob action or rioting.

Yet Smelser's theory contains some of the same circularity of argument found in Kornhauser's analysis. A social movement is caused by strain, says Smelser, but the only evidence of underlying strain appears to be the social movement itself. Finally, structural-strain theory is incomplete, overlooking the important role that resources like the mass media or international alliances play in the success or failure of a social movement (Oberschall, 1973; Jenkins & Perrow, 1977; McCarthy & Zald, 1977; Olzak & West, 1991).

Resource-Mobilization Theory

Resource-mobilization theory points out that no social movement is likely to succeed—or even get off the ground—without substantial resources, including

DISCUSS: Illustrating the importance of resources to social movements, consider the contribution academics have made to the growing success of the feminist movement.

Q: "You cannot put a rope around the neck of an idea . . ." Sean O'Casey

Q: "I assert that there is no country in Europe in which the public administration has not become, not only more centralized, but more inquisitive and more minute; it everywhere interferes in private concerns more than it did . . ." Alexis de Tocqueville (*The Old Regime and the French Revolution*, Book IV, Chapter V)

NOTE: A Marxist view of "new social movements" sees people and the state as entering more and more areas of private life in an effort to resolve the contradictions of late 20th-century capitalist economies.

money, human labor, office and communications facilities, access to the mass media, and a positive public image. In short, any social movement rises or falls on its ability to attract resources, mobilize people, and forge alliances. The collapse of socialism in Eastern Europe was largely the work of dissatisfied people in those countries. But to topple their leaders, Poles and others needed the fax machines, copiers, telecommunications gear, money, and moral support provided by other nations.

In other words, according to resource-mobilization theory, outsiders are as important as insiders to the outcome of a social movement. Since socially disadvantaged people, by definition, lack the money, contacts, leadership skills, and organizational know-how that a successful movement requires, sympathetic outsiders fill the resource gap. In our own country, well-to-do white people, including college students, performed a vital service to the black civil rights movement in the 1960s, and affluent men as well as women have taken a leading role in the current women's movement (Snow, Zurcher, & Ekland-Olson, 1980; Killian, 1984; Snow, Rochford, Jr., Worden, & Benford, 1986; Baron, Mittman, & Newman, 1991; Burstein, 1991; Meyer & Whittier, 1994; Valocchi, 1996).

On the other side of the coin, a lack of resources limits efforts to bring about change. The history of the AIDS epidemic is a case in point. Initially, in the early 1980s, the government ignored the rising incidence of AIDS, leaving gay communities in San Francisco, New York, and other cities to shoulder the responsibility for treatment and educational programs. Gradually, as the general public began to grasp the scope of the problem, pressure prompted local, state, and federal governments to allocate more resources for research, education, and treatment. Members of the entertainment industry in particular lent their money, visibility, and prestige to the movement. These resources were crucial in transforming a fledgling social movement into a well-organized, global coalition of political leaders, educators, and medical specialists.

Critical evaluation. Resource-mobilization theory recognizes that resources as well as discontent are necessary to the success of a social movement. Research has confirmed that forging alliances to gain resources is especially important, and notes that movements with few resources may, in desperation, turn to violence to call attention to their cause (Grant & Wallace, 1991).

Critics of this theory counter that even relatively powerless segments of a population can promote change if they are able to organize effectively and have strongly committed members. Research by Aldon

One example of a "new social movement" is the worldwide effort to eliminate land mines. Years after hostilities cease, these mines remain in place and take a staggering toll on innocent civilians. At a protest in Berlin, Germany, a mountain of shoes created a memorial to tens of thousands who have been crippled or died as a result of stepping on underground mines.

Morris (1981) shows that people of color drew largely on their own skills and resources to fuel the civil rights movement of the 1950s and 1960s. A second problem with this theory is that it overstates the extent to which powerful people are willing to challenge the status quo. Some rich white people did provide valuable resources to the black civil rights movement, but, probably more often, elites were indifferent or opposed to significant change (McAdam, 1982, 1983; Pichardo, 1995).

Overall, the success or failure of a social movement is decided by political struggle. A strong and united establishment (perhaps aided by a countermovement) reduces the odds that a social movement will succeed. If, however, the established powers are divided, the movement's chances of success improve.

New Social Movements Theory

A final, more recent theoretical approach addresses the changing character of social movements. *New social movements theory* emphasizes the distinctive features of recent social movements in postindustrial societies of North America and Western Europe (Melucci, 1980; McAdam, McCarthy, & Zald, 1988; Kriesi, 1989; Pakulski, 1993).

A key contention of new social movements theory is that recruitment into social movements is based more on symbolism (in Weberian terms) than on class interests (in Marxist terms). Indeed, Stanley Aronowitz (1992) suggests that minorities, lesbians, and environmentalists—adherents of the new social movements of the left—may take over the working classes' historic mission to overthrow capitalism. "New social movements" are found in postindustrial societies; conventional social movements in industrial societies.

DIVERSITY: Although some social movements that challenge the status quo have been dominated by men, not all have—the abolition movement, suffrage movement, child-care movements, and anti-drunk driving movements are only a few examples.

TABLE 23–1 Theories of Social Movements: A Summary

Deprivation Theory	People experiencing relative deprivation begin social movements. The social movement is a means of seeking change that brings participants greater benefits. Social movements are especially likely when rising expectations are frustrated.
Mass-Society Theory	People who lack established social ties are mobilized into social movements. Periods of social breakdown are likely to spawn social movements. The social movement gives members a sense of belonging and social participation.
Structural-Strain Theory	People come together because of their shared concern about the inability of society to operate as they believe it should. The growth of a social movement reflects many factors, including a belief in its legitimacy and some precipitating event that provokes action.
Resource-Mobilization Theory	People may join for all the reasons noted above and also because of social ties to existing members. The success or failure of a social movement depends largely on the resources available to it. Also important is the extent of opposition within the larger society.
New Social Movements Theory	People who become part of social movements are motivated by "quality of life" issues, not necessarily economic concerns. Mobilization is national or international in scope. New social movements arise in response to the expansion of the mass media and new information technology.

Most of today's social movements are international, focusing on global ecology, the social standing of women and gay people, animal rights, and reducing the risks of war. As the process of globalization connects the world's nations in more and more ways, in other words, social movements, too, are becoming global.

Second, while traditional social movements such as labor organizations are concerned mostly with economic issues, new social movements tend to focus on cultural change and improving our social and physical surroundings. The international environmental movement, for example, opposes practices that aggravate global warming and other environmental dangers.

Third, whereas most social movements of the past drew strong support from working-class people, new social movements, with their noneconomic agendas, usually draw support from the middle class. Furthermore, in the United States and other rich nations, the number of highly educated professionals—the people who most support "new social movements"—is increasing, which suggests that these movements will grow (Jenkins & Wallace, 1996).

Critical evaluation. One clear strength of this theory is its recognition that social movements have increased in scale in response to the development of a global economy and international political connections. This theory also highlights the power of the mass media to unite people around the world in pursuit of political goals.

Critics, however, claim that this approach exaggerates the differences between past and present social movements. The women's movement, for example, focuses on many of the same issues—workplace conditions and pay—that have concerned labor organizations for decades.

Each of the five theories we have presented offers some explanation for the emergence of social movements; no single theory can stand alone (Kowalewski & Porter, 1992). Table 23–1 summarizes the theories.

GENDER AND SOCIAL MOVEMENTS

Gender figures prominently in the operation of social movements. In keeping with traditional ideas about gender in the United States, men more than women tend to take part in public life—including spearheading social movements.

Investigating "Freedom Summer," a 1964 voter registration project in Mississippi, Doug McAdam (1992) found that most people viewed the job of registering African American voters in the midst of considerable hostility from whites dangerous, and therefore "men's work" unsuitable for women. He also discovered that project leaders were likely to assign women volunteers to clerical and teaching assignments, leaving the actual field activities to men. This was so even though women who participated in Freedom Summer were more qualified than their male counterparts in terms of years of activism and organizational affiliations. McAdam concluded that only the most committed women were able to overcome the movement's gender

SOCIAL SURVEY: "Should organizing protest marches and demonstrations against the government be allowed?" (GSS 1996, N = 1,332; *Codebook*, 1996:639)

"Definitely allowed"   45.8%   "Definitely not allowed" 8.2%
"Probably allowed"   29.8%   DK/NR   5.6%
"Probably not allowed"   10.5%

NOTE: In some cases, the failure of a social movement to establish and sustain a social identity leads to its demise. For example, the American Indian Movement, which lasted from about 1968 to 1973, never succeeded in fostering a pan-tribal identity (Stotok, Shriver, & Cable, 1994).

Q: "Mass movements can rise and spread without belief in a God, but never without belief in a devil." Eric Hoffer

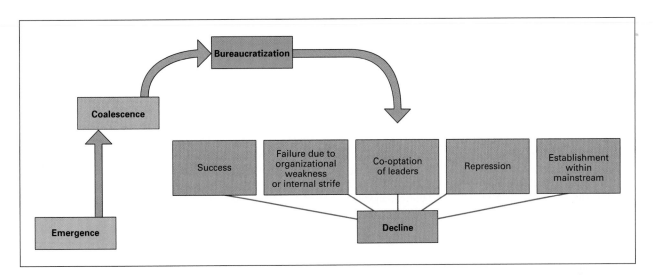

FIGURE 23–3 Stages in the Lives of Social Movements

barriers. In short, while women have played leading roles in many social movements (including the abolitionist and feminist movements in the United States), male dominance has been the norm even in social movements that otherwise oppose the status quo.

STAGES IN SOCIAL MOVEMENTS

Despite the many differences that set one social movement off from another, all unfold in roughly the same way, as shown in Figure 23–3. Researchers have identified four stages in the life of the typical social movement (Blumer, 1969; Mauss, 1975; Tilly, 1978).

Stage 1: Emergence. Social movements are driven by the perception that all is not well. Some, such as the civil rights and women's movements, are born of widespread dissatisfaction. Others emerge only as a small vanguard group increases public awareness of some issue. Gay activists, for example, initially raised public concern about the threat posed by AIDS.

Stage 2: Coalescence. After emerging, a social movement must define itself and develop a strategy for "going public." Leaders must determine policies, decide on tactics, build morale, and recruit new members. At this stage, the movement may engage in collective action like rallies or demonstrations to attract media attention and thereby public notice. The movement may also form alliances with other organizations to gain necessary resources.

Stage 3: Bureaucratization. To become a political force, a social movement must take on bureaucratic traits, described in Chapter 7 ("Groups and Organizations"). Thus, as it becomes established, the social movement depends less on the charisma and talents of a few leaders and relies more on a capable staff. When social movements do not become established in this way, they risk dissolving. For example, many activist organizations on college campuses during the late 1960s were energized by a single charismatic leader and, consequently, did not last long. On the other hand, the National Organization for Women (NOW), despite its changing leadership, is well-established and offers a steady voice on behalf of feminists.

Even so, bureaucratization can sometimes hinder a social movement. In reviewing social movements in U.S. history, Frances Piven and Richard Cloward (1977) found that leaders can become so engrossed in building an organization that they neglect the need to keep people "fired up" for change. In such cases, the radical edge of protest is lost.

Stage 4: Decline. Eventually, most social movements lose their influence. Frederick Miller (1983) suggests four reasons that this can occur.

First, if members have met their goals, decline may simply signal success. For example, the women's suffrage movement disbanded after it won women in the United States the right to vote. Such clear-cut successes are rare, however, since few social movements have a single goal. More commonly, winning one victory leads

SOCIAL SURVEY: "In general, would you say that people should obey the law without exception, or are there exceptional occasions on which people should follow their consciences even if it means breaking the law?" (GSS 1996, N = 1,332; *Codebook*, 1996:638)

"Obey the law"   40.2%   DK/NR   6.0%
"Follow conscience"   53.8%

SOCIAL SURVEY: "Should organizing a nationwide strike of all workers against the government be allowed or not?" (GSS 1996, N = 1,332; *Codebook*, 1996:640)

"Definitely allowed"   16.4%   "Definitely not allowed" 27.6%
"Probably allowed"   20.4%   DK/NR   8.6%
"Probably not allowed"   27.0%

CONTROVERSY & DEBATE

Are You Willing to Take a Stand?

Are you satisfied with our society as it is? Surely, everyone would change some things about our way of life. Indeed, surveys show that, if they could, a lot of people would change plenty! There is considerable pessimism about the state of U.S. society: Two-thirds of U.S. adults think that the average person's situation "is getting worse, not better," and three-fourths of respondents state that most government officials are "not interested" in the average person's problems (NORC, 1996:190).

But, in light of such concerns, few people are willing to stand up and try to bring about change. Only 10 percent of adults in the United States have ever picketed during a labor strike; just 5 percent say they have ever taken part in any other kind of demonstration (NORC, 1996:221).

Many college students probably suspect age has something to do with such apathy. That is, young people have the interest and idealism to challenge the status quo, while older adults worry only about their families and their job security. Indeed, one of the popular sayings of the activist decade of the 1960s was "You can't trust anyone over thirty!" But the facts today tell us otherwise: Students entering college in 1995 expressed no greater interest in political issues than their parents.

Asked to select important goals in life from a list, the figure shows less than one-third of first-year students included "keeping up with political affairs," and just 23 percent checked off "participating in community action programs." Only a handful of students (16 percent) say they often discuss politics and an even smaller share (5 percent) expect to join a demonstration while in college.

Certainly, people cite some good reasons to avoid political controversy. Any time we challenge the system—whether on campus or in the national political arena—we risk making enemies, losing a job, or perhaps even sustaining physical injury.

But the most important reason that people in the United States avoid joining in social movements may have to do with cultural norms about how change should occur. In our individualistic culture, people favor taking personal responsibility over collective action as a means of addressing social problems. For example, when asked about the best way for women or African Americans to improve their social position, most U.S. adults say that individuals should become better trained and otherwise improve their occupational qualifications. By contrast, only a small

to new campaigns. Because issues related to gender extend far beyond voting, the women's movement has recast itself time and again.

Second, a social movement may flag because of organizational factors, such as poor leadership, loss of interest among members, insufficient funds, or repression by authorities. Some people lose interest when the excitement of early efforts is replaced by day-to-day routine. Fragmentation due to internal conflicts over goals and strategies is another common problem. Students for a Democratic Society (SDS), a student movement promoting participatory democracy and opposing the war in Vietnam, splintered into several small factions by the end of the 1960s, as members disagreed over strategies for social change.

Third, a social movement can fall apart if the established power structure, through offers of money, prestige, and other rewards, diverts leaders from their goals. Co-optation—that is, "selling out"—is one facet of the iron law of oligarchy, discussed in Chapter 7 ("Groups

and Organizations"). That is, organizational leaders use their positions to enrich themselves. For example, Vernon Jordan, once head of the National Urban League, is now a close advisor to President Clinton—and a rich and powerful Washington "insider." But this process can also work the other way: Some people leave lucrative, high-prestige occupations to become activists. Cat Stevens, a rock star of the 1970s, became a Muslim, changed his name to Yusuf Islam, and now promotes the spread of his religion.

Fourth, a social movement can collapse because of repression. Officials may crush a social movement by frightening away participants, discouraging new recruits, and even imprisoning leaders. In general, the more revolutionary the social movement, the more officials try to repress it. Until 1990, the government of South Africa, for example, banned the African National Congress (ANC), a political organization seeking to overthrow the state-supported system of apartheid. Even suspected members of the ANC were

SOCIAL SURVEY: In 1973, the following proportion of adults responded that they had taken part in various kinds of protest actions: (GSS 1973, N = 1,504; *Codebook,* 1996:221–22)
Picketing for a labor strike, 9.5%
A civil rights demonstration, 4.3%
An anti-war demonstration, 4.9%
A pro-war demonstration, 0.4%

A school-related demonstration, 5.3%

NOTE: Many social movements fall into one of two categories: *equality movements* seeking social equality for various categories of people (based on class, race, sexual orientation, etc.), and specific *protest movements* targeting gun control, nuclear power, animal experimentation, etc. (Caplow, 1991).

minority point to women's groups or civil rights activism as the best way to bring about change (NORC, 1996: 323–24). This individualistic orientation explains why U.S. adults are half as likely as their European counterparts to join in lawful demonstrations (*World Values Survey,* 1994).

Sociology, of course, poses a counterpoint to our cultural individualism. As C. Wright Mills (1959) explained decades ago, many of the problems we encounter as individuals are caused by the structure of society. Thus, said Mills, solutions to many of life's problems depend on collective effort—that is, people willing to take a stand for what they believe.

Continue the debate . . .

1. *Do you think the reluctance of people in the United States to address*

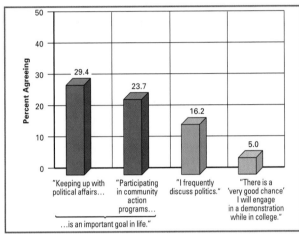

Political Involvement of Students Entering College in 1996: A Survey
Source: Sax et al. (1996).

problems through collective action shows that they are basically satisfied with their lives? Or that they think individuals acting together can't make a difference?

2. *Have you ever participated in a political demonstration? What were its goals? What did it accomplish?*

3. *Identify ways that life today has been affected by people who took a stand in the past (think about race relations, the state of the environment, the standing of women).*

subject to arrest. In 1990, the government lifted the decades-old ban and released ANC leader Nelson Mandela from prison; in 1994, Mandela became president of a country now moving away from apartheid.

Beyond the reasons noted by Miller, a fifth cause of decline is that a social movement may "go mainstream." Some movements become an accepted part of the system—typically after realizing some of their goals—so they no longer challenge the status quo. The U.S. labor movement, for example, is now well established; its leaders control vast sums of money and, according to some critics, now have more in common with the business tycoons they opposed in the past than with rank-and-file workers.

SOCIAL MOVEMENTS AND SOCIAL CHANGE

Social movements exist to encourage—or to resist—social change. Whatever the intention, their success varies from case to case. The civil rights movement has certainly

pushed this country toward racial equality, despite opposition from a handful of white supremacist countermovements like the Aryan Nation and the Ku Klux Klan.

Sometimes we overlook the success of past social movements and take for granted the changes that other people struggled so hard to win. Beginning a century ago, workers' movements in the United States fought to end child labor in factories, limit working hours, make the workplace safer, and establish the right to bargain collectively with employers. Laws protecting the environment are another product of successful social movements during this century. And women today have greater legal rights and economic opportunities won by earlier generations of women.

Seen one way, major social transformations such as the Industrial Revolution and capitalism give rise to social movements, including those involving workers and women. On the other hand, the efforts of workers, women, racial and ethnic minorities, and gay people have sent ripples of change throughout our society.

Thus, social change is both the cause and the consequence of social movements.

LOOKING AHEAD: SOCIAL MOVEMENTS IN THE TWENTY-FIRST CENTURY

Especially since the turbulent 1960s—a decade marked by widespread social protests—U.S. society has been pushed and pulled by many social movements and countermovements. Sometimes tension explodes into violence, as with the 1992 Los Angeles riots after the first trial of the police accused of beating Rodney King. In other cases, the struggles are more restrained, as with political debate between Congressional Democrats supporting social "safety nets" and Republicans opposed to "big government." Yet people agree that many of this nation's most pressing problems—racial tension, the size of government, and crime—remain unresolved. In addition, of course, new issues—including the state of the family and gay rights—have moved to center stage.

Social movements have always been part of U.S. society, although their focus, tactics, and intensity change with time. There is little doubt, therefore, that social movements will continue to shape our way of life. Indeed, for three reasons, the scope of social movements is likely to increase. First, protest should increase as women, African Americans and other historically excluded categories of people gain a greater political voice. Second, at a global level, the technology of the Information Revolution means that anyone with a satellite dish, personal computer, or fax machine can stay abreast of political events, often as they happen. Third, new technology and the emerging global economy mean that social movements are now uniting people throughout the entire world. Moreover, since many problems are global in scope, only international cooperation can solve them.

SUMMARY

1. A collectivity differs from a social group in its limited social interaction, vague social boundaries, and weak and often unconventional norms.

2. Crowds, a type of collective behavior, take various forms: casual crowds, conventional crowds, expressive crowds, acting crowds, and protest crowds.

3. Crowds that become emotionally intense spawn violence in the form of mobs and riots. Mobs pursue a specific goal; rioting involves undirected destructiveness.

4. Crowds have figured heavily in social change throughout history, although the value of their action depends on one's political outlook.

5. Contagion theory views crowds as anonymous, suggestible, and subject to rising emotions. Convergence theory links crowd behavior to the traits of participants. Emergent-norm theory suggests that crowds develop their own behavioral norms.

6. Rumor, a form of mass behavior, thrives in a climate of ambiguity. Rumor involves public issues, gossip deals with personal issues.

7. Public opinion consists of people's positions on important, controversial issues. Public attitudes change over time; at any time on any given issue, a small share of people hold no opinion at all.

8. A panic (in a local area) or mass hysteria (across an entire society) are types of collective behavior by which people respond to a significant event, real or imagined, with irrational, frantic, and often self-destructive behavior.

9. In industrial societies, people use fashion as a source of social prestige. A fad is more unconventional than a fashion and is also of shorter duration, although people embrace fads with greater enthusiasm.

10. Social movements exist to promote or discourage change. Sociologists classify social movements according to the range of people they seek to involve and the extent of the change they seek.

11. According to deprivation theory, social movements arise as people feel deprived in relation to some standard of well-being.

12. Mass-society theory holds that people join social movements to gain a sense of belonging and moral direction.

13. Structural-strain theory explains the development of a social movement as a cumulative effect of six factors. Well-formulated grievances and goals encourage the formation of social movements; undirected anger, by contrast, promotes rioting.

14. Resource-mobilization theory ties the success or failure of a social movement to the availability of resources such as money, human labor, and alliances with other organizations.

15. New social movements theory focuses on quality-of-life issues usually international in scope.

16. A typical social movement proceeds through consecutive stages: emergence (defining the public issue), coalescence (entering the public arena), bureaucratization (becoming formally organized), and decline (due to failure or, sometimes, success).

17. Past social movements have shaped society in ways that people now take for granted. Just as movements produce change, so change itself causes social movements.

KEY CONCEPTS

social movement organized activity that encourages or discourages social change

collective behavior activity involving a large number of people, often spontaneous, and usually in violation of established norms

collectivity a large number of people whose minimal interaction occurs in the absence of well-defined conventional norms

crowd a temporary gathering of people who share a common focus of attention and whose members influence one another

mob a highly emotional crowd that pursues a violent or destructive goal

riot a social eruption that is highly emotional, violent, and undirected

mass behavior collective behavior among people dispersed over a wide geographical area

rumor unsubstantiated information spread informally, often by word of mouth

gossip rumor about people's personal affairs

propaganda information presented with the intention of shaping public opinion

panic a form of localized collective behavior by which people react to a threat or other stimulus with irrational, frantic, and often self-destructive behavior

mass hysteria a form of dispersed collective behavior by which people react to a real or imagined event with irrational, frantic, and often self-destructive behavior

fashion a social pattern favored by a large number of people

fad an unconventional social pattern that people embrace briefly but enthusiastically

relative deprivation a perceived disadvantage arising from a specific comparison

CRITICAL-THINKING QUESTIONS

1. The concept of collective behavior encompasses a broad range of social patterns. What traits do they all have in common?

2. Imagine the aftermath of a football game where revelry turns into destructive rampage. What insights into this event do contagion theory, convergence theory, and emergent-norm theory provide?

3. The 1960s was a decade of both great affluence and widespread social protest. What sociological insights help to explain this apparent paradox?

4. In what respects do some recent social movements (those concerned with the environment, animal rights, and gun control) differ from older crusades (focusing on, say, civil rights and gender equality)?

LEARNING EXERCISES

1. If you have access to the Internet, visit the Web site for the National Organization for the Reform of Marijuana Laws: http://www.natlnorml.org What are the goals of this organization? How is it trying to expand the social movement in favor of legalizing marijuana use?

2. With ten friends, try a fascinating experiment: One person writes down a detailed "rumor" about someone and whispers it to the second person, who whispers it to a third, and so on. The last person to hear the rumor writes it down again. Compare the two versions of the rumor.

3. With other members of the class, identify "fad" products, from hula hoops to Beanie Babies. What makes people want them? Why do they drop from favor so quickly?

4. What social movements are represented by organizations on your campus? Your class might invite several leaders to describe their groups' goals and strategies.

5. Install the CD-ROM packaged inside the back cover of your text and complete the activities designed to accompany this chapter.

Joan Truckenbrod, *Sociotecture*, 1991
Courtesy of The Williams Gallery, Princeton, N.J. © Joan Truckenbrod, 1997.

CHAPTER 24

SOCIAL CHANGE: TRADITIONAL, MODERN, AND POSTMODERN SOCIETIES

The firelight flickers in the gathering darkness as Chief Kanhonk sits, as he has done at the end of the day for many years, ready to begin an evening of animated talk and storytelling (Simons, 1998). This is the hour when the Kaiapo, a small society in Brazil's lush Amazon region, celebrate their heritage. Because the Kaiapo are a traditional people with no written language, the elders rely on evenings by the fire to pass along their culture to their children and grandchildren. In the past, evenings like this have been filled with tales of brave Kaiapo warriors fighting off Portuguese traders in pursuit of slaves and gold.

But as the minutes pass, only a few older villagers assemble for the evening ritual. "It is the Big Ghost," one man grumbles, explaining the poor turnout. The "Big Ghost" has indeed descended upon them; its bluish glow spills from windows throughout the village. The Kaiapo children—and many adults as well—are watching television.

Installing a satellite dish in the village several years ago has had consequences far greater than anyone imagined. In the end, what their enemies failed to do with guns, the Kaiapo may well do to themselves with prime-time programming.

The Kaiapo are among the 230,000 native peoples who inhabit the country we call Brazil. They stand out because of their striking body paint and ornate ceremonial dress. Recently, they have become rich from gold mining and harvesting mahogany trees. Now they must decide if their new-found fortune is a blessing or a curse.

To some, affluence means the opportunity to learn about the outside world through travel and television. Others, like Chief Kanhonk, are not so sure. Sitting by the fire, he thinks aloud, "I have been saying that people must buy useful things like knives and fishing hooks. Television does not fill the stomach. It only shows our children and grandchildren white people's things." Bebtopup, the oldest priest, nods in agreement: "The night is the time the old people teach the young people. Television has stolen the night" (Simons, 1998:495).

The Kaiapo story raises profound questions about the causes of change and whether change is always for the better. The Kaiapo may be edging toward modernity, but is a higher standard of living necessarily better than their traditional way of life? Moreover, the drama of the Kaiapo is being played out around the globe as more and more traditional cultures are being lured by the affluence and materialism of rich societies away from their heritage.

This chapter examines social change as a process with both positive and negative consequences. Of

SUPPLEMENTS: An outline of this chapter, supplementary lecture material, and suggested discussion topics are included in the *Data File*.
SOCIAL SURVEY: "One trouble with science is that it makes our way of life change too fast." (GSS 1988, N = 1,481; *Codebook*, 1996:325)
"Agree"   40.2%   "Disagree"   57.7%   DK/NR   2.1%

DISCUSS: Are "great people" or "average people" primarily responsible for social change? Historically, conservatives argued the former, since this individualistic position favored traditional hierarchy and elites. Liberals tended toward the more egalitarian, collectivist view.
DISCUSS: Consider ways in which the university diffuses knowledge, thereby promoting social change (cf. Wilkinson, 1994).

particular interest to people in the United States is what sociologists call *modernity*, changes brought about by the Industrial Revolution, and *postmodernity*, recent transformations caused by the Information Revolution and the postindustrial economy.

WHAT IS SOCIAL CHANGE?

In earlier chapters, we examined relatively *static* social patterns, including status and role, social stratification, and social institutions. The *dynamic* forces that have shaped our way of life range from innovations in technology to the growth of bureaucracy and the expansion of cities. These are all dimensions of **social change,** *the transformation of culture and social institutions over time*. The process of social change has four major characteristics:

1. **Social change is inevitable.** "Nothing is constant except death and taxes," goes the old saying. Yet even our thoughts about death have changed dramatically as life expectancy in the United States has doubled since 1850. Taxes, meanwhile, were unknown through most of human history, beginning only as societies grew in size several thousand years ago. In short, there is virtually nothing that is not subject to the twists and turns of change.

    Still, some societies change faster than others. As Chapter 4 ("Society") explained, hunting and gathering societies change quite slowly; members of modern, complex societies, on the other hand, experience significant change within a single lifetime.

    Moreover, in a given society, some cultural elements change faster than others. William Ogburn's (1964) theory of *cultural lag* (see Chapter 3) states that material culture (that is, things) usually changes faster than nonmaterial culture (ideas and attitudes). For example, medical technology that prolongs life has developed more rapidly than ethical standards for deciding when and how to use it.

2. **Social change is sometimes intentional but often unplanned.** Industrial societies actively encourage many kinds of change. For example, scientists seek more efficient forms of energy, and advertisers try to convince us that life is incomplete without this or that new gadget. Yet rarely can anyone envision all the consequences of the changes they set in motion.

    Early automobile manufacturers understood that cars would allow people to travel in a single day distances that had previously required weeks or months. But no one could see how profoundly the mobility provided by automobiles would alter life in the United States, scattering family members, threatening the environment, and reshaping cities and suburbs. Neither could automotive pioneers have predicted the 50,000 deaths each year in car accidents in the United States alone.

3. **Social change is controversial.** As the history of the automobile demonstrates, social change yields both good and bad consequences. Capitalists welcomed the Industrial Revolution because advancing technology increased productivity and swelled profits. Many workers, however, feared that machines would make their skills obsolete and resisted the push towards "progress."

    In the United States, changing social patterns between black people and white people, between women and men, and between gays and heterosexuals give rise to both celebration and backlash as people disagree about how we ought to live.

4. **Some changes matter more than others.** Some changes (such as clothing fads) have only passing significance, whereas other innovations (like computers) unleash changes that transform the entire world and last for generations. Looking ahead, will the Information Revolution turn out to be as pivotal as the Industrial Revolution? Like the automobile and television, computers will have both positive and negative effects, providing new kinds of jobs while eliminating old ones, isolating people in offices while linking people in global electronic networks, offering vast amounts of information while threatening personal privacy.

CAUSES OF SOCIAL CHANGE

Social change has many causes. And in a world linked by sophisticated communication and transportation technology, change in one place often begets change elsewhere.

CULTURE AND CHANGE

Chapter 3 ("Culture") identified three important sources of cultural change. First, *invention* produces new objects,

NOTE: In light of how quickly today's information becomes obsolete, note that Euclidian mathematics texts remained up-to-date and more or less unchanged for 23 centuries.

NOTE: In modern, rapidly changing societies, the origins of cultural elements are often forgotten. Lucky Strike cigarettes were named for a California gold strike; Baby Ruth candy bars were named for the birth of Grover Cleveland's daughter.

Q: "All of us are taking a journey into the future that will last every day of our lives. What will we be seeing and doing? How will we live?" Isaac Asimov

Q: "The philosophers have attempted to understand the world. The point, however, is to change it." Karl Marx

NOTE: Two sections of Chapter 4 ("Society") introduced Marx's materialist analysis of change and Weber's idealist analysis.

ideas, and social patterns. Rocket propulsion research, which began in the 1940s, has produced spacecraft that can reach toward the stars. Today we take such technology for granted; during the next century a significant number of people may well travel in space.

Second, *discovery* occurs when people take note of existing elements of the world. Medical advances, for example, offer a growing understanding of the human body. Beyond their direct effects upon human health, medical discoveries have stretched life expectancy, setting in motion the "graying" of our society (see Chapter 14, "Aging and the Elderly").

Third, *diffusion* creates change as products, people, and information spread from one culture to another. Ralph Linton (1937) recognized that many familiar elements of our culture came from other lands. For example, cloth (developed in Asia), clocks (invented in Europe), and coins (created in Turkey) have all become part of our way of life. In general, material objects diffuse more readily than cultural ideas. The Kaiapo, described at the beginning of this chapter, have been quick to adopt television, but they have been reluctant to embrace the materialism and individualism at the core of Western commercial programming.

Throughout our history, immigrants have brought change to the United States. In recent decades, people from Latin America and Asia have introduced new cultural patterns, clearly evident in the sights, smells, and sounds of cities across the country. Conversely, the global power of the United States ensures that much of our culture—from cheeseburgers to rap music to M.B.A. degrees—is being diffused to other societies.

CONFLICT AND CHANGE

Tension and conflict in a society also produce change. Karl Marx saw class conflict as the engine that drives societies from one historical era to another (see Chapter 4, "Society," and Chapter 9, "Social Stratification"). In industrial-capitalist societies, he explained, struggle between capitalists and workers propels society toward a socialist system of production.

In the century since Marx's death, this model has proven simplistic. Yet, Marx correctly foresaw that social conflict arising from inequality (involving race and gender as well as class) would force changes in every society, including our own.

IDEAS AND CHANGE

Max Weber, too, contributed to our understanding of social change. Weber acknowledged that conflict

Today, most of the people with access to computers live in rich countries such as the United States. But the number of people in agrarian societies going "online" is on the rise. How do you think the introduction of new information technology will change more traditional societies? Are all the changes likely to be for the good?

could bring about change, but he traced the roots of most social change to ideas. For example, people with charisma can carry a message that sometimes changes the world.

Weber highlighted the importance of ideas by showing how the religious beliefs of early Protestants set the stage for the spread of industrial capitalism (see Chapter 4, "Society"). The fact that industrial capitalism developed primarily in areas of Western Europe where the Protestant work ethic was strong proved to Weber (1958; orig. 1904–5) the power of ideas to bring about change.

Ideas also play a major role in the direction of social movements. Chapter 23 ("Collective Behavior and Social Movements") explained how change comes from the determination of men and women acting together to, say, clean up the environment or make the world more just by improving the lives of poor and oppressed people. The gay rights movement, for example, draws strength from people who believe that lesbians and gay men should enjoy the same rights and opportunities as the heterosexual majority.

THE MAP: Signaling the mobility and growth of U.S. society: The average age of housing stock is 26 years—below the median age of the population (34 years). The counties with relatively more long-term residents typically have an older population, and they are also places where economic growth is limited or stagnant. Many of them have lost young people to urban areas offering greater economic prospects. Thus few counties have escaped change of one kind or another. The trend from 1985 to 1995 was toward less moving.

NOTE: Census data point to Johnstown, Penn., as the most settled U.S. community, where 25% of residents have not moved since 1959 (U.S. average: 8.4%); Bryan-College Station, Tex., is the most mobile—41% moved in the 18 months before the data were collected (U.S. average: 21.7%).

SEEING OURSELVES

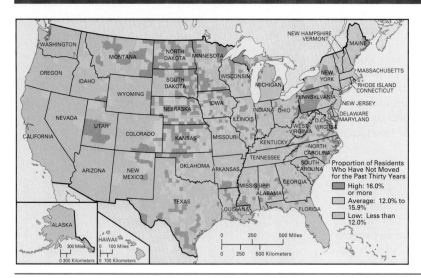

NATIONAL MAP 24–1
Who Stays Put? Residential Stability Across the United States

Overall, only about 9 percent of U.S. residents have not moved during the last thirty years. Counties with a higher proportion of "long-termers" typically have experienced less change over recent decades: Many neighborhoods have been in place since before World War II, and many of the same families live in them. Looking at the map, what can you say about these relatively stable areas? Why are most of these counties rural and some distance from the coasts?

Source: U.S. Bureau of the Census (1996).

DEMOGRAPHIC CHANGE

Population growth is yet another important dimension of social change, since it alters many related social patterns. In the Netherlands, a nation that has one of the highest population densities in the world, homes are small and narrow and people climb extremely steep staircases to make the most efficient use of space. In Japan, another high-density nation, urban commuters crowd into subways in ways that would challenge the patience of a lifelong New Yorker.

Profound change is also taking place as our population, collectively speaking, grows older. As Chapter 14 ("Aging and the Elderly") explained, 13 percent of the U.S. population was over age sixty-five in 1996, triple the proportion back in 1900. By the year 2030, seniors will account for 20 percent of the total (U.S. Bureau of the Census, 1997). Medical research and health-care services already focus extensively on the elderly, and life will change in countless additional ways as homes and household products are redesigned to meet the needs of growing ranks of older consumers.

Migration within and among societies is another demographic factor that promotes change. Between 1870 and 1930, tens of millions of immigrants entered the industrial cities in the United States. Millions more from rural areas joined the rush. As a result, farm communities declined, cities expanded, and, for the first time, the United States became a predominantly urban nation. Similar changes are taking place today as people move from the Snowbelt to the Sunbelt and mix with new immigrants from Latin America and Asia.

Where in the United States have demographic changes been greatest and which areas have been least affected? National Map 24–1 provides one answer, showing counties where the largest share of people have lived in their present homes for thirty years or more.

MODERNITY

A central concept in the study of social change is **modernity,** *social patterns linked to industrialization.* In everyday usage, modernity (its Latin root means "lately") designates the present in relation to the past. Sociologists include in this catch-all concept the social patterns set in motion by the Industrial Revolution beginning in Western Europe in the mid-eighteenth century. **Modernization,** then, is *the process of social change initiated by industrialization.* The time line inside the front cover of this text highlights important events that mark the emergence of modernity.

FOUR DIMENSIONS OF MODERNIZATION

Peter Berger (1977), in his influential study of social change, has identified four major characteristics of modernization:

In response to the accelerated pace of change in the late nineteenth century, Paul Gauguin (1848–1903) left his native France for the South Seas where he was captivated by a simpler and seemingly timeless way of life.

He romanticized this environment in his 1894 painting The Day of the God *(Mahana no Atua).*

Paul Gauguin, *The Day of the God* (Mahana no Atua), 1894, oil on canvas (68.3 x 91.5 cm), Helen Birch Bartlett Memorial Collection, 1926. Photograph © 1994, The Art Institute of Chicago. All rights reserved.

1. **The decline of small, traditional communities.** Modernity involves "the progressive weakening, if not destruction, of the . . . relatively cohesive communities in which human beings have found solidarity and meaning throughout most of history" (Berger 1977:72). For thousands of years, in hunting and gathering camps and the agrarian villages of Europe and North America, people lived in small-scale communities where social life revolved around family and neighborhood. Such traditional worlds give each person a well-defined place that, although limiting range of choice, offers a strong sense of identity, belonging, and purpose.

   Small, isolated communities still exist in the United States, of course, but they are home to only a small percentage of our nation's people. Even so, cars, telephones, and television give most rural families the pulse of the larger society and connect them to the entire world.

2. **The expansion of personal choice.** Members of traditional, preindustrial societies view their lives as shaped by forces beyond human control—gods, spirits, or, simply, fate. But as the power of tradition erodes, people come to see their lives as a series of options, a process Berger calls *individualization*. Many people in the United States, for example, adopt one "lifestyle" or another, showing an openness to change.

3. **Increasing social diversity.** In preindustrial societies, strong family ties and powerful religious beliefs enforce conformity while discouraging diversity and change. Modernization promotes a more rational, scientific world view as tradition loses its hold and people gain more and more individual choice. The growth of cities, expansion of impersonal bureaucracy, and the social mix of people from various backgrounds combine to foster diverse beliefs and behavior.

4. **Future orientation and growing awareness of time.** While premodern people focus on the past, people in modern societies think more about the future. Modern people are not only forward-looking but optimistic that new inventions and discoveries will improve their lives.

   Modern people also organize their daily routines down to the very minute. With the introduction of clocks in the late Middle Ages, Europeans began to think not in terms of sunlight and seasons but in terms of hours and minutes. Preoccupied with personal gain, modern people demand precise measurement of time and are likely to agree that "Time is money." Berger points out that one good indicator of a society's degree of modernization is the proportion of people wearing wristwatches.

Finally, recall that modernization touched off the development of sociology itself. As Chapter 1 ("The

RESOURCE: Emile Durkheim's "Anomy and Modern Life" and Max Weber's "The Disenchantment of Modern Life" are among the "classics" in the 4th edition of *Seeing Ourselves*.

DISCUSS: Consider the limits of science implied by Leo Tolstoy's observation that "Science is meaningless because it gives no answer to the question, the only question of importance for us: 'What shall we do and how shall we live?'"

DISCUSS: Pose to the class the Weberian irony that the more we learn about the natural world, the more uncertainty we feel about ultimate cause and meaning.

Q: "The bourgeoisie, during its rule of scarcely one hundred years, has created more massive and more colossal productive forces than have all preceding generations together." Karl Marx and Friedrich Engels

Max Weber maintained that the distinctive character of modern society was its rational world view. Virtually all of Weber's work on modernity centered on types of people he considered typical of their age: the scientist, the capitalist, and the bureaucrat. Each is rational to the core: The scientist is committed to the orderly discovery of truth, the capitalist to the orderly pursuit of profit, and the bureaucrat to orderly conformity to a rational system of rules.

Weber studied various modern "types"—the capitalist, the scientist, the bureaucrat—all of whom share the rational world view that Weber believed was coming to dominate humanity.

Critical evaluation. Compared with Tönnies, and especially Durkheim, Weber was critical of modern society. He knew that science could produce technological and organizational wonders, but he worried that science was turning us away from more basic questions about the meaning and purpose of human existence. Weber feared that rationalization, especially in bureaucracies, would erode the human spirit with endless rules and regulations.

Finally, some of Weber's critics think that the alienation he attributed to bureaucracy actually stemmed from social inequality. This criticism leads us to the ideas of Karl Marx.

KARL MARX: CAPITALISM

For Karl Marx, modern society was synonymous with capitalism; he saw the Industrial Revolution as primarily a *capitalist revolution*. Marx traced the emergence of the bourgeoisie in medieval Europe to expanding commerce. The bourgeoisie gradually displaced the feudal aristocracy as the Industrial Revolution placed a powerful new system of production under its control.

Marx agreed that modernity weakened small-scale communities (as described by Tönnies), sharpened the division of labor (as noted by Durkheim), and fostered a rational world view (as Weber claimed). But he saw all these simply as conditions necessary for capitalism to flourish. Capitalism, according to Marx, draws population from farms and small towns into an ever-expanding market system centered in cities; specialization is needed for efficient factories; and rationality is exemplified by the capitalists' relentless pursuit of profit.

Earlier chapters have painted Marx as a spirited critic of capitalist society, but his vision of modernity also has a considerable amount of optimism. Unlike Weber, who viewed modern society as an "iron cage" of bureaucracy, Marx believed that social conflict in capitalist societies would sow seeds of revolutionary change, leading to an egalitarian socialism. Such a society, as he saw it, would harness the wonders of industrial technology to enrich people's lives and also rid the world of social classes, the source of social conflict and dehumanization. While Marx's evaluation of modern capitalist society was highly negative, then, he imagined a future of human freedom, creativity, and community.

Critical evaluation. Marx's theory of modernization is a complex theory of capitalism. But he underestimated the dominance of bureaucracy in modern societies. In socialist societies, in particular, the stifling effects of

TABLE 24–1 Traditional and Modern Societies: The Big Picture

Elements of Society	Traditional Societies	Modern Societies
Cultural Patterns		
Values	Homogeneous; sacred character; few subcultures and countercultures	Heterogeneous; secular character; many subcultures and countercultures
Norms	High moral significance; little tolerance of diversity	Variable moral significance; high tolerance of diversity
Time orientation	Present linked to past	Present linked to future
Technology	Preindustrial; human and animal energy	Industrial; advanced energy sources
Social Structure		
Status and role	Few statuses, most ascribed; few specialized roles	Many statuses, some ascribed and some achieved; many specialized roles
Relationships	Typically primary; little anonymity and privacy	Typically secondary; considerable anonymity and privacy
Communication	Face to face	Face-to-face communication supplemented by mass media
Social control	Informal gossip	Formal police and legal system
Social stratification	Rigid patterns of social inequality; little mobility	Fluid patterns of social inequality; considerable mobility
Gender patterns	Pronounced patriarchy; women's lives centered on the home	Declining patriarchy; increasing number of women in the paid labor force
Economy	Based on agriculture; much manufacturing in the home; little white-collar work	Based on industrial mass production; factories become centers of production; increasing white-collar work
State	Small-scale government; little state intervention in society	Large-scale government; considerable state intervention in society
Family	Extended family as the primary means of socialization and economic production	Nuclear family retains some socialization functions but is more a unit of consumption than of production
Religion	Religion guides world view; little religious pluralism	Religion weakens with the rise of science; extensive religious pluralism
Education	Formal schooling limited to elites	Basic schooling becomes universal, with growing proportion receiving advanced education
Health	High birth and death rates; short life expectancy because of low standard of living and simple medical technology	Low birth and death rates; longer life expectancy because of higher standard of living and sophisticated medical technology
Settlement patterns	Small scale; population typically small and widely dispersed in rural villages and small towns	Large scale; population typically large and concentrated in cities
Social Change	Slow; change evident over many generations	Rapid; change evident within a single generation

bureaucracy turned out to be as bad as—or even worse than—the dehumanizing aspects of capitalism. The recent upheavals in Eastern Europe and the former Soviet Union reveal the depth of popular opposition to oppressive state bureaucracies.

THEORETICAL ANALYSIS OF MODERNITY

The rise of modernity is a complex process involving many dimensions of change, described in previous chapters and summarized in Table 24–1. How can we make sense of so many changes going on all at once? Sociologists have devised two broad explanations of modern society, one guided by the structural-functional paradigm and one based on social-conflict theory.

STRUCTURAL-FUNCTIONAL THEORY: MODERNITY AS MASS SOCIETY

One broad approach—drawing on the ideas of Ferdinand Tönnies, Emile Durkheim, and Max Weber—depicts modernization as the emergence of *mass society* (Dahrendorf, 1959; Kornhauser, 1959; Nisbet, 1966,

GLOBAL: Tourism was all but unknown a century ago; today, the entire world copes with hundreds of millions of tourists. This change is one effect of technological advances.
NOTE: Many large charities ceased collecting at home and began soliciting in the workplace several decades ago, recognizing that people were more responsive to co-workers than to neighbors.
NOTE: The conservative implication of mass-society theory is that

social inequality still persists, but it is not as severe a problem as it was in the 19th century. Instead, the growing state is problematic.
DISCUSS: Most psychiatrists and psychologists agree that our society is witnessing a rise in mild personality disorders. Do you think that the weaker moral structure of today's society, which fails to provide the guidance and support found in earlier times, plays a part in this rise?

1969; Stein, 1972; Berger, Berger, & Kellner, 1974; Pearson, 1993). A **mass society** is *a society in which industry and expanding bureaucracy have eroded traditional social ties.* A mass society is marked by weak kinship and impersonal neighborhoods, so individuals are socially isolated. This isolation, in turn, leaves people feeling morally uncertain and personally powerless.

The Mass Scale of Modern Life

Mass-society theory argues, first, that the scale of modern life has greatly increased. Before the Industrial Revolution, Europe and North America formed a mosaic of countless rural villages and small towns. In these small communities, which inspired Tönnies's concept of *Gemeinschaft*, people lived out their lives surrounded by kin and guided by a shared heritage. Gossip was an informal, yet highly effective, way to ensure conformity to community standards. These small communities, with their strong moral values, tolerated little social diversity—the state of mechanical solidarity described by Durkheim.

For example, before 1690 English law demanded that everyone regularly participate in the Christian ritual of Holy Communion (Laslett, 1984). On this continent, only Rhode Island among the New England colonies tolerated any religious dissent. Because social differences were repressed, subcultures and countercultures rarely arose and change proceeded slowly.

Increasing population, the growth of cities, and specialized economic activity driven by the Industrial Revolution gradually altered this pattern. People came to know one another by their jobs (for example, as "the doctor" or "the bank clerk") rather than by their kinship group or home town. People looked on most others simply as strangers. The face-to-face communication of the village was eventually replaced by the impersonal mass media—newspapers, radio, television, and more recently, computer networks. Large organizations steadily assumed more and more responsibility for seeing to the daily tasks that had once been carried out by family, friends, and neighbors; public education drew more and more people to schools; police, lawyers, and formal courts supervised a formal criminal justice system. Even charity became the work of faceless bureaucrats working for various social welfare agencies.

Geographic mobility, mass communications, and exposure to diverse ways of life all erode traditional values. People become more tolerant of social diversity, defending individual rights and freedom of choice. Subcultures and countercultures multiply. Treating people differently based on their race, sex, or religion comes to be defined as backward and unjust. In the process, minorities at the margin of society gain greater power and broader participation in public life. Yet, mass-society theorists fear that transforming people of various backgrounds into a generic mass may end up dehumanizing everyone.

The Ever-Expanding State

In the small-scale, preindustrial societies of Europe, government amounted to little more than a local noble. A royal family formally reigned over an entire nation, but without efficient transportation or communication, the power of even absolute monarchs fell far short of the power wielded by today's political leaders.

As technological innovation allowed government to expand, the centralized state grew in size and importance. At the time the United States gained independence from Great Britain, the federal government was a tiny organization whose prime function was national defense. Since then, government has entered more and more areas of social life—schooling the population, regulating wages and working conditions, establishing standards for products of all sorts, and offering financial assistance to the ill and the unemployed. To pay for such programs, taxes have soared: Today's average worker labors four months each year just to pay for the broad array of services the government provides.

In a mass society, power resides in large bureaucracies, leaving people in local communities little control over their lives. For example, state officials mandate that local schools must have a standardized educational program, local products must be government certified, and every citizen must maintain extensive tax records. While such regulations may protect people and advance social equality, they also force us to deal more and more with nameless officials in distant and often unresponsive bureaucracies, and they undermine the autonomy of families and neighborhoods.

Critical evaluation. The theory of mass society concedes that the transformation of small-scale communities has positive aspects, but only at the cost of losing our cultural heritage. Modern societies increase individual rights, tolerate greater social differences, and raise standards of living. But they are prone to what Weber feared most—excessive bureaucracy—as well as Tönnies's self-centeredness and Durkheim's anomie. Their size, complexity, and tolerance of diversity all but doom traditional values and family patterns, leaving

Q: "The need for a constantly expanding market for its products chases the bourgeoisie over the whole surface of the globe. It must nestle everywhere, settle everywhere, establish connections everywhere." Karl Marx and Friedrich Engels

Q: "Time is a river of passing events, and its current is strong. No sooner is a thing brought to sight than it is swept by and another takes its place—and this too will be swept away." Marcus Aurelius

Q: "The bourgeoisie . . . has pitilessly torn asunder the motley feudal ties that bound man to his 'natural superiors,' and has left remaining no other nexus between man and man than naked self-interest, than callous 'cash payment.'" Karl Marx and Friedrich Engels

Q: "The major advances in civilization are processes that all but wreck the societies in which they occur." Alfred North Whitehead

individuals isolated, powerless, and materialistic. As Chapter 16 ("Politics and Government") noted, voter apathy has become a serious problem in the United States. But should we be surprised that individuals in vast, impersonal societies think no one person can make a difference?

Critics, however, contend that mass-society theory romanticizes the past. They remind us that many people in small towns were actually eager to set out for the excitement and higher standard of living found in cities. Moreover, mass-society theory ignores problems of social inequality. Critics say this theory attracts social and economic conservatives who defend conventional morality and are indifferent to the historical plight of women and other minorities.

SOCIAL-CONFLICT THEORY: MODERNITY AS CLASS SOCIETY

The second interpretation of modernity derives largely from the ideas of Karl Marx. From a social-conflict perspective, modernity takes the form of a **class society,** *a capitalist society with pronounced social stratification.* That is, while agreeing that modern societies have expanded to a mass scale, this approach views the heart of modernization to be an expanding capitalist economy, rife with inequality (Miliband, 1969; Habermas, 1970; Polenberg, 1980; Blumberg, 1981; Harrington, 1984).

Capitalism

Class-society theory follows Marx in claiming that the increasing scale of social life in modern society results from the insatiable appetite of capitalism. Because a capitalist economy pursues ever-increasing profits, both production and consumption steadily increase.

According to Marx, capitalism rests on "naked self-interest" (Marx & Engels, 1972:337; orig. 1848). This self-centeredness erodes the social ties that once cemented small-scale communities. Capitalism also treats people as commodities: as a source of labor and a market for capitalist products.

Capitalism also supports science, not just as the key to greater productivity but as an ideology that justifies the status quo. That is, modern societies encourage people to view human well-being as a *technical* puzzle to be solved by engineers and other experts rather than through the pursuit of *social* justice (Habermas, 1970). A capitalist culture, for example, seeks to improve health through scientific medicine rather than by eliminating poverty, which threatens many people's health in the first place.

Many people marveled at new industrial technology that was changing the world a century ago. But some, including Norwegian painter Edvard Munch, could see that the social consequences of the Industrial Revolution were not all positive. Looking at Workers on Their Way Home, *which Munch completed in 1915, what do you think are his criticisms of modern industrial society?*

Business also raises the banner of scientific logic, trying to increase profits through greater efficiency. As Chapter 15 ("The Economy and Work") explains, capitalist corporations have reached enormous size and control almost unimaginable wealth as a result of "going global" as multinationals. From the class-society point of view, then, the expanding scale of life is less a function of *Gesellschaft* than the inevitable and destructive consequence of capitalism.

Persistent Inequality

Modernity has gradually worn away the rigid categories that set nobles apart from commoners in preindustrial societies. But class-society theory maintains that elites persist—albeit now as capitalist millionaires rather than nobles born to wealth and power. In the United States, we may have no hereditary monarchy, but the richest 5 percent of the population nevertheless controls half of all property.

What of the state? Mass-society theorists contend that the state works to increase equality and combat social problems. Marx was skeptical that the state could accomplish more than minor reforms because, as he

Q: "Identity is a coherent sense of self. It depends upon the awareness that one's endeavors and one's life make sense, that they are meaningful in the context in which life is lived. It depends also upon stable values, and upon the conviction that one's actions and values are harmoniously related. It is a sense of wholeness, of integration, of knowing what is right and what is wrong and of being able to choose." Alan Wheelis (1958:18)

NOTE: Following Wheelis's argument, we might say that conformity in traditional societies reflects unchanging morality; what we call morality in modern societies is more a matter of conformity to changing public opinion.

NOTE: For mass-society theorists, the essential problem of modernity is *anomie* (as noted by Durkheim); for class-society theorists, it is *alienation* (following Marx).

TABLE 24–2 Two Interpretations of Modernity: A Summary

	Process of Modernization	Effects of Modernization
Mass-Society Theory	Industrialization; growth of bureaucracy	Increasing scale of life; rise of the state and other formal organizations
Class-Society Theory	Rise of capitalism	Expansion of the capitalist economy; persistence of social inequality

saw it, the real power lies in the hands of capitalists who control the economy. Other class-society theorists add that, to the extent that working people and minorities do have greater political rights and enjoy a higher standard of living today, these changes are the fruits of political struggle, not expressions of government goodwill. In short, they conclude, despite our pretensions of democracy, most people are all but powerless in the face of wealthy elites.

Critical evaluation. Table 24–2 summarizes the interpretations of modernity offered by mass-society theory and class-society theory. While the former focuses on the increasing scale of life and the growth of government, the latter stresses the expansion of capitalism and the persistence of inequality.

Class-society theory also dismisses Durkheim's argument that people in modern societies suffer from anomie, claiming instead that they suffer from alienation and powerlessness. Not surprisingly, then, the class-society interpretation of modernity enjoys widespread support among liberals (and radicals) who favor greater equality and call for extensive regulation (or abolition) of the capitalist marketplace.

A basic criticism of class-society theory is that it overlooks the many ways that equality in modern societies has increased. For example, discrimination based on race, ethnicity, and gender is now illegal and widely regarded as a social problem. Further, most people in the United States favor unequal rewards, at least insofar as they reflect differences in personal talent and effort.

Moreover, few observers think a centralized economy would cure the ills of modernity in light of socialism's failure to generate a high overall standard of living. Many other problems in the United States—from unemployment, homelessness, and industrial pollution to unresponsive government—are also found in socialist nations such as the former Soviet Union.

MODERNITY AND THE INDIVIDUAL

Both mass- and class-society theories look at the broad societal changes that have taken place since the Industrial Revolution. But from these macro-level approaches we can also draw micro-level insights into how modernity shapes individual lives.

Mass Society: Problems of Identity

Modernity liberated individuals from small, tightly knit communities of the past. Most people in modern societies, therefore, have privacy and freedom to express their individuality. Mass-society theory suggests, however, that extensive social diversity, isolation, and rapid social change make it difficult for people to establish any coherent identity at all (Wheelis, 1958; Riesman, 1970; Berger, Berger, & Kellner, 1974).

Chapter 5 ("Socialization") explained that people's personalities are largely a product of their social experiences. The small, homogeneous, and slowly changing societies of the past provided a firm (if narrow) foundation for building a meaningful identity. Even today, the Amish communities that flourish in the United States and Canada teach young men and women "correct" ways to think and behave. Not everyone born into an Amish community can tolerate strict demands for conformity, but most members establish a well-integrated and satisfying personal identity (cf. Hostetler, 1980; Kraybill & Olshan, 1994).

Mass societies, socially diverse and rapidly changing, offer only shifting sands on which to build a personal identity. Left to make many life decisions on their own, many people—especially those with greater affluence—face a bewildering range of options. Choice has little value without standards to guide our selections, and in a tolerant mass society, people may find one path no more compelling than the next. Not surprisingly, many people shuttle from one identity to another, changing their lifestyle, relationships, and even religion in search of an elusive "true self." Beset by the widespread "relativism" of modern societies, people without a moral compass lack the security and certainty once provided by tradition.

To David Riesman (1970; orig. 1950), modernization brings changes in **social character**, *personality patterns common to members of a particular society*. Preindustrial societies foster what Riesman calls **tradition-directedness**, *rigid conformity to time-honored ways of living*. Members of traditional societies model their

NOTE: David Reisman used the term "social character" to mean "mode of conformity." Tradition-direction is conformity based on categorical memberships; inner-direction (not addressed in this chapter) is conformity to inwardly held values in the absence of strong tradition; other-direction is conformity to one's contemporaries.

NOTE: In cross-national research, David John Frank et al. (1994) concludes that societies placing a great deal of emphasis on individualism have a much higher proportion of psychologists and psychiatrists.

NOTE: The "lonely crowd" thesis includes the argument that the family has lost its socialization function to schools, various specialists, and the mass media, prompting more other-direction in children.

Mass-society theory attributes feelings of anxiety, isolation, and lack of meaning in the modern world to rapid social change that washes away tradition. Edvard Munch captured this vision of modern emptiness in his painting The Scream. *Class-society theory, by contrast, ties such feelings to social inequality, by which some categories of people have power and privileges denied to others. Paul Marcus portrays modern injustice in the painting* Musical Chairs.

Edvard Munch, *The Scream*, Oslo, National Gallery (left); © Paul Marcus, *Musical Chairs*, oil painting on wood, 48 in. × 72 in. (right).

lives on those of their ancestors, so that living the "good life" amounts to "doing what our people have always done."

Tradition-directedness corresponds to Tönnies's *Gemeinschaft* and Durkheim's mechanical solidarity. Culturally conservative, tradition-directed people think and act alike. Unlike the conformity sometimes found in modern societies, the uniformity of tradition-directedness is not an effort to mimic one another. Instead people are alike because they all draw on the same solid cultural foundation. Amish women and men exemplify tradition-directedness; in Amish culture, tradition ties everyone to ancestors and descendants in an unbroken chain of righteous living.

Members of diverse and rapidly changing societies define a tradition-directed personality as deviant because it seems so rigid. Modern people, by and large, prize personal flexibility and sensitivity to others. Riesman describes this type of social character as **other-directedness,** *a receptiveness to the latest trends and fashions, often expressed in the practice of imitating others.* Because their socialization occurs within societies that are constantly in flux, other-directed people develop fluid identities marked by superficiality, inconsistency, and change. They try on different "selves," almost like so many pieces of new clothing, seek out "role models,"

and engage in varied "performances" as they move from setting to setting (Goffman, 1959). In a traditional society, such "shiftiness" makes a person untrustworthy, but in a changing, modern society, the chameleon-like ability to fit in virtually anywhere is very useful.

In societies that value the up-to-date rather than the traditional, people anxiously solicit the approval of others, looking to members of their own generation rather than to elders as significant role models. "Peer pressure" can be irresistible to people with no enduring standards to guide them. Our society urges individuals to be true to themselves. But when social surroundings change so rapidly, how can people develop the self to which they should be true? This problem lies at the root of the identity crisis so widespread in industrial societies today. "Who am I?" is a nagging question that many of us struggle to answer. In truth, this problem is not so much psychological as sociological, reflecting the inherent instability of modern mass society.

Class Society: Problems of Powerlessness

Class-society theory paints a different picture of modernity's effects on individuals. This approach maintains that persistent social inequality undermines modern society's promise of individual freedom. For some,

RESOURCE: Georg Simmel's classic about modernity, "The Metropolis and Mental Life," is included in the Macionis and Benokraitis reader, *Seeing Ourselves*.

NOTE: Maureen T. Hallinan (1997) suggests that we begin thinking about social change without assuming that trends are continuous and linear in an effort to better explain "dramatic social upheavals."

Q: "The people who are always hankering loudest for some golden yesteryear usually drive new cars." Russell Baker

DISCUSS: We often describe changes in shorthand terms—for instance, the "activist 1960s" or the "go-go and greedy 1980s." How do students characterize recent decades of our history?

NOTE: Humorist Mark Twain claimed the opposite of progress was Congress.

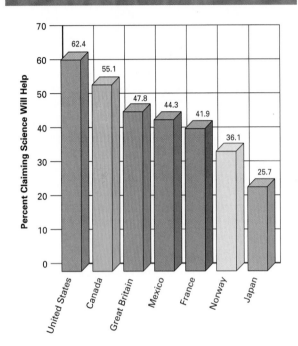

GLOBAL SNAPSHOT

FIGURE 24–1 Support for Science: A Global Survey

Survey Question: "In the long run, do you think the scientific advances we are making will help or harm humankind?"

Source: *World Values Survey* (1994).

modernity serves up great privilege, but, for many, everyday life means coping with economic uncertainty and a gnawing sense of powerlessness (Newman, 1993).

For minorities, the problem of relative disadvantage looms even larger. Similarly, although women enjoy increasing participation in modern societies, they continue to run up against traditional barriers of sexism. In short, this approach rejects mass-society theory's claim that people suffer from too much freedom. Instead, class-society theory holds that our society still denies a majority of people full participation in social life.

On a global scale, as Chapter 11 ("Global Stratification") explained, the expanding scope of world capitalism has placed more of the earth's population in the shadow of multinational corporations. As a result, more than half of the world's income is concentrated

in the rich, industrial nations, where only 15 percent of its people live. Is it any wonder, class-society theorists ask, that people in poor nations seek greater power to shape their own lives?

The problem of widespread powerlessness led Herbert Marcuse (1964) to challenge Max Weber's statement that modern society is rational. Marcuse condemned modern society as irrational for failing to meet the needs of so many people. While modern capitalist societies produce unparalleled wealth, poverty remains the daily plight of more than a billion people. Moreover, Marcuse argues, technological advances further reduce people's control over their own lives. High technology confers great power on a core of specialists—not the majority of people—who now control events and dominate the public agenda, whether the issue is computing, energy production, or health care. Countering the common view that technology *solves* the world's problems, Marcuse believed that science actually *causes* them. In sum, class-society theory claims that people suffer because modern, scientific societies concentrate both wealth and power in the hands of a privileged few.

MODERNITY AND PROGRESS

In modern societies, most people expect—and applaud—social change. We link modernity to the idea of *progress* (from Latin, meaning "moving forward"), a state of continual improvement. At the same time, we see stability as stagnation.

This chapter began by describing the Kaiapo of Brazil, for whom affluence has expanded opportunities but weakened traditional heritage. In studying the Kaiapo, we see that social change, with all its beneficial and detrimental consequences, is too complex simply to equate with progress.

More precisely, whether or not we see a given change as progress depends on our values. A rising standard of living among the Kaiapo—or, historically, among people in the United States—has helped make lives longer and more comfortable. In global context, as Figure 24–1 shows, the U.S. population has considerable confidence in science to improve our lives. But surveys also show that many adults in the United States also feel that science "makes our way of life change too fast" (NORC, 1996:325).

Social change, then, is both complex and controversial. We in the United States are proud of our pursuit of basic human rights, for example. Yet, as Chapter 3 ("Culture") explained, we now have something of a "culture of rights" that emphasizes our freedoms but

Q: "Change is one thing, progress is another. Change is scientific; progress is ethical; change is indubitable, whereas progress is a matter of controversy." Bertrand Russell

GLOBAL: "Honor" in medieval Europe, "wa" in Japan, and "dharma" in India all express the power of the community to direct the thoughts and behavior of individuals. With modernization, all have tended to erode in favor of "dignity," "choice," and "individual rights."

DISCUSS: Honor is a matter of specific status; dignity is generically human. One loses honor by violating normative roles; one loses dignity by giving up (or giving away) autonomy. Discuss the differences between "dying with honor" and "dying with dignity."

NOTE: Another implication of the loss of traditional honor in modern societies is the decline of public civility.

SOCIOLOGY OF EVERYDAY LIFE

Whatever Happened to Honor?

Honor occupies about the same place in contemporary usage as chastity. An individual asserting it hardly invites admiration, and one who claims to have lost it is an object of amusement rather than sympathy. (1974:83)

Honor is a human virtue that seems out of place in modern society. Honor refers to acting in accordance with traditional cultural norms. Since norms used to be quite different for various categories of people, men claimed honor by acting in masculine ways and women by being feminine. Honor, in short, is acting like the category of person you are in a world that rigidly distinguishes between females and males, nobles and serfs, family and outsiders.

Through observing the rules, everyone can claim honor. During the Middle Ages, European nobles acted honorably when they fulfilled their feudal obligations to protect "commoners" and showed proper respect to other aristocrats. Similarly, commoners acted honorably by fulfilling their duties to the nobles and observing common decency to each other. Honorable men followed the cultural ideal by taking a fatherly, protective role toward women

and never "taking advantage" of them. For their part, honorable women observed proper morals and manners in the presence of men.

With modernization, cultural norms have become weaker and more variable, and categorical distinctions among people have been challenged by drives for social equality. Modern culture holds that all people should treat others as equals. Therefore, although the concept of honor survives in some ethnic communities and traditional occupations

like the military, it has less appeal for most of us.

But modernization does increase our concern for people as *individuals*, which we describe with the concept of *dignity*. Whereas various categories of people have distinctive codes of honor, dignity is a universal statement that all people have inherent value. We recognize the dignity of others by acknowledging our common humanity and ignoring social differences.

In the spirit of modern individualism, women may object to men's treating them as *women* rather than as *people*. The traditional male practice of holding open a door for a woman or paying for a shared meal may bring the man honor, but today's women may view such behavior as an affront to their dignity.

As a result, honor is fading from industrial societies. The cultural diversity and rapid social change sweeping across the modern world call into question all traditional scripts for living. In contrast to codes of honor that guided people in the past, human beings now value individual self-worth and self-determination—the essence of dignity.

Source: Based on Berger, Berger, & Kellner (1974).

tends to overlook our obligations to others. The box sharpens the distinction between obligations and rights by contrasting the traditional concept of honor with the modern idea of dignity.

In principle, almost everyone in our society supports the idea that individuals should have considerable autonomy in shaping their own lives. Thus, many people applaud the decline of traditional codes of honor as a sign of progress. Yet, as people exercise their freedom of choice, they inevitably challenge

social patterns cherished by those who maintain a more traditional way of life. For example, people may choose not to marry, to live with someone without marrying, perhaps even to form a partnership with someone of their own sex. To those who support individual choice, such changes symbolize progress; to those who value traditional family patterns, however, these developments signal societal decline.

New technology, too, provokes controversy. More rapid transportation and more efficient communication

NOTE: Postmodernism recognizes that, with the onset of the Information Revolution, ideas are gaining in importance as things decline in significance (New Age thinking as well as fundamentalist religious revival are examples). Such a change prompts us to look critically at the emphasis on material possessions that came with modern, industrial culture.

Q: "'Postmodernism' usually refers to a certain constellation of styles and tones in cultural works; pastiche; blankness; a sense of exhaustion; a mixture of levels, forms, styles; a relish for copies and repetitions; a knowingness that dissolves commitment into irony; acute self-consciousness about the constructed nature of the work; pleasure in the play of surfaces; a rejection of history." Todd Gitlin ("Postmodernism: Roots and Politics," *Dissent*, Winter 1989:100–8)

In today's world, people can find new ways to express age-old virtues such as concern for their neighbors. Habitat for Humanity, an organization with chapters in cities and towns across the United States, is made up of people who want to lend a helping hand to those in need. This Washington, D.C., chapter is helping local families realize their dream of owning a home.

may improve our lives in many ways. But complex technology has also weakened traditional attachments to hometowns and even to families. Moreover, industrial technology has unleashed an unprecedented threat to the natural environment. In short, we all know that social change comes faster all the time, but we may disagree about whether a particular change is progress or a step backwards.

MODERNITY: GLOBAL VARIATION

`October 1, 1994, Kobe, Japan.` Riding the computer-controlled monorail high above the streets of Kobe or the 200-mile-per-hour bullet train to Tokyo, we see Japan as the society of the future, in love with high technology. Yet the Japanese remain strikingly traditional in other respects: Few corporate executives and almost no senior politicians are women; young people still accord seniors considerable respect; and public orderliness contrasts with the turmoil of U.S. cities.

Japan is a nation at once traditional and modern. This contradiction reminds us that, while it is useful to contrast traditional and modern societies, the old and the new often coexist in unexpected ways. In the People's Republic of China, ancient Confucian principles are mixed with contemporary socialist thinking. Similarly, in Mexico and much of Latin America, people observe centuries-old Christian rituals even as they struggle to move ahead economically.

The description of Brazil's Kaiapo that opened this chapter points up the tension that typically accompanies the introduction of modern social patterns in a traditional society. The broader point is that combinations of traditional and modern patterns are far from unusual—indeed, they are found throughout the world.

POSTMODERNITY

If modernity was the product of the Industrial Revolution, is the Information Revolution creating a postmodern era? A number of scholars think so, and use the term **postmodernity** to refer to *social patterns characteristic of a postindustrial society.*

Precisely what postmodernism is remains a matter of debate. The term has been used for decades in literary, philosophical, and even architectural circles. It moved into sociology on a wave of social criticism that has been building since the spread of left-leaning politics in the 1960s. Although there are many variants of postmodern thinking, all share the following five themes (Bernstein, 1992; Borgmann, 1992; Crook, Pakulski, & Waters, 1992; Hall & Neitz, 1993):

1. **In important respects, modernity has failed.** The promise of modernity was a life free from want. As postmodernist critics see it, however, the twentieth century was unsuccessful in solving social problems like poverty and providing everyone with financial security.

2. **The bright light of "progress" is fading.** Modern people look to the future, expecting that their lives will improve in significant ways. Members (even leaders) of postmodern societies, however, are less confident about what the future holds. Furthermore, the buoyant optimism that carried society into the modern era more than a century ago has given way to stark pessimism; most U.S. adults think life is getting worse (NORC, 1996:190).

3. **Science no longer holds the answers.** The defining trait of the modern era was a scientific outlook and a confident belief that

DISCUSS: Other postmodern changes include: the collapse of culture into various "lifestyles"; the dissolution of social stratification into a mosaic of class and gender and racial categories; weakening political parties; the rise of smaller organizational work groups, suggesting the erosion of traditional bureaucracy; weakening faith in science. (Cf. Stephen Crook, Jan Pakulski, and Malcolm Waters, *Postmodernization: Change in Advanced Societies*, Thousand Oaks,

Calif.: Sage, 1992)

Q: "We must become the change we want to see." Mahatma Ghandi

THEN AND NOW: Is the United States the greatest country in the world? Answering "yes," *1955:* 66%; *1995:* 37% (Russell, 1995b).

Q: "A man cannot get rich if he takes care of his family." Navajo saying

CRITICAL THINKING

The United States: A Nation in Decline?

Asked what was his greatest concern about the future of his country, U.S. novelist Walker Percy responded:

Probably the fear of seeing America, with all its great strength and beauty and freedom . . . gradually subside into decay and be defeated . . . from within by weariness, boredom, cynicism, greed and in the end helplessness before its great problems. . . .

Are we, in fact, a nation in decline? William Bennett (U.S. Secretary of Education between 1985 and 1988) points out that, by some measures, the United States is thriving. Between 1960 and 1995, for example, economic output tripled and median family income (controlled for inflation) climbed by more than one-third. During the same period, the official poverty rate dropped by half.

Nonetheless, Bennett thinks other indicators of well-being paint a very different—and disturbing—picture of life in the United States at the end of this century. Between 1960 and 1995, violent crime shot up fourfold; the number of children born to single mothers as well as the number of children supported by welfare rose more than fivefold; the divorce rate doubled; and teen suicide tripled. Television viewing has increased by 35 percent and College Board scores have fallen by an average of seventy-five points.

Government spending (in constant dollars) rose fivefold between 1960 and 1995, even as our population increased by just 45 percent. Clearly, then, a wide range of serious social problems continues to plague the United States despite (or, possibly, because of) government efforts to address them. As a result, Bennett concludes that our nation's decline is primarily moral—a matter of weakening individual character:

Our society now places less value than before on what we owe to others as a matter of moral obligation; less value on sacrifice as a moral good; less value on social conformity and respectability; and less value on correctness and restraint in matters of physical pleasure and sexuality.

Our current dilemma—that even as we make government bigger and more powerful, many social problems are getting worse—rests on the fact that government, even at its best, can do little to build individual character. Bennett continues:

Our social institutions—families, churches, schools, neighborhoods, and civic associations—have traditionally taken on the responsibility of providing our children with love, order, and discipline—of teaching self-control, compassion, tolerance, civility, honesty, and respect for authority. . . . The social regression of the past thirty years is due in large part to the enfeebled state of our social institutions and their failure to carry out these critical and time-honored tasks.

From Bennett's point of view, the primary values of any society are set not by government but by people living in communities and, especially, by families raising their children. In effect, he concludes, we must not assume that affluence is the best—or even the only—measure of a society's well-being. Moreover, we cannot afford to ignore—nor can we hand over to the government our basic responsibility to sustain civilization.

Source: Based on Bennett (1993) and various data sources.

technology would make life better. But postmodern critics contend that science has not solved many old problems (like poor health) and has even created new problems (such as degrading the environment).

More generally, postmodernist thinkers discredit the very foundation of science: that objective reality and truth exist at all. Reality amounts to so much "social construction," they say; moreover, we can "deconstruct"

NOTE: For a summary of the proliferation of rights, look back at the box about the culture of victimization in Chapter 3, page 72.

Q: Communitarians are "people committed to creating a new moral, social, and political order based on restored communities, without allowing puritanism or oppression." Amitai Etzioni

DISCUSS: Etzioni maintains that U.S. moral revival is possible without the new puritanism of the right or the danger of totalitarianism

from the left. While he believes that family is vital, he supports women's equal access to the workplace. He also proposes that schools teach morality, but with no indoctrination.

Q: Mahatma Gandhi notes seven great dangers to human virtue: wealth without work; pleasure without conscience; knowledge without character; business without ethics; science without humanity; religion without sacrifice; politics without principle.

CONTROVERSY & DEBATE

Personal Freedom and Social Responsibility: Can We Have It Both Ways?

Shortly after midnight on a crisp March evening in 1964, a car pulled to a stop in the parking lot of a New York apartment complex. Kitty Genovese turned off the headlights, locked the doors of her vehicle, and headed across the blacktop toward the entrance to her building. Moments from safety, she was attacked by a man wielding a knife; as she shrieked in terror, he stabbed her repeatedly. Windows opened above, as curious neighbors searched for the cause of the commotion. But the attack continued—for more than thirty minutes—until Genovese lay dead in the doorway. The police never identified her assailant but they did discover a stunning fact: *Not one of dozens of neighbors who witnessed the attack on Kitty Genovese went to her aid or even called police.*

More than any other event in recent decades, the Genovese tragedy forced us to confront the question of what we owe

others. Members of modern societies prize their individual rights and personal privacy, sometimes to the point of withdrawing from public responsibility and turning a cold shoulder to people in need. When a cry for help is met by indifference, have we pushed our modern idea of personal autonomy too far? In a cultural climate of expanding individual rights, can we sustain a sense of human community?

These questions point up the tension between traditional and modern social systems, which we can see in the writings of all the sociologists discussed in this chapter. Tönnies, Durkheim, and others concluded that, in some respects, traditional community and modern individualism are incompatible. That is, society can unite its members in a moral community but only to the extent that it limits their range of personal choices about how to live. In short, while we

value both community and autonomy, we can't have it both ways.

In recent years, sociologist Amitai Etzioni (1993, 1996) has tried to strike a middle ground. The "communitarian movement" rests on the simple premise that "strong rights presume strong responsibilities." Or, put otherwise, an individual's pursuit of self-interest must be balanced by a commitment to the larger community.

As Etzioni sees it, modern people have become too concerned with individual rights. That is, people expect the system to work for them, but they are reluctant to support the system. For example, while we believe in the principle of trial by a jury of one's peers, fewer and fewer people today are willing to perform jury duty; similarly, the public is quick to accept government services, but reluctant to pay for these services with taxes.

---

science to see how it has been widely used for political purposes, especially by powerful segments of society.

4. **Cultural debates are intensifying.** Modernity was to be an era of enhanced individuality and expanding tolerance. But it has fallen short here as well. Feminism points out that patriarchy continues to limit the lives of women, and multiculturalism seeks to empower minorities who remain at the margins of social life.

5. **Social institutions are changing.** Just as industrialization brought sweeping transformation to social institutions, the rise of a postindustrial society is remaking society all over again. For example, just as the Industrial Revolution placed *material things* at the center of productive life, now the Information Revolution emphasizes

ideas. Similarly, the postmodern family no longer conforms to any singular pattern; on the contrary, individuals are choosing among many new family forms.

Critical evaluation. Analysts who claim that the United States and other high-income societies are entering a postmodern era criticize modernity for failing to meet human needs. Yet few think that modernity has failed completely; after all, we have seen marked increases in longevity and living standards over the course of this century. Moreover, even if we accepted postmodernist views that science is bankrupt and progress is a sham, what are the alternatives?

Finally, many voices offer very different understandings of recent social trends. The box on page 645 provides one case in point.

NOTE: After the Genovese murder, the *New York Times* asked, "Does residence in a great city destroy all sense of personal responsibility for one's neighbors?"

DISCUSS: What do changes in popular magazines suggest about social change? In the 1950s, *Life* was big; by 1974, *People* was out; by 1979, *Self* was launched; in 1986, *Child*. Does this trend show a narrowing of our interests?

Q: "So the journey is over and I am back again where I started, richer by much experience and poorer by many exploded convictions, many perished certainties. . . . Those who like to feel they are always right and to attach a high importance to their own opinions should stay at home. When one is traveling, convictions are mislaid as easily as spectacles; but, unlike spectacles, they are not easily replaced." Aldous Huxley, *Jesting Pilate*

Specifically, the communitarians advance four proposals to balance individual rights and public responsibilities. First, our society should halt the expanding "culture of rights" by which people put their own interests ahead of social responsibility (nothing in the Constitution allows us to do whatever we want to). Second, communitarians remind us, all rights involve responsibilities (we cannot simply take from society without giving something back). Third, there are certain responsibilities that no one is free to ignore (such as upholding the law and protecting the natural environment). And, fourth, defending some community interests may require limiting individual rights (protecting public safety, for example, might mean subjecting workers to drug tests).

The communitarian movement appeals to many people who, along with Etzioni, seek to balance personal freedom with social responsibility. But critics have attacked this initiative from both sides of the political spectrum. To those on the left, problems such as voter apathy and street crime cannot be solved with some vague notion of "social reintegration." Instead, we need expanded government programs to ensure equality in U.S. society. Specifically, these critics say, we must curb the political influence of the rich and actively combat racism and sexism.

Conservatives on the political right also find fault with Etzioni's proposals, but for different reasons (cf. Pearson, 1995). To these critics, the communitarian movement amounts to little more than a rerun of the leftist agenda of the 1960s. That is, the communitarian vision of a good society favors liberal goals (such as protecting the environment) but skims over conservative goals such as allowing prayer in school or restoring the strength of traditional families. Moreover, conservatives ask whether a free society should permit the kind of social engineering that Etzioni advocates to build social responsibility (such as institutionalizing anti-prejudice programs in schools and requiring people to perform a year of national service).

Perhaps, as Etzioni himself has suggested, the fact that both the left and the right find fault with his views shows that he has found a moderate, sensible answer to a serious problem. But it may also be that, in a society as diverse as the United States, people will not readily agree on what they owe to themselves—or each other.

Continue the debate . . .

1. *Have you ever failed to come to the aid of someone in need or danger? Why?*

2. *President Kennedy admonished us to "Ask not what your country can do for you, ask what you can do for your country." Do you think people today support this idea? What makes you think so?*

3. *Do you agree or disagree that our society needs to balance rights with more responsibility? Explain your position.*

LOOKING AHEAD: MODERNIZATION AND OUR GLOBAL FUTURE

Back in Chapter 1, we imagined the entire world reduced to a village of 1,000 people. About 150 residents of this "global village" live in high-income countries, while about half the people receive less than ideal nourishment. Most seriously, 200 people are so poor that they are at risk for their lives.

Chapter 11 ("Global Stratification") presented two competing views of why 1 billion people the world over are poor. *Modernization theory* claims that in the past the entire world was poor and that technological change, especially the Industrial Revolution, enhanced human productivity and raised living standards. From this point of view, the solution to global poverty is to promote technological development in poor nations.

For reasons suggested earlier, however, global modernization may be difficult. Recall that David Riesman portrayed preindustrial people as *tradition-directed* and likely to resist change. So modernization theorists advocate that the world's rich societies help poor countries to grow economically. Specifically, industrial nations can export technology to poor regions, welcome students from abroad, and provide foreign aid to stimulate economic growth.

The discussion of modernization theory in Chapter 11 points to some limited success with policies in Latin America and, especially, in the small Asian countries of Taiwan, South Korea, Singapore, and Hong Kong. But jump-starting development in the poorest countries of the world poses greater challenges. And even where dramatic change has occurred, modernization entails a tradeoff. Traditional people, such as Brazil's Kaiapo, may acquire wealth through economic

Q: "While I take inspiration from the past, like most Americans, I live for the future." Former President Ronald Reagan (1992)
Q: "The road leading out from our bewilderment and despair is of course political." Olof Palme
Q: "The powerful play goes on, and you and I may contribute a verse." Walt Whitman
Q: "Only the wisest and the stupidest do not change." Confucius

Q: "Somewhere ages and ages hence:
Two roads diverged in a wood, and I—
I took the one less traveled by,
And that has made all the difference."
Robert Frost
Q: "Nobody makes a greater mistake than he who does nothing because he could only do a little." Edmund Burke

development, but they lose their cultural identity and values as they are drawn into global "McCulture," which is based on Western materialism, pop music, trendy clothes, and fast food. One Brazilian anthropologist expressed hope about the future of the Kaiapo: "At least they quickly understood the consequences of watching television. . . . Now [they] can make a choice" (Simons, 1998:495).

But not everyone thinks that modernization is really an option. According to a second approach to global stratification, *dependency theory*, today's poor societies have little ability to modernize, even if they want to. From this point of view, the major barrier to economic development is not traditionalism but global domination by rich, capitalist societies. Initially, this dominance took the form of colonialism whereby European societies seized much of Latin America, Africa, and Asia. Trade relationships soon enriched England, Spain, and other colonial powers, and their colonies became poorer and poorer. Almost all societies that were colonized are now politically independent, but colonial-style ties continue in the form of multinational corporations operating throughout the world.

In effect, dependency theory asserts that rich nations achieved their modernization at the expense of poor ones, by plundering poor nations' natural resources and exploiting their human labor. Even today, the world's poorest countries remain locked in a disadvantageous economic relationship with rich nations, dependent on wealthy countries to buy their raw materials and in return provide them with whatever manufactured products they can afford. Overall, dependency theorists conclude, ties with rich societies only perpetuate current patterns of global inequality.

Whichever approach one finds more convincing, we can no longer isolate changes in the United States from those in the rest of the world. At the beginning of the twentieth century, most people in today's high-income countries lived in relatively small settlements with limited awareness of the larger world. Now, at the threshold of the twenty-first century, the entire world has become one human village because the lives of all people are increasingly linked.

The century now coming to a close has witnessed unprecedented human achievement. Yet solutions to many problems of human existence—including finding meaning in life, resolving conflicts between nations, and eradicating poverty—have eluded us. To this list of pressing matters new concerns have been added, such as controlling population growth and establishing a sustainable society by living in harmony with the natural environment. In the next century, we must be prepared to tackle such problems with imagination, compassion, and determination. Our unprecedented understanding of human society gives us reason to look to the task ahead with optimism.

SUMMARY

1. Every society changes continuously, although at varying speeds. Social change often generates controversy.

2. Social change results from invention, discovery, and diffusion as well as social conflict.

3. Modernity refers to the social consequences of industrialization, which, according to Peter Berger, include the erosion of traditional communities, expanding personal choice, increasingly diverse beliefs, and a keen awareness of the future.

4. Ferdinand Tönnies described modernization as the transition from *Gemeinschaft* to *Gesellschaft*, which signifies the progressive loss of community amid growing individualism.

5. Emile Durkheim saw modernization as a function of a society's expanding division of labor. Mechanical solidarity, based on shared activities and beliefs, gradually gives way to organic solidarity, in which specialization makes people interdependent.

6. According to Max Weber, modernity replaces tradition with a rational world view. Weber feared the dehumanizing effects of rational organization.

7. Karl Marx saw modernity as the triumph of capitalism over feudalism. Viewing capitalist societies as fraught with social conflict, Marx advocated revolutionary change to achieve a more egalitarian, socialist society.

8. According to mass-society theory, modernity increases the scale of life, enlarging the role of government and other formal organizations in carrying out tasks previously performed by family members and neighbors. Cultural diversity and rapid social change make it difficult for people in modern societies to develop stable identities and to find meaning in their lives.

9. Class-society theory states that capitalism is central to Western modernization. This approach charges that, by concentrating wealth in the hands of a

few, capitalism generates widespread feelings of powerlessness.

10. Social change is too complex and controversial simply to be equated with social progress.

11. Postmodernity refers to cultural traits of postindustrial societies. Postmodern criticism of society centers on the failure of modernity, and specifically science, to fulfill its promise of prosperity and well-being.

12. In a global context, modernization theory links global poverty to the power of tradition. Therefore, some modernization theorists advocate intentional intervention by rich societies to stimulate the economic development of poor nations.

13. Dependency theory explains global poverty as the product of the world economic system. The operation of multinational corporations ensures that poor nations will remain economically dependent on rich nations.

KEY CONCEPTS

social change the transformation of culture and social institutions over time

modernity social patterns linked to industrialization

modernization the process of social change initiated by industrialization

mass society a society in which industry and expanding bureaucracy have eroded traditional social ties

class society a capitalist society with pronounced social stratification

social character personality patterns common to members of a particular society

tradition-directedness rigid conformity to time-honored ways of living

other-directedness a receptiveness to the latest trends and fashions, often expressed in the practice of imitating others

postmodernity social patterns characteristic of postindustrial societies

CRITICAL-THINKING QUESTIONS

1. How well do you think Tönnies, Durkheim, Weber, and Marx predicted the character of modern society? How do their visions of modernity differ?

2. What traits lead some to call the United States a "mass society"? Why do other analysts describe the United States as a "class society"?

3. What is the difference between *anomie* (a trait of mass society) and *alienation* (a characteristic of class society)? Among which categories of the U.S. population would you expect each to be pronounced?

4. What developments lead some analysts to say the United States has become a postmodern society?

LEARNING EXERCISES

1. Have you an elderly relative or friend? If asked, most older people will be happy to tell you about the social changes they have seen in their lifetimes.

2. Ask people in your class to make five predictions about U.S. society in the year 2050, when today's twenty-year-olds will be senior citizens. Compare notes: On what issues is there agreement?

3. If you have computer access, install the CD-ROM packaged inside the back cover of your text and complete the activities designed to accompany this chapter.

4. Visit the Web site for the Communitarian Network at http://www.gwu.edu/~ccps/ Explore the changes this organization is seeking and how they propose to achieve them.

5. Finally, on a personal note, I hope this book has helped you and will be a useful resource for courses later on. Please feel free to send an e-mail message (macionis@kenyon.edu) with your thoughts and suggestions. And, yes, I *will* write back!

PART V
NEW INFORMATION TECHNOLOGY AND SOCIAL CHANGE

Chapter 3 ("Culture") presented William Ogburn's (1964) concept of *cultural lag*, the pattern by which some elements of culture change faster than others. Usually, Ogburn explained, technology changes fastest; getting used to new technology, on the other hand, takes people much longer. This cultural pattern of "lagging behind" probably explains why we use old terminology to describe new developments, such as measuring the "horsepower" of gasoline engines or, more recently, exploring the "superhighway" of cyberspace (Newmann, 1991).

The fact that developments in science and technology outpace our ability to comprehend them makes many people uneasy about social change. In a national survey, about 40 percent of U.S. adults agreed with the statement: "One trouble with science is that it makes our way of life change too fast" (NORC, 1996:325). But most people are more optimistic, expecting that new technology will improve our lives.

The reason that many people see social change as both bad and good is that change disrupts established social patterns while creating new possibilities. This final Cyber.Scope highlights how the computer age is altering the shape of cities, forming new kinds of human communities, and bringing people together in new ways to form social movements.

The New Shape of Cities

The metropolis, as Chapter 21 ("Population and Urbanization") explains, stands as the greatest monument to the Industrial Era. A

century ago, factories full of huge machines offered jobs that drew people from across the countryside to form cities of unprecedented size. Industrial metropolises such as New York, Chicago, Philadelphia, and Detroit churned with activity, and new buildings of mortar, steel, and glass stretched skyward.

These cities became busier and denser as industrial technology centralized people. Businesses fused together into a "central business district," where executives and managers could easily establish face-to-face communication. Factories, too, were situated together near rivers and railroads, which brought them fuel and raw materials and took away their finished products.

The industrial cities of the United States reached their peak populations by 1950, just as scientists were building the first computers. Computer technology helped push the economy from industry to service and information work, and this shift spurred the decentralization of cities. Population began radiating farther away from the central city so that, by 1970, most city-dwellers were actually living in suburbs. Businesses followed suit, deserting the downtowns for industrial parks and outlying shopping malls.

Why have the old central cities lost much of their attraction? One important reason is that, in the business world, having a central city address is no longer so important. That is, with new information technology, people can communicate efficiently without working in the same area. Thus, the new shape of cities is sprawling and decentralized, with

cities growing "out" more than "up." The urban scene at the end of the twentieth century includes swelling suburbs and rapidly growing "edge cities"—clusters of office buildings, shopping malls, hotels, and entertainment complexes miles from the old "downtowns."

Change in the shape of cities highlights, once again, one of the most important consequences of new information technology: Physical distance no longer separates people the way it used to. Thus, people who work together do not need to share an office building or even to live in the same city. The other side of the same coin is that, in the cyber-age, we may not pay very much attention to the people who are—physically speaking—all around us. In short, new information technology is forming new kinds of human communities while eroding older ones.

The Rise of Virtual Communities

Consider some dramatic changes taking place at Dartmouth College, in Hanover, New Hampshire, one of the country's most academically competitive schools and a college at the forefront of the Information Revolution. Ever since all dormitory rooms were hooked up to the college's computer network—sometimes called the "one plug per pillow" model—life on campus has not been the same. In the cyber-age, students such as Arthur Desrosiers have discovered that they have fewer and fewer reasons to leave their rooms. Desrosiers, a Dartmouth sophomore, relies on his

650

NOTE: Sunbelt cities, which came of age in the postindustrial era, continue to increase in population (see Table 21–2).
DIVERSITY: A positive effect of cyber-education is helping students who, because they speak English as a second language or are simply shy, avoid speaking up in class. These students are usually comfortable using e-mail to contact faculty and other students.
DISCUSS: Does e-mail allow students more access to faculty? Or less, since face-to-face contact is less common? What differences can students see in the range and content of personal conversations versus cyber-conversations?
CYBER: Computer technology has made many recent social movements global in scope. The French Revolution of 1789, by contrast, was limited to people in personal contact with one another, and was carried out entirely within the city of Paris.

computer to browse the college library, write papers, ask questions of his professors, send notes to his girlfriend, keep up with old high school friends, and even order pizza while joining in 2:00 A.M. online bull sessions. Perhaps strangest of all, Desrosiers often fires messages back and forth to his two roommates, who happen to be staring silently at screens of their own just a few feet away in the same room!

It may be another sign of the times that a once-popular restaurant just down the street from dorms that house 3,000 students has closed its doors. Similarly, the student union is far less busy than it was just a few years ago. There, some of the space once used for socializing now accommodates—you guessed it—computer terminals for students who want to check their e-mail between classes.

At Dartmouth, computers have never been more popular. All together, the 8,000 students, faculty, and staff send and receive some 250,000 messages each day. No one doubts that new information technology has expanded the possibilities for accessing more information than ever before and contacting people almost anywhere in the world. But, some people are beginning to see that an older form of local community is being lost in the process. Some faculty worry that they see less and less of their students. And some students are beginning to think that they ought to see more of each other. As senior Abigail Butler puts it, "I know people who sit home Friday and Saturday night and e-mail back and forth to people they only know by nicknames, while the rest of the world is going by. After a while it starts to be really unfulfilling. It's easier to just meet someone in person and actually talk . . ." (Gabriel, 1996).

Social Movements: New Ways to Connect

New ways to connect with people means a rising potential for starting and expanding social movements. Today, anyone with an interest in some issue and a computer can make contact, ask questions, and spread ideas—in short, play a role in intentional social change. In addition, computers offer access to almost unlimited information, through countless Web pages posted by organizations and individuals with programs for change.

Perhaps most important, computer technology has made it easy to make connections on a global scale. Take the students at the Redemptorist Vocational School in Pattaya, Thailand. These young men and women have physical disabilities, which, before the Information Age, might have kept them from learning at all. But using their school's computers, the students have established contact with hundreds of other people with disabilities in dozens of countries, including the United States. From these contacts, and from visiting the Web sites of national and international organizations representing people with disabilities, the students have received a rich education, indeed. They have been surprised to learn that many countries have laws that protect people with disabilities from discrimination and that mandate access ramps for sidewalks and buildings; they have discovered that cities abroad feature buses that "kneel" to permit entry by people in wheelchairs, as well as public restrooms designed to accommodate everyone. Armed with their new knowledge, the students at the Redemptorist Vocational School are now taking the lead in their own country, using the Internet to educate people about disabilities and lobbying government officials to make changes in Thailand's laws.

The Internet represents a powerful communication resource for anyone. But it is especially important for people whose ability to make contact with others is otherwise limited, including people with disabilities. As one Thai student reports, "On the 'Net, I don't feel like a handicapped person" (Smolan & Erwitt, 1996:150). And even though computer access is far from equal in the United States and around the world, the Internet is providing more and more people in poor countries with the power of a "global reach."

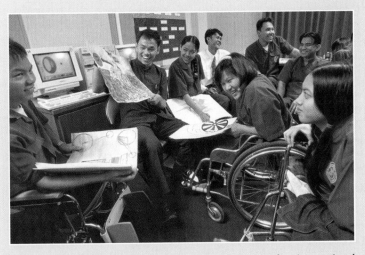

With access to the Internet, these Thai students have joined an international social movement to advance the opportunities of people with disabilities.

GLOSSARY

absolute poverty a deprivation of resources that is life-threatening

achieved status a social position that someone assumes voluntarily and that reflects personal ability and effort

acid rain precipitation, made acidic by air pollution, that destroys plant and animal life

activity theory the proposition that a high level of activity enhances personal satisfaction in old age

Afrocentrism the dominance of African cultural patterns

ageism prejudice and discrimination against the elderly

age-sex pyramid a graphic representation of the age and sex of a population

age stratification the unequal distribution of wealth, power, and privilege among people at different stages of the life course

agriculture the technology of large-scale farming using plows harnessed to animals or more powerful sources of energy

alienation the experience of isolation and misery resulting from powerlessness

animism the belief that elements of the natural world are conscious forms of life that affect humanity

anomie Durkheim's term for a condition in which society provides little moral guidance to individuals

anticipatory socialization social learning directed toward gaining a desired position

ascribed status a social position that someone receives at birth or assumes involuntarily later in life

assimilation the process by which minorities gradually adopt patterns of the dominant culture

authoritarianism a political system that denies popular participation in government

authority power that people perceive as legitimate rather than coercive

beliefs specific statements that people hold to be true

bilateral descent a system tracing kinship through both men and women

blue-collar occupations lower-prestige work involving mostly manual labor

bureaucracy an organizational model rationally designed to perform complex tasks efficiently

bureaucratic inertia the tendency of bureaucratic organizations to perpetuate themselves

bureaucratic ritualism a preoccupation with rules and regulations to the point of thwarting an organization's goals

capitalism an economic system in which natural resources and the means of producing goods and services are privately owned

capitalists people who own factories and other productive enterprises

caste system a system of social stratification based on ascription

cause and effect a relationship in which change in one variable (the independent variable) causes change in another (the dependent variable)

charisma extraordinary personal qualities that can turn an audience into followers

charismatic authority power legitimized through extraordinary personal abilities that inspire devotion and obedience

church a type of religious organization well integrated into the larger society

civil religion a quasi-religious loyalty binding individuals in a basically secular society

class conflict antagonism between entire classes over the distribution of wealth and power in society

class consciousness Marx's term for the recognition by workers of their unity as a social class in opposition to capitalists and to capitalism itself

class society a capitalist society with pronounced social stratification

class system a system of social stratification based largely on individual achievement

cohabitation the sharing of a household by an unmarried couple

cohort a category of people with a common characteristic, usually their age

collective behavior activity involving a large number of people, often spontaneous, and usually in violation of established norms

collectivity a large number of people whose minimal interaction occurs in the absence of well-defined conventional norms

colonialism the process by which some nations enrich themselves through political and economic control of other countries

communism a hypothetical economic and political system in which all members of a society are socially equal

concept a mental construct that represents some part of the world, inevitably in a simplified form

concrete operational stage Piaget's term for the level of human development at which individuals first perceive causal connections in their surroundings

conglomerate a giant corporation composed of many smaller corporations

control holding constant all variables except one in order to clearly see its effect

corporation an organization with a legal existence, including rights and liabilities, apart from its members

correlation a relationship in which two (or more) variables change together

counterculture cultural patterns that strongly oppose those widely accepted within a society

credentialism evaluating a person on the basis of educational degrees

crime the violation of norms a society formally enacts into criminal law

crimes against the person (violent crimes) crimes that direct violence or the threat of violence against others

crimes against property (property crimes) crimes that involve theft of property belonging to others

criminal justice system a formal response to alleged violations of the law on the part of police, courts, and prison officials

criminal recidivism subsequent offenses by people previously convicted of crimes

crowd a temporary gathering of people who share a common focus of attention and whose members influence one another

crude birth rate the number of live births in a given year for every thousand people in a population

crude death rate the number of deaths in a given year for every thousand people in a population

cult a religious organization that is substantially outside a society's cultural traditions

cultural conflict political opposition, often accompanied by social hostility, rooted in different cultural values

cultural ecology a theoretical paradigm that explores the relationship of human culture and the natural environment

cultural integration the close relationship among various elements of a cultural system

cultural lag the fact that cultural elements change at different rates, which may disrupt a cultural system

cultural relativism the practice of judging a culture by its own standards

cultural transmission the process by which one generation passes culture to the next

cultural universals traits that are part of every known culture

culture the values, beliefs, behavior, and material objects that constitute a people's way of life

culture shock personal disorientation that comes from experiencing an unfamiliar way of life

Davis-Moore thesis the assertion that social stratification is a universal pattern that has beneficial consequences for the operation of a society

deductive logical thought reasoning that transforms general ideas into specific hypotheses suitable for scientific testing

democracy a political system in which power is exercised by the people as a whole

demographic transition theory a thesis linking population patterns to a society's level of technological development

demography the study of human population

denomination a church, independent of the state, that accepts religious pluralism

dependency theory a model of economic and social development that explains global inequality in terms of the historical exploitation of poor societies by rich societies

dependent variable a variable that is changed by another (independent) variable

descent the system by which members of a society trace kinship over generations

deterrence the attempt to discourage criminality through punishment

deviance the recognized violation of cultural norms

direct-fee system a medical-care system in which patients pay directly for the services of physicians and hospitals

discrimination treating various categories of people unequally

disengagement theory the proposition that society enhances its orderly operation by disengaging people from positions of responsibility as they reach old age

division of labor specialized economic activity

dramaturgical analysis Erving Goffman's term for the investigation of social interaction in terms of theatrical performance

dyad a social group with two members

dysfunctions (*see* social dysfunction)

eating disorder an intense form of dieting or other kind of weight control in pursuit of being very thin

ecclesia a church that is formally allied with the state

ecologically sustainable culture a way of life that meets the needs of the present generation without threatening the environmental legacy of future generations

ecology the study of the interaction of living organisms and the natural environment

economy the social institution that organizes the production, distribution, and consumption of goods and services

ecosystem a system composed of the interaction of all living organisms and their natural environment

education the social institution guiding a society's transmission of knowledge—including basic facts, job skills, and also cultural norms and values—to its members

ego Freud's designation of a person's conscious efforts to balance innate pleasure-seeking drives with the demands of society

empirical evidence information we can verify with our senses

endogamy marriage between people of the same social category

environmental deficit profound and negative long-term harm to the natural environment caused by humanity's focus on short-term material affluence

environmental racism the pattern by which environmental hazards are greatest in proximity to poor people, especially minorities

ethnicity a shared cultural heritage

ethnocentrism the practice of judging another culture by the standards of one's own culture

ethnomethodology Harold Garfinkel's term for the study of the way people make sense of their everyday lives

Eurocentrism the dominance of European (particularly English) cultural patterns

euthanasia (mercy killing) assisting in the death of a person suffering from an incurable disease

exogamy marriage between people of different social categories

experiment a research method for investigating cause and effect under highly controlled conditions

expressive leadership group leadership that emphasizes collective well-being

extended family (consanguine family) a family unit including parents and children, but also other kin

fad an unconventional social pattern that people embrace briefly but enthusiastically

faith belief anchored in conviction rather than scientific evidence

false consciousness Marx's term for explanations of social problems in terms of the shortcomings of individuals rather than the flaws of society

family a social institution, found in all societies, that unites individuals into cooperative groups that oversee the bearing and raising of children

family unit a social group of two or more people, related by blood, marriage, or adoption, who usually live together

family violence emotional, physical, or sexual abuse of one family member by another

fashion a social pattern favored by a large number of people

feminism the advocacy of social equality for men and women, in opposition to patriarchy and sexism

feminization of poverty the trend by which women represent an increasing proportion of the poor

fertility the incidence of childbearing in a country's population

folkways a society's customs for routine, casual interaction

formal operational stage Piaget's term for the level of human development at which individuals think abstractly and critically

formal organization a large secondary group organized to achieve its goals efficiently

functional illiteracy reading and writing skills insufficient for everyday living

fundamentalism a conservative religious doctrine that opposes intellectualism and worldly accommodation in favor of restoring a traditional, otherworldly spirituality

Gemeinschaft a type of social organization by which people are bound closely together by kinship and tradition

gender the significance that members of a society attach to being female or male

gender roles (sex roles) attitudes and activities that a society links to each sex

gender stratification a society's unequal distribution of wealth, power, and privilege between men and women

generalized other George Herbert Mead's term for the general cultural norms and values shared by us and others that we use as a point of reference in evaluating ourselves

genocide the systematic annihilation of one category of people by another

gerontocracy a form of social organization in which the elderly have the most wealth, power, and prestige

gerontology the study of aging and the elderly

Gesellschaft a type of social organization by which people come together only on the basis of individual self-interest

global economy economic activity spanning many nations of the world with little regard for national borders

global perspective the study of the larger world and our society's place in it

gossip rumor about people's personal affairs

government a formal organization that directs the political life of a society

greenhouse effect a rise in the earth's average temperature (global warming) due to an increasing concentration of carbon dioxide in the atmosphere

groupthink the tendency of group members to conform by adopting a narrow view of some issue

hate crime a criminal act against a person or person's property by an offender motivated by racial or other bias

Hawthorne effect a change in a subject's behavior caused simply by the awareness of being studied

health a state of complete physical, mental, and social well-being

health maintenance organization (HMO) an organization that provides comprehensive medical care to subscribers for a fixed fee

hermaphrodite a human being with some combination of female and male genitalia

hidden curriculum subtle presentations of political or cultural ideas in the classroom

high culture cultural patterns that distinguish a society's elite

high-income countries industrial nations in which most people have an abundance of material goods

holistic medicine an approach to health care that emphasizes prevention of illness by taking account of a person's entire physical and social environment

homogamy marriage between people with the same social characteristics

horticulture technology based on using hand tools to cultivate plants

humanizing bureaucracy fostering a more democratic organizational atmosphere that recognizes and encourages the contributions of everyone

hunting and gathering simple technology for hunting animals and gathering vegetation

hypothesis an unverified statement of a relationship between variables

id Freud's designation of the human being's basic drives

ideal culture (as opposed to real culture) social patterns mandated by cultural values and norms

ideal type an abstract statement of the essential characteristics of any social phenomenon

ideology cultural beliefs that serve to justify social stratification

incest taboo a cultural norm forbidding sexual relations or marriage between certain kin

income wages or salaries from work and earnings from investments

independent variable a variable that causes change in another (dependent) variable

inductive logical thought reasoning that transforms specific observations into general theory

industrialism technology that powers sophisticated machinery with advanced sources of energy

infant mortality rate the number of deaths among infants under one year of age for each thousand live births in a given year

ingroup a social group commanding a member's esteem and loyalty

institutional prejudice or discrimination bias in attitudes or action inherent in the operation of society's institutions

instrumental leadership group leadership that emphasizes the completion of tasks

intergenerational social mobility upward or downward social mobililty of children in relation to their parents

interview a series of questions a researcher administers in person to respondents

intragenerational social mobility a change in social position occurring within a person's lifetime

juvenile delinquency the violation of legal standards by the young

kinship a social bond, based on blood, marriage, or adoption, that joins individuals into families

labeling theory the assertion that deviance and conformity result, not only from what people do, but from how others respond to those actions

labor unions worker organizations that seek to improve wages and working conditions through various strategies, including negotiation and strikes

language a system of symbols that allows members of a society to communicate with one another

latent functions the unrecognized and unintended consequences of a social pattern

liberation theology a fusion of Christian principles with political activism, often Marxist in character

life expectancy the average life span of a society's population

looking-glass self Cooley's term for the image people have of themselves based on how they suppose others perceive them

low-income countries nations with little industrialization in which severe poverty is the rule

macro-level orientation a focus on broad social structures that shape society as a whole

mainstreaming integrating special students into the overall educational program

manifest functions the recognized and intended consequences of a social pattern

marriage a legally sanctioned relationship, involving economic cooperation as well as normative sexual activity and childbearing, that people expect to be enduring

Marxist political-economy model an analysis that explains politics in terms of the operation of a society's economic system

mass behavior collective behavior among people dispersed over a wide geographical area

mass hysteria a form of dispersed collective behavior by which people react to a real or imagined event with irrational, frantic, and often self-destructive behavior

mass media impersonal communications directed toward a vast audience

mass society a society in which industry and expanding bureaucracy have eroded traditional social ties

master status a status that has exceptional importance for social identity, often shaping a person's entire life

material culture the tangible things created by members of a society

matriarchy a form of social organization in which females dominate males

matrilineal descent a system tracing kinship through women

matrilocality a residential pattern in which a married couple lives with or near the wife's family

mean the arithmetic average of a series of numbers

measurement the process of determining the value of a variable in a specific case

mechanical solidarity Durkheim's term for social bonds, based on shared morality, that unite members of preindustrial societies

median the value that occurs midway in a series of numbers arranged in order of magnitude or, simply, the middle case

medicalization of deviance the transformation of moral and legal issues into medical matters

medicine a social institution concerned with combating disease and improving health

megalopolis a vast urban region containing a number of cities and their surrounding suburbs

meritocracy a system of social stratification based on personal merit

metropolis a large city that socially and economically dominates an urban area

micro-level orientation a focus on patterns of social interaction in specific situations

middle-income countries nations with limited industrialization and moderate personal income

migration the movement of people into and out of a specified territory

military-industrial complex the close association among the federal government, the military, and defense industries

minority any category of people, set apart by physical or cultural difference, that is socially disadvantaged

miscegenation biological reproduction by partners of different racial categories

mob a highly emotional crowd that pursues a violent or destructive goal

mode the value that occurs most often in a series of numbers

modernity social patterns linked to industrialization

modernization the process of social change initiated by industrialization

modernization theory a model of economic and social development that explains global inequality in terms of technological and cultural differences among societies

monarchy a political system in which a single family rules from generation to generation

monogamy a form of marriage joining two partners

monopoly domination of a market by a single producer

monotheism belief in a single divine power

mores a society's standards of proper moral conduct

mortality the incidence of death in a country's population

multiculturalism an educational program recognizing past and present cultural diversity in U.S. society and promoting the equality of all cultural traditions

multinational corporation a large corporation that operates in many countries

natural environment the earth's surface and atmosphere, including various living organisms, air, water, soil, and other resources necessary to sustain life

neocolonialism a new form of global power relationships that involves not direct political control but economic exploitation by multinational corporations

neolocality a residential pattern in which a married couple lives apart from the parents of both spouses

network a web of social ties that links people who identify and interact little with one another

nonmaterial culture the intangible world of ideas created by members of a society

nonverbal communication communication using body movements, gestures, and facial expressions as opposed to speech

norms rules and expectations by which a society guides the behavior of its members

nuclear family (conjugal family) a family unit composed of one or two parents and their children

nuclear proliferation the acquisition of nuclear-weapons technology by more and more nations

objectivity a state of personal neutrality in conducting research

oligarchy the rule of the many by the few

oligopoly domination of a market by a few producers

operationalize a variable specifying exactly what one is to measure in assigning a value to a variable

organic solidarity Durkheim's term for social bonds, based on specialization, that unite members of industrial societies

organizational environment a range of factors external to an organization that affects its operation

other-directedness a receptiveness to the latest trends and fashions, often expressed in the practice of imitating others

outgroup a social group toward which one feels competition or opposition

panic a form of localized collective behavior by which people react to a threat or other stimulus with irrational, frantic, and often self-destructive behavior

paradigm, see theoretical paradigm

participant observation a method by which researchers systematically observe people while joining in their routine activities

pastoralism technology that supports the domestication of animals

patriarchy a form of social organization in which males dominate females

patrilineal descent a system tracing kinship through men

patrilocality a residential pattern in which a married couple lives with or near the husband's family

peer group a social group whose members have interests, social position, and age in common

personality a person's fairly consistent patterns of thinking, feeling, and acting

personal space the surrounding area to which an individual makes some claim to privacy

plea bargaining a legal negotiation in which the state reduces a defendant's charge in exchange for a guilty plea

pluralism a state in which racial and ethnic minorities are distinct but have social parity

pluralist model an analysis of politics that views power as dispersed among many competing interest groups

political action committee (PAC) an organization formed by a special-interest group, independent of political parties, to pursue political aims by raising and spending money

political revolution the overthrow of one political system in order to establish another

politics the social institution that distributes power, sets a society's agenda, and makes decisions

polyandry a form of marriage uniting one female with two or more males

polygamy a form of marriage uniting three or more people

polygyny a form of marriage uniting one male with two or more females

polytheism belief in many gods

popular culture cultural patterns that are widespread among a society's population

population the people who are the focus of research

positivism an approach to understanding the world based on science

postindustrial economy a productive system based on service work and extensive use of information technology

postindustrialism technology that supports an information-based economy

postmodernity social patterns characteristic of postindustrial societies

power the ability to achieve desired ends despite resistance

power-elite model an analysis of politics that views power as concentrated among the rich

prejudice a rigid and irrational generalization about an entire category of people

preoperational stage Piaget's term for the level of human development in which individuals first use language and other symbols

presentation of self an individual's effort to create specific impressions in the minds of others

primary group a small social group in which relationships are both personal and enduring

primary labor market occupations that provide extensive benefits to workers

primary sector the part of the economy that generates raw materials directly from the natural environment

primary sex characteristics the genitals, organs used to reproduce the human species

profane that which is defined as an ordinary element of everyday life

profession a prestigious white-collar occupation that requires extensive formal education

proletariat people who provide the labor necessary to operate factories and other productive enterprises

propaganda information presented with the intention of shaping public opinion

qualitative research investigation in which a researcher gathers impressionistic, not numerical, data

quantitative research investigation in which a researcher collects numerical data

questionnaire a series of written questions that a researcher presents to subjects

race a category composed of people who share biologically transmitted traits that members of a society deem socially significant

racism the belief that one racial category is innately superior or inferior to another

rain forests regions of dense forestation, most of which circle the globe close to the equator

rationality deliberate, matter-of-fact calculation of the most efficient means to accomplish a particular goal

rationalization of society Weber's term for the historical change from tradition to rationality as the dominant mode of human thought

rational-legal authority (also **bureaucratic authority**) power legitimized by legally enacted rules and regulations

real culture (as opposed to ideal culture) actual social patterns that only approximate cultural expectations

reference group a social group that serves as a point of reference in making evaluations or decisions

rehabilitation a program for reforming the offender to prevent subsequent offenses

relative deprivation a perceived disadvantage arising from a specific comparison

relative poverty the deprivation of some people in relation to those who have more

reliability consistency in measurement

religion a social institution involving beliefs and practices based upon a conception of the sacred

religiosity the importance of religion in a person's life

replication repetition of research by other investigators

research method a systematic plan for conducting research

resocialization radically altering an inmate's personality through deliberate manipulation of the environment

retribution an act of moral vengeance by which society inflicts suffering on an offender comparable to that caused by the offense

riot a social eruption that is highly emotional, violent, and undirected

ritual formal, ceremonial behavior

role behavior expected of someone who holds a particular status

role conflict incompatibility among roles corresponding to two or more statuses

role set a number of roles attached to a single status

role strain incompatibility among roles corresponding to a single status

routinization of charisma the transformation of charismatic authority into some combination of traditional and bureaucratic authority

rumor unsubstantiated information spread informally, often by word of mouth

sacred that which is defined as extraordinary, inspiring a sense of awe, reverence, and even fear

sample a part of a population researchers select to represent the whole

Sapir-Whorf thesis the thesis that people perceive the world through the cultural lens of language

scapegoat a person or category of people, typically with little power, whom people unfairly blame for their own troubles

schooling formal instruction under the direction of specially trained teachers

science a logical system that bases knowledge on direct, systematic observation

secondary analysis a research method in which a researcher uses data collected by others

secondary group a large and impersonal social group devoted to some specific interest or activity

secondary labor market jobs that provide minimal benefits to workers

secondary sector the part of the economy that transforms raw materials into manufactured goods

secondary sex characteristics bodily development, apart from the genitals, that distinguishes biologically mature females and males

sect a type of religious organization that stands apart from the larger society

secularization the historical decline in the importance of the supernatural and the sacred

segregation the physical and social separation of categories of people

self George Herbert Mead's term for a dimension of personality composed of an individual's self-awareness and self-image

sensorimotor stage Piaget's term for the level of human development in which individuals experience the world only through sensory contact

sex the biological distinction between females and males

sexism the belief that one sex is innately superior to the other

sex ratio the number of males for every hundred females in a given population

sexual harassment comments, gestures, or physical contact of a sexual nature that are deliberate, repeated, and unwelcome

sexual orientation an individual's preference in terms of sexual partners: same sex, other sex, either sex, neither sex

sick role patterns of behavior defined as appropriate for those who are ill

social change the transformation of culture and social institutions over time

social character personality patterns common to members of a particular society

social conflict struggle between segments of society over valued resources

social-conflict paradigm a framework for building theory that sees society as an arena of inequality that generates conflict and change

social construction of reality the process by which people creatively shape reality through social interaction

social control various means by which members of a society encourage conformity to norms

social dysfunction the undesirable consequences of any social pattern for the operation of society

social epidemiology the study of how health and disease are distributed throughout a society's population

social function the consequences of any social pattern for the operation of society

social group two or more people who identify and interact with one another

social institution a major sphere of social life, or societal subsystem, organized to meet a basic human need

social interaction the process by which people act and react in relation to others

socialism an economic system in which natural resources and the means of producing goods and services are collectively owned

socialization the lifelong social experience by which individuals develop human potential and learn patterns of their culture

socialized medicine a health-care system in which the government owns and operates most medical facilities and employs most physicians

social mobility change in people's position in a social hierarchy

social movement organized activity that encourages or discourages social change

social stratification a system by which a society ranks categories of people in a hierarchy

social structure relatively stable patterns of social behavior

societal protection a means by which society renders an offender incapable of further offenses temporarily through incarceration or permanently by execution

society people who interact in a defined territory and share culture

sociobiology a theoretical paradigm that explores ways in which biology affects how humans create culture

sociocultural evolution the Lenskis' term for the changes that occur as a society gains new technology

socioeconomic status (SES) a composite ranking based on various dimensions of social inequality

sociology the systematic study of human society

special-interest group a political alliance of people interested in some economic or social issue

spurious correlation an apparent, although false, relationship between two (or more) variables caused by some other variable

state capitalism an economic and political system in which companies are privately owned although they cooperate closely with the government

status a recognized social position that an individual occupies

status consistency the degree of consistency of a person's social standing across various dimensions of social inequality

status set all the statuses a person holds at a given time

stereotype an exaggerated generalization applied to every person in some category

stigma a powerfully negative social label that radically changes a person's self-concept and social identity

structural-functional paradigm a framework for building theory that sees society as a complex system whose parts work together to promote solidarity and stability

structural social mobility a shift in the social position of large numbers of people due more to changes in society itself than to individual efforts

subculture cultural patterns that set apart some segment of a society's population

suburbs urban areas beyond the political boundaries of a city

superego Freud's designation of the operation of culture within the individual in the form of internalized values and norms

survey a research method in which subjects respond to a series of items in a questionnaire or an interview

symbolic-interaction paradigm a framework for building theory that sees society as the product of the everyday interactions of individuals

symbols anything that carries a particular meaning recognized by people who share culture

technology knowledge that a society applies to the task of living in a physical environment

terrorism random acts of violence or the threat of such violence employed by an individual or group as a political strategy

tertiary sector the part of the economy that produces services rather than goods

theoretical paradigm a basic image of society that guides sociological thinking and research

theory a statement of how and why specific facts are related

Thomas theorem W. I. Thomas's assertion that situations we define as real become real in their consequences

total institution a setting in which people are isolated from the rest of society and manipulated by an administrative staff

totalitarianism a political system that extensively regulates people's lives

totem an object in the natural world collectively defined as sacred

tracking the assignment of students to different types of educational programs

tradition sentiments and beliefs passed from generation to generation

traditional authority power legitimized through respect for long-established cultural patterns

tradition-directedness rigid conformity to time-honored ways of living

transsexuals people who feel they are one sex though biologically they are the other

triad a social group with three members

underground economy economic activity involving income that is not reported to the government as required by law

urban ecology the study of the link between the physical and social dimensions of cities

urbanization the concentration of humanity into cities

validity measuring precisely what one intends to measure

values culturally defined standards of desirability, goodness, and beauty that serve as broad guidelines for social living

variable a concept whose value changes from case to case

victimless crimes violations of law in which there are no readily apparent victims

war organized, armed conflict among the people of various societies

wealth the total value of money and other assets, minus outstanding debts

welfare capitalism an economic and political system that combines a mostly market-based economy with government programs to provide for people's basic needs

welfare state a range of government agencies and programs that provides benefits to the population

white-collar crime crimes committed by persons of high social position in the course of their occupations

white-collar occupations higher-prestige work involving mostly mental activity

zero population growth the level of reproduction that maintains population at a steady state

REFERENCES

ABBOTT, ANDREW. *The System of Professions: An Essay on the Division of Expert Labor*. Chicago: University of Chicago Press, 1988.

ABERLE, DAVID F. *The Peyote Religion Among the Navaho*. Chicago: Aldine, 1966.

ABRAHAMSON, PAUL R. "Postmaterialism and Environmentalism: A Comment on an Analysis and a Reappriasal." *Social Science Quarterly*. Vol. 78, No. 1 (March 1997):21–23.

ADELSON, JOSEPH. "Splitting Up." Article on divorce in the Sept 1996 issue of *Commentary*.

ADLER, JERRY. "When Harry Called Sally . . ." *Newsweek* (October 1, 1990):74.

ADORNO, T. W., ET AL. *The Authoritarian Personality*. New York: Harper & Brothers, 1950.

AGUIRRE, BENIGNO E., and E. L. QUARANTELLI. "Methodological, Ideological, and Conceptual-Theoretical Criticisms of Collective Behavior: A Critical Evaluation and Implications for Future Study." *Sociological Focus*. Vol. 16, No. 3 (August 1983):195–216.

AGUIRRE, BENIGNO E., E. L. QUARANTELLI, and JORGE L. MENDOZA. "The Collective Behavior of Fads: Characteristics, Effects, and Career of Streaking." *American Sociological Review*. Vol. 53, No. 4 (August 1988):569–84.

AIDS (1997). Data cited in Gorman, Christine, "When Did AIDS Begin?" *Time* (February 16, 1998):64.

AKERS, RONALD L., MARVIN D. KROHN, LONN LANZA-KADUCE, and MARCIA RADOSEVICH. "Social Learning and Deviant Behavior." *American Sociological Review*. Vol. 44, No. 4 (August 1979):636–55.

ALAM, SULTANA. "Women and Poverty in Bangladesh." *Women's Studies International Forum*. Vol. 8, No. 4 (1985):361–71.

ALBA, RICHARD D. *Italian Americans: Into the Twilight of Ethnicity*. Englewood Cliffs, N.J.: Prentice Hall, 1985.

———. *Ethnic Identity: The Transformation of White America*. Chicago: University of Chicago Press, 1990.

ALBON, JOAN. "Retention of Cultural Values and Differential Urban Adaptation: Samoans and American Indians in a West Coast City." *Social Forces*. Vol. 49, No. 3 (March 1971):385–93.

ALFORD, RICHARD. "The Structure of Human Experience: Expectancy and Affect; The Case of Humor." Unpublished paper, Department of Sociology, University of Wyoming, 1979.

ALLAN, EMILIE ANDERSEN, and DARRELL J. STEFFENSMEIER. "Youth, Underemployment, and Property Crime: Differential Effects of Job Availability and Job Quality on Juvenile and Young Adult Arrest Rates." *American Sociological Review*. Vol. 54, No. 1 (February 1989):107–23.

ALLEN, MICHAEL PATRICK, and PHILIP BROYLES. "Campaign Finance Reforms and the Presidential Campaign Contributions of Wealthy Capitalist Families." *Social Science Quarterly*. Vol. 72, No. 4 (December 1991):738–50.

ALLEN, WALTER R. "African American Family Life in Social Context: Crisis and Hope." *Sociological Forum*. Vol. 10, No. 4 (December 1995):569–92.

ALLSOP, KENNETH. *The Bootleggers*. London: Hutchinson and Company, 1961.

ALTER, JONATHAN. "Down to Business." *Newsweek* (May 12, 1997):58–60.

ALTMAN, DREW, ET AL. "Health Care for the Homeless." *Society*. Vol. 26, No. 4 (May–June 1989):4–5.

AMERICAN COUNCIL ON EDUCATION. "Thirteenth Annual Status Report on Minorities in Higher Education." Washington, D.C.: The Council, 1995.

———. Response to telephone inquiry, 1996.

AMERICAN MEDICAL ASSOCIATION (AMA). Executive Summary of Media Violence Survey Analysis. [Online] Available http://www.ama-assn.org/ad-com/releases/1996/mvan1909.htm, 1997.

AMERICAN SOCIOLOGICAL ASSOCIATION. "Code of Ethics." Washington, D.C.: 1984.

ANDERSON, JOHN WARD. "Early to Wed: The Child Brides of India." *Washington Post* (May 24, 1995):A27, A30.

ANDERSON, JOHN WARD, and MOLLY MOORE. "World's Poorest Women Suffer in Common." *Columbus Dispatch* (April 11, 1993):4G.

ANDO, FAITH H. "Women in Business." In Sara E. Rix, ed., *The American Woman: A Status Report 1990–91*. New York: Norton, 1990:222–30.

ANG, IEN. *Watching Dallas: Soap Opera and the Melodramatic Imagination*. London: Methuen, 1985.

ANGELO, BONNIE. "The Pain of Being Black" (an interview with Toni Morrison). *Time*. Vol. 133, No. 21 (May 22, 1989):120–22.

———. "Assigning the Blame for a Young Man's Suicide." *Time*. Vol. 138, No. 2 (November 18, 1991):12–14.

ANGIER, NATALIE. "Scientists, Finding Second Idiosyncracy in Homosexuals' Brains, Suggest Orientation is Physiological." *New York Times* (August 1, 1992):A7.

APA. *Violence and Youth: Psychology's Response*. Washington, D.C.: American Psychological Association, 1993.

APPLEBOME, PETER. "70 Years After Scopes Trial, Creation Debate Lives." *New York Times* (March 10, 1996):1, 10.

ARCHER, DANE, and ROSEMARY GARTNER. *Violence and Crime in Cross-National Perspective*. New Haven, Conn.: Yale University Press, 1987.

ARENDT, HANNAH. *The Origins of Totalitarianism*. Cleveland, Ohio: Meridian Books, 1958.

———. *Between Past and Future: Six Exercises in Political Thought*. Cleveland, Ohio: Meridian Books, 1963.

ARIÈS, PHILIPPE. *Centuries of Childhood: A Social History of Family Life*. New York: Vintage Books, 1965.

———. *Western Attitudes Toward Death: From the Middle Ages to the Present*. Baltimore, Md.: Johns Hopkins University Press, 1974.

ARJOMAND, SAID AMIR. *The Turban for the Crown: The Islamic Revolution in Iran*. New York: Oxford University Press, 1988.

ARMEY, DICK. "How Taxes Corrupt." *Wall Street Journal* (June 19, 1996):A20.

ASANTE, MOLEFI KETE. *The Afrocentric Idea*. Philadelphia: Temple University Press, 1987.

———. *Afrocentricity*. Trenton, N.J.: Africa World Press, 1988.

ASCH, SOLOMON. *Social Psychology*. Englewood Cliffs, N.J.: Prentice Hall, 1952.

ASHFORD, LORI S. "New Perspectives on Population: Lessons From Cairo." *Population Bulletin*. Vol. 50, No. 1 (March 1995).

ASTONE, NAN MARIE, and SARA S. McLANAHAN. "Family Structure, Parental Practices and High School Completion." *American Sociological Review*. Vol. 56, No. 3 (June 1991):309–20.

ATCHLEY, ROBERT C. "Retirement as a Social Institution." *Annual Review of Sociology*. Vol. 8. Palo Alto, Calif.: Annual Reviews, 1982:263–87.

———. *Aging: Continuity and Change*. Belmont, Calif.: Wadsworth, 1983; 2d ed., 1987.

AUSTER, CAROL J., and MIND MACRONE. "The Classroom as a Negotiated Social Setting: An Empirical Study of the Effects of Faculty Members' Behavior on Students' Participation." *Teaching Sociology*. Vol. 22, No. 4 (October 1994):289–300.

AXTELL, ROGER E. *Gestures: The DOs and TABOOs of Body Language Around the World*. New York: Wiley, 1991.

AYENSU, EDWARD S. "A Worldwide Role for the Healing Powers of Plants." *Smithsonian*. Vol. 12, No. 8 (November 1981):87–97.

BABBIE, EARL. *The Practice of Social Research*. 7th ed. Belmont, Calif.: Wadsworth, 1995.

BACHMAN, RONET. *Violence Against Women*. U.S. Bureau of Justice Statistics. Washington, D.C.: U.S. Government Printing Office, 1994.

BACHRACH, PETER, and MORTON S. BARATZ. *Power and Poverty*. New York: Oxford University Press, 1970.

BACKMAN, CARL B., and MURRAY C. ADAMS. "Self-Perceived Physical Attractiveness, Self-Esteem, Race, and Gender." *Sociological Focus*. Vol. 24, No. 4 (October 1991):283–90.

BAHL, VINAY. "Caste and Class in India." Paper presented to the Southern Sociological Society, Atlanta, April, 1991.

BAILEY, WILLIAM C. "Murder, Capital Punishment, and Television: Execution Publicity and Homicide Rates." *American Sociological Review*. Vol. 55, No. 5 (October 1990):628–33.

BAILEY, WILLIAM C., and RUTH D. PETERSON. "Murder and Capital Punishment: A Monthly Time-Series Analysis of Execution Publicity." *American Sociological Review*. Vol. 54, No. 5 (October 1989):722–43.

BAKER, MARY ANNE, CATHERINE WHITE BERHEIDE, FAY ROSS GRECKEL, LINDA CARSTARPHEN GUGIN, MARCIA J. LIPETZ, and MARCIA TEXLER SEGAL. *Women Today: A Multidisciplinary Approach to Women's Studies*. Monterey, Calif.: Brooks/Cole, 1980.

BAKER, ROSS. "Business as Usual." *American Demographics*. Vol. 19, No. 4 (April 1997):28.

BALES, ROBERT F. "The Equilibrium Problem in Small Groups." In Talcott Parsons et al., eds., *Working Papers in the Theory of Action*. New York: Free Press, 1953:111–15.

BALES, ROBERT F., and PHILIP E. SLATER. "Role Differentiation in Small Decision-Making Groups." In Talcott Parsons and Robert F. Bales, eds., *Family, Socialization and Interaction Process*. New York: Free Press, 1955:259–306.

BALTES, PAUL B., and K. WARNER SCHAIE. "The Myth of the Twilight Years." *Psychology Today*. Vol. 7, No. 10 (March 1974):35–39.

BALTZELL, E. DIGBY. *The Protestant Establishment: Aristocracy and Caste in America*. New York: Vintage Books, 1964.

———. "Introduction to the 1967 Edition." In W. E. B. Du Bois, *The Philadelphia Negro: A Social Study*. New York: Schocken, 1967; orig. 1899.

———, ED. *The Search for Community in Modern America*. New York: Harper & Row, 1968.

———. "The Protestant Establishment Revisited." *The American Scholar*. Vol. 45, No. 4 (Autumn 1976):499–518.

———. *Philadelphia Gentlemen: The Making of a National Upper Class*. Philadelphia: University of Pennsylvania Press, 1979; orig. 1958.

———. *Puritan Boston and Quaker Philadelphia*. New York: Free Press, 1979.

———. "The WASP's Last Gasp." *Philadelphia Magazine*. Vol. 79 (September 1988):104–7, 184, 186, 188.

———. *Sporting Gentlemen: From the Age of Honor to the Cult of the Superstar*. New York: Free Press, 1995.

BANDON, ALEXANDRA. "Longer, Healthier, Better." *New York Times Magazine* (March 9, 1997):44–45.

BANFIELD, EDWARD C. *The Unheavenly City Revisited*. Boston: Little, Brown, 1974.

BARASH, DAVID. *The Whispering Within*. New York: Penguin Books, 1981.

BARKER, EILEEN. "Who'd Be a Moonie? A Comparative Study of Those Who Join the Unification Church in Britain." In Bryan Wilson, ed., *The Social Impact of New Religious Movements*. New York: The Rose of Sharon Press, 1981:59–96.

———. *New Religious Movements: A Practical Introduction*. London: Her Majesty's Stationery Office, 1989.

BARON, JAMES N., BRIAN S. MITTMAN, and ANDREW E. NEWMAN. "Targets of Opportunity: Organizational and Environmental Determinants of Gender Integration Within the California Civil Service, 1979–1985." *American Journal of Sociology*. Vol. 96, No. 6 (May 1991): 1362–1401.

BARONE, MICHAEL, and GRANT UJIFUSA. *The Almanac of American Politics*. Washington, D.C.: Barone and Co., 1981.

BARRY, KATHLEEN. "Feminist Theory: The Meaning of Women's Liberation." In Barbara Haber, ed., *The Women's Annual 1982–1983*. Boston: G. K. Hall, 1983:35–78.

BASSUK, ELLEN J. "The Homelessness Problem." *Scientific American*. Vol. 251, No. 1 (July 1984):40–45.

BAUER, P. T. *Equality, the Third World, and Economic Delusion*. Cambridge, Mass.: Harvard University Press, 1981.

BAYDAR, NAZLI, and JEANNE BROOKS-GUNN. "Effect of Maternal Employment and Child-Care Arrangements on Preschoolers' Cognitive and Behavioral Outcomes: Evidence From Children From the National Longitudinal Survey of Youth." *Developmental Psychology*. Vol. 27 (1991):932–35.

BECKER, HOWARD S. *Outside: Studies in the Sociology of Deviance*. New York: Free Press, 1966.

BEDELL, GEORGE C., LEO SANDON, JR., and CHARLES T. WELLBORN. *Religion in America*. New York: Macmillan, 1975.

BEEGHLEY, LEONARD. *The Structure of Social Stratification in the United States*. Needham Heights, Mass.: Allyn & Bacon, 1989.

BEGLEY, SHARON. "Gray Matters." *Newsweek* (March 7, 1995):48–54.

———. "How to Beat the Heat." *Newsweek* (December 8, 1997):34–38.

BEINS, BARNEY, cited in "Examples of Spuriousness." *Teaching Methods*. No. 2 (Fall 1993):3.

BELL, ALAN P., MARTIN S. WEINBERG, and SUE KIEFER-HAMMERSMITH. *Sexual Preference: Its Development in Men and Women*. Bloomington: Indiana University Press, 1981.

BELL, DANIEL. *The Coming of Post-Industrial Society: A Venture in Social Forecasting*. New York: Basic Books, 1973.

BELLAH, ROBERT N. *The Broken Covenant*. New York: Seabury Press, 1975.

BELLAH, ROBERT N., RICHARD MADSEN, WILLIAM M. SULLIVAN, ANN SWIDLER, and STEVEN M. TIPTON. *Habits of the Heart: Individualism and Commitment in American Life*. New York: Harper & Row, 1985.

BELLAS, MARCIA L. "Comparable Worth in Academia: The Effects on Faculty Salaries of the Sex Composition and Labor-Market Conditions of Academic Disciplines." *American Sociological Review*. Vol. 59, No. 6 (December 1994):807–21.

BELSKY, JAY, RICHARD M. LERNER, and GRAHAM B. SPANIER. *The Child in the Family*. Reading, Mass.: Addison-Wesley, 1984.

BEM, SANDRA LIPSITZ. "Gender Schema Theory: A Cognitive Account of Sex-Typing." *Psychological Review*. Vol. 88, No. 4 (July 1981):354–64.

———. *The Lenses of Gender: Transforming the Debate on Sexual Inequality*. New Haven, Conn.: Yale University Press, 1993.

BENEDICT, RUTH. "Continuities and Discontinuities in Cultural Conditioning." *Psychiatry*. Vol. 1 (May 1938):161–67.

———. *The Chrysanthemum and the Sword: Patterns of Japanese Culture*. New York: New American Library, 1974; orig. 1946.

BENET, SULA. "Why They Live to Be 100, or Even Older, in Abkhasia." *New York Times Magazine* (December 26, 1971):3, 28–29, 31–34.

BENJAMIN, BERNARD, and CHRIS WALLIS. "The Mortality of Widowers." *The Lancet*. Vol. 2 (August 1963):454–56.

BENJAMIN, LOIS. *The Black Elite: Facing the Color Line in the Twilight of the Twentieth Century*. Chicago: Nelson-Hall, 1991.

BENNETT, NEIL G., DAVID E. BLOOM, and PATRICIA H. CRAIG. "The Divergence of Black and White Marriage Patterns." *American Journal of Sociology*. Vol. 95, No. 3 (November 1989):692–722.

BENNETT, STEPHEN EARL. "Left Behind: Exploring Declining Turnout Among Noncollege Young Whites, 1964–1988." *Social Science Quarterly*. Vol. 72, No. 2 (June 1991):314–33.

BENNETT, WILLIAM J. "Quantifying America's Decline." *Wall Street Journal* (March 15, 1993).

———. "Redeeming Our Time." *Imprimis*. Vol. 24, No. 11 (November 1995). Hillsdale, Mich.: Hillsdale College.

———. "School Reform: What Remains to Be Done." *Wall Street Journal* (September 2, 1997):A18.

BENOKRAITIS, NIJOLE, and JOE FEAGIN. *Modern Sexism: Blatant, Subtle, and Overt Discrimination*. 2d ed. Englewood Cliffs, N.J.: Prentice Hall, 1995.

BERARDO, F. M. "Survivorship and Social Isolation: The Case of the Aged Widower." *The Family Coordinator*. Vol. 19 (January 1970):11–25.

BERGAMO, MONICA, and GERSON CAMAROTTI. "Brazil's Landless Millions." *World Press Review*. Vol. 43, No. 7 (July 1996):46–47.

BERGEN, RAQUEL KENNEDY. "Interviewing Survivors of Marital Rape: Doing Feminist Research on Sensitive Topics." In Claire M. Renzetti and Raymond M. Lee, *Researching Sensitive Topics*. Thousand Oaks, Calif.: Sage, 1993.

BERGER, PETER L. *Invitation to Sociology*. New York: Anchor Books, 1963.

———. *The Sacred Canopy: Elements of a Sociological Theory of Religion*. Garden City, N.Y.: Doubleday, 1967.

———. *Facing Up to Modernity: Excursions in Society, Politics, and Religion*. New York: Basic Books, 1977.

———. *The Capitalist Revolution: Fifty Propositions About Prosperity, Equality, and Liberty*. New York: Basic Books, 1986.

BERGER, PETER, BRIGITTE BERGER, and HANSFRIED KELLNER. *The Homeless Mind: Modernization and Consciousness*. New York: Vintage Books, 1974.

BERGER, PETER L., and HANSFRIED KELLNER. *Sociology Reinterpreted: An Essay on Method and Vocation*. Garden City, N.Y.: Anchor Books, 1981.

BERGESEN, ALBERT, ED. *Crises in the World-System*. Beverly Hills, Calif.: Sage, 1983.

BERK, RICHARD A. *Collective Behavior*. Dubuque, Iowa: Wm. C. Brown, 1974.

BERNARD, JESSIE. *The Female World*. New York: Free Press, 1981.

———. *The Future of Marriage*. New Haven, Conn.: Yale University Press, 1982; orig. 1973.

BERNARD, LARRY CRAIG. "Multivariate Analysis of New Sex Role Formulations and Personality." *Journal of Personality and Social Psychology*. Vol. 38, No. 2 (February 1980):323–36.

BERNHARDT, ANNETTE, MARTINA MORRIS, and MARK S. HANDCOCK. "Women's Gains or Men's Losses? A Closer Look at the Shrinking Gender Gap in Earnings." *American Journal of Sociology*. Vol. 101, No. 1 (September 1995):302–28.

BERNSTEIN, NINA. "On Frontier of Cyberspace, Data Is Money, and a Threat." *New York Times* (June 12, 1997):A1, B14–15.

BERNSTEIN, RICHARD J. *The New Constellation: The Ethical-Political Horizons of Modernity/Postmodernity*. Cambridge, Mass.: MIT Press, 1992.

BERRILL, KEVIN T. "Anti-Gay Violence and Victimization in the United States: An Overview." In Gregory M. Herek and Kevin T. Berrill, *Hate Crimes: Confronting Violence Against Lesbians and Gay Men*. Newbury Park, Calif.: Sage, 1992:19–45.

BERRY, BRIAN L., and PHILIP H. REES. "The Factorial Ecology of Calcutta." *American Journal of Sociology*. Vol. 74, No. 5 (March 1969):445–91.

BERSCHEID, ELLEN, and ELAINE HATFIELD. *Interpersonal Attraction*. 2d ed. Reading, Mass.: Addison-Wesley, 1983.

BESHAROV, DOUGLAS J., and LISA A. LAUMANN. "Child Abuse Reporting." *Society*. Vol. 34, No. 4 (May/June 1996):40–46.

BEST, JOEL. "Victimization and the Victim Industry." *Society*. Vol. 34, No. 2 (May/June 1997):9–17.

BEST, RAPHAELA. *We've All Got Scars: What Boys and Girls Learn in Elementary School*. Bloomington: Indiana University Press, 1983.

BIANCHI, SUZANNE M., and DAPHNE SPAIN. "Women, Work, and Family in America." *Population Bulletin*. Vol. 51, No. 3 (December 1996).

———. "U.S. Women Make Workplace Progress." *Population Today*. Vol. 25, No. 1 (January 1997):1–2.

BIBLARZ, TIMOTHY J., and ADRIAN E. RAFTERY. "The Effects of Family Disruption on Social Mobility." *American Sociological Review*. Vol. 58, No. 1 (February 1993):97–109.

BILLSON, JANET MANCINI, and BETTINA J. HUBER. *Embarking Upon a Career With an Undergraduate Degree in Sociology*. 2d ed. Washington, D.C.: American Sociological Association, 1993.

BLANKENHORN, DAVID. *Fatherless America: Confronting Our Most Urgent Social Problem*. New York: HarperCollins, 1995.

BLAU, JUDITH R., and PETER M. BLAU. "The Cost of Inequality: Metropolitan Structure and Violent Crime." *American Sociological Review*. Vol. 47, No. 1 (February 1982):114–29.

BLAU, PETER M. *Exchange and Power in Social Life*. New York: Wiley, 1964.

———. *Inequality and Heterogeneity: A Primitive Theory of Social Structure*. New York: Free Press, 1977.

BLAU, PETER M., TERRY C. BLUM, and JOSEPH E. SCHWARTZ. "Heterogeneity and Intermarriage." *American Sociological Review*. Vol. 47, No. 1 (February 1982):45–62.

BLAU, PETER M., and OTIS DUDLEY DUNCAN. *The American Occupational Structure*. New York: Wiley, 1967.

BLAUSTEIN, ALBERT P., and ROBERT L. ZANGRANDO. *Civil Rights and the Black American*. New York: Washington Square Press, 1968.

BLOOM, LEONARD. "Familial Adjustments of Japanese-Americans to Relocation: First Phase." In Thomas F. Pettigrew, ed., *The Sociology of Race Relations*. New York: Free Press, 1980:163–67.

BLUM, LINDA M. *Between Feminism and Labor: The Significance of the Comparable Worth Movement*. Berkeley: University of California Press, 1991.

BLUMBERG, PAUL. *Inequality in an Age of Decline*. New York: Oxford University Press, 1981.

BLUMER, HERBERT G. "Fashion." In David L. Sills, ed., *International Encyclopedia of the Social Sciences*. Vol. 5. New York: Macmillan and Free Press, 1968:341–45.

———. "Collective Behavior." In Alfred McClung Lee, ed., *Principles of Sociology*. 3d ed. New York: Barnes & Noble Books, 1969:65–121.

BLUMSTEIN, PHILIP, and PEPPER SCHWARTZ. *American Couples*. New York: William Morrow, 1983.

BOBO, LAWRENCE, and VINCENT L. HUTCHINGS. "Perceptions of Racial Group Competition: Extending Blumer's Theory of Group Position to a Multiracial Social Context." *American Sociological Review*. Vol. 61, No. 6 (December 1996):951–72.

BODENHEIMER, THOMAS S. "Health Care in the United States: Who Pays?" In Vicente Navarro, ed., *Health and Medical Care in the U.S.: A Critical Analysis*. Farmingdale, N.Y.: Baywood Publishing Co., 1977:61–68.

BOERNER, CHRISTOPHER, and THOMAS LAMBERT. "Environmental Injustice." *The Public Interest*. Vol. 118 (Winter 1995):61–82.

BOFF, LEONARD and CLODOVIS. *Salvation and Liberation: In Search of a Balance Between Faith and Politics*. Maryknoll, N.Y.: Orbis Books, 1984.

BOGARDUS, EMORY S. "Comparing Racial Distance in Ethiopia, South Africa, and the United States." *Sociology and Social Research*. Vol. 52, No. 2 (January 1968):149–56.

BOHANNAN, CECIL. "The Economic Correlates of Homelessness in Sixty Cities." *Social Science Quarterly*. Vol. 72, No. 4 (December 1991):817–25.

BOHANNAN, PAUL. *Divorce and After*. Garden City, N.Y.: Doubleday, 1970.

BOHM, ROBERT M. "American Death Penalty Opinion, 1936–1986: A Critical Examination of the Gallup Polls." In Robert M. Bohm, ed., *The Death Penalty in America: Current Research*. Cincinnati: Anderson Publishing Co., 1991:113–45.

BOLI, JOHN, and GEORGE M. THOMAS. "World Culture in the World Polity: A Century of International Non-Governmental Organization." *American Sociological Review*. Vol. 62, No. 2 (April 1997):171–90.

BONCZAR, THOMAS P., and ALLAN J. BECK. *Lifetime Likelihood of Going to State or Federal Prison*. Washington, D.C.: U.S. Bureau of Justice Statistics, 1997.

BONILLA-SANTIAGO, GLORIA. "A Portrait of Hispanic Women in the United States." In Sara E. Rix, ed., *The American Woman 1990–91: A Status Report*. New York: Norton, 1990:249–57.

BONNER, JANE. Research presented in "The Two Brains." Public Broadcasting System telecast, 1984.

BOO, KATHERINE. "Two Women, Two Responses to Change." *Washington Post* (December 15, 1996):A1, A28–29.

BOOTH, ALAN, and LYNN WHITE. "Thinking About Divorce." *Journal of Marriage and the Family*. Vol. 42, No. 3 (August 1980):605–16.

BORGMANN, ALBERT. *Crossing the Postmodern Divide*. Chicago: University of Chicago Press, 1992.

BORMANN, F. HERBERT. "The Global Environmental Deficit." *BioScience*. Vol. 40 (1990):74.

BORMANN, F. HERBERT, and STEPHEN R. KELLERT. "The Global Environmental Deficit." In Bormann, F. Herbert and Stephen R. Kellert, eds., *Ecology, Economics, and Ethics: The Broken Circle*. New Haven, Conn.: Yale University Press, 1991:ix–xviii.

BOSWELL, TERRY E. "A Split Labor Market Analysis of Discrimination Against Chinese Immigrants, 1850–1882." *American Sociological Review*. Vol. 51, No. 3 (June 1986):352–71.

BOSWELL, TERRY E., and WILLIAM J. DIXON. "Marx's Theory of Rebellion: A Cross-National Analysis of Class Exploitation, Economic Development, and Violent Revolt." *American Sociological Review*. Vol. 58, No. 5 (October 1993): 681–702.

BOTT, ELIZABETH. *Family and Social Network*. New York: Free Press, 1971; orig. 1957.

BOULDING, ELISE. *The Underside of History*. Boulder, Colo.: Westview Press, 1976.

BOWLES, SAMUEL, and HERBERT GINTIS. *Schooling in Capitalist America: Educational Reform and the Contradictions of Economic Life*. New York: Basic Books, 1976.

BOYER, ERNEST L. *College: The Undergraduate Experience in America*. Prepared by The Carnegie Foundation for the Advancement of Teaching. New York: Harper & Row, 1987.

BRAITHWAITE, JOHN. "The Myth of Social Class and Criminality Reconsidered." *American Sociological Review*. Vol. 46, No. 1 (February 1981):36–57.

BRANEGAN, JAY. "Is Singapore a Model for the West?" *Time*. Vol. 141, No. 3 (January 18, 1993):36–37.

BREEN, LEONARD Z. "The Aging Individual." In Clark Tibbitts, ed., *Handbook of Social Gerontology*. Chicago: University of Chicago Press, 1960:145–62.

BRIGHTMAN, JOAN. "Why Hillary Chooses Rodham Clinton." *American Demographics*. Vol. 16, No. 3 (March 1994):9–11.

BRINTON, CRANE. *The Anatomy of Revolution*. New York: Vintage Books, 1965.

BRINTON, MARY C. "The Social-Institutional Bases of Gender Stratification: Japan as an Illustrative Case." *American Journal of Sociology*. Vol. 94, No. 2 (September 1988):300–34.

BRODER, JOHN M. "Big Social Changes Revive False God of Numbers." *New York Times* (August 17, 1997): section 4, pp. 1, 4.

BROWN, CLAIR, and JOSEPH PECHMAN, eds. *Gender in the Workplace*. Washington, D.C.: Brookings, 1987.

BROWN, LESTER R. "Reassessing the Earth's Population." *Society*. Vol. 32, No. 4 (May–June 1995):7–10.

BROWN, LESTER R., ET AL., EDS. *State of the World 1993: A Worldwatch Institute Report on Progress Toward a Sustainable Society*. New York: Norton, 1993.

BROWN, MARY ELLEN, ED. *Television and Women's Culture: The Politics of the Popular*. Newbury Park, Calif.: Sage, 1990.

BRUNO, MARY. "Abusing the Elderly." *Newsweek* (September 23, 1985):75–76.

BUCKLEY, STEPHEN. "A Spare and Separate Way of Life." *Washington Post* (December 18, 1996):A1, A32–33.

BUMPASS, LARRY, and JAMES A. SWEET. 1992–1994 National Survey of Families and Households. Reported in "Report From PPA." *Population Today*. Vol. 23, No. 6 (June 1995):3.

BURAWAY, MICHAEL. "Review Essay: The Soviet Descent Into Capitalism." *American Journal of Sociology*. Vol. 102, No. 5 (March 1997):1430–44.

BURCH, ROBERT. Testimony to House of Representatives Hearing in "Review: The World Hunger Problem." October 25, 1983, Serial 98–38.

BURKE, TOM. "The Future." In Sir Edmund Hillary, ed., *Ecology 2000: The Changing Face of the Earth*. New York: Beaufort Books, 1984:227–41.

BURSTEIN, PAUL. "Legal Mobilization as a Social Movement Tactic: The Struggle for Equal Employment Opportunity." *American Journal of Sociology*. Vol. 96, No. 5 (March 1991):1201–25.

BUSBY, LINDA J. "Sex Role Research on the Mass Media." *Journal of Communications*. Vol. 25 (Autumn 1975):107–13.

BUTLER, ROBERT N. *Why Survive? Being Old in America*. New York: Harper & Row, 1975.

BUTTERFIELD, FOX. "Prison: Where the Money Is." *New York Times* (June 2, 1996):E16.

———. "The Wisdom of Children Who Have Known Too Much." *New York Times* (June 8, 1997): section 4, pp. 1, 4.

BUTTERWORTH, DOUGLAS, and JOHN K. CHANCE. *Latin American Urbanization*. Cambridge: Cambridge University Press, 1981.

CAHNMAN, WERNER J., and RUDOLF HEBERLE. "Introduction." In *Ferdinand Toennies on Sociology: Pure, Applied, and Empirical*. Chicago: University of Chicago Press, 1971:vii–xxii.

CALLAHAN, DANIEL. *Setting Limits: Medical Goals in an Aging Society*. New York: Simon & Schuster, 1987.

CALMORE, JOHN O. "National Housing Policies and Black America: Trends, Issues, and Implications." In *The State of Black America 1986*. New York: National Urban League, 1986:115–49.

CAMERON, WILLIAM BRUCE. *Modern Social Movements: A Sociological Outline*. New York: Random House, 1966.

CANCIO, A. SILVIA, T. DAVID EVANS, and DAVID J. MAUME, JR. "Reconsidering the Declining Significance of Race: Racial Differences in Early Career Wages." *American Sociological Review*. Vol. 61, No. 4 (August 1996):541–56.

CANETTI, ELIAS. *Crowds and Power*. New York: Seabury Press, 1978.

CANTOR, MURIAL G., and SUZANNE PINGREE. *The Soap Opera*. Beverly Hills, Calif.: Sage, 1983.

CANTRIL, HADLEY, HAZEL GAUDET, and HERTA HERZOG. *Invasion From Mars: A Study in the Psychology of Panic*. Princeton, N.J.: Princeton University Press, 1947.

CAPLOW, THEODORE, ET AL. *Middletown Families*. Minneapolis: University of Minnesota Press, 1982.

CAPLOW, THEODORE, HOWARD M. BAHR, JOHN MODELL, and BRUCE A. CHADWICK. *Recent Social Trends in the United States, 1960–1990.* Montreal: McGill-Queen's University Press, 1991.

CARLEY, KATHLEEN. "A Theory of Group Stability." *American Sociological Review.* Vol. 56, No. 3 (June 1991):331–54.

CARLSON, MARGARET. "The Real Money Train." *Time.* Vol. 146, No. 24 (December 11, 1995):93.

CARLSON, NORMAN A. "Corrections in the United States Today: A Balance Has Been Struck." *The American Criminal Law Review.* Vol. 13, No. 4 (Spring 1976):615–47.

CARMICHAEL, STOKELY, and CHARLES V. HAMILTON. *Black Power: The Politics of Liberation in America.* New York: Vintage Books, 1967.

CARR, LESLIE G. "Colorblindness and the New Racism." Paper presented at the annual meeting, American Sociological Association, Washington, D.C., 1995.

CARROLL, GINNY. "Who Foots the Bill?" *Newsweek.* Special Issue (Fall–Winter 1990):81–85.

CASTELLS, MANUEL. *The Urban Question.* Cambridge, Mass.: MIT Press, 1977.
———. *The City and the Grass Roots.* Berkeley: University of California Press, 1983.

CASTRO, JANICE. "Disposable Workers." *Time.* Vol. 131, No. 14 (March 29, 1993):43–47.

CENTER FOR MEDIA AND PUBLIC AFFAIRS. 1991 report by Robert Lichter, Linda Lichter, and Stanley Rothman.

CENTER FOR RESPONSIVE POLITICS. The Big Picture. [Online] Available http://www.crp.org/crpdocs/bigpicture/default.htm, February 12, 1998.

CENTER FOR THE STUDY OF SPORT IN SOCIETY. *1997 Racial Report Card: A Study in the NBA, NFL, and Major League Baseball.* Boston: Northeastern University, 1998.

CHAGNON, NAPOLEON A. *Yąnomamö: The Fierce People.* 4th ed. New York: Holt, Rinehart & Winston, 1992.

CHANDLER, TERTIUS, and GERALD FOX. *3000 Years of Urban History.* New York: Academic Press, 1974.

CHANGE, KWANG-CHIH. *The Archaeology of Ancient China.* New Haven, Conn.: Yale University Press, 1977.

CHAPPELL, NEENA L., and BETTY HAVENS. "Old and Female: Testing the Double Jeopardy Hypothesis." *The Sociological Quarterly.* Vol. 21, No. 2 (Spring 1980):157–71.

CHARLES, MARIA. "Cross-National Variation in Occupational Segregation." *American Sociological Review.* Vol. 57, No. 4 (August 1992):483–502.

CHAVES, MARK. "Ordaining Women: The Diffusion of an Organizational Innovation." *American Journal of Sociology.* Vol. 101, No. 4 (January 1996):840–73.

CHERLIN, ANDREW. *Marriage, Divorce, Remarriage.* Rev. ed. Cambridge, Mass.: Harvard University Press, 1990.

CHERLIN, ANDREW, and FRANK F. FURSTENBERG, JR. "The American Family in the Year 2000." *The Futurist.* Vol. 17, No. 3 (June 1983):7–14.
———. *The New American Grandparent: A Place in the Family, A Life Apart.* New York: Basic Books, 1986.

CHESNAIS, JEAN-CLAUDE. "The Demographic Sunset of the West?" *Population Today.* Vol. 25, No. 1 (January 1997):4–5.

CHILDREN'S DEFENSE FUND. *The State of America's Children Yearbook, 1995.* Washington, D.C.: Children's Defense Fund, 1995.

CHOWN, SHEILA M. "Morale, Careers and Personal Potentials." In James E. Birren and K. Warner Schaie, eds., *Handbook of the Psychology of Aging.* New York: Van Nostrand Reinhold, 1977:672–91.

The Christian Science Monitor. Women and Power (September 6, 1995):1, 9, 10, 11.

CHURCH, GEORGE J. "Unions Arise—With New Tricks." *Time.* Vol. 143, No. 24 (June 13, 1994):56–58.
———. "Ripping Up Welfare." *Time.* Vol. 148, No. 8 (August 12, 1996):18–22.

CLARK, CURTIS B. "Geriatric Abuse: Out of the Closet." In *The Tragedy of Elder Abuse: The Problem and the Response.* Hearings before the Select Committee on Aging, House of Representatives (July 1, 1986):49–50.

CLARK, JUAN M., JOSE I. LASAGA, and ROSE S. REGUE. *The 1980 Mariel Exodus: An Assessment and Prospect: Special Report.* Washington, D.C.: Council for Inter-American Security, 1981.

CLARK, MARGARET S., ED. *Prosocial Behavior.* Newbury Park, Calif.: Sage, 1991.

CLARK, THOMAS A. *Blacks in Suburbs.* New Brunswick, N.J.: Rutgers University Center for Urban Policy Research, 1979.

CLARKE, JAMES W. "Black-on-Black Violence." *Society.* Vol. 33, No. 5 (July/August 1996):46–50.

CLARKE, ROBIN. "Atmospheric Pollution." In Sir Edmund Hillary, ed., *Ecology 2000: The Changing Face of the Earth.* New York: Beaufort Books, 1984a:130–48.

———. "What's Happening to Our Water?" In Sir Edmund Hillary, ed., *Ecology 2000: The Changing Face of the Earth.* New York: Beaufort Books, 1984b:108–29.

CLINARD, MARSHALL, and DANIEL ABBOTT. *Crime in Developing Countries.* New York: Wiley, 1973.

CLOWARD, RICHARD A., and LLOYD E. OHLIN. *Delinquency and Opportunity: A Theory of Delinquent Gangs.* New York: Free Press, 1966.

CLYMER, ADAM. "Class Warfare? The Rich Win by Default." *New York Times* (August 11, 1996): section 4, pp. 1, 14.

COE, MICHAEL D., and RICHARD A. DIEHL. *In the Land of the Olmec.* Austin: University of Texas Press, 1980.

COHEN, ADAM. "A New Push for Blind Justice." *Time.* Vol. 145, No. 7 (February 20, 1995):39–40.

COHEN, ALBERT K. *Delinquent Boys: The Culture of the Gang.* New York: Free Press, 1971; orig. 1955.

COHEN, LLOYD R. "Sexual Harassment and the Law." *Society.* Vol. 28, No. 4 (May–June 1991):8–13.

COHN, RICHARD M. "Economic Development and Status Change of the Aged." *American Journal of Sociology.* Vol. 87, No. 2 (March 1982):1150–61.

COLEMAN, JAMES S. "Rational Organization." *Rationality and Society.* Vol. 2, (1990):94–105.
———. "The Design of Organizations and the Right to Act." *Sociological Forum.* Vol. 8, No. 4 (December 1993):527–46.

COLEMAN, JAMES S., and THOMAS HOFFER. *Public and Private High Schools: The Impact of Communities.* New York: Basic Books, 1987.

COLEMAN, JAMES, THOMAS HOFFER, and SALLY KILGORE. *Public and Private Schools: An Analysis of Public Schools and Beyond.* Washington, D.C.: National Center for Education Statistics, 1981.

COLEMAN, RICHARD P., and BERNICE L. NEUGARTEN. *Social Status in the City.* San Francisco: Jossey-Bass, 1971.

COLEMAN, RICHARD P., and LEE RAINWATER. *Social Standing in America.* New York: Basic Books, 1978.

COLLINS, RANDALL. "A Conflict Theory of Sexual Stratification." *Social Problems.* Vol. 19, No. 1 (Summer 1971):3–21.
———. *The Credential Society: An Historical Sociology of Education and Stratification.* New York: Academic Press, 1979.
———. *Sociological Insight: An Introduction to Nonobvious Sociology.* New York: Oxford University Press, 1982.

COLLOWAY, N. O., and PAULA L. DOLLEVOET. "Selected Tabular Material on Aging." In Caleb Finch and Leonard Hayflick, eds., *Handbook of the Biology of Aging.* New York: Van Nostrand Reinhold, 1977:666–708.

COMTE, AUGUSTE. *Auguste Comte and Positivism: The Essential Writings.* Gertrud Lenzer, ed. New York: Harper Torchbooks, 1975.

CONNETT, PAUL H. "The Disposable Society." In F. Herbert Bormann and Stephen R. Kellert, eds., *Ecology, Economics, and Ethics: The Broken Circle.* New Haven, Conn.: Yale University Press, 1991:99–122.

CONTRERAS, JOSEPH. "A New Day Dawns." *Newsweek* (March 30, 1992):40–41.

COOK, RHODES. "House Republicans Scored a Quiet Victory in '92." *Congressional Quarterly Weekly Report.* Vol. 51, No. 16 (April 17, 1993):965–68.

COOLEY, CHARLES HORTON. *Social Organization.* New York: Schocken Books, 1962; orig. 1909.
———. *Human Nature and the Social Order.* New York: Schocken Books, 1964; orig. 1902.

COONEY, MARK. "From Warfare to Tyranny: Lethal Conflict and the State." *American Sociological Review.* Vol. 62, No. 2 (April 1997):316–38.

CORLEY, ROBERT N., O. LEE REED, PETER J. SHEDD, and JERE W. MOREHEAD. *The Legal and Regulatory Environment of Business.* 9th ed. New York: McGraw-Hill, 1993.

COSER, LEWIS A. *Masters of Sociological Thought: Ideas in Historical and Social Context.* 2d ed. New York: Harcourt Brace Jovanovich, 1977.

COTTLE, THOMAS J. "What Tracking Did to Ollie Taylor." *Social Policy.* Vol. 5, No. 2 (July–August 1974):22–24.

COTTRELL, JOHN, and THE EDITORS OF TIME-LIFE. *The Great Cities: Mexico City.* Amsterdam: 1979.

COUNCIL ON FAMILIES IN AMERICA. *Marriage in America: A Report to the Nation.* New York: Institute for American Values, 1995.

COUNCIL ON INTERNATIONAL EDUCATIONAL EXCHANGE. *Educating for Global Competence: The Report of the Advisory Committee for International Educational Exchange.* New York: The Council, 1988.

COUNTS, G. S. "The Social Status of Occupations: A Problem in Vocational Guidance." *School Review.* Vol. 33 (January 1925):16–27.

COURTNEY, ALICE E., and THOMAS W. WHIPPLE. *Sex Stereotyping in Advertising.* Lexington, Mass.: D.C. Heath, 1983.

COURTWRIGHT, DAVID T. *Violent Land: Single Men and Social Disorder From the Frontier to the Inner City.* Cambridge, Mass.: Harvard University Press, 1996.

COVINGTON, JEANETTE. "Racial Classification in Criminology: The Reproduction of Racialized Crime." *Sociological Forum*. Vol. 10, No. 4 (December 1995):547–68.

COWAN, CAROLYN POPE. *When Partners Become Parents*. New York: Basic Books, 1992.

COWGILL, DONALD, and LOWELL HOLMES. *Aging and Modernization*. New York: Appleton-Century-Crofts, 1972.

COWLEY, GEOFFREY. "The Prescription That Kills." *Newsweek* (July 17, 1995): 54.

COX, HARVEY. *The Secular City*. Rev. ed. New York: Macmillan, 1971; orig. 1965.

———. *Turning East: The Promise and Peril of the New Orientalism*. New York: Simon & Schuster, 1977.

———. "Church and Believers: Always Strangers?" In Thomas Robbins and Dick Anthony, *In Gods We Trust: New Patterns of Religious Pluralism in America*. 2d ed. New Brunswick, N.J.: Transaction, 1990:449–62.

CRENSHAW, EDWARD M., and J. CRAIG JENKINS. "Social Structure and Global Climate Change: Sociological Propositions Concerning the Greenhouse Effect." *Sociological Focus*. Vol. 29, No. 4 (October 1996):341–58.

CRISPELL, DIANE. "Grandparents Galore." *American Demographics*. Vol. 15, No. 10 (October 1993):63.

———. "Speaking in Other Tongues." *American Demographics*. Vol. 19, No. 1 (January 1997):12–15.

———. "Lucky to be Alive." *American Demographics*. Vol. 19, No. 4 (April 1997):25.

CROOK, STEPHAN, JAN PAKULSKI, and MALCOLM WATERS. *Postmodernity: Change in Advanced Society*. Newbury Park, Calif.: Sage, 1992.

CROSSEN, CYNTHIA, and ELLEN GRAHAM. "Good News—and Bad—About America's Health." *Wall Street Journal* (June 28, 1996):R1.

CROSSETTE, BARBARA. "Female Genital Mutilation by Immigrants Is Becoming Cause for Concern in the U.S." *New York Times International* (December 10, 1995):11.

CROUSE, JAMES, and DALE TRUSHEIM. *The Case Against the SAT*. Chicago: University of Chicago Press, 1988.

CUFF, E. C., and G. C. F. PAYNE, EDS. *Perspectives in Sociology*. London: Allen and Unwin, 1979.

CUMMING, ELAINE, and WILLIAM E. HENRY. *Growing Old: The Process of Disengagement*. New York: Basic Books, 1961.

CURRIE, ELLIOTT. *Confronting Crime: An American Challenge*. New York: Pantheon Books, 1985.

CURRY, GEORGE E., ed. *The Affirmative Action Debate*. Reading, Mass.: Addison-Wesley, 1996.

CURTIS, JAMES E., EDWARD G. GRABB, and DOUGLAS BAER. "Voluntary Association Membership in Fifteen Countries: A Comparative Analysis." *American Sociological Review*. Vol. 57, No. 2 (April 1992):139–52.

CURTISS, SUSAN. *Genie: A Psycholinguistic Study of a Modern-Day "Wild Child."* New York: Academic Press, 1977.

CUTLER, DAVID M., and LAWRENCE F. KATZ. "Rising Inequality? Changes in the Distribution of Income and Consumption in the 1980s." Working Paper No. 3964. Cambridge, Mass.: National Bureau of Economic Research, 1992.

CUTRIGHT, PHILLIP. "Occupational Inheritance: A Cross-National Analysis." *American Journal of Sociology*. Vol. 73, No. 4 (January 1968):400–16.

CYLKE, F. KURT, JR. *The Environment*. New York: HarperCollins, 1993.

DAHL, ROBERT A. *Who Governs?* New Haven, Conn.: Yale University Press, 1961.

———. *Dilemmas of Pluralist Democracy: Autonomy vs. Control*. New Haven, Conn.: Yale University Press, 1982.

DAHRENDORF, RALF. *Class and Class Conflict in Industrial Society*. Stanford, Calif.: Stanford University Press, 1959.

DALY, MARTIN, and MARGO WILSON. *Homicide*. New York: Aldine, 1988.

DANIELS, ROGER. "The Issei Generation." In Amy Tachiki et al., eds., *Roots: An Asian American Reader*. Los Angeles: UCLA Asian American Studies Center, 1971:138–49.

DANNEFER, DALE. "Adult Development and Social Theory: A Reappraisal." *American Sociological Review*. Vol. 49, No. 1 (February 1984):100–16.

DARNTON, JOHN. "The Battle Cry of 'Reform' Rocks the House of Lords." *New York Times* (April 21, 1996):1, 8.

DARNTON, NINA, and YURIKO HOSHIA. "Whose Life Is It, Anyway?" *Newsweek*. Vol. 113, No. 4 (January 13, 1989):61.

DAVIDSON, JAMES D., RALPH E. PYLE, and DAVID V. REYES. "Persistence and Change in the Protestant Establishment, 1930–1992." *Social Forces*. Vol. 74, No. 1 (September 1995):157–75.

DAVIES, CHRISTIE. *Ethnic Humor Around the World: A Comparative Analysis*. Bloomington: Indiana University Press, 1990.

DAVIES, JAMES C. "Toward a Theory of Revolution." *American Sociological Review*. Vol. 27, No. 1 (February 1962):5–19.

DAVIES, MARK, and DENISE B. KANDEL. "Parental and Peer Influences on Adolescents' Educational Plans: Some Further Evidence." *American Journal of Sociology*. Vol. 87, No. 2 (September 1981):363–87.

DAVIS, DONALD M., cited in "T.V. Is a Blonde, Blonde World." *American Demographics*, special issue: *Women Change Places*. Ithaca, N.Y.: 1993.

DAVIS, KINGSLEY. "Extreme Social Isolation of a Child." *American Journal of Sociology*. Vol. 45, No. 4 (January 1940):554–65.

———. "Final Note on a Case of Extreme Isolation." *American Journal of Sociology*. Vol. 52, No. 5 (March 1947):432–37.

DAVIS, KINGSLEY. "The Myth of Functional Analysis as a Special Method in Sociology and Anthropology." *American Sociological Review*. Vol. 24, No. 1 (February 1959):75ff.

DAVIS, KINGSLEY, and WILBERT MOORE. "Some Principles of Stratification." *American Sociological Review*. Vol. 10, No. 2 (April 1945):242–49.

DAVIS, NANCY, and ROBERT V. ROBINSON. "Are the Rumors of War Exaggerated? Religious Orthodoxy and Moral Progressivism in America." *American Journal of Sociology*. Vol. 102, No. 3 (November 1996):756–87.

DAVIS, SHARON A., and EMIL J. HALLER. "Tracking, Ability, and SES: Further Evidence on the 'Revisionist-Meritocratic Debate.'" *American Journal of Education*. Vol. 89 (May 1981):283–304.

DECKARD, BARBARA SINCLAIR. *The Women's Movement: Political, Socioeconomic, and Psychological Issues*. 2d ed. New York: Harper & Row, 1979.

DEDRICK, DENNIS K., and RICHARD E. YINGER. "MAD, SDI, and the Nuclear Arms Race." Manuscript in development. Georgetown, Ky.: Georgetown College, 1990.

DELACROIX, JACQUES, and CHARLES C. RAGIN. "Structural Blockage: A Cross-national Study of Economic Dependency, State Efficacy, and Underdevelopment." *American Journal of Sociology*. Vol. 86, No. 6 (May 1981):1311–47.

DELLA CAVA, MARCO R. "For Dutch, It's as Easy as Asking a Doctor." *USA Today* (January 7, 1997):4A.

DEMERATH, N. J., III. "Who Now Debates Functionalism? From *System, Change, and Conflict* to 'Culture, Choice, and Praxis'." *Sociological Forum*. Vol. 11, No. 2 (June 1996):333–45.

DEMOTT, JOHN S. "Wreaking Havoc on Spring Break." *Time*. Vol. 127, No. 14 (April 7, 1986):29.

DENT, DAVID J. "African-Americans Turning to Christian Academies." *New York Times*, Education Life supplement (August 4, 1996):26–29.

DEPARLE, JASON. "Painted by Numbers, 1980s are Rosy to G.O.P., While Democrats See Red." *New York Times* (September 26, 1991a):B10.

DERSHOWITZ, ALAN. *The Vanishing American Jew*. Boston: Little, Brown, 1997.

Der Spiegel. "Third World Metropolises Are Becoming Monsters; Rural Poverty Drives Millions to the Slums." In *World Press Review* (October 1989).

DEVINE, JOEL A. "State and State Expenditure: Determinants of Social Investment and Social Consumption Spending in the Postwar United States." *American Sociological Review*. Vol. 50, No. 2 (April 1985):150–65.

DIAMOND, MILTON. "Sexual Identity, Monozygotic Twins Reared in Discordant Sex Roles and a BBC Follow-Up." *Archives of Sexual Behavior*. Vol. 11, No. 2 (April 1982):181–86.

DICKENS, CHARLES. *The Adventures of Oliver Twist*. Boston: Estes and Lauriat, 1886; orig. 1837–39.

DIMAGGIO, PAUL, JOHN EVANS, and BETHANY BRYSON. "Have Americans' Social Attitudes Become More Polarized?" *American Journal of Sociology*. Vol. 102, No. 3 (November 1996):690–755.

DIXON, WILLIAM J., and TERRY BOSWELL. "Dependency, Disarticulation, and Denominator Effects: Another Look at Foreign Capital Penetration." *American Journal of Sociology*. Vol. 102, No. 2 (September 1996):543–62.

DIZARD, JAN E., and HOWARD GADLIN. *The Minimal Family*. Amherst: The University of Massachusetts Press, 1990.

DOBSON, RICHARD B. "Mobility and Stratification in the Soviet Union." *Annual Review of Sociology*. Vol. 3. Palo Alto, Calif.: Annual Reviews, 1977:297–329.

DOBYNS, HENRY F. "An Appraisal of Techniques with a New Hemispheric Estimate." *Current Anthropology*. Vol. 7, No. 4 (October 1966):395–446.

DOLLARD, JOHN, ET AL. *Frustration and Aggression*. New Haven, Conn.: Yale University Press, 1939.

DOMHOFF, G. WILLIAM. *Who Rules America Now? A View of the '80s*. Englewood Cliffs, N.J.: Prentice Hall, 1983.

DONOVAN, VIRGINIA K., and RONNIE LITTENBERG. "Psychology of Women: Feminist Therapy." In Barbara Haber, ed., *The Women's Annual 1981: The Year in Review*. Boston: G. K. Hall, 1982:211–35.

DOUGLASS, RICHARD L. "Domestic Neglect and Abuse of the Elderly: Implications for Research and Service." *Family Relations*. Vol. 32 (July 1983):395–402.

DOYLE, JAMES A. *The Male Experience*. Dubuque, Iowa: Wm. C. Brown, 1983.

DOYLE, RICHARD F. *A Manifesto of Men's Liberation*. 2d ed. Forest Lake, Minn.: Men's Rights Association, 1980.

DU BOIS, W. E. B. *Dusk of Dawn*. New York: Harcourt, Brace & World, 1940.

———. *The Philadelphia Negro: A Social Study*. New York: Schocken Books, 1967; orig. 1899.

DUBOS, RENÉ. *Man Adapting*. New Haven, Conn.: Yale University Press, 1980; orig. 1965.

DUHL, LEONARD J. "The Social Context of Health." In Arthur C. Hastings et al., eds., *Health for the Whole Person: The Complete Guide to Holistic Medicine*. Boulder, Colo.: Westview Press, 1980:39–48.

DUNLAP, DAVID W. "Fearing a Toehold for Gay Marriages, Conservatives Rush to Bar the Door." *New York Times* (March 3, 1996):A13.

DUNLAP, RILEY E., GEORGE H. GALLUP, JR., and ALEC M. GALLUP. *The Health of the Planet Survey*. Princeton, N.J.: The George H. Gallup International Institute, 1992.

DUNLAP, RILEY E., and ANGELA G. MERTIG. "The Evolution of the U.S. Environmental Movement From 1970 to 1990: An Overview." In Riley E. Dunlap and Angela G. Mertig, eds., *American Evironmentalism: The U.S. Environmental Movement, 1970–1990*. New York: Taylor & Francis, 1992:1–10.

DUNN, ASHLEY. "Ancient Chinese Craft Shifts Building Designs in the U.S." *New York Times* (September 22, 1994):A1, B4.

DUNN, JOHN. "Peddling Big Brother." *Time*. Vol. 137, No. 25 (June 24, 1991):62.

DURKHEIM, EMILE. *The Division of Labor in Society*. New York: Free Press, 1964a; orig. 1895.

———. *The Rules of Sociological Method*. New York: Free Press, 1964b; orig. 1893.

———. *The Elementary Forms of Religious Life*. New York: Free Press, 1965; orig. 1915.

———. *Suicide*. New York: Free Press, 1966; orig. 1897.

———. *Selected Writings*. Anthony Giddens, ed. Cambridge: Cambridge University Press, 1972.

———. *Sociology and Philosophy*. New York: Free Press, 1974; orig. 1924.

DURNING, ALAN THEIN. "Supporting Indigenous Peoples." In Lester R. Brown et al., eds., *State of the World 1993: A Worldwatch Institute Report on Progress Toward a Sustainable Society*. New York: Norton, 1993:80–100.

DWORKIN, ANDREA. *Intercourse*. New York: Free Press, 1987.

EBAUGH, HELEN ROSE FUCHS. *Becoming an EX: The Process of Role Exit*. Chicago: University of Chicago Press, 1988.

ECKHOLM, ERIK. "Malnutrition in Elderly: Widespread Health Threat." *New York Times* (August 13, 1985):19–20.

ECKHOLM, ERIK, and JOHN TIERNEY. "AIDS in Africa: A Killer Rages On." *New York Times* (September 16, 1990):A1, 14.

The Economist. "Worship Moves in Mysterious Ways." Vol. 326, No. 7802 (March 13, 1993):65, 70.

———. "Cockfighting: 'Til Death Us Do Part." Vol. 330, No. 7851 (February 19, 1994):30.

———. "Japan's Missing Children." Vol. 333, No. 7889 (November 12, 1994):46.

EDIN, KATHRYN, and LAURA LEIN. "Work, Welfare, and Single Mothers' Economic Survival Strategies." *American Sociological Review*. Vol. 62, No. 2 (April 1996):253–66.

EDMONDSON, BRAD. "The Great Money Grab." *American Demographics*. Vol. 17, No. 2 (February 1995):2.

———. "Fountains of Youth." *American Demographics*. Vol. 18, No. 7 (July 1996):60.

———. "The Facts of Death." *American Demographics*. Vol. 49, No. 4 (April 1997):47–53.

———. "The Wired Bunch." *American Demographics*. Vol. 49, No. 6 (June 1997):10–15.

EDWARDS, DAVID V. *The American Political Experience*. 3d ed. Englewood Cliffs, N.J.: Prentice Hall, 1985.

EDWARDS, RICHARD. *Contested Terrain: The Transformation of the Workplace in the Twentieth Century*. New York: Basic Books, 1979.

EGGEBEEN, DAVID J., and DANIEL T. LICHTER. "Race, Family Structure and Changing Poverty Among American Children." *American Sociological Review*. Vol. 56, No. 6 (December 1991):801–17.

EHRENREICH, BARBARA. *The Hearts of Men: American Dreams and the Flight From Commitment*. Garden City, N.Y.: Anchor Books, 1983.

EHRENREICH, JOHN. "Introduction." In John Ehrenreich, ed., *The Cultural Crisis of Modern Medicine*. New York: Monthly Review Press, 1978:1–35.

EICHLER, MARGRIT. *Nonsexist Research Methods: A Practical Guide*. Winchester, Mass.: Unwin Hyman, 1988.

EISEN, ARNOLD M. *The Chosen People in America: A Study of Jewish Religious Ideology*. Bloomington: Indiana University Press, 1983.

EISENSTEIN, ZILLAH R., ED. *Capitalist Patriarchy and the Case for Socialist Feminism*. New York: Monthly Review Press, 1979.

EISLER, BENITA. *The Lowell Offering: Writings by New England Mill Women 1840–1845*. Philadelphia and New York: J. B. Lippincott, 1977.

EKMAN, PAUL. "Biological and Cultural Contributions to Body and Facial Movements in the Expression of Emotions." In A. Rorty, ed., *Explaining Emotions*. Berkeley: University of California Press, 1980a:73–101.

———. *Face of Man: Universal Expression in a New Guinea Village*. New York: Garland Press, 1980b.

———. *Telling Lies: Clues to Deceit in the Marketplace, Politics, and Marriage*. New York: Norton, 1985.

EKMAN, PAUL, WALLACE V. FRIESEN, and JOHN BEAR. "The International Language of Gestures." *Psychology Today* (May 1984):64–69.

EL-ATTAR, MOHAMED. Personal communication, 1991.

ELIAS, ROBERT. *The Politics of Victimization: Victims, Victimology and Human Rights*. New York: Oxford University Press, 1986.

ELKIND, DAVID. *The Hurried Child: Growing Up Too Fast Too Soon*. Reading, Mass.: Addison-Wesley, 1981.

ELLIOT, DELBERT S., and SUZANNE S. AGETON. "Reconciling Race and Class Differences in Self-Reported and Official Estimates of Delinquency." *American Sociological Review*. Vol. 45, No. 1 (February 1980):95–110.

ELLISON, CHRISTOPHER G., JOHN P. BARTKOWSKI, and MICHELLE L. SEGAL. "Do Conservative Protestant Parents Spank More Often? Further Evidence From the National Survey of Families and Households." *Social Science Quarterly*. Vol. 77, No. 3 (September 1996):663–73.

ELLISON, CHRISTOPHER G., and DARREN E. SHERKAT. "Conservative Protestantism and Support for Corporal Punishment." *American Sociological Review*. Vol. 58, No. 1 (February 1993):131–44.

ELMER-DEWITT, PHILIP. "The Revolution That Fizzled." *Time*. Vol. 137, No. 20 (May 20, 1991):48–49.

———. "First Nation in Cyberspace." *Time*. Vol. 142, No. 24 (December 6, 1993):62–64.

———. "The Genetic Revolution." *Time*. Vol. 143, No. 3 (January 17, 1994):46–53.

———. "Battle for the Internet." *Time*. Vol. 144, No. 4 (July 25, 1994):50–56.

EMBER, MELVIN, and CAROL R. EMBER. "The Conditions Favoring Matrilocal Versus Patrilocal Residence." *American Anthropologist*. Vol. 73, No. 3 (June 1971):571–94.

———. *Anthropology*. 6th ed. Englewood Cliffs, N.J.: Prentice Hall, 1991.

EMBREE, AINSLIE T. *The Hindu Tradition*. New York: Vintage Books, 1972.

EMERSON, JOAN P. "Behavior in Private Places: Sustaining Definitions of Reality in Gynecological Examinations." In H. P. Dreitzel, ed., *Recent Sociology*. Vol. 2. New York: Collier, 1970:74–97.

ENDICOTT, KAREN. "Fathering in an Egalitarian Society." In Barry S. Hewlett, ed., *Father-Child Relations: Cultural and Bio-Social Contexts*. New York: Aldine, 1992:281–96.

ENGELS, FRIEDRICH. *The Origin of the Family*. Chicago: Charles H. Kerr & Company, 1902; orig. 1884.

ENGLAND, PAULA. *Comparable Worth: Theories and Evidence*. Hawthorne, N.Y.: Aldine, 1992.

EPPS, EDGAR G. "Race, Class, and Educational Opportunity: Trends in the Sociology of Education." *Sociological Forum*. Vol. 10, No. 4 (December 1995):593–608.

ERIKSON, ERIK H. *Childhood and Society*. New York: Norton, 1963; orig. 1950.

———. *Identity and the Life Cycle*. New York: Norton, 1980.

ERIKSON, KAI T. *Wayward Puritans: A Study in the Sociology of Deviance*. New York: Wiley, 1966.

ERIKSON, ROBERT, and JOHN H. GOLDTHORPE. *The Constant Flux: A Study of Class Mobility in Industrial Societies*. Oxford: Clarendon Press, 1992.

ERIKSON, ROBERT S., NORMAN R. LUTTBEG, and KENT L. TEDIN. *American Public Opinion: Its Origins, Content, and Impact*. 2d ed. New York: Wiley, 1980.

ETZIONI, AMITAI. *A Comparative Analysis of Complex Organization: On Power, Involvement, and Their Correlates*. Rev. and enlarged ed. New York: Free Press, 1975.

———. "Too Many Rights, Too Few Responsibilities." *Society*. Vol. 28, No. 2 (January–February 1991):41–48.

———. "How to Make Marriage Matter." *Time*. Vol. 142, No. 10 (September 6, 1993):76.

———. "The Responsive Community: A Communitarian Perspective." *American Sociological Review*. Vol. 61, No. 1 (February 1996):1–11.

ETZIONI-HALEVY, EVA. *Bureaucracy and Democracy: A Political Dilemma*. Rev. ed. Boston: Routledge & Kegan Paul, 1985.

EVANS, M. D. R. "Immigrant Entrepreneurship: Effects of Ethnic Market Size and Isolated Labor Pool." *American Sociological Review*. Vol. 54, No. 6 (December 1989):950–62.

EXTER, THOMAS G. "The Costs of Growing Up." *American Demographics*. Vol. 13, No. 8 (August 1991):59.

FALK, GERHARD. Personal communication, 1987.

FALKENMARK, MALIN, and CARL WIDSTRAND. "Population and Water Resources: A Delicate Balance." *Population Bulletin*. Vol. 47, No. 3 (November 1992). Washington, D.C.: Population Reference Bureau.

FALLON, A. E., and P. ROZIN. "Sex Differences in Perception of Desirable Body Shape." *Journal of Abnormal Psychology*. Vol. 94, No. 1 (1985):100–5.

FALLOWS, JAMES. "Immigration: How It's Affecting Us." *The Atlantic Monthly*. Vol. 252 (November 1983):45–52, 55–62, 66–68, 85–90, 94, 96, 99–106.

FANTINI, MARIO D. *Regaining Excellence in Education*. Columbus, Ohio: Merrill, 1986.

FARLEY, CHRISTOPHER JOHN. "Winning the Right to Fly." *Time*. Vol. 146, No. 9 (August 28, 1995):62–64.

FARLEY, REYNOLDS, and WILLIAM H. FREY. "Changes in the Segregation of Whites From Blacks During the 1980s: Small Steps Toward a More Integrated Society." *American Sociological Review*. Vol. 59, No. 1 (February 1994):23–45.

FARRELL, MICHAEL P., and STANLEY D. ROSENBERG. *Men at Midlife*. Boston: Auburn House, 1981.

FEAGIN, JOE. *The Urban Real Estate Game*. Englewood Cliffs, N.J.: Prentice Hall, 1983.

——. "The Continuing Significance of Race: Antiblack Discrimination in Public Places." *American Sociological Review*. Vol. 56, No. 1 (February 1991):101–16.

——. "Death By Discrimination?" *Newsletter*, Society for the Study of Social Problems. Vol. 28, No. 1 (Winter 1997):15–16.

FEATHERMAN, DAVID L., and ROBERT M. HAUSER. *Opportunity and Change*. New York: Academic Press, 1978.

FEATHERSTONE, MIKE, ED. *Global Culture: Nationalism, Globalization, and Modernity*. London: Sage, 1990.

FEDARKO, KEVIN. "Who Could Live Here?" *Time*. Vol. 139, No. 3 (January 20, 1992):20–23.

——. "Land Mines: Cheap, Deadly, and Cruel." *Time*. Vol. 147, No. 20 (May 13, 1996):54–55.

FELLMAN, BRUCE. "Taking the Measure of Children's T.V." *Yale Alumni Magazine* (April 1995):46–51.

FENNELL, MARY C. "The Effects of Environmental Characteristics on the Structure of Hospital Clusters." *Administrative Science Quarterly*. Vol. 29, No. 3 (September 1980):489–510.

FERGUSON, TOM. "Medical Self-Care: Self Responsibility for Health." In Arthur C. Hastings et al., eds., *Health for the Whole Person: The Complete Guide to Holistic Medicine*. Boulder, Colo.: Westview Press, 1980:87–109.

FERGUSSON, D. M., L. J. HORWOOD, and F. T. SHANNON. "A Proportional Hazards Model of Family Breakdown." *Journal of Marriage and the Family*. Vol. 46, No. 3 (August 1984):539–49.

FERREE, MYRA MARX, and ELAINE J. HALL. "Rethinking Stratification From a Feminist Perspective: Gender, Race, and Class in Mainstream Textbooks." *American Sociological Review*. Vol. 61, No. 6 (December 1996):929–50.

FIND/SVP. *The 1997 American Internet Users Survey: Realities Behind the Hype*. Reported in *Society*, Vol. 43, No. 5 (July/August 1997):2.

FINKELSTEIN, NEAL W., and RON HASKINS. "Kindergarten Children Prefer Same-Color Peers." *Child Development*. Vol. 54, No. 2 (April 1983):502–8.

FIORENTINE, ROBERT. "Men, Women, and the Premed Persistence Gap: A Normative Alternatives Approach." *American Journal of Sociology*. Vol. 92, No. 5 (March 1987):1118–39.

FIORENTINE, ROBERT, and STEPHEN COLE. "Why Fewer Women Become Physicians: Explaining the Premed Persistence Gap." *Sociological Forum*. Vol. 7, No. 3 (September 1992):469–96.

FIREBAUGH, GLENN. "Growth Effects of Foreign and Domestic Investment." *American Journal of Sociology*. Vol. 98, No. 1 (July 1992):105–30.

——. "Does Foreign Capital Harm Poor Nations? New Estimates Based on Dixon and Boswell's Measures of Capital Penetration." *American Journal of Sociology*. Vol. 102, No. 2 (September 1996):563–75.

FIREBAUGH, GLENN, and FRANK D. BECK. "Does Economic Growth Benefit the Masses? Growth, Dependence, and Welfare in the Third World." *American Sociological Review*. Vol. 59, No. 5 (October 1994):631–53.

FIREBAUGH, GLENN, and KENNETH E. DAVIS. "Trends in Antiblack Prejudice, 1972–1984: Region and Cohort Effects." *American Journal of Sociology*. Vol. 94, No. 2 (September 1988):251–72.

FISCHER, CLAUDE S., ET AL. *Networks and Places: Social Relations in the Urban Setting*. New York: Free Press, 1977.

FISHER, ELIZABETH. *Woman's Creation: Sexual Evolution and the Shaping of Society*. Garden City, N.Y.: Anchor/Doubleday, 1979.

FISHER, ROGER, and WILLIAM URY. "Getting to YES." In William M. Evan and Stephen Hilgartner, eds., *The Arms Race and Nuclear War*. Englewood Cliffs, N.J.: Prentice Hall, 1988:261–68.

FISKE, ALAN PAIGE. "The Cultural Relativity of Selfish Individualism: Anthropological Evidence That Humans Are Inherently Sociable." In Margaret S. Clark, ed., *Prosocial Behavior*. Newbury Park, Calif.: Sage, 1991:176–214.

FISKE, EDWARD B. "Adults: The Forgotten Illiterates." *Christian Science Monitor* (May 30, 1997):18.

FITZPATRICK, JOSEPH P. "Puerto Ricans." In *Harvard Encyclopedia of American Ethnic Groups*. Cambridge, Mass.: Harvard University Press, 1980:858–67.

FITZPATRICK, MARY ANNE. *Between Husbands and Wives: Communication in Marriage*. Newbury Park, Calif.: Sage, 1988.

FLAHERTY, MICHAEL G. "A Formal Approach to the Study of Amusement in Social Interaction." *Studies in Symbolic Interaction*. Vol. 5. New York: JAI Press, 1984:71–82.

——. "Two Conceptions of the Social Situation: Some Implications of Humor." *The Sociological Quarterly*. Vol. 31, No. 1 (Spring 1990).

FLORIDA, RICHARD, and MARTIN KENNEY. "Transplanted Organizations: The Transfer of Japanese Industrial Organization to the U.S." *American Sociological Review*. Vol. 56, No. 3 (June 1991):381–98.

FLYNN, PATRICIA. "The Disciplinary Emergence of Bioethics and Bioethics Committees: Moral Ordering and its Legitimation." *Sociological Focus*. Vol. 24, No. 2 (May 1991):145–56.

FOBES, RICHARD. "Creative Problem Solving." *The Futurist*. Vol. 30, No. 1 (January–February 1996):19–22.

Forbes. "Forbes 400." Vol. 160, No. 8 (October 13, 1997):418–22.

FORD, CLELLAN S., and FRANK A. BEACH. *Patterns of Sexual Behavior*. New York: Harper & Row, 1951.

FORREST, HUGH. "They Are Completely Inactive . . ." *The Gambier Journal*. Vol. 3, No. 4 (February 1984):10–11.

Fortune. "The Fortune 500." Vol. 131, No. 9 (May 15, 1995): Special issue.

FORTUNE 500. [Online] Available http://www.pathfinder.com/fortune/fortune500/, January 19, 1998.

FOST, DAN. "American Indians in the 1990s." *American Demographics*. Vol. 13, No. 12 (December 1991):26–34.

FRANK, ANDRÉ GUNDER. *On Capitalist Underdevelopment*. Bombay: Oxford University Press, 1975.

——. *Crisis: In the World Economy*. New York: Holmes & Meier, 1980.

——. *Reflections on the World Economic Crisis*. New York: Monthly Review Press, 1981.

FRANKLIN, JOHN HOPE. *From Slavery to Freedom: A History of Negro Americans*. 3d ed. New York: Vintage Books, 1967.

FRANKLIN ASSOCIATES. *Characterization of Municipal Solid Waste in the United States, 1960–2000*. Prairie Village, Kans.: Franklin Associates, 1986.

FRAZIER, E. FRANKLIN. *Black Bourgeoisie: The Rise of a New Middle Class*. New York: Free Press, 1965.

FREDRICKSON, GEORGE M. *White Supremacy: A Comparative Study in American and South African History*. New York: Oxford University Press, 1981.

FREE, MARVIN D. "Religious Affiliation, Religiosity, and Impulsive and Intentional Deviance." *Sociological Focus*. Vol. 25, No. 1 (February 1992):77–91.

FREEDOM HOUSE. *Freedom in the World*. New York: Freedom House, 1998.

FRENCH, MARILYN. *Beyond Power: On Women, Men, and Morals*. New York: Summit Books, 1985.

FRIEDAN, BETTY. *The Fountain of Age*. New York: Simon and Schuster, 1993.

FRIEDMAN, MEYER, and RAY H. ROSENMAN. *Type A Behavior and Your Heart*. New York: Fawcett Crest, 1974.

FRIEDRICH, CARL J., and ZBIGNIEW BRZEZINSKI. *Totalitarian Dictatorship and Autocracy*. 2d ed. Cambridge, Mass.: Harvard University Press, 1965.

FRIEDRICH, OTTO. "A Proud Capital's Distress." *Time*. Vol. 124, No. 6 (August 6, 1984):26–30, 33–35.

——. "United No More." *Time*. Vol. 129, No. 18 (May 4, 1987):28–37.

FRUM, DAVID, and FRANK WOLFE. "If You Gotta Get Sued, Get Sued in Utah." *Forbes*. Vol. 153, No. 2 (January 1994):70–73.

FUCHS, VICTOR R. "Sex Differences in Economic Well-Being." *Science*. Vol. 232 (April 25, 1986):459–64.

FUGITA, STEPHEN S., and DAVID J. O'BRIEN. "Structural Assimilation, Ethnic Group Membership, and Political Participation Among Japanese Americans: A Research Note." *Social Forces*. Vol. 63, No. 4 (June 1985):986–95.

FUJIMOTO, ISAO. "The Failure of Democracy in a Time of Crisis." In Amy Tachiki et al., eds., *Roots: An Asian American Reader*. Los Angeles: UCLA Asian American Studies Center, 1971:207–14.

FULLER, REX, and RICHARD SCHOENBERGER. "The Gender Salary Gap: Do Academic Achievement, Intern Experience, and College Major Make a Difference?" *Social Science Quarterly*. Vol. 72, No. 4 (December 1991):715–26.

FURSTENBERG, FRANK F., JR. "The New Extended Family: The Experience of Parents and Children After Remarriage." Paper presented to the Changing Family Conference XIII: The Blended Family. University of Iowa, 1984.

FURSTENBERG, FRANK F., JR., J. BROOKS-GUNN, and S. PHILIP MORGAN. *Adolescent Mothers in Later Life*. New York: Cambridge University Press, 1987.

FURSTENBERG, FRANK F., JR., and ANDREW CHERLIN. *Divided Families: What Happens to Children When Parents Part*. Cambridge, Mass.: Harvard University Press, 1991.

FUSFELD, DANIEL R. *Economics: Principles of Political Economy*. Glenview, Ill.: Scott, Foresman, 1982.

GABRIEL, TRIP. "Computers Help Unite Campuses but Also Drive Some Students Apart." *New York Times* (November 11, 1996).

GAGLIANI, GIORGIO. "How Many Working Classes?" *American Journal of Sociology*. Vol. 87, No. 2 (September 1981):259–85.

GALLUP, GEORGE, JR. *Religion in America*. Princeton, N.J.: Princeton Religion Research Center, 1982.

GALLUP POLL. *The Gallup Poll Monthly*. December, 1993.

GALSTER, GEORGE. "Black Suburbanization: Has It Changed the Relative Location of Races?" *Urban Affairs Quarterly*. Vol. 26, No. 4 (June 1991):621–28.

GALSTON, WILLIAM A., and DAVID WASSERMAN. "Gambling Away Our Moral Capital." *The Public Interest*. Vol. 123 (Spring 1996):58–71.

GAMBLE, ANDREW, STEVE LUDLAM, and DAVID BAKER. "Britain's Ruling Class." *The Economist*. Vol. 326, No. 7795 (January 23, 1993):10.

GAMORAN, ADAM. "The Variable Effects of High-School Tracking." *American Sociological Review*. Vol. 57, No. 6 (December 1992):812–28.

GANS, HERBERT J. *People and Plans: Essays on Urban Problems and Solutions*. New York: Basic Books, 1968.

———. *Popular Culture and High Culture*. New York: Basic Books, 1974.

———. *Deciding What's News: A Study of CBS Evening News, NBC Nightly News, Newsweek and Time*. New York: Vintage Books, 1980.

———. *The Urban Villagers: Group and Class in the Life of Italian-Americans*. New York: Free Press, 1982; orig. 1962.

GARFINKEL, HAROLD. "Conditions of Successful Degradation Ceremonies." *American Journal of Sociology*. Vol. 61, No. 2 (March 1956):420–24.

———. *Studies in Ethnomethodology*. Cambridge: Polity Press, 1967.

GARREAU, JOEL. *Edge City*. New York: Doubleday, 1991.

GEERTZ, CLIFFORD. "Common Sense as a Cultural System." *The Antioch Review*. Vol. 33, No. 1 (Spring 1975):5–26.

GEIST, WILLIAM. *Toward a Safe and Sane Halloween and Other Tales of Suburbia*. New York: Times Books, 1985.

GELLES, RICHARD J., and CLAIRE PEDRICK CORNELL. *Intimate Violence in Families*. 2d ed. Newbury Park, Calif.: Sage, 1990.

GELMAN, DAVID. "Who's Taking Care of Our Parents?" *Newsweek* (May 6, 1985):61–64, 67–68.

———. "Born or Bred?" *Newsweek* (February 24, 1992):46–53.

GEORGE, SUSAN. *How the Other Half Dies: The Real Reasons for World Hunger*. Totowa, N.J.: Rowman & Allanheld, 1977.

GERLACH, MICHAEL L. *The Social Organization of Japanese Business*. Berkeley and Los Angeles: University of California Press, 1992.

GERSTEL, NAOMI. "Divorce and Stigma." *Social Problems*. Vol. 43, No. 2 (April 1987):172–86.

GERTH, H. H., and C. WRIGHT MILLS, EDS. *From Max Weber: Essays in Sociology*. New York: Oxford University Press, 1946.

GESCHWENDER, JAMES A. *Racial Stratification in America*. Dubuque, Iowa: Wm. C. Brown, 1978.

GEWERTZ, DEBORAH. "A Historical Reconsideration of Female Dominance Among the Chambri of Papua New Guinea." *American Ethnologist*. Vol. 8, No. 1 (1981):94–106.

GIBBONS, DON C., and MARVIN D. KROHN. *Delinquent Behavior*. 4th ed. Englewood Cliffs, N.J.: Prentice Hall, 1986.

GIBBS, NANCY. "When Is It Rape?" *Time*. Vol. 137, No. 22 (June 3, 1991a):48–54.

———. "The Clamor on Campus." *Time*. Vol. 137, No. 22 (June 3, 1991b):54–55.

———. "How Much Should We Teach Our Children About Sex?" *Time*. Vol. 141, No. 21 (May 24, 1993):60–66.

———. "The Vicious Cycle." *Time*. Vol. 143, No. 25 (June 20, 1994):24–33.

———. "The Blood of Innocents." *Time*. Special Issue. No. 25 (June 1, 1995):57–64.

———. "Cause Celeb." *Time*. Vol. 147, No. 25 (June 17, 1996):28–30.

GIDDENS, ANTHONY. *Sociology: A Brief but Critical Introduction*. New York: Harcourt Brace Jovanovich, 1982.

GIELE, JANET Z. "Gender and Sex Roles." In Neil J. Smelser, ed., *Handbook of Sociology*. Newbury Park, Calif.: Sage, 1988:291–323.

GIGLIOTTI, RICHARD J., and HEATHER K. HUFF. "Role Related Conflicts, Strains, and Stresses of Older-Adult College Students." *Sociological Focus*. Vol. 28, No. 3 (August 1995):329–42.

GILBERT, NEIL. "Realities and Mythologies of Rape." *Society*. Vol. 29, No. 4 (May–June 1992):4–10.

GILBERTSON, GRETA A., and DOUGLAS T. GURAK. "Broadening the Enclave Debate: The Dual Labor Market Experiences of Dominican and Colombian Men in New York City." *Sociological Forum*. Vol. 8, No. 2 (June 1993):205–20.

GILL, RICHARD T. "What Happened to the American Way of Death?" *The Public Interest*. Vol. 127 (Spring 1996):105–17.

GILLIGAN, CAROL. *In a Different Voice: Psychological Theory and Women's Development*. Cambridge, Mass.: Harvard University Press, 1982.

———. *Making Connections: The Relational Worlds of Adolescent Girls at Emma Willard School*. Cambridge, Mass.: Harvard University Press, 1990.

GIMENEZ, MARTHA E. "Silence in the Classroom: Some Thoughts About Teaching in the 1980s." *Teaching Sociology*. Vol. 17, No. 2 (April 1989):184–91.

GINDA, JOHN J. "Teaching 'Nature Versus Nurture': The Case of African American Athletic Success." *Teaching Sociology*. Vol. 23, No. 4 (October 1995):389–95.

GINSBURG, FAYE, and ANNA LOWENHAUPT TSING, EDS. *Uncertain Terms: Negotiating Gender in American Culture*. Boston: Beacon Press, 1990.

GIOVANNINI, MAUREEN. "Female Anthropologist and Male Informant: Gender Conflict in a Sicilian Town." In John J. Macionis and Nijole V. Benokraitis, eds., *Seeing Ourselves: Classic, Contemporary, and Cross-Cultural Readings in Sociology*. 2d ed. Englewood Cliffs, N.J.: Prentice Hall, 1992:27–32.

GLAAB, CHARLES N. *The American City: A Documentary History*. Homewood, Ill.: Dorsey Press, 1963.

GLADUE, BRIAN A., RICHARD GREEN, and RONALD E. HELLMAN. "Neuroendocrine Response to Estrogen and Sexual Orientation." *Science*. Vol. 225, No. 4669 (September 28, 1984):1496–99.

GLAZER, NATHAN, and DANIEL P. MOYNIHAN. *Beyond the Melting Pot*. 2d ed. Cambridge, Mass.: MIT Press, 1970.

GLEICK, ELIZABETH. "The Marker We've Been Waiting For." *Time*. Vol. 149, No. 14 (April 7, 1997):28–42.

GLEICK, SHARON. "Who Are They?" *Time*. Special Issue (June 1, 1995):44–51.

GLENN, NORVAL D., and BETH ANN SHELTON. "Regional Differences in Divorce in the United States." *Journal of Marriage and the Family*. Vol. 47, No. 3 (August 1985):641–52.

GLOCK, CHARLES Y. "The Religious Revival in America." In Jane Zahn, ed., *Religion and the Face of America*. Berkeley: University of California Press, 1959:25–42.

———. "On the Study of Religious Commitment." *Religious Education*. Vol. 62, No. 4 (1962):98–110.

GLUCK, PETER R., and RICHARD J. MEISTER. *Cities in Transition*. New York: New Viewpoints, 1979.

GLUECK, SHELDON, and ELEANOR GLUECK. *Unraveling Juvenile Delinquency*. New York: Commonwealth Fund, 1950.

GOETTING, ANN. "Divorce Outcome Research." *Journal of Family Issues*. Vol. 2, No. 3 (September 1981):350–78.

———. Personal communication, 1989.

GOFFMAN, ERVING. *The Presentation of Self in Everyday Life*. Garden City, N.Y.: Anchor Books, 1959.

———. *Asylums: Essays on the Social Situation of Mental Patients and Other Inmates*. Garden City, N.Y.: Anchor Books, 1961.

———. *Stigma: Notes on the Management of Spoiled Identity*. Englewood Cliffs, N.J.: Prentice Hall, 1963.

———. *Interactional Ritual: Essays on Face to Face Behavior*. Garden City, N.Y.: Anchor Books, 1967.

———. *Gender Advertisements*. New York: Harper Colophon, 1979.

GOLDBERG, STEVEN. *The Inevitability of Patriarchy*. New York: William Morrow, 1974.

———. Personal communication, 1987.

GOLDEN, FREDERIC. "Here Come the Microkids." *Time*. Vol. 119, No. 18 (May 3, 1982):50–56.

GOLDFARB, JEFFREY C. *Beyond Glasnost: The Post-Totalitarian Mind*. Chicago: University of Chicago Press, 1989.

GOLDFARB, WILLIAM. "Groundwater: The Buried Life." In F. Herbert Bormann and Stephen R. Kellert, eds., *Ecology, Economics, and Ethics: The Broken Circle*. New Haven, Conn.: Yale University Press, 1991:123–35.

GOLDSBY, RICHARD A. *Race and Races*. 2d ed. New York: Macmillan, 1977.

GOLDSMITH, H. H. "Genetic Influences on Personality From Infancy." *Child Development*. Vol. 54, No. 2 (April 1983):331–35.

GOODE, WILLIAM J. "The Theoretical Importance of Love." *American Sociological Review*. Vol. 24, No. 1 (February 1959):38–47.

———. "Encroachment, Charlatanism, and the Emerging Profession: Psychology, Sociology and Medicine." *American Sociological Review*. Vol. 25, No. 6 (December 1960):902–14.

GORDON, JAMES S. "The Paradigm of Holistic Medicine." In Arthur C. Hastings et al., eds., *Health for the Whole Person: The Complete Guide to Holistic Medicine*. Boulder, Colo.: Westview Press, 1980:3–27.

GORING, CHARLES BUCKMAN. *The English Convict: A Statistical Study*. Montclair, N.J.: Patterson Smith, 1972; orig. 1913.

GORMAN, CHRISTINE. "Mexico City's Menacing Air." *Time*. Vol. 137, No. 13 (April 1, 1991):61.

GOTTFREDSON, MICHAEL R., and TRAVIS HIRSCHI. "National Crime Control Policies." *Society*. Vol. 32, No. 2 (January–February 1995):30–36.

GOTTMANN, JEAN. *Megalopolis*. New York: Twentieth Century Fund, 1961.

GOUGH, KATHLEEN. "The Origin of the Family." *Journal of Marriage and the Family*. Vol. 33, No. 4 (November 1971):760–71.

GOULD, STEPHEN J. "Evolution as Fact and Theory." *Discover* (May 1981):35–37.

GOULDNER, ALVIN. *Enter Plato*. New York: Free Press, 1965.

———. "The Sociologist as Partisan: Sociology and the Welfare State." In Larry T. Reynolds and Janice M. Reynolds, eds., *The Sociology of Sociology*. New York: David McKay, 1970a:218–55.

———. *The Coming Crisis of Western Sociology*. New York: Avon Books, 1970b.

GRAHAM, JOHN W., and ANDREA H. BELLER. "Child Support in Black and White: Racial Differentials in the Award and Receipt of Child Support During the 1980s." *Social Science Quarterly*. Vol. 77, No. 3 (September 1996):528–42.

GRANOVETTER, MARK. "The Strength of Weak Ties." *American Journal of Sociology*. Vol. 78, No. 6 (May 1973):1360–80.

GRANT, DON SHERMAN, II, and MICHAEL WALLACE. "Why Do Strikes Turn Violent?" *American Journal of Sociology*. Vol. 96, No. 5 (March 1991):1117–50.

GRANT, DONALD L. *The Anti-Lynching Movement*. San Francisco: R and E Research Associates, 1975.

GRANT, KAREN R. "The Inverse Care Law in the Context of Universal Free Health Insurance in Canada: Toward Meeting Health Needs Through Public Policy." *Sociological Focus*. Vol. 17, No. 2 (April 1984):137–55.

GRAY, PAUL. "Whose America?" *Time*. Vol. 137, No. 27 (July 8, 1991):12–17.

GREELEY, ANDREW M. *Ethnicity in the United States: A Preliminary Reconnaissance*. New York: Wiley, 1974.

———. *Religious Change in America*. Cambridge, Mass.: Harvard University Press, 1989.

GREEN, JOHN C. "Pat Robertson and the Latest Crusade: Resources and the 1988 Presidential Campaign." *Social Sciences Quarterly*. Vol. 74, No. 1 (March 1993):156–68.

GREENBERG, DAVID F. *The Construction of Homosexuality*. Chicago: University of Chicago Press, 1988.

GREENHOUSE, LINDA. "Justices Uphold Stiffer Sentences for Hate Crimes." *New York Times* (June 12, 1993):1, 8.

GREENWALD, JOHN. "The New Service Class." *Time*. Vol. 144, No. 20 (November 14, 1994):72–74.

GREER, SCOTT. *Urban Renewal and American Cities*. Indianapolis, Ind.: Bobbs-Merrill, 1965.

GREGORY, PAUL R., and ROBERT C. STUART. *Comparative Economic Systems*. 2d ed. Boston: Houghton Mifflin, 1985.

GREGORY, SOPHFRONIA SCOTT. "The Knife in the Book Bag." *Time*. Vol. 141, No. 6 (February 8, 1993):37.

GROSS, JANE. "New Challenge of Youth: Growing Up in a Gay Home." *New York Times* (February 11, 1991):A1, B7.

GRUENBERG, BARRY. "The Happy Worker: An Analysis of Educational and Occupational Differences in Determinants of Job Satisfaction." *American Journal of Sociology*. Vol. 86, No. 2 (September 1980):247–71.

GUP, TED. "What Makes This School Work?" *Time*. Vol. 140, No. 25 (December 21, 1992):63–65.

GUTFELD, ROSE. "Eight of Ten Americans are Environmentalists." *Wall Street Journal* (August 2, 1991):A1.

GUTMAN, HERBERT G. *The Black Family in Slavery and Freedom, 1750–1925*. New York: Pantheon Books, 1976.

GWARTNEY-GIBBS, PATRICIA A. "The Institutionalization of Premarital Cohabitation: Estimates From Marriage License Applications, 1970 and 1980." *Journal of Marriage and the Family*. Vol. 48, No. 2 (May 1986):423–34.

GWARTNEY-GIBBS, PATRICIA A., JEAN STOCKARD, and SUSANNE BOHMER. "Learning Courtship Agression: The Influence of Parents, Peers, and Personal Experiences." *Family Relations*. Vol. 36, No. 3 (July 1987):276–82.

GWYNNE, S. C., and JOHN F. DICKERSON. "Lost in the E-Mail." *Time*. Vol. 149, No. 15 (April 21, 1997):88–90.

HABERMAS, JÜRGEN. *Toward a Rational Society: Student Protest, Science, and Politics*. Jeremy J. Shapiro, trans. Boston: Beacon Press, 1970.

HACKER, HELEN MAYER. "Women as a Minority Group." *Social Forces*. Vol. 30 (October 1951):60–69.

———. "Women as a Minority Group: 20 Years Later." In Florence Denmark, ed., *Who Discriminates Against Women?* Beverly Hills, Calif.: Sage, 1974:124–34.

HACKEY, ROBERT B. "Competing Explanations of Voter Turnout Among American Blacks." *Social Science Quarterly*. Vol. 73, No. 1 (March 1992):71–89.

HACKMAN, J. R. "The Design of Work Teams." In J. Lorch, ed., *Handbook of Organizational Behavior*. Englewood Cliffs, N.J.: Prentice Hall, 1988:315–42.

HADAWAY, C. KIRK, PENNY LONG MARLER, and MARK CHAVES. "What the Polls Don't Show: A Closer Look at U.S. Church Attendance." *American Sociological Review*. Vol. 58, No. 6 (December 1993):741–52.

HADDEN, JEFFREY K., and CHARLES E. SWAIN. *Prime Time Preachers: The Rising Power of Televangelism*. Reading, Mass.: Addison-Wesley, 1981.

HAFNER, KATIE. "Making Sense of the Internet." *Newsweek* (October 24, 1994):46–48.

HAGAN, JOHN, and PATRICIA PARKER. "White-Collar Crime and Punishment: The Class Structure and Legal Sanctioning of Securities Violations." *American Sociological Review*. Vol. 50, No. 3 (June 1985):302–16.

HAIG, ROBIN ANDREW. *The Anatomy of Humor: Biopsychosocial and Therapeutic Perspectives*. Springfield, Ill.: Charles C. Thomas, 1988.

HALBERSTAM, DAVID. *The Reckoning*. New York: Avon Books, 1986.

HALEDJIAN, DEAN. "How to Tell a Businessman From a Businesswoman." Annandale, Va.: Northern Virginia Community College, 1997.

HALL, JOHN R., and MARY JO NEITZ. *Culture: Sociological Perspectives*. Englewood Cliffs, N.J.: Prentice Hall, 1993.

HALLINAN, MAUREEN T. "The Sociological Study of Social Change." *American Sociological Review*. Vol. 62, No. 1 (February 1997):1–11.

HALLINAN, MAUREEN T., and RICHARD A. WILLIAMS. "Interracial Friendship Choices in Secondary Schools." *American Sociological Review*. Vol. 54, No. 1 (February 1989):67–78.

HAMBLIN, DORA JANE. *The First Cities*. New York: Time-Life Books, 1973.

HAMEL, RUTH. "Raging Against Aging." *American Demographics*. Vol. 12, No. 3 (March 1990):42–45.

HAMMOND, PHILIP E. "Introduction." In Philip E. Hammond, ed., *The Sacred in a Secular Age: Toward Revision in the Scientific Study of Religion*. Berkeley: University of California Press, 1985:1–6.

HAMRICK, MICHAEL H., DAVID J. ANSPAUGH, and GENE EZELL. *Health*. Columbus, Ohio: Merrill, 1986.

HANDGUN CONTROL, INC. Data cited in *Time* (December 20, 1993) and various newspaper reports (March 2, 6, 1994).

———. [Online] Available http://www.handguncontrol.org, 1998.

HANDLIN, OSCAR. *Boston's Immigrants 1790–1865: A Study in Acculturation*. Cambridge, Mass.: Harvard University Press, 1941.

HANEY, CRAIG, CURTIS BANKS, and PHILIP ZIMBARDO. "Interpersonal Dynamics in a Simulated Prison." *International Journal of Criminology and Penology*. Vol. 1 (1973):69–97.

HARBERT, ANITA A., and LEON H. GINSBERG. *Human Services for Older Adults*. Columbia: University of South Carolina Press, 1991.

HAREVEN, TAMARA K. "The Life Course and Aging in Historical Perspective." In Tamara K. Hareven and Kathleen J. Adams, eds., *Aging and Life Course Transitions: An Interdisciplinary Perspective*. New York: Guilford Press, 1982:1–26.

HARLAN, WILLIAM H. "Social Status of the Aged in Three Indian Villages." In Bernice L. Neugarten, ed., *Middle Age and Aging: A Reader in Social Psychology*. Chicago: University of Chicago Press, 1968:469–75.

HARLOW, CAROLINE WOLF. *Female Victims of Violent Crime*. Bureau of Justice Statistics report. Washington, D.C.: U.S. Government Printing Office, 1991.

HARLOW, HARRY F., and MARGARET KUENNE HARLOW. "Social Deprivation in Monkeys." *Scientific American*. Vol. 207 (November 1962):137–46.

HARRIES, KEITH D. *Serious Violence: Patterns of Homicide and Assault in America*. Springfield, Ill.: Charles C. Thomas, 1990.

HARRINGTON, MICHAEL. *The New American Poverty*. New York: Penguin Books, 1984.

HARRIS, CHAUNCEY D., and EDWARD L. ULLMAN. "The Nature of Cities." *The Annals*. Vol. 242 (November 1945):7–17.

HARRIS, JACK DASH. Lecture on cockfighting in the Philippines. Semester at Sea (October 27, 1994).

HARRIS, MARVIN. *Cows, Pigs, Wars and Witches: The Riddles of Culture*. New York: Vintage Books, 1975.

———. "Why Men Dominate Women." *New York Times Magazine* (November 13, 1977):46, 115–23.

———. *Cultural Anthropology*. 2d ed. New York: Harper & Row, 1987.

HARRISON, PAUL. *Inside the Third World: The Anatomy of Poverty*. 2d ed. New York: Penguin Books, 1984.

HARTMANN, BETSY, and JAMES BOYCE. *Needless Hunger: Voices From a Bangladesh Village*. San Francisco: Institute for Food and Development Policy, 1982.

HARVEY, DAVID. "Labor, Capital, and Class Struggle Around the Built Environment." *Politics and Society*. Vol. 6 (1976):265–95.

HAVIGHURST, ROBERT J., BERNICE L. NEUGARTEN, and SHELDON S. TOBIN. "Disengagement and Patterns of Aging." In Bernice L. Neugarten, ed.,

Middle Age and Aging: A Reader in Social Psychology. Chicago: University of Chicago Press, 1968:161–72.

HAYNEMAN, STEPHEN P., and WILLIAM A. LOXLEY. "The Effect of Primary-School Quality on Academic Achievement Across Twenty-nine High- and Low-Income Countries." *American Journal of Sociology*. Vol. 88, No. 6 (May 1983):1162–94.

HEALTH INSURANCE ASSOCIATION OF AMERICA. *Source Book of Health Insurance Data*. Washington, D.C.: The Association, 1991.

HEATH, JULIA A., and W. DAVID BOURNE. "Husbands and Housework: Parity or Parody?" *Social Science Quarterly*. Vol. 76, No. 1 (March 1995):195–202.

HEILBRONER, ROBERT L. *The Making of Economic Society*. 7th ed. Englewood Cliffs, N.J.: Prentice Hall, 1985.

HELGESEN, SALLY. *The Female Advantage: Women's Ways of Leadership*. New York: Doubleday, 1990.

HELIN, DAVID W. "When Slogans Go Wrong." *American Demographics*. Vol. 14, No. 2 (February 1992):14.

HELMUTH, JOHN W. "World Hunger Amidst Plenty." *USA Today*. Vol. 117, No. 2526 (March 1989):48–50.

HENLEY, NANCY, MYKOL HAMILTON, and BARRIE THORNE. "Womanspeak and Manspeak: Sex Differences in Communication, Verbal and Nonverbal." In John J. Macionis and Nijole V. Benokraitis, eds., *Seeing Ourselves: Classic, Contemporary, and Cross-Cultural Readings in Sociology*, 2d ed. Englewood Cliffs, N.J.: Prentice Hall, 1992:10–15.

HENRY, WILLIAM A., III. "Gay Parents: Under Fire and On the Rise." *Time*. Vol. 142, No. 12 (September 20, 1993):66–71.

HERMAN, DIANNE. "The Rape Culture." In John J. Macionis and Nijole V. Benokraitis, eds., *Seeing Ourselves: Classic, Contemporary, and Cross-Cultural Readings in Sociology*. 4th ed. Upper Saddle River, N.J.: Prentice Hall, 1998.

HERMAN, EDWARD S. *Corporate Control, Corporate Power: A Twentieth Century Fund Study*. New York: Cambridge University Press, 1981.

HERRNSTEIN, RICHARD J. *IQ and the Meritocracy*. Boston: Little, Brown, 1973.

HERRNSTEIN, RICHARD J., and CHARLES MURRAY. *The Bell Curve: Intelligence and Class Structure in American Life*. New York: Free Press, 1994.

HERRSTROM, STAFFAN. "Sweden: Pro-Choice on Child Care." *New Perspectives Quarterly*. Vol. 7, No. 1 (Winter 1990):27–28.

HERSCH, JONI, and SHELLY WHITE-MEANS. "Employer-Sponsored Health and Pension Benefits and the Gender/Race Wage Gap." *Social Science Quarterly*. Vol. 74, No. 4 (December 1993):850–66.

HESS, STEPHEN. "Reporters Who Cover Congress." *Society*. Vol. 28, No. 2 (January–February 1991):60–65.

HEWLETT, BARRY S. "Husband-Wife Reciprocity and the Father-Infant Relationship Among Aka Pygmies." In Barry S. Hewlett, ed., *Father-Child Relations: Cultural and Bio-Social Contexts*. New York: Aldine, 1992:153–76.

HEWLETT, SYLVIA ANN. "The Feminization of the Work Force." *New Perspectives Quarterly*. Vol. 7, No. 1 (Winter 1990):13–15.

HIROSHI, MANNARI. *The Japanese Business Leaders*. Tokyo: University of Tokyo Press, 1974.

HIRSCHI, TRAVIS. *Causes of Delinquency*. Berkeley: University of California Press, 1969.

HOCHSCHILD, ARLIE, with ANNE MACHUNG. *The Second Shift: Working Parents and the Revolution at Home*. New York: Viking Books, 1989.

HODGE, ROBERT W., DONALD J. TREIMAN, and PETER H. ROSSI. "A Comparative Study of Occupational Prestige." In Reinhard Bendix and Seymour Martin Lipset, eds., *Class, Status, and Power: Social Stratification in Comparative Perspective*. 2d ed. New York: Free Press, 1966:309–21.

HOERR, JOHN. "The Payoff From Teamwork." *Business Week*. No. 3114 (July 10, 1989):56–62.

HOGAN, DENNIS P., and EVELYN M. KITAGAWA. "The Impact of Social Status and Neighborhood on the Fertility of Black Adolescents." *American Journal of Sociology*. Vol. 90, No. 4 (January 1985):825–55.

HOGGARTH, RICHARD. "The Abuses of Literacy." *Society*. Vol. 55, No. 3 (March–April 1995):55–62.

HOLLANDER, PAUL. "We Are All (Sniffle, Sniffle) Victims Now." *Wall Street Journal* (January 18, 1995):A14.

HOLM, JEAN. *The Study of Religions*. New York: Seabury Press, 1977.

HOLMES, MALCOLM D., HARMON M. HOSCH, HOWARD C. DAUDISTEL, DOLORES PEREZ, and JOSEPH B. GRAVES. "Judges, Ethnicity and Minority Sentencing: Evidence Among Hispanics." *Social Science Quarterly*. Vol. 74, No. 3 (September 1993):496–506.

HOLMES, STEVEN A. "Income Disparity Between Poorest and Richest Rises." *New York Times* (June 20, 1996):A1, A18.

————. "For Hispanic Poor, No Silver Lining." *New York Times* (October 13, 1996): section 4, p. 5.

HOLMSTROM, DAVID. "Abuse of Elderly, Even by Adult Children, Gets More Attention and Official Concern." *Christian Science Monitor* (July 28, 1994):1.

HONEYWELL, ROY J. *The Educational Work of Thomas Jefferson*. Cambridge, Mass.: Harvard University Press, 1931.

HOROWITZ, IRVING LOUIS. *The Decomposition of Sociology*. New York: Oxford University Press, 1993.

HOSTETLER, JOHN A. *Amish Society*. 3d ed. Baltimore: Johns Hopkins University Press, 1980.

HOUT, MICHAEL, and ANDREW M. GREELEY. "The Center Doesn't Hold: Church Attendance in the United States, 1940–1984." *American Sociological Review*. Vol. 52, No. 3 (June 1987):325–45.

HOUT, MIKE, CLEM BROOKS, and JEFF MANZA. "The Persistence of Classes in Post-Industrial Societies." *International Sociology*. Vol. 8, No. 3 (September 1993):259–77.

HOWE, NEIL, and WILLIAM STRAUSS. "America's 13th Generation." *New York Times* (April 16, 1991).

HOWLETT, DEBBIE. "Cruzan's Struggle Left Imprint: 10,000 Others in Similar State." *USA Today* (December 27, 1990):3A.

HOYT, HOMER. *The Structure and Growth of Residential Neighborhoods in American Cities*. Washington, D.C.: Federal Housing Administration, 1939.

HSU, FRANCIS L. K. *The Challenge of the American Dream: The Chinese in the United States*. Belmont, Calif.: Wadsworth, 1971.

HUBER, JOAN, and GLENNA SPITZE. "Considering Divorce: An Expansion of Becker's Theory of Marital Instability." *American Journal of Sociology*. Vol. 86, No. 1 (July 1980):75–89.

HUCHINGSON, JAMES E. "Science and Religion." *The Herald* (Dade County, Florida). December 25, 1994:1M, 6M.

HUET-COX, ROCIO. "Medical Education: New Wine in Old Wine Skins." In Victor W. Sidel and Ruth Sidel, eds., *Reforming Medicine: Lessons of the Last Quarter Century*. New York: Pantheon Books, 1984:129–49.

HUFFMAN, MATT L., STEVEN C. VELASCO, and WILLIAM T. BIELBY. "Where Sex Composition Matters Most: Comparing the Effects of Job Versus Occupational Sex Composition of Earnings." *Sociological Focus*. Vol. 29, No. 3 (August 1996):189–207.

HULS, GLENNA. Personal communication, 1987.

HUMPHREY, CRAIG R., and FREDERICK R. BUTTEL. *Environment, Energy, and Society*. Belmont, Calif.: Wadsworth, 1982.

HUMPHREY, DEREK. *Final Exit: The Practicalities of Self-Deliverance and Assisted Suicide for the Dying*. Eugene, Ore.: The Hemlock Society, 1991.

HUMPHRIES, HARRY LEROY. *The Structure and Politics of Intermediary Class Positions: An Empirical Examination of Recent Theories of Class*. Unpublished Ph.D. dissertation. Eugene: University of Oregon, 1984.

HUNNICUT, BENJAMIN K. "Are We All Working Too Hard? No Time for God or Family." *Wall Street Journal* (January 4, 1990).

HUNT, MORTON. *Sexual Behavior in the 1970s*. Chicago: Playboy Press, 1974.

HUNTER, FLOYD. *Community Power Structure*. Garden City, N.Y.: Doubleday, 1963; orig. 1953.

HUNTER, JAMES DAVISON. *American Evangelicalism: Conservative Religion and the Quandary of Modernity*. New Brunswick, N.J.: Rutgers University Press, 1983.

————. "Conservative Protestantism." In Philip E. Hammond, ed., *The Sacred in a Secular Age*. Berkeley: University of California Press, 1985:50–66.

————. *Evangelicalism: The Coming Generation*. Chicago: University of Chicago Press, 1987.

————. *Culture Wars: The Struggle to Define America*. New York: Basic Books, 1991.

HURLEY, ANDREW. *Environmental Inequalities: Class, Race, and Industrial Pollution in Gary, Indiana, 1945–1980*. Chapel Hill: University of North Carolina Press, 1995.

HURN, CHRISTOPHER. *The Limits and Possibilities of Schooling*. Needham Heights, Mass.: Allyn & Bacon, 1978.

HWANG, SEAN-SHONG, STEVEN H. MURDOCK, BANOO PARPIA, and RITA R. HAMM. "The Effects of Race and Socioeconomic Status on Residential Segregation in Texas, 1970–1980." *Social Forces*. Vol. 63, No. 3 (March 1985):732–47.

HYMAN, HERBERT H., and CHARLES R. WRIGHT. "Trends in Voluntary Association Memberships of American Adults: Replication Based on Secondary Analysis of National Sample Survey." *American Sociological Review*. Vol. 36, No. 2 (April 1971):191–206.

HYMOWITZ, CAROL. "World's Poorest Women Advance by Entrepreneurship." *Wall Street Journal* (September 9, 1995):B1.

IANNACCONE, LAURENCE R. "Why Strict Churches Are Strong." *American Journal of Sociology*. Vol. 99, No. 5 (March 1994):1180–1211.

IDE, THOMAS R., and ARTHUR J. CORDELL. "Automating Work." *Society*. Vol. 31, No. 6 (September–October 1994):65–71.

ILLICH, IVAN. *Medical Nemesis: The Expropriation of Health*. New York: Pantheon Books, 1976.

INTER-PARLIAMENTARY UNION. *Men and Women in Politics: Democracy in the Making.* Geneva: 1997.

ISAY, RICHARD A. *Being Homosexual: Gay Men and Their Development.* New York: Farrar, Straus, & Giroux, 1989.

JACOB, JOHN E. "An Overview of Black America in 1985." In James D. Williams, ed., *The State of Black America 1986.* New York: National Urban League, 1986:i–xi.

JACOBS, DAVID, and RONALD E. HELMS. "Toward a Political Model of Incarceration: A Time-Series Examination of Multiple Explanations for Prison Admission Rates." *American Journal of Sociology.* Vol. 102, No. 2 (September 1996):323–57.

JACOBS, JAMES B. "Should Hate Be a Crime?" *The Public Interest.* No. 113 (Fall 1993):3–14.

JACOBS, JANE. *The Death and Life of Great American Cities.* New York: Random House, 1961.

———. *The Economy of Cities.* New York: Vintage Books, 1970.

JACOBSON, JODI L. "Closing the Gender Gap in Development." In Lester R. Brown et al., eds., *State of the World 1993: A Worldwatch Institute Report on Progress Toward a Sustainable Society.* New York: Norton, 1993:61–79.

JACOBY, RUSSELL, and NAOMI GLAUBERMAN, EDS. *The Bell Curve Debate.* New York: Random House, 1995.

JACQUET, CONSTANT H., and ALICE M. JONES. *Yearbook of American and Canadian Churches 1991.* Nashville, Tenn.: Abingdon Press, 1991.

JAGAROWSKY, PAUL A., and MARY JO BANE. *Neighborhood Poverty: Basic Questions.* Discussion paper series H-90-3. John F. Kennedy School of Government. Cambridge, Mass.: Harvard University Press, 1990.

JAGGER, ALISON. "Political Philosophies of Women's Liberation." In Laurel Richardson and Verta Taylor, eds., *Feminist Frontiers: Rethinking Sex, Gender, and Society.* Reading, Mass.: Addison-Wesley, 1983.

JAMES, DAVID R. "City Limits on Racial Equality: The Effects of City-Suburb Boundaries on Public-School Desegregation, 1968–1976." *American Sociological Review.* Vol. 54, No. 6 (December 1989):963–85.

JANIS, IRVING. *Victims of Groupthink.* Boston: Houghton Mifflin, 1972.

———. *Crucial Decisions: Leadership in Policymaking and Crisis Management.* New York: Free Press, 1989.

JANUS, CHRISTOPHER G. "Slavery Abolished? Only Officially." *Christian Science Monitor* (May 17, 1996):18.

JARRETT, ROBIN L. "Living Poor: Family Life Among Single Parent, African-American Women." *Social Problems.* Vol. 41, No. 1 (February 1994):30–49.

JEFFERSON, THOMAS. Letter to James Madison, October 28, 1785. In Julian P. Boyd, ed., *The Papers of Thomas Jefferson.* Princeton, N.J.: Princeton University Press, 1953:681–83; orig. 1785.

JENCKS, CHRISTOPHER. "Genes and Crime." *The New York Review* (February 12, 1987):33–41.

JENCKS, CHRISTOPHER, ET AL. *Inequality: A Reassessment of the Effect of Family and Schooling in America.* New York: Basic Books, 1972.

JENKINS, BRIAN M. "Terrorism Remains a Threat." Syndicated column, *The Columbus Dispatch* (January 14, 1990):D1.

JENKINS, HOLMAN, JR. "The 'Poverty' Lobby's Inflated Numbers." *Wall Street Journal* (December 14, 1992):A10.

JENKINS, J. CRAIG, and CHARLES PERROW. "Insurgency of the Powerless: Farm Worker Movements (1946–1972)." *American Sociological Review.* Vol. 42, No. 2 (April 1977):249–68.

JENKINS, J. CRAIG, and MICHAEL WALLACE. "The Generalized Action Potential of Protest Movements: The New Class, Social Trends, and Political Exclusion Explanations." *Sociological Forum.* Vol. 11, No. 2 (June 1996):183–207.

JENSEN, LIEF, DAVID J. EGGEBEEN, and DANIEL T. LICHTER. "Child Policy and the Ameliorative Effects of Public Assistance." *Social Science Quarterly.* Vol. 74, No. 3 (September 1993):542–59.

JOHNSON, CATHRYN. "Gender, Legitimate Authority, and Leader-Subordinate Conversations." *American Sociological Review.* Vol. 59, No. 1 (February 1994):122–35.

JOHNSON, DIRK. "Census Finds Many Claiming New Identity: Indian." *New York Times* (March 5, 1991):A1, A16.

JOHNSON, NORRIS R. "Panic at 'The Who Concert Stampede': An Empirical Assessment." *Social Problems.* Vol. 34, No. 4 (October 1987):362–73.

JOHNSON, PAUL. "The Seven Deadly Sins of Terrorism." In Benjamin Netanyahu, ed., *International Terrorism.* New Brunswick, N.J.: Transaction Books, 1981:12–22.

JOHNSTON, DAVID CAY. "Voting, America's Not Keen On. Coffee Is Another Matter." *New York Times* (November 10, 1996): section 4, p. 2.

JOHNSTON, R. J. "Residential Area Characteristics." In D. T. Herbert and R. J. Johnston, eds., *Social Areas in Cities. Vol. 1: Spatial Processes and Form.* New York: Wiley, 1976:193–235.

JOINT ECONOMIC COMMITTEE. *The Concentration of Wealth in the United States: Trends in the Distribution of Wealth Among American Families.* Washington, D.C.: United States Congress, 1986.

JOSEPHY, ALVIN M., JR. *Now That the Buffalo's Gone: A Study of Today's American Indians.* New York: Alfred A. Knopf, 1982.

JOURNAL OF THE AMERICAN MEDICAL ASSOCIATION. Data cited in Pollack, Andrew, "Overseas, Smoking Is One of Life's Small Pleasures." *New York Times* (August 17, 1996).

KADUSHIN, CHARLES. "Friendship Among the French Financial Elite." *American Sociological Review.* Vol. 60, No. 2 (April 1995):202–21.

KAELBLE, HARTMUT. *Social Mobility in the 19th and 20th Centuries: Europe and America in Comparative Perspective.* New York: St. Martin's Press, 1986.

KAIN, EDWARD L. "A Note on the Integration of AIDS Into the Sociology of Human Sexuality." *Teaching Sociology.* Vol. 15, No. 4 (July 1987):320–23.

———. *The Myth of Family Decline: Understanding Families in a World of Rapid Social Change.* Lexington, Mass.: Lexington Books, 1990.

KAIN, EDWARD L., and SHANNON HART. "AIDS and the Family: A Content Analysis of Media Coverage." Presented to National Council on Family Relations, Atlanta, 1987.

KALISH, RICHARD A. "The New Ageism and the Failure Models: A Polemic." *The Gerontologist.* Vol. 19, No. 4 (August 1979):398–402.

———. *Late Adulthood: Perspectives on Human Development.* 2d ed. Monterey, Calif.: Brooks/Cole, 1982.

KALISH, SUSAN. "Interracial Births Increase as U.S. Ponders Racial Definitions." *Population Today.* Vol. 23, No. 4 (April 1995):1–2.

KALLEBERG, ARNE L., and MARK E. VAN BUREN. "Is Better Better? Explaining the Relationship Between Organization Size and Job Rewards." *American Sociological Review.* Vol. 61, No. 1 (February 1996):47–66.

KAMINER, WENDY. "Volunteers: Who Knows What's in It for Them." *Ms.* (December 1984):93–94, 96, 126–28.

———. "Demasculinizing the Army." *New York Times Review of Books* (June 15, 1997):7.

KANAMINE, LINDA. "School Operation Fails For-Profit Test." *USA Today* (November 24, 1995):6A.

KANTER, ROSABETH MOSS. *Men and Women of the Corporation.* New York: Basic Books, 1977.

———. *The Change Masters: Innovation and Entrepreneurship in the American Corporation.* New York: Simon & Schuster, 1983.

———. *When Giants Learn to Dance: Mastering the Challenges of Strategy, Management, and Careers in the 1990s.* New York: Simon & Schuster, 1989.

KANTER, ROSABETH MOSS, and BARRY A. STEIN. "The Gender Pioneers: Women in an Industrial Sales Force." In R. M. Kanter and B. A. Stein, eds., *Life in Organizations.* New York: Basic Books, 1979:134–60.

———. *A Tale of "O": On Being Different in an Organization.* New York: Harper & Row, 1980.

KAPFERER, JEAN-NOEL. "How Rumors Are Born." *Society.* Vol. 29, No. 5 (July–August 1992):53–60.

KAPLAN, ELAINE BELL. "Black Teenage Mothers and Their Mothers: The Impact of Adolescent Childbearing on Daughters' Relations With Mothers." *Social Problems.* Vol. 43, No. 4 (November 1996):427–43.

KAPLAN, ERIC B., ET AL. "The Usefulness of Preoperative Laboratory Screening." *Journal of the American Medical Association.* Vol. 253, No. 24 (June 28, 1985):3576–81.

KAPTCHUK, TED. "The Holistic Logic of Chinese Medicine." In Shepard Bliss et al., eds., *The New Holistic Health Handbook.* Lexington, Mass.: The Steven Greene Press/Penguin Books, 1985:41.

KARATNYCKY, ADRIAN. "Democracies on the Rise, Democracies at Risk." *Freedom Review.* Vol. 26, No. 1 (January–February 1995):5–10.

KARP, DAVID A., and WILLIAM C. YOELS. "The College Classroom: Some Observations on the Meaning of Student Participation." *Sociology and Social Research.* Vol. 60, No. 4 (July 1976):421–39.

KATES, ROBERT W. "Ending Hunger: Current Status and Future Prospects." *Consequences.* Vol. 2, No. 2 (1996):3–11.

KATZ, JAMES E. "The Social Side of Information Networking." *Society.* Vol. 34, No. 3 (March/April 1997):9–12.

KATZ, MICHAEL B. *In the Shadow of the Poorhouse.* New York: Basic Books, 1986.

KAUFMAN, MARC. "Becoming 'Old Old'." *Philadelphia Inquirer* (October 28, 1990):1-A, 10-A.

KAUFMAN, ROBERT L., and SEYMOUR SPILERMAN. "The Age Structures of Occupations and Jobs." *American Journal of Sociology.* Vol. 87, No. 4 (January 1982):827–51.

KAUFMAN, WALTER. *Religions in Four Dimensions: Existential, Aesthetic, Historical and Comparative.* New York: Reader's Digest Press, 1976.

KEITH, PAT M., and ROBERT B. SCHAFER. "They Hate to Cook: Patterns of Distress in an Ordinary Role." *Sociological Focus.* Vol. 27, No. 4 (October 1994):289–301.

KELLER, HELEN. *The Story of My Life*. New York: Doubleday, Page, 1903.

KELLER, SUZANNE. *The Urban Neighborhood*. New York: Random House, 1968.

KELLERT, STEPHEN R., and F. HERBERT BORMANN. "Closing the Circle: Weaving Strands Among Ecology, Economics, and Ethics." In F. Herbert Bormann and Stephen R. Kellert, eds., *Ecology, Economics, and Ethics: The Broken Circle*. New Haven, Conn.: Yale University Press, 1991:205–10.

KELLEY, JONATHAN, and M. D. R. EVANS. "Class and Class Conflict in Six Western Nations." *American Sociological Review*. Vol. 60, No. 2 (April 1995):157–78.

KEMP, ALICE ABEL, and SHELLEY COVERMAN. "Marginal Jobs or Marginal Workers: Identifying Sex Differences in Low-Skill Occupations." *Sociological Focus*. Vol. 22, No. 1 (February 1989):19–37.

KENNICKELL, ARTHUR, and JANICE SHACK-MARQUEZ. "Changes in Family Finances From 1983 to 1989: Evidence From the Survey of Consumer Finances." *Federal Reserve Bulletin* (January 1992):1–18.

KENYON, KATHLEEN. *Digging Up Jericho*. London: Ernest Benn, 1957.

KERCKHOFF, ALAN C., RICHARD T. CAMPBELL, and IDEE WINFIELD-LAIRD. "Social Mobility in Great Britain and the United States." *American Journal of Sociology*. Vol. 91, No. 2 (September 1985):281–308.

KIDD, QUENTIN, and AIE-RIE LEE. "Postmaterialist Values and the Environment: A Critique and Reappraisal." *Social Science Quarterly*. Vol. 78, No. 1 (March 1997):1–15.

KIDRON, MICHAEL, and RONALD SEGAL. *The New State of the World Atlas*. New York: Simon & Schuster, 1991.

KILBOURNE, BROCK K. "The Conway and Siegelman Claims Against Religious Cults: An Assessment of Their Data." *Journal for the Scientific Study of Religion*. Vol. 22, No. 4 (December 1983):380–85.

KILGORE, SALLY B. "The Organizational Context of Tracking in Schools." *American Sociological Review*. Vol. 56, No. 2 (April 1991):189–203.

KING, KATHLEEN PIKER, and DENNIS E. CLAYSON. "The Differential Perceptions of Male and Female Deviants." *Sociological Focus*. Vol. 21, No. 2 (April 1988):153–64.

KING, MARTIN LUTHER, JR. "The Montgomery Bus Boycott." In Walt Anderson, ed., *The Age of Protest*. Pacific Palisades, Calif.: Goodyear, 1969:81–91.

KINKEAD, GWEN. *Chinatown: A Portrait of a Closed Society*. New York: HarperCollins, 1992.

KINSEY, ALFRED, ET AL. *Sexual Behavior in the Human Male*. Philadelphia: Saunders, 1948.

———. *Sexual Behavior in the Human Female*. Philadelphia: Saunders, 1953.

KIPP, RITA SMITH. "Have Women Always Been Unequal?" In Beth Reed, ed., *Towards a Feminist Transformation of the Academy: Proceedings of the Fifth Annual Women's Studies Conference*. Ann Arbor, Mich.: Great Lakes Colleges Association, 1980:12–18.

KIRK, MARSHALL, and PETER MADSEN. *After the Ball: How America Will Conquer its Fear and Hatred of Gays in the '90s*. New York: Doubleday, 1989.

KISER, EDGAR, and JOACHIM SCHNEIDER. "Bureaucracy and Efficiency: An Analysis of Taxation in Early Modern Prussia." *American Sociological Review*. Vol. 59, No. 2 (April 1994):187–204.

KISHOR, SUNITA. "'May God Give Sons to All': Gender and Child Mortality in India." *American Sociological Review*. Vol. 58, No. 2 (April 1993):247–65.

KITANO, HARRY H. L. "Japanese." In *Harvard Encyclopedia of American Ethnic Groups*. Cambridge, Mass.: Harvard University Press, 1980:561–71.

KITSON, GAY C., and HELEN J. RASCHKE. "Divorce Research: What We Know, What We Need to Know." *Journal of Divorce*. Vol. 4, No. 3 (Spring 1981):1–37.

KITTRIE, NICHOLAS N. *The Right To Be Different: Deviance and Enforced Therapy*. Baltimore: Johns Hopkins University Press, 1971.

KLUCKHOHN, CLYDE. "As An Anthropologist Views It." In Albert Deuth, ed., *Sex Habits of American Men*. New York: Prentice Hall, 1948.

KMITCH, JANET, PEDRO LABOY, and SARAH VAN DAMME. "International Comparisons of Manufacturing Compensation." *Monthly Labor Review*. Vol. 118, No. 10 (October 1995):3–9.

KOCH, HOWARD. *The Panic Broadcast: Portrait of an Event*. Boston: Little, Brown, 1970.

KOELLN, KENNETH, ROSE M. RUBIN, and MARION SMITH PICARD. "Vulnerable Elderly Households: Expenditures on Necessities by Older Americans." *Social Science Quarterly*. Vol. 76, No. 3 (September 1995):619–33.

KOHLBERG, LAWRENCE. *The Psychology of Moral Development: The Nature and Validity of Moral Stages*. New York: Harper & Row, 1981.

KOHLBERG, LAWRENCE, and CAROL GILLIGAN. "The Adolescent as Philosopher: The Discovery of Self in a Postconventional World." *Daedalus*. Vol. 100 (Fall 1971):1051–86.

KOHN, MELVIN L. *Class and Conformity: A Study in Values*. 2d ed. Homewood, Ill.: Dorsey Press, 1977.

KOHN, MELVIN L., and CARMI SCHOOLER. "Job Conditions and Personality: A Longitudinal Assessment of Their Reciprocal Effects." *American Journal of Sociology*. Vol. 87, No. 6 (May 1982):1257–83.

KOLATA, GINA. "When Grandmother Is the Mother, Until Birth." *New York Times* (August 5, 1991):1, 11.

KOMAROVSKY, MIRRA. *Blue Collar Marriage*. New York: Vintage Books, 1967.

———. "Cultural Contradictions and Sex Roles: The Masculine Case." *American Journal of Sociology*. Vol. 78, No. 4 (January 1973):873–84.

———. *Dilemmas of Masculinity: A Study of College Youth*. New York: Norton, 1976.

KORNHAUSER, WILLIAM. *The Politics of Mass Society*. New York: Free Press, 1959.

KOSTERS, MARVIN. "Looking for Jobs in All the Wrong Places." *The Public Interest*. Vol. 125 (Fall 1996):125–31.

KOWALEWSKI, DAVID, and KAREN L. PORTER. "Ecoprotest: Alienation, Deprivation, or Resources." *Social Sciences Quarterly*. Vol. 73, No. 3 (September 1992):523–34.

KOZOL, JONATHAN. *Prisoners of Silence: Breaking the Bonds of Adult Illiteracy in the United States*. New York: Continuum, 1980.

———. "A Nation's Wealth." *Publisher's Weekly* (May 24, 1985a):28–30.

———. *Illiterate America*. Garden City, N.Y.: Doubleday, 1985b.

———. *Rachel and Her Children: Homeless Families in America*. New York: Crown Publishers, 1988.

———. *Savage Inequalities: Children in America's Schools*. New York: Harper Perennial, 1992.

KRAFFT, SUSAN. "¿Quién es Numero Uno?" *American Demographics*. Vol. 15, No. 7 (July 1993):16–17.

KRAMARAE, CHERIS. *Women and Men Speaking*. Rowley, Mass.: Newbury House, 1981.

KRANTZ, MICHAEL. "Say It With a :-)." *Time*. Vol. 149, No. 15:29.

KRASKA, PETER B., and VICTOR E. KAPPELER. "Militarizing American Police: The Rise and Normalization of Paramilitary Units." *Social Problems*. Vol. 44, No. 1 (February 1997):1–18.

KRAYBILL, DONALD B. *The Riddle of Amish Culture*. Baltimore: Johns Hopkins University Press, 1989.

———. "The Amish Encounter With Modernity." In Donald B. Kraybill and Marc A. Olshan, eds., *The Amish Struggle With Modernity*. Hanover, N.H.: University Press of New England, 1994:21–33.

KRAYBILL, DONALD B., and MARC A. OLSHAN, EDS. *The Amish Struggle With Modernity*. Hanover, N.H.: University Press of New England, 1994.

KRIESI, HANSPETER. "New Social Movements and the New Class in the Netherlands." *American Journal of Sociology*. Vol. 94, No. 5 (March 1989):1078–116.

KRISTOF, NICHOLAS D. "Baby May Make Three, But in Japan, That's Not Enough." *New York Times* (October 6, 1996):A3.

KRISTOL, IRVING. "Life Without Father." *Wall Street Journal* (November 3, 1994):A18.

———. "Age Before Politics." *Wall Street Journal* (April 25, 1996):A20.

KÜBLER-ROSS, ELISABETH. *On Death and Dying*. New York: Macmillan, 1969.

KUHN, THOMAS. *The Structure of Scientific Revolutions*. 2d ed. Chicago: University of Chicago Press, 1970.

KUZNETS, SIMON. "Economic Growth and Income Inequality." *The American Economic Review*. Vol. XLV, No. 1 (March 1955):1–28.

———. *Modern Economic Growth: Rate, Structure, and Spread*. New Haven, Conn.: Yale University Press, 1966.

LABOVITZ, PRICISSA. "Immigration—Just the Facts." *New York Times* (March 25, 1996).

LACAYO, RICHARD. "Blood in the Stands." *Time*. Vol. 125, No. 23 (June 10, 1985):38–39, 41.

LADD, JOHN. "The Definition of Death and the Right to Die." In John Ladd, ed., *Ethical Issues Relating to Life and Death*. New York: Oxford University Press, 1979:118–45.

LADNER, JOYCE A. "Teenage Pregnancy: The Implications for Black Americans." In James D. Williams, ed., *The State of Black America 1986*. New York: National Urban League, 1986:65–84.

LAI, H. M. "Chinese." In *Harvard Encyclopedia of American Ethnic Groups*. Cambridge, Mass.: Harvard University Press, 1980:217–33.

LAMAR, JACOB V., JR. "Redefining the American Dilemma." *Time*. Vol. 126, No. 19 (November 11, 1985):33, 36.

LAMBERG-KARLOVSKY, C. C., and MARTHA LAMBERG-KARLOVSKY. "An Early City in Iran." In *Cities: Their Origin, Growth, and Human Impact*. San Francisco: Freeman, 1973:28–37.

LANDERS, ANN. Syndicated column: *Dallas Morning News* (July 8, 1984):4F.

LANDERS, RENE M. "Gender, Race, and the State Courts." *Radcliffe Quarterly*. Vol. 76, No. 4 (December 1990):6–9.

LANE, DAVID. "Social Stratification and Class." In Erik P. Hoffman and Robbin F. Laird, eds., *The Soviet Polity in the Modern Era*. New York: Aldine, 1984:563–605.

LANG, KURT, and GLADYS ENGEL LANG. *Collective Dynamics*. New York: Thomas Y. Crowell, 1961.

LAPPÉ, FRANCES MOORE, and JOSEPH COLLINS. *World Hunger: Twelve Myths*. New York: Grove Press/Food First Books, 1986.

LAPPÉ, FRANCES MOORE, JOSEPH COLLINS, and DAVID KINLEY. *Aid as Obstacle: Twenty Questions about Our Foreign Policy and the Hungry*. San Francisco: Institute for Food and Development Policy, 1981.

LARMER, BROOK. "Dead End Kids." *Newsweek* (May 25, 1992):38–40.

LASLETT, PETER. *The World We Have Lost: England Before the Industrial Age*. 3d ed. New York: Charles Scribner's Sons, 1984.

LAUMANN, EDWARD O., JOHN H. GAGNON, ROBERT T. MICHAEL, and STUART MICHAELS. *The Social Organization of Sexuality: Sexual Practices in the United States*. Chicago: University of Chicago Press, 1994.

LEACOCK, ELEANOR. "Women's Status in Egalitarian Societies: Implications for Social Evolution." *Current Anthropology*. Vol. 19, No. 2 (June 1978):247–75.

LEAVITT, JUDITH WALZER. "Women and Health in America: An Overview." In Judith Walzer Leavitt, ed., *Women and Health in America*. Madison: University of Wisconsin Press, 1984:3–7.

LE BON, GUSTAVE. *The Crowd: A Study of the Popular Mind*. New York: Viking Press, 1960; orig. 1895.

LEE, BARRETT A., R. S. OROPESA, BARBARA J. METCH, and AVERY M. GUEST. "Testing the Decline of Community Thesis: Neighborhood Organization in Seattle, 1929 and 1979." *American Journal of Sociology*. Vol. 89, No. 5 (March 1984):1161–88.

LEE, SHARON M. "Poverty and the U.S. Asian Population." *Social Science Quarterly*. Vol. 75, No. 3 (September 1994):541–59.

LEERHSEN, CHARLES. "Unite and Conquer." *Newsweek* (February 5, 1990):50–55.

LEFEBVRE, HENRI. *The Production of Space*. Oxford: Blackwell, 1991.

LELAND, JOHN. "Bisexuality." *Newsweek* (July 17, 1995):44–49.

LEMERT, EDWIN M. *Social Pathology*. New York: McGraw-Hill, 1951.

———. *Human Deviance, Social Problems, and Social Control*. 2d ed. Englewood Cliffs, N.J.: Prentice Hall, 1972.

LENGERMANN, PATRICIA MADOO, and RUTH A. WALLACE. *Gender in America: Social Control and Social Change*. Englewood Cliffs, N.J.: Prentice Hall, 1985.

LENNON, MARY CLARE, and SARAH ROSENFELD. "Relative Fairness and the Doctrine of Housework: The Importance of Options." *American Journal of Sociology*. Vol. 100, No. 2 (September 1994):506–31.

LENSKI, GERHARD. *Power and Privilege: A Theory of Social Stratification*. New York: McGraw-Hill, 1966.

LENSKI, GERHARD, PATRICK NOLAN, and JEAN LENSKI. *Human Societies: An Introduction to Macrosociology*. 7th ed. New York: McGraw-Hill, 1995.

LEONARD, EILEEN B. *Women, Crime, and Society: A Critique of Theoretical Criminology*. New York: Longman, 1982.

LERNER, DANIEL. *The Passing of Traditional Society: Modernizing the Middle East*. New York: Free Press, 1958.

LESLIE, GERALD R., and SHEILA K. KORMAN. *The Family in Social Context*. 7th ed. New York: Oxford University Press, 1989.

LESTER, DAVID. *The Death Penalty: Issues and Answers*. Springfield, Ill.: Charles C. Thomas, 1987.

LEVER, JANET. "Sex Differences in the Complexity of Children's Play and Games." *American Sociological Review*. Vol. 43, No. 4 (August 1978):471–83.

LEVINE, DONALD N. *Georg Simmel: On Individuality and Social Forms*. Chicago: University of Chicago Press, 1971; orig. 1904:294–323.

LEVINE, MICHAEL. "Reducing Hostility Can Prevent Heart Disease." *Mount Vernon News* (August 7, 1990):4A.

LEVINE, MICHAEL P. *Student Eating Disorders: Anorexia Nervosa and Bulimia*. Washington, D.C.: National Educational Association, 1987.

LEVINE, ROBERT V. "Is Love a Luxury?" *American Demographics*. Vol. 15, No. 2 (February 1993):27–28.

LEVINSON, DANIEL J., with CHARLOTTE N. DARROW, EDWARD B. KLEIN, MARIA H. LEVINSON, and BRAXTON MCKEE. *The Seasons of a Man's Life*. New York: Alfred A. Knopf, 1978.

LEVITAN, SARA, and ISAAC SHAPIRO. *Working but Poor: America's Contradiction*. Baltimore: Johns Hopkins University Press, 1987.

LEVY, FRANK. *Dollars and Dreams: The Changing American Income Distribution*. New York: Russell Sage Foundation, 1987.

LEWIS, FLORA. "The Roots of Revolution." *New York Times Magazine* (November 11, 1984):70–71, 74, 77–78, 82, 84, 86.

LEWIS, OSCAR. *The Children of Sanchez*. New York: Random House, 1961.

LEWIS, PEIRCE, CASEY MCCRACKEN, and ROGER HUNT. "Politics: Who Cares?" *American Demographics*. Vol. 16, No. 10 (October 1994):20–26.

LEWTHWAITE, GILBERT A., and GREGORY KANE. "Bought and Freed." *Sun* (Baltimore: June 18, 1996):A1, A8.

LI, JIANG HONG, and ROGER A. WOJTKIEWICZ. "A New Look at the Effects of Family Structure on Status Attainment." *Social Science Quarterly*. Vol. 73, No. 3 (September 1992):581–95.

LIAZOS, ALEXANDER. "The Poverty of the Sociology of Deviance: Nuts, Sluts and Preverts." *Social Problems*. Vol. 20, No. 1 (Summer 1972):103–20.

LICHTER, DANIEL R. "Race, Employment Hardship, and Inequality in the American Nonmetropolitan South." *American Sociological Review*. Vol. 54, No. 3 (June 1989):436–46.

LICHTER, S. ROBERT, STANLEY ROTHMAN, and LINDA R. ROTHMAN. *The Media Elite: America's New Powerbrokers*. Bethesda, Md.: Adler & Adler, 1986.

LICHTER, S. ROBERT, STANLEY ROTHMAN, and LINDA S. LICHTER. *The Media Elite: America's New Powerbrokers*. New York: Hastings House, 1990.

LIEBOW, ELLIOT. *Tally's Corner*. Boston: Little, Brown, 1967.

LIN, GE, and PETER ROGERSON. Research reported in Diane Crispell, "Sons and Daughters Who Keep in Touch." *American Demographics*. Vol. 16, No. 8 (August 1994):15–16.

LIN, NAN, and WEN XIE. "Occupational Prestige in Urban China." *American Journal of Sociology*. Vol. 93, No. 4 (January 1988):793–832.

LINDEN, EUGENE. "Can Animals Think?" *Time*. Vol. 141, No. 12 (March 22, 1993):54–61.

———. "More Power to Women, Fewer Mouths to Feed." *Time*. Vol. 144, No. 13 (September 26, 1994):64–65.

LINDSTROM, BONNIE. "Chicago's Post-Industrial Suburbs." *Sociological Focus*. Vol. 28, No. 4 (October 1995):399–412.

LING, PYAU. "Causes of Chinese Emigration." In Amy Tachiki et al., eds., *Roots: An Asian American Reader*. Los Angeles: UCLA Asian American Studies Center, 1971:134–38.

LINK, BRUCE G., BRUCE P. DOHRENWEND, and ANDREW E. SKODOL. "Socio-Economic Status and Schizophrenia: Noisome Occupational Characteristics As a Risk Factor." *American Sociological Review*. Vol. 51, No. 2 (April 1986):242–58.

LINN, MICHAEL. Noted in *Cornell Alumni News*. Vol. 99, No. 2 (September 1996):25.

LINTON, RALPH. "One Hundred Percent American." *The American Mercury*. Vol. 40, No. 160 (April 1937):427–29.

———. *The Study of Man*. New York: D. Appleton-Century, 1937.

LIPSET, SEYMOUR MARTIN. *Political Man: The Social Bases of Politics*. Garden City, N.Y.: Anchor/Doubleday, 1963.

LIPSET, SEYMOUR MARTIN, and REINHARD BENDIX. *Social Mobility in Industrial Society*. Berkeley: University of California Press, 1967.

LISKA, ALLEN E. *Perspectives on Deviance*. 3d ed. Englewood Cliffs, N.J.: Prentice Hall, 1991.

LISKA, ALLEN E., and MARK TAUSIG. "Theoretical Interpretations of Social Class and Racial Differentials in Legal Decision Making for Juveniles." *Sociological Quarterly*. Vol. 20, No. 2 (Spring 1979):197–207.

LISKA, ALLEN E., and BARBARA D. WARNER. "Functions of Crime: A Paradoxical Process." *American Journal of Sociology*. Vol. 96, No. 6 (May 1991):1441–63.

LITTMAN, DAVID L. "2001: A Farm Odyssey." *Wall Street Journal* (September 14, 1992):A10.

LO, CLARENCE Y. H. "Countermovements and Conservative Movements in the Contemporary U.S." *Annual Review of Sociology*. Vol. 8. Palo Alto, Calif.: Annual Reviews, 1982:107–34.

LOFLAND, LYN. *A World of Strangers*. New York: Basic Books, 1973.

LOGAN, JOHN R., and MARK SCHNEIDER. "Racial Segregation and Racial Change in American Suburbs, 1970–1980." *American Journal of Sociology*. Vol. 89, No. 4 (January 1984):874–88.

LOHR, STEVE. "British Health Service Faces a Crisis in Funds and Delays." *New York Times* (August 7, 1988):1, 12.

———. "Leashes Get Shorter for Executives." *New York Times* (July 18, 1997):D1, D6.

LONGINO, JR., CHARLES F. "Myths of An Aging America." *American Demographics*. Vol. 16, No. 8 (August 1994):36–42.

LORD, WALTER. *A Night to Remember*. Rev. ed. New York: Holt, Rinehart & Winston, 1976.

LORENZ, FREDERICK O., and BRENT T. BRUTON. "Experiments in Surveys: Linking Mass Class Questionnaires to Introductory Research Methods." *Teaching Sociology*. Vol. 24, No. 3 (July 1996):264–71.

LORENZ, KONRAD. *On Aggression*. New York: Harcourt, Brace & World, 1966.

LOY, PAMELA HEWITT, and LEA P. STEWART. "The Extent and Effects of Sexual Harassment of Working Women." *Sociological Focus*. Vol. 17, No. 1 (January 1984):31–43.

LUBENOW, GERALD C. "A Troubling Family Affair." *Newsweek* (May 14, 1984):34.

LUND, DALE A. "Conclusions about Bereavement in Later Life and Implications for Interventions and Future Research." In Dale A. Lund, ed., *Older Bereaved*

Spouses: Research With Practical Applications. London: Taylor-Francis-Hemisphere, 1989:217–31.

LUND, DALE A., MICHAEL S. CASERTA, and MARGARET F. DIMOND. "Gender Differences Through Two Years of Bereavement Among the Elderly." *The Gerontologist*. Vol. 26, No. 3 (1986):314–20.

LUTZ, CATHERINE A. *Unnatural Emotions: Everyday Sentiments on a Micronesia Atoll and Their Challenge to Western Theory*. Chicago: University of Chicago Press, 1988.

LUTZ, CATHERINE A., and GEOFFREY M. WHITE. "The Anthropology of Emotions." In Bernard J. Siegel, Alan R. Beals, and Stephen A. Tyler, eds., *Annual Review of Anthropology*. Palo Alto, Calif.: Annual Reviews, Vol. 15 (1986):405–36.

LUTZ, WILLIAM. Presented in "The Two Sides of Warspeak." *Time* (February 25, 1991):13.

LYNCH, BARBARA DEUTSCH. "The Garden and the Sea: U.S. Latino Environmenta; Discourses and Mainstream Environmentalism." *Social Problems*. Vol. 40, No. 1 (February 1993):108–24.

LYND, ROBERT S. *Knowledge For What? The Place of Social Science in American Culture*. Princeton, N.J.: Princeton University Press, 1967.

LYND, ROBERT S., and HELEN MERRELL LYND. *Middletown in Transition*. New York: Harcourt, Brace & World, 1937.

LYNOTT, PATRICIA PASSUTH, and BARBARA J. LOGUE. "The 'Hurried Child': The Myth of Lost Childhood on Contemporary American Society." *Sociological Forum*. Vol. 8, No. 3 (September 1993):471–91.

MA, LI-CHEN. Personal communication, 1987.

MABRY, MARCUS. "New Hope for Old Unions?" *Newsweek* (February 24, 1992):39.

MCADAM, DOUG. *Political Process and the Development of Black Insurgency, 1930–1970*. Chicago: University of Chicago Press, 1982.

———. "Tactical Innovation and the Pace of Insurgency." *American Sociological Review*. Vol. 48, No. 6 (December 1983):735–54.

———. *Freedom Summer*. New York: Oxford University Press, 1988.

———. "The Biographical Consequences of Activism." *American Sociological Review*. Vol. 54, No. 5 (October 1989):744–60.

———. "Gender as a Mediator of the Activist Experience: The Case of Freedom Summer." *American Journal of Sociology*. Vol. 97, No. 5 (March 1992):1211–40.

MCADAM, DOUG, JOHN D. MCCARTHY, and MAYER N. ZALD. "Social Movements." In Neil J. Smelser, ed., *Handbook of Sociology*. Newbury Park, Calif.: Sage, 1988:695–737.

MCBROOM, WILLIAM H., and FRED W. REED. "Recent Trends in Conservatism: Evidence of Non-Unitary Patterns." *Sociological Focus*. Vol. 23, No. 4 (October 1990):355–65.

MCCARTHY, JOHN D., and MAYER N. ZALD. "Resource Mobilization and Social Movements: A Partial Theory." *American Journal of Sociology*. Vol. 82, No. 6 (May 1977):1212–41.

MACCOBY, ELEANOR EMMONS, and CAROL NAGY JACKLIN. *The Psychology of Sex Differences*. Palo Alto, Calif.: Stanford University Press, 1974.

MCCOLM, R. BRUCE, JAMES FINN, DOUGLAS W. PAYNE, JOSEPH E. RYAN, LEONARD R. SUSSMAN, and GEORGE ZARYCKY. *Freedom in the World: Political Rights & Civil Liberties, 1990–1991*. New York: Freedom House, 1991.

MCCONNELL, SCOTT. "New Liberal Fear: Hyperdemocracy." *The New York Post* (January 18, 1995):19.

MACDONALD, J. FRED. *Blacks and White TV: African Americans in Television Since 1948*. Chicago: Nelson-Hall, 1992.

MACE, DAVID, and VERA MACE. *Marriage East and West*. Garden City, N.Y.: Doubleday (Dolphin), 1960.

MCGUIRE, MEREDITH B. *Religion: The Social Context*. 2d ed. Belmont, Calif.: Wadsworth, 1987.

MCHENRY, SUSAN. "Rosabeth Moss Kanter." In *Ms*. Vol. 13 (January 1985):62–63, 107–8.

MACIONIS, JOHN J. "Intimacy: Structure and Process in Interpersonal Relationships." *Alternative Lifestyles*. Vol. 1, No. 1 (February 1978):113–30.

———. "The Search for Community in Modern Society: An Interpretation." *Qualitative Sociology*. Vol. 1, No. 2 (September 1978):130–43.

———. "A Sociological Analysis of Humor." Presentation to the Texas Junior College Teachers Association, Houston, 1987.

———. "Making Society (and, Increasingly, the World) Visible." In Earl Babbie, ed., *The Spirit of Sociology*. Belmont, Calif.: Wadsworth, 1993:221–24.

MACIONIS, JOHN J., and VINCENT N. PARRILLO. *Cities and Urban Life*. Upper Saddle River, N.J.: Prentice Hall, 1998.

MACKAY, DONALD G. "Prescriptive Grammar and the Pronoun Problem." In Barrie Thorne, Cheris Kramarae, and Nancy Henley, eds., *Language, Gender and Society*. Rowley, Mass.: Newbury House, 1983:38–53.

MACKINNON, CATHARINE A. *Feminism Unmodified: Discourses on Life and Law*. Cambridge, Mass.: Harvard University Press, 1987.

MACKLIN, ELEANOR D. "Nonmarital Heterosexual Cohabitation: An Overview." In Eleanor D. Macklin and Roger H. Rubin, eds., *Contemporary Families and Alternative Lifestyles: Handbook on Research and Theory*. Beverly Hills, Calif.: Sage, 1983:49–74.

MCLANAHAN, SARA. "Family Structure and the Reproduction of Poverty." *American Journal of Sociology*. Vol. 90, No. 4 (January 1985):873–901.

MCLEOD, JANE D., and MICHAEL J. SHANAHAN. "Poverty, Parenting, and Children's Mental Health." *American Sociological Review*. Vol. 58, No. 3 (June 1993):351–66.

MCLEOD, JAY. *Ain't No Makin' It: Aspirations and Attainment in a Low-Income Neighborhood*. Boulder, Colo.: Westview Press, 1995.

MCLUHAN, MARSHALL. *The Gutenberg Galaxy*. New York: New American Library, 1969.

MCNEIL, DONALD G., JR. "Should Women Be Sent Into Combat?" *New York Times* (July 21, 1991):E3.

MCNULTY, PAUL J. "Who's in Jail and Why They Belong There." *Wall Street Journal* (November 9, 1994):A23.

MCPHAIL, CLARK. *The Myth of the Maddening Crowd*. New York: Aldine, 1991.

MCPHAIL, CLARK, and RONALD T. WOHLSTEIN. "Individual and Collective Behaviors Within Gatherings, Demonstrations, and Riots." *Annual Review of Sociology*. Vol. 9. Palo Alto, Calif.: Annual Reviews, 1983:579–600.

MCRAE, SUSAN. *Cross-Class Families: A Study of Wives' Occupational Superiority*. New York: Oxford University Press, 1986.

MCROBERTS, HUGH A., and KEVIN SELBEE. "Trends in Occupational Mobility in Canada and the United States: A Comparison." *American Sociological Review*. Vol. 46, No. 4 (August 1981):406–21.

MADDOX, SETMA. "Organizational Culture and Leadership Style: Factors Affecting Self-Managed Work Team Performance." Paper presented at the annual meeting of the Southwest Social Science Association, Dallas, February, 1995.

MADSEN, AXEL. *Private Power: Multinational Corporations for the Survival of Our Planet*. New York: William Morrow, 1980.

MAJKA, LINDA C. "Sexual Harassment in the Church." *Society*. Vol. 28. No. 4 (May-June 1991):14–21.

MALTHUS, THOMAS ROBERT. *First Essay on Population 1798*. London: Macmillan, 1926; orig. 1798.

MARCUSE, HERBERT. *One-Dimensional Man*. Boston: Beacon Press, 1964.

MARE, ROBERT D. "Five Decades of Educational Assortative Mating." *American Sociological Review*. Vol. 56, No. 1 (February 1991):15–32.

MARGOLICK, DAVID. "Rape in Marriage Is No Longer Within the Law." *New York Times* (December 13, 1984):6E.

MARÍN, GERARDO, and BARBARA VANOSS MARÍN. *Research With Hispanic Populations*. Newbury Park, Calif.: Sage, 1991.

MARKOFF, JOHN. "Remember Big Brother? Now He's a Company Man." *New York Times* (March 31, 1991):7.

MARKSON, ELIZABETH W. "Moral Dilemmas." *Society*. Vol. 29, No. 5 (July-August 1992):4–6.

MARQUAND, ROBERT. "Worship Shift: Americans Seek Feeling of 'Awe'." *Christian Science Monitor* (May 28, 1997):1, 8.

MARQUAND, ROBERT, and DANIEL B. WOOD. "Rise in Cults as Millennium Approaches." *Christian Science Monitor* (March 28, 1997):1, 18.

MARRIOTT, MICHAEL. "Fathers Find that Child Support Means Owing More than Money." *New York Times* (July 20, 1992):A1, A13.

MARSDEN, PETER. "Core Discussion Networks of Americans." *American Sociological Review*. Vol. 52, No. 1 (February 1987):122–31.

MARSHALL, SUSAN E. "Ladies Against Women: Mobilization Dilemmas of Antifeminist Movements." *Social Problems*. Vol. 32, No. 4 (April 1985):348–62.

MARTIN, DOUGLAS. "The Medicine Woman of the Mohegans." *New York Times* (June 4, 1997):B1, B7.

MARTIN, JOHN M., and ANNE T. ROMANO. *Multinational Crime: Terrorism, Espionage, Drug and Arms Trafficking*. Newbury Park, Calif.: Sage, 1992.

MARTIN, RICHARD C. *Islam: A Cultural Perspective*. Englewood Cliffs, N.J.: Prentice Hall, 1982.

MARTIN, WILLIAM. "The Birth of a Media Myth." *The Atlantic*. Vol. 247, No. 6 (June 1981):7, 10, 11, 16.

MARTINEZ, VALERIE J., R. KENNETH GODWIN, FRANK R. KEMERER, and LAURA PERNA. "The Consequences of School Choice: Who Leaves and Who Stays in the Inner City." *Social Science Quarterly*. Vol. 76, No. 1 (September 1995):485–501.

MARULLO, SAM. "The Functions and Dysfunctions of Preparations for Fighting Nuclear War." *Sociological Focus*. Vol. 20, No. 2 (April 1987):135–53.

MARX, GARY T., and JAMES L. WOOD. "Strands of Theory and Research in Collective Behavior." In Alex Inkeles et al., eds., *Annual Review of Sociology*. Vol. 1. Palo Alto, Calif.: Annual Reviews, 1975:363–428.

MARX, KARL. Excerpt from "A Contribution to the Critique of Political Economy." In Karl Marx and Friedrich Engels, *Marx and Engels: Basic Writings on Politics and Philosophy*. Lewis S. Feurer, ed. Garden City, N.Y.: Anchor Books, 1959:42–46.

———. *Karl Marx: Early Writings*. T. B. Bottomore, ed. New York: McGraw-Hill, 1964a.

———. *Karl Marx: Selected Writings in Sociology and Social Philosophy*. T. B. Bottomore, trans. New York: McGraw-Hill, 1964.

———. *Capital*. Friedrich Engels, ed. New York: International Publishers, 1967; orig. 1867.

———. "Theses on Feuer." In Robert C. Tucker, ed., *The Marx-Engels Reader*. New York: Norton, 1972:107–9; orig. 1845.

MARX, KARL, and FRIEDRICH ENGELS. "Manifesto of the Communist Party." In Robert C. Tucker, ed., *The Marx-Engels Reader*. New York: Norton, 1972:331–62; orig. 1848.

———. *The Marx-Engels Reader*. Robert C. Tucker, ed. New York: Norton, 1977.

MARX, LEO. "The Environment and the 'Two Cultures' Divide." In James Rodger Fleming and Henry A. Gemery, eds., *Science, Technology, and the Environment: Multidisciplinary Perspectives*. Akron, Ohio: University of Akron Press, 1994:3–21.

MASSEY, DOUGLAS S. Review of *The Bell Curve: Intelligence and Class Structure in American Life* by Richard J. Herrnstein and Charles Murray. *American Journal of Sociology*. Vol. 101, No. 3 (November 1995):747–53.

MASSEY, DOUGLAS S., and NANCY A. DENTON. "Hypersegregation in U.S. Metropolitan Areas: Black and Hispanic Segregation Along Five Dimensions." *Demography*. Vol. 26, No. 3 (August 1989):373–91.

MASTERS, WILLIAM H., VIRGINIA E. JOHNSON, and ROBERT C. KOLODNY. *Human Sexuality*. 3d ed. Glenview, Ill.: Scott, Foresman/Little, Brown, 1988.

MATTHIESSEN, PETER. *In the Spirit of Crazy Horse*. New York: Viking Press, 1983.

———. *Indian Country*. New York: Viking Press, 1984.

MAUER, MARC. *Americans Behind Bars: The International Use of Incarceration, 1992–1993*. Washington, D.C.: The Sentencing Project, 1994.

MAURO, TONY. "Cruzan's Struggle Left Imprint: Private Case Triggered Public Debate." *USA Today* (December 27, 1990):3A.

MAURO, TONY. "Ruling Likely Will Add Fuel to Already Divisive Debate." *USA Today* (January 7, 1997):1A, 2A.

MAUSS, ARMAND L. *Social Problems of Social Movements*. Philadelphia: Lippincott, 1975.

MAY, ELAINE TYLER. "Women in the Wild Blue Yonder." *New York Times* (August 7, 1991):21.

MAYO, KATHERINE. *Mother India*. New York: Harcourt, Brace, 1927.

MEAD, GEORGE HERBERT. *Mind, Self, and Society*. Charles W. Morris, ed. Chicago: University of Chicago Press, 1962; orig. 1934.

MEAD, MARGARET. *Coming of Age in Samoa*. New York: Dell, 1961; orig. 1928.

———. *Sex and Temperament in Three Primitive Societies*. New York: William Morrow, 1963; orig. 1935.

MEADOWS, DONELLA H., DENNIS L. MEADOWS, JORGAN RANDERS, and WILLIAM W. BEHRENS, III. *The Limits to Growth: A Report on the Club of Rome's Project on the Predicament of Mankind*. New York: Universe, 1972.

MELTZER, BERNARD N. "Mead's Social Psychology." In Jerome G. Manis and Bernard N. Meltzer, eds., *Symbolic Interaction: A Reader in Social Psychology*. 3d ed. Needham Heights, Mass.: Allyn & Bacon, 1978.

MELUCCI, ALBERTO. "The New Social Movements: A Theoretical Approach." *Social Science Information*. Vol. 19, No. 2 (May 1980):199–226.

———. *Nomads of the Present: Social Movements and Individual Needs in Contemporary Society*. Philadelphia: Temple University Press, 1989.

MERGENBAGEN, PAULA. "Rethinking Retirement." *American Demographics*. Vol. 16, No. 6 (June 1994):28–34.

———. "Sun City Gets Boomerized." *American Demographics*. Vol. 18, No. 8 (August 1996):16–20.

MERTON, ROBERT K. "Social Structure and Anomie." *American Sociological Review*. Vol. 3, No. 6 (October 1938):672–82.

———. *Social Theory and Social Structure*. New York: Free Press, 1968.

———. "Discrimination and the American Creed." In *Sociological Ambivalence and Other Essays*. New York: Free Press, 1976:189–216.

MEYER, DAVIS S. and NANCY WHITTIER. "Social Movement Spillover." *Social Problems*. Vol. 41, No. 2 (May 1994):277–98.

MEYER, DAVID S., and SUZANNE STAGGENBORG. "Movements, Countermovements, and the Structure of Political Opportunity." *American Journal of Sociology*. Vol. 101, No. 6 (May 1996):1628–60.

MEYROWITZ, JOSHUA, and JOHN MAGUIRE. "Media, Place, and Multiculturalism." *Society*. Vol. 30, No. 5 (July-August 1993):41–48.

MICHELS, ROBERT. *Political Parties*. Glencoe, Ill.: Free Press, 1949; orig. 1911.

MILBRATH, LESTER W. *Envisioning A Sustainable Society: Learning Our Way Out*. Albany: State University of New York Press, 1989.

MILGRAM, STANLEY. "Behavioral Study of Obedience." *Journal of Abnormal and Social Psychology*. Vol. 67, No. 4 (1963):371–78.

———. "Group Pressure and Action Against a Person." *Journal of Abnormal and Social Psychology*. Vol. 69, No. 2 (August 1964):137–43.

———. "Some Conditions of Obedience and Disobedience to Authority." *Human Relations*. Vol. 18 (February 1965):57–76.

MILIBAND, RALPH. *The State in Capitalist Society*. London: Weidenfield and Nicolson, 1969.

MILLER, ARTHUR G. *The Obedience Experiments: A Case of Controversy in Social Science*. New York: Praeger, 1986.

MILLER, BERNA. "The Quest for Lifelong Learning." *American Demographics*. Vol. 19, No. 3 (March 1997):20, 22.

———. "Population Update for April." *American Demographics*. Vol. 19, No. 4 (April 1997):18.

MILLER, DAVID L. *Introduction to Collective Behavior*. Belmont, Calif.: Wadsworth, 1985.

MILLER, FREDERICK D. "The End of SDS and the Emergence of Weatherman: Demise Through Success." In Jo Freeman, ed., *Social Movements of the Sixties and Seventies*. New York: Longman, 1983:279–97.

MILLER, G. TYLER, JR. *Living in the Environment: An Introduction to Environmental Science*. Belmont, Calif.: Wadsworth, 1992.

MILLER, MICHAEL. "Lawmakers Begin to Heed Calls to Protect Privacy." *Wall Street Journal* (April 11, 1991):A16.

MILLER, WALTER B. "Lower Class Culture as a Generating Milieu of Gang Delinquency." In Marvin E. Wolfgang, Leonard Savitz, and Norman Johnston, eds., *The Sociology of Crime and Delinquency*. 2d ed. New York: Wiley, 1970:351–63; orig. 1958.

MILLET, KATE. *Sexual Politics*. Garden City, N.Y.: Doubleday, 1970.

MILLMAN, JOEL, NINA MUNK, MICHAEL SCHUMAN, and NEIL WEINBERG. "The World's Wealthiest People." *Forbes*. Vol. 152, No. 1 (July 5, 1993):66–69.

MILLS, C. WRIGHT. *White Collar: The American Middle Classes*. New York: Oxford University Press, 1951.

———. *The Power Elite*. New York: Oxford University Press, 1956.

———. *The Sociological Imagination*. New York: Oxford University Press, 1959.

MINK, BARBARA. "How Modernization Affects Women." *Cornell Alumni News*. Vol. III, No. 3 (April 1989):10–11.

MINTZ, BETH, and MICHAEL SCHWARTZ. "Interlocking Directorates and Interest Group Formation." *American Sociological Review*. Vol. 46, No. 6 (December 1981):851–69.

MIROWSKY, JOHN. "The Psycho-Economics of Feeling Underpaid: Distributive Justice and the Earnings of Husbands and Wives." *American Journal of Sociology*. Vol. 92, No. 6 (May 1987):1404–34.

MIROWSKY, JOHN, and CATHERINE ROSS. "Working Wives and Mental Health." Presentation to the American Association for the Advancement of Science, New York, 1984.

———. *The Social Causes of Psychological Distress*. Hawthorne, N.Y.: Aldine, 1989.

MOGELONSKY, MARCIA. "Reconfiguring the American Dream (House)." *American Demographics*. Vol. 19, No. 1 (January 1997):31–35.

MOLM, LINDA D. "Risk and Power Use: Constraints on the Use of Coercion in Exchange." *American Sociological Review*. Vol. 62, No. 1 (February 1997):113–33.

MOLOTCH, HARVEY. "The City as a Growth Machine." *American Journal of Sociology*. Vol. 82, No. 2 (September 1976):309–33.

MONEY, JOHN, and ANKE A. EHRHARDT. *Man and Woman, Boy and Girl*. New York: New American Library, 1972.

MONK-TURNER, ELIZABETH. "The Occupational Achievement of Community and Four-Year College Graduates." *American Sociological Review*. Vol. 55, No. 5 (October 1990):719–25.

MONTAGU, ASHLEY. *The Nature of Human Aggression*. New York: Oxford University Press, 1976.

MOODY, JOHN. "Safe? You Bet Your Life." *Time*. Vol. 126, No. 24 (July 24, 1995):35.

MOORE, GWEN. "The Structure of a National Elite Network." *American Sociological Review*. Vol. 44, No. 5 (October 1979):673–92.

———. "Structural Determinants of Men's and Women's Personal Networks." *American Sociological Review*. Vol. 55, No. 5 (October 1991):726–35.

———. "Gender and Informal Networks in State Government." *Social Science Quarterly*. Vol. 73, No. 1 (March 1992):46–61.

MOORE, JOAN, and HARRY PACHON. *Hispanics in the United States*. Englewood Cliffs, N.J.: Prentice Hall, 1985.

MOORE, MIKE. "14 Minutes to Nuclear Midnight." *Chronicle of Higher Education*. Vol. XLII, No. 30 (April 5, 1996):A52.

MOORE, WILBERT E. "Modernization as Rationalization: Processes and Restraints." In Manning Nash, ed., *Essays on Economic Development and Cultural Change in Honor of Bert F. Hoselitz*. Chicago: University of Chicago Press, 1977:29–42.

———. *World Modernization: The Limits of Convergence.* New York: Elsevier, 1979.

MORAN, JOHN S., S. O. ARAL, W. C. JENKINS, T. A. PETERMAN, and E. R. ALEXANDER. "The Impact of Sexually Transmitted Diseases on Minority Populations." *Public Health Reports.* Vol. 104, No. 6 (November-December 1989):560–65.

MORRIS, ALDON. "Black Southern Sit-in Movement: An Analysis of Internal Organization." *American Sociological Review.* Vol. 46, No. 6 (December 1981):744–67.

MORRISON, DENTON E. "Some Notes Toward Theory on Relative Deprivation, Social Movements, and Social Change." In Louis E. Genevie, ed., *Collective Behavior and Social Movements.* Itasca, Ill.: Peacock, 1978:202–9.

MORROW, LANCE. "The Temping of America." *Time.* Vol. 131, No. 14 (March 29, 1993):40–41.

MORTON, JACKSON. "Census on the Internet." *American Demographics.* Vol. 17, No. 3 (March 1995):52–53.

MOSKOS, CHARLES C. "Female GIs in the Field." *Society.* Vol. 22, No. 6 (September-October 1985):28–33.

MOSLEY, W. HENRY, and PETER COWLEY. "The Challenge of World Health." *Population Bulletin.* Vol. 46, No. 4 (December 1991). Washington, D.C.: Population Reference Bureau.

MOYNIHAN, DANIEL PATRICK. *The Negro Family: The Case for National Action.* Washington, D.C.: U.S. Department of Labor, 1965.

———. "Toward a New Intolerance." *The Public Interest.* No. 112 (Summer 1993):119–22.

MUELLER, DANIEL P., and PHILIP W. COOPER. "Children of Single Parent Families: How Do They Fare as Young Adults?" Presentation to the American Sociological Association, San Antonio, Texas, 1984.

MUFSON, STEVEN. "China's Growing Inequality." *Washington Post* (January 1, 1997):A1, A26–A27.

MULLER, EDWARD N. *Aggressive Political Participation.* Princeton, N.J.: Princeton University Press, 1979.

MUMFORD, LEWIS. *The City in History: Its Origins, Its Transformations, and Its Prospects.* New York: Harcourt, Brace & World, 1961.

MURDOCK, GEORGE PETER. "Comparative Data on the Division of Labor by Sex." *Social Forces.* Vol. 15, No. 4 (May 1937):551–53.

———. "The Common Denominator of Cultures." In Ralph Linton, ed., *The Science of Man in World Crisis.* New York: Columbia University Press, 1945:123–42.

———. *Social Structure.* New York: Free Press, 1965; orig. 1949.

MURRAY, CHARLES. *Losing Ground: American Social Policy 1950–1980.* New York: Basic Books, 1984.

———. "Keeping Priorities Straight on Welfare Reform." *Society.* Vol. 33, No. 5 (July/August 1996):10–12.

MURRAY, MEGAN BALDRIDGE. "Innovation Without Geniuses." In *Yale Alumni Magazine and Journal.* Vol. XLVII, No. 6 (April 1984):40–43.

MURRAY, PAULI. *Proud Shoes: The History of an American Family.* New York: Harper & Row, 1978.

MYERS, NORMAN. "Humanity's Growth." In Sir Edmund Hillary, ed., *Ecology 2000: The Changing Face of the Earth.* New York: Beaufort Books, 1984a:16–35.

———. "The Mega-Extinction of Animals and Plants." In Sir Edmund Hillary, ed., *Ecology 2000: The Changing Face of the Earth.* New York: Beaufort Books, 1984b:82–107.

———. "Disappearing Cultures." In Sir Edmund Hillary, ed., *Ecology 2000: The Changing Face of the Earth.* New York: Beaufort Books, 1984c:162–69.

———. "Biological Diversity and Global Security." In F. Herbert Bormann and Stephen R. Kellert, eds., *Ecology, Economics, and Ethics: The Broken Circle.* New Haven, Conn.: Yale University Press, 1991:11–25.

MYERS, SHEILA, and HAROLD G. GRASMICK. "The Social Rights and Responsibilities of Pregnant Women: An Application of Parsons' Sick Role Model." Paper presented to Southwestern Sociological Association, Little Rock, Arkansas, March 1989.

NAGEL, JOANE. "Constructing Ethnicity: Creating and Recreating Ethnic Identity and Culture." *Social Problems.* Vol. 41, No. 1 (February 1994):152–76.

———. *American Indian Ethnic Renewal: Red Power and the Resurgence of Identity and Culture.* New York: Oxford University Press, 1996.

NAJAFIZADEH, MEHRANGIZ, and LEWIS A. MENNERICK. "Sociology of Education or Sociology of Ethnocentrism: The Portrayal of Education in Introductory Sociology Textbooks." *Teaching Sociology.* Vol. 20, No. 3 (July 1992):215–21.

NASH, J. MADELEINE. "To Know Your Own Fate." *Time.* Vol. 145, No. 14 (April 3, 1995):62.

NATIONAL CENTER FOR EDUCATION STATISTICS. *Digest of Education Statistics: 1991.* Washington, D.C.: U.S. Government Printing Office, 1992.

———. *Digest of Education Statistics: 1994.* Washington, D.C.: U.S. Government Printing Office, 1995.

NATIONAL CENTER FOR HEALTH STATISTICS. *Monthly Vital Statistics Report.* Vol. 44, No. 4 (April 1995). Washington, D.C.: U.S. Government Printing Office.

NATIONAL COMMISSION ON EXCELLENCE IN EDUCATION. *A Nation at Risk.* Washington, D.C.: U.S. Government Printing Office, 1983.

NAVARRO, VICENTE. "The Industrialization of Fetishism or the Fetishism of Industrialization: A Critique of Ivan Illich." In Vicente Navarro, ed., *Health and Medical Care in the U.S.: A Critical Analysis.* Farmingdale, N.Y.: Baywood Publishing Co., 1977:38–58.

NEIDERT, LISA J., and REYNOLDS FARLEY. "Assimilation in the United States: An Analysis of Ethnic and Generation Differences in Status and Achievement." *American Sociological Review.* Vol. 50, No. 6 (December 1985):840–50.

NELAN, BRUCE W. "Crimes Without Punishment." *Time.* Vol. 141, No. 2 (January 11, 1993):21.

NELSON, JOEL I. "Work and Benefits: The Multiple Problems of Service Sector Employment." *Social Problems.* Vol. 42, No. 2 (May 1994):240–55.

NEUGARTEN, BERNICE L. "Grow Old with Me. The Best Is Yet to Be." *Psychology Today.* Vol. 5 (December 1971):45–48, 79, 81.

———. "Personality and the Aging Process." *The Gerontologist.* Vol. 12, No. 1 (Spring 1972):9–15.

———. "Personality and Aging." In James E. Birren and K. Warner Schaie, eds., *Handbook of the Psychology of Aging.* New York: Van Nostrand Reinhold, 1977:626–49.

NEUHOUSER, KEVIN. "The Radicalization of the Brazilian Catholic Church in Comparative Perspective." *American Sociological Review.* Vol. 54, No. 2 (April 1989):233–44.

New Haven Journal-Courier. "English Social Structure Changing." November 27, 1986.

NEWMAN, KATHERINE S. *Declining Fortunes: The Withering of the American Dream.* New York: Basic Books, 1993.

NEWMAN, WILLIAM M. *American Pluralism: A Study of Minority Groups and Social Theory.* New York: Harper & Row, 1973.

NIELSEN, FRANCOIS, and ARTHUR S. ALDERSON. "The Kuznets Curve: The Great U-Turn: Income Inequality in U.S. Counties, 1970 to 1990." *American Sociological Review.* Vol. 62, No. 1 (February 1997):12–33.

NIELSEN, JOYCE MCCARL, ED. *Feminist Research Methods: Exemplary Readings in the Social Sciences.* Boulder, Colo.: Westview Press, 1990.

1991 Green Book. U.S. House of Representatives. Washington, D.C.: U.S. Government Printing Office, 1991.

NISBET, ROBERT A. *The Sociological Tradition.* New York: Basic Books, 1966.

———. *The Quest for Community.* New York: Oxford University Press, 1969.

———. "Sociology as an Art Form." In *Tradition and Revolt: Historical and Sociological Essays.* New York: Vintage Books, 1970.

NOLAN, JAMES L., JR., ed. *The American Culture Wars: Current Contests and Future Prospects.* Charlottesville, Va.: University Press of Virginia, 1996.

NORBECK, EDWARD. "Class Structure." In *Kodansha Encyclopedia of Japan.* Tokyo: Kodansha, 1983:322–25.

NORC. *General Social Surveys, 1972–1991: Cumulative Codebook.* Chicago: National Opinion Research Center, 1991.

———. *General Social Surveys, 1972–1992: Cumulative Codebook.* Chicago: National Opinion Research Center, 1992.

———. *General Social Surveys, 1972–1994: Cumulative Codebook.* University of Chicago: National Opinion Research Center, 1994.

———. *General Social Surveys, 1972–1996: Cumulative Codebook.* Chicago: National Opinion Research Center, 1996.

———. *GSS News* (August 1997):3.

NORDHEIMER, JON. "Downsized, But Not Out: A Mill Town's Tale." *New York Times* (March 9, 1997): section 3, pp. 1, 12, 13.

NUNN, CLYDE Z., HARRY J. CROCKETT, JR., and J. ALLEN WILLIAMS, JR. *Tolerance for Nonconformity.* San Francisco: Jossey-Bass, 1978.

OAKES, JEANNIE. "Classroom Social Relationships: Exploring the Bowles and Gintis Hypothesis." *Sociology of Education.* Vol. 55, No. 4 (October 1982):197–212.

———. *Keeping Track: How High Schools Structure Inequality.* New Haven, Conn.: Yale University Press, 1985.

OBERSCHALL, ANTHONY. *Social Conflict and Social Movements.* Englewood Cliffs, N.J.: Prentice Hall, 1973.

O'BRIEN, DAVID J., EDWARD W. HASSINGER, and LARRY DERSHEM. "Size of Place, Residential Stability, and Personal Social Networks." *Sociological Focus.* Vol. 29, No. 1 (February 1996):61–72.

O'CONNOR, RORY J. "Internet Declared Protected Speech." *Post-Star* (Glens Fall, N.Y.: June 27, 1997):A1–A2.

O'DEA, THOMAS F., and JANET O'DEA AVIAD. *The Sociology of Religion.* 2d ed. Englewood Cliffs, N.J.: Prentice Hall, 1983.

OFFIR, CAROLE WADE. *Human Sexuality*. New York: Harcourt Brace Jovanovich, 1982.

OGBURN, WILLIAM F. *On Culture and Social Change*. Chicago: University of Chicago Press, 1964.

O'HARE, WILLIAM P. "In the Black." *American Demographics*. Vol. 11, No. 11 (November 1989):25–29.

———. "The Rise of Hispanic Affluence." *American Demographics*. Vol. 12, No. 8 (August 1990):40–43.

O'HARE, WILLIAM P., WILLIAM H. FREY, and DAN FOST. "Asians in the Suburbs." *American Demographics*. Vol. 16, No. 9 (May 1994):32–38.

OLSEN, GREGG M. "Re-Modeling Sweden: The Rise and Demise of the Compromise in a Global Economy." *Social Problems*. Vol. 43, No. 1 (February 1996):1–20.

OLSEN, MARVIN E., DORA G. LODWICK, and RILEY E. DUNLAP. *Viewing the World Ecologically*. Boulder, Colo.: Westview Press, 1992.

OLZAK, SUSAN. "Labor Unrest, Immigration, and Ethnic Conflict in Urban America, 1880–1914." *American Journal of Sociology*. Vol. 94, No. 6 (May 1989):1303–33.

OLZAK, SUSAN, and ELIZABETH WEST. "Ethnic Conflict and the Rise and Fall of Ethnic Newspapers." *American Sociological Review*. Vol. 56, No. 4 (August 1991):458–74.

O'REILLY, JANE. "Wife Beating: The Silent Crime." *Time*. Vol. 122, No. 10 (September 5, 1983):23–24, 26.

ORLANSKY, MICHAEL D., and WILLIAM L. HEWARD. *Voices: Interviews With Handicapped People*. Columbus, Ohio: Merrill, 1981:85, 92, 133–34, 172.

ORSHANSKY, MOLLIE. "How Poverty Is Measured." *Monthly Labor Review*. Vol. 92, No. 2 (February 1969):37–41.

ORWIN, CLIFFORD. "All Quiet on the Western Front?" *The Public Interest*. Vol. 123 (Spring 1996): 3–9.

OSGOOD, D. WAYNE, JANET K. WILSON, PATRICK M. O'MALLEY, JERALD G. BACHMAN, and LLOYD D. JOHNSTON. "Routine Activities and Individual Deviant Behavior." *American Sociological Review*. Vol. 61, No. 4 (August 1996):635–55.

OSTLING, RICHARD N. "Jerry Falwell's Crusade." *Time*. Vol. 126, No. 9 (September 2, 1985):48–52, 55, 57.

———. "Technology and the Womb." *Time*. Vol. 129, No. 12 (March 23, 1987):58–59.

OSTRANDER, SUSAN A. "Upper Class Women: The Feminine Side of Privilege." *Qualitative Sociology*. Vol. 3, No. 1 (Spring 1980):23–44.

———. *Women of the Upper Class*. Philadelphia: Temple University Press, 1984.

OUCHI, WILLIAM. *Theory Z: How American Business Can Meet the Japanese Challenge*. Reading, Mass.: Addison-Wesley, 1981.

OWEN, DAVID. *None of the Above: Behind the Myth of Scholastic Aptitude*. Boston: Houghton Mifflin, 1985.

PAKULSKI, JAN. "Mass Social Movements and Social Class." *International Sociology*. Vol. 8, No. 2 (June 1993):131–58.

PALMORE, ERDMAN. "Predictors of Successful Aging." *The Gerontologist*. Vol. 19, No. 5 (October 1979a):427–31.

———. "Advantages of Aging." *The Gerontologist*. Vol. 19, No. 2 (April 1979b):220–23.

———. "What Can the USA Learn from Japan About Aging?" In Steven H. Zarit, ed., *Readings in Aging and Death: Contemporary Perspectives*. New York: Harper & Row, 1982:166–69.

PAMPEL, FRED C., KENNETH C. LAND, and MARCUS FELSON. "A Social Indicator Model of Changes in the Occupational Structure of the United States: 1947–1974." *American Sociological Review*. Vol. 42, No. 6 (December 1977):951–64.

PARCEL, TOBY L., CHARLES W. MUELLER, and STEVEN CUVELIER. "Comparable Worth and Occupational Labor Market: Explanations of Occupational Earnings Differentials." Paper presented to the American Sociological Association, New York, 1986.

PARENTI, MICHAEL. *Inventing Reality: The Politics of the Mass Media*. New York: St. Martin's Press, 1986.

PARK, ROBERT E. *Race and Culture*. Glencoe, Ill.: Free Press, 1950.

———. "The City: Suggestions for the Investigation of Human Behavior in the Human Environment." In Robert E. Park and Ernest W. Burgess, *The City*. Chicago: University of Chicago Press, 1967; orig. 1925:1–46.

PARKINSON, C. NORTHCOTE. *Parkinson's Law and Other Studies in Administration*. New York: Ballantine Books, 1957.

PARRILLO, VINCENT N. "Diversity in America: A Sociohistorical Analysis." *Sociological Forum*. Vol. 9, No. 4 (December 1994):42–45.

PARROTT, JULIE. "The Effects of Culture on Eating Disorders." Paper presented to Southwestern Social Science Association, Dallas, Texas, March 1987.

PARSONS, TALCOTT. "Age and Sex in the Social Structure of the United States." *American Sociological Review*. Vol. 7, No. 4 (August 1942):604–16.

———. *Essays in Sociological Theory*. New York: Free Press, 1954.

———. *The Social System*. New York: Free Press, 1964; orig. 1951.

———. *Societies: Evolutionary and Comparative Perspectives*. Englewood Cliffs, N.J.: Prentice Hall, 1966.

PARSONS, TALCOTT, and ROBERT F. BALES, EDS. *Family, Socialization and Interaction Process*. New York: Free Press, 1955.

PAUL, ELLEN FRANKEL. "Bared Buttocks and Federal Cases." *Society*. Vol. 28, No. 4 (May-June, 1991):4–7.

PEAR, ROBERT. "Women Reduce Lag in Earnings, But Disparities With Men Remain." *New York Times* (September 4, 1987):1, 7.

PEAR, ROBERT, with ERIK ECKHOLM. "When Healers Are Entrepreneurs: A Debate Over Costs and Ethics." *New York Times* (June 2, 1991):1, 17.

PEARSON, DAVID E. "Post-Mass Culture." *Society*. Vol. 30, No. 5 (July-August 1993):17–22.

———. "Community and Sociology." *Society*. Vol. 32, No. 5 (July-August 1995):44–50.

PENNINGS, JOHANNES M. "Organizational Birth Frequencies: An Empirical Investigation." *Administrative Science Quarterly*. Vol. 27, No. 1 (March 1982):120–44.

PEREZ, LISANDRO. "Cubans." In *Harvard Encyclopedia of American Ethnic Groups*. Cambridge, Mass.: Harvard University Press, 1980:256–60.

PERROLLE, JUDITH A. "Comments from the Special Issue Editor: The Emerging Dialogue on Environmental Justice." *Social Problems*. Vol. 40, No. 1 (February 1993):1–4.

PERSELL, CAROLINE HODGES. *Education and Inequality: A Theoretical and Empirical Synthesis*. New York: Free Press, 1977.

———. "The Interdependence of Social Justice and Civil Society." *Sociological Forum*. Vol. 12, No. 2 (June 1997):149–72.

PESSEN, EDWARD. *Riches, Class, and Power: America Before the Civil War*. New Brunswick, N.J.: Transaction Books, 1990.

PETER, LAURENCE J., and RAYMOND HULL. *The Peter Principle: Why Things Always Go Wrong*. New York: William Morrow, 1969.

Peters Atlas of the World. New York: Harper & Row, 1990.

PETERS, THOMAS J., and ROBERT H. WATERMAN, JR. *In Search of Excellence: Lessons From America's Best-Run Companies*. New York: Warner Books, 1982.

PETERSILIA, JOAN. "Probation in the United States: Practices and Challenges." *National Institute of Justice Journal*. No. 233 (September 1997):4.

PETERSON, RICHARD R. "A Re-Evaluation of the Economic Consequences of Divorce." *American Sociological Review*. Vol. 61, No. 3 (June 1996):528–36.

PETERSON, SCOTT. "Women Live on Own Terms Behind the Veil." *Christian Science Monitor* (July 31, 1996):1, 10.

PHELAN, JO, BRUCE G. LINK, ANN STUEVE, and ROBERT E. MOORE. "Education, Social Liberalism, and Economic Conservatism: Attitudes Toward Homeless People." *American Sociological Review*. Vol. 60, No. 1 (February 1995):126–40.

PHILIPSON, ILENE J., and KAREN V. HANSEN. "Women, Class, and the Feminist Imagination." In Karen V. Hansen and Ilene J. Philipson, eds., *Women, Class, and the Feminist Imagination: A Socialist-Feminist Reader*. Philadelphia: Temple University Press, 1992:3–40.

PHILLIPS, KEVIN. *Arrogant Capital: Washington, Wall Street, and the Frustration of American Politics*. Boston: Little, Brown and Company, 1994.

PHILLIPSON, CHRIS. *Capitalism and the Construction of Old Age*. London: Macmillan, 1982.

PHYSICIANS' TASK FORCE ON HUNGER IN AMERICA. "Hunger Reaches Blue-Collar America." Report issued 1987.

PICHARDO, NELSON A. "The Power Elite and Elite-Driven Countermovements: The Associated Farmers of California During the 1930s." *Sociological Forum*. Vol. 10, No. 1 (March 1995):21–49.

PILLEMER, KARL. "Maltreatment of the Elderly at Home and in Institutions: Extent, Risk Factors, and Policy Recommendations." In U.S. Congress. House, Select Committee on Aging and Senate, Special Committee on Aging. *Legislative Agenda for an Aging Society: 1988 and Beyond*. Washington, D.C.: U.S. Government Printing Office, 1988.

PINES, MAYA. "The Civilization of Genie." *Psychology Today*. Vol. 15 (September 1981):28–34.

PIRANDELLO, LUIGI. "The Pleasure of Honesty." In *To Clothe the Naked and Two Other Plays*. New York: Dutton, 1962:143–98.

PITNEY, JOHN J., JR. "What Scholars Don't Know About Term Limits." *The Chronicle of Higher Education*. Vol. XLI, No. 33 (April 28, 1995):A76.

PITT, MALCOLM. *Introducing Hinduism*. New York: Friendship Press, 1955.

PIVEN, FRANCES FOX, and RICHARD A. CLOWARD. *Poor People's Movements: Why They Succeed, How They Fail*. New York: Pantheon Books, 1977.

———. *Why Americans Don't Vote*. New York: Pantheon Books, 1988.

PLOMIN, ROBERT, and TERRYL T. FOCH. "A Twin Study of Objectively Assessed Personality in Childhood." *Journal of Personality and Social Psychology*. Vol. 39, No. 4 (October 1980):680–88.

POHL, RUDIGER. "The Transition From Communism to Capitalism in East Germany." *Society*. Vol. 33, No. 4 (June 1996):62–65.

POLENBERG, RICHARD. *One Nation Divisible: Class, Race, and Ethnicity in the United States Since 1938*. New York: Pelican Books, 1980.

POLLACK, ANDREW. "Happy in the East (^-^) or Smiling :-) in the West." *New York Times* (August 12, 1996).

———. "Overseas, Smoking Is One of Life's Small Pleasures." *New York Times* (August 17, 1997):E5.

POLLACK, PHILIP H., III, and M. ELLIOT VITTAS. "Who Bears the Burdens of Environmental Pollution: Race, Ethnicity, and Environmental Equity in Florida." *Social Science Quarterly*. Vol. 76, No. 2 (June 1995):294–310.

POLLARD, KELVIN. "Play Ball! Demographics and Major League Baseball." *Population Today*. Vol. 24, No. 4 (April 1996):3.

———. "Speaking Graphically: Per Capita Fresh Water Availability . . ." *Population Today*. Vol. 24, No. 12 (December 1996):6.

POLSBY, NELSON W. "Three Problems in the Analysis of Community Power." *American Sociological Review*. Vol. 24, No. 6 (December 1959):796–803.

POMER, MARSHALL I. "Labor Market Structure, Intragenerational Mobility, and Discrimination: Black Male Advancement Out of Low-Paying Occupations, 1962–1973." *American Sociological Review*. Vol. 51, No. 5 (October 1986):650–59.

POOLEY, ERIC. "Death or Life?" *Time*. Vol. 149, No. 24 (June 16, 1997):30–36.

POPENOE, DAVID. *Disturbing the Nest: Family Change and Decline in Modern Societies*. New York: Aldine, 1988.

———. "Family Decline in the Swedish Welfare State." *The Public Interest*. No. 102 (Winter 1991):65–77.

———. "The Controversial Truth: Two-Parent Families Are Better." *New York Times* (December 26, 1992):21.

———. "American Family Decline, 1960–1990: A Review and Appraisal." *Journal of Marriage and the Family*. Vol. 55, No. 3 (August 1993):527–55.

———. "Parental Androgyny." *Society*. Vol. 30, No. 6 (September-October 1993):5–11.

———. "Scandinavian Welfare." *Society*. Vol. 31, No. 6 (September-October, 1994):78–81.

———. Review of John Snarey's *How Fathers Care for the Next Generation: A Four Decade Study*, in *Contemporary Sociology*. Vol. 23, No. 5 (September 1994):698–700.

POPKIN, SUSAN J. "Welfare: Views From the Bottom." *Social Problems*. Vol. 17, No. 1 (February 1990):64–79.

POPULATION REFERENCE BUREAU. *1995 World Population Data Sheet*. Washington, D.C.: Population Reference Bureau, Inc., 1995.

———. "Past and Future Population Doubling Times, Selected Countries." *Population Today*. Vol. 23, No. 2 (February 1995):6.

———. "Kids Count." Washington, D.C.: 1997.

Population Today. "Majority of Children in Poverty Live with Parents Who Work." Vol. 23, No. 4 (April 1995):6.

PORTES, ALEJANDRO. "The Rise of Ethnicity: Determinants of Ethnic Perceptions Among Cuban Exiles in Miami." *American Sociological Review*. Vol. 49, No. 3 (June 1984):383–97.

PORTES, ALEJANDRO, and LEIF JENSEN. "The Enclave and the Entrants: Patterns of Ethnic Enterprise in Miami Before and After Mariel." *American Sociological Review*. Vol. 54, No. 6 (December 1989):929–49.

POSTEL, SANDRA. "Facing Water Scarcity." In Lester R. Brown et al., eds., *State of the World 1993: A Worldwatch Institute Report on Progress Toward a Sustainable Society*. New York: Norton, 1993:22–41.

POWELL, CHRIS, and GEORGE E. C. PATON, EDS. *Humour in Society: Resistance and Control*. New York: St. Martin's Press, 1988.

PRESSER, HARRIET B. "The Housework Gender Gap." *Population Today*. Vol. 21, No. 7/8 (July-August 1993):5.

PRESSLEY, SUE ANNE, and NANCY ANDREWS. "For Gay Couples, the Nursery Becomes the New Frontier." *Washington Post* (December 20, 1992):A1, A22–23.

PRIMEGGIA, SALVATORE, and JOSEPH A. VARACALLI. "Southern Italian Comedy: Old to New World." In Joseph V. Scelsa, Salvatore J. LaGumina, and Lydio Tomasi, eds., *Italian Americans in Transition*. New York: The American Italian Historical Association, 1990:241–52.

PRINDLE, DAVID F. *Risky Business: The Political Economy of Hollywood*. Boulder, Colo.: Westview Press, 1993.

———. "Take Three on Hollywood Liberalism." *Social Science Quarterly*. Vol. 75, No. 2 (June 1994):458–59.

PRINDLE, DAVID F., and JAMES W. ENDERSBY. "Hollywood Liberalism." *Social Science Quarterly*. Vol. 74, No. 1 (March 1993):136–49.

PUTERBAUGH, GEOFF, ED. *Twins and Homosexuality: A Casebook*. New York: Garland, 1990.

PUTKA, GARY. "SAT To Become A Better Gauge." *Wall Street Journal* (November 1, 1990):B1.

PUTKA, GARY, and STEVE STECKLOW. "Do For-Profit Schools Work? These Seem to for One Entrepreneur." *Wall Street Journal* (June 8, 1994):A1, A4.

QUEENAN, JOE. "The Many Paths to Riches." *Forbes*. Vol. 144, No. 9 (October 23, 1989):149.

QUICK, REBECCA. "Wanna Earn as Much as the Boss? Stop Surfing the Net, Get to Work." *Wall Street Journal* (April 11, 1997):B1.

QUINNEY, RICHARD. *Class, State and Crime: On the Theory and Practice of Criminal Justice*. New York: David McKay, 1977.

RABKIN, JEREMY. "The Supreme Court in the Culture Wars." *The Public Interest*. Vol. 125 (Fall 1996):3–26.

RADEMACHER, ERIC W. "The Effect of Question Wording on College Students." *The Pittsburgh Undergraduate Review*. Vol. 8, No. 1 (Spring 1992):45–81.

RADEMAEKERS, WILLIAM, and RHEA SCHOENTHAL. "Iceman." *Time*. Vol. 140, No. 17 (October 26, 1992):62–66.

RALEY, R. KELLY. "A Shortage of Marriageable Men? A Note on the Role of Cohabitation in Black-White Differences in Marriage Rates." *American Journal of Sociology*. Vol. 61, No. 6 (December 1996):973–83.

RAMO, JOSHUA COOPER. "Finding God on the Web." *Time* (December 16, 1996):60–67.

RANDALL, VICKI. *Women and Politics*. London: Macmillan, 1982.

RAPHAEL, RAY. *The Men From the Boys: Rites of Passage in Male America*. Lincoln and London: University of Nebraska Press, 1988.

RATAN, SUNEEL. "A New Divide Between Haves and Have-Nots?" *Time*. Special Issue. Vol. 145, No. 12 (Spring 1995):25–26.

RAVITCH, DIANE, and JOSEPH VITERITTI. "A New Vision for City Schools." *The Public Interest*. Vol. 122 (Winter 1996):3–16.

RAY, PAUL H. "The Emerging Culture." *American Demographics*. Vol 19, No. 2 (February 1997):29–34, 56.

RECKLESS, WALTER C., and SIMON DINITZ. "Pioneering With Self-Concept as a Vulnerability Factor in Delinquency." *Journal of Criminal Law, Criminology, and Police Science*. Vol. 58, No. 4 (December 1967):515–23.

REICH, ROBERT B. "As the World Turns." *The New Republic* (May 1, 1989):23, 26–28.

———. *The Work of Nations: Preparing Ourselves for 21st-Century Capitalism*. New York: Alfred A. Knopf, 1991.

REID, SUE TITUS. *Crime and Criminology*. 6th ed. Fort Worth, Tex.: Holt, Rinehart & Winston, 1991.

REINHARZ, SHULAMIT. *Feminist Methods in Social Research*. New York: Oxford University Press, 1992.

REMOFF, HEATHER TREXLER. *Sexual Choice: A Woman's Decision*. New York: Dutton/Lewis, 1984.

RICE, TOM W., and MEREDITH L. PEPPER. "Region, Migration, and Attitudes in the United States." *Social Science Quarterly*. Vol. 78, No. 1 (March 1997):83–95.

RICHARDSON, JAMES T. "Definitions of Cult: From Sociological-Technical to Popular Negative." Paper presented to the American Psychological Association, Boston, August 1990.

RIDGEWAY, CECILIA L. *The Dynamics of Small Groups*. New York: St. Martin's Press, 1983.

RIEFF, PHILIP. "Introduction." In Charles Horton Cooley, *Social Organization*. New York: Schocken Books, 1962.

RIESMAN, DAVID. *The Lonely Crowd: A Study of the Changing American Character*. New Haven, Conn.: Yale University Press, 1970; orig. 1950.

RILEY, MATILDA WHITE, ANNE FONER, and JOAN WARING. "Sociology of Age." In Neil J. Smelser, ed., *Handbook of Sociology*. Newbury Park, Calif.: Sage, 1988:243–90.

RILEY, NANCY E. "Gender, Power, and Population Change." *Population Bulletin*. Vol. 52, No. 1 (May 1997).

RITZER, GEORGE. *Sociological Theory*. New York: Alfred A. Knopf, 1983:63–66.

———. *The McDonaldization of Society: An Investigation Into the Changing Character of Contemporary Social Life*. Thousand Oaks, Calif.: Pine Forge Press, 1993.

RITZER, GEORGE, and DAVID WALCZAK. *Working: Conflict and Change*. 4th ed. Englewood Cliffs, N.J.: Prentice Hall, 1990.

RIVERA-BATIZ, FRANCISCO L., and CARLOS SANTIAGO, cited in Sam Roberts, "Puerto Ricans on Mainland Making Gains, Study Finds." *New York Times* (October 19, 1994):A20.

ROBERTS, J. DEOTIS. *Roots of a Black Future: Family and Church*. Philadelphia: Westminster Press, 1980.

ROBERTS, J. TIMMONS. "Psychosocial Effects of Workplace Hazardous Exposures: Theoretical Synthesis and Preliminary Findings." *Social Problems*. Vol. 40, No. 1 (February 1993):74–89.

ROBERTS, STEVEN V. "Open Arms for Online Democracy." *U.S. News and World Report*. Vol. 118, No. 2 (January 16, 1995):10.

ROBINSON, DAWN. "Toward a Synthesis of Sociological and Psychological Theories of Eating Disorders." Paper presented to Southwestern Social Science Association, Dallas, Texas, March 1987.

ROBINSON, JOYCE, and GLENNA SPITZE. "Whistle While You Work? The Effect of Household Task Performance on Women's and Men's Well-Being." *Social Science Quarterly*. Vol. 73, No. 4 (December 1992):844–61.

ROBINSON, VERA M. "Humor and Health." In Paul E. McGhee and Jeffrey H. Goldstein, eds., *Handbook of Humor Research, Vol. II, Applied Studies*. New York: Springer-Verlag, 1983:109–28.

ROCKETT, IAN R. H. "Population and Health: An Introduction to Epidemiology." *Population Bulletin*. Vol. 49, No. 3 (November 1994). Washington, D.C.: Population Reference Bureau.

RODGERS, JOAN R. "An Empirical Study of Intergenerational Transmission of Poverty in the United States." *Social Science Quarterly*. Vol. 76, No. 1 (March 1995):178–94.

ROESCH, ROBERTA. "Violent Families." *Parents*. Vol. 59, No. 9 (September 1984):74–76, 150–52.

ROETHLISBERGER, F. J., and WILLIAM J. DICKSON. *Management and the Worker*. Cambridge, Mass.: Harvard University Press, 1939.

ROGERS, ALISON. "The World's 101 Richest People." *Fortune*. Vol. 127, No. 13 (June 28, 1993):36–66.

ROHLEN, THOMAS P. *Japan's High Schools*. Berkeley: University of California Press, 1983.

ROKOVE, MILTON L. *Don't Make No Waves, Don't Back No Losers*. Bloomington: Indiana University Press, 1975.

ROMAN, MEL, and WILLIAM HADDAD. *The Disposable Parent: The Case for Joint Custody*. New York: Holt, Rinehart & Winston, 1978.

RÓNA-TAS, ÁKOS. "The First Shall Be Last? Entrepreneurship and Communist Cadres in the Transition From Socialism." *American Journal of Sociology*. Vol. 100, No. 1 (July 1994):40–69.

ROOF, WADE CLARK. "Socioeconomic Differentials Among White Socioreligious Groups in the United States." *Social Forces*. Vol. 58, No. 1 (September 1979):280–89.

———. "Unresolved Issues in the Study of Religion and the National Elite: Response to Greeley." *Social Forces*. Vol. 59, No. 3 (March 1981):831–36.

ROOF, WADE CLARK, and WILLIAM MCKINNEY. *American Mainline Religion: Its Changing Shape and Future*. New Brunswick, N.J.: Rutgers University Press, 1987.

ROOS, PATRICIA. "Marriage and Women's Occupational Attainment in Cross-Cultural Perspective." *American Sociological Review*. Vol. 48, No. 6 (December 1983):852–64.

ROPER CENTER FOR PUBLIC OPINION RESEARCH. Grading the Schools. [Online] Available http://www.pdkintl.org/kappan/kpoll97d.htm, 1998.

RORTY, RICHARD. "The Unpatriotic Academy." *New York Times* (February 13, 1994):15.

ROSE, JERRY D. *Outbreaks*. New York: Free Press, 1982.

ROSEN, ELLEN ISRAEL. *Bitter Choices: Blue-Collar Women In and Out of Work*. Chicago: University of Chicago Press, 1987.

ROSENBAUM, DAVID E. "Americans Want a Right to Die. Or So They Think." *New York Times* (June 8, 1997):E3.

ROSENFELD, RACHEL A., and ARNE L. KALLEBERG. "A Cross-National Comparison of the Gender Gap in Income." *American Journal of Sociology*. Vol. 96, No. 1 (July 1990):69–106.

ROSENTHAL, ELIZABETH. "Canada's National Health Plan Gives Care to All, With Limits." *New York Times* (April 30, 1991):A1, A16.

ROSENTHAL, JACK. "The Rapid Growth of Suburban Employment." In Lois H. Masotti and Jeffrey K. Hadden, eds., *Suburbia in Transition*. New York: New York Times Books, 1974:95–100.

ROSNOW, RALPH L., and GARY ALAN FINE. *Rumor and Gossip: The Social Psychology of Hearsay*. New York: Elsevier, 1976.

ROSS, CATHERINE E., JOHN MIROWSKY, and JOAN HUBER. "Dividing Work, Sharing Work, and In-Between: Marriage Patterns and Depression." *American Sociological Review*. Vol. 48, No. 6 (December 1983):809–23.

ROSS, JOHN. "To Die in the Street: Mexico City's Homeless Population Boom as Economic Crisis Shakes Social Protections." *SSSP Newsletter*. Vol. 27, No. 2 (Summer 1996):14–15.

ROSSI, ALICE S. "Gender and Parenthood." In Alice S. Rossi, ed., *Gender and the Life Course*. New York: Aldine, 1985:161–91.

ROSSI, PETER H. Review of Christopher Jencks, *The Homeless* (Cambridge, Mass.: Harvard University Press). *Society*. Vol. 32, No. 4 (May-June 1995):80–81.

ROSTOW, WALT W. *The Stages of Economic Growth: A Non-Communist Manifesto*. Cambridge: Cambridge University Press, 1960.

———. *The World Economy: History and Prospect*. Austin: University of Texas Press, 1978.

ROSZAK, THEODORE. *The Cult of Information: The Folklore of Computers and the True Art of Thinking*. New York: Pantheon Books, 1986.

ROTHMAN, STANLEY, STEPHEN POWERS, and DAVID ROTHMAN. "Feminism in Films." *Society*. Vol. 30, No. 3 (March-April 1993):66–72.

ROUDI, NAZY. "The Demography of Islam." *Population Today*. Vol. 16, No. 3 (March 1988):6–9.

ROWE, DAVID C. "Biometrical Genetic Models of Self-Reported Delinquent Behavior: A Twin Study." *Behavior Genetics*. Vol. 13, No. 5 (1983):473–89.

ROWE, DAVID C., and D. WAYNE OSGOOD. "Heredity and Sociological Theories of Delinquency: A Reconsideration." *American Sociological Review*. Vol. 49, No. 4 (August 1984):526–40.

RUBENSTEIN, ELI A. "The Not So Golden Years." *Newsweek* (October 7, 1991):13.

RUBIN, BETH A. "Class Struggle American Style: Unions, Strikes and Wages." *American Sociological Review*. Vol. 51, No. 5 (October 1986):618–31.

RUBIN, LILLIAN BRESLOW. *Worlds of Pain: Life in the Working-Class Family*. New York: Basic Books, 1976.

RUDÉ, GEORGE. *The Crowd in History: A Study of Popular Disturbances in France and England, 1730–1848*. New York: Wiley, 1964.

RUGGLES, STEVEN. "The Origins of African-American Family Structure." *American Sociological Review*. Vol. 59, No. 1 (February 1994):136–51.

RULE, JAMES, and PETER BRANTLEY. "Computerized Surveillance in the Workplace: Forms and Delusions." *Sociological Forum*. Vol. 7, No. 3 (September 1992):405–23.

RUSSELL, CHERYL. "The Master Trend." *American Demographics*. Vol. 15, No. 10 (October 1993):28–37.

———. "Overworked? Overwhelmed?" *American Demographics*. Vol. 17, No. 3 (March 1995):8.

———. "Are We In the Dumps?" *American Demographics*. Vol. 17, No. 1 (January 1995):6.

———. "True Crime." *American Demographics*. Vol. 17, No. 8 (August 1995):22–31.

RUSSELL, DIANA E. H. *Rape in Marriage*. New York: Macmillan, 1982.

RYAN, WILLIAM. *Blaming the Victim*. Rev. ed. New York: Vintage Books, 1976.

RYMER, RUSS. *Genie*. New York: HarperPerennial, 1994.

RYTINA, JOAN HUBER, WILLIAM H. FORM, and JOHN PEASE. "Income and Stratification Ideology: Beliefs About the American Opportunity Structure." *American Journal of Sociology*. Vol. 75, No. 4 (January 1970):703–16.

SABATO, LARRY J. *PAC Power: Inside the World of Political Action Committees*. New York: Norton, 1984.

SAGAN, CARL. *The Dragons of Eden*. New York: Ballantine, 1977.

SALE, KIRKPATRICK. *The Conquest of Paradise: Christopher Columbus and the Columbian Legacy*. New York: Alfred A. Knopf, 1990.

SALHOLZ, ELOISE. "The Future of Gay America." *Newsweek* (March 12, 1990):20–25.

SALTMAN, JULIET. "Maintaining Racially Diverse Neighborhoods." *Urban Affairs Quarterly*. Vol. 26, No. 3 (March 1991):416–41.

SAMPSON, ANTHONY. *The Changing Anatomy of Britain*. New York: Random House, 1982.

SAMPSON, ROBERT J. "Urban Black Violence: The Effects of Male Joblessness and Family Disruption." *American Journal of Sociology*. Vol. 93, No. 2 (September 1987):348–82.

SAMPSON, ROBERT J., and JOHN H. LAUB. "Crime and Deviance Over the Life Course: The Salience of Adult Social Bonds." *American Sociological Review*. Vol. 55, No. 5 (October 1990):609–27.

SÀNDOR, GABRIELLE. "The Other Americans." *American Demographics*. Vol. 16, No. 6 (June 1994):36–41.

SANTOLI, AL. "Fighting Child Prostitution." *Freedom Review*. Vol. 25, No. 5 (September-October 1994):5–8.

SAPIR, EDWARD. "The Status of Linguistics as a Science." *Language*. Vol. 5 (1929):207–14.

———. *Selected Writings of Edward Sapir in Language, Culture, and Personality*. David G. Mandelbaum, ed. Berkeley: University of California Press, 1949.

SAX, LINDA J., ALEXANDER W. ASTIN, WILLIAM S. KORN, and KATHRYN M. MAHONEY. *The American Freshman: National Norms for Fall 1996*. Los Angeles: UCLA Higher Education Research Institute, 1996.

SCAFF, LAWRENCE A. "Max Weber and Robert Michels." *American Journal of Sociology*. Vol. 86, No. 6 (May 1981):1269–86.

SCANLON, JAMES P. "The Curious Case of Affirmative Action for Women." *Society*. Vol. 29, No. 2 (January-February 1992):36–42.

SCHAIE, I. WARNER. "Intelligence and Problem Solving." In James E. Birren and R. Bruce Sloane, eds., *Handbook of Mental Health and Aging*. Englewood Cliffs, N.J.: Prentice Hall, 1980:262–84.

SCHEFF, THOMAS J. *Being Mentally Ill: A Sociological Theory*. 2d ed. New York: Aldine, 1984.

SCHELLENBERG, JAMES A. *Masters of Social Psychology*. New York: Oxford University Press, 1978:38–62.

SCHERER, RON. "Worldwide Trend: Tobacco Use Grows." *Christian Science Monitor* (July 17, 1996):4, 8.

SCHILLER, BRADLEY. "Who Are the Working Poor?" *The Public Interest*. Vol. 155 (Spring 1994):61–71.

SCHLESINGER, ARTHUR. "The City in American Civilization." In A. B. Callow, Jr., ed., *American Urban History*. New York: Oxford University Press, 1969:25–41.

SCHLESINGER, ARTHUR, JR. "The Cult of Ethnicity: Good and Bad." *Time*. Vol. 137, No. 27 (July 8, 1991):21.

SCHMIDT, ROGER. *Exploring Religion*. Belmont, Calif.: Wadsworth, 1980.

SCHOOLER, CARMI, JOANNE MILLER, KAREN A. MILLER, and CAROL N. RICHTAND. "Work for the Household: Its Nature and Consequences for Husbands and Wives." *American Journal of Sociology*. Vol. 90, No. 1 (July 1984):97–124.

SCHUMANN, HANS WOLFGANG. *Buddhism: An Outline of Its Teachings and Schools*. Wheaton, Ill.: The Theosophical Publishing House/Quest Books, 1974.

SCHUTT, RUSSELL K. "Objectivity Versus Outrage." *Society*. Vol. 26, No. 4 (May-June 1989):14–16.

SCHWARTZ, BARRY. "Memory As a Cultural System: Abraham Lincoln in World War II." *American Sociological Review*. Vol. 61, No. 5 (October 1996):908–27.

SCHWARTZ, FELICE N. "Management, Women, and the New Facts of Life." *Harvard Business Review*. Vol. 89, No. 1 (January-February 1989):65–76.

SCHWARTZ, JOE. "Rising Status." *American Demographics*. Vol. 11, No. 1 (January 1989):10.

SCHWARTZ, JOHN E., and THOMAS J. VOLGY. *The Forgotten Americans: Thirty Million Working Poor in the Land of Opportunity*. New York: Norton, 1992.

SCHWARTZ, MARTIN D. "Gender and Injury in Spousal Assault." *Sociological Focus*. Vol. 20, No. 1 (January 1987):61–75.

SCHWARTZ-NOBEL, LORETTA. *Starving in the Shadow of Plenty*. New York: McGraw-Hill, 1981.

SCOMMEGNA, PAOLA. "Teens' Risk of AIDS, Unintended Pregnancies Examined." *Population Today*. Vol. 24, No. 8 (August 1996):1–2.

SCOTT, JOHN, and CATHERINE GRIFF. *Directors of Industry: The British Corporate Network, 1904–1976*. New York: Blackwell, 1985.

SCOTT, W. RICHARD. *Organizations: Rational, Natural, and Open Systems*. Englewood Cliffs, NJ: Prentice Hall, 1981.

SEARS, DAVID O., and JOHN B. MCCONAHAY. *The Politics of Violence: The New Urban Blacks and the Watts Riot*. Boston: Houghton Mifflin, 1973.

SEBASTIAN, TIM. "Massacred: 1,000; Tried, 0." *World Press Review* (June 1996):6–10.

SEGAL, MADY WECHSLER, and AMANDA FAITH HANSEN. "Value Rationales in Policy Debates on Women in the Military: A Content Analysis of Congressional Testimony, 1941–1985." *Social Science Quarterly*. Vol. 73, No. 2 (June 1992):296–309.

SEKULIC, DUSKO, GARTH MASSEY, and RANDY HODSON. "Who Were the Yugoslavs? Failed Sources of Common Identity in the Former Yugoslavia." *American Sociological Review*. Vol. 59, No. 1 (February 1994):83–97.

SELIMUDDIN, ABU K. "The Selling of America." *USA Today*. Vol. 117, No. 2525 (March 1989):12–14.

SELLIN, THORSTEN. *The Penalty of Death*. Beverly Hills, Calif.: Sage, 1980.

SELTZER, ROBERT M. *Jewish People, Jewish Thought: The Jewish Experience in History*. New York: Macmillan, 1980.

SEN, K. M. *Hinduism*. Baltimore: Penguin Books, 1961.

SENNETT, RICHARD, and JONATHAN COBB. *The Hidden Injuries of Class*. New York: Vintage Books, 1973.

SHAPIRO, JOSEPH P. "Welfare: The Myth of Reform." *U.S. News and World Report*. Vol. 188, No. 2 (January 16, 1995):30–40.

SHAPIRO, JOSEPH P., and JOANNIE M. SCHROF. "Honor Thy Children." *U.S. News and World Report*. Vol. 118, No. 8 (February 27, 1995):39–49.

SHAPIRO, NINA. "Botswana Test Case." *Chicago Tribune* (September 15, 1991):1.

SHARPE, ANITA. "The Rich Aren't So Different After All." *Wall Street Journal* (November 12, 1996):B1, B10.

SHAWCROSS, WILLIAM. *Sideshow: Kissinger, Nixon and the Destruction of Cambodia*. New York: Pocket Books, 1979.

SHEEHAN, TOM. "Senior Esteem as a Factor in Socioeconomic Complexity." *The Gerontologist*. Vol. 16, No. 5 (October 1976):433–40.

SHEEHY, GAIL. *Passages: Predictable Crises of Adult Life*. New York: Dutton, 1976.

SHELDON, WILLIAM H., EMIL M. HARTL, and EUGENE McDERMOTT. *Varieties of Delinquent Youth*. New York: Harper, 1949.

SHELEY, JAMES F., JOSHUA ZHANG, CHARLES J. BRODY, and JAMES D. WRIGHT. "Gang Organization, Gang Criminal Activity, and Individual Gang Members' Criminal Behavior." *Social Science Quarterly*. Vol. 76, No. 1 (March 1995):53–68.

SHENON, PHILIP. "A Pacific Island Nation Is Stripped of Everything." *New York Times* (December 10, 1995):3.

SHERMAN, LAWRENCE W., and DOUGLAS A. SMITH. "Crime, Punishment, and Stake in Conformity: Legal and Informal Control of Domestic Violence." *American Sociological Review*. Vol. 57, No. 5 (October 1992):680–90.

SHERRID, PAMELA. "Hot Times in the City of London." *U.S. News & World Report* (October 27, 1986):45–46.

SHEVKY, ESHREF, and WENDELL BELL. *Social Area Analysis*. Stanford, Calif.: Stanford University Press, 1955.

SHIBUTANI, TAMOTSU. *Improvised News: A Sociological Study of Rumor*. Indianapolis, Ind.: Bobbs-Merrill, 1966.

SHIPLER, DAVID K. *Russia: Broken Idols, Solemn Dreams*. New York: Penguin Books, 1984.

SHIPLEY, JOSEPH T. *Dictionary of Word Origins*. Totowa, N.J.: Roman & Allanheld, 1985.

SHIVELY, JOELLEN. "Cowboys and Indians: Perceptions of Western Films Among American Indians and Anglos." *American Sociological Review*. Vol. 57, No. 6 (December 1992):725–34.

SHUPE, ANSON, WILLIAM A. STACEY, and LONNIE R. HAZLEWOOD. *Violent Men, Violent Couples: The Dynamics of Domestic Violence*. Lexington, Mass.: Lexington Books, 1987.

SIDEL, RUTH, and VICTOR W. SIDEL. *A Healthy State: An International Perspective on the Crisis in United States Medical Care*. Rev. ed. New York: Pantheon Books, 1982a.

———. *The Health Care of China*. Boston: Beacon Press, 1982b.

SILLS, DAVID L. "The Succession of Goals." In Amitai Etzioni, ed., *A Sociological Reader on Complex Organizations*. 2d ed. New York: Holt, Rinehart & Winston, 1969:175–87.

SILVERBERG, ROBERT. "The Greenhouse Effect: Apocalypse Now or Chicken Little?" *Omni* (July 1991):50–54.

SILVERSTEIN, MICHAEL. In Jon Snodgrass, ed., *A Book of Readings for Men Against Sexism*. Albion, Calif.: Times Change Press, 1977:178–79.

SIMMEL, GEORG. *The Sociology of Georg Simmel*. Kurt Wolff, ed. New York: Free Press, 1950:118–69.

———. "The Metropolis and Mental Life." In Kurt Wolff, ed., *The Sociology of Georg Simmel*. New York: Free Press, 1964:409–24; orig. 1905.

———. "Fashion." In Donald N. Levine, ed., *Georg Simmel: On Individuality and Social Forms*. Chicago: University of Chicago Press, 1971; orig. 1904.

SIMONS, CAROL. "Japan's *Kyoiku* Mamas." In John J. Macionis and Nijole V. Benokraitis, eds., *Seeing Ourselves: Classic, Contemporary, and Cross-Cultural Readings in Sociology*. Englewood Cliffs, N.J.: Prentice Hall, 1993.

SIMONS, MARLISE. "The Price of Modernization: The Case of Brazil's Kaiapo Indians." In John J. Macionis and Nijole V. Benokraitis, eds., *Seeing Ourselves: Classic, Contemporary, and Cross-Cultural Readings in Sociology*. 4th ed. Upper Saddle River, N.J.: Prentice Hall, 1998:494–500.

SIMPSON, GEORGE EATON, and J. MILTON YINGER. *Racial and Cultural Minorities: An Analysis of Prejudice and Discrimination*. 4th ed. New York: Harper & Row, 1972.

SIMPSON, JANICE C. "Buying Black." *Time*. Vol. 140, No. 9 (August 31, 1992):52–53.

SINGER, JEROME L., and DOROTHY G. SINGER. "Psychologists Look at Television: Cognitive, Developmental, Personality, and Social Policy Implications." *American Psychologist*. Vol. 38, No. 7 (July 1983):826–34.

SIVARD, RUTH LEGER. *World Military and Social Expenditures, 1987–88*. 12th ed. Washington, D.C.: World Priorities, 1988.

SIZER, THEODORE R. *Horace's Compromise: The Dilemma of the American High School*. Boston: Houghton Mifflin, 1984.

SKINNER, DAVID. "Computers: Good for Education?" *The Public Interest*. No. 128 (Summer 1997):98–109.

SKOCPOL, THEDA. *States and Social Revolutions: A Comparative Analysis of France, Russia, and China*. Cambridge: Cambridge University Press, 1979.

SKOLNICK, ARLENE. *The Psychology of Human Development*. New York: Harcourt Brace Jovanovich, 1986.

SLATER, PHILIP E. "Contrasting Correlates of Group Size." *Sociometry*. Vol. 21, No. 2 (June 1958):129–39.

———. *The Pursuit of Loneliness*. Boston: Beacon Press, 1976.

SMALL BUSINESS ADMINISTRATION. News release on census data for women-owned businesses. January 1996.

SMART, NINIAN. *The Religious Experience of Mankind*. New York: Charles Scribner's Sons, 1969.

SMELSER, NEIL J. *Theory of Collective Behavior*. New York: Free Press, 1962.

SMITH, ADAM. *An Inquiry Into the Nature and Causes of the Wealth of Nations*. New York: The Modern Library, 1937; orig. 1776.

SMITH, DOUGLAS A. "Police Response to Interpersonal Violence: Defining the Parameters of Legal Control." *Social Forces*. Vol. 65, No. 3 (March 1987):767–82.

SMITH, DOUGLAS A., and PATRICK R. GARTIN. "Specifying Specific Deterrence: The Influence of Arrest on Future Criminal Activity." *American Sociological Review*. Vol. 54, No. 1 (February 1989):94–105.

SMITH, DOUGLAS A., and CHRISTY A. VISHER. "Street-Level Justice: Situational Determinants of Police Arrest Decisions." *Social Problems*. Vol. 29, No. 2 (December 1981):167–77.

SMITH, ROBERT B. "Health Care Reform Now." *Society*. Vol. 30, No. 3 (March-April 1993):56–65.

SMITH, ROBERT ELLIS. *Privacy: How to Protect What's Left of It*. Garden City, N.Y.: Anchor/Doubleday, 1979.

SMITH, TOM W. Research results reported in "Anti-Semitism Decreases But Persists." *Society*. Vol. 33, No. 3 (March/April 1996):2.

SMITH-LOVIN, LYNN, and CHARLES BRODY. "Interruptions in Group Discussions: The Effects of Gender and Group Composition." *American Journal of Sociology*. Vol. 54, No. 3 (June 1989):424–35.

SMOLAN, RICK, and JENNIFER ERWITT. *24 Hours in Cyberspace*. New York: Que* Macmillan Publishing, 1996.

SMOLOWE, JILL. "A Heavenly Host in Georgia." *Time*. Vol. 141, No. 3 (January 18, 1993):55.

———. "When Violence Hits Home." *Time*. Vol. 144, No. 1 (July 4, 1994):18–25.

SNELL, MARILYN BERLIN. "The Purge of Nurture." *New Perspectives Quarterly*. Vol. 7, No. 1 (Winter 1990):1–2.

SNOW, DAVID A., E. BURKE ROCHFORD, JR., STEVEN K. WORDEN, and ROBERT D. BENFORD. "Frame Alignment Processes, Micromobilization, and Movement Participation." *American Sociological Review*. Vol. 51, No. 4 (August 1986):464–81.

SNOW, DAVID A., LOUIS A. ZURCHER, JR., and SHELDON EKLAND-OLSON. "Social Networks and Social Movements: A Macrostructural Approach to Differential Recruitment." *American Sociological Review*. Vol. 45, No. 5 (October 1980):787–801.

SNOWMAN, DANIEL. *Britain and America: An Interpretation of Their Culture 1945–1975*. New York: Harper Torchbooks, 1977.

SOUTH, SCOTT J., and STEVEN F. MESSNER. "Structural Determinants of Intergroup Association: Interracial Marriage and Crime." *American Journal of Sociology*. Vol. 91, No. 6 (May 1986):1409–30.

SOWELL, THOMAS. *Ethnic America*. New York: Basic Books, 1981.

———. *Race and Culture*. New York: Basic Books, 1994.

———. "Ethnicity and IQ." In Steven Fraser, ed., *The Bell Curve Wars: Race, Intelligence and the Future of America*. New York: Basic Books, 1995:70–79.

———. *Migrations and Cultures: A World View*. New York: Basic Books, 1996. (check year)

SOYINKA, WOLE. "Africa's Culture Producers." *Society*. Vol. 28, No. 2 (January-February 1991):32–40.

SPATES, JAMES L. "Sociological Overview." In Alan Milberg, ed., *Street Games*. New York: McGraw-Hill, 1976a:286–90.

———. "Counterculture and Dominant Culture Values: A Cross-National Analysis of the Underground Press and Dominant Culture Magazines." *American Sociological Review*. Vol. 41, No. 5 (October 1976b):868–83.

———. "The Sociology of Values." In Ralph Turner, ed., *Annual Review of Sociology*. Vol. 9. Palo Alto, Calif.: Annual Reviews, 1983:27–49.

SPATES, JAMES L., and JOHN J. MACIONIS. *The Sociology of Cities*. 2d ed. Belmont, Calif.: Wadsworth, 1987.

SPATES, JAMES L., and H. WESLEY PERKINS. "American and English Student Values." *Comparative Social Research*. Vol. 5. Greenwich, Conn.: JAI Press, 1982:245–68.

SPECTOR, LEONARD S. "Nuclear Proliferation Today." In William M. Evan and Stephen Hilgartner, eds., *The Arms Race and Nuclear War*. Englewood Cliffs, N.J.: Prentice Hall, 1988:25–29.

SPECTER, MICHAEL. "Plunging Life Expectancy Puzzles Russia." *New York Times* (August 2, 1995):A1, A2.

———. "Moscow on the Make." *New York Times Magazine* (June 1, 1997):48–55, 72, 75, 80, 84.

———. "Deep in the Russian Soul, a Lethal Darkness." *New York Times* (June 8, 1997): section 4, pp. 1, 5.

SPEER, JAMES A. "The New Christian Right and Its Parent Company: A Study in Political Contrasts." In David G. Bromley and Anson Shupe, eds., *New Christian Politics*. Macon, Ga.: Mercer University Press, 1984:19–40.

SPEER, TIBBETT L. "Are College Costs Cutting Enrollment?" *American Demographics*. Vol. 16, No. 11 (November 1994):9–10.

———. "Digging Into the Underground Economy." *American Demographics*. Vol. 17, No. 2 (February 1995):15–16.

———. "A Nation of Students." *American Demographics*. Vol. 48, No. 8 (August 1996):32–39.

———. "Taxing Times." *American Demographics*. Vol. 49, No. 4 (April 1997):41–44.

SPENCER, MARTIN E. "Multiculturalism, 'Political Correctness,' and the Politics of Identity." *Sociological Forum*. Vol. 9, No. 4 (December 1994):547–67.

SPENDER, DALE. *Man Made Language*. London: Routledge & Kegan Paul, 1980.

SPITZER, STEVEN. "Toward a Marxian Theory of Deviance." In Delos H. Kelly, ed., *Criminal Behavior: Readings in Criminology*. New York: St. Martin's Press, 1980:175–91.

STACEY, JUDITH. *Patriarchy and Socialist Revolution in China*. Berkeley: University of California Press, 1983.

———. *Brave New Families: Stories of Domestic Upheaval in Late Twentieth-Century America*. New York: Basic Books, 1990.

———. "Good Riddance to 'The Family': A Response to David Popenoe." *Journal of Marriage and the Family*. Vol. 55, No. 3 (August 1993):545–47.

STACK, CAROL B. *All Our Kin: Strategies for Survival in a Black Community*. New York: Harper & Row, 1975.

STAHURA, JOHN M. "Suburban Development, Black Suburbanization and the Black Civil Rights Movement Since World War II." *American Sociological Review*. Vol. 51, No. 1 (February 1986):131–44.

STANLEY, LIZ, ED. *Feminist Praxis: Research, Theory, and Epistemology in Feminist Sociology*. London: Routledge & Kegan Paul, 1990.

STANLEY, LIZ, and SUE WISE. *Breaking Out: Feminist Consciousness and Feminist Research*. London: Routledge & Kegan Paul, 1983.

STAPLES, ROBERT, and ALFREDO MIRANDE. "Racial and Cultural Variations Among American Families: A Decennial Review of the Literature on Minority Families." *Journal of Marriage and the Family*. Vol. 42, No. 4 (August 1980):157–72.

STARK, RODNEY. *Sociology*. Belmont, Calif.: Wadsworth, 1985.

STARK, RODNEY, and WILLIAM SIMS BAINBRIDGE. "Of Churches, Sects, and Cults: Preliminary Concepts for a Theory of Religious Movements." *Journal for the Scientific Study of Religion*. Vol. 18, No. 2 (June 1979):117–31.

———. "Secularization and Cult Formation in the Jazz Age." *Journal for the Scientific Study of Religion*. Vol. 20, No. 4 (December 1981):360–73.

STARK, RODNEY, and CHARLES Y. GLOCK. *American Piety: The Nature of Religious Commitment*. Berkeley: University of California Press, 1968.

STARR, PAUL. *The Social Transformation of American Medicine*. New York: Basic Books, 1982.

Statistics of Income Bulletin. Vol. 11, No. 3 (Winter 1991–92).

STAVRIANOS, L. S. *A Global History: The Human Heritage*. 3d ed. Englewood Cliffs, N.J.: Prentice Hall, 1983.

STEARNS, LINDA BREWSTER, and KENNETH D. ALLAN. "Economic Behavior in Institutional Environments: The Corporate Merger Wave of the 1980s." *American Sociological Review*. Vol. 61, No. 4 (August, 1996):699–718.

STEELE, SHELBY. *The Content of Our Character: A New Vision of Race in America*. New York: St. Martin's Press, 1990.

STEIN, MAURICE R. *The Eclipse of Community: An Interpretation of American Studies*. Princeton, N.J.: Princeton University Press, 1972.

STEINBERG, LAURENCE. "Failure Outside the Classroom." *Wall Street Journal* (July 11, 1996):A14.

STEPHENS, JOHN D. *The Transition From Capitalism to Socialism*. Urbana: University of Illinois Press, 1986.

STERNLIEB, GEORGE, and JAMES W. HUGHES. "The Uncertain Future of the Central City." *Urban Affairs Quarterly*. Vol. 18, No. 4 (June 1983):455–72.

STEVENS, GILLIAN, and GRAY SWICEGOOD. "The Linguistic Context of Ethnic Endogamy." *American Sociological Review*. Vol. 52, No. 1 (February 1987):73–82.

STIEHM, JUDITH HICKS. *Arms and the Enlisted Woman*. Philadelphia: Temple University Press, 1989.

STIER, HAYA. "Continuity and Change in Women's Occupations Following First Childbirth." *Social Science Quarterly*. Vol. 77, No. 1 (March 1996):60–75.

STODDARD, SANDOL. *The Hospice Movement: A Better Way to Care for the Dying*. Briarcliff Manor, N.Y.: Stein and Day, 1978.

STONE, LAWRENCE. *The Family, Sex and Marriage in England 1500–1800*. New York: Harper & Row, 1977.

STONE, ROBYN, GAIL LEE CAFFERATA, and JUDITH SANGL. *Caregivers of the Frail Elderly: A National Profile*. Washington, D.C.: U.S. Department of Health and Human Services, 1987.

STOUFFER, SAMUEL A., ET AL. *The American Soldier: Adjustment During Army Life*. Princeton, N.J.: Princeton University Press, 1949.

STRAUS, MURRAY A., and RICHARD J. GELLES. "Societal Change and Change in Family Violence From 1975 to 1985 as Revealed by Two National Surveys." *Journal of Marriage and the Family*. Vol. 48, No. 4 (August 1986):465–79.

STREIB, GORDON F. "Are the Aged a Minority Group?" In Bernice L. Neugarten, ed., *Middle Age and Aging: A Reader in Social Psychology*. Chicago: University of Chicago Press, 1968:35–46.

STRIEGEL-MOORE, RUTH, LISA R. SILBERSTEIN, and JUDITH RODIN. "Toward an Understanding of Risk Factors for Bulimia." *American Psychologist*. Vol. 41, No. 3 (March 1986):246–63.

Student CHIP Social Survey Software. Data sets by Bruner & Macionis. Hanover, N.H.: Zeta Data. © 1992 by James A. Davis.

SUDNOW, DAVID N. *Passing On: The Social Organization of Dying*. Englewood Cliffs, N.J.: Prentice Hall, 1967.

SUMNER, WILLIAM GRAHAM. *Folkways*. New York: Dover, 1959; orig. 1906.

SUNG, BETTY LEE. *Mountains of Gold: The Story of the Chinese in America*. New York: Macmillan, 1967.

SUTHERLAND, EDWIN H. "White Collar Criminality." *American Sociological Review*. Vol. 5, No. 1 (February 1940):1–12.

SUTHERLAND, EDWIN H., and DONALD R. CRESSEY. *Criminology*. 10th ed. Philadelphia: J.B. Lippincott, 1978.

SWARTZ, STEVE. "Why Michael Milken Stands to Qualify for Guinness Book." *Wall Street Journal*. Vol. LXX, No. 117 (March 31, 1989):1, 4.

SYZMANSKI, ALBERT. *Class Structure: A Critical Perspective*. New York: Praeger, 1983.

SZASZ, THOMAS S. *The Manufacturer of Madness: A Comparative Study of the Inquisition and the Mental Health Movement*. New York: Dell, 1961.

———. *The Myth of Mental Illness: Foundations of a Theory of Personal Conduct*. New York: Harper & Row, 1970; orig. 1961.

———. "Mental Illness Is Still a Myth." *Society*. Vol. 31, No. 4 (May-June 1994):34–39.

———. "Idleness and Lawlessness in the Therapeutic State." *Society*. Vol. 32, No. 4 (May/June 1995):30–35.

TAEUBER, KARL, and ALMA TAEUBER. *Negroes in Cities*. Chicago: Aldine, 1965.

TAJFEL, HENRI. "Social Psychology of Intergroup Relations." *Annual Review of Psychology*. Palo Alto, Calif.: Annual Reviews, 1982:1–39.

TANNEN, DEBORAH. *You Just Don't Understand Me: Women and Men in Conversation*. New York: Wm. Morrow, 1990.

———. *Talking from 9 to 5: How Women's and Men's Conversational Styles Affect Who Gets Heard, Who Gets Credit, and What Gets Done at Work*. New York: Wm. Morrow, 1994.

TANNENBAUM, FRANK. *Slave and Citizen: The Negro in the Americas*. New York: Vintage Books, 1946.

TANNER, MICHAEL, and STEPHEN MOORE. "Why Welfare Pays." *Wall Street Journal* (September 28, 1995):A20.

TARROW, SIDNEY. *Social Movements, Collective Action and Politics*. New York: Cambridge University Press, 1994.

TAVRIS, CAROL, and SUSAN SADD. *The Redbook Report on Female Sexuality*. New York: Delacorte Press, 1977.

TAX FOUNDATION. [Online] Available http://www.taxfoundation.org/prtaxfree.html, 1997.

TAYLOR, JOHN. "Don't Blame Me: The New Culture of Victimization." *New York Magazine* (June 3, 1991):26–34.

TERKEL, STUDS. *Working*. New York: Pantheon Books, 1974:1–2, 57–59, 65, 66, 69, 221–22. Copyright © 1974 by Pantheon Books, a division of Random House, Inc.

TERRY, DON. "In Crackdown on Bias, A New Tool." *New York Times* (June 12, 1993):8.

THEEN, ROLF H. W. "Party and Bureaucracy." In Erik P. Hoffmann and Robbin F. Laird, eds., *The Soviet Polity in the Modern Era*. New York: Aldine, 1984:131–65.

THEILMANN, JOHN, and ALLEN WILHITE. "Congressional Turnover: Negating the Incumbent Advantage." *Social Science Quarterly*. Vol. 76, No. 3 (September 1995):594–606.

THERNSTROM, STEPHAN. "The Minority Majority Will Never Come." *Wall Street Journal* (July 26, 1990):A16.

THOMAS, EDWARD J. *The Life of Buddha as Legend and History*. London: Routledge & Kegan Paul, 1975.

THOMAS, PAULETTE. "Success at a Huge Personal Cost." *Wall Street Journal* (July 26, 1995):B1, B6.

THOMAS, PIRI. *Down These Mean Streets*. New York: Signet, 1967.

THOMAS, W. I. "The Relation of Research to the Social Process." In Morris Janowitz, ed., *W. I. Thomas on Social Organization and Social Personality*. Chicago: University of Chicago Press, 1966:289–305; orig. 1931.

THOMMA, STEVEN. "Christian Coalition Demands Action From GOP." *Philadelphia Inquirer* (September 14, 1997):A2.

THOMPSON, LARRY. "The Breast Cancer Gene: A Woman's Dilemma." *Time*. Vol. 143, No. 3 (January 17, 1994):52.

———. "Fertility With Less Fuss." *Time*. Vol. 144, No. 20 (November 14, 1994):79.

THOMPSON, MARK. "Offensive Maneuvers." *Time*. Vol. 149, No. 18 (May 5, 1997):40–42.

THORNBERRY, TERRANCE, and MARGARET FARNSWORTH. "Social Correlates of Criminal Involvement: Further Evidence on the Relationship Between Social Status and Criminal Behavior." *American Sociological Review*. Vol 47, No. 4 (August 1982):505–18.

THORNE, BARRIE, CHERIS KRAMARAE, and NANCY HENLEY, EDS. *Language, Gender and Society*. Rowley, Mass.: Newbury House, 1983.

THORNTON, ARLAND. "Changing Attitudes Toward Separation and Divorce: Causes and Consequences." *American Journal of Sociology*. Vol. 90, No. 4 (January 1985):856–72.

THUROW, LESTER C. "A Surge in Inequality." *Scientific American*. Vol. 256, No. 5 (May 1987):30–37.

TIGER, LIONEL, and JOSEPH SHEPHER. *Women in the Kibbutz*. New York: Harcourt Brace Jovanovich, 1975.

TILLY, CHARLES. *From Mobilization to Revolution*. Reading, Mass.: Addison-Wesley, 1978.

———. "Does Modernization Breed Revolution?" In Jack A. Goldstone, ed., *Revolutions: Theoretical, Comparative, and Historical Studies*. New York: Harcourt Brace Jovanovich, 1986:47–57.

TITTLE, CHARLES R., and WAYNE J. VILLEMEZ. "Social Class and Criminality." *Social Forces*. Vol. 56, No. 22 (December 1977):474–502.

TITTLE, CHARLES R., WAYNE J. VILLEMEZ, and DOUGLAS A. SMITH. "The Myth of Social Class and Criminality: An Empirical Assessment of the Empirical Evidence." *American Sociological Review*. Vol. 43, No. 5 (October 1978):643–56.

TOBIN, GARY. "Suburbanization and the Development of Motor Transportation: Transportation Technology and the Suburbanization Process." In Barry Schwartz, ed., *The Changing Face of the Suburbs*. Chicago: University of Chicago Press, 1976.

TOCH, THOMAS. "The Exodus." *U.S. News & World Report*. Vol. 111, No. 24 (December 9, 1991):68–77.

TOCQUEVILLE, ALEXIS DE. *The Old Regime and the French Revolution*. Stuart Gilbert, trans. Garden City, N.Y.: Anchor/Doubleday Books, 1955; orig. 1856.

TOENNIES, FERDINAND. *Community and Society (Gemeinschaft und Gesellschaft)*. New York: Harper & Row, 1963; orig. 1887.

TOFANI, LORETTA. "AIDS Ravages a Continent, and Sweeps a Family." *Philadelphia Inquirer* (March 24, 1991):1, 15–A.

TOFFLER, ALVIN, and HEIDI TOFFLER. *War and Anti-war: Survival at the Dawn of the 21st Century*. Boston: Little, Brown, 1993.

TOLSON, JAY. "The Trouble With Elites." *The Wilson Quarterly*. Vol. XIX, No. 1 (Winter 1995):6–8.

TOOMEY, BEVERLY, RICHARD FIRST, and JOHN RIFE. Research described in "Number of Rural Homeless Greater Than Expected." Ohio State *Quest* (Autumn 1990):2.

TOWNSEND, BICKLEY. "Room at the Top for Women." *American Demographics*. Vol. 18, No. 7 (July 1996):28–37.

TREAS, JUDITH. "Socialist Organization and Economic Development in China: Latent Consequences for the Aged." *The Gerontologist*. Vol. 19, No. 1 (February 1979):34–43.

———. "Older Americans in the 1990s and Beyond." *Population Bulletin*. Vol. 50, No. 2 (May 1995). Washington, D.C.: Population Reference Bureau.

TREIMAN, DONALD J. "Industrialization and Social Stratification." In Edward O. Laumann, ed., *Social Stratification: Research and Theory for the 1970s*. Indianapolis, Ind.: Bobbs-Merrill, 1970.

TRENT, KATHERINE. "Family Context and Adolescents' Expectations About Marriage, Fertility, and Nonmarital Childbearing." *Social Science Quarterly*. Vol. 75, No 2 (June 1994):319–39.

TROELTSCH, ERNST. *The Social Teaching of the Christian Churches*. New York: Macmillan, 1931.

TROIDEN, RICHARD R. *Gay and Lesbian Identity: A Sociological Analysis*. Dix Hills, N.Y.: General Hall, 1988.

TUMIN, MELVIN M. "Some Principles of Stratification: A Critical Analysis." *American Sociological Review*. Vol. 18, No. 4 (August 1953):387–94.

———. *Social Stratification: The Forms and Functions of Inequality*. 2d ed. Englewood Cliffs, N.J.: Prentice Hall, 1985.

TUCKER, M. BELINDA, and CLAUDIA MITCHELL-KERNAN, eds. *The Decline of Marriage Among African Americans*. New York: Russell Sage Foundation, 1995.

TURNER, RALPH H., and LEWIS M. KILLIAN. *Collective Behavior*. 2d ed. Englewood Cliffs, N.J.: Prentice Hall, 1972; 3d ed., 1987; 4th ed., 1993.

TYGIEL, JULES. *Baseball's Great Experiment: Jackie Robinson and His Legacy*. New York: Oxford University Press, 1983.

TYLER, S. LYMAN. *A History of Indian Policy*. Washington, D.C.: United States Department of the Interior, Bureau of Indian Affairs, 1973.

TYREE, ANDREA, MOSHE SEMYONOV, and ROBERT W. HODGE. "Gaps and Glissandos: Inequality, Economic Development, and Social Mobility in 24 Countries." *American Sociological Review*. Vol. 44, No. 3 (June 1979):410–24.

UCHITELLE, LOUIS. "But Just Who is That Fairy Godmother?" *New York Times* (September 29, 1991): Section 4, p. 1.

UNITED NATIONS DEVELOPMENT PROGRAMME. *Human Development Report 1990*. New York: Oxford University Press, 1990.

———. *Human Development Report 1991*. New York:Oxford University Press, 1991.

———. *Human Development Report 1993*. New York:Oxford University Press, 1993.

———. *Human Development Report 1994*. New York: Oxford University Press, 1994.

———. *Human Development Report 1995*. New York: Oxford University Press, 1995.

———. *Human Development Report 1996*. New York: Oxford University Press, 1996.

———. *Human Development Report 1997*. New York: Oxford University Press, 1997.

UNIVERSITY OF AKRON RESEARCH CENTER. *National Survey of Religion and Politics 1992*. Akron, Ohio: University of Akron Research Center, 1993.

UNNEVER, JAMES D., CHARLES E. FRAZIER, and JOHN C. HENRETTA. "Race Differences in Criminal Sentencing." *The Sociological Quarterly*. Vol. 21, No. 2 (Spring 1980):197–205.

UNRUH, JOHN D., JR. *The Plains Across*. Urbana: University of Illinois Press, 1979.

U.S. BUREAU OF THE CENSUS. *Statistical Abstract of the United States 1970*. 90th ed. Washington, D.C.: U.S. Government Printing Office, 1970.

———. Press release on homeless count (CB91–117). Washington, D.C.: U.S. Government Printing Office, 1991.

———. *Statistical Abstract of the United States: 1992*. 112th ed. Washington, D.C.: U.S. Government Printing Office, 1992.

———. *Money Income of Households, Families, and Persons in the United States: 1992*. Current Population Reports, Series P-60, No. 184. Washington, D.C.: U.S. Government Printing Office, 1993.

———. *Poverty in the United States: 1992*. Current Population Reports, Series P-60, No. 185. Washington, D.C.: U.S. Government Printing Office, 1993.

———. *Statistical Abstract of the United States: 1993*. 113th ed. Washington, D.C.: U.S. Government Printing Office, 1993.

———. *Educational Attainment in the United States: March 1993 and 1992*. Current Population Reports, Series P-20, No. 476. Washington, D.C.: U.S. Government Printing Office, 1994.

———. *School Enrollment—Social and Economic Characteristics of Students: October 1993*. Current Population Reports, Series P-20, No. 479. Washington, D.C.: U.S. Government Printing Office, 1994.

———. *Statistical Abstract of the United States: 1994*. 114th ed. Washington, D.C.: U.S. Government Printing Office, 1994.

———. *Asset Ownership of Households: 1993*. Current Population Reports, Series P-70, No. 47. Washington, D.C.: U.S. Government Printing Office, 1995.

———. *Current Population Reports*. Series P-60, No. 188. Washington, D.C.: U.S. Government Printing Office, 1995.

———. *Household and Family Characteristics: March 1994*. Current Population Reports, Series P-20, No. 483, Washington, D.C.: U.S. Government Printing Office, 1995.

———. *Income, Poverty, and Valuation of Noncash Benefits: 1993*. Current Population Reports, Series P-60, No. 188. Washington, D.C.: U.S. Government Printing Office, 1995.

———. *Statistical Abstract of the United States: 1995*. 115th ed. Washington, D.C.: U.S. Government Printing Office, 1995.

———. *Marital Status and Living Arrangements: March 1995*. PPL-52. Washington, D.C.: U.S. Government Printing Office, 1996.

———. *Money Income in the United States 1995*. Current Population Reports, P60–193. Washington, D.C.: U.S. Government Printing Office, 1996.

———. *Population Projections of the United States by Age, Sex, Race, and Hispanic Origin: 1995 to 2050*. P25–1130. Washington, D.C.: U.S. Government Printing Office, 1996.

———. Prepublication data on income and wealth provided by the Census Bureau, 1996.

———. Press release on women-owned businesses, 1996.

———. Response to telephone query, 1996.

———. *Women-Owned Businesses*. Washington, D.C.: U.S. Government Printing Office, 1996.

———. *World Population Profile 1996*. WP/96. Washington, D.C.: U.S. Government Printing Office, 1996.

———. Data on educational achievement. [Online] Available http://www.census.gov/population/socdemo/education/educ96cps.dat, 1997.

———. Data on mixed marriages. [Online] Available http://www.census.gov/population/socdemo/ms-la/95his04.tx, 1997.

———. *Educational Attainment in the United States: March 1996 (Update)*. Current Population Reports, P20–493. Washington, D.C.: U.S. Government Printing Office, 1997.

———. *Health Insurance Coverage: 1996*. Current Population Reports, P60–199. Washington, D.C.: U.S. Government Printing Office, 1997.

———. *Household and Family Characteristics: March 1996*. PPL-66. Washington, D.C.: U.S. Government Printing Office, 1997.

———. *Money Income in the United States 1996 (With Separate Data on Valuation of Noncash Benefits)*. Current Population Reports, P60–197. Washington, D.C.: U.S. Government Printing Office, 1997.

———. *Poverty in the United States: 1996*. Current Population Reports, P60–198. Washington, D.C.: U.S. Government Printing Office, 1997.

———. *School Enrollment—Social and Economic Characteristics of Students: October 1995 (Update)*. PPL-55: The Bureau, 1997.

———. *Statistical Abstract of the United States 1997*. Washington, D.C.: U.S. Government Printing Office, 1997.

———. Table F-1: Income Limits for Each Fifth and Top 5 Percent of Families (All Races): 1947 to 1996. [Online] Available http://www.census.gov/hhes/income/histinc/f01.htm, December 31, 1997.

———. Table F-3: Mean Income Received by Each Fifth and Top 5 Percent of Families (All Races): 1966 to 1996. [Online] Available http://www.census.gov/hhes/income/histinc/f03.htm, December 31, 1997.

———. Table F-5: Race and Hispanic Origin of Householder—Families by Median and Mean Income: 1947 to 1996. [Online] Available http://www.census.gov/hhes/income/histinc/f05.htm, December 31, 1997.

———. "Who's Minding Our Preschoolers?" Fall 1994 (Update). P70–62. Washington, D.C.: U.S. Government Printing Office, 1997.

———. Estimated Median Age at First Marriage, by Sex: 1890 to the Present. [Online] Available http://www.census.gov/population/socdemo/ms-la/95his06.txt, January 2, 1998.

———. International Database. [Online] Available http://www.census.gov/cgi-bin/ipc/idbsum, January 8, 1998.

———. Historical Income Tables—Persons. Table P-9: Age—All Persons 15 Years Old and Over by Median and Mean Income and Sex: 1974 to 1996. [Online] Available http://www.census.gov/hhes/income/histinc/p09.htm, January 18, 1998.

———. Resident Population of the United States: Estimates by Sex, Race, and Hispanic Origin, With Median Age. [Online] Available http://www.census.gov/population/estimates/nation/intfile3–1.tx, January 19, 1998.

———. Historical Income Tables—Families. Table F-2B: Share of Aggregate Income Received by Each Fifth and Top 5 Percent of Black Families: 1966 to 1996. [Online] Available http://www.census.gov/hhes/income/histinc/f02b.htm, February 8, 1998.

U.S. BUREAU OF ECONOMIC ANALYSIS. Foreign Direct Investment in the United States: Selected Items, by Country of Foreign Parent and by Industry of Affiliate, 1994–96. [Online] Available http://www.bea.doc.gov/bea/di/fdius-d.htm#fdius-1, January 19, 1998.

U.S. BUREAU OF JUSTICE STATISTICS. *Sourcebook of Criminal Justice Statistics 1990*. Timothy J. Flanagan and Kathleen Maguire, eds. Washington, D.C.: U.S. Government Printing Office, 1991.

———. *Compendium of Federal Justice Statistics, 1989*. Washington D.C.: U.S. Government Printing Office, 1992.

———. *Violence Against Women*. Washington, D.C.: U.S. Government Printing Office, 1994.

———. *National Crime Victimization Survey, 1992–1993*. Washington, D.C.: U.S. Government Printing Office, 1995.

———. *Criminal Victimization 1994*. Washington, D.C.: U.S. Government Printing Office, 1996.

———. *Correctional Populations in the United States 1995*. Washington, D.C.: The Bureau, 1997.

———. *Criminal Victimization 1996*. Washington, D.C.: The Bureau, 1997.

———. *Sourcebook of Criminal Justice Statistics 1996*. Washington, D.C.: The Bureau, 1997.

U.S. BUREAU OF LABOR STATISTICS. *Employment and Earnings*. Vol. 41, No. 1 (January). Washington, D.C.: U.S. Government Printing Office, 1994.

———. *Employment and Earnings*. Vol. 42, No. 1 (January). Washington, D.C.: U.S. Government Printing Office, 1995.

———. Unpublished data on U.S. labor force, 1995.

———. *Employment and Earnings*. Vol. 43, No. 1 (January 1996).

———. Response to telephone query, 1996.

U.S. CENTERS FOR DISEASE CONTROL AND PREVENTION. Response to telephone query, 1994.

———. *HIV/AIDS Surveillance Report*. Vol. 7, No. 1. Rockville, Md.: CDC National AIDS Clearinghouse, 1995.

———. *HIV/AIDS Surveillance Report. Vol. 9, No. 1 (Midyear ed., 1997)*: 8.

———. *Morbidity and Mortality Weekly Report*. Vol. 46, No. 51 (December 26, 1997).

U.S. Department of Agriculture. Agricultural Research Service. Family Economics Research Group. *Expenditures on a Child by Families, 1992.* Hyattsville, Md.: The Group, 1993.

U.S. Department of Justice. Press release, June 22, 1994.

U.S. Department of Labor. Bureau of Labor Statistics. "Portability of Pension Benefits Among Jobs." Washington, D.C.: U.S. Government Printing Office, 1994.

————. Bureau of Labor Statistics. *Employment and Earnings.* Vol. 44, No. 1 (January). Washington, D.C.: U.S. Government Printing Office, 1997.

————. Bureau of Labor Statistics. "Looking for a Job While Employed." Summary 97–14. Washington, D.C.: U.S. Government Printing Office, 1997.

————. Bureau of Labor Statistics. *Employment and Earnings.* Vol. 45, No. 1 (January). Washington, D.C.: U.S. Government Printing Office, 1998.

Useem, Bert. "Disorganization and the New Mexico Prison Riot of 1980." *American Sociological Review.* Vol. 50, No. 5 (October 1985):677–88.

Useem, Michael. "Corporations and the Corporate Elite." In Alex Inkeles et al., eds., *Annual Review of Sociology.* Vol. 6. Palo Alto, Cal.: Annual Reviews, 1980:41–77.

Useem, Michael, and Jerome Karabel. "Pathways to Corporate Management." *American Sociological Review.* Vol. 51, No. 2 (April 1986):184–200.

U.S. Equal Employment Opportunity Commission. *Job Patterns for Minorities and Women in Private Industry 1994.* Washington, D.C.: The Commission, 1995.

————. Response to personal query, 1996.

————. *Job Patterns for Minorities and Women in Private Industry, 1996.* Washington, D.C.: The Commission, 1997.

U.S. Federal Bureau of Investigation. *Crime in the United States 1993.* Washington, D.C.: U.S. Government Printing Office, 1994.

————. *Crime in the United States 1994.* Washington, D.C.: U.S. Government Printing Office, 1995.

————. *Uniform Crime Reports for the United States 1995.* Washington, D.C.: U.S. Government Printing Office, 1996.

————. *Uniform Crime Reports for the United States 1996.* Washington, D.C.: U.S. Government Printing Office, 1997.

U.S. Federal Election Commission. *1994 Congressional Funding Sets New Record.* Washington, D.C.: The Commission, 1995.

————. "Congressional Fundraising and Spending Up Again in 1996." Washington, D.C.: The Commission, 1997.

————. "FEC Releases Semiannual Federal PAC Count." [Online] Available http://www.fec.gov/press/count98.htm, February 7, 1998.

U.S. House of Representatives. "Street Children: A Global Disgrace." Hearing on November 7, 1991. Washington, D.C.: U.S. Government Printing Office, 1992.

U.S. Immigration and Naturalization Service. *Statistical Yearbook.* Washington, D.C.: U.S. Government Printing Office, 1995.

————. Table 3: Immigrants Admitted by Region and Selected Country of Birth, Fiscal Years 1984–94. Fax received from INS January 1996.

————. Immigrants Admitted by Region and Selected Country of Birth. [Online] Available http://www.ins.doj.gov/stats/annual/fy94/744.htm, December 5, 1997.

————. Table 5: Immigrants Admitted by Region and Selected Country of Birth, Fiscal Years 1994–96. [Online] Available http://www.ins.doj.gov/stats/annual/fy96/1005.htm, December 5, 1997.

U.S. Internal Revenue Service. *Statistics of Income Bulletin* (Spring 1993).

U.S. National Center for Education Statistics. *Digest of Education Statistics 1996.* Washington, D.C.: The Center, 1996.

————. *Digest of Education Statistics 1997.* Washington, D.C.: U.S. Government Printing Office, 1997.

U.S. National Center for Health Statistics. *Vital Statistics of the United States, 1988, Vol. 1, Natality.* Washington, D.C.: U.S. Government Printing Office, 1990.

————. *Current Estimates From the National Health Interview Survey United States, 1993.* Vital and Health Statistics. Series 10, No. 190. Hyattsville, Md.: The Center, 1994.

————. "Annual Summary of Births, Marriages, Divorces, and Deaths: United States, 1994." *Monthly Vital Statistics Report.* Vol. 43, No. 13 (October 23, 1995). Hyattsville, Md.: The Center, 1995.

————. *Current Estimates From the National Health Interview Survey 1994.* Hyattsville, Md.: The Center, 1995.

————. *Advance Report of Final Mortality Statistics, 1993.* Hyattsville, Md.: The Center, 1996.

————. *Advance Report of Final Mortality Statistics, 1994.* Hyattsville, Md.: The Center, 1996.

————. *Monthly Vital Statistics Report.* Vol. 45, No. 11 (June 10, 1997).

————. *Monthly Vital Statistics Report.* Vol. 45, No. 12 (July 17, 1997):1.

————. "Births and Deaths: United States, 1996." *Monthly Vital Statistics Report.* Vol. 46, No. 1, Suppl. 2 (September 11, 1997).

U.S. State Department. 1996 Patterns of Global Terrorism Report. [Online] Available http://www.state.gov/www/global/terrorism/1996report/1996index.htm, February 7, 1998.

Vallas, Stephen P., and John P. Beck. "The Transformation of Work Revisited: The Limits of Flexibility in American Manufacturing." *Social Problems.* Vol. 43, No. 3 (August 1996):339–61.

Valocchi, Steve. "The Emergence of the Integrationist Ideology in the Civil Rights Movement." *Social Problems.* Vol. 43, No. 1 (February 1996):116–30.

Van Biema, David. "Parents Who Kill." *Time.* Vol. 144, No. 20 (November 14, 1994):50–51.

————. "Sparse At Seder?" *Time.* Vol. 149, No. 17 (April 28, 1997):67.

————. "Buddhism in America." *Time.* Vol. 150, No. 15 (October 13, 1997):71–81.

van den Haag, Ernest, and John P. Conrad. *The Death Penalty: A Debate.* New York: Plenum Press, 1983.

Vaughan, Mary Kay. "Multinational Corporations: The World as a Company Town." In Ahamed Idris-Soven et al., eds., *The World as a Company Town: Multinational Corporations and Social Change.* The Hague: Mouton Publishers, 1978:15–35.

Vayda, Eugene, and Raisa B. Deber. "The Canadian Health Care System: An Overview." *Social Science and Medicine.* Vol. 18, No. 3 (1984):191–97.

Veblen, Thorstein. *The Theory of the Leisure Class.* New York: The New American Library, 1953; orig. 1899.

Veum, Jonathan R. "Accounting for Income Mobility Changes in the United States." *Social Science Quarterly.* Vol. 73, No. 4 (December 1992):773–85.

Viguerie, Richard A. *The New Right: We're Ready to Lead.* Falls Church, Va.: The Viguerie Company, 1981.

Vines, Gail. "Whose Baby Is It Anyway?" *New Scientist.* No. 1515 (July 3, 1986):26–27.

Vinovskis, Maris A. "Have Social Historians Lost the Civil War? Some Preliminary Demographic Speculations." *Journal of American History.* Vol. 76, No. 1 (June 1989):34–58.

Vogel, Ezra F. *The Four Little Dragons: The Spread of Industrialization in East Asia.* Cambridge, Mass.: Harvard University Press, 1991.

Vogel, Lise. *Marxism and the Oppression of Women: Toward a Unitary Theory.* New Brunswick, N.J.: Rutgers University Press, 1983.

Vold, George B., and Thomas J. Bernard. *Theoretical Criminology.* 3d ed. New York: Oxford University Press, 1986.

von Hirsh, Andrew. *Past or Future Crimes: Deservedness and Dangerousness in the Sentencing of Criminals.* New Brunswick, N.J.: Rutgers University Press, 1986.

Vonnegut, Kurt, Jr. "Harrison Bergeron." In *Welcome to the Monkey House.* New York: Delacorte Press/Seymour Lawrence, 1968:7–13; orig. 1961.

Waite, Linda J., Gus W. Haggstrom, and David I. Kanouse. "The Consequences of Parenthood for the Marital Stability of Young Adults." *American Sociological Review.* Vol. 50, No. 6 (December 1985):850–57.

Walder, Andrew G. "Career Mobility and the Communist Political Order." *American Sociological Review.* Vol. 60, No. 3 (June 1995):309–28.

Waldfogel, Jane. "The Effect of Children on Women's Wages." *American Sociological Review.* Vol. 62, No. 2 (April 1997):209–17.

Waldman, Steven. "Deadbeat Dads." *Newsweek* (May 4, 1992):46–52.

Walker, Karen. "'Always There For Me': Friendship Patterns and Expectations Among Middle- and Working-Class Men and Women." *Sociological Forum.* Vol. 10, No. 2 (June 1995):273–96.

Wall, Thomas F. *Medical Ethics: Basic Moral Issues.* Washington, D.C.: University Press of America, 1980.

Wallace, Ruth A., and Alison Wolf. *Contemporary Sociological Theory: Continuing the Classic Tradition.* 4th ed. Englewood Cliffs, N.J.: Prentice Hall, 1995.

Waller, Douglas. "Onward Cyber Soldiers." *Time.* Vol. 146, No. 8 (August 21, 1995):38–44.

Wallerstein, Immanuel. *The Modern World-System: Capitalist Agriculture and the Origins of the European World-Economy in the Sixteenth Century.* New York: Academic Press, 1974.

————. *The Capitalist World-Economy.* New York: Cambridge University Press, 1979.

————. "Crises: The World Economy, the Movements, and the Ideologies." In Albert Bergesen, ed., *Crises in the World-System.* Beverly Hills, Calif.: Sage, 1983:21–36.

————. *The Politics of the World Economy: The States, the Movements, and the Civilizations.* Cambridge: Cambridge University Press, 1984.

Wallerstein, Judith S., and Sandra Blakeslee. *Second Chances: Men, Women, and Children a Decade After Divorce.* New York: Ticknor & Fields, 1989.

WALLIS, DAVID. "After Cyberoverkill Comes Cyberburnout." *New York Times* (August 4, 1996):43, 46.

WALTERS, LAUREL SHAPER. "World Educators Compare Notes." *The Christian Science Monitor: Global Report* (September 7, 1994):8.

WALTON, JOHN, and CHARLES RAGIN. "Global and National Sources of Political Protest: Third World Responses to the Debt Crisis." *American Sociological Review*. Vol. 55, No. 6 (December 1990):876–90.

WARNER, R. STEPHEN. "Work in Progress Toward a New Paradigm for the Sociological Study of Religion in the United States." *American Journal of Sociology*. Vol. 98, No. 5 (March 1993):1044–93.

WARNER, SAM BASS, JR. *Streetcar Suburbs*. Cambridge, Mass.: Harvard University and MIT Presses, 1962.

WARNER, W. LLOYD, and J. O. LOW. *The Social System of the Modern Factory*. Yankee City Series, Vol. 4. New Haven, Conn.: Yale University Press, 1947.

WARNER, W. LLOYD, and PAUL S. LUNT. *The Social Life of a Modern Community*. New Haven, Conn.: Yale University Press, 1941.

WASKUL, DENNIS. "Selfhood in the Age of Computer Mediated Symbolic Interaction." Paper presented to the annual meeting of the Southwest Social Science Association, New Orleans, La., March, 1997.

WATERS, MELISSA S., WILL CARRINGTON HEATH, and JOHN KEITH WATSON. "A Positive Model of the Determination of Religious Affiliation." *Social Science Quarterly*. Vol. 76, No. 1 (March 1995):105–23.

WATSON, JOHN B. *Behaviorism*. Rev. ed. New York: Norton, 1930.

WAXMAN, CHAIM I. *The Stigma of Poverty: A Critique of Poverty Theories and Policies*. 2d ed. New York: Pergamon Press, 1983.

WATTENBERG, BEN J. "The Population Explosion Is Over." *New York Times Magazine* (November 23, 1997):60–63.

WEBER, ADNA FERRIN. *The Growth of Cities*. New York: Columbia University Press, 1963; orig. 1899.

WEBER, MAX. *The Protestant Ethic and the Spirit of Capitalism*. New York: Charles Scribner's Sons, 1958; orig. 1904–5.

———. "Science as a Vocation." In H. H. Gerth and C. Wright Mills, *From Max Weber: Essays in Sociology*. New York: Oxford University Press, 1958:129–56; orig. 1918.

———. *Economy and Society*. G. Roth and C. Wittich, eds. Berkeley: University of California Press, 1978.

WEBSTER, PAMELA S., TERRI ORBUCH, and JAMES S. HOUSE. "Effects of Childhood Family Background on Adult Marital Quality and Perceived Stability." *American Journal of Sociology*. Vol. 101, No. 2 (September 1995):404–32.

WEEKS, JOHN R. "The Demography of Islamic Nations." *Population Bulletin*. Vol. 43, No. 4 (December 1988). Washington, D.C.: Population Reference Bureau.

WEICHER, JOHN C. "Getting Richer (At Different Rates)." *Wall Street Journal* (June 14, 1995):A18.

WEIDENBAUM, MURRAY. "The Evolving Corporate Board." *Society*. Vol. 32, No. 3 (March/April 1995):9–20.

WEINBERG, GEORGE. *Society and the Healthy Homosexual*. Garden City, N.Y.: Anchor Books, 1973.

WEINER, TIM. "Head of C.I.A. Plans Center to Protect U.S. Cyberspace." *New York Times* (June 26, 1996):B7.

WEINRICH, JAMES D. *Sexual Landscapes: Why We Are What We Are, Why We Love Whom We Love*. New York: Charles Scribner's Sons, 1987.

WEISBURD, DAVID, STANTON WHEELER, ELIN WARING, and NANCY BODE. *Crimes of the Middle Class: White Collar Defenders in the Courts*. New Haven, Conn.: Yale University Press, 1991.

WEISNER, THOMAS S., and BERNICE T. EIDUSON. "The Children of the '60s as Parents." *Psychology Today* (January 1986):60–66.

WEITZMAN, LENORE J. *The Divorce Revolution: The Unexpected Social and Economic Consequences for Women and Children in America*. New York: Free Press, 1985.

———. "The Economic Consequences of Divorce Are Still Unequal: Comment on Peterson." *American Sociological Review*. Vol. 61, No. 3 (June 1996):537–38.

WEITZMAN, LENORE J., DEBORAH EIFLER, ELIZABETH HODAKA, and CATHERINE ROSS. "Sex-Role Socialization in Picture Books for Preschool Children." *American Journal of Sociology*. Vol. 77, No. 6 (May 1972):1125–50.

WELLER, JACK M., and E. L. QUARANTELLI. "Neglected Characteristics of Collective Behavior." *American Journal of Sociology*. Vol. 79, No. 3 (November 1973):665–85.

WELLFORD, CHARLES. "Labeling Theory and Criminology: An Assessment." In Delos H. Kelly, ed., *Criminal Behavior: Readings in Criminology*. New York: St. Martin's Press, 1980:234–47.

WELLMAN, BARRY. "The Community Question: Intimate Networks of East Yorkers." *American Journal of Sociology*. Vol. 84, No. 5 (March 1979):1201–31.

WENKE, ROBERT J. *Patterns of Prehistory*. New York: Oxford University Press, 1980.

WERMAN, JILL. "Who Makes What?" *Working Woman* (January 1989):72–76, 80.

WERTHEIMER, BARBARA MAYER. "The Factory Bell." In Linda K. Kerber and Jane De Hart Mathews, eds., *Women's America: Refocusing the Past*. New York: Oxford University Press, 1982:130–40.

WESOLOWSKI, WLODZIMIERZ. "Transition From Authoritarianism to Democracy." *Social Research*. Vol. 57, No. 2 (Summer 1990):435–61.

WESTERN, BRUCE. "Postwar Unionization in Eighteen Advanced Capitalist Countries." *American Sociological Review*. Vol. 58, No. 2 (April 1993):266–82.

———. "A Comparative Study of Working-Class Disorganization: Union Decline in Eighteen Advanced Capitalist Countries." *American Sociological Review*. Vol. 60, No. 2 (April 1995):179–201.

WESTERN, MARK, and ERIK OLIN WRIGHT. "The Permeability of Class Boundaries to Intergenerational Mobility Among Men in the United States, Canada, Norway and Sweden." *American Sociological Review*. Vol. 59, No. 4 (August 1994):606–29.

WHALEN, JACK, and RICHARD FLACKS. *Beyond the Barricades: The Sixties Generation Grows Up*. Philadelphia: Temple University Press, 1989.

WHEELIS, ALLEN. *The Quest for Identity*. New York: Norton, 1958.

WHITAKER, MARK. "Ten Ways to Fight Terrorism." *Newsweek* (July 1, 1985):26–29.

WHITE, JACK E. "I'm Just Who I Am." *Time*. Vol. 149, No. 18 (May 5, 1997):32–36.

WHITE, RALPH, and RONALD LIPPITT. "Leader Behavior and Member Reaction in Three 'Social Climates.'" In Dorwin Cartwright and Alvin Zander, eds., *Group Dynamics*. Evanston, Ill.: Row, Peterson, 1953:586–611.

WHITE, WALTER. *Rope and Faggot*. New York: Arno Press and *New York Times*, 1969; orig. 1929.

WHITMAN, DAVID. "Shattering Myths About the Homeless." *U.S. News & World Report* (March 20, 1989):26, 28.

WHORF, BENJAMIN LEE. "The Relation of Habitual Thought and Behavior to Language." In *Language, Thought, and Reality*. Cambridge, Mass.: The Technology Press of MIT/New York: Wiley, 1956:134–59; orig. 1941.

WHYTE, WILLIAM FOOTE. *Street Corner Society*. 3d ed. Chicago: University of Chicago Press, 1981; orig. 1943.

WHYTE, WILLIAM H., JR. *The Organization Man*. Garden City, N.Y.: Anchor Books, 1957.

WIARDA, HOWARD J. "Ethnocentrism and Third World Development." *Society*. Vol. 24, No. 6 (September-October 1987):55–64.

WIATROWSKI, MICHAEL A., DAVID B. GRISWOLD, and MARY K. ROBERTS. "Social Control Theory and Delinquency." *American Sociological Review*. Vol. 46, No. 5 (October 1981):525–41.

WIDOM, CATHY SPATZ. "Childhood Sexual Abuse and Its Criminal Consequences." *Society*. Vol. 33, No. 4 (May/June 1996):47–53.

WILCOX, CLYDE. "Race, Gender, and Support for Women in the Military." *Social Science Quarterly*. Vol. 73, No. 2 (June 1992):310–23.

WILES, P. J. D. *Economic Institutions Compared*. New York: Halsted Press, 1977.

WILLIAMS, RHYS H., and N. J. DEMERATH, III. "Religion and Political Process in an American City." *American Sociological Review*. Vol. 56, No. 4 (August 1991):417–31.

WILLIAMS, ROBIN M., JR. *American Society: A Sociological Interpretation*. 3d ed. New York: Alfred A. Knopf, 1970.

WILLIAMSON, JEFFREY G., and PETER H. LINDERT. *American Inequality: A Macroeconomic History*. New York: Academic Press, 1980.

WILSON, BRYAN. *Religion in Sociological Perspective*. New York: Oxford University Press, 1982.

WILSON, EDWARD O. *Sociobiology: The New Synthesis*. Cambridge, Mass.: Belknap Press of the Harvard University Press, 1975.

———. *On Human Nature*. New York: Bantam Books, 1978.

———. "Biodiversity, Prosperity, and Value." In F. Herbert Bormann and Stephen R. Kellert, eds., *Ecology, Economics, and Ethics: The Broken Circle*. New Haven, Conn.: Yale University Press, 1991:3–10.

WILSON, JAMES Q. *Bureaucracy: What Government Agencies Do and Why They Do It*. New York: Basic Books, 1991.

———. "Crime, Race, and Values." *Society*. Vol. 30, No. 1 (November-December 1992):90–93.

WILSON, JAMES Q., and RICHARD J. HERRNSTEIN. *Crime and Human Nature*. New York: Simon and Schuster, 1985.

WILSON, LOGAN. *American Academics Then and Now*. New York: Oxford University Press, 1979.

WILSON, THOMAS C. "Urbanism and Tolerance: A Test of Some Hypotheses Drawn From Wirth and Stouffer." *American Sociological Review*. Vol. 50, No. 1 (February 1985):117–23.

———. "Urbanism and Unconventionality: The Case of Sexual Behavior." *Social Science Quarterly*. Vol. 76, No. 2 (June 1995):346–63.

WILSON, WILLIAM JULIUS. *The Declining Significance of Race*. Chicago: University of Chicago Press, 1978.

———. "The Black Underclass." *The Wilson Quarterly*. Vol. 8 (Spring 1984):88–99.

———. "Studying Inner-City Social Dislocations: The Challenge of Public Agenda Research." *American Sociological Review*. Vol. 56, No. 1 (February 1991):1–14.

———. *When Work Disappears: The World of the New Urban Poor*. New York: Alfred A. Knopf, 1996.

———. "Work." *New York Times Magazine* (August 18, 1996):26–31, 40, 48, 52, 54.

WINKLER, KAREN J. "Scholar Whose Ideas of Female Psychology Stir Debate Modifies Theories, Extends Studies to Young Girls." *Chronicle of Higher Education*. Vol. XXXVI, No. 36 (May 23, 1990):A6–A8.

WINN, MARIE. *Children Without Childhood*. New York: Pantheon Books, 1983.

WINNICK, LOUIS. "America's 'Model Minority'." *Commentary*. Vol. 90, No. 2 (August 1990):22–29.

WIRTH, LOUIS. "Urbanism As a Way of Life." *American Journal of Sociology*. Vol. 44, No. 1 (July 1938):1–24.

WITKIN-LANOIL, GEORGIA. *The Female Stress Syndrome: How to Recognize and Live With It*. New York: Newmarket Press, 1984.

WOLF, DIANE L., ed. *Feminist Dilemma of Fieldwork*. Boulder, Colo.: Westview Press, 1996.

WOLF, NAOMI. *The Beauty Myth: How Images of Beauty Are Used Against Women*. New York: William Morrow, 1990.

WOLFE, DAVID B. "Targeting the Mature Mind." *American Demographics*. Vol. 16, No. 3 (March 1994):32–36.

WOLFE, TOM. *Radical Chic*. New York: Bantam, 1970.

WOLFGANG, MARVIN E., ROBERT M. FIGLIO, and THORSTEN SELLIN. *Delinquency in a Birth Cohort*. Chicago: University of Chicago Press, 1972.

WOLFGANG, MARVIN E., TERRENCE P. THORNBERRY, and ROBERT M. FIGLIO. *From Boy to Man, From Delinquency to Crime*. Chicago: University of Chicago Press, 1987.

WOLFINGER, RAYMOND E., and STEVEN J. ROSENSTONE. *Who Votes?* New Haven, Conn.: Yale University Press, 1980.

WOLFINGER, RAYMOND E., MARTIN SHAPIRO, and FRED J. GREENSTEIN. *Dynamics of American Politics*. 2d ed. Englewood Cliffs, N.J.: Prentice Hall, 1980.

WOLKOMIR, MICHELLE, MICHAEL FUTREAL, ERIC WOODRUM, and THOMAS HOBAN. "Substantive Religious Belief and Environmentalism." *Social Science Quarterly*. Vol. 78, No. 1 (March 1997):96–108.

WONG, BUCK. "Need for Awareness: An Essay on Chinatown, San Francisco." In Amy Tachiki et al., eds., *Roots: An Asian American Reader*. Los Angeles: UCLA Asian American Studies Center, 1971:265–73.

WOODWARD, C. VANN. *The Strange Career of Jim Crow*. 3d rev. ed. New York: Oxford University Press, 1974.

WOODWARD, KENNETH L. "Feminism and the Churches." *Newsweek*. Vol. 13, No. 7 (February 13, 1989):58–61.

———. "Talking to God." *Newsweek*. Vol. 119, No. 1 (January 6, 1992):38–44.

———. "The Elite, and How to Avoid It." *Newsweek* (July 20, 1992):55.

WOOLEY, ORLAND W., SUSAN C. WOOLEY, and SUE R. DYRENFORTH. "Obesity and Women—II: A Neglected Feminist Topic." *Women's Studies International Quarterly*. Vol. 2 (1979):81–92.

The World Almanac and Book of Facts 1998. Mahwah, N.J.: World Almanac Books, 1998.

THE WORLD BANK. *World Development Report 1991: The Challenge of Development*. New York: Oxford University Press, 1991.

———. *World Development Report 1993*. New York: Oxford University Press, 1993.

———. *World Development Report 1995: Workers in an Integrating World*. New York: Oxford University Press, 1995.

———. *World Development Report 1997: The State in a Changing World*. New York: Oxford University Press, 1997.

WORLD HEALTH ORGANIZATION. *Constitution of the World Health Organization*. New York: World Health Organization Interim Commission, 1946.

———. Data cited in Pollack, Andrew, "Overseas, Smoking Is One of Life's Small Pleasures," *New York Times* (August 12, 1996).

World Values Survey, 1990–1993. Ann Arbor, Mich.: Inter-university Consortium for Political and Social Research, 1994.

WORSLEY, PETER. "Models of the World System." In Mike Featherstone, ed., *Global Culture: Nationalism, Globalization, and Modernity*. Newbury Park, Calif.: Sage, 1990:83–95.

WREN, CHRISTOPHER S. "In Soweto-by-the-Sea, Misery Lives On as Apartheid Fades." *New York Times* (June 9, 1991):1, 7.

WRIGHT, ERIK OLIN. *Classes*. London: Verso, 1985.

WRIGHT, ERIK OLIN, ANDREW LEVINE, and ELLIOTT SOBER. *Reconstructing Marxism: Essays on Explanation and the Theory of History*. London: Verso, 1992.

WRIGHT, ERIK OLIN, and BILL MARTIN. "The Transformation of the American Class Structure, 1960–1980." *American Journal of Sociology*. Vol. 93, No. 1 (July 1987):1–29.

WRIGHT, ERIC R. "Personal Networks and Anomie: Exploring the Sources and Significance of Gender Composition." *Sociological Focus*. Vol. 28, No. 3 (August 1995):261–82.

WRIGHT, JAMES D. "Address Unknown: Homelessness in Contemporary America." *Society*. Vol. 26, No. 6 (September-October 1989):45–53.

———. "Ten Essential Observations On Guns in America." *Society*. Vol. 32, No. 3 (March-April 1995):63–68.

WRIGHT, QUINCY. "Causes of War in the Atomic Age." In William M. Evan and Stephen Hilgartner, eds., *The Arms Race and Nuclear War*. Englewood Cliffs, N.J.: Prentice Hall, 1987:7–10.

WRIGHT, RICHARD A. *In Defense of Prisons*. Westport, Conn.: Greenwood Press, 1994.

WRIGHT, STUART A. "Social Movement Decline and Transformation: Cults in the 1980s." Paper presented at the Southwestern Social Science Association, Dallas, Texas, March 1987.

WRIGHT, STUART A., and WILLIAM V. D'ANTONIO. "The Substructure of Religion: A Further Study." *Journal for the Scientific Study of Religion*. Vol. 19, No. 3 (September 1980):292–98.

WU, LAWRENCE L. "Effects of Family Instability, Income, and Income Instability on the Risk of a Premarital Birth." *American Sociological Review*. Vol. 61, No. 3 (June 1996):386–406.

WYNTER, LEON E. "Business and Race." *Wall Street Journal* (May 10, 1995):B1.

YANDLE, TRACY, and DUDLEY BURTON. "Reexamining Environmental Justice: A Statistical Analysis of Historical Hazardous Waste Landfill Sitting in Metropolitan Texas." *Social Science Quarterly*. Vol. 77, No. 3 (September 1996):477–92.

YANKELOVICH, DANIEL. "How Changes in the Economy Are Reshaping American Values." In Henry J. Aaron, Thomas E. Mann, and Timothy Taylor, eds., *Values and Public Policy*. Washington, D.C.: The Brookings Institution, 1994:20.

YATES, RONALD E. "Growing Old in Japan; They Ask Gods for a Way Out." *Philadelphia Inquirer* (August 14, 1986):3A.

YEATTS, DALE E. "Self-Managed Work Teams: Innovation in Progress." *Business and Economic Quarterly* (Fall-Winter 1991):2–6.

———. "Creating the High Performance Self-Managed Work Team: A Review of Theoretical Perspectives." Paper presented at the annual meeting of the Social Science Association, Dallas, February 1995.

YODER, JAN D., and ROBERT C. NICHOLS. "A Life Perspective: Comparison of Married and Divorced Persons." *Journal of Marriage and the Family*. Vol. 42, No. 2 (May 1980):413–19.

YOELS, WILLIAM C., and JEFFREY MICHAEL CLAIR. "Laughter in the Clinic: Humor in Social Organization." *Symbolic Interaction*. Vol. 18, No. 1 (1995):39–58.

YOUNG, MICHAEL. "Meritocracy Revisited." *Society*. Vol. 31, No. 6 (September-October 1994):85–89.

ZACHARY, G. PASCAL. "Not So Fast: Neo-Luddites Say an Unexamined Cyberlife is a Dangerous One." *Wall Street Journal* (June 16, 1997):R18.

ZALMAN, MARVIN, and STEVEN STACK. "The Relationship Between Euthanasia and Suicide in the Netherlands: A Time Series Analysis, 1950–1990." *Social Science Quarterly*. Vol. 77, No. 3 (September 1996):576–93.

ZANGWILL, ISRAEL. *The Melting Pot*. Macmillan, 1921; orig. 1909.

ZASLAVSKY, VICTOR. *The Neo-Stalinist State: Class, Ethnicity, and Consensus in Soviet Society*. Armonk, N.Y.: M. E. Sharpe, 1982.

ZEITLIN, IRVING M. *The Social Condition of Humanity*. New York: Oxford University Press, 1981.

ZHOU, MIN, and JOHN R. LOGAN. "Returns of Human Capital in Ethnic Enclaves: New York City's Chinatown." *American Sociological Review*. Vol. 54, No. 5 (October 1989):809–20.

ZIMBARDO, PHILIP G. "Pathology of Imprisonment." *Society*. Vol. 9 (April 1972):4–8.

ZIPP, JOHN F. "Perceived Representativeness and Voting: An Assessment of the Impact of 'Choices' vs. 'Echoes'." *The American Political Science Review*. Vol. 79, No. 1 (March 1985):50–61.

ZIPP, JOHN F., and JOEL SMITH. "A Structural Analysis of Class Voting." *Social Forces*. Vol. 60, No. 3 (March 1982):738–59.

ZUBOFF, SHOSHANA. "New Worlds of Computer-Mediated Work." *Harvard Business Review*. Vol. 60, No. 5 (September-October 1982):142–52.

ZURCHER, LOUIS A., and DAVID A. SNOW. "Collective Behavior and Social Movements." In Morris Rosenberg and Ralph Turner, eds., *Social Psychology: Sociological Perspectives*. New York: Basic Books, 1981:447–82.

PHOTO CREDITS

Frontispiece: Mark Peters

CHAPTER 1: Albina Kosiec Felski, *The Circus*, 1971, oil on canvas, 48 x 48 in. (121.9 x 121.9 cm), National Museum of American Art, Smithsonian Institution, Washington, DC/Art Resource, NY, *xxviii*; Robert Burke/Gamma-Liaison, Inc., *1*; Paul W. Liebhardt, *2, 3*; Luc Delahaye/Magnum Photos, Inc., *8*; Corbis-Bettmann, *12*; Simon Bening, *April: Farmyard with woman milking cow*, from *Da Costa Book of Hours*, Bruges, c.1515, © The Piermont Morgan Library, NY, M.399,F.5V/Art Resource, NY, *14 (left)*; Archive Photos, *14 (right)*; Corbis-Bettmann, *15 (left)*; Brown Brothers, *15 (right)*; Amy Jones, *St. Regis Indian Reservation*, 1937, photo courtesy Janet Marqusee Fine Arts Ltd., *17*; Brown Brothers, *18*; © Paul Marcus 1995, oil on panel, *Dinner Is Served, 19*; Louis Schanker (1903–1981), *Three Men on a Bench*, © Christie's Images, *20*; Jacob Lawrence, American, b.1917, *Munich Olympic Games*, poster, 1972, courtesy of the artist and Francine Seders Gallery, Seattle, photo Spike Mafford, *22*.

CHAPTER 2: © Harvey Dinnerstein, *Underground Together*, 1996, oil on canvas, 90 x 107 1/4 in. photograph courtesy of Gerold Wunderlich & Co., New York, NY, *26*; Photo by Ruben Burrell, courtesy of Hampton University, *27*; Paul Gauguin (French, 1848–1903), *Where Do We Come From? What Are We? Where Are We Going?*, 1897, oil on canvas, 139.1 x 374.6 cm. (54 3/4 x 147 1/2 in.) Tompkins collections, courtesy of Museum of Fine Arts, Boston, *29*; John Eastcott/Yva Momatiuk/The Image Works, *30*; Bob Daemmrich/Stock Boston, *32*; Steve McCurry/Magnum Photos, Inc., *35 (left)*; Argas/Gamma-Liaison, Inc., *35 (right)*; Mark Richards/PhotoEdit, *37*; Tony Freeman/PhotoEdit, *39*; Mike Greenbar/The Image Works, *40*; Bob Daemmrich/Stock Boston, *41*; David Wells/The Image Works, *43*; David Bradnum/Robert Estall Photo Agency, *46 (left)*; Carol Beckwith & Angela Fisher/Robert Estall Photo Agency, *46 (right)*.

CYBER.SCOPE PART I: Gabe Palmer/Mugshots/The Stock Market, *56*.

CHAPTER 3: Larsen & Larsen Studio, Inc., *60*; Jim Estrin/New York Times Permissions, *62*; Tomas Friedmann/Photo Researchers, Inc., *62*; Paul W. Liebhardt, *63 (top, left; center, left; bottom, middle)*; Carlos Humberto/TDC/Contact/The Stock Market, *63 (top, middle)*; Mireille Vautier/Woodfin Camp & Associates, *63 (top, right)*; David Austen/Stock Boston, *63 (center, middle)*; J. Du Boisberran/The Image Bank, *63 (center, right)*; Jack Fields/Photo Researchers, Inc., *63 (bottom, right)*; G. Humer/Gamma-Liaison, Inc., *64*; Alighierio e Boetti, *Mappa (Map)*, 1971–89, embroidery on canvas, 118 x 236 3/4 in. Collection Caterina Boetti, Rome, photo credit Cathy Carver/Dia Center for the Arts, *66*; Jeff Greenberg/Picture Cube, Inc., *67 (left)*; Pedrick/The Image Works, *67 (middle)*; CLEO Photo/Jeroboam, Inc., *67 (right)*; *Mrs. Van Gogh Makes the Bed*, from *Great Housewives of Art* by Sally Swain, © 1988 by Sally Swain, used by permission of Viking Penguin, a division of Penguin Putnam Inc., *70*; Jeff Greenberg/PhotoEdit, *72*; Reprinted by permission of Margaret Courtney-Clarke, © 1990, *73*; A. Berliner/Gamma-Liaison, Inc., *75*; Photo by Henry Chalfant, from *Spraycan Art* by Henry Chalfant and James Prigoff, Thames and Hudson Ltd. 1987, London, *77*; J.P Laffont/Sygma, *82*; Inge Morath/Magnum Photos, Inc., *83*; Paul Kuroda/The Orange County Register, *84*; Paul W. Liebhardt, *85*; Andre Gallant/The Image Bank, *86 (top, left)*; Pete Turner/The Image Bank, *86 (top, middle)*; Brun/Photo Researchers, Inc., *86 (top, right)*; Bruno Hadjih/Gamma-Liaison, Inc., *86 (bottom, left)*; Elliot Erwitt/Magnum Photos, Inc., *86 (bottom, middle)*; George Holton/Photo Researchers, Inc., *86 (bottom, right)*.

CHAPTER 4: Walter Greaves (1846–1930) *Hammersmith Bridge on Boat Race Day* 1862, Tate Gallery, London, Great Britain/Art Resource, NY, *92*; © 1996, *The Washington Post*, photo by Carol Guzy, reprinted with permission, *93*; Patrick Bordes/Photo Researchers, Inc., *94*; Victor Englebert/Photo Researchers, Inc., *95*; Robert Frerck/Woodfin Camp & Associates, *96*; Rosenfeld Images Ltd./Science Photo Library/Photo Researchers, Inc., *99 (left)*; Cameramann/The Image Works, *99 (right)*; Culver Pictures, Inc., *102*; Ben Shahn, *Organize? With 1,250,000 Workers Backing Us*, original oil on canvas for a poster, late 1930's, © Estate of Ben Shahn/Licensed by VAGA, NY, The Granger Collection, *104*; Norbert Goeneutte *The Paupers' Meal on a Winter Day in Paris*, Waterhouse and Dodd, London, Fine Art Photographic Library, London/Art Resource, NY, *105*; Charles Steiner/The Image Works, *107*; The Granger Collection, *110*; George Tooker, *Landscape with Figures* 1963, egg tempera on gesso panel, 26 x 30 inches, *111*; Elliot Landy/Magnum Photos, Inc., *113 (a,c,d)*; Robert Sorbo/AP/Wide World Photos, *113 (b)*; Paul W. Liebhardt, *114*.

CHAPTER 5: Hale Woodruff, *Girls Skipping*, 1949, oil on canvas, 24 x 32 inches, courtesy of Michael Rosenfeld Gallery, New York, *120*; Blair Seitz/Photo Researchers, Inc., *121*; Ted Horowitz/The Stock Market, *122 (left)*; Henley & Savage/The Stock Market, *122 (middle)*; Tom Pollack/Monkmeyer Press, *122 (right)*; A. Ramsey/Woodfin Camp & Associates, *124*; UPI/Corbis-Bettmann, *125*;

Lee Malerich, *Act Out Your Id*, 1994, embroidery on pieced fabric, 6 7/8 x 5 in., *126*; Elizabeth Crews/Elizabeth Crews Photography, *127*; Keith Carter, *129*; Rimma Gerlovina and Valeriy Gerlovin, *Manyness* 1990, © the artists, Pomona, NY, *130*; Henry Ossawa Tanner, *The Banjo Lesson*, 1893, oil on canvas, Hampton University Museum, Hampton, Virginia, *133*; Monty Brinton/CBS Photo Archive, *136*; Bernstein/Spooner/Gamma-Liaison, Inc., *138*; Constance Stuart Larrabee (American, b. 1914) *Witwatersand Goldminer Watching Sunday Mine Dance, Johannesburg, South Africa* 1946, silver gelatin print, 11 7/8 x 11 3/4 in., The National Museum of Women in the Arts, gift of the artist, *141*; Danny Lyon/Magnum Photos, Inc., *142*.

CHAPTER 6: Paul Cadmus (b. 1904) *Man With False Noses: An Allegory on Promiscuity*, 1955, pen, ink, and egg tempera on paper, 19 1/4 x 12 inches, courtesy DC Moore Gallery, NYC, © Christie's images, *146*; John Macionis, *147*; Jim Anderson/Woodfin Camp & Associates, *148*; AP/Wide World Photos, *149*; Ian Berry/Magnum Photos, Inc., *150*; Dimaggio/Kalish/The Stock Market, *152*; Wesley Bocxe/Photo Researchers, Inc., *154*; Paul W. Liebhardt, *157*; David Cooper/Gamma-Liaison, Inc., *159 (top, left)*; Alan Weiner/Gamma-Liaison, Inc., *159 (top, middle)*; Lynn McLaren/Picture Cube, Inc., *159 (top, right)*; Guido Rossi/The Image Bank, *159 (bottom, left)*; Richard Pan, *159 (bottom, middle)*; Costa Manos/Magnum Photos, Inc., *159 (bottom, right)*; Duke University/Hartman Center with permission of Pepsi-Cola Company, *161*; Paul W. Liebhardt, *162*; Tony Freeman/PhotoEdit, *164*; Harry Langdon/Shooting Star International Photo Agency, © All Rights Reserved, *167*.

CHAPTER 7: Ed McGowin, *Society Telephone Society*, 1989, oil on canvas with carved and painted wood frame, 54 in. x 54 in. © Ed McGowin 1997, *170*; Tony Freeman/PhotoEdit, *171*; Jean-Marc Giboux/Gamma-Liaison, Inc., *172*; Carol Beckwith & Angela Fisher/Robert Estall Photo Agency, *177*; Paul W. Liebhardt, *179*; Dan Habib/Impact Visuals Photo & Graphics, Inc., *180*; Biblioteque Nationale de France, Paris. From *The Horizon History of China* by the editors of Horizon Magazine, The Horizon Publishing Co., Inc., 551 5th Ave., NY 10017, © 1969, *185*; Paul W. Liebhardt, *187*; George Tooker *Government Bureau* 1956, egg tempera on gesso panel, 19 5/8 x 29 5/8 in., The Metropolitan Museum of Art, George A. Hearn Fund, 1956 (56.78), photograph © 1984 The Metropolitan Museum of Art, *188*; Gabe Palmer/The Stock Market, *191*; Bartholomew/Gamma-Liaison, Inc., *193*; Karen Kasmauski/Woodfin Camp & Associates, *195*.

CHAPTER 8: Private Collection/Christian Pierre/SuperStock, *200*; LeRoy Woodson/Woodfin Camp & Associates, *201*; SIPA Press, *202*; Cliff Owen/UPI/Corbis-Bettmann, *204*; The Granger Collection, *205*; Paul W. Liebhardt, *207*; Edward Gargan/New York Times Permissions, *208*; Jon Levy/Gamma-Liaison, Inc., *209*; Frank Romero, *Freeway Wars* 1990, serigraph (edition of 99), 31 1/2 x 38 in. Frank Romero © Serigraph, Nicolas and Cristina Hernandez Trust collection, Pasadena, PA, *212*; Danny Hellman, *213*; Mark Peterson/SABA Press Photos, Inc., *216*; John Giordano/SABA Press Photos, *218*; Campbell/Sygma, *219*; Steve Liss/Gamma-Liaison, Inc., *220*.

CYBER.SCOPE PART II: T. Crosby/Gamma-Liaison, Inc., *232*; Peter Steiner © 1993 from the New Yorker Collection, All Rights Reserved, *233*.

CHAPTER 9: Antonio Ruiz, *Verano* 1937, oil on wood 29 x 35 cm, collection of Acervo Patrimonial, SHCP, Mexico, *234*; Painting by Ken Marshall © 1992 from *Titanic: An Illustrated History*, a Hyperion/Madison Press Book, *235*; Sebastiao Salgado/Magnum Photo, Inc., *236*; Antonio Berni (1905–1981) *Los Emigrantes*, © Christie's Images, *237*; Haviv/SABA Press Photos, Inc., *238*; Fujifotos/The Image Works, *241*; Robert Wallis/SABA Press Photos, Inc., *242*; Limbourg Brothers, *August* from *Tres Riches Heures du duc de Berry*, Musee Conde, Chantilly, France, Giraudon/Art Resource, NY, *246*; Michael Grecco/Sygma, *247*; The Granger Collection, *248*; Egyptian Museum, Cairo, Hirmer Fotoarchive, *251*.

CHAPTER 10: William Gropper, *Sweat Shop*, oil on canvas, 18 x 30 in. (45.7 x 76.2 cm), © Christie's Images, *258*; © 1966, *The Washington Post*, photo by Juana Arias, reprinted with permission, *259*; Bachmann/The Image Works, *266*; Grapes/Michaud/Photo Researchers, Inc., *267 (left)*; Burt Glinn/Magnum Photos, Inc., *267*; Kenneth Meyer, *268*; Camilio Jose Vergara, *269*; Pipes, Richard, *Campaign 1960*, gelatin-silver print, 14 x 11 (35.6 x 28 cm), The Museum of Modern Art, New York, gift of the photographer, copy print © 1997 The Museum of Modern Art, New York, *271*; Tony Freeman/PhotoEdit, *272*; Tim Carlson/Stock Boston, *277*; University of Chicago Department of Sociology, *281*; Diego Rivera *Our Bread* (El pan nuestro), 1928, mural 2.04 x 1.58 m, Court of Fiestas, Level 3, South Wall, Secretaria de Educación Publica, Mexico City, Mexico, Schalkwijk/Art Resource, NY, © Estate of Diego Rivera/Licensed by VAGA, NY, *282*; Mary Ellen Mark Library, *283*.

CHAPTER 11: Diego Rivera *Formation of Revolutionary Leadership* (*Los Explotatores*), 1926–27, mural, 3.43 x 5.55 m, Chapel, Universidad Autonoma

Chapingo, Chapingo, Mexico, Schalkwijk/Art Resource, NY, © Estate of Diego Rivera/Licensed by VAGA, NY, *288*; Photo by Gregory Kane, *Baltimore Sun*, *289*; Ron Haviv/SABA Press Photos, Inc., *291* (*left*); Bartholomew/Gamma-Liaison, Inc., *291* (*right*); Martin Benjamin/The Image Works, *292* (*top, left*); Peter Turnley/Black Star, *292* (*top, right*); Pablo Bartholomew/Gamma-Liaison, Inc., *292* (*bottom*); David Stewart-Smith/ SABA Press Photos, Inc., *294*; Viviane Moos/SABA Press Photos, Inc., *298*; Charlesworth/SABA Photos, Inc., *300*; Steve Maines/Stock Boston, *302*; Tom Stodart/Katz/SABA Press Photos, Inc., *303*; Sean Sprague/Impact Visuals Photo & Graphics, Inc., *305*; Hernando Cortes, *Capture of Mexico City*, August 1521, colored engraving, 19th cent., The Granger Collection, *306*.

CHAPTER 12: Romare Bearden (American, 1914–1988) *SHE-BA* 1970, collage on composition board, 48 x 35 7/8 in., Ella Gallup Sumner and Mary Catlin Sumner *Collection* Fund, © Wadsworth Atheneum, Hartford, © Romare Bearden Foundation/Licensed by VAGA, NY, *314*; Catherine Leroy/SIPA Press, *315*; Richard J. Haier, Ph.D., *316*; James D. Wilson/Gamma-Liaison, Inc., *317*; Aspect Picture Library/The Stock Market, *320*; Joseph B. Brignolo/The Image Bank, *321*; Explorer/Y. Layma/Photo Researchers, Inc., *322*; Jacques M. Chenet/Gamma-Liaison, Inc., *326*; Ed Malitsky/Picture Cube, Inc., *327*; Natsuko Utsumi/Gamma-Liaison, Inc., *335*; Net Nanny Ltd., *337*; Drew Friedman, *338*; Sophia Smith Collection, Smith College, *339*; Jay Silverman/The Image Bank, *341*.

CHAPTER 13: Harry Roseland, *Beach Scene, Coney Island* 1891, © Christie's Images, *346*; AP/Wide World Photos, *347*; Joel Gordon/Joel Gordon Photography, *349* (*top, left*); Leong Ka Tai/Material World, *349* (*top, middle*); Robert Caputo/Stock Boston, *349* (*top, right*); Paul W. Liebhardt, *349* (*bottom, left, and middle*); Lisi Dennis/The Image Bank, *349* (*bottom, right*); Raveendran/Agence France-Presse, *353*; Corbis-Bettmann, *355* (*left*); Culver Pictures, Inc., *355* (*left center*); Photographic and Prints Division, Schomburg Center for Research in Black Culture/The New York Public Library/Astor, Lenox and Tilden Foundations, *355* (*right center*); UPI/Corbis-Bettmann, *355* (*right*); Archive Photos, *358* (*left*); Sygma, *358* (*right*); Sheldon Preston, *359*; UPI/Corbis-Bettmann, *362*, *366*; A. Ramey/Woodfin Camp & Associates, *364*; Jeff Greenberg/Stock Boston, *368*; © Nick Quijano 1997, *La Vida en Broma*, 1988: Street life in Old San Juan, *370*.

CHAPTER 14: *Gifts* © Deidre Scherer, 1966, from the collection of St. Mary's Foundation, Rochester, NY, *376*; Rob Crandall/Rob Crandall Photographer, *377*; Elliot Erwitt/Magnum Photo, Inc., *382* (*left*); Bruno Barbey/ Magnum Photos, Inc., *382* (*right*); Eve Arnold/Magnum Photos, Inc., *385*; Alese and Mort Pechter/The Stock Market, *389*; Patrick Zachmann/ Magnum Photos, Inc., *391*; Reuters/Dutch TV/Archive Photos, *393*; Ira Wyman/Sygma, *394*.

CYBER.SCOPE PART III: John Agee © 1995 from The New Yorker Collection, All Rights Reserved, *398*; Beth Kreiser/AP/World Wide Photos, *399* (*top*); Matthew McVay/Stock Boston, *399* (*bottom*).

CHAPTER 15: The Grand Design/SuperStock, Inc., *400*; Scott Perry/New York Times Permissions, *401*; American Textile History Museum, Lowell, MA, *403*; Bob Schatz/Gamma-Liaison, Inc., *404*; Bellavia/REA/SABA Press Photos, Inc., *408* (*left*); John Bryson/Sygma, *408* (*right*); Patrick Ward/Stock Boston, *410*; Owen Franken/Stock Boston, *414*; Jose Clemente Orozco, *The Unemployed*, © Christie's Images, © Estate of Jose Clemente Orozco/Licensed by VAGA, NY, *415*; Eric Miller/Impact Visuals Photo & Graphics, Inc., *419*; Z. Bzdak/The Image Works, *421*.

CHAPTER 16: O. Louis Mazzatenta/National Geographic Society, *426*; Tomas Muscionico/Contact Press Images Inc., *427*; Philip Evergood, *American Tragedy* 1936, oil on canvas, 29 1/2 x 39 1/2 in. Terry Dintenfass Gallery, NY, *429*; David Ball/Picture Cube, Inc., *433*; A. Ramey/Woodfin Camp & Associates, *436* (*left*); Joel Gordon/Joel Gordon Photography, *436* (*right*); Barry Iverson/Woodfin Camp & Associates, *442*; Peter Northall/Black Star, *444*; Baldeu/Sygma, *445*; Joe McNally, Life Magazine © Time Inc., *446*.

CHAPTER 17: Frida Kahlo, *My Grandparents, My Parents, and I (Family Tree)*, 1936, oil and tempera on metal panel 12 1/8 x 13 5/8 in. (30.7 x 35.5 cm), The Museum of Modern Art, NY, *452*; Brooks Kraft/Sygma, *453*; Bob Daemmrich/Stock Boston, *454*; Bo Zaunders/The Stock Market, *456*; Marc Chagall *Scene Paysanne*, © 1999 Artists Rights Society (ARS), New York/ADAGP, Paris, *459*; Christian Pierre, B. 1962, *I Do*, American Private Collection, SuperStock, Inc., *461*; Raghu Rai/Magnum Photos, *462*; © 1989 Carmen Lomas Garza, *Cumpleanos de Lala y Tudi*, oil on canvas, 17 x 15 in. collection of the artist, photo Wolfgang Dietze, *466*; D. Young-Wolfe/PhotoEdit, *468*; Edward Hopper (1882–1967) *Room in New York*, 1932, oil on canvas, 29 x 36 in. Sheldon Memorial Art Gallery, University of Nebraska-Lincoln, F.M. Hall Collection, 1932.H-1666, *470*; Stern (Ullah)/Black Star, *475*.

CHAPTER 18: © 1994 Dinh Le, *Interconfined*, C-print and Linen Tape, 55 x 39 in., *480*; Mark Peterson/SABA Press Photos, Inc., *481*; SuperStock, *482*; T. Matsumoto/Sygma, *484*; Mathieu Polak/Sygma, *485*; Gilles Peress/Magnum Photos Inc., *487*; Anna Belle Lee Washington/SuperStock, *489*; Hans Hoefer/Woodfin Camp & Associates, *491*; Hans Kemp/Sygma, *492*; Bradshaw/SABA Press Photos, Inc., *494*; Thomas Hart Benton, *Arts of the South*, tempera with oil glaze, 8 x 13 feet, Harriet Russell Stanley Fund/New Britain Museum of American Art, CT, © T.H. Benton and R.P. Benton Testamentary Trusts/Licensed by VAGA, NY, *500*; Nick Kelsh/Kelsh Wilson Design Inc., *501*.

CHAPTER 19: Romare Bearden, *The Piano Lesson*, 1983, collage and watercolor, 29 x 22 in. © Romare Bearden Foundation/Licensed by VAGA, NY, *506*; Richard Kalvar/Magnum Photos, Inc., *507*; Alan Oddie/PhotoEdit, *509*; Stephen Ferry/Gamma-Liaison, Inc., *514* (*left*); James D. Wilson/Gamma-Liaison, Inc., *514* (*right*); Gabe Palmer/Mugshots/The Stock Market, *518*; D. Young-Wolff/PhotoEdit, *520*; David Young Wolff/PhotoEdit, *524* (*left*); Jay Dickman, *524* (*right*).

CHAPTER 20: The Granger Collection, *528*; Susan Rosenberg/Photo Researchers, Inc., *529*; The Granger Collection, *530*; W. Campbell/Sygma, *536* (*left*); Steve Lehman/SABA Press Photos, Inc., *536* (*right*); Tony Freeman/ PhotoEdit, *536*; John Coletti/Picture Cube, Inc., *538*; Gaslight Advertising Archives, Inc., NY, *540*; A.F. Seligmann, *Allgemeines Krankenhaus* (General Hospital) 19th cent. painting, canvas, *Professor Theodor Billroth Lectures at the General Hospital, Vienna, 1880*, Erich Lessing/Art Resource, NY, *542*; Peter Menzel/Peter Menzel Photography, *543*; Bob Strong/The Image Works, *544*; ABC Television/Globe Photos, *547* (*left*); Lauren Greenfield/Sygma, *547* (*right*); Joseph Nettles/Stock Boston, *548*; Steve Murez/Black Star, *549*.

CYBER.SCOPE PART IV: Dirck Halstead/Gamma-Liaison, Inc., *554*; © Tara Sosrowardoyo/Indo-pix, *555*.

CHAPTER 21: Ernest Fiene (1894–1965) *Nocturne*, © Christie's Images, *556*; Charles Gupton/Stock Boston, *557*; Peter Menzel/Material World, *565* (*top*); David Reed/Material, *565* (*bottom*); Najlah Feany/SABA Press Photos, Inc., *566*; Cotton Coulson/Woodfin Camp & Associates, *567*; The Granger Collection, *568*; Valley Forge Historical Society, *572*; Peter Breughel the Elder (c. 1525/30–1569), *Peasant Dance*, c. 1565, Kunsthistorisches Museum, Vienna/Superstock, *573* (*left*); Fernand Leger, *The City*, 1919, oil on canvas, 90 3/4 x 117 1/4, Philadelphia Museum of Art, A.E. Gallatin Collection, © 1999 Artists Rights Society (ARS), New York/ADAGP, Paris, *573* (*right*); Ron Haviv/SABA Press Photos, Inc., *575*; Jonathan Nourok/PhotoEdit, *578*.

CHAPTER 22: © Anatoly Shdanow/UNEP/The Image Works, *582*; Michael Friedel/Woodfin Camp & Associates, *583*; Peter Martens/Magnum Photos, Inc., *585*; Frances/Sygma, *587*; Culver Pictures, Inc., *591*; Thomas Hartwell/Sygma, *593*; Paul W. Liebhardt, *595*; Tony Freeman/PhotoEdit, *598* (*left*); Gregory G. Dimijian/Photo Researchers, *598* (*right*); Eric Pasquier/ Sygma, *599*; Elizabeth Mangelsdorf/S.F. Examiner/SABA Press Photos, Inc., *600*; Rick Gerharter/Impact Visuals Photo & Graphics, Inc., *601*.

CHAPTER 23: Harvey Dinnerstein, *Walking Together, Montgomery*, 1956, collection of the Parrish Art Museum, Southampton, NY, photograph courtesy of the artist, *606*; James Leynse/SABA Press Photos, Inc., *607*; Archive Photos, *609*; The Granger Collection, *610*; David Butow/SABA Press Photos, Inc., *611*; Sabina Dowell, *613*; Patrick Durand/Sygma, *615*; Tom Kelly/FPG International, *616* (*top, left*); Inge Morath/Magnum Photos, Inc., *616* (*top, middle*); Owen Franken/Stock Boston, *616* (*top, right*); Willie L. Hill, Jr./Stock Boston, *616* (*bottom, left*); Michael Grecco/ Stock Boston, *616* (*bottom, middle*); Michael Schumann/SABA Press Photos, Inc., *619*; J.L. Atlan/Sygma, *620*; Hans Edinger/AP/Wide World Photos, *621*.

CHAPTER 24: *Sociotecture*, 1991, Joan Truckenbrod, courtesy of The Williams Gallery, Princeton, NJ, © Joan Truckenbrod 1997, *628*; Mauri Rautkari/World Wide Fund for Nature, *629*; Mark Peters, *631*; Paul Gauguin, *The Day of the God (Mahana no Atua)*, 1894, oil on canvas (68.3 x 91.5 cm.), Helen Birch Bartlett Memorial Collection, 1926, photograph © 1994, The Art Institute of Chicago, All Rights Reserved, *633*; George Tooker, *The Subway*, 1950, egg tempera on composition board, 18 1/8 x 36 1/8 in., Whitney Museum of American Art, NY, purchased with funds from the Juliana Force Purchase Award, 50.23, *635*; Simon & Schuster/PH College, *636*; Edvard Munch *Workers on Their Way Home* 1913–1915, canvas, Expressionism Painting 20th Cent., Munch Musset, Oslo, Norway, Erich Lessing/Art Resource, N.Y., *639*; Edvard Munch, *The Scream*, Oslo, National Gallery, Scala/Art Resource, NY, *641* (*left*); © Paul Marcus, *Musical Chairs*, oil painting on wood, 48 in. x 72 in., *641* (*right*); Donna Kraebel, *643*; R. Crandall/The Image Works, *644*; Rafael Macia/ Photo Researchers, Inc., *645*.

CYBER.SCOPE PART V: Peter Charlesworth/SABA Press Photos, Inc., *651*.

NAME INDEX

Wright, Stuart A., 483, 619
Wu, Lawrence L., 474
Wynter, Leon E., 398

X, Malcolm, 18
Xie, Nan, 262

Yandle, Tracy, 601

Yankelovich, Daniel, 72, 274, 476
Yates, Ronald E., 384, 388
Yeatts, Dale E., 191, 192
Yeltsin, Boris, 243
Yinger, Richard E., 446
Yoder, Jan D., 471
Yoels, William C., 521

Zachary, G. Pascal, 233
Zald, Mayer N., 607, 610, 618, 620, 621
Zalman, Marvin, 540
Zangrando, Robert L., 363
Zangwill, Israel, 357
Zaslavsky, Victor, 243
Zborowski, Mark, 530

Zeitlin, Irving M., 104
Zhou, Min, 365
Zimbardo, Philip, 38, 40, 41, 50
Zipp, John F., 439
Zuboff, Shoshana, 417
Zurcher, Louis A., 612, 621

SUBJECT INDEX

Degradation ceremony, 210
Deindustrialization, 275–76
De jure segregation, 358
Democracy:
 defined, 430
 political freedom, global map, 431
 as value, 70
Democratic leadership, 175, 186
Demographic transition theory, 563–64
Demography, 557–62
 life expectancy, global map, 383
 population growth, global map, 560
 and social change, 632
Denial, dying and, 141, 394
Denmark, 74, 430, 434, 473, 474, 511
Denomination, religious, 487
Dependency theory of development,
 301, 305–9, 420, 563–64, 578, 648
Dependent variable, 32, 38
Deprivation theory of social
 movements, 617–18, 622
Descent, patterns of, 456–57
Deterrence:
 of crime, 226, 227
 of war, 446
Development, human, 122–23
Deviance, 201–31
 and biology, 202–3
 and crime (*see* Crime)
 defined, 201
 Durkheim on, 204–5, 208
 functions of, 204–5, 208
 and gender, 215–17
 medicalization of, 210–11
 and personality, 203
 primary and secondary, 210
 social-conflict analysis of, 213–15
 and social diversity, 215–19
 social foundations, 203–4
 strain theory of, 206–8, 216
 structural-functional analysis, 204–8,
 215
 subcultures, 207–8
 symbolic-interaction analysis of,
 208–13, 215
Deviant career, 210
Dharma, 302, 493
Differential association theory
 (Sutherland), 211–12, 213, 228
Diffusion, of culture, 81, 631
Dignity, versus honor, 643
Diplomacy, 446
Direct-fee medicine, 545
Disabled people, 9, 150, 524
Disarmament, 446–47
Discovery, 81, 631
Discrimination:
 and gender, 332
 institutional, 356
 and race, 22, 355–57
 reverse, 373
Disengagement theory of aging, 390
Dispersed collectivities, 608
Disposable society, 590–91
Diversity (*see* Cultural diversity)
Division of labor, 114–15, 292–93, 337,
 634–35
Divorce, 1, 10, 116, 453, 469–72, 476
Djibouti, 322
DNA (deoxyribonucleic acid), 551
Domestic violence, 335, 472–73
Double standards, 36–37, 87, 88
Downsizing, 276, 281, 401, 416
Downward social mobility, 272
Dramaturgical analysis, 155–63
Dred Scott case (1857), 362–63
Dropping out, 521–22
Drugs, 201, 212, 214, 224
Dyads, 179, 180

Early adulthood, 139–40
Earnings (*see* Income)
Eastern Europe, 99, 107, 225, 293, 406,
 411, 441, 620 (*see also* specific
 countries)
East Germany, 293, 411
Eating disorders, 529, 537
Ecclesia, 487, 489–90
Ecologically sustainable culture, 602–3
Ecology (*see also* Natural environment)
 cultural, 599–600

defined, 583
 urban, 574–75
Economy, 401–25 (*see also* Work)
 agricultural employment, global map,
 406
 and corporations, 417–20
 dependency theory, 301, 305–9
 development, global map, 7
 global, 8, 84, 275–76, 290–93, 307–8,
 405, 419–21
 and government, 422–23
 in high-income countries, 6, 290–93
 historical overview of, 401–5
 industrial employment, global map,
 406
 inequality in selected countries
 (1980–1996), 243
 in low-income countries, 7, 8, 293
 in middle-income countries, 293
 modernization theory, 301–5
 postindustrial, 403–4, 411–17, 554
 sectors of, 404–5
 symbolic, 554
 types of systems, 405–11
 underground, 416–17
Ecosystem, 584
 sustainable, 602–3
Ecuador, 86
Edge cities, 571–72, 650
Education, 1, 3, 16–17, 263–64, 507–27
 academic standards, 522–23
 achievement in U.S., 263–64, 510–11
 adult, 524–25
 and African Americans, 3–4, 363,
 372, 515, 517, 521
 and Asian Americans, 364, 365
 desegregation of schools, 347, 356
 of disabled, 524
 and discipline, 519–21
 dropping out, 521–22
 and economic development, 507–9
 and functional illiteracy, 522
 functions of, 511–13
 and gender, 325, 332–33
 in global perspective, 507–11
 in Great Britain, 509–10
 hidden curriculum, 133, 513
 and Hispanic Americans, 4, 517, 521
 in India, 509
 and Information Revolution, 523
 intelligence and, 254–55
 in Japan, 241, 507, 509–10
 and multiculturalism, 78–80
 and political correctness, 81
 public versus private schools, 515–16
 and segregation, 347, 356
 and social inequality, 513–18
 and socialization, 132–33, 133–34,
 511
 standardized testing, 513–14
 and stratification, 515–18
 structural-functional analysis of,
 511–13
 student attitudes, 81
 and student passivity, 519–21
 tracking in, 18, 514–15
 in twenty-first century, 525–26
 in U.S., 510–11
 and women, 509, 510, 517
Efficiency, as value, 70
Ego, 125
Egypt, 96, 340, 442, 491, 566, 575–76,
 592–93
Elderly (*see also* Aging)
 as share of population, global map,
 379
 as share of population, national map,
 380
Elections, 41
Electronic church, 502
Electronic mail, 42, 58, 182, 187
Electronic town meetings, 448
El Salvador, 293
Embarrassment, 162
Emergent-norm theory of crowd
 behavior, 611–12
Emigration, 559
Emotions, 158
Empirical evidence, 28
Empty nest, 464
Enclosure movement, 13

Endogamous marriage, 237, 455, 460
Energy consumption, 585
 global map, 586
 inventions, 402
England (*see* Great Britain)
English language, 68, 79, 84, 163–64,
 349
Enlightenment, 227
Environment (*see* Natural environment)
Environment, organizational, 192
Environmental deficit, 587, 602
Environmental movement, 603
Environmental Protection Agency, 596
Environmental racism, 601
Equality, value of, 260
Equal opportunity, 70, 511
Equal Rights Amendment (ERA), 340,
 341
Eros, 125
Eskimos, 351
Espionage, 224
Estate system, 239
Estonia, 411
Ethics:
 and death, 392–93, 541
 health, 392–93, 541
 and reproductive technology, 475
 and research, 37–38
Ethiopia, 295, 296, 299, 308, 311, 432,
 531
Ethnicity (*see also* specific categories of
 people)
 categories, 350
 defined, 349
 and Information Revolution, 399
 minority-majority population,
 national map, 352
 and poverty, 277
 and religion, 497–98
 and social mobility, 273
 and social stratification, 264–65
Ethnocentrism, 81–83, 305
Ethnographies, 45
Ethnomethodology, 153–54
Eurocentrism, 79
Europe (*see* specific countries)
Euthanasia, 392–94, 541
Evolution, 87, 245, 502
 sociocultural, 94–102, 252
Exogamy, 455
Experiment, 38, 50
Experimental group, 38–39
Expressive crowds, 608
Expressive leadership, 174, 175
Extended family, 454, 455, 468
Extinction, 597–98
Eye contact, 157, 160

Facial expressions, 157, 159
Facsimile (fax) machines, 56, 108, 404
 global map, 109
Factory system, 13, 56, 57, 402, 403,
 412
Fads, 615–16
Faith, 482
False consciousness, 103
Family, 86, 110, 453–79
 African American, 222–23, 264,
 467–68, 474
 and aging, 464–65
 alternative forms, 473–76
 Asian American, 223, 467, 474
 and authority, 428
 basic concepts, 454–55
 and child rearing, 330–32, 463–64
 defined, 454
 and divorce, 1, 10, 116, 453, 469–72,
 476
 divorce rates, national map, 471
 female-headed, 277–79, 370, 467,
 473–74
 and gender, 324, 468–69
 in global perspective, 455–57
 Hispanic American, 39, 467, 474
 and industrial technology, 99
 and Information Revolution, 555
 in later life, 464–65
 and new reproductive technology,
 475
 patterns of descent, 456–57
 and race and ethnicity, 466–68

recent trends in, 453–54
 and remarriage, 472
 and residential patterns, 455–56
 single-parent, 222, 264, 277–79,
 473–74
 size, 464
 and social class, 271–72, 466
 social-conflict analysis of, 459–60
 social-exchange analysis of, 460
 and socialization, 132–33, 458
 stages of life, 461–65
 structural-functional analysis of,
 457–59
 in Sweden, 456–57, 474
 symbolic-interaction analysis of, 460
 traditional, 476–77
 violence in, 335, 472–73
Family and Medical Leave Act, 341,
 464
Family of affinity, 455
Family of orientation, 454
Family of procreation, 454
Family unit, 454
"Family values" agenda, 436
Fascism, 432
Fashions, 615–16
Fecundity, 558
Female genital mutilation, 315
Female-headed families, 277–79, 370,
 467, 473–74
Female infanticide, 300, 455
Feminine traits, 320, 324 (*see also*
 Gender)
Feminism, 646 (*see also* Women's
 movement)
 basic ideas, 340
 defined, 339
 opposition to, 342
 and religion, 485
 variations within, 340–42
Feminist research, 37
Feminization of poverty, 278
Fertility, 558, 564, 566
Feudalism, 104, 240–41
Fieldwork, 45
Filipino Americans, 364, 368–69, 373
Finland, 134, 322, 333
First estate, 239
Flirting, 152
Folkways, 73
Food production, 304, 308
Foot-binding, 322
Force, 427
Foreign aid, 304
Foreign debt, 308
Formal operational stage (Piaget), 127
Formal organizations, 171 (*see also*
 Bureaucracy)
 compared to small groups, 186
 and gender, 189–91
 in Japan, 194–96, 198
 and personal privacy, 196, 197
 and race, 190
 size of, 186
 types of, 181–84
France, 74, 285, 340, 420, 434, 445,
 545, 642
Freedom:
 culture as, 88
 economic (capitalism vs. socialism),
 410–11
 global map, 431
 and socialization, 143
 versus social responsibility, 646–47
 value of, 71
Free enterprise, as value, 70–71
Free will, 1
French Revolution, 13, 441, 618
Function, social, 112–15 (*see also*
 Structural-functional paradigm)
Functional illiteracy, 522
Fundamentalism, religious, 499,
 500–502
Funerals, 85–86

Gambling, 203, 209
Games, 71, 131
 and gender, 324–25
Gay people, 9, 340 (*see also*
 Homosexuality)
 and AIDS, 317, 538–41, 550, 621

Urban political economy, 575
Urban renewal, 570
Urban revolutions, 568, 576–77
USSR (see Commonwealth of
    Independent States; Soviet Union)
Utilitarian organizations, 182, 183
Utopia, 409

Validity, of measurement, 31–32
Values:
    conflict of, 71
    cultural, 69–71
    inconsistency in, 71
    language and, 163
    and scientific study, 34
    and social class, 270–71
Variable, 30–34, 38
VCRs, 135
Venereal disease, 538–41
Venezuela, 261
Veto group, 439
Victimization, culture of, 71, 72
Victimization survey, 220
Victimless crimes, 219–20
Vietnam, 432, 443, 537
Vietnamese Americans, 368
Vietnam War, 176, 406, 407, 484
Violence:
    against children, 121, 203, 473
    elderly abuse, 388
    in families, 472–73
    and mass media, 137
    in prison, 40, 50
    in schools, 519, 520
    terrorism, 442
    against women, 322, 335–37, 340,
        472–73
Violent crime, defined, 219–20
Virtual communities, 650–51
Virtual culture, 75
Voluntary associations, 182
Voter apathy, 427, 438–39

Wage labor, 402
War, 104
    casualties, 443
    causes and costs of, 443–45
War crimes, 444
WASP (see White Anglo-Saxon
    Protestant)
Water consumption, global map, 594
Water pollution, 595
Water supply, 532, 592–94
Wealth (see also Income; Power)
    distribution in U.S., 261–62
    and gender, 332
Weddings (see Marriage)
Welfare, 43, 214, 245, 259, 280
    debate concerning, 284–85
Welfare capitalism, 409, 448
Welfare state, 434–35
White Anglo-Saxon Protestant
    (WASP), 361–62
    concentration of, national map, 361
White-collar crime, 214–15, 600
White-collar occupations, 249, 262–64,
    413–15
White ethnic Americans, 371–72
Who's Who in America, 268, 497
Wodaabe of Africa, 320
Women (see also Family, Feminism,
    Gender; individual topics;
    Marriage)
    and aging, 140, 386, 391
    athletic performance, 319
    and beauty myth, 326, 327
    and child rearing, 330–32, 463–64
    and cigarette smoking, 537
    and college degrees, 332–33, 517
    and development of sociology, 14
    and eating disorders, 529, 537
    and education, 509, 510, 517
    feminine traits, 320, 324
    and gender distinctions, 318–21
    and genital mutilation, 315

and housework, 329–30
and housework, global map, 331
and intelligence, 319
Japanese, 241, 365
labor force participation of, 160,
    326–28, 403, 411, 415–16, 418
and life expectancy, 319
national map, 534
in medicine, 543
and middle age, 140
and the military, 334
as minority, 334–35
and modernization, 305
Muslim, 491
occupations of, 262–63, 273, 327–28,
    330
paid employment, global map, 329
in politics, 333–34
and population control, 566
and pornography, 336–37
and poverty, 298–99
and power, global map, 323
and religion, 485
sex ratio, 561
and sexual harassment, 202, 216, 336,
    342
and sexual slavery, 300
and singlehood, 474
technology and changing status of, 97
upper class, 267
violence against, 322, 335–37, 340,
    472–73
and work, global map, 329
Women's movement, 87, 621, 622, 625
Women's networks, 181
Work:
    agricultural employment, global map,
        406
    and alienation, 105–7
    changing patterns of, 98, 404, 413
    dual labor market, 413

and gender, 160, 326–27, 329, 403,
    411, 412, 415–16, 418
and gender, global map, 329
and global economy, 275–76
industrial employment, global map,
    406
and introduction of factories, 13, 56,
    57, 402, 403, 412
labor force, U.S., 412
national map, 412
and occupational prestige, 148,
    262–63
postindustrialism and, 99–100,
    403–4, 411–17
professions, 414–15
self-employment, 415–16
and technology, 417
temporary, 414
unemployment, 416
value of, 70
Work ethic, 110, 361, 486, 631
Working class, 104, 269–72
Working poor, 282
Workplace, social diversity in, 417, 418
Work teams, self-managed, 192
World religions, 489–95
World War II, 334, 359
Writing, 97

Xenophobia, 373

Yanomamö, 62, 64, 74, 96, 443
Yonsei, 368
Yugoslavia, 77, 444

Zaire, 295, 309
Zambia, 445
Zebaleen of Egypt, 592–93
Zero population growth, 564
Zimbabwe, 243, 508

USING THE ANNOTATIONS

This revision of *Sociology* continues to incorporate the Annotated Instructor's Edition that was introduced in previous editions. The AIE is a professional version of the text that provides additional marginal information for the instructor. These annotations are prepared by John J. Macionis and feature a wealth of data, ideas, and resources to enhance classroom teaching and discussion. Annotations are of twelve types:

Supplements: Cross-references to material in the *Data File*, video library, or other supplementary material.

Global: Facts or observations placing the topic at hand in a global context.

Diversity: Data or insights analyzing the issue in terms of race, ethnicity, gender, or socioeconomic status.

Cyber: Material concerning the social implications of new information technology.

Social Survey: Pertinent data, from the National Opinion Research Center's *General Social Surveys, 1972–1996*, that enrich class discussions.

The Map: Additional insights into the data portrayed in the global maps ("Windows on the World") and national maps ("Seeing Ourselves").

Quotations (Q): Noteworthy comments made by sociologists, literary figures, and current news makers.

Then and Now: Data revealing the extent of sociological changes during recent decades.

Note: A theoretical or methodological comment, the etymology of a term, or information about the text's artwork or photography.

Resource: An article or book useful for further investigation of a specific topic.

Discuss: Topical information or a suggestion likely to provoke class discussion.

Exercise: An instructional activity for students.

These annotations have been developed with the intention of providing a wide range of useful material to instructors of diverse backgrounds and interests. Of course, any particular annotation is likely to be more useful to some instructors than to others. We encourage you to review the annotations and identify those that meet the needs of your specific course.

Finally, we invite your suggestions for future editions of the Annotated Instructor's Edition. Please write to John Macionis, Kenyon College, Gambier, OH 43022, or send e-mail to MACIONIS@KENYON.EDU Appropriate attribution will be made for any material that is used in subsequent editions of this book.

GRANT OF LICENSE

In consideration of your payment of the license fee, which is part of the price you paid for this product, and your agreement to abide by the terms and conditions of this Agreement, the Company grants to you

- For the data disk – a nonexclusive right to use and display the copy of the enclosed data disk (hereinafter the DATA).

- For the program disk – a nonexclusive, nontransferable, permanent license to use and display the copy of the enclosed software program (hereinafter the PROGRAM) on a single computer (i.e., with a single CPU) at a single location so long as you comply with the terms of this Agreement. The Company reserves all rights not expressly granted to you under this Agreement. Together, the PROGRAM AND THE DATA ARE CALLED THE SOFTWARE.

OWNERSHIP OF SOFTWARE

You own only the magnetic or physical media (the enclosed disk) on which the SOFTWARE is recorded or fixed, but the Company retains all the rights, title, and ownership to the SOFTWARE recorded on the original disk copy(ies) and all subsequent copies of the SOFTWARE, regardless of the form or media on which the original or other copies may exist. This license is not a sale of the original SOFTWARE or any copy to you.

RESTRICTIONS ON COPYING, USE, AND TRANSFER

This SOFTWARE and the accompanying printed materials and user manual (the Documentation) are the subject of copyright and are licensed to you only.

- For the Program – You may not copy the documentation or the PROGRAM except that you may make a single copy of the PROGRAM for backup or archival purposes only.

You may not network the PROGRAM or otherwise use it on more than one computer or computer terminal at the same time. You may physically transfer the PROGRAM from one computer to another provided that the PROGRAM is used on only one computer at a time. You may not distribute copies of the PROGRAM DISK or Documentation to others. You may not reverse engineer, disassemble, decompile, modify, adapt, translate, or create derivative works based on the PROGRAM or the Documentation without the prior written consent of the Company.

The enclosed PROGRAM may not be transferred to anyone else without the prior written consent of the Company. Any unauthorized transfer of the PROGRAM shall result in the immediate termination of this Agreement.

For the DATA – You may not sell or license copies of the DATA or the documentation to others and you may not transfer or distribute it, except to instructors and students in your school who are users of the Company textbook that accompanies this SOFTWARE.

You may be held legally responsible for any copying or copyright infringement which is caused or encouraged by your failure to abide by the terms of these restrictions.

TERMINATION

This license is effective until terminated. This license will terminate automatically without notice from the Company and become null and void if you fail to comply with any provisions or limitations of this license. Upon termination, you shall destroy the Documentation and all copies of the SOFTWARE. All provisions of this Agreement as to warranties, limitation of liability, remedies or damages, and our ownership rights shall survive termination.

MISCELLANEOUS

THIS AGREEMENT SHALL BE CONSTRUED IN ACCORDANCE WITH THE LAWS OF THE UNITED STATES OF AMERICA AND THE STATE OF NEW YORK, APPLICABLE TO CONTRACTS MADE IN NEW YORK, AND SHALL BENEFIT THE COMPANY, ITS AFFILIATES, AND ASSIGNEES.

ACKNOWLEDGMENT

YOU ACKNOWLEDGE THAT YOU HAVE READ THIS AGREEMENT, UNDERSTAND IT, AND AGREE TO BE BOUND BY ITS TERMS AND CONDITIONS. YOU ALSO AGREE THAT THIS AGREEMENT IS THE COMPLETE AND EXCLUSIVE STATEMENT OF THE AGREEMENT BETWEEN YOU AND THE COMPANY AND SUPERSEDES ALL PROPOSALS OR PRIOR AGREEMENTS, ORAL OR WRITTEN, AND ANY OTHER COMMUNICATIONS BETWEEN YOU AND THE COMPANY OR ANY REPRESENTATIVE OF THE COMPANY RELATING TO THE SUBJECT MATTER OF THIS AGREEMENT.

Should you have any questions concerning this agreement or if you wish to contact the Company for any reason, please contact in writing: Executive Manager, New Media, Prentice Hall, One Lake Street, Upper Saddle River, NJ 07458.

SYSTEM REQUIREMENTS

MACINTOSH: minimum 68040/33MHz, System 7.5 or above, 12mb RAM (16mb recommended), 1mb free HD space, 2x CD-ROM, 640X480 screen resolution, color monitor (thousands of colors required). QuickTime 3.0 installed from CD.

PC: minimum 486/DX25, Windows 3.x (minimum 8mb RAM) or Windows 95/98 (minimum 16mb RAM), 1 mb free HD space, 2X CD-ROM, SVGA monitor, thousands of colors, sound and video cards required. For Windows 3.x, Video for Windows installed from CD.